PRINCIPLES AND PRACTICES OF NEW JERSEY REAL ESTATE

Frank W. Kovats, DREI

To Emily, Frank, Keith, Katrina, Kyle, Kristi, Kirsten and Keely

Library of Congress Catalog Card Number: **00 130058**
ISBN: 0-9678430-1-4

Fifteenth Edition, Second Printing

Copyright © 1978, 1980, 1982, 1983, 1984, 1985, 1986, 1987, 1988, 1989, 1990, 1992, 1993, 1995, 1997, 1998, 2000, 2003 and 2004 by Kovco Publications, Inc., Maywood, NJ 07652

All rights reserved.

This book, or any part thereof, may not be reproduced in any form or by any means, including electronic, photographic, or mechanical, or by any sound recording system or by any device for storage and retrieval of information, without the written consent of the Publisher.

Home office: 230 West Passaic Street, Maywood, NJ 07607-1267

Cover design: Michele O'Hagan, 1106 Design, Phoenix, AZ

All State Statutes found in this book are current as of this printing, but are subject to change according to State Laws. It is therefore recommended that the reader verify with the New Jersey Real Estate Commission any changes in these statutes since the date of this publication.

While diligent efforts have been made in compiling this publication, the author and publisher make no warranties and assume no responsibility for accuracy or completeness of the information contained herein.

ABOUT THE AUTHOR

Frank W. Kovats has been developing and teaching license preparation courses since 1961. Born in Belleville, New Jersey, he graduated from Upsala College in 1959 and for several years served as Chairman of the Rental Housing Committee for the New Jersey Association of Realtors. He has also served as President, New Jersey Chapter One, Institute of Real Estate Management; a member of the Ad Hoc Committee on education to the New Jersey Real Estate Commission; a member of the faculty of the Realtor Institute; President of the New Jersey Association of Real Estate Educators; and Vice President of the Real Estate Educators Association. He has been awarded the DREI (Distinguished Real Estate Instructor) designation by the Real Estate Educators Association.

CONSULTING EDITORS

I would like to thank the following reviewers for their helpful comments on early drafts of this edition. The inclusion of their names should not be construed to represent their approval of the finished product, as the responsibility for any error or omission is mine.

Lawrence Danks, Camden County College
Robert A. Gaccione, Esq., Gaccione, Pomaco and Beck, Belleville, NJ
Dennis Gaglione, Esq., Gaccione, Pomaco and Beck, Belleville, NJ
Don Haven, The Real Estate School, Cherry Hill, NJ
Barry S. Jones, PLS, Albert A. Fralinger, Jr., P.A.
Joseph Kliminski, Bloomfield Savings Bank of New Jersey, Bloomfield, NJ
Howard Krohnengold, Staff Instructor, Kovats Real Estate and Insurance Schools, Maywood, NJ
Mel Lissner, Director, The Mel Lissner Real Estate School, Edison, NJ
Vivian Lopez, Esq., Rahway, NJ
Robert J. Mulligan, Valley National Bank, Wayne, NJ
Michael Muscarella, Esq., Acusearch Title Services, Inc., Hackensack, NJ
Gustave A. Peduto, Esq., Iselin, NJ
Dominick Zagaroli, GAA, Westchester Community College

Frank W. Kovats, DREI
Maywood, New Jersey

PREFACE

The economic importance of real estate today demands a higher professional level for all persons dealing in real estate, with an increased emphasis on educational requirements. Also, every state requires that a person engaging professionally in the real estate business, either as a broker or as a salesperson, must be licensed, and in each case, a state examination is a prerequisite for a license.

Principles and Practices of New Jersey Real Estate has been written to serve as an educational guide for students and for persons desiring to take New Jersey's real estate licensing examination, as a quick reference for those already in the profession, and for use by the many other professionals dealing with various aspects of real estate.

Since this book is not intended to be an in-depth study on each particular chapter theme, the author strongly recommends, when needed, one of the many excellent books written on each specific subject area covered in this book, and the use of legal, accounting or other professional services if legal advice or other assistance is needed.

The material used in compiling this publication comes from the many sources listed in the back of the book, with an emphasis on New Jersey's State laws. Every effort has been made to organize the material in a manner most beneficial to the serious real estate student, with the quizzes on each chapter serving as a study guide to the State examination. Although these quizzes have been assembled by general subject in each chapter, occasionally the reference to the answers will be found in other sections or in the definitions in the back of the book.

No implication is made that these questions have been, or will be, contained in the examination, but they are of the content and type usually found therein.

It may be argued that some questions are unfair or "tricky" . . . perhaps with some degree of justification. However, many of these questions are similar in content and format to State examination questions. After familiarization, discussion and practice, most of these questions will lose the "tricky" label. Their primary purpose is to assist you in learning the material and not to have you memorize answers.

A practice examination for salesperson and broker candidates has been included at the end of the book to assist you in preparing for the State licensing examination.

Please note: You are not expected to answer the questions after your first study of each chapter. It is important to proceed at the pace directed by your instructor. The questions do, however, serve as an excellent review of the material covered and should be clearly understood prior to sitting for the State licensing examination.

Any comments, criticisms or suggestions for future editions would be welcomed and appreciated. The mailing address of the author is:

Frank W. Kovats, DREI
230 West Passaic Street
Maywood, New Jersey 07607

Phone (201) 843-PASS

ACKNOWLEDGMENTS

The contributions of many friends, colleagues and former students have gone into this book. I am particularly indebted to John W. Reilly and Paige Bovee Vitousek for the liberal use of "Principles and Practices of Hawaiian Real Estate" as a source for the first edition of this book in 1978. I am also grateful to Mel Lissner, Director of The Mel Lissner Real Estate School, for the many helpful suggestions he made during the evolution of this text, and to Ted Schwartz for his guidance with the chapter on Environmental Laws. Bob Kenner, Herbert M. Tanzman Realtors, generously made available material which he had gathered on the subject of New Jersey's Environmental laws. Special thanks are also due Ed Rust, Rust Communications Group, for the graphics work and his personal interest in the production of this Fifteenth Edition, and to Fran Janosco, Courier Corporation, Westford, MA.

The illustration of the State of New Jersey on the title page, depicting the tremendous variety of our state, is by the late *Star-Ledger* artist William Canfield and was reproduced here with his very kind permission.

Permission for the reproduction of legal forms has been kindly granted by the All-State Legal Supply Co. (Deed), the Garden State Multiple Listing Service LLC (Real Estate Listing Contract), the New Jersey Association of Realtors (Real Estate Sales Contract), and the Color Process Printing Co. (Apartment Lease). These forms are copyrighted and may not be reproduced without the express permission of the copyright holders.

The maps of the Hackensack Meadowlands District (page 474) and the New Jersey Coastal Zone (page 475) are from "Rules on Coastal Resources and Development," published by the New Jersey Department of Environmental Protection, Division of Coastal Resources. The map of the New Jersey Pinelands (page 473) was provided courtesy of the Pinelands Commission.

And finally, I want to most sincerely thank my friend Larry Danks for permission to use portions of his excellent book, *New Jersey Real Estate*.

F.W.K.

TABLE OF CONTENTS

Chapter **Page**

LIST OF FIGURES

Figure **Page**

CHAPTER ONE

HISTORICAL DEVELOPMENT OF NEW JERSEY REAL ESTATE

When the Dutch and Swedish settlers arrived in the section of the New World now known as New Jersey at the beginning of the seventeenth century and projected the establishment of settlements upon the Delaware and the Hudson, they found on those rivers an independent nation of the far-reaching Algonquin family known as the Lenni-Lenape, later known as the Delawares. Lenni means pure or original and Lenape means people, hence their name may mean "the first people." Although their number probably never exceeded 3,000, they were more numerous in the southern and central than in the northern parts of the state. Other tribes, including the Powhatan-Renape, also lived here.

In 1758 the first Indian reservation in the country was established in the "Pines" of Burlington County in a town called Brotherton when 200 Lenni-Lenape Indians were settled on 3,000 acres of land. They remained there until 1802, when they were removed to New York State. Later they were transported to Green Bay, Wisconsin, and finally to Indian Territory. Today, except for the retention of place names like Communipaw, Crosswicks, Hackensack, Hoboken, Ho-Ho-Kus, Passaic, Pompton, Rahway, Secaucus, Succasunna and Watchung, hardly any trace of the Lenni-Lenape remains in New Jersey. In 1832 the State of New Jersey appropriated $2,000 to extinguish the "right, title, and interest which the Lenni-Lenape held or might have held against the colony or the State."

Disputes over land, and confusion over boundaries of not only the colony itself with its neighbors, but also of the scope of the respective land grants within the colony, dominated much of New Jersey's early history. Following the early explorations by Giovanni de Verrazano, Henry Hudson, Cornelius May and others, the exploration and settlement of New Jersey in the seventeenth century was marked by competition among various nations to secure their land claims to the region. The first settlements were principally military outposts to assert the respective national claims against other nations and the Native Americans. From their base on Manhattan Island at New Amsterdam, settled in 1626, the Dutch expanded across the river by building a fort and village at Pavonia in 1630 in the area of present-day Jersey City. In 1655, they also took over New Sweden's forts along the Delaware River, including Fort Elfsborg near present-day Salem on the New Jersey side of the river. Dutch control of what is now New York and New Jersey was lost to the English in 1664, when they surrendered to a naval fleet which was sent by James, the Duke of York, to seize the lands between the Connecticut and Delaware Rivers which had been granted to the Duke by his brother, King Charles II.

On June 23, 1664, the Duke of York granted the New Jersey portion of his lands to Lord John Berkeley and Sir George Carteret, who both had been loyal supporters of the Crown during the English civil wars. But questions over the legality of the grant and the ambiguous boundary definitions of the area would continue to provoke disputes well into the next century. The Duke had previously appointed Richard Nicolls (the commander of the fleet that captured New Amsterdam) as governor of his colonial holdings, and Nicolls had also granted lands to others without knowledge of the grants to Berkeley and Carteret. Thus, the first governors of New Jersey were agents who were appointed by the proprietary landowners. The settlement of the colony was pursued primarily for the revenues that the proprietors and their agents sought to gain from the sale, rental and development of their properties.

In 1665, to encourage immigration by those of other nations as well as by the English, Berkeley and Carteret issued a document entitled Concessions and Agreement. The document promised settlers religious freedom, liberal land grants and other incentives. They also encouraged settlement from those of religious faiths that had been the target of discrimination in other colonies, such as Puritans, Quakers, Calvinists, Catholics, Baptists and Presbyterians. New England colonists were persuaded to relocate to New Jersey by the promise of religious freedom, liberal land incentives, a milder climate and more fertile soil. These settlers were prominent in the founding of such early towns as Elizabeth, Middletown, Shrewsbury, Woodbridge, Piscataway and Newark. The Dutch, however, also continued to establish villages even after the assumption of English political control, adding to the towns they had settled in present Bergen and Hudson counties by entering the

Raritan Valley. Some of these settlements included Protestants from other European countries, particularly France, who had previously emigrated to Holland.

Following a brief retaking of control by the Dutch of their former colony in 1673, a treaty signed in London in February 1674 restored control of New York and New Jersey to the English. However, it further complicated the questions of the validity and scope of the earlier land grants from the Duke of York. Apparently frustrated in his hopes of gaining a return from his colonial grant, a month after the signing of the treaty Berkeley sold his portion of the colony, which was located in the southwestern part of the present state, to John Fenwick and Edward Byllinge for the bargain price of 1,000 pounds. Fenwick and Byllinge were Quakers who were soon joined by others of the same beliefs who shared the lands under common ownership. The portion sold by Berkeley represented well over half of the total acreage of the colony.

In 1676, an agreement recognizing a formal division of the holdings of the Quakers and of Carteret was reached with the execution of the "Quintipartite Deed," named for the fact that it was signed by Carteret on one side and four Quakers (including William Penn) on the other. The Deed established the boundary between Carteret's lands comprising 2,981 square miles, now known as the Province of East Jersey, and the Province of West Jersey, a larger area of 4,595 square miles owned by the Quakers, by drawing a line from Little Egg Harbor in present Atlantic County to the Delaware Water Gap. Later disputes, however, challenged the validity of this boundary, and conflicts over the exact location of the terminus of the boundary along the Delaware would continue for many years. Various conflicting claims contended that the line ended in an area ranging from Hunterdon County north to Sussex County in the vicinity of the present town of Newton, thus leaving a large "wedge" of disputed lands between East and West Jersey. Remnants of these competing boundaries exist today.

Following the death of Carteret in 1682, the Quakers bought East Jersey from his widow. As contemporary experts have noted, however, confusion and conflict over land rights continued because of uncertainty about boundaries, inaccurate surveying and poor record-keeping. The Quakers soon recognized that East Jersey already had too many non-Quaker residents to allow a purely Quaker community. Accordingly, they decided to sell off half of their interests, in twenty-fourths, to 12 other speculators who were primarily Scottish. The new ownership group organized itself into the East Jersey Board of Proprietors. The group continued to sell land to new settlers and took steps to increase revenue from existing landowners and tenants. Resentment by settlers against the proprietors soon provoked unrest and sporadic violence, leading the proprietors to pursue ways to give up their claims to govern in return for confirmation of their property rights. The proprietors thus voluntarily gave up their governmental role in 1702, when the administration of the colony was voluntarily ceded to the British monarch in return for the reaffirmation of their land claims.

New Jersey became a royal colony under a common governor with New York until 1738, when Lewis Morris was named as the first governor of New Jersey alone. The real estate role of the proprietors and their successors continued into modern times in the legal control over ungranted real estate. It was not until 1998 that the proprietors of East Jersey dissolved their corporation, then the oldest corporation in continuing existence in the United States. However, its sister Council of West Jersey Proprietors (which was first organized as an informal society not formally incorporated under a royal charter) continues to convene each April in Burlington City, as it has every year since 1688, and still occasionally is involved in asserting or resolving title claims to property. In 1719, an act was passed which provided that former surveys which were not recorded within a named time would be void against succeeding surveys of the same land which were duly recorded.

The feudal concept of service to the king, wherein certain "tenures" were granted to individuals in exchange for a grant of land, never prevailed in New Jersey. Settlers obtained title to real estate by purchasing it from the Indians or through grants from local proprietary authorities. In essence Berkeley and Carteret were real estate promoters. They were responsible for the development of the colony, as were other proprietors, and there was no direct expense to the British treasury. When, after the Revolutionary War, the new United States government claimed all of the land in New Jersey by reason of conquest, the land was sold to citizens at very low prices and every effort was made to have the original occupants retain ownership. Thus, New Jersey's lands progressed from a system of government and royalty ownership to the **allodial system** which gave people the right to own full and complete property rights in land subject only to the various public and private restrictions such as zoning, taxation and deed restrictions. Today, accurately defined boundaries and official maps of all lands in the state are made a part of the public records in each of our 21 counties.

Geographically, New Jersey today contains a total area of 8,204.37 square miles: 7,504.80 square miles of land and 699.57 square miles of water. The population as of mid-1998 was estimated to be 8,115,011, made up of 2,898,000 households. (Population by county is included in the appendix). Of New Jersey's total land, 43% is forested and 24.1% is in farms. The greatest length is 166 miles from High Point to Cape May and the narrowest width is 32 miles from Trenton to Raritan Bay. We have 125 miles of coastline, more than 800 lakes and ponds, and more than 100 rivers and creeks, 1,400 miles of trout streams and approximately 19,000 industrial establishments represented in 90% of all industries. Our civil divisions are made up of 21 counties and 566 municipalities.

In contemporary New Jersey, the colonial heritage of the importance of land and the control of its use, regulation and taxation continues in the context of the modern state—the most densely populated of all states and the fifth-smallest state in land area. Conflicts and competition over how the state's available land should be utilized remain as primary issues at all levels of government.

CHAPTER TWO

NATIONAL ASSOCIATION OF REALTORS®

The national real estate body, which was the leader in adopting ethical standards, is the NATIONAL ASSOCIATION OF REALTORS® (NAR.), formerly called the National Association of Real Estate Boards, which was founded in 1908. From this organization came the development of state associations, which were then broken down into local real estate boards. In New Jersey, these are the New Jersey Association of REALTORS® and the various local boards.

The purpose of a real estate board is to provide for its members the benefits of united efforts and concentrated action toward any end which may tend to strengthen the stability and the dignity of the real estate profession. The term "REALTOR®" is a trade name, and is to be used only by those brokers who belong to the NATIONAL ASSOCIATION OF REALTORS®. Members display the word in their offices so the public may know they follow a prescribed set of ethics and business standards.

The REALTOR® Code of Ethics printed on the following pages was first adopted by the NATIONAL ASSOCIATION OF REALTORS® in 1913, and has been extensively amended since that time. In 1963 the N.A.R. Committee on Professional Standards published a book entitled *Interpretations of the Code of Ethics* which applies the rules stated in the Code to actual situations. This book offers a superb insight into the purpose, meaning and application of the Code, and is highly recommended to all real estate agents concerned with elevating the professional standards of the industry.

The REALTOR® Code of Ethics is, of course, obligatory only upon members of the NATIONAL ASSOCIATION OF REALTORS® and constituent local boards. However, since it is the only nationally recognized code of its kind, it serves equally as well as a guide for nonmembers. The Real Estate Commission strongly recommends its use to all those licensed to engage in the Real Estate business. Many of the rules of conduct of New Jersey's state laws are based on this Code of Ethics.

In adhering to this Code, REALTORS® have pledged themselves to the proposition that the welfare and interests of their clients and the public will be placed above any profit or advantage for themselves.

Code of Ethics and Standards of Practice of the NATIONAL ASSOCIATION OF REALTORS®

Effective January 1, 2004

Where the word REALTORS® is used in this Code and Preamble, it shall be deemed to include REALTOR-ASSOCIATE®s.

While the Code of Ethics establishes obligations that may be higher than those mandated by law, in any instance where the Code of Ethics and the law conflict, the obligations of the law must take precedence.

Preamble

Under all is the land. Upon its wise utilization and widely allocated ownership depend the survival and growth of free institutions and of our civilization. REALTORS® should recognize that the interests of the nation and its citizens require the highest and best use of the land and the widest distribution of land ownership. They require the creation of adequate housing, the building of functioning cities, the development of productive industries and farms, and the preservation of a healthful environment.

Such interests impose obligations beyond those of ordinary commerce. They impose grave social responsibility and a patriotic duty to which REALTORS® should dedicate themselves, and for which they should be diligent in preparing themselves. REALTORS®, therefore, are zealous to maintain and improve the standards of their calling and share with their fellow REALTORS® a common responsibility for its integrity and honor.

In recognition and appreciation of their obligations to clients, customers, the public, and each other, REALTORS® continuously strive to become and remain informed on issues affecting real estate and, as knowledgeable professionals, they willingly share the fruit of their experience and study with others. They identify and take steps, through enforcement of this Code of Ethics and by assisting appropriate regulatory bodies, to eliminate practices which may damage the public or which might discredit or bring dishonor to the real estate profession. REALTORS® having direct personal knowledge of conduct that may violate the Code of Ethics involving misappropriation of client or customer funds or property, willful discrimination, or fraud resulting in substantial economic harm, bring such matters to the attention of the appropriate Board or Association of REALTORS®. *(Amended 1/00)*

Realizing that cooperation with other real estate professionals promotes the best interests of those who utilize their services, REALTORS® urge exclusive representation of clients; do not attempt to gain any unfair advantage over their competitors; and they refrain from making unsolicited comments about other practitioners. In instances where their opinion is sought, or where REALTORS® believe that comment is necessary, their opinion is offered in an objective, professional manner, uninfluenced by any personal motivation or potential advantage or gain.

The term REALTOR® has come to connote competency, fairness, and high integrity resulting from adherence to a lofty ideal of moral conduct in business relations. No inducement of profit and no instruction from clients ever can justify departure from this ideal.

In the interpretation of this obligation, REALTORS® can take no safer guide than that which has been handed down through the centuries, embodied in the Golden Rule, "Whatsoever ye would that others should do to you, do ye even so to them."

Accepting this standard as their own, REALTORS® pledge to observe its spirit in all of their activities and to conduct their business in accordance with the tenets set forth below.

Duties to Clients and Customers

Article 1

When representing a buyer, seller, landlord, tenant, or other client as an agent, REALTORS® pledge themselves to protect and promote the interests of their client. This obligation to the client is primary, but it does not relieve REALTORS® of their obligation to treat all parties honestly. When serving a buyer, seller, landlord, tenant or other party in a non-agency capacity, REALTORS® remain obligated to treat all parties honestly. *(Amended 1/01)*

- **Standard of Practice 1-1**
  REALTORS®, when acting as principals in a real estate transaction, remain obligated by the duties imposed by the Code of Ethics. *(Amended 1/93)*

- **Standard of Practice 1-2**
  The duties the Code of Ethics imposes are applicable whether REALTORS® are acting as agents or in legally recognized non-agency capacities except that any duty imposed exclusively on agents by law or regulation shall not be imposed by this Code of Ethics on REALTORS® acting in non-agency capacities.

  As used in this Code of Ethics, "client" means the person(s) or entity(ies) with whom a REALTOR® or a REALTOR®'s firm has an agency or legally recognized non-agency relationship; "customer" means a party to a real estate transaction who receives information, services, or benefits but has no contractual relationship with the REALTOR® or the REALTOR®'s firm; "prospect" means a purchaser, seller, tenant, or landlord who is not subject to a representation relationship with the REALTOR® or REALTOR®'s firm; "agent" means a real estate licensee (including brokers and sales associates) acting in an agency relationship as defined by state law or regulation; and

NATIONAL ASSOCIATION OF REALTORS®

The Voice for Real Estate®

Real Strength. Real Advantages.

"broker" means a real estate licensee (including brokers and sales associates) acting as an agent or in a legally recognized non-agency capacity. *(Adopted 1/95, Amended 1/04)*

- **Standard of Practice 1-3**
REALTORS®, in attempting to secure a listing, shall not deliberately mislead the owner as to market value.

- **Standard of Practice 1-4**
REALTORS®, when seeking to become a buyer/tenant representative, shall not mislead buyers or tenants as to savings or other benefits that might be realized through use of the REALTOR®'s services. *(Amended 1/93)*

- **Standard of Practice 1-5**
REALTORS® may represent the seller/landlord and buyer/tenant in the same transaction only after full disclosure to and with informed consent of both parties. *(Adopted 1/93)*

- **Standard of Practice 1-6**
REALTORS® shall submit offers and counter-offers objectively and as quickly as possible. *(Adopted 1/93, Amended 1/95)*

- **Standard of Practice 1-7**
When acting as listing brokers, REALTORS® shall continue to submit to the seller/landlord all offers and counter-offers until closing or execution of a lease unless the seller/landlord has waived this obligation in writing. REALTORS® shall not be obligated to continue to market the property after an offer has been accepted by the seller/landlord. REALTORS® shall recommend that sellers/landlords obtain the advice of legal counsel prior to acceptance of a subsequent offer except where the acceptance is contingent on the termination of the pre-existing purchase contract or lease. *(Amended 1/93)*

- **Standard of Practice 1-8**
REALTORS®, acting as agents or brokers of buyers/tenants, shall submit to buyers/tenants all offers and counter-offers until acceptance but have no obligation to continue to show properties to their clients after an offer has been accepted unless otherwise agreed in writing. REALTORS®, acting as agents or brokers of buyers/tenants, shall recommend that buyers/tenants obtain the advice of legal counsel if there is a question as to whether a pre-existing contract has been terminated. *(Adopted 1/93, Amended 1/99)*

- **Standard of Practice 1-9**
The obligation of REALTORS® to preserve confidential information (as defined by state law) provided by their clients in the course of any agency relationship or non-agency relationship recognized by law continues after termination of agency relationships or any non-agency relationships recognized by law. REALTORS® shall not knowingly, during or following the termination of professional relationships with their clients:
1) reveal confidential information of clients; or
2) use confidential information of clients to the disadvantage of clients; or
3) use confidential information of clients for the REALTOR®'s advantage or the advantage of third parties unless:
    a) clients consent after full disclosure; or
    b) REALTORS® are required by court order; or
    c) it is the intention of a client to commit a crime and the information is necessary to prevent the crime; or
    d) it is necessary to defend a REALTOR® or the REALTOR®'s employees or associates against an accusation of wrongful conduct.

Information concerning latent material defects is not considered confidential information under this Code of Ethics. *(Adopted 1/93, Amended 1/01)*

- **Standard of Practice 1-10**
REALTORS® shall, consistent with the terms and conditions of their real estate licensure and their property management agreement, competently manage the property of clients with due regard for the rights, safety and health of tenants and others lawfully on the premises. *(Adopted 1/95, Amended 1/00)*

- **Standard of Practice 1-11**
REALTORS® who are employed to maintain or manage a client's property shall exercise due diligence and make reasonable efforts to protect it against reasonably foreseeable contingencies and losses. *(Adopted 1/95)*

- **Standard of Practice 1-12**
When entering into listing contracts, REALTORS® must advise sellers/landlords of:
1) the REALTOR®'s company policies regarding cooperation and the amount(s) of any compensation that will be offered to subagents, buyer/tenant agents, and/or brokers acting in legally recognized non-agency capacities;
2) the fact that buyer/tenant agents or brokers, even if compensated by listing brokers, or by sellers/landlords may represent the interests of buyers/tenants; and
3) any potential for listing brokers to act as disclosed dual agents, e.g. buyer/tenant agents. *(Adopted 1/93, Renumbered 1/98, Amended 1/03)*

- **Standard of Practice 1-13**
When entering into buyer/tenant agreements, REALTORS® must advise potential clients of:
1) the REALTOR®'s company policies regarding cooperation;
2) the amount of compensation to be paid by the client;
3) the potential for additional or offsetting compensation from other brokers, from the seller or landlord, or from other parties; and
4) any potential for the buyer/tenant representative to act as a disclosed dual agent, e.g. listing broker, subagent, landlord's agent, etc. *(Adopted 1/93, Renumbered 1/98, Amended 1/04)*

- **Standard of Practice 1-14**
Fees for preparing appraisals or other valuations shall not be contingent upon the amount of the appraisal or valuation. *(Adopted 1/02)*

- **Standard of Practice 1-15**
REALTORS®, in response to inquiries from buyers or cooperating brokers shall, with the sellers' approval, divulge the existence of offers on the property. *(Adopted 1/03)*

Article 2

REALTORS® shall avoid exaggeration, misrepresentation, or concealment of pertinent facts relating to the property or the transaction. REALTORS® shall not, however, be obligated to discover latent defects in the property, to advise on matters outside the scope of their real estate license, or to disclose facts which are confidential under the scope of agency or non-agency relationships as defined by state law. *(Amended 1/00)*

- **Standard of Practice 2-1**
  REALTORS® shall only be obligated to discover and disclose adverse factors reasonably apparent to someone with expertise in those areas required by their real estate licensing authority. Article 2 does not impose upon the REALTOR® the obligation of expertise in other professional or technical disciplines. *(Amended 1/96)*
- **Standard of Practice 2-2**
  (Renumbered as Standard of Practice 1-12 1/98)
- **Standard of Practice 2-3**
  (Renumbered as Standard of Practice 1-13 1/98)
- **Standard of Practice 2-4**
  REALTORS® shall not be parties to the naming of a false consideration in any document, unless it be the naming of an obviously nominal consideration.
- **Standard of Practice 2-5**
  Factors defined as "non-material" by law or regulation or which are expressly referenced in law or regulation as not being subject to disclosure are considered not "pertinent" for purposes of Article 2. *(Adopted 1/93)*

Article 3

REALTORS® shall cooperate with other brokers except when cooperation is not in the client's best interest. The obligation to cooperate does not include the obligation to share commissions, fees, or to otherwise compensate another broker. *(Amended 1/95)*

- **Standard of Practice 3-1**
  REALTORS®, acting as exclusive agents or brokers of sellers/landlords, establish the terms and conditions of offers to cooperate. Unless expressly indicated in offers to cooperate, cooperating brokers may not assume that the offer of cooperation includes an offer of compensation. Terms of compensation, if any, shall be ascertained by cooperating brokers before beginning efforts to accept the offer of cooperation. *(Amended 1/99)*
- **Standard of Practice 3-2**
  REALTORS® shall, with respect to offers of compensation to another REALTOR®, timely communicate any change of compensation for cooperative services to the other REALTOR® prior to the time such REALTOR® produces an offer to purchase/lease the property. *(Amended 1/94)*
- **Standard of Practice 3-3**
  Standard of Practice 3-2 does not preclude the listing broker and cooperating broker from entering into an agreement to change cooperative compensation. *(Adopted 1/94)*
- **Standard of Practice 3-4**
  REALTORS®, acting as listing brokers, have an affirmative obligation to disclose the existence of dual or variable rate commission arrangements (i.e., listings where one amount of commission is payable if the listing broker's firm is the procuring cause of sale/lease and a different amount of commission is payable if the sale/lease results through the efforts of the seller/landlord or a cooperating broker). The listing broker shall, as soon as practical, disclose the existence of such arrangements to potential cooperating brokers and shall, in response to inquiries from cooperating brokers, disclose the differential that would result in a cooperative transaction or in a sale/lease that results through the efforts of the seller/landlord. If the cooperating broker is a buyer/tenant representative, the buyer/tenant representative must disclose such information to their client before the client makes an offer to purchase or lease. *(Amended 1/02)*
- **Standard of Practice 3-5**
  It is the obligation of subagents to promptly disclose all pertinent facts to the principal's agent prior to as well as after a purchase or lease agreement is executed. *(Amended 1/93)*
- **Standard of Practice 3-6**
  REALTORS® shall disclose the existence of accepted offers, including offers with unresolved contingencies, to any broker seeking cooperation. *(Adopted 5/86, Amended 1/04)*
- **Standard of Practice 3-7**
  When seeking information from another REALTOR® concerning property under a management or listing agreement, REALTORS® shall disclose their REALTOR® status and whether their interest is personal or on behalf of a client and, if on behalf of a client, their representational status. *(Amended 1/95)*
- **Standard of Practice 3-8**
  REALTORS® shall not misrepresent the availability of access to show or inspect a listed property. *(Amended 11/87)*

Article 4

REALTORS® shall not acquire an interest in or buy or present offers from themselves, any member of their immediate families, their firms or any member thereof, or any entities in which they have any ownership interest, any real property without making their true position known to the owner or the owner's agent or broker. In selling property they own, or in which they have any interest, REALTORS® shall reveal their ownership or interest in writing to the purchaser or the purchaser's representative. *(Amended 1/00)*

- **Standard of Practice 4-1**
  For the protection of all parties, the disclosures required by Article 4 shall be in writing and provided by REALTORS® prior to the signing of any contract. *(Adopted 2/86)*

Article 5

REALTORS® shall not undertake to provide professional services concerning a property or its value where they have a present or contemplated interest unless such interest is specifically disclosed to all affected parties.

Article 6

REALTORS® shall not accept any commission, rebate, or profit on expenditures made for their client, without the client's knowledge and consent.

When recommending real estate products or services (e.g., homeowner's insurance, warranty programs, mortgage financing, title insurance, etc.), REALTORS® shall disclose to the client or customer to whom the recommendation is made any financial benefits or fees, other than real estate referral fees, the REALTOR® or REALTOR®'s firm may receive as a direct result of such recommendation. *(Amended 1/99)*

- **Standard of Practice 6-1**
  REALTORS® shall not recommend or suggest to a client or a customer the use of services of another organization or business entity in which they have a direct interest without disclosing such interest at the time of the recommendation or suggestion. *(Amended 5/88)*

Article 7

In a transaction, REALTORS® shall not accept compensation from more than one party, even if permitted by law, without disclosure to all parties and the informed consent of the REALTOR®'s client or clients. *(Amended 1/93)*

Article 8

REALTORS® shall keep in a special account in an appropriate financial institution, separated from their own funds, monies coming into their possession in trust for other persons, such as escrows, trust funds, clients' monies, and other like items.

Article 9

REALTORS®, for the protection of all parties, shall assure whenever possible that all agreements related to real estate transactions including, but not limited to, listing and representation agreements, purchase contracts, and leases are in writing in clear and understandable language expressing the specific terms, conditions, obligations and commitments of the parties. A copy of each agreement shall be furnished to each party to such agreements upon their signing or initialing. *(Amended 1/04)*

- **Standard of Practice 9-1**
  For the protection of all parties, REALTORS® shall use reasonable care to ensure that documents pertaining to the purchase, sale, or lease of real estate are kept current through the use of written extensions or amendments. *(Amended 1/93)*

Duties to the Public

Article 10

REALTORS® shall not deny equal professional services to any person for reasons of race, color, religion, sex, handicap, familial status, or national origin. REALTORS® shall not be parties to any plan or agreement to discriminate against a person or persons on the basis of race, color, religion, sex, handicap, familial status, or national origin. *(Amended 1/90)*

REALTORS®, in their real estate employment practices, shall not discriminate against any person or persons on the basis of race, color, religion, sex, handicap, familial status, or national origin. *(Amended 1/00)*

- **Standard of Practice 10-1**
  REALTORS® shall not volunteer information regarding the racial, religious or ethnic composition of any neighborhood and shall not engage in any activity which may result in panic selling. REALTORS® shall not print, display or circulate any statement or advertisement with respect to the selling or renting of a property that indicates any preference, limitations or discrimination based on race, color, religion, sex, handicap, familial status, or national origin. *(Adopted 1/94)*

- **Standard of Practice 10-2**
  As used in Article 10 "real estate employment practices" relates to employees and independent contractors providing real-estate related services and the administrative and clerical staff directly supporting those individuals. *(Adopted 1/00)*

Article 11

The services which REALTORS® provide to their clients and customers shall conform to the standards of practice and competence which are reasonably expected in the specific real estate disciplines in which they engage; specifically, residential real estate brokerage, real property management, commercial and industrial real estate brokerage, real estate appraisal, real estate counseling, real estate syndication, real estate auction, and international real estate.

REALTORS® shall not undertake to provide specialized professional services concerning a type of property or service that is outside their field of competence unless they engage the assistance of one who is competent on such types of property or service, or unless the facts are fully disclosed to the client. Any persons engaged to provide such assistance shall be so identified to the client and their contribution to the assignment should be set forth. *(Amended 1/95)*

- **Standard of Practice 11-1**
  When REALTORS® prepare opinions of real property value or price, other than in pursuit of a listing or to assist a potential purchaser in formulating a purchase offer, such opinions shall include the following:
  1) identification of the subject property
  2) date prepared
  3) defined value or price
  4) limiting conditions, including statements of purpose(s) and intended user(s)
  5) any present or contemplated interest, including the possibility of representing the seller/landlord or buyers/tenants
  6) basis for the opinion, including applicable market data
  7) if the opinion is not an appraisal, a statement to that effect
  (Amended 1/01)

- **Standard of Practice 11-2**
The obligations of the Code of Ethics in respect of real estate disciplines other than appraisal shall be interpreted and applied in accordance with the standards of competence and practice which clients and the public reasonably require to protect their rights and interests considering the complexity of the transaction, the availability of expert assistance, and, where the REALTOR® is an agent or subagent, the obligations of a fiduciary. *(Adopted 1/95)*

- **Standard of Practice 11-3**
When REALTORS® provide consultive services to clients which involve advice or counsel for a fee (not a commission), such advice shall be rendered in an objective manner and the fee shall not be contingent on the substance of the advice or counsel given. If brokerage or transaction services are to be provided in addition to consultive services, a separate compensation may be paid with prior agreement between the client and REALTOR®. *(Adopted 1/96)*

- **Standard of Practice 11-4**
The competency required by Article 11 relates to services contracted for between REALTORS® and their clients or customers; the duties expressly imposed by the Code of Ethics; and the duties imposed by law or regulation. *(Adopted 1/02)*

Article 12

REALTORS® shall be careful at all times to present a true picture in their advertising and representations to the public. REALTORS® shall also ensure that their professional status (e.g., broker, appraiser, property manager, etc.) or status as REALTORS® is clearly identifiable in any such advertising. *(Amended 1/93)*

- **Standard of Practice 12-1**
REALTORS® may use the term "free" and similar terms in their advertising and in other representations provided that all terms governing availability of the offered product or service are clearly disclosed at the same time. *(Amended 1/97)*

- **Standard of Practice 12-2**
REALTORS® may represent their services as "free" or without cost even if they expect to receive compensation from a source other than their client provided that the potential for the REALTOR® to obtain a benefit from a third party is clearly disclosed at the same time. *(Amended 1/97)*

- **Standard of Practice 12-3**
The offering of premiums, prizes, merchandise discounts or other inducements to list, sell, purchase, or lease is not, in itself, unethical even if receipt of the benefit is contingent on listing, selling, purchasing, or leasing through the REALTOR® making the offer. However, REALTORS® must exercise care and candor in any such advertising or other public or private representations so that any party interested in receiving or otherwise benefiting from the REALTOR®'s offer will have clear, thorough, advance understanding of all the terms and conditions of the offer. The offering of any inducements to do business is subject to the limitations and restrictions of state law and the ethical obligations established by any applicable Standard of Practice. *(Amended 1/95)*

- **Standard of Practice 12-4**
REALTORS® shall not offer for sale/lease or advertise property without authority. When acting as listing brokers or as subagents, REALTORS® shall not quote a price different from that agreed upon with the seller/landlord. *(Amended 1/93)*

- **Standard of Practice 12-5**
REALTORS® shall not advertise nor permit any person employed by or affiliated with them to advertise listed property without disclosing the name of the firm. *(Adopted 11/86)*

- **Standard of Practice 12-6**
REALTORS®, when advertising unlisted real property for sale/lease in which they have an ownership interest, shall disclose their status as both owners/landlords and as REALTORS® or real estate licensees. *(Amended 1/93)*

- **Standard of Practice 12-7**
Only REALTORS® who participated in the transaction as the listing broker or cooperating broker (selling broker) may claim to have "sold" the property. Prior to closing, a cooperating broker may post a "sold" sign only with the consent of the listing broker. *(Amended 1/96)*

Article 13

REALTORS® shall not engage in activities that constitute the unauthorized practice of law and shall recommend that legal counsel be obtained when the interest of any party to the transaction requires it.

Article 14

If charged with unethical practice or asked to present evidence or to cooperate in any other way, in any professional standards proceeding or investigation, REALTORS® shall place all pertinent facts before the proper tribunals of the Member Board or affiliated institute, society, or council in which membership is held and shall take no action to disrupt or obstruct such processes. *(Amended 1/99)*

- **Standard of Practice 14-1**
REALTORS® shall not be subject to disciplinary proceedings in more than one Board of REALTORS® or affiliated institute, society or council in which they hold membership with respect to alleged violations of the Code of Ethics relating to the same transaction or event. *(Amended 1/95)*

- **Standard of Practice 14-2**
REALTORS® shall not make any unauthorized disclosure or dissemination of the allegations, findings, or decision developed in connection with an ethics hearing or appeal or in connection with an arbitration hearing or procedural review. *(Amended 1/92)*

- **Standard of Practice 14-3**
REALTORS® shall not obstruct the Board's investigative or professional standards proceedings by instituting or threatening to institute actions for libel, slander or defamation against any party to a professional standards proceeding or their witnesses based on the filing of an arbitration request, an ethics complaint, or testimony given before any tribunal. *(Adopted 11/87, Amended 1/99)*

- **Standard of Practice 14-4**
  REALTORS® shall not intentionally impede the Board's investigative or disciplinary proceedings by filing multiple ethics complaints based on the same event or transaction. *(Adopted 11/88)*

Duties to REALTORS®

Article 15

REALTORS® shall not knowingly or recklessly make false or misleading statements about competitors, their businesses, or their business practices. *(Amended 1/92)*

- **Standard of Practice 15-1**
  REALTORS® shall not knowingly or recklessly file false or unfounded ethics complaints. *(Adopted 1/00)*

Article 16

REALTORS® shall not engage in any practice or take any action inconsistent with exclusive representation or exclusive brokerage relationship agreements that other REALTORS® have with clients. *(Amended 1/04)*

- **Standard of Practice 16-1**
  Article 16 is not intended to prohibit aggressive or innovative business practices which are otherwise ethical and does not prohibit disagreements with other REALTORS® involving commission, fees, compensation or other forms of payment or expenses. *(Adopted 1/93, Amended 1/95)*

- **Standard of Practice 16-2**
  Article 16 does not preclude REALTORS® from making general announcements to prospects describing their services and the terms of their availability even though some recipients may have entered into agency agreements or other exclusive relationships with another REALTOR®. A general telephone canvass, general mailing or distribution addressed to all prospects in a given geographical area or in a given profession, business, club, or organization, or other classification or group is deemed "general" for purposes of this standard. *(Amended 1/04)*

  Article 16 is intended to recognize as unethical two basic types of solicitations:

  First, telephone or personal solicitations of property owners who have been identified by a real estate sign, multiple listing compilation, or other information service as having exclusively listed their property with another REALTOR®; and

  Second, mail or other forms of written solicitations of prospects whose properties are exclusively listed with another REALTOR® when such solicitations are not part of a general mailing but are directed specifically to property owners identified through compilations of current listings, "for sale" or "for rent" signs, or other sources of information required by Article 3 and Multiple Listing Service rules to be made available to other REALTORS® under offers of subagency or cooperation. *(Amended 1/04)*

- **Standard of Practice 16-3**
  Article 16 does not preclude REALTORS® from contacting the client of another broker for the purpose of offering to provide, or entering into a contract to provide, a different type of real estate service unrelated to the type of service currently being provided (e.g., property management as opposed to brokerage) or from offering the same type of service for property not subject to other brokers' exclusive agreements. However, information received through a Multiple Listing Service or any other offer of cooperation may not be used to target clients of other REALTORS® to whom such offers to provide services may be made. *(Amended 1/04)*

- **Standard of Practice 16-4**
  REALTORS® shall not solicit a listing which is currently listed exclusively with another broker. However, if the listing broker, when asked by the REALTOR®, refuses to disclose the expiration date and nature of such listing; i.e., an exclusive right to sell, an exclusive agency, open listing, or other form of contractual agreement between the listing broker and the client, the REALTOR® may contact the owner to secure such information and may discuss the terms upon which the REALTOR® might take a future listing or, alternatively, may take a listing to become effective upon expiration of any existing exclusive listing. *(Amended 1/94)*

- **Standard of Practice 16-5**
  REALTORS® shall not solicit buyer/tenant agreements from buyers/tenants who are subject to exclusive buyer/tenant agreements. However, if asked by a REALTOR®, the broker refuses to disclose the expiration date of the exclusive buyer/tenant agreement, the REALTOR® may contact the buyer/tenant to secure such information and may discuss the terms upon which the REALTOR® might enter into a future buyer/tenant agreement or, alternatively, may enter into a buyer/tenant agreement to become effective upon the expiration of any existing exclusive buyer/tenant agreement. *(Adopted 1/94, Amended 1/98)*

- **Standard of Practice 16-6**
  When REALTORS® are contacted by the client of another REALTOR® regarding the creation of an exclusive relationship to provide the same type of service, and REALTORS® have not directly or indirectly initiated such discussions, they may discuss the terms upon which they might enter into a future agreement or, alternatively, may enter into an agreement which becomes effective upon expiration of any existing exclusive agreement. *(Amended 1/98)*

- **Standard of Practice 16-7**
  The fact that a prospect has retained a REALTOR® as an exclusive representative or exclusive broker in one or more past transactions does not preclude other REALTORS® from seeking such prospect's future business. *(Amended 1/04)*

- **Standard of Practice 16-8**
  The fact that an exclusive agreement has been entered into with a REALTOR® shall not preclude or inhibit any other REALTOR® from entering into a similar agreement after the expiration of the prior agreement. *(Amended 1/98)*

- **Standard of Practice 16-9**
  REALTORS®, prior to entering into a representation agreement, have an affirmative obligation to make reasonable efforts to determine whether the prospect is subject to a current, valid exclusive agreement to provide the same type of real estate service. *(Amended 1/04)*
- **Standard of Practice 16-10**
  REALTORS®, acting as buyer or tenant representatives or brokers, shall disclose that relationship to the seller/landlord's representative or broker at first contact and shall provide written confirmation of that disclosure to the seller/landlord's representative or broker not later than execution of a purchase agreement or lease. *(Amended 1/04)*
- **Standard of Practice 16-11**
  On unlisted property, REALTORS® acting as buyer/tenant representatives or brokers shall disclose that relationship to the seller/landlord at first contact for that buyer/tenant and shall provide written confirmation of such disclosure to the seller/landlord not later than execution of any purchase or lease agreement. *(Amended 1/04)*

  REALTORS® shall make any request for anticipated compensation from the seller/landlord at first contact. *(Amended 1/98)*
- **Standard of Practice 16-12**
  REALTORS®, acting as representatives or brokers of sellers/landlords or as subagents of listing brokers, shall disclose that relationship to buyers/tenants as soon as practicable and shall provide written confirmation of such disclosure to buyers/tenants not later than execution of any purchase or lease agreement. *(Amended 1/04)*
- **Standard of Practice 16-13**
  All dealings concerning property exclusively listed, or with buyer/tenants who are subject to an exclusive agreement shall be carried on with the client's representative or broker, and not with the client, except with the consent of the client's representative or broker or except where such dealings are initiated by the client.

  Before providing substantive services (such as writing a purchase offer or presenting a CMA) to prospects, REALTORS® shall ask prospects whether they are a party to any exclusive representation agreement. REALTORS® shall not knowingly provide substantive services concerning a prospective transaction to prospects who are parties to exclusive representation agreements, except with the consent of the prospects' exclusive representatives or at the direction of prospects. *(Adopted 1/93, Amended 1/04)*
- **Standard of Practice 16-14**
  REALTORS® are free to enter into contractual relationships or to negotiate with sellers/landlords, buyers/tenants or others who are not subject to an exclusive agreement but shall not knowingly obligate them to pay more than one commission except with their informed consent. *(Amended 1/98)*
- **Standard of Practice 16-15**
  In cooperative transactions REALTORS® shall compensate cooperating REALTORS® (principal brokers) and shall not compensate nor offer to compensate, directly or indirectly, any of the sales licensees employed by or affiliated with other REALTORS® without the prior express knowledge and consent of the cooperating broker.
- **Standard of Practice 16-16**
  REALTORS®, acting as subagents or buyer/tenant representatives or brokers, shall not use the terms of an offer to purchase/lease to attempt to modify the listing broker's offer of compensation to subagents or buyer/tenant representatives or brokers nor make the submission of an executed offer to purchase/lease contingent on the listing broker's agreement to modify the offer of compensation. *(Amended 1/04)*
- **Standard of Practice 16-17**
  REALTORS®, acting as subagents or as buyer/tenant representatives or brokers, shall not attempt to extend a listing broker's offer of cooperation and/or compensation to other brokers without the consent of the listing broker. *(Amended 1/04)*
- **Standard of Practice 16-18**
  REALTORS® shall not use information obtained from listing brokers through offers to cooperate made through multiple listing services or through other offers of cooperation to refer listing brokers' clients to other brokers or to create buyer/tenant relationships with listing brokers' clients, unless such use is authorized by listing brokers. *(Amended 1/02)*
- **Standard of Practice 16-19**
  Signs giving notice of property for sale, rent, lease, or exchange shall not be placed on property without consent of the seller/landlord. *(Amended 1/93)*
- **Standard of Practice 16-20**
  REALTORS®, prior to or after terminating their relationship with their current firm, shall not induce clients of their current firm to cancel exclusive contractual agreements between the client and that firm. This does not preclude REALTORS® (principals) from establishing agreements with their associated licensees governing assignability of exclusive agreements. *(Adopted 1/98)*

Article 17

In the event of contractual disputes or specific non-contractual disputes as defined in Standard of Practice 17-4 between REALTORS® (principals) associated with different firms, arising out of their relationship as REALTORS®, the REALTORS® shall submit the dispute to arbitration in accordance with the regulations of their Board or Boards rather than litigate the matter.

In the event clients of REALTORS® wish to arbitrate contractual disputes arising out of real estate transactions, REALTORS® shall arbitrate those disputes in accordance with the regulations of their Board, provided the clients agree to be bound by the decision.

The obligation to participate in arbitration contemplated by this Article includes the obligation of REALTORS® (principals) to cause their firms to arbitrate and be bound by any award. *(Amended 1/01)*

- **Standard of Practice 17-1**
  The filing of litigation and refusal to withdraw from it by REALTORS® in an arbitrable matter constitutes a refusal to arbitrate. *(Adopted 2/86)*
- **Standard of Practice 17-2**
  Article 17 does not require REALTORS® to arbitrate in those circumstances when all parties to the dispute advise the Board in writing that they choose not to arbitrate before the Board. *(Amended 1/93)*
- **Standard of Practice 17-3**
  REALTORS®, when acting solely as principals in a real estate transaction, are not obligated to arbitrate disputes with other REALTORS® absent a specific written agreement to the contrary. *(Adopted 1/96)*
- **Standard of Practice 17-4**
  Specific non-contractual disputes that are subject to arbitration pursuant to Article 17 are:

  1) Where a listing broker has compensated a cooperating broker and another cooperating broker subsequently claims to be the procuring cause of the sale or lease. In such cases the complainant may name the first cooperating broker as respondent and arbitration may proceed without the listing broker being named as a respondent. Alternatively, if the complaint is brought against the listing broker, the listing broker may name the first cooperating broker as a third-party respondent. In either instance the decision of the hearing panel as to procuring cause shall be conclusive with respect to all current or subsequent claims of the parties for compensation arising out of the underlying cooperative transaction. *(Adopted 1/97)*

  2) Where a buyer or tenant representative is compensated by the seller or landlord, and not by the listing broker, and the listing broker, as a result, reduces the commission owed by the seller or landlord and, subsequent to such actions, another cooperating broker claims to be the procuring cause of sale or lease. In such cases the complainant may name the first cooperating broker as respondent and arbitration may proceed without the listing broker being named as a respondent. Alternatively, if the complaint is brought against the listing broker, the listing broker may name the first cooperating broker as a third-party respondent. In either instance the decision of the hearing panel as to procuring cause shall be conclusive with respect to all current or subsequent claims of the parties for compensation arising out of the underlying cooperative transaction. *(Adopted 1/97)*

  3) Where a buyer or tenant representative is compensated by the buyer or tenant and, as a result, the listing broker reduces the commission owed by the seller or landlord and, subsequent to such actions, another cooperating broker claims to be the procuring cause of sale or lease. In such cases the complainant may name the first cooperating broker as respondent and arbitration may proceed without the listing broker being named as a respondent. Alternatively, if the complaint is brought against the listing broker, the listing broker may name the first cooperating broker as a third-party respondent. In either instance the decision of the hearing panel as to procuring cause shall be conclusive with respect to all current or subsequent claims of the parties for compensation arising out of the underlying cooperative transaction. *(Adopted 1/97)*

  4) Where two or more listing brokers claim entitlement to compensation pursuant to open listings with a seller or landlord who agrees to participate in arbitration (or who requests arbitration) and who agrees to be bound by the decision. In cases where one of the listing brokers has been compensated by the seller or landlord, the other listing broker, as complainant, may name the first listing broker as respondent and arbitration may proceed between the brokers. *(Adopted 1/97)*

The Code of Ethics was adopted in 1913. Amended at the Annual Convention in 1924, 1928, 1950, 1951, 1952, 1955, 1956, 1961, 1962, 1974, 1982, 1986, 1987, 1989, 1990, 1991, 1992, 1993, 1994, 1995, 1996, 1997, 1998, 1999, 2000, 2001, 2002 and 2003.

Explanatory Notes

The reader should be aware of the following policies which have been approved by the Board of Directors of the National Association:

In filing a charge of an alleged violation of the Code of Ethics by a REALTOR®, the charge must read as an alleged violation of one or more Articles of the Code. Standards of Practice may be cited in support of the charge.

The Standards of Practice serve to clarify the ethical obligations imposed by the various Articles and supplement, and do not substitute for, the Case Interpretations in *Interpretations of the Code of Ethics*.

Modifications to existing Standards of Practice and additional new Standards of Practice are approved from time to time. Readers are cautioned to ensure that the most recent publications are utilized.

© 2004, NATIONAL ASSOCIATION OF REALTORS®, All Rights Reserved
Form No. 166-288 (12/03)

Published with the consent of the NATIONAL ASSOCIATION OF REALTORS®, author of and owner of all rights in the Code of Ethics of the NATIONAL ASSOCIATION OF REALTORS®, © NATIONAL ASSOCIATION OF REALTORS® 2004—All Rights Reserved.

The NATIONAL ASSOCIATION OF REALTORS® reserves exclusively unto itself the right to officially comment on and interpret the CODE and particular provisions thereof. For the NATIONAL ASSOCIATION'S official interpretations of the CODE see INTERPRETATIONS OF THE CODE OF ETHICS; NATIONAL ASSOCIATION OF REALTORS®.

CHAPTER THREE

NEW JERSEY LICENSE LAWS

INTRODUCTION

This selective summary contains highlights of The New Jersey Real Estate License Act and The Rules and Regulations of the New Jersey Real Estate Commission. **It is meant only to assist you in focusing your study and should not be thought of as a substitute for reviewing the entire applicable statutes and regulations.** It should also be noted that this is a restructured summary and does not appear in statutory or regulatory order, and is not always written in statutory language. Interpretive comments and examples contained in it are the author's.

As a consumer, it is beneficial to know the safeguards that have been enacted by the Legislature and the Real Estate Commission to protect the public with respect to real estate transactions. An informed consumer is better able to protect his own interest by knowing what a licensee should and should not be doing. Prospective licensees will benefit from learning this information, as it will alert them to their responsibilities and serve as important preparatory material for the New Jersey real estate license examinations.

The New Jersey Real Estate License Act (1921) was designed to license and regulate brokers and salespersons and to establish a Real Estate Commission, further empowered to develop rules and regulations to protect the public. All licensees are bound by the provisions of the License Act and by the Rules and Regulations of the New Jersey Real Estate Commission.

REAL ESTATE COMMISSION

The New Jersey Real Estate Commission (NJREC) operates as a Division of the Department of Banking and Insurance, which is responsible for providing the Commission with personnel and operating funds. The day-to-day business of this Division is under the control of an executive secretary (executive director) who is appointed by the governor and who receives a salary. The Division maintains records, which are open to public inspection, handles licensing matters and public inquiries, investigates complaints, provides for licensee regulation and monitors out-of-state land sales to our residents.

The Commission consists of eight members, all appointed by the governor for a term of three years except the governmental designee. Five of the members must be real estate brokers who have been both brokers and state residents for ten years prior to appointment. Two are public members who may not be real estate licensees, and the final member is the governmental designee who is an employee of an appropriate state department and serves at the pleasure of the governor. All members have voting power and a majority of the members constitutes a quorum. The commissioners select one of their members to serve as president of the Commission, who serves as presiding officer at all hearings. Commissioners receive compensation for their service, which is on a part-time basis, with the president receiving higher compensation than the other members. The governmental designee does not receive compensation, as he or she is already a state employee.

The Commission functions as a quasi-judicial body and may issue a subpoena to any person, administer oaths and conduct hearings in the aid of its investigations. The Commission may call upon any licensee to produce records pertinent to its investigations. The Commission may initiate an investigation based upon a complaint or upon its own motion. The Commission serves to develop rules and regulations, provides interpretations of current rules and regulations affecting licensees, holds public hearings, hears appeals of decisions made by the full-time Commission staff and decides upon disciplinary action which may affect licensees. The Commission is assisted in its work by the full-time efforts of the Division's administrative, managerial and secretarial staff.

TYPES OF REAL ESTATE LICENSES

Unless exempt, a person cannot engage in any aspect of handling real estate belonging to others without a license. The Commission issues three types of real estate licenses:

A licensed **broker** is any person or *firm* who, for a commission or other valuable consideration, engages in listing, selling, buying, renting, negotiating, exchanging or auctioning the real estate of others. The use of the term "broker" refers to one who operates his or her own business. Every resident real estate broker not licensed as a broker-salesperson must maintain a main office for the transaction of business in New Jersey, which must be open to the public during normal business hours. The main office must have prominently displayed therein the license certificate of the broker and all licensed persons in his employ. The broker must give the pocket card that accompanies the license to all licensees and they must have the card in their possession at all times when engaging in the business of real estate.

If a broker maintains more than one place of business, a separate **branch office license** is required for each office, and the branch office must be under proper supervision of a licensed broker-salesperson.

A **broker-salesperson** is any individual who has satisfied the experience requirement (explained below) and has passed the state examination for broker, but is employed by and operates under the supervision of a licensed real estate broker in a sales capacity.

A **salesperson** is any individual who, for a commission or valuable consideration, is employed by a broker to buy, sell, rent or negotiate the real estate of others. Salespersons must work under the supervision of a broker and may not normally work for more than one broker at the same time. A salesperson may not accept a commission or other compensation from anyone other than his or her employing broker. A salesperson may never function in the real estate business on his own, but must work under the supervision and control of a broker.

A salesperson may transfer his license to another broker by paying a minimal transfer fee. A new license will be issued showing the name of the salesperson and the new employing broker.

If a salesperson is terminated, discharged or otherwise leaves the employ of the broker, the employing broker must return the license to the Commission within five days. The broker must advise the salesperson that this has been done by writing to his last known address. A copy of this letter must accompany the returned license when forwarded to the Commission. (Provisions for expediting license transfers are discussed below.)

Licenses for salespersons and broker-salespersons may only be issued to natural persons and not in the name of a firm. The term **licensee**, as used in this chapter, refers to anyone who holds a real estate license, regardless of type.

EXEMPTIONS

The following are exempt from the requirement of having to obtain a license:

- owners, lessors (landlords) and New Jersey attorneys;
- all persons acting in a legal capacity such as receivers, trustees, executors, administrators or persons selling real estate under the order of any court or the terms of a deed or trust;
- banks, trust companies and insurance companies located within the state; and
- an employee engaged by an owner to "manage" his property, providing:
  - the employee engages in property management activity in pursuit of the employer's general business;
  - the employee performs additional activities for the employer such as bookkeeping, purchasing, etc.; and
  - the employee is paid based upon the employer's obligation to pay compensation in the absence of any rental activity.

Such persons and entities are exempt from the provisions of the License Act only insofar as they are acting within their usual capacities, For example, the exemption for attorneys only authorizes attorneys to sell or rent real estate incidental to their normal practice of law. If an attorney wishes to open a real estate office and solicit listings, he would have to qualify for real estate licensure. Unlicensed persons may not represent themselves as being licensed.

ACTIVITIES REQUIRING LICENSURE

Anyone engaging in the real estate business on a full- or part-time basis must be licensed, and any single act constitutes engaging in the real estate business. The following activities are covered:

- listing real estate for sale;
- selling, exchanging, purchasing, renting or auctioning real estate;
- collecting rent and managing income-producing properties;
- negotiating a loan to be secured by a mortgage;
- selling businesses that involve an interest in real estate, including negotiation of a new lease or the assignment of an existing lease;
- selling lots for an owner for a salary or commission; or
- attempting to do any of the above.

LICENSING PROCEDURE

Qualifications

Salesperson—18 years of age, high school education or equivalent, successfully complete 75 hours of instruction in an approved school, pass a state examination, furnish evidence of good moral character and sponsored for licensure by a New Jersey broker. The Commission recommends that a complete investigative report be made of the applicant's background. A salesperson candidate must be a legal resident of the United States, but does not have to be a citizen.

Broker—18 years of age, high school education or equivalent, three years full-time experience under the supervision of a broker immediately preceding date of application for broker's license, successfully complete 150 hours of instruction in an approved school concurrent with the holding of a salesperson's license and pass a state examination. A broker candidate must be a legal resident of the United States, but need not be a citizen. The three-year experience required to qualify for licensure as a broker must be full-time during normal business hours, meaning at least 40 hours per week, between the hours of approximately 10 A.M. to 8 P.M. any five of seven days in the week. However, no more than 25 hours per week of non-real estate employment may be engaged in during this three-year period.

Criminal History Record Check

All applicants for licensure must submit a "Request for Criminal History Record Information" to the Commission, accompanied by the required fee. Conviction for certain crimes may preclude licensure, as is detailed later.

Examinations

Applicants for broker and salesperson licenses must pass a licensing examination, designated by the Commission, which is administered weekly by an independent testing service. If required, the applicant may repeat the examination without the need of further instruction. The applicant may only sit for the examination, however, after having presented evidence of satisfactory completion of an appropriate approved course of instruction or if an educational waiver has been obtained. Such evidence is good for only one year from the date the applicant has completed such instruction. An applicant who fails to pass the examination and make application for licensure during that time must complete the required instruction again in order to requalify.

Waiver of Educational Requirement

The educational requirement may be waived at the discretion of the Commission if: the applicant holds a broker's license in another state; was previously licensed as a New Jersey real estate broker within the last five years; presents evidence of equivalent real estate courses in college; or is a New Jersey attorney. The waiver, when granted, is for the educational requirement only. There is no test waiver.

Payment of Fees

Applicants for licensure shall pay application and license fees and a Guaranty Fund payment to the Commission as required by current regulation. All real estate licenses must be renewed biennially on July 1, in odd-numbered years. Licenses renewed after this date require an additional payment of a late fee.

Failure to Renew License

If a broker or salesperson license is not renewed for two consecutive years from the expiration date of the license last held, the license would be cancelled. Such persons will have to requalify for licensure as if they had never been licensed. A license is active only when the license fee is paid and the license is being held by a broker. Licenses returned to the Commission are deemed to be inactive.

Licensing of Particular Veterans

Veterans who were wounded or disabled in the line of duty may qualify for a broker's license by completing an approved program in real estate and passing the broker's test. The experience requirement and all license fees are waived. Veterans should contact the Commission prior to embarking on any such program to determine if they qualify and to obtain approval for the course work they intend to pursue.

Temporary Broker's License

Upon the death or mental or physical incapacity of the broker of record or employing broker, if no other person in the firm holds a broker's license, the Commission may issue a temporary broker's license to a salesperson with three years full-time experience immediately preceding the date of application. The application for the temporary license must be made within 30 days of the broker's death or incapacity. The temporary license is valid for one year, with no extensions of time permitted.

Partnerships and Corporations

Broker's licenses issued to entities shall require at least one of the partners or corporate officers to qualify as **broker of record**. If such person leaves the employ of the firm, a new qualified broker of record must be named. All real estate activities of the corporation or partnership and its salespersons shall be under the supervision of the broker of record.

Non-resident Licensing

Residents of other states may be licensed, but are required to provide an executed irrevocable consent form agreeing to be open to suit in our state courts if they violate our license laws or rules and regulations.

Substitute Sponsor

The Commission grants to brokers of record or employing brokers the right to have initial applications for licenses of salespersons and broker-salespersons sponsored by one person other than the broker of record or employing broker. This other person must be a licensed broker and an officer of the corporation or a partner in the partnership, as the case may be. If the employing broker is a sole proprietor, the designee must be a licensed broker-salesperson in the employ of the employing broker. A formal **power of attorney** must be filed with the Commission if a broker wishes to authorize another person to execute initial license documents on his or her behalf.

Employing broker or broker of record may also designate one employee to execute on his behalf documents required to effectuate the transfer of the license of a salesperson or broker-salesperson, or to sign the license of terminating employees who are not transferring their license. The employing broker or broker of record must, on a form provided by the Commission, notify the Commission of the person so authorized. Such person does not have to be the holder of a real estate license. Designees may not sign experience reports for broker applicants.

License Lending

Lending of license for the benefit of another or attempting to circumvent statute or regulation by such action is forbidden. Lending of license shall be construed to include any arrangement whereby the broker fails to personally oversee and direct the operations of the business for which he is broker of record. Oversight requires the broker to be physically present in the main office location of the firm at least one day each week (excluding vacations and emergencies). Extended communication by telephone or mail may be considered as evidence of license lending.

Refusal to Issue License

The Commission may refuse to issue a license to anyone convicted of "money offenses" within five years of application for licensure. Such offenses include forgery, burglary, any theft and related offense with the exception of shoplifting, criminal conspiracy to defraud or other like offenses. "Like offenses" have been construed by the Real Estate Commission to include offenses involving dishonesty, particularly in business relationships. Candidates may also be refused licensure if their background includes such offenses which would not meet the test of good moral character, such as crimes of violence.

The Rehabilitated Convicted Offenders Act supersedes the five-year prohibition against licensure. If an applicant can submit sufficient evidence of rehabilitation under standards provided by this act and can demonstrate good moral character, a license may be issued.

Applicants who have been convicted of crimes, misdemeanors or disorderly person offenses must reveal them on their license application. Applicants convicted of offenses in the past whose records have been expunged are not required to disclose such offenses on a real estate license application.

Display of Licenses

All licenses must be conspicuously displayed in the main office of the firm and shall be available for inspection.

Pocket Cards

When a new license or a license renewal is issued, a wallet-size card identifying the holder as a real estate licensee accompanies it. The Real Estate Commission requires that the licensee obtain this pocket card from the broker, sign it and carry it when conducting real estate business. The public has been advised by the Commission to seek this identification as evidence of licensure and also as a safety precaution prior to allowing one purporting to be a licensee to enter the premises.

License Transfer Procedures

If a licensee transfers from one broker to another and requests that the license be given to him instead of being returned to the Commission, the procedure is as follows:

- The rear of the license is signed and dated by the terminating broker before it is given to the departing licensee.
- When the license is given to the departing licensee, the termination section of the license, showing the date of termination, is completed, signed and retained by the employing broker.
- Within five days of delivery of the license to the departing licensee, the terminating broker must mail to the Commission the completed and signed termination section of the license and send a copy of it to the departing licensee at his last known address. When the transferring licensee receives the license from the terminating broker, he may then take the license to the new employing broker.

Before the licensee can start to work for the new broker, that broker must:

- Enter on the license, in the appropriate spot, the effective date of the individual's employment with that broker and sign the license as the new employing broker;
- Detach the temporary license stub portion and display it with the other persons licensed with that broker; and
- Mail to the Commission the dated and signed license of the transferring individual with a check for $25 to cover the license transfer fee.

GUARANTY FUND

The Guaranty Fund is a state-regulated fund used to indemnify aggrieved participants in real estate transactions. The law provides for recovery from the fund for any person who suffers a loss due to the embezzlement, conversion or unlawful obtaining of money or property by a licensed real estate broker, broker-salesperson or real estate salesperson or an unlicensed employee of a real estate broker. To provide money to sustain the fund, brokers are assessed a one-time fee of $20 and salespersons $10 upon the initial issuance or first renewal of a license.

An aggrieved party could recover from the fund after a civil action against the broker or salesperson resulted in an unsatisfied judgment and the court then ordered the Real Estate Guaranty Fund to pay. No order shall be entered unless the claimant files a certification affirming that a criminal complaint alleging misappropriation of funds by the licensee or unlicensed employee has been filed with a law enforcement agency in New Jersey. The suit must be commenced within six years from the date of the fraudulent act, and the Real Estate Commission would be joined as a necessary party to any such civil action.

Upon issuance of a court order for payment from the fund, the license of the broker or salesperson responsible for the claim would be revoked and would not be eligible for reinstatement until the judgment was satisfied in full, including reimbursement to the fund together with interest. Reasonable attorney fees and costs may also be included as part of the judgment and attorneys may request an advance fee from the fund when bringing an action on a client's behalf. Special assessments may be made from time to time to replenish the fund if it becomes too seriously depleted. There is a $20,000 limitation on recovery for any one claim against the fund.

Excess funds which accumulate beyond projected need may be used for educational and research purposes at the discretion of the Commission.

GENERAL OPERATION OF THE REAL ESTATE BUSINESS

Places of Business

Every resident broker not licensed as a broker-salesperson must maintain an approved place of business in this state. The office must be open during normal business hours. The name of the broker of record or employing broker and the words "Licensed Real Estate Broker" must be conspicuously displayed on the outside of the building. If a broker's place of business is located at his residence, the office must be separated from the living quarters and have its own exterior entrance which is visible from the street on which the building fronts. No broker may have an office at the home of any of his salespersons or broker-salespersons.

Branch Offices

A duplicate license must be obtained for each branch office showing the name of the broker and the address of the branch office. The license must be conspicuously displayed at all times in the office. Each branch must be under the supervision of a broker employed as a broker-salesperson by the employing broker or broker of record of the firm, who shall devote full time to the management of the office during normal business hours. The individual supervising the office must have his name prominently displayed with the title "Office Supervisor," and the name must be recorded at the Commission. The names of all other licensees doing business at the branch office shall be similarly displayed.

It is not acceptable for one supervisor to simply visit several branches a few times each week. Regular on-site management is required at each office. The branch office supervisor is required to be physically present in the office at least five days per week, during which time he may not otherwise be employed in a job that requires him to be present in another location during that time. When the supervising broker is away from the office, he must provide sufficient information to allow personnel to communicate with him at all times.

Change of Business Location

The broker must notify the Commission of any change of business location. A minimal transfer fee is required for the new license to the broker and all persons licensed under the broker, each of which will show the new authorized address. Failure to notify the Commission of change of address will result in cancellation of the broker's license.

Employment Agreements

No salesperson may commence operations for a broker and no broker may authorize a salesperson to act on his or her behalf until a written employment agreement has been signed by the broker and the salesperson (or broker-salesperson). Such terms must include, but need not be limited to, the following:

- rate of compensation to be paid the salesperson;
- promise by the broker to pay commissions owed within 10 business days of their receipt or as soon thereafter as the funds have cleared the broker's bank (broker shall provide written explanation to salesperson for the failure to pay any such monies as provided);
- rate of compensation to be paid on transactions which close subsequent to salesperson's termination with the broker; and
- provision that any future changes in the agreement will not be binding unless they are contained in writing signed by both parties.

A copy of the agreement must be provided to the salesperson upon commencement of employment ,and the broker must maintain the original as a business record. Compensation paid to brokers must be deposited in the broker's general business account within five business days.

Upon termination of employment, broker shall provide a complete accounting in writing of all monies due the salesperson as of the date of termination and/or those which may become due in the future. In the event any sums so accounted for are not in accord with the terms of the post-termination agreement, the broker must give a complete and comprehensive written explanation of any difference to the salesperson with the accounting not later than 30 days after termination.

The broker shall maintain all the records cited above, along with adequate proof of delivery to the salesperson, for **six years**. In situations where the Commission confirms that a broker has complied with all requirements imposed, the Commission will not further investigate a complaint alleging non-payment of a commission by a broker to a salesperson unless accompanied by a copy of an arbitration decision or the equivalent, or a copy of a judgment of a court secured by the salesperson against the broker. Unless appealed, the failure of the broker to pay monies awarded to a salesperson under terms of such decision or judgment within 30 days of its effective date shall subject the broker to disciplinary action.

Prohibition against Discrimination in Provision of Services

No licensee shall deny real estate brokerage services to any person for reasons of race, religion, sex, marital status, national origin or because a person is handicapped. "Handicapped" is defined as anyone having a physical or mental impairment that substantially limits one or more major life activities. This has been interpreted to include persons with AIDS or HIV infection, but does not include current, illegal use of or addiction to a controlled substance. The definitions of "handicapped" are consistent under state and federal laws.

Office Closing Procedures

When a broker of record or employing broker ceases to be active in the operation of a real estate office, the broker must immediately return his license to the Commission and the licenses of all salespersons and broker-salespersons for cancellation, accompanied by a copy of the requisite termination letter described above. Procedures also describe requirements for closing out and disbursing contents of trust accounts, payments of commissions owed, notification to principals that the business is ceasing operation and the location at which permanent transaction records will be stored for six years. Similar procedures are also specified when the ownership of a business is being transferred from one licensee to another. In cases of office closing or transfer, the licensee(s) involved must certify by affidavit to the Real Estate Commission that all requirements have been met.

COMMISSIONS

Brokers may not sue for commissions unless they were licensed at all times during the transaction. The Real Estate Commission will not intervene in contractual disputes between licensees regarding commissions and it does not regulate the fees that licensees charge for their services. Salespersons and broker-salespersons are prohibited from accepting a commission from any person except their employer, who must be a licensed broker.

Commission regulations deal with the broker's compensation agreements in three categories: (a) brokers and the general public; (b) brokers and other brokers; and (c) brokers and licensees in their employ.

General Public

The listing agreement must contain, in large type, the following statement:

"As seller you have the right to individually reach an agreement on any fee, commission or valuable consideration with your broker. No fee, commission or valuable consideration has been fixed by any governmental authority or by any trade association or the multiple listing service."

To this end, no listing or contract of sale shall contain a pre-printed fee or commission rate, nor shall any such writing contain a commission clause that suggests a rate or fee, such as the use of a pre-printed percent sign next to a blank space, which would imply that the commission would have to be a percentage of the sale price, when it could be a negotiated flat fee instead. The listing broker must disclose to the seller the rate or amount of commission split with other licensees.

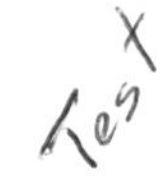

Net listings are expressly forbidden. A net listing is a listing in which the broker's commission is equal to the difference between the sale price and an agreed upon (net) price specified by the seller. This type of arrangement is prohibited in New Jersey.

Salespersons and broker-salespersons have no ability to sue the client for a commission. The principal is only obligated to pay a commission to the broker.

Other Brokers

Price Fixing. Licensees must not conspire, suggest or recommend to any other licensee(s) that any rate, commission or fee charged by them be fixed, maintained, established or otherwise stabilized. Such activity is also a violation of the Sherman Antitrust Act, which will be discussed in Chapter 12.

Broker Cooperation. All brokers, whether residential, industrial or commercial, must fully cooperate with all other brokers through normal cooperation arrangements, which must promote the seller's interest. Listing brokers shall not place unreasonable restrictions on listed property for co-op brokers. An owner who does not wish the listing broker to cooperate must so state in writing by signing a **Waiver of Broker Cooperation** form (see page 214). This form must be made available for inspection by other brokers upon request.

While there may be some special circumstances which might cause a property not to be made available for broker cooperation, generally it is clearly in the seller's best interest to permit broker cooperation. Brokers may not suggest noncooperation simply because they want to get the full commission on the sale. Such self-centered, unethical action is clearly not in the seller's best interest and is cause for disciplinary action by the Commission.

Discriminatory Commission Splits. Licensees shall not discriminate in commission splits paid to other brokers and shall maintain a written file showing why such commission splits varied from the company norm.

Commissions to Non-resident Brokers. A commission or referral fee may be paid to, and received from, a non-resident broker, as long as the nonresident is a duly licensed broker in another jurisdiction in which he maintains an office.

Salesperson Compensation

No salesperson may accept a fee or a valuable consideration from any person for performing real estate activities other than his licensed employing broker. All commissions due salespersons must be paid within ten days after they are received by the broker from the client unless the salesperson and broker have an agreement to the contrary. In all other cases, commission disputes between brokers and salespersons must be resolved between the parties themselves, as the Commission will not act in these matters.

ADVERTISING

The purpose of the advertising regulations is to protect the public against advertising that might serve to be false and misleading.

General Regulations

Advertising regulations are designed to protect the public from being misled. The regulations apply to all types of advertising including publications, radio and television broadcasts, E-mail and the Internet, business cards and stationery, signs and billboards.

Ads placed by licensees must show the broker's regular business name and contain words that would indicate that the ad was placed by a person engaged in the real estate business such as broker, real estate broker, real estate agency, Realtor® or Realtist®. Ads that omit the names and addresses of the persons placing them (blind ads) are prohibited.

No advertisement or application may directly or indirectly specify any limitation regarding race, religion, creed, color, sex, affectional or sexual orientation, marital status, familial status, national origin, ancestry or physical or mental handicap.

Ads that refer to amounts, down payments, monthly payments, taxes or mortgage money available must contain the words "to a qualified buyer," so that the buyer-borrower will clearly understand that the advertised terms are available only under certain conditions. In addition, the amounts must be followed by the words "approximate" or "estimated." If such amounts are mentioned, the broker must maintain proof of the validity of the statements for one year.

No free offering, including the offering of a free appraisal, may be made in any advertisement or promotional material. Words such as "included" or "included in the purchase price" may be used when referring to items included by the owner when selling or renting real estate. Free offers that are ancillary to the real estate transaction, such as the offering of a free comparative market analysis (CMA) or items of token value such as calendars or pens, are not prohibited. An appraisal is defined as a complete study and analysis of property value by a licensed appraiser and is not synonymous with a competitive market analysis or market study. Such CMAs may be advertised and are frequently offered by licensees in order to assist in obtaining listings.

A recent amendment to NJSA 45:15-17 (g) provides that, subject to certain restrictions, licensees may include offers of free or discounted products or services in their advertising and promotional material. Licensees who intend to include such offers in their advertising or promotional material should be aware that the amended law prohibits:

1. making the receipt of any free or discounted products or services contingent upon a consumer signing a listing agreement, a sale contract, or other type of real estate contract;
2. offering a lot or parcel or lots or parcels for advertising purposes; and
3. offering free or discounted products or services as part of a lottery, a contest, a drawing or a game.

In addition, licensees must disclose in writing any compensation received for such promotion or offer. Such disclosure must be provided no later than when the promotion or offer is extended by the broker to the consumer.

Brokers may not indicate in any ad or sign that a property has been "sold" until after the closing has taken place and the title has been transferred. Words like "too late," "gone" or "sale pending" are misleading and must not be used.

Except for magazine or newspaper ads under municipality headings, all ads must specify the municipality within which the property is located. If a vicinity has been mentioned in an ad, the exact municipal location of the property must also be shown, so that the prospect is not misled.

Advertisements containing the name of a salesperson should use care to ensure that the salesperson is not thought to be the broker. With the exception of business cards, all advertisements that contain the name of a salesperson must also include, in larger print, the regular business name of the broker.

The business card of a licensed salesperson must indicate that the licensee is a salesperson by use of the words "salesperson" or "sales associate" or "sales representative," or where permitted by law, "realtor associate" or "realtist associate." The business card of a broker must indicate that the licensee is a broker by use of the word broker or, where permitted by law, Realtor® or Realtist®.

No licensee shall publish any advertisement or place any sign which makes reference to the availability of a specific property which is exclusively listed for sale by another broker unless the licensee obtains the prior written consent of the listing broker. Such consent shall not be given or withheld by the listing broker without the knowledge of the owner.

Licensees shall not conspire to boycott media who advertise commissions or fees of other licensees that are of a competitive or discount nature.

If a Web page is established by a salesperson or broker-salesperson and it is not linked electronically to the Web page of the broker under which he or she is licensed, it must display the telephone number and may display the street address of the brokerage office from which the individual operates. If the Web page of a salesperson or broker-salesperson is linked to the Web page of the broker under whose supervision he or she operates, it must display information that clearly indicates how to link to the broker.

The only location that can be advertised is the licensed main office or a licensed branch office from which the advertising licensee conducts real estate business. Salespersons and broker-salespersons are prohibited from making any reference to a "home office" in any advertising.

Franchisee and Trade Name Advertising

Insignia or trade names may not imply common management or ownership unless this is actually the case.

Licensees using a franchise trade name must include the legend "Each office independently owned and operated" in all advertising except sale signs and small classified (spot) ads.

Advertising referring to membership in a Multiple Listing Service must specify the complete name of the listing service in all advertising, except for sale signs, small classified ads, business cards and business signs.

Home Warranty Advertising

Home warranty advertising shall specify whether the warranty is by inspection or non-inspection, whether the warranty is mandatory and whether the purchaser is responsible for the payment of the warranty.

SAFEGUARDING FUNDS

Trust (Escrow) Accounts

Brokerage firms are required to maintain a trust account for the purpose of holding funds belonging to others relative to transactions in which they are engaged. Otherwise the broker would be considered guilty of commingling. Trust accounts may be maintained only in Commission-approved depository institutions physically located and authorized to do business in this state. The names and addresses of all financial institutions holding broker trust accounts, accompanied by all account numbers, must be filed with the Commission by affidavit or certification with application or renewal for broker's license.

A broker may maintain one trust account into which all qualified monies may be deposited, so long as careful accounting is kept as to the amounts belonging to each party. Separate interest-bearing trust accounts are also permitted, so long as the account is clearly identified as being related to a particular transaction. Brokers acting as temporary custodians of such funds may not receive, obtain or use any interest earned on such funds for their own business or personal use. Depository institutions will only be approved upon providing the Commission with written confirmation that they will immediately notify the Commission in writing if a check or other instrument drawn on a broker's trust account is dishonored or returned for insufficient funds.

Every broker is responsible for maintaining a ledger book detailing all actions involving funds received and disbursed in his capacity as an escrow agent. Commission rules proscribe the proper procedure for maintenance of the ledger book and the trust account checkbook. Records must indicate the date, amount, payee and purpose of each disbursement and fully detail each separate trust account transaction. Trust account records, banking records and other transaction documents are subject to unannounced inspection by NJREC investigative staff.

When making an inspection, a Commission investigator will carefully scrutinize the trust account ledger book. Under NJAC 11:5-5.4, all New Jersey real estate brokers are required to maintain a ledger book recording the activity in their trust accounts in addition to notations made in the checkbooks of such accounts. A sample page from a trust account ledger book is shown as Figure 3.1.

Every licensee who is paid monies to be held in trust by a broker shall only accept such monies if they are in the form of cash or a negotiable instrument payable to the trust account of the broker through whom the individual is licensed. (A check cannot be accepted when it is made payable to a broker-salesperson or a salesperson.) The licensee shall immediately upon the receipt of the funds account for or deliver them to the broker for deposit into the trust account.

The principal broker is responsible for all trust fund monies, however, he may authorize a salesperson in writing to deposit client monies on his behalf. The broker may also authorize a person other than himself to make withdrawals, but in

FIGURE 3.1

Trust/Escrow Ledger

Reproduced below is a sample page from a trust (escrow) account ledger book. Pursuant to Commission rule 11.5-5.4, all New Jersey real estate brokers are required to maintain a ledger book recording the activity in their trust accounts in addition to notations made in checkbooks of such accounts. The sample below provides for the entry of all of the information required to be maintained in the ledger book. The sample was prepared by the Real Estate Commission in an effort to assist brokers in complying with the requirements of the rule.

STREET ADDRESS	TOWN	COUNTY	STATE	ZIP CODE	☐ SALE ☐ RENTAL

SELLER/LANDLORD	PURCHASER/TENANT
NAME ____________	NAME ____________
ADDRESS ____________	ADDRESS ____________
CITY ____________ STATE ______ ZIP ______	CITY ____________ STATE ______ ZIP ______
TELEPHONE (HOME) ____________ (WORK) ____________	TELEPHONE (HOME) ____________ (WORK) ____________

MISC. COMMENTS

DATE	RECEIVED FROM/ON BEHALF OF OR PAID TO	AMOUNT RECEIVED	RECEIVED BY	CHECK NO.	AMOUNT PAID	BALANCE

this case, the Commission must grant written permission.

Earnest Money Deposits

If a licensee believes that a seller may not be able to perform under the terms of the contract or be able to return funds paid on deposit, he must act to protect the purchaser's deposit by:

- placing the funds in the trust account; or
- having the purchaser sign a statement confirming his awareness of any risk involved in allowing the seller to hold the deposit directly, recognizing that the licensee made no representations as to the solvency of the seller or his ability to return the deposit funds.

It is difficult to envision when it would not be in the buyer's best interest to have the deposit held in trust and it is standard practice in real estate resale transactions. Earnest money deposits may be held by a broker, an attorney, a financial institution, a title company or the owner of the property.

Commingling

Licensees are not permitted to commingle (mix) their personal or business funds with those of clients. Any of the following actions constitute commingling:

- failing to maintain a separate account for client and customer funds in an authorized institution;

- failing to promptly deposit monies received into this account ("promptly" is defined as within five business days after receipt of such funds); or
- failing to promptly segregate property belonging to others.

A nominal amount of business funds kept in the trust account to maintain continuity of the account does not constitute commingling.

Advance Fees

Brokers who collect advance fees in excess of $25.00 must give the client an itemized listing of expenditures and statement of account within 90 days.

OTHER LICENSEE RESPONSIBILITIES

Duplicate Originals—A duplicate original of all executed instruments must be delivered to all parties to the transaction immediately.

Obligation to Learn Pertinent Facts—Every licensee must make reasonable effort to ascertain pertinent facts about any property he lists or for which he accepts an agency, including, but not limited to, the general condition of the property and the financial qualifications of every person for whom he submits an offer to his client.

A reasonable effort to ascertain pertinent facts must include at least inquiries to the seller or seller's agent about physical conditions that may affect the property, and a visual inspection of the property. The licensee therefore should not take listings sight unseen and when listing the property should make careful observation of the entire premises. While it is not the function of the licensee to perform the duties of a professional property inspector, he is bound to learn such things which could be known through a reasonable inspection of the property and by a thorough and detailed consultation with the owner.

Absolute Fidelity to Principal—As agent, the licensee is expected to represent the principal's interest. He owes absolute fidelity to the principal and honest dealing to all other parties to the transaction.

Submit All Written Offers Immediately—Licensees must transmit all formal written offers on a property within **24 hours** of receipt, and are encouraged to get written acknowledgment from the person receiving the offer indicating the date and time the offer was submitted. Licensees may never refuse to present offers, nor may they withhold them. If a prospect makes an oral offer, licensees should advise him that they are only bound to present formal offers reduced to writing. (While this is the procedure called for by regulation, the safest course for the licensee is simply to present all offers, either oral or written, promptly, as the licensee is always required to keep the principal informed of all pertinent facts regarding the transaction.)

Recommend Legal Counsel When Appropriate—Licensees must recommend legal counsel when it is in the interest of either party to the transaction. When in doubt, the licensee should err on the side of caution and recommend that counsel be consulted.

Provide Attorney General's Memorandum—A copy of the Attorney General's Memorandum on the Law against Discrimination must be given to the owner when a listing is taken. The licensee must refuse the listing if the owner gives any indication that he will not comply with the law.

Agency Law—Licensees are subject to the law of agency. This important relationship will be covered in Chapter 12.

Written Reaffirmation for Homeowner's Insurance—If a broker includes in his contract that he is authorized to obtain the buyer's homeowner's insurance, he must obtain a separate written reaffirmation of that fact not less than five days prior to settlement. A real estate broker must be the holder of a property and casualty insurance license to be paid a fee for placing the insurance.

Permanent Transaction Records—Permanent records of all funds and property of others received, along with all other transaction details and documentation, must be retained for **six years** after the transaction. Expired listings and rejected offers must be kept for only **six months**. Office files are the property of the broker. Licensees are prohibited from taking such records from the office upon termination of their employment. They may obtain copies of such records, but only with the written consent of the broker.

Attorney Review Clause—All licensee-prepared contracts of sale and leases with a term of one year or more must contain the required Attorney Review Clause. This important provision will be discussed in Chapter 14.

GROUNDS FOR SUSPENSION AND REVOCATION OF LICENSE

1. Making false promises or any substantial misrepresentation.

2. Acting for more than one party in a transaction without the knowledge of all (acting as an undisclosed dual agent).

3. Flagrant and continued misrepresentation or false promises through advertising, salespersons, agents or otherwise.

4. Failure to account for or to pay over funds belonging to others.

5. Any conduct which demonstrates unworthiness, incompetence, bad faith or dishonesty. The failure of any person to cooperate with the Commission in the performance of its duties or to comply with a subpoena issued by the Commission compelling the production of materials in the course of an investigation, or the failure to give a written or verbal statement concerning a matter under investigation, may be construed as conduct demonstrating unworthiness.

6. Failure to provide the client with a fully executed copy of any exclusive listing or rental agreement at the time of execution or failure to specify a definite, unqualified termination date therein. ("Automatic renewal" clauses are not permitted, but the owner may extend a listing by signing an extension to a current, unexpired listing.)

7. Using methods such as games, lotteries, prizes, drawings and the like or offering lots for advertising purposes.

8. Being convicted of a crime and withholding such information from the Commission after the issuance of a license. A licensee may also face disciplinary action for failing to advise the Commission within 30 days of having been convicted of any crime, misdemeanor or disorderly persons offense, or of having been indicted, or failing to reveal the filing of any formal criminal charges or of the suspension or revocation of any real estate license issued by another state, or of the initiation of formal disciplinary hearings in another state affecting any real estate license held, or for failing to supply any documentation available to the licensee that the Commission may request in connection with such matters.

9. Collecting a fee or other consideration for acting as the real estate broker in a transaction, when at the same time representing either party in the same transaction in a different capacity (e.g., as attorney, executor) for a fee.

10. Using a trade name or insignia of an organization of which the licensee is not a member. For example, one may not use the term Realtor® as a synonym for "real estate broker." While this is done frequently by the public in general, the term Realtor® is a registered trademark of the National Association of Realtors (NAR) and may only be used to refer to its members.

11. Paying any rebate, profit, compensation or commission to anyone not possessed of a real estate license, except that free, discounted or other services or products provided for in NJSA 45:15 -17 (g) are not deemed to be rebates.

12. Commingling (as previously described).

13. Selling a property in which the licensee has an interest without first disclosing to the purchaser in the contract of sale his interest therein. A licensee is permitted to sell a prospect property in which he holds an interest, but the buyer must know that he holds the interest. The licensee cannot hide behind a corporate or partnership name or use any other ruse to hide his identity or interest. A real estate licensee must also disclose his status as a real estate broker, broker-salesperson or salesperson in the contract of sale any time he is purchasing or selling any real property. This requirement applies whether the transaction is being handled through his/her office or not.

14. Any conduct that constitutes fraud or dishonest dealing, whether mentioned expressly in the statute or not. Examples include: lying to a seller about the true value of a property so that the licensee might purchase it himself, inducing a buyer to lie on a mortgage application, attempting to perpetrate a fraud against the FHA, VA or any governmental agency, and the creation of a **dual contract**. A dual contract is a situation created when a licensee prepares two contracts, one with the true purchase price and terms and another with an inflated price or differing terms with the intent of defrauding a party to the transaction. A dual contract is also sometimes referred to as "kiting a deal" or "ballooning."

15. A salesperson's accepting a commission or other valuable consideration from any person other than his licensed employing broker. Salespersons may only accept compensation from their employing broker, and never directly from other brokers, sellers, buyers or others.

16. Procuring a license for himself or another through fraud or deceit, such as one's lying on a license application, attempting to hide a previous criminal conviction or a broker's submitting a false apprenticeship report for a broker candidate.

17. Violation of any provisions of the article dealing with causes for suspension and revocation of license.

It is important to reiterate that the grounds for suspension and revocation include not only circumstances specifically named here, but also any actions by a licensee which would demonstrate dishonest or incompetent behavior.

DISCIPLINARY ACTION

Hearings

The opportunity must be given for the licensee to be heard either in person or to be represented by counsel before the Commission prior to suspension or revocation of license. The licensee must be notified at least ten days prior to the hearing date. If the licensee is a broker-salesperson or salesperson, the Commission must also notify the broker employing him.

Penalties for Violations

Suspension of License—Suspension of license involves a period less than the entire remaining license term. The Commission has the authority, with at least 24 hours notice, to suspend a license without a hearing upon finding that *prima facie* evidence of commingling or failure to pay over monies exists. A full hearing must be held within 30 days of any order imposing such a temporary suspension. Upon entering an order to temporarily suspend the license of any broker, the Commission may also issue an order directing that some or all of the accounts maintained by the broker in any depository institution in the state be temporarily frozen.

Revocation of License—Revocation of license is the termination of a license for its entire remaining term. License revocation precludes a person whose license has been revoked from being an officer, director, partner or owner of a controlling interest in a licensed corporation or partnership. It also precludes such person from being employed or compensated by, or sharing office space with a licensed broker during the period of revocation.

Fines

First violation—Not more than $5,000.
Subsequent violations—Not more than $10,000.

An order for restitution may also be made if appropriate. Note that these maximum fines are assessable for each count of the offense, so if a licensee were found guilty of three counts of an offense at the same time, the maximum fine would be $25,000 ($5,000 + $10,000 + $10,000).

If a licensee is found guilty of a third violation, whether the same or separate offenses, the Commission may deem that person a repeat offender and may direct that no license as a real estate salesperson or broker shall henceforth be issued to that person.

Fees, fines and penalties collected by the Commission are not used to support Commission operations, but must be remitted to the State Treasurer. Commission decisions are reviewable by the Superior Court. Under order of the court, a defendant found guilty of violation, and refusing to pay the fines assessed, may be committed to the county jail for a period of time not to exceed 30 days. (Violations of the license law are misdemeanors, not felonies.) When a licensee is indicted for a crime, the license may be suspended at the discretion of the Commission. If convicted of a money offense, the license must be revoked. A licensee may further be required to submit to written examination after disciplinary action to regain the license.

NJREC disciplinary actions appear regularly in the *Banking and Insurance Quarterly*, citing the name of the disciplined licensee, the name of the firm if applicable, a citation of the violated section(s), a description of the offense and the penalty given. Examples of several recently cited actions are shown below:

- After a full hearing at which the licensee failed to appear, the Commission found that the licensee had violated: NJSA 45:15-17 (a), making a substantial misrepresentation; 17(e), unworthiness, bad faith or dishonesty; and 17(n), procuring a license by fraud, misrepresentation or deceit, by failing to disclose two criminal convictions for theft on an application for licensure. The Commission revoked the licensee's eligibility to hold a license for seven years and imposed a $3,000 fine.

- After a full hearing at which respondent failed to appear, the Commission found the licensee guilty of violations of NJSA 45:15-1 and 45:15-3, unlicensed activity and NJSA 45:15-17 (a) and (t) for misrepresenting himself as a licensed real estate broker. The Commission ordered the licensee to cease and desist from all real estate brokerage activity in New Jersey and imposed a fine of $10,000. He was also ordered to make restitution to several victims.

- After a hearing, the Commission approved a settlement wherein the licensee admitted to violations of: NJSA 45:15-17(d), failing to account for or to pay over monies belonging to others which came into his possession as escrow agent of the funds of others in real estate and rental transactions; 17 (e), unworthiness; and 17 (o), for commingling and misappropriation of escrow deposit monies. The licensee consented to a lifetime revocation of his broker's license and a fine of $5,000. He will be eligible to apply for a salesperson's license in five years, which would be held on a probationary basis for a period of two years. He must also make restitution to numerous clients on sale and rental transactions and must divest himself of his ownership interest in any licensed entity. If he fails to make restitution, the Commission can impose further penalties. The licensee admitted having diverted to his own business use over $200,000 of rent receipts and escrow deposit monies.

Copies of the *Banking and Insurance Quarterly* are mailed to all real estate offices and approved schools throughout the state.

Automatic Suspension of Salesperson's License

If a broker has his license suspended or revoked, all other licensees operating under him will have their licenses automatically suspended, pending a change of employing broker and the issuance of a new license. The licenses of such licensees are temporarily suspended without prejudice. There is no presumption of wrongdoing on their part. The license is only being suspended because they have no broker of record or employing broker.

If a salesperson is found guilty of violating the license law or the rules and regulations, the license of his broker will not be suspended or revoked unless the broker had guilty knowledge of the salesperson's activities. Guilty knowledge means that the broker was actively involved in the wrongdoing himself or was aware of it and took no appropriate action to correct it.

Blockbusting

Blockbusting regulations are intended to foster equal housing opportunity for all. Licensees may never engage in actions which would serve to harm the rights of minority persons in their search for housing. Blockbusting under this regulation is defined as any attempt by a broker or salesperson to solicit a sale or rental listing by alleging that a change in property value is likely because of the projected entry into the neighborhood of persons of another race, creed or ethnic origin. Soliciting is defined as the use of any means to advance these purposes, including but not limited to personal communication, telephoning, advertising or direct mail.

Brokers and salespersons who solicit three or more prospects in the same block in any one month must maintain records of each solicitation for at least one year from the date of the solicitation, producing it upon request from the Commission.

RESIDENTIAL RENTAL REFERRAL SERVICES

Every person engaged in the business of referring prospective residential tenants to possible rental units must be licensed. Licensees must enter into a written contract with prospective tenants. The contract must accurately state the services to be performed, the fee charged, the date and duration of the contract, the refund policy and a statement that the New Jersey Real Estate Commission licenses the business.

Prospective tenants must not be referred to rental units or locations unless the lessor has given the referral agency written or oral authorization to do so. Oral authorization must be confirmed in writing within 24 hours. The availability of units advertised in media must be verified each day the ad appears, and units to which prospective tenants are referred must be verified as available every three business days. Prior to the prospective tenant obtaining rental property, no licensee may charge a fee in excess of $25.00.

REAL ESTATE SALES FULL DISCLOSURE ACT

The New Jersey Real Estate License Laws regulate the sale of out-of-state properties under the **Real Estate Sales Full Disclosure Act**. The law is a consumer protection law that is intended to discourage fraud, deceit, and misrepresentations in the sale of properties located in other states. The **Bureau of Subdivided Land Sales Control** within the New Jersey Real Estate Commission administers the Act.

The Act applies to all **offers** and **dispositions** of residential subdivided land, condominiums, time shares and properties subject to a "homeowners' association" offered through a common promotional plan.

Offerings. An offering is any sales promotions conducted physically in New Jersey. This includes the publication or mailing into New Jersey of any promotional materials for the purpose of inducing the purchase of an interest in a regulated subdivision, as well as telemarketing activities.

Conditions for Issuance of Registration. An offering involving subdivisions located outside New Jersey is illegal unless the subdivision is registered with the Bureau of Subdivided Land Sales Control. Upon receipt of an application for registration, accompanied by a **statement of record** (see page 48), the Commission will initiate an investigation to determine that:

- the subdivider can convey the interest in the subdivided lands if the purchaser complies with the terms of the offer;
- there is reasonable assurance that the improvements will be completed as promised;
- the advertising is not false, misleading or discriminatory, and complies with Commission advertising regulations; and
- the subdivider, or if a corporation, its officers or directors, have not been convicted of a crime or civil offense involving land sales in New Jersey or any other jurisdiction.

Exemptions from the Act. The Real Estate Sales Full Disclosure Act does not apply to certain situations unless the method of disposition is used to evade the Act. The exemptions are as follows:

- Subdivisions of fewer than 100 lots, parcels, units or interests.
- Sales pursuant to court order.
- Sales wholly for industrial or commercial purposes.
- Sales by any governmental agency.
- Sales of cemetery lots or interests.
- Commercial properties
- Individual listings.
- Communities consisting wholly of rental units (this exemption does not apply to time shares).

Brokers of Record. Out-of-state developers must designate a currently licensed New Jersey broker as a "Broker of Record" in the initial registration application. The developer may also designate additional or "Supplemental Brokers" to offer and market registered property in New Jersey. Authorized brokers are issued a special license called a "Broker's Release." Only authorized brokers may offer regulated properties in New Jersey. Brokers should determine the status of a project before offering or advertising any regulated properties.

Filing Fees. The fee for an initial registration is $500, plus an additional $35 per lot, parcel or unit. Filing fees are capped at $3,000.

Public Offering Statement. The subdivider must give all purchasers a copy of a current Public Offering Statement prior to their signing any contract, and they must be given an opportunity to examine it. The statement includes the name and address of the developer, the name of the authorized broker, a general description of the subdivision stating the number of lots, etc., a statement of existing and proposed taxes, encumbrances, and the estimated cost and completion date of improvements.

Rescission (Cooling-off) Period. Any contract for the purchase or lease of a lot may be rescinded (canceled) by the purchaser or lessee without cause of any kind by sending or delivering a notice of cancellation by midnight of the seventh calendar day following the day on which the contract or lease was executed.

Penalties. Any person who violates any provision of this Act shall be fined not less than $250 and not more than $50,000 per violation. In addition, any real estate licensee who violates any provision of the Act is subject to the penalties as prescribed in the license laws and rules and regulations.

Statutory Authority

License laws have been enacted in all of the states and the District of Columbia to provide the authority for licensing real estate brokers and salespersons and to define disciplinary action for violations of the law.

The laws have been challenged in every state on the grounds that the requirement deprives one of the right to earn a livelihood without due process of law. The courts, however, have unanimously ruled that the states, under the police powers, have not only the right but also the responsibility to require that persons who wish to engage in the real estate business demonstrate a certain degree of character and competence because of their fiduciary status.

The New Jersey Real Estate Commission has been given statutory authority to supplement the license law with rules and regulations. These rules and regulations must fall within the framework of the law and cannot add to it.

It is most important that you possess a thorough understanding of the license laws and rules and regulations, since this is the basic authority which will govern your conduct in the real estate business. The New Jersey license laws and rules and regulations of the New Jersey Real Estate Commission are reprinted verbatim next.

This section contains the New Jersey License Law and the Rules and Regulations of the New Jersey Real Estate Commission. The page numbers in the original document furnished by the Commission have been changed to conform to the design of this book, but the Statute section numbers remain the same as in the original text.

NEW JERSEY REAL ESTATE COMMISSION
20 WEST STATE STREET, CN 328, TRENTON, NEW JERSEY 08625-0328

PROFESSIONS AND OCCUPATIONS

TITLE 45, CHAPTER 15
REAL ESTATE BROKERS, SALESPERSONS AND AUCTIONEERS LICENSING LAW

ARTICLE 1. REAL ESTATE BROKERS AND SALESMEN

ARTICLE 3. REAL ESTATE GUARANTY FUND

RULES AND REGULATIONS ADMINISTATIVE CODE 11:5

SUBCHAPTER 1: ORGANIZATIONAL RULES

SUBCHAPTER 2: EDUCATION

SUBCHAPTER 3: LICENSING

SUBCHAPTER 4: EMPLOYMENT PRACTICES/OFFICE AND LICENSEE SUPERVISION

SUBCHAPTER 5: TRUST ACCOUNTS/RECORDS OF BROKERAGE ACTIVITY

SUBCHAPTER 6: CONDUCT OF BUSINESS

SUBCHAPTER 7: PROHIBITED ACTIVITIES

SUBCHAPTER 8: DISCIPLINARY ACTIONS/CONDITIONS FOR RESTORATION OF LICENSE/REAL ESTATE GUARANTY FUND CLAIMS

SUBCHAPTER 9: RULES INTERPRETING AND IMPLEMENTING THE REAL ESTATE SALES FULL DISCLOSURE ACT, N.J.S.A. 45:15-16.27, ET SEQ.

SUBCHAPTER 10: PETITIONS FOR RULEMAKING

SUBCHAPTER 11: PROCEDURES ON DISCIPLINARY ACTIONS, CONTESTED APPLICATIONS, DECLARATORY RULING REQUESTS

NEW JERSEY STATUTES ANNOTATED

CHAPTER 15

REAL ESTATE BROKERS AND SALESMEN

ARTICLE 1. REAL ESTATE BROKERS AND SALESMEN

45:15–1. License required to engage in business of real estate broker, broker-salesperson or salesperson

No person shall engage either directly or indirectly in the business of a real estate broker, broker-salesperson or salesperson, temporarily or otherwise, and no person shall advertise or represent himself as being authorized to act as a real estate broker, broker-salesperson or salesperson, or to engage in any of the activities described in R.S. 45:15–3, without being licensed so to do as hereinafter provided.

Amended by L.1953, c. 229, § 1; L.1993, c. 51, § 1, eff. May 20, 1993.

45:15–1.1. Housing referral aide in CETA program; exemption

A person employed in a participant position as a housing referral aide under any program established and funded pursuant to the Comprehensive Employment and Training Act of 1973, Pub.L. 93–203, 29 U.S.C. § 801 et seq., while performing his duties in such position, shall not be deemed to be engaged in the business of a real estate broker, broker-salesperson or salesperson under the provisions of chapter 15 of Title 45 of the Revised Statutes.

L.1978, c. 5, § 1, eff. March 15, 1978. Amended by L.1993, c. 51, § 2, eff. May 20, 1993.

45:15–1.2. Unauthorized acceptance of fee or commission for assistance in locating rental housing; disorderly persons offense; exceptions

Any person who, before a lease has been fully executed or, where no lease is drawn, before possession is taken by the tenant, charges or accepts any fee, commission or compensation in exchange for providing assistance in locating rental housing, including providing written lists or telephone information on purportedly available rental units, without being licensed pursuant to this act shall be a disorderly person and shall be subject to a fine of not less than $200 or to imprisonment for not more than 30 days or both.

The provisions of this section shall not be construed to prohibit a licensed real estate broker, or an owner of rental properties or his agents and employees, from requiring the payment of a deposit to reserve a particular unit or from charging and accepting a fee for processing an application to rent an apartment or for performing a credit check or other investigation upon prospective tenants prior to the execution of a lease or the taking of possession of a rental unit by a prospective tenant.

L.1993, c. 51, § 41, eff. May 20, 1993.

45:15–2. "Engaging in business" defined

Any single act, transaction or sale shall constitute engaging in business within the meaning of this article.

45:15–3. "Real estate broker", "real estate salesperson" and "real estate broker–salesperson" defined; license required to bring action for compensation

A real estate broker, for the purposes of this article, is defined to be a person, firm or corporation who, for a fee, commission or other valuable consideration, or by reason of a promise or reasonable expectation thereof, lists for sale, sells, exchanges, buys or rents, or offers or attempts to negotiate a sale, exchange, purchase or rental of real estate or an interest therein, or collects or offers or attempts to collect rent for the use of real estate or solicits for prospective purchasers or assists or directs in the procuring of prospects or the negotiation or closing of any transaction which does or is contemplated to result in the sale, exchange, leasing, renting or auctioning of any real estate or negotiates, or offers or attempts or agrees to negotiate a loan secured or to be secured by mortgage or other encumbrance upon or transfer of any real estate for others, or any person who, for pecuniary gain or expectation of pecuniary gain conducts a public or private competitive sale of lands or any interest in lands. In the sale of lots pursuant to the provisions of this article, the term "real estate broker" shall also include any person, partnership, association or corporation employed by or on behalf of the owner or owners of lots or other parcels of real estate, at a stated salary, or upon a commission, or upon a salary and commission, or otherwise, to sell such real estate, or any parts thereof, in lots or other parcels, and who shall sell or exchange, or offer or attempt or agree to negotiate the sale or exchange, of any such lot or parcel of real estate.

A real estate salesperson, for the purposes of this article, is defined to be any person who, for compensation, valuable consideration or commission, or other thing of value, or by reason of a promise or reasonable expectation thereof, is employed by and operates under the supervision of a licensed real estate broker to sell or offer to sell, buy or offer to buy or negotiate the purchase, sale or exchange of real estate, or offers or attempts to negotiate a loan secured or to be secured by a mortgage or other encumbrance upon or transfer of real estate, or to lease or rent, or offer to lease or rent any real estate for others, or to collect rents for the use of real estate, or to solicit for prospective purchasers or lessees of real estate, or who is employed by a licensed real estate broker to sell or offer to sell lots or other parcels of real estate, at a stated salary, or upon a commission, or upon a salary and commission, or otherwise to sell real estate, or any parts thereof, in lots or other parcels.

A real estate broker-salesperson, for the purposes of this amendatory and supplementary act, is defined to be any person who is qualified to be licensed as a real estate broker but who, for compensation, valuable consideration or commission, or other thing of value, or by reason of a promise or reasonable expectation thereof, is employed by and operates under the supervision of a licensed real estate broker to perform the functions of a real estate salesperson as defined herein.

No person, firm, partnership, association or corporation shall bring or maintain any action in the courts of this State for the collection of compensation for the performance of any of the acts mentioned in this article without alleging and proving that he was a duly licensed real estate broker at the time the alleged cause of action arose.

No person claiming to be entitled to compensation as a salesperson or broker-salesperson for the performance of any of the acts mentioned in chapter 15 of Title 45 of the Revised Statutes shall bring or maintain any action in the courts of this State for the collection of compensation against any person, firm, partnership or corporation other than the licensed broker with whom the salesperson or broker-salesperson was employed at the time the alleged cause of action arose and no action shall be brought or maintained without the claimant alleging and proving that he was a duly licensed real estate salesperson or broker-salesperson at the time the alleged cause of action arose.

Amended by L.1953, c. 229, § 2; L.1993, c. 51, § 3, eff. May 20, 1993.

45:15–3.1. Referral fee or commission; payment to unlicensed nonresident broker if licensed in other jurisdiction

A duly licensed real estate broker of this State may pay a referral fee or referral commission to a person not licensed if the person is a licensed real estate broker of another jurisdiction in which the licensed broker maintains a bona fide office. A licensed real estate broker of another jurisdiction may make a referral, receive a referral fee or referral commission, and bring or maintain an action in the courts of this State against a duly licensed real estate broker of this State for the collection of the fee or commission.

For the purposes of this section, "referral" means the introduction, assisting, or directing of a person by one broker to another broker for real estate brokerage services, aid, or information; "referral fee" or "referral commission" means the compensation paid or received for the referral.

L.1979, c. 322, § 1, eff. Jan. 18, 1980. Amended by L.1993, c. 51, § 4.

45:15–4. Application of provisions of article limited

The provisions of this article shall not apply to any person, firm, partnership, association or corporation who, as a bona fide owner or lessor, shall perform any of the aforesaid acts with reference to property owned by him, nor shall they apply to or be construed to include attorneys at law, receivers, trustees in bankruptcy, executors, administrators or persons selling real estate under the order of any court or the terms of a deed of trust, state banks, federal banks, savings banks and trust companies located within the state, or to insurance companies incorporated under the insurance laws of this state.

45:15–5. New Jersey real estate commission; membership; appointment; terms of office; quorum; vacancies; removals

The New Jersey Real Estate Commission, hereinafter in this article designated as the "commission," created and established by an act entitled "An act to define, regulate and license real estate brokers and salesmen, to create a State real estate commission and to provide penalties for the violation of the provisions hereof," approved April 5, 1921 (P.L.1921, c. 141, s. 370), as amended by an act approved April 23, 1929 (P.L.1929, c. 168, s. 310), is continued. The commission shall constitute the division of the New Jersey Real Estate Commission in the Department of Insurance. The commission shall consist of eight members, appointed by the Governor pursuant to the provisions of P.L.1971, c. 60 (C. 45:1–2.1 et seq.), each of whom shall have been a resident of this State for a period of at least 10 years. Five members shall have been real estate brokers for a period of at least 10 years; two members shall be public members; and one member shall be a representative of an appropriate department. The department representative shall serve at the pleasure of the Governor. Upon the expiration of the term of office of any other member, his successor shall be appointed by the Governor for a term of 3 years. A majority of the voting members of the commission shall constitute a quorum thereof. Each member shall hold his office until his successor has qualified. Members to fill vacancies shall be appointed by the Governor for the unexpired term. The Governor may remove any commissioner for cause, upon notice and opportunity to be heard.

Amended by L.1948, c. 88, p. 501, § 4; L.1977, c. 331, § 1, eff. Jan. 11, 1978; L.1993, c. 51, § 5, eff. May 20, 1993.

45:15–6. President; rules and regulations; compensation

The commission shall select from its members a president, and may do all things necessary and convenient for carrying into effect the provisions of this article, and may promulgate necessary rules and regulations pursuant to the "Administrative Procedure Act," P.L.1968, c. 410 (C. 52:14B–1 et seq.). The president shall receive a salary of $15,000.00 per year and each other member of the commission shall receive a salary of $10,000.00 per year, except the department representative who serves without compensation pursuant to section 2 of P.L.1971, c. 60 (C. 45:1–2.2). No commissioner shall receive any other compensation, either directly or indirectly, for his services.

Amended by L.1954, c. 193, § 1; L.1985, c. 137, § 1, eff. April 12, 1985.

45:15-7. Personnel; duties and compensation; office space; supplies

The Commissioner of Insurance shall provide the commission with such personnel as he shall deem necessary, after consultation with the commission, for the proper discharge of the duties imposed by the provisions of this article. The Commissioner of Insurance shall prescribe the duties of persons thus assigned to the commission, and shall fix their compensation, within the limits of available appropriations therefor. The Commissioner of Insurance shall provide the commission with such office space, furniture and stationery as he shall determine, after consultation with the commission, to be reasonably necessary for carrying out the provisions of this article.

Amended by L.1948, c. 88, p. 502, § 5; L.1993, c. 51, § 6, eff. May 20, 1993.

45:15-8. Seal; certified copies of records as evidence; public inspection of records

The commission shall adopt a common seal by which it shall authenticate its proceedings. Copies of all records and papers in the office of the commission, duly certified and authenticated by its seal, shall be received in evidence in all courts with like effect as the original. All records kept in the office of the commission under the authority of this article shall be open to public inspection under regulations prescribed by the commission.

45:15-9. Applications for licenses; fees; qualifications of applicants; consent to service by nonresidents; change in status; failure to renew

All persons desiring to become real estate brokers, broker-salespersons or salespersons shall apply to the commission for a license under the provisions of this article. Every applicant for a license as a broker, broker-salesperson or salesperson shall be of the age of 18 years or over, and in the case of an association or a corporation the directors thereof shall be of the age of 18 years or over. Application for a license, whether as a real estate broker, broker-salesperson or a salesperson, shall be made to the commission upon forms prescribed by it and shall be accompanied by an application fee of $25 which fee shall not be refundable. Every applicant for a license whether as a real estate broker, broker-salesperson or salesperson shall have the equivalent of a high school education. The issuance of a license to an applicant who is a nonresident of this State shall be deemed to be his irrevocable consent that service of process upon him as a licensee in any action or proceeding may be made upon him by service upon the secretary of the commission or the person in charge of the office of the commission. The applicant shall furnish evidence of good moral character, and in the case of an association, partnership or corporation, the members, officers or directors thereof shall furnish evidence of good moral character. The commission may make such investigation and require such proof as it deems proper and in the public interest as to the honesty, trustworthiness, character and integrity of an applicant. Every applicant for a license as a broker or broker-salesperson shall have first been the holder of a New Jersey real estate salesperson's license and have been actively engaged on a full-time basis in the real estate brokerage business in this State for three years immediately preceding the date of application, which requirement may be waived by the commission where the applicant has been the holder of a broker's license in another state and actively engaged in the real estate brokerage business for at least three years immediately preceding the date of his application, meets the educational requirements and qualifies by examination. No license as a broker shall be granted to a general partnership or corporation unless at least one of the partners or officers of said general partnership or corporation qualifies as and holds a license as a broker to transact business in the name and on behalf of said general partnership or corporation as its authorized broker and no such authorized broker shall act as a broker on his own individual account unless he is also licensed as a broker in his individual name; the license of said general partnership or corporation shall cease if at least one partner or officer does not hold a license as its authorized broker at all times. A change in the status of the license of an authorized broker to an individual capacity or vice versa shall be effected by application to the commission accompanied by a fee of $25. No license as a broker shall be granted to a limited partnership unless its general partner qualifies as and holds a license as a broker to transact business in the name of and on behalf of the limited partnership. In the event that a corporation is a general partner of a limited partnership, no license as a broker shall be granted to the limited partnership unless the corporation is licensed as a broker and one of the officers of the corporation qualifies as and holds a license as the corporation's authorized broker.

In the event that any person to whom a broker's or broker-salesperson's license has been or shall have been issued shall fail to renew such license or obtain a new license for a period of more than two but less than five consecutive years after the expiration of the last license held, prior to issuing another broker or broker-salesperson license to the person, the commission shall require such person to work as a licensed salesperson on a full-time basis for one full year, to pass an examination, and to successfully complete a 90-hour general broker's pre-licensure course at a licensed real estate school, as the commission shall prescribe by regulation. In the event that any person to whom a broker's or broker-salesperson's license has been or shall have been issued fails to maintain or renew the license or obtain a new license for a period of more than five consecutive years after the expiration of the last license held, prior to issuing another broker or broker-salesperson license to the person the commission shall require the person to pass the salesperson's license examination and then to work as a licensed salesperson on a full-time basis for three years, to fulfill all of the educational requirements applicable to first time applicants for a broker or broker-salesperson license and to pass the broker's license examination. The commission may, in its discretion, approve for relicensure the former holder of a broker or broker-salesperson license who has not renewed the license or obtained a new license for two or more consecutive years upon a sufficient showing that the applicant was medically unable to do so. All applicants so approved shall pass the broker's license examination prior to being relicensed. This paragraph shall not apply to a person reapplying for a broker's or broker-salesperson's license who was licensed as a broker or broker-salesperson and who allowed his license to expire due to subsequent employment in a public agency in this State with responsibility for dealing with matters relating to real estate if the person reapplying does so within one year of termination of that employment.

In the event that any person to whom a salesperson's license has been or shall have been issued shall fail to maintain or renew such license or obtain a new license for a period of two consecutive years or more after the expiration of the last license held, the commission shall require such person to attend a licensed school and pass the State examination prior to issuance of a further license. The commission may, in its discretion, approve for relicensure a salesperson applicant who has not renewed his license or obtained a new license for two or more consecutive years upon a sufficient showing that the applicant was medically unable to do so. All salesperson applicants so approved shall pass the salesperson's license examination prior to being relicensed. This paragraph shall not apply to a person reapplying for a salesperson's license who was a licensed salesperson and who allowed his license to expire due to subsequent employment in a public agency in this State with responsibility for dealing with matters relating to real estate if the person reapplying does so within one year of termination of that employment.

Amended by L.1938, c. 227, p. 523, § 1; L.1953, c. 77, p. 995, § 1; L.1953, c. 229, p. 1688, § 3; L.1966, c. 10, § 1, eff. April 1, 1966; L.1977, c. 331, § 2, eff. Jan. 11, 1978; L.1983, c. 456, § 1, eff. May 1, 1983; L.1989, c. 126, § 1, eff. July 3, 1989; L.1993, c. 51, § 7.

45:15–10. Examinations; granting and biennial renewal of licenses; expiration

Before any such license shall be granted the applicant, and in the case of a partnership, association or corporation the partners, directors or officers thereof actually engaged in the real estate business as a broker, broker-salesperson or salesperson, shall submit to an examination to be conducted under the supervision of the commission which examination shall test the applicant's general knowledge of the statutes of New Jersey concerning real property, conveyancing, mortgages, agreements of sale, leases and of the provisions of this article, the rules and regulations of the commission and such other subjects as the commission may direct. The commission may make rules and regulations for the conduct of such examinations. Upon satisfactorily passing such examination and fulfilling all other qualifications a license shall be granted by the commission to the successful applicant therefor as a real estate broker, broker-salesperson or salesperson, and the applicant upon receiving the license is authorized to conduct in this State the business of a real estate broker, broker-salesperson or salesperson, as the case may be. Such license shall expire on the last day of a two-year license term as established by the commission ; such license shall be renewed, without examination, biennially thereafter, upon the payment of the fee fixed by R.S. 45:15–15.

Amended by L.1972, c. 94, § 1, eff. July 18, 1972; L.1977, c. 331, § 3, eff. Jan. 11, 1978; L.1993, c. 51, § 8; L.1996, c. 38, § 1, eff. Dec. 18, 1996.

45:15–10.1. Prerequisite to admission to examination

a. As a prerequisite to admission to an examination, every individual applicant for licensure as a real estate salesperson shall give evidence of satisfactory completion of 75 hours in the aggregate of such courses of education in real estate subjects at a school licensed by the commission as the commission shall by regulation prescribe. At least three hours of that course of study shall be on the subject of ethics and ethical conduct in the profession of a real estate salesperson.

b. As a prerequisite to admission to an examination, every individual applicant for licensure as a real estate broker or broker-salesperson shall give evidence of satisfactory completion of 150 hours in the aggregate of such courses of education in real estate and related subjects at a school licensed by the commission as the commission shall by regulation prescribe. Thirty hours of that course of study shall be on the subject of ethics and ethical conduct in the profession of a real estate broker.

The commission may approve courses in specialized aspects of the real estate brokerage business offered by providers who are not the holders of a real estate school license pursuant to section 47 of P.L.1993, c. 51 (C. 45:15–10.4), the completion of which may be recognized as fulfilling a portion of the total broker pre-licensure education requirements.

L.1966, c. 227, § 1. Amended by L.1977, c. 331, § 4, eff. July 1, 1978; L.1983, c. 456, § 2, eff. May 1, 1983; L.1989, c. 126, § 2, eff. July 3, 1989; L.1993, c. 51, § 9.

45:15–10.2. Waiver of educational requirements

The commission may waive some or all of the educational requirements for licensure established pursuant to subsection a. of section 1 of P.L.1966, c. 227 (C. 45:15–10.1) in the case of an applicant whose education or experience is in the judgment of the commission substantially equivalent to those educational requirements. The commission shall prescribe by regulation the requirements which an applicant shall meet in order to qualify for the waiver of educational requirements pursuant to this section.

L.1966, c. 227, § 2. Amended by L.1993, c. 51, § 10.

45:15-10.3. Bureau of Real Estate Education established

There is established within the Division of the New Jersey Real Estate Commission in the Department of Insurance a Bureau of Real Estate Education which shall be responsible for the licensure of real estate pre-licensure schools and instructors.

L.1993, c. 51, § 46.

45:15-10.4. License required for real estate schools; qualifications for school licensure

a. No school shall conduct real estate education courses, the attendance and successful completion of which shall constitute the fulfillment of the educational prerequisites for licensure established pursuant to section 1 of P.L.1966, c. 227 (C. 45:15-10.1) unless licensed as a real estate school pursuant to P.L.1993, c. 51 (C. 45:15-12.3 et al.).

b. A school shall not be licensed as a real estate school unless its owners, management and facilities meet all of the qualifications for licensure established pursuant to this amendatory and supplementary act and which the commission may by regulation prescribe. An applicant for a license to operate a real estate school, and in the case of a partnership or corporation the members, officers, directors and owners of a controlling interest thereof, shall affirmatively demonstrate their good moral character to the commission. The commission may make such investigation and require such proof as it deems proper and in the public interest as to the honesty, trustworthiness, character and integrity of an applicant.

L.1993, c. 51, § 47.

45:15-10.5. License as real estate instructor required; qualifications

a. No person, with the exception of a guest lecturer, may teach real estate education courses, the attendance and successful completion of which shall constitute the fulfillment of the educational prerequisites for licensure established pursuant to section 1 of P.L.1966, c. 227 (C. 45:15-10.1) unless licensed as a real estate instructor pursuant to this amendatory and supplementary act.

b. A person shall not be licensed as a real estate instructor unless the person affirmatively demonstrates to the commission his good moral character, successfully completes a real estate instructor course approved by the commission, successfully completes a written examination conducted under the auspices of the commission, and meets all other qualifications as the commission may prescribe by regulation.

L.1993, c. 51, § 48.

45:15-10.6. Application for real estate school license; fees; renewals; exemptions from fee requirements

a. Every application for licensure as a real estate school shall be accompanied by an application fee of $50 and a criminal history record check fee for all individual owners, members of a partnership, or officers, directors and owners of a controlling interest in a corporation, which fees shall be non-refundable.

b. All licenses issued to real estate schools shall expire on a date fixed by the commission which date shall not be more than two years from the date of issuance of the license. The license fee for each real estate school license issued in the first 12 months of any two-year real estate school license term established by the commission shall be $200 for the first location and $100 for each additional location licensed. The license fee for each real estate school license issued in the second 12 months of any two-year real estate school license term established by the commission shall be $100 for the first location and $50 for each additional location licensed. The fee for the renewal of each real estate school license for an additional two-year license term shall be $200 for the first location and $100 for each additional location.

c. Any accredited college or university located in this State or any public adult education program conducted by a board of education in this State which otherwise qualifies for licensure as a real estate school shall be issued a license without the payment of any license or license renewal fee.

L.1993, c. 51, § 49.

45:15-10.7. Application for licensure as a real estate instructor; nonrefundable fees; renewals

Every application for licensure as a real estate instructor shall be accompanied by an application fee of $25 and a criminal history record check fee, which fees shall be non-refundable. All licenses issued to real estate instructors shall expire on a date fixed by the commission which shall be no more than two years from the date of issuance of the license. The license fee for each real estate instructor license issued in the first 12 months of any two-year real estate instructor license term established by the commission shall be $100 and the fee for an instructor license issued in the second 12 months of the cycle shall be $50. The fee for the renewal of each real estate instructor license for an additional two-year license term shall be $50. Upon payment of the renewal fee and the submission of evidence of satisfactory completion of any continuing education requirements which the commission may by regulation prescribe, the commission shall renew the license of a real estate instructor for a two-year period.

L.1993, c. 51, § 50.

45:15–10.8. Qualifications of directors of licensed real estate schools; temporary authorization of unlicensed person upon death or incapacity of director

A school shall not be licensed as a real estate school unless it is under the management and supervision of a director who is approved by the commission and who is licensed as a real estate instructor in accordance with the provisions of this act. In the event of the death or mental or physical incapacity of the director of a licensed real estate school, which leaves no other owner or employee of the school licensed as a real estate instructor and willing to assume the responsibilities of the director on an interim or permanent basis, the commission may issue temporary authorization to another person to enable that person to carry on the duties of the director until such time as either another licensed instructor is designated by the school and approved by the commission as the director, or until such time as the real estate courses in progress at the time of the former director's death or incapacity are completed. A school shall not commence any new real estate courses until a qualified licensee is designated and approved as the school's director.

The provisions of this section shall not apply to any public adult education program conducted under the auspices of a board of education in this State or any accredited college or university licensed as real estate schools.

L.1993, c. 51, § 51.

45:15–10.9. Qualifications for directors of pre-licensure program of public adult education programs and accredited colleges and universities; temporary authorization of an unlicensed person upon the death or incapacity of director

No public adult education program conducted under the auspices of a board of education in this State and no accredited college or university in this State shall be licensed as a real estate school unless its real estate pre-licensure education program is under the supervision of a director who is a licensed real estate instructor or an individual who has affirmatively demonstrated to the commission his good moral character and has attended a real estate instructor course approved by the commission within two years of applying to the commission for approval as the director of the real estate program. In the event of the death or physical or mental incapacity of the director of a public adult education program or the director of a college or university licensed as a real estate school, which leaves no other employee licensed as a real estate instructor or otherwise qualified to be the director of the program and willing to assume the responsibilities of the director on an interim or permanent basis, the commission may issue a temporary authorization to another person to enable that person to carry on the duties of the director until such time as either another licensed instructor or qualified person is designated by the school and approved by the commission as the director, or until such time as the real estate courses in progress at the time of the former director's death or incapacity are completed. New courses shall not be commenced by the school until a qualified person is designated and approved as the director of the school.

L.1993, c. 51, § 52.

45:15–10.10. Licensing of previously approved schools and instructors; requirements for issuance of license

Upon application to the commission and payment of the prescribed license fee no later than January 1, 1994, any school and instructor then designated by the commission as an approved school or instructor shall, subject to the results of the commission's investigation into the good moral character of the applicant, be issued a real estate school or instructor license.

L.1993, c. 51, § 53, eff. May 20, 1993.

45:15–10.11. Revocation or suspension of real estate school or instructor licenses

The commission may suspend or revoke the license of any real estate school or instructor or impose fines as provided in R.S. 45:15–17 upon satisfactory proof that the licensee is guilty of:

a. Making any false promise or substantial misrepresentation;

b. Pursuing a flagrant and continued course of misrepresentation or making false promises through agents, advertisements or otherwise;

c. Engaging in any conduct which demonstrates unworthiness, incompetency, bad faith or dishonesty;

d. Failing to provide a student with a copy of a written agreement which designates the total tuition charges for attendance at a real estate pre-licensure course offered by a licensed school, or other charges imposed upon students who enroll in the course, and the refund policy of the school in regard to tuition and other charges;

e. Using any plan, scheme or method of attracting students to enroll in a real estate pre-licensure course which involves a lottery, contest, game, prize or drawing;

f. Being convicted of a crime, knowledge of which the commission did not have at the time of last issuing a license to the licensee;

g. Procuring a real estate license for himself or anyone else by fraud, misrepresentation or deceit;

h. Making any verbal or written statement which falsely indicates that a person attended or successfully completed any real estate pre-licensure course conducted by the licensee; or

i. Any other conduct whether of the same or of a different character than specified in this section which constitutes fraud or dishonest dealing.

L.1993, c. 51, § 54.

45:15–10.12. Revocation of license; prohibited acts and employments

A person whose license has been revoked pursuant to section 54 of P.L.1993, c. 51 (C. 45:15–10.11) shall not be a general partner, officer, director or owner, either directly or indirectly, of a controlling interest in any licensed school, nor shall the person be retained or employed in any capacity, or compensated in any manner by a licensed school, nor shall the person occupy or share office space in a licensed school location for any purpose during the period of revocation.

L.1993, c. 51, § 55.

45:15–10.13. Revocation of real estate school license upon revocation of instructor's license of partner, officer, director, or owner of a controlling interest in school unless certain conditions fulfilled

Upon the revocation of the instructor license issued to any partner, officer, director or owner of a controlling interest in any licensed school, the commission shall revoke the license of the school unless, within a period of time fixed by the commission, the following conditions are fulfilled: a. in the case of a licensed school owned by a partnership, the connection of the partner whose instructor license has been revoked to the school shall be severed and his interest in the school shall be divested; or b. in the case of a licensed school owned by a corporation, the officer, director or owner of a controlling interest whose instructor license has been revoked shall be terminated from the position and, where an owner of a controlling interest, his ownership of the interest shall be divested; or c. in the case of a limited partnership, if the person whose instructor license has been revoked was a general partner, his interest in the school shall be divested or, if the person whose instructor license was revoked was a limited partner, his interest in the school shall be divested if it constituted a controlling interest as defined herein. For the purposes of this section, the term "controlling interest" means 5% or more of the equity of a licensed corporation or of the ownership of a partnership.

L.1993, c. 51, § 56.

45:15–10.14. Rules and regulations

The commission is expressly vested with the power and authority to promulgate and enforce all necessary rules and regulations for the conduct of the business of real estate schools offering pre-licensure and continuing education courses consistent with the provisions of this amendatory and supplementary act.

L.1993, c. 51, § 57, eff. May 20, 1993.

45:15–11. Grant of license to certain wounded or disabled war veterans

Any citizen of New Jersey who has served in the armed forces of the United States or who served as a member of the American Merchant Marine during World War II and is declared by the United States Department of Defense to be eligible for federal veterans' benefits, who has been honorably discharged, and who, having been wounded or disabled in the line of duty, has completed a program of courses in real estate approved by the New Jersey Real Estate Commission, and who has successfully passed an examination conducted by said commission qualifying him to operate as a real estate broker, broker-salesperson or salesperson, may, upon presentation of a certificate certifying that he has completed such program of courses as aforesaid, obtain without cost from the commission and without qualification through experience as a salesperson, a license to operate as a real estate broker, broker-salesperson or a real estate salesperson, as the case may be, which licenses shall be the same as other licenses issued under this article. Renewal of licenses may be granted under this section for each ensuing license term, upon request, without fees therefor.

Amended by L.1953, c. 77, p. 996, § 2; L.1977, c. 331, § 6, eff. Jan. 11, 1978; L.1991, c. 389, § 33, eff. Jan. 14, 1992; L.1993, c. 51, § 11; L.1996, c. 38, § 2, eff. Dec. 18, 1996.

45:15–11.1, 45:15–11.2. Repealed by L.1970, c. 255, § 2, eff. Nov. 2, 1970

45:15–11.3. Temporary broker's license for salesperson on death or incapacity of licensed broker or broker-salesperson

In the event of the death or mental or physical incapacity of a licensed real estate broker where no other member or officer in the agency, copartnership, association or corporation of which he was a member or officer is the holder of a broker-salesperson's license or where an individual broker operating as a sole proprietor dies or is mentally or physically incapacitated leaving no employee holding a real estate broker-salesperson's license, then the Real Estate Commission may issue a temporary broker's license on a special form to another person for the purpose of enabling such other person to continue the real estate activities on behalf of and under the same designation of said agency, copartnership, association, corporation or individual, as the case may be, upon the filing of an application and a certified copy of the death certificate or a certification of mental or physical incapacity executed by a duly licensed physician or officer of a medical institution, together with payment of the regular license fee; provided such other person has been the holder of a real estate salesperson's license for at least three years immediately preceding the date of the application and provided that said application shall have been made within 30 days from date of the demise or incapacity of said broker.

Such temporary license shall continue only until the licensee is afforded an opportunity of pursuing the approved broker's course in accordance with the provisions of subsection b. of section 1 of P.L.1966, c. 227 (C. 45:15–10.1)and qualifying by examination. Such license may be issued and effective for a period of one year from the date of issuance. Such temporary license shall not be extended or renewed.

L.1970, c. 255, § 1, eff. Nov. 2, 1970. Amended by L.1993, c. 51, § 12, eff. May 20, 1993.

45:15–12. Places of business; duplicate licenses; display of words "Licensed Real Estate Broker"

Every real estate broker shall maintain a designated main office open to the public. A real estate broker's main office shall have prominently displayed therein the license certificate of the broker and all licensed persons in his employ and shall be deemed the business address of all licensed persons for all purposes under chapter 15 of Title 45 of the Revised Statutes. In case a real estate broker maintains more than one place of business, a branch office license shall be issued to such broker for each branch office so maintained in this State; provided, however, that the said branch office or offices are under the direct supervision of a broker-salesperson. The branch office license or licenses shall be issued upon the payment of a fee of $25 for each license so issued. Every place of business maintained by a real estate broker shall have conspicuously displayed on the exterior thereof the name in which the broker is authorized to operate and, in the case of a corporation or partnership, the name of the individual licensed as its authorized broker, and the words Licensed Real Estate Broker. A real estate broker whose main office is located in another state shall maintain a valid real estate broker's license in good standing in the state where the office is located.

Amended by L.1953, c. 229, p. 1689, § 4; L.1966, c. 11, § 1; L.1993, c. 51, § 13.

45:15–12.1. No license to be issued to person convicted of certain offenses; revocation of license of partnership, association or corporation

No license shall be issued by the commission to any person known by it to have been, within five years theretofore, convicted of forgery, burglary, robbery, any theft offense other than shoplifting, criminal conspiracy to defraud, or other like offense or offenses, or to any copartnership of which such person is a member, or to any association or corporation of which said person is an officer, director, or employee, or in which as a stockholder such person has or exercises a controlling interest either directly or indirectly.

L.1953, c. 229, p. 1692, § 8. Amended by L.1989, c. 126, § 6, eff. July 3, 1989; L.1993, c. 51, § 14, eff. May 20, 1993.

45:15–12.2. Repeal

Sections 45:15–30 to 45:15–33, inclusive, of the Revised Statutes are repealed.

L.1953, c. 229, p. 1693, § 9.

45:15–12.3. Revocation of license; acts and employments prohibited

A person whose license has been revoked pursuant to R.S. 45:15–17 or section 6 of P.L.1953, c. 229 (C. 45:15–19.1) shall not be a general partner, officer, director or owner, either directly or indirectly, of a controlling interest in a licensed partnership, limited partnership or corporation, nor shall the person be retained or employed in any capacity, or compensated in any manner by a licensee, nor shall the person occupy or share office space in a licensed office location for any purpose during the period of revocation.

L.1993, c. 51, § 21, eff. May 20, 1993.

45:15–12.4. License of partnership or corporation revoked upon the revocation of license of a partner, officer, director, or owner of a controlling interest unless certain conditions fulfilled

Upon the revocation of the license issued to any partner, officer, director or owner of a controlling interest in any licensed partnership, limited partnership or corporation, the commission shall revoke the license of the partnership or corporation unless, within a period fixed by the commission, the following conditions are fulfilled: a. in the case of a partnership, the connection of the partner whose license has been revoked to the licensee shall be severed and his interest in the licensee shall be divested; b. in the case of a corporation, the officer, director or owner of a controlling interest whose license has been revoked shall be terminated from the position and, where an owner of a controlling interest, his ownership of the interest shall be divested; or c. in the case of a limited partnership, if the person whose license has been revoked is the general partner, the connection of that person to the licensee shall be severed and his interest in the licensee shall be divested or, if the person whose license was revoked is a limited partner, his interest in the licensee shall be divested if it constituted a controlling interest as defined herein. For the purposes of this section, the term "controlling interest" means 5% or more of the equity of a licensed corporation or of the ownership of a partnership.

L.1993, c. 51, § 22, eff. May 20, 1993.

45:15–12.5. Maintenance of escrow account required; special accounts authorized for specific transactions

a. Every individual, partnership or corporation licensed as a real estate broker shall maintain in a State or federally chartered bank, savings bank, savings and loan association or other depository institution physically located and authorized to transact business in this State and approved by the commission a special account into which the broker shall deposit and maintain all monies received while acting in the capacity of a real estate broker, or as escrow agent, or as the temporary custodian of funds of others in real estate transactions in this State. The account shall be maintained in the name in which the individual, partnership or corporation is licensed to do business as a broker and shall be designated as either the broker's "trust account" or "escrow account" and shall be maintained separate and apart from all other personal and business accounts. All checks and deposit slips produced as a result of the establishment of the account shall contain the words "trust account" or "escrow account." The provisions of this subsection shall not apply to an individual licensed as a broker-salesperson.

b. A real estate broker may establish a special interest bearing escrow account under the broker's control in a depository institution approved by the commission for the deposit of monies from a specific transaction provided the account is clearly identified as pertaining to that transaction. Such accounts shall be maintained separate and apart from all other escrow, business and personal funds.

L.1993, c. 51, § 42, eff. May 20, 1993.

45:15–12.6. Approval of depository institutions by commission; written notice of dishonored checks

The commission shall approve a depository institution as required pursuant to section 42 of this amendatory and supplementary act [1] upon the institution providing written confirmation to the commission that it shall immediately notify the commission of any issuance of a notice to a licensed broker that a check or other instrument written upon the broker's escrow or trust account has been dishonored or returned for insufficient funds.

L.1993, c. 51, § 43, eff. May 20, 1993.

[1] Section 45:15–12.5.

45:15–12.7. Real estate broker acting as escrow agent or temporary custodian of funds prohibited from using interest earned on such funds for personal or business use

A real estate broker acting in the capacity of an escrow agent or as the temporary custodian of the funds of others in any real estate transaction shall not receive, obtain or use any interest earned on the funds for the broker's own personal or business use.

L.1993, c. 51, § 44, eff. May 20, 1993.

45:15–12.8. Real estate broker acting as escrow agent or temporary custodian of the funds to accept only cash or negotiable instrument payable to broker; delivery

Every real estate licensee who, in the performance of any of the activities described in R.S. 45:15–3, receives any monies of others as a representative of a broker acting as an escrow agent or as the temporary custodian of the funds of others in a real estate transaction, shall only accept the monies if they are in the form of cash or a negotiable instrument payable to the broker through whom the individual is licensed. The licensee shall, immediately upon receipt of the funds, account for and deliver the funds to the broker for deposit into the escrow or trust account maintained by the broker, or for such other disposition as is required by the escrow agreement under the terms of which the funds were provided to the licensee.

L.1993, c. 51, § 45, eff. May 20, 1993.

45:15–13. Form, contents and display of licenses; notice of change of places of business

All licenses shall be issued by the commission in such form as it shall prescribe. Each license shall show the name and address of the licensee and shall have imprinted thereon the seal of the commission. Notice in writing shall be given to the commission by each licensed broker of any change of business address, whereupon the commission shall issue new licenses to the broker and to all persons licensed through the broker for the unexpired period, upon the payment of a fee of $25 for the issuance of the new broker license and a fee of $5.00 for each additional new license certificate so issued. A change of business address without notification to the commission, and without the issuance of a new broker's license, shall automatically cancel the license theretofore issued.

Amended by L.1961, c. 88, p. 637, § 1; L.1966, c. 11, § 2; L.1993, c. 51, § 15.

45:15–14. Custody of salesmen's licenses; return of license upon termination of employment; new license upon re-employment

All licenses issued to real estate brokers, broker-salespersons and salespersons shall be kept by the broker by whom such real estate licensee is employed, and the pocket card accompanying the same shall be delivered by the broker to the licensee who shall have the card in his possession at all times when engaged in the business of a real estate broker, broker-salesperson or salesperson. When any real estate licensee is terminated or resigns his employment with the real estate broker by whom he was employed at the time of the issuing of such license to him, notice of the termination shall be given in writing by the broker to the terminated licensee with the effective date of the termination reflected thereon, or notice of the resignation shall be given in writing by the resigning licensee to the broker with the effective date of the resignation reflected thereon. Upon the issuance of a written notice of termination by a broker or his authorized representative, or upon receipt of a written resignation by a broker or his authorized representative, such employer shall within five business days of the effective date of the termination or resignation, either: a. deliver, or send by registered mail, to the commission, such real estate licensee's license and, at the same time, send a written communication to such real estate licensee at his last known residence, advising him that his license has been delivered or mailed to the commission. A copy of such communication to the licensee shall accompany the license when mailed or delivered to the commission; or, b. deliver to the departing licensee and to the commission any other materials as the commission may prescribe by regulation to accomplish the transfer of the licensee to another employing broker. No real estate licensee shall perform any of the acts contemplated by this article, either directly or indirectly, under the authority of such license, from and after the effective date of the licensee's termination or resignation until authorized to do so by the commission. A new license may be issued to such licensee, upon the payment of a fee of $25, and upon the submission of satisfactory proof that he has obtained employment with another licensed broker. A broker-salesperson or salesperson must be licensed under a broker; he cannot be licensed with more than one broker at the same time.

Amended by L.1961, c. 88, p. 637, § 2; L.1966, c. 11, § 3; L.1993, c. 51, § 16.

45:15-15. License fees; authority of licensees; renewals; refusal or revocation of licenses

The biennial fee for each real estate broker's license shall be $100, the biennial fee for each real estate broker-salesperson's license shall be $100 and the biennial fee for each real estate salesperson's license shall be $50. The biennial fee for a branch office license shall be $50. Each license granted under this article shall entitle the licensee to perform all of the acts contemplated herein during the period for which the license is issued, as prescribed by this article. If a licensee fails to apply for a renewal of his license prior to the date of expiration of such license, the commission may refuse to issue a renewal license except upon the payment of a late renewal fee in the amount of $10 for a salesperson or broker-salesperson and $20 for a broker; provided, however, the commission may, in its discretion, refuse to renew any license upon sufficient cause being shown. The commission shall refuse to renew the license of any licensee convicted of any offense enumerated in section 6 of P.L.1953, c. 229 (C. 45:15-19.1) during the term of the last license issued by the commission unless the conviction was previously the subject of a revocation proceeding. Renewed licenses may be granted for each ensuing two years upon request of licensees and the payment of the full fee therefor as herein required. Upon application and payment of the fees provided herein, initial licenses and licenses reinstated pursuant to R.S. 45:15-9 may be issued, but the commission may, in its discretion, refuse to grant or reinstate any license upon sufficient cause being shown. The license fees for initial or reinstated licenses shall be determined based upon the biennial fees established herein, with a full biennial fee payable for the license term in which application is received. The revocation or suspension of a broker's license shall automatically suspend every real estate broker-salesperson's and salesperson's license granted to employees of the broker whose license has been revoked or suspended, pending a change of employer and the issuance of a new license. The new license shall be issued without additional charge, if the same is granted during the license term in which the original license was granted.

A real estate broker who maintains a main office or branch office licensed by the commission which is located in another state shall maintain a valid real estate broker's license in good standing in the state where the office is located and shall maintain a real estate license in that other state for each office licensed by the commission. Upon request, the real estate broker shall provide a certification of his license status in the other state to the commission. Any license issued by the commission to a real estate broker for a main or branch office located outside this State shall be automatically suspended upon the revocation, suspension or refusal to renew the real estate broker's license issued by the state where the office is located. The licenses issued by the commission to every broker-salesperson or salesperson employed by the broker shall be automatically suspended pending a change of employer and the issuance of a new license. The new license shall be issued without additional charge if granted during the license term in which the original license was granted.

Amended by L.1953, c. 77, p. 997, § 3; L.1966, c. 11, § 4; L.1983, c. 532, § 5; L.1993, c. 51, § 17; L.1996, c. 38, § 3, eff. Dec. 18, 1996.

45:15-16. Salesperson's or broker-salesperson's commissions to be paid only by employer

No real estate salesperson or broker-salesperson shall accept a commission or valuable consideration for the performance of any of the acts herein specified, from any person except his employer, who must be a licensed real estate broker.

Amended by L.1993, c. 51, § 18, eff. May 20, 1993.

45:15-16.1. Repealed by L.1975, c. 235, § 25, eff. Dec. 23, 1975

45:15-16.2. Educational and information programs

The Division of the New Jersey Real Estate Commission in the State Department of Insurance, within the limits of appropriations available or to be made available to it for the purpose, may conduct educational and information programs relating to the real estate brokerage business and real estate brokers, broker-salespersons and salespersons for the information, education, guidance and protection of the general public, licensees, and applicants for licensure. The educational and information programs may include preparation, printing and distribution of publications and articles and the conduct of conferences, forums, lectures, and a public information service.

L.1955, c. 238, p. 907, § 1. Amended by L.1993, c. 51, § 19, eff. May 20, 1993.

45:15-16.3 to 45:15-16.26. Repealed by L.1989, c. 239, § 24, eff. Jan. 2, 1990

45:15-16.27. Short title

This act shall be known and may be cited as the "Real Estate Sales Full Disclosure Act."[1]

L.1989, c. 239, § 1, eff. Jan. 2, 1990.

[1] Section 45:15-16.27 et seq.

45:15-16.28. Definitions

As used in this act:

"Advertising" means the publication, or causing to be published, of any information offering for sale, or for the purpose of causing or inducing any other person to purchase or acquire, an interest in the title to subdivided lands, including the land sales contract to be used and any photographs or drawings or artist's representation of physical conditions or facilities on the property existing or to exist by means of any:

(1) Newspaper or periodical;

(2) Radio or television broadcast;

(3) Written or printed or photographic matter produced by any duplicating process producing 10 copies or more;

(4) Billboards or signs;

(5) Display of model homes or units;

(6) Material used in connection with the disposition or offer of subdivided lands by radio, television, telephone or any other electronic means; or

(7) Material used by subdividers or their agents to induce prospective purchasers to visit the subdivision; particularly vacation certificates which require the holders of those certificates to attend or submit to a sales presentation by a subdivider or its agents.

"Advertising" does not mean: stockholder communications such as annual reports and interim financial reports, proxy materials, registration statements, securities prospectuses, applications for listing securities on stock exchanges, or similar documents; prospectuses, property reports, offering statements, or other documents required to be delivered to a prospective purchaser by an agency of any other state or the Federal Government; all communications addressed to and relating to the account of any person who has previously executed a contract for the purchase of the subdivider's lands except when directed to the sale of additional lands.

"Blanket encumbrance" means a trust deed, mortgage, judgment, or any other lien or encumbrance, including an option or contract to sell or a trust agreement, affecting a subdivision or affecting more than one lot offered within a subdivision, except that term shall not include any lien or other encumbrance arising as the result of the imposition of any tax assessment by any public authority.

"Broker" or "salesperson" means any person who performs within this State as an agent or employee of a subdivider any one or more of the services or acts as set forth in this act, and includes any real estate broker or salesperson licensed pursuant to R.S. 45:15-1 et seq. or any person who purports to act in any such capacity.

"Commission" means the New Jersey Real Estate Commission.

"Common promotional plan" means any offer for the disposition of lots, parcels, units or interests of real property by a single person or group of persons acting in concert, where those lots, parcels, units or interests are contiguous, or are known, designated or advertised as a common entity or by a common name regardless of the number of lots, parcels, units or interests covered by each individual offering.

"Disposition" means the sale, lease, assignment, award by lottery, or any other transaction concerning a subdivision if undertaken for gain or profit.

"Notice" means a communication by mail from the commission executed by its secretary or other duly authorized officer. Notice to subdividers shall be deemed complete when mailed to the subdivider's address currently on file with the commission.

"Offer" means every inducement, solicitation or attempt to encourage a person to acquire an interest in a subdivision if undertaken for gain or profit.

"Person" means an individual, corporation, government or governmental subdivision or agency, business trust, estate, trust, partnership, unincorporated association, two or more of any of the foregoing having a joint or common interest, or any other legal or commercial entity.

"Purchaser" means a person who acquires or attempts to acquire or succeeds to an interest in a subdivision.

"Time-share estates" includes both "fee simple" and "right to use" time-share interests and means:

(1) An "interval estate" meaning a combination of an estate for years in a lot, parcel or unit, during the term of which title rotates among the time-share owners, coupled with a vested undivided fee simple interest in the remainder in that unit as established by the declaration or deed creating the interval estate; or

(2) A "time-span estate" meaning a combination of an undivided interest in a present estate in fee simple in a lot, parcel or unit established by the declaration or deed creat-

ing the time-span estate, coupled with the exclusive right to possession and occupancy of the parcel or unit during a regularly recurring period; or

(3) A "vacation license" meaning the exclusive right to possession and occupancy of a lot, unit or parcel during a regularly recurring period established by club membership, lease or license.

"Subdivider" or "developer" means any owner of subdivided lands or the agent of that owner who offers the subdivided lands for disposition.

"Subdivision" and "subdivided lands" mean any land situated outside the State of New Jersey whether contiguous or not, if one or more lots, parcels, units or interests are offered as a part of a common promotional plan of advertising and sale and expressly means and includes such units or interests commonly referred to as a "condominium," defined in the "Condominium Act," P.L.1969, c. 257 (C. 46:8B–1 et seq.). In addition to condominiums, this definition shall also specifically include, but shall not be limited to, any form of homeowners association, any housing cooperative, any community trust, or other trust device and any form of time-sharing.

L.1989, c. 239, § 2, eff. Jan. 2, 1990.

45:15–16.29. Bureau of subdivided land sales control; continuation

The Bureau of Subdivided Land Sales Control within the Division of the New Jersey Real Estate Commission in the Department of Insurance, established pursuant to section 3 of P.L.1975, c. 235 (C. 45:15–16.5), shall continue.

L.1989, c. 239, § 3, eff. Jan. 2, 1990.

45:15–16.30. Offer, disposition or participation in disposition of subdivided lands; requirements

Unless the subdivided lands or the transaction is exempt pursuant to section 6 of this act:[1]

a. No person may offer, dispose or participate in this State in the disposition of subdivided lands or of any interest in subdivided lands unless in accordance with the provisions of this act.

b. No person may dispose or participate in the disposition of any interest in subdivided lands unless a current public offering statement, disclosing fully all information required in section 12 of this act,[2] is delivered to the purchaser and the purchaser is afforded a reasonable opportunity to examine the public offering statement prior to the disposition.

L.1989, c. 239, § 4, eff. Jan. 2, 1989.

[1] Section 45:15–16.32.
[2] Section 45:15–16.38.

45:15–16.31. Disposition of subdivision or subdivided lands subject to act

Disposition of subdivision or subdivided lands are subject to this act if:

a. Any offer or disposition of subdivided lands is made in this State; or

b. Any offer of subdivided land originating outside this State is directed by the subdivider or his agent to a person or resident within this State.

L.1989, c. 239, § 5, eff. Jan. 2, 1990.

45:15–16.32. Exempt transactions

a. Unless the method of disposition is adopted for the purpose of evasion of this act, the provisions of this act are not applicable to offers or dispositions of an interest in a subdivision:

(1) By an owner for his own account in a single or isolated transaction;

(2) Wholly for industrial or commercial purposes;

(3) Pursuant to court order;

(4) By any governmental agency;

(5) As cemetery lots or interests;

(6) Of less than 100 lots, parcels, units or interests; but, this exemption shall not apply to condominiums, cooperatives, time-shares, retirement communities and offers or dispositions by entities comprised of or acting on behalf of the owners of other units in the subdivision, including, but not limited to entities designated as homeowners associations, regardless of the number of lots, parcels, units or interests offered or disposed of;

(7) Where the common elements or interests, which would otherwise subject the offering to this act, are limited to the provision of unimproved, unencumbered open space, except where registration is required by the "Interstate Land Sales Full Disclosure Act," Pub.L. 90–448 (15 U.S.C. § 1701 et seq.) with the Office of Interstate Land Sales Registration, in the Department of Housing and Urban Development; or

(8) In a development comprised wholly of rental units, where the relationship created is one of landlord and tenant; but this exemption shall not apply to time-shares, regardless of the manner in which an interest in such a time-share subdivision is evidenced.

b. Unless the method of disposition is adopted for the purpose of evasion of this act, the provisions of this act are not applicable to:

(1) Offers or dispositions of evidences of indebtedness secured by a mortgage or deed of trust of real estate;

(2) Offers or dispositions of securities or units of interest issued by a real estate investment trust regulated under any State or federal statute;

(3) Offers or dispositions of securities currently registered with the Bureau of Securities in the Department of Law and Public Safety; or

(4) Offers or dispositions of any interest in oil, gas or other minerals or any royalty interest therein if the offers or dispositions of such interests are regulated as securities by federal law or by the State Bureau of Securities.

c. The commission may, from time to time, pursuant to any rules and regulations promulgated pursuant to this act, exempt from any of the provisions of this act any subdivision or any lots in a subdivision, if it finds that the enforcement of this act with respect to that subdivision or the lots therein, is not necessary in the public interest, or required for the protection of purchasers, by reason of the small amount involved or the limited character of the offering.

L.1989, c. 239, § 6, eff. Jan. 2, 1990.

45:15–16.33. Registration; application; notice of filing; order of registration; notice of need to correct

a. Upon the filing of an application for registration at the offices of the commission, naming the brokers licensed as real estate brokers pursuant to R.S. 45:15–1 et seq. who are the authorized representatives of the subdivider, and accompanied by the proper registration fee in the proper form, and a statement of record as provided for in section 10 of this act, and the proposed public offering statement, the commission shall issue a notice of filing to the applicant. Within 90 days from the date of the notice of filing, the commission shall enter an order registering the subdivision or subdivided lands or rejecting the registration. If no order of rejection is entered within 90 days from the date of notice of filing, the subdivisions or subdivided lands shall be deemed registered unless the applicant has consented in writing to a delay.

b. If the commission affirmatively determines upon inquiry and examination that the requirements of section 9 of this act [1] have been met, it shall enter an order registering the subdivision or subdivided lands and shall designate the form of the public offering statement.

c. If the commission determines upon inquiry and examination that any of the requirements of section 9 of this act have not been met, the commission shall notify the applicant that the application for registration must be corrected in the particulars specified within 30 days from the date the notice is received by the applicant. These findings shall be the result of the commission's preliminary inquiry and examination and no hearing shall be required as the basis for those findings. The receipt of a written request for a hearing shall stay the order of rejection until a hearing has been held and a determination has been made.

L.1989, c. 239, § 7, eff. Jan. 2, 1990.

[1] Section 45:15–16.35.

45:15–16.34. Fees; form for application for registration; onsite inspection

a. (1) The fee for an initial registration shall be $500 plus $35 for each lot, parcel, unit or interest which fee shall not exceed $3,000. The initial registration shall be valid for a period of one year from the date of approval of the registration. If the fees are insufficient to defray the cost of rendering services required by the provisions of this act, the commission may, by regulation, establish a revised fee schedule. Any revised fee schedule shall assure that the fees collected reasonably cover, but do not exceed, the expenses of administering the provisions of this act.

(2) Annual renewal of registration shall be made in accordance with the provisions of section 14 of this act.[1]

(3) Any current registration filed with and approved by the commission pursuant to the provisions of P.L.1975, c. 235 (C. 45:15–16.3 et seq.) prior to the date of enactment of this act shall be exempt from initial registration under this act.

b. The application for registration shall be made on forms prescribed by the commission and shall be accompanied by the appropriate filing fee. As provided in subsection f. of section 15 of this act,[2] the commission may determine, at its discretion, that an onsite investigation or inspection is required. The commission shall advise the registrant of the amount of the cost of travel from New Jersey to the location of the subdivided lands and return and any additional expenses of an inspection, which shall be the amount of the inspection fee. All inspection fees shall be accounted for to the applicant.

c. The fee for a consolidated filing, filed pursuant to section 13 of this act,[3] shall be the same as set forth in subsection a. of this section.

L.1989, c. 239, § 8, eff. Jan. 2, 1990.

[1] Section 45:15–16.40.
[2] Section 45:15–16.41.
[3] Section 45:15–16.39.

45:15–16.35. Conditions for issuance of registration

Upon receipt of an application for registration in proper form, accompanied by a statement of record, the commission shall initiate an examination to determine that:

a. The subdivider can convey or cause to be conveyed the interest in subdivided lands offered for disposition if the purchaser complies with the terms of the offer, and when appropriate, that release clauses, conveyances in trust or other safeguards have been provided;

b. There is reasonable assurance that all proposed improvements will be completed as represented;

c. The advertising material and the general promotional plan are not false, misleading, or discriminatory and comply with the standards prescribed by the commission in its rules and regulations and afford full and fair disclosure;

d. The subdivider has not, or if a corporation, its officers, directors, and principals have not, been convicted of a crime or civil offense involving land dispositions or any aspect of the land sales business in this State, the United States, or any other state or foreign country; and that the developer has not been subject to any permanent injunction or final administrative order restraining a false or misleading promotional plan involving real property dispositions, the seriousness of which in the opinion of the commission warrants the denial of registration; and

e. The public offering statement requirements of section 12 of this act [1] have been satisfied.

L.1989, c. 239, § 9, eff. Jan. 2, 1990.

[1] Section 45:15-16.38.

45:15-16.36. Statement of record; contents; accompanying documents

The statement of record shall contain the information and be accompanied by the documents specified as follows:

a. The name and address of each person having an interest in the lots in the subdivision to be covered by the statement of record and the extent of that interest;

b. A legal description of, and a statement of the total area included in, the subdivision and a statement of the topography, together with a map showing the subdivision proposed and the dimensions of the lots, parcels, units, or interests to be covered by the statement of record and their relation to existing streets, roads and other improvements. The map shall be drawn to scale, signed and sealed, by a licensed professional engineer or land surveyor;

c. A statement of the condition of the title to the land comprising the subdivision, including all encumbrances and deed restrictions and covenants applicable thereto;

d. A statement of the general terms and conditions proposed to dispose of the lots in the subdivision;

e. A statement of the present condition of access to the subdivision, the existence of any unusual conditions relating to noise or safety, which affect the subdivision and are known or should reasonably be known to the developer, the availability of sewage disposal facilities and other public utilities, including water, electricity, gas, and telephone facilities, in the subdivision to nearby municipalities, and the nature of any improvements to be installed by the developer and his estimated schedule for completion;

f. A statement as to whether the property or any portion thereof is regularly or periodically subject to natural forces that would tend to adversely affect the use or enjoyment of the property and whether the property or any portion thereof is located in a federally designated flood hazard area;

g. In the case of any subdivision or portion thereof against which there exists a blanket encumbrance, a statement of the consequences for an individual purchaser of a failure, by the persons bound, to fulfill obligations under the instruments creating such encumbrances and the steps, if any, taken to protect the purchaser in such eventuality;

h. (1) Copy of its articles of incorporation, with all amendments thereto, if the developer is a corporation; (2) copies of all instruments by which the trust is created or declared, if the developer is a trust; (3) copies of its articles of partnership or association and all other papers pertaining to its organization, if the developer is a partnership, unincorporated association, joint stock company, or any other form of organization; and (4) if the purported holder of legal title is a person other than the developer, copies of the appropriate documents required pursuant to this subsection for that person;

i. Copies of the deed or other instrument establishing title to the subdivision in the developer or other person and copies of any instrument creating a lien or encumbrance upon the title of developer or other person or copies of the opinion of counsel in respect to the title to the subdivision in the developer or other person or companies of the title insurance policy guaranteeing that title;

j. Copies of all forms of conveyance to be used in selling or leasing lots to purchasers;

k. Copies of instruments creating easements or other restrictions;

l. Certified and uncertified financial statements of the developer as required by the commission;

m. Copies of any management contract, lease of recreational areas, or similar contract or agreement affecting the use, maintenance, or access of all or any part of the subdivision;

n. A statement of the status of compliance with the requirements of all laws, ordinances, regulations, and other requirements of governmental agencies, including the federal government, having jurisdiction over the premises;

o. The developer shall immediately report any material changes in the information contained in an application for registration. The term "material changes" shall be further defined by the commission in its regulations; and

p. Any other information and any other documents and certification as the commission may require as being reasonably necessary for the protection of purchasers.

L.1989, c. 239, § 10, eff. Jan. 2, 1990.

45:15–16.37. Statement of record; availability to public

The information contained in any statement of record and any additions or corrections required by section 10 of this act [1] shall be made available to the public under regulations promulgated by the commission pursuant to this act and copies shall be furnished to every applicant at a reasonable charge prescribed by the commission.

L.1989, c. 239, § 11, eff. Jan. 2, 1990.

[1] Section 45:15–16.36.

45:15–16.38. Public offering statement; contents; form; use; amendment or consolidation; cancellation clause in contract; availability to public

a. A public offering statement shall disclose fully and accurately the physical characteristics of the subdivided lands offered and shall make known to prospective purchasers all unusual and material circumstances or features affecting those lands. The proposed public offering statement submitted to the commission shall be in a form prescribed by the rules and regulations promulgated pursuant to this act and shall include the following:

(1) The name and principal address of the developer and his authorized New Jersey representative who shall be a licensed real estate broker licensed to maintain offices within this State;

(2) A general description of the subdivision or subdivided lands stating the total number of lots, parcels, units or interests in the offering;

(3) A summary of the terms and conditions of any management contract, lease of recreational areas, or similar contract or agreement affecting the use, maintenance, or access of all or any part of the subdivision or subdivided lands, the effect of each agreement upon a purchaser, and a statement of the relationship, if any, between the developer or subdivider and the managing agent or firm;

(4) The significant terms of any encumbrances, easements, liens and restrictions, including zoning and other regulations affecting the lands and each unit or lot, and a statement of all existing taxes and existing or proposed special taxes or assessments which affect the lands;

(5) A statement of the use for which the property is offered, including, but not limited to:

(a) Information concerning improvements, including hospitals, health and recreational facilities of any kind, streets, water supply, levees, drainage control systems, irrigation systems, sewage disposal facilities and customary utilities; and

(b) The estimated cost, date of completion and responsibility for construction and maintenance of existing and proposed improvements which are referred to in connection with the offering or disposition of any interest in the subdivision or subdivided lands;

(6) The notice, as required in subsection d. of this section, shall, in addition to being contained in all contracts or agreements, be conspicuously located and simply stated in the public offering statement; and

(7) Additional information required by the commission to assure full and fair disclosure to prospective purchasers.

b. The public offering statement shall not be used for any promotional purposes before registration of the subdivided lands and afterwards only if it is used in its entirety. No person may advertise or represent that the commission approves or recommends the subdivided lands or the disposition thereof. No portion of the public offering statement may be underscored, italicized, or printed in larger or heavier or different color type than the remainder of the statement unless the commission requires or permits it.

c. The commission may require the subdivider to alter or amend the proposed public offering statement in order to assure full and fair disclosure to prospective purchasers, and no change in the substance of the promotional plan or plan of disposition or development of the subdivision may be made after registration without notifying the commission and without making an appropriate amendment to the public offering statement. A public offering statement is not current unless all amendments or consolidations are incorporated.

d. Any contract or agreement for the purchase or the leasing of a lot may be rescinded by the purchaser or lessee without cause of any kind by sending or delivering written notice of cancellation by midnight of the seventh calendar day following the day on which the purchaser has executed the contract or agreement. Every contract or agreement shall be in writing and shall contain the following notice in 10–point bold type or larger, directly above the space provided for the signature of the purchaser or lessee:

> NOTICE to PURCHASER or LESSEE: You are entitled to the right to cancel this contract by midnight of the seventh calendar day following the day on which you have executed this contract or agreement.

e. The subdivider shall make copies of the public offering statement available to prospective purchasers prior to their signing any contract or agreement.

L.1989, c. 239, § 12, eff. Jan. 2, 1990.

45:15–16.39. Registration; additional subdivided lands under common promotional plan

A subdivider may register additional subdivided lands pursuant to the same common promotional plan as those previously registered by submitting an additional filing providing the additional information necessary to register the additional lots, parcels, units or interests which shall be designated as "a consolidated filing."

L.1989, c. 239, § 13, eff. Jan. 2, 1990.

45:15–16.40. Annual report by subdivider; amendments to registration; review of requests; fee; order terminating responsibilities of developer

a. Within 30 days after each annual anniversary date of an order registering the subdivided lands, or on or before a date set by the commission, and while the subdivider retains any interest therein, the subdivider of these lands shall file a report in the form prescribed by the rules and regulations promulgated by the commission. The report shall reflect any material changes in the information contained in the original application for registration; except that, with respect to any registration filed with and approved by the commission prior to the date of enactment of this act, no additional information shall be required on the subdivided land covered by such registration other than that necessary to indicate any material changes in information contained in the original application for registration.

b. The commission shall process and review requests for amendments to a registration in accordance with the standards and procedures established in this act for review of applications for registration. Requests for amendment, other than price changes and advertising, shall be accompanied by a fee as the commission may prescribe by rule.

c. Upon a determination by the commission that an annual report is no longer necessary for the protection of the public interest or that the developer no longer retains any interest and no longer has any contractual, bond or other obligations in the subdivision, the commission shall issue an order terminating the responsibilities of the developer under this act.

L.1989, c. 329, § 14, eff. Jan. 2, 1990.

45:15–16.41. Powers of commission

The commission may:

a. Accept registrations filed in this State, in other states or with the federal government;

b. Contract with similar agencies in this State or other jurisdictions to perform investigative functions;

c. Accept grants in aid from any governmental or other source;

d. Cooperate with similar agencies or commissions in this State or other jurisdictions to establish uniform filing procedures and forms, uniform public offering statements, advertising standards, rules and common administrative practices;

e. Grant exemptions pursuant to the rules and regulations adopted pursuant to section 23 of this act;[1]

f. Make any necessary public or private investigations within or outside of this State to determine whether any person has violated or is about to violate any provision of this act, or to aid in the enforcement of this act or in the prescribing of rules and regulations and forms hereunder;

g. Require or permit any person to file a statement in writing, under oath or otherwise, as the commission determines, as to all the facts and circumstances concerning the matter to be investigated;

h. For the purpose of any investigation or proceeding under this act, the commission or any officer designated by rule, may administer oaths, or affirmations, and upon its own motion or upon request of any party may subpoena witnesses and compel their attendance, take evidence, and require the production of any matter which is relevant to the investigation, including the existence, description, nature, custody, condition and location of any books, documents, or other tangible things and the identity and location of persons having knowledge of relevant facts or any other matter reasonably calculated to lead to the discovery of material evidence; and

i. Upon failure to obey a subpoena or to answer questions propounded by the investigating officer and upon reasonable notice to all persons affected thereby, the commission may apply to the Superior Court for an order compelling compliance.

L.1989, c. 239, § 15, eff. Jan. 2, 1989.

[1] Section 45:15–16.49.

45:15–16.42. Cease and desist orders; notice and hearing; temporary orders

a. If the commission determines after notice and hearing that a person has:

(1) Violated any provision of this act;

(2) Directly or through an agent or employee engaged in any false, deceptive, or misleading advertising, promotional or sales methods in the State of New Jersey to offer or dispose of an interest in the subdivision or subdivided lands;

(3) Made any material change in the plan of disposition and development of the subdivision or subdivided lands subsequent to the order of registration without first complying with the provisions of subsection *o.* of section 10 of this act;

(4) Disposed of any subdivision or subdivided lands which have not been registered with the commission; or

(5) Violated any lawful order or rule or regulation of the commission;

the commission may issue an order requiring the person to cease and desist from the unlawful practice and to take such affirmative action as in the judgment of the commission will carry out the purposes of this act.

b. If the commission makes a finding of fact in writing that the public interest will be irreparably harmed by delay in issuing an order, it may issue a temporary cease and desist order. Every temporary cease and desist order shall include in its terms a provision that upon request a hearing will be held within 15 days of the receipt of the request.

L.1989, c. 239, § 16, eff. Jan. 2, 1990.

45:15–16.43. Revocation of registration; notice and hearing; grounds

a. A registration may be revoked after notice and hearing upon a written finding of fact that the subdivider has:

(1) Failed to comply with the terms of a cease and desist order issued pursuant to subsection a. of section 16 of this act;[1]

(2) Been convicted in any court for a crime or civil offense involving fraud, deception, false pretenses, misrepresentation, false advertising, dishonest dealing, or other like offense subsequent to the filing of the application for registration;

(3) Disposed of, concealed, or diverted any funds or assets of any person so as to defeat the rights of subdivision purchasers;

(4) Failed faithfully to perform any stipulation or agreement made with the commission as an inducement to grant any registration, to reinstate any registration, or to approve any promotional plan or public offering statement;

(5) Advertised his subdivision or responded to applications for his subdivision in a manner which was discriminatory on the basis of marital status, sex, race, creed, color, religion or national origin;

(6) Willfully violated any provision of this act or of a rule or regulation promulgated pursuant to section 23 of this act;[2] or

(7) Made intentional misrepresentation or concealed material facts in the documents and information submitted in the application filed for registration. Findings of fact, if set forth in statutory language, shall be accompanied by a concise and explicit statement of the underlying facts supporting the findings.

b. If the commission finds, after notice and hearing, that the subdivider has been guilty of a violation for which revocation could be ordered, it may, in lieu thereof, issue a cease and desist order pursuant to subsection a. of section 16 of this act.

L.1989, c. 239, § 17, eff. Jan. 2, 1990.

[1] Section 45:15–16.42.

[2] Section 45:15–16.49.

45:15–16.44. Injunctions or temporary restraining orders; intervention in actions involving subdivided lands

a. If it appears that a person has engaged, or is about to engage, in an act or practice constituting a violation of a provision of this act, the commission, with or without prior administrative proceedings, may bring an action in the Superior Court to enjoin the acts or practices and to enforce compliance with this act or any rule, regulation or order hereunder. Upon proper showing, injunctive relief or temporary restraining orders shall be granted, and a receiver may be appointed. The commission shall not be required to post a bond in any court proceeding.

b. The commission may intervene in a suit involving any subdivision. In any such suit, by or against the developer or subdivider, the developer or subdivider shall promptly furnish the commission with notice of the suit and copies of all pleadings.

L.1989, c. 239, § 18, eff. Jan. 2, 1990.

45:15–16.45. Jurisdiction of courts; service of process

a. For purposes of this act, an applicant for registration submitted to the commission shall be deemed as submission, by the applicant, to the jurisdiction of the Courts of the State of New Jersey.

b. In addition to the methods of service provided for in the Rules Governing the Courts of the State of New Jersey, service may be made by delivering a copy of the process to the person in charge of the office of the commission at its office, but that service shall not be effective unless the plaintiff, which may be the commission in a proceeding instituted by it:

(1) Sends a copy of the process and the pleading by certified mail to the defendant or respondent at his last known address; and

(2) The plaintiff's affidavit of compliance with this section is filed in the case on or before the return day of the process, if any, or within the time as the court allows.

c. If any person, including any nonresident of this State, engaged in conduct prohibited by this act and has not filed a consent of service of process and personal jurisdiction over him cannot otherwise be obtained in this State, that conduct authorizes the commission to receive service of process in any noncriminal proceedings against him or his successor which grows out of that conduct and which is brought under this act with the same force and validity as if served on him personally. Notice shall be given as provided in subsection a. of this section.

L.1989, c. 239, § 19, eff. Jan. 2, 1990.

45:15–16.46. Violations; penalties; hearing and finding; action to recover; compromise of penalty

a. Any broker or salesperson who violates any of the provisions of this act shall, in addition to the penalties set forth herein, be subject to the penalties as set forth in R.S. 45:15–17.

b. Any person who violates any provision of this act or any person who, in an application for registration filed with the commission, makes any untrue statement of a material fact or omits to state a material fact shall be fined not less than $250, nor more than $50,000, per violation.

c. The commission may levy and collect the penalties set forth in subsection b. of this section after affording the person alleged to be in violation of this act an opportunity to appear before the commission and to be heard personally or through counsel on the alleged violations and a finding by the commission that said person is guilty of the violation. When a penalty levied by the commission has not been satisfied within 30 days of the levy, the penalty may be sued for and recovered by, and in the name of, the commission in a summary proceeding pursuant to "the penalty enforcement law" (N.J.S.2A:58–1 et seq.).

d. The commission may, in the interest of justice, compromise any civil penalty, if in its determination the gravity of the offense or offenses does not warrant the assessment of the full fine.

L.1989, c. 239, § 20, eff. Jan. 2, 1990.

45:15–16.47. Action by person who suffers loss due to failure to comply with act; remedies; award of costs and attorney fees; joint and several liability; invalidity of waiver of compliance clauses; notice to and intervention by commissioner

a. Any person who suffers any ascertainable loss of moneys as a result of the failure of another to comply fully with the provisions of this act may bring an action or assert a counterclaim in any court of competent jurisdiction. In any action filed under this section in which a defendant is found to have knowingly engaged in any false, deceptive, misleading promotional or sales methods or discriminatory advertising on the basis of race, sex, creed, color, marital status, national origin or religion, concealed or fraudulently diverted any funds or assets so as to defeat the rights of subdivision purchasers, made an intentional misrepresentation or concealed a material fact in an application for registration, or disposed of any subdivision or subdivided lands required to be registered under section 7 of this act which are not so registered, the court shall, in addition to any other appropriate legal or equitable remedy, award double the damages suffered, and court costs expended, including reasonable attorney's fees. In the case of an untruth, omission, or misleading statement the developer sustains the burden of proving that the purchaser knew of the untruth, omission or misleading statement, or that he did not rely on such information, or that the developer did not know, and in the exercise of reasonable care could not have known, of the untruth, omission, or misleading statement.

b. The court may, in addition to the remedies provided in this act, frame any other relief that may be appropriate under the circumstances including, in the court's discretion, restitution of all monies paid and, where a subdivider has failed to provide to a purchaser a copy of the current public offering statement approved by the commission prior to execution of the contract or agreement, rescission of the contract. If the purchaser fails to establish a cause of action, and the court further determines that the action was wholly without merit, the court may award attorney's fees to the developer or subdivider.

c. Every person who directly or indirectly controls a subdivision or developer and violates the provisions of subsection a. of this section, every general partner, officer, or director of a developer, and every person occupying a similar status or performing a similar function, shall be jointly and severally liable with and to the same extent as the developer. The person otherwise liable pursuant to this subsection sustains the burden of proof that he did not know, and in the exercise of reasonable care could not have known, of the existence of the facts by reason of which the liability is alleged to exist. There is a right to contribution among persons found liable.

d. Any stipulation or provision purporting to bind any purchaser acquiring a parcel, lot, unit, or interest in any development subject to the provisions of this act to a waiver of compliance with the provisions of this act, shall be void.

e. Any party to an action asserting a claim, counterclaim or defense based upon any violation of this act shall mail a copy of the initial or responsive pleading containing the claim, counterclaim or defense to the commission within 10 days of the filing of the pleading with court. Upon application to the court where the matter is pending, the commission shall be permitted to intervene or to appear in any status appropriate to the matter.

L.1989, c. 239, § 21, eff. Jan. 2, 1990.

45:15–16.48. Registration of subdivision under Land Sales Full Disclosure Act; duration

Any registration of a subdivision or amendment thereto, or consolidation, or renewal thereof approved by the commission prior to August 2, 1989, under the "Land Sales Full

Disclosure Act," P.L.1975, c. 235 (C. 45:15–16.3 et seq.) shall, upon the enactment of this act, be deemed in force and effect for the remainder of the 12–month period for which it was issued.

L.1989, c. 239, § 22, eff. Jan. 2, 1990.

45:15–16.49. Rules and regulations

The commission shall, pursuant to the provisions of the "Administrative Procedure Act," P.L.1968, c. 410 (C. 52:14B–1 et seq.), promulgate rules and regulations necessary to effectuate the provisions of this act. The rules may include, but shall not be limited to: a. provisions for advertising standards to insure full and fair disclosure; b. provisions for adequate bondings or access to some escrow or trust fund not otherwise required by the municipal governing body to be located within this State, or the state or country where the property is located, so as to insure compliance with the provisions of this act, and to compensate purchasers for failure of the registrant to perform in accordance with the terms of any contract or public statement; c. provisions that require a registrant to deposit purchaser down payments, security deposits or other funds in an escrow account, or with an attorney licensed to practice law in this State, or the state or country where the property is located, until such time as the commission by its rules and regulations deems it appropriate to permit such funds to be released; d. provisions to insure that all contracts between developer and purchaser are fair and reasonable; e. provisions that the developer must give a fair and reasonable warranty on construction of any improvements; f. provisions that the budget for the operation and maintenance of the common or shared elements or interest shall provide for adequate reserves for depreciation and replacement of the improvements; g. provisions for operating procedures; and h. other rules and regulations necessary to effectuate the purposes of this act, and taking into account and providing for, the broad range of development plans and devises, management mechanisms, and methods of ownership, permitted under the provisions of this act.

L.1989, c. 239, § 23, eff. Jan. 2, 1990.

45:15–17. Probation, suspension or revocation of licenses; investigations; jurisdiction; cause

The commission may, upon its own motion, and shall, upon the verified complaint in writing of any person, investigate the actions of any real estate broker, broker-salesperson or salesperson, or any person who assumes, advertises or represents himself as being authorized to act as a real estate broker, broker-salesperson or salesperson or engages in any of the activities described in R.S. 45:15–3 without being licensed so to do. The lapse or suspension of a license by operation of law or the voluntary surrender of a license by a licensee shall not deprive the commission of jurisdiction to proceed with any investigation as herein provided or prevent the commission from taking any regulatory action against such licensee, provided, however, that the alleged charges arose while said licensee was duly licensed. Each transaction shall be construed as a separate offense.

In conducting investigations, the commission may take testimony by deposition as provided in R.S. 45:15–18, require or permit any person to file a statement in writing, under oath or otherwise as the commission determines, as to all the facts and circumstances concerning the matter under investigation, and, upon its own motion or upon the request of any party, subpoena witnesses, compel their attendance, take evidence, and require the production of any material which is relevant to the investigation, including any and all records of a licensee pertaining to his activities as a real estate broker, broker-salesperson or salesperson. The commission may also require the provision of any information concerning the existence, description, nature, custody, condition and location of any books, documents, or other tangible material and the identity and location of persons having knowledge of relevant facts of any other matter reasonably calculated to lead to the discovery of material evidence. Upon failure to obey a subpoena or to answer questions posed by an investigator or legal representative of the commission and upon reasonable notice to all affected persons, the commission may commence an administrative action as provided below or apply to the Superior Court for an order compelling compliance.

The commission may place on probation, suspend for a period less than the unexpired portion of the license period, or may revoke any license issued under the provisions of this article, or the right of licensure when such person is no longer the holder of a license at the time of hearing, or may impose, in addition or as an alternative to such probation, revocation or suspension, a penalty of not more than $5,000 for the first violation, and a penalty of not more than $10,000 for any subsequent violation, which penalty shall be sued for and recovered by and in the name of the commission and shall be collected and enforced by summary proceedings pursuant to "the penalty enforcement law" (N.J.S. 2A:58–1 et seq.), where the licensee or any person, in performing or attempting to perform any of the acts mentioned herein, is deemed to be guilty of:

a. Making any false promises or any substantial misrepresentation; or

b. Acting for more than one party in a transaction without the knowledge of all parties thereto; or

c. Pursuing a flagrant and continued course of misrepresentation or making of false promises through agents, broker-salespersons or salespersons, advertisements or otherwise; or

d. Failure to account for or to pay over any moneys belonging to others, coming into the possession of the licensee; or

e. Any conduct which demonstrates unworthiness, incompetency, bad faith or dishonesty. The failure of any person to cooperate with the commission in the performance of its duties or to comply with a subpoena issued by the commission compelling the production of materials in the course of an investigation, or the failure to give a verbal or written statement concerning a matter under investigation may be construed as conduct demonstrating unworthiness; or

f. Failure to provide his client with a fully executed copy of any sale or exclusive sales or rental listing contract at the time of execution thereof, or failure to specify therein a definite terminal date which terminal date shall not be subject to any qualifying terms or conditions; or

g. Using any plan, scheme or method for the sale or promotion of the sale of real estate which involves a lottery, a contest, a game, a prize, a drawing, or the offering of a lot or parcel or lots or parcels for advertising purposes; or

h. Being convicted of a crime, knowledge of which the commission did not have at the time of last issuing a real estate license to the licensee; or

i. Collecting a commission as a real estate broker in a transaction, when at the same time representing either party in a transaction in a different capacity for a consideration; or

j. Using any trade name or insignia of membership in any real estate organization of which the licensee is not a member; or

k. Paying any rebate, profit, compensation or commission to anyone not possessed of a real estate license; or

l. Any other conduct, whether of the same or a different character than specified in this section, which constitutes fraud or dishonest dealing; or

m. Accepting a commission or valuable consideration as a real estate broker-salesperson or salesperson for the performance of any of the acts specified in this act, from any person, except his employing broker, who must be a licensed broker; or

n. Procuring a real estate license, for himself or anyone else, by fraud, misrepresentation or deceit; or

o. Commingling the money or other property of his principals with his own or failure to maintain and deposit in a special account, separate and apart from personal or other business accounts, all moneys received by a real estate broker, acting in said capacity, or as escrow agent, or the temporary custodian of the funds of others, in a real estate transaction; or

p. Selling property in the ownership of which he is interested in any manner whatsoever, unless he first discloses to the purchaser in the contract of sale his interest therein and his status as a real estate broker, broker-salesperson or salesperson; or

q. Purchasing any property unless he first discloses to the seller in the contract of sale his status as a real estate broker, broker-salesperson or salesperson; or

r. Charging or accepting any fee, commission or compensation in exchange for providing information on purportedly available rental housing, including lists of such units supplied verbally or in written form, before a lease has been executed or, where no lease is drawn, before the tenant has taken possession of the premises without complying with all applicable rules promulgated by the commission regulating these practices; or

s. Failing to notify the commission within 30 days of having been convicted of any crime, misdemeanor or disorderly persons offense, or of having been indicted, or of the filing of any formal criminal charges, or of the suspension or revocation of any real estate license issued by another state, or of the initiation of formal disciplinary proceedings in another state affecting any real estate license held, or failing to supply any documentation available to the licensee that the commission may request in connection with such matter; or

t. The violation of any of the provisions of this article or of the administrative rules adopted by the commission pursuant to the provisions of this article. The commission is expressly vested with the power and authority to make, prescribe and enforce any and all rules and regulations for the conduct of the real estate brokerage business consistent with the provisions of chapter 15 of Title 45 of the Revised Statutes.

If a licensee is deemed to be guilty of a third violation of any of the provisions of this section, whether of the same provision or of separate provisions, the commission may deem that person a repeat offender, in which event the commission may direct that no license as a real estate broker, broker-salesperson or salesperson shall henceforth be issued to that person.

Amended by L.1948, c. 155, p. 889, § 2; L.1953, c. 229, p. 1690, § 5; L.1954, c. 193, p. 724, § 2; L.1966, c. 11, § 5; L.1977, c. 331, § 5, eff. Jan. 11, 1978; L.1989, c. 126, § 3, eff. July 3, 1989; L.1993, c. 51, § 20, eff. May 20, 1993.

45:15-17.1. Temporary suspension of license; notice required; evidentiary hearing

The commission may, on its own motion, enter an order temporarily suspending the license of any licensee upon making a finding that prima facie evidence exists that the licensee has violated subsection d. or subsection *o.* of R.S. 45:15-17. At least 24 hours prior to entering the order, the commission shall give notice to the licensee of the application for the order and shall provide the licensee with an opportunity to be heard. The notice may be given either by telephone or in writing and may be served personally or sent by certified mail to the last known business address of the licensee.

When the commission orders the temporary suspension of a license, it shall advise the licensee of the date upon which the commission shall hold an evidentiary hearing on the violations upon which the temporary suspension is based, which date shall be no more than 30 days following the date of the order entering the temporary suspension.

L.1993, c. 51, § 23, eff. May 20, 1993.

45:15–17.2. Assets of broker with temporarily suspended license to be frozen; notice; payment of monies into the court upon continuation of suspension or revocation of license

Upon entering an order temporarily suspending the license of any broker, the commission may also enter an order directing that some or all of the accounts maintained by the broker in any depository institution in the State be temporarily frozen. The commission shall serve copies of the order upon the institution either in person or by certified mail within ten days and, where a broker's trust or escrow account is frozen, upon all persons known to the commission for whom the broker was acting as escrow agent or trustee. In the event the commission subsequently determines that the suspension shall not be continued, it shall immediately notify the depository institution and other interested parties that the temporary freeze order is dissolved. If the commission orders that the license suspension shall continue for more than 30 days or that a license revocation shall be imposed, the commission shall, within 10 days of that ruling, make application to Superior Court for payment into the court of all funds in the accounts temporarily frozen by order of the commission. The commission shall provide notice of the application to the broker and all known interested parties. Following payment into court, the monies or any portion of them shall thereafter only be released upon court order obtained by the broker or other interested party, upon notice to the commission and in compliance with court rules.

L.1993, c. 51, § 24, eff. May 20, 1993.

45:15–17.3. Failure by agent to comply with requirements for sale of mobile home; conduct demonstrating incompetency

A real estate licensee who acts as an agent or broker in the sale of a mobile or manufactured home, as defined in subsection a. of R.S. 39:10–19, in a manner which does not comply with all requirements of R.S. 39:10–1 et seq. applicable to the sale of any such mobile or manufactured home, shall, pursuant to R.S. 45:15–17, be subject to sanctions by the New Jersey Real Estate Commission for engaging in conduct which demonstrates incompetency.

L.1994, c. 150, § 2, eff. Dec. 2, 1994.

45:15–17.4. Rules and regulations

The New Jersey Real Estate Commission, after consultation with the Director of the Division of Motor Vehicles, shall, pursuant to the provisions of the "Administrative Procedure Act," P.L.1968, c. 410 (C. 52:14B–1 et seq.), promulgate rules and regulations to effectuate the provisions of this act.

L.1994, c. 150, § 3, eff. Dec. 2, 1994.

45:15–18. Notice of proposed suspension or revocation of license; witnesses and depositions; review

With the exception of a temporary suspension imposed by the commission pursuant to section 23 of P.L.1993, c. 51 (C. 45:15–17.1), the commission shall, before suspending or revoking any license, and at least ten days prior to the date set for the hearing, notify in writing the licensee of any charges made, and afford him an opportunity to be heard in person or by counsel. Such written notice may be served either personally or sent by certified mail to the last known business address of the licensee. If the licensee is a broker-salesperson or salesperson, the commission shall also notify the broker employing him, specifying the charges made against such licensee, by sending a notice thereof by certified mail to the broker's last known business address. The commission shall have power to bring before it any licensee or any person in this State pursuant to subpoena served personally or by certified mail; or the commission may take testimony by deposition in the same manner as prescribed by law in judicial proceedings in the courts of this State. Any final decision or determination of the commission shall be reviewable by the Appellate Division of the Superior Court.

Amended by L.1953, c. 43, p. 816, § 73; L.1993, c. 51, § 25, eff. May 20, 1993.

45:15–19. Revocation of salesperson's or broker-salesperson's license not to affect employer's license; exception

Any unlawful act or violation of any of the provisions of this article, by any real estate broker-salesperson or salesperson, shall not be cause for the revocation of any real estate broker's license, unless it shall appear to the satisfaction of the commission that the real estate broker employing such licensee had guilty knowledge thereof.

Amended by L.1993, c. 51, § 26, eff. May 20, 1993.

45:15–19.1. Revocation of license upon conviction of certain offenses

When, during the term of any license issued by the commission, the licensee shall be convicted in a court of competent jurisdiction in the State of New Jersey or any state (including federal courts) of forgery, burglary, robbery, any theft or related offense with the exception of shoplifting, criminal conspiracy to defraud, or other like offense or offenses, or any crime involving, related to or arising out of the licensee's activities as a real estate broker, broker-salesperson or salesperson, and a duly certified or exemplified copy of the judgment of conviction shall be obtained by the commission, the commission shall revoke forthwith the license by it theretofore issued to the licensee so convicted.

L.1953, c. 229, p. 1692, § 6. Amended by L.1989, c. 126, § 4, eff. July 3, 1989; L.1993, c. 51, § 27, eff. May 20, 1993.

45:15–19.2. Suspension of license

In the event that any licensee shall be indicted in the State of New Jersey or any state or territory (including federal courts) for murder, kidnapping, aggravated sexual assault, robbery, burglary, arson, any theft offense, bribery, racketeering, distribution of a controlled dangerous substance or conspiracy to distribute a controlled dangerous substance, forgery, criminal conspiracy to defraud, or other like offense or offenses, or any crime involving, related to or arising out of the licensee's activities as a real estate broker, broker-salesperson or salesperson, and a certified copy of the indictment is obtained by the commission, or other proper evidence thereof be to it given, the commission shall have authority, in its discretion, to suspend the license issued to such licensee pending trial upon such indictment.

L.1953, c. 229, p. 1692, § 7. Amended by L.1989, c. 126, § 5, eff. July 3, 1989; L.1993, c. 51, § 28, eff. May 20, 1993.

45:15–20. Licensing nonresidents; reciprocal privilege in certain cases; form of license

A nonresident may become a real estate broker, broker-salesperson or salesperson by conforming to all of the provisions of this article. All nonresident licenses issued by the commission prior to July 1, 1994 may be renewed upon payment of the renewal fees established pursuant to R.S. 45:15–15. All nonresident licenses so renewed shall be issued by the commission in the same form as a resident license. In the event that any person to whom a nonresident license is issued fails to maintain or renew the license or to obtain a new license from the commission for a period of two or more consecutive years, the person shall be required to fulfill the requirements for initial licensure established pursuant to R.S. 45:15–9 prior to the issuance of any further license.

A licensed broker whose main office is not located within this State shall only provide brokerage services concerning real estate located within this State either personally or through persons in the broker's employ who are the holders of real estate broker-salesperson or salesperson licenses issued by the commission. In the event that a broker maintains one or more branch offices in this State, no person shall engage in the business of a real estate broker, broker-salesperson or salesperson at those offices unless the person is a holder of a license issued by the commission authorizing him to do so.

Amended by L.1938, c. 227, p. 524, § 2; L.1949, c. 214, p. 693, § 1; L.1961, c. 88, p. 638, § 3; L.1993, c. 51, § 29.

45:15–21. Nonresident licensees; filing of consent as to service of process and pleadings

Every applicant for a license whose business address is outside this State shall file an irrevocable consent that suits and actions may be commenced against such applicant by the commission or by any person in any of the courts of record of this State, by the service of any process or pleading authorized by the laws of this State, in any county in which the plaintiff may reside, by serving the same on the secretary of the commission, said consent stipulating and agreeing that such service of such process or pleadings on said secretary shall be taken and held in all courts to be as valid and binding as if due service had been made personally upon the applicant in this State. This consent shall be duly acknowledged, and, if made by a corporation, shall be authenticated by its seal. The consent from a corporation shall be accompanied by a duly certified copy of the resolution of the board of directors, authorizing the proper officers to execute it. In all cases where process or pleadings shall be served, under the provisions of this article, upon the secretary of the commission, such process or pleadings shall be served in duplicate, one of which shall be filed in the office of the commission and the other shall be forwarded immediately by the secretary of the commission, by registered mail, to the last known business address of the licensee against which such process or pleadings are directed.

Every licensee whose business address is outside this State shall, by acceptance of a license for that out-of-state address, automatically and irrevocably consent to the commission's jurisdiction over and investigative authority regarding the licensed business premises, and all records and conduct of the licensee both within and outside of the State. The licensee shall also automatically and irrevocably consent that service of any pleading or subpoena issued by the secretary of the commission pursuant to R.S. 45:15–17 or R.S. 45:15–18 which is delivered by certified mail to the licensee's last known address, shall constitute valid and binding service of the subpoena or pleading upon the licensee as if service had been made personally upon the licensee in this State.

Amended by L.1993, c. 51, § 30.

45:15–22. Repealed by L.1993, c. 51, § 58, eff. May 20, 1993

45:15–23. Repealed by L.1989, c. 126, § 7, eff. July 3, 1989

45:15–24. Commitment for nonpayment of judgment

The trial shall be with a jury upon the demand of any party to the action. The court shall, if judgment be rendered for the plaintiff, cause any such defendant, who refuses or neglects to pay forthwith the amount of the judgment rendered against him and all costs and charges incident thereto, to be committed to the county jail for a period not exceeding thirty days.

Amended by L.1953, c. 43, p. 817, § 75.

45:15-25, 45:15-26. Repealed by L.1953, c. 43, §§ 76, 77

45:15-27. Disposition of penalties

Any penalty recovered for any violation of this article shall be applied by the commission to the same purpose as other funds of the commission collected in accordance with the provisions of this article.

Amended by L.1953, c. 43, p. 817, § 78.

45:15-28. Repealed by L.1953, c. 43, § 79

45:15-29. Payment of moneys into state treasury; payment of expenses of commission

a. All fines and penalties received by the commission pursuant to the provisions of this article shall be paid by it into the State treasury monthly. The payments shall be made on or before the tenth day of each month following their receipt, and at the time of payment a statement thereof shall be filed with the Director of the Division of Budget and Accounting.

b. All expenses incurred by the commission shall be paid from fees collected by the commission pursuant to the provisions of article I of chapter 15 of Title 45 of the Revised Statutes. Monies collected annually pursuant to this subsection shall be dedicated to the commission for the purposes of funding its incurred expenses for the current fiscal year, which expenses shall include, in addition to the direct cost of personal service, the cost of maintenance and operation, the cost of employee benefits and the workers' compensation paid for and on account of personnel, rentals for space occupied in State-owned or State-leased buildings and all other direct and indirect costs of the administration thereof.

Amended by L.1995, c. 156, § 15, eff. July 1, 1995.

45:15-29.1. Transfer of employees

Such employees of the New Jersey Real Estate Commission, as the Commissioner of Insurance may determine are needed for the proper performance of the work of the division of the New Jersey Real Estate Commission in the Department of Insurance, are hereby transferred to the Department of Insurance. Persons so transferred shall be assigned to such duties as the Commissioner of Insurance shall determine.

L.1948, c. 88, p. 502, § 6. Amended by L.1993, c. 51, § 31, eff. May 20, 1993.

45:15-29.2. Rights under Title 11A and under pension laws not affected

Nothing in this act shall be construed to deprive any person of any right or protection provided him by Title 11 [1] of the Revised Statutes, Civil Service, or under any pension law or retirement system.

L.1948, c. 88, p. 502, § 7.

[1] Now Title 11A.

45:15-29.3. Orders, rules and regulations previously made

The orders, rules and regulations heretofore made or promulgated by the New Jersey Real Estate Commission shall continue with full force and effect until amended or repealed by the New Jersey Real Estate Commission constituted hereunder as the Division of the New Jersey Real Estate Commission in the Department of Insurance.

L.1948, c. 88, p. 503, § 9. Amended by L.1993, c. 51, § 32, eff. May 20, 1993.

45:15-29.4. "New Jersey real estate commission," references to

Whenever the term "New Jersey Real Estate Commission" occurs or any reference is made thereto, in any law, contract or document, the same shall be deemed to mean or refer to the New Jersey Real Estate Commission constituted hereunder as the Division of the New Jersey Real Estate Commission in the Department of Insurance.

L.1948, c. 88, p. 503, § 10. Amended by L.1993, c. 51, § 33, eff. May 20, 1993.

45:15-29.5. Pending actions or proceedings

This act shall not affect actions or proceedings, civil or criminal, brought by or against the New Jersey Real Estate Commission and pending on the effective date of this act, and such actions or proceedings may be prosecuted or defended in the same manner and to the same effect by the New Jersey Real Estate Commission constituted hereunder as the Division of the New Jersey Real Estate Commission in the Department of Insurance as if the foregoing provisions had not taken effect; nor shall any of the foregoing provisions affect any order or recommendation made by, or other matters or proceedings before, the New Jersey Real Estate Commission; and all such matters or proceedings pending before the New Jersey Real Estate Commission on the effective date of this act shall be continued by the New Jersey Real Estate Commission constituted hereunder as the Division of the New Jersey Real Estate Commission in the Department of Insurance.

L.1948, c. 88, p. 503, § 11. Amended by L.1993, c. 51, § 34, eff. May 20, 1993.

ARTICLE 2. REAL ESTATE AUCTIONEERS [REPEALED]

45:15–30 to 45:15–33. Repealed by L.1953, c. 229, § 9

ARTICLE 3. REAL ESTATE GUARANTY FUND

45:15–34. Establishment; administration; recovery for embezzlement, conversion or unlawful obtaining of money or property by broker salesman; limit on claims

A real estate guaranty fund is established as a special trust fund to be maintained by the State Treasurer and administered by the New Jersey Real Estate Commission in accordance with the provisions of this act to provide a fund from which recovery may be obtained by any person aggrieved by the embezzlement, conversion or unlawful obtaining of money or property in a real estate brokerage transaction by a licensed real estate broker, broker-salesperson or salesperson or an unlicensed employee of a real estate broker; provided, however, that the amount of such recovery shall not exceed in the aggregate the sum of $10,000 in connection with any one transaction regardless of the number of claims, persons aggrieved, or parcels of, or interests in real estate involved in the transaction. The maximum amount recoverable per transaction shall be increased to $20,000 for claims filed on the basis of causes of action which accrue after the effective date of P.L.1993, c. 51 (C. 45:15–12.3 et al.).

L.1976, c. 112, § 1, eff. Feb. 1, 1977. Amended by L.1993, c. 51, § 35, eff. May 20, 1993.

45:15–35. Additional amount paid by brokers, broker-salesperson and salesperson upon initial issuance of license

Upon the initial issuance of a biennial license as a real estate broker, broker-salesperson or salesperson the licensee shall pay to the commission, in addition to the license fee fixed by R.S. 45:15–15, an additional amount to be forwarded by the commission to the State Treasurer and accounted for and credited by him to the real estate guaranty fund. The additional amount payable by a broker or broker-salesperson shall be $20 and by a salesperson, $10.

L.1976, c. 112, § 2, eff. Feb. 1, 1977. Amended by L.1993, c. 51, § 36, eff. May 20, 1993.
Amended by L.1996, c. 38, § 4, eff. Dec. 18, 1996.

45:15–36. Management and investment of funds

The State Treasurer shall hold, manage and through the Division of Investment, invest and reinvest funds of the real estate guaranty fund and credit all interest and other income earned thereon to the real estate guaranty fund in the same manner as provided by law with respect to investment of pension and retirement funds administered by the State. The Real Estate Commission shall keep the State Treasurer advised of the anticipated cash demands for payment of claims against the fund.

L.1976, c. 112, § 3, eff. Feb. 1, 1977.

45:15–37. Payment of claim; final judgment and order of court

No claim shall be made for payment from the real estate guaranty fund except upon the reduction to final judgment, which shall include reasonable attorney fees and costs, of a civil action against the broker, broker-salesperson or salesperson or unlicensed employee of a broker, and, where the judgment creditor has pursued all available remedies, made all reasonable searches, and has been unable to satisfy the judgment from the licensee's assets, the entry of a court order which directs the Real Estate Commission to make payment from the fund. No such order shall authorize a payment to the spouse or personal representative of the spouse of the judgment debtor.

No order shall be entered unless the claimant, either at the time of filing the civil action or thereafter, files a certification affirming that a criminal complaint alleging the misappropriation of funds by the broker, broker-salesperson, salesperson or unlicensed employee has been filed with a law enforcement agency of this State or of a county or municipality in this State. The criminal complaint shall refer to the same conduct to which reference is made in the civil action as forming the basis for a claim against the real estate guaranty fund. The certification shall specify the date on which the criminal complaint was filed and the law enforcement agency with which it was filed. A copy of the certification shall be provided to the Real Estate Commission upon its being filed. The requirement to file a certification shall apply prospectively only to claims seeking reimbursement from the fund filed on the basis of causes of action which accrue after the effective date of P.L.1993, c. 51 (C. 45:15–12.3 et al.).

Upon delivery by the Real Estate Commission to the State Treasurer of a certified copy of the court order together with an assignment to the Real Estate Commission of the judgment creditor's right, title and interest in the judgment to the extent of the amount of the court order, the State Treasurer shall make payment to the claimant from the real estate guaranty fund.

L.1976, c. 112, § 4, eff. Feb. 1, 1977. Amended by L.1993, c. 51, § 37, eff. May 20, 1993.

45:15–38. Civil action which may result in court order for payment; limitations of action; joinder of commission

Any civil action which may result in a court order for payment from the real estate guaranty fund shall be instituted within six years of the accrual of the cause of action and the New Jersey Real Estate Commission shall be joined as a necessary party to any such civil action. Nothing in this section shall affect the right of any aggrieved person to pursue other rights or remedies authorized by law.

L.1976, c. 112, § 5, eff. Feb. 1, 1977. Amended by L.1984, c. 124, § 1, eff. Aug. 8, 1984.

45:15-39. Designation of agent for acceptance of process by broker-salesperson or salesperson for civil proceedings under this act

Any person to whom is issued a license to be a real estate broker, broker-salesperson or salesperson shall, by the securing of said license, make and constitute the secretary of the commission or the person in charge of the office of the commission as agent for the acceptance of process in any civil proceeding hereunder.

L.1976, c. 112, § 6, eff. Feb. 1, 1977. Amended by L.1993, c. 51, § 38, eff. May 20, 1993.

45:15-40. Insufficient funds to pay claims; priority of payment; additional assessment to replenish; surplus; use

a. If at any time the funds available in the real estate guaranty fund are insufficient to satisfy in full court orders for payment therefrom, payment shall be made in the order in which such court orders were issued; and the Real Estate Commission shall by regulation impose further additional amounts to be paid by brokers, broker-salespersons and salespersons to replenish the guaranty fund. No such additional amount assessed at any one time shall exceed the amounts specified in section 2 of this act.[1]

b. If at any time the funds available in the real estate guaranty fund are, in the opinion of the Real Estate Commission, in excess of amounts anticipated to be necessary to meet claims for a period of at least 2 years, the commission may, with the approval of the Commissioner of Insurance, allocate and receive from the guaranty fund a specified amount thereof for research and educational projects to increase the proficiency and competency of real estate licensees.

L.1976, c. 112, § 7, eff. Feb. 1, 1977. Amended by L.1993, c. 51, § 39, eff. May 20, 1993.

[1] Section 45:15-35.

45:15-41. Revocation of license of broker-salesperson or salesperson whose act gave rise to claim; reinstatement

Upon the issuance of a court order for payment from the real estate guaranty fund the license of the broker, broker-salesperson or salesperson, whose acts gave rise to the claim, shall be revoked and no such broker, broker-salesperson or salesperson shall be eligible for reinstatement of his license until he shall have satisfied the judgment in full including reimbursement of the real estate guaranty fund together with interest.

L.1976, c. 112, § 8, eff. Feb. 1, 1977. Amended by L.1993, c. 51, § 40, eff. May 20, 1993.

45:15-42. Rules and regulations

The Real Estate Commission is authorized to issue rules and regulations to implement the provisions of this act.

L.1976, c. 112, § 9, eff. Feb. 1, 1977.

ADOPTED LICENSE LAW AMENDMENTS

AMENDMENT TO 45:15-12.8

Effective on April 30, 1999, N.J.S.A. 45:15-12.8 was amended to empower the Real Estate Commission to adopt rules specifying forms of payment, in addition to cash and negotiable instruments payable to brokers, through which monies to be held by brokers in trust or in escrow, or as the temporary custodians of such funds, may be accepted.

Subsequently, the Commission enacted amendments to N.J.A.C. 11:5-5.1 and 11:5.4 authorizing brokers involved in short term rental transactions to, under limited circumstances, accept such payments made on credit cards. A separate detailed notice with respect to those rule amendments was issued shortly after their enactment.

The text of N.J.S.A. 45:15-12.8 as amended in 1999 reads as follows:

Every real estate licensee who, in the performance of any of the activities described in R.S. 45:15-3, receives any monies of others as a representative of a broker acting as an escrow agent or as the temporary custodian of the funds of others in a real estate transaction, shall only accept the monies if they are in the form of cash or a negotiable instrument payable to the broker through whom the individual is licensed, or such other form as the commission may prescribe by rule. The licensee shall, immediately upon receipt of the funds, account for and deliver the funds to the broker for deposit into the escrow or trust account maintained by the broker, or for such other disposition as is required by the escrow agreement under the terms of which the funds were provided to the licensee.

AMENDMENTS TO 45:15-17 (g) and (k)

On April 19, 2001 P.L. 2000, c. 68 was enacted. Effective on that date this legislation amended sections 17(g) and 17(k) of New Jersey's Real Estate licensing law (N.J.S.A. 45:15-17g and 17k).

As amended the law provides that, subject to certain restrictions, licensees may include offers of free or discounted products or services in their advertising and promotional material. Licensees who intend to include such offers in their advertising or promotional material should be aware that the amended law prohibits:

1 making the receipt of any free or discounted products or services contingent upon a consumer signing a listing agreement, a sale contract, or other type of real estate contract;
2 offering a lot or parcel or lots or parcels for advertising purposes; and
3 offering free or discounted products or services as part of a lottery, a contest, a drawing or a game.

In addition, licensees must comply with the disclosure requirements imposed by the amended law in situations where the licensee has received any compensation for their participation in the promotion or offer.

The Commission is in the process of formulating proposed amendments to its advertising rule, N.J.A.C. 11:5-6.1, which have been made necessary by the enactment of this legislation. Further information on the proposed rule amendments will be posted on this website at the time an official notice of their proposal is published in the New Jersey Register.

The pertinent text of N.J.S.A. 45:15-17 as amended appears below.

". . .The Commission may place on probation, suspend for a period less than the unexpired portion of the license period, or may revoke any license issued under the provisions of this article, or the right of licensure when such person is no longer the holder of a license at the time of hearing, or may impose, in addition or as an alternative to such probation, revocation or suspension, a penalty of not more than $5,000 for the first violation, and a penalty of not more than $10,000 for any subsequent violation, which penalty shall be sued for a recovered by an in the name of the Commission and shall be collected and enforced by summary proceedings pursuant to the "Penalty Enforcement Law of 1999," P.L. 1999, c.274 (C:2A:58-10 et seq.). Where the licensee or any person, in performing or attempting to perform any of the acts mentioned herein, is deemed to be guilty of. . . .

g. Using any plan, scheme or method for the sale or promotion of the sale of real estate which involves a lottery, a contest, a game, a prize, a drawing, or the offering of a lot or parcel or lots or parcels for advertising purposes provided, however, that a promotion or offer of free, discounted or other services or products which does not require that the recipient of any free, discounted or other services or products enter into a sale, listing or other real estate contract as a condition of the promotion or offer shall not constitute a violation of this subsection if that promotion or offering does not involve a lottery, a contest, a game, a drawing or the offering of a lot or parcel or lots or parcels for advertising purposes. A broker shall disclose in writing any compensation received for such promotion or offer in the form and substance as required by the federal "Real Estate Settlement Procedures Act of 1974," 12 U.S.C. ss.2601 et seq. except that, notwithstanding the provisions of that federal act, written disclosure shall be provided no later than when the promotion or offer is extended by the broker to the consumer; or. . . .

k. Paying any rebate, profit, compensation or commission to anyone not possessed of a real estate license, except that free, discounted or other services or products provided for in subsection g. of this section shall not constitute a violation of this subsection; or. . . .

CHAPTER 5

REAL ESTATE COMMISSION

Authority

N.J.S.A. 45:15-6, 45:15-10.4, 45:15-16.49, 45:15-17(t) and 45:15-17.4.

Source and Effective Date

R.1998 d.497, effective September 14, 1998.
See: 30 N.J.R. 2333(a), 30 N.J.R. 3646(a).

Executive Order No. 66(1978) Expiration Date

Chapter 5, Real Estate Commission, expires on September 14, 2003.

Chapter Historical Note

Chapter 5, Real Estate Commission, was filed and became effective prior to September 1, 1969. Pursuant to Executive Order No. 66(1978), Chapter 5 expired on August 2, 1983.

Chapter 5, Real Estate Commission, was adopted as new rules by R.1983 d.471, effective November 7, 1983. See: 15 N.J.R. 1343(a), 15 N.J.R. 1865(c).

Pursuant to Executive Order No. 66(1978), Chapter 5, Real Estate Commission, was readopted as R.1988 d.555, effective October 28, 1988. See: 20 N.J.R. 2184(a), 20 N.J.R. 3019(a).

Subchapter 2, Organizational Rules, was adopted as R.1989 d.258, effective April 19, 1989. See: 21 N.J.R. 1364(a).

Subchapter 3, Petitions for Rulemaking, Subchapter 4, Proceedings before the Commission, and Subchapter 5, Appeals of Initial Denials of Licensing Applications, were adopted as R.1989 d.429, effective August 21, 1989. See: 21 N.J.R. 1315(a), 21 N.J.R. 2524(a).

Subchapter 6, Rules Interpreting and Implementing the Real Estate Sales Full Disclosure Act, N.J.S.A. 45:15-16.27 et seq., was adopted as R.1990 d.455, effective September 17, 1990. See: 22 N.J.R. 1421(a), 22 N.J.R. 2969(d).

Pursuant to Executive Order No. 66(1978), Chapter 5, Real Estate Commission, was readopted as R.1993 d.552, effective October 15, 1993. See: 25 N.J.R. 3597(b), 25 N.J.R. 5229(a).

Pursuant to Executive Order No. 66(1978), Chapter 5, Real Estate Commission, was readopted as R.1998 d.497, effective September 14, 1998. As a part of R.1998 d.497, effective October 5, 1998, sections 1.1 through 1.44 of Subchapter 1, Rules and Regulations, were recodified as Subchapter 2, Education; Subchapter 3, Licensing; Subchapter 4, Employment Practices/Office and Licensee Supervision; Subchapter 5, Trust Accounts/Records of Brokerage Activity; Subchapter 6, Conduct of Business; Subchapter 7, Prohibited Activities; and Subchapter 8, Disciplinary Actions/Conditions for Restoration of License/Real Estate Guaranty Fund Claims. Also as a part of R.1998 d.497, effective October 5, 1998, Subchapter 2, Organizational Rules, was recodified as Subchapter 1; Subchapter 6, Rules Interpreting and Implementing the Real Estate Sales Full Disclosure Act, N.J.S.A. 45:15-16.27 et seq., was recodified as Subchapter 9; Subchapter 3, Petitions for Rulemaking, was recodified as Subchapter 10; Subchapter 4, Proceedings before the Commission, was recodified as Subchapter 11, Procedures on Disciplinary Actions, Contested Applications, Declaratory Ruling Requests; and Subchapter 5, Appeals of Initial Denials of Licensing Applications, was recodified as section 11.10. See: Source and Effective Date. See, also, section annotations.

CHAPTER TABLE OF CONTENTS

proper as to the honesty, trustworthiness, character and integrity of an applicant.

(e) When a school is to be conducted in the name of a corporation, a certified copy of its certificate of incorporation shall accompany the application for licensure. When a school is to be conducted under a trade name, whether a sole proprietorship, firm, general partnership, or limited partnership, a true copy of the certificate of trade name or articles of the general or limited partnership as filed in the office of the county clerk shall accompany the application. A school shall not use the designation of "College" or "University," as part of its name or in any other manner, unless it, in fact, meets the standards and qualifications of the State agency having jurisdiction and has been approved by that agency.

(f) Every school licensed by the Commission shall maintain a bona fide office open to the public during normal business hours for the purpose of assisting former and current students. Schools shall provide adequate space, seating, equipment and instructional materials for their students. The premises, equipment and facilities of the school shall comply with all local, city, county and State regulations, such as fire codes, building and sanitation codes. A certificate from proper authority covering these requirements shall accompany an application for school licensure. The Commission may require proof of ownership or a copy of the lease if the facility is rented. Public adult education programs conducted under the auspices of a board of education in this State and any college or university accredited as such by the State Department of Higher Education, the facilities of which have been approved by a State agency, shall be presumed to have met the requirements of this paragraph, so long as the real estate courses offered are held at the approved facility.

1. Any additional teaching locations must be licensed by the Commission and must comply with all the requirements applicable to licensed schools, their directors and instructors as set forth in the Act and this rule. School directors shall have oversight responsibility for these locations. All courses conducted at such locations must be taught by licensed instructors or guest lecturers, pursuant to N.J.S.A. 45:15-10.5 and this rule.

(g) All schools shall furnish to the Commission at the time of application for initial licensure the school policy and regulations pertaining to standards for satisfactory completion of the courses offered at the school and the issuance of a Certificate, conditions for dismissal of a student and conditions for reinstatement.

1. Any changes in school policy and regulations, as set forth in paragraph (g) above, from the information submitted with the original application for school licensure or as otherwise previously supplied, shall be promptly disclosed to the Commission in writing, or on a form which the Commission prescribes.

(h) When a school fulfills all of the requirements for licensure, then a license shall be executed by the President of the Commission as attested by the Executive Director. School licensure shall be limited to the specific ownership and school locations identified on the license document(s).

(i) An individual seeking approval as a director of a licensed real estate school administered by a public adult education program or an accredited college or university who is not licensed as a real estate instructor may nevertheless qualify as the director of such a school, so long as he or she is at least 18 years of age; has a background of good moral character, including the absence of any conviction for the crimes or other offenses specified under the provisions of N.J.S.A. 45:15-12.1; and has fulfilled all of the education requirements imposed upon candidates for licensure as real estate instructors within two years of applying to the Commission for approval to be the director of such a school.

(j) In order to enable the Commission to confirm that courses offered by real estate schools include the required number of hours of instruction as prescribed in N.J.S.A. 45:15-10.1(a) and (b) and N.J.A.C. 11:5-2.1, every six months, each school director shall submit data on courses to be offered by their school in the forthcoming six month period, the starting and ending dates of the courses, the days and hours of class sessions and teaching locations. Such course information shall be provided on forms prescribed by the Commission and shall be retained as permanent records for not less than three years after submission.

(k) No person, other than a guest lecturer, shall teach real estate education courses, the attendance and successful completion of which shall constitute the fulfillment of the educational prerequisites for licensure established under N.J.S.A. 45:15-10.1, unless that person is licensed as an instructor pursuant to N.J.S.A. 45:15-10.5 and this section.

1. Each applicant for licensure as a real estate instructor shall be 18 years of age or older and shall have a background of good moral character, including the absence of any conviction for those certain crimes or other like offenses referred to in N.J.S.A. 45:15-12.1, subject to the applicant's ability to affirmatively demonstrate his or her rehabilitation from such conviction. In order to confirm the absence of any such conviction, the Commission shall require all non-attorney applicants to submit with their application for instructor licensure a New Jersey State Police Request for Criminal History Record Information Form and a certified check or money order in the amount established by the New Jersey State Police as the processing fee for such forms.

2. Each applicant for licensure must hold a bachelor's degree from an accredited college or university, except for the following applicants:

i. New Jersey licensed brokers who have been continuously licensed as such for the two years immediately preceding their application; and

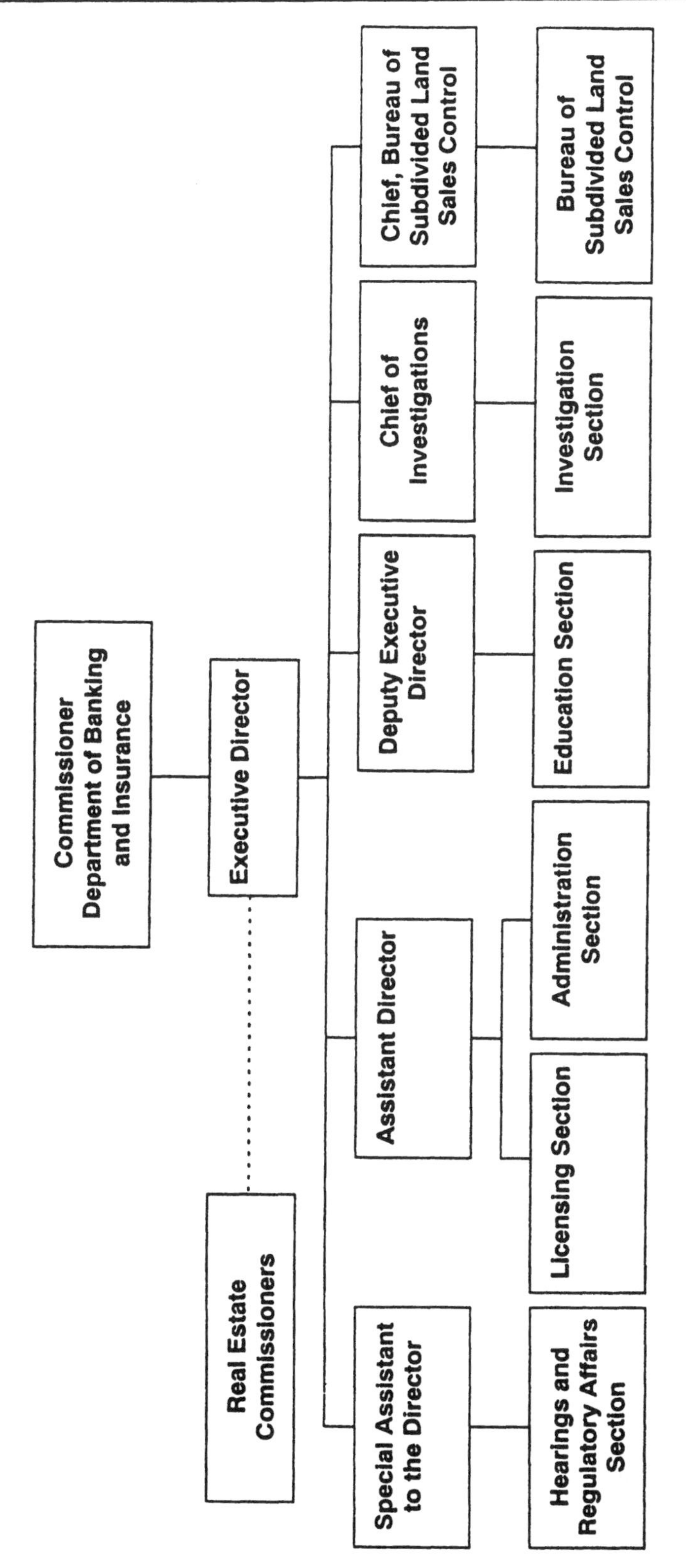

Amended by R.1989 d.324, effective May 24, 1989.
See: 21 N.J.R. 1364(a), 21 N.J.R. 1709(a).
Amended by R.1998 d.497, effective October 5, 1998.
See: 30 N.J.R. 2333(a), 30 N.J.R. 3646(a).

Updated the Commission Organization Chart.

11:5–1.3 Functions of the Commission

(a) The Commission is comprised of six sections whose functions are as follows:

1. The Licensing Section is responsible for processing license applications, transfers, terminations, renewals and upgrades, and for providing licensing information to the public and to licensees.

2. The Investigations Section is responsible for investigating the qualifications of applicants for licensure, and for investigating complaints against licensed brokers or sales-persons or individuals who have allegedly engaged in the business of a real estate broker or a salesperson without being licensed to do so.

3. The Real Estate Education Section is responsible for reviewing the qualifications of real estate school and instructor applicants and for regulating their activities as such through the Education Subsection.

4. The Bureau of Subdivided Land Sales Control within the Investigations Section is responsible for enforcing the provisions of the Land Sales Full Disclosure Act. Its duties include, but are not limited to reviewing applications for the registration of new projects, conducting inspections of conditionally registered projects, and reviewing applications for the renewal of projects.

5. The Administration Section is responsible for the budget and accounting functions and also for ensuring that personnel operate in a manner which will accomplish their designated duties in conjunction with the staff of the Department of Banking and Insurance. It is also responsible for other functions including administration of the Real Estate Guaranty Fund.

6. The Hearings and Regulatory Affairs Section is responsible for processing the rulemaking activity of the Commission, the scheduling and processing of contested cases, the prosecution of certain contested matters, and other functions.

Amended by R.1989 d.324, effective May 24, 1989.
See: 21 N.J.R. 1709(a).
At (a)3, reference to Education Subsection added to end of sentence.
Amended by R.1998 d.497, effective October 5, 1998.
See: 30 N.J.R. 2333(a), 30 N.J.R. 3646(a).
Rewrote (a).

11:5–1.4 Information available to the public

With the exception of the records designated as non-public in N.J.A.C. 11:5–2.5(g), the public may obtain information or make submissions or requests concerning any Commission functions by contacting the Real Estate Commission, Department of Banking and Insurance, PO Box 328, Trenton, New Jersey 08625–0328.

Amended by R.1998 d.497, effective October 5, 1998.
See: 30 N.J.R. 2333(a), 30 N.J.R. 3646(a).
Rewrote the section.

11:5–1.5 Commission records open to public inspection; investigative files not open to the public

(a) The New Jersey Real Estate Commission makes, maintains and keeps records as listed in (b) through (g) below.

(b) Current and computerized public licensing records are available at the Commission's office for inspection and copying during normal business hours upon sufficient notice to the Commission staff. The Commission staff may require several weeks notice to locate records other than computerized records. Except as otherwise noted in this section, records are maintained for a minimum of three years. Older records may be unavailable. Copies of records can be purchased from the Commission at the fees established in the Right to Know Law, N.J.S.A. 47:1A–2.

(c) Requests for certified copies of the Commission's public licensing records (or for a certificate of the absence of a public record) shall be submitted in writing and must specify which records are requested and the time period covered by the request. The Commission staff requires at least 10 working days to provide certified copies of public records.

(d) The following records are maintained pursuant to the Real Estate Licensing Act:

1. Certifications of license history and status based upon computerized licensing records;

2. Real estate broker, broker-salesperson, salesperson, school and instructor license applications, and materials submitted therewith to obtain, transfer, reinstate or renew such licenses, and the final disposition of such applications. However, criminal history information obtained by the Commission pursuant to N.J.A.C. 11:5–3.3 and personal data on a licensee such as home address, home telephone number and date of birth are considered confidential;

3. Real Estate Commission meeting minutes;

4. Orders to Show Cause and complaints issued by the Attorney General's office charging that a licensee or an unlicensed person has violated provisions of the Real Estate License Act or the Commission's administrative rules; documents accepted into the agency record in any such proceeding; and the final disposition of such proceedings including settlements; and

5. Notices, proposals and other records concerning rulemaking required to be kept or distributed to the public by the Commission pursuant to the Administrative Procedure Act, N.J.S.A. 52:14B–1 et seq. and N.J.A.C. 1:30–3 and 4 et seq. Complete records of unadopted proposals are available for one year after publication of the proposal. Complete records of adopted rules are available for three years after each rule's effective date.

(e) The following records are maintained by the Bureau of Subdivided Land Sales Control, pursuant to the Real Estate Full Disclosure Act, N.J.S.A. 45:15–16.27 et seq.:

1. Statements of record and additions or corrections thereto filed with the Bureau pursuant to N.J.S.A. 45:15–16.33, 16.36, 16.39 and 16.41(a);

2. Annual reports submitted by a subdivider pursuant to N.J.S.A. 45:15–16.40;

3. Public offering statements and amended public offering statements prepared pursuant to N.J.S.A. 45:15–16.38;

4. Orders to Show Cause and other pleadings charging violations of N.J.S.A. 45:15–16.27 et seq. and the final disposition of such orders, including Orders to Cease and Desist and/or imposing penalties or sanctions; documents accepted into the agency record in any such proceedings; and

5. Applications for exemption of a subdivision filed with the Bureau pursuant to N.J.S.A. 45:15–16.32(c) and N.J.A.C. 11:5–9.18 and the final disposition of any such exemption application.

(f) The following records are maintained pursuant to the Real Estate Guaranty Fund Act, N.J.S.A. 45:15–34 et seq.:

1. Court orders for payment from the Real Estate Guaranty Fund; and

2. Pleadings served upon the Commissioner of Insurance or any duly authorized agent or employee of the Department of Insurance pursuant to N.J.S.A. 45:15–39.

(g) The following licensee records are nonpublic in accordance with N.J.S.A. 47:1A–1 et seq.:

1. Criminal complaints, indictments, judgments of conviction and other separate documents submitted in connection with a license application concerning whether an applicant is disqualified by reason of indictment for or conviction of a crime;

2. Criminal history records obtained as the result of any criminal history check;

3. Petitions or discharges in bankruptcy, complaints, orders or other pleadings in actions for assignment to creditors and other separate documents submitted in connection with a license application concerning whether the applicant is disqualified by reason of unworthiness;

4. Copies of orders of suspension or revocation issued by professional or occupational licensing authorities, and other separate documents submitted in connection with a license application concerning whether the applicant is disqualified from licensure;

5. Records concerning the medical disability of any licensee;

6. Investigative files in any matter pending investigation, or in any completed investigation in which no formal disciplinary action was taken;

7. Personal data on a licensee such as home address, home telephone number and date of birth; and

8. The Social Security numbers of any applicants or licensees which were submitted to the Commission on a license application or otherwise obtained by the Commission.

New Rule, R.1994 d.269, effective June 20, 1994 (operative July 1, 1994).
See: 26 N.J.R. 736(a), 26 N.J.R. 1222(a), 26 N.J.R. 2585(b).
Amended by R.1998 d.497, effective October 5, 1998.
See: 30 N.J.R. 2333(a), 30 N.J.R. 3646(a).
In (d)2 and (e)5, changed N.J.A.C. references.

SUBCHAPTER 2. EDUCATION

11:5–2.1 Educational requirements for salespersons and brokers in making application for licensure examination

(a) All applicants for a salesperson's or broker's license shall present with their license application evidence of their satisfactory completion of a course of education in real estate subjects taught in accordance with N.J.S.A. 45:15–10.1 and as required by this section.

1. This requirement shall also apply to disabled veterans making application for licensure pursuant to N.J.S.A. 45:15–11. However, the Commission shall approve a program of studies in real estate completed by such a veteran offered by a provider other than a licensed school if the program consisted of at least 75 hours in the case of an applicant for a salesperson's license, or 225 hours in the case of an applicant for a broker's license and the program was offered by an accredited college or university for credit.

2. No person shall receive credit toward the fulfillment of the salesperson prelicensure education requirement for attendance at a broker's prelicensure course and no person shall receive credit toward the fulfillment of the broker's prelicensure education requirements for attendance at a salesperson's prelicensure course.

(b) To qualify to challenge the real estate salesperson license examination, a candidate must first successfully complete a course of study in real estate at a school licensed by the Commission pursuant to N.J.S.A. 45:15–10.4 consisting of a minimum of 75 hours as specified in (f) below. To qualify to challenge the real estate broker's license exam, a candidate must first successfully complete courses of study in real estate consisting of a minimum of 150 hours as specified in (g) below, offered by a licensed school or, with respect to those certain courses specified in (g)5 below, offered by some other Commission-approved provider.

(c) No person with the exception of qualified disabled veterans shall receive credit for satisfactory completion of the prescribed 150 hours of broker's courses unless that person was the holder of a salesperson's license at the time of enrollment in said course.

(d) The time allotted by any school for a final examination covering real estate subjects shall be applicable toward the minimum hours of course study. No more than five minutes of each course hour may be utilized for breaks in the actual classroom instruction being conducted at any given session of a pre-licensure course. During the time in which actual classroom instruction is conducted, in addition to covering the substantive material mandated by (f) and (g) below, instructors are to provide thorough instruction on the State license examination and license issuance procedures for salesperson and broker license candidates, as applicable, and to perform all reasonably required administrative functions such as taking attendance and making announcements of general interest.

(e) The requirements that broker license candidates complete the general 90 hour broker prelicensure education course and that salesperson license candidates complete the 75 hour salesperson prelicensure education course shall not apply to:

1. Applicants for licensure as a broker or salesperson who have held a real estate broker's license issued by another state and who were actively engaged in the real estate brokerage business for three years or more immediately preceding the date of application;

2. Applicants for licensure as a broker who are attorneys at law admitted to the practice in the State of New Jersey and applicants for licensure as a salesperson who are attorneys at law admitted to practice in New Jersey or in any other state at the time of making application;

3. Applicants for licensure as a salesperson who have earned a college degree from any accredited institution of higher education, provided that:

i. The total number of college level classroom hours devoted to real estate and related subjects was 75 or more, and such courses were completed within three years of making application;

ii. The applicant received a bachelor or associate degree in real estate regardless of how long prior to their application for a waiver they received that degree; or

iii. The applicant satisfactorily completed 75 or more classroom hours of course work in real estate or related subjects, at least 45 hours of which consisted of instruction on real estate conducted as part of a post-graduate program and that such post-graduate studies were completed within three years of making application.

4. Applicants for licensure as a salesperson who hold or held a real estate license issued by another state, provided that:

i. The applicant has satisfactorily completed a prelicensure course of real estate education at a proprietory school, college or university in that other state;

ii. The prelicensure course was sanctioned by the real estate licensing authority of that state;

iii. The total number of classroom hours included in the course was 75 or more;

iv. The applicant qualified for licensure in that state by examination; and

v. The applicant was actively licensed in that state within three years of applying for the waiver.

5. Applicants for licensure as a salesperson who previously held a license as a New Jersey real estate broker and whose last license expired more than two but less than five years prior to making application.

(f) The salesperson's course of 75 hours shall include:

1. Property rights (9 hours);

2. Contracts and other property instruments (12 hours);

3. Leases and landlord-tenant relations (6 hours);

4. Mortgages and other liens (12 hours);

5. Business opportunity sales (2 hours);

6. The laws of agency (12 hours);

7. Appraising (2 hours);

8. License Act and regulations (9 hours);

9. Other state, Federal and municipal laws and regulations, including N.J.S.A. 17:16C–1 et seq., 39:1–1 et seq., 46:8–43 et seq. and 46:8C–1 et seq. as they pertain to the resale of mobile and manufactured housing units which bear or are required to bear motor vehicle titles (5 hours);

10. Salesperson duties and pitfalls in the real estate business (3 hours);

11. Quizzes and final examination (3 hours).

(g) The 150 hours of prelicensure education required of candidates for licensure as a broker or broker-salesperson by N.J.S.A. 45:15–10 shall be acquired as provided in this subsection. A 90 hour general broker's prelicensure course shall first be completed in accordance with the following syllabus and directives. Thereafter, two 30 hour broker courses as described in (g)5, 6 and 7 below shall be completed. All three courses, totaling 150 hours of instruction, must be successfully completed within a period of two years. Where the three courses are not so completed, a candidate must again successfully complete any previously taken course and all courses not previously taken within the two year time frame, and again fulfill the experience requirement established at N.J.S.A. 45:15–9 and N.J.A.C. 11:5–3.8 in order to qualify to challenge the broker license examination.

1. The 90 hour general broker's prelicensure course may be taught in blocks or modules of material. The maximum number of modules into which the course may be divided is 23, with their content corresponding to the 23 subject matter areas identified in the syllabus below. Schools offering courses in modules may include more than one subject matter in a given module. No student may commence a course which is offered in modules on a date other than the starting date of any module. No student shall be given credit for the successful completion of a 90 hour general broker's prelicensure course unless and until they have received instruction in all of the subject matter areas identified below for approximately the number of hours indicated, and passed a comprehensive final examination. The 90 hour general broker's prelicensure course shall be conducted in accordance with the following syllabus and directives. Substantive instruction shall be provided on the following topics for approximately the number of hours indicated:

i. Review license laws and regulations including provisions of the Real Estate Sales Full Disclosure Act and N.J.A.C. 11:5–9 (six hours);

ii. Listing contracts—sales and rentals (three hours);

iii. Sale contracts (three hours);

iv. Deeds and real property rights and interests including nature of ownership, legal description, chain of title, restrictions, consideration, various types, acknowledgments and recording, land and land elements, water rights (including riparian rights), state claims regarding tidelands estates and other interests, methods of ownership, dower and curtesy, wills and descent, adverse possession and fixtures (three hours);

v. Advanced financing techniques including qualification formulae, various types, typical prerequisites (insurance, flood insurance, if applicable, certificate of occupancy, etc.) and income tax ramifications (six hours);

vi. Liens, foreclosures and redemptions (one hour);

vii. Easements, restrictions, etc. (one hour);

viii. Condemnation (one hour);

ix. Zoning, including non-conforming uses, variances, subdivisions, planning, zoning issues raised by condominium construction or conversion and other types of real estate development (five hours);

x. Surveys (non-government type) and legal descriptions (one hour);

xi. Property taxes, assessment, re-valuations, assessment appeals and special appeals (three hours);

xii. Real estate valuation including techniques and distinctions between comparative market analyses and formal appraisals (three hours);

xiii. Settlement/closing procedures, RESPA forms (six hours);

xiv. Mathematics relative to real estate (six hours);

xv. Laws: Federal Fair Housing and the New Jersey Law Against Discrimination, New Jersey "Mount Laurel" requirements, RESPA, Truth in Lending, rent control, New Jersey Land Use Law, New Jersey's Truth in Renting Law, and the provisions in that law, in N.J.S.A. 17:16C–1 et seq., in N.J.S.A. 39:1–1 et seq. and in N.J.S.A. 46:8C–1 et seq. which pertain to the resale of mobile and manufactured housing units which bear or are required to bear motor vehicle titles (total three hours);

xvi. Business and management practices (total of six hours for (g)1xvi(1) through (6) below), including:

(1) Company structure including single ownership, partnership, corporate, requirements to establish, employees vs. independent contractors;

(2) Office management including bookkeeping and accounting relative to real estate, escrow responsibilities, company dollars, ledgers, records and computers;

(3) Personnel management including recruiting, hiring, training, supervising, compensation and termination;

(4) Advertising and promotions;

(5) Community involvement by the company, broker and salespersons; and

(6) Insurance including errors and omissions, etc.

xvii. Principles of agency including ethics and legal liability, disclosure requirements and case studies (six hours);

xviii. Commercial and industrial real estate including small scale, large scale, leasing, financing, site analysis, advertising, remuneration, bulk sales, U.C.C., considerations in franchise transactions, E.C.R.A., BOCA Code, construction financing and other commercial construction concerns (three hours);

xix. Property management including responsibilities and information regarding repairs and maintenance, public relations, collection of rents, government regulations, business trends, personnel, recordkeeping, advertising, etc. (three hours);

xx. Residential real estate development including requirements of New Jersey's Planned Real Estate Development Act including time-sharing, the Home Owner's Warranty program and other concerns regarding single-family and condo/co-op development, conversion, marketing and financing (two hours);

xxi. Leases and landlord/tenant laws including Truth in Renting Law (four hours);

xxii. Real estate investments, syndications, REIT's, limited partnerships and S.E.C. licensing requirements (two hours); and

xxiii. Income tax considerations and ramifications of various real estate transactions (three hours).

2. Within the 90 hour general broker prelicensure course instruction will also be provided on the following topics for the hours indicated. These topics shall be taught in such a manner as to familiarize students with the basic elements of the listed topics and to impart to students an awareness of their scope and effect. The coverage on these topics will also inform students of the sources which can be contacted in order to obtain additional general information and/or specific data concerning the topics' applicability to or impact upon particular locations, and to educate students on their obligations and responsibilities as licensees to ascertain and disclose such information. The topics to be taught are:

i. Radon contamination, which instruction shall also include testing techniques, remediation techniques and the New Jersey DEP confidentiality statute (one hour);

ii. Ground water contamination, which instruction shall also include testing and remediation techniques (one hour);

iii. Problems posed by a property's proximity to solid waste disposal and/or toxic waste sites (one hour);

iv. Ground water percolation and private sewage disposal systems, which instruction shall also include testing methods (one hour);

v. Problems posed by lands officially designed as Wetlands, Pinelands, or within any other special classifications (one hour); and

vi. New Jersey's Coastal Areas Facilities Review Act (one hour).

3. Instructors conducting 90 hour general broker prelicensure courses shall provide general information to their students concerning the procedures through which students can arrange to sit for the State license examination and through which licenses are issued by the Commission, and shall give at least two spot quizzes and a comprehensive final exam on the material covered in the course (four hours).

4. In addition to classroom instruction and assigned reading from a general textbook, in the 90 hour broker course students shall also be assigned additional outside reading on various topics which shall include, but not be limited to, informational publications of the New Jersey Department of Environmental Protection on the various environmental topics covered, those sections of the New Jersey Law Against Discrimination which directly relate to the activities of real estate professionals, and other topics as directed by the New Jersey Real Estate Commission.

5. After having successfully completed the 90 hour broker course, all candidates for licensure as a broker or broker-salesperson must successfully complete a 30 hour prelicensure course on brokers' ethics and agency law and relationships, and a second 30 hour prelicensure course on office management and related topics.

i. All such agency/ethics and office management courses shall be taught by licensed instructors at licensed schools.

ii. All such agency/ethics courses shall be taught utilizing methods which maximize the use of case studies of recent Commission decisions in disciplinary actions, demonstration models and other non-lecture techniques.

iii. A final examination of not less than one hour shall be administered in all such courses on which students must receive a passing grade in order to be deemed to have successfully completed such courses.

iv. No school shall allow students to commence any 30 hour agency/ethics course or office management course at a time other than the starting date of such courses.

6. The 30 hours of instruction in the ethics/agency course shall be devoted to:

i. The fiduciary duties owed by agents to their principals;

ii. Disclosed and undisclosed dual agency;

iii. Conflicts of interest and self-dealing;

iv. The risks and benefits of sub-agency to the principal and the agent;

v. Restrictions on and disclosure requirements regarding acting for more than one party to a transaction, including those pertaining to licensees providing mortgage services;

vi. Disclosure requirements to non-principals;

vii. Issues raised by licensees involved in transactions as non-agents; and

viii. The obligations to properly qualify or pre-qualify prospective purchasers and related issues.

7. The 30 hours of instruction in the office management and related topics course shall be devoted to:

i. Office management requirements imposed upon supervising brokers of main and branch offices;

ii. Recordkeeping requirements, with particular emphasis upon and extensive coverage of escrow account records;

iii. The importance of adequate supervision and training of other licensees to assure their compliance with the license law and the rules of the Commission;

iv. Instruction on proper qualification and pre-qualification techniques, including requiring demonstrations by the students, and with emphasis upon the significance of training and oversight of other licensees;

v. Statutory and rule requirements pertaining to contracts, leases and listing agreements and to broker advertising;

vi. Closings;

vii. Environmental concerns; and

viii. Instruction on licensure requirements and procedures applicable to license applications, transfers, changes of broker address, branch offices, etc., and office closing requirements.

(h) A complete syllabus for the salesperson and broker courses shall be maintained at the offices of the Real Estate Commission and be open to the public for inspection.

(i) All course hours are suggested and may be modified at the discretion of the director of the approved school subject to written notice to and written approval by the Real Estate Commission.

As amended, R.1974 d.307, effective November 13, 1974.
See: 6 N.J.R. 246(c), 6 N.J.R. 478(e).
As amended, R.1978 d.135, effective April 27, 1978.
See: 10 N.J.R. 163(b), 10 N.J.R. 256(d).
As amended, R.1978 d.271, effective August 2, 1978.
See: 10 N.J.R. 256(b), 10 N.J.R. 399(b).
As amended, R.1979 d.52, effective February 8, 1979.
See: 10 N.J.R. 498(c), 11 N.J.R. 142(b).
As amended, R.1983 d.471, effective November 7, 1983.
See: 15 N.J.R. 1343(a), 15 N.J.R. 1865(c).
"Salesman" replaced by "salesperson"; subsection (k) deleted.
As amended, R.1984 d.218, effective June 4, 1984.
See: 16 N.J.R. 489(a), 16 N.J.R. 1352(a).
Section substantially amended.
Amended by R.1988 d.411, effective September 6, 1988.
See: 20 N.J.R. 725(b), 20 N.J.R. 2296(a).
Subsections (d) and (e) substantially amended.
Amended by R.1988 d.254, effective June 6, 1988 (operative December 1, 1989).
See: 19 N.J.R. 1051(a), 20 N.J.R. 1205(b).
At (g) old text deleted, new (g) added; brokers pre-licensure syllabus revised.
Notice of Correction, effective May 4, 1992.
See: 24 N.J.R. 1799(a).
Amended by R.1994 d.58, effective February 7, 1994 (operative July 1, 1994).
See: 25 N.J.R. 4852(a), 26 N.J.R. 799(b).
Notice of Correction, effective August 15, 1994.
See: 26 N.J.R. 3442(a).
Amended by R.1997 d.27, effective January 21, 1997.
See: 28 N.J.R. 3065(a), 29 N.J.R. 366(a).
In (f)9, added N.J.S.A. references; in (g)1xv, inserted reference to New Jersey Truth in Renting Law; and inserted N.J.S.A. references.
Amended by R.1998 d.497, effective October 5, 1998.
See: 30 N.J.R. 2333(a), 30 N.J.R. 3646(a).
In (g), changed the N.J.A.C. references throughout and substituted "Real Estate" for "Land" in 1i; and deleted former (j).

Case Notes

Real Estate Commission did not deny real estate sales person due process by failing to notify her that her real estate license had expired. Coyle v. New Jersey Real Estate Com'n, 280 N.J.Super. 93, 654 A.2d 986 (A.D.1994).

Applicants (real estate salespersons) who were denied relicensure upon their failure to apply for renewal within a two-year period after expiration of their last licenses were not deprived of vested property right in violation of due process by statutory amendment which required school and test for relicensure following a 90–day grace period. Graham v. N.J. Real Estate Commission, 217 N.J.Super. 130, 524 A.2d 1321 (App.Div.1987).

Real estate licensing law exemption for attorneys held only to authorize attorneys to sell or rent real estate incidental to their normal practice of law; denial of broker's license to attorney who did not meet statutory apprenticeship and testing requirements upheld. Spirito v. State, New Jersey Real Estate Commission, 180 N.J.Super. 180, 434 A.2d 623 (App.Div.1981).

11:5–2.2 Licensed schools and instructors; requirements

(a) The following regulations are applicable to schools and instructors licensed to conduct courses of education in real estate subjects pursuant to N.J.S.A. 45:15–10.4 and 10.5 and to applicants for such licenses.

1. The original license term for pre-licensure course instructors and schools shall begin on July 1, 1994 and terminate on February 28, 1997. Thereafter, each two-year license term for school and instructor licenses shall run from March 1 to the last day of February of the second following year.

(b) The Commission shall require any school or instructor in making application for licensure to submit certain documents, statements and forms which shall form the basis for the Commission's judgment whether to grant a license. Where the Commission initially denies an application for a school or instructor license, it shall provide to the applicant notification in writing with reasons for such action. The applicant may appeal such a decision to the full Commission. N.J.A.C. 11:5–11.10 shall be applicable to all such appeals.

(c) Public adult education programs conducted under the auspices of a board of education in this State and any college or university accredited as such by the State Department of Higher Education shall be presumed to be qualified providers of real estate courses, so long as their real estate prelicensure education program is under the direction of a licensed instructor or other qualified individual who has affirmatively demonstrated to the Commission his or her good moral character and has met the other requirements of N.J.S.A. 45:15–10.9.

(d) Except as provided in (c) above, all other applicants for a license to operate a real estate prelicensure school, and in the case of a corporation, or limited or general partnership, the members, officers, directors and owners of a controlling interest thereof, shall demonstrate their good moral character, including the absence of any conviction for the crimes or other offenses specified under the provisions of N.J.S.A. 45:15–12.1. The Commission may make such further investigation and require such proof as it deems proper as to the honesty, trustworthiness, character and integrity of an applicant.

(e) When a school is to be conducted in the name of a corporation, a certified copy of its certificate of incorporation shall accompany the application for licensure. When a school is to be conducted under a trade name, whether a sole proprietorship, firm, general partnership, or limited partnership, a true copy of the certificate of trade name or articles of the general or limited partnership as filed in the office of the county clerk shall accompany the application. A school shall not use the designation of "College" or "University," as part of its name or in any other manner, unless it, in fact, meets the standards and qualifications of the State agency having jurisdiction and has been approved by that agency.

(f) Every school licensed by the Commission shall maintain a bona fide office open to the public during normal business hours for the purpose of assisting former and current students. Schools shall provide adequate space, seating, equipment and instructional materials for their students. The premises, equipment and facilities of the school shall comply with all local, city, county and State regulations, such as fire codes, building and sanitation codes. A certificate from proper authority covering these requirements shall accompany an application for school licensure. The Commission may require proof of ownership or a copy of the lease if the facility is rented. Public adult education programs conducted under the auspices of a board of education in this State and any college or university accredited as such by the State Department of Higher Education, the facilities of which have been approved by a State agency, shall be presumed to have met the requirements of this paragraph, so long as the real estate courses offered are held at the approved facility.

1. Any additional teaching locations must be licensed by the Commission and must comply with all the requirements applicable to licensed schools, their directors and instructors as set forth in the Act and this rule. School directors shall have oversight responsibility for these locations. All courses conducted at such locations must be taught by licensed instructors or guest lecturers, pursuant to N.J.S.A. 45:15–10.5 and this rule.

(g) All schools shall furnish to the Commission at the time of application for initial licensure the school policy and regulations pertaining to standards for satisfactory completion of the courses offered at the school and the issuance of a Certificate, conditions for dismissal of a student and conditions for reinstatement.

1. Any changes in school policy and regulations, as set forth in paragraph (g) above, from the information submitted with the original application for school licensure or as otherwise previously supplied, shall be promptly disclosed to the Commission in writing, or on a form which the Commission prescribes.

(h) When a school fulfills all of the requirements for licensure, then a license shall be executed by the President of the Commission as attested by the Executive Director. School licensure shall be limited to the specific ownership and school locations identified on the license document(s).

(i) An individual seeking approval as a director of a licensed real estate school administered by a public adult education program or an accredited college or university who is not licensed as a real estate instructor may nevertheless qualify as the director of such a school, so long as he or she is at least 18 years of age; has a background of good moral character, including the absence of any conviction for the crimes or other offenses specified under the provisions of N.J.S.A. 45:15–12.1; and has fulfilled all of the education requirements imposed upon candidates for licensure as real estate instructors within two years of applying to the Commission for approval to be the director of such a school.

(j) In order to enable the Commission to confirm that courses offered by real estate schools include the required number of hours of instruction as prescribed in N.J.S.A. 45:15–10.1(a) and (b) and N.J.A.C. 11:5–2.1, every six months, each school director shall submit data on courses to be offered by their school in the forthcoming six month period, the starting and ending dates of the courses, the days and hours of class sessions and teaching locations. Such course information shall be provided on forms prescribed by the Commission and shall be retained as permanent records for not less than three years after submission.

(k) No person, other than a guest lecturer, shall teach real estate education courses, the attendance and successful completion of which shall constitute the fulfillment of the educational prerequisites for licensure established under N.J.S.A. 45:15–10.1, unless that person is licensed as an instructor pursuant to N.J.S.A. 45:15–10.5 and this section.

1. Each applicant for licensure as a real estate instructor shall be 18 years of age or older and shall have a background of good moral character, including the absence of any conviction for those certain crimes or other like offenses referred to in N.J.S.A. 45:15–12.1, subject to the applicant's ability to affirmatively demonstrate his or her rehabilitation from such conviction. In order to confirm the absence of any such conviction, the Commission shall require all non-attorney applicants to submit with their application for instructor licensure a New Jersey State Police Request for Criminal History Record Information Form and a certified check or money order in the amount established by the New Jersey State Police as the processing fee for such forms.

2. Each applicant for licensure must hold a bachelor's degree from an accredited college or university, except for the following applicants:

i. New Jersey licensed brokers who have been continuously licensed as such for the two years immediately preceding their application; and

ii. Licensed brokers from other states who have been continuously licensed as such for the three years immediately preceding their application.

3. Except as provided in (*l*)3i and ii below, all instructor license applicants must successfully complete all of the education requirements for licensure as a New Jersey broker established at N.J.A.C. 11:5–2.1, totaling 150 hours, not more than one year prior to passing the instructor license examination and applying for an instructor license.

i. New Jersey broker licensees who have been licensed as such for at least the two years immediately preceding the application and who have completed the full 150 hours of broker prelicensure courses established at N.J.A.C. 11:5–2.1 shall be deemed to have fulfilled the education requirements for licensure as an instructor.

ii. The following individuals will not be required to take the 90–hour general broker course but must successfully complete the two 30–hour broker prelicensure courses referred to in N.J.A.C. 11:5–2.1 in order to fulfill the instructor prelicensure education requirements:

(1) New Jersey broker licensees who have been licensed as such for the two years preceding their application for an instructor license but who have not previously completed those two courses; and

(2) Licensed brokers from other states who have been licensed as such for the three years immediately preceding application.

4. All instructor license applicants shall successfully complete an instructor license examination as established by the Commission. The examination shall extensively test the applicant's general real estate knowledge and shall include questions on teaching methods. Applicants are advised to engage in independent study and/or to take courses offered by independent providers on teaching methods.

5. Subsequent to passing the instructor license examination, as a prerequisite to being issued an instructor license, all applicants must attend a seminar conducted by or under the direction of the Commission staff covering Commission and licensing procedures. Such seminars shall not exceed one day in length.

(*l*) Regulations applicable to the renewal of school and instructor licenses are as follows:

1. Pursuant to N.J.S.A. 45:15–10.7, the fee for the renewal of a real estate instructor license for an additional two-year license term shall be $50.00. The fee for the renewal of a real estate school license shall be $200.00 for the first teaching location licensed and $100.00 for each additional licensed location to be renewed.

2. As a prerequisite for the renewal of an instructor license, an instructor must attend a Commission-sponsored seminar updating them on recent developments affecting the real estate brokerage business in New Jersey. Such seminars shall be offered on a minimum of two dates, each in a different location throughout the state, during the second year of each two-year license term. Persons initially licensed as instructors in the last six months of the two-year license term are exempt from this seminar attendance requirement for the first renewal of their instructor license.

3. In the event that any person to whom an instructor's license has been or shall have been issued shall fail to renew such license or obtain a new license for a period of two consecutive years or more after the expiration of the last license held, the Commission shall require such person to again fulfill all the qualifications for initial licensure as an instructor prior to issuance of a further instructor's license. This requirement shall not apply to a person reapplying for an instructor's license who was a licensed instructor and who allowed their license to expire due to subsequent employment in a public agency in this State with responsibility for dealing with matters relating to real estate if the person reapplying does so within one year of termination of that employment.

(m) The maximum teaching load per instructor or guest lecturer shall not exceed the ratio of one instructor or guest lecturer to 60 students per class. Each prelicensure course offered by a licensed school shall be under the supervision of an instructor licensed pursuant to N.J.S.A. 45:15–10.5 and N.J.A.C. 11:5–2.2(k). At least one licensed instructor shall be present in the classroom at all sessions. However, additional instructors or guest lecturers may be utilized for instruction so long as not more than 25 percent of the required instruction is done by guest lecturers. Broker prelicensure courses may be taught by up to three instructors, provided that one licensed instructor is designated as having the responsibility for the quality of instruction in that course. School directors shall maintain as a business record the names of any persons teaching as guest lecturers or as a group of instructors, with an indication of the designated supervising instructor.

(n) All tuition charged by a school shall be specified separately. If additional fees are to be charged for supplies, materials or books needed in course of work, they shall be itemized by the school and such items shall become the property of the student upon payment.

(*o*) The tuition and fees shall be specifically set forth in a student contract. The contract shall expressly state the school's policy regarding the return of unearned tuition when a student is dismissed or withdraws voluntarily or because of hardship.

(p) Any person who has a permanent disability or physical handicap which precludes that person from attending regular scheduled classes at a licensed school may request Commission approval to receive special instruction through a licensed school provided this request is supported by sworn statements of doctors or other persons having knowledge of the facts and provided a licensed school is willing to undertake such an agreement.

(q) No school shall, without the approval of the Commission, accept for enrollment as a transfer student any person concurrently enrolled with any other licensed school, unless upon the showing of good cause by said student to the Commission in writing.

(r) Every school shall permanently establish and maintain for each student, complete, accurate and detailed records for a period of not less than three years after student matriculation. Such records shall be available for inspection during regular school hours by the Commission and shall contain the following information:

1. The total number of hours of instruction undertaken by the student;

2. Completed areas of study in real estate subjects prescribed by the Act and these regulations;

3. The student's attendance record; and

4. The names of all supervising instructors and guest lecturers.

(s) To satisfactorily complete any prelicensure course, a student must receive a passing grade and attend at least 80 percent of the class session hours required for the course by N.J.A.C. 11:5–2.1.

(t) Upon a student's satisfactory completion of a course in real estate, the school shall issue to the student a Certificate.

(u) The director of a real estate school shall be responsible for properly closing the school in compliance with this subsection.

1. No later than 10 days after the date on which the school ceases operations, the director shall return the school license, stamp, and all education certificates to the Commission and shall advise the Commission in writing of the date on which the school closed.

2. Within 30 days of the date on which the school ceases operations, the director shall submit an affidavit to the Commission certifying the following:

i. The location where student records are to be kept in compliance with (r) above and the name of the person who is to act as custodian of the records. The Commission shall be notified immediately of any change in such information. Records shall be kept for a period of not less than three years;

ii. The name of the owner or authorized representative of the school and the address where he or she may be contacted by the Commission;

iii. That the school license and school stamp have been returned to the Commission;

iv. That all students have been timely notified of the school closing, and any tuition received by the school for future courses or courses which were not completed has been returned to the students;

v. That all signs have been removed, and all advertisements and trade materials which refer to the school have been recalled;

vi. That the appropriate telephone services have been advised that the school is closed and that future telephone directories should not contain the name of the school; and

vii. That there are no outstanding fees, fines or penalties due and owing the Commission.

(v) No school shall use any name other than the name in which it is licensed for advertising or publicity purposes; nor shall any school advertise or imply that it is "recommended," "endorsed," "accredited," or "approved" by the Commission, but a licensed school may indicate that it has been "licensed" to conduct courses of education in real estate subjects to qualify applicants for licensure examination. No school shall make any warranties or guarantees that a student will pass the State license examination as a result of taking its course.

(w) (Reserved)

(x) The purpose of this subsection is to assure that there is a total separation between instructional activity conducted by licensed schools and any solicitation of students, which, as defined in (x)2ii below, means any recruiting efforts or brokerage activity directed at students. These provisions will be construed in a manner consistent with that regulatory objective. A violation of any of these provisions will be considered by the Commission as conduct demonstrating unworthiness for licensure, thereby subjecting the offending licensee to sanctions pursuant to N.J.S.A. 45:15–17(e) and (t). The Commission may also impose sanctions for a violation of these provisions pursuant to N.J.S.A. 45:15–10.11. Requirements regulating the involvement of licensed schools in soliciting students to become salespersons for particular real estate brokers are as follows:

1. At the beginning of the first class session of all salesperson prelicensure courses, all licensed schools shall distribute to all students in writing the following:

NOTICE

TO: ALL SALESPERSON COURSE STUDENTS
FROM: NEW JERSEY REAL ESTATE COMMISSION
RE: SOLICITATION OF SALESPERSON LICENSE CANDIDATES AT PRE-LICENSURE SCHOOLS

It is the policy of the New Jersey Real Estate Commission that there be a complete and total separation between the instruction you receive in your prelicensure education course and any efforts by brokers to recruit you to join the firm and/or to secure listings or offers on listed properties from you. This policy is reflected in Commission rule N.J.A.C. 11:5-2.2(x), which is reproduced in its entirety below.

If you are subjected to any recruitment efforts or are solicited for listings or offers during class time you should immediately notify your instructor, the Director of your school, and the New Jersey Real Estate Commission by writing to:

New Jersey Real Estate Commission
20 West State Street
PO Box 328
Trenton, New Jersey 08625-0328
Attn: Director, Real Estate Education

You are free to negotiate the terms of your employment with any broker. It is in your own best interest to talk to several prospective employing brokers before deciding which offers the best compensation plan, including post-termination payment provisions, and support package for you. You should also consider a prospective employer's professionalism and reputation for honesty and integrity when deciding which broker to work for.

In the event an enrolled student does not attend the first session of a salespersons course, a copy of the foregoing notice shall be delivered to that student at the commencement of the first class session which that student does attend.

2. For the purposes of this subsection, the following definitions shall apply:

i. The phrase "brokerage activity" means any activity which, pursuant to N.J.S.A. 45:15–1 and 15–3 would require the person engaging in such activity to hold a license as a real estate broker or real estate salesperson;

ii. The term "solicit" means to recruit, invite or urge a student to seek employment with a particular broker, or to list, purchase or lease through, or to make referrals of listing, purchaser or lessee prospects to a particular broker; and

iii. The phrase "successful completion" means the receipt by the student of a Real Estate Commission school certificate form, duly signed by the instructor and the school director and stamped by the licensed school, certifying to the student's having completed and passed a prelicensure course conducted by that school.

3. With the exception of posting, distributing written materials as provided in (x)5 below, no school director, instructor, guest lecturer or staff member shall, prior to, nor within seven days following, a student's successful completion of a course, solicit a student to become a salesperson for any particular real estate broker, nor shall any such person at any time accept any fee or other compensation for soliciting or recruiting students attending their school to apply for employment with a particular real estate broker.

4. No in-person or electronic solicitation of students to apply for employment as salespersons with a particular real estate broker or any referral program shall be permitted at a licensed school location during the prescribed class hours, nor in the breaks between such class hours. Such soliciting may be scheduled and held at licensed schools before, after or separate from the prescribed class hours, for example as a "career night" for students, provided that students are notified in writing in advance that their attendance at such recruitment functions is completely voluntary. However, no school director, instructor, guest lecturer or staff member shall engage in such activity at any time prior to, nor within seven days following, a student's successful completion of a course. Licensed instructors who are also licensed brokers or salespersons may conduct prelicensure courses, and licensees who are not licensed instructors may appear as guest lecturers in such courses, so long as their presentations do not include the solicitation of students.

5. Any licensed school which posts, distributes or displays written material which solicits students to inquire about employment as a salesperson with a particular broker must similarly post, distribute or display comparable written material from any real estate broker who requests the school to do so. However, no written material soliciting students to apply for employment with a particular real estate broker or any referral program shall be distributed during the prescribed class hours.

6. No licensed school may offer a reduced tuition rate to students where eligibility for the lower tuition is contingent upon a student making a commitment to becoming licensed through a particular broker subsequent to their qualifying for licensure and no licensed school may otherwise make or imply any promise or guarantee of employment to any student.

7. No oral statements or written text referring to a licensed school may be included or contained in any advertisement by a real estate licensee, and no advertisement of a licensed school may refer to the brokerage operation or include the telephone number of any licensee except that a school which is owned by a real estate licensee or franchisor may use that name in its school name.

i. Any advertisement by a school whose name includes the name of an affiliated licensed real estate broker or franchisor shall include the following disclosure legend:

> Attending this school will not obligate you to become employed with our affiliated real estate broker(s), nor guarantee you an interview or a job with our affiliated real estate broker(s).

ii. No advertisement referring to a licensed school may be placed in the Help Wanted classified section of any newspaper or periodical.

8. No licensed school shall conduct prelicensure course sessions in any area which is part of a location which is licensed as a main or branch office of a real estate broker. For the purposes of this paragraph, an area will be considered as part of a licensed office location if any brokerage activity is conducted in that area at any time.

i. Where space on two or more floors in a multi-story building is licensed as a main or branch office location, it is permissible for prelicensure courses to be conducted in such a building, provided that the primary means of access to and egress from the floor where the courses are conducted does not require the students to walk through any area of the licensed office location wherein brokerage activity occurs.

ii. Where only one floor in a building is licensed as a main or branch office, it is permissible for prelicensure courses to be conducted in another area on that floor, provided that there is a separate entrance to that area either from the exterior of the building or from a common foyer or lobby and provided that the primary means of access to and egress from the area wherein the courses will be conducted does not require students to walk through a portion of the licensed premises wherein brokerage activity takes place.

iii. In all situations where prelicensure courses are conducted in the same building in which brokerage activity occurs under the authority of a broker in any way affiliated with the licensed school conducting such courses, the broker shall post signs either on the exterior of the building or in any common foyer or lobby, directing students either to the separate exterior entrance to the school location or to the primary route of access to the school location from such foyer or lobby.

9. No licensed school shall allow any person to, solicit students enrolled in, or considering enrolling in, a prelicensure course to list, purchase or lease any property; or for referrals of prospective sellers, purchasers or lessees at any time while such students are on school premises.

R.1972 d.127, effective June 28, 1972.
See: 4 N.J.R. 71(a).
Amended by R.1972 d.150, effective July 27, 1972.
See: 4 N.J.R. 160(d), 4 N.J.R. 190(a).
Amended by R.1980 d.441, effective October 10, 1980.
See: 12 N.J.R. 341(a), 12 N.J.R. 665(e).
(e) and (f): New text.
Amended by R.1983, d.471, effective November 7, 1983.
See: 15 N.J.R. 1343(a), 15 N.J.R. 1865(c).
Language simplified.
Amended by R.1984, d.218, effective June 4, 1984.
See: 16 N.J.R. 489(a), 16 N.J.R. 1352(a).
Section substantially amended.
Amended by R.1986 d.63, effective March 17, 1986.
See: 17 N.J.R. 376(a), 18 N.J.R. 566(b).
(*o*)-(p) deleted; old (q) recodified to (p) with text added "instructor(s) name and . . . after student matriculation."; (r)-(w) recodified to (q)-(v).
Amended by R.1988 d.409, effective September 6, 1988.
See: 20 N.J.R. 1161(a), 20 N.J.R. 2298(a).
Substantially amended (j) and (k); added new (*l*) and recodified (*l*)-(v) as (m)-(w).
Amended by R.1990 d.378, effective August 6, 1990.
See: 22 N.J.R. 777(a), 22 N.J.R. 2323(a).
Added new x.
Amended by R.1993 d.11, effective January 4, 1993.
See: 24 N.J.R. 3488(a), 25 N.J.R. 180(a).
Subsection (e) deleted and reserved.
Amended by R.1994 d.59, effective February 7, 1994 (operative July 1, 1994).
See: 25 N.J.R. 4855(a), 26 N.J.R. 801(a).
Amended by R.1994 d.267, effective June 20, 1994 (operative July 1, 1994).
See: 26 N.J.R. 730(a), 26 N.J.R. 1194(b), 26 N.J.R. 1222(a), 26 N.J.R. 2581(c).
Amended by R.1998 d.497, effective October 5, 1998.
See: 30 N.J.R. 2333(a), 30 N.J.R. 3646(a).
Changed N.J.A.C. references throughout.

SUBCHAPTER 3. LICENSING

11:5–3.1 Terms of real estate licenses

Commencing July 1, 1997, broker, broker-salesperson, salesperson and branch office licenses shall be issued on the basis of two year license terms. All licenses issued during each biennial term shall run from the date of issuance to the end of the biennial term. All licenses shall expire on June 30 of the second year following the year in which the license term commenced.

New Rule, R.1997 d.159, effective April 7, 1997.
See: 29 N.J.R. 299(a), 29 N.J.R. 1324(b).

11:5–3.2 Payment of fees as prescribed by statute

Any and all fees prescribed by the Real Estate License Act shall be paid by broker's business account check, certified or bank check or money order payable to the State Treasurer of New Jersey. No cash or currency shall be accepted.

Amended by R.1986 d.92, effective April 7, 1986.
See: 17 N.J.R. 2353(a), 18 N.J.R. 702(a).
Added text, "brokers business account check, certified or bank".

11:5–3.3 Criminal history record check

(a) The applicant, if a natural person, shall submit with his or her application for salesperson's or broker's license a New Jersey State Police Request for Criminal History Record Information and a certified check or money order to pay for its processing.

(b) The applicant, if a corporation or partnership, shall submit with its application for license New Jersey State Police Requests for Criminal History Record Information, and certified checks or money orders to pay for their processing, for each officer, director, partner, or owner of a controlling interest.

(c) The Commission may require an individual licensee or any officer, director, partner or owner of a controlling interest of a licensed corporation or partnership to complete and submit to the Commission a New Jersey State Police fingerprint card, and submit a certified check or money order in payment of the processing fee for the card.

R.1971 d.83, effective May 27, 1971.
See: 2 N.J.R. 42(e), 3 N.J.R. 110(d).
Amended by R.1976 d.19, effective January 13, 1976.
See: 7 N.J.R. 567(e), 8 N.J.R. 70(e).
Amended by R.1983 d.471, effective November 7, 1983.
See: 15 N.J.R. 1343(a), 15 N.J.R. 1865(c).

Subsections (c) and (e) deleted, recodification.
New Rule, R.1985 d.601, effective November 18, 1985.
See: 17 N.J.R. 2230(a), 17 N.J.R. 2779(a).
Repealed this section dealing with "Fingerprinting" and adopted New Rule.
Amended by R.1995 d.23, effective January 17, 1995.
See: 26 N.J.R. 3111(a), 27 N.J.R. 370(a).

11:5–3.4 Examination rules

(a) In the administration of examinations for licensure as a real estate broker, broker-salesperson or salesperson, the following examination rules shall apply:

1. Examinees shall not be permitted to refer to any notes, books, or memoranda.

2. The copying of questions or making of notes for personal use is strictly prohibited.

3. No examinee shall leave the examining room except at the discretion of the examiner.

4. The real estate broker license and salesperson license examinations, required by N.J.S.A. 45:15–10 to be taken and successfully passed by all applicants for a real estate broker, broker-salesperson or salesperson license before said license may be issued, shall be in the form of a multiple choice examination prepared by a testing service as designated by the Commission. Fees charged applicants to take the real estate examinations shall be considered service fees to be paid directly to the testing service separate and apart from any fee required by N.J.S.A. 45:15–9 to be paid to the Commission at the time of the license application.

(b) A request for special accommodations may be made if the applicant qualifies for such accommodations as provided in the Americans With Disabilities Act or any other applicable law. Such requests shall initially be made to the firm administering the licensing examinations. The Commission shall retain final authority to determine whether such requests shall be granted.

As amended, R.1972 d.168, effective August 26, 1972.
See: 4 N.J.R. 160(d), 4 N.J.R. 190(a).
As amended, R.1973 d.43, effective February 5, 1973.
See: 5 N.J.R. 13(b), 5 N.J.R. 86(b).
As amended, R.1973 d.306, effective October 25, 1973.
See: 5 N.J.R. 350(a), 5 N.J.R. 338(a).
As amended, R.1983 d.471, effective November 7, 1983.
See: 15 N.J.R. 1343(a), 15 N.J.R. 1865(c).
"Salesman" replaced by "salesperson".
Amended by R.1995 d.23, effective January 17, 1995.
See: 26 N.J.R. 3111(a), 27 N.J.R. 370(a).
Amended by R.1998 d.497, effective October 5, 1998.
See: 30 N.J.R. 2333(a), 30 N.J.R. 3646(a).
Rewrote (b).

11:5–3.5 Requests for disclosure of social security numbers

(a) The Commission may request that licensees and license applicants, including registrants for license examinations, submit their social security numbers to the Commission. All such requests shall either include or be accompanied by a notice stating:

1. The purpose or purposes for which the Commission intends to use the social security numbers;

2. That disclosure made pursuant to the request is either voluntary or mandatory; and

3. That the request is authorized by this section and by such other law as may be applicable.

New Rule, R.1994 d.268, effective June 20, 1994 (operative July 1, 1994).
See: 26 N.J.R. 735(a), 26 N.J.R. 1222(a), 26 N.J.R. 2585(a).
Repeal and New Rule, R.1997 d.160, effective April 7, 1997.
See: 29 N.J.R. 302(a), 29 N.J.R. 1324(c).
Section was "Collection of Social Security numbers of licenses'.

11:5–3.6 Salesperson's license; age requirement

(a) No salesperson's license shall be issued to any person who has not attained the age of 18 years.

(b) Every applicant for licensure as a salesperson shall present with his/her application for licensure a certificate of satisfactory completion of a course of education in real estate subjects at a school licensed by the Commission pursuant to N.J.S.A. 45:15–10.1(a) and 10.4 and N.J.A.C. 11:5–2.2, unless waived by the Commission in accordance with the provisions of N.J.S.A. 45:15–10.2.

(c) An applicant must apply for and request the issuance of a salesperson's license not later than one year after the date of successful completion of the course prescribed at N.J.A.C. 11:5–2.1. Any person who fails to apply for the issuance of a salesperson's license within the one year period shall be required to retake and successfully complete the prescribed course in real estate and the examination.

(d) All applicants for licensure as a salesperson shall certify that they possess a high school education or equivalency. The Commission may require the production of evidence of such education or equivalency as a condition to issuing a license to any applicant.

As amended, R.1973 d.214, effective August 2, 1973.
See: 5 N.J.R. 228(f), 5 N.J.R. 316(a).
As amended, R.1974 d.307, effective November 13, 1974.
See: 6 N.J.R. 246(c), 6 N.J.R. 478(e).
As amended, R.1981 d.261, effective July 9, 1981.
See: 13 N.J.R. 306(a), 13 N.J.R. 440(c).
(b) "On or after September 1, 1967" deleted; "for licensure as a salesman" added.
(d) added.
As amended, R.1983 d.471, effective November 7, 1983.
See: 15 N.J.R. 1343(a), 15 N.J.R. 1865(c).
"Salesman" changed to "salesperson".
As amended, R.1984 d.218, effective June 4, 1984.
See: 16 N.J.R. 489(a), 16 N.J.R. 1352(a).
New subsections (d) through (f) added.
Amended by R.1995 d.23, effective January 17, 1995.
See: 26 N.J.R. 3111(a), 27 N.J.R. 370(a).
Amended by R.1998 d.497, effective October 5, 1998.
See: 30 N.J.R. 2333(a), 30 N.J.R. 3646(a).
In (b) and (c), changed N.J.S.A. and N.J.A.C. references; rewrote (d); and deleted former (e) through (f).

11:5–3.7 Employment of salesperson sponsored by broker

No broker shall knowingly sponsor an applicant for licensure as a real estate salesperson who does not bear a good reputation for honesty and fair dealings.

As amended, R.1983 d.471, effective November 7, 1983.
See: 15 N.J.R. 1343(a), 15 N.J.R. 1865(c).
"Salesman" replaced by "salesperson".
Amended by R.1998 d.497, effective October 5, 1998.
See: 30 N.J.R. 2333(a), 30 N.J.R. 3646(a).
Rewrote (a); and deleted former (b).

11:5–3.8 Qualifications for licensing; broker and broker-salesperson

(a) All references in this section to "brokers" shall include broker-salespersons. The experience requirement for licensure as a broker imposed by N.J.S.A. 45:15–9 is construed to require a demonstration by the applicant of their commitment to real estate brokerage as their primary vocation, as evidenced by their involvement in the real estate brokerage business on a full-time basis.

1. With the exception of persons licensed as brokers in other states, all applicants for licensure as a broker must have been continuously licensed and employed on a full-time basis as a real estate salesperson during the three years immediately preceding their application. Such full-time employment shall be demonstrated by a showing that:

i. The applicant has worked as a salesperson under the authority of the broker(s) with whom they were licensed for at least 40 hours per week and during the hours of approximately 10:00 A.M. to 8:00 P.M.;

ii. Such work in (a)1i above was performed during any five days in each week of the three year period; and

iii. If the applicant was employed in any other occupation during the three year period, such other employment was on a part-time basis and did not exceed 25 hours per calendar week.

2. No applications for approval of an applicant's experience to qualify for licensure as a broker shall be made until an applicant:

i. Has been continuously licensed as a salesperson for at least the three years immediately preceding such application;

ii. Has completed the 90–hour general broker's prelicensure course and the two 30–hour courses referred to in N.J.A.C. 11:5–2.1(g).

(b) The Commission shall give due consideration to the following in reviewing the experience of an applicant:

1. Evidence of having been actively involved in the real estate brokerage business as a real estate salesperson on a full-time basis during each year of the three year period. Written statements by the brokers with whom the applicant was licensed during the three year period which certify the applicant's activity as a salesperson while licensed through those brokers must be submitted.

2. Applicants and/or brokers may also be required to submit supporting documentation relating to the closed transactions on which the applicant received compensation as a salesperson from the broker, or to supply other evidence of full-time activity, such as extensive involvement in a specialized field of real estate brokerage.

3. In no event will an applicant whose brokerage activity was limited to solely making referrals to other licensees be deemed to have fulfilled the full-time, active involvement in the brokerage business requirement for licensure.

(c) Broker-salespersons shall meet the same qualifications as brokers, including the qualifications as set forth in (a) and (b) above. A person licensed as a broker-salesperson must be employed by and act under the supervision of a duly licensed real estate broker and shall not independently maintain an office or escrow account. A broker-salesperson may be authorized to serve as an office supervisor or a branch office in accordance with the provisions of N.J.S.A. 45:15–12.

(d) Every applicant for licensure as a broker or broker-salesperson shall present with his or her application for licensure examination a certificate of satisfactory completion of courses in real estate and related subjects at a school licensed by the Commission or offered by another approved provider pursuant to N.J.S.A. 45:15–10.1(b) and N.J.A.C. 11:5–2.1 and 2.2, unless waived by the Commission in accordance with the provisions of N.J.S.A. 45:15–10.2 and N.J.A.C. 11:5–2.1.

(e) An applicant must pass the State broker license examination and apply for and request the issuance of a license as a broker or broker-salesperson not later than one year after successful completion of the 150–hour broker prelicensure education requirements. Any person who fails to apply for the issuance of a license as a broker or broker-salesperson within the said one year time period shall be required to retake and successfully complete all prescribed courses and the examination and must submit evidence of having again fulfilled the experience requirement during the three years immediately preceding the new application.

As amended, R.1972 d.150, effective July 27, 1972.
See: 4 N.J.R. 160(d), 4 N.J.R. 190(a).
As amended, R.1974 d.307, effective November 13, 1974.
See: 6 N.J.R. 246(c), 6 N.J.R. 478(e).
As amended, R.1981 d.261, effective July 9, 1981.
See: 13 N.J.R. 306(a), 13 N.J.R. 440(c).
Substantially amended.
As amended, R.1983 d.471, effective November 7, 1983.
See: 15 N.J.R. 1343(a), 15 N.J.R. 1865(c).

Former subsections (a) and (f) deleted, recodified, "salesman" changed to "salesperson".
Amended by R.1987 d.68, effective January 20, 1987.
See: 18 N.J.R. 1782(a), 19 N.J.R. 232(a).
Deleted text in (a) "full-time during his apprenticeship as a salesperson" and added text "on a full ... per calendar week."
Amended by R.1994 d.56, effective February 7, 1994 (operative July 1, 1994).
See: 25 N.J.R. 4849(b), 26 N.J.R. 798(a).
Amended by R.1998 d.497, effective October 5, 1998.
See: 30 N.J.R. 2333(a), 30 N.J.R. 3646(a).
In (a)2ii and (d), changed N.J.A.C. references.

Case Notes

Real estate salesman was not authorized to sue to collect commission to which employer may have been entitled. Harper-Lawrence, Inc. v. United Merchants and Mfrs., Inc., 261 N.J.Super. 554, 619 A.2d 623 (A.D.1993), certification denied 134 N.J. 478, 634 A.2d 525.

Real estate licensing law exemption for attorneys held only to authorize attorneys to sell or rent real estate incidental to their normal practice of law; denial of broker's license to attorney who did not meet statutory apprenticeship and testing requirements upheld. Spirito v. State, New Jersey Real Estate Commission, 180 N.J.Super. 180, 434 A.2d 623 (App.Div.1981).

11:5-3.9 Return of license when broker ceases to be active; office closing; change of broker of record

(a) Each broker who ceases to be active shall immediately return to the Commission his license, and licenses of all salespersons and broker-salespersons for cancellation.

(b) Each employee's license must be accompanied by a letter terminating employment in compliance with N.J.S.A. 45:15-14.

(c) No broker engaging in the real estate brokerage business as a sole proprietor, as a broker of record of a partnership or as a broker of record of a corporation shall be relicensed as broker or salesperson unless within 30 days of the date of which the broker ceases engaging in the real estate brokerage business he or she shall complete and submit an affidavit to the Commission certifying that:

1. The broker's license, the corporate or partnership license, and the licenses of all salespersons and broker-salespersons have been returned to the Commission for cancellation;

2. The broker's trust account has been closed and that all funds held in trust for others have been disbursed to proper parties;

3. All commissions owed to salespersons and broker-salespersons have been paid, or, if not yet received by the broker, will be paid upon receipt;

4. No further commissions are due the broker except that any commissions for services previously rendered and payable in the future upon the occurrence of specified events are described on a list ättached to the affidavit. The list shall describe the nature and amounts of such outstanding commissions with sufficient information to identify each transaction;

5. The broker has notified all principals in ongoing transactions, in writing, that the broker has ceased engaging in the real estate brokerage business or that the broker will hereinafter engage in the real estate brokerage business in another capacity. The notice shall describe the disposition of pending transactions and the name of custodian and place of deposit of any funds received from principals;

6. The broker has removed from the licensed premises all signs indicating that the premises contains the office of a licensed real estate broker;

7. The broker has recalled all signs and other advertisements or trade materials indicating that the broker is engaged in the real estate brokerage business;

8. The broker has advised the appropriate telephone services that the firm is no longer engaged in the real estate brokerage business, and that further telephone directories should not contain the name of the individual or firm as licensed brokers;

9. There are no outstanding fines or penalties due and owing the Real Estate Commission;

10. The broker acknowledges his or her responsibility to maintain records as required in N.J.A.C. 11:5-5.4. The broker must provide the address of the place of depository of such records and acknowledge responsibility to advise the Commission of any change in the name of the custodian or place of depository for a period of six years.

(d) When a new broker of record of a corporation or partnership is being substituted for the existing broker of record, the existing broker of record satisfies the certification requirements of (c) above when in compliance with the substitution procedures of (e) below.

(e) No new broker of record of a corporation or partnership shall be substituted unless the new broker of record and the former broker of record prepare and submit a joint affidavit to the Commissioner certifying that:

1. Custody of all funds held in trust for principals has been assumed by the new broker of record;

2. The new broker of record has reviewed all pending transactions and is satisfied that all funds held in trust have been accounted for;

3. All salespersons' commissions are paid to date;

4. The new broker acknowledges responsibility to pay salespersons' commissions in accordance with the policy for payment existing on the date of substitution;

5. No fines are presently owed to the Real Estate Commission, and if any fines are assessed after the date of substitution for actions occurring prior to substitution, both the former broker and new broker are jointly and severally responsible for payment;

6. All signs and advertisements have been changed to reflect the broker now authorized to transact business in the name of the firm;

7. All records required to be maintained pursuant to N.J.A.C. 11:5–5.4 have been turned over to the new broker, and the new broker acknowledges responsibility to maintain such records for a period of six years;

8. The new broker acknowledges that he or she will be responsible to transact business in the name and on behalf of the firm.

As amended, R.1983 d.471, effective November 7, 1983.
See: 15 N.J.R. 1343(a), 15 N.J.R. 1865(c).
"Salesman" changed to "salesperson", language simplified.
Amended by R.1985 d.186, effective April 15, 1985.
See: 16 N.J.R. 2228(b), 17 N.J.R. 970(b).
Amended by R.1998 d.497, effective October 5, 1998.
See: 30 N.J.R. 2333(a), 30 N.J.R. 3646(a).
In (c), changed N.J.A.C. reference and deleted "permanent type" following "maintain" in 10; and in (e), changed N.J.A.C. reference in 7.

11:5–3.10 Sponsoring of license applications or transfers of license

(a) The New Jersey Real Estate Commission, Department of Insurance, hereby grants to brokers of record or employing brokers the right to have initial applications for licenses of salespersons or broker-salespersons who will be in their employ sponsored by one other person, other than the authorized broker of record or employing broker. This other person must be the holder of a broker's license and an officer of the broker of record's corporation or a member of his or her partnership, as the case may be. In the event the employing broker is a sole proprietor, such a designee shall be licensed as a broker-salesperson in the employ of the employing broker. The broker of record or employing broker, as applicable, shall file with the New Jersey Real Estate Commission a power of attorney granting this authority to the designated person at least 10 days prior to delegating performance of the function of that person.

(b) Any employing broker or broker of record may authorize one individual in their employ to sign and surrender to the Real Estate Commission, in accordance with the requirements of N.J.S.A. 45:15–14, the real estate salesperson or broker-salesperson license of any licensee whose employment relationship with that employing broker or broker of record is terminated. The employing broker or broker of record shall, on a form to be provided by the Commission, notify the Commission in writing of the designation of the employee so authorized, which person need not be the holder of a real estate license. The form designating the authorized person shall be filed with the Real Estate Commission at least 10 days prior to delegating performance of the function of that person. The employing broker or broker of record shall immediately notify the Real Estate Commission in writing in the event that, for any reason, the authority of the person so designated to perform that function is revoked, and shall indicate whether a new designee is to be named. Only the employing broker or broker of record and one other person duly designated and identified to the Real Estate Commission as provided in this section may perform the said license transfer functions at any one time.

R.1972 d.127, effective June 28, 1972.
See: 4 N.J.R. 71(a).
Amended by R.1983 d.471, effective November 7, 1983.
See: 15 N.J.R. 1343(a), 15 N.J.R. 1865(c).
"Salesman" replaced by "salesperson".
Amended by R.1987 d.119, effective March 2, 1987.
See: 18 N.J.R. 2418(a), 19 N.J.R. 409(b).
Substantially amended.

11:5–3.11 Expediting of license issuance and transfer procedures

(a) For the purpose of expediting the right of licensees to engage in real estate activities, where license certificates cannot be issued without delay after all conditions have been fulfilled, the Commission directs that a certificate of authority in the form of a letter to the licensee be sent to serve as a temporary license for a limited period of time.

(b) In cases where a licensee who is transferring from one broker to another requests that their current broker deliver their license to them, rather than return it to the Commission, so as to expedite the transfer process, the license shall be so delivered, provided that:

1. The rear of the license certificate is signed and dated by the terminating broker in the appropriate location prior to the delivery of the license to the departing licensee;

2. At the time of the delivery of the license to the departing licensee, the termination confirmation section of the license, reflecting the effective date of the licensee's separation from that broker, has been completed, signed and retained by the terminating broker; and

3. Within five business days of the delivery of the license to the departing licensee, the terminating broker shall mail to the Commission the completed and signed termination confirmation section of the license and send a copy of it to the departing licensee at their last known residence address.

(c) A transferring licensee who receives their license from the terminating broker after that broker has signed the license and entered the date of termination on it may then take that license to their new employing broker. Prior to the transferring person commencing work as a licensee for the new employing broker, that broker shall:

1. Enter on the license in the appropriate location the effective date of the individual's employment with that broker and sign the license as the new employing broker;

2. Detach the temporary license stub portion from the main license document and place it with the licenses of the other persons licensed with that broker; and

3. Mail to the Commission the dated and signed license of the transferring individual with the required transfer fee (see N.J.S.A. 45:15–14) in the form of a certified or cashier's check or money order or broker's business account check. See N.J.A.C. 11:5–3.2.

R.1972 d.127, effective June 28, 1972.
See: 4 N.J.R. 17(a).
Amended by R.1983 d.471, effective November 7, 1983.
See: 15 N.J.R. 1343(a), 15 N.J.R. 1865(c).
Reference to a letter and its contents was deleted.
Amended by R.1994 d.60, effective February 7, 1994 (operative July 1, 1994).
See: 25 N.J.R. 4858(a), 26 N.J.R. 803(a).
Amended by R.1998 d.497, effective October 5, 1998.
See: 30 N.J.R. 2333(a), 30 N.J.R. 3646(a).
In (c), changed N.J.A.C. reference in 3.

SUBCHAPTER 4. EMPLOYMENT PRACTICES/OFFICE AND LICENSEE SUPERVISION

11:5–4.1 Employment agreements; commissions; accounting to salespersons; actions for collection of compensation

(a) No salesperson may commence operations as such for a broker and no broker may authorize a salesperson to act as such on his or her behalf until a written agreement as provided in this subsection has been signed by the broker and salesperson. Prior to an individual's commencement of activity as a salesperson under the authority of a broker, the broker and salesperson shall both sign a written agreement which recites the terms under which the services of the salesperson have been retained by the broker. Such terms shall include, but need not be limited to, the following:

1. The rate of compensation to be paid to the salesperson during his or her affiliation with the broker;

2. A promise by the broker to pay to the salesperson his or her portion of commissions earned within 10 business days of their receipt by the broker or as soon thereafter as such funds have cleared the broker's bank, or in accordance with another payment schedule explicitly set forth in the employment agreement;

3. The rate of compensation payable to the salesperson on transactions which close and, if applicable, on renewals which occur subsequent to the termination of the salesperson's affiliation with the broker; and

4. A provision that any future changes to the agreement will not be binding unless the changes are contained in a writing signed by both parties.

(b) A copy of the fully executed agreement shall be provided to the salesperson upon the commencement of his or her affiliation with the broker, and the original thereof shall be maintained by the broker as a business record in accordance with N.J.A.C. 11:5–5.5.

(c) All compensation paid to brokers shall, unless debited from funds held in escrow in accordance with N.J.A.C. 11:5–5.1(d), be deposited into the general business account of the broker within five business days of their receipt by the broker.

(d) In the event that any monies due a salesperson under the terms of the written agreement with their broker are not paid within 10 business days of the broker's receipt of such funds or promptly thereafter upon their having cleared the broker's account, the broker shall provide to the salesperson a complete and comprehensive written explanation of the failure to pay such monies.

(e) Upon the termination of the affiliation of a salesperson with a broker, the broker shall make a complete accounting in writing of all monies due the salesperson as of the date of termination and/or which may become due in the future. In the event any sums so accounted for are not in accord with the terms of the post-termination compensation clause in the written agreement between the broker and the salesperson, the broker shall give a complete and comprehensive written explanation of any difference to the salesperson with the accounting. Such accounting shall be delivered to the salesperson not later than 30 days after termination.

(f) Copies of all written agreements as described in (a) above, of all written explanations of the failure to pay compensation due a salesperson on a timely basis as described in (e) above, and of all accountings and written explanations regarding compensation due a salesperson subsequent to the termination of their affiliation with a broker as described in (f) above shall be maintained by the broker, with adequate proof of the delivery of the same to the salesperson, for a period of six years.

(g) In situations where the Commission confirms that a broker has complied with all of the requirements imposed by this section, the Commission will not further investigate a complaint alleging the non-payment of a commission by a broker to a salesperson unless such complaint is accompanied by a copy of an arbitration decision or the equivalent, or a copy of a judgment of a court of competent jurisdiction secured by the salesperson against the broker. Unless appealed, the failure by a broker to pay monies awarded to a salesperson under the terms of any such decision or judgment within 30 days of its effective date shall subject the broker to sanctions pursuant to N.J.S.A. 45:15–17.

(h) Broker and salesperson licensees may only bring or maintain actions in the courts of New Jersey for the payment of compensation due them for brokerage services performed as provided in N.J.S.A. 45:15–3.

1. The Commission interprets the language "at the time the alleged cause of action arose" as used in N.J.S.A. 45:15–3 to mean at the time that the brokerage services which form the basis for the alleged claim to compensation were rendered. For example, at the time when a property was listed for sale or rental by a licensee.

2. The Commission does not interpret the language "at the time the alleged cause or action arose" as requiring that the licensee must have been actively licensed at the time that the compensation allegedly due was to have been paid. For example, the Commission does not construe this language as requiring licensure at the time of the renewal of a lease to enable a claimant to sue for compensation based upon a promise, made or in effect when the lease was originally executed, to pay additional consideration to the claimant in the event that the lease was renewed.

(i) All references to "salesperson" in this section shall be construed to also include individuals licensed as broker-salespersons. All references to "non-payment of a commission" in this section shall be construed to include the non-payment of other forms of compensation.

As amended, R.1976 d.254, eff. August 16, 1976.
See: 8 N.J.R. 336(b), 8 N.J.R. 422(a).
As amended, R.1983 d.471, eff. November 7, 1983.
See: 15 N.J.R. 1343(a), 15 N.J.R. 1865(c).
"Salesman" replaced by "salesperson".
Amended by R.1989 d.424, effective August 21, 1989 (operative November 19, 1989).
See: 21 N.J.R. 1308(b), 21 N.J.R. 2519(a).
Language entirely deleted and replaced with more detailed requirements including essential provisions which must be included in all contracts between brokers and salespersons.
Amended by R.1994 d.57, effective February 7, 1994.
See: 25 N.J.R. 4851(a), 26 N.J.R. 799(a).
Amended by R.1998 d.497, effective October 5, 1998.
See: 30 N.J.R. 2333(a), 30 N.J.R. 3646(a).
In (a), rewrote 2; deleted former (c); recodified former (d) through (j) as (c) through (i); and changed N.J.A.C. references throughout.

Case Notes

Real Estate Commission regulation is reasonable interpretation of statute governing actions for recovery of real estate commissions, which requires that claimant be duly authorized real estate broker at time commission was earned. Prestia Realty Inc. V. Hartz Mountain Industries, Inc., 303 N.J.Super. 140, 696 A.2d 95 (N.J.Super.A.D. 1997).

Regulation stating that real estate broker suing for commissions must have been duly licensed when broker performed all necessary brokerage services does not require broker to be licensed at time of closing. Atlantic Commercial Group, Inc. v. Dunham, 303 N.J.Super. 122, 696 A.2d 85 (N.J.Super.A.D. 1997).

Issues of fact precluded summary judgment on issue whether claimed agent was an employee of real estate agency for purposes of wrongful discharge claim. MacDougall v. Weichert, 144 N.J. 380, 677 A.2d 162 (1996).

Commingling of funds, accounting failures, as well as other violations, warranted permanent revocation of broker/salesperson license and imposition of fine. New Jersey Real Estate Commission v. Duffy, 93 N.J.A.R.2d (REC) 13.

Commingling trust monies and failing to maintain separate account for escrow funds, as well as other violations, warranted revocation of broker's license, suspension of salesperson's license, and assessment of fine. New Jersey Real Estate Commission v. Woods. 92 N.J.A.R.2d (REC) 25.

Failing to maintain as separate funds monies held as escrow agent, and other violations, warranted revocation of broker's license and assessment of fine. New Jersey Real Estate Commission v. Brown. 92 N.J.A.R.2d (REC) 21.

11:5–4.2 Broker supervision and oversight of individual licensees, office operations and escrowed monies

(a) The following apply to individual broker licensees operating as sole proprietors (employing brokers) or as the authorized broker (broker of record) of a corporation or other entity licensed as a New Jersey real estate broker. As used in this section, the term "individual broker" shall refer to employing brokers and brokers of record and the term "broker licensee" shall refer to sole proprietors and corporations or other entities licensed as brokers.

1. The Commission will hold responsible individual brokers for any actions of the broker licensee or any person employed by or licensed through the broker licensee taken in the pursuit of its real estate brokerage business which violate any of the provisions of the real estate license law, N.J.S.A. 45:15–1 et seq., or the regulations promulgated thereunder.

i. This responsibility shall apply regardless of where the persons licensed through the broker licensee engage in actions in pursuit of the broker licensee's real estate brokerage business.

2. Every real estate transaction in which a broker licensee participates as a broker shall be under the ultimate supervision of the individual broker.

3. The individual broker shall, in addition to ascertaining that a separate account is maintained for the funds of others coming into the possession of the broker licensee, make certain that no such funds of others are disbursed or utilized without his or her express authorization and knowledge.

4. The provisions of this subsection do not apply to brokers licensed as broker-salespersons.

As amended, R.1983 d.471, effective November 7, 1983.
See: 15 N.J.R. 1343(a), 15 N.J.R. 1865(c).
Subsections (a) and (c) deleted; subsection (b) recodified as (a).
Amended by R.1995 d.23, effective January 17, 1995.
See: 26 N.J.R. 3111(a), 27 N.J.R. 370(a).
Amended by R.1998 d.246, effective May 18, 1998.
See: 30 N.J.R. 278(a), 30 N.J.R. 1827(a).
Rewrote (a).

11:5–4.3 Use of license for the benefit of others

(a) No arrangement, direct or indirect, shall be entered into by any licensee whereby an individual licensee lends his name or license for the benefit of another person, firm or corporation, or whereby the provisions of the real estate statute and rules relating to licensing are circumvented.

(b) Lending a broker's license for the benefit of another person, firm or corporation shall be construed as including any arrangement whereby a broker fails to personally oversee and direct the operations of the business of which he or she is licensed as broker of record or employing broker. For the purposes of this section, personal oversight and direction of the business shall be construed as requiring the broker to be physically present in the main office or branch office locations of the business at least one day each week (excluding vacations and emergencies). Communication via telephone and/or mail alone for an extended period of time may be considered by the Commission as evidence of prohibited license lending.

(c) Nothing in this section shall be construed to limit a broker's responsibility to insure the adequate supervision of all offices in accordance with the requirements of N.J.A.C. 11:5–4.4 and 4.5.

As amended, R.1982 d.101, effective April 5, 1982.
See: 13 N.J.R. 302(b), 14 N.J.R. 345(b).
Deleted existing text of (b) and added new (b) through (b)2.
As amended, R.1983 d.471, effective November 7, 1983.
See: 15 N.J.R. 1343(a), 15 N.J.R. 1865(c).
Amended by R.1989 d.426, effective August 21, 1989 (operative November 19, 1989).
See: 20 N.J.R. 2184(a), 20 N.J.R. 3019(a), 21 N.J.R. 1311(a), 21 N.J.R. 2522(a).
Established the minimum amount of personal contact which brokers must maintain with their offices and salespeople, deleted (b) and added new (b) and (c).
Amended by R.1998 d.497, effective October 5, 1998.
See: 30 N.J.R. 2333(a), 30 N.J.R. 3646(a).
In (c), changed N.J.A.C. references.

11:5–4.4 Maintained offices

(a) Every resident real estate broker not licensed as a broker-salesperson shall maintain a main office for the transaction of business in the State of New Jersey, which shall be open to the public during usual business hours. This main office and the activities of the licensees working from it shall be under the direct supervision of either the broker himself or herself, or of a person licensed as a broker-salesperson. Such supervision shall be maintained on a full time basis. Maintaining full-time supervision shall not be construed as requiring the person performing the supervisory functions to be present at the office location continuously during usual business hours. However, the person performing the supervisory functions shall provide sufficient information so as to allow the personnel at the main office to make communication with that person at all times. Further, the licensee supervising the main office shall be so employed on a full-time basis and, when not required to be away from the office for reasons related to the business of the office, shall be physically present at that office during usual business hours at least five days per calendar week (excluding vacations and emergencies) and shall not be otherwise employed during such time.

1. In the event the main office of a broker is under the direct supervision of a broker-salesperson, the broker who maintains such a main office shall be ultimately responsible for all activities conducted by licensees and employees. Such a broker shall also provide sufficient information to the personnel at such offices so as to allow them to make communication with such broker at all times. Nothing in this section shall be construed to limit a broker's responsibility to comply with the requirements of N.J.A.C. 11:5–4.3.

(b) If such office is located in a residence, it shall be independent of living quarters and shall have a separate exterior entrance plainly visible from the street upon which the licensed premises shall have frontage. This subsection shall not apply to offices in existence prior to December 1, 1963.

(c) No broker's maintained place or places of business shall be in the dwelling premises of any salesperson in that broker's employ.

(d) Sole proprietor employing brokers and persons licensed as a broker of record for a licensed entity are responsible to supervise, track and oversee the brokerage activity of persons licensed under their authority regardless of where such activity takes place.

As amended, R.1983 d.471, effective November 7, 1983.
See: 15 N.J.R. 1343(a), 15 N.J.R. 1865(c).
"Salesman" replaced by "salesperson".
Amended by R.1989 d.427, effective August 21, 1989 (operative November 19, 1989).
See: 20 N.J.R. 1160(a), 21 N.J.R. 1312(b), 21 N.J.R. 2523(a).
Clarification obligation of brokers of record to supervise their main office on a full time basis and unusual business hours, added to (a) and new (a)1.
Amended by R.1998 d.246, effective May 18, 1998.
See: 30 N.J.R. 278(a), 30 N.J.R. 1827(a).
Inserted a new (d).
Amended by R.1998 d.497, effective October 5, 1998.
See: 30 N.J.R. 2333(a), 30 N.J.R. 3646(a).
In (a)1, changed N.J.A.C. reference.

Case Notes

Regulation of the New Jersey real estate commission which states holders of reciprocal licenses for non-resident brokers are not permitted to maintain offices in New Jersey is invalid as there is no statutory prohibition on the maintenance of a branch office by a reciprocally licensed non-resident broker in New Jersey which is under the direct, full-time supervision of a competent New Jersey licensee. Atty.Gen. F.O.1977, No. 14.

11:5–4.5 Branch office compliance with N.J.A.C. 11:5–4.4 (Maintained offices)

(a) In the event a real estate broker maintains a branch office or offices, every such place of business shall comply with the provisions of N.J.A.C. 11:5–4.4 (Maintained offices).

(b) No license shall be issued for a branch office situated in the dwelling premises of a salesperson or broker-salesperson.

(c) Any branch office shall be under the direct supervision of a licensed broker employed as a broker salesperson by the broker maintaining the branch office.

(d) Such individual shall devote his or her full time to management of said office during the usual business hours.

(e) The name of the individual responsible for the supervision of the branch office shall be recorded at all times with the Commission.

(f) When a branch office license is issued to a broker it shall specifically set forth the name of the broker and the address of the branch office, and shall be conspicuously displayed at all times in the branch office. The branch office shall also prominently display the name of the broker-salesperson licensee in charge as "office supervisor" and the names of all other broker-salespersons and the salespersons doing business at that branch office.

(g) The said branch office license shall be returned for cancellation or correction upon the change of an "office supervisor".

As amended, R.1983 d.471, effective November 7, 1983.
See: 15 N.J.R. 1343(a), 15 N.J.R. 1865(c).
Correct N.J.A.C. citations added.
Amended by R.1985 d.187, effective April 15, 1985.
See: 16 N.J.R. 2228(a), 17 N.J.R. 970(a).
(f): Substantially amended.
Amended by R.1989 d.428, effective August 21, 1989 (operative February 21, 1990).
See: 21 N.J.R. 1313(a), 21 N.J.R. 2523(a).
Required that branch offices be supervised by broker-salespersons.
Amended by R.1995 d.23, effective January 17, 1995.
See: 26 N.J.R. 3111(a), 27 N.J.R. 370(a).
Amended by R.1998 d.497, effective October 5, 1998.
See: 30 N.J.R. 2333(a), 30 N.J.R. 3646(a).
In (a), changed the N.J.A.C. reference and deleted "of this subchapter" from the end.

Case Notes

Regulation of the New Jersey real estate commission which states holders of reciprocal licenses for non-resident brokers are not permitted to maintain offices in New Jersey is invalid as there is no statutory prohibition on the maintenance of a branch office by a reciprocally licensed non-resident broker in New Jersey which is under the direct, full-time supervision of a competent New Jersey licensee. Atty.Gen. F.O.1977, No. 14.

SUBCHAPTER 5. TRUST ACCOUNTS/RECORDS OF BROKERAGE ACTIVITY

11:5-5.1 Special accounts for funds of others; commingling

(a) Every resident real estate broker shall establish and maintain, in an authorized financial institution in New Jersey, and every reciprocally licensed Real Estate broker shall establish and maintain in an authorized financial institution in New Jersey or the State wherein he has a resident real estate broker's license, a special account or special accounts, separate and apart from other business or personal accounts, for the deposit of all moneys or others received by the broker acting in said capacity, or as escrow agent, or as temporary custodian, in a real estate transaction.

(b) Every real estate broker shall file with the broker's application for licensure or license renewal an affidavit or certificate setting forth the name or names of the financial institution or institutions where said special account or accounts have been established and shall identify any and all account numbers. Any change in an existing account or the establishment of any new account shall be immediately reported to the Real Estate Commission in the form of an affidavit or certification.

(c) In construing N.J.S.A. 45:15-17(*o*), the following shall be considered to constitute commingling by a licensee:

1. Mingling the money of his principals with his own;

2. Failure to maintain and deposit promptly in a special account in an authorized financial institution, separate and apart from personal or other business accounts, all moneys received by a real estate broker acting in said capacity, or as escrow agent, or as the temporary custodian of the funds of others in a real estate transaction; or

3. Failure to promptly segregate any moneys received which are to be held for the benefit of others.

(d) Where the nature of a given real estate transaction is such that the commissions earned by a broker in connection with services rendered in said transaction are included among the funds deposited to the broker's trust account, the portion of such funds deposited to the broker's trust account which constitute the broker's commission shall be promptly paid from the trust account, with appropriate annotations to the broker's business records to indicate the amount and source of such commissions; provided, however, that such broker shall have been previously authorized to make such disbursement.

(e) Within the meaning of this section, the word "promptly" means not more than five business days next following the receipt of the money or property of another. However, where monies are received by a licensee as provided in (c)2 above as a good faith or earnest money deposit accompanying an offer to buy or lease property, if during the five business day period next following the date of the licensee's receipt of those funds the offer is withdrawn prior to acceptance by the offeree or is rejected with no counteroffer made by the offeree, the licensee need not deposit those funds into an escrow or trust account but may, upon the request of the offerer, return them in the same form in which they were received to the offerer. In all other cases, the licensee must deposit such monies within five business days of receipt. Examples of such cases include transactions where negotiations are ongoing, or if a contract or lease is being reviewed by an attorney, or if subsequently to the rejection of an offer the offerer has requested the licensee to retain the monies in the event that the offerer determines to submit another offer on the same or a different property.

(f) The maintenance of clearly nominal amounts of the licensee's funds in trust accounts solely to provide continuity in such account or to meet bank service charges shall not be construed to be commingling.

(g) Where any law or governmental regulation compels maintenance of a fixed amount of the funds of a licensee is a trust account for the purpose of providing a safety factor, the maintenance of such fixed amount shall not be construed to be commingling.

(h) Every person licensed as a broker of record or as a sole proprietor broker shall be a signatory on the escrow or trust account(s) of their brokerage firm. Only individuals who are actively licensed by the Commission as a real estate broker-salesperson or salesperson may be additional signatories on escrow or trust accounts.

As amended, R.1982 d.101, effective April 5, 1982.
See: 13 N.J.R. 302(b), 14 N.J.R. 345(b).
New (a) and (b) added, (c) marked "Reserved"; old (a)-(e) numbered as (d)-(h).
As amended, R.1983 d.471, effective November 7, 1983.
See: 15 N.J.R. 1343(a), 15 N.J.R. 1865(c).
Subsections (d) through (h) recodified as (c) through (g).
Amended by R.1993 d.8, effective January 4, 1993.
See: 24 N.J.R. 3483(a), 25 N.J.R. 118(a).
Exception allowed to deposit of funds entrusted to real estate broker as escrow agent.
Amended by R.1998 d.497, effective October 5, 1998.
See: 30 N.J.R. 2333(a), 30 N.J.R. 3646(a).
In (c), deleted "or other property" following "money" in 1, and substituted "moneys" for "properties" in 3; in (d), deleted ", the portion of such funds" preceding "which constitute" and substituted "indicate" for "define" following "records to"; and added (h).

Case Notes

Real estate guaranty fund held liable for misconduct of broker in sale of his own property, where purchaser relied on broker's licensed status in depositing money in broker's escrow account; purchaser required to exhaust writ of execution remedies against broker before executing judgment against fund. Brody v. Alfieri, 179 N.J.Super. 485, 432 A.2d 567 (Ch.Div.1981).

Relationship between listing broker and selling broker under multiple listing arrangement held not to constitute a joint venture so as to provide a basis for holding listing broker liable for selling broker's defalcation. Sullivan v. Jefferson, Jefferson & Vaida, 167 N.J.Super. 282, 400 A.2d 836 (App.Div.1979).

Failure to maintain separate escrow account and lending broker's license justifies license revocation. New Jersey Real Estate Commission v. Mertz and Dragotta, 97 N.J.A.R.2d (REC) 13.

Real estate salesperson loses license by demonstrating unworthiness and dishonesty through criminal conviction and using escrow monies for personal use. New Jersey Real Estate Commission v. Santoro and Miller, 97 N.J.A.R.2d (REC) 6.

Broker was subject to license revocation and monetary penalty for commingling business and personal funds and for failing to maintain separate account to hold real estate transaction funds. Real Estate Commission v. Potok and Island RMS, Inc., 96 N.J.A.R.2d (REC) 42.

Making false representation as being owner of real estate brokerage, collecting commission from person other than employing broker, and commingling of funds; revocation of salespersons' licenses and imposition of fines. New Jersey Real Estate Commission v. Ballman, 93 N.J.A.R.2d (REC) 17.

Commingling of funds, making misrepresentations to investigator, as well as other violations, warranted revocation of broker's license and imposition of fine. New Jersey Real Estate Commission v. Eberhardt. 92 N.J.A.R.2d (REC) 53.

Misrepresentations, misappropriation of monies, unlawful taking of monies, and other violations, warranted broker/salesperson license revocation, restitution, and fine. New Jersey Real Estate Commission v. Allen. 92 N.J.A.R.2d (REC) 45.

Improprieties regarding deposit monies and mortgage application; suspension of broker's license and imposition of fine. New Jersey Real Estate Commission v. Daniel Mullen and Holly Beach Realty, Inc. 92 N.J.A.R.2d (REC) 38.

Failure to account for deposit monies, commingling of funds, and engaging in business without license; salesperson's license revoked and fine imposed. New Jersey Real Estate Commission v. Groff. 92 N.J.A.R.2d (REC) 31.

Commingling trust monies and failing to maintain separate account for escrow funds, as well as other violations, warranted revocation of broker's license, suspension of salesperson's license, and assessment of fine. New Jersey Real Estate Commission v. Woods. 92 N.J.A.R.2d (REC) 25.

Failing to maintain as separate funds monies held as escrow agent, and other violations, warranted revocation of broker's license and assessment of fine. New Jersey Real Estate Commission v. Brown. 92 N.J.A.R.2d (REC) 21.

11:5–5.2 Funds of others; safeguards

(a) No licensee shall accept funds or deposits from a prospective purchaser without ascertaining that there have been established by escrow, or otherwise, adequate precautions to safeguard such funds or deposits where the licensee knows, or conditions are such as to palpably give him reason to know, any facts which would tend to reasonably create a doubt:

1. As to the ability of the seller to perform his contractual obligations; or

2. As to the ability of the seller to return such funds or deposits in the event of the failure of a contingency contained in a real estate contract.

(b) The provisions of subsection (a) shall not apply to a licensee who, before accepting such funds or deposits, has adequately informed the prospective purchaser of any risk entailed and has secured from him a separate signed writing in which the purchaser has acknowledged:

1. His awareness of any risk or contingency;

2. The disposition of his funds or deposits; and

3. The absence of any representations by the licensee as to the solvency of the seller and his ability to return such funds.

(c) Funds or deposits placed in escrow pursuant to this regulation may be held by any person or entity legally authorized to hold funds in that capacity, such as, but not limited to, the real estate broker himself, lawyers or banks.

Case Notes

Real estate guaranty fund held liable for misconduct of broker in sale of his own property, where purchaser relied on broker's licensed status in depositing money in broker's escrow account; purchaser required to exhaust writ of execution remedies against broker before executing judgment against fund. Brody v. Alfieri, 179 N.J.Super. 485, 432 A.2d 567 (Ch.Div.1981).

Relationship between listing broker and selling broker under multiple listing arrangement held not to constitute a joint venture so as to provide a basis for holding listing broker liable for selling broker's defalcation. Sullivan v. Jefferson, Jefferson & Vaida, 167 N.J.Super. 282, 400 A.2d 836 (App.Div.1979).

11:5–5.3 Advance fees; accounting

(a) Any broker who charges or collects an advance fee in excess of $25.00 for services to be rendered, such as, but not limited to advertising costs, under an advance fee agreement, shall within 90 days after such charge or collection furnish his principal with an accounting as to the use of such moneys.

(b) Such accounting shall set forth the actual amount of each individual expenditure, including date of insertion and name of newspaper or periodical, and similarly detail any other type of promotional expenditure if the funds are spent for other than newspaper or periodical advertising.

Case Notes

Failure to list default judgment in Office Closing Affidavit not violation of law but real estate company's failure to defend against action legally deficient. New Jersey Real Estate Commission v. Burke, 97 N.J.A.R.2d (REC) 4.

Fraud and failure to comply with record-keeping requirements warrant license revocation and imposition of fines. New Jersey Real Estate Commission v. Tumolo and Rossell, 97 N.J.A.R.2d (REC) 1.

11:5–5.4 Records to be maintained by broker

(a) Every broker shall keep records as prescribed herein of all funds of others received by him or her for not less than six years from the date of receipt of any such funds. All such funds shall be deposited by the broker in accordance with the requirements of N.J.A.C. 11:5–5.1.

1. Whenever a broker receives funds to be held in trust in cash, a written receipt signed by the licensee to whom the funds were paid and specifying the date, amount, purpose and from whom those funds were received shall be issued to the payor of the funds. A copy of that receipt shall be retained by the broker as prescribed in this section.

(b) The records required to be kept pursuant to (a) above shall include:

1. Written references on the checkbook stubs or checkbook ledger pages to all deposits into and withdrawals from the account(s) maintained by the broker in accordance with N.J.A.C. 11:5–5.1, which shall specifically identify the date, amount and payor of each item deposited, the property to which the monies pertain and the reason for their being held by the broker. Such records shall also specify the date, amount, payee and purpose of each disbursement. All trust or escrow account withdrawals shall be only by authorized intrastate or interstate bank transfer or by check payable to a named payee and not to cash;

2. An appropriate ledger book for all trustee accounts or escrow accounts showing, in one location in that ledger book for each separate trust transaction, the payor of all funds deposited in such accounts, the date of deposit, the names of all persons for whom the funds are or were held, the amount of such funds, the amounts and dates of all disbursements of such moneys, and the names of all persons to whom such funds were disbursed. The Commission will not deem a regular checkbook ledger as sufficient to constitute an appropriate ledger book. Such a ledger book may be maintained in a computer or similar device, so long as it is capable of reproducing the electronically stored data on paper so as to depict the complete history of all activity in each separate trust transaction, and the data can be maintained in an easily accessible form for the required six year period. A regular running balance of the individual transaction ledger sheets shall be maintained. The total of the running balance must agree with the control figure computed by taking the beginning balance, adding the total of moneys received in trust on that transaction, and deducting the total of all moneys disbursed;

3. Copies of all records, showing that at least quarterly a reconciliation has been made of the checkbook balance, the bank statement balance and the client trust ledger sheet balances;

4. All bank statements, cancelled checks and duplicate deposit slips;

5. Copies of all offers, contracts of sale and sale or rental listing agreements;

6. Copies of all leases and property management agreements;

7. Copies of all statements to owners, sellers, purchasers and tenants showing the disbursement of funds to them or on their behalf, which statements shall identify the property and unit, if applicable, for which the disbursement was made and the reason for the disbursement;

8. Copies of all bills paid for owners, sellers, purchasers or tenants by the broker from escrowed funds, which payments may only be made pursuant to written authorization;

9. Copies of all records showing payments to persons licensed with the paying broker and to cooperating brokers, which records shall contain all information required by N.J.A.C. 11:5–5.1(d); and

10. Copies of all receipts issued for all security deposits accepted from tenants, and of checks for and letters accompanying the release of such funds, and/or the duplicate deposit slips evidencing the deposit of such funds by the broker.

(c) With the exception of the materials described in (d) below, on transactions where a broker has not received the property or funds of others, the following records shall be maintained for six years from the earlier of the date of the listing or property management agreement or of the contract or lease:

1. Copies of all fully executed leases, contracts of sale, property management and listing agreements;

2. Copies of bills for brokerage services rendered in such transactions;

3. Copies of all records showing payments to persons licensed with the paying broker and to co-operating brokers; and

4. Copies of all bank statements, cancelled checks and duplicate deposit slips pertaining to the broker's general business account.

(d) Unaccepted offers and expired listing agreements during the term of which no contract of sale was executed or no tenancy was entered into shall be maintained for six months from the date of the offer or the expiration date of the listing agreement.

(e) The financial books and other records as described in (a), (b), (c) and (d) above shall be maintained in accordance with generally accepted accounting practice. They shall be located at the main New Jersey office of each broker or, in situations where separate general business and/or trust or escrow accounts are maintained at licensed branch offices, either at that branch office or at the main office of the broker. Paper copies of all items designated as records in (a) through (d) above shall be maintained by brokers as provided in this section. This requirement shall apply to all such records, including any items generated through E-mail or any other means which does not require the creation of a paper document. All such records shall be available for inspections, checks for compliance with this section and copying by a duly authorized representative of the New Jersey Real Estate Commission.

Amended by R.1989 d.425, effective August 21, 1989 (operative November 19, 1989).
See: 21 N.J.R. 1310(a), 21 N.J.R. 2520(a).
Clear specifications added regarding the type of business records brokers are required to maintain, new (a)1, new (b)1–10, and new (c)-(e).
Amended by R.1998 d.246, effective May 18, 1998.
See: 30 N.J.R. 278(a), 30 N.J.R. 1827(a).
In (e), inserted new third and fourth sentences.
Amended by R.1998 d.497, effective October 5, 1998.
See: 30 N.J.R. 2333(a), 30 N.J.R. 3646(a).
In (a), changed N.J.A.C. reference and deleted references to property; and in (b), changed N.J.A.C. references.

Case Notes

Fraud and failure to comply with record-keeping requirements warrant license revocation and imposition of fines. New Jersey Real Estate Commission v. Tumolo and Rossell, 97 N.J.A.R.2d (REC) 1.

Revocation of real estate broker's license was justified. New Jersey Real Estate Commission v. Roth, 94 N.J.A.R.2d (REC) 17.

Commingling of funds, accounting failures, as well as other violations, warranted permanent revocation of broker/salesperson license and imposition of fine. New Jersey Real Estate Commission v. Duffy, 93 N.J.A.R.2d (REC) 13.

Commingling of funds, making misrepresentations to investigator, as well as other violations, warranted revocation of broker's license and imposition of fine. New Jersey Real Estate Commission v. Eberhardt. 92 N.J.A.R.2d (REC) 53.

Commingling trust monies and failing to maintain separate account for escrow funds, as well as other violations, warranted revocation of broker's license, suspension of salesperson's license, and assessment of fine. New Jersey Real Estate Commission v. Woods. 92 N.J.A.R.2d (REC) 25.

Failing to maintain as separate funds monies held as escrow agent, and other violations, warranted revocation of broker's license and assessment of fine. New Jersey Real Estate Commission v. Brown. 92 N.J.A.R.2d (REC) 21.

11:5–5.5 Inspection of records

(a) Every licensee shall make available for inspection by the Commission or its designated representatives all records of transactions, books of account, instruments, documents and forms utilized or maintained by such licensee in the conduct of the licensed business, which may be pertinent to the conduct of the investigation of any specific complaint.

(b) To accomplish the objectives and carry out the duties prescribed by this Act, especially the provisions of N.J.S.A. 45:15–17, the Commission may issue subpoenas to any person, administer an oath or affirmation to any person, and conduct hearings in aid of any investigation or inquiry.

(c) All files on pending and closed sale, exchange or lease transactions, all files on listings for sales or rentals, and all property management files shall be maintained or stored at the offices of brokers licensed as employing brokers or corporate or partnership brokers. Upon terminating their employment with such a broker, and/or transferring to the employ of another such broker, no salesperson or broker-salesperson shall remove or cause to be removed any of the contents of such files from the offices of the broker. The term "files" as used herein shall be construed to mean all transaction records required to be kept by brokers pursuant to N.J.A.C. 11:5–5.4.

As amended, R.1983 d.471, effective November 7, 1983.
See: 15 N.J.R. 1343(a), 15 N.J.R. 1865(c).
Language citing statute deleted in subsection (a).
Amended by R.1988 d.410, effective September 6, 1988.
See: 20 N.J.R. 883(a), 20 N.J.R. 2295(a).
Added (c).
Petition for Rulemaking: Upon termination from employment with a broker, no salesperson or broker salesperson may remove files from the office pertaining to sale or rental listings.
See: 23 N.J.R. 1968(e).
Public Notice: Petition to amend subsection (c).
See: 23 N.J.R. 2191(b).

Amended by R.1992 d.107, effective March 2, 1992.
See: 23 N.J.R. 3428(a), 23 N.J.R. 3739(a), 24 N.J.R. 852(b).
Meaning of "files" specified at (c).
Amended by R.1998 d.497, effective October 5, 1998.
See: 30 N.J.R. 2333(a), 30 N.J.R. 3646(a).
In (b), deleted ", in addition to other powers conferred upon it by the Act" following "Commission"; and in (c), changed N.J.A.C. reference.

Case Notes

Real estate licensing law exemption for attorneys held only to authorize attorneys to sell or rent real estate incidental to their normal practice of law; denial of broker's license to attorney who did not meet statutory apprenticeship and testing requirements upheld. Spirito v. State, New Jersey Real Estate Commission, 180 N.J.Super. 180, 434 A.2d 623 (App.Div.1981).

SUBCHAPTER 6. CONDUCT OF BUSINESS

11:5–6.1 Advertising rules

(a) Unless otherwise set forth herein, subsections (b) through (n) below shall apply to all categories of advertising including all publications, radio or television broadcasts, all electronic media including E-mail and the Internet, business stationery, business cards, business and legal forms and documents, and signs and billboards.

1. Individuals operating as sole proprietors and licensed as employing brokers shall conspicuously display on the exterior of their maintained place of business their name and the words "Licensed Real Estate Broker".

2. Firms licensed as corporate or partnership brokers shall conspicuously display on the exterior of their maintained place of business their regular business name and the name of the individual licensed as their broker of record and the words "Licensed Real Estate Broker".

(b) All advertising of any licensed individual, partnership, firm, or corporate broker shall include their regular business name which for the purposes of these rules, shall mean the name in which that individual, partnership, firm or corporation is on record with the Commission as doing business as a real estate broker. All advertising by a salesperson or broker-salesperson shall include the name in which they are licensed and the regular business name of the individual, partnership, firm or corporate broker through whom they are licensed. If such advertisements contain a reference to the licensed status of the person placing the ad, their status as a salesperson or broker-salesperson must be indicated through inclusion of a descriptive term as provided in (e) below. A salesperson may not indicate in any advertisement or otherwise that he or she is licensed as a broker-salesperson.

1. With the exception of business cards, in all advertisements which contain the name of a salesperson or broker-salesperson the regular business name of the individual, partnership, firm or corporate broker through whom that person is licensed shall appear in larger print or be displayed in a more prominent manner than the name of the salesperson or broker-salesperson.

2. Where a webpage on the worldwide web established by a salesperson, a broker-salesperson, or a team of such licensees is not linked electronically to the webpage of the broker through whom the person or team is licensed, the webpage shall display the telephone number and may display the street address of the licensed brokerage office from which the individual or team operates as real estate licensees. That information shall appear in wording as large as the predominant size wording on the webpage.

3. Where a webpage of an individual or team is linked electronically to the webpage of the broker through whom such person or persons are licensed, the webpage of the nonbroker licensee(s) shall display information which clearly indicates how to link to the broker. That information shall appear in wording as large as the predominant size wording on the webpage.

(c) All advertising, with the exception of lawn signs placed on residential properties containing four or fewer units, shall clearly indicate after the licensee's regular business name that the advertising licensee is engaged in the real estate brokerage business. Except as prescribed by N.J.S.A. 45:15–17(j), examples of permissible language shall include, but are not limited to, "Realtor," "Realtist," "real estate broker," "broker," or "real estate agency". Examples of prohibited language when used alone shall include, but are not limited to, "realty," "real estate," "land sales," and "land investments." This provision shall not apply when the word "agency" appears in the advertisement as part of the licensee's regular business name or when the licensee has legal or equitable ownership of the property.

(d) With the exception of business cards, any advertising which contains a home telephone number, cell-phone number, beeper or pager number, home fax number, or E-mail address of an individual salesperson or broker-salesperson, or a team of such licensees, shall also include the telephone number and may include the street address of the licensed brokerage office from which the advertising licensee(s) operate. All such advertising shall also contain language identifying each number included in the advertising. For example, a home telephone number may be followed or preceded by the word "home" or the abbreviation "res."

1. No advertising shall represent that a location is a place at which the business of a real estate licensee is conducted unless that location is the licensed main office or a licensed branch office of the broker through whom the advertising licensee is licensed. Salespersons and broker-salespersons shall not include in their advertisements any reference to a "home office."

(e) The business card of any licensed salesperson shall indicate that this licensee is a salesperson by the use of the words salesperson or sales representative, or sales associate, or where permitted by law, realtor-associate or realtist associate. The business card of any licensed broker-salesperson shall indicate that this licensee is a broker-salesperson by the use of any of the aforementioned words or by the use of the words broker-salesperson. The business card of any licensed broker shall indicate that this licensee is a broker by use of the word broker or, where permitted by law, Realtor or Realtist.

(f) Any advertising which refers to amounts of down payment, monthly payment, or carrying charges, or which indicates that a mortgage is obtainable (where the mortgage referred to is not already a lien against the premises advertised), shall contain the words "to a qualified buyer".

(g) Any advertisement which sets forth amounts of down payment, monthly payment, carrying charges, taxes or mortgage money obtainable shall contain appropriate qualifying words such as "approximate" or "estimated," which qualifying words shall be clearly associated with the amounts set forth. If such amounts are mentioned the broker shall maintain written proof of the validity of these statements in the broker's files. Such written proof shall be maintained for a period of 12 months from the date upon which an advertisement containing such unqualified references shall have last appeared in any publication.

(h) With the exception of magazine or newspaper advertisements published under municipality headings, any advertisement for the sale, exchange or rental of real property, or any interest therein, shall designate the geographical area containing that property by specifying the municipality within which that property is located.

(i) No licensed individual, limited or general partnership, firm or corporation shall advertise or use any form of application or make any inquiry which expresses directly or indirectly any limitation, specification or discrimination as to race, religion, creed, color, sex, affectional or sexual orientation, marital status, national origin, ancestry or as to whether a person is handicapped as that term is defined in N.J.A.C. 11:5–6.4(h).

(j) Any use of an insignia, emblem, logo, trade name or other form of identification in any advertising or other public utterance, either by a single licensee or any group of licensees, which suggests or otherwise implies common ownership or common management among such licensees, shall be prohibited except in the case of branch offices controlled by a single broker or licensee and duly licensed as branch offices pursuant to the provision of N.J.S.A. 45:1–1 et seq. Nothing herein provided is intended to preclude or inhibit the use, advertising or display of any insignia, emblem, logo or trade name of any bona fide trade association by any licensee provided that such licensee is a member of such trade association.

1. Any franchised licensee using in any advertising the trade name of a franchisor shall include in such advertising in a manner reasonably calculated to attract the attention of the public the franchised licensee's regular business name.

2. Any licensee including the franchisor using the trade name of franchisor in any advertising shall also include in a manner reasonably calculated to attract the attention of the public the following legend or a substantially similar legend: "each office is independently owned and operated", except in the following categories of advertising:

i. "For sale" signs located on the premises of specific properties for sale;

ii. Small "spot" classified advertising by a licensee in newspapers, magazines or other publications advertising properties. A small spot classified advertisement is defined as an advertisement which is no more than one column wide and 20 lines long and which describes no more than two properties; a line is defined as a standard newspaper classified advertising line of the newspaper, magazine or other publication in which the advertisement is published;

iii. Business cards; and

iv. Advertising placed or distributed by offices which are wholly owned by the franchisor, which contains the office address and contains language which identifies the office as being wholly owned or the franchisor.

3. The intent of this subsection is to further promote the general purpose of the Real Estate License Act of ensuring that all individuals, firms or corporations are clearly identifiable to the public as the licensed brokers who are financially and otherwise responsible to the consuming public for their real estate brokerage activities. It is not the intent of this subsection to limit or otherwise inhibit the operation of branch offices as set forth in N.J.S.A. 45:15–12 and sections 18 and 19 of this subchapter, nor is it the intent of this subsection to prevent the franchising of any group of licensees provided such franchising or other association is not inconsistent with the purpose of the Real Estate License Act as expressed herein.

(k) Any advertising by any licensed individual, partnership, firm or corporation referring generally to membership in any real estate multiple listing service operation shall specify the complete name of the listing service in which membership is held, except in the following categories of advertising:

1. "For sale" signs and small "spot" classified advertising of any licensee as described in (j) above;

2. Business cards;

3. All business signs.

(*l*) Any home warranty offer contained in any advertisement shall comply with all Federal and State warranty legislation, including the New Home Warranty and Builder's Registration Act, c.467, L.1977, N.J.S.A. 46:3B–1, et seq., and the Magnuson-Moss Warranty Act, P.L. 93–637, 15 U.S.C. 2301 et seq. Such advertising shall specify clearly whether the warranty is by inspection or non-inspection of the premises, whether the warranty is mandatory, and whether the purchaser or the seller is responsible for payment for the warranty. No advertisement shall contain an offer for a warranty unless a warranty may be secured for the property being advertised.

(m) Except as herein provided, no free offering, including the offering of a free appraisal, shall be made in any advertisement or promotional material. "Appraisal" as used herein is given its technical meaning as a complete study and analysis by a certified or licensed appraiser to ascertain fair market value by using a process in which all factors that would fix price in the market place must be considered.

1. Nothing herein shall be construed as prohibiting the use of such words as "included" or "included in the purchase price" in reference to items included by the owner in the sale of any real property or interest therein.

2. Free offerings ancillary to the real estate transaction process and that are informational or educational in nature, including, but not limited to, offerings of market studies or seminars, and offerings in the nature of promotional items of token value, such as calendars or pens, are not prohibited. A market study is not an appraisal as herein defined.

i. The prohibition upon licensees from making free offerings of items of more than token value applies to all offerings which confer upon consumers a monetary benefit of a value of more than $5.00 retail. Examples of prohibited free offerings include free or subsidized homeowners warranties, property, radon and pest inspections, surveys, mortgage fees, offers to pay other costs typically incurred by parties to real estate transactions, and coupons offering discounts on commissions charged by brokerage firms.

ii. Any written comparative market study or analysis (CMA) provided by a licensee to a consumer shall include a statement indicating that the CMA is not an appraisal and should not be considered the equivalent of an appraisal. The said statement shall appear in print as large as the predominant size print in any writing reporting the results of the CMA.

(n) No licensee shall publish or cause to be published any advertisement or place any sign which makes reference to the availability of a specific property which is exclusively listed for sale by another broker unless the licensee obtains the prior written consent of the broker with whom the property is exclusively listed. Such consent shall not be given or withheld by the listing broker without the knowledge of the owner.

As amended, R.1976 d.276, effective August 31, 1976.
See: 8 N.J.R. 387(a), 8 N.J.R. 482(a).
As amended, R.1977 d.84, effective March 10, 1977.
See: 9 N.J.R. 91(d), 9 N.J.R. 178(a).
As amended, R.1978 d.42, effective January 31, 1978.
See: 9 N.J.R. 534(c), 10 N.J.R. 116(c).
As amended, R.1979 d.461, effective November 26, 1979.
See: 10 N.J.R. 499(a), 12 N.J.R. 44(b).
As amended, R.1980 d.52, effective January 31, 1980.
See: 12 N.J.R. 44(a), 12 N.J.R. 128(a).
As amended, R.1980 d.213, effective May 14, 1980.
See: 12 N.J.R. 44(a), 12 N.J.R. 343(a).
As amended, R.1980 d.279, effective June 26, 1980.
See: 12 N.J.R. 340(b), 12 N.J.R. 484(d).
As amended, R.1983 d.471, effective November 7, 1983.
See: 15 N.J.R. 1343(a), 15 N.J.R. 1865(c).
Time limits on compliance deleted.
As amended, R.1986 d.91, effective April 7, 1986.
See: 17 N.J.R. 666(a), 18 N.J.R. 699(a).
(m)3.–5. deleted.
Amended by R.1987 d.69, effective January 20, 1987.
See: 18 N.J.R. 1679(a), 19 N.J.R. 232(b).
Amended (d) and (e).
Petition: Notice of Action upon petition for Declaratory Ruling and/or Rulemaking limiting the scope of Advertising Rules.
See: 19 N.J.R. 570(d), 19 N.J.R. 664(a).
Amended by R.1988 d.237, effective June 6, 1988.
See: 20 N.J.R. 497(a), 20 N.J.R. 1205(a).
Substantially amended subsection (j).
Amended by R.1989 d.447, effective August 21, 1989.
See: 21 N.J.R. 1312(a), 21 N.J.R. 2552(b).
Exempted residential lawn sign advertisement for properties of four or fewer units, corrected spelling of realtist and added new (n) regarding consent of exclusive listing broker.
Amended by R.1993 d.9, effective January 4, 1993 (operative May 4, 1993).
See: 24 N.J.R. 3484(a), 25 N.J.R. 178(b).
Requirements for signs, cards, etc. amended to show name of broker, identified as such.
Amended by R.1994 d.266, effective June 20, 1994 (operative July 1, 1994).
See: 26 N.J.R. 729(a), 26 N.J.R. 1194(a), 26 N.J.R. 1222(a), 26 N.J.R. 2581(b).
Amended by R.1997 d.26, effective January 21, 1997.
See: 28 N.J.R. 3064(a), 29 N.J.R. 365(a).
In (*l*), inserted reference to the seller regarding warranty payment; in (m)2, inserted reference to informational or educational; and added (m)2i.
Amended by R.1998 d.246, effective May 18, 1998.
See: 30 N.J.R. 278(a), 30 N.J.R. 1827(a).
In (a), inserted "all electronic media including E-mail and the Internet," in the introductory paragraph; in (b), added new 1 through 3; rewrote (d); and in (m), substituted "certified or licensed appraiser" for "specialist or expert" in the introductory paragraph, added ", and coupons offering discounts on commissions charged by brokerage firms" at the end of 1i, and inserted a new 1ii.
Amended by R.1998 d.497, effective October 5, 1998.
See: 30 N.J.R. 2333(a), 30 N.J.R. 3646(a).
In (g), deleted "without qualification," following "mentioned" in the second sentence; and in (i), changed N.J.A.C. reference.

Case Notes

New Jersey Land Sales Full Disclosure Act discriminated in its plain effect against interstate commerce and violated dormant commerce clause. Old Coach Development Corp., Inc. v. Tanzman, C.A.3 (N.J.)1989, 881 F.2d 1227.

Barring real estate broker's merchandise coupon program pursuant to statute was not improper regulation of competition. Coldwell Banker Residential Real Estate Services, Inc. v. New Jersey Real Estate Com'n, 242 N.J.Super. 354, 576 A.2d 938 (A.D.1990).

Statute prohibiting real estate brokers from using promotions involving "prizes" did not deprive broker that wished to use merchandise coupon program of property without due process. Coldwell Banker Residential Real Estate Services, Inc. v. New Jersey Real Estate Com'n, 242 N.J.Super. 354, 576 A.2d 938 (A.D.1990).

Commingling trust monies and failing to maintain separate account for escrow funds, as well as other violations, warranted revocation of broker's license, suspension of salesperson's license, and assessment of fine. New Jersey Real Estate Commission v. Woods. 92 N.J.A.R.2d (REC) 25.

11:5–6.2 Contracts of sale, leases and listing agreements

(a) The following paragraphs specify licensees' obligations to obtain written confirmation of the intentions of, and to deliver copies of documents to, parties to a real estate transaction.

1. Where a licensee memorializes the terms of an offer or counter-offer on a writing which will itself become an "instrument" as defined in (a)3 below, the licensee shall deliver to the maker of such an offer or counter-offer a clear copy of the executed offer or counter-offer immediately upon its being signed, and initialed if necessary as provided in this section, by the maker of the offer or counter-offer. Any addition, deletion, or other change in any such offer or counter-offer shall be initialed by the party proposing such a revision and, if accepted, by the other party to the transaction.

2. Where a licensee records the terms of an offer or counter-offer on a writing which is not intended to be binding upon either party, and which so states on its face, in the event that the licensee secures the signature and/or initials of any party on such a writing, the licensee shall provide to the signing and/or initialing party a clear copy of the writing as signed and/or initialed by them.

3. As used in this subsection, the term "instrument" means any complete and fully executed written contract of sale, lease, option agreement, or other writing affecting an interest in real estate, or any complete and fully executed addendum or amendment to any such contract, lease, option agreement or writing. The term instrument as used in this subsection does not include listing agreements and buyer brokerage agreements.

4. Licensees shall immediately deliver to all parties to any fully executed instrument a clear copy with original signatures of any such fully executed instrument. Licensees shall provide their clients with a fully executed copy of any sale or exclusive sale or rental listing contract at the time of execution thereof.

5. Licensee-prepared revisions or additions reflected on the instrument itself shall be initialed by all parties to the transaction. Licensee-prepared revisions or additions to an instrument not memorialized by changes on the instrument itself shall be reflected on amendments or addenda to the instrument signed by all parties to the transaction.

i. Licensees shall immediately deliver to the party proposing a revision or addition to an instrument a clear copy of any proposed revised instrument initialed by that party and a clear copy of any proposed amendment or addendum signed by that party.

ii. All revisions, amendments and addenda to any fully executed instrument which are prepared by licensees must comply with New Jersey law as it pertains to the attorney review of contract and lease documents prepared by real estate licensees.

6. This rule is to ensure prompt communication of the executed evidence of a transaction to all interested parties.

(b) No listing agreement or contract for the sale of real property, or any interest therein, shall contain a prescribed or predetermined fee, commission rate, or commission amount; nor shall any such writing contain a commission clause or provision which suggests (such as with a small blank space and percent sign) to a seller that the commission is a prescribed rate or amount.

(c) The commission clause or provision in all listing agreements for the sale of one to four family dwelling units or interest therein, or in all contracts for such sale, if there is no listing agreement, shall contain in print larger than the predominant size print in the writing, the language: "As seller you have the right to individually reach an agreement on any fee, commission, or other valuable consideration with any broker. No fee, commission or other consideration has been fixed by any governmental authority or by any trade association or multiple listing service." Nothing herein is intended to prohibit an individual broker from independently establishing a policy regarding the amount of fee, commission or other value consideration to be charged in transaction by the broker.

(d) Upon request, the listing broker shall advise the seller of the rate or amount of any commission split or distribution.

(e) All listing agreements of any licensed individual, partnership, firm or corporation which provide for the listing of property with any real estate multiple listing service operation shall specify the complete name of that listing service.

(f) No licensed individual, partnership, firm or corporation shall enter into a "net listing" contract for the sale of real property, or any interest therein. A "net listing" is defined as an agency agreement in which a prospective seller lists real estate for sale with an authorization to a broker to sell at a specified net dollar return to the seller, and which provides that the broker may retain as commission the difference between the specified dollar return to the seller and the actual sales price.

(g) Licensees shall comply with the following provisions:

1. All contracts prepared by licensees for the sale of residential real estate containing one to four dwelling units and for the sale of vacant one-family lots in transactions in which the licensee has a commission or fee interest shall contain, at the top of the first page and in print larger than the predominant size print in the writing, the following language:

THIS IS A LEGALLY BINDING CONTRACT THAT WILL BECOME FINAL WITHIN THREE BUSINESS DAYS. DURING THIS PERIOD YOU MAY CHOOSE TO CONSULT AN ATTORNEY WHO CAN REVIEW AND CANCEL THE CONTRACT. SEE SECTION ON ATTORNEY REVIEW FOR DETAILS.

2. The contract shall also contain the following language within the text of every such contract.

ATTORNEY REVIEW:

1. Study by Attorney

The Buyer or the Seller may choose to have an attorney study this contract. If an attorney is consulted, the attorney must complete his or her review of the contract within a three-day period. This contract will be legally binding at the end of this three-day period unless an attorney for the Buyer or Seller reviews and disapproves of the contract.

2. Counting the Time

You count the three days from the date of delivery of the signed contract to the Buyer and the Seller. You do not count Saturdays, Sundays or legal holidays. The Buyer and the Seller may agree in writing to extend the three-day period for attorney review.

3. Notice of Disapproval

If an attorney for the Buyer or the Seller reviews and disapproves of this contract, the attorney must notify the Broker(s) and the other party named in this contract within the three-day period. Otherwise this contract will be legally binding as written. The attorney must send the notice of disapproval to the Broker(s) by certified mail, by telegram, or by delivering it personally. The telegram or certified letter will be effective upon sending. The personal delivery will be effective upon delivery to the Broker's office. The attorney may but need not also inform the Broker(s) of any suggested revisions in the contract that would make it satisfactory.

3. The contract shall also contain the names and full addresses of all persons to whom a Notice of Disapproval must be sent in order to be effective as provided in item three of the Attorney Review Provision.

4. All leases prepared by licensees for a term of one year or more for residential dwelling units in transactions in which they have a commission or fee interest shall, at the top of the first page and in print larger than the predominant size print of the writing, contain the following language:

THIS IS A LEGALLY BINDING LEASE THAT WILL BECOME FINAL WITHIN THREE BUSINESS DAYS. DURING THIS PERIOD YOU MAY CHOOSE TO CONSULT AN ATTORNEY WHO CAN REVIEW AND CANCEL THE LEASE. SEE SECTION ON ATTORNEY REVIEW FOR DETAILS.

5. The lease shall also contain the following language within the text of every such lease.

ATTORNEY REVIEW:

1. Study by Attorney

The Tenant or the Landlord may choose to have an attorney study this lease. If an attorney is consulted, the attorney must complete his or her review of the lease within a three-day period. This lease will be legally binding at the end of this three-day period unless an attorney for the Tenant or the Landlord reviews and disapproves of the lease.

2. Counting the Time

You count the three days from the date of delivery of the signed lease to the Tenant and the Landlord. You do not count Saturdays, Sundays or legal holidays. The Tenant and the Landlord may agree in writing to extend the three-day period for attorney review.

3. Notice of Disapproval

If an attorney for the Tenant or the Landlord reviews and disapproves of this lease, the attorney must notify the Broker(s) and the other party named in the lease within the three-day period. Otherwise this lease will be legally binding as written. The attorney must send the notice of disapproval to the Broker(s) by certified mail, by telegram, or by delivering it personally. The telegram or certified letter will be effective upon sending. The personal delivery will be effective upon delivery to the Broker's office. The attorney may but need not also inform the Broker(s) of any suggested revisions in the lease that would make it satisfactory.

6. The lease shall also contain the names and full addresses of all persons to whom a Notice of Disapproval must be sent in order to be effective, as provided in item three of the Attorney Review Provision.

7. The failure of any licensee to include such language in any such contract of sale or lease agreement prepared by the licensee shall be construed by the Commission as engaging in the unauthorized practice of law and shall be considered by the Commission as conduct which demonstrates the licensee's unworthiness and incompetency, thereby subjecting the licensee to sanctions pursuant to N.J.S.A. 45:15–17(e).

Amended by R.1977 d.84, effective March 10, 1977.
See: 9 N.J.R. 91(d), 9 N.J.R. 178(a).
Amended by R.1977 d.391, effective October 19, 1977.
See: 9 N.J.R. 344(a), 9 N.J.R. 536(a).
Amended by R.1979 d.461, effective November 26, 1979.

See: 10 N.J.R. 499(a), 12 N.J.R. 44(b).
Amended by R.1980 d.51, effective January 31, 1980.
See: 12 N.J.R. 127(e).
Amended by R.1980 d.214, effective May 14, 1980.
See: 12 N.J.R. 342(d).
Amended by R.1980 d.274, effective June 19, 1980.
See: 12 N.J.R. 423(d).
Amended by R.1980 d.408, effective September 23, 1980.
See: 12 N.J.R. 340(b), 12 N.J.R. 665(c).
(c) substantially amended.
Amended by R.1980 d.409, effective September 24, 1980.
See: 12 N.J.R. 665(d).
(c) compliance date amended from November 1, 1981 to January 2, 1981.
Amended by R.1983 d.471, effective November 7, 1983.
See: 15 N.J.R. 1343(a), 15 N.J.R. 1865(c).
Time limits on compliance deleted.
Amended by R.1987 d.159, effective April 6, 1987.
See: 18 N.J.R. 1677(a), 18 N.J.R. 2112(a), 19 N.J.R. 551(a).
Added (g).
Amended by R.1987 d.359, effective September 8, 1987.
See: 19 N.J.R. 503(b), 19 N.J.R. 1646(a).
Added (h) "Agreement to Honor".
Invalidity Annotation
N.J.A.C. 11:5–1.16(h) held invalid as an intrusion upon the State Supreme Court's constitutional authority to regulate the practice of law. Carmagnola v. Hann, 233 N.J.Super. 547 (App. Div. June 12, 1989), 559 A.2d 478.
Amended by R.1989 d.539, effective October 16, 1989.
See: 21 N.J.R. 2438(b), 21 N.J.R. 3299(a).
Subsection (h) deleted due to Appellate Court decision ___ N.J.Super. ___, Dkt. No. A–2211–88T2F (App.Div.1989).
Amended by R.1993 d.10, effective January 4, 1993.
See: 24 N.J.R. 3485(a), 25 N.J.R. 179(a).
Text at (a) substantially amended to specify licensees' obligations to parties in a real estate transaction involving offers or counter-offers.
Petition for Rulemaking.
See: 25 N.J.R. 4523(c), 26 N.J.R. 505(b).

Case Notes

Statute giving terminated agents full commission rights if they continued to service policies would prevail over strict terms of contract settlement between insurance company and terminated agents. Matter of Terminated Aetna Agents, 248 N.J.Super. 255, 590 A.2d 1189 (A.D.1990), certification denied 126 N.J. 319, 598 A.2d 880.

Regulation requiring that all real estate contracts subject to attorney review contain an "agreement to honor," was void. Carmagnola v. Hann, 233 N.J.Super. 547, 559 A.2d 478 (A.D.1989).

11:5–6.3 Broker insurance placement provision

Where a contract provided by a real estate broker contains a provision to the effect that such broker, in his capacity as a licensed insurance agent or broker, is authorized to place or procure insurance on the property being sold, the licensee benefitting by such a provision shall obtain separate written reaffirmation of such provision by the prospective insured not less than five days prior to the closing of title.

11:5–6.4 Obligations of licensees to public and to each other

(a) All licensees are subject to and shall strictly comply with the laws of agency and the principles governing fiduciary relationships. In accepting employment as an agent, the licensee pledges himself to protect and promote, as he would his own, the interests of the client or principal he has undertaken to represent; this obligation of absolute fidelity to the client's or principal's interest is primary but does not relieve the licensee from the obligation of dealing fairly with all parties to the transaction.

(b) Every licensee shall make reasonable effort to ascertain all material information concerning the physical condition of every property for which he or she accepts an agency or which he or she is retained to market as a transaction broker, and concerning the financial qualifications of every person for whom he or she submits an offer to his or her client or principal. Information about social conditions and psychological impairments as defined in (d) below is not considered to be information which concerns the physical condition of a property.

1. A reasonable effort to ascertain material information shall include at least:

i. Inquiries to the seller or seller's agent about any physical conditions that may affect the property; and

ii. A visual inspection of the property to determine if there are any readily observable physical conditions affecting the property.

2. As used in this section, information is "material" if a reasonable person would attach importance to its existence or non-existence in deciding whether or how to proceed in the transaction, or if the licensee knows or has reason to know that the recipient of the information regards, or is likely to regard it as important in deciding whether or how to proceed, although a reasonable person would not so regard it.

(c) Licensees shall disclose all information material to the physical condition of any property which they know or which a reasonable effort to ascertain such information would have revealed to their client or principal and when appropriate to any other party to a transaction. Licensees shall also disclose any actual or potential conflicts of interest which the licensee may reasonably anticipate.

1. With respect to off-site conditions which may materially affect the value of the residential real estate, in all sales contracts involving newly constructed residential real estate they prepare, licensees shall include a statement as set forth below. By including this statement in a contract of sale prepared by the licensee, the licensee shall be deemed to have fulfilled his or her disclosure obligations under (c) above with respect to such off-site conditions. The statement shall be in print as large as the predominant size print in the document and shall read as follows:

"NOTIFICATION REGARDING
OFF-SITE CONDITIONS

Pursuant to the New Residential Construction Off-Site Conditions Disclosure Act, P.L. 1995, c.253 (C.46:3C–1 et seq.), sellers of newly constructed residential real estate are required to notify purchasers of the availability of lists disclosing the existence and location of off-site conditions which may affect the value of the residential real estate being sold. The lists are to be made available by the municipal clerk of the municipality within which the residential real estate is located and in other municipalities which are within one-half mile of the residential real estate. The address(es) and telephone number(s) of the municipalities relevant to this project and the appropriate municipal offices where the lists are made available are listed below. Purchasers are encouraged to exercise all due diligence in order to obtain any additional or more recent information that they believe may be relevant to their decision to purchase the residential real estate. Purchasers are also encouraged to undertake an independent examination of the general area within which the residential real estate is located in order to become familiar with any and all conditions which may affect the value of the residential real estate.

The purchaser has five (5) business days from the date the contract is executed by the purchaser and the seller to send notice of cancellation of the contract to the seller. The notice of cancellation shall be sent by certified mail. The cancellation will be effective upon the notice of cancellation being mailed. If the purchaser does not send a notice of cancellation to the seller in the time or manner described above, the purchaser will lose the right to cancel the contract as provided in this notice.

Municipality ______________________

Address ______________________

Telephone Number ______________________"

The statement shall either be included in the text of the contract itself or attached to the contract as an Addendum.

2. In all residential real estate sale contracts they prepare except contracts for newly constructed residential real estate, licensees shall include a statement as set forth below. The statement shall be in print as large as the predominant size print in the document and shall read as follows:

"NOTICE ON OFF–SITE CONDITIONS

Pursuant to the New Residential Construction Off-site Conditions Disclosure Act, P.L. 1995, c.253 the clerks of municipalities in New Jersey maintain lists of off-site conditions which may affect the value of residential properties in the vicinity of the off-site condition. Purchasers may examine the lists and are encouraged to independently investigate the area surrounding this property in order to become familiar with any off-site conditions which may affect the value of the property. In cases where a property is located near the border of a municipality, purchasers may wish to also examine the list maintained by the neighboring municipality."

The statement shall either be included in the text of the contract itself or attached to the contract as an Addendum.

i. Licensees who possess actual knowledge of an off-site condition which may materially affect the value of residential real estate other than newly constructed properties shall disclose that information to prospective purchasers of such residential real estate affected by the condition. That disclosure shall be made prior to the signing of the contract by a prospective purchaser.

ii. In cases where the licensee did not possess actual knowledge of the presence of an off-site condition which might materially affect the value of the residential real estate, by virtue of including the foregoing statement in a contract of sale prepared by him or her, the licensee shall be deemed to have fulfilled his or her disclosure obligations under (c) above with respect to such off-site conditions.

3. As used in this subsection, the following words and terms shall have the following meanings:

i. "Newly constructed" means any dwelling unit not previously occupied, excluding dwelling units constructed solely for lease and units governed by the National Manufactured Housing Construction and Safety Standards Act of 1974, 42 U.S.C. §§ 5402 et seq.

ii. "Off-site conditions" refers to the following conditions as set forth in the New Residential Construction Off–Site Conditions Disclosure Act, N.J.S.A. 46:3C–3 (P.L. 1995 c.253), or as amended:

(1) The latest Department of Environmental Protection listing of sites included on the National Priorities List pursuant to the "Comprehensive Environmental Response, Compensation and Liability Act of 1980," 42 U.S.C. §§ 9601 et seq.;

(2) The latest sites known to and confirmed by the Department of Environmental Protection and included on the New Jersey master list of known hazardous discharge sites, prepared pursuant to P.L. 1982, c.202 (N.J.S.A. 58.10–23.15 et seq.);

(3) Overhead electric utility transmission lines conducting 240,000 volts or more;

(4) Electrical transformer substations;

(5) Underground gas transmission lines as defined in 49 C.F.R. 192.3;

(6) Sewer pump stations of a capacity equal to, or in excess of 0.5 million gallons per day and sewer trunk lines in excess of 15 inches in diameter;

(7) Sanitary landfill facilities as defined pursuant to section 3 of P.L. 1970, c.39 (N.J.S.A. 13:1E–3);

(8) Public wastewater treatment facilities; and

(9) Airport safety zones as defined pursuant to section 3 of P.L. 1983, c.260 (N.J.S.A. 6:1–82).

iii. "Residential real estate" means a property or structure or both which will serve as a residence for the purchaser.

(d) Information about social conditions or psychological impairments of a property is not considered information which affects the physical condition of a property. Subject to (d)3 below, licensees are not required by (c) above to disclose such information.

1. As used in this section, the term "social conditions" includes, but is not limited to, neighborhood conditions such as barking dogs, boisterous neighbors, and other conditions which do not impact upon or adversely affect the physical condition of the property.

2. As used in this section, the term "psychological impairments" includes, but is not limited to, a murder or suicide which occurred on a property, or a property purportedly being haunted.

3. Except as provided below, upon receipt of an inquiry from a prospective purchaser or tenant about whether a particular property may be affected by a social condition or psychological impairment, licensees shall provide whatever information they know about the social conditions or psychological impairments that might affect the property.

i. In accordance with N.J.S.A. 10:5–1 et seq. (the "Law Against Discrimination"), licensees shall make no inquiry and provide no information on the racial composition of, or the presence of a group home in, a neighborhood. In response to requests for such information, licensees shall inform the persons making the inquiry that they may conduct their own investigation. This paragraph does not apply to the owner of a multiple dwelling or his agent to the extent that such inquiries are necessary for compliance with N.J.A.C. 13:10.

ii. In accordance with N.J.S.A. 2C:7–6 through 11 ("Megan's Law") and the guidelines promulgated thereunder, licensees shall make no inquiry about and provide no information on notifications from a county prosecutor issued pursuant to that law. In response to requests for such information, licensees shall inform the person making the inquiry that information about registered sex offenders is maintained by the county prosecutor.

(e) In all contracts and leases on residential real estate they prepare, licensees shall include the following statement in print as large as the predominant size print in the document:

MEGAN'S LAW STATEMENT—Under New Jersey law, the county prosecutor determines whether and how to provide notice of the presence of convicted sex offenders in an area.

In their professional capacity, real estate licensees are not entitled to notification by the county prosecutor under Megan's Law and are unable to obtain such information for you. Upon closing the county prosecutor may be contacted for such further information as may be disclosable to you.

(f) Every licensee shall fully cooperate with all other New Jersey licensees utilizing cooperation arrangements which shall protect and promote the interests of the licensee's client or principal. Commission splits shall be governed by the provisions of N.J.A.C. 11:5–7.5 and 7.6. Full cooperation requires a listing broker to transmit to their principal(s) all written offers submitted through the offices of other licensees on properties listed with the listing broker. Full cooperation also requires listing brokers not to place restrictions upon the showing of properties listed with them to prospective purchasers who are working through cooperating brokers. This obligation shall be a continuing one unless the client or principal, with full knowledge of all relevant facts, expressly relieves his agent from this responsibility. Should the client or principal direct the licensee not to cooperate with all other licensees, evidence of this intent shall be in writing in the form of a WAIVER OF BROKER COOPERATION as set forth below and signed by the client or principal. Copies of this WAIVER OF BROKER COOPERATION and the listing agreement to which it relates shall be provided to the client or principal and to their authorized representative by the Broker. This waiver shall become a part of the listing agreement at the time it is signed, and shall be made available for inspection by other Brokers upon request. However, no direction or inducement from the client or principal shall relieve the licensee of his responsibility of dealing fairly and exercising integrity with all other licensees.

WAIVER OF BROKER COOPERATION

I UNDERSTAND THAT COOPERATION AMONGST BROKERS PRODUCES WIDER EXPOSURE OF MY PROPERTY AND MAY RESULT IN IT BEING SOLD OR LEASED SOONER AND AT A HIGHER PRICE THAN WOULD BE THE CASE WERE MY BROKER NOT TO COOPERATE WITH OTHER BROKERS. I FURTHER UNDERSTAND THAT WHEN MY BROKER COOPERATES WITH OTHER BROKERS, I CAN STILL HAVE THE ARRANGEMENTS FOR THE SHOWING OF THE PROPERTY AND ALL NEGOTIATIONS WITH ME OR MY ATTORNEY MADE ONLY THROUGH MY LISTING BROKER'S OFFICE, SHOULD I SO DESIRE.

However, despite my awareness of these factors, I direct that this property is to be marketed only through the efforts of the Listing Broker. This listing is not to be published in any multiple listing service. I will only consider offers on this property which are obtained by, and I will only allow showings of this property to be conducted by the Listing Broker or his or her duly authorized representatives. THE LISTING BROKER IS HEREBY DIRECTED NOT TO COOPERATE WITH ANY OTHER BROKER.

By signing below, the parties hereto confirm that no pressure or undue influence has been exerted upon the owners as to how this property is to be marketed by the Listing Broker.
The owner(s) further confirm receipt of a fully executed copy of the listing agreement on this property, and of this Waiver of Broker Cooperation form.
Dated: ________ Owner ________________
Owner ________________
Listing Broker ________________
By: Authorized Licensee or Broker ________________

(g) If any offer on any real property or interest therein is made orally, the licensee shall advise the offeror that he is not obligated to present to the owner or his authorized representative any offer unless the offer is in writing, and the licensee shall secure forthwith the offer in writing. Unless a writing containing or confirming the terms of the listing agreement otherwise provides, the licensee shall transmit forthwith every written offer on any real property or interest therein presented to or obtained by the licensee during the term of the listing to the owner or his authorized representative. For the purposes of this section, the term of a listing shall be deemed to expire either on the termination date established in the listing agreement, or upon the closing of a pending sale or lease. If any acceptance of an offer is given orally, the licensee shall secure forthwith the acceptance in writing.

(h) Back-up offers shall be handled as follows:

1. As used in this subsection, the term "back-up offer" shall mean a written and signed offer to purchase or lease an interest in real estate which is received by a licensee at a time when a previously executed contract or lease pertaining to the same interest in real estate is pending and in effect, having survived attorney review if it was subject to such review. Offers obtained while a previously executed contract or lease is still pending attorney review are not considered back-up offers and must be presented as provided in (g) above.

2. Whenever a licensee transmits a back-up offer to an owner, the licensee shall advise the owner in writing to consult an attorney before taking any action on the back-up offer, and shall retain a copy of such written notice as a business record in accordance with N.J.A.C. 11:5–5.4.

3. Whenever a licensee receives a back-up offer, the licensee shall notify the offeror in writing that the property to which the offer pertains is the subject of a pending contract of sale or lease and, in the event that the licensee receiving the back-up offer is not licensed with the listing broker, a copy of that notice shall be delivered to the listing broker at the time the offer is presented. The said notice shall not disclose the price and terms of the pending contract or lease. A copy of such written notice shall be retained by the licensee as a business record in accordance with N.J.A.C. 11:5–5.4.

(i) It shall be the duty of a licensee to recommend that legal counsel be obtained whenever the interests of any party to a transaction seem to require it.

(j) At the time of the taking of any listing of residential property, a licensee shall furnish to the owner a copy of a summary of the New Jersey Law Against Discrimination N.J.S.A. 10:5–1 et seq. which summary shall have been prepared and furnished by the Attorney General of the State of New Jersey, shall state the provisions of the Law Against Discrimination, and shall state which properties are covered by this law and which properties are exempt from this law. Should the owner profess an unwillingness to abide by or an intention to violate this law then the licensee shall not accept these listings.

(k) No licensee shall deny real estate brokerage services to any person for reasons of race, religion, color, sex, affectional or sexual orientation, marital status, national origin or because a person is handicapped; and no licensee shall participate or otherwise be a party to any plan, scheme or agreement to discriminate against any person on the basis of race, religion, color, sex, affectional or sexual orientation, marital status, national origin or because a person is handicapped. For the purposes of this subsection, the term "handicapped" means suffering from physical disability, infirmity, malformation or disfigurement which is caused by bodily injury, birth defect or illness including epilepsy, and which shall include, but not be limited to, any degree of paralysis, amputation, lack of physical coordination, blindness or visual impediment, deafness or hearing impediment, muteness or speech impediment or physical reliance on a service or guide dog, wheelchair, or other remedial appliance or device, or from any mental, physiological or developmental disability resulting from anatomical, psychological, physiological or neurological conditions which prevents the normal exercise of any bodily or mental functions or is demonstrable, medically or psychologically, by accepted clinical or laboratory diagnostic techniques. Handicapped shall also mean suffering from AIDS or HIV infection, as defined in N.J.S.A. 10:5–5(ff) and (gg).

(*l*) Licensees may engage in brokerage activity in transactions involving the resale of mobile and manufactured homes as provided in N.J.S.A. 39:10–19. Licensees who do so shall be familiar with all laws applicable to such transactions. These laws include N.J.S.A. 39:1–1 et seq. as it applies to the resale of and the transfer of the titles to such motor vehicle units, N.J.S.A. 46:8C–1 et seq., as it applies to the resale of such units when situated in Mobile Home Parks, N.J.S.A. 17:16C–1 et seq., as it applies to the financing of purchases of personal property and New Jersey's Truth in Renting Act, N.J.S.A. 46:8–43 et seq. Licensees who, when involved in transactions of this type, evidence a lack of familiarity with these laws either through acts of omission or commission shall be subject to sanctions by the Commission for having engaged in conduct demonstrating incompetency, in violation of N.J.S.A. 45:15–17(e).

As amended, R.1975 d.260, effective August 28, 1975.
See: 7 N.J.R. 333(d), 7 N.J.R. 469(c).
As amended, R.1976 d.10, effective January 13, 1976.
See: 7 N.J.R. 567(e), 8 N.J.R. 70(e).
As amended, R.1979 d.461, effective November 26, 1979.
See: 10 N.J.R. 499(a), 12 N.J.R. 44(b).
As amended, R.1983 d.471, effective November 7, 1983.
See: 15 N.J.R. 1343(a), 15 N.J.R. 1865(c).
Statutory cite added.
Amended by R.1988 d.69, effective February 16, 1988 (operative March 1, 1988).
See: 19 N.J.R. 1621(a), 20 N.J.R. 402(a).
Amended to clearly define full cooperation.
Amended by R.1988 d.412, effective September 6, 1988.
See: 20 N.J.R. 725(a), 20 N.J.R. 2295(b).
Added text to (g) that is favorable to handicapped individuals.
Amended by R.1993 d.365, effective July 19, 1993.
See: 24 N.J.R. 3486(a), 25 N.J.R. 3219(a).
Amended by R.1994 d.266, effective June 20, 1994 (operative July 1, 1994).
See: 26 N.J.R. 729(a), 26 N.J.R. 1194(a), 26 N.J.R. 1222(a), 26 N.J.R. 2581(b).
Amended by R.1997 d.27, effective January 21, 1997.
See: 28 N.J.R. 3065(a), 29 N.J.R. 366(a).
Added (i).
Amended by R.1997 d.275, effective July 7, 1997.
See: 29 N.J.R. 300(a), 29 N.J.R. 2849(a).
Substantially amended (b); recodified former second sentence of (b) as (c) and amended; added (c)1 through 3, (d) and (e); and recodified former (c) through (i) as (f) through (*l*).
Administrative correction.
See: 29 N.J.R. 3260(a).
In (c)1, in the second paragraph, inserted "shall be sent by certified mail. The cancellation".
Amended by R.1998 d.497, effective October 5, 1998.
See: 30 N.J.R. 2333(a), 30 N.J.R. 3646(a).
In (f) and (h), changed N.J.A.C. references.

Case Notes

Builder-developer of residential real estate or broker representing it may be liable for nondisclosure of off-site physical conditions known to it and unknown and not readily observable by purchaser if the existence of those conditions is of sufficient materiality to affect the habitability, use, or enjoyment of the property. Strawn v. Canuso, 140 N.J. 43, 657 A.2d 420 (1995).

Transaction where vendor and purchaser are not represented by counsel; broker required to identify when independent counsel needed; duty to inform either vendor or purchaser of that fact; same duty applies to title officer. In re Opinion No. 26 of Committee on Unauthorized Practice of Law, 139 N.J. 323, 654 A.2d 1344 (1995).

Purchasers of new homes stated cause of action against home builders and selling brokers for violation of Consumer Fraud Act. Strawn v. Canuso, 271 N.J.Super. 88, 638 A.2d 141 (A.D.1994), leave to appeal granted 137 N.J. 303, 645 A.2d 134, affirmed 140 N.J. 43, 657 A.2d 420.

Real Estate broker who receives a commission from a seller for negotiating a sale held statutorily barred from also earning a consideration from the buyer in the same transaction for assistance and obtaining the necessary financing. Mortgage Bankers Ass'n of New Jersey v. New Jersey Real Estate Commission, 200 N.J.Super. 584, 491 A.2d 1317 (App.Div.1985), reversed 102 N.J. 176, 506 A.2d 733 (1986).

Real estate agent held not liable for damages for any tortious interference with vendors' existing or prospective contracts where agent transmitted to vendor each bidder's offer on property as they were submitted to her, and secured for vendors a purchaser at the highest price obtainable through competitive bidding. Melveney v. McCrane, 138 N.J.Super. 456, 351 A.2d 385 (App.Div.1976).

Real estate broker's license; revocation for failure to file federal tax returns. N.J.S.A. 45:15–17. New Jersey Real Estate Com'n v. McLeod, 93 N.J.A.R.2d (REC) 9.

Failure to disclose material information; license of broker revoked; fines imposed on both broker and salesperson. New Jersey Real Estate Commission v. Hunt, 93 N.J.A.R.2d (REC) 1.

Broker's failure to pay commission after receiving advice of legality to pay it constituted bad faith; penalty imposed. New Jersey Real Estate Commission v. Latour, 92 N.J.A.R.2d (REC) 50.

Developer's failure to submit annual reports; registration revoked, fine imposed, order to cease and desist marketing of project issued. New Jersey Real Estate Commission v. Cepco, Inc., 92 N.J.A.R.2d (REC) 49.

Misrepresentations, misappropriation of monies, unlawful taking of monies, and other violations, warranted broker/salesperson license revocation, restitution, and fine. New Jersey Real Estate Commission v. Allen, 92 N.J.A.R.2d (REC) 45.

Improprieties regarding deposit monies and mortgage application; suspension of broker's license and imposition of fine. New Jersey Real Estate Commission v. Daniel Mullen and Holly Beach Realty, Inc., 92 N.J.A.R.2d (REC) 38.

Salespersons' misrepresentations regarding offer warranted license revocations and assessment of fines. New Jersey Real Estate Commission v. Ahuja, 92 N.J.A.R.2d (REC) 7.

11:5–6.5 Residential rental referral agencies

(a) Every person engaged in the business of referring, for a fee, prospective residential tenants to possible rental units shall be licensed in accordance with the New Jersey Real Estate License Act, N.J.S.A. 45:15–1 et seq., and shall comply with the provisions of this section in addition to the obligations imposed by the Act, and other rules contained in this chapter.

(b) Every licensee subject to this section shall enter into a written contract with the prospective tenant and give such person a copy of the contract. The contract shall accurately state:

1. The services to be performed by the agency;

2. The fee charged;

3. The date and duration of the contract;

4. The affirmative actions required of the prospective tenant to utilize the service;

5. The refund policy; and

6. A statement that the business is licensed by the New Jersey Real Estate Commission.

(c) No licensee shall advertise or refer to a prospective residential tenant to:

1. A non-existent address;

2. A property not verified as available as provided in (e) below;

3. A possible rental unit or location for which the licensee does not have the lessor's, or the duly authorized agent of the lessor's, oral or written consent to refer prospective tenants.

(d) Oral consent of the lessor or his duly authorized agent to refer prospective tenants to a possible rental unit or location shall be confirmed by the licensee in writing within 24 hours of the licensee's receipt of such consent.

(e) Every licensee subject to this section shall verify the continuing availability of the rental unit with the lessor or agent as follows:

1. All units advertised in media shall be verified each day the advertisement appears; and

2. All units to which prospective tenants are referred shall be verified as available every three working days.

(f) In the event a diligent effort by the licensee to verify availability of the rental unit is unsuccessful because of a failure of a lessor or agent to respond, the prospective tenant shall be specifically advised of the date and time the unit was last verified as available.

1. Every prospective tenant shall upon request be advised of the date and time any particular unit was last verified as available.

2. No licensee subject to this section shall refer a prospective tenant to any rental unit not verified as available within the previous seven calendar days.

(g) Every licensee subject to this section shall maintain sufficient telephone lines and staff to receive and answer inquiries from contract consumers.

(h) Prior to the prospective tenant obtaining rental property through the services of the licensee, no licensee shall charge or accept a fee in excess of $25.00 unless:

1. Any fee charged, collected or received in excess of $25.00 is deposited promptly in the broker's escrow account until the services described by the contract are fully performed; or

2. The licensee posts with an approved escrow agent cash security in an amount approved by the Commission, based upon the following criteria:

i. The rental referral fees;

ii. The volume of rental referral business of the licensee;

iii. The duration of the rental referral contract; and

iv. The prior performance of the licensee or its principals in the rental referral business.

(i) Any licensee subject to this section shall maintain for one year the following records:

1. Written consent or written confirmation of oral consent of a lessor or agent to refer prospective tenants;

2. Records of the verification of availability of rental units as set forth in (e) above; and

3. Copies of contracts with prospective tenants.

(j) Every licensee subject to this section shall prominently post a copy of this regulation in its office for the information of its customers, and provide customers a copy upon request.

Repealed by R.1983 d.471, effective November 7, 1983.
See: 15 N.J.R. 1343(a), 15 N.J.R. 1865(c).
Section was "Rental location and operations".
New Rule, R.1985 d.93, effective March 4, 1985.
See: 16 N.J.R. 2952(a), 17 N.J.R. 600(a).
Amended by R.1998 d.497, effective October 5, 1998.
See: 30 N.J.R. 2333(a), 30 N.J.R. 3646(a).
In (b), deleted an address at the end of 6.

Case Notes

Rule governing rental location licenses held valid against challenges of unlawful rate-making by the Commission, arbitrary nature and confiscatory effect (citing former rule). In re N.J.A.C. 11:5–1.32, 179 N.J.Super. 294, 431 A.2d 855 (App.Div.1981).

11:5–6.6 Participation in trade associations or listing services

(a) No licensed individual, partnership, firm or corporation shall become a member of or otherwise participate in the activities or operation of any trade association or organization or of any multiple listing service operation which engages in the following policies and practices:

1. Places requirements, obligations, or standards upon licensed members or participants which conflict with the Real Estate License Act, N.J.S.A. 45:15–1 et seq., the Real Estate Sales Full Disclosure Act, N.J.S.A. 45:15–16.27 et seq., the New Jersey Antitrust Act, N.J.S.A. 56:9–1 et seq., or the New Jersey Law Against Discrimination, N.J.S.A. 10:5–1 et seq., or which otherwise relate to the comprehensive scheme of regulation already preempted by the State of New Jersey.

2. Interferes with the licensee's obligation of fidelity to his client's interests, his obligation of dealing fairly with all other parties in a transaction, or his obligation of fully cooperating with any other New Jersey licensee, as more fully set forth in N.J.A.C. 11:5–6.4;

3. Directly or indirectly imposes or attempts to impose prescribed or predetermined fees or commission rates or commission amounts, or prescribed or predetermined commission splits, between the listing broker and the selling broker.

Amended by R.1979 d.461, effective November 26, 1979.
See: 10 N.J.R. 499(a), 12 N.J.R. 44(b).
Amended by R.1998 d.497, effective October 5, 1998.
See: 30 N.J.R. 2333(a), 30 N.J.R. 3646(a).
In (a), substituted "Real Estate Sales Full Disclosure Act" for "Land Sales Disclosure Act" and changed an N.J.S.A. reference in 1, and changed N.J.A.C. reference in 2; and deleted a former (b).

11:5–6.7 Disclosures by licensees providing mortgage financing services to buyers for a fee

(a) Every real estate licensee who provides mortgage financing services to buyers must provide written disclosure to the buyer/borrower and to the seller as required in this rule as a condition to receiving, in addition to a share of the brokerage commission on the sale, any compensation, reimbursement or thing of value from the buyer, or any other source. These disclosures are required whenever the real estate brokerage agency, any division therein, or any individual licensed or employed by the agency will receive compensation or reimbursement for providing mortgage financing services related to the sales transaction, even if that particular division or individual will not share in the sales commission. Copies of all written disclosures required by this rule must be retained by the broker as business records pursuant to N.J.A.C. 11:5–5.4. The broker shall maintain records of such related mortgage transactions which shall be available to the Commission for inspection pursuant to N.J.A.C. 11:5–5.5.

(b) The licensee must provide written disclosure as required by (a) above to the buyer/borrower before charging or accepting or contracting for any fees for mortgage financing services and providing such services other than prequalification. The written disclosure to the buyer must include the following information:

1. The amount of all fees which the buyer will be expected to pay to the licensee for mortgage services, and whether and under what circumstances such fees are refundable;

2. The amount and source of any compensation or reimbursement which the licensee will receive for providing mortgage financing services to the buyer;

3. Where the licensee takes applications for or places loans exclusively with any three or fewer lenders, or is affiliated with any lender or mortgage broker as defined in N.J.A.C. 11:5–6.8, the disclosure must advise the buyer of that fact, give the names of such lenders and state:

YOU ARE UNDER NO OBLIGATION TO USE THE MORTGAGE SERVICES OFFERED BY THIS REAL ESTATE LICENSE. YOU MAY OBTAIN YOUR MORTGAGE LOAN FROM ANOTHER SOURCE.

4. Where the licensee or agency is also representing the seller in the sales transaction, the disclosure to the buyer/borrower must include the statement set forth in (e) below.

(c) Real estate licensees who are dually licensed as mortgage bankers or brokers may combine the disclosures to buyers required in this rule with the written disclosure to borrowers required by the Department of Banking and Insurance pursuant to its rules mandating such disclosures.

(d) A listing broker who represents only the seller and who offers to provide mortgage financing services to buyers for compensation or reimbursement shall provide written disclosure to the seller by including the following statement in the listing agreement. A selling broker who represents only the seller as subagent of the listing broker, and who offers to provide mortgage financing services to buyers for compensation or reimbursement, shall provide the following disclosure statement to the seller, with a copy to the listing broker, at the time any written offer is presented.

THIS REAL ESTATE AGENCY MAY OFFER TO PROVIDE MORTGAGE FINANCING SERVICES TO THE BUYER FOR A FEE IN ADDITION TO THE SALES COMMISSION. AS AGENT OF THE SELLER, THIS REAL ESTATE AGENCY HAS A FIDUCIARY DUTY TO YOU, THE SELLER, WHICH WILL NOT CHANGE SHOULD MORTGAGE FINANCING SERVICES BE PROVIDED. IN THE EVENT THAT MORTGAGE FINANCING SERVICES ARE PROVIDED TO THE BUYER, THIS AGENCY SHALL NOT UNDERTAKE REPRESENTATION OF THE BUYER IN THIS REAL ESTATE SALE.

(e) Where the licensee or agency does provide mortgage financing services to the buyer for compensation or reimbursement and also represents only the seller in the sales transaction, the following statement must be included in the written disclosure to the buyer required by (b) or (c) above. The licensee or agency must also promptly send or deliver the following written disclosure statement to the seller, with a copy to the listing broker, at the time a mortgage application is submitted on behalf of the buyer/ borrower.

____

(name of licensee and brokerage agency)

REPRESENTS THE SELLER IN THE REAL ESTATE SALES TRANSACTION. UPON CLOSING OF TITLE, THIS REAL ESTATE AGENCY WILL RECEIVE A SALES COMMISSION FOR REPRESENTING THE SELLER. THIS REAL ESTATE AGENCY ALSO PROVIDES MORTGAGE FINANCING SERVICES TO THE BUYER FOR A FEE IN THE AMOUNT OF _. AS AGENT OF THE SELLER, THIS REAL ESTATE AGENCY HAS A FIDUCIARY DUTY TO THE SELLER WHICH IS NOT CHANGED BY PROVIDING MORTGAGE SERVICES TO THE BUYER. THIS AGENCY DOES NOT REPRESENT THE BUYER IN THIS REAL ESTATE SALE.

Where the precise amount of the compensation to the licensee or agency for providing mortgage services has not yet been established, the maximum estimated amount of compensation should be included in this disclosure. The compensation received by the licensee may not be increased above the amount disclosed here without written notice to both parties, with a copy to the listing broker.

New Rule, R.1992 d.232, effective June 1, 1992.
See: 23 N.J.R. 3424(b), 24 N.J.R. 2058(b).
Amended by R.1998 d.497, effective October 5, 1998.
See: 30 N.J.R. 2333(a), 30 N.J.R. 3646(a).

Rewrote (c); in (b), (d), and (e), deleted references to stylistic requirements; and changed N.J.A.C. references throughout the section.

Case Notes

Requiring real estate brokers give vendors and purchasers notice and disclosure and accept no more than $250 for providing mortgage related services was consistent with statute. Mortgage Bankers Ass'n of New Jersey v. New Jersey Real Estate Com'n, 283 N.J.Super. 233, 661 A.2d 832 (A.D.1995).

11:5–6.8 Disclosure of licensee's affiliation with a mortgage lender or mortgage broker to whom the licensee refers buyers

(a) Whenever a real estate licensee refers a buyer/borrower to a mortgage lender or mortgage broker with whom the licensee is affiliated, the licensee must provide written disclosure of the affiliation to the buyer. This disclosure must be made even though the licensee will receive no fees or compensation for the referral, see N.J.A.C. 11:5–7.2, and even though the licensee also refers the buyer to other, unaffiliated sources of mortgage financing. The disclosure must include the following statement:

YOU ARE UNDER NO OBLIGATION TO USE THE MORTGAGE SERVICES OF ________ WHO/WHICH IS AFFILIATED WITH THIS REAL ESTATE LICENSEE. YOU MAY OBTAIN YOUR MORTGAGE LOAN FROM ANOTHER SOURCE.

(b) For the purposes of this rule, a real estate licensee is considered to be affiliated with a mortgage lender or mortgage broker when:

1. The licensee, or the licensee's spouse, parent or child, is an officer, director or employee of the lender or mortgage broker, or works as a solicitor for the lender or mortgage broker;

2. The licensee, either alone or with spouse, parent or child, owns more than one percent of the lender or mortgage broker; the licensee is more than one percent owned by the lender or mortgage broker; or the licensee owns more than one percent or is more than one percent owned by a corporate parent, holding company or other business entity which is a majority shareholder in the lender or mortgage broker;

3. The licensee is a franchisee of a franchiser which owns more than one percent of the lender or mortgage broker or the licensee itself is the franchiser or franchisee of a mortgage lending franchise; or

4. The licensee shares office space or other facilities, or staff, with the lender or mortgage broker.

(c) Where an employing broker or broker of record of a real estate agency has an individual or corporate affiliation with a lender or mortgage broker, all licensees licensed with that real estate broker must provide the required disclosures to buyers referred to the affiliate.

1. Where an office manager has such an individual affiliation, the manager and all licensees working under his or her supervision must provide the disclosure to all buyers referred to the affiliate by that office.

2. Where a salesperson or broker-salesperson has such an individual affiliation, he or she must provide the disclosure to all buyers he or she refers to the affiliate.

(d) The disclosure required by this section may be combined with the disclosure of affiliation required under RESPA, 12 U.S.C. §§ 2601 et seq. Copies of all written disclosures required by this rule must be retained by the broker as business records available for inspection pursuant to N.J.A.C. 11:5–5.4 and 5.5.

New Rule, R.1992 d.232, effective June 1, 1992.
See: 23 N.J.R. 3424(b), 24 N.J.R. 2058(b).
Amended by R.1998 d.497, effective October 5, 1998.
See: 30 N.J.R. 2333(a), 30 N.J.R. 3646(a).
In (a) and (d), changed N.J.A.C. references; and in (a), deleted a reference to stylistic requirements in the introductory paragraph.

Case Notes

Requiring real estate brokers give vendors and purchasers notice and disclosure and accept no more than $250 for providing mortgage related services was consistent with statute. Mortgage Bankers Ass'n of New Jersey v. New Jersey Real Estate Com'n, 283 N.J.Super. 233, 661 A.2d 832 (A.D.1995).

11:5–6.9 Consumer Information Statement

(a) When applied to rental transactions which are not exempt from this rule, references to sellers and buyers, and to the various types of brokerage agreements and business relationships mentioned throughout this rule should be construed as indicating their appropriate counterparts in rental transactions. For example, references to sellers should be read as lessors or owners and references to buyers should be read as lessees or tenants, etc. As used in this rule, the following terms or phrases shall have the following meanings:

1. "Brokerage agreement" means a written agreement between a brokerage firm and a party describing the terms under which that firm will perform brokerage services as specified in N.J.S.A. 45:15–3. Brokerage agreements include, but are not limited to, sale and rental listing agreements, buyer-broker, lessee-broker, transaction broker, and dual agency agreements.

2. "Brokerage firm" means a licensed corporate, partnership or sole proprietor broker, and all individuals licensed with that broker.

3. Consumer Information Statement" means the Consumer Information Statement on New Jersey Real Estate Relationships as prescribed in (h) below.

4. "Informed consent to dual agency" means the written authorization by a party for the brokerage firm which represents them as their agent in a real estate transaction to also represent the other party to that transaction as an agent. Informed consent can only be obtained after the brokerage firm has disclosed to the consenting party all material facts which might reasonably impact on that party's decision to authorize dual agency, including the extent of the conflicts of interests involved and the specific ways in which each consenting party will receive less than full agency representation from the dual agent. In order to obtain informed consent it is also necessary for the licensee to first advise the consenting party of the other business relationships offered by that licensee and of those not offered by that licensee, and of that party's right to consult an attorney.

5. "Party" shall mean actual or prospective sellers, lessors, buyers or lessees of an interest in real estate.

6. "Short term rental" shall mean the rental of a residential property for not more than the 125 consecutive day time period specified in N.J.S.A. 46:8–19 as constituting the "seasonal use or rental" of real property, under the terms of an oral rental agreement or written lease which contains a specific termination date. Month-to-month tenancies are not considered short term rentals.

7. "Transaction broker" shall mean a brokerage firm which works with both parties in an effort to arrive at an agreement on the sale or rental of real estate and facilitates the closing of a transaction, but does not represent either party, and has no agency relationship with either party to the transaction. The New Jersey Real Estate License Law, N.J.S.A. 45:15–1 et seq., and the administrative rules promulgated thereunder do not mandate that licensees must act as agents when rendering real estate brokerage services.

8. "Business relationship(s)" means real estate licensees working as a seller's agent; a buyer's agent; a disclosed dual agent; or a transaction broker.

(b) Prior to acting as a dual agent, a brokerage firm must have the written informed consent of the parties to the transaction. Informed consent is not acquired through distribution of the Consumer Information Statement on New Jersey Real Estate Relationships as required by (e) and (k) below alone. At a minimum, licensees must also secure the signature of the party on a separate writing which confirms the party's informed consent to the licensee acting as a Disclosed Dual Agent for that party. Such a writing may be part of, or an attachment to a brokerage agreement.

(c) Licensees shall supply information with regard to their working relationship with parties to real estate transactions as provided in this section.

(d) Licensees shall comply with all requirements of this section when involved in:

1. Transactions which involve the sale of residential real estate containing one to four dwelling units or the sale of vacant one-family lots;

2. Residential lease transactions other than short term rentals. However, in short-term rental transactions, licensees shall include in all leases prepared by them a statement indicating that they are acting in the transaction either as an agent of the landlord, an agent of the tenant, a disclosed dual agent or a transaction broker; and

3. The securing of brokerage agreements on residential properties, including rental listing agreements on residential properties to be offered for short term rentals.

(e) All licensees shall supply information on business relationships to buyers and sellers in accordance with the following:

1. With respect to buyers:

i. All licensees shall verbally inform buyers of the four business relationships described in this section prior to the first discussion at which a buyer's motivation or financial ability to buy is discussed.

ii. If the first such discussion occurs during a business meeting on the buyer's real estate needs, licensees shall deliver the written Consumer Information Statement to the buyers prior to such a discussion. If the first such discussion is telephonic or in a social setting, licensees shall, after having verbally informed the buyer of the four business relationships, deliver the written Consumer Information Statement to the buyer at their next meeting. However, if prior to their first business meeting after such a discussion, any material is mailed, faxed or delivered by the licensee to the buyer, the Consumer Information Statement shall be included with such material.

iii. Where the written Consumer Information Statement has not been delivered to buyers as provided in (e)1ii above, licensees shall deliver the written statement to buyers no later than the first showing and, if no showing is conducted, no later than the preparation of an initial offer or contract.

iv. Those licensees who intend to enter into a buyer-brokerage relationship with such persons shall deliver the Consumer Information Statement no later than the commencement of their buyer-brokerage agreement presentation.

2. With respect to sellers:

i. All licensees shall verbally inform sellers of the four business relationships described in this section prior to the first discussion at which the seller's motivation or desired selling price is discussed.

ii. If the first such discussion occurs during a business meeting on the seller's real estate needs, licensees shall deliver the written Consumer Information Statement to the sellers prior to such a discussion. If the first such discussion is telephonic or in a social setting, licensees shall, after having verbally informed the seller of the four business relationships, deliver the written Consumer Information Statement to the seller at their next meeting. However, if prior to their first business meeting after such a discussion, any material is mailed, faxed or delivered by the licensee to the seller, the Consumer Information Statement shall be included with such material.

iii. On unlisted properties where the written Consumer Information Statement has not been delivered to sellers as provided in (e)2ii above, licensees shall deliver the written statement to sellers no later than their first showing of the property, and if no showing is conducted, no later than the presentation of an initial offer or contract.

iv. Those licensees who intend to enter into a listing or transaction brokerage agreement with a seller shall deliver the Consumer Information Statement no later than the commencement of their listing or transaction brokerage agreement presentation.

(f) The purpose of (e) above and (h) below is to require licensees to provide basic and introductory information to the public in a convenient and consistent manner, rather than a comprehensive explanation of agency law.

(g) The statement as supplied by the Commission shall be reproduced and delivered by licensees as required in this section as a separate item, with no deletions or additions, other than the optional additional text referred to in (g)1 and 2 below, and recited in (h) below.

1. Brokerage firms may acknowledge delivery of the Statement by procuring the signature of the party to whom it was delivered and the date of delivery in the appropriate place at the bottom of the Statement.

i. On transactions which result in fully executed contracts of sale or consummated rental transactions, copies of Consumer Information Statements on which receipt has been acknowledged as set forth in (g)1 above, shall be maintained as business records for six years in accordance with N.J.A.C. 11:5–5.4(c).

2. Brokerage firms may also indicate on the Statement the capacity in which they intend to work with the party to whom they deliver the Statement.

3. Regardless of whether brokerage firms choose to include on the Statement the additional information referred to in (g)1 and 2 above, all brokerage firms, as is required by (i) and (j) below, shall:

i. Indicate in all brokerage agreements the business relationship they intend to have with the other party to the agreement; and

ii. Indicate in all offers, contracts, or leases prepared by licensees the business relationship the firm has with respect to the parties named in those documents.

(h) The mandatory text of the Consumer Information Statement to be delivered by licensees as provided in (e) above is as follows:

CONSUMER INFORMATION STATEMENT ON NEW JERSEY REAL ESTATE RELATIONSHIPS

In New Jersey, real estate licensees are required to disclose how they intend to work with buyers and sellers in a real estate transaction. (In rental transactions, the terms "buyers" and "sellers" should be read as "tenants" and "landlords," respectively.)

1. AS A SELLER'S AGENT OR SUBAGENT, I, AS A LICENSEE, REPRESENT THE SELLER AND ALL MATERIAL INFORMATION SUPPLIED TO ME BY THE BUYER WILL BE TOLD TO THE SELLER.

2. AS A BUYER'S AGENT, I, AS A LICENSEE, REPRESENT THE BUYER AND ALL MATERIAL INFORMATION SUPPLIED TO ME BY THE SELLER WILL BE TOLD TO THE BUYER.

3. AS A DISCLOSED DUAL AGENT, I, AS A LICENSEE, REPRESENT BOTH PARTIES. HOWEVER, I MAY NOT, WITHOUT EXPRESS PERMISSION, DISCLOSE THAT THE SELLER WILL ACCEPT A PRICE LESS THAN THE LISTING PRICE OR THAT THE BUYER WILL PAY A PRICE GREATER THAN THE OFFERED PRICE.

4. AS A TRANSACTION BROKER, I, AS A LICENSEE, DO NOT REPRESENT EITHER THE BUYER OR THE SELLER. ALL INFORMATION I ACQUIRE FROM ONE PARTY MAY BE TOLD TO THE OTHER PARTY.

Before you disclose confidential information to a real estate licensee regarding a real estate transaction, you should understand what type of business relationship you have with that licensee.

There are four business relationships: (1) seller's agent; (2) buyer's agent; (3) disclosed dual agent; and (4) transaction broker. Each of these relationships imposes certain legal duties and responsibilities on the licensee as well as on the seller or buyer represented. These four relationships are defined in greater detail below. Please read carefully before making your choice.

SELLER'S AGENT

A seller's agent WORKS ONLY FOR THE SELLER and has legal obligations, called fiduciary duties, to the seller. These include reasonable care, undivided loyalty, confidentiality and full disclosure. Seller's agents often work with buyers, but do not represent the buyers. However, in working with buyers a seller's agent must act honestly. In dealing with both parties, a seller's agent may not make any misrepresentation to either party on matters material to the transaction, such as the buyer's financial ability to pay, and must disclose defects of a material nature affecting the physical condition of the property which a reasonable inspection by the licensee would disclose.

Seller's agents include all persons licensed with the brokerage firm which has been authorized through a listing agreement to work as the seller's agent. In addition, other brokerage firms may accept an offer to work with the listing broker's firm as the seller's agents. In such cases, those firms and all persons licensed with such firms are called "sub-agents." Sellers who do not desire to have their property marketed through sub-agents should so inform the seller's agent.

BUYER'S AGENT

A buyer's agent WORKS ONLY FOR THE BUYER. A buyer's agent has fiduciary duties to the buyer which include reasonable care, undivided loyalty, confidentiality and full disclosure. However, in dealing with sellers a buyer's agent must act honestly. In dealing with both parties, a buyer's agent may not make any misrepresentations on matters material to the transaction, such as the buyer's financial ability to pay, and must disclose defects of a material nature affecting the physical condition of the property which a reasonable inspection by the licensee would disclose.

A buyer wishing to be represented by a buyer's agent is advised to enter into a separate written buyer agency contract with the brokerage firm which is to work as their agent.

DISCLOSED DUAL AGENT

A disclosed dual agent WORKS FOR BOTH THE BUYER AND THE SELLER. To work as a dual agent, a firm must first obtain the informed written consent of the buyer and the seller. Therefore, before acting as a disclosed dual agent, brokerage firms must make written disclosure to both parties. Disclosed dual agency is most likely to occur when a licensee with a real estate firm working as a buyer's agent shows the buyer properties owned by sellers for whom that firm is also working as a seller's agent or subagent.

A real estate licensee working as a disclosed dual agent must carefully explain to each party that, in addition to working as their agent, their firm will also work as the agent for the other party. They must also explain what effect their working as a disclosed dual agent will have on the fiduciary duties their firm owes to the buyer and to the seller. When working as a disclosed dual agent, a brokerage firm must have the express permission of a party prior to disclosing confidential information to the other party. Such information includes the highest price a buyer can afford to pay and the lowest price a seller will accept and the parties' motivation to buy or sell. Remember, a brokerage firm acting as a disclosed dual agent will not be able to put one party's interests ahead of those of the other party and cannot advise or counsel either party on how to gain an advantage at the expense of the other party on the basis of confidential information obtained from or about the other party.

If you decide to enter into an agency relationship with a firm which is to work as a disclosed dual agent, you are advised to sign a written agreement with that firm.

TRANSACTION BROKER

The New Jersey Real Estate Licensing Law does not require licensees to work in the capacity of an "agent" when providing brokerage services. A transaction broker works with a buyer or a seller or both in the sales transaction without representing anyone. A TRANSACTION BROKER DOES NOT PROMOTE THE INTERESTS OF ONE PARTY OVER THOSE OF THE OTHER PARTY TO THE TRANSACTION. Licensees with such a firm would be required to treat all parties honestly and to act in a competent manner, but they would not be required to keep confidential any information. A transaction broker can locate qualified buyers for a seller or suitable properties for a buyer. They can then work with both parties in an effort to arrive at an agreement on the sale or rental of real estate and perform tasks to facilitate the closing of a transaction. A transaction broker primarily serves as a manager of the transaction, communicating information between the parties to assist them in arriving at a mutually acceptable agreement and in closing the transaction, but cannot advise or counsel either party on how to gain an advantage at the expense of the other party. Owners considering working with transaction brokers are advised to sign a written agreement with that firm which clearly states what services that firm will perform and how it will be paid. In addition, any transaction brokerage agreement with a seller or landlord should specifically state whether a notice on the property to be rented or sold will or will not be circulated in any or all Multiple Listing System(s) of which that firm is a member.

YOU MAY OBTAIN LEGAL ADVICE ABOUT THESE BUSINESS RELATIONSHIPS FROM YOUR OWN LAWYER.

THIS STATEMENT IS NOT A CONTRACT AND IS PROVIDED FOR INFORMATIONAL PURPOSES ONLY.

(END OF MANDATORY CONSUMER INFORMATION STATEMENT TEXT)

(OPTIONAL ACKNOWLEDGEMENT OF RECEIPT AFTER TEXT OF CONSUMER INFORMATION STATEMENT.)

FOR SELLERS AND LANDLORDS

"By signing this Consumer Information Statement, I acknowledge that I received this Statement from (Name of Brokerage Firm) prior to discussing my motivation to sell or lease or my desired selling or leasing price with one of its representatives."

FOR BUYERS AND TENANTS

"By signing this Consumer Information Statement, I acknowledge that I received this Statement from (Name of Brokerage Firm) prior to discussing my motivation or financial ability to buy or lease with one of its representatives."

(OPTIONAL INDICATION OF IN WHAT CAPACITY FIRM INTENDS TO WORK WITH RECIPIENT OF

CONSUMER INFORMATION STATEMENT AS PERMITTED BY (g)2 ABOVE):

I, ____________________, as an authorized representative of ________________________, intend, as of this time, to work with you as a

(indicate one of the following):
seller's agent only
buyer's agent only
seller's agent and disclosed dual agent if the opportunity arises
buyer's agent and disclosed dual agent if the opportunity arises
transaction broker only
seller's agent on properties on which this firm is acting as the seller's agent and transaction broker on other properties

(i) In all brokerage agreements, brokerage firms must include the following:

1. A statement acknowledging receipt of the Consumer Information Statement; and

2. A declaration of business relationship indicating the regular business name of the broker and in what capacity the licensee servicing the agreement and their firm will operate as real estate licensees with respect to the other party to the brokerage agreement. The declaration of business relationship in all brokerage agreements shall contain, in print larger than the predominant size print in the writing, the following language:

I, ____________________, as an authorized representative of ________________________, intend, as of this time, to work with you as a

(indicate one of the following):
seller's agent only
buyer's agent only
seller's agent and disclosed dual agent if the opportunity arises
buyer's agent and disclosed dual agent if the opportunity arises
transaction broker only
seller's agent on properties on which this firm is acting as the seller's agent and transaction broker on other properties

3. Where brokerage firms secure a written acknowledgement of receipt of the Consumer Information Statement on the Statement itself as provided in (g)1 above and include on the Consumer Information Statement a declaration of the business relationship they intend to have with the other party to the brokerage agreement as provided in (g)2 above, the attachment of a copy of the Consumer Information Statement to the brokerage agreement and the inclusion of a reference to the receipt of the Consumer Information Statement in the brokerage agreement shall constitute compliance with this section.

(j) Licensees shall disclose to consumers what type of brokerage services they will provide in the following manner:

1. Buyer-brokers shall verbally disclose to sellers that they are acting on behalf of a buyer prior to their first communication with the seller during which the seller's motivation to sell or desired price is discussed.

2. All offers, contracts or leases not exempt by this rule which are prepared by licensees shall include the following statements:

"By signing below the sellers (or landlords as applicable) and purchasers (or tenants as applicable) acknowledge they received the Consumer Information Statement on New Jersey Real Estate Relationships from the brokerage firms involved in this transaction prior to the first showing of the property."

3. In all offers, contracts, or leases, including leases for short-term rentals, prepared by licensees as permitted by N.J.A.C. 11:5–6.2(g), licensees shall include the regular business name of the broker with whom they are licensed and a declaration of business relationship indicating in what capacity they and their firm are operating as real estate licensees in that real estate transaction. The declaration of business relationship in all offers to purchase or to lease property, including those made on contracts of sale or lease documents prepared by licensees, shall contain, in print as large as the predominant size print in the writing, the following language:

______________ and ____________________ as its authorized
(Name of firm) (Name(s) of licensee(s))
representative(s) are working in this transaction as ________
(indicate one of the following):

seller's agents
buyer's agents
disclosed dual agents
transaction brokers

i. In transactions in which more than one firm is involved, all licensee-prepared offers, contracts and leases, including leases on short-term rentals, shall contain, in the same size type and immediately following the declaration of business relationship set forth above, the following clause:

Information supplied by ____________________
(Name of firm)
has indicated that it is operating in this transaction as a__
(indicate one of the following):

seller's agent only

buyer's agent only

transaction broker

ii. The requirement to include the clause cited in (j)3i above in licensee-prepared offers, contracts and leases shall not apply with respect to firms whose involvement in a transaction was limited to merely referring a party to another firm.

(k) Licensees shall disclose to other licensees what type of business relationship they have with the party with whom they have a brokerage agreement, and with any other parties with whom they may be working, in the following manner:

1. In all written or computer generated notices directed to other brokerage firms through a Multiple Listing Service or otherwise, the listing broker shall indicate whether they are working as a seller's agent or as a transaction broker. On listings where the listing broker is operating as a seller's agent, such notices shall also state:

i. Whether subagency is offered;

ii. Whether the seller has authorized the sharing of the listing broker's compensation with cooperating subagents and/or transaction brokers and/or buyer brokers; and

iii. The amount of compensation offered to cooperating subagents and/or transaction brokers and/or buyer brokers.

2. When a licensee with a listing broker receives an inquiry about a particular property from any other licensee, the licensee with the broker shall, before providing any information to the inquiring licensee beyond general information previously circulated about the listing, verbally ascertain from the inquiring licensee the capacity in which that licensee is operating or intends to operate (buyer-broker, subagent, disclosed dual agent or transaction broker). Inquiries from other licensees in the listing broker's firm shall also be responded to as set forth in this subsection.

(*l*) In transactions where brokers seek compensation for their brokerage services from a party to the transaction whom they are not representing or working with, the business relationship with the party they are representing or working with and the compensation arrangement shall also be disclosed to both parties as required by N.J.A.C. 11:5–7.1.

(m) Notwithstanding anything appearing in (g) and (h) above to the contrary, where a brokerage firm is itself the owner of the property being sold by individuals licensed through the broker-owner of the property, a Consumer Information Statement, revised as provided in this section, shall be delivered to prospective purchasers in accordance with the provisions of this rule.

1. On the line immediately below the title of the Consumer Information Statement, the following text shall appear in print larger than the predominant size print in the writing:

As the holder of a New Jersey real estate license, I am required by law to inform you how I will operate in this transaction, should you pursue it, and to provide this statement to you.

My employer is the owner of the property(s) in which you have expressed an interest. For the purposes of its business relationship disclosure rules, the New Jersey Real Estate Commission deems brokers selling property they own and licensees employed or retained by such broker-owners to be operating as seller's agents when they sell property owned by the broker. The statements which follow with regard to licensees who act as sellers' agents apply to me and other persons employed or retained by the owner, particularly those statements concerning the obligation of sellers' agents to pass on to the sellers all material information they obtain with regard to the buyers' ability to pay.

New Rule, R.1995 d.110, effective February 21, 1995 (operative July 1, 1995).
See: 26 N.J.R. 3113(a), 27 N.J.R. 697(a).
Administrative corrections.
See: 27 N.J.R. 1191(a); 27 N.J.R. 1618(b).
Public Notice: Petition for rulemaking; Agency disclosure.
See: 27 N.J.R. 5058(b).
Public Notice: Notice of action on petition for rulemaking.
See: 28 N.J.R. 1412(d).
Public Notice: Notice of Action on Petition for Rulemaking.
See: 29 N.J.R. 385(a).
Amended by R.1998 d.245, effective May 18, 1998.
See: 29 N.J.R. 1663(b), 30 N.J.R. 1829(a).
Rewrote (a)6; in (e), rewrote 1iii, 2iii and inserted a new iv; in (h), amended the "Consumer Information Statement"; and in (j), amended the "declaration of business relationship" document and added a new (m).
Amended by R.1998 d.497, effective October 5, 1998.
See: 30 N.J.R. 2333(a), 30 N.J.R. 3646(a).
In (g), (j) and (*l*), changed N.J.A.C. references.

Case Notes

Builder-developer of residential real estate or broker representing it may be liable for nondisclosure of off-site physical conditions known to it and unknown and not readily observable by purchaser if the existence of those conditions is of sufficient materiality to affect the habitability, use, or enjoyment of the property. Strawn v. Canuso, 140 N.J. 43, 657 A.2d 420 (1995).

SUBCHAPTER 7. PROHIBITED ACTIVITIES

11:5–7.1 Prohibition against licensees receiving dual compensation for dual representation in the sale or rental transaction

(a) Real estate licensees are prohibited from receiving compensation from both a seller and a buyer for representing both seller and buyer in the same real estate sales transaction. This prohibition applies even when the dual agency has been fully disclosed by the licensee to both parties.

(b) Real estate licensees are prohibited from receiving compensation from both a landlord and a tenant for representing both the landlord and the tenant in the same rental transaction. This prohibition applies even when the dual agency has been fully disclosed by the licensee to both parties.

(c) Within the meaning of this section, the phrases "sales transaction" and "rental transaction" do not include any related transactions whether or not they are contingencies in the contract or lease. For example, where there is a mortgage contingency in a contract of sale, the mortgage loan is a related transaction between the buyer and lender; it is not the same transaction as the sale.

(d) A licensee who represents only one party to a sale or rental transaction may receive the entire compensation for such representation from either party or a portion of that compensation from both parties to the transaction, provided that where a licensee prepares a contract or lease full written disclosure of the agency relationship and of the compensation arrangement is made to both parties to the transaction in the contract or lease. Where a licensee does not prepare the contract or lease, but seeks compensation from a party whom he or she does not represent, that licensee's agency relationship and proposed compensation arrangement shall be disclosed to all parties in a separate writing prior to execution of the contract or lease.

(e) A licensee who represents any party to a sale or rental transaction may receive compensation from either party for providing actual services in related transactions, provided that the licensee discloses the related services, sources and amounts of compensation in writing to the parties to the sale or rental transaction. Where the related services to be provided by the licensee are mortgage financing services provided to the buyer for compensation or reimbursement, the written disclosures must comply with N.J.A.C. 11:5-6.7. The broker shall maintain records of such related transactions including all required written disclosures, which records shall be available to the Commission for inspection pursuant to N.J.A.C. 11:5-5.5.

(f) Except as provided in (g) below, when providing mortgage financing services related to the purchase or sale of a one to six family residential dwelling, a portion of which may be used for non-residential purposes, located in New Jersey:

1. A real estate broker shall not solicit or receive compensation or reimbursement pursuant to (e) above greater than the expense amount permitted at closing by rule of the Department of Banking and Insurance unless licensed as a mortgage broker or mortgage banker by the Department of Banking and Insurance pursuant to the New Jersey Licensed Lenders Act, N.J.S.A. 17:11C-1 et seq.; and

2. A real estate salesperson or broker-salesperson shall not solicit or receive any compensation or reimbursement pursuant to (e) above from any person other than his or her employing real estate broker unless licensed as a mortgage broker or mortgage banker by the Department of Banking and Insurance pursuant to the New Jersey Licensed Lenders Act, N.J.S.A. 17:11C-1 et seq.

(g) Any real estate licensee who is individually employed as a mortgage solicitor by a licensed mortgage banker or mortgage broker and registered in compliance with applicable law and the rules of the Department of Banking and Insurance may solicit and accept compensation from his or her licensed mortgage employer for providing mortgage services in residential mortgage transactions.

New Rule, R.1992 d.232, effective June 1, 1992.
See: 23 N.J.R. 3424(b), 24 N.J.R. 2058(b).
Amended by R.1992 d.468, effective November 16, 1992.
See: 24 N.J.R. 1957(a), 24 N.J.R. 2129(a), 24 N.J.R. 4268(a).
Added (f), limiting solicitation and receipt of compensation for mortgage financing services to $250.00; and (g), permitting solicitation of mortgage banker or broker by real estate licensee who is also employed as a mortgage solicitor by said banker or broker.
Amended by R.1998 d.497, effective October 5, 1998.
See: 30 N.J.R. 2333(a), 30 N.J.R. 3646(a).
In (e), changed N.J.A.C. references; and rewrote (f) and (g).

11:5-7.2 Prohibition against kickbacks for related business referrals

(a) Any real estate licensee who solicits or accepts any fee, kickback, compensation or thing of value merely for referring a customer or client to a lender, mortgage broker, or other provider of related services, shall be subject to sanction by the Commission for engaging in conduct demonstrating unworthiness, bad faith and dishonesty. Any compensation received by a real estate licensee, pursuant to N.J.A.C. 11:5-7.1(e), for services in related transactions must be for services actually performed by the licensee beyond mere referral. Compliance with the anti-kickback provisions of the Federal Real Estate Settlement Procedures Act ("RESPA"), 12 U.S.C. § 2607, the regulations thereunder, or any opinion regarding RESPA issued by the Federal Department of Housing and Urban Development will be considered to be in compliance with this subsection.

(b) Real estate brokers are prohibited from offering incentives to the salespersons or broker-salespersons licensed under them for merely referring clients or customers to a particular lender, mortgage broker or other provider of related services. Any compensation paid by a real estate broker to a salesperson for services in transactions related to a sale or rental transaction must be for services actually performed by the salesperson beyond mere referral. For example, a real estate broker who provides in-house mortgage services may compensate a salesperson licensed with that broker who performs actual mortgage services. However, the broker is prohibited from offering bonuses or any extra consideration of any kind to salespersons for merely referring buyers to the in-house mortgage service or any particular lender or mortgage broker. For example, a real estate broker shall not offer or pay a salesperson a higher commission rate on a real estate transaction because the mortgage is placed through the in-house mortgage service or affiliated lender. A broker shall not award prizes or bonuses to salespersons based upon the number of customer referrals made to the in-house mortgage service or to a particular lender.

New Rule, R.1992 d.232, effective June 1, 1992.
See: 23 N.J.R. 3424(b), 24 N.J.R. 2058(b).
Amended by R.1998 d.497, effective October 5, 1998.
See: 30 N.J.R. 2333(a), 30 N.J.R. 3646(a).
In (a), changed N.J.A.C. reference.

Case Notes

Requiring real estate brokerage offices to be Mortgage Bankers and Brokers Act licensee branches was arbitrary. Mortgage Bankers Ass'n of New Jersey v. New Jersey Real Estate Com'n, 283 N.J.Super. 233, 661 A.2d 832 (A.D.1995).

11:5-7.3 Licensees with in-house mortgage services prohibited from excluding all outside mortgage solicitors

Real estate brokers who provide mortgage financing services to buyer/borrowers in-house, whether through computerized loan origination systems, or affiliated lenders or affiliated mortgage brokers, etc., are prohibited from limiting buyer's choices by denying outside lenders reasonable access to solicit mortgage loans in their real estate offices. Reasonable access will be presumed where three or more outside, non-affiliated lenders are permitted to send solicitors into the real estate office during business hours to contact salespersons. The reasonableness of the broker's overall office policy concerning rate sheets, and access by outside lenders, other visitors and solicitors, will also be considered. In no event shall this rule be interpreted to require any real estate broker to permit any one specific lender to solicit loans inside the real estate office or to require the real estate broker to set aside any particular space or facilities inside the real estate office for the use of outside mortgage solicitors.

New Rule, R.1992 d.232, effective June 1, 1992.
See: 23 N.J.R. 3424(b), 24 N.J.R. 2058(b).
Public Notice: Petition for Rulemaking.
See: 28 N.J.R. 1412(c).
Public Notice: Action on petition for rulemaking.
See: 28 N.J.R. 2414(a).
Public Notice: Action on petition for rulemaking.
See: 28 N.J.R. 4816(a).

11:5-7.4 Blockbusting; solicitation

(a) No broker or salesman shall affirmatively solicit the sale, lease or the listing for sale or lease of residential property on the grounds of alleged change of value due to the presence or prospective entry into the neighborhood of a person or persons of another race, religion or ethnic origin, nor shall distribute, or cause to be distributed, material, or make statements designed to include a residential property owner to sell or lease his property due to such change in the neighborhood.

(b) Every real estate broker who, in a personal meeting, solicits the sale, lease or the listing for sale or lease of three or more residential properties fronting on either side of any street between intersecting or cross streets or between a cul-de-sac or other like termination point and an intersecting or cross street within the same month, whether directly or through personal meetings attended by his or her salespersons, shall maintain a permanent record for at least one year from the date of said solicitation, which shall be available for inspection by the Commission or any representative thereof upon request, setting forth the name and address of each person so solicited, the address of the property involved, the name of the licensee actually making such solicitation, and the date upon which the solicitation took place. At the request of the Commission or any representative thereof, any such broker shall file with the Commission a copy of the permanent record, or a statement containing the same information as set forth in the permanent record. Such filing shall be made with the Commission no later than ten days following the request therefore.

As amended, R.1972 d.127, effective June 28, 1972.
See: 4 N.J.R. 71(a).
Amended by R.1998 d.497, effective October 5, 1998.
See: 30 N.J.R. 2333(a), 30 N.J.R. 3646(a).
In (b), substituted "who, in a personal meeting, solicits" for "soliciting" and "personal meetings attended by his or her salespersons," for "his salesman," in the first sentence; and deleted a former (c).

11:5-7.5 Proscription of price-fixing and agreements in regard to methods of arriving at commission

(a) No licensee shall combine, conspire, suggest, or recommend to, or with any other licensee(s) that any rate, commission or fee to be charged by them, or any division of such commission by them be fixed, established, maintained, suggested or stabilized. Nothing in this section shall prohibit any intra-office communications with regard to the establishment of commissions or division of commissions.

(b) No licensee shall directly or indirectly recommend or suggest to any other licensee(s) that such person(s) adhere to any schedule or recommendation of another concerning the rates, commissions or fees to be charged or the methodology or approach by which a commission, rate or fee is arrived at, or division of fees to be made, in the conduct of business. Nothing in this section shall prohibit any intra-office communications with regard to the establishment of commissions or division of commissions. Information imparted solely for the purposes of instruction, and not for the purpose of recommending guidelines or a preferred method of pricing, at any bona fide trade association seminar or educational courses shall be excepted from the proscription set forth in this section.

New Rule, R.1981 d.261, effective July 9, 1981.
See: 13 N.J.R. 306(a), 13 N.J.R. 440(c).

11:5-7.6 Proscription of certain discriminatory commission splits

No licensee shall directly or indirectly take any punitive or retaliatory action against any other licensee(s) where such action is based upon the failure or refusal to adhere or to adopt any commission. No licensee shall adopt a discriminatory commission split against another broker because of such other broker's failure or refusal to adhere to or adopt any commission; if a listing broker varies his commission split policy with any selling broker on a cooperative sale, the listing broker shall maintain a file at his place of business which shall contain in writing an explanation for the variation and which reflects who made the decision and why it was made. Nothing in this section shall prohibit a listing broker from varying his commission split policy with respect to any one or more selling brokers in order to achieve equality of commission splits with such other selling broker or brokers in connection with their commission split policy with such listing broker.

New Rule, R.1981 d.261, effective July 9, 1981.
See: 13 N.J.R. 306(a), 13 N.J.R. 440(c).

11:5–7.7 Proscription on pressuring media

No licensee shall agree, combine or conspire with another to boycott, or threaten to boycott, or refuse to do business with any promotional medium where such refusal or boycott is based on the acceptance by any medium of advertising of price or commissions of a competitive or discount nature.

New Rule, R.1981 d.261, effective July 9, 1981.
See: 13 N.J.R. 306(a), 13 N.J.R. 440(c).

SUBCHAPTER 8. DISCIPLINARY ACTIONS/CONDITIONS FOR RESTORATION OF LICENSE/REAL ESTATE GUARANTY FUND CLAIMS

11:5–8.1 Disciplinary action; restitution

(a) Violation of any of these rules and regulations, or of any real estate statute, shall be sufficient cause for any disciplinary action permitted by statute.

(b) In accordance with the provisions of N.J.S.A. 45:15–9 and N.J.S.A. 45:15–17, the Commission, in appropriate circumstances, will exercise its authority to impose restitution of moneys owed others as a condition to the issuance of a license or to the reinstatement of a license after revocation or suspension.

(c) The Commission may, where the nature of the offense so warrants, impose as a condition to any future license restoration, the successful accomplishment of a written examination of the same type normally given to applicants for initial licenses.

As amended, R.1977 d.392, effective October 19, 1977.
See: 9 N.J.R. 438(a), 9 N.J.R. 536(b).
As amended, R.1983 d.471, effective November 7, 1983.
See: 15 N.J.R. 1343(a), 15 N.J.R. 1865(c).
Added (c).

Case Notes

Broker's disclosure to Real Estate Commission of appellate court's decision that competing broker had tortiously interfered with exclusive contract and with prospective economic advantage implicated the public interest so as to be protected by Conscientious Employee Protection Act. Barratt v. Cushman & Wakefield of New Jersey, Inc., 144 N.J. 120, 675 A.2d 1094 (1966).

No sanctions imposed against agent when evidence did not establish she had submitted falsified documents. New Jersey Real Estate Commission v. Ross, 97 N.J.A.R.2d (REC) 11.

Licensed real estate salesperson's deceit in course of REC investigation was deemed not sufficiently material to set aside settlement reached in matter. Real Estate Commission v. Mosseri, 96 N.J.A.R.2d (REC) 39.

Broker's license was revoked for failure to disclose pending criminal charges. New Jersey Real Estate Commission v. Diaz, 96 N.J.A.R.2d (REC) 35.

Broker's license was properly revoked for misconduct as insurance producer. New Jersey Real Estate Commission v. Lopez, 96 N.J.A.R.2d (REC) 31.

Formerly licensed agent engaging in real estate transactions was fined and penalized for sales activities. New Jersey Real Estate Commission v. Abad, 96 N.J.A.R.2d (REC) 26.

Real estate salesperson's failure to respond honestly to application question concerning prior professional license revocation justified revocation of salesperson's license. New Jersey Real Estate Commission v. Rolston, 96 N.J.A.R.2d (REC) 24.

Theft conviction supported revocation of real estate salesperson's license, even where conviction was unrelated to license. New Jersey Real Estate Commission v. Kanoff, 96 N.J.A.R.2d (REC) 23.

Real estate salesperson's license on probation for failure to disclose prior felony conviction. New Jersey Real Estate Commission v. Irizarry, 96 N.J.A.R.2d (REC) 17.

Licensed real estate salesperson's failure to disclose prior convictions justifies license suspension. New Jersey Real Estate Commission, 96 N.J.A.R.2d (REC) 16.

Real estate salesperson fined and permanently barred from licensure for unlicensed transactions and falsifying license. New Jersey Real Estate Commission v. Fernandes, 96 N.J.A.R.2d (REC) 11.

Real estate license revoked where salesperson impersonates broker during agency inspection. New Jersey Real Estate Commission v. Cron, 96 N.J.A.R.2d (REC) 8.

Pending criminal theft charges involving insurance license justify denial of real estate license. New Jersey Real Estate Commission v. Nelson, 96 N.J.A.R.2d (REC) 7.

Working as real estate broker after license expired and while conducting fraudulent activities compels permanent ban from licensure. New Jersey Real Estate Commission v. Pinilis, 96 N.J.A.R.2d (REC) 1.

Real estate brokers suspended and fined; failure to maintain accounts. New Jersey Real Estate Commission v. Bailey, 94 N.J.A.R.2d (REC) 33.

Criminal conviction did not warrant revocation of broker-salesperson license. Real Estate Commission of New Jersey v. McLeod, 94 N.J.A.R.2d (REC) 29.

Revocation of real estate license and assessment of penalties were appropriate. New Jersey Real Estate Commission v. Sabia, 94 N.J.A.R.2d (REC) 23.

Real estate broker license placed on probation and fine imposed. Real Estate Commission v. Zappia, 94 N.J.A.R.2d (REC) 11.

Six-month suspension and imposition of penalty was justified. New Jersey Real Estate Commission v. Donnon, 94 N.J.A.R.2d (REC) 1.

Making false representation as being owner of real estate brokerage, collecting commission from person other than employing broker, and commingling of funds; revocation of salespersons' licenses and imposition of fines. New Jersey Real Estate Commission v. Ballman, 93 N.J.A.R.2d (REC) 17.

Commingling of funds, accounting failures, as well as other violations, warranted permanent revocation of broker/salesperson license and imposition of fine. New Jersey Real Estate Commission v. Duffy, 93 N.J.A.R.2d (REC) 13.

Failure to file income tax return; broker/salesperson license revoked. New Jersey Real Estate Commission v. McLeod, 93 N.J.A.R.2d (REC) 9.

Developer's failure to submit annual reports; registration revoked, fine imposed, order to cease and desist marketing of project issued. New Jersey Real Estate Commission v. Cepco, Inc. 92 N.J.A.R.2d (REC) 49.

Failure to account for deposit monies, commingling of funds, and engaging in business without license; salesperson's license revoked and fine imposed. 'New Jersey Real Estate Commission v. Groff. 92 N.J.A.R.2d (REC) 31.

Salesperson's failure to file answer to order to show cause or to make appearance before New Jersey Real Estate Commission warranted license suspension. New Jersey Real Estate Commission v. Grennor. 92 N.J.A.R.2d (REC) 29.

Salesperson procured real estate license by fraud, misrepresentation and deceit by failing to reveal having pled guilty to charge one week before executing application and licensing form; suspension and fine. New Jersey Real Estate Commission v. Cordaro. 92 N.J.A.R.2d (REC) 17.

Failure to disclose convictions; salesperson's license suspended. New Jersey Real Estate Commission v. Fields. 92 N.J.A.R.2d (REC) 15.

Criminal convictions warranted revocation of real estate salesperson's license. New Jersey Real Estate Commission v. Szatkowski. 92 N.J.A.R.2d (REC) 13.

Federal conspiracy to falsify claims and statements and of fraud warranted salesperson's license revocation. New Jersey Real Estate Commission v. Lanza. 92 N.J.A.R.2d (REC) 5.

Theft conviction warranted two-year revocation of salesperson's license. New Jersey Real Estate Commission v. Rosko. 92 N.J.A.R.2d (REC) 2.

False voter registration and tampering with public records convictions warranted suspension of real estate salesperson's license. New Jersey Real Estate Commission v. Federico. 92 N.J.A.R.2d (REC) 1.

11:5–8.2 Real estate guaranty fund

(a) Every licensed real estate broker and licensed broker-salesperson shall pay an additional amount as specified in N.J.S.A. 45:15–35 and every licensed real estate salesperson shall pay an additional amount as specified in N.J.S.A. 45:15–35 with their application for license renewal next following January 1, 1993.

1. Said fees shall be paid into the real estate guaranty fund and be utilized in accordance with N.J.S.A. 45:15–34 et seq.

(b) Before making a request for the entry of a court order directing payment from the real estate guaranty fund, a judgment credit shall have a writ of execution issued and prior to its return shall make a bona fide effort to examine the judgment debtor under oath and make any and all other reasonable searches and inquiries to ascertain whether the judgment debtor possesses real or personal property or other assets, liable to be sold or applied in satisfaction of the judgment in whole or in part. Information regarding any personal or real property or other assets liable to be sold or applied in satisfaction of the judgment which are discovered must be reported in writing to the officer to whom the writ of execution is directed.

New Rule, R.1981 d.252, effective July 9, 1981.
See: 13 N.J.R. 306(a), 13 N.J.R. 441(a).
Amended by R.1991 d.114, effective March 4, 1991.
See: 22 N.J.R. 3688(a), 23 N.J.R. 701(a).
Imposed special assessment on license renewals after January 1, 1991.
Amended by R.1993 d.153, effective April 5, 1993.
See: 25 N.J.R. 56(b), 25 N.J.R. 1548(a).
In (a), specified assessment amounts established by N.J.S.A. 45:15–35.

SUBCHAPTER 9. RULES INTERPRETING AND IMPLEMENTING THE REAL ESTATE SALES FULL DISCLOSURE ACT, N.J.S.A. 45:15–16.27 ET SEQ.

11:5–9.1 Applicability and scope

(a) The rules in this subchapter are promulgated by the New Jersey Real Estate Commission (hereinafter, the Commission) to implement the provisions of the Real Estate Sales Full Disclosure Act (hereinafter, the Act), N.J.S.A. 45:15–16.27 et seq. These rules are applicable to all applications and matters pertaining to and/or effected by the provisions of this Act.

(b) All registration and exemption applications and all correspondence and inquiries should be directed to: New Jersey Real Estate Commission, Bureau of Subdivided Land Sales Control, 20 West State Street, PO Box 328, Trenton, New Jersey 08625–0328.

Amended by R.1998 d.497, effective October 5, 1998.
See: 30 N.J.R. 2333(a), 30 N.J.R. 3646(a).
In (b), updated the address at the end.

11:5–9.2 Definitions

The following words and terms, as used in this subchapter, shall have the following meanings, unless the context clearly indicates otherwise.

"Advertising" means the publication or causing to be published, of any information offering for sale or for the purpose of causing or inducing any other person to purchase or acquire, an interest in the title to subdivided lands, including the sales contract to be used and any photographs or drawings or artist's representation of physical conditions or facilities on the property existing or to exist by means of any:

1. Newspaper or periodical;

2. Radio or television broadcast;

3. Written or printed or photographic matter produced by any duplicating process producing 10 copies or more;

4. Billboards or signs;

5. Display of model homes or units;

6. Material used in connection with the disposition or offer of subdivided lands by radio, television, telephone or any other electronic means; or

7. Material used by subdividers or their agents to induce prospective purchasers to visit the subdivision; particularly vacation certificates which require the holders of those certificates to attend or submit to a sales presentation by a subdivider or its agents.

"Advertising" does not mean: stockholder communications such as annual reports and interim financial reports, proxy materials, registration statements, securities prospectuses, applications for listing securities on stock exchanges, or similar documents, prospectuses, property reports, offering statements or other documents required to be delivered to a prospective purchaser by an agency of any other state or the Federal Government; all communications addressed to and relating to the account of any person who has previously executed a contract for the purchase of the subdivider's lands except when directed to the sale of additional lands.

"Applicant" means a person who or entity which has applied for the registration of real property of interests therein with the Commission pursuant to the Act or for a total or limited exemption from those registration requirements.

"Blanket encumbrance" means a trust deed, mortgage, judgment, or any other lien or encumbrance, including an option or contract to sell, or a trust agreement affecting a subdivision or affecting more than one lot offered within a subdivision, except that term shall not include any lien or other encumbrance arising as the result of the imposition of any tax assessment by any public authority.

"Broker" or "salesperson" means any person who performs within this State as an agent or employee of a subdivider any one or more of the services or acts as set forth in this Act, and includes any real estate broker or salesperson licensed pursuant to N.J.S.A. 45:15-1 et seq. or any person who purports to act in any such capacity.

"Broker's Release" means the document issued by the Commission affirming that the broker to whom it is issued has been approved by the Commission as the designated New Jersey broker of record or as a supplemental broker of a registrant, and has been authorized by the Commission to commence solicitation and sales efforts on behalf of that registrant in New Jersey.

"Commission" means the New Jersey Real Estate Commission.

"Common promotional plan" means any offer for the disposition of lots, parcels, units or interests of real property by a single person or group of persons acting in concert, where those lots, parcels, units or interests are contiguous, or are known, designated or advertised as a common entity or by a common name regardless of the number of lots, parcels, units or interests covered by each individual offering.

"Deed in trust" means a written instrument, in recordable form and conforming to all applicable laws of the situs state, under the terms of which title to a property passes to a trustee who is independent of and unaffiliated with the applicant/registrant, and which title is to be held by that trustee on behalf of the purchaser pursuant to a trust agreement or equivalent instrument between the registrant and the trustee obligating the trustee to convey title to the purchaser promptly upon the purchaser's fulfillment of their obligations under an installment contract for the purchase of such property by the purchaser from the registrant.

"Disposition" means the sale, lease, assignment, award by lottery, or any other transaction concerning a subdivision if undertaken for gain or profit.

"Notice" means a communication by mail from the Commission executed by its secretary or other duly authorized officer. Notice to subdividers shall be deemed complete when mailed to the subdivider's address currently on file with the Commission.

"Offer" means every inducement, solicitation or attempt to encourage a person to acquire an interest in a subdivision if undertaken for gain or profit.

"Person" means an individual, corporation, government or governmental subdivision or agency, business trust, estate, trust, partnership, unincorporated association, two or more of any of the foregoing having a joint or common interest, or any other legal or commercial entity.

"Principal" means all individual applicants or subdividers; all general partners of applicants or subdividers that are partnerships; all officers, directors and shareholders of corporate applicants or subdividers who are actively involved in the planning, management or promotion of the offering; and all other individuals who either own or control an interest of 10 percent or more in an applicant or subdivider, or who will actively participate in the planning, management or promotion of the offering, regardless of the form of organization of the applicant or subdivider.

"Purchaser" means a person who acquires or attempts to acquire or succeeds to an interest in a subdivision.

"Situs state" means the state, province, territory, protectorate, country or other jurisdiction situated outside of the State of New Jersey within which a subdivision is located.

"Time-share estates" includes both "fee simple" and "right to use" time-share interests and means:

1. An "interval estate" meaning a combination of an estate for years in a lot, parcel or unit, during the term of which title rotates among the time-share owners, coupled with a vested undivided fee simple interest in the remainder in that unit as established by the declaration or deed creating the interval estate; or

2. A "time-span estate" meaning a combination of an undivided interest in a present estate in fee simple in a lot, parcel or unit established by the declaration or deed creating the time-span estate, coupled with the exclusive right to possession and occupancy of the parcel or unit during a regularly recurring period; or

3. A "vacation license" meaning the exclusive right to possession and occupancy of a lot, unit or parcel during a regularly recurring period established by club membership, lease or license.

"Subdivider" or "developer" means any owner of subdivided lands or the agent of that owner who offers the subdivided lands for disposition.

"Subdivision" and "subdivided lands" mean any land situated outside the State of New Jersey whether contiguous or not, if one or more lots, parcels, units or interests are offered as part of a common promotional plan of advertising and sale and expressly means and includes such units or interests commonly referred to as a "condominium" defined in the "Condominium Act" P.L. 1969, c.257 (N.J.S.A. 46:8B–1 et seq.). In addition to condominiums, this definition shall also specifically include, but shall not be limited to, any form of homeowners association, any housing cooperative, any community trust or other trust device and any form of time-sharing.

Amended by R.1998 d.497, effective October 5, 1998.
See: 30 N.J.R. 2333(a), 30 N.J.R. 3646(a).
In "Advertising", deleted "land" preceding "sales contract".

11:5–9.3 Forms of documents

(a) Rules concerning documents with respect to the registration of subdivisions with the Commission and to the sale of interests in out-of-State subdivisions pursuant to the Act are as follows:

1. All statements of record submitted to the Commission shall be bound, referenced and properly indexed with the exception of those received from the Office of Interstate Land Sales Registration, U.S. Department of Housing and Urban Development.

2. All documents submitted to the Commission for filing shall, wherever possible, be typewritten on one side of the paper only. One copy of each exhibit or document shall be submitted, unless the Commission requests more than one copy. All documents submitted to the Commission shall not exceed 8½ x 14 inches. The Commission will make exceptions for documents which an applicant for registration cannot reasonably reduce, such as topographical maps, plat maps and surveys, if such documents can be folded to 8½ x 14 inches. Where the Commission requires certified documents and the applicant cannot obtain reduced certified documents, the applicant may reduce such documents and submit therewith an affidavit verifying such document. All documents submitted pursuant to these rules shall become part of the Commission's public records.

3. An applicant may submit photographs as part of the application for registration. Photographs shall not be used in lieu of the legal description of the registered property or any other required written documents.

4. An applicant may submit verified copies of original documents.

5. An affidavit or affirmation as prescribed in the Commission's forms shall be executed for each of the following documents:

i. Statement of record, partial statement of record;

ii. Application for consolidated registration;

iii. Application for amendment to Order of Registration;

iv. Annual report of registered properties;

v. Partner, officer, director or principal disclosure;

vi. Consent(s) to service of process; and

vii. Broker's Affidavit and application for release.

6. A certified property report and statement of record of the Office of Interstate Land Sales Registration, Department of Housing and Urban Development, may be filed as a statement of record conforming to the requirements of the Act, provided the following documentation shall also be submitted:

i. Consent(s) to service of process;

ii. Audited financial statement(s) as provided in N.J.A.C. 11:5–6.4(a)15;

iii. A statement detailing any bonding or security agreements entered into;

iv. Copies of all plats pertinent to the subdivision;

v. A copy of each contract to be used in the sale of property in the development to New Jersey purchasers;

vi. A list of the officers of the corporation;

vii. A copy of the articles or certificate of incorporation;

viii. Application/ affidavit of developer; and

ix. Such other additional documents or proofs that may be requested.

7. The acceptance of the certified report and statement of record of the Office of Interstate Land Sales Registration may be conditioned upon an acceptable on-site inspection by the Commission or its designee. No marketing or sales activity will be permitted in New Jersey until all the proper authorizations have been received by the applicant and broker from the Commission.

ii. By means of evidence acceptable to the Commission, that a bond, irrevocable bank letter of credit, or other financial assurances acceptable to the Commission, but in no event bonds issued by the applicant or any affiliated company, in an amount sufficient to ensure all monies paid by New Jersey purchasers prior to the delivery of a deed or deed in trust has been posted by an acceptable third party surety or entity on behalf of the applicant. In order for a surety or entity to be deemed acceptable, it shall be authorized to do business in the situs state and engaged in the general business of providing financial assurances on the open market. Such a bond or other financial assurance shall provide that the New Jersey Real Estate Commission on behalf of all New Jersey purchasers, or the appropriate regulatory agency of the situs state on behalf of all purchasers, is the insured and shall ensure all purchasers' deposits paid and/or all installment payment made prior to the delivery of a deed in recordable form to the purchaser or trustee. Whether the amount of such instruments is acceptable shall be determined based upon past and projected sales, purchase price and other contract terms and shall be reviewed annually by the Commission if it is a named insured;

4. An irrevocable appointment of the Commission to accept, on behalf of the applicant, service of any lawful process in any proceeding arising under the Act against the applicant or his agents;

5. A statement as to the states or other jurisdictions, including the Federal government, in which an application for registration, or similar documents, have been filed, and copies of any adverse orders, judgments or decrees by any regulatory agency, court, or administrative body, with the exception of orders approving advertising, entered against the applicant, any parent or subsidiary of the applicant, or any company related to or affiliated with the applicant with respect to the property for which the application for registration is being filed;

6. The name, address and principal occupation for the past five years of every principal officer and director of the applicant, and of every partner who owns a 10 percent or greater interest in the applicant, and of every shareholder who owns 10 percent or more of the stock of the applicant as of 30 days prior to the filing of the application for registration, with an indication of the nature and extent of their interest in the applicant;

7. Copies of the certificate or articles of incorporation, with all amendments thereto, if the applicant is a corporation; copies of all instruments by which the trust is created or declared, if the developer is a trust; copies of the articles of partnership or association and all other organization papers if the applicant is organized under another form. In the event the applicant is not the legal title holder to the property being registered, the above documents shall be submitted for both the applicant and the legal title holder;

8. A legal description by metes and bounds or by lot and block numbers, section, township and range designation, or other acceptable means of the lands to be registered, together with a map showing the proposed or actual subdivision and showing the dimensions of the lots, parcels, units or interests, as available, and the relation of such lands to existing streets, roads and other improvements. The aforesaid map or plat shall be drawn to scale, signed and sealed by a licensed professional engineer or land surveyor;

9. Copies of the deed or other instruments establishing title in the developer or other record owner and any escrow agreement required pursuant to (a)3 above, and a current title search, title report, title insurance policy, title opinion from an independent attorney, or certificate or binder issued by a licensed title insurance company. The Commission may also require a copy of any agreement which grants the applicant the rights to dispose of the property interest on behalf of the title holder;

10. A statement or listing of any pending litigation, court orders, judgments or decrees which materially affect the sale or development of the offering or the financial stability of the applicant;

11. A statement that the lots, parcels, units or interests in the development will be offered to the public and sold or alienated without regard to marital status, sex, race, handicap, religion, familial status, color, ancestry, creed or national origin;

12. A statement of the present condition of access to the development and of the existence of any adverse conditions that affect the development, or unusual conditions relating to noise or safety which affect the development that are known to the applicant, or should reasonably be known, or are readily ascertainable;

13. Copies of all contracts, agreements and acknowledgements which a purchaser or lessee may be required to execute in connection with this offering;

14. In the event there is, or will be, a blanket encumbrance affecting the development or a portion thereof, a copy of the document creating it and a statement of the consequences to a purchaser of a failure of the person bound to fulfill the obligations under the instrument, and of the manner in which the interest of the purchaser is to be protected in the event of such eventuality;

15. The audited financial statements of the applicant for the fiscal year. The term "financial statements" includes, but is not limited to, the following statements: auditor's report, balance sheet, statement of income, statement of changes in retained earnings, statement of changes in financial position, statement of changes in owner's equity, notes to financial statements and current profit and loss statement. The filing of the audited consolidated financial statements of a parent company of an applicant may be permitted if the parent company is the registrant, applicant, co-registrant or guarantor. In

the discretion of the Commission, it may accept or require alternative information evidencing the applicant's ability to complete the promised improvements to the development in lieu of the audited financial statements;

16. A statement concerning any filing for or adjudication of bankruptcy during the last five years by or with regard to the applicant, its predecessor, parent or subsidiary company and any principal owning more than a 10 percent interest in the subdivision at the time of the filing of the application for registration. These requirements shall not extend to limited partners or those whose interests are solely those of passive investors;

17. Copies of all easements and restrictions of record and any easements or restrictions not of record which are within the applicant's knowledge;

18. A statement as to the status of all applications for permits and/or compliance with any permits required or issued by any Federal, state, or local agencies or similar organizations which have the authority to regulate development or issue permits, approvals or licenses which may be material to the development, sale or other disposition of the lots, units, parcels or interests to be registered and the existing or proposed facilities, common areas or improvements thereof;

19. A statement indicating whether the applicant, or a parent or subsidiary of the applicant, or any of their current officers or principals have, during the past 10 years, or any of their former officers or principals have during the last two years been convicted of a crime involving any aspect of the real estate sales or real estate securities business in this State, the United States or any other state or foreign jurisdiction and whether the applicant has been subject to any permanent injunction or final administrative order restraining a false or misleading promotional plan involving real property disposition, or any final administrative order or judgement by any court finding that the applicant or any such persons have engaged in any unfair acts and/or fraudulent or deceptive practices involving the disposition of real property or of other products or services;

20. A copy of the proposed budget for the operation and maintenance of the common elements and facilities based upon full occupancy together with the estimated annual assessment and monthly charges to be assessed to each type of unit. If the proposed offering is a condominium, time-share or homeowners association, or involves any common ownership interest, the budget shall specifically state the amount set aside as reserves for the replacement of the common elements and facilities, as certified by an independent public accountant, or property manager or other independent expert. The budget should also indicate whether the applicant is subsidizing the maintenance fee or plans to subsidize the maintenance fee during sales prior to transfer of control to any association, and if so, the amount of the subsidy and the probable effect of the applicant's discontinuing the making of such payments upon the maintenance fee payable by each owner. The budget shall be accompanied by a letter of adequacy issued by an independent public accountant, or certified property manager, attesting that the budget was prepared in good faith and a letter from an independent insurance agent or broker confirming that the insurance coverage meets any standards required in the project documents and as required by situs state law;

21. A covering letter specifying the following information with regard to the project:

i. The nature of the project;

ii. Identifying to whom all correspondence should be directed, with an address; and

iii. Identifying to whom Annual Report Notices and forms should be sent, with an address and telephone number; and

22. Such other additional information as the Commission may require, after review of an application for registration, to assure full and fair disclosure.

Amended by R.1998 d.497, effective October 5, 1998.
See: 30 N.J.R. 2333(a), 30 N.J.R. 3646(a).
In (a), rewrote 3 and 21.

Case Notes

New Jersey Land Sales Full Disclosure Act discriminated in its plain effect against interstate commerce and violated dormant commerce clause. Old Coach Development Corp., Inc. v. Tanzman, C.A.3 (N.J.)1989, 881 F.2d 1227.

11:5–9.5 Public Offering Statements

(a) No registrant may dispose of any lot, parcel, unit or interest in a registered subdivision unless said registrant delivers to the purchaser a current New Jersey Public Offering Statement or approved equivalent, and affords the purchaser a reasonable opportunity to read the same before the purchaser signs the contract or purchase agreement.

the discretion of the Commission, it may accept or require alternative information evidencing the applicant's ability to complete the promised improvements to the development in lieu of the audited financial statements;

16. A statement concerning any filing for or adjudication of bankruptcy during the last five years by or with regard to the applicant, its predecessor, parent or subsidiary company and any principal owning more than a 10 percent interest in the subdivision at the time of the filing of the application for registration. These requirements shall not extend to limited partners or those whose interests are solely those of passive investors;

17. Copies of all easements and restrictions of record and any easements or restrictions not of record which are within the applicant's knowledge;

18. A statement as to the status of all applications for permits and/or compliance with any permits required or issued by any Federal, state, or local agencies or similar organizations which have the authority to regulate development or issue permits, approvals or licenses which may be material to the development, sale or other disposition of the lots, units, parcels or interests to be registered and the existing or proposed facilities, common areas or improvements thereof;

19. A statement indicating whether the applicant, or a parent or subsidiary of the applicant, or any of their current officers or principals have, during the past 10 years, or any of their former officers or principals have during the last two years been convicted of a crime involving any aspect of the real estate sales or real estate securities business in this State, the United States or any other state or foreign jurisdiction and whether the applicant has been subject to any permanent injunction or final administrative order restraining a false or misleading promotional plan involving real property disposition, or any final administrative order or judgement by any court finding that the applicant or any such persons have engaged in any unfair acts and/or fraudulent or deceptive practices involving the disposition of real property or of other products or services;

20. A copy of the proposed budget for the operation and maintenance of the common elements and facilities based upon full occupancy together with the estimated annual assessment and monthly charges to be assessed to each type of unit. If the proposed offering is a condominium, time-share or homeowners association, or involves any common ownership interest, the budget shall specifically state the amount set aside as reserves for the replacement of the common elements and facilities, as certified by an independent public accountant, or property manager or other independent expert. The budget should also indicate whether the applicant is subsidizing the maintenance fee or plans to subsidize the maintenance fee during sales prior to transfer of control to any association, and if so, the amount of the subsidy and the probable effect of the applicant's discontinuing the making of such payments upon the maintenance fee payable by each owner. The budget shall be accompanied by a letter of adequacy issued by an independent public accountant, or certified property manager, attesting that the budget was prepared in good faith and a letter from an independent insurance agent or broker confirming that the insurance coverage meets any standards required in the project documents and as required by situs state law;

21. A covering letter specifying the following information with regard to the project:

i. The nature of the project;

ii. Identifying to whom all correspondence should be directed, with an address; and

iii. Identifying to whom Annual Report Notices and forms should be sent, with an address and telephone number; and

22. Such other additional information as the Commission may require, after review of an application for registration, to assure full and fair disclosure.

Amended by R.1998 d.497, effective October 5, 1998.
See: 30 N.J.R. 2333(a), 30 N.J.R. 3646(a).
In (a), rewrote 3 and 21.

Case Notes

New Jersey Land Sales Full Disclosure Act discriminated in its plain effect against interstate commerce and violated dormant commerce clause. Old Coach Development Corp., Inc. v. Tanzman, C.A.3 (N.J.)1989, 881 F.2d 1227.

11:5–9.5 Public Offering Statements

(a) No registrant may dispose of any lot, parcel, unit or interest in a registered subdivision unless said registrant delivers to the purchaser a current New Jersey Public Offering Statement or approved equivalent, and affords the purchaser a reasonable opportunity to read the same before the purchaser signs the contract or purchase agreement.

1. In all cases where a New Jersey purchaser has not had contact with an authorized New Jersey broker, registrants shall maintain the signed and dated receipt for the New Jersey Public Offering statement and a copy of the contract which the New Jersey purchaser signed for a period of seven years.

(b) The Public Offering Statement shall disclose fully and accurately the characteristics of the subdivision and the lots, parcels, units or interests offered and shall make known to prospective purchasers all unusual and material circumstances and features affecting the subdivision. The Public Offering Statement shall be in clear and concise language and combine simplicity and accuracy in order to fully advise purchasers of their rights, privileges, obligations and restrictions.

1. The Public Offering Statement shall be in a form designated by the Commission. No change in form may be made without the consent of the Commission.

(c) The Commission may require an applicant to alter or amend the proposed Public Offering Statement in order to assure full and fair disclosure to prospective purchasers and may require the revision of a Public Offering Statement which it finds to be unnecessarily complex, confusing, illegible or incomplete.

(d) A Public Offering Statement shall not be deemed current unless it contains all amendments approved by the Commission.

(e) The Public Offering Statement shall contain the following information:

1. The name and address of the subdivision being offered, the name and principal address of the applicant and the name and address of the New Jersey broker of record;

2. A narrative description of the interest to be offered including; but not limited to; the rights and obligations of purchasers in their lots, parcels, units or interests and in the common elements;

3. A narrative description of the subdivision including, but not limited to, specific designation of the total number of lots, parcels, units or interests contained in the offering, the total number of lots, parcels, units or interests which will or may be constructed in the entire project, the present and proposed access to the development and the promised completion date of the present offering for sale and the estimated completion date of the entire development;

4. Relevant community information including, but not limited to, the existence and location of hospitals, health and recreational facilities, schools, fire and police protection, places of worship, streets, water supplies, levees, drainage control systems, irrigation systems, customary utilities, etc.;

5. A statement of the nature, type and capacity of improvements to be installed by the developer and the proposed dates of completion for sections offered for sale and estimated dates of completion for sections not yet offered for sale. The developer may indicate that the estimated dates of completion of improvements in sections not yet offered for sale are subject to market conditions and other variables, or similar qualifying language. Also, a statement of any approvals not yet obtained, the acquisition of which is a precondition to the completion of such improvements, and whether the identified improvements will be dedicated to public use;

6. A statement of the proposed method of operation and management of the common elements and facilities, and of all fixed, estimated or proposed fees, assessments, and reserves for future replacement and repair of common elements. If there are no provisions for reserves, a statement indicating same shall be included. If the proposed offering is a condominium, time-share or homeowners association, or involves any common ownership interest, in addition to the amount set aside as reserves for the replacement or repair of the common elements and facilities, the risk to purchasers if the applicant fails to sell out shall also be stated. A statement indicating whether the applicant is subsidizing the maintenance fee or plans to subsidize the maintenance fee during sales prior to transfer of control to any association, and if so, the amount of the subsidy and the probable effect of the cessation of the payment of the subsidy upon the maintenance fee payable by each owner shall also be included;

7. A description of any management or service contract, lease or other contract or agreement affecting the use, maintenance or access from and to any and all of the common elements or community facilities, together with a statement as to the effect of each upon the purchaser;

8. A statement of the relationship, if any, between the applicant and any management or servicing agent or firm;

9. A statement explaining any restrictions on occupancy, on the right of alienation and on the right of alteration of the lot, parcel, unit or interest, and on the use of any common facilities or amenities;

10. The significant terms of any encumbrances, easements, liens and restrictions including, but not limited to, zoning regulations affecting such lands and each lot, parcel, unit or interest, as well as the uses on and the zoning classification of adjoining lands at the time of registration, consolidation or the last filed annual report;

11. A statement as to whether the property or any portion thereof is regularly or periodically subject to natural forces that would tend to adversely affect the use or enjoyment of the property and whether the property or any portion thereof is located in a Federally designated flood hazard area;

12. A statement as to whether the property or any portion thereof is subject to man-made forces that would

tend to adversely affect the use or enjoyment of the property such as, but not limited to, the property's proximity to airports or flight paths, railroads, noisy or polluting industrial use, landfills, dumps, nuclear or toxic waste facilities or other similar forces;

13. A statement of all current or estimated taxes;

14. A statement of all existing or proposed special taxes and proposed assessments or assessments of record and identifying who shall be responsible for payment thereof;

15. A statement of all of the estimated title closing or settlement costs to be paid by the purchaser, including, but not limited to, all costs that are charged by the applicant and its agents and any person or entity controlled by the applicant;

16. A statement explaining the warranty or guarantee given by the applicant, if any, and the rights and remedies of the purchaser;

17. A statement by the applicant confirming that all monies paid by New Jersey residents to the applicant or his agents prior to closing will be held in escrow or in trust or guaranteed by some other means acceptable to the Commission, and which shall include all of the information required to be provided in applications for registration by N.J.A.C. 11:5–9.4(a)3.

18. A statement printed in 10–point boldface type or larger, conspicuously located, which states that the purchaser has the right to cancel any contract or agreement for the purchase of any lot, parcel, unit or interest in the development, without cause, by sending or delivering written notice of cancellation to the developer or his agent by midnight of the seventh calendar day following the day on which such contract or agreement was executed and that all monies paid will be promptly refunded, and further stating that the purchaser should read the Public Offering Statement in its entirety before signing any contracts or paying any monies;

19. A statement indicating that, regardless of whether the registrant offers or recommends financing the purchase of an interest in the subdivision through a particular lender or lenders, alternate sources of financing are available;

20. Where applicable, a statement explaining the nature, type and amount of hazard and liability insurance supplied or to be supplied by the applicant or association and what the insurance covers and an explanation of the nature and type of hazard and liability insurance available to the owner, and the necessity of flood or hazard insurance; and

21. Any additional information required by the Commission to assure full and fair disclosure to prospective purchasers.

(f) Applicants and registrants shall immediately report to the Commission any material change, as defined in N.J.A.C. 11:5–9.10(b), in the information contained in any proposed or approved Public Offering Statement and shall simultaneously submit a request for approval of the appropriate amendment.

(g) The Commission shall process and review requests for amendments to Public Offering Statements in accordance with the standards and procedures established in N.J.A.C. 11:5–9.10.

(h) The Public Offering Statement shall not be used for any promotional purposes before registration of the project, and thereafter only if used in its entirety.

1. No Public Offering Statement shall indicate, and no person shall represent or imply, that the Commission approves the merits of, or recommends the purchase of, an interest in the properties described in the offering.

(i) Prior to distributing a Public Offering Statement as required by N.J.A.C. 11:5–9.14(i) written in a language other than English, registrants who advertise in a language other than English shall file with the Commission copies of the Public Offering Statement approved by the Commission printed in both English and in the language in which the advertising appears. That filing shall be accompanied by a certification attesting to the accuracy of the translation of the text of the Public Offering Statement. The certification shall be in a form as specified by the Commission and signed by an authorized representative of the registrant and a qualified translator.

Amended by R.1997 d.161, effective April 7, 1997 (operative July 1, 1997).
See: 29 N.J.R. 303(a), 29 N.J.R. 1325(a).
Added (i).
Amended by R.1998 d.497, effective October 5, 1998.
See: 30 N.J.R. 2333(a), 30 N.J.R. 3646(a).
Rewrote the section.

Case Notes

New Jersey Land Sales Full Disclosure Act discriminated in its plain effect against interstate commerce and violated dormant commerce clause. Old Coach Development Corp., Inc. v. Tanzman, C.A.3 (N.J.)1989, 881 F.2d 1227.

11:5–9.6 Representation of applicants and registrants by New Jersey real estate brokers

(a) The applicant shall designate a currently licensed New Jersey real estate broker as its original broker of record with the initial application for registration, and such broker and any substituted or supplemental brokers must comply with the New Jersey Real Estate Brokers and Salesmen Act, N.J.S.A. 45:15–1 et seq., and the rules promulgated thereunder. An applicant/registrant may substitute another broker for the one initially designated. The initially designated broker and all substituted brokers shall execute an affidavit in accordance with N.J.A.C. 11:5–9.4(a)1.

1. The applicant may designate, in addition to the broker of record, other brokers who may join in the disposition of the registered property subject to filing the proper application with the Commission. The additional brokers, known as supplemental brokers, shall also execute an affidavit as required by N.J.A.C. 11:5–9.4(a). Nothing herein shall prevent any New Jersey broker from cooperating with any other New Jersey broker in any transaction, in accordance with N.J.A.C. 11:5–6.4(c). For the purposes of this section, persons who are licensed as New Jersey real estate brokers, and who have been designated by the applicant/registrant and approved by the Commission as the broker of record or as a supplemental broker for a particular subdivision, and who have been issued a current brokers release for that subdivision, are considered authorized brokers.

(b) Only authorized brokers may receive commissions from the registrant for the sale of interests in registered properties within New Jersey.

(c) Only authorized brokers and persons licensed under them may distribute literature on, or personally or via telephone solicit for prospective purchasers or offer or attempt to negotiate the sale or rental of an interest in a registered property, or provide or prepare contracts in New Jersey pertaining to registered property.

1. Where permitted by local law, unlicensed employees of a registrant working in the situs state and/or from the offices of the registrant may mail to New Jersey purchasers promotional literature on registered properties and may make appointments for New Jersey purchasers to inspect registered properties, provided that such persons make no material representations about such properties.

2. An authorized broker or a person licensed under them shall be present at any promotional booth maintained by a registrant or an agent of a registrant at any trade show or similar exhibition in New Jersey, and at any seminar promoting the sale or rental of registered property conducted by a registrant or any agent of a registrant in this State.

(d) All authorized brokers shall:

1. Prominently display the current broker's release;

2. Provide a copy of the current New Jersey Public Offering Statement to all New Jersey purchasers with whom they have had contact prior to the signing of any contract;

3. Obtain a signed and dated receipt for the same from the purchaser in all cases where the broker provides the Public Offering Statement to the purchaser, which receipt shall be maintained as a business record by the broker in accordance with N.J.A.C. 11:5–5.4; and

4. In all cases where the broker provides or prepares a contract which is signed by a New Jersey purchaser, the broker shall maintain a copy of that contract as a business record in accordance with N.J.A.C. 11:5–5.4.

(e) New Jersey brokers may not represent unregistered subdivisions or sections of unregistered subdivisions unless such projects are exempted from registration pursuant to N.J.S.A. 45:15–16.32 and N.J.A.C. 11:5–9.18.

Amended by R.1998 d.497, effective October 5, 1998.
See: 30 N.J.R. 2333(a), 30 N.J.R. 3646(a).
Deleted former (e); recodified former (f) as (e); and changed N.J.A.C. references throughout the section.

Case Notes

New Jersey Land Sales Full Disclosure Act discriminated in its plain effect against interstate commerce and violated dormant commerce clause. Old Coach Development Corp., Inc. v. Tanzman, C.A.3 (N.J.)1989, 881 F.2d 1227.

11:5–9.7 Fees with respect to the sale of interstate properties

(a) All applicants for registration shall pay application fees as prescribed in N.J.S.A. 45:15–16.34.

(b) All applicants for an exemption or a limited exemption shall pay application fees as prescribed in N.J.A.C. 11:5–9.18.

(c) Any request for approval of a material change in, or an amendment to, an application for registration and/or an Order of Registration and/or a Public Offering Statement shall be accompanied by a fee of $250.00. No fee shall be charged for amendments to applications or proposed Public Offering Statements made prior to the issuance of an Order of Registration.

1. If applications for approval of a material change in and/or for an amendment to an Order of Registration and/or an amendment to a Public Offering Statement are made simultaneously, only one fee will be payable;

2. If applications are made for approval of multiple material changes, and/or multiple amendments to an Order of Registration, and/or multiple amendments to a Public Offering Statement simultaneously, only one fee will be payable.

(d) The Commission shall maintain a copy of every application for registration, together with all amendments thereto, that has been approved and shall make them reasonably available for public inspection during ordinary business hours at the Commission's office.

1. The Commission will furnish to the public, upon request, a copy of the statement of record of any registered subdivision at a cost of $0.50 per page.

(e) All fees paid are non-refundable.

Amended by R.1998 d.497, effective October 5, 1998.
See: 30 N.J.R. 2333(a), 30 N.J.R. 3646(a).
In (b), changed N.J.A.C. reference; and in (c), deleted former 3.

11:5–9.8 Issuance by the Commission of a Notice of Filing

(a) Upon receipt of an application for registration in proper form and accompanied by payment of the required filing fee in the correct amount as prescribed by N.J.S.A. 45:15–16.34, the Commission shall, within 10 business days of its receipt of the same, issue a Notice of Filing to the applicant. The notice of filing shall not be construed as an approval of the registration or any portion thereof.

1. The date of filing shall be considered as the date when all required documents have been submitted in proper form and all fees, including the inspection fee, if requested, have been paid.

11:5–9.9 Inspection of properties by the Commission

(a) As provided in N.J.S.A. 45:15–16.41, the Commission, at its discretion, may make on-site inspections of any subdivision which is the subject of an application for registration, either before an Order of Registration has been issued or thereafter. In any instance where an Order of Registration has been issued prior to the subdivision being inspected by the Commission, such Order shall be considered conditional and subject to the results of the Commission's inspection of the premises. The Commission may at its discretion conduct subsequent on-site inspections.

(b) The costs of inspections shall be paid by the applicant who shall provide a deposit when requested by the Commission. After the inspection the Commission shall provide the applicant/registrant with a statement of costs incurred and a refund of any portion of the deposit not expended or a request for additional funds if required.

11:5–9.10 Amendments to registration applications and Public Offering Statements

(a) The registrant shall immediately file with the Commission amendments to its registration application and/or Public Offering Statement reflecting any material change(s) in previously supplied information or documents, in order that the information provided purchasers is current.

(b) Material change means, but is not limited to, any significant change in the size or character of the development or interest being offered or anything having a significant effect on the rights, duties or obligations of the developer or purchaser.

1. Changes in selling prices and advertising, the identity of the officers and directors of a registrant, and notice of the completion of improvements on a timely basis as represented in a previously approved Public Offering Statement are not considered material changes.

2. The transfer of control of any association responsible for the maintenance of common areas and/or the operation of common facilities or amenities by the registrant to the owners of interests in the subdivision is a material change.

(c) Subsequent to the Commission having approved a Public Offering Statement, no revised Public Offering Statement shall be given to prospective purchasers without the approval of the Commission.

1. Applications for approval of an amended or corrected Public Offerings Statement shall be made by filing a red-lined copy of the proposed Revised Public Offering Statement with the Commission and an application update.

(d) The Commission shall process and review requests for amendments to Orders of Registration and Public Offering Statements in accordance with the standards and procedures established in the Act and this subchapter for the review of applications for registration. Requests for amendments shall be accompanied by a fee of $250.00, as provided in N.J.A.C. 11:5–9.7.

Amended by R.1998 d.497, effective October 5, 1998.
See: 30 N.J.R. 2333(a), 30 N.J.R. 3646(a).
Rewrote (b) and (c); and in (d), changed N.J.A.C. reference.

11:5–9.11 Annual reporting upon and the termination of registrations

(a) No later than 30 days after the anniversary date of the latest Order of Registration, and while the registrant retains any interest in the subdivision, the registrant shall file, on a form designated by the Commission, an annual report reflecting any material changes in the information contained in the original application for registration or in the most recent Annual Report previously filed.

1. This requirement shall not diminish the obligation of the registrant to notify the Commission of material changes as they occur.

2. The annual report shall contain an audited financial statement or compilation prepared by an independent public accountant showing the receipts and expenditures of any association serving the project and under the control of the registrant, which financial statements shall be compiled on a yearly basis, and certified if required by the situs state.

3. The yearly audit submitted with the annual report shall be the most current audit available. In no event may the date of the yearly audit be earlier than 18 months prior to the date of the annual report. The registrant will not have to file a separate audit with the Commission for any association controlled by the owners of interests in the subdivision.

(b) The registrant may file an application for termination of its obligations with the Commission in which the registrant shall certify the grounds for termination.

1. Upon a determination by the Commission that an annual report is no longer necessary for the protection of the public interest because the registrant no longer retains any interest and no longer has any contractual, bond or other obligations to New Jersey purchasers in the subdivision, including having fulfilled all undertakings referred to in the Public Offering Statement, and the registrant has ceased all marketing activity in New Jersey, the Commission shall issue an order terminating the responsibilities of the registrant under the Act upon the registrant making application for the issuance of an Order of Termination, accompanied by acceptable proofs that the above requirements have been met.

11:5–9.12 Home builders

Unless exempt pursuant to N.J.S.A. 45:15–16.32, a home builder selling house and lot packages offered as part of a common promotional plan, regardless of whether the lots are contiguous, is a "subdivider" as defined in N.J.S.A. 45:15–16.28, and therefore such offerings are subject to the Act and to this subchapter.

11:5–9.13 Grounds for denial of registration applications and for the revocation of Orders of Registration

A finding that an applicant or registrant has previously been determined to have engaged in unfair acts and/or fraudulent or deceptive practices by the Federal Trade Commission, or as set forth in the Federal Interstate Land Sales Full Disclosure Act (82 Stat. 590; 15 U.S.C. § 1701 et seq.), or to have violated the Act and/or similar acts in other States, may constitute grounds for the Commission, after providing the applicant or registrant with the opportunity for a hearing pursuant to the Administrative Procedure Act, N.J.S.A. 52:14B–1 et seq., and the Uniform Administrative Procedure Rules, N.J.A.C. 1:1, to refuse to issue or to revoke an Order of Registration.

11:5–9.14 Advertising and sales promotions with respect to the sale and marketing of registered properties

(a) Advertisements that refer to the purchase price of any lot, unit, parcel or interest in real estate shall state the full purchase price and shall disclose any known or estimated additional assessments or costs to the purchaser.

1. In order to eliminate fictitious pricing or illusionary discounts, no certificates shall be distributed indicating that a discount from the advertised price shall be given. This shall not preclude the giving of a discount on the basis of any reasonable criteria.

2. Advertising shall not refer to a price increase unless the amount and date of the increase are indicated.

(b) Advertising that contains statements regarding taxes shall not use terms such as "low" and "stable", but shall state what the current taxes are, or an accurate estimate of such taxes based on current tax rates or value ratios.

1. Any reference to proposed improvements for which the purchaser will be assessed shall clearly set forth the facts of the assessment and the estimated amount of the assessment.

2. Advertising shall not state that items or services are free when the cost thereof is included in the assessment.

(c) Advertising shall not refer to any common element or facility that does not presently exist unless that fact is prominently stated in the advertising, accompanied by the proposed date of completion, which shall also appear prominently in the advertising.

(d) Advertising shall not contain photographs, sketches or artist's conceptions unless the fact that these are conceptions are stated immediately adjacent to them in the advertisement.

(e) Advertising shall not refer in wording, photograph, sketch or conception to any recreation, medical, social, shopping or other facility that is not located within the subdivision unless it clearly states that the facilities are not located in the subdivision and states the approximate distance therefrom in miles via paved roads.

(f) Any model unit that is used as part of a promotional plan shall be in substantial conformity with the units that are subsequently constructed unless otherwise noted in the contract of sale. If changes are to be made in the units other than landscaping, appliances, furnishings, heating, air conditioning, electrical or plumbing, a legible notice shall be conspicuously placed in the model, or picture photo or rendering of the model, advertising prospective purchasers of the change. In the event that there are items in the model that are available only at additional cost, legible notice informing purchasers that the items are available only at additional cost should be posted in a prominent place in the model.

(g) When properties or interests therein are not registered with the Commission, nor wholly or partially exempt from the Act, and advertisements regarding such properties or interests are placed in any media which is distributed in or broadcast into the State of New Jersey, a disclaimer shall be included, indicating that the properties or interests are not registered with the New Jersey Real Estate Commission, and that the advertisement is not an offer to New Jersey residents.

1. As a result of their failure to register such properties or interests pursuant to N.J.S.A. 45:15–16.27 et seq., the owners of such properties or interests may not make, or cause to be made, an offer or disposition of the properties or interests in this State, nor direct any offer of such properties or interests originating outside of this State to a person or resident within this State.

(h) Advertisements which contain offers of premiums or of reimbursement of travel expenses in cash or merchandise shall be subject to the following:

1. The promotional material shall clearly and conspicuously state the necessity of attendance at or submission to a sales promotion, the minimum length of time required to be spent at such sales promotion in order to qualify for reimbursement or other premium or inducement, the terms and conditions of the offer, and the retail value of any premiums offered;

i. Such advertisements shall also include a statement indicating that the promotion is a solicitation for the sale of timeshares, condominiums, lots, or other interests in real estate as applicable, the name of the project and the registration number assigned to the project by the Commission preceded by: "N.J. Reg. No."

2. "Travel expenses" may be reimbursed in cash or by merchandise;

3. Any advertisements, including those which contain offers of reimbursement of travel expenses, offers of premiums, or other inducements must also comply with the provisions of the New Jersey Consumer Fraud Act (N.J.S.A. 56:8–1 et seq.).

(i) Registrants who advertise in a language other than English shall make available to prospective purchasers all disclosure documents, including, but not limited to, the Public Offering Statement, and the sales contract written in the same language as that used in the registrant's advertisements.

Amended by R.1997 d.161, effective April 7, 1997 (operative July 1, 1997).
See: 29 N.J.R. 303(a), 29 N.J.R. 1325(a).
Added (i).
Amended by R.1998 d.497, effective October 5, 1998.
See: 30 N.J.R. 2333(a), 30 N.J.R. 3646(a).
Rewrote (g) and (h).

11:5–9.15 Compliance with situs state requirements

Any instrument evidencing the sale or disposition of an interest in a registered property shall be executed in accordance with the laws of the situs state. An applicant/registrant may be required to submit proof of compliance.

11:5–9.16 Improvements to be made at registered properties

(a) A property in a subdivision, or any part thereof, on which construction of a promised improvement for public use, convenience or necessity has not been completed, shall not be registered for disposition unless completion of the improvement is assured by a court order, or government approved improvement district with sufficient taxing or other authority to raise adequate capital to assure completion, or a substantial completion bond or similar undertaking acceptable to the Commission as provided in (c) below, or by adequate reserves established and maintained in a trust or escrow account meeting the following criteria:

1. Such funds shall be kept and maintained in an escrow account separate and apart from the registrant's funds and from any other escrowed funds;

2. The account shall be established in a bank or trust company doing business in this State or the situs state, and approved by the Commission; and

3. The trust or escrow agreement shall have as its purpose the protection of the purchaser or prospective purchaser in the event of a failure to complete construction of promised improvements or a failure to satisfy any obligations or liens encumbering the purchaser's title by reason of the construction.

(b) A property in a subdivision, or a part thereof, on which construction of a promised improvement not for public use, convenience or necessity is represented or implied, shall not be registered for disposition to the public where such improvement has not been completed, unless completion is assured by:

1. An adequate plan of development, including financial resources committed to carry out the plan as provided in (c) below, which plan is subject to the Commission's continuing review and approval; or

2. Adequate funds maintained in a trust or escrow account, or an irrevocable bank letter of credit.

(c) The Commission may accept surety bonds, escrow accounts, irrevocable bank letters of credit, or any other financial security adequate to assure a plan of development. In determining the security required, the Commission shall examine the status of improvements, the overall cost of improvements, the terms of purchaser contracts, the financial condition of the subdivider and such other data as it considers necessary. The Commission may consider whatever financial security has been posted with other governmental authorities in making its determination.

11:5–9.17 Contracts for the purchase of an interest in a registered property

(a) All contracts or agreements for the disposition of a lot, parcel, unit or interest in a registered subdivision shall not impose undue restrictions or hardships upon the purchaser. All contracts shall be in accordance with the laws of the situs state, except that they shall conform to the Real Estate Sales Full Disclosure Act and to this subchapter, and all conflicts shall be resolved to the satisfaction of the Commission.

(b) Any contract or agreement for the purchase of any lot, parcel, unit or interest in a registered subdivision may be cancelled without cause, by the purchaser sending or delivering written notice of cancellation by midnight of the seventh calendar day following the date on which such contract or agreement was executed. Upon receipt of such a notice of cancellation, the developer or his agent shall promptly refund all monies to the purchaser.

(c) Every contract or agreement shall contain the following notice in 10–point boldfaced type or larger, directly above the space provided for the signature of the purchaser:

> NOTICE to PURCHASER or LESSEE: You have the right to cancel this contract by midnight of the seventh calendar day following the day on which you have executed this contract or agreement. You should read this entire contract and the Public Offering Statement on this project before signing any documents or paying any monies.

(d) All contracts which contain provisions requiring the payment of deposit monies shall contain a statement describing how the deposit moneys will be maintained in escrow or otherwise secured as provided in N.J.A.C. 11:5–9.4(a)3.

(e) Prior to using a contract or an agreement for the disposition of a lot, parcel, unit or interest in a registered subdivision that is written in a language other than English, as required by N.J.A.C. 11:5–9.14(i), registrants who advertise in a language other than English shall file with the Commission copies of the contract accepted by the Commission that are printed in both English and in the language in which the advertising appears. That filing shall be accompanied by a certification attesting to the accuracy of the translation of the text of the contract. The certification shall be in a form as specified by the Commission and signed by an authorized representative of the registrant and a qualified translator.

Amended by R.1997 d.161, effective April 7, 1997 (operative July 1, 1997).
See: 29 N.J.R. 303(a), 29 N.J.R. 1325(a).
Added (e).
Amended by R.1998 d.497, effective October 5, 1998.
See: 30 N.J.R. 2333(a), 30 N.J.R. 3646(a).
Rewrote (d); and in (e), changed N.J.A.C. reference.

Case Notes

New Jersey Land Sales Full Disclosure Act discriminated in its plain effect against interstate commerce and violated dormant commerce clause. Old Coach Development Corp., Inc. v. Tanzman, C.A.3 (N.J.)1989, 881 F.2d 1227.

11:5–9.18 Exemptions from the provisions of N.J.S.A. 45:15–16.27 et seq.

(a) Any person who believes that property may be exempt from the provisions of the Act, or who is contemplating marketing property in New Jersey which he believes may be exempt, may apply to the Commission for a Letter of Exemption. Such application shall be in written affidavit form and shall list the reasons why such property or proposed project may be exempt from the Act. Such an application for exemption shall be accompanied by a nonrefundable fee of $80.00.

1. In the event the Commission shall determine that such property is exempt from the Act, it shall issue a Letter of Exemption setting forth the facts upon which the determination is based.

2. In the event the Commission shall determine that such property is not exempt from the provisions of the Act, it shall deny the request for exemption in writing, setting forth therein the facts upon which the determination is based, and shall send such writing to the applicant via certified mail, return receipt requested.

3. Any person who is aggrieved by such a determination is entitled to a hearing on such determination, provided said hearing is requested in writing no later than 30 days from the date of the applicant's receiving notice of such determination.

4. The Commission shall issue a determination as to whether a property is, or is not, exempt within 30 days of its receipt of a complete request for exemption, with the appropriate fee.

(b) If the nature of the property and/or of the proposed offering indicate that the applicant would be subject to the registration requirements of the Act, the applicant may apply to the Commission for a limited exemption. If the commission determines that enforcement of the entire Act and of all of these rules is not necessary in the public interest or for the protection of purchasers, due to the small amounts involved or the limited character of the offering, it may issue a "Limited Exemption" from registration to the applicant.

1. A limited exemption may be granted by reason of the small number of lots, parcels, units or interests to be offered only if all improvements necessary for the use of the property have been completed, or adequate surety and/or financial assurances for completion of promised improvements and amenities has been established. No limited exemption may be granted with regard to property contiguous or reasonably contiguous to property for which a limited exemption has previously been granted and which is being offered by the same applicant, or by a predecessor or successor in title to or an affiliate of that applicant.

2. A limited exemption may be granted by reason of the limited character of the offering where the nature of the property, or of the prospective purchasers to whom the property will be offered, is such that it is likely prospective purchasers will have expert advice concerning the purchase independent of that supplied by the applicant or his agents. An application for a limited exemption for this reason shall include a copy of any prospectus, offering statement or other such solicitation. A limited exemption granted for this reason shall be confined to the group of offerees specified in the application.

3. An application for a limited exemption shall specify the particular lots, parcels, units or interests for which exemption is sought. Any limited exemption granted

shall be confined to those lots, parcels, units or interests so specified.

4. An application for a limited exemption shall include a narrative description that clearly describes the nature of the subdivision and the factual basis and reasons why the limited exemption should be granted.

5. The Commission shall assign a New Jersey exemption number beginning with the prefix "N.J.E." to each project to which a limited exemption is issued. This number shall thereafter appear on all publications or broadcasts of advertisements of the exempted project which include offers of a premium or to provide or reimburse the cost of travel which are directed to citizens of this State, or which appear in national or regional advertising circulated within this State.

6. Any limited exemption granted shall remain in effect for a period of two years from the date of issuance indicated in the Letter of Exemption, unless revoked as described below.

7. Any limited exemption granted shall permit the recipient to offer the property to New Jersey residents without obtaining an Order of Registration. A limited exemption shall not deprive the Commission of jurisdiction to enforce any other provision of the Act or this subchapter, or to revoke the limited exemption after notice and an opportunity to be heard.

8. A $250.00 non-refundable fee shall be tendered with any application for a limited exemption.

9. All applications for a limited exemption shall comply with the following minimum requirements:

i. The filing of an exemption application affidavit-questionnaire;

ii. The filing of proof of title and a plat map specifying the lots or units to be exempted, with colored shading;

iii. The requirements for the securing of all deposits, down payments, or funds of others as prescribed in this subchapter;

iv. The filing of satisfactory proof of surety and/or financial assurances for any promised improvements or amenities;

v. The advertisement standards and procedures established at N.J.A.C. 11:5–9.14; and

vi. The filing of any other documents that the Commission may deem necessary.

10. Any applicant granted a limited exemption by the Commission, pursuant to this subchapter, shall comply with the annual reporting requirements of N.J.S.A. 45:15–16.40 and N.J.A.C. 11:5–9.11.

11. No limited exemption granted hereunder shall be effective until a Letter of Limited Exemption is issued by the Commission to the applicant for the exemption.

12. A copy of the New Jersey Letter of Limited Exemption, or of a Public Offering Statement approved by the Commission, shall be provided to each New Jersey purchaser prior to their signing any contract for the purchase of an interest in property included within the limited exemption issued by the Commission, and a receipt obtained for the same shall be kept on file for seven years by the recipient of the limited exemption.

13. Any material change in the information reflected on the application for a limited exemption or on any documentation submitted in support of such application, shall immediately void any exemption issued based upon such application.

Amended by R.1998 d.497, effective October 5, 1998.
See: 30 N.J.R. 2333(a), 30 N.J.R. 3646(a).
In (b), rewrote 5, deleted "The Commission shall determine what constitutes a material change" from the end of 13, and changed N.J.A.C. references throughout.

SUBCHAPTER 10. PETITIONS FOR RULEMAKING

11:5–10.1 Petitions for rulemaking—scope

This subchapter shall apply to all petitions made by interested persons for the promulgation, amendments or repeal of any rule by the New Jersey Real Estate Commission, as required by N.J.S.A. 52:14B–4(f).

11:5–10.2 Procedure for the submission of petitions for rulemaking

(a) Any interested person may petition the Real Estate Commission to promulgate, amend or repeal a rule. Such petition shall state clearly and concisely:

1. The full name and address of the petitioner;

2. The substance or nature of the rulemaking which is requested;

3. The reasons for the request;

4. The petitioner's interest in the request, including, without limitation, any relevant organizational affiliation or economic interest; and

5. References to the Commission's authority to take the requested action.

(b) Petitions should be sent to the following address:

New Jersey Real Estate Commission
PO Box 328
Trenton, New Jersey 08625–0328

(c) Filing a petition shall be made by forwarding an original and two copies to the Commission at the address indicated in (b) above.

(d) Any document submitted to the Real Estate Commission which is not in substantial compliance with (a) above shall not be deemed to be a petition for a rule requiring further Commission action pursuant to N.J.S.A. 52:14B(f).

(e) Within 30 days of its receipt of a petition for rulemaking, the Commission shall review the same to ascertain if the submission complies with the requirements of (a) above and, in the event that the Commission determines that the submission is not in substantial compliance with (a) above, the Commission shall notify the petitioner of such noncompliance and of the particular deficiency or deficiencies in the submission on which the decision of the Commission was based. The Commission shall also advise the petitioner that any deficiencies may be corrected and the petition may be re-submitted for further consideration.

11:5–10.3 Procedure for the consideration and disposition of rulemaking petitions

(a) Upon receipt of a petition in compliance with N.J.A.C. 11:5–10.2, the Commission will file a notice of petition with the Office of Administrative Law for publication in the New Jersey Register. The notice will include:

1. The name of the petitioner;

2. The substance or nature of the rulemaking action which is requested;

3. The problem or purpose which is the subject of the request; and

4. The date the petition was received.

(b) Within 30 days of receiving the petition, the Commission will consider the petition and decide upon an action on the petition. The petitioner may be requested to attend a Commission meeting and answer questions concerning the petition. The Commission will mail to the petitioner, and file with the Office of Administrative Law for publication in the New Jersey Register, a notice of action on the petition which will include:

1. The name of the petitioner;

2. The New Jersey Register citation for the notice of petition, if that notice appeared in a previous Register;

3. Certification by the Commission that the petition was duly considered pursuant to law;

4. The nature or substance of the Commission's action upon the petition; and

5. A brief statement of reasons for the Commission's action.

(c) Commission action on a petition may include:

1. Denying the petition;

2. Filing a notice of proposed rule or a notice of pre-proposal for a rule with the Office of Administrative Law; or

3. Referring the matter for further deliberations, the nature of which will be specified and which will conclude upon a specified date. The results of these further deliberations will be mailed to the petitioner and submitted to the OAL for publication in the New Jersey Register.

Amended by R.1998 d.497, effective October 5, 1998.
See: 30 N.J.R. 2333(a), 30 N.J.R. 3646(a).
In (a), changed N.J.A.C. reference.

11:5–10.4 Public hearings for promulgation, amending or repealing rules

(a) The Commission may hold a public hearing to gather information concerning any proposed rule, amendment, or repeal.

(b) The Commission shall publish a notice of the place, date and time of the hearing at least 15 business days before the date of the hearing.

SUBCHAPTER 11. PROCEDURES ON DISCIPLINARY ACTIONS, CONTESTED APPLICATIONS, DECLARATORY RULING REQUESTS

11:5–11.1 Pleadings enumerated and defined

(a) Pleadings before the Commission shall be orders to show cause, complaints, answers, petitions, and motions, which for purposes of these rules are defined as follows:

1. "Orders to show cause" means orders issued by the Director on behalf of the New Jersey Real Estate Commission compelling the persons to whom the order is directed to appear and show cause before the Commission why certain actions, including but not limited to the imposition of sanctions, should not be taken by the Commission pursuant to the Real Estate Licensing Act, N.J.S.A. 45:15–1 et seq. and the rules promulgated thereunder.

2. "Complaint" means a filing by the Office of the Attorney General of New Jersey alleging violations of one or more of the provisions of N.J.S.A. 45:15–1 et seq. and/or of the Commission's rules.

3. "Answer" means the pleading filed by a licensee or other party against whom an order to show cause or complaint is directed which sets forth the respondent's position with the respect to each factual and legal allegation in the order or complaint and specifies all affirmative defenses raised by the respondent.

4. "Petition" means the pleading filed by an interested person to request a rulemaking action or declaratory ruling by the Commission or the pleading filed by an interested person seeking to intervene in any rulemaking or declaratory ruling proceeding.

5. "Motion" means the application filed incidental to an action before the Commission for the purpose of obtaining a ruling or order directing that some action be taken in favor of the movant.

(b) Documents, affidavits or other evidentiary matter submitted with or attached to a pleading other than a motion shall not be deemed evidentiary. Such materials must be offered into evidence at a hearing and admitted as such in order to be considered as part of the evidentiary record.

11:5–11.2 Answers

(a) Any party against whom an order to show cause or complaint is directed and who desires to contest the same or make any representation to the Commission in connection therewith shall file an answer in writing with the Commission.

(b) The answer shall apprise the Commission fully and completely of the nature of all defenses and shall admit or deny specifically and in detail all material allegations of the order to show cause or complaint.

(c) Matters alleged by way of affirmative defense shall be separately stated and numbered in the answer.

(d) An Answer must be filed within 20 days after service of the Order to Show Cause or complaint unless the deputy attorney general or staff member who represents the complainant consents, or the Commission orders an extension of time to Answer.

(e) Filing of an Answer shall be made by forwarding an original and two copies to the Director of the Commission and a copy to the deputy attorney general or staff member who is representing the complainant in the matter.

Amended by R.1998 d.497, effective October 5, 1998.
See: 30 N.J.R. 2333(a), 30 N.J.R. 3646(a).
In (d), inserted "or staff member" following "attorney general"; and rewrote (e).

11:5–11.3 Adversary hearing determination by the Commission

(a) Promptly after the answer is filed, the Commission will review the pleadings at a Commission meeting and decide whether any material fact or issue of law is contested. If the Commission determines that a matter is contested, a hearing will be scheduled. On its own motion or at the request of either party, the Commission may, in its discretion, transmit the case to the Office of Administrative Law for hearing and initial decision.

(b) If, upon review of the pleadings, the Commission determines that no material facts or issues of law are contested, the Commission shall afford the respondent an opportunity to be heard and to present witnesses and documentary evidence, which presentation shall be limited to the issue of the severity of any sanction or penalty to be imposed. By stipulation or other means, the deputy attorney general or staff member representing the complainant shall present evidence sufficient to establish the factual basis for all alleged violations and may present documentary evidence or witnesses in rebuttal of any mitigation testimony or evidence presented by the respondent.

Amended by R.1998 d.497, effective October 5, 1998.
See: 30 N.J.R. 2333(a), 30 N.J.R. 3646(a).
In (b), inserted "or staff member" following "attorney general" in the second sentence.

11:5–11.4 Motions

(a) In all matters heard by the Commission, motions and replies shall be made in the manner and form prescribed by the rules which establish the procedures for motion practice before the Office of Administrative Law, N.J.A.C. 1:1–12. In construing those rules, the terms "Executive Director" and "Commission" are substituted for the terms "Clerk" and "Judge", respectively.

(b) Filing of a motion or reply shall be made by forwarding an original and 15 copies to the Director of the Commission and a copy to all other attorneys and pro se parties, if any, in the matter.

(c) A motion shall be considered by the Commission at a regularly scheduled meeting pursuant to the requirements of N.J.A.C. 1:1–12.

(d) Oral argument on a motion when permitted or directed by the Commission shall be presented to the Commission by the parties or their representatives in person at a Commission meeting; motions will not be heard by telephone conference.

(e) Motions for the reconsideration of sanctions imposed by the Commission must be filed within 30 days of the date upon which notice of the decision imposing sanctions was provided to the movant. Such motions must be accompanied by a recitation of the particular facts and legal basis which purportedly support the application.

Amended by R.1998 d.497, effective October 5, 1998.
See: 30 N.J.R. 2333(a), 30 N.J.R. 3646(a).
In (a), changed N.J.A.C. reference.

11:5–11.5 Conference hearing procedure

(a) The Director may, on behalf of the Commission, issue an Order to Show Cause requiring a licensee or other person to appear before the Commission for a conference hearing as defined in N.J.A.C. 1:1–2.1 in circumstances where violations of N.J.S.A. 45:15–17d, 17n, 17o and/or 19.1 are alleged to have occurred or where there is danger of imminent harm to the public.

(b) The order to show cause shall be served upon the respondent at least 10 days prior to the hearing.

(c) The respondent shall not be required to file a written answer, but shall be required to appear on the return date of the order to show cause and admit or deny the allegations in the order to show cause and present all defenses to the alleged violations.

(d) The respondent may notify the Commission by telephone or letter of any witnesses to be subpoenaed on the respondent's behalf and shall provide to the Commission the addresses at which such witnesses can be served.

(e) Discovery and motions in conference hearings shall be limited in accordance with N.J.A.C. 1:1–10.6 and 1:1–12.1, respectively.

Amended by R.1998 d.497, effective October 5, 1998.
See: 30 N.J.R. 2333(a), 30 N.J.R. 3646(a).
In (a), added an N.J.S.A. reference.

11:5–11.6 Sanctions: failure to answer or appear; default

(a) In all matters heard by the Commission, the imposition of sanctions for the failure to appear and/or to comply with any order of the Commission or the requirements of these procedural rules shall be governed by the procedures established for the imposition of sanctions in matters heard by the Office of Administrative Law at N.J.A.C. 1:1–14.4.

(b) The Commission shall have the discretionary authority to grant extensions of the time to file an answer or appear.

11:5–11.7 Settlements

(a) The parties to a proposed settlement shall present the settlement to the Commission pursuant to the requirements of N.J.A.C. 1:1–19.1.

(b) Such a settlement shall be presented to the Commission during the public session of a Commission meeting. Should a proposed settlement be rejected by the Commission, the proposal shall not be considered or used for any purpose in any subsequent hearing. Any settlement approved by the Commission shall be a public record.

11:5–11.8 Decisions in enforcement actions

All final decisions of the Real Estate Commission on contested and uncontested matters shall be reduced to writing, in the form of an Order of the Commission, which shall be served upon all parties to the matter either personally or by registered or certified mail sent to the last known business address of all parties. Unless otherwise ordered, all fines imposed by order of the Commission shall be payable within 30 days of the effective date of the order as established by the Administrative Procedure Act, N.J.S.A. 52:14B–1 et seq.

Amended by R.1998 d.497, effective October 5, 1998.
See: 30 N.J.R. 2333(a), 30 N.J.R. 3646(a).
Added a new last sentence.

11:5–11.9 Applications for temporary suspension

(a) The Commission may on its own motion, and upon the terms and conditions as set forth in N.J.S.A. 45:15–17.1 and as the Commission deems appropriate, enter an order temporarily suspending the license of any licensee upon making a finding that prima facie evidence exists that:

1. The licensee has failed to account for or to pay over any moneys belonging to others that have come into the possession of the licensee, in violation of N.J.S.A. 45:15–17(d); or

2. The licensee has commingled his or her personal money or property with the money or property of others or has failed to maintain and deposit such moneys in a special account, separate and apart from personal or other business accounts, when acting in the capacity of a real estate broker, or escrow agent, or as the temporary custodian of the funds of others, in a real estate transaction, in violation of N.J.S.A. 45:15–17(*o*).

(b) At least 24 hours prior to ordering a temporary suspension, the Commission shall give notice to the licensee of the application for the order and provide the licensee an opportunity to appear before the Commission to show cause why the license should not be suspended pending a full hearing of the matter. Such notice shall be given in writing or telephonically.

1. Written notice shall be served personally or sent by certified mail to the last known business address of the licensee.

2. Telephonic notice shall be confirmed in a writing sent to the licensee's last known business address as soon as practicable after the delivery of the telephonic notice.

3. The person who personally or telephonically delivers notice of an application for a temporary suspension shall execute a certification confirming that he or she has provided the notice, which certification shall be submitted into the record of the proceeding on the application for the temporary suspension.

(c) At the hearing on the application for the temporary suspension, the Commission shall consider evidence presented by the licensee to explain, disprove or rebut the prima facie evidence upon which the application for the temporary suspension is based. Unless otherwise provided in N.J.S.A. 45:15–17.1, the provisions of N.J.A.C. 1:1–12.6(f) shall apply to proceedings on applications for temporary suspensions.

(d) Prior to entering any order imposing a temporary suspension as provided in (a) above, the Commission shall also make findings that:

1. An adequate good faith effort to provide notice to the licensee was made and that the licensee was afforded an opportunity to be heard. Submission of the certifica-

tion referred to in (b) above shall be sufficient to establish that an adequate good faith effort was made to provide notice of the proceeding;

2. Based on the evidence presented, there is a substantial likelihood that the charging party will prevail on the merits when the matter is fully argued before the Commission; and

3. Immediate and irreparable harm will probably result before the licensee can be fully heard. Prima facie evidence of a violation of N.J.S.A. 45:15–17(d) or (*o*) shall be considered sufficient to satisfy this criterion.

(e) All orders imposing temporary suspensions shall advise the suspended licensee of the date upon which the Commission shall hold a full evidentiary hearing on the violations upon which the temporary suspension is based, which date shall be no more than 30 days following the effective date of the temporary suspension. Such a hearing shall be a plenary hearing, conducted in accordance with N.J.A.C. 1:1–14.1 through 14.7.

(f) The temporary suspension shall become effective upon issuance by the Commission, and the licensee and his or her broker shall promptly be notified of its issuance, whereupon the license of the suspended person shall immediately be returned to the Commission. The Commission shall confirm the suspension in a written order which shall be served upon the licensee and his or her broker via personal service or by certified mail, return receipt requested at the licensee's last known business address.

(g) In order to entertain applications for temporary suspensions made during time periods when the Commission is not scheduled to meet, or when a quorum cannot be obtained, the Commission may delegate to three commissioners, at least one of whom shall be either the President or Vice–President of the Commission and at least one of whom shall be a public member, the authority to temporarily suspend a license as provided in (a) through (f) above. In such circumstances, all references in these rules to the Commission shall be construed as referring to the three commissioners so designated by the Commission.

New Rule, R.1994 d.270, effective June 20, 1994 (operative July 1, 1994).
See: 26 N.J.R. 737(a), 26 N.J.R. 1222(a), 26 N.J.R. 2586(a).

Case Notes

Conviction of crime of theft compelled revocation of real estate salesperson's license. NJREC v. Belle, 96 N.J.A.R.2d (REC) 22.

Pending criminal trial for theft justified suspension of real estate salesperson's license. NJREC v. Reich, 96 N.J.A.R.2d (REC) 21.

11:5–11.10 Procedures applicable to appeals of initial denials of licensing applications

(a) Initial denials of the following applications may be appealed to the full Real Estate Commission through compliance with all of the requirements established in (b) below:

1. License applications, with the exception of reinstatement applications submitted beyond the statutorily established time limitations upon such reinstatements;

2. Applications from disabled veterans for education waivers and/or broker experience requirement waivers;

3. Applications for the issuance of education waivers by persons other than disabled veterans;

4. Applications for the issuance of broker experience requirement waivers by broker licensees of other states; and

5. Applications by broker license candidates for the Commission's approval of their experience as a salesperson so as to qualify to challenge the broker license examination.

(b) All appeals to the full Real Estate Commission provided for in (a) above shall be filed by the appealing applicant submitting to the Commission within 45 days of the date of the notice of denial an original and 15 copies of all of the documentation noted below:

1. A covering letter stating the factual and legal basis of the appeal, to which shall be attached a copy of the application and the denial letter which forms the basis of the appeal. The said covering letter shall also state whether the applicant desires to appear and present oral argument and/or testimony when the appeal is considered by the Commission;

2. Where the denial was based upon an applicant's prior criminal history and/or their loss of a professional license, all judgments of conviction on the convictions which form the basis of the denial and a letter from their probation or parole officer, if within one year of making the application they were under such supervision, which letter shall state the extent of the applicant's compliance with the terms and conditions of his or her probationary sentence or parole supervision, and/or a copy of the order or memorandum of settlement evidencing the loss of the professional license;

3. On all applications as described in (b)2 above, a letter from the broker with whom the applicant intends to be licensed, evidencing that person's full knowledge of the factors which formed the basis of the initial denial;

4. Any other relevant documentation which the applicant desires the Commission to consider when hearing the appeal; and

5. Any other documentation which the Commission determines is required in order to allow it to make a fully informed decision on the appeal.

(c) Upon the proper filing of an appeal as described in (b) above, the appeal package shall be reviewed and the applicant advised of the following:

1. The date, time and place at which the appeal will be considered by the full Real Estate Commission; or

2. That based upon the content of the appeal documents a determination has been made to approve the application; or

3. The appeal package is deficient in certain respects, which shall be specified to the applicant, with an indication that upon receipt of the missing documentation the appeal will be given further consideration.

(d) All applicants have the opportunity to be represented by counsel when submitting an appeal and/or appearing before the Real Estate Commission and to call witnesses to testify on their behalf at the time of its consideration of their appeal.

(e) Upon the conclusion of a hearing on an appeal, the Commission shall either render a decision or take the matter under advisement and render a decision at a future date. The ruling of the Commission shall be communicated to the applicant in written form promptly upon the decision being rendered.

Amended by R.1998 d.497, effective October 5, 1998.
See: 30 N.J.R. 2333(a), 30 N.J.R. 3646(a).
Rewrote (a).

ADOPTED RULE AMENDMENTS

The following amended rules became effective December 20, 1999. The rules prescribe the forms of payment which New Jersey real estate brokers may accept when receiving monies to be held in trust or in escrow by them, or which monies they are to hold as a temporary custodian. The rules impose specific disclosure and procedural requirements upon brokers who accept credit card charges in payment of deposits or rent on short-term rental transactions. Short-term rentals are the only type of transaction where brokers may accept credit card charges in payment of deposits or rent.

11:5-5.1 Special accounts for funds of others; commingling

(a) – (h) No change.

(i) Brokers may accept payments to be held in trust or in escrow, or as the temporary custodian of the funds of others in any real estate transaction in the following forms: cash; a negotiable instrument payable to the broker's firm; a charge against a check debit card resulting in a credit to the broker's trust or escrow account; or a wire transfer of funds directly from an account of the payor to the trust or escrow account of the broker. As provided herein, brokers may also accept deposit and rent payments to be held by them in trust or in escrow or as a temporary custodian in the form of charges made upon the credit cards of tenants in short term rental transactions.

1. All payments to be held by a broker in trust or in escrow, or as the temporary custodian of monies in a real estate transaction made in the form of cash, negotiable instruments, wire transfers or by charges made upon credit cards or check debit cards shall be recorded in the broker's trust or escrow account ledger and as otherwise required by N.J.A.C. 11:5-5.4.

2. Brokers shall not accept payments made through credit card charges in any real estate transaction other than a short-term rental. For the purposes of this rule a "short term rental" is a rental of a residential property for not more than 125 consecutive days with a specific termination date.

3. Brokers who accept payments in the form of credit card charges in short term rentals shall cause those payments to be credited to a special trust or escrow account, distinct from the escrow or trust account(s) maintained by the broker for other purposes. Brokers who accept such payments shall also maintain a business account, separate and apart from all trust or escrow accounts including the account to which the credit card charges will be credited. The said business account may be the same business account maintained by the broker for general purposes.

4. Before accepting any payment in the form of a credit card charge on a short term rental a broker shall inform the owner in writing of the potential for such payments to be "charged-back" by the tenant and obtain written authorization signed by the owner for the broker to accept such payments.

i. For the purposes of this rule "charged-back" means the re-crediting of previously charged payment to the account of a cardholder through the electronic debiting of an account of the broker.

ii. Where an owner's written authorization is secured by the listing broker it shall be made a part of or an addendum to a listing agreement.

iii. In all cases the owner's written authorization shall be retained by the broker to whom it was given as a business record in accordance with N.J.A.C. 11:5-5.4.

5. In the event that a dispute concerning a charged-back payment arises between a broker and a consumer, under no circumstances shall the broker apply or set-off against the disputed amount any monies paid to the broker on another transaction in which the same consumer is a party.

6. Brokers who accept credit card charges in payment

of deposits or rent on short-term rentals shall formulate a written statement of their policy on credit card payment cancellations. All such cancellation policies shall include:

i. an indication of the time period during which the cardholder may cancel the charged payment made to the broker; and

ii. a statement that, in the event a cancellation request is not received by the broker within the specified cancellation time period the request will not be honored and the disposition of the monies credited to the broker will be governed by the terms of the lease or rental agreement between the landlord and the cardholder.

7. In no event shall the cancellation period terminate prior to the delivery to the cardholder of a fully executed written lease containing the final terms of the rental agreement, or the full acceptance by the parties of the final terms of a verbal rental agreement.

8. Brokers shall provide copies of the written cancellation policy in the following manner:

i. to property owners upon the earlier of the broker obtaining a listing on the rental property or presenting an offer to rent the property; and

ii. to prospective tenants at the time of first accepting a payment in the form of a credit card charge. In the event that the same tenant makes subsequent payments on the same rental transaction through charges against a credit card, the broker accepting such payments shall not be required to provide additional copies of the written cancellation policy.

9. Except as otherwise provided in (j) below, brokers who accept payments in the form of credit card charges shall comply with all restrictions and requirements imposed by N.J.S.A. 45:15-17(o) and this rule with regard to the deposit and maintenance of such funds.

j. In all cases the amount credited to a broker's special escrow or trust account as a result of a charged payment on a short term rental transaction shall be the full amount of the payment made by the tenant to the broker. All transaction fees payable by the broker to the company which issued the credit card shall not be paid before the full amount of the charged payment is credited to the broker's special escrow or trust account. Brokers who accept payments through charges on credit cards shall also comply with one of the procedures specified in subparagraphs 1 and 2, below.

1. A business account of the broker shall be designated in the contract between the broker and any company whose credit card charges the broker will accept as the sole source of funds for the payment by the broker of all credit card transaction fees due to the company, and the sole source of funds for all charge-backs which may be assessed against the broker by the company; or

2. The broker shall maintain a reserve amount of the broker's funds in the special escrow or trust account to which charged payments will be credited. The said reserve shall be sufficient to cover all transaction fees incurred by the broker on charged transactions and all estimated charge-backs of payments by cardholders. The maintenance of such reserve funds in the said special escrow or trust account shall not be construed as commingling. In all cases where brokers utilize this procedure:

i. Transaction fees debited from the said reserve amount shall be replenished by the broker on at least a monthly basis; and

ii. In the event that a broker is notified that a charge-back has occurred after some or all of the funds received through the charged-back payment have been disbursed, the broker shall, within one business day of receipt of such notice, replenish the reserve funds in the special escrow or trust account in an amount equal to the amount debited from the reserve through the charge-back; and

iii. Brokers may replenish or increase the said reserve amount as often as necessary. Brokers may only reduce the said reserve amount on an annual basis. All credits to and debits from the special escrow or trust account made by the broker to replenish, increase or decrease the reserve amount shall be duly noted in the business records of the broker and maintained as such as required by N.J.A.C. 11:5-5.4.

11:5.4 Records to be maintained by broker.

(a) No change.

(b) the records required to be maintained by (a) above shall include:

1. No change.

2. An appropriate ledger book for all trustee accounts or escrow accounts showing, in one location in that ledger book for each separate trust transaction, the payor of all funds deposited in such accounts, the date of deposit, the names of all persons for whom the funds are or were held, the amount of such funds, the amounts and dates of all disbursements of such moneys, and the names of all persons to whom such funds were disbursed. The Commission will not deem a regular checkbook ledger as sufficient to constitute an appropriate ledger book. Such a ledger book may be maintained in a computer or similar device, so long as it is capable of reproducing the electronically stored data on paper so as to depict the complete history of all activity in each separate trust transaction, and the data can be maintained in an easily accessible form for the required six year period. A regular running balance of the individual transaction ledger sheets shall be maintained. The total of the running balance must agree with the control figure computed by taking the beginning balance, adding the total of moneys received in trust on that transaction, and deducting the total of all moneys disbursed;

i. Brokers who accept credit card charges on short term rental transactions and who maintain a reserve in their special trust or escrow account to which funds received through such charges are credited as provided in N.J.A.C. 11:5-5.1(j) shall record in one location in their ledger book, entries specifying deposits made to establish, replenish, and increase the reserve amount and all withdrawals made to reduce the reserve amount.

Brokers who maintain reserves in such special escrow or trust accounts shall not be required to make an entry in their ledger for each transaction fee debited from the said account as a result of their acceptance of a payment through a charge on a credit card.

3. No change.

4. All bank statements, cancelled checks [and] duplicate deposit slips and if the broker accepts credit card charges on short term rental transactions as provided in N.J.A.C. 11:5-5.1, all confirmation slips or other written material reflecting the broker's acceptance of such payment.

I. The Commission has adopted amendments to its advertising rule, N.J.A.C. 11:5-6.1.

The amendments to this rule became operative on October 15, 2001. These amendments primarily affect business cards and when licensees can advertise that a property has been sold. Such advertising includes placing signs on properties.

After reviewing the comments submitted subsequent to the proposal of these amendments, the Commission declined to adopt a provision in the proposal that would have banned firms and their licensees who participated in the sale of another broker's listing from advertising that they had sold the property. Consequently, so long as the content of the advertisement is truthful, the Commission's rules continue to contain no prohibition upon cooperating firms and licensees advertising that they sold a property that had been listed by another broker at the time of the transaction once a closing has occurred and title has been transferred.

The text of the amended sections of N.J.A.C. 11:5-6.1 follows:

11:5-6.1 Advertising Rules

(a) Unless otherwise set forth herein, subsections (b) through (o) below shall apply to all categories of advertising including all publications, radio or television broadcasts, all electronic media including e-mail and the Internet, business stationery, business cards, business and legal forms and documents, and signs and billboards.

(b) All advertising of any licensed individual, partnership, firm, or corporate broker shall include their regular business name which for the purposes of these rules, shall mean the name in which that individual, partnership, firm or corporation is on record with the Commission as doing business as a real estate broker. All advertising as a salesperson or broker-salesperson shall include the name in which they are licensed and the regular business name of the individual, partnership, firm or corporate broker through whom they are licensed. If such advertisements contain a reference to the licensed status of the person placing the ad, their status as a salesperson or broker-salesperson must be indicated through inclusion of a descriptive term as provided in (c) below. A salesperson may not indicate in any advertisement or otherwise that he or she is licensed as a broker-salesperson.

1. In all advertisements which contain the name of the salesperson, the regular business name of the individual, partnership firm or corporate broker through whom that person is licensed shall appear in larger print or be displayed in a more prominent manner than the name of the salesperson or broker-salesperson.

2. – 3. (No change)

(c) (No change)

(d) Any advertising which contains a home telephone number, cell-phone number, beeper or pager number, home fax number, or e-mail address of an individual salesperson or broker-salesperson, or a team of such licensees, shall also include the telephone number and may include the street address of the licensed brokerage office from which the advertising licensee(s) operate. All such advertising shall also contain language identifying each number included in the advertising. For example, a home telephone number may be followed or preceded by the word "home" or the abbreviation "res."

(e) – (f) (No change)

(g) Any advertisement which sets forth amounts of down payment, monthly payment, carrying charges, taxes or mortgage money obtainable shall contain appropriate qualifying words such as "approximate" or "estimated," which qualifying words shall be clearly associated with the amounts set forth. If such amounts are mentioned, the broker shall maintain written proof of the validity of these statements in the broker's files. Such written proof shall be maintained for a period of 12 months from the date upon which an advertisement containing such references shall have last appeared in any publication.

(h) – (m) (No changes)

(n) No licensee shall publish or cause to be published any advertisement or place any sign which makes reference to the availability of a specific property which is exclusively listed for sale by another broker unless the licensee obtains the prior written consent of the broker with whom the property is exclusively listed. Such consent shall not be given or withheld by the listing broker without the knowledge of the owner.

1. With regard to information on listings disseminated through the Internet by licensees other than the listing broker, listing brokers shall be deemed to have given the consent referred to in (n) above with the knowledge of the owner where:

i. A written listing agreement contains the seller's authorization for information on the listing to be posed on the website of the broker, or of a multiple listing service to which the broker belongs, or of another party to which the broker or such an MLS submits information on listings; and

ii. The website on which the listing information shall initially appear has instituted no measures to prevent other parties with websites from utilizing an electronic link to enable consumers to view that information while remaining in the website of the other party.

(o) No licensee shall indicate in any advertisement that a property has been sold, or that they participated in the sale of a property, until a closing has occurred at which title to the property was transferred from the seller to the buyer.

1. For the purposes of this subsection, the term "advertisement" shall include communications to other licensees through notices submitted to a multiple listing service or otherwise.

2. In the time period after a contract prepared by a licensee emerges from Attorney Review or a contract not subject to Attorney Review is fully executed and delivered to all parties, but before closing occurs at which title is transferred, unless such a contract is cancelled and the seller authorizes the listing broker to renew efforts to market the property, any advertisement of the property which is the subject of the contract shall include the term "under contract".

II. The amendments to N.J.A.C. 11:5-6.4(f) address the obligation of brokers to fully cooperate with each other, using arrangements which protect and promote the interests of the client or principal. The amendments to N.J.A.C. 11:5-6.4(g) relate to the listing firm's obligation to promptly submit all written offers received by that firm to the seller. The full text of the amended subsections follows:

11:5-6.4 Obligation of licensees to public and to each other

(a) – (e) (No change)

(f) Unless directed not to do so in writing by an owner as provided herein, every licensee shall fully cooperate with all other New Jersey licensees utilizing cooperation arrangements which shall protect and promote the interests of the licensee's client or principal. Collusion and discrimination with respect to commission rates and splits are prohibited as provided in N.J.A.C. 11:5-7.5 and 7.6.

1. The obligation to fully cooperate with all other licensees includes the requirements that listing brokers:

i. Notify any Multiple Listing System to which a listing is to be submitted of having acquired the listing with 48 hours of the effective date of the listing;

ii. Transmit to their principal(s) all written offers on their listings submitted by licensees with other firms within 24 hours of receipt of the written offer by their firm; and

iii. Place no unreasonable restrictions upon the showing of properties listed with them to prospective purchasers who are working through cooperating brokers. A requirement that all appointments for showings must be made through the listing broker's office is not considered an unreasonable restriction upon showings.

2. All requirements imposed by the obligation to fully cooperate shall be complied with on all listings unless the client or principal, with full knowledge of all relevant facts, expressly relieves the listing broker from one or more of those requirements in writing. Such writing shall be signed by the owner and made an attachment to the listing agreement. Such writing shall be made available for inspection by other brokers upon request.

3. All written listing agreements prepared by licensees shall include a provision as set forth below, which provision shall be in print larger than the predominant size print in the agreement. The provision may be included with the body of the listing agreement or attached to the listing as an addendum to it. Where the provision is made an addendum to the listing agreement it shall be signed by the owner at the same time that the owner signs the listing agreement. Prior to securing the owner's signature on the listing agreement, the listing broker shall specify the complete formula for determining the commission split in the indicated location in the provision.

COMMISSION SPLITS

LISTING BROKERS USUALLY COOPERATE WITH OTHER BROKERAGE FIRMS BY SHARING INFORMATION ABOUT THEIR LISTINGS AND OFFERING TO PAY PART OF THEIR COMMISSION TO THE FIRM THAT PRODUCES A BUYER. THIS IS GENERALLY REFERRED TO AS THE "COMMISSION SPLIT."

SOME LISTING BROKERS OFFER TO PAY COMMISSION SPLITS OF A PORTION OF THE GROSS COMMISSION USUALLY EXPRESSED AS A PERCENTAGE OF THE SELLING PRICE, LESS A SIGNIFICANT DOLLAR AMOUNT. OTHER LISTING BROKERS OFFER A PORTION OF THE GROSS COMMISSION LESS ONLY A MINIMAL LISTING FEE OR LESS ZERO.

THE AMOUNT OF COMMISSION SPLIT YOUR BROKER OFFERS CAN AFFECT THE EXTENT TO WHICH YOUR PROPERTY IS EXPOSED TO PROSPECTIVE BUYERS WORKING WITH LICENSEES FROM OTHER BROKERAGE FIRMS.

ON THIS LISTING, THE BROKER IS OFFERING A COMMISSION SPLIT OF MINUS TO POTENTIAL COOPERATING BROKERS.

IF YOU FEEL THAT THIS MAY RESULT IN YOUR PROPERTY RECEIVING LESS THAN MAXIMUM EXPOSURE TO BUYERS, YOU SHOULD DISCUSS THOSE CONCERNS WITH THE LISTING SALESPERSON OR HIS/HER SUPERVISING BROKER.

BY SIGNING THIS LISTING AGREEMENT THE OWNER(S) ACKNOWLEDGE HAVING READ THIS STATEMENT ON COMMISSION SPLITS.

4. Should the client or principal direct the listing broker not to cooperate at all with all other licensees, evident of this intent shall be in writing in the form of a WAIVER OF BROKER COOPERATION as set forth below and signed by the client or principal. Copies of this WAIVER OF BROKER COOPERATION and the listing agreement to which it relates shall be provided to the client or principal and to their authorized representative by the broker. This waiver shall become a part of the listing agreement at the time it is signed, and shall be made available for inspection by other brokers upon request. However, no direction or inducement from the client or principal shall relieve the list-

ing broker of his responsibility of dealing fairly and exercising integrity with all other licensees.

WAIVER OF BROKER COOPERATION

I UNDERSTAND THAT COOPERATION AMONGST BROKERS PRODUCES WIDER EXPOSURE OF MY PROPERTY AND MAY RESULT IN IT BEING SOLD OR LEASED SOONER AND AT A HIGHER PRICE THAN WOULD BE THE CASE WERE MY BROKER NOT TO COOPERATE WITH OTHER BROKERS. I FURTHER UNDERSTAND THAT WHEN MY BROKER COOPERATES WITH OTHER BROKERS, I CAN STILL HAVE THE ARRAGEMENTS FOR THE SHOWING OF THE PROPERTY AND ALL NEGOTIATIONS WITH ME OR MY ATTORNEY MADE ONLY THROUGH MY LISTING BROKER'S OFFICE, SHOULD I SO DESIRE.

However, despite my awareness of these factors, I direct that the property be marketed only through the efforts of the listing broker. This listing is not to be published in any multiple listing service. I will only consider offers on this property which are obtained by, and I will only allow showings of this property to be conducted by the listing broker or his or her duly authorized representative. THE LISTING BROKER IS HEREBY DIRECTED NOT TO COOPERATE WITH ANY OTHER BROKER.

By signing below, the parties hereto confirm that no pressure or undue influence has been exerted upon the owners as to how this property is to be marketed by the Listing Broker.

The owner(s) further confirm receipt of fully executed copies of the listing agreement on this property and of this Waiver of Broker Cooperation form.

Dated: ______________________

Owner ______________________

Owner ______________________

Listing Broker ______________________

By: Authorized Licensee
or Broker______________________

(g) If any offer on any real property or interest therein is made orally, the licensee shall advise the offeror that he is not obligated to present to the owner or his authorized representative any offer unless the offer is in writing. Unless a writing containing or confirming the terms of the listing agreement otherwise provides, the licensee shall transmit every written offer on any real property or interest therein presented to or obtained by the licensee during the term of the listing to the owner or his authorized representative within 24 hours of receipt of the written offer by their firm. For the purposes of this section, the term of a listing shall be deemed to expire either on the termination date established in the listing agreement, or upon the closing of a pending sale or lease. If any acceptance of an offer is given orally, the licensee shall secure forthwith the acceptance in writing.

(h) – (l) (No change)

KEY WORDS

Apprenticeship
Associate Broker
Attorney General's Memorandum
Attorney Review
Back-up Offer
Branch Office
Broker
Broker-salesperson
Commingling
Criminal History Record Check
Cul-de-sac
Dual Capacity
Employing Broker
Employment Agreement
Escrow Account
Fiduciary
Fraud
Guaranty Fund
Irrevocable Consent
License Lending
Misdemeanor
Misrepresentation
Moral Turpitude
Net Listing
Non-resident License
Office Supervisor
Prospectus
Real Estate Commission
Real Estate Sales Full Disclosure Act
Realtor
Receiver
Revoked
Rules and Regulations
S.B.I. Form 212
Suspended
Temporary License

CHAPTER 3
Review Questions
(Answers on page 551)

1. When money is deposited in a client trust account:
   (A) the maintenance of nominal amounts of the licensees' funds in the trust account to meet service charges constitutes commingling.
   (B) the deposit cannot be released without written authorization of the seller.
   (C) deposit money must be promptly returned to the buyer if the offer is not accepted.
   (D) interest must be paid to the buyer until closing.

2. Which of the following would NOT be a cause for disciplinary action under Title 45, Chapter 15?
   (A) Making promises of a nature likely to persuade or induce a prospective buyer.
   (B) Failure to include a specific termination date in an exclusive listing.
   (C) Acquiring a listing in which the broker gets to keep all monies in the purchase price above a specified amount.
   (D) Failure to submit to an owner, before his acceptance of an offer, all written offers received for property listed for sale.

3. If the broker terminates employment of a salesperson, he must:
   (A) state reason for termination on the back of the license.
   (B) immediately return the salesperson's license to the REC.
   (C) return the license within ten days.
   (D) give the salesperson his license.

4. When there is a first violation of the licensing act, the REC is empowered to:
   (A) impose monetary fines.
   (B) revoke the license.
   (C) suspend the license.
   (D) All of the above.

5. A broker's records must be made available:
   (A) to agents of the Commission providing broker receives 10 days' notice of inspection.
   (B) to members of the public as they contain public information.
   (C) to members of the Commission without notice.
   (D) to agents of the Commission upon receipt of 30 days' notice by registered or certified mail.

6. Fiduciary relationship refers to:
   (A) the relationship between two brokers.
   (B) the relationship created between plaintiff and defendant.
   (C) the position of trust between broker and his principal.
   (D) None of the above.

7. A broker incorporates his business and subsequently dies, and another person becomes the broker for the corporation.
   (A) Any listings he has secured are immediately terminated.
   (B) All his listings may be canceled by the principals without further cause.
   (C) New listings must be secured from the owners of all properties being handled by the office.
   (D) Contracts with principals do not terminate upon death of the broker under these circumstances.

8. A newly licensed broker can maintain an office in ALL BUT ONE of the following:
   (A) His residence, provided that it is zoned for that use.
   (B) A commercial building.
   (C) The home of a salesperson in his employ.
   (D) A marina.

9. When a licensee is guilty of violating the New Jersey Real Estate License Act or the Rules and Regulations of the New Jersey Real Estate Commission, the Commission may, for the first violation:
   (A) impose a fine of not more than $500.
   (B) impose a fine of not more than $5,000.
   (C) impose a fine of not more than $2,000.
   (D) The Real Estate Commission cannot impose fines.

10. A real estate broker typically can:
    (A) prepare an abstract of title.
    (B) prepare a deed.
    (C) prepare a purchase and sale agreement.
    (D) None of the above.

11. Unless otherwise agreed to in writing, the employing broker must pay all commissions due a salesperson within how many days after receipt by the broker?
    (A) Ten days.
    (B) Thirty days.
    (C) Immediately.
    (D) Seven calendar days.

(Quiz continues on next page)

12. After completion of the real estate license preparation course, what period of time does the applicant have in which to pass the state examination and request issuance of his license?
    (A) Six months.
    (B) One year.
    (C) Five years.
    (D) The applicant can apply anytime.

13. Regarding a dispute between licensees concerning the division of commissions, which of the following is correct?
    (A) The Real Estate Commission can demand an accounting (explanation).
    (B) The Real Estate Commission is responsible for settling disputes between licensees.
    (C) A salesperson cannot sue his broker for a commission he feels he has earned but not been paid.
    (D) Only the broker can file a complaint with the Real Estate Commission.

14. Real estate licenses are renewed:
    (A) annually on January 1st.
    (B) biennially on July 1st, in odd-numbered years.
    (C) one year from the date they are issued for the first time.
    (D) every five years.

15. Pertaining to the salesperson's license, which of the following is true?
    (A) It must be prominently displayed in the broker's main office.
    (B) It must be prominently displayed in the branch office where the salesperson is employed.
    (C) The salesperson must carry it.
    (D) It is a right and not a privilege.

16. A salesperson may accept a commission from which of the following?
    (A) The employing broker.
    (B) The employing broker or another salesperson.
    (C) Any licensed real estate broker.
    (D) Only the seller or employing broker.

17. Which of the following statements concerning branch offices is correct?
    (A) The branch office must be open to the public during normal business hours.
    (B) The branch office can be open only during evening hours or weekends.
    (C) The broker can have one manager in charge of several offices.
    (D) The branch office manager must be licensed as a salesperson for two years.

18. Broker's real estate ads in New Jersey must include:
    (A) the address.
    (B) the name of the brokerage firm.
    (C) the name of the listor.
    (D) the name of the agent showing the property.

19. When a real estate broker advertises in the local newspaper, he must:
    (A) state the price of the house.
    (B) give the address of the house.
    (C) specify the municipality within which the property is located.
    (D) give the name of the authorized broker.

20. Should the employing broker die, a temporary broker license may be issued to a salesperson provided:
    (A) that the request is made within six months of the broker's death.
    (B) that the request is made within 30 days of the broker's death and that the applicant has three years' prior experience.
    (C) that the application is made within two weeks of the broker's death.
    (D) A salesperson cannot be issued a temporary license under any condition.

21. Which of the following requires licensees to provide owners with a copy of the Attorney General's Memorandum on the Law Against Discrimination?
    (A) The New Jersey Law Against Discrimination.
    (B) The Rules and Regulations of the New Jersey Real Estate Commission.
    (C) The New Jersey Division of Civil Rights.
    (D) All of the above.

22. The REC may suspend or revoke a license:
    (A) when a broker charges more than 6% commission.
    (B) for splitting commission with a broker from out of state.
    (C) for using the insignia of membership in a real estate organization of which licensee is not a member.
    (D) for being committed for observation in a mental institution.

23. In advertising a listed property for sale, a broker may NOT legally:
    (A) run an ad which does not give the listing price of the property.
    (B) state the kind of financing available.
    (C) fail to state the street address of the property.
    (D) run an ad giving the impression that he is the owner of the property.

24. The Realtor® Code of Ethics is:
    (A) a code put into law by the Real Estate Commission of New Jersey.
    (B) a code obligatory upon members of the National Association of Realtors®.
    (C) part of an act pertaining to prevention of discrimination in real property transactions.
    (D) part of the Statutes of New Jersey pertaining to licensed real estate salespersons and brokers.

25. Who is required to comply with the State licensing laws?
    (A) An individual employed to handle the sale of units in a condominium building.
    (B) One who for compensation effects an "exchange" of real estate.
    (C) One who auctions real estate.
    (D) All of the above.

26. A principal broker for a corporation must be:
    (A) a citizen of the United States.
    (B) a New Jersey resident.
    (C) responsible for every licensee and clothed with full authority even if he has no ownership interest.
    (D) given a contract for a fixed term unless he has a substantial ownership interest.

27. A salesperson who has completed a sale would ordinarily receive his commission from the:
    (A) seller.
    (B) buyer.
    (C) seller and buyer with their permission.
    (D) None of the above.

28. A real estate deal is made between a seller and buyer, without the services of a broker. They arrange with a licensed broker, for a fee, to prepare certain instruments. He may lawfully prepare:
    (A) agreement of sale.
    (B) deed.
    (C) purchase money mortgage.
    (D) None of the above.

29. If a licensee is convicted of forgery, the REC will NOT grant a license within:
    (A) one year.
    (B) two years.
    (C) three years.
    (D) five years.

30. To be licensed as a broker, you must be:
    (A) of legal age.
    (B) a citizen of the United States.
    (C) a resident of New Jersey.
    (D) All of the above.

31. A broker may properly advertise:
    (A) free appraisal.
    (B) free cooking gas.
    (C) free parking.
    (D) free market study.

32. With regard to the maintenance of trust accounts, which of the following statements is NOT true?
    (A) The account may be designated "trust account."
    (B) The account may be designated "escrow account."
    (C) A broker may establish a special interest-bearing account for the deposit of monies from a specific transaction.
    (D) The depository institution may be located in another state if it is an approved depository in the other state.

33. A real estate licensee brings a prospective buyer to see a property and the property owner requests identification from the licensee indicating her licensure status. The proper identification for the licensee to produce is a:
    (A) driver's license.
    (B) real estate license.
    (C) Realtor® membership card.
    (D) pocket card.

34. Monies may be paid out of the Guaranty Fund in the event:
    (A) a seller suffers a monetary loss due to the embezzlement of money by a licensed broker, a licensed real estate salesperson or an unlicensed employee of a real estate broker.
    (B) a salesman does not get paid by his broker in accordance with his written agreement.
    (C) an aggrieved party did not sue.
    (D) a co-broker did not honor his agreement.

35. The responsibilities of the Real Estate Commission include:
    (A) setting the fees for licensing exams.
    (B) promulgating real estate laws.
    (C) setting license fees.
    (D) None of the above.

36. A real estate salesperson may lawfully accept a bonus for the completion of a difficult sale:
    (A) if the sellers wish to give one.
    (B) if they pay taxes on the income.
    (C) only from his or her employing broker.
    (D) if he or she receives it from the buyer.

(Quiz continues on next page)

37. The broker owes an obligation to:
    (A) divide the commission with another broker chosen or preferred by the buyer.
    (B) divulge to the buyer the lowest price at which the seller will sell.
    (C) present to his principal all written offers he receives, including all of the terms and conditions of each offer signed by a prospective buyer.
    (D) nobody.

38. You are the seller's broker negotiating a difficult sales contract between an experienced seller of real estate and a novice purchaser.
    (A) You have no concern about the buyer's lack of experience.
    (B) You refuse to continue to negotiate with purchaser.
    (C) You recommend that purchaser employ an attorney.
    (D) You suggest that purchaser consider employing another broker.

39. A real estate broker hires a secretary who does not have a real estate license and agrees to pay her a fixed salary. Which of the following duties may be performed by her?
    (A) Giving information over the telephone as to selling price of the office listings.
    (B) Collecting rents from lessees of property managed by the broker.
    (C) Telephone solicitation of listings from prospective sellers.
    (D) Typing contracts for the salespersons in the broker's office.

40. A salesperson may advertise a property for sale only:
    (A) if he personally listed the property.
    (B) if the name of his broker is included in the ad.
    (C) if his broker is entitled to use the term "Realtor®."
    (D) if he pays for the ad himself out of his commission.

41. A broker must keep permanent records of how he handled other persons' funds for:
    (A) 60 days.
    (B) two years.
    (C) six years.
    (D) ten years.

42. A broker must transmit to his principal:
    (A) all offers.
    (B) all offers to purchase at the listed price.
    (C) all offers reasonably near the listed price.
    (D) all written offers.

43. Residential rental referral agencies must include which of the following in their contract with a prospective tenant?
    (A) The date and duration of the contract.
    (B) The refund policy.
    (C) A statement that the business is licensed by the New Jersey Real Estate Commission.
    (D) All of the above.

44. With regard to the Real Estate Sales Full Disclosure Act, which of the following statements is NOT true?
    (A) Cemetery lots are exempt from the law.
    (B) The display of model homes is considered a form of advertising.
    (C) The rescission period is three days.
    (D) Subdivisions containing fewer than 100 lots are generally exempt from the Act.

45. A salesperson has listed a house for sale and has knowledge of a latent defect in the building. His responsibility is to:
    (A) ignore it.
    (B) disclose it to the buyer.
    (C) report it to the building department.
    (D) correct the condition.

46. A New Jersey broker named I.M. First listed a house at 326 Cove Drive in Mantoloking. She may refuse to cooperate with another licensee if:
    (A) she has an exclusive right to sell listing.
    (B) she has an exclusive agency listing.
    (C) the other broker refused to cooperate with her last month.
    (D) the owner of the home signs a statement directing her not to cooperate.

47. The maximum fine for violations of the Real Estate Sales Full Disclosure Act is:
    (A) $250 per violation.
    (B) $2,000 per violation.
    (C) $5,000 per violation.
    (D) $50,000 per violation.

48. When a broker prepares a document pertaining to a real estate transaction:
    (A) he must give a copy to all parties signing it at the time the signature is obtained.
    (B) he must sign the document himself.
    (C) he is violating the law.
    (D) he should record the contract.

49. Funds received for deposit in the Guaranty Fund:
    (A) may not exceed $150,000.
    (B) may be used for educational purposes by the Board of Realtors.
    (C) may be used to settle commission disputes between licensees.
    (D) are used to indemnify aggrieved participants in real estate transactions.

50. Every broker must maintain records of all funds and property of others for not less than six years, except in two cases where records have to be kept for only six months. Name the two exceptions.
    (A) Unaccepted offers and expired listings that did not sell.
    (B) Copies of leases and property management agreements.
    (C) Copies of all offers and contracts of sale.
    (D) All bank statements and duplicate deposit slips.

CHAPTER FOUR

LAND, LAND ELEMENTS AND WATER

LAND

Land is generally thought of as the earth's surface. However, from a legal standpoint, it extends downward to the center of the earth and upward to the sky, including natural things that are attached such as trees, shrubs or water, plus the minerals below the surface and the air rights above it.

Real estate, or **real property**, includes land as defined above, and the rights that go with the land such as easements, rents and profits and all man-made things attached to the land, such as buildings, fences, patios, fixtures, etc. **Personal property** comprises all other things that do not meet the definition of real property. Personal property will be discussed in Chapter 5.

Improvements are permanent, man-made attachments to land that increase its value or improve its usefulness, such as buildings, fences and driveways. Land to which there are no man-made additions is referred to as "unimproved" or "raw" land.

Bundle of Rights Theory. The bundle of rights theory proposes that ownership of real estate implies a group of rights, the total of which establish absolute ownership. Under this theory, since the land itself cannot be physically transferred, it is made up of a set of separate and distinct rights, each of which can be transferred separately. These rights include the right to occupy and use the property for any legal purpose; to build on the property; to pass the property to heirs by will; to lease; to mortgage; to keep other people from using the property; to sell or refuse to sell; to grant a license or an easement; to mine, drill or farm; to encumber the land and to restrict the use of the property.

These rights, however, are not unqualified. They are limited by the power of the state to raise **taxes**; the state's **police power** to restrict, regulate and control (without compensation) an individual's free use of land and buildings through public health and building codes, zoning ordinances, policy and fire department regulations, environmental controls and, in some jurisdictions, rent control; the right to take private property by exercising the power of **eminent domain** through the act of condemnation; and to take property if the owner dies with no will and no heirs (escheat).

LAND ELEMENTS

Gas, Oil and Minerals. When real property is transferred, the rights to the gas, oil and minerals beneath the ground go with the land unless specified otherwise.

Air Rights. An owner may own, sell or lease the air space above his property, for it is considered to be part of his real estate. The government, however, has the right to regulate the use of the air over all private lands for the benefit of public air transportation. In large cities, the air space nearest the ground that would not generally be used by aircraft is frequently sold, along with rights of support, to large corporations. A well-known example of this is the Pan American Building, built over the New York Central Railway's tracks in New York City.

Plantings. Plantings are separated into two categories: perennial plantings and annual plantings.

Perennial Plantings. Trees, shrubs, bushes, etc., which are of natural growth and do not require annual cultivation and planting are considered to be part of the land, and are deemed to be **real property**. Intentional severance, however, as in the case of timber, will render the cut trees as personal property.

Annual Plantings. The harvest of crops such as grain, corn, etc. that are planted and harvested annually, and are produced by man's labor, are considered to be **personal property**. Therefore, because of the "emblement rights," a tenant may take the harvest of an annual crop, even if the harvest occurs after the tenancy has ended.

WATER RIGHTS

Water is considered to be a part of real property, whether above or below the ground. Under the federal Constitution, Congress has control over all navigable waters in the United States, and any rights of private individuals are subordinate thereto. Congress also has full power to regulate and control the building of bridges over such waters, as well as the building of dams that would affect them.

Whenever boundaries or uses of water are discussed the term " riparian land" is used and the owners are said to have certain **riparian** (having to do with water) rights. Land that borders the sea, especially land washed by waves and coastal currents, is referred to as **littoral land**. The distinction between littoral and riparian land is that the latter refers to the bank of a river. However, the terms are often used interchangeably, because the rules dealing with both are consistent.

1. Navigable and Non-navigable Waters and Streams. Waters or streams are said to be navigable if they are identified as such on a federal survey map. The public has no right to travel over individual owners' own streams which are non-navigable. These streams are under the jurisdiction of the Division of Water Resources.

In New Jersey all land under navigable waters and all land washed by the mean high water line is owned by the state unless the rights to these lands (riparian rights) have been sold by the state. Riparian rights may be purchased in fee or leased from the Bureau of Marine Lands Management, a division of the Department of Environmental Protection. If the owner of the land adjoining the water does not purchase the rights the state may sell or lease them to other parties after proper notice. A typical lease term is 15 years.

Under the Wetlands Act of 1970, the Department of Environmental Protection regulates certain activities in designated wetland areas. A permit must be obtained from the Commissioner of Environmental Protection before a riparian owner can remove soil, or before filling, grading, construction, draining, dredging or similar activities can take place.

Where a stream flows within the boundaries of a property, it is owned by the landowners. If such a stream serves as a boundary for two separately held properties, the centerline of the normal streambed serves as the boundary line and each owner has jurisdiction up to that centerline.

2. Underground Water. Most ordinary wells in New Jersey are fed by percolating ground water that is normally formed by rain or melting snow. In the case of underground water, the general rule used in deciding who owns it and how it is to be used provides that an owner can rightfully use the water under his property for use on the land where it has been found, but that he should not pipe this water off to other lands, for this may cause an adjoining landowner to be deprived of his water supply.

3. Accretion. Another important riparian right is the determination of private ownership of lands that have been formed by accretion. Accretion is the gaining of additional land through the process of either **alluvion** or **reliction**.

Alluvion. The gradual and imperceptible deposit of additional soil attaching itself to existing property through natural causes such as deposits of soil carried by streams. The additional land attached is also referred to as alluvion. Land created by alluvion normally belongs to the owner of the land to which it has been added. Thus, title may be given by nature through alluvion to owners who have land adjoining lakes, rivers or oceans.

Reliction. Where the water recedes gradually from an area and new land is exposed, the land is said to have been formed by reliction. Generally, the exposed land belongs to the party who owned the rights to the water area. The site of our Meadowlands Sports Complex offers a classic example of reliction.

4. Avulsion. Avulsion refers to a sudden change in the course of a stream due to an earthquake or flood. If the stream served as the boundary line for the adjoining owners, the property line does not change. This is not true when land is lost by erosion, which is a gradual wearing away of land by natural causes such as wind and rain, which causes its loss.

BEACH RIGHTS

Ancient English Law recognized the Crown as having dominion over all navigable waters. However, our courts have gradually been transforming this concept into the public trust doctrine, and the state holds title to waters and other public lands as a trustee for the benefit of the people. The State Supreme Court invoked this doctrine as the basis for opening up certain privately owned beachfront property to general public access and use in *Matthews v. Bayhead Improvement Association*, 95 NJ 306 (1984).

The court did not, however, extend the public trust doctrine to all oceanfront property. It said, "Considerable uncertainty will continue to surround the question of the public's right to cross private land and to use a portion of the dry sand." In the future, as demand grows for privately owned recreational land, the public trust doctrine will undoubtedly be used to expand public rights of access and use.

KEY WORDS

- Accretion
- Air Rights
- Alluvion
- Avulsion
- Bundle of Rights
- Condemnation
- Emblement
- Eminent Domain
- Escheat
- Improvements
- Land
- Littoral
- Navigable Waters
- Police Power
- Real Estate
- Reliction
- Riparian Rights

CHAPTER 4
Review Questions
(Answers on page 551)

1. All of the following are synonymous with land and improvements and rights therein EXCEPT:
   (A) real estate.
   (B) real property.
   (C) Realtor.
   (D) realty.

2. Trees, shrubs, bushes, etc. which grow naturally and do not require annual planting are:
   (A) emblements.
   (B) personalty.
   (C) realty.
   (D) intangible.

3. The right of ownership, the right to use, possess, enjoy and dispose of a thing in every legal way and to exclude everyone else without rights from interfering is called:
   (A) corporeal ownership.
   (B) incorporeal ownership.
   (C) bundle of rights.
   (D) survivorship.

4. A riparian owner is one who owns land bounding on:
   (A) municipal property.
   (B) a waterway.
   (C) a national forest.
   (D) unsurveyed public lands.

5. Real estate includes all of these EXCEPT:
   (A) a garage.
   (B) stone piled on a property.
   (C) an in-ground swimming pool.
   (D) a screened patio or porch.

6. The legal rights attached to real property are referred to as the:
   (A) situs.
   (B) bundle of rights.
   (C) severance rights.
   (D) reliction rights.

7. Rights in real property can include all of the following, EXCEPT:
   (A) surface rights.
   (B) subsurface rights.
   (C) water rights.
   (D) avulsion rights.

8. When a New Jersey farmer sells his property:
   (A) the mineral rights will automatically pass to the buyer unless they are specifically reserved by the seller.
   (B) the air rights must be specifically described in the deed for the buyer to get title thereto.
   (C) he must record the deed.
   (D) he must report the sale to the Farmers Home Administration.

9. The boundary of your property line can be changed by:
   (A) accretion.
   (B) amortization.
   (C) avulsion.
   (D) acceleration.

10. Crops which grow on land and require annual planting and cultivation are:
    (A) personalty.
    (B) realty.
    (C) real property.
    (D) improvements.

11. Which of the following is NOT a part of the owner's "bundle of rights"?
    (A) The right to evict a tenant for cause.
    (B) The right to pass title by will.
    (C) The right to absolute control of the property.
    (D) The right to dispose of the property.

12. When the course of a stream is suddenly changed by natural forces, it is called:
    (A) erosion.
    (B) alluvion.
    (C) avulsion.
    (D) dereliction.

13. When title is gained because a portion of a water course permanently dries up, exposing land, it is called:
    (A) reliction.
    (B) erosion.
    (C) accretion.
    (D) alluvion.

14. Air rights may:
    (A) be sold or leased.
    (B) be leased only.
    (C) be sold only.
    (D) not be retained by the seller when the land is sold.

CHAPTER FIVE

PERSONAL PROPERTY AND FIXTURES

PERSONAL PROPERTY

Personal property consists of every kind of property that is not real property and would include most man-made property, money, and movable goods or chattels. Some distinguishing characteristics of personal property as compared to real property are:

1. Tangible personal property is called a **chattel** and is financed by way of a **security agreement** (formerly called a chattel mortgage). Real property is usually financed by a mortgage.

2. In the case of a foreclosure, personal property may be foreclosed upon with relative ease, merely by canceling the contract and taking back possession of the property. However, a foreclosure proceeding on real property is an involved and time-consuming process.

3. The sale of personal property is accomplished with a **bill of sale**, while real property is conveyed by means of a deed or assignment of lease.

4. Tax laws make many important distinctions between real and personal property.

It is important to understand the difference between real and personal property. All real property is automatically included in the sale unless specifically excluded in the listing and sale contract. Personal property, on the other hand, is automatically excluded from the sale unless it has been specifically included in the listing and sale contract. It is the responsibility of attorneys and real estate licensees to assure that contracts properly reflect the intention of the parties. Careful inspection of the property and consultation with the seller should result in the proper determination of what is to be included and excluded. Carelessness by licensees in taking listings which improperly represent the intention of the parties with respect to included and excluded items can be a cause of needless problems at settlement.

FIXTURES

A **fixture** is an article or item of personal property that has become affixed to land or a building in such a manner that it has become an actual part of the real property. However, if the article is attached in such a way to retain its original character, and as such, is easily removable, it may then still be considered a chattel or personal property. Fixtures pass with the land, whereas chattels must be mentioned in the deed or sold by a bill of sale in order to pass with the sale of a property.

There are four basic criteria or "tests of a fixture" that are used in determining whether or not an article is a fixture. These are: (1) the method of attachment; (2) adaptation of the article to the property; (3) relationship of the parties; and (4) intention of the parties. Let us examine these in more detail.

1. Method of Attachment. If the article is attached to the realty in such a permanent fashion as to cause considerable damage if the article were removed, it is usually held to be a fixture and is considered part of the real estate.

2. Adaptation of the Article to the Property. If the article were constructed or designed especially for a particular building, and was essential to the use of the building, it would indicate the intention was to make it a permanent part of the building, and it would be deemed a fixture. Examples would include custom-made storm windows and church pews.

3. Relationship of the Parties. If the person attaching the object were the owner of the building, it would appear that the intention was for the personal property to become a fixture. On the other hand, when a tenant installs an object, it might be assumed that the article was intended to remain personal property, to be taken when the lease is terminated.

4. Intention of the Parties. The factor of intention tends to be the most important test of a fixture. The intent must be clear, as would be shown by oral statements or actions of the parties. For example, a seller might post a "not included" sign on certain articles when the house is shown to a prospective buyer.

If the parties have not expressly indicated their intention, the courts will use the above facts and circumstances to determine whether or not a fixture was intended. However, by mutual agreement, the buyer and seller (or landlord and tenant) can agree that articles of real property may be removed and/or that some articles of personalty may remain. The real estate professional must be able to distinguish between real and personal property and can minimize problems by including an **itemization of items** considered personal property which will remain with the seller unless otherwise negotiated.

TRADE FIXTURES

Trade fixtures are articles attached by the tenant to the building for use in conducting a trade or business. Trade fixtures are **personal property** and can be removed by the tenant when the lease expires, but the tenant is responsible for damage to the property caused by their removal. Examples include bar and restaurant equipment, ovens and walk-in refrigerators used in restaurants, barber chairs, hair washing sinks in beauty salons, display cases and floor-mounted shelving in retail stores, etc. Such fixtures have to be removed prior to or within a reasonable period of time after expiration of the lease or they would become property of the landlord.

It should be noted that there is little uniformity in the courts as to what constitutes a fixture or trade fixture. The prudent licensee should attempt to put into writing all items that are to be included and sold as part of the real estate, particularly if there is any doubt as to whether or not they could be considered fixtures.

APPURTENANCES

A conveyance of land carries with it any appurtenances to the land. An appurtenance is anything attached to the land or used with it that will pass to the new owner upon conveyance of the land. Some common forms of appurtenances include:

Improvements. Additions to land that increase its value or improve its usefulness, such as buildings, fences and driveways.

Air Rights. Rights to the air space over land.

Mineral Rights. Rights to all or specific minerals on or under the land.

Water Rights. Rights to the use of the water located on the land or which runs through, under or bounds the land.

KEY WORDS

Appurtenance
Bill of Sale
Chattel
Chattel Mortgage
Fixture
Personalty
Security Agreement
Trade Fixture

CHAPTER 5
Review Questions
(Answers on page 551)

1. An example of personal property is:
   (A) a household furnishing.
   (B) a gas range.
   (C) a built-in dishwasher.
   (D) a disposal.

2. Which of the following does NOT apply to real property?
   (A) Chattel mortgage.
   (B) Fee simple.
   (C) Fixture.
   (D) Appurtenances.

3. Which of the following is personal property?
   (A) Mineral rights.
   (B) Water rights.
   (C) A beneficiary's rights under a trust involving real property.
   (D) Trees.

4. Generally, things or objects of a temporary or easily movable nature are:
   (A) fixtures.
   (B) included.
   (C) personalty.
   (D) appurtenances.

5. An example of a fixture is a:
   (A) portable dishwasher.
   (B) dining room china cabinet.
   (C) ceiling fan.
   (D) refrigerator.

6. When the contract for the sale of real property includes the sale of certain removable items, such as refrigerators and furniture, upon delivery of the deed the seller should also deliver:
   (A) a bill of sale.
   (B) an estoppel certificate.
   (C) a chattel mortgage.
   (D) a satisfaction piece.

7. Which of the following is NOT an appurtenance?
   (A) A barn.
   (B) An orchard.
   (C) A fence.
   (D) A trade fixture.

8. Which of the following is a factor in determining whether an article of property is a fixture?
   (A) The value of the article.
   (B) Its size.
   (C) Its weight.
   (D) The method of annexation.

9. Property is:
   (A) real if it is tangible.
   (B) personal if a fixture.
   (C) personal if not real.
   (D) All of the above.

10. Which of the following is (are) personal property?
    (A) Fixtures.
    (B) Mortgages.
    (C) Air rights.
    (D) Water rights.

11. Property classed as real property:
    (A) must always remain real property.
    (B) may, under certain circumstances, become personal property.
    (C) is never, under any circumstances, exempt from taxes.
    (D) may not be owned by aliens.

12. Regarding property:
    (A) A trade fixture is real property.
    (B) Personal property is anything that is not real property.
    (C) A fixture is personalty.
    (D) Chattels are realty.

13. Which of the following types of property is normally NOT real property?
    (A) Appurtenances.
    (B) Furniture.
    (C) Fixtures.
    (D) Shrubs.

14. Which of the following statements is (are) true?
    (A) A bill of sale is used to transfer title to a fixture.
    (B) Refrigerators are not considered fixtures in private homes.
    (C) A chattel mortgage is used to finance the purchase of land.
    (D) Chattels automatically pass with a sale of land.

CHAPTER SIX

ESTATES AND INTERESTS IN REAL PROPERTY

Rights in property range from complete ownership to comparatively lesser rights. There are two types of rights in real estate: estates and interests. An estate (tenancy, tenement) is an ownership or possessory interest that one has in land. An interest is any right that one has in property, and is less than an estate in land. The terms estate and interest are often used interchangeably, as we will use them, although while all estates constitute interests in land, not all interests in land are estates. The rights one is entitled to depend on the kind of estate held.

There are two categories of interests: **present interests**, those in which the holder takes possession of the property now, such as a fee simple or leasehold interest, and **future interests**, those in which possession is postponed until sometime in the future, such as a remainder or reversion. (We will discuss all of these interests shortly.)

Property, property estates and interests are also classified as:

Corporeal. Property that is tangible, that may be seen or touched, such as land and buildings, and trees and shrubs.

Incorporeal. Property that is intangible, which cannot be seen or touched, such as an easement. An easement conveys the right of use in another's land, but is neither visible nor tangible.

Property interests that are inheritable are called **hereditaments**. When property, or an interest in it, is passed from one party to another, it is accomplished by the signing of a conveyance, a legal document, such as a deed, easement or mortgage. The word "conveys" means to transfer an interest in real property. The party making or granting the conveyance is called the grantor, and the one receiving the conveyance is called the grantee. Under specific instruments to be covered later, you will see that these parties are often given names that more specifically define their roles under particular instruments being used.

ESTATES

An estate is an ownership or possessory interest one has in property. There are two kinds of estates: freeholds and leaseholds (non-freehold estates). Estates are classified by the length of time they last.

Freehold Estates

Freehold estates are estates that last for an indefinite period of time, that is, at least as long as a lifetime. Such estates last for the indefinite terms of a lifetime or forever. The estate in land that lasts forever is called a fee simple estate and the one that lasts for a lifetime is called a life estate.

Fee Simple Estates

Most deeds now in use pass a **fee simple absolute (fee simple, fee)** estate. It is the highest degree of ownership recognized by law since there is no limitation on the ability of the owner to dispose of the land during his lifetime, and upon death, the property will automatically pass to the owner's heirs either by will or by descent. A fee simple estate includes all possible rights of ownership and is limited only by the public restrictions of taxation, eminent domain, police power and escheat. It may, however, be owned subject to other interests, such as easements, mortgages, etc.

Since a fee interest may be passed on through conveyance or inheritance without end, it is said to last "forever." Virtually all real estate is owned "in fee." Property transfers are automatically presumed to be in fee unless otherwise stated. Fee owners also have the right of **alienation**, meaning the right to convey or transfer the property or interests in it freely without any limitation or restriction upon conveyance. A fee simple interest may also be divided into smaller interests granted to others, such as a life estate, future interest or leasehold.

While fee simple absolute estates are by far the most common, there are several other types of fee simple estates, including: **fee simple subject to a condition subsequent** and **fee simple determinable**. These estates are not final and absolute as the fee simple absolute estate is, but have a "string attached" or condition to the conveyance and are based upon the occurrence or non-occurrence of some named event. They are characterized by the use of conditional words in the instrument of conveyance such as "so long as," "provided that," "conditioned upon" or "until." (Evidence of intent, rather than the use of a specific word or words, would be used by a court to determine which estate had been created.) The clause in the instrument that provides for the property to revert or come back to the grantor if the named condition is violated or left unfulfilled is called a **reverter**. Such estates would be conveyed when the grantor wishes to have some specific requirement fulfilled as a condition of the conveyance, most particularly when the conveyance is a gift.

Example

Mary Jackson conveys 100 acres of land to the Reservoir Ridge Bird Sanctuary, so long as the land is used for a sanctuary. In every sense, this conveyance has the same effect as if it were a fee simple absolute conveyance. However, in a fee simple conditional or fee simple determinable conveyance, if the land were to be used for purposes unrelated to the bird sanctuary, Ms. Jackson or her heirs could seek to have the land revert to them because the condition had been violated. Had the conveyance been in fee simple absolute, the conveyance would have indeed been final and absolute and Mary would not be able to recover the land, even if deed restrictions she created had been violated.

As noted above, the clause in the deed that provides for the property to return to the original owner is called a reverter. In short, a fee simple conditional or determinable conveyance is one with "strings attached," and a fee simple absolute conveyance is one without any "strings attached." The difference between a fee simple conditional and fee simple determinable estate is that the fee simple conditional estate gives the original owner and his heirs the right to terminate the estate through court action because of a violation of the condition contained in the conveyance. In a fee simple determinable estate the estate would be automatically terminated.

Because these two estates are subject to defeat, they are also defeasible fees. **Defeasible** means capable of being defeated. On the other hand, a fee simple absolute estate is **indefeasible**, or not capable of being defeated. (For the balance of the text, and in practice, when the term fee simple is used, it should be presumed to mean fee simple absolute ownership.)

Life Estate

A life estate is an estate in land that is limited to the life of a natural person. This characteristic distinguishes the life estate from the estates discussed above, all of which can be passed on by will or by descent. The party conveying the life estate is called the grantor, and the recipient is called a **life tenant**. The life tenant is entitled to possession of the property, and all profits derived from it, during the period of his tenancy. Once granted, a life estate cannot be revoked, except through court action or as otherwise provided by statute. The most common type of life estate is one based on the life of the life tenant. The estate of such a life tenant is not an estate of inheritance; that is, it cannot be passed on to the owner's heirs, because it terminates upon the death of the life tenant.

A life estate **pur autre vie**, however, is based upon "the life of another" other than the life tenant, and is inheritable until the measuring life ends.

Example

Arnold conveys a parcel of land to his son Bill, for the life of his daughter, Claire. When Claire dies, Bill's life estate is terminated. It should be noted, however, that if Bill dies before Claire, the estate belongs to Bill's heirs during the life of Claire.

The deed used to create the life estate would include words such as "for life," indicating that it is the grantor's intention to create a life estate. A life tenant may sell or lease his life interest, but cannot convey fee simple ownership. (One may never convey to another a right he does not hold himself.) Any interest conveyed by a life tenant would terminate at the end of the measuring life. Life tenants must maintain the property and make reasonable repairs to it, pay taxes and not commit waste. Waste is harm caused to the value of a property by a tenant due to abuse, failure to make repairs if required to do so, or making unreasonable use of the property's resources.

Life estates may be created in the following ways:

Grant. Edward conveys a life estate in a property he owns to Marie by deed.

Reservation. Joe and Helen Travers convey the property where they reside to their son Patrick in fee, but in the deed reserve a life estate for themselves, giving them the right to live in the property for as long as either of them live. (It is most important that one never convey title to his property to anyone else for the purpose of "saving estate taxes" or "protecting us against creditors" without the advice of an attorney. There have been cases where such persons have lost their homes to "trusted" friends and relatives.)

Will. Daisy Smith specifies in her will that when she dies her son Matty is to be given a life interest in a named property. (Life estates created by grant, by reservation or by will are referred to as **conventional life estates**).

Operation of Law. Statute formerly created marital

rights of **dower and curtesy**. While these life estates may no longer be created in New Jersey, many of those previously created remain in existence. Life estates created by law are called **legal life estates**. Legal life estates will be discussed in Chapter 8.

Life estates may take different forms. Some life estates create a **reversion** or reversionary interest in the grantor. In this case, possession of the property will revert to the grantor upon the death of the life tenant. From the moment of the conveyance of the life estate to the life tenant, the grantor immediately gains the right to regain possession of the property on an unknown date in the future. The **future interest** thus created is called a reversion. In other life estates, the grantor may indicate that when the life tenancy ends, possession and title are to pass to some named **third party** called a **remainderman**, since he "gets what remains" after the life tenant's use of the property. The future interest that a remainderman holds is called a remainder. The remainderman may only take possession upon the death of the life tenant and has no right of use in the property until then. A future interest is a present right, which will or may permit the holder to come into possession in the future. This is contrasted with a present interest, such as a fee simple interest, in which possession is held currently.

Rights and Duties of a Life Tenant

The holder of a life estate is entitled to all income from the property during the life tenancy. The life tenant can exploit the natural resources so long as the exploitation does not permanently damage the interests of those who will enjoy the property on termination of the life estate. In other words, he may not commit **waste**. The life tenant must preserve the property, maintain it and keep structures in good repair, but he is under no obligation to improve it. The life tenant must pay all property taxes on the land during the existence of the life estate.

The life tenant may sell, mortgage or lease his life interest. However, upon his death, the rights of all others, whether by sale, mortgage or lease, will be automatically terminated. Consequently, the life tenant cannot **devise** the life estate, as a devise is a gift of real property by will.

LEASEHOLD ESTATES (Nonfreehold Estates, Estates of Less than Freehold)

Leasehold estates are estates in land that last less than a lifetime. Tenants hold these interests. A tenant is one who holds the exclusive right to use the named premises and who possesses an interest in real estate. A tenant's rights contrast sharply with those of a boarder or hotel or motel guest who simply holds a license (permission) to use, which does not constitute an interest in real estate. A leasehold estate is the personal property of the tenant. The various types of leasehold estates will be covered in Chapter 22.

KEY WORDS

Conventional Life Estate	Leasehold Estate	Qualified Fee
Defeasible Fee	Legal Life Estate	Remainder
Devise	Less-than-freehold	Remainderman
Estate	Life Estate	Reservation
Fee Simple	Life Tenant	Reversion
Freehold Estate	Non-freehold	Waste

CHAPTER 6
Review questions
(Answers on page 552)

1. Which of the following is NOT a type of life estate?
   (A) Legal.
   (B) Conventional.
   (C) Indefeasible.
   (D) Pur autre vie.

2. The duration of a life estate is:
   (A) a fixed term.
   (B) potentially infinite.
   (C) a life or the lives of one or more persons.
   (D) not to exceed 99 years.

3. An owner of a life estate can do ALL BUT ONE of the following:
   (A) Sell her interest.
   (B) Mortgage her interest.
   (C) Devise her interest.
   (D) Lease her interest.

4. A widow who is willed the use of the family home for the rest of her natural life, with provision that title shall go to the children upon her death, holds:
   (A) a fee simple estate.
   (B) a leasehold.
   (C) an easement.
   (D) a life estate.

5. Which of the following is correct regarding a life estate?
   (A) Must be measured by the life of the grantee only.
   (B) Because it is based on life, the holder may not encumber it.
   (C) It may be created by will or deed.
   (D) Requires that the holder make principal payments on any encumbrances.

6. In a life estate, the interest held by someone other than the grantor is called a:
   (A) fee simple conditional.
   (B) fee simple determinable.
   (C) remainder interest.
   (D) reversionary interest.

7. An ownership interest in real property is known as:
   (A) an estate.
   (B) a dower.
   (C) a curtesy.
   (D) a possession.

8. The return of land to the grantor or his heirs when the grant is over is:
   (A) remainder.
   (B) reversion.
   (C) kickback.
   (D) status quo.

9. An estate in land vested in a grantee "until he marries" is properly classifiable as:
   (A) an estate in equity.
   (B) a defeasible fee.
   (C) a less-than-freehold estate.
   (D) a life estate.

10. Duffy sells his property to Gilligan, retaining a life interest for himself. He later sells his life estate to Thompson. Gilligan objects to the sale and sues for possession.
    (A) Duffy must cancel the sale of the life estate to protect his interest.
    (B) Gilligan is entitled to immediate possession.
    (C) Thompson may keep the property as long as Duffy lives.
    (D) A life estate may be leased, but not sold. Gilligan is not entitled to possession but can get the sale rescinded.

11. A life estate is conveyed to A for the life of X. A dies. Title:
    (A) reverts back to the grantor.
    (B) passes on to X.
    (C) goes to A's heirs until the death of X.
    (D) None of the above.

12. A conveyance of a life estate where the fee at the end of the life estate goes to someone other than the grantor is a life estate with a:
    (A) remainder.
    (B) reversion.
    (C) reservation.
    (D) restriction.

13. Magna grants a life estate to Carter with the stipulation that the property will go back to Magna when Carter dies. In this case, Magna has:
    (A) a remainder.
    (B) a right of reentry.
    (C) a life estate.
    (D) a reversion.

14. If Jones holds a fee simple estate in property, which of the following acts will result in his being left with a less-than-freehold estate?
    (A) assigning a right of way to a utility company.
    (B) deciding to lease the land on a long-term lease.
    (C) selling the mineral and oil rights to another party.
    (D) None of the above.

15. A life estate is an estate in real property. It:
    (A) can only come into being by grant.
    (B) can exist with another estate in the same property at the same time.
    (C) is not a freehold estate.
    (D) is always limited to the life of the grantee.

16. If Alan deeded 40 acres of land to Bill for the life of Ceil, which of the following statements would be true?
    (A) Bill holds a life estate; Alan, an estate in remainder.
    (B) Bill holds a life estate; Alan, an estate in reversion.
    (C) Bill holds a fee simple estate; Ceil, a life estate.
    (D) Ceil holds a life estate; Bill, an estate in reversion.

17. If Charlotte Roose owns property in fee simple she can do all of the following with the property EXCEPT:
    (A) mortgage it.
    (B) lease it.
    (C) sell it.
    (D) condemn it.

18. Faith conveys a house to Hope for life, then to Charity. Hope's heirs have:
    (A) no estate or interest.
    (B) the same interest Hope had.
    (C) a reversion.
    (D) a remainder.

19. Full and complete ownership of land as recognized today exists most nearly in:
    (A) a life estate.
    (B) an estate in remainder.
    (C) a fee simple estate.
    (D) an estate in reversion.

20. An example of a freehold estate is:
    (A) a life estate.
    (B) a periodic estate.
    (C) an estate at will.
    (D) an estate for years.

CHAPTER SEVEN

METHODS OF OWNERSHIP

TYPES OF TENANCY

All property has an owner, the federal, state or local government, or some private institution or party. It is this latter category, ownership by a private party, that is identified legally through various forms of tenancy. The four principal types of tenancies, or ownership interests, are (1) tenancy in severalty; (2) joint tenancy; (3) tenancy by the entirety; and (4) tenancy in common (see Figures 7.1 and 7.3).

1. Tenancy in Severalty. When one person, single or married, or a legal entity such as a corporation owns property, it is referred to as sole ownership, or **ownership in severalty**. It simply means that the property is owned by one person only and that person alone can use, mortgage or dispose of the property as he or she desires. The word severalty does not mean "several," as one might think, but rather that the interest of the owner is "severed" and is separate and apart from the interest of any other person.

2. Joint Tenancy. A joint tenancy is an interest in land held by two or more persons with rights of **survivorship**. Property held in joint tenancy does not pass to the heirs of the decedent. Instead, it passes to the surviving owner or owners, without the need for probate proceedings. Probate is the process of establishing the validity of the will of a deceased person.

Example
Adam, Bob and Carl are brothers who agree to become joint tenants in a property they are buying. After obtaining ownership, Carl dies. Carl's share of the property automatically passes to Adam and Bob, the survivors. Later, Adam dies. The joint tenancy is now dissolved and Bob owns the property in severalty.

A joint tenancy may only be created through direct action of the parties involved and never through operation of law or by descent (gaining title as an heir when the owner dies intestate). A joint tenancy may not be presumed and can only be created by a clear statement of intent in the deed that the parties are taking title as "joint tenants with the right of survivorship, and not as tenants in common."

Four "unities" or simultaneous happenings are necessary to create a joint tenancy: (1) time; (2) title; (3) interest; and (4) possession.

Unity of time means the parties must have taken title at the same time. Once a joint tenancy is formed, a new joint tenant cannot be added at a later time unless a new joint tenancy is formed between the existing co-owners and the new co-owner.

Unity of title means that the joint tenants must acquire their interests by way of the same deed or will.

Unity of interest means that the joint tenants must own equal ownership interests. For example, one owner cannot have a one-third interest and the other two-thirds.

Unity of possession means that each joint tenant is entitled to the same undivided possession of the entire property, and no action for trespass can be brought by one owner against the other. (One owner cannot specify he owns the south 40 acres, while his co-owner owns the north 40.)

In certain cases the unities of time and title have been eliminated, allowing a husband, for example, who is the sole owner of property to convey that property to himself and his wife as joint tenants or tenants by the entirety, rather than abiding by the former necessity of first conveying ownership to an outsider (straw man) and then having that outsider reconvey ownership back to him and his wife as joint tenants.

A joint tenant may sell his interest in the property without the consent of the other owner, but this will break his joint tenancy and make the new owner a tenant in common with the remaining owner. If there are more than two parties to the tenancy, the death of one owner will not affect the title, since it is automatically vested in the remaining owners. However, the survivor(s), as a matter of good practice, should record a death certificate in the county clerk's office. One joint tenant may also encumber his interest and not break the tenancy, but if a mortgage is foreclosed, it then severs the joint tenancy relationship.

The following actions will sever a joint tenancy:

a. In the case of two owners, a conveyance by one joint tenant breaks the joint tenancy, and the new owner becomes a tenant in common with the previous owner.

b. If A, B and C own property as joint tenants, and A conveys his interest to Z, then B and C remain as joint tenants, but Z holds his 1/3 interest in the property as a tenant in common with B and C.

c. **Partition** is a legal proceeding by which an estate held by tenants in common or joint tenants is divided and title in severalty to a designated portion given to each of the previous owners. If the owners cannot agree to an equitable subdivision of their interests (partition in kind), the court has the power to direct a sale and will divide the proceeds among the co-owners according to their respective interests (judicial partition).

d. If a husband and wife jointly owning property as joint tenants are divorced and their divorce decree states that their jointly held land shall be sold, with the proceeds being divided equally, the joint tenancy would be severed.

e. Involuntary transfer of title, such as one party going into bankruptcy, would sever the tenancy, because title to all his property would automatically be transferred to a trustee in bankruptcy.

Certain events do not sever the joint tenancy. For example:

a. A will by one joint tenant does not break the joint tenancy, due to the right of survivorship by the remaining tenant. Thus, the will is partially ineffective, and title to the property will automatically go to the survivor without the necessity of probate.

b. An easement granted to a third party by one of the joint tenants does not break the joint tenancy, but again dies with the joint tenant granting it.

During the lifetime of a joint tenant, the undivided fractional interest he owns is subject to the rights, claims, liens and judgments of his creditors. However, legal action to enforce the claims must be instituted during the lifetime of the debtor-joint tenant. After the death of the debtor, the creditors lose their rights in the property because any surviving owners take the property free from the claims of the deceased joint tenant's creditors.

A natural person and a corporation cannot co-own a property as joint tenants because the natural person will never be able to be the surviving owner.

3. Tenancy by the Entirety. Tenancy by the entirety is similar to joint tenancy, with the exception that there are only two persons in the ownership and they must be husband and wife. Upon the death of either, the survivor automatically acquires title to the share of the deceased spouse free and clear of the claims of heirs and creditors of the deceased spouse. If they become divorced, however, the parties would then become tenants in common. This tenancy is recognized in New Jersey, but not in all states. Under this type of ownership, creditors cannot attach the real estate for the debt of one of the spouses. In other words, a creditor of one spouse cannot force a sale of one-half of the property to satisfy a judgment against that spouse. However, a creditor of both spouses could take legal action to force a sale of the property to satisfy a joint obligation.

The principal difference between tenancy by the entirety and joint tenancy is that neither husband nor wife acting alone can alter the ownership or rights of the other. A transfer by one without the consent of the other is no good. Likewise, neither could mortgage the property alone. The right of survivorship of either one cannot be defeated by the other, by will or otherwise.

A tenancy by the entirety is automatically created when a deed conveys property to a husband and wife, unless an express provision indicates an intention to create some other form of co-ownership.

If they represent themselves as husband and wife when, in fact, they are not married, the conveyance will be deemed to have created a tenancy in common. If, however, they have specifically stated that they want rights of survivorship, it would appear that their actual intention was to form a joint tenancy.

When a conveyance or devise is made to a husband and wife and to a third party, the husband and wife generally hold a 50% interest as tenants in common with the other party. Take, for example, a conveyance to "A and B, husband and wife, and C." The husband and wife own their half as tenants by the entireties. A similar result occurs when a conveyance is made to "A and B, husband and wife, and C and D, husband and wife." A and B and C and D are each tenants by the entireties with regard to their 50% interests, but each couple is a tenant in common as to the other couple.

4. Tenancy in Common. This type of tenancy exists when an estate of land is held by two or more persons, with the outstanding feature that upon the death of one party there is no right of survivorship among the other owners. When a tenant in common dies, his interest in the property passes to his heirs, not to the surviving co-owners. A tenancy in common is formed whenever two or more unmarried people take title together, unless specified otherwise. The share of each tenant in common descends to his heirs or to parties named in his will. A tenant in common holds an estate in land by separate and distinct title, but with the unity of possession. Thus, even though the tenant does not necessarily have the same proportionate share of interest (as in a joint tenancy), he will still be possessed of an individual undivided share of the whole. Stated otherwise, he is entitled to undivided possession of the property regardless of the size of his share of the whole. Since one tenant in common has no right of exclusive possession of any portion of the property, if two married couples purchase a two-family home as tenants in common, they should expressly modify this rule so that each couple can have exclusive possession of one apartment. Under this type of ownership, one is free to sell his interest as he sees fit and the new owner simply becomes a new tenant in common with the other owner or owners. If one tenant mortgages his interest in the land it does not bind the others, it merely creates a lien on the mortgagor's interest.

Example
Alice, Bertha and Cathy purchase a property together as tenants in common. Alice dies. Alice's interest in the property will not go to Bertha and Cathy because as tenants in common they have

FIGURE 7.1
Interests in Real Property

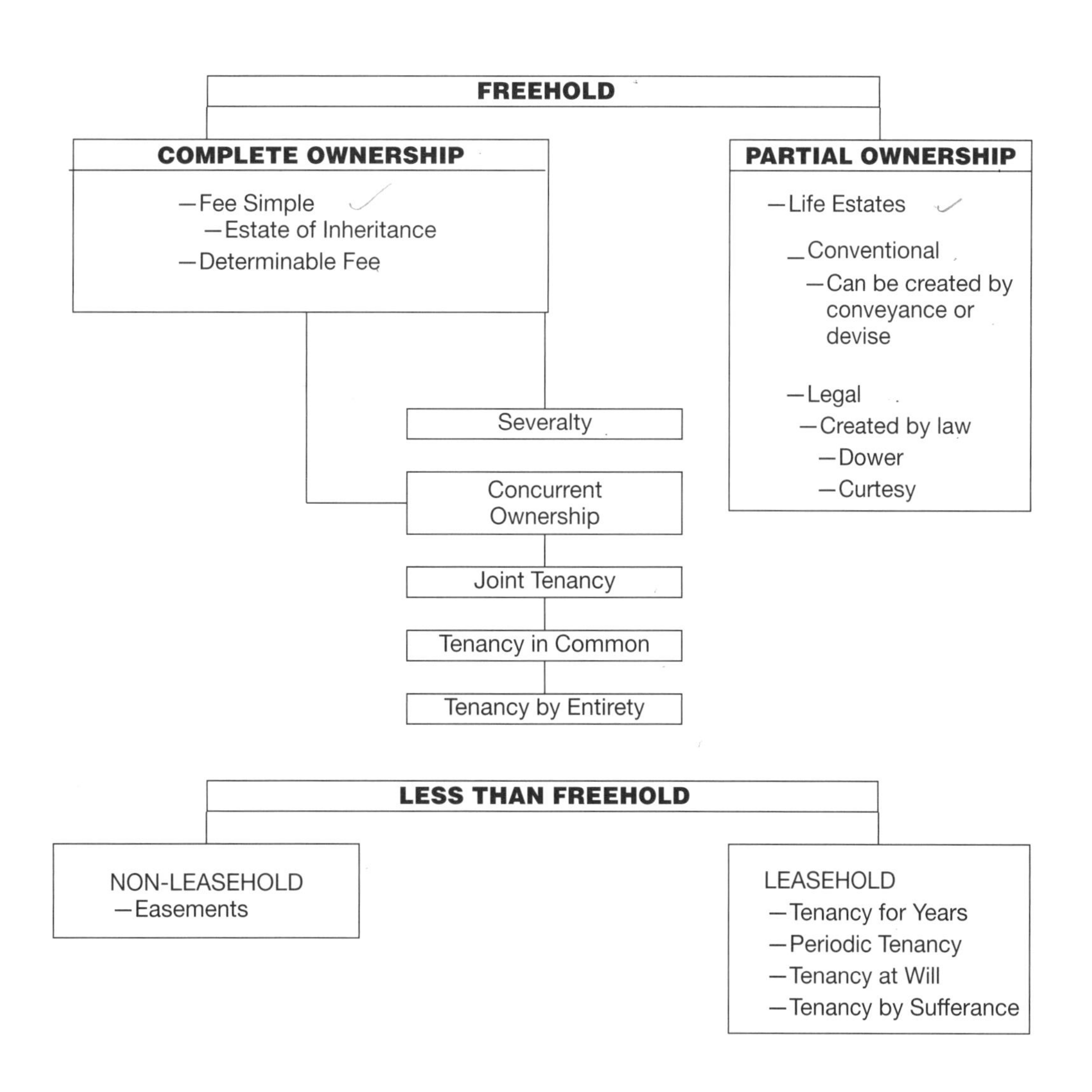

no rights of survivorship. Instead. Alice's interest will pass according to the terms of her will, or to her legally recognized heirs if she dies intestate. Alice's heirs, along with Bertha and Cathy, will now be co-owners of the property as tenants in common.

OTHER FORMS OF MULTIPLE OWNERSHIP

In addition to being owned individually, ownership interests in real estate may also be by various legal entities, as described below:

1. Partnership. A partnership is an association of two or more persons to carry on a business for profit. There are two types of partnerships: **general** and **limited**. In a general partnership all partners participate to some extent in the management and operation of the partnership affairs and share in the profits and losses. A limited partnership is composed of one or more general partners and one or more limited partners. The general partners are in charge of the limited partnership. The limited partners are passive investors who are not permitted to participate in the operations of the partnership. Their liability is limited to the amount of their investment as stated in the partnership agreement, and they cannot bind the entity by their acts or conduct.

Under the Uniform Partnership Act, title to real estate can be held in the name of the **partners** or in the name of the **partnership**. If title is taken in the partnership's name, it is a "tenancy in partnership." Title is conveyed by the partner holding proper authority or by all the partners signing the agreement to sell. The death of one partner either dissolves the partnership or his interests in the partnership property will go to the surviving partners, depending on the terms of the partnership agreement. The heirs of the deceased partner have no dower or curtesy interest in the property of the partnership.

2. Joint Venture. The joining of two or more parties in a specific business enterprise is called a **joint venture**. Joint ventures are often used in large-scale construction projects such as the development and sale of real estate subdivisions. This is a business form similar to a general partnership, and, in fact, is treated as such for tax purposes. The main difference between the two is that a joint venture is a special joining of the parties for a specific project with no intention on the part of the parties to enter into any continuing partnership relationship. When the purpose of the joint venture has been accomplished, the entity ceases to exist. Also, while a general partner can bind the partnership to a contract, one party to a joint venture agreement cannot bind the other joint venturers to a contract. Where the parties combine their efforts on several different projects, the relationship becomes more like a general partnership than a joint venture.

3. Co-operative Apartments (Co-op). A cooperative apartment, commonly called a co-op, is a form of ownership in which a corporation is established to hold title to property and to lease the property to shareholders in the corporation. Persons wishing to occupy units which are owned by the corporation sign a **subscription agreement** for stock and receive a **proprietary lease** on a specific unit, subject to certain conditions and obligations as to its use and right to sublease.

In the proprietary lease, the shareholder agrees to pay a proportionate share of expenses incurred by the corporation for maintenance, property taxes and debt service. The cooperative is usually managed by a property manager under the direction of a board of directors elected by the shareholders. Federal income tax law allows the shareholder to deduct the portion of each payment that represents property taxes and interest. The shareholder's right or interest in the co-op is considered to be personal property, not real property. He owns shares of stock in the corporation (personal property) and has a leasehold interest (personal property).

Stock in the corporation may provide for the possibility of further assessment and may have further restrictions upon its transferability. The corporation may retain a right of first refusal and may require that the occupant sell the shares for the original price paid.

4. Condominium. The legislation authorizing the creation and regulation of condominiums in New Jersey is embodied in two acts—the **Horizontal Property Act** of 1963 and the Condominium Act of 1969.

A condominium is a system of ownership of individual units in a multi-unit structure, combined with joint ownership of common areas. Each owner receives a unit deed to his own unit entitling him to a proportionate share in the common areas.

Common areas (common elements) are areas that are owned by all unit owners. Examples include exterior walls, beams, roof, stairwells, plumbing, heating and wiring, elevators, parking lots, tennis courts and other recreational areas. All the owners as tenants in common normally own the common areas. For example, in a 50-unit condominium, if all units were the same size, each owner would own a 1/50 interest in the common areas, and a 1/50 share in maintenance and other condominium expenses.

Condominiums can be developed for any purpose—residential, commercial or industrial. However, all would have the following common characteristics:

- Title is conveyed by a **unit deed** conveying title to both the unit and the common areas.
- There is a reserve fund for capital improvements (e.g., new roof, boiler) and liability for special assessments when reserves are less than required.
- Each unit may be separately mortgaged.
- Taxes are assessed against each unit separately and each unit owner receives a separate tax bill.
- Each unit owner pays a monthly maintenance fee, non-payment of which creates a lien against the unit.
- Each unit is eligible for title insurance as a separate piece of property.
- Unit owners are responsible for providing property and liability insurance for their individual dwelling units.
- Insurance coverage for common areas is provided by the association and paid for out of the monthly maintenance charge.
- A board of directors is elected from the unit owners to regulate and administer the condominium in accordance with the condominium bylaws.

The recording of a **declaration** and **master deed** in the county clerk's or registrar's office creates the condominium. The party filing or causing the filing of the master deed is known as the **sponsor**, who must also be the owner of the land or a party having a contract to purchase it. Recorded along with the declaration and master deed is a **condominium map**, a "scale drawing" prepared by a licensed professional surveyor showing the layout of the complex and the exact location and dimensions of each unit and the common elements (see Figure 7.2).

All owners of the fee simple estate covered by the master deed must execute the master deed. If the condominium is formed from land held as leasehold, all lessees must execute the master deed, in addition to the fee owners.

The master deed must contain: (1) a statement of dedication of the land to condominium ownership; (2) the name of the project, including the word "condominium"; (3) a legal description of the

FIGURE 7.2
Franklin Court Condominium Map

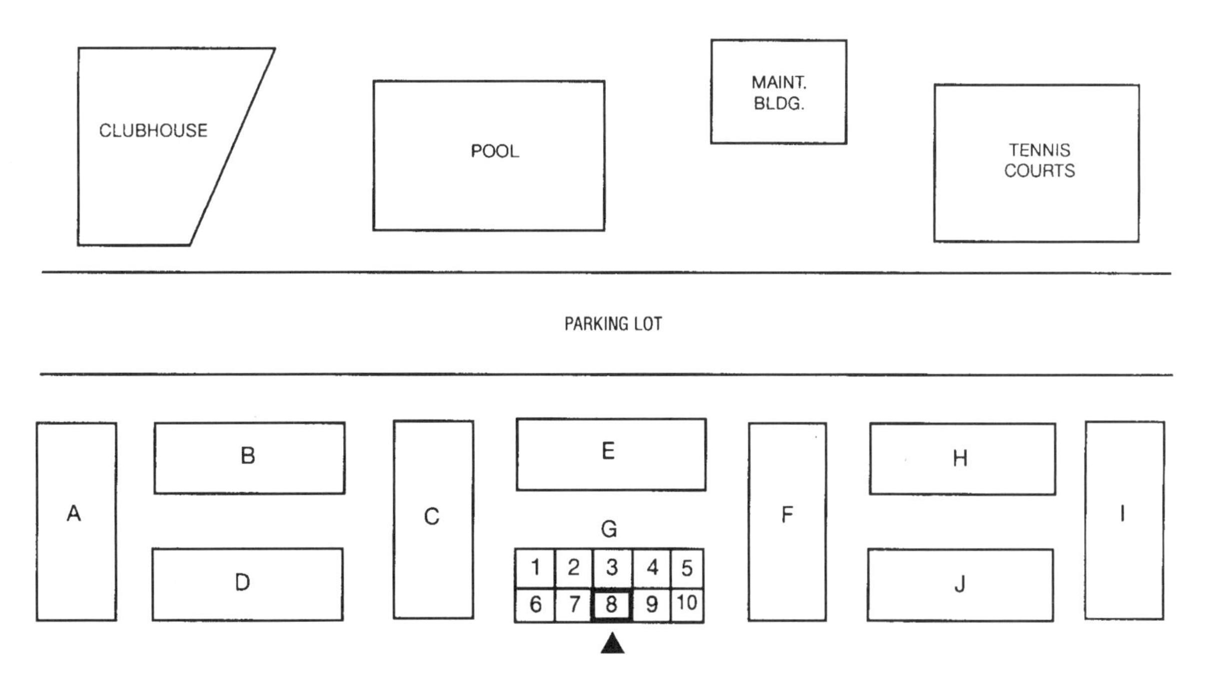

There are ten buildings in the Franklin Court complex, lettered A through I. Each building contains two floors, so there are 20 units per building, for a total of 200 units. Downstairs units in G building and other buildings are numbered from 1 to 10, and from 11 to 20 for upstairs units. Randolph and Sue Veck own unit G-8, along with a 1/200 interest in the common areas. Each of the other 200 units is similarly owned, with their owners sharing a similar 1/200 interest in the common areas and a 1/200 share in maintenance and other condominium expenses.

land; (4) a survey of the land; (5) plans of the improvements, showing location and dimensions of each unit and thc common elements, with each unit required to be designated by letter, name or number; (6) a description of the common elements and limited common elements (parking spaces, storage bins, etc.); (7) the proportionate undivided interests in the common elements and limited common elements appurtenant to each unit, totaling 100%; (8) the voting rights of the unit owners; (9) the bylaws; (10) the method of amending and supplementing the master deed; (11) the name and nature of the condominium association; (12) the manner of sharing common expenses and owning common surplus; and (13) such other provisions as may be desired, including, but not limited to, restrictions or limitations upon the use, occupancy, transfer, leasing or other disposition of any unit.

Condominium Owners Association. A developer who records a master deed also creates a legal framework so that unit owners can govern themselves. This is the condominium owners association, and each unit purchaser automatically becomes a member. The main functions of the association are to control, regulate and maintain the common elements for the good of its members and to enforce the condominium's bylaws.

Bylaws. The condominium bylaws establish the rules under which the association operates. They are prepared by the developer's attorney and are recorded with the master deed. The bylaws stipulate the procedure for election of the board of directors and define its power and authority. They also provide how maintenance fees are established and collected, how contracts will be awarded for maintenance and management, and how personnel will be hired.

In creating a condominium, if the Planned Real Estate Development Full Disclosure Act, N.J.S.A.. 45:22A-21 *et seq.*, is not followed in every detail, there will be no exclusive ownership of the units and the entire property will be owned as a tenancy in common. The Division of Housing and Urban Renewal of the State Department of Community Affairs administer the Act. Among other things, the Act provides that all contracts for the purchase of a condominium unit must contain a clause giving the purchaser the right to cancel the contract within seven calendar days after signing of the contract by the purchaser.

Shareholders in co-ops and condominium unit owners can deduct mortgage interest and real estate taxes for federal income tax purposes. Upon default of a mortgage in a condominium, the purchaser at a foreclosure sale would acquire title to the apartment and it would generally have no effect on the other apartment owners. In a co-op, however, the apartment owner is responsible together with the other owners for the payment of all the expenses of the entire building, which may include the mortgage. Therefore, if one owner defaults, the other owners must together share his unpaid expenses. Obviously, if too many tenants default, the corporation may find itself in serious financial trouble.

5. Real Estate Investment Trust (REIT). A REIT is a real estate mutual fund that allows small investors to invest in real estate. A trust is formed and investors purchase real estate investment trust certificates issued by the REIT. The trust then uses the funds to purchase real estate and mortgages.

REITs are not subject to double taxation (discussed below) if the following requirements are met: the trust must have at least 100 investors, it must be in unincorporated form, it must distribute 90% of its annual income to the beneficiaries, 75% of the trust's income must be from "passive" real estate investments such as mortgage interest and rentals, and no five persons may own more than 50% of the beneficial title.

6. Corporation. A corporation is a separate, artificial entity, created and regulated by state law, that has perpetual existence and the right to sell or distribute shares of ownership to the public. Receiving a charter from the state creates it. It also has the right to own, encumber, sell or convey realty and personal property in its own name, or to do any acts incidental to the transaction of its business, or expedient for the attainment of its corporate purposes. These rights are limited only by state regulations and the restrictions imposed in its own charter and bylaws. When dealing with a corporation, it is important to determine that the officer representing the corporation has been authorized to act for the corporation through a corporate resolution passed by the board of directors.

Some distinctions of a corporation are that it is considered a separate legal entity; it has perpetual existence; it is unaffected by change of personnel or officers, by death, or by the personal financial disaster of one individual; the shareholders have practically no direct control over its affairs; the shareholders are not liable for the firm's debts and it can usually better handle large properties because it can attract capable, diversified and skilled help in management.

The major disadvantage of a corporation is that its income is subject to **double taxation**. The corporation must file a tax return and pay tax on its profits, and the stockholders must also pay tax when they receive dividends. In addition, any loss suffered by the corporation may not be passed to the shareholders. Thus, a shareholder cannot use the corporation's losses on his or her personal tax return to offset income from other sources.

Since a corporation cannot hold title in joint tenancy because of its perpetual existence (it would always survive a co-owner), corporations generally hold title to property in severalty, or as a tenant in common.

7. Limited Liability Corporation. A limited liability corporation (LLC) is a hybrid between a corporation and a partnership that combines the tax advantages of a partnership with the limited liability afforded to corporate shareholders. Unlike a corporation that can be formed with one shareholder, an LLC must have two or more members (owners). Generally, only the LLC is responsible for the company's debts, but if a member personally guarantees the obligations of the LLC, he or she will be liable. For example, a landlord who leases space to a newly formed LLC that has no credit history would likely require a personal guarantee before executing a lease.

8. Syndicate. A syndicate is a joining together of two or more people for the purpose of making and operating an investment. One or more of the parties takes an active role in the creation and managing of the investment while others take a passive role, usually limited to supplying capital. It is not a true legal ownership, but is rather a term used to describe multiple ownership of an investment. Most real estate syndications are organized as limited partnerships. This enables the partnership to act as a conduit and pass through high-depreciation deductions directly to the individual investors and thus avoid the double taxation aspects of corporate ownership.

TIME-SHARING OWNERSHIP

Time-sharing ownership, commonly known as "vacation ownership," is an innovative method of marketing resort and vacation condominiums. It can be broadly described as a form of property ownership under which a property is held by a number of people, each with a right of possession for a specified time interval. Time shares are structured either as right-to-use projects or fee simple ownership.

Right-to-Use Projects. These projects are typically structured as:

- Vacation leases
- Vacation licenses
- Club memberships
- Right-to-use time shares

In such arrangements the purchaser does not acquire any interest in real property. The purchaser merely acquires a license or contracts the right to use and occupy a specific unit, apartment or room during a certain period of time (days or weeks) for a predetermined number of years. The cost for the entire period is paid in advance.

Time-share Estates (Fee Projects). This type of arrangement includes an estate in the property. A fee interest in the real estate and improvements is conveyed to the purchaser by a deed. The purchaser acquires, as a tenant in common with other owners, an undivided fee simple interest in a unit, parcel or the entire project. Generally, individual use periods of time are established or allocated by separate legal instruments.

Time shares are marketed using typical condominium documentation, with the addition of a time-sharing agreement which specifically outlines the rights, responsibilities, and periods of occupancy to which the buyer is entitled. Some of the items detailed in the time-sharing documents are use periods, ownership interests, exclusive occupancy, management, collection and payment of costs, voting rights, enforcement, prohibition of partition, damage or destruction of the unit or project and insurance.

Developers selling time-share units located outside of New Jersey must comply with the provisions of the Real Estate Sales Full Disclosure Act (45:15-16.27) if they market the units in New Jersey.

KEY WORDS

Common Element
Common Expense
Common Interest
Condominium
Cooperative Apartment (Co-op)
Corporation
Horizontal Property Act
Joint Tenancy
Joint Venture
Limited Partnership
Partition
Partnership
Proprietary Lease
Right of Survivorship
Tenancy by the Entirety
Tenancy by Severalty
Tenancy in Common
Unities of Title
Undivided Interest

Figure 7.3

Types of Tenancy

	Tenancy in Severalty	Tenancy in Common	Joint Tenancy	Tenancy by Entireties
Definition	Property held by one person, severed from all others.	Property held by two or more persons, with no right of survivorship.	Property held by two or more (not corporation) with right of survivorship.	Property held by husband and wife with right of survivorship.
Creation	Any transfer to one person.	By express act; also by failure to express the tenancy.	Express intention plus four unities of time, title, interest and possession (with statutory exceptions).	Divorce automatically results in tenancy in common.
Possession	Total.	Equal right of possession.	Equal right of possession.	Equal right of possession.
Title	One title in one person.	Equal co-owner has a separate legal title to his undivided interest; will be equal interests unless expressly made unequal.	One title to the whole property since each tenant is theoretically deemed owner of whole; must be equal undivided interests.	One title in the marital unit.
Conveyance	No restrictions (check release of marital rights if any).	Each co-owner's interest may be conveyed separately by its owner; purchaser becomes tenant in common.	Conveyance of one co-owner's interest breaks his tenancy; purchaser becomes tenant in common.	Cannot convey without consent of spouse.
Effect of Death	Entire property subject to probate and included in gross estate for Federal and state death taxes.	Decedent's fractional interest subject to probate and included in gross estate for Federal and state death taxes. The property passes by will to devisees or heirs, who take as tenants in common. No survivorship rights.	No probate and can't be disposed of by will; property automatically belongs to surviving co-tenants (last one holds in severalty). Entire property included in decedent's gross estate for Federal estate tax purposes, minus percent attributable to survivor's contribution.	Right of survivorship so no probate. Same death taxes as joint tenancy.
Creditor's Rights	Subject to creditor claims.	Co-owner's fractional interest may be sold to satisfy his creditor, who then becomes tenant in common.	Joint tenant's interest also subject to execution sale, joint tenancy is broken and creditor becomes tenant in common. Creditor gets nothing if debtor tenant dies before sale.	Only a creditor of both spouses can execute on property.
Presumption	None.	Favored in doubtful cases; presumed to be equal interests.	Not favored, so must be expressly stated.	Automatically created when names of both spouses appear on the deed.

CHAPTER 7
Review Questions
(Answers on page 552)

1. A conveys property to B and C who are unrelated and not joint tenants. If B dies:
   (A) C is the sole owner.
   (B) B's share goes to his heirs.
   (C) the property reverts back to A.
   (D) E comes into the picture.

2. Which of the following statements apply equally to joint tenants and tenants by the entirety?
   (A) There is no right to file a partition suit.
   (B) The survivor becomes owner.
   (C) A deed signed by one will convey a fractional interest.
   (D) A deed will not convey any interest unless signed by both spouses.

3. When a person owns property to the exclusion of all other persons, he is said to hold the property in:
   (A) personalty.
   (B) common.
   (C) severalty.
   (D) secret.

4. A tenancy in common must have unity of:
   (A) time.
   (B) title.
   (C) interest.
   (D) possession.

5. Co-ownership of property by a husband and wife can take any of the following forms EXCEPT a:
   (A) tenancy in common.
   (B) tenancy by the entirety.
   (C) joint tenancy.
   (D) tenancy in severalty.

6. When used in connection with ownership interests, the term "partition" means:
   (A) a formal written request signed by a group of petitioners.
   (B) court action by which owners of property seek to sever their common ownership.
   (C) a bearing wall in a building.
   (D) a non-bearing wall in a building.

7. A joint tenant may NOT:
   (A) sell his interest.
   (B) give away his interest.
   (C) encumber his interest.
   (D) devise his interest.

8. Your customer plans to get divorced shortly before closing of a property she and her boyfriend just purchased and asks you about how to hold title to the property. You should suggest she:
   (A) get divorced first.
   (B) conceal the pending divorce.
   (C) consult an attorney.
   (D) choose joint tenancy.

9. When purchasing real estate, the form or method of ownership (severalty, tenants in common or joint tenants) should be determined by:
   (A) the broker.
   (B) the buyer and his attorney.
   (C) the seller.
   (D) the law of the state in which the real estate is located.

10. If title to a farm is held as tenants by the entirety, which of the following is true?
    (A) A valid contract of sale on the farm must be signed by both of the spouses that are selling.
    (B) A creditor of one spouse can assert a valid lien on the farm.
    (C) The husband can devise his interest.
    (D) Spouses have no survivorship rights.

11. When a person who owns real estate in severalty dies testate, his property:
    (A) goes entirely to the surviving joint tenant.
    (B) is probated and distributed according to the will.
    (C) would be solely vested in the remaining tenant in common.
    (D) reverts to the county by escheat.

12. Property purchased by a brother and sister with full survivorship would be:
    (A) tenancy in common.
    (B) joint tenancy.
    (C) tenancy by entirety.
    (D) severalty.

13. One of the features of owning real property as tenants in common is:
    (A) each co-owner must have equal interest.
    (B) each owner may not will his interest.
    (C) each co-owner may acquire interest at different times.
    (D) the last survivor owns property in severalty.

(Quiz continues on next page)

14. Two sisters, Mary and Rose, inherit real estate from their mother with no stipulation except that 1/3 is to go to Mary and 2/3 to Rose. Which of the following is true?
    (A) Mary and Rose are joint tenants of the property.
    (B) Rose may not mortgage her interest in the property without Mary's consent.
    (C) Upon Mary's death her part of the property reverts to Rose.
    (D) Upon Rose's death, her share passes to her heirs or devisees.

15. A woman and her brother hold property in joint tenancy. The woman deeded her part to herself and her husband. Therefore,
    (A) the deed to the husband is invalid.
    (B) the joint tenancy is broken.
    (C) all three now hold title in joint tenancy.
    (D) joint tenancy remains the same.

16. One of the advantages of joint tenancy is:
    (A) it cannot be terminated without the consent of each tenant.
    (B) tenants may own different fractional shares.
    (C) it avoids delays and expenses of probate.
    (D) it can only exist between husband and wife.

17. Property owned by a tenant in common passes at death:
    (A) to his co-tenant or tenants.
    (B) to his estate.
    (C) by right of survivorship.
    (D) by escheat.

18. A joint tenant may NOT:
    (A) sell his interest.
    (B) give away his interest.
    (C) encumber his interest.
    (D) sell the property.

19. Where two brothers hold title to property, one with a 1/3 interest and the other a 2/3 interest, title would most likely be held as:
    (A) joint tenancy.
    (B) tenancy by the entirety.
    (C) tenancy in common.
    (D) tenancy in severalty.

20. A corporation cannot hold title to real property in New Jersey with another as a joint tenant because:
    (A) it is a violation of the Securities Act.
    (B) of its perpetual existence.
    (C) it is difficult to list all stockholders in the deed.
    (D) a corporation cannot convey title to real property.

21. A, B and C own property as joint tenants. C dies and B sells his interest in the property to D. The property is now owned:
    (A) as joint tenants by A, D and C's widow, E, his sole heir.
    (B) A and D as joint tenants.
    (C) A and D as tenants in common, each with a 1/2 interest.
    (D) A and D and B's wife.

22. Hanna Marsh and Max Haver buy a house together. They are a young, unmarried couple and want to know how they should take title so that if one of them dies, that person's heirs will inherit the property interest. Their attorney will most likely recommend:
    (A) joint tenancy.
    (B) tenancy at will.
    (C) tenancy by the entirety.
    (D) tenancy in common.

23. A deed in favor of Norman and Rosalie with the stated proportionate interests of 2/3 and 1/3 respectively:
    (A) creates a tenancy in common.
    (B) creates a valid joint tenancy.
    (C) creates a severalty interest for each.
    (D) is void.

24. A tenancy by the entirety exists:
    (A) automatically when names of husband and wife appear on the deed.
    (B) whenever there is right of survivorship among concurrent owners.
    (C) when two or more people own the entire property.
    (D) after the owners have been divorced.

25. Dower rights are extinguished by:
    (A) separation.
    (B) death of the husband.
    (C) assignment.
    (D) divorce.

26. Tenants by the entirety:
    (A) each own a portion of the property.
    (B) may seek an action for partition.
    (C) have the right of survivorship.
    (D) may share unequal interests.

27. In New Jersey, condominiums are regulated by:
    (A) the NJ Real Estate Commission.
    (B) the NJ Condominium Bureau.
    (C) the NJ Department of Community Affairs.
    (D) the Horizontal Property Act.

CHAPTER EIGHT

DOWER, CURTESY, WILLS AND DESCENT

DOWER

Dower is the interest given to a wife by state law in the property of her husband upon his death. It is a life estate in a one-half part of all lands owned by the husband at any time during the continuance of the marriage. This right is said to be an inchoate dower interest before her husband's death, because during his life the wife's rights consist only of a possibility that she will receive anything upon his death. It becomes a consummate interest upon his death, for only then does it change into an actual possession, usually when a court assigns the wife her separate dower interest.

The necessary requirements for the existence of dower are: (1) a valid marriage (New Jersey does not recognize common law marriage); (2) the husband owns the property during the marriage; and (3) the husband must die prior to his wife.

A wife cannot convey her inchoate dower interest to another, nor can that interest be sold in a forced sale to pay the wife's debts. She may release her dower interest by joining her husband in a deed conveying the realty to a third party or by a separate document, executed at the same time as the conveyance. The wife's dower interests are superior to any claims of the husband's creditors, however, her dower is subject to liens or encumbrances to which the land was subject at the time of the marriage, or at the time the husband acquired the land. A wife has no dower in lands owned by her husband in joint tenancy or partnership with another, only those owned by him in tenancy in common or severalty.

During the marriage, then, there is a one-half inchoate dower interest in all real estate owned in severalty by a married man. It therefore becomes necessary to have the wife release her dower interest in any real property the husband has acquired, whether by purchase, gift, or inheritance, that is held at any time during the marriage. Thus, any real property transferred during the husband's lifetime without the wife's signature will be transferred with a cloud on the title. If she has not released her dower rights, she may, upon his death, step in and rightfully claim her interest in such property. In other words, the person to whom the property is transferred takes it subject to her dower rights.

As of May 28, 1980, no new dower and curtesy interests may be created in this state. Chapter 485 of the Laws of New Jersey, 1979, provides for the abolition of the interest as to any real property acquired after the effective date of the Act, which is May 28, 1980. It is extremely important to focus upon the prospective effect of the Act, because dower and curtesy interests existing prior to the effective date of the Act are not affected by the Act.

Right of Possession

A new right has been established by the Act called the **right of possession**. Each spouse has the right of joint possession during marriage with the other spouse of the property occupied as their **principal matrimonial residence** acquired after the effective date of the Act. The right of possession may not be released, extinguished or sold without the consent of both the husband and the wife, except by judgment of a court of competent jurisdiction.

It is important to keep in mind that the right of possession is limited to the time that the persons are married. A widow, or widower, will not have a right of possession, because death terminates the marriage.

The Act will be of concern when a husband or wife owns property individually, and not jointly. The following rules should be considered when dealing with the applicability of the law:

1. In all cases where the family home is being sold, both spouses must consent to the sale and release their interest, be it dower, curtesy or right of possession.

2. All property acquired prior to May 28, 1980 by one spouse will be subject to the dower or curtesy interest of the other spouse, which must be released in order to convey clear title.

3. All property acquired on or after May 28, 1980 which is not in the family home may be sold

without regard to the interests of dower, curtesy and the right of possession.

In 1988, a New Jersey court permitted an award of damages in favor of a husband, and against the wife's grantee, resulting from the wife's conveyance of the marital residence without the husband's consent. The wife had conveyed the property (title to which had been acquired by her through inheritance) while a divorce action filed by the husband was pending. The Court held that, notwithstanding the fact that the husband moved out of the marital residence during the pendency of the divorce, his joint right of possession was not extinguished. Accordingly, only a final judgment of divorce will terminate this marital right.

CURTESY

Curtesy is the one-half life estate given to a widowed husband, by state law, in the lands owned by his wife during the marriage. The requirements are: a valid marriage; that the property be owned during the marriage; and that the wife die prior to the husband. Both dower and curtesy are terminated by divorce.

ELECTIVE SHARE AND THE AUGMENTED ESTATE

For many years, New Jersey was one of the few states in the country which did not provide some form of elective share to a surviving spouse. Consequently, the surviving spouse's rights were limited to dower and curtesy. These rights often did not provide sufficient protection because they did not include any interest in personal property owned by the deceased spouse such as stocks, bonds, bank accounts, etc.

On May 28, 1980, as a part of a major reform of our probate law, the New Jersey Legislature enacted an elective share law which introduced the concept of the augmented estate. The **augmented estate** is the net probate estate of a deceased spouse plus certain transfers he made during his lifetime to his spouse and to others. The surviving spouse can then take one-third of the augmented estate, unless the provisions which the decedent made during his lifetime and by will, plus property owned by the surviving spouse, exceed this one-third amount.

The New Jersey law differs from the elective share law of most other states because it includes all property owned by the surviving spouse at the time of the deceased spouse's death, not only property acquired from the deceased spouse. Consequently, a surviving spouse having substantial assets of his or her own will not be able to elect in many cases.

Suppose a married man died leaving a probate estate in his name of $400,000, joint bank accounts with children of $100,000 and a $100,000 house owned jointly with his wife. If the wife owned nothing else in her own name, she would be entitled to an elective share of one-third of $600,000, or $200,000. If the husband did not provide for her in his will, she could take the $100,000 house as the surviving owner, and in addition, she could elect against his will for another $100,000. If, however, she had assets in her own name of $100,000 from personal savings, inheritance, etc., she would not be entitled to an elective share for the following reasons: The augmented estate ($600,000) and her elective share ($200,000) remain the same. But the value of the house ($100,000) and her other assets ($100,000) count against the elective share and she would not be entitled to make an election. Insurance proceeds, pensions and annuities payable to someone other than the surviving spouse are excluded when computing the assets of the augmented estate.

WILLS AND DESCENT

Property accumulated during life may be disposed of to designated beneficiaries effective upon death. The instrument used to achieve this disposition is called a "last will and testament," most commonly called a **will**. The execution of a will during life has no effect, for the instrument only becomes effective at death. This is the distinguishing feature between wills and other instruments such as deeds and contracts which convey and create property interests.

When a person dies with a will, title to the decedent's real property passes directly to the beneficiaries named in the will. If there is no will, property will pass to the decedent's heirs by the state **Law of Descent** (see Figure 8.1).

While the beneficiaries or heirs may immediately convey or encumber such legal title, their title is not legally marketable, since the law provides that upon death all property is subject to the temporary possession of an executor or administrator. However, a beneficiary holding title as a tenant by the entirety or a joint tenant would immediately have a marketable title.

Legal title is subject to the control of the probate court. Probate is the legal process of determining the validity of a will, paying off the debts of the estate and determining who gets the remainder of the estate. If the decedent is a resident of New Jersey, the will should be filed for probate with the surrogate court of the county where the decedent resided, regardless of where in the state the property is located. If the decedent is a non-resident, the will should be filed in the surrogate court of the county where the real estate is located.

The deceased person is said to have died **testate** if he leaves a will, or intestate if there is no will. The party making the will is the testator (if male), or testatrix (if female), and must be of legal age (18) and sound mind. When there is an **intestacy**, an **administrator** (or **administratrix**) is appointed to administer the decedent's affairs. If the decedent left a will, the person named in the will to administer the decedent's estate is known as the executor (or executrix). When a person dies without a will, or intestate, and if there are no heirs capable of inheriting his estate, the estate then reverts to the state. This is called **escheat**.

The testator should, and usually does, appoint an executor to carry out the provisions and duties specified in the will. If the testator fails to appoint an executor, or the executor is unable or unwilling to serve, a substitute administrator takes his place. The administrator's duties are to obey the directions of the court and to properly dispose of the estate in question.

Formerly, a gift of real estate by will was called a devise, and a gift of personal property was called a bequest. Today, a testamentary gift of real or personal property is a devise, and the term bequest has been eliminated. A **codicil** is a supplement or addition to a will that adds, subtracts or qualifies the provisions of the will. Both the will and the codicil are formal written instruments signed by the testator and declared to be his last will and testament in the presence of at least two disinterested persons who sign as witnesses. A codicil may be endorsed on the will or it may form a separate document, but in either case it must be executed and attested in the same way as the will to which it is added. It then forms a part of that will and the two documents are read together. The document should be prepared by an attorney, for a will may be declared partially or completely invalid because of failure to comply with any one of a number of legal requirements.

A **holographic will** (an unwitnessed will that is written entirely in the handwriting of the person under whose name it appears) is valid in New Jersey. However, failure to seek professional assistance in preparing a will may result in disagreements and litigation later on. People often intend to say something in a letter or conversation, but somehow manage to convey a different impression to the reader or listener. Usually, it is not too difficult to clear up a misunderstanding that stems from imprecise language, but when the confusion concerns a will, the heirs can only speculate as to what the decedent intended.

If a person dies without a will (intestate), the **New Jersey Law of Descent and Distribution** determines the manner in which New Jersey real estate will be distributed. (See chart next page.)

Any property held in joint tenancy will pass to the surviving owner(s), and if held in tenancy by the entirety, it will go to the surviving spouse. Although jointly held property avoids the delay and expense of probate, the full value of the joint property (except to the extent the survivor can prove his or her contributions) is included in the decedent's estate for estate tax purposes.

ALIENATION

The transfer of property and possession of lands, or other things, from one person to another is called **alienation**. Property is usually conveyed by voluntary alienation, as with a deed, will or lease assignment. However, involuntary alienation (without the owner's consent) can result from court action as in escheat, condemnation, foreclosure, tax sales, etc.

KEY WORDS

Administrator	Codicil	Elective Share	Intestate
Administratrix	Curtesy	Escheat	Legacy
Alienation	Descent	Executor	Probate
Augmented Estate	Devise	Executrix	Testate
Bequest	Dower	Inchoate	Testator
Cloud on Title			

FIGURE 8.1
Descent of Real Property in New Jersey

On and after September 1,1978

Decedent dies survived by:	Real **and** personal property pass as follows:
1. Spouse and no surviving issue or parent of decedent.	To spouse.
2. Spouse and parent(s) of decedent, but no surviving issue.	Spouse receives first $50,000 plus 1/2 of balance. Remaining 1/2 as in No. 7.
3. Spouse and surviving issue (all of whom are also issue of surviving spouse).	Spouse receives first $50,000 plus 1/2 of balance. Remaining 1/2 as in No. 5 or No. 6.
4. Spouse and surviving issue (one or more of whom are not issue of surviving spouse).	Spouse receives 1/2. Remaining 1/2 as in No. 5 or No. 6.
5. Only one child or the issue of only one child.	To such child, if living, otherwise in equal parts as tenants in common to such issue stirpes.
6. Two or more children and/or issue of deceased children.	In equal parts as tenants in common to the children per stirpes to the issue of deceased children.
7. Parent(s).	To parent or parents equally as tenants in common.
8. Brothers or sisters of the whole or half blood or their issue (i.e., issue of decedent's parents or either of them).	In equal parts as tenants in common to such brothers and sisters and per stirpes to the issue of deceased brothers and sisters.
9. Paternal and/or maternal grandparents (or their issue in the event at least one grandparent survives).	One-half to the paternal grandparents equally as tenants in common or the entire 1/2 to the surviving paternal grandparent. The other 1/2 to the maternal grandparents equally as tenants in common or the entire 1/2 to the survivor. If one set of grandparents is dead but one or both of the other set survive, the 1/2 share which would have gone to the deceased grandparents passes to their issue per stirpes. If no such issue, the entire estate passes to the surviving grandparent or grandparents equally as tenants in common.
10. Collateral heirs (other than brothers or sisters of the whole or half-blood or their issue). In determining collateral heirs, no common ancestor beyond a grandparent may be considered.	In equal parts as tenants in common to the issue grandparents per stirpes.
11. If none of the above.	To the State of New Jersey.

Sources: P.L. 1977, Chapter 412, Secs. 36-46; N.J.S.A. 3A:2A-33-43; P.L. 1978, c. 30

CHAPTER 8
Review Questions
(Answers on page 552)

1. When a person dies without a will, he is said to have died:
   (A) testate.
   (B) intestate.
   (C) in escheat.
   (D) without heirs.

2. In probating an estate, which of the following is the last to receive payments, if any?
   (A) Second mortgagee.
   (B) Creditors.
   (C) Heirs.
   (D) Government for taxes.

3. A will takes effect:
   (A) upon signing.
   (B) upon recording.
   (C) upon delivery.
   (D) upon death of testator.

4. Which of the following would NOT be a party to a will?
   (A) Testator.
   (B) Administrator.
   (C) Executor.
   (D) Devisee.

5. An executrix is appointed by the:
   (A) probate court.
   (B) heirs of the deceased.
   (C) deceased's attorney.
   (D) testator.

6. When a person dies testate, his real property:
   (A) escheats and is sold at auction by the state.
   (B) passes by descent.
   (C) passes by devise.
   (D) goes to his administrator.

7. The word "escheat" refers to:
   (A) the feudal custom of the king's seizure of land.
   (B) the right of the government to take private property for a public purpose upon payment.
   (C) the acquisition of title by adverse possession.
   (D) the right of the state to acquire title where the owner dies without a will and without heirs.

8. Title to the owner's real estate can be transferred at the death of the owner by which one of the following?
   (A) Warranty deed.
   (B) Quitclaim deed.
   (C) Trustee's deed.
   (D) Last will and testament.

9. A wife's interest in her husband's pre-1980 estate upon his death is best described as:
   (A) right of descendency.
   (B) curtesy.
   (C) right of possession.
   (D) dower.

10. In 1990 John bought a house in his own name, and when he married Mary the following year, she moved into the house. The marital rights affecting this residence include:
    (A) right of possession.
    (B) dower rights.
    (C) curtesy rights.
    (D) the right to partition.

11. The word "devise" is used in connection with which of the following?
    (A) Lease.
    (B) Will.
    (C) Purchase and sale agreement.
    (D) Option.

12. A sale of property is considered transfer of title by:
    (A) descent.
    (B) will.
    (C) voluntary alienation.
    (D) involuntary alienation.

13. Which of the following statements is true?
    (A) There must be children from the marriage in order for a husband to claim his curtesy rights.
    (B) A testator is appointed by the decedent in his last will and testament.
    (C) Descent refers to goodly or personable.
    (D) A holographic will is valid in New Jersey.

(Quiz continues on next page)

14. Which of the following statements is true?
    (A) A married woman's dower rights may be terminated by her husband's execution of a deed.
    (B) A demise is a gift of realty by will.
    (C) Intestate refers to the crossing of state lines.
    (D) A wife cannot convey her inchoate dower interest to another.

15. A minor could legally act in the capacity of a:
    (A) vendee.
    (B) vendor.
    (C) grantee.
    (D) grantor.

CHAPTER NINE

EASEMENTS, RESTRICTIONS AND RIGHTS OF ADJOINING OWNERS

EASEMENTS

We now direct our attention to encumbrances that affect the physical condition or use of property. An **easement** (the most common of this type of encumbrance) is a right one has in the land of another, giving the holder of the easement the right to do certain things on the owner's land. Easements are divided into two classes: **easements appurtenant** and **easements in gross**.

Easement Appurtenant. An easement appurtenant is a right acquired by the owner of one parcel of land to use an adjacent parcel of land for a special purpose (for example, the right to cross an adjoining property). In order to create an easement appurtenant, there must be two tracts of land owned by different parties. One tract is called the **servient premises**, and is the tract which is burdened by the easement. The other is called the **dominant premises**, and is the land receiving the benefit of the easement. An easement appurtenant "runs with the land," meaning that it is not revocable and will be automatically transferred to any subsequent purchaser even though it might not be stated in the deed.

Easement in Gross. An easement in gross does not benefit a particular parcel. Thus, there is no dominant premises, only a servient one. Examples are a railroad easement, or an easement given to a telephone company or utility company to install and maintain poles and wires on, across and over the grantor's land. Since an easement in gross exists without a dominant premises and cannot pass as an appurtenance to the land, it must be expressly transferred.

Creation of Easements

Easements are most commonly created by: express grant or reservation; implied grant or reservation; prescription; condemnation; necessity; and dedication.

Express Grant or Reservation. An express grant or an express reservation is one of the most common means of creating an easement. Because an easement conveys an interest in land, the instrument conveying it must contain the essential elements of any conveyance of land—namely, the names of the grantor and grantee, operative words of conveyance, a legal description of the servient premises, the nature of the easement and the means of ingress and egress. Execution by the grantor and delivery to the grantee are also essential to make it effective. The grant may be by deed or written agreement, and it should be acknowledged and recorded. Recording is not a necessity, but as with most other legal documents, it is strongly recommended. Often an owner will sell only a part of his land, such as the portion fronting on the street, and reserve in the deed an easement in the portion retained. This is called an **express reservation**.

Example

Paul conveys 10 acres of land to Jim by deed, but in it Paul reserves the right to continue to cross over Jim's land to gain access to an adjoining property he owns at the rear of Jim's property. When Jim accepts the conveyance from Paul, he does so with the understanding that his title will be encumbered in this manner.

Implied Grant or Reservation. Occasionally an owner sells part of his land, and fails to mention the necessity of an easement for the remaining tract. As a result of the transaction, an easement may be created because a court would consider that the owner intended to create one, even though he failed to mention it. To support the implied easement the following conditions must exist:

- The prior use of one part of the land must have been such that it would be discovered by a reasonable inspection of the premises.
- The two parcels must have been owned by one party when the use began and ownership of the land separated after the use began, so that one party owns the burdened parcel and the other owns the benefited parcel.
- The easement must be necessary, meaning that a substitute for the easement cannot be obtained without unreasonable trouble and expense.
- The prior use must have been continuous.

Example
Martin, who owns lots 1 and 2, conveys lot 1, (facing the street) to Abraham. At the time Martin signed and delivered the deed, a driveway over a portion of lot 1 was being openly used and was reasonably necessary for access to lot 2. An easement over lot 1 would ordinarily be created by implied grant with the deed of lot 1.

Prescription. An easement by prescription arises when a person makes use of another's land for an extensive period of time (20 years in New Jersey). In order to obtain an easement by prescription, persons claiming the easement must meet the same requirements as if they were claiming title by adverse possession, i.e., the use must be adverse, meaning without the owner's consent; continuous; uninterrupted; and visible, open and notorious, meaning that an ordinary owner of land, diligent in the protection of his interests, would have a reasonable opportunity to be aware of it.

Condemnation. Condemnation is the taking of private property for public use with compensation to the owner under eminent domain. See Chapter 16, Condemnation and Adverse Possession.

Necessity. When a grantor conveys a part of his land that is entirely surrounded by his remaining lands, thus leaving the grantee landlocked, and there is no outlet to a highway except over his remaining land, a right of way by necessity is created by implied grant over the remaining land of the seller. A way of necessity may also arise by implied reservation in favor of the grantor who conveys a part of his land in such a manner as to leave the land retained by him inaccessible except over the land conveyed.

Although a way of necessity in many ways is the same thing as an easement created by implied grant or implied reservation, one major difference necessary in its creation is that an easement by necessity is not dependent upon the existence, at the time of the conveyance, of a continuous prior use over the servient estate.

Sale by Reference to Subdivision Plat. Where a landowner subdivides his land into lots, blocks, streets and alleys, and then sells lots in the subdivision, each purchaser of a lot automatically acquires an easement for use of the streets and alleys shown on the recorded plat even though the deed to the lot may not have mentioned such right. A **plat** is a map on file at the recording office showing the boundaries and location of individual properties within a development. The plat also gives the municipality rights in the streets. In some cases, the municipality acquires full ownership of the streets. In other instances it acquires only an easement. When an owner transfers complete ownership of the streets to a community as a gift, the process is referred to as a **dedication**. By accepting the roads, the community assumes responsibility for their upkeep and the developer is relieved of a property tax liability on the dedicated land. If the subdivider does not intend to dedicate the land to the municipality, the plat should indicate that the streets will remain private property.

Termination of Easement

Easements can be terminated in several ways. These include by express release; by merger; by abandonment; by the terms of the instrument that created the easement; and termination of purpose.

Express Release. A release of right or claim will terminate the easement. The customary method of such express release is a quitclaim given by the owner of the easement to the owner of the servient premises.

Merger. Merger of the dominant and servient premises will terminate an easement because one cannot have an easement over one's own property.

Abandonment. When the owner of an easement, with actual intention to do so, permanently abandons the easement, it will then no longer exist. For example, if a manufacturing company has an easement for railroad purposes allowing it to transport finished products to a warehouse for shipping, and it tears up the tracks and demolishes the warehouse, the easement will be terminated. Mere non-use is insufficient evidence of intent to abandon.

By the Terms of the Instrument that Created the Easement. If an easement agreement states that the easement will only be granted for a certain period of time, it is automatically terminated at the end of that period.

Termination of Purpose. An easement is created for a specific purpose, therefore when that purpose ceases, so does the easement. Thus, if an easement is created as a right to pass over certain property to fish in the lake, the easement is terminated if the lake is drained and used as a parking lot.

Easement and License Distinguished

An easement is usually created in writing, for a specific purpose. It is of a permanent nature, is transferred with the conveyance of the land, and is irrevocable. A license, on the other hand, is created in writing or orally, and is for a temporary period. It is a personal, revocable and nonassignable permission to enter upon the land of another for a specified purpose, but without granting any interest in the land itself. Thus, a license is less than an estate in land. A license to occupy land, being a personal arrangement, ceases upon the death of either party.

RESTRICTIONS

Public Restrictions. A restriction, another common encumbrance, is a limitation on the rights of the owner to use or enjoy the land. Restrictions are usually public, and are regulated by some governmental entity, being considered necessary for public interest or purpose. Such public restrictions most commonly would be: (1) police power, regulating ownership through city planning, zoning and building codes; (2) the law of eminent domain, which is exercised by the act of condemnation; (3) the right of the government to taxation; and (4) the right of escheat.

Private Restrictions. In addition to the right to acquire and possess property, owners also have the right to dispose of it and to keep some degree of control over the future use of the property as long as it is not a violation of the law. This is accomplished by placing a **deed restriction** in the deed. These restrictions are binding not only on the immediate parties, but on all subsequent owners as well.

There are two types of deed restrictions:

1. Restrictions imposed by subdividers or developers, which may be for the purpose of making a subdivision more attractive, or restricting the homes in cost, number, size, height, etc. These types of restrictions are often referred to as **neighborhood schemes**. Restrictions made in conformance with neighborhood schemes are for the benefit of all the purchasers of the lots, and the owner of one lot may enforce the restrictions against the owners of the other lots.

2. Restrictions created when a private landowner or seller places restrictions in the deed of the property she has sold.

Common examples of such restrictions include: limiting improvements to a particular type of structure; specification of minimum square footage for the structure; type of exterior construction materials and exterior colors; stipulation of setback distances; whether or not garages may face the street, etc. These restrictions are binding not only on the immediate parties, but on all subsequent owners as well. The restrictions must not be against public policy. Thus, if a racial deed restriction appeared in a deed, the deed would not be void, but that provision would be ineffective.

Termination of Restrictions

Deed restrictions may be terminated in a number of ways:

- By release from the party that placed the restriction.
- By expiration of a time limit contained in the restriction.
- By merger of ownership of all lots affected.
- By abandonment of a restriction by frequent violations without enforcement by beneficiaries.
- By material change in the nature of a neighborhood or other circumstances that would cause the courts to deny enforcement.
- By act of public authorities, such as condemnation.
- By the terms of the instrument that created the restriction, (i.e., lapse of time.)
- By mutual agreement of all parties entitled to enforce the restriction.
- By final judgment in an action to quiet title or an action to determine the validity of the restriction.

RIGHTS OF ADJOINING OWNERS

The three situations that most commonly affect adjoining owners are (1) encroachments; (2) lateral support; and (3) party walls.

Encroachments. An encroachment exists when a part of one property, such as a house, building, fence, wall, eaves of a garage, or tree branches encroaches on or extends over a neighboring property. An encroachment on the property of another, if significant, can affect the marketability of title to a property. Encroachments can only be detected by an inspection of the property, or by a current property **survey**.

If left uncorrected, an encroachment upon the property of another could result in the encroaching party's gaining either ownership of, or continuing rights of use in, the neighboring property.

Lateral and Subjacent Support; Subsidence. Where neighbors own adjoining lands, each owes the other certain duties of lateral support. Each owner has the right to have his land supported in its natural condition by the land of his neighbor. Therefore, if A excavates near the property line, causing B's land to subside or fall into the excavation, B may sue A and recover damages. If

A's title is a separate estate below B's land, then B has a similar right known as *subjacent support*. Therefore, in the case of mining operations, if A was the holder of subsurface mineral rights below B's property, he may be liable for damage to the property and for **subsidence** caused by the activities. Subsidence is the lowering of the land-surface elevation from changes that take place underground. Common causes of subsidence from human activity include pumping water, oil and gas from underground reservoirs and the collapse of underground mines.

If an owner erects a building or structure that will damage his neighbor's land, such as gathering and discharging water or waste materials, he will be liable to his neighbor for damages.

Party Walls. Where adjoining property owners each have buildings that abut the common boundary line, they may agree to use the same wall for both of their buildings. This is called a "party wall," and both owners are equally responsible for the cost of its building and maintenance. Technically, each owns the section of the wall that rests on his land, and each has an easement of support in the wall of the other. Since an easement is an interest or right in the land of another, a party wall agreement should be in writing. In the event one owner decides to demolish his building, he may do so, but must leave the party wall intact for the support of the adjoining owner's building. Party walls are common in modern tract housing and in older cities where buildings and townhouses were often constructed immediately next to one another. **Party driveways**, with corresponding rights and obligations, are also common in older municipalities with small lot sizes.

KEY WORDS

Abandonment
Adjoining Owner
Condition
Dedication
Dominant Estate
Easement
Easement Appurtenant
Easement in Gross
Encroachment
Encumbrance
Lateral Support
License
Party Driveway
Party Wall
Plat
Prescription
Reservation
Restriction
Run with the Land
Servient Estate
Subsidence

CHAPTER 9
Review Questions
(Answers on page 553)

1. An easement created by adverse use is said to have been created by:
   (A) express grant.
   (B) implication of law.
   (C) reservation.
   (D) prescription.

2. When an easement appurtenant exists between two parcels of land which are separately owned:
   (A) both the dominant tenement and servient tenement are benefited by the easement.
   (B) the servient tenement is benefited by the easement.
   (C) the dominant tenement is benefited by the easement.
   (D) the servient tenement may revoke the use of easement by giving proper notice.

3. Which of the following creates deed restrictions?
   (A) Local building inspector.
   (B) Authorized authorities.
   (C) Planning commission.
   (D) Grantor.

4. Which of the following restrictions is NOT a governmental restriction?
   (A) Police power.
   (B) Covenant.
   (C) Escheat.
   (D) Eminent domain.

5. A restriction is considered to be:
   (A) a lien.
   (B) a color of title.
   (C) an encumbrance.
   (D) an abstract.

6. An appropriation of land for some public use made by the owner and accepted for such use by or on behalf of the public, as streets in a plotted subdivision, is called:
   (A) easement.
   (B) dedication.
   (C) public grant.
   (D) condemnation.

7. If, after you purchase a property, you have a survey made and find that your neighbor, through error, has built an ornamental fence two feet over on your land, this would be a basic example of:
   (A) an easement.
   (B) an encroachment.
   (C) an appurtenance.
   (D) adverse possession.

8. A license to use another person's property:
   (A) runs with the land.
   (B) is less than an estate in land.
   (C) may be assigned to another licensee.
   (D) can be devised to the licensee's heirs.

9. The right of a water company to lay and maintain water mains along the rear of a lot is called:
   (A) an appurtenance.
   (B) riparian right.
   (C) easement in gross.
   (D) a right of encroachment.

10. A personal right which can be used by the person granted the privilege, but which does NOT run with the land, is called a:
    (A) profit.
    (B) license.
    (C) deed restriction.
    (D) easement.

11. A recorded easement may be removed from the records by:
    (A) recording a quitclaim deed signed by the owner of the dominant property.
    (B) a marginal release.
    (C) a release signed by the servient owner.
    (D) liberation.

12. The words "ingress" and "egress" have a relationship with:
    (A) streams.
    (B) easements.
    (C) birds.
    (D) license laws.

13. An easement given to a utility company to maintain its equipment is:
    (A) an easement by necessity.
    (B) a gross easement.
    (C) an electric easement.
    (D) a prescriptive easement.

14. Which of the following techniques would be used to determine whether or not an encroachment exists?
    (A) Title search.
    (B) Suit to quiet title.
    (C) Title insurance.
    (D) Survey.

CHAPTER TEN

ACKNOWLEDGMENTS, RECORDING AND CONSTRUCTIVE NOTICE

ACKNOWLEDGMENTS

An acknowledgment is a formal declaration, made before a notary public or some other duly authorized officer of the court, that a particular document is genuine and that the person who is signing it enters into it freely and voluntarily. The officer also witnesses the signature as being a genuine signature of the person signing.

The certificate of acknowledgment is either filled in, or attached onto the instrument by the officer before whom the declaration is made, and states that the party actually appeared before him and acknowledged that his execution of the instrument was done as his free act and will. This process guards against, but does not prevent, having defective instruments entered into the record. Responsibility of the notary lies in determining that the person appearing before him to acknowledge the document is satisfactorily identified as such. A person who takes an acknowledgement cannot be an "interested person," i.e., the spouse, partner, etc. of the party giving an acknowledgement.

The reason for an acknowledgment is not to make an instrument valid, but to enable it to be recorded, and thus to import constructive notice of its contents and to enable the instrument to be used as evidence without further proof.

If the certificate of acknowledgment is sufficient in other respects, a mistake in the date, or even omission of the date, will not invalidate it. However, the signature of the officer taking the acknowledgment must appear.

Duly Authorized Officers. Duly authorized officers include:

- Attorneys-at-law of New Jersey;
- Notaries public of New Jersey;
- County clerks and deputy county clerks;
- Registrars and deputy registrars of deeds; and
- Surrogates and deputy surrogates.

RECORDING

Recording is the process of writing or entering certain documents into the public records, thereby giving notice of their existence. It was designed as a safeguard to the ownership of land, so that those planning to purchase or otherwise deal with land might be more fully informed as to the ownership and condition of the title.

Records and documents relating to real estate transfers are maintained in a central place for convenient reference. Recording offices are located in the county seat in each of New Jersey's 21 counties. The registrar of deeds or county clerk in the county where the property is located maintains deeds and other legal instruments affecting title.

The effect of a properly recorded instrument is to give **constructive notice** to the world of its existence. Constructive notice is notice that is deemed to be given because the facts to which it relates are readily available; or would be obvious from inspection; or could reasonably have been determined by prudent inquiry. Examples are notice that would come to the attention of a purchaser who made a proper search of the public records, or from a proper visual inspection of the property. Once an instrument has been recorded all persons are legally presumed to know of its existence, whether they actually do or not.

When one knows a fact concerning a property through direct knowledge or observation, or when notice is expressly or actually given, it is called **actual notice**. For example, if A informs B that he sold his house to C, then B would have actual notice of the sale to C. However, if A sold his house to C and C recorded the deed in the recording office, then B—and everyone else—would have constructive notice of the sale to C.

In addition to recording deeds, many other legal instruments which can affect title status such as mortgages, satisfactions of mortgage, easements, restrictions, options, agreements of sale, leases, assignments and mechanic's notices should also be recorded.

The actual process for recording a deed is accomplished by photocopying the original deed and filing it in one of many deed books. The deeds are indexed for reference in a grantor-grantee index in which deeds and other instruments are indexed alphabetically by the name of the grantor in a grantor index and alphabetically by the name of a grantee in a grantee index. Each index will list the name of the corresponding grantee or grantor, describe the property, indicate the type of instrument and provide a book and page number where the instrument may be found. The recording system makes it possible to ascertain certain facts relevant to determining the condition of title by reference to a "library" of title records.

One could learn for example, that a certain piece of land is apparently owned by Margaret J. Young, is under a three-year option to Astute Investors Inc., is subject to easements held by Titan Electric Company, is encumbered by a "no fence" restriction and is mortgaged to Progressive Savings and Loan Association. Any one of a variety of instruments can thus serve to assist in creating an individualized portrait of the current status of record title. Review of the actual documents themselves can serve to further clarify and define the quality of it. Examination of title records will be discussed in detail in Chapter 11.

Prerequisites to recording include the following:

1. The instrument must be in English or accompanied by an English translation.
2. The instrument must bear a signature. A signature includes any mark made on a document by a person who thereby intends to give legal effect to the document. A signature also includes any mark made on a document on behalf of a person, with that person's authority and to effectuate that person's intent (N.J.S.A. 46, 14-4.2).
3. The instrument must contain an acknowledgement.
4. The names of the signatories and of the officer taking the acknowledgement must be typed or printed underneath.
5. The recording fee must be paid.
6. If the instrument is a deed it must contain:
    a. Information as to consideration for realty transfer tax purposes.
    b. The name and signature of the preparer on the first page.
    c. The tax block and lot designation.

Recording has a twofold effect: first, it provides a means of protecting existing estates or other interests in real estate; and second, it protects the interests of subsequent purchasers against secret, unrecorded interests. Not all interests in land need to be recorded, however. Title acquired through adverse possession, and easements by prescription, implication or necessity, are still effective against a purchaser even if unrecorded and even though the purchaser may have been unaware of them.

An unrecorded instrument is valid between the parties to it; however, a subsequent bona fide purchaser acquiring an interest in the property will take priority over a prior unrecorded interest. While there is no specific time limit within which a person must record a document relating to his purchase of real estate, timing is very important. Often a bona fide purchaser is protected only if he records first. If a conflict arises with regard to the condition of title to a property, **priority of recordation** will usually determine the rights of the parties involved.

Example

A sells a parcel of land to B, who fails to record the deed and provide constructive notice of his purchase. A then sells the same parcel of land to C, who immediately records the deed, giving constructive notice of his purchase. B would have difficulty proving to a court of law that he was the rightful owner only because he said he purchased the land first. C would normally be declared the rightful owner because he recorded first. Although B would have recourse against A to recover his money, he would in all likelihood never get ownership of the property.

The recording law only protects a **bona fide purchaser** who first records. A bona fide purchaser is a party who has paid value for an estate or other interest in real property without actual or constructive notice of an already existing estate or interest in the same parcel. In addition, the law accords constructive notice of any adverse interests of the parties in possession of real estate. This is true even though a subsequent purchaser fails to inspect the premises and investigate the possible rights of those in possession. Thus, in the above example, if C had knowledge of the transfer to B, or if C had received a gift of the property from A, or if B had taken possession of the property, the court would recognize B as the rightful owner.

A document is generally considered recorded when it is acknowledged by the person signing it and attested to by a notary public or other qualified officer, and is then given to the recorder or registrar in the county clerk's office. It then becomes the duty of this person to copy it, to give it proper identification, and then, making note of the year, month, day, hour and minute it was received, to enter it into the public records. When this has been done, the original document is then returned to the party who left it for recordation.

KEY WORDS

Acknowledgment
Actual Notice
Bona fide Purchaser
Constructive Notice
Donee
Notary Public
Recording

CHAPTER 10
Review Questions
(Answers on page 553)

1. Mr. X, a bona fide purchaser for value who records his deed, would take precedence over a grantee with a prior unrecorded deed:
   (A) where Mr. X has actual knowledge of the prior unrecorded deed.
   (B) where the prior unrecorded deed's grantee has taken possession of the property and was living in a house on the property.
   (C) where Mr. X had no knowledge of the previous transaction and the prior grantee did not take possession.
   (D) under no circumstances.

2. Documents are entered into the public record by recording them at:
   (A) tax office.
   (B) borough hall.
   (C) county seat.
   (D) municipal recording office.

3. Constructive notice means that:
   (A) all parties with an interest in the property have been notified, by certified or registered mail, of existing defects to title.
   (B) if an encumbrance against a title were recorded, but the buyer was not aware of it, he would still be subject to its effects when he became the owner, if it had not been removed prior to purchase.
   (C) all parties who seek to acquire an interest in real estate are not bound by the information in public records if they choose not to make a search.
   (D) All of the above.

4. An acknowledgement is given by:
   (A) an attorney-at-law.
   (B) the party signing the instrument.
   (C) a notary public.
   (D) the registrar of deeds.

5. Which of the following has access to the records in the recording offices in each county?
   (A) Prospective buyers.
   (B) The general public.
   (C) Prospective lenders.
   (D) All of the above.

6. Actual notice is:
   (A) notice that has been received by direct communication, either oral or written.
   (B) the same as constructive notice.
   (C) recorded notice.
   (D) implied notice.

7. Deeds are recorded to provide:
   (A) actual notice.
   (B) constructive notice.
   (C) consummate notice.
   (D) conspicuous notice.

8. Constructive notice of a fact is established by:
   (A) entering it on public record.
   (B) acting openly in accordance with the fact.
   (C) direct communication of the fact to each interested party.
   (D) testifying to the existence of the fact under oath in open court.

9. Recording an instrument is:
   (A) mandatory.
   (B) permitted only if the instrument is acknowledged.
   (C) necessary to make it legal.
   (D) always free.

10. If A sells a property to B and B takes possession but does not record his deed and subsequently A sells the property to C and C records his deed, who owns the property?
    (A) A
    (B) B
    (C) C
    (D) None of the above.

11. Which of the following parties is in the weakest position against a claim of title by a stranger?
    (A) Holder of warranty deed.
    (B) One who holds an unrecorded deed and who does not live on the property.
    (C) One who holds an unrecorded deed.
    (D) One who holds a recorded quitclaim deed to the property.

12. Which of the following statements is true?
    (A) Recording a deed guarantees its validity.
    (B) In New Jersey, recording offices for eligible instruments are located in each of the 566 municipalities.
    (C) Month-to-month leases are usually recorded.
    (D) Recording of documents provides constructive notice.

13. Which of the following statements is NOT true:
    (A) An instrument cannot be recorded unless it is in English or accompanied by an English translation.
    (B) Recording offices for eligible instruments are located in each of the 21 New Jersey counties.
    (C) Month-to-month leases are usually recorded.
    (D) Recording of documents provides constructive notice.

14. Recording a deed is to the greatest benefit of the:
    (A) grantor.
    (B) public trustee.
    (C) attorney.
    (D) grantee.

15. In real estate transactions in New Jersey all of the following documents are usually recorded in the county clerk's office EXCEPT a(n):
    (A) deed.
    (B) offer to purchase.
    (C) mortgage.
    (D) purchase money mortgage.

16. The recording of a deed:
    (A) guarantees title.
    (B) insures ownership.
    (C) verifies title.
    (D) constitutes constructive notice of ownership.

CHAPTER ELEVEN

TITLE INSURANCE

The fact that a seller can produce a deed to property naming himself as owner is not always adequate proof of his ownership. The deed may be defective, the previous owner's title may have been defective, or the seller's degree of ownership may be uncertain. The title may be free and clear of any encumbrances, but still be legally unmarketable. Thus, the purchaser's attorney has to ascertain that the seller's title meets the standards established in the sales contract. This is generally established through the use of title insurance. Similarly, the mortgagee who takes a mortgage on the property as security for the repayment of a loan is also greatly concerned with the condition of the title.

Historical Background

In 1868, the need for title insurance drew public attention in the Pennsylvania Supreme Court case of *Watson v. Muirhead* (57 Pa. State 161). After losing his investment at a sheriff's sale as a result of an outstanding judgment, Watson sued his conveyancer, Charles Muirhead. Muirhead had discovered the judgment, but represented the title as clear after an attorney advised that the judgment was not valid.

The court eventually ruled that conveyancers and attorneys could not be held liable for erroneous opinions based on professional standards of evaluation, and Watson lost his investment. As a result of the case, it became clear that something was needed to protect innocent investors from similar hazards and to encourage land development and American growth.

On March 28, 1876, a group of conveyancers led by Joshua H. Morris met in a small office opposite Philadelphia's Independence Hall to incorporate the world's first title insurance company, The Real Estate Title Insurance Company of Philadelphia. They pledged that their new firm would "insure the purchasers of real estate and mortgages against losses from defective titles, liens and encumbrances," and they guaranteed that "through these facilities, transfer of real estate and real estate securities can be made more speedily and with greater security than heretofore."

A short time later, the first title insurance policy was purchased by Morris' aunt, Martha Morris, who took out a $1,500 policy to protect her loan on a home on North 43rd Street in Philadelphia. In that first year of business, The Real Estate Title Insurance Company of Philadelphia issued 169 policies.

Title Insurance Defined

A title insurance policy may be defined as a contract of indemnity under which a title insurance company, for a one-time payment, agrees to indemnify the insured, not in excess of the policy amount, and subject to the exceptions, exclusions, conditions and stipulations of the policy, against any defect in the title which existed and affected the property being insured when the policy was issued, and was either omitted from the policy or erroneously stated therein. Thus, the risk of loss, as in other insurance policies, is transferred from the property owner or other beneficiary to an insurance company. The title company also agrees to defend, at its own expense, any lawsuit attacking the title which is based on a defect covered by the policy and which existed prior to the policy date.

Examination of Title Records Prior to Purchase

Prior to the closing of title, title records should be examined to determine if the seller holds the interest that he alleges to hold and to ascertain the quality of title. By the act of conveyance itself, the seller does not covenant that the title is good. It is the buyer's responsibility to protect himself. (By standard contractual agreement, the seller usually states that the property is free of substantial encumbrance. This is no guarantee of clear title, however.) The buyer, being unskilled in searching title and needing an independent search as a condition of insuring it, asks a title company directly or through his attorney to research the property's title status for him for a fee. The search of the public record includes documents recorded in the county clerk's or registrar of deeds office, state records, municipal tax and utility records, New Jersey Superior Court and U.S. District Court records. If an estate is found in the chain of title, the searcher must conduct a search at the surrogate's office and, if a corporation is found in the chain of title within the last ten years, corporate status and franchise tax searches must be ordered from both the departments of State and Treasury. Additional searchers may include LLC status reports, and riparian searches.

A detailed explanation of the search process is beyond the scope of this text. However, the potential number of various types of records within these broad categories is large and the search is a detailed process requiring care and experience.

An abstractor will, as a result of research into the record, produce an **abstract of title**, a condensed historical record of all grants affecting the property including all deeds, mortgages, wills and judicial proceedings together with all other recorded liens and encumbrances affecting title. Using information relevant to property transfers, a **chain of title** will be "run" which will attempt to trace an unbroken chain of former owners back for **60 years**.

If there is a "break" or "gap" in the chain of title, the title of all those who subsequently owned the property, including the seller(s), would be in question, and clear title could not be passed until the problem was corrected. Such gaps might be caused, for example, by discovering an incompetent grantor or a substantial difference between the name of a previous grantee and a subsequent grantor. Gaps will be investigated. Some will have explanations that can lead to relatively simple correction. Others will involve serious title questions that may have to be settled by a court action. Until corrected, such gaps will cause the title to be unmarketable and uninsurable.

Examination of Title

Examination of title is the process by which the information discovered in a search or abstract is analyzed by an attorney or a title insurance officer who will prepare a **commitment** (title report, binder) on a form prescribed by the title insurance company. The issuance of a commitment is based on the result of an examination of the title search, the judgment search, the tax assessment search, a location survey of the property and the information furnished in the application. By the terms of the commitment, the company promises to write a specific policy of title insurance in favor of a named insured in a specific amount, subject to the requirements, exceptions, conditions and stipulations contained in the form.

The commitment is not only a statement of all matters shown in the public records that may affect a title, but also a statement about the conditions that must be complied with before the issuance of the title policy, and about the exceptions to the title that will appear in the policy. It shows the attorney what the present condition (state of the title) is as shown by the public records, but does not include every document in the chain of title.

A review of the commitment in Figure 11.1 discloses that it does not guarantee clear title to the property. Part 1 lists all recorded objections that could be found to the title. In Part 2, the company stipulates that there may be items that were not researched or could not be researched in preparing the report. (Think of a commitment as a medical history and of a report of title as a statement regarding the condition of current health.)

The issuing of a commitment is a critical juncture in a real estate transaction because refusal of the title company to insure generally means that a settlement will not occur unless the defects can be cleared. It is important to recognize that a commitment is not the same as a title insurance policy. It can be used to verify that the seller is in fact the owner of the property, and it informs the lender, seller, and buyer of the state of the title before the transaction is closed, but it does not guarantee title. Therefore, the commitment identifies what has to be done to bring the title to the condition specified in the sales contract. The liability and obligation under the commitment terminate nine months from its effective date or when the policy is issued, whichever occurs first. Any reliance on an expired commitment is at the risk of the proposed insured.

If the commitment indicates that title is clear, the buyer will accept title. If, however, the commitment points out defects or otherwise indicates that title is clouded, the buyer is given notice and must act accordingly. Depending on the terms of the sales contract, he may insist that the cloud be removed prior to the purchase, accept the risk involved or refuse to proceed with the purchase.

The first nine exceptions shown in the commitment are standard, meaning they would appear on any report of title issued by the company. Those that follow, and many other exceptions that could potentially be named, would only be cited if the circumstances warrant it. The sample commitment in Figure 11.1 discloses that there was a mortgage on the property, a *lis pendens* had been filed relative to a pending suit, exceptions were cited relevant to the death of one of the owners of the property and a judgment was reported. Many of these exceptions would be removed by the title company, and they would insure against their preventing any future title problems to the buyer, but only after the company had received proof that the matters would not encumber the title. Examples would include evidence that debts in question had been paid or shown not to be owed; receipt of a waiver showing that no estate or inheritance taxes were owed or through swearing by affidavit by the seller(s) that judgments of same and similar name were not theirs.

FIGURE 11.1 Sample Title Insurance Commitment

CITY WIDE TITLE INSURANCE COMPANY

COMMITMENT for TITLE INSURANCE

AGREEMENT TO ISSUE POLICY

We agree to issue a policy to you according to the terms of this Commitment. When we show the policy amount and your name as the proposed insured in Schedule A. this Commitment will become effective as of the Commitment Date shown in Schedule A.

If the requirements shown in this Commitment have not been met within the time period shown after the Commitment Date in Schedule A, our obligation under this Commitment will end. Also, our obligation under this Commitment will end when the Policy is issued and then our obligation to you will be under the policy.

Our obligation under this Commitment is limited by the following:

The Provisions of Schedule A
The Requirements in Schedule B
The Exceptions in Schedule B-II
The Conditions Stated

This Commitment is not valid without Schedule A and Sections I and II of Schedule B.

In Witness Whereof CITY WIDE TITLE INSURANCE COMPANY has caused this Commitment to be signed and sealed as of the effective date shown in Schedule A: the Commitment to become valid when countersigned by an authorized signatory.

CITY WIDE TITLE INSURANCE COMPANY

By ______________________________ President

Attest ____________________________ Secretary

FIGURE 11.1 (cont'd)

SCHEDULE A

Commitment Number ABC - 12345

1. Commitment Date: October 2, 2002

2. Policy (or policies) to be issued:

ALTA Residential Title Insurance Policy.
Amount: $100,000 Proposed Insured: Calvin H. Young and Janine R. Young, husband and wife

ALTA Loan Policy
Policy Amount: $60,000 Proposed Insured: Mightyfine Bank. Inc.

3. Fee Simple Interest in the land described in this Commitment is owned at the Commitment date by:

JOHN J. SMITH and MARY R. SMITH, husband and wife, by deed from Wilbert W. Wallace, dated December 2, 1982, recorded December 5, 1982 in Deed Book 4517. Page 34. Thereafter, the said John J. Smith departed from this life on November 15, 2001, whereupon title became vested in Mary R. Smith by right of survivorship.

4. The land referred to in this Commitment is described as Follows:

PROPERTY ADDRESS: 6714 Revolution Street, City of Burlington (A full legal description of the property would follow)

SCHEDULE B - Section 1 - Requirements

The following requirements must be met:

a) Pay the agreed amounts for interest in the land and/or mortgage to be insured
b) Pay us the premiums, fees and charges for the policy
c) You must tell us in writing the name of anyone not referred to in this Commitment who will get an interest in the land or who will make a loan on the land. We may then make additional requirements or exceptions.
d) Documents satisfactory to us creating the interest in the land and/or mortgage to be issued must be signed, delivered and recorded:

Deed from: Mary R. Smith, widow
To: Calvin H. Young and Janine R. Young, husband and wife

Mortgage from: Calvin H. Young and Janine R. Young, husband and wife
To: Mightyfine Bank, Inc.

NOTICE: New Jersey law requires that the title company give notice to the proposed insured(s) that "there may be conditions, exceptions and limitations of the insurance liability of the title company contained in the commitment to insure, and that the proposed insured is entitled to review the commitment to insure before transfer of title with an attorney at law of the insured's own choosing".

FIGURE 11.1 (cont'd)

SCHEDULE B - Section II - Exceptions

Any policy we issue will have the following exceptions unless they are taken care of to our satisfaction:

1. Rights or claims of parties in possession of the land not shown on the public record.
2. Easements, or claims of easements not shown by the public record.
3. Any facts about the land which a correct survey would disclose, and which are not shown by the public record.
4. Any liens on your title, arising now or later, for labor or material, not shown by the public record.
5. Proof as to past marital status of present owner and buyer.
6. Taxes and municipal claims.
7. Possible additional assessment for real property taxes.
8. Possible liability for municipal improvements such as curbing, paving, sidewalks, sewers, etc., constructed or being constructed, but not yet assessed.
9. New Jersey Superior Court and United States District Court judgments and bankruptcies.
10. Restrictions as contained in Deed Book 521, page 409.
11. MORTGAGE covering subject premises: John J. Smith and Mary R. Smith to Futurity Savings and Loan Association dated December 2, 1982, recorded December 6.1982 Mortgage Book 2101, page S4, to secure $41, 500.
ASSIGNED TO: Big Mortgage Corporation, dated November 10, 1983, recorded November 13, 1983 in Assignment Book 445, page 114.
12. LIS PENDENS: Superior Court of New Jersey, Chancery Division, Burlington County, Docket No. D-I 0 114-80, Civil Action Notice of Lis Pendens: ABC Corporation vs. Mary J. Smith filed August 4. 1999 as File # LP-S7278.
13. Proof that there were no children born to or adopted by John J. Smith after the making of a Will dated January 9, 1987, proved in Burlington County Will Book Docket No. 87 -1046-03. .
14, Decedent's Debts due by the Estate of John J.Smith, who died within one year past, viz.: November 15, 2001.
15. New Jersey Inheritance Tax, if any, payable upon the Estate of John J. Smith.
16. Federal Estate Tax, if any, payable upon the Estate of John J. Smith.
17. JUDGMENT: -vs.- Mary R. Smith, Judgment # Dj-81967-87

SUPERIOR COURT OF NEW JERSEY
JUDGMENT # J-13071-90

DEBT: $492.95
COSTS: $58.64

DATE ENTERED: 06-23-90
TYPE OF ACTION: CONTRACT
VENUE: BURLINGTON

INT: 88.32
DCKG: 2.00

CREDITOR(S): AMERICAN MAGAZINE INC., A DELA WARE CORPORATION, and DOING BUSINESS IN NEW JERSEY

DEBTOR(S): MARY R. SMITH ATTORNEY FOR CREDITOR(S): ROBERT BLACKACRE

END OF JUDGMENT

Title Insurance Coverage

A title insurance policy in practical effect (1) insures the accuracy and sufficiency of the abstract; (2) insures the correctness and sufficiency of the examination of the title; and (3) insures against unknown and hidden defects. These unknown defects can be classified into two groups:

1. *Technical errors* such as mistakes in recording or indexing, erroneous city and county tax department notations, or omissions by title searchers; and

2. *Off-record risks* which would not be revealed by a search of the title or which predate the starting point of the search. A partial list of off-record risks includes:

- Rights originating or existing by reason of a forged instrument or forged release of a mortgage;
- Name similarity in the execution of papers;
- Incapacity of a grantor through mental incompetence, infancy or other legal disability;
- Deeds executed under an invalid power of attorney (e.g., one that has expired);
- Lack of an essential formality in the execution of an instrument, such as lack of delivery or lack of acknowledgment;
- Unrecorded outstanding mortgages;
- Undisclosed judgments against the seller;
- Unpaid real estate taxes and other tax liens not yet recorded;
- Fraud, misrepresentation or undue influence in the transfer of title;
- Prescriptive easements;
- Creditor claims on former owners in bankruptcy;
- Undiscovered marriages and divorces with resultant dower and curtesy rights; and
- Undiscovered wills that name additional or different devisees.

One company has compiled a list of over 60 different causes of loss or damage in this hidden defect category.

Affirmative Insurance

The title search will often reveal **known defects** in title such as building and use restrictions in deeds appearing in the chain of title. As long as the restrictions appear of record and have not expired, the title insurance company cannot insure the title outright without reference to the restrictions. If, however, the setback restrictions have not been violated, the company may refer to them and guarantee that the building conforms to the restrictions and that a future violation will not result in forfeiture or reversion of title. If the restrictions have been violated, the company may insure against actual loss being suffered by the purchaser by reason of the violation and further insure that the restrictions contain no provision for forfeiture or reversion of title. This is called **affirmative insurance**. This coverage always appears in the lender's policy, but is written on a case-by-case basis for the owner's policy (discussed below). When minor boundary disputes arise, the risk of loss from affirmative insurance is unlikely in a lender's policy, because the problem would not manifest itself until the lender takes title and suffers a monetary loss. On the other hand, in an owner's policy the risk of this type of loss is high because minor disputes between neighbors often ripen into claims unless clearly excepted and not affirmatively insured.

From the above, it is easy to understand that there can be a great deal of legal risk associated with acquiring title to real estate. It should be noted that unknown defects do not arise very often and only a small portion of premiums collected is used to pay claims based on them. Most of the premium dollar is spent on loss prevention in identifying, avoiding, preventing and curing title problems before closing of title.

Run-down Search

Subsequent to the initial search, but immediately prior to closing, a continuation or "run down" search is also conducted to reveal any matters of record which have occurred between the time of the initial search and the closing of title.

In a typical transaction, any actual or potential **cloud on title** that remains unresolved will cause title not to close. A cloud on title is an outstanding claim or encumbrance which would impair the seller's ability to pass clear title. If a potential cloud manifests itself, until it is clarified it has the same effect as if it actually existed until proven to the contrary. If legal action is necessary to clarify the status of title, the action is called an **action to quiet title**.

Since no one can guarantee that a title is free from defects, even after a title search and examination have been done, it is necessary for the buyer to protect title to the property through the purchase of a title insurance policy. This is true even if a family member or a trusted friend conveys title. The presumption may be that title insurance is not necessary in such cases because "I know my mother (brother, cousin, friend) wouldn't cheat me." Since no one can know the true status of title, unmarketable title can be inadvertently passed by a family member or friend just as easily as it could be by a stranger.

TITLE INSURANCE POLICY

Title insurance differs significantly from other forms of insurance in many respects. First, only a one-time premium is paid for the entire term of the policy. No other premium ever has to be paid. Second, it is the only policy of insurance that protects against loss or damage arising out of matters that have occurred in the past rather than those that may occur in the future. The risks of title insurance end where the risks of other types of insurance begin. Therefore, only those title defects that occurred prior to a conveyance are insured. Third, total policy coverage diminishes as damage payments are made to the insured. The amount coincides with the amount of each payment. Therefore, if the insured collects $25,000 in damages under a $100,000 policy, only $75,000 would remain in force for protection against future contingencies.

In other respects, title insurance has a number of similarities to other insurance, and the courts have applied the same rules as are applied to other types of insurance policies. For example, the title policy is subject to the same rules of construction as other insurance policies, and the policy provisions will always be interpreted liberally in favor of the insured. The company agrees to pay for any losses up to the face amount of the policy that a policyowner suffers, except for those defects specifically excluded. The loss may be the loss of the title itself or the cost of legal fees and other costs to make the title good. Although title insurance can be bought at any time, it is most often purchased when an interest in real property is acquired.

Limitations of Title Insurance

Title insurance is not without limitations. Each policy contains **exclusions** and **exceptions** which exclude liability with regard to certain defects, liens or other encumbrances. Exclusions are those matters that the policy expressly indicates are not within the coverage provided. Common exclusions include:

- Governmental police power, including building and zoning ordinances and other land use regulations;
- The right to take land by condemnation;
- Title risks created, allowed or agreed to by the insured;
- Defects known to the insured but not the agent;
- Risks that result in no loss to the insured; and
- Risks that arise after the policy date.

Common policy exceptions include tax liens remaining unpaid at the date of the policy; hazardous waste and environmental liens that do not appear as a matter of record on the policy date; survey matters; easements and other matters that do not appear of record, such as deed restrictions or water or mineral rights, and rights of parties in possession of property other than those having record interest.

An exclusion should not be confused with an exception. Exclusions relate to matters that were never intended to be the subject of title insurance, whether or not the problem exists. The word "exception" means that coverage under a policy may exist, and, but for the fact an exception has been placed in the policy, there probably would be coverage. They are matters that the title company cannot insure because they constitute objections to title.

Marketable Title

A marketable (clear, merchantable) title is a title that is free from reasonable doubts or objections; one that the courts would compel a purchaser to accept under the terms of a sales contract. Marketability of title may be affected by chain of title problems such as a conveyance made under duress, by encumbrances such as significant encroachments, mineral reservations, various types of liens and recorded instruments, by "loss of title" problems such as eminent domain, and by any of the other potential hazards previously mentioned.

Virtually all real estate transactions are tied to the necessity of having title protected by title insurance. Without that precaution, a lender will refuse to lend the funds necessary to complete the transaction, since both buyer and lender would be exposing their investments to potential risk.

FORMS OF TITLE INSURANCE

There are two commonly used forms of title policies: an owner's policy, which protects the new owner's interest in the property, and a lender's policy, which insures the mortgagee's interest. Each of these policies is described below.

Owner's (Fee) Policy. The primary assurance offered by the owner's policy is that the title to the insured land is wholly in the name of the insured. The owner's policy affords coverage equal to the sale price, and the policy remains in force as long as the owner (buyer) or his heirs have an interest in the property. The policy does not protect the insured from loss arising from matters specifically excluded in the policy, nor from the insured's own liability, such as judgments against him or conditions created by him. However, undiscovered and hidden defects not specifically excluded are covered. The owner's policy is not assignable, so a new policy must be purchased each time the property changes hands. The fee paid for an owner's policy is a one-time fee, paid when the policy is issued. An owner's policy is optional, but only a foolish or uninformed purchaser would fail to obtain title protection.

An owner's policy provides protection for as long as the insured owns the interest covered by the policy. Upon the insured's death, the policy's coverage continues in favor of anyone who acquired the insured's interest. For a corporate insured, any successor to the corporate entity by way of dissolution, merger or receivership becomes an insured under the existing owner's policy.

The protection of the owner's policy continues for as long as the named insured is subject to liability that might arise from any title warranties made by the insured in any transfer or conveyance of the insured interest. Coverage also continues when the insured conveys the insured's interest to a purchaser and takes back a mortgage. Thus, an insured that sells his or her interest and takes back a mortgage continues to be protected by the original owner's policy. In other words, the insured is protected as long as he has an interest in the property, or reacquires his interest.

Back-title Information. Occasionally a client provides "back title" information in the form of a prior policy. If the policy is issued by a reputable company, the searcher will begin the search at the point the old policy left off and provide copies of any easements, restrictions, etc., set forth in that policy. If the policy is ten years old or less, the insurer can give the client a reduced premium. The discount applies only to the face amount of insurance on the original policy and not to any increase. Although back titles of all major companies are accepted, the insuring company assumes the risk for any errors made by the company that insured the back title.

Mortgagee's (Lender's) Policy. The mortgagee's policy provides exclusive protection for lenders who take real estate as security for a loan. In such cases, this policy will insure the mortgagee's security interest in the collateral property. However, the protection only applies to situations in which the security claim proves legally invalid. It will not cover losses created by a borrower's defaults. The fee paid for a mortgagee's policy is a one-time charge but, unlike the owner's policy, coverage continues with the life of the mortgage, even if the mortgage is assigned to another lender. In addition to the named insured, a number of notable differences exist between an owner's and mortgagee's policy. For example, the mortgagee's policy covers only the outstanding balance due on the mortgage. So as the loan amount is reduced over time, coverage decreases, and ends when the loan is satisfied.

Notice of Availability of Owner's Policy

When purchasing a lender's policy, the owner can, for a nominal charge, also purchase an owner's title policy to protect his interest. To protect an uninformed owner when only a loan policy has been requested, New Jersey law requires that the purchaser be given written notice of the availability of owner's title insurance coverage when a loan title policy is being issued. The law covers mortgage transactions involving one- to four-family dwellings with terms of over two years.

Other Policy Forms

In addition to insuring the interests of lenders and owners, title insurers are also prepared to insure **leasehold estates** and the interest of vendees who purchase real estate under a **land contract**. Tenants (lessees) with long-term leases buy leasehold policies to insure that the landlord (lessor) has clear title to the leased premises. A tenant would want this kind of protection before investing substantial amounts in remodeling. A land contract involves a real estate installment sale under which the buyer may use and occupy the land, but will not receive a deed from the seller until all or a specified part of the purchase price has been paid. Land contracts will be discussed in Chapter 19.

Title Insurance Rates

The charge for title insurance is composed of several elements, including searching, examination, underwriting premium, agent's commission and determining insurability. The greatest portion of the charge for title insurance is allocated to abstracting, examination and closing services, which are normally incurred in all real estate transactions.

Sample Title Insurance Premiums

Coverage	Basic	Reissue	Refinance	Modification
$ 50,000	$ 262.50	$ 212.50	$ 200.00	$ 200.00
$100,000	$ 525.00	$ 425.00	$ 250.00	$ 200.00
$200,000	$ 925.00	$ 750.00	$ 475.00	$ 325.00
$300,000	$1,325.00	$1,075.00	$ 700.00	$ 475.00
$400,000	$1,725.00	$1,400.00	$ 925.00	$ 625.00

Title insurance rates are somewhat involved. Starting with the basic rate for an original policy, there are a number of rate reduction formulas, all designed to give the customer a reduced cost as long as the reduction is consistent with reduced exposure and the cost of processing. These reduced rates apply to reissue policies, refinance policies, simultaneously issued owner's and lender's policies, modification policies and many other situations.

Title companies must file a schedule of fees and classifications with the Department of Banking and Insurance. They must justify their bases and obtain the Department's approval.

The basic rate is used for both the lender's policy and the owner's policy. When policies are issued simultaneously, the premium will be based on the higher amount (normally the purchase price) and the lender's policy (with coverage up to the loan balance) costs only $25. In rare instances, the higher amount may be the loan amount, for example where a property is considerably improved and the purchase price is lower than normal. The modification rate usually applies to the lender's policy, wherein the lender modifies the original loan in some manner, i.e., rate, loan amount or terms of loan.

Affidavits of Title

When a title insurer agrees to insure title, it does so not only on the basis of its own research, but also on the basis of representations made by the seller and buyer. These representations are contained in the affidavit of title.

An affidavit is a sworn statement given by a deponent (affiant) in which the deponent deposes that or affirms the truth of the statements contained therein. A "seller's affidavit" of title is one in which the seller makes statements which clarify matters that could affect the passage of clear title. Among the facts the grantor(s) affirms in the seller's affidavit are that: he is of legal age and in possession of the interest to be conveyed, his marital status is as designated on the affidavit, and judgments reported in the judgment search which showed a name the same as or similar to his, are not his, and that he has done nothing to encumber the title which does not appear in the public record, such as having knowledge of unrecorded contracts, deeds and mortgages or having any unpaid bills for repairs or improvements to the property.

When a title insurer pays a claim under a title insurance policy it is entitled to step into the shoes of the insured and it acquires, under the right of **subrogation**, the right to take legal action against a third party responsible for a loss to an insured for which a claim has been paid. For example, a title company pays a claim for damages to an insured property owner for a loss caused by a seller who forged a co-owner's signature on a deed of conveyance. The subrogation clause gives the company the right to take on—as its own—the property owner's claim and sue the seller for damages. Subrogation prevents the policyowner from collecting twice for the same loss—once from the insurance company, and then from the party that caused the loss.

Endorsements

An endorsement is a written statement that is used to modify, add, reduce or delete any or some of the contents and coverages of a title insurance policy or commitment. The number, contents and coverages relative to endorsements are unlimited, subject only to the willingness of the title company to assume the additional risk, the permissibility of the risk under state law, and full compliance with the pertinent statutory provisions for filing, approval and use of the endorsement forms. The New Jersey Department of Banking and Insurance regulates policy forms and endorsements as well as premiums and charges.

TIDAL LANDS

A substantial title problem affecting many properties throughout the state involves the matter of tidal lands. By law (NJSA 12 and 13) and court decision, the state holds title in fee simple to all lands currently or formerly flowed by the tide, whether or not part of or connected with a navigable waterway. Many such lands have been illegally developed, sold and resold. Through intensive surveys and investigations, the state has determined the lands affected. Seventeen of New Jersey's 21 counties are affected by tidelands claims. Only the four counties located in the northwestern corner of the State are exempt: Morris, Sussex, Warren and Hunterdon. A fifth county (Somerset) has very few tidelands claims. Since the state has an interest in all or a portion of such properties, the current owners cannot pass clear title to them without paying the value of the state's interest. There are, however, a number of exceptions, including the following:

- Lands conveyed by the state through a riparian grant;
- Lands which had ceased being tide-flowed on November 3, 1941 and for which the state had not filed a claim map by November 3, 1982, or which thereafter may cease being tide-flowed for 40 years and for which the state has not filed a claim map;
- Lands which had ceased to be tide-flowed through accretion; and

- Lands to which the State has relinquished its interest by legislative grant.

The state's Tidelands Resource Council (TRC) has the responsibility of conveying, leasing or licensing the use of tidal lands. Law commits the income derived from the grants to the Fund for the Support of Free Public Schools, which guarantees the financial obligations of local school boards. It is required by law to charge the current market value of the state's interest in affected lands. The amount due to clear the owner's title of this cloud will vary depending upon the value of the property and the extent of the state's interest in it.

The title company should analyze every title in each of the 17 counties affected to determine if the state has asserted a claim. This may be done by reference to a tidelands claim map. The searcher should also be instructed to check, as a matter of course, the copics of the maps filed with the county clerk or registrar. Once it has been determined that the state is indeed asserting a tidelands claim, an appropriate exception should be shown in Schedule B. Failure to set up the exception could lead to substantial liability. The owner will be advised as part of the title review process whether such tidal land rights affect his property.

American Land Title Association (ALTA)

The trade association of the land title industry is the American Land Title Association (ALTA). More than 2,000 members representing every state, the District of Columbia, Puerto Rico and Canada belong to the American Land Title Association and use standardized ALTA title insurance policies.

KEY WORDS

Abstract of Title
ALTA
Chain of Title
Commitment
County Clerk's Office
Mortgagee's Policy
Owner's Policy
Quiet Title Proceeding
Subrogation
Title Insurance
Title Report
Title Search

CHAPTER 11
Review Questions
(Answers on page 553)

1. A lender's title policy protects:
   (A) the mortgagee only.
   (B) the owner only.
   (C) both the owner and the lender.
   (D) neither the owner nor the mortgagee.

2. Title insurance premiums are paid:
   (A) annually.
   (B) once—at the issuance of the policy.
   (C) by the seller, usually.
   (D) monthly.

3. The county clerk does which of the following?
   (A) Confirms the accuracy of the legal description in the deed.
   (B) Attests to the accuracy of the survey.
   (C) Gives an acknowledgment.
   (D) Enters the document into the public records.

4. The cost of the mortgagee's policy of title insurance is usually borne by:
   (A) broker.
   (B) seller.
   (C) borrower.
   (D) lender.

5. Common exclusions in title insurance policies include:
   (A) zoning.
   (B) rights of parties in possession.
   (C) taxes and assessments not yet due.
   (D) All of the above.

6. An abstract of title is:
   (A) a brief digest of the title to a particular property.
   (B) a summary of each deed in a title search.
   (C) an appraisal of the lands and the improvements.
   (D) a summary of all the improvements and encroachments on the property.

7. Which of the following statements is NOT true?
   (A) The mortgagee's policy protects the lender.
   (B) The mortgagee's policy is paid for by the grantee.
   (C) The fee policy protects the owner.
   (D) Title defects arising after closing are protected.

8. To what does the term "chain of title" refer?
   (A) Recording law.
   (B) Will beneficiaries.
   (C) Title evidence.
   (D) A succession of owners.

9. The best evidence of title is provided by:
   (A) title search.
   (B) title insurance.
   (C) abstract of title.
   (D) warranty deed.

10. An owner's title policy protects:
    (A) the owner for as long as he or his heirs own the property.
    (B) a subsequent purchaser that the owner sells to so long as the term of the owner's policy has not expired.
    (C) the mortgagee up to the amount of the loan.
    (D) the owner if he receives an assignment of the policy from the previous owner.

11. Which of the following is NOT an objective of a title search?
    (A) Establish relative value.
    (B) Verify ownership.
    (C) Find money encumbrances.
    (D) Find non-money encumbrances.

12. A brief history of the title to a tract of land, consisting of a summary of all instruments affecting title to such land, is called a (an):
    (A) affidavit of title.
    (B) abstract of title.
    (C) cloud on title.
    (D) title insurance policy.

13. Three of the following real estate terms are closely associated. Which term is out of place?
    (A) Seller.
    (B) Grantor.
    (C) Vendor.
    (D) Abstract.

14. To alienate title to property, one:
    (A) clouds the title.
    (B) transfers ownership of property.
    (C) must contact the Immigration Department.
    (D) must be acting voluntarily.

CHAPTER TWELVE

AGENCY

Agency is the legal relationship between two parties who agree that one party, the **agent**, will act on behalf of the other party, the **principal**, subject to the principal's reasonable direction and control. In practice, real estate agents seldom refer to the party they represent as their "principal." Generally, they refer to the principal as their "client" and parties with whom they negotiate on behalf of the principal as "customers."

Minors and mentally ill people cannot be principals because they lack contractual capacity to act for themselves. However, corporations and partnerships are legal entities that do have the capacity to contract and therefore can be principals. In a real estate transaction, the agency relationship is formed between the brokerage firm (not the listing salesperson) and the principal. The brokerage firm includes the broker and all licensees who are licensed under the broker in one or more actual locations.

Parties to the Agency Relationship

Principal—A person who appoints another to act on his behalf.

Agent—A person authorized by another (the principal) to act on the latter's behalf, or in his place, in establishing a legal relationship with a third party. An agent must keep his principal informed about any matter that affects the subject matter of the agency, and must avoid any conflict of interest, any kind of self-dealing, or making a secret profit at the expense of the principal.

Customer—The third party in the agency relationship. The buyer is the customer of the seller's agent, and the seller is the customer of the buyer's agent. When the licensee acts as a *transaction broker* (discussed below) the parties on both sides of the transaction are customers.

Subagent—A person who is authorized to act on behalf of an agent by a principal. In other words, an agent for an agent. Before 1995, this was the predominant brokerage business relationship in New Jersey. Today, subagency is rarely used as a business relationship between brokerage offices.

Agents may be classified as *general agents* and *special agents*.

General Agent—A general agent is one who has *broad authority* to represent his principal in a series of transactions of a continuous nature. An example of a general agent is a real estate property manager who has the authority to hire and fire employees, to purchase supplies, to pay bills, to contract for maintenance and so on.

Special Agent—A special agent is one who acts with *limited authority* in conducting a specific task for a principal. For example, a real estate broker who is engaged by a property owner to find a buyer or a tenant, and who is not authorized to sell the property or to bind the owner to a sales contract, is a special agent.

Creation of the Agency Relationship

There are two primary agency relationships that you will encounter in the real estate business: the broker-salesperson relationship, and the client-broker relationship.

Broker (Principal)-Salesperson (Agent)

An agency relationship is created between the broker and his salespersons through a written **employment agreement**.

Client (Principal)-Broker (Agent)

Although a real estate broker may represent a buyer or seller, or a landlord or tenant, the most common agency agreement is one of two kinds. It is either a written agreement evidenced by the **listing contract**, in which the property owner lists his property for sale with the broker, or it is the relationship that exists when a buyer seeks the services of a broker to find, and negotiate for her, in the purchase of a particular piece of property **(buyer agency contract)**. Listing contracts will be discussed in Chapter 13. Buyer agency agreements will be discussed later in this chapter.

The above contracts empower the broker to act

as the client's special agent to find a buyer, a tenant or a suitable property. When a salesperson signs a listing or buyer agency contract, he does so in the name of the broker, thereby binding the broker just as firmly as if the broker had signed the contract himself.

Duties of an Agent to the Principal

Agents are considered by law to be **fiduciaries**. A fiduciary is a person who handles the money or property of another person in a position of confidence and trust. As a fiduciary, the agent has a duty to place the principal's interest ahead of all other interests, including his or her own.

An agent owes to the principal the following fiduciary duties:

Undivided Loyalty. An agent's loyalty and trust can be rightfully expected by a principal, for any adverse or opposed interests would be contradictory to the agency relationship. This also means that the agent must not represent another with opposing interests in the same transaction without the written consent of both parties. Even with written consent, it must be made abundantly clear to all that the agent has this duty of loyalty, and will therefore pass on all information to his principal. This is true even if the third party has related it in confidence. Thus, when a broker representing a seller talks with a potential buyer (perhaps while sitting at an open house) who thinks the agent will also act in his behalf, and thus reveals confidences to him, the broker must make his true position known. If, by the conversation, the reasonable assumption is made that the broker would act on the buyer's behalf, the broker might be liable to the buyer for any damages sustained. He might also lose his license, and forfeit any commission the seller had agreed to pay.

Duty of Obedience. The agent must obey, promptly and efficiently, all *lawful instructions* of the client, even if he disagrees with the client's judgment.

Duty of Disclosure. An agent must disclose to the principal all relevant and material information concerning the transaction except for information obtained through a previous fiduciary relationship. This disclosure requirement does not include information protected by law (fair housing, etc.).

The agent must present all written offers brought to the principal, regardless of the amount or terms of the offer, for it is his obligation to put forth his best efforts to obtain the most advantageous offer for the principal. The agent must attempt to keep himself fully informed on all matters of concern to his principal, and inform the principal of any changes that might affect the subject matter of the agency.

Duty of Confidentiality. The agent must safeguard the principal's confidences and personal information unless the principal releases the agent from this duty. Without authorization of the principal, a seller's agent may never tell or imply to a buyer customer the lowest price that a seller will accept. By the same token, a buyer's agent must not reveal to a seller customer the highest price that the buyer is willing to pay.

Duty of Reasonable Care and Diligence. The agent has the duty to use reasonable care and diligence in handling the client's transaction, using the same care as he would if the property were his own or following recognized professional standards existing in the community. An agent representing himself to the public as possessing certain abilities and skills has the duty of possessing or having continuing access to such abilities or skills. An agent must never deliberately overprice a property to ensure that he will be given the listing. If it happens, and it can be demonstrated that the excessive price inhibited a sale, the agent is subject to a suit for damages.

The agent must also carefully "qualify" any prospects to be as sure as possible that only serious and financially able prospects are shown the property. The agent should also advise the seller of the soundness and quality of offers received to assist the seller's judgment. Brokers must be careful and thorough in the qualifying process. Simply accepting information from the buyer and not questioning it further can lead to difficulty. Sellers have the right to expect expert advice and assistance in finding a buyer who will be able to close title.

Duty to Account. The agent must keep the principal informed, disclosing all material facts regarding the transaction and maintain accurate records of all monies entrusted to him in accordance with state licensing laws. Any monies received by a salesperson must be immediately turned over to the broker, who in turn must deposit them into a client's trust account. The broker may at no time commingle these funds with his own or that of his firm, and to do so could result in suspension or revocation of his license.

A breach of fiduciary duties to a client often leads the third party to believe that the agent was acting for him. This creates an undisclosed dual agency, which is considered an act of fraud. The implications of an undisclosed dual agency are discussed below.

Agent's Duties to Third Parties

The agent's responsibilities to third parties with whom he deals on behalf of a principal are also of paramount importance. Since the agent can be held responsible to the third party for any fraud he commits (with or without his principal's permission), he should exercise due caution when relating any material facts concerning the property. If, to the buyer's detriment, an agent misrepresents, or makes a false statement of fact, he can be held liable. Naturally, if any of these things are done with the consent of the principal, the third party may have the choice of recovering his loss from either the principal or the agent. The prudent agent should attempt to ascertain all material facts about a property to his own satisfaction, and should not rely exclusively upon information supplied by the principal. It should be noted, however, that the agent is justified in relying on a statement of fact if something beyond a reasonable investigation would be required to discover the truth. Thus, if a principal intentionally misleads an agent, the third party would look to the principal for recovery of any loss sustained.

The agent's duties to third parties also requires that the buyer be advised of any factors that could negatively affect the value or use of a property to be purchased in a material way, such as the fact that the highway fronting the property is soon to be widened, that the county landfill is to be located next to the property or that there is to be a zoning change which could adversely affect value. Buyers must be advised of any material fact that could affect their decision to purchase. In short, if a typical buyer would want to know such information, the agent must disclose it.

Property Condition Disclosure

Approximately two-thirds of all lawsuits against real estate licensees involve claims alleging misrepresentation or failure to disclose property defects. As a result, many brokers are now requiring sellers to fill out a property condition disclosure form at the time a listing agreement is signed. Although the forms do not replace the broker's responsibility to disclose known material property defects, they add a measure of protection to all parties in the transaction. Mandatory property condition disclosure is the law in 29 states, but in New Jersey it is practiced voluntarily. It is important that the property owner, not the broker, fill out the form. It is strongly recommended that licensees use these forms (See Figure 12.1).

Agency Disclosure

In recent years it became apparent that most prospective buyers thought that the real estate agent that was trying to find them a home was working for them, when in fact the broker was the agent for the seller. To protect buyers and sellers, New Jersey regulations require agency disclosure. Under the regulations, before an agent can discuss with a buyer or tenant any confidential aspects of a sale or rental such as personal finances, the agent must present to the client or customer a written disclosure form called a **Consumer Information Statement** (CIS) that describes their business relationship in the transaction. If the conversation is held over the telephone, an oral explanation of the agency alternatives will suffice, followed by a written explanation.

Buyers, sellers, landlords and tenants must be given a copy of the CIS when involved in transactions for the sale or rental of all one- to four-family residential properties or vacant one-family lots. Rentals for not more than 125 days (short-term rentals) with a specific termination date are exempt from the disclosure requirement, although licensees still must disclose their business relationship in the transaction. Month-to-month tenancies are not considered short-term rentals. The CIS (reprinted in Figure 12.2) should be reviewed at this time.

All "brokerage agreements" must contain a statement that the client has received a copy of the disclosure statement prior to signing the agreement. By signing the agreement, the parties acknowledge receipt of the CIS. Brokerage agreements include, but are not limited to, listing agreements, buyer-broker, lessee-broker, and transaction broker and dual agency agreements. If more than one firm is involved, the agreement must contain a statement that describes the agency status of the cooperating broker and the manner in which the commission will be shared.

The Five Business Relationships

The Consumer Information Statement describes the five business relationships that a real estate broker can enter into with a customer or client:

1. Seller's Agent;
2. Buyer's Agent;
3. Disclosed Dual Agent;
4. Transaction Broker; and
5. Seller's Agent on properties for which this firm is acting as Seller's Agent, and Transaction Broker on other properties.

Business relationship No. 5 will not appear as a

FIGURE 12.1
Property Condition Disclosure Form

NEW JERSEY ASSOCIATION OF REALTORS® STANDARD FORM OF SELLER'S PROPERTY CONDITION DISCLOSURE STATEMENT

1 **Property Address:** ______________________________
2 ______________________________
3 **Seller:** ______________________________
4
5 The purpose of this Disclosure Statement is to disclose, to the best of Seller's knowledge, the condition of the Property, as
6 of the date set forth below. The Seller acknowledges that he/she is under an obligation to disclose any known material defects
7 in the Property even if not addressed in this printed form. The Seller represents that he/she has completed this form <u>without</u>
8 <u>the assistance of any licensed real estate broker or salesperson</u>. Any prospective buyer of the Property is cautioned to inspect
9 the Property carefully. Moreover, this Disclosure Statement is not intended to be a substitute for prospective buyer's hiring of
10 qualified experts to inspect the Property.
11
12 **OCCUPANCY**
13 Yes No Unknown
14 [ ] [ ] [ ] 1. Does the Seller currently occupy this property? If not how long has it been since
15 Seller occupied the property?______________________
16
17 **ROOF**
18 2. Age of roof______________________
19 [ ] [ ] [ ] 3. Has roof been replaced or repaired during your ownership?
20 [ ] [ ] [ ] If yes were the shingles removed?
21 [ ] [ ] [ ] 4. Does the roof leak?
22 5. Explain any "yes" answers that you give in this section: ______________________
23 ______________________
24 ______________________
25
26 **BASEMENTS AND CRAWL SPACES** (Complete only if applicable)
27 [ ] [ ] [ ] 6. Does the property have a sump pump?
28 [ ] [ ] 7. Are you aware of any water leakage, accumulation, or dampness within the basement
29 or crawl spaces or other structures?
30 [ ] [ ] 8. Are you aware of any repairs or other attempts to control any water or dampness
31 problem in the basement or crawlspace? If "Yes" describe the location, extent, date,
32 and name of the person who did the repair or control effort:______________________
33 ______________________
34 ______________________
35 [ ] [ ] 9. Are you aware of any cracks or bulges in the floor or foundation walls? If yes, are they
36 horizontal__________or vertical__________
37 10. Explain any "yes" answers that you give in this section: ______________________
38 ______________________
39 ______________________
40
41 **TERMITES/WOOD DESTROYING INSECTS, DRY ROT, PESTS**
42 [ ] [ ] [ ] 11. Are you aware of any termites/wood destroying insects, dry rot, pests affecting the
43 property?
44 [ ] [ ] [ ] 12. Are you aware of any damage to the property caused by termites/wood destroying
45 insects, dry rot, or pests?
46 [ ] [ ] 13. If yes, has the damage been repaired?
47 [ ] [ ] 14. Is your property currently under contract by a licensed pest control company? If
48 "yes", name and address of licensed pest control company______________________
49 ______________________
50 [ ] [ ] 15. Are you aware of any termite/pest control inspections or treatments for the property
51 in the past?
52 16. Explain any "yes" answer that you give in this section:______________________
53 ______________________

FIGURE 12.1 (cont'd)

55
56 **STRUCTURAL ITEMS**
57 [ ] [ ] [ ] 17. Are you aware of any movement, shifting, or other problems with walls or
58 foundations?
59 [ ] [ ] [ ] 18. Are you aware if the property or improvements theron have ever been damaged by
60 fire, smoke, wind or flood?
61 [ ] [ ] [ ] 19. Are you aware of any fire retardant plywood used in the construction?
62 [ ] [ ] [ ] 20. Are you aware of any current or past problems with driveways, walkways, patios,
63 sinkholes, or retaining walls on the property?
64 21. Explain any "yes answers that you give in this section. When explaining efforts to
65 control or repair, please describe the location and extent of the problem and the date
66 and person by whom the work was done, if known:________________
67 ____
68 ____
69 ____
70
71
72 **ADDITIONS/REMODELS**
73 Yes No Unknown
74 [ ] [ ] 22. Are you aware of any additions, structural changes or other alterations to the property.
75 [ ] [ ] 22a. Were the proper building permits and approvals obtained? Explain any "yes" answers
76 you give in this section:______________________________
77 ____
78
79 **WATER AND SEWAGE**
80 23. What is the source of your drinking water?
81 [ ] Public [ ] Community System [ ] Well on Property
82 [ ] Other (explain)____________________________
83 [ ] [ ] 24. If your drinking water supply is not public; has it been tested?____________
84 When? __________ Did it pass? _____ If not explain______________
85 ____
86 [ ] 25. When was well installed?____________________________
87 [ ] Location of well? ______________________________
88 [ ] [ ] 26. Do you have a softener, filter, or other purification system?
89 [ ] Leased [ ] Owned
90 27. What is the type of sewage system?
91 [ ] Public Sewer [ ] Private Sewer [ ] Septic System [ ] Cesspool
92 [ ] Other (explain): ____________________________
93 [ ] 28. If Septic System when was it installed?________________________
94 Location? __________________________________
95 [ ] 29. When was the Septic System or Cesspool last cleaned and/or serviced? __________
96 by whom? __________________________________
97 [ ] [ ] [ ] 30. Are you aware of any abandoned Septic Systems or Cesspool on your property? If
98 "yes" is the closure in accordance with the township ordinance? Explain__________
99 ____
100 [ ] [ ] 31. Are you aware of any leaks, backups, or other problems relating to any of the
101 plumbing systems, fixtures water and sewage related items? If "yes" explain:
102 ____
103 [ ] [ ] 32. Are you aware of any shut off, disconnected, or abandoned wells, underground water
104 or sewage tanks, or dry wells on the property?
105 [ ] [ ] [ ] 33. Is either the private water or sewage system shared? If "yes" explain____________
106 ____
107 34. Water Heater: [ ] Electric [ ] Fuel Oil [ ] Gas Age of Water Heater____________
108 35. Explain any "yes" answers you give in this section____________________
109 ____
110
111 **HEATING AND AIR CONDITIONING**
112 36. Type of air conditioning: [ ] Central Electric [ ] Central Gas
113 [ ] Wall/Window Unit [ ] None
114 37. List any areas of the house that are not air conditioned:__________________
115 ____
116
117 [ ] 38. What is the age of Air Conditioning System______________
118 39. Type of heat: [ ] Electric [ ] Fuel Oil [ ] Natural Gas [ ] Propane [ ] Unheated
119 [ ] Other

FIGURE 12.1 (cont'd)

120				40. What is the type of heating system? (e.g. forced air, hot water or base board, radiator,
121				steam heat) ______
122				41. Age of furnace______ Date of last service______
123				42. List any areas of the house that are not heated:______
124	[ ]	[ ]		43. Are you aware of any underground fuel tanks on the property?
125	[ ]	[ ]		If tank is not in use do you have a closure certificate?
126	[ ]	[ ]		44. Are you aware if any problems with any item in this section? If "yes" explain ______
127				______
128				
129	**WOOD BURNING STOVE OR FIREPLACE**			
130	[ ]	[ ]		45. Do you have [ ] wood burning stove? [ ] fireplace? [ ] insert? [ ] Other
131	[ ]	[ ]		45a. If you have a fireplace, was the flu cleaned by a chimney sweep company?
132				When______
133	[ ]	[ ]		46. Are you aware of any problems? If "yes" please explain:______
134				______
135				
136	**ELECTRICAL SYSTEM**			
137				47. What type of wiring is in this structure? [ ] Copper
138				[ ] Aluminum [ ] Other [ ] Unknown
139				48. What amp service does it have? [ ] 60 [ ] 100
140				[ ] 150 [ ] 200 [ ] Other [ ] Unknown
141	[ ]	[ ]	[ ]	49. Does it have 220 volt service? Which is present?
142				[ ] Circuit Breakers [ ] Fuses
143	[ ]	[ ]		50. Are you aware of any additions to the original service? If "yes" were the additions
144				done by a licensed electrician? Name and address______
145				______
146	[ ]	[ ]	[ ]	51. If yes, were proper building permits and approvals obtained?
147	[ ]	[ ]		52. Are you aware of any wall switches, light fixtures or electrical outlets in need of repair?
148				53. Explain any "yes" answers you give in this section:______
149				
151	**MAJOR APPLIANCES AND OTHER ITEMS** (For informational purposes only)			
152	Are the following items, that may be included in the sale, in working order? (Mark only if included in sale)			
153	Yes	No	Unknown	
154	[ ]	[ ]		54. Electric Garage Door Opener No. of Transmitters______
155	[ ]	[ ]		55. Smoke Detectors Battery[ ] Electric[ ] Both[ ] How Many______
156				Carbon Monoxide Detectors How Many______
157				Location______
158				56. Swimming Pool [ ] Pool Heater [ ] Spa/Hot Tub [ ]
159	[ ]	[ ]		Were proper permits and approvals obtained?______
160	[ ]	[ ]		57. Are the following in working order? (Check only those included in the sale)
161				Y for yes N for no [ ] Refrigerator [ ] Range [ ] Microwave Oven
162				[ ] Dishwasher [ ] Trash Compactor [ ] Garbage Disposal
163				[ ] Washer [ ] Dryer [ ] Intercom [ ] Other
164				If no, please explain?______
165	[ ]	[ ]		58. Are you aware of any items in this section in need of repair or replacement? If "yes"
166				explain:______
167				______
168				
169	**LAND** (Soils, Drainage and Boundaries)			
170	[ ]	[ ]		59. Are you aware of any fill or expansive soil on the property?
171	[ ]	[ ]	[ ]	60. Is the property located in a flood hazard zone?
172	[ ]	[ ]	[ ]	61. Is the property located in a delineated wetlands?
173	[ ]	[ ]		62. Are you aware of any drainage or flood problems affecting the property?
174	[ ]	[ ]		63. Are you aware of any encroachments, utility easements, boundary line disputes, or
175				easements affecting the property?
176	[ ]	[ ]		64. Are you aware if any part of the property is being claimed by the State of New Jersey
177				as land presently or formerly covered by tidal water (Riparian claim or lease grant)?
178				Explain:______
179				______
180	[ ]	[ ]		65. Are you aware of any shared or common areas (e.g. driveways bridges, docks, walls,
181				bulkheads, etc.) or maintenance agreements? Explain any "yes" answers that you give
182				in this section______
183				______
184				

FIGURE 12.1 (cont'd)

Line				
185	**ENVIRONMENTAL HAZARDS**			
186	[ ]	[ ]	[ ]	67. Are you aware of any present or previous underground storage (UST) tanks or toxic
187				substances present on this property or adjacent property (structure or soil), such as
188				polychlorinated biphenyl (PCB), solvents, hydraulic fluid, petro-chemicals,
189				hazardous wastes, or others? If "yes" Explain:__________
190				__________
191	[ ]	[ ]	[ ]	68. Are you aware if the underground storage tank, has been tested? (Attach copy of each
192				test report or closure certificate if available).
193	[ ]	[ ]	[ ]	69. Are you aware if the property has been tested for radon gas. (Attach copy of each test
194				report if available).
195	[ ]	[ ]	[ ]	70. Are you aware if the property has been tested for any other toxic substances? (e.g.
196				urea-formaldehyde foam insulation, asbestos-containing materials, pesticides in land)
197				(Attach copy of each test report if available).
198				71. If "yes" to any of the above, was remediation undertaken? Explain:__________
199				__________
200				
201	**DEED RESTRICTION, HOMEOWNERS ASSOCIATIONS/CONDOMINIUMS AND CO-OPS**			
202	[ ]	[ ]		72. Are you aware if the property is subject to any deed restrictions?
203	[ ]	[ ]	[ ]	73. Is the property part of a condominium or other common interest ownership? If so,
204				what is the Associations's name and telephone number?__________
205				__________
206	[ ]	[ ]	[ ]	74. If so, are there any dues or assessments involved? If "yes" how much?__________
207				__________
208	[ ]	[ ]		75. Are you aware of any defect, damage, or problem with any common elements or
209				common areas that materially affects the property?
210	[ ]	[ ]		76. Are you aware of any condition or claim which may result in an increase in
211				assessments or fees?
212	[ ]	[ ]		77. Are you aware if the property is subject to covenants, conditions, or restrictions as
213				part of a condominium, homeowners association, or other form of common interest
214				ownership?
215	[ ]	[ ]		77a. Have there been any rule changes that impact the property?
216				78. Explain any "yes" answers you give in this section:__________
217				__________
218				
219	**MISCELLANEOUS**			
220	[ ]	[ ]		79. Are you aware of any existing or threatened legal action affecting the property?
221	[ ]	[ ]		80. Are you aware of any violations of federal, state, or local laws or regulations relating
222				to this property?
223	[ ]	[ ]		81. Are you aware of any zoning violations, non-conforming uses, or set-back violations
224				relating to this property?
225	[ ]	[ ]		82. Are you aware of any public improvement, condominium or homeowner association
226				assessments against the property that remain unpaid or of any violations of zoning,
227				housing, building, safety or fire ordinances that remain uncorrected?
228	[ ]	[ ]		83. Are you aware of any reason, including a defect in title encumbrance and lien that
229				would prevent you from conveying title?
230	Yes	No	Unknown	
231	[ ]	[ ]		84. Are you aware of any material defects to the property dwelling, or fixtures which are
232				not disclosed elsewhere on this form? (A material defect is a defect with the property
233				or any portion of it that would have a significant adverse impact on the value or
234				desirability of the residential real property.) If "yes" explain:__________
235				__________
236				__________
237				__________
238				85. Explain any other "yes" answers you give in this section:__________
239				__________
240				__________
241				__________
242				

FIGURE 12.1 (cont'd)

243 **ACKNOWLEDGMENT OF SELLER**
244 The undersigned Seller acknowledges that the information set forth in this Disclosure Statement is accurate and complete
245 to the best of Seller's knowledge, but is neither a warranty nor a representation as to the condition of the Property. Seller hereby
246 authorizes its real estate agent to provide this Disclosure statement to any prospective buyer of the Property, and to other real
247 estate agents. Seller alone is responsible for the accuracy of the information contained in this statement. This Disclosure
248 Statement has been completed by the seller without assistance from any licensed broker or salesperson.
249
250 ______________________ ______________________
251 SELLER DATE
252 ______________________ ______________________
253 SELLER DATE
254
255
256 **EXECUTOR, ADMINISTRATOR, TRUSTEE**
257 The undersigned has never occupied the property and lacks personal knowledge necessary to complete this Disclosure
258 Statement.
259
260 ______________________ ______________________
261 NAME DATE
262 ______________________ ______________________
263 NAME DATE
264
265
266 **RECEIPT AND ACKNOWLEDGMENT BY PROSPECTIVE BUYER**
267 The Undersigned Prospective Buyer acknowledges receipt of this Disclosure Statement prior to the signing of a Contract
268 of Sale pertaining to this Property. Prospective Buyer acknowledges that this Disclosure Statement is not a warranty or
269 representation by Seller and that, unless stated otherwise in the Contract of Sale, which may be entered into between Seller and
270 Prospective Buyer, the Property shall be purchased in its present condition. It is Prospective Buyer's responsibility to satisfy
271 himself/herself as to the condition of the Property. Prospective Buyer acknowledges that the Property may be inspected by
272 qualified professionals, at Prospective Buyer's expense, to determine the actual condition of the Property.
273
274 ______________________ ______________________
275 PROSPECTIVE BUYER DATE
276 ______________________ ______________________
277 PROSPECTIVE BUYER DATE

separate relationship on the Consumer Information Statement because it is a combination of two other relationships that are listed.

Timing of the Disclosure

Licensees must verbally inform the parties of the five business relationships prior to the first discussion involving:

- The buyer's motivation or financial ability to buy; or
- The seller's motivation to sell or desired selling price.

Licensees must deliver the disclosure statement to the parties prior to any business meeting at which a discussion of their real estate needs will take place. If the discussion is held over the telephone or in a social setting, licensees must, after verbally explaining the agency alternatives, deliver the CIS to the parties prior to their next meeting. In the meantime, if any material is mailed, faxed or delivered to the parties, the disclosure statement must be included with such material.

In cases where there have been no discussions on motivation or financial ability the agent must deliver the CIS no later than the first showing of any listed or unlisted properties.

A licensee who intends to act as a buyer's agent must deliver the disclosure statement to the buyer no later than the commencement of the buyer-agent agreement presentation.

Acknowledging Receipt of the CIS

The regulations do not require the parties to acknowledge receipt of the CIS by signing it. However, the CIS provides optional language that the brokerage firm can use to acknowledge delivery of the disclosure statement if it chooses to do so.

Regardless of whether brokerage firms choose to include on the disclosure statement the optional language referred to above, buyers, sellers, landlords and tenants must acknowledge receipt of the CIS on all offers, contracts or leases prepared by licensees.

Buyers who wish to be represented by a buyer's agent should enter into a separate written **buyer agency contract** with the brokerage firm that is to work as their agent. (See Figure 12.3). These agreements may be similar to exclusive right to sell listing agreements, which we will discuss in Chapter 13. The broker may be entitled to a commission even if the buyer purchases a house without the assistance of the broker. In addition, the buyer could be liable for a payment of more than one commission if he enters into buyer agency contracts with more than one broker.

Disclosed Dual Agent

Dual agency is a limited agency relationship where the brokerage firm represents both the buyer and the seller in the same real estate transaction. It is both unethical and illegal for a broker to represent both parties without the consent of both.

A "dual agency" in which the broker represents both parties at the same time is **legal** with the **informed consent** of all parties. A *Consent to Dual Agency Agreement* is shown as Figure 12.4. "Informed consent" means the written authorization by a party for the brokerage firm that represents them as their agent in a real estate transaction to also represent the other to that transaction as an agent. Informed consent can only be obtained after the brokerage firm has disclosed to the consenting parties all facts that might impact their decision to authorize dual agency, including the extent of the conflicts involved and *the specific ways in which each consenting party will receive less than full agency representation from the dual agent.* In order to obtain informed consent it is also necessary for the licensee to first advise the consenting party of the alternatives to dual agency which are available to that party (seller's agent; buyer's agent; transaction broker).

When working as a disclosed dual agent, a brokerage firm must have the express permission of a party to disclose confidential information to the other party. As noted earlier, such information includes the highest price a buyer can afford to pay, the lowest price a seller will accept and the parties' motivation to buy or sell.

Undisclosed Dual Agent

An undisclosed dual agency relationship is created when a real estate brokerage company has an express agency with a seller and an implied agency with a buyer or an express agency with a buyer and an implied agency with a seller. An undisclosed dual agency is a violation of the license laws and the agent can be liable for damages and forfeiture of compensation as well as loss of a real estate license. Furthermore, the principal can rescind any transaction procured by the dual agent without any showing of injury to the principal or bad faith by the agent.

Dual agency, intended or not, is the basis for an increasing number of lawsuits being brought against real estate brokers as the public learns more about how real estate business is conducted

FIGURE 12.2 Consumer Information Statement

STATE OF NEW JERSEY

DEPARTMENT

OF

BANKING AND INSURANCE

REAL ESTATE COMMISSION

CONSUMER INFORMATION STATEMENT

FOR
OWNERS
BUYERS &
RENTERS
OF NEW JERSEY REAL ESTATE

CONSUMER INFORMATION STATEMENT ON NEW JERSEY REAL ESTATE RELATIONSHIPS

In New Jersey, real estate licensees are required to disclose how they intend to work with buyers and sellers in a real estate transaction. (In rental transactions, the terms "buyers" and "sellers" should be read as "tenants" and "landlords," respectively.)

1. AS A SELLER'S AGENT OR SUBAGENT I, AS A LICENSEE, REPRESENT THE SELLER AND ALL MATERIAL INFORMATION SUPPLIED TO ME BY THE BUYER WILL BE TOLD TO THE SELLER.

2. AS A BUYER'S AGENT I, AS A LICENSEE, REPRESENT THE BUYER AND ALL MATERIAL INFORMATION SUPPLIED TO ME BY THE SELLER WILL BE TOLD TO THE BUYER.

3. AS A DISCLOSED DUAL AGENT I, AS A LICENSEE, REPRESENT BOTH PARTIES. HOWEVER, I MAY NOT, WITHOUT EXPRESS PERMISSION, DISCLOSE THAT THE SELLER WILL ACCEPT A PRICE LESS THAN THE LISTING PRICE OR THAT THE BUYER WILL PAY A PRICE GREATER THAN THE OFFERED PRICE.

4. AS A TRANSACTION BROKER I, AS A LICENSEE, DO NOT REPRESENT EITHER THE BUYER OR THE SELLER. ALL INFORMATION I ACQUIRE FROM ONE PARTY MAY BE TOLD TO THE OTHER PARTY.

Before you disclose confidential information to a real estate licensee regarding a real estate transaction, you should understand what type of business relationship you have with that licensee.

There are four business relationships: (1) seller's agent; (2) buyer's agent; (3) disclosed dual agent; and (4) transaction broker. Each of these relationships imposes certain legal duties and responsibilities on the licensee as well as on the seller or buyer represented. These four relationships are defined in greater detail on the following pages. Please read carefully before making your choice.

SELLER'S AGENT

A seller's agent WORKS ONLY FOR THE SELLER and has legal obligations, called fiduciary duties, to the seller. These include reasonable care, undivided loyalty, confidentiality and full disclosure. Seller's agents often work with buyers, but do not represent the buyers. However, in working with buyers a seller's agent must act honestly. In dealing with both parties, a seller's agent may not make any misrepresentation to either party on matters material to the transaction, such as the buyer's financial ability to pay, and must disclose defects of a material nature affecting the physical condition of the property which a reasonable inspection by the licensee would disclose. Seller's agents include all persons licensed with the brokerage firm which has been authorized through a listing agreement to work as the seller's agent. In addition, other brokerage firms may accept an offer to work with the listing broker's firm as the seller's agents. In such cases, these firms, and all persons licensed with such firms, are called "sub-agents." Sellers who do not desire to have their property marketed through sub-agents should so inform the seller's agent.

BUYER'S AGENT

A buyer's agent WORKS ONLY FOR THE BUYER. A buyer's agent has fiduciary duties to the buyer which include reasonable care, undivided loyalty, confidentiality and full

---

and society becomes more litigious. Much of this results from the confusion among buyers and sellers concerning the agency status of a broker and the broker not understanding the difference in the terms "clients" and "customers." A **client** is a principal (buyer or seller) who is represented by a broker through a salesperson in the broker's office. A **customer** is a buyer working with a salesperson who represents the seller, or a seller working with a salesperson who represents the buyer. In other words, an agent works "for" the client and "with" the customer.

The law is clear that a broker who shows a prospective purchaser certain properties offered for sale and transmits offers from the prospective purchaser to the owner does not become the agent of the prospective purchaser. An agency relationship with such a customer ordinarily does not result when the broker only shows

FIGURE 12.2 (cont'd)

disclosure. However, in dealing with sellers a buyer's agent must act honestly. In dealing with both parties, a buyer's agent may not make any misrepresentations on matters material to the transaction, such as the buyer's financial ability to pay, and must disclose defects of a material nature affecting the physical condition of the property which a reasonable inspection by the licensee would disclose.

A buyer wishing to be represented by a buyer's agent is advised to enter into a separate written buyer agency contract with the brokerage firm which is to work as their agent.

DISCLOSED DUAL AGENT

A disclosed dual agent WORKS FOR BOTH THE BUYER AND THE SELLER. To work as a dual agent, a firm must first obtain the informed written consent of the buyer and the seller. Therefore, before acting as a disclosed dual agent, brokerage firms must make written disclosure to both parties. Disclosed dual agency is most likely to occur when a licensee with a real estate firm working as a buyer's agent shows the buyer properties owned by sellers for whom that firm is also working as a seller's agent or sub-agent. A real estate licensee working as a disclosed dual agent must carefully explain to each party that, in addition to working as their agent, their firm will also work as the agent for the other party. They must also explain what effect their working as a disclosed dual agent will have on the fiduciary duties their firm owes to the buyer and to the seller. When working as a disclosed dual agent, a brokerage firm must have the express permission of a party prior to disclosing confidential information to the other party. Such information includes the highest price a buyer can afford to pay and the lowest price a seller will accept and the parties' motivation to buy or sell. Remember, a brokerage firm acting as a disclosed dual agent will not be able to put one party's interests ahead of those of the other party and cannot advise or counsel either party on how to gain an advantage at the expense of the other party on the basis of confidential information obtained from or about the other party.

If you decide to enter into an agency relationship with a firm which is to work as a disclosed dual agent, you are advised to sign a written agreement with that firm.

TRANSACTION BROKER

The New Jersey Real Estate Licensing Law does not require licensees to work in the capacity of an "agent" when providing brokerage services. A transaction broker works with a buyer or a seller or both in the sales transaction without representing anyone. A TRANSACTION BROKER DOES NOT PROMOTE THE INTERESTS OF ONE PARTY OVER THOSE OF THE OTHER PARTY TO THE TRANSACTION. Licensees with such a firm would be required to treat all parties honestly and to act in a competent manner, but they would not be required to keep confidential any information. A transaction broker can locate qualified buyers for a seller or suitable properties for a buyer. They can then work with both parties in an effort to arrive at an agreement on the sale or rental of real estate and perform tasks to facilitate the closing of a transaction. A transaction broker primarily serves as a manager of the transaction, communicating information between the parties to assist them in arriving at a mutually acceptable agreement and in closing the transaction, but cannot advise or counsel either party on how to gain an advantage at the expense of the other party. Owners considering working with transaction brokers are advised to sign a written agreement with that firm which clearly states what services that firm will perform and how it will be paid. In addition, any transaction brokerage agreement with a seller or landlord should specifically state whether a notice on the property to be rented or sold will or will not be circulated in any or all Multiple Listing System(s) of which that firm is a member.

YOU MAY OBTAIN LEGAL ADVICE ABOUT THESE BUSINESS RELATIONSHIPS FROM YOUR OWN LAWYER.

THIS STATEMENT IS NOT A CONTRACT AND IS PROVIDED FOR INFORMATIONAL PURPOSES ONLY.

ACKNOWLEDGEMENT OF RECEIPT OF CONSUMER INFORMATION STATEMENT (CIS)

FOR SELLERS AND LANDLORDS

"By signing this Consumer Information Statement, I acknowledge that I received this Statement from ______________________ (Name of Brokerage Firm) prior to discussing my motivation to sell or lease or my desired selling or leasing price with one of its representatives."

Signed______________________

FOR BUYERS AND TENANTS

"By signing this Consumer Information Statement, I acknowledge that I received this Statement from ______________________(Name of Brokerage Firm) prior to discussing my motivation or financial ability to buy or lease with one of its representatives."

Signed______________________

####

DECLARATION OF BUSINESS RELATIONSHIP

I, ______________________,
(name of licensee)
as an authorized representative of
______________________,
(name of brokerage firm)
intend, as of this time, to work with you as a:
(indicate one of the following)

o seller's agent only   o buyer's agent only

o seller's agent and disclosed dual agent if the opportunity arises

o buyers agent and disclosed dual agent if the opportunity arises

o transaction broker only

o seller's agent on properties on which this firm is acting as the seller's agent and transaction broker on other properties

DATE ______________________

available property, describing the amenities and attributes of the subject property. These activities are typically deemed to be ancillary to the broker's obligation to procure a ready, willing and able buyer. But it is in this phase that the broker or sales associate may begin to refer to the buyer as "my client" and may say something like "This house has been on the market for a long time and I think it is overpriced, so try a lower offer." In so doing, the agent has created an inadvertent, undisclosed dual agency.

Real estate licensees can avoid undisclosed dual agency relationships, with their legal and economic consequences, by following three simple rules:

1. Choose whom they will represent.
2. Fully disclose the agency relationship to all involved.

3. Act in such a manner as to represent the primary interest of the chosen principal.

Agents Buying from Owner

Licensees who are employed to sell properties must not purchase the property for themselves unless the principal's consent to do so has been received. The New Jersey Real Estate License Law (45:15-17) includes among prohibited practices the purchasing of property by licensees for themselves without first making full disclosures thereof and obtaining the approval of the owner. If licensees conceal the fact that they are the purchasers, they violate the duty of loyalty even though paying the going market price for the property. And they cannot circumvent the prohibition against buying listed property without disclosure by having a spouse or someone else buy the property for their benefit. Brokers cannot do indirectly what may not be done directly.

A broker cannot accept an opportunity to profit from a sale without the knowledge and consent of the principal. It would be a conflict of interest, for example, for a broker to agree to manage purchased property for the buyer without full disclosure to the seller/client.

Termination of the Agency Relationship

The agency relationship can be terminated under the following conditions:

1. Acts of the parties, such as mutual agreement, justifiable revocation by the principal and justifiable renunciation by the agent.
2 Accomplishment of the objective.
3. Expiration of an agreed-upon time limit.
4. Operation of law, such as death, insanity or bankruptcy of either the principal or the agent, destruction of the subject matter of the agency, or a change of law making the purpose of the agency illegal.

Agency Coupled with an Interest. An agency coupled with an interest is a relationship in which the agent has an interest in the property that forms the subject matter of the relationship. Such a relationship cannot be automatically revoked, at least as long as the agent retains his interest. Also, it does not terminate automatically on the death of the principal, but may subsist until the agent has fulfilled his duties in respect to the property under the terms of his appointment. A typical example involves a joint venture in which a broker and a developer agree to develop a residential subdivision, with the developer handling the construction while the broker lists and sells the homes. Since the broker will have an ownership interest, his listing cannot be revoked by the developer or terminated if the developer dies.

Power of Attorney

A power of attorney is a written instrument authorizing a person to act as an official agent of the person granting it. The person giving the power is called the **principal** or grantor and the person to whom the authority is given is called the **attorney-in-fact**, or agent.

Example

Morey is retiring and moving to North Carolina. He has not yet sold his house in New Jersey. He gives his nephew, Gordon, a power of attorney so Gordon may sign an agreement of sale and deed while Morey is in North Carolina.

A general power of attorney would authorize the agent to act for his principal in all matters, whereas a specific power of attorney generally authorizes the agent to only act on behalf of his principal on certain matters. Thus, the extent of the authorization would be indicated in the instrument. Highlights of powers of attorney used in real estate activities in New Jersey are: (1) one acting under a power of attorney from an owner of real estate does not need a real estate license to sell the owner's property except if the attorney-in-fact is engaged in real estate development or brokerage and is purposely evading the licensing laws; (2) the power of attorney should be acknowledged and recorded, otherwise a signed document, such as a deed, would be ineffective against third parties; (3) in the conveyance of real estate, a specific, rather than a general power of attorney should be used; (4) any instruments signed under a power of attorney should be executed in this style: "John Paul Principal, by Charles Edward Agent, his attorney-in-fact"; (5) while in most instances one spouse can be the attorney-in-fact for the other, the release of a wife's dower rights, accomplished when she signs a deed, must have as the attorney-in-fact someone other than her husband; (6) normally, the death of either the principal or the attorney-in-fact terminates the power of attorney; and (7) since any real estate documents to be signed must be in writing, so must the power of attorney.

Broker Compensation

When is the commission earned? The brokerage commission has been earned when the broker does what he was hired to do—provide a ready, willing and able buyer in accordance with terms set by the seller. "Ready and willing" means the buyer is prepared to enter into a contract in

FIGURE 12.3
Exclusive Buyer Agency Agreement

NEW JERSEY ASSOCIATION OF REALTORS® STANDARD FORM OF

EXCLUSIVE BUYER AGENCY AGREEMENT

1. **Agency**.____________________ and ____________________ referred to in this
Buyer Buyer
Agreement as "Buyer" hereby designate ____________________ as Buyer's exclusive agent,
Brokerage Firm
referred to in this Agreement as "Buyer's Agent", for the purpose of searching for, locating, and purchasing real estate by Buyer, pursuant to all of the terms and conditions set forth below.

2. **Declaration of Business Relationship**. The real estate license law of the state of New Jersey requires every real estate licensee to declare the basis of the business relationship being established between such licensee and Buyer. Accordingly, **I,** ____________________ **AS AN AUTHORIZED REPRESENTATIVE**
Name of Licensee
OF ____________________ **INTEND, AS OF THIS TIME, TO WORK WITH YOU (buyer)**
Name of Firm
AS A: (choose one) _______ **BUYER'S AGENT ONLY** _______ **BUYER'S AGENT AND DISCLOSED DUAL AGENT IF THE OPPORTUNITY ARISES.**

3. **Term**. This Agency Agreement shall commence on ________________ and shall expire at midnight on the ____________ day of ____________________ or three (3) days after receipt by Buyer's Agent of a written termination notice from Buyer, whichever shall first occur.

4. **Brokerage Fee**. In consideration of the services rendered by Buyer's Agent in behalf of Buyer, Buyer agrees to pay to Buyer's Agent a brokerage fee of ______________________________. The brokerage fee shall be earned, due and payable by Buyer to Buyer's Agent if any property introduced by Buyer's Agent to Buyer during the term of this Agreement is purchased by Buyer prior to the expiration of this Agreement, or within_________ days after the termination of this Agreement. However, if the seller of such property authorizes the listing broker to pay a portion of the listing broker's brokerage fee to Buyer's Agent, that portion of such brokerage fee shall be credited against Buyer's obligation to Buyer's Agent as set forth above. In such event, Buyer agrees to pay to Buyer's Agent, at the time of title closing, the difference between the amount so received from the listing broker and the total brokerage fee due to Buyer's Agent as referred to in this paragraph.

5. **Buyer's Agent's Duty.** Buyer's Agent shall:
   a. Use diligence in its search to locate a property which is acceptable to the Buyer
   b. Use professional knowledge and skills to assist Buyer to negotiate for the purchase of such property
   c. Assist the Buyer throughout the transaction and to represent Buyer's best interests

6. **Buyer's Duty**. Buyer shall:
   a. Provide accurate and relevant personal information to Buyer's Agent regarding Buyer's financial ability to purchase real estate
   b. Advise Buyer's Agent of any home offered for sale to Buyer where Buyer may have an interest in purchasing such property.
   c. Submit through Buyer's Agent, any offer to purchase or contract on a property which was shown to Buyer by Buyer's Agent

7. **Other Buyers**. Other potential buyers may be interested in the same properties as Buyer. It is agreed that Buyer's Agent may represent such other potential buyers whether such representation arises prior to, during, or after the termination of this Agreement. In any such situation, Buyer agrees that Buyer's Agent will not disclose to any other potential buyer the terms of the Buyer's offer or any other confidential information concerning the Buyer and also will not disclose to Buyer the terms of any other buyer's offer or any other confidential information concerning the other buyer(s).

8. **Dual Agency**. Buyer understands that Buyer's Agent may elect to represent a seller as well as Buyer in the sale and purchase of such seller's property. If such event, Buyer acknowledges that Buyer's Agent will be a dual agent, and pursuant to law, will have to obtain the written informed consent of both the seller and Buyer for the Buyer's Agent to be a Disclosed Dual Agent. Buyer understands that by consenting to the Buyer's Agent to be a Disclosed Dual Agent, there will be a limitation on the Buyer's Agent's ability to represent either the Buyer or seller fully and exclusively. Buyer's Agent, when acting as a Disclosed Dual Agent, will not be able to put either the seller's interests ahead of the Buyer's nor the Buyer's interests ahead of the seller's. **Buyer's consent to Buyer's Agent being a Disclosed Dual Agent shall be deemed to have been given only when the "Informed Consent to Dual Agency" which appears on the reverse of this Agreement is signed by the Buyer.**

9. Buyer represents to Buyer's Agent that no other buyer's agency agreement is presently in effect. Buyer agrees not to enter into any such agreement during the term of this Agreement.

10. Buyer acknowledges receipt of the Consumer Information Statement on New Jersey Real Estate Relationships.

11. Buyer hereby acknowledges receipt of a signed copy of this legally binding Agreement and agrees to be bound by and comply with its terms and conditions.

IF BUYER DOES NOT UNDERSTAND ALL OF THE TERMS OF THIS AGREEMENT, LEGAL ADVICE SHOULD BE SOUGHT BEFORE SIGNING.

By:____________________ Buyer ____________________
Buyer's Agent Date
Buyer ____________________
Date

NJAR-121-4/99

accordance with terms set by the seller. "Able" means financially able.

A broker is also entitled to compensation if the refusal or neglect of the buyer or seller to consummate the transaction as agreed upon defeated the transaction. If the seller defaults, the broker could sue the seller. If the buyer defaults, the broker can take a direct action against the buyer. If, however, the buyer made the offer to buy contingent on some event such as the ability to obtain certain financing, the buyer may rightfully cancel the contract and obtain a return of the deposit should the contingency fail. In this case, the broker would not be entitled to any commission.

In the event of competing claims by selling brokers who are part of a co-operative agreement to split the commission, the broker who was the procuring cause shall prevail. The **procuring cause** is the proximate cause originating a series of events which, without break in their continuity, results in the accomplishment of the objective. A real estate broker will be regarded as the procuring cause of a sale if his efforts are the foundation on which negotiations resulting in a sale are begun.

The seller has a right to know the identity of the buyer, and if the broker refuses to disclose the name of the buyer, or has another act as strawman or dummy for an undisclosed buyer, the seller has the right to decline the offer, and the broker cannot claim a commission. In the event the seller accepts the offer of an undisclosed buyer, and that buyer then defaults, the broker would be personally liable for any loss suffered by the seller.

It is common for listings to provide that if, within 90 days after the expiration of the listing, the property is sold to any party with whom the listing broker negotiated and whose name was registered and revealed to the owner by the broker, the owner must pay the broker his commission.

Disbursement of the Commission

After the sale has been closed, and the commission has been paid to the firm(s) involved in the transaction, each firm will then divide the commission with its salespersons according to the employment contract between the salespersons and the firm. Example: A $100,000 home is listed with Black Realty for a 6% sales commission, and is sold through Multiple Listing Service by a salesperson with White Realty. At the closing, the seller will disburse checks to White Realty for $3,000 and to Black Realty for $3,000. The way each company pays its own salespersons will be determined by each brokerage firm's employment contract. As an example, Black Realty might pay the salesperson who obtained the listing 40% of the $3,000 taken in by that firm, while White Realty might pay its salesperson who sold the listing 50% of the $3,000 it received.

Another common situation arises when a home is listed by a salesperson from Grey Realty, and is sold by another salesperson from the same firm. In this case, the entire $6,000 commission would go to Grey Realty. They might then divide it by giving 25% of the $6,000 to the salesperson who obtained the listing and 25% of the $6,000 to the salesperson who made the sale.

Prohibition Against Dual Compensation for Dual Representation

The Rules and Regulations of the New Jersey Real Estate Commission prohibit licensees from receiving compensation from both a buyer and seller (or landlord and tenant) for representing both parties in the same real estate transaction. The prohibition exists even if the licensee fully discloses the dual representation to both parties. (See 11:5-1.38)

Advising Sellers and Purchasers

Licensees should render advice only on real estate matters in their area of expertise and should not engage in providing opinions on legal or tax matters beyond the scope of their legitimate responsibilities. The parties must be directed to obtain appropriate advice when in the client's or customer's best interest. Licensees should not render opinions about the condition of the property, except to advise of defects or of such information that the seller has provided. Provision of incorrect information relied upon by the client or customer can make licensees liable for their errors. It is essential that brokers carry errors and omissions insurance (discussed below) to protect them against liability for errors made or for information which should have been provided but wasn't. Such policies do not protect against unlawful acts, concealment of facts or breach of fiduciary duty, however.

Employee or Independent Contractor

Another area of importance to both brokers and their salespersons is whether or not salespersons fall into the category of independent contractors or employees. In New Jersey it is mandatory that every broker have a written agreement with licensees whether they are licensed as salespersons or broker-salespersons. The agreement must be dated and signed by the parties and cover the main aspects of the agreement, including com-

FIGURE 12.4 Informed Consent to Dual Agency

NEW JERSEY ASSOCIATION OF REALTORS® STANDARD FORM OF

INFORMED CONSENT TO DUAL AGENCY

(BUYER)

This Agreement evidences Buyer's consent that the Brokerage Firm, as Buyer's Agent, may act as a Disclosed Dual Agent in order to represent both Buyer and Seller in the same real estate transaction, and seeks Buyer's consent to allow Buyer's Agent to act as a Disclosed Dual Agent when the opportunity arises. Buyer should be aware that a real estate licensee may legally act as a Disclosed Dual Agent only with Buyer's and Seller's informed written consent.

Buyer understands that Disclosed Dual Agency (representing more than one party to a transaction) has the potential of creating a conflict of interest in that both Seller and Buyer may intend to rely on the Buyer's Agent's advice, and their respective interests may be adverse to each other. Therefore, when acting as a Disclosed Dual Agent, Buyer's Agent will not represent the interests of Buyer to the exclusion or detriment of the interests of a Seller; nor will Buyer's Agent represent the interests of Seller to the exclusion and detriment of the interests of Buyer.

As a Disclosed Dual Agent of both the Seller and the Buyer, Buyer's Agent will be working equally for both parties to the real estate transaction, and will provide services to complete the transaction **without** the full range of fiduciary duties ordinarily owed by an agent who represents Buyer alone, or the Seller alone. In the preparation of offers and counteroffers between Buyer and Seller, Buyer's Agent will act only as an intermediary to facilitate the transaction rather than as an active negotiator representing either the Buyer or Seller in a fiduciary capacity. By consenting to this dual agency, Buyer is giving up the right to undivided loyalty and will be owed only limited duties of disclosure, obedience and confidentiality by the Buyer's Agent.

For example, Buyer acknowledges that Buyer's Agent, as a Disclosed Dual Agent, is not permitted, under law, to disclose to either Buyer or Seller any confidential information which has been or will be communicated to Buyer's Agent by either of the parties to the transaction. Moreover, Buyer's Agent is not permitted to disclose (without the express written permission of the Seller) to the Buyer that such Seller will accept a price less than the full listing price. Nor will Buyer's Agent disclose (without the express written permission of the Buyer) to the Seller that Buyer will pay a sum greater than the price offered by Buyer. It is also impermissible for Buyer's Agent to advise or counsel either the Buyer or Seller on how to gain an advantage at the expense of the other party on the basis of confidential information obtained from or about the other party.

Buyer acknowledges receipt of the Consumer Information Statement on New Jersey Real Estate Relationships.

I, ________________________________ AS AN AUTHORIZED REPRESENTATIVE OF
Name of Licensee

________________________________ INTEND, AS OF THIS TIME, TO WORK WITH YOU (BUYER)
Name of Firm

AS A BUYER'S AGENT AND DISCLOSED DUAL AGENT IF THE OPPORTUNITY ARISES.

If Buyer does not understand all of the provisions of this Informed Consent to Dual Agency, legal advice should be sought before signing.

By signing below, Buyer acknowledges that Buyer has read and understood this Informed Consent to Dual Agency and gives consent to Buyer's Agent to act as a Disclosed Dual Agent.

Buyer's Signature	Brokerage Firm
Buyer's Signature	Address
	City, State, Zip Code
Date	Salesperson's Signature

NJAR-122A-9/95

FIGURE 12.5 Informed Consent to Dual Agency

NEW JERSEY ASSOCIATION OF REALTORS® STANDARD FORM OF
INFORMED CONSENT TO DUAL AGENCY
(SELLER)

©2001, New Jersey Association of Realtors®, Inc.

1 PROPERTY ADDRESS: ____________________
2
3
4 This Agreement evidences Seller's consent that the Brokerage Firm, as Seller's Agent, may act as a Disclosed Dual Agent in
5 order to represent both Seller and Buyer in the same real estate transaction, and seeks Seller's consent to allow Seller's Agent
6 to act as a Disclosed Dual Agent when the opportunity arises. Seller should be aware that a real estate licensee may legally act
7 as a Disclosed Dual Agent only with Seller's and Buyer's informed written consent.
8
9 Seller understands that Disclosed Dual Agency (representing more than one party to a transaction) has the potential of creating
10 a conflict of interest in that both Seller and Buyer may intend to rely on the Seller's Agent's advice, and their respective interests
11 may be adverse to each other. Therefore, when acting as a Disclosed Dual Agent, Seller's Agent will not represent the interests
12 of Buyer to the exclusion or detriment of the interests of a Seller; nor will Seller's Agent represent the interests of Seller to the
13 exclusion and detriment of the interests of Buyer.
14
15 As a Disclosed Dual Agent of both the Seller and the Buyer, Seller's Agent will be working equally for both parties to the real
16 estate transaction and will provide services to complete the transaction **without** the full range of fiduciary duties ordinarily
17 owed by an agent who represents Seller alone, or the Buyer alone. In the preparation of offers and counteroffers between Seller
18 and Buyer, Seller's Agent will act only as an intermediary to facilitate the transaction rather than as an active negotiator
19 representing either the Seller or Buyer in a fiduciary capacity. By consenting to this dual agency, Seller is giving up the right
20 to undivided loyalty and will be owed only limited duties of disclosure and obedience by the Seller's Agent.
21
22 For example, Seller acknowledges that Seller's Agent, as a Disclosed Dual Agent, is not permitted, under law, to disclose to
23 either Seller or Buyer any confidential information which has been, or will be communicated to Seller's Agent by either of the
24 parties to the transaction. Moreover, Seller's Agent is not permitted to disclose (without the express written permission of the
25 Seller) to the Buyer that such Seller will accept a price less than the full listing price. Nor will Seller's Agent disclose (without
26 the express written permission of the Buyer) to the Seller that Buyer will pay a sum greater than the price offered by Buyer. It
27 is also impermissible for Seller's Agent to advise or counsel either the Seller or Buyer on how to gain an advantage at the
28 expense of the other party on the basis of confidential information obtained from or about the other party.
29
30 Seller acknowledges receipt of the Consumer Information Statement on New Jersey Real Estate Relationships.
31
32 I, ____________________ AS AN AUTHORIZED REPRESENTATIVE OF
33 (Name of Licensee)
34 ____________________ INTEND, AS OF THIS TIME, TO WORK WITH YOU
35 (Name of Firm)
36 (SELLER) AS A SELLER'S AGENT AND DISCLOSED DUAL AGENT IF THE OPPORTUNITY ARISES.
37
38 **If Seller does not understand all of the provisions of this Informed Consent to Dual Agency, legal advice should be**
39 **sought before signing.**
40
41 By signing below, Seller acknowledges that Seller has read and understood this Informed Consent to Dual Agency and gives
42 consent to Seller's Agent to act as a Disclosed Dual Agent.
43
44
45 ____________________ ____________________
46 SELLER'S SIGNATURE BROKERAGE FIRM
47
48 ____________________ ____________________
49 SELLER'S SIGNATURE ADDRESS
50
51 ____________________
52 CITY, STATE, ZIP CODE
53
54 ____________________ ____________________
55 DATE SALESPERSON'S SIGNATURE
56
57
58
59
60
61
62
63
64
65
66
67
68
69
70
71

NJAR Form-122B-1/01

pensation, duties and termination.

In common practice, real estate salespersons are referred to as independent contractors. However, what the parties call the relationship is not the determining factor. Instead, it is the degree of control that the broker has over the salesperson's activities.

Independent Contractors. If sales personnel are treated as independent contractors, the following factors are required to maintain such status: the salesperson must pay his own federal and self-employment taxes; the salespeople must pay for their own license fees and board membership fees; the broker may not reimburse the salespeople for business-related auto, transportation or entertainment expenses; the broker may not require attendance during any set office hours nor at any sales meetings; the broker may not require the salespeople to meet any sales or listing quotas; the salesperson may receive no minimum salary; and cannot be covered under employee plans such as medical reimbursement or group term life insurance plans, pension plans or profit-sharing plans.

Employees. An employee, unlike an independent contractor, acts when, how and in the manner prescribed by the employer. If sales personnel are treated as employees, their employing broker must withhold income tax, social security and unemployment tax from wages; provide workers compensation and temporary disability Insurance; and may provide employee benefits such as those described above.

Because New Jersey's licensing law makes the broker responsible for all activities of his salespersons, many brokers attempt to exercise a high degree of control over their salespeople. If the broker decides to treat licensees as independent contractors, great care should be taken to structure the relationship to insure that the requirements necessary for such classification have been met. If the IRS successfully challenges the broker's treatment of his salespeople as independent contractors, he might not only be required to start paying federal withholding and FICA, but also be required to pay back taxes not withheld.

Safe Harbor Provisions

The IRS has three requirements for independent contractor status: (1) the person must have a valid real estate license; (2) there must be a written agreement with that person stating that he or she will not be treated as an employee; and (3) at least 90% of the person's income must be based on sales rather than the number of hours worked. Activities that satisfy these three requirements fall under "safe harbor provisions."

Concerning written contract agreements, the Internal Revenue Code makes it clear that an agreement will not fit within the safe harbor provisions if it provides that "an individual will not be treated as an employee" but does not specifically state "for tax purposes."

Therefore, brokers intending to establish independent contractor relationships should have agreements stating, "The parties hereto agree that the salesperson is providing services in his capacity as an independent contractor. Accordingly, the salesperson will not be treated as an employee for federal tax purposes with respect to services performed in accordance with the terms of this agreement."

NOTE: In May, 1997, a trial court in Atlantic County ruled that for purposes of the New Jersey Workers Compensation Law, salespersons are employees of brokerage firms under which they are licensed. When the ruling was appealed, the Appellate Division upheld the trial court's decision. Accordingly, brokers who are not providing workers compensation insurance are advised to consult with their insurance carrier, or attorney, or both about this important matter.

Unlicensed Real Estate Assistants

Recently, real estate licensees have made it a practice to hire unlicensed employees or personal assistants to help with some of the routine tasks involved in real estate transactions. These unlicensed assistants are allowed to engage in office activities that are not directly related to sales, but they cannot engage in the real estate business.

The New Jersey Real Estate Commission has defined the activities that may be performed by a personal assistant who does not hold a real estate license. Specifically, an unlicensed assistant, employee or secretary **CAN**:

- Answer phones and forward calls
- Process and submit listings and changes to an MLS system.
- Follow up on loan applications after contracts have been fully executed.
- Set up file procedures, track and secure documents, etc.
- Have keys made for company listings at the direction of a licensee.
- Write ads for approval of a licensee and place ads as directed.
- Keep records of, and deposit payments of, earnest money, security deposits and rent.
- Type contract forms for approval by a licensee.
- Monitor files and report findings to a licensee.

- Compute commission checks.
- Place signs on properties.
- Order items or inspections as directed by a licensee.
- Prepare flyers and promotional material for approval by licensee.
- Act as a courier for delivering documents or picking up keys, etc. (Licensee is responsible for delivery of contracts or closing materials).
- Schedule appointments with the seller or seller's agent in order for a licensee to show listed property.
- Be present at open houses to provide security.

An unlicensed assistant, employee or secretary **CANNOT**:

- Make cold calls by telephone or in person to potential listers, purchasers, tenants or landlords.
- In the absence of a licensee, host open houses, and booths at home shows, malls or fairs, or distribute promotional material at such locations.
- Prepare promotional material or ads without the review and approval of a licensee.
- Show property.
- Answer any questions on listings, title, financing or closings from either the public or other licensees.
- Discuss or explain a contract, listing, lease agreement or other real estate document with anyone outside the firm.
- Work as a licensee/secretary in one firm and do real estate-related activities with that firm, while licensed with another firm.
- Negotiate or agree to any commission, commission split, management fee or referral fee on behalf of a licensee.
- Make telephone calls for the purpose of collecting or attempting to collect late rent payments.
- Be present during home inspections in the absence of a licensee.

In addition, the compensation of an unlicensed assistant or secretary should not be based on the success of their activity, i.e., a percentage of commission, but should be directly related to the duties being performed. If a licensee is using another licensee to act as his or her personal assistant/secretary, both should be aware that they are employees or independent contractors of their broker and compensation must be paid by the broker. All licensees are cautioned to research and adhere to federal and state income tax and employment requirements.

Antitrust Laws

Antitrust laws were born in 1890 when Congress enacted the Sherman Antitrust Act. "Trust" in this context means a combination of producers or sellers of a product, the purpose which is to control prices and suppress competition. The Act declared illegal every contract, combination in the form of a trust or otherwise, or conspiracy in restraint of interstate and foreign trade. Its purpose was to preserve competition in the marketplace and prevent monopolies. In a 1950 case, *U.S. v. National Association of Real Estate Boards* (NAREB), the Supreme Court held that the business of real estate brokerage was included under the concept of "trade" as used in the Sherman Act.

Real estate brokers and sales associates must be careful to avoid the following activities that constitute antitrust violations:

- Price Fixing. A real estate brokerage firm can establish an intraoffice policy on fees or division of fees, but it cannot combine with or suggest to any other licensee that rates be fixed, established or maintained.
- Boycotting other brokers (e.g., discount brokers) by refusing to cooperate or cooperating on less favorable terms.
- Boycotting or refusing to do business with any promotional medium because it advertises commissions of a discount nature.
- "Tying agreements," such as: (a) a clause in a sales contract that requires someone who buys a lot in a subdivision from a broker/developer to "list back" the property with the developer upon resale, and (b) a property management agreement in which the owner promises to list the property with the broker/manager when the owner sells.
- Allocating customers or markets by dividing their markets geographically or according to price range and agreeing not to compete along those lines. The rationale for this rule is that an agreement among competitors to divide the market gives each an effective monopoly in its share of the market.
- Conspiring to fix the duration of listing agreements.
- Excluding brokers from membership in local boards or MLS systems by imposing unfair membership requirements such as unreasonably high fees.

Errors and Omissions (E&O) Insurance

In the past decade, court decisions have exposed real estate brokers and other professionals to enormous liabilities. Consequently, the importance of having errors and omissions insurance is obvious. This is a form of insurance which covers liabilities for mistakes, errors and negligence in the listing and selling activities of a real estate office. E&O

insurance does not cover punitive damages, and does not cover negligence or misrepresentation when buying for one's own account.

Examples of the kind of things for which real estate brokers are being held liable include, but are not limited to: improper qualifications of buyers or tenants; not disclosing an offer; representing that a property is "safe and sound"; not making a reasonable effort to sell the listed property; and failure to reveal a termite condition.

A typical E & O policy will cover claims made against the insured during the policy period for acts, errors and omissions in professional services rendered during or prior to the policy period (with exceptions).

It is essential that the real estate practitioner seek competent advice on insurance coverage in this most important area.

NEW JERSEY CASES ON AGENCY*

New Jersey court rulings have made it imperative that real estate agents take extra precautions in their dealings with vendors and purchasers of real property. Commissions have been denied to agents who, whether intentionally or accidentally, fail to adhere to some basic ethical and professional standards. Indeed, in some instances, actual and punitive damages may be assessed against these agents. The following summary will attempt to outline some of the most significant cases in order that you may better serve your clients and protect yourself from liability and judgment.

Duty of Loyalty

It is well established that, as a fiduciary in the relationship, a real estate broker has a duty to act in good faith on behalf of his principal. *Rothman Realty Corp. v. Bereck*, 73 NJ 590 (1977). He must exercise fidelity and primary devotion to his principal and he cannot permit his interests to interfere with those of his principal. *Ellsworth Dobbs, Inc. v. Johnson*, 50 NJ 528 (1967). In most cases, a broker's principal is the owner vendor. In those instances, a broker is required to transmit increasingly favorable offers to the vendor as they are submitted to him. *Melveney v. McCrane*, 138 NJ Super. 456 (App. Div. 1976). He is required to disclose to the vendor any and all conflicts of interest that he may have as a representative of the vendor. For example, in the case of *Thompson v. Hoagland*, 100 NJ Super. 478 (App. Div. 1968), the court held that a real estate broker's relationship with a proposed purchaser with whom the broker had a number of joint investments in real estate was of a character requiring full apprisal of the owners thereof and their consent, express or implied, to the submission of an offer by that proposed purchaser.

Duty of Disclosure

While the issue of disclosure may be simple on its face, it can often be confusing in practice. Most notably, the matter of *Silverman v. Bresnahan*, 35 NJ Super. 390 (App. Div. 1955), involved a real estate broker who undertook to find a purchaser for a vendor's property and failed to disclose to the vendor that he was representing the prospective purchaser for her property and would receive a commission from the purchaser. In that case, the broker remained silent even when he tendered her the contract of sale and deposit from the purchaser. The court, in denying the broker his right to a commission, held that, unless a principal has knowledge of and consents to other representation, an agent for the sale or purchase of real estate can represent but one—to be employed by another in the same transaction prevents him from obtaining the best terms for his original principal. In fact, it was of no consequence to the court in that case that injury did not result to the principal by reason of the agent's concealment of facts. It was enough that the agent has breached the basic public policy of absolute fidelity and good faith to the principal. The court was quick to reference the case of *Ledirk Amusement Co., Inc. v. Schechner*, 133 NJ Eq. 602 (Ch. 1943), aff'd. 135 NJ Eq. 209 (E. & A. 1944), however, which stated:

In some instances, there is no legal or practical impediment to one person acting as broker for both parties, but there must be the fullest disclosure to each principal that the broker is acting for both in order that the principals may deal at arm's length. . . .

Duty of Reasonable Care and Diligence

The case of *Farrell v. Janik*, 225 NJ Super. 282 (Law Div. 1988), illustrates another area in which a real estate broker may incur liability in assisting a purchaser even though the purchaser may not be the agent's principal. In that case, the real estate broker introduced the purchasers to the lending institution. The court, while reiterating its previous rulings that a real estate agent has an obligation to periodically review the status of an executed contract for sale of land to see if purchasers are tending to their obligations under

* The New Jersey cases are excerpts from a risk reduction seminar sponsored by the Passaic County Board of Realtors and are reprinted with permission of the writer, Mary Keane-Kosarek, P.C.

the contract, stated further that where an agent introduces the purchasers to the lending institution he must periodically communicate with the mortgagors to ascertain if the application is proceeding smoothly. The court held that where the agent did not inform the lending institution that purchasers could close title without securing financing of their present residence for less than the amount required by the lending institution, the vendor has established a negligence claim against the agent.

Sub-agency and Vicarious Liability

Finally, the relationship between listing and selling brokers has, of late, come before the courts. It is clear that a listing broker is agent for the vendor. It is equally clear that a selling broker, who secures a purchaser while acting in consort with the listing broker, by virtue of membership with the Multiple Listing Service, also owes his allegiance to the vendor. This is true unless purchaser makes alternate arrangements for payment of commission to selling agent, and severance by the selling agent of his relationship with the listing agent prior to showing the property to the prospective purchaser. But to what extent can one agent be held responsible for the acts of another in a multiple listing arrangement? The court in *Sullivan v. Jefferson, Jefferson & Vaida*, 167 NJ Super. (App. Div. 1979), stated that a joint venture was not created by reason of joint participation of the listing and selling brokers in a multiple listing arrangement where the joint participation resulted from the effect of operation of law and not from a voluntary consensual undertaking between them arising out of the multiple listing service. In that case, the selling broker, who was not a member in that county's multiple listing service, fraudulently converted deposit monies and it was determined that the listing broker should not be held responsible for the defalcation of the selling broker. Beware, however, that the court has left open the question of the liability of one agent for the acts of another in a relationship established by virtue of membership in the multiple listing service. Indeed, you may find yourself liable for the acts of the participating broker in that situation. It is wise, therefore, to fully apprise yourself of the actions of the participating broker in a multiple listing relationship during the course of the transaction.

KEY WORDS

Agency
Agent
Attorney in Fact
Buyer's Agent
Client
Consumer Information Statement
Disclosed Dual Agent
Fiduciary
Independent Contractor
Listing
Power of Attorney
Principal
Procuring Cause
Ready, Willing and Able
Seller's Agent
Special Agent
Sherman Antitrust Act
Transaction Broker
Undisclosed Dual Agent

CHAPTER 12
Review Questions
(Answers on page 554)

1. All but one of the following owes a fiduciary obligation:
   (A) executor.
   (B) guardian.
   (C) attorney.
   (D) mortgagor.

2. One who has the right to sign the name of his principal to a contract of sale is:
   (A) a real estate broker.
   (B) a special agent.
   (C) an attorney-in-fact.
   (D) an attorney-at-law.

3. A real estate salesperson might lawfully accept an extra commission in a difficult sale from:
   (A) an appreciative seller.
   (B) a thankful buyer.
   (C) a broker-employer.
   (D) the mortgage lender.

4. Any person, partnership, association or corporation who authorizes or employs another, called the agent, to perform certain acts on his behalf is the:
   (A) agent.
   (B) broker.
   (C) principal.
   (D) assignor.

5. An agent is considered to have earned his commission:
   (A) only if title is transferred.
   (B) if he secures an offer from a prospective buyer.
   (C) if he produces a ready, willing and able buyer on the principal's terms.
   (D) when the principal signs a contract of sale.

6. A broker is:
   (A) a principal to the salesperson.
   (B) the agent of a seller under a listing contract.
   (C) the agent of a buyer in a buyer-agency agreement.
   (D) All of the above.

7. Salespersons may accept compensation of their predetermined share:
   (A) as indicated and given by the multiple listing service.
   (B) from the owner of the property.
   (C) from their employing broker.
   (D) from the cooperating broker.

8. The commission rate for the sale of real estate is determined by:
   (A) seller.
   (B) fixed schedules approved by the Real Estate Commission.
   (C) scarcity of real estate for sale.
   (D) negotiation.

9. Which of the following persons would NOT have fiduciary duties to a principal?
   (A) Trustees.
   (B) Administrators.
   (C) Employees.
   (D) Receivers.

10. The position of trust assumed by the broker as an agent for the principal is described most accurately as:
    (A) trustee relationship.
    (B) trustor relationship.
    (C) confidential relationship.
    (D) fiduciary relationship.

11. Known hidden defects in a property must be disclosed by:
    (A) seller only.
    (B) broker only.
    (C) salesperson only.
    (D) seller, broker and salesperson.

12. An owner requests a broker to list his property for sale at $70,000. Upon inspection, the broker believes the property is worth $80,000. The broker should:
    (A) get a net listing for the property at $70,000.
    (B) buy the property himself for $70,000.
    (C) inform the seller that his property is worth $80,000.
    (D) suggest that the owner list the property for $75,000 so that he will have room for bargaining.

13. A principal-agent relationship exists between the:
    (A) broker and his salespersons.
    (B) salesperson and customer.
    (C) broker and cooperating broker.
    (D) broker and customer.

14. A person who is given authority to perform a specific legal duty by another is:
    (A) a power of attorney.
    (B) an attorney-in-fact.
    (C) an attorney-at-law.
    (D) an executor.

15. A salesperson employed by a real estate broker to show and sell property to a customer:
(A) is an agent for the broker, who is an agent for the principal.
(B) is himself the primary agent for the principal.
(C) is a principal party to the transaction.
(D) is a general agent.

16. All BUT which of the following are fiduciaries?
(A) Principal.
(B) Trustee.
(C) Guardian.
(D) Receiver.

17. The best description of a special agent would be a person who:
(A) is an attorney.
(B) is a broker.
(C) has limited authority.
(D) has contractual authority.

18. It would NOT be the responsibility of the broker to inform the purchaser of which of the following?
(A) The basement floods.
(B) The property, according to a map 100 years old, is located in a flood area.
(C) The price paid by the seller.
(D) The house is infested with termites.

19. In a typical real estate listing contract, the broker would best be described as:
(A) a general agent.
(B) a special agent.
(C) the principal for the agent.
(D) the principal for the sub-agent.

20. A Power of Attorney is NOT necessarily revoked if:
(A) the principal dies.
(B) the attorney-in-fact fails to use it for 90 days.
(C) the principal records a declaration revoking it.
(D) the attorney-in-fact dies.

21. A declaration made by a person to an official that he freely and voluntarily executed a deed is called an:
(A) acknowledgment.
(B) authorization.
(C) authentication.
(D) execution.

22. Death of either the principal or agent terminates the:
(A) listing contract.
(B) contract for sale.
(C) deed.
(D) mortgage.

23. An agency agreement will be terminated by:
(A) the death of the agent.
(B) the bankruptcy of the principal.
(C) the death of the principal.
(D) all of the above.

24. Which of the following will NOT terminate an agency relationship?
(A) Revocation by the principal.
(B) Mutual consent.
(C) Reciprocity.
(D) Renunciation by the agent.

25. Responsibilities of an agent in an agency relationship include all of the following EXCEPT:
(A) exercise of due care.
(B) accountability.
(C) obedience.
(D) patience.

26. To enforce his right to a commission a broker must:
(A) act under written authorization.
(B) have an exclusive listing.
(C) belong to the MLS.
(D) be a Realtor.®

27. Apollo Creed lists his house with the XYZ Realty Corp., for which Justin Case is the authorized broker. Which of the following statements is true?
(A) Mr. Creed's death will terminate the listing agreement.
(B) Mr. Case's death will terminate the listing agreement.
(C) The XYZ Realty Corp. is a general agent.
(D) The listing is automatically renewable if it is an exclusive.

28. Which of the following is/are required to create an agency relationship?
(A) Written agreement.
(B) Compensation by principal.
(C) Consent of principal and agent.
(D) All of the above.

29. A customer may best be described as:
(A) always the buyer.
(B) someone you work "with."
(C) someone you work "for."
(D) the person to whom a fiduciary duty is owed.

30. If a broker acts as a dual agent without disclosure, which of the following may occur?
(A) Loss of license.
(B) Rescission of contract.
(C) Forfeiture of commission.
(D) All of the above.

CHAPTER THIRTEEN

LISTINGS

A real estate broker is ordinarily a special agent authorized to conduct a single transaction for his principal, who is generally the owner of the real estate, or a buyer seeking a special property. Our discussion in this chapter shall deal with the broker-owner relationship.

The authority to act as agent is given to the real estate broker by means of a **listing contract**, which is a written agreement of employment with the property owner, whereby the owner lists his property for sale with the broker. A listing contract is called a bilateral contract in that both parties have reciprocal obligations towards each other; the seller promises to pay a commission in return for the broker's promise to put forth his best efforts toward finding a ready, willing and able buyer.

The listing contract contains the name and address of the seller(s) and the seller's broker, a description of the property, the terms of the sale (price, etc.), the duration of the broker's employment, the commission to be paid the broker and the signature of the party to be bound by the listing.

The real estate license law provides that brokers and salespersons must give copies of documents and agreements to the persons signing them immediately after the signature is obtained. This law applies to copies of the agreement of sale, lease, option or any other document pertaining to any of the acts for which one is required to hold a license.

There are three types of listing contracts that may legally be used in New Jersey: (1) open listing; (2) exclusive agency; and (3) exclusive right to sell.

Open Listing. An open listing not only allows the seller to list the property with more than one broker, but also allows him the privilege of selling the property himself (unless he specifically agrees not to do so), without being liable to anyone for a commission. If the property is sold by any broker holding the open listing, the full commission goes to that broker.

Under the Statute of Frauds, an open listing must be in writing and is not enforceable unless it: contains authority for the broker to sell; identifies the property for sale; and states the sales price and conditions of the sale and the amount of commission to be paid to the broker. If a licensee acts upon an authorization contained in a letter written by an owner in response to an inquiry by a licensee as to whether a property is for sale, the licensee should be sure the aforementioned essentials are contained in the authorization.

An open listing does not require a definite termination date, and the sale of the property terminates the listing. The owner usually does not need to notify the other agents, for the sale itself will cancel all outstanding listings, automatically protecting him from paying more than one commission.

Since an open listing is one given to several brokers, it cannot be submitted to a Multiple Listing Service, nor is any broker likely to spend much money advertising such a listing, since he has little assurance that he will recover his expenses. Thus, instead of getting a greater amount of service and exposure by listing with several brokers, the inexperienced seller may find that he has done exactly the opposite by selecting an open listing contract.

Exclusive Agency Listing. An exclusive agency listing is a written agreement that gives one broker only the right to sell a property for a specified time, but gives the owner the right to sell the property himself without owing a commission. The listing broker is entitled to a commission if he or she sells the property or if it is sold by anyone who is not the owner. The Multiple Listing Service must accept exclusive agency listings submitted by members.

Exclusive Right to Sell Listing. This type of listing not only makes the broker the sole and exclusive agent for the seller for a definite time, but also assures the named broker that he will receive a commission even if the landowner sells the property himself. Essentially, the broker will receive a commission if the property is sold "by you, by me, or by anyone." A broker can apply his best efforts, confident in the knowledge that he will obtain a commission, and will recover his expenses for advertising and soliciting, if he or anyone else, including the owner, sells the property during the listing period. This is the most common type of listing contract used in New Jersey.

Oral Listing. An oral listing is created when an owner orally authorizes a broker to sell or rent his property at a specified price, under specific terms and conditions, and for a stated commission. An oral listing is unenforceable and the broker may find he has rendered his services without compensation.

However, a special provision in the Statute of Frauds protects the broker's rights to a commission. Any real estate agent who sells, exchanges or leases property pursuant to an oral agreement with the owner, and who actually performs before the authority is repudiated or terminated by the owner in writing, may recover from the owner the amount of commission payable, provided the broker shall, within five days after the making of the oral listing, serve upon the owner a notice in writing or by registered mail setting forth the terms of the oral listing. To be enforceable the notice must comply with the essentials previously mentioned under Open Listing, such as authority, price, terms and amount of commission payable. Notice must be given within five days after making the oral agreement, not within five days of presenting an offer or within five days after execution of a contract of sale.

Net Listing. A net listing is one where the owner specifies a net price he wants for his property, and the amount over and above that price is the commission paid the selling broker for his services. **This type of listing is prohibited in New Jersey.** It is one that is contrary to the basic premise of the laws of agency, which require that a broker make every effort on behalf of his principal to obtain the most benefit for his client and have no personal interest in the transaction. Since obtaining a high price for the property would obviously be to the broker's advantage (by increasing the amount of his commission), a price level could be set that would be a deterrent to the sale, and thus not in the best interest of the owner.

Multiple Listing Service

The Multiple Listing Service (MLS) is an arrangement, generally among real estate board members, whereby each broker pools his listings, bringing them to the attention of other member brokers. A standard MLS form (Figure 13.1) must be used by all members participating in the service. The form provides for an exclusive right to sell agreement between the seller and the broker; when a sale results, the commission is divided between the listing broker and the selling broker. The commission split varies considerably but is often 50% of the total commission to the listing broker and selling broker, respectively.

In the event that the owner does not wish to have his broker cooperate with other brokers, the broker must have the owner sign a Waiver of Broker Cooperation (as shown below) indicating that he is aware of the potential disadvantages of non-cooperation in the sale of property. This waiver becomes part of the listing agreement and a copy of it must be provided to the owner. The waiver must be made available for inspection by other brokers upon request.

WAIVER OF BROKER COOPERATION

I UNDERSTAND THAT COOPERATION AMONGST BROKERS PRODUCES WIDER EXPOSURE OF MY PROPERTY AND MAY RESULT IN IT BEING SOLD OR LEASED SOONER AND AT A HIGHER PRICE THAN WOULD BE THE CASE WERE MY BROKER NOT TO COOPERATE WITH OTHER BROKERS. I FURTHER UNDERSTAND THAT WHEN MY BROKER COOPERATES WITH OTHER BROKERS, I CAN STILL HAVE THE ARRANGEMENTS FOR THE SHOWING OF THE PROPERTY AND ALL NEGOTIATIONS WITH ME OR MY ATTORNEY MADE ONLY THROUGH MY LISTING BROKER'S OFFICE, SHOULD I SO DESIRE.

However, despite my awareness of these factors, I direct that this property is to be marketed only through the efforts of the Listing Broker. This listing is not to be published in any multiple listing service. I will only consider offers on this property which are obtained by, and I will only allow showings of this property to be conducted by, the Listing Broker or his or her duly authorized representatives. THE LISTING BROKER IS HEREBY DIRECTED NOT TO COOPERATE WITH ANY OTHER BROKER.

By signing below, the parties hereto confirm that no pressure or undue influence has been exerted upon the owners as to how this property is to be marketed by the Listing Broker.

The owner(s) further confirm receipt of a fully executed copy of the listing agreement on this property, and of this Waiver of Broker Cooperation form.

DATED:

Owner______________________________

Owner______________________________

Listing Broker______________________________

By: Authorized Licensee or Broker

____

FIGURE 13.1 Sample Listing Agreement

REAL ESTATE LISTING/COMMISSION AGREEMENT (Page 1 of 2)

ABC MULTIPLE LISTING SERVICE

1. THE FOLLOWING TERMS ARE DEFINED IN THE BOX BELOW AND WHEN MENTIONED IN THIS AGREEMENT SHALL MEAN:

INFORMATION BOX:

"Owner(s) ("You") Rocco Balboa SS# 123-23-1235 Owner's Address 114 Yantacaw Brook Road

Adrian Balboa SS# 135-16-7890 Wyckoff, New Jersey 07481

Owner's Tele # 201-555-1234 Fax # - - LB Tele# 201 - 567 - 8910 Fax # 201 - 555 - 3546

"Listing Broker" New Jersey Good Realty, Inc. "Property" 114 Yantacaw Brook Road

Broker's Add. 735 Elm Avenue Wyckoff, New Jersey 07481

Wyckoff, New Jersey ZIP 07481 "Listing Price" SALE $ 185,000.00

"Service" ABC MULTIPLE LISTING SERVICE RENTAL $ ______

TERM OF AGREEMENT:

From "Commencement Date" March 21, 2002 To "Expiration Date" September 30, 2002

DISCLOSURE OF BUSINESS RELATIONSHIP BOX:

I, ______ (Name of Licensee) as an authorized representative of New Jersey Good Realty, Inc. (Name of Listing Broker) Intend as of this time, to work with you as a: *(Check only one line)*

___ Seller's / Landlord's Agent only

X Seller's / Landlord's Agent and Disclosed Dual Agent if the opportunity arises.

___ Transaction Broker

TABLE FOR COMPUTER
Seller Agent = "SA"
Disclosed Dual Agent= "DD"
Transaction Broker = "TB"

OFFER OF COOPERATION / COMPENSATION BOX:

The Seller / Landlord authorizes and the Listing Broker offers Cooperation / Compensation as follows:

(Check and Complete Appropriate Line(s))

	YES: (Cooperation)	(Compensation)	NO:
TO: SUBAGENTS	____	____	X
TO: BUYER BROKERS	X	@ 3%-100	____
TO: TRANSACTION BROKERS	X	@ 3%-100	____

The Owner X does ___ does not authorize the Listing Broker to place a Lockbox on the Property to aid in the showing of the Property.

2. GRANT OF EXCLUSIVE RIGHT TO SELL, LEASE, EXCHANGE OR OTHERWISE TRANSFER AND TO MULTIPLE LIST PROPERTY.
In consideration of the Listing Broker listing and endeavoring to find Buyers/Tenants for the Property at the Listing Price, the OWNER, (or their legally authorized representative) grants the Listing Broker the exclusive right to sell, lease, exchange or otherwise transfer the Property, at the Listing Price and on the terms as stated in this Agreement, or upon such other Price and/or terms as may be acceptable to the Owner. The Listing Broker is directed by the Owner to list the Property with the SERVICE and to distribute this listing to Service participants.

3. COMMISSION OR FEE DISCLOSURE.
"AS SELLER, YOU HAVE THE RIGHT TO INDIVIDUALLY REACH AN AGREEMENT ON ANY FEE, COMMISSION, OR OTHER VALUABLE CONSIDERATION WITH ANY BROKER, NO FEE, COMMISSION OR OTHER CONSIDERATION HAS BEEN FIXED BY ANY GOVERNMENTAL AUTHORITY OR BY ANY TRADE ASSOCIATION OR MULTIPLE LISTING SERVICE." Nothing herein is intended to prohibit an individual Broker from independently establishing a policy regarding the amount of fee, commission or other valuable consideration to be charged in transactions by the Broker.

4. PAYMENT OF COMMISSION FOR SALE/LEASE, AGENCY ARRANGEMENTS.
The Owner agrees to pay the Listing Broker (or as the Listing Broker may direct) a commission if the Property is sold, leased, exchanged or otherwise transferred by/through the Listing Broker, or through any other source (including the direct sale/lease by the Owner) before the Expiration Date. The Commission shall be as follows:

The "Sale Commission:" 6% of sales price **The "Rental Commission:"** ______

The Commission shall be earned when a ready, willing and able Buyer/Tenant is produced and shall be paid at the time of the transfer of the Property or signing of the lease. By signing this Agreement the Owner instructs the title agent/attorney to pay the commission at such time. In the event the Property is sold to the Tenant during the term of its Tenancy, the Sale Commission shall be paid by the Owner to the Listing Broker if sold to the Tenant by ______. The listing Broker agrees that the Commission may be shared with any **REALTOR**® or Broker who assists Listing Broker in causing a sale, lease, exchange or transfer of the Property as indicated in the offer of Cooperation/Compensation Box.

5. BROKER PROTECTION
Owner agrees to pay the Listing Broker the Commission if the Owner, acting on the Owner's own behalf, within 90 days after the Expiration Date conveys or agrees to convey the Property to any Buyer shown the Property by the Listing Broker or any person during the term of this Listing Agreement. This clause shall not apply if the property has been listed by the Owner with another broker by written agreement.

6. OWNER(S) LIABILITY.
This agreement shall not release Owner(s) from any liability to Listing Broker resulting from the Owner's use of the Property or the Owner's acts in showing and inspection of the Property. The OWNER(S) hold harmless and indemnify the Broker against loss or damage resulting directly from any condition of the Property not disclosed to the Broker or from the Owner's use of/or acts in the showing and inspection of the Property.

(ADDITIONAL CONTRACTUAL PROVISIONS ARE ON THE REVERSE SIDE OF THIS PAGE, PLEASE REVIEW)

ListingAgent New Jersey Good Realty, Inc. (L.S.) Owner Rocco Balboa (L.S.) March 21, 2002 Date

(Print Name)

LA ID # 100053286 Owner Adrian Balboa (L.S.) March 21, 2002 Date

______ (L.S.) Owner ______ (L.S.) Date

Accepted By Authorized Representative

(Print Name)

Broker ID # ______ Owner ______ (L.S.) Date

BROKER COPY /WHITE SERVICE COPY /CANARY OWNER COPY /PINK

FIGURE 13.1 (cont'd)

7. OWNERSHIP, LIENS AND MORTGAGES. *(Page 2 of 2)*
The Owner(s) represent that they are the sole owner(s) of the Property, the Owner(s) have the legal right to sell or lease the Property and that to the best of their knowledge they have Marketable Title to the Property. The Owner(s) further represent that Owner(s) do not know of any mortgages, other liens (including unpaid taxes) or encumbrances outstanding against the Property except as stated on the Listing Input Sheets under Mortgage Balances and after a sale at the Listing Price there will be sufficient proceeds to discharge all liens and encumbrances and to pay the Commission stated in this Agreement. The Owner(s) are not aware of any environmental hazards or proceedings regarding such hazards which are now pending or threatened with regard to the Property.

8. ACKNOWLEDGEMENT OF COPY OF ATTORNEY GENERAL'S LETTER.
The Owner acknowledges that the Attorney General's Summary of the New Jersey Law Against Discrimination is printed below and Owner has reviewed and agrees to the terms and conditions of the law.

9. SIGN AUTHORIZATION.
The Owner authorizes the Broker to place a real estate sign on the Property. The Owner agrees not to place Owner's or any other "For Sale/For Lease" sign on the Property during the term of this Agreement.

10. REFERRING INTERESTED BUYERS TO BROKER/NEGOTIATIONS THROUGH LISTING BROKER.
The Owner shall refer to the Listing Broker every prospective Buyer/Tenant who contacts the Owner during the term of this Agreement. The Owner directs that all negotiations for the purchase or lease of the Property shall be conducted through the Listing Broker.

11. NOT CURRENTLY LISTED.
The Owner represents that the Property is not currently listed with any other **REALTOR**® or Broker.

12. ACCURACY OF INFORMATION.
The information contained in this Agreement and on the attached Listing Input Sheets has been furnished by the Owner who states it is correct to the best of Owner's knowledge and belief, and the compilation by the Broker for the SERVICE is not to be deemed a representation as to the accuracy of the information provided.

13. ACKNOWLEDGEMENT OF RECEIPT OF FULLY SIGNED AGREEMENT.
The Owner acknowledges that this Agreement has been read by the Owner. The Owner understands its contents, has received a copy of this Agreement and the Consumer Information Statement on New Jersey Real Estate Relationships at the time Owner has signed this Agreement. The attached Listing Input Sheet(s) (2) have been read by and are approved as accurate by the Owner.

State of New Jersey
DEPARTMENT OF LAW AND PUBLIC SAFETY
OFFICE OF THE ATTORNEY GENERAL
PO Box 080
TRENTON, NJ 08625-0080
(609) 292-4925

JAMES E. MCGREEVEY
Governor

DAVID SAMSON
Attorney General

TO: Owners of Real Property
SUBJECT: New Jersey Law Against Discrimination and Federal Fair Housing Laws

The rules of the New Jersey Real Estate Commission require every licensed broker or salesperson with whom you are listing your property for sale or for rent to give you a copy of this legal memorandum. The purpose of this is to help you comply with New Jersey Law Against Discrimination ("LAD") and federal laws which prohibit discrimination in the sale or rental of real property. Together, the LAD and the Fair Housing Amendments Act of 1988 prohibit you from discriminating against a prospective buyer or tenant because of his/her race, creed, color, national origin, sex, marital status, affectional or sexual orientation, familial status, actual or perceived physical or mental handicap, ancestry or nationality. (Note: "familial status" refers to families with a child or children under 18 years old and /or pregnant women. "Handicapped" includes persons afflicted with AIDS or HIV or perceived to be afflicted with AIDS.)

The following are some of the requirements which apply to the sale or rental of your property:

1. All persons, regardless of their membership in one of the protected classes stated above, are entitled to equal treatment in the terms, conditions or privileges of the sale or rental of any real property (e.g. it is illegal to deny that housing is available for inspection, sale or rent when it really is available.
2. No discriminatory advertising of any kind relating to the proposed sale or rental is permitted.
3. The broker or salesperson with whom you list your property must refuse the listing if you indicate any intention of discriminating on any of the aforesaid bases.
4. The broker or salesperson with whom you list your property must transmit to you every written offer he/she receives on your property.
5. Any provision in any lease or rental agreement prohibiting maintenance of a pet or pets on the premises is not applicable to a service or guide dog owned by a handicapped, blind or deaf tenant.
6. A landlord may not charge a handicapped, blind or deaf tenant an extra fee for keeping a service or guide dog.
7. As landlord, you must permit a handicapped tenant, at his/her own expense, to make reasonable modifications to the existing premise if such modifications are necessary to afford such a person full enjoyment on the premises.

The sale or rental of all property including open land, whether for business or residential purposes, is covered by the LAD, with the following exceptions:

1. The rental of a single apartment or flat in a two-family dwelling, the other occupancy unit of which is occupied by the owner as his/her residence or the household of his/her family at the time of such rentals.
2. The rental of a rooms or rooms to another person or persons by the owner or occupant of a one-family dwelling occupied by him/her as his/her residence or the household of his/her family at the time of such rental.
3. In the sale, lease or rental of real property, preference given to persons of the same religion by a religious organization.

However, these exceptions do not apply if the dwelling was built or substantially rebuilt with the use of public funds, or financed in whole or part by a loan, or a commitment for a loan, guaranteed or insured by any agency of the federal government. The term "any agency of the federal government" includes, but is not limited to, the Federal Housing Administration (FHA) or Veterans Administration (VA), which are commonly used in such matters. In addition, discrimination in connect with some of the transactions covered by the above exceptions is nevertheless prohibited under the Federal Civil Rights Act of 1866 (42 U.S.C. 1981, 1982). However, the prohibition against discrimination on the basis of familial status does not apply to housing for older persons (as defined in the "Law Against Discrimination" at N.J.S.A. 10:5-5mm) where at least one occupant of the dwelling is at least 55 years old.

Brokers and salespersons are licensed by the New Jersey Real Estate Commission. Their activities are subject to the general real estate laws of the state and the Commission's own rules and regulations. The New Jersey Law against Discrimination apples to all people in the State and is enforced by the Division on Civil Rights in the Department of Law and Public Safety.

Should you require additional information or have any questions, please contact the Division on Civil Rights, Bureau of Prevention and Citizens' Rights at (609) 292-2918.

Sincerely yours,

DAVID SAMSON
ATTORNEY GENERAL OF NEW JERSEY

Revised April, 2002

The New Jersey Real Estate Commission requires the use of the waiver to protect owners against brokers encouraging unwarranted "office exclusives" for their own selfish ends, rather than in the client's best interest. There are legitimate circumstances when non-cooperation may promote the client's best interest, but such cases are rare. An "office exclusive" is not another type of listing, but simply a general industry term used to refer to any exclusive listing where the listing broker alone will show the property and where broker cooperation is not permitted by the owner.

Termination of Listing Contract

The most common ways to terminate a listing contract are: (1) expiration; (2) death, insanity or bankruptcy of broker or principal; (3) mutual agreement; (4) regulation; (5) destruction of the property; (6) revocation; (7) renunciation; and (8) accomplishment of the objective.

1. **Expiration.** A listing will expire after the period specified in the listing contract.

2. **Death, Insanity or Bankruptcy.** If either the broker or the principal dies, or is adjudged insane or goes through bankruptcy, the listing is automatically terminated. However, if the principal or broker dies after entering into a binding contract with a purchaser, it may still be closed, with the broker or his estate being entitled to a commission.

3. **Mutual Agreement.** Any listing may be terminated by mutual agreement between the principal and the broker.

4. **Regulation.** A regulation, such as exercise of the right of eminent domain through condemnation of the property, would terminate the listing. Also, the agent is not entitled to his commission if the property is sold in a foreclosure sale.

5. **Destruction.** Termination would result if the property were destroyed, as by fire, making it impossible to fulfill the Listing Contract.

6. **Revocation.** The principal may at any time revoke or cancel the Listing Contract. However, unless he has justification, the agent may hold him liable for breach of contract.

7. **Renunciation.** The agent may renounce or cancel the Listing Contract, but may be held liable by the principal for breach of contract unless he can show he has justifiable grounds for his actions.

8. **Accomplishment of Objective.** When the house is sold, the objective has been achieved, and the listing is terminated.

KEY WORDS

Commission
Exclusive Agency Listing
Exclusive Right to Sell Listing
Multiple Listing
Net Listing
Open Listing

CHAPTER 13
Review Questions
(Answers on page 554)

(Answers on page 554)

1. To a real estate broker, the listing property owner is known as:
   (A) agent.
   (B) fiduciary.
   (C) prospect.
   (D) principal.

2. After showing the property to a prospect, the broker with an exclusive agency listing should:
   (A) make a record of it in the broker's files.
   (B) notify seller of the prospect's identity.
   (C) send office memo to buyer.
   (D) wait until prospect makes a deal with seller.

3. Which type of listing gives a broker the greatest protection?
   (A) An open listing.
   (B) A net listing.
   (C) An exclusive right to sell listing.
   (D) An exclusive agency listing.

4. If Betty Broker holds two listings, an open listing on one property and an exclusive listing on another, and one week after both listings expire the two owners get together and exchange properties without previously being shown the properties, Betty Broker may:
   (A) sue for full commissions on both.
   (B) sue for commission on the open listing.
   (C) demand full commission on the exclusive listing.
   (D) receive no commission from their listing.

5. Upon completion of a sale, the selling broker was paid $6,000. The portion paid to the salesperson responsible for the sale would be:
   (A) always 50%.
   (B) established by the Board of Realtors.
   (C) determined by the employment agreement between the broker and the salesperson.
   (D) specified in the sales contract.

6. A property is listed with a broker at $65,000. The owner tells the broker that he is willing to sell for $62,000. A buyer is willing to sign an offer for $62,000, but indicates he will pay up to $65,000. The broker should:
   (A) refuse to submit the $62,000 offer.
   (B) suggest compromise of $63,500.
   (C) persuade the buyer to make a $65,000 offer.
   (D) persuade the buyer to go to another broker.

7. Warren gave a listing to Great Benefits Realtors, Expert Realty Co. and All Star Real Estate Agency. The type of listing he gave them was a (an):
   (A) exclusive agency listing.
   (B) exclusive right to sell listing.
   (C) open listing.
   (D) multiple listing.

8. Except under specific conditions, an agent may serve only one principal at a time. However, a principal may have more than one agent. Which of the following would best describe such a situation?
   (A) Multiple listing.
   (B) Open listing.
   (C) Exclusive agency.
   (D) Exclusive right to sell.

9. In a multiple listing, a salesperson who negotiates a sale is directly responsible to:
   (A) the listing broker.
   (B) his employing broker.
   (C) the cooperating salesperson.
   (D) the seller.

10. A listing agreement in which the owner promises to pay a commission under all circumstances of sale except if he sells the property himself is known as:
    (A) an exclusive right to sell.
    (B) an exclusive agency.
    (C) a net listing.
    (D) a sole and exclusive listing.

11. The usual listing gives the broker authority to:
    (A) sign a contract for the seller.
    (B) reject offers less than the list price.
    (C) convey title.
    (D) None of the above.

12. An owner who wants to employ more than one broker should give each broker:
    (A) a multiple listing.
    (B) an exclusive agency.
    (C) an open listing.
    (D) a net listing.

13. Which statement is FALSE regarding an exclusive agency listing agreement?
    (A) The owner must receive a copy when the agreement is signed.
    (B) The listing broker is not required to cooperate with other brokers.
    (C) It must have a definite, unqualified termination date.
    (D) The owner may employ only one broker.

14. An exclusive agency contract:
    (A) is only terminated if the property is sold by the seller.
    (B) must be in writing.
    (C) can be listed by the owner with more than one broker.
    (D) does not require a termination date.

15. In an exclusive right to sell, the property owner:
    (A) can still sell the property himself without obligation to pay a fee.
    (B) would pay a commission even if the property were not sold.
    (C) is obligated to pay the listing broker a commission even if another broker finds a buyer.
    (D) can list the property with more than one broker.

16. When a broker has an exclusive right to sell listing:
    (A) the seller may sell the property himself without obligation to pay the broker his commission.
    (B) the broker receives a commission regardless of whether the property is sold.
    (C) the broker is entitled to his fee no matter who procures a buyer for the property.
    (D) only the broker who procures the buyer is entitled to a fee.

17. Broker Smith has a listing on a house which contains a provision that the house is to be sold in an "as is" condition. Smith learns of a major hidden defect in the property and, when showing a prospective purchaser, should:
    (A) advise the buyer of the defect.
    (B) point out that the house will be sold in an "as is" condition.
    (C) mention the defect to the buyer only if asked.
    (D) inform the buyer that the seller has told him of no defects.

18. Which of the following events will NOT result in termination of the listing contract?
    (A) Death of seller.
    (B) Bankruptcy of broker.
    (C) Insanity of seller.
    (D) Marriage of seller.

19. A listing agreement may be terminated by:
    (A) the expiration of the time limit contained in the listing.
    (B) mutual agreement.
    (C) revocation by the property owner.
    (D) All of the above.

20. After the sale, the listing broker refused to split the commission with the selling broker. Who is responsible to pay the selling broker?
    (A) The listor.
    (B) The listing broker.
    (C) The seller.
    (D) The MLS.

21. In an exclusive agency listing, the owner sells the property. Broker gets:
    (A) full commission.
    (B) 1/3 commission.
    (C) no commission.
    (D) 1/2 commission.

22. An owner wishes to list her property but does not want to pay a commission if she finds the buyer herself. She should negotiate which of the following?
    (A) Open listing.
    (B) Exclusive agency listing.
    (C) Neither (A) nor (B).
    (D) Either (A) or (B).

23. An unconfirmed oral listing is:
    (A) unlawful.
    (B) unenforceable.
    (C) a violation of the statute of limitations.
    (D) usually submitted to the MLS.

24. Which of the following statements is true?
    (A) A definite termination date must be provided in all exclusive listings.
    (B) The term "Multiple Listing" is the listing of property with a number of different brokers.
    (C) There is only one type of exclusive listing.
    (D) To be enforceable the listing must be signed by the buyer.

25. In a typical real estate transaction, the buyer's agent is:
    (A) the listing broker.
    (B) the participating broker.
    (C) the listing broker and selling broker.
    (D) neither broker.

NOTE: Upon completion of Chapters 1-13, you should answer the questions in Review Quiz One, page 509, and check your solutions with the Quiz Answers at the back of the book.

CHAPTER FOURTEEN

CONTRACTS

A **contract** may be defined as a voluntary agreement between two or more legally competent parties, supported by consideration, wherein the parties agree to do, or refrain from doing, some legal act. Simply put, a contract is a promise enforceable by law. Thus, for a valid contract to exist there must be both an agreement and a resulting legal obligation. A solid, clearly defined contract insures the performance of the parties to their agreements by requiring that they either perform, or pay for all loss or damage caused by their non-performance.

In New Jersey, the Statute of Frauds governs most real estate contracts. The statute was created to prevent perjury, forgery and dishonest conduct on the part of unscrupulous persons in proving the existence and terms of contractual obligations.

In 1996, the New Jersey Legislature amended the Statute in a substantive manner. Formerly, contracts for the sale of real estate, and leases for longer than three years, had to be written and signed in order to be legal, binding and enforceable. Such is no longer the case.

Oral agreements for the sale of real estate and oral leases for longer than three years may now be enforced provided the party seeking enforcement can prove the contract by "clear and convincing evidence." Clear and convincing evidence is a standard of proof that is greater than the "preponderance of evidence" test used in civil matters, but less than the criminal standard of "beyond a reasonable doubt" required to convict defendants in criminal cases. Under the new statute, in order to enforce an oral contract for the above described transactions, there must be clear and convincing evidence that the buyer and seller had orally agreed on: (a) the existence of the agreement; (b) the nature of the interest to be transferred (fee simple, life estate, easement, etc.); (c) the precise real estate to be transferred; and (d) the identity of the transferor and transferee.

A real estate broker's authorization must be in writing and signed for either a sale or lease transaction, regardless of whether the broker is acting on behalf of the seller, the buyer, the landlord or the tenant. In addition, written authorization is required for the sale of a business *even if the business does not involve an interest in real estate.*

Although certain agreements may be exempt from the Statute of Frauds, a written contract that clearly spells out the rights and obligations of each party is highly recommended. A written contract will support the terms of the agreement and minimize subsequent misunderstandings between the contracting parties.

TYPES OF CONTRACTS

Contracts may be classified as (1) unilateral; (2) bilateral; (3) valid; (4) void; (5) voidable; (6) unenforceable or enforceable; or (7) executed or executory.

Unilateral Contract. A unilateral contract is one in which a promise is made by one party to induce some act or performance on the part of the other. The performance of the act thus denotes acceptance of the offer, and by that consummates the obligations of the contract. For example, in an option contract, one party promises to deliver title to his property, if the other party pays the option price and exercises the option. Although the buyer is not obligated to perform, the seller must deliver title if the buyer does decide to exercise the option and buy the property.

Bilateral Contract. A bilateral contract is one in which both parties mutually exchange the promises, and the contract becomes binding at the time of the agreement. For example, a buyer promises to pay a certain price for a piece of property, and the seller promises to deliver free and clear title. Most real estate contracts are bilateral.

Valid Contract. A valid contract is one that satisfies all the legal requirements of a contract; one that has all the essential elements required by law.

Void Contract. This is a contract that has no effect legally, with the parties in the same position they would have been if no contract existed at all. The term "void contract" is somewhat self-contradictory, since an agreement that produces no legal obligation cannot properly be called a contract. Thus, it may be said that a void contract is a nullity that can be neither ratified nor enforced (i.e., a contract for an illegal purpose, such as a **dual contract**). A dual contract is an arrangement whereby a buyer and seller of property agree to different terms than those of the original contract to benefit fraudulently from the transaction, for example, a contract drawn at a higher price than the true contract to obtain a larger mortgage loan.

Voidable Contract. A voidable contract is one that may be enforced or rejected by one party to the contract, and at the same time is unenforceable against that same party. An example is a contract between a minor (one under 18 years of age) and an adult. Although the minor can hold the adult to his contractual promise, treating the contract as valid, the adult cannot do the same, since the minor has the right to disaffirm his obligation because of his infancy. A minor's contracts for necessaries, such as food and clothing, however, are not voidable by the minor.

Unenforceable Contract. An unenforceable contract is a valid contract that cannot be enforced. Examples include contracts where enforcement is sought after the statute of limitations has expired, oral contracts which are required by the Statute of Frauds to be written, and contracts the terms of which are unconscionable.

Executed and Executory Contracts. An executed contract refers to a contract where both parties have performed all that is required of them by the contract. When the buyer and seller perform under the contract of sale, and the deed is delivered in exchange for the purchase price, the contract is said to be "executed."

An executory contract is a contract under which one or more parties has not yet performed, as when a contract for the sale of real estate is made with the closing in six months, or where a lender makes a loan at a certain interest rate, payable at a future time.

ESSENTIAL ELEMENTS OF A CONTRACT

To be binding and enforceable at law, all contracts must have five essential elements: (1) offer and acceptance; (2) consideration; (3) competent parties; (4) reality of consent; and (5) legal purpose. The absence of any element would make the contract void or voidable. In a real estate contract, there are two additional elements: description of the property and signature of the party to be charged.

Offer and Acceptance

The first element for any contract is that there must be an offer and an acceptance. The party making the offer is the offeror (usually the buyer), and the party to whom the offer is made is the offeree (usually the seller). To be effective, an offer must be communicated to the offeree by a means selected by the offeror, must actually be intended as an offer, and must be definite and certain as to its terms.

After an offer has been made, it may be: (a) terminated by lapse of time; (b) withdrawn or revoked by the offeror; (c) rejected by the offeree; (d) accepted by the offeree; (e) accepted by the offeree, but on different conditions (this is called a counteroffer and constitutes a rejection of the original offer); (f) terminated by death or insanity of either the offeror or offeree; (g) terminated by the destruction of the subject matter of the offer; or (h) terminated by any change in law making the object of the offer illegal.

An offer should state a specified period of time during which it is to remain effective. If no time is specified, the offer terminates upon the expiration of a reasonable length of time, determined by the surrounding circumstances. A person making an offer can withdraw the offer at any time prior to acceptance, even if he or she previously stated that the offer would be held open for a certain period. If a seller signs a contract after the specified time of an offer has lapsed it would merely constitute a counteroffer, because the original offer was terminated at the expiration of the specified time limit.

An offer is normally deemed accepted when the acceptance has been communicated back to the offeror before the expiration of the time limit stated in the offer. If no time limit is contained, the offer expires at the end of a reasonable time. The time begins when the offeree receives the offer. Acceptance by mail or telegram is effective upon sending.

An offer may be revoked by the offeror any time prior to its acceptance being communicated back to him, even before the time limit originally specified for the offeree to accept it. An offer must contain definite terms and indicate a present intention to enter into a contract. An invitation to make offers (bids) on a property by listing it for sale or advertising it, for example, would not normally meet the definition of an offer. An example of an offer and acceptance follows.

Example

Sidney lists his home with Action Real Estate for $199,900. Herbert inquires about the property, is shown through it, and makes a written offer of

$190,000 to buy the property. Sidney accepts Herbert's offer in its entirety under the terms proposed and communicates his acceptance back to Herbert through his salesperson by signing and accepting the offer. This constitutes offer and acceptance. In this case Herbert is the offeror, since he has made the offer to purchase, and Sidney is the offeree, since he has received the offer.

A **counteroffer** is a rejection of an offer combined with a return proposal which creates a new offer. A counteroffer always terminates the original offer. Counteroffers are quite common in real estate, as there is a good deal of back and forth negotiation between the parties before final agreement is reached. The negotiation usually centers upon agreeing to a mutually acceptable sale price, but may involve negotiation on other terms such as the amount of the earnest money deposit, settlement date, type of financing or personal property items to be included.

Example

John's home is listed for sale with Woodbury Real Estate for $119,900. Mary offers to buy John's home for $116,500. Mary is the offeror and John is the offeree. John rejects Mary's offer, but makes a return proposal, agreeing to sell the property for $119,000. John's proposal to Mary is a counteroffer, and since John is now making the offer, he is the offeror and Mary, who is the receiver of this offer, is the offeree.

Once an offer is rejected, it is immediately terminated. Even if the offeree later decides that its terms would be acceptable, the offeror is not bound by it and could not be forced to re-initiate it. Sellers should consider each offer they receive as if it will be their last or best offer, because sometimes it is. There is no relationship between the number and dollar amounts of offers received and those likely to be received in the future. Each offer should be evaluated carefully upon its own merits.

Example

Paul offers $285,000 for Edwin's property listed at $307,500. Edwin considers accepting Paul's offer, but rejects it in the hope that Paul will respond with a higher bid. Paul decides not to make another offer. Edwin now tells his agent that he will accept Paul's offer of $285,000. Paul cannot be held to this offer as Edwin has already rejected it. Effectively, a rejected offer is a dead offer. (Paul may, however, reinstitute his offer if he wishes. In this case, Paul's offer would constitute a new offer).

Consideration

An agreement alone does not make an enforceable contract. There must be consideration supporting the agreement. Consideration means that each party must exchange with the other something of value such as the exchange of a promise for a promise, money for a promise or money for a **forbearance**. A forbearance is a voluntary agreement to refrain from doing something that you have a legal right to do. In a real estate sales contract, the consideration usually consists of an exchange of promises. The seller promises to transfer title to the buyer in exchange for the buyer's promise to pay the purchase price to the seller. Usually, the law will not inquire into the fairness of the consideration unless there is evidence of fraud, undue influence or other factors affecting reality of consent. Reality of consent is explained below.

People often confuse the earnest money deposit with consideration. In the sale of real estate the consideration would be the exchange of promises to buy and sell at a set price, not the earnest money deposit. Earnest money, although customary (and important), is not essential to a valid contract.

Competent Parties

All parties to a valid contract must have legal capacity in order for the contract to be binding. Certain persons who lack contractual capacity are minors, insane persons and intoxicated persons. Should any of these persons enter into a contract, either they or their guardians could void the agreement. Thus, such contracts are voidable by the incompetent party but not by the other party to the agreement.

A contract with a minor should be entered into with caution, for the minor can cancel or disaffirm the contract with no liability. The courts will generally find that based on age, a minor does not have the experience, judgment or ability to properly evaluate a contractual agreement. A minor may either cancel or ratify a contract upon reaching legal age.

Highly intoxicated persons are considered to be incapable of understanding the nature of the transaction, and are thus given the same protection as that given to minors.

Insane persons are protected in the same way as minors or highly intoxicated persons. However, contracts of persons legally adjudged insane are considered void instead of voidable and can never have any legal effect.

Reality of Consent

Before a valid contract can exist, the parties must enter into an agreement knowingly and voluntarily, and they must mutually consent to be bound by its terms. This mutual consent is frequently referred to as a "meeting of the minds." In addition, a valid contract must be free from mistake, misrepresentation, fraud, undue influence or duress.

Mistakes. Mistakes made in the preparation of a contract have different effects, depending on the kind of mistake. If a **unilateral mistake** is made regarding the substance of the contract, it may be voidable by the injured party. A mistake regarding one's misunderstanding of the law's applicability or one made as a result of the party's own carelessness would not affect the status of an otherwise valid contract. In other words, ignorance of the law is no excuse.

Example
When Arnold signs a contract to purchase real estate, he does not realize that the balance must be paid at the closing and he fails to include a financing contingency clause. If he cannot produce the balance in cash at settlement he will be in default. His unilateral mistake will not be grounds for rescission.

Mutual mistakes occur when both parties assume something to be true, when in fact it is incorrect, and the parties rely on such information when forming the agreement. If there is a mutual mistake, a "meeting of the minds " never took place and the contract would be void.

Example
Barney and Barry reach an agreement for the sale of a particular house, which unknown to either party had burned down prior to the closing. The contract can be rescinded on the basis of the mutual mistake because the parties acted under an erroneous assumption concerning the subject matter of the agreement.

Fraud is a deliberate and intentional misstatement of fact.

Example
Henry Hankin goes to a real estate broker to find a building in which he can operate his accounting service. The broker shows Henry a building, which he owns, and tells him that zoning will permit his intended use. He does this to induce Henry to sign the sales contract hoping that no subsequent problem will arise, but knowing that the property is located in a residential zone where Henry's use is not permitted. Henry, relying upon the broker's statement, signs the contract but later discovers that his proposed use is impermissible. Henry may cancel the contract with the broker on the basis of the broker's fraud against him and sue for damages in a civil action. The broker could also be subject to criminal action and/or fine, and suspension or revocation of license by the NJ Real Estate Commission.

Misrepresentation is an unknowing or innocent misstatement of fact. A contract is voidable whenever there is a material misstatement of fact.

Example
Leo signed a contract to sell Homer and Dottie a 25-acre parcel of land. A subsequent survey revealed that the parcel contained only 15 acres. Leo honestly believed that he had 25 acres to sell. Homer and Dottie may cancel the contract because of Leo's substantial misrepresentation.

Undue influence arises when, in a close and confidential relationship, one party has taken advantage of another to such a degree that freely given consent and understanding have been seriously impaired.

Example
Eighty-eight-year-old Uncle Pat has been living with his nephew Tom. Uncle Pat owns some timberland and Tom, for his own selfish ends, induces his sick and confused uncle to sign a deed so he can misappropriate the proceeds for his own use. Uncle Pat himself, or others acting on his behalf, could seek to have the contract voided because of Tom's undue influence when the instrument was signed.

Duress indicates the compelling of a person, through fear, to perform or agree to perform an act. Contracts obtained under duress are voidable by the aggrieved party.

Legal Purpose

All contracts must have a legal purpose. Any contract formed to accomplish an illegal end in violation of any statute, administrative regulation or court decision was never a contract at all, and is void on its face.

Example
Albert, who is not licensed, agrees to find tenants for Betty's apartment building and Betty agrees in writing to pay him a fee of $100 each time he finds a suitable tenant. Albert finds five tenants but Betty re-fuses to pay him, so Albert sues her

for breach of contract. No contract ever existed, since Albert was engaging in the practice of real estate without being licensed. Albert therefore never had any legal right to be paid a fee.

Contracts that were for a legal purpose when formed, but which prior to performance have subsequently become illegal due to a change in the law, are similarly void due to supervening illegality.

Description of the Property

The property to be conveyed or encumbered must be at least sufficiently described in the contract so that the land involved may be adequately determined. This requirement is normally met by the use of a recognized legal description of the property. Evidence may be introduced which serves to clarify a written description, but not which serves to furnish a description not contained in the contract. An indeterminate property description, in the face of a disagreement between the parties over what parcel(s) was involved in the contract, would void the contract.

Signature of the Parties

The full names of all parties should be clearly stated in the contract and their signatures affixed. The Statute of Frauds does not require the contract to be signed by all parties. It need only be signed by the party "to be charged" (the party sued). Accordingly, the signature of the party seeking enforcement is not required. If a contract fails to include the signature of the seller's spouse (or co-owner), and the seller does not carry out his promise to convey the realty, the buyer could not force conveyance of the property, but would only have the right to bring a suit against the seller for the value of his lost bargain. It is therefore strongly recommended that all pertinent signatures be obtained at the time of the agreement.

ASSIGNMENT OF CONTRACT

An **assignment** is a legal instrument that passes all the rights and obligations under a contract from one party to another. The party who makes the assignment is the assignor and the party receiving the assignment is the assignee.

Example

On April 15 Bill signed an agreement of sale with Jim agreeing to buy his home on or before July 15. On May 1 Bill assigned all his rights and obligations under the contract to George. George will now purchase the property from Jim on July 15. Bill is the assignor and George is the assignee. If George fails to perform as agreed, Bill will be in breach of contract with Jim.

Contracts are assignable unless their terms specifically forbid it or unless it is a personal service contract. Personal service contracts such as an entertainer's contract to perform or a listing contract are not assignable under the presumption that such services contracted for are unique and incapable of being performed in the same manner by anyone else. Contracts such as mortgages and leases are assigned frequently.

OPTIONS

An **option** is a written contract supported by consideration under which a prospective purchaser, called the optionee, is given the option or right to purchase the property, for a stated price and terms, within a fixed period of time, but without imposing any obligation to purchase. Since an option is an offer secured by a consideration, it cannot be revoked. It is a binding promise to keep an offer open for a stated period of time. The buyer/optionee generally puts up a deposit (option money) which is commonly 5 to 10% of the purchase price. The optionee then has the choice of exercising the option, receiving delivery of the property, and having the option money applied to the purchase price, or refusing to consummate the transaction, thereby forfeiting the deposit.

Thus, the buyer, by exercising the option, may compel the seller to convey the property, but the seller must be content only with the option money if the buyer decides not to purchase. Generally under such an agreement, if the premises are destroyed, the risk of loss remains with the seller until the deal is consummated.

RISK OF LOSS BEFORE CLOSING

When a buyer and seller have signed a contract for the sale of real estate, the buyer does not acquire legal title to the property because that will not happen until later, when a deed is signed and delivered at the closing. However, the buyer does acquire equitable title, which means the law recognizes some ownership rights, even though the buyer is not yet the owner of record. This raises an important question. Who is responsible if the house burns down, or a tree falls through the roof after the contract is signed and prior to the closing? Generally, the contract provides that the seller is responsible for the risk of loss or damage to the property by fire or otherwise, except ordinary wear and tear, until the closing. In the absence of such a provision, the buyer would bear the risk of loss during this time under New Jersey law.

EARNEST MONEY

Earnest money is the money paid (either initially or by additional deposits) as a token of good faith by a prospective purchaser to indicate both the ability and intent to carry out the contract. It is frequently called a **binder**. As noted earlier, earnest money is not essential to make a sales contract binding, as long as the buyer and seller both exchange mutual promises of performance. If the buyer performs, the earnest money is applied toward the purchase price. Default by the buyer will generally result in the earnest money being paid to the seller as damages.

If a broker feels that unusual circumstances exist in connection with disputed trust monies, the advice of an attorney should be sought. However, in the absence of any unusual circumstances the Real Estate Commission suggests the following possible course of action:

1. A broker who receives a demand to release deposit monies and is satisfied that the agreement provides for such a release, should, to protect himself, notify the other party to the transaction, by certified mail, of the demand. The broker should further advise the other party that the funds will be released unless a written claim or notice of claim is received by the broker from the other party within a reasonable period of time, say, 15-20 days from the date the certified letter is received. If the broker receives no claim or notice of intent to make claim the funds may be released. In this situation, specific written consents to the release are not necessarily required.

2. If a claim or notice of intent to make a claim is received, as a response to the broker's certified letter in (1.) above, the broker may hold the disputed funds pending resolution of the disagreement. The disagreement may be settled amicably between the parties, or by court order, if the matter is litigated. In either case, upon appropriate notification of the resolution of the problem, the broker may release the disputed funds. If during the time the problem is being amicably resolved or litigated the broker feels he does not want to continue holding the monies, he may initiate an interpleader action through the courts and place the monies at the discretion of the court.

3. If the broker claims any portion of the deposit monies on account of commission earned or for other reasons, he should notify both parties by certified mail of such claim, and initiate appropriate litigation to pursue his claim.

4. The Real Estate Commission, as a regulatory body, is neither empowered nor authorized to settle civil disputes between parties concerning deposit monies. The Commission does, however, routinely audit escrow accounts of brokers to determine that escrow funds are being properly held and accounted for.

BREACH OF CONTRACT

When a party to a contract, without legal cause or excuse, fails to perform, it is a breach or default, and the party who is not in default has certain legal rights or remedies. Contracting parties have the following remedies in case of breach by the other:

Breach by Seller (Buyer's Remedies)

Rescission of the Contract. The basic and minimal remedy available to the purchaser if the seller defaults is to rescind and recover the deposit paid under the contract. In addition, the purchaser is entitled to be reimbursed for the reasonable expenses of the title search.

Sue for Compensatory Damages. The purchaser is allowed to sue for loss of bargain along with recovery of the deposit. Usually, the loss of bargain damages will consist of the difference between the contract price and the market price of the property at the time of the seller's breach. Compensatory damges may also include the additional cost of acquiring a substantially equivalent property and the additional expenses incurred during the search for the substitute property.

Specific Performance. The above remedies available to the purchaser for the seller's default may be inadequate, because the purchaser may have a particular need for the property involved. In this case, the purchaser may turn to the remedy of specific performance. By this action the purchaser asks the court for an order compelling the seller to convey title upon receiving the purchase price from the purchaser.

Breach by Buyer (Seller's Remedies)

Forfeiture of Deposit. Prior to 1991, if a buyer defaulted, the seller could retain the deposit as damages, consider the matter terminated, and so inform the buyer. If the contract was silent as to damages for its breach, the buyer could not recover the deposit, regardless of the damages actually suffered by the seller. Such is no longer the case. Today, the seller is not entitled to retain the deposit of the buyer under a contract to purchase unless the contract contains a well-drafted **liquidated damages** clause. In the absence of such a provision, the seller is entitled only to the actual damages suffered and the buyer may recover that portion of the deposit that exceeds the seller's actual damages. If, however, the buyer paid a deposit simply as a step in a transaction and the parties fail to execute a contract, the buyer may recover the full deposit.

Liquidated damages are a legally recoverable amount, agreed upon in good faith, that one party agrees to pay the other in the event of a breach of contract, based upon probable and foreseeable damages resulting from a breach. Courts will carefully scrutinize the amount agreed upon to determine whether it is actually liquidated damages or a penalty. A penalty is an arbitrary amount which is not related to probable damages, and is designed to serve as a threat to prevent a breach. The courts will not enforce penalty provisions as a remedy for breach of contract.

Suit for Compensatory Damages. A seller may bring an action for actual damages sustained as a result of the breach. The measure of damages is the difference between the contract price and the market value of the property at the time of the breach, less credit for any deposit made on account of the purchase price. When the purchaser defaults, the seller may sell to a third party without losing the right to sue the purchaser for damages. In a declining market, the measure of damages would be the difference between the contract price and the value of the property at the time of the *resale* rather than at the time of the *breach*.

Specific Performance. A seller seldom seeks the remedy of specific performance because it is costly and time-consuming. However, if the purchaser has paid only a token deposit, the seller may seek specific performance in an effort to convince the purchaser to make a money settlement.

STATUTE OF LIMITATIONS

A contract can be discharged by full performance, or by breach of contract, giving the injured party a choice of remedies, but civil actions must be commenced within the periods prescribed by law. The time varies, depending on the nature of the action. In New Jersey, the statute of limitations will bar any action seeking relief for a breach of contract after *six years*.

PAROL EVIDENCE RULE

Parol evidence is oral evidence. It is that which is given by word of mouth. An example is the kind of evidence given by witnesses in court. Under the Parol Evidence Rule, when parties put their agreement in writing, all previous oral agreements merge into the written agreement and are therefore not admissible into evidence. A contract as written cannot be modified or changed by parol evidence unless there was a mistake or fraud in the preparation of the agreement. The "entire contract" clause in the form sales contract used by Realtors® illustrates the parol evidence rule by stating: "This contract contains the entire agreement of the parties. No representations have been made by any of the parties, the Broker(s) or his/her/their agents except as set forth in this agreement." (See paragraph 25, Figure 14.1).

CASH TRANSACTIONS

An IRS regulation requires all business organizations (including real estate offices) to report the receipt of more than $10,000 in cash in one or more related transactions.

The report to the IRS must be made within 15 days of the receipt of the cash and the office must keep a copy of the report for five years. The form (No. 8300) may be obtained from the local IRS office. A copy of the form or a written statement acknowledging receipt of the cash must be given to the person from whom the cash was received. Anyone failing to comply with the regulation will be subject to civil and/or criminal prosecution or penalty.

PREPARATION OF CONTRACTS BY LICENSEES

Real estate agents are recognized to have limited authority in the preparation of contracts and in the rendering of advice relative to their area of expertise. Any person who engages in the practice of law without a license is a disorderly person. The Supreme Court of New Jersey has exclusive jurisdiction over the practice of law in our state.

In *NJ Bar Association v. NJ Association of Realtors*, the court granted a consent judgment confirming an agreement between the parties, providing that real estate brokers would be permitted to fill in the blank spaces in approved standard contract forms for the following types of residential sales and lease agreements:

1. Contracts for the sale of one- to four-family dwellings and vacant one-family lots involving

transactions in which the broker has a fee or commission interest.

2. Leases for residential dwellings with a term of one year or more in which the broker has a fee or commission interest.

All residential sales contracts and residential leases prepared by real estate licensees must contain, at the top of the first page, the following language:

THIS IS A LEGALLY BINDING CONTRACT THAT WILL BECOME FINAL WITHIN THREE BUSINESS DAYS. DURING THIS PERIOD YOU MAY CHOOSE TO CONSULT AN ATTORNEY WHO CAN REVIEW AND CANCEL THE CONTRACT. SEE SECTION ON ATTORNEY REVIEW FOR DETAILS.

The contract must also contain the following language within the text of every such contract:

ATTORNEY REVIEW

1. **Study by Attorney.** The Buyer or the Seller may choose to have an attorney study this contract. If an attorney is consulted, the attorney must complete his or her review of the contract within a three-day period. This contract will be legally binding at the end of this three-day period unless an attorney for the Buyer or Seller reviews and disapproves of the contract.

2. **Counting the Time.** You count the three days from the date of delivery of the signed contract to the Buyer and the Seller. You do not count Saturdays, Sundays or legal holidays. The Buyer and the Seller may agree in writing to extend the three-day period for attorney review.

3. **Notice of Disapproval.** If an attorney for the Buyer or the Seller reviews and disapproves of this contract, the attorney must notify the Broker(s) and the other party named in this contract within the three-day period. Otherwise this contract will be legally binding as written. The attorney must send the notice of disapproval to the Broker(s) by certified mail, by telegram, or by delivering it personally. The telegram or certified letter will be effective upon sending. The personal delivery will be effective upon delivery to the Broker's office. The attorney may, but need not also inform the Broker(s) of any suggested revisions in the contract that would make it satisfactory.

4. The contract shall also contain the names and full addresses of all persons to whom a Notice of Disapproval must be sent in order to be effective as provided in item three of the Attorney Review Provision.

All residential leases prepared by licensees for a term of one year or more must contain the same attorney review clause, substituting the term "tenant" for "buyer," and "landlord" for "seller." Residential leases for a term of less than one year do not require attorney review language. Real estate licensees are specifically prohibited from preparing commercial leases and contracts for the sale of commercial property.

IMPORTANT NOTE: To avoid potential civil liability, and a violation of Commission Rules, licensees should include all of the attorney review language in all post-contract addenda (riders) or revisions they prepare in sale or lease transactions to which the attorney review requirements apply, regardless of whether the original contract was or was not prepared by a licensee. A contract revision prepared by a real estate licensee is void unless the revision contains the attorney review clause.

WHY THE ATTORNEY REVIEW CLAUSE WAS CREATED*

The preparation of contracts, including real estate contracts, historically has been considered to be the practice of law, which only attorneys may undertake. As a result, the New Jersey State Bar Association filed suit seeking to stop real estate licensees from preparing contracts, contending that it constitutes the unauthorized practice of law. After years of litigation, the Bar Association and NJAR reached a settlement that created the attorney review clause.

The purpose of the attorney review clause is to permit real estate licensees to prepare a contract for the sale of residential property while providing the buyer and seller with three business days to consult an attorney about the transaction. Thus, the preparation and signing of the contract will not be delayed because an attorney was not available, but the parties have the right to have an attorney review the contract to protect their interests.

Interpretation of Attorney Review by the Courts

- Early decisions held that attorneys who properly and timely serve a notice of disapproval can disapprove of the contract for any reason or no reason at all. [*Desnevich v. Moran*, 211 Super. 554,556 (App. Div. 1986)].

- The attorney review provision only has to be

***Source:** "Maneuvering Through the Attorney Review Minefield," by Barry S. Goodman, *NJ REALTOR® Magazine*, August, 2001.

included in a contract (or an amendment to the contract) if a real estate licensee prepares it. Thus, if an attorney prepares the contract, the attorney review provision does not have to be included.

- There must be literal compliance with the terms of attorney review. For example, in one case a licensee did not include the addresses of the buyer and seller in the contract. The court stated that it understood that such a practice was intended "to protect the identity of their buyers and sellers from other brokers and parties," but that such a practice violated the REC's regulations. The court explained that such information was essential for an attorney to send the notice of disapproval to the other party. [*Kargen v. Kerr*, 248 NJ, Super. 91, 97 (Ch. Div. 1991)].

- A notice of disapproval is ineffective if the seller's attorney sends the notice to the broker but not to the buyer. If this happens, the contract will be binding at the end of the three-day period. [*Desnevich v. Moran*, 211 Super. 554,556 (App. Div. 1986)].

- The notice must be sent to the brokers for both parties by certified mail, telegram or personal delivery and the "better practice" is to send it to the buyer, as well as the buyer's attorney. Where the seller's attorney sent a letter by ordinary mail to the buyer's broker (with a copy to the buyer's attorney), the court ruled that the contract had not been disapproved and was legally binding at the end of attorney review. [*Kutzin v. Pirnie*, 124 NJ 500, 507-508 (1991)].

- A party's new attorney can disapprove the contract even though the party's prior attorney had approved it. In one case, the sellers' attorney had approved the contract during attorney review by signing the contract for the sellers pursuant to a power of attorney. However, the court held that the sellers could have a second attorney disapprove the contract as long as the disapproval properly was sent within the three-day period. [*Levison v. Weintraub*, 215 NJ Super. 273 (App. Div. 1987)].

- The signed contract must be delivered to the seller. In a recent case, the seller instructed the broker to forward the signed contract directly to her attorney. As a result, the broker sent the contract to the seller's attorney but not to the seller. Since the signed contract never was delivered to the seller, the court held that the review period never commenced. [*Peterson v. Estate of Pursell*, Appellate Division, Docket No. A-3973-99 T5 (decided April 10, 2001)].

- Brokers are not entitled to a commission if the contract properly is disapproved by the attorney for one of the parties, or if the broker does not comply with the attorney review requirements. [*Century 21-Candid Realty v. Cliett*, 203 NJ Super. 78 (Law Div. 1985)].

Offers Received During and After Attorney Review

During attorney review, written offers are not "back-up offers" and must be presented to the owner. After attorney review has been completed, written offers are treated as "back-up offers" and the licensee must provide the following written notices:

1. to the owner to consult an attorney before taking any action concerning the back-up offer;
2. to the offeror that the property is the subject of a pending contract of sale or lease; and
3. if the licensee is not licensed with the listing broker, a copy of the notice to the offeror must be sent to the listing broker when the back-up offer is presented. [NJAC 11:5-6.4 (h)].

After the contract is out of attorney review, the licensee still must present all written and signed offers to the sellers or their authorized representative. [NJAC 11:5-6.4 (g) and (h)].

Possible Penalties for Noncompliance with Attorney Review Requirements

In addition to a licensee not earning a commission if he/she fails to comply with the requirements of attorney review, the Real Estate Commission's regulations specify that the failure of any licensee to include the mandated language in a contract is conduct that demonstrates "unworthiness and incompetence." A licensee also can be criminally prosecuted for the unauthorized practice of law for failing to comply with the requirements of attorney review (NJSA 2C:21-22). Under this statute, a person is guilty of a disorderly person's offense if the person knowingly engages in the unauthorized practice of law. Criminal penalties for such an offense may include (1) a fine of up to $1,000, or two times the economic gain of the licensee or loss to the victim, whichever is the highest; and (2) up to six months in prison (NJSA 2C:43-3.8).

Conclusion

The attorney review clause clearly has provided opportunities for real estate licensees to prepare contracts that otherwise would be prohibited as the practice of law. However, licensees must comply with all of the requirements of attorney review in order to avoid a charge that they are committing the unauthorized practice of law. Each licensee, therefore, is encouraged to carefully read the attorney review clause and understand its nuances.

NEW JERSEY SUPREME COURT NOTICE REGARDING CLOSINGS WITHOUT ATTORNEYS

In October 1996 the New Jersey Supreme Court ruled on the challenge to Opinion 26 of the Court's Committee on the Unauthorized Practice of Law. That Opinion had been widely interpreted as requiring parties to be represented by counsel at real estate closings.

In its ruling, the court reaffirmed its March 1995 decision holding that, so long as certain disclosures were made and other procedures adhered to, the practice of conducting real estate closings without attorneys to represent the parties present would not constitute the unauthorized practice of law. To achieve such a result, the broker must notify both parties of the conflicting interests of brokers and title companies in real estate transactions and of the general risk attendant upon their not being represented by counsel.

The court prescribed a Notice requirement (See Figure 14.1) with which licensees must comply by attaching it to proposed contracts as their cover pages.

Licensees are required to inform buyers and sellers that they must read the notice before signing the contract. At the closing, the title company employee in charge must ask both parties whether, how and when they received the notice, and maintain a record of their responses. Brokers who fail to comply with these conditions will have engaged in the unauthorized practice of law.

The court's rulings also hold that brokers may order title searches and abstracts and that an attorney retained by a broker may draft conveyance documents only upon the written request of the party on whose behalf the document is to be prepared. The court also concluded that brokers who fail to comply with these conditions will have engaged in the unauthorized practice of law.

Finally, the court also concluded that brokers have a duty to inform the seller or buyer of a situation where independent counsel is needed.

The Rules and Regulations of the New Jersey Real Estate Commission require real estate licensees to recommend that legal counsel be obtained where the interests of any party to a transaction seem to require it [11:5-6.4(I)].

CONTRACTS FOR THE SALE OF REAL ESTATE

In addition to the essential elements of a contract discussed earlier, contracts for the sale of real estate should provide the following:

Purchase Price. In addition to the full purchase price, the amount of the earnest money deposit should be stated. If a token deposit is given, provision for payment of the balance should be stipulated. For the buyer's protection, the contract should provide that the earnest money be held in escrow by a third party (broker, attorney) pending the closing.

Brokerage Commission. The brokerage commission, if any, should be stated as a percent of the sale price or a fixed dollar amount. The commission is normally paid out of the settlement proceeds, at the closing.

Financing Contingencies.

- **Procurement of Mortgage.** Often a contract will contain a clause making it subject to some contingency, e.g., "Contract contingent on buyer being able to procure a mortgage loan in the amount of $________." Then, the amount of commitment, date of procurement, kind of mortgage (VA, FHA, Conventional), term of loan, and rate of interest should be stated.
- **Assumption of Mortgage.** If the buyer is taking over the seller's mortgage by assumption, the contract should state the name of the lending institution, the balance to be assumed, and the terms and conditions of assumption.
- **Taking Subject to Existing Mortgage.** If the real estate is subject to an existing mortgage, the buyer may agree to buy the property subject to such existing mortgages. If, however, the contract is silent about existing mortgages, the buyer is under no obligation to accept title subject to mortgage.

Conditions and Stipulations

- **Other Contingencies.** Contracts may also be contingent upon the buyer procuring a variance, zoning change or building permit, or on buyer's approval of the results of a structural, mechanical and electrical inspection of the house and buyer's approval of the results of a termite inspection. When a contingency clause is included in a contract, it is essential that the terms be absolutely definite. A vague or ambiguous contingency can be a grievous and costly mistake in that it will provide a "loop-hole" for the parties. The buyer may waive or dispense with any contingency clause placed for his benefit.

- **Easements and Restrictive Covenants.** Unless otherwise provided, the buyer is not required to accept a title encumbered with restrictive covenants or easements that interfere with the use and enjoyment of the premises. In such cases, the title is rendered unmarketable.

- **Existing Leases.** Because property is sold subject to the rights of tenants, the seller should be required to include a list of all leases including expiration dates, security deposits, rentals, tenants and any special agreements such as options, concessions (such as last month's rent free), rights of first refusal and so forth. Contracts generally provide that the seller agrees to convey title subject to leases existing as of the date of the contract. The seller should be cautioned against signing any leases subsequent to signing the contract, as the buyer need not accept a title subject to tenancies not mentioned in the contract.

- **Closing.** The date and place for closing should be mentioned. Many buyers and sellers believe that the date set in the contract is the exact date on which title will change hands. It should be made clear that the closing date in the contract is only a tentative date unless a "time is of the essence" provision is agreed upon. The phrase "time is of the essence" in a contract means that punctual performance by one party is essential to require counter-performance by the other party. If time is not of the essence in the contract, a reasonable lapse of time will not render the contract unenforceable. But lapse of an unreasonable time period will be fatal to enforceability.

- **Delivery of Marketable Title.** Unless otherwise provided, the seller must convey a marketable title (also called merchantable title), which is a title free of undisclosed defects such as mortgages and other liens, easements, restrictive covenants, leases, encroachments and substantial existing violations of zoning ordinances. Proof of marketability is covered in Chapter 11.

- **Kind of Deed to Be Delivered at Closing.** The type of deed to be given at closing should be specified in the contract, although the absence of such a provision will not affect the enforceability of the agreement. If the contract is silent about the type of deed, a "Bargain and Sale Deed without Covenants " must be given under New Jersey law.

KEY WORDS

Assignment	Deposit	Optionor
Binder	Duress	Parol
Breach of Contract	Earnest Money	Rescission
Closing	Equitable Owner	Specific Performance
Competent Parties	Executed Contract	Statute of Frauds
Consideration	Executory Contract	Statute of Limitations
Contract	Marketable Title	Time is of the Essence
Contractual Capacity	Meeting of the Minds	Unilateral
Counteroffer	Offer	Valid
Damages	Option	Void
Default	Optionee	Voidable

FIGURE 14.1

Sample Contract of Sale

NOTICE

TO BUYER AND SELLER

READ THIS NOTICE BEFORE SIGNING THE CONTRACT

The Law requires real estate brokers to give you the following information before you sign this contract. It requires us to tell you that you must read all of it before you sign. The purpose is to help you in this purchase or sale.

1) As a real estate broker, I represent: ☐ the seller, not the buyer; ☒ the buyer, not the seller; ☐ both the seller and the buyer; ☐ neither the seller nor the buyer. The title company does not represent either the seller or the buyer.

2) You will not get any legal advice unless you have your own lawyer. Neither I nor anyone from the title company can give legal advice to either the buyer or the seller. If you do not hire a lawyer, no one will represent you in legal matters now or at the closing. Neither I nor the title company will represent you in those matters.

3) The contract is the most important part of the transaction. It determines your rights, risks, and obligations. Signing the contract is a big step. A lawyer would review the contract, help you to understand it, and to negotiate its terms.

4) The contract becomes final and binding unless your lawyer cancels it within the following three business days. If you do not have a lawyer, you cannot change or cancel the contract unless the other party agrees. Neither can the real estate broker nor the title insurance company change the contract.

5) Another important service of a lawyer is to order a survey, title report, or other important reports. The lawyer will review them and help to resolve any questions that may arise about the ownership and condition of the property. These reports and survey can cost you a lot of money. A lawyer will also prepare the documents needed to close title and represent you at the closing.

6) A buyer without a lawyer runs special risks. Only a lawyer can advise a buyer about what to do if problems arise concerning the purchase of this property. The problems may be about the seller's title, the size and shape of the property, or other matters that may affect the value of the property. If either the broker or the title company knows about the problems, they should tell you. But they may not recognize the problem, see it from your point of view, or know what to do. Ordinarily, the broker and the title company have an interest in seeing that the sale is completed, because only then do they usually receive their commissions. So, their interests may differ from yours.

7) Whether you retain a lawyer is up to you. It is your decision. The purpose of this notice is to make sure that you have the information needed to make your decision.

Seller Rocco Balboa	Buyer Apollo Creed
Seller Adrian Balboa	Buyer Ruby Creed
Date	Date

Selling Broker Tryde and Trew Realty, Inc.

Date

NJAR Form-118-11/02 Page 1 of 6

FIGURE 14.1 (cont'd)

REALTOR®

NEW JERSEY ASSOCIATION OF REALTORS® STANDARD FORM OF REAL ESTATE CONTRACT

©1996 New Jersey Association of REALTORS®, Inc.

THIS FORM MAY BE USED ONLY IN THE SALE OF A ONE TO FOUR FAMILY RESIDENTIAL PROPERTY OR VACANT ONE FAMILY LOTS.
THIS FORM IS SUITABLE FOR USE ONLY WHERE THE SELLER HAS PREVIOUSLY EXECUTED A WRITTEN LISTING AGREEMENT.

EQUAL HOUSING OPPORTUNITY

THIS IS A LEGALLY BINDING CONTRACT THAT WILL BECOME FINAL WITHIN THREE BUSINESS DAYS. DURING THIS PERIOD YOU MAY CHOOSE TO CONSULT AN ATTORNEY WHO CAN REVIEW AND/OR CANCEL THE CONTRACT. SEE SECTION ON ATTORNEY REVIEW FOR DETAILS.

CONTRACT OF SALE

1 **1. PURCHASE AGREEMENT AND PROPERTY DESCRIPTION:**
2
3 Apollo Creed and Ruby Creed, husband and wife, **Buyer,**
4
5 Soc. Sec. # 135-22-7001 Soc. Sec. # 123-22-6412
6
7 whose address is 116 Elm Avenue, Ramsey, New Jersey 07746
8
9 **AGREES TO PURCHASE FROM**
10
11 Rocco Balboa and Adrian Balboa, husband and wife, **Seller,**
12
13 Soc. Sec. # 123-23-1235 No see. Soc. Sec. # 135-16-7890
14
15 whose address is 114 Yantacaw Brook Road, Wyckoff, New Jersey 07481
16 **THROUGH THE BROKER(S) NAMED IN THIS AGREEMENT AT THE PRICE AND TERMS STATED BELOW,**
17 **THE FOLLOWING PROPERTY:**
18 Property Address: 114 Yantacaw Brook Road, Wyckoff, New Jersey 07481
19 Shown on the municipal tax map of Wyckoff, New Jersey County Bergen
20 As Lot M Block 10 Approximate size of lot 120' X 90'
21 **THE WORDS "BUYER" AND "SELLER" INCLUDE ALL BUYERS AND SELLERS LISTED ABOVE.**
22
23 **2. PURCHASE PRICE: THE TOTAL PURCHASE PRICE IS:** $ 185,000
24
25 **3. MANNER OF PAYMENT:**
26 (A) **Deposit paid** by Buyer on signing of this Agreement to ❑ Listing Broker or ❑ Participating $ 1,000 earnest money
27 Broker, by ❑ cash or ☒ check, for which this is a receipt:
28
29 (B) **Additional deposit** to be paid by Buyer on or before April 25, 2002 (date): $ 17,500
30 **All deposit monies paid by the Buyer shall be held in escrow in the NON-INTEREST**
31 **BEARING TRUST ACCOUNT of** Tryde and Trew Realty, Inc., **Escrowee,**
32 **until closing of title, at which time all monies shall be paid over to the Seller.** The deposit monies shall
33 not be paid over to the Seller prior to the closing of title, unless agreed in writing by both the Buyer and Seller.
34 In the event the Buyer and Seller cannot agree on the disbursement of these escrow monies, the Escrowee may
35 place the deposit monies in Court requesting the Court to resolve the dispute.
36
37 (C) **IF PERFORMANCE BY BUYER IS CONTINGENT UPON OBTAINING A MORTGAGE.**
38 The Buyer agrees to apply immediately for a mortgage loan through any lending institution of the Buyer's
39 choice or the office of the Listing Broker or the Participating Broker. The application shall be furnished by the
40 Buyer in writing on an application form prescribed by the lending institution to which the application shall be
41 submitted. Buyer shall also furnish, in a timely manner, such other documents and information as is usually
42 required by said lending institution. Failure of Buyer to comply with the foregoing, in good faith, shall be
43 deemed a breach of this Contract of Sale. The amount of mortgage loan required by the Buyer is
44 $ 129,500.00 and will be what is commonly known as the
45 (F.H.A.) (V.A.) (Conventional) (A.R.M.) 25 year direct reduction plan with interest at not
46 more than 9 % and not more than 2 Points. Buyer agrees to pay not
47 more than 2 Points. Seller agrees to pay not more than ______ Points.
48 **IF THE MORTGAGE LOAN HAS NOT BEEN ARRANGED, OR IF THE BUYER HAS NOT**
49 **NOTIFIED SELLER OF BUYER'S DECISION TO COMPLETE THE TRANSACTION**
50 **WITHOUT OBTAINING A MORTGAGE COMMITMENT, ON OR BEFORE**
51 May 5 **(Date) THEN EITHER BUYER OR SELLER MAY VOID**
52 **THIS AGREEMENT BY WRITTEN NOTICE TO THE OTHER PARTY.** The method of notifying
53 the other party shall be in accordance with Section 21 of the Agreement. $ 129,500. 00
54
55 (D) **BALANCE OF PURCHASE PRICE.** The balance of the purchase price shall be paid by cash,
56 certified check or Attorney's Trust Account check on delivery of a Bargain and Sale W/C/A/G (Type
57 of Deed). Title to the Property will be free from all claims or rights of others, except as described in Sections
58 6, 7 and 8 of this Agreement. The deed shall contain the full legal description of the Property. Payment of the
59 balance of the purchase price by Buyer and delivery of the deed and affidavit of title by Seller occur at the
60 "Closing." The Closing will take place on or before May 15, 2002, at the office of
61 New Jersey Good Realty, Inc. or such other place as the Seller and the Buyer may agree. $ 37,000.00
62
63 **TOTAL PURCHASE PRICE:** $ 185,000.00
64
65 **4. BUYER FINANCIALLY ABLE TO CLOSE:**
66 Buyer represents that Buyer has sufficient cash available (together with the mortgage referred to in Section 3) to complete
67 this purchase.

NJAR Form-118-11/02 Page 2 of 6

Buyer's Initials: ________ **Seller's Initials:** ________

FIGURE 14.1 (cont'd)

68 **5. ACCURATE DISCLOSURE OF SELLING PRICE:**
69 The Buyer and Seller certify that this Contract accurately reflects the gross sale price as indicated on line sixty-three (63) of this
70 Contract. The Buyer and Seller **UNDERSTAND AND AGREE** that **THIS INFORMATION SHALL BE DISCLOSED** to the
71 Internal Revenue Service as required by law.
72
73 **6. TENANTS, IF ANY:**
74 This sale is made subject to the following tenancies. The Seller warrants that these tenancies are not in violation of existing
75 Municipal, County, State or Federal rules, regulations or laws.
76 **NAME LOCATION RENT SECURITY DEPOSIT TERM**
77
78
79
80 **7. QUALITY OF TITLE:**
81 This sale will be subject to easements and restrictions of record, if any, and such state of facts as an accurate survey might disclose.
82 Generally, an easement is a right of a person other than the owner of Property to use a portion of the Property for a special purpose. A
83 restriction is a recorded limitation on the manner in which a Property owner may use his/her/their Property. The Buyer does not have
84 to complete the purchase, however, if any easement, restriction, or facts disclosed by an accurate survey would substantially interfere
85 with the use of the Property for residential purposes. The sale will also be made subject to applicable zoning ordinances.
86 Title to the Property shall be good, marketable and insurable, at regular rates, by any title insurance company licensed to
87 do business in the State of New Jersey, subject only to the claims and rights described in this section and Section 6. Buyer agrees
88 to order title insurance commitment (title search) and survey if necessary and to furnish copies to Seller. In the event Seller's
89 title shall contain any exceptions other than as set forth in this paragraph, Buyer shall notify Seller and Seller shall have 30 days
90 within which to eliminate those exceptions. If Seller cannot remove those exceptions, Buyer shall have the option to void this
91 Contract or to proceed with closing of title without any reduction in the purchase price. If Buyer elects to void this Contract, as
92 provided in the preceding sentence, the deposit money shall be returned to Buyer and Seller shall reimburse Buyer for search and
93 survey expenses not exceeding ___1,000.00___ dollars.
94
95 **8. BUILDING AND ZONING LAWS:**
96 The Buyer intends to use the Property as a ___single___ family home. The Seller states, to the best of the
97 Seller's knowledge, that this use does not violate any applicable zoning ordinance, building code or other law. The Seller will pay for
98 and obtain Certificate of Occupancy, Certificate of Land Use Compliance or other similar document required by law and will arrange
99 and pay for all inspections required to obtain such document. **SELLER AGREES TO CORRECT ALL VIOLATIONS, AT**
100 **THE SELLER'S OWN EXPENSE, PRIOR TO THE CLOSING OF TITLE.**
101
102 **9. ITEMS INCLUDED IN SALE:**
103 Gas and electric fixtures, cooking ranges and ovens, hot water heaters, linoleum, T.V. antenna, screens, storm sash, shades, blinds,
104 awnings, radiator covers, heating apparatus and sump pump, if any, except where owned by tenants, are included in this sale. All of
105 the appliances shall be in working order as of the closing of title. **This provision shall not survive closing of title.** This means
106 that the Seller **DOES NOT GUARANTEE** the condition of the appliances **AFTER** the deed and affidavit of title have been
107 delivered to the Buyer at the "Closing". **The following items are also specifically included:**
108
109
110
111 **10. ITEMS EXCLUDED FROM SALE:**
112
113 Wall to wall carpeting, chandeliers in dining room and entrance foyer.
114
115 **11. ASSESSMENTS:**
116 All confirmed assessments and all unconfirmed assessments which may be imposed by the municipality for public improvements
117 which have been completed as of the date of Closing are to be paid in full by the Seller or credited to the Buyer at the Closing. A
118 confirmed assessment is a lien (legal claim) against the Property. An unconfirmed assessment is a potential lien (legal claim) which,
119 when approved by the appropriate governmental body, will become a legal claim against the Property.
120
121 **12. FINAL INSPECTION:**
122 Seller agrees to permit the Buyer or the Buyer's duly authorized representative to examine the interior and exterior of the Property
123 at any reasonable time immediately before Closing.
124
125 **13. NEW JERSEY HOTEL AND MULTIPLE DWELLING HEALTH AND SAFETY ACT:**
126 If the New Jersey Hotel and Multiple Dwelling Health and Safety Act applies to the Property, the Seller represents that the
127 Property complies with the requirements of the Act.
128
129 **14. NO ASSIGNMENT:**
130 This Agreement shall not be assigned without the written consent of the Seller. This means that the Buyer may not transfer to
131 anyone else his/her/their rights under this Agreement to buy the Property.
132
133 **15. RISK OF LOSS:**
134 The risk of loss or damage to the Property by fire or otherwise, except ordinary wear and tear, is on the Seller until the Closing.
135
136 **16. ADJUSTMENTS AT CLOSING; RIGHTS TO POSSESSION:**
137 Rents, water charges, sewer charges, real estate taxes, interest on any existing mortgage to be assumed by Buyer, and fuel are to
138 be apportioned as of the date of actual closing of title. The Buyer shall be entitled to possession of the Property and any rents or
139 profits from the Property, immediately upon the delivery of the deed and closing of title. The Seller shall have the privilege of paying
140 off any person with a claim or right affecting the Property from the proceeds of this sale at the time of Closing.
141
142 **17. MAINTENANCE AND CONDITION OF PROPERTY:**
143 The Seller agrees to maintain the grounds, buildings and improvements, in good condition, subject to ordinary wear and tear. The
144 premises shall be in "broom clean" condition and free of debris on the date of Closing. Seller represents that all electrical, plumbing,
145 heating and air conditioning systems (if applicable), together with all fixtures included within the terms of the Agreement now work

NJAR Form-118-11/02 Page 3 of 6 **Buyer's Initials:** ______ **Seller's Initials:** ______

FIGURE 14.1 (cont'd)

and shall be in proper working order at the time of Closing. Seller further states, that to the best of Seller's knowledge, there are currently no leaks or seepage in the roof, walls or basement **UNLESS OTHERWISE INDICATED IN THE ADDITIONAL CONTRACTUAL PROVISIONS SECTION (Section 33) OF THIS AGREEMENT. ALL REPRESENTATIONS AND/OR STATEMENTS MADE BY THE SELLER, IN THIS SECTION, SHALL NOT SURVIVE CLOSING OF TITLE.** This means that the Seller **DOES NOT GUARANTEE** the condition of the premises **AFTER** the deed and affidavit of title have been delivered to the Buyer at the "Closing".

18. LEAD-BASED PAINT DOCUMENT ACKNOWLEDGMENT: (Applies to dwellings built before 1978)

Buyer acknowledges receipt of the EPA pamphlet entitled "Protect Your Family From Lead In Your Home." Moreover, a copy of a document entitled "Disclosure of Information and Acknowledgment Lead-Based Paint and Lead-Based Paint Hazards" has been fully completed and signed by Buyer, Seller and Broker(s) and is appended to this Agreement as Addendum "A" and is part of this Agreement.

19. LEAD-BASED PAINT AND/OR LEAD-BASED PAINT HAZARD CONTINGENCY CLAUSE:

(This paragraph is applicable to all dwellings built prior to 1978. The law requires that unless the Buyer and Seller agree to a longer or shorter period, Seller must allow Buyer a ten-day (10) period within which to complete an inspection and/or risk assessment of the Property. Buyer, however, has the right to waive this clause in its entirety.)

This Agreement is contingent upon an inspection and/or risk assessment (the "Inspection") of the Property by a certified inspector/risk assessor for the presence of lead-based paint and/or lead-based paint hazards. The Inspection shall be ordered and obtained by the Buyer at the Buyer's expense, within ten (10) calendar days after the termination of the Attorney Review period set forth in Section 24 of this Agreement (the "Completion Date"). If the Inspection indicates that no lead-based paint or lead-based paint hazard is present at the Property, this contingency clause shall be deemed to be null and void. If the Inspection indicates that lead-based paint or lead-based paint hazard is present at the Property, this contingency clause will terminate at the time set forth above unless within (5) days from the Completion Date, the Buyer delivers a copy of the inspection and/or risk assessment report to the Seller and Broker(s) and (a) advises Seller and Broker(s) , in writing, that Buyer is voiding this Agreement; or (b) delivers to Seller and Broker(s) a written amendment (the "Amendment") to this Agreement listing the specific existing deficiencies and corrections required by the Buyer. The Amendment shall provide that the Seller agrees to (a) correct the deficiencies; and (b) furnish the Buyer with a certification from a certified inspector/risk assessor that the deficiencies have been corrected, before the date of Closing. The Seller shall have __10__ days after receipt of the Amendment to sign and return it to Buyer or send a written counter-proposal to Buyer. If Seller does not sign and return the Amendment or fails to offer a counter-proposal, this Agreement shall be null and void. In the event Seller offers a counter-proposal, Buyer shall have __10__ days after receipt of the counter-proposal to accept it. If the Buyer fails to accept the counter-proposal within the time limit provided, this Agreement shall be null and void.

20. INSPECTION CONTINGENCY CLAUSE:

(a) **Responsibilities of Home Ownership**

The Buyer and Seller acknowledge and agree that because the purchase of a home is one of the most significant investments a person can make in a lifetime, all aspects of this transaction require considerable analysis and investigation by Buyer before closing title to the Property. While the Broker(s) and Salesperson(s) who are involved in this transaction are trained as licensees under the License Law of the State of New Jersey, they readily acknowledge that they have had no special training or experience with respect to the complexities pertaining to the multitude of structural, topographical and environmental components of this Property. For example, and not by way of limitation, the Broker(s) and Salesperson(s) have no special training, knowledge or experience with regard to discovering and/or evaluating physical defects including structural defects, roof, basement, mechanical equipment such as heating, air conditioning, electrical systems, sewage, plumbing, exterior drainage, termite and other types of insect infestation or damage caused by such infestation. Moreover, the Broker(s) and Salesperson(s) similarly have no special training, knowledge or experience with regard to evaluation of possible environmental conditions which might affect the Property pertaining to the dwelling such as the existence of radon gas, formaldehyde gas, airborne asbestos fibers, toxic chemicals, underground storage tanks, lead, mold or other pollutants in the soil, air or water.

(b) **Radon Testing and Reports**

If the Property has been tested for radon, Seller agrees to provide the Buyer, at the time this Agreement is entered into, with a copy of the results of the radon test and evidence of any subsequent radon mitigation or treatment of the Property. Buyer shall have the right to conduct a radon inspection/test as provided in paragraph (c) below.

(c) **Buyer's Rights To Inspections**

The Buyer acknowledges that the Property is being sold in an "**AS IS**" condition and that this Agreement is entered into based upon the knowledge of the Buyer as to the value of the land and whatever buildings are upon the Property, and not on any representation made by the Seller, the named Broker(s) or their agents as to character or quality. Therefore, the Buyer, at the Buyer's sole cost and expense, is granted the right to have the dwelling and all other aspects of the Property, inspected and evaluated by "qualified inspectors" (as the term is defined in paragraph (f) below) for the purpose of determining the existence of any physical defects or environmental conditions such as outlined above. If Buyer chooses to make the inspections referred to in this paragraph, such inspections must be completed, and written reports must be furnished to the Seller listed in Section 1 and Broker(s) listed in Section 26 of this Agreement within __14__ calendar days after the end of the Attorney Review Period set forth in Section 24 of this Agreement. If Buyer shall fail to furnish such written reports to the Seller and Broker(s) within the time period specified in this paragraph, this contingency clause shall be deemed waived by Buyer, and the Property shall be deemed acceptable by Buyer. The time period for furnishing the inspection reports is referred to as the "Inspection Time Period."

(d) **Responsibilities to Cure**

If any physical defects, or environmental conditions are reported by the inspectors to the Seller within the Inspection Time Period, the Seller shall then have seven (7) calendar days after the receipt of such reports to notify the Buyer in writing that the Seller shall correct or cure any of the defects set forth in such reports. If Seller shall fail to notify Buyer of Seller's agreement to so cure and correct, such failure to so notify shall be deemed to be a refusal by Seller to cure or correct such defects. If Seller shall fail to agree to cure or correct such defects within said seven (7) day period, or if any part of the dwelling is found to be located within a flood hazard area, or if the environmental condition at the Property is incurable and is of such significance as to unreasonably endanger the health of the Buyer, the Buyer shall then have the right to void this Contract by notifying the Seller in writing within seven (7) calender days thereafter. If Buyer shall fail to void this Contract within the seven (7) day period, the Buyer shall have waived his right to cancel this Contract and this Contract shall remain in full force, and Seller shall be under no obligation to correct or cure any of the defects set forth in the inspections. If Seller shall agree to correct or cure such defects, all such repair work shall be completed by Seller prior to the closing of title.

Buyer's Initials: ________ Seller's Initials: ________

NJAR Form-118-11/02 Page 4 of 6

FIGURE 14.1 (cont'd)

(e) **Flood Hazard Area (delete if not applicable)**

Buyer acknowledges that the Property is within a flood hazard area, and Buyer waives Buyer's right to void this Agreement for such reason.

(f) **Qualifications of Inspectors**

Where the term "qualified inspectors" is used in this Contract, it is intended to refer to persons who are licensed by the State of New Jersey for such purpose or who are regularly engaged in the business of inspecting residential properties for a fee and who generally maintain good reputations for skill and integrity in their area of expertise.

21. NOTICES:

All notices as required in this Contract must be in writing. All notices shall be by certified mail, by telegram, telefax or by delivering it personally. The telegram, certified letter or telefax will be effective upon sending. The personal delivery will be effective upon delivery to the other party. Notices to the Seller shall be addressed to the address that appears on line fifteen (15) of this Contract. Notice to the Buyer shall be addressed to the address that appears on line seven (7) of this Contract.

22. MEGAN'S LAW STATEMENT:

UNDER NEW JERSEY LAW, THE COUNTY PROSECUTOR DETERMINES WHETHER AND HOW TO PROVIDE NOTICE OF THE PRESENCE OF CONVICTED SEX OFFENDERS IN AN AREA. IN THEIR PROFESSIONAL CAPACITY, REAL ESTATE LICENSEES ARE NOT ENTITLED TO NOTIFICATION BY THE COUNTY PROSECUTOR UNDER MEGAN'S LAW AND ARE UNABLE TO OBTAIN SUCH INFORMATION FOR YOU. UPON CLOSING, THE COUNTY PROSECUTOR MAY BE CONTACTED FOR SUCH FURTHER INFORMATION AS MAY BE DISCLOSABLE TO YOU.

23. NOTICE ON OFF-SITE CONDITIONS: (Applicable to all resale transactions)

PURSUANT TO THE NEW RESIDENTIAL CONSTRUCTION OFF-SITE CONDITIONS DISCLOSURE ACT, P.L. 1995, C. 253, THE CLERKS OF MUNICIPALITIES IN NEW JERSEY MAINTAIN LISTS OF OFF-SITE CONDITIONS WHICH MAY AFFECT THE VALUE OF RESIDENTIAL PROPERTIES IN THE VICINITY OF THE OFF-SITE CONDITION. PURCHASERS MAY EXAMINE THE LISTS AND ARE ENCOURAGED TO INDEPENDENTLY INVESTIGATE THE AREA SURROUNDING THIS PROPERTY IN ORDER TO BECOME FAMILIAR WITH ANY OFF-SITE CONDITIONS WHICH MAY AFFECT THE VALUE OF THE PROPERTY. IN CASES WHERE A PROPERTY IS LOCATED NEAR THE BORDER OF A MUNICIPALITY, PURCHASERS MAY WISH TO ALSO EXAMINE THE LIST MAINTAINED BY THE NEIGHBORING MUNICIPALITY.

24. ATTORNEY REVIEW CLAUSE:

(1) **Study by Attorney**

The Buyer or the Seller may choose to have an attorney study this Contract. If an attorney is consulted, the attorney must complete his or her review of the Contract within a three-day period. This Contract will be legally binding at the end of this three-day period unless an attorney for the Buyer or the Seller reviews and disapproves of the Contract.

(2) **Counting the Time**

You count the three days from the date of delivery of the signed Contract to the Buyer and Seller. You do not count Saturdays, Sundays or legal holidays. The Buyer and the Seller may agree in writing to extend the three-day period for attorney review.

(3) **Notice of Disapproval**

If an attorney for the Buyer or the Seller reviews and disapproves of this Contract, the attorney must notify the REALTOR®(S) and the other party named in this Contract within the three-day period. Otherwise this Contract will be legally binding as written. The attorney must send the notice of disapproval to the REALTOR®(S) by certified mail, by telegram, or by delivering it personally. The telegram or certified letter will be effective upon sending. The personal delivery will be effective upon delivery to the REALTOR®(S) office. The attorney may also, but need not, inform the REALTOR®(S) of any suggested revision(s) in the Contract that would make it satisfactory.

25. ENTIRE AGREEMENT; PARTIES LIABLE:

This Agreement contains the entire agreement of the parties. No representations have been made by any of the parties, the Broker(s) or his/her/their agents except as set forth in this Agreement. This Agreement is binding upon all parties who sign it and all who succeed to their rights and responsibilities.

26. BROKER'S COMMISSION:

The commission, in accord with the previously executed listing agreement, shall be due and payable at the time of actual closing of title and payment by Buyer of the purchase consideration for the Property. The Seller hereby authorizes and instructs the Buyer's attorney, or the Buyer's title insurance company or whomever is the disbursing agent to pay the full commission as set forth below to the below mentioned Broker/Brokers out of the proceeds of sale prior to the payment of any such funds to the Seller. Buyer consents to the disbursing agent making the said disbursements.

New Jersey Good Realty, Inc. ______ **COMMISSION IN ACCORD WITH PREVIOUSLY EXECUTED LISTING AGREEMENT, LESS PARTICIPATING BROKER'S COMMISSION (IF ANY)**

Listing Broker

735 Elm Avenue, Wyckoff, New Jersey ______

Address and Telephone #

Tryde and Trew Realty, Inc. ______ 3% - $100 ______

Participating Broker ______ Commission

______

Address and Telephone #

27. FAILURE OF BUYER OR SELLER TO SETTLE:

In the event the Seller willfully fails to close title to the Property in accordance with this Contract, the Buyer may commence any legal or equitable action to which the Buyer may be entitled. In the event the Buyer fails to close title in accordance with this Contract, the deposit monies paid on account, at the Seller's option, shall be paid over to the Seller as liquidated damages. In the alternative, the Seller may commence an action for damages it has suffered, and, in such case, the deposit monies paid on account of the purchase

NJAR Form-118-11/02 Page 5 of 6

Buyer's Initials: ______ **Seller's Initials:** ______

FIGURE 14.1 (cont'd)

price shall be applied against such damages. Liquidated damages means the Seller will keep the money paid on account and not commence any legal action for the Buyer's failure to close title. In the event the Seller breaches this Contract, Seller will, nevertheless, be liable to the Broker for commissions as otherwise set forth in this Contract.

28. CONSUMER INFORMATION STATEMENT ACKNOWLEDGMENT:

By signing below the sellers and purchasers acknowledge they received the Consumer Information Statement on New Jersey Real Estate Relationships from the brokerage firms involved in this transaction prior to the first showing of the property.

29. DECLARATION OF LICENSEE BUSINESS RELATIONSHIP(S):

(a) New Jersey Good Realty, Inc.________________, **(name of firm) AND**

Charles Wilbert________________ **(name(s) of licensee(s)), AS ITS AUTHORIZED REPRESENTATIVE(S), ARE WORKING IN THIS TRANSACTION AS (choose one)** ☒ **SELLER'S AGENTS** ☐ **BUYER'S AGENTS** ☐ **DISCLOSED DUAL AGENTS** ☐ **TRANSACTION BROKERS.**

(b) **INFORMATION SUPPLIED BY** Tryde and Trew Realty, Inc.________ **(name of other firm) HAS INDICATED THAT IT IS OPERATING IN THIS TRANSACTION AS A (choose one)** ☐ **SELLER'S AGENT** ☒ **BUYER'S AGENT** ☐ **DISCLOSED DUAL AGENT** ☐ **TRANSACTION BROKER.**

30. NEW CONSTRUCTION RIDER:

If the property being sold consists of a lot and a detached single family home (the "House") to be constructed upon the lot by the Seller, the "Rider To Contract of Sale of Real Estate – New Construction" has been signed by Buyer and Seller and is appended to and made a part of this Agreement.

31. PRIVATE WELL TESTING:

(This section is applicable if the property's potable water supply is provided by a private well located on the property (or the potable water supply is a well that has less than 15 service connections or does not regularly serve an average of at least 25 individuals daily at least 60 days a year).)

Pursuant to the Private Well Testing Act (N.J.S.A. 58:12A-26 to 37) and regulations (N.J.A.C. 7:9E – 3.1 to 5.1), if this Contract is for the sale of real property whose potable water supply is provided from a private well and the analytical results of prior water tests no longer are valid, a test on the water supply must be performed by a laboratory certified by NJDEP. Seller agrees to procure the test, at Seller's sole cost and expense and to provide a copy of the test results to Buyer within seven (7) calendar days after receiving the report(s). Seller shall order the new test or, if applicable, provide Buyer with the valid prior water test within seven (7) calendar days after the end of the Attorney Review Period set forth in Section 24 of this Agreement. The test shall cover the parameters set forth in the Act and regulations. As required in the Act, prior to closing of title, Seller and Buyer shall each certify in writing that they have received and read a copy of the water test results.

If any of the water tests do not meet applicable standards at the time Seller provides the water test results to the Buyer, Seller shall notify Buyer, in writing, that Seller agrees to cure or correct said conditions in the water test results. If Seller shall fail to notify Buyer of Seller's agreement to cure or correct, such failure to so notify shall be deemed to be a refusal by Seller to cure or correct. If Seller shall fail to agree to cure or correct any of the conditions set forth in the water test results within seven (7) calendar days or if the condition is incurable and is of such significance as to unreasonably endanger the health of the Buyer, the Buyer shall then have the right to void this Contract by notifying the Seller in writing within seven (7) calendar days thereafter. If Buyer shall fail to void this Contract within the seven (7) day period, the Buyer shall have waived his right to cancel this Contract and this Contract shall remain in full force, and the Seller shall be under no obligation to correct or cure any of the conditions set forth in the water test results. If Seller shall agree to correct or cure such conditions, all such remediation shall be completed by Seller prior to the closing of title.

32. MEGAN'S LAW REGISTRY:

Buyer is notified that New Jersey law establishes an Internet Registry of Sex Offenders that may be accessed at www.njsp.org.

33. ADDITIONAL CONTRACTUAL PROVISIONS (if any):

34. INDEX:

IN THE PRESENCE OF:

________________	4/15/02 Date	________________ BUYER	(L.S.)
________________	4/15/02 Date	________________ BUYER	(L.S.)
________________	4/15/02 Date	________________ SELLER	(L.S.)
________________	4/15/02 Date	________________ SELLER	(L.S.)

NJAR Form-118-11/02 Page 6 of 6

Buyer's Initials: ________ **Seller's Initials:** ________

FIGURE 14.1 (cont'd)

ADDENDUM A

DISCLOSURE OF INFORMATION AND ACKNOWLEDGMENT ABOUT LEAD-BASED PAINT AND/OR LEAD-BASED PAINT HAZARDS

I. LEAD PAINT WARNING

Every purchaser of any interest in residential real property on which a residential dwelling was built prior to 1978 is notified that such property may present exposure to lead from lead-based paint that may place young children at risk of developing lead poisoning. Lead poisoning in young children may produce permanent neurological damage, including learning disabilities, reduced intelligence quotient, behavioral problems, and impaired memory. Lead poisoning also poses a particular risk to pregnant women. The seller of any interest in residential real property is required to provide the buyer with any information on lead-based paint hazards from risk assessments or inspections in the seller's possession and notify the buyer of any known lead-based paint hazards. A risk assessment or inspection for possible lead-based paint hazards is recommended prior to purchase.

II. PROPERTY ADDRESS: ____

____

III. SELLER'S DISCLOSURE (initial) (**To be completed and signed at time of listing**)

_______ (a) Presence of lead-based paint and/or lead-based paint hazards (check one below):

❑ Known lead-based paint and/or lead-based paint hazards are present in the housing (explain):

____

____

❑ Seller has no knowledge of lead-based paint and/or lead-based paint hazards in the housing.

_______ (b) Records and Reports available to the seller (check one below):

❑ Seller has no reports or records pertaining to lead-based paint and/or lead-based hazards in the housing.

❑ Seller has the following reports or records pertaining to lead-based paint and/or lead-based paint hazards in the housing, all of which seller has provided to its listing agent, and has directed its listing agent to provide purchaser or purchaser's agent with these records and reports **prior to seller accepting any offer to purchase** (list documents below):

____

____

_______ (c) **If there is any change in the above information prior to seller accepting an offer from the purchaser to purchase, seller will disclose all changes to the purchaser prior to accepting the offer.**

IV. SELLER'S CERTIFICATION OF ACCURACY

Seller(s) have reviewed the Seller's Disclosure in Section III and certify, to the best of his/her/their knowledge, that the information they have provided is true and accurate.

Seller ____________________ Date / / Seller ____________________ Date / /

V. LISTING AGENT'S CERTIFICATION OF ACCURACY

Listing Agent certifies that he/she has informed the seller of the seller's obligations under 42 U.S.C. 4852d and is aware of his/her responsibility to ensure compliance.

Listing Agent ______________________________________ Date / /

VI. PURCHASER'S ACKNOWLEDGMENT (initial) (**The Seller's Disclosure in Section III and Certification in Section IV and the Listing Agent's Certification in Section V to be completed and signed prior to purchaser signing this Addendum A.**)

_______ (a) Purchaser has received copies of all information listed in Section III above.

_______ (b) Purchaser has received the pamphlet Protect Your Family From Lead in Your Home.

_______ (c) Purchaser has (check one below):

❑ Received a 10-day opportunity (or mutually agreed upon period) to conduct a risk assessment or inspection for the presence of lead-based paint and/or lead-based paint hazards; or

❑ Waived the opportunity to conduct a risk assessment or inspection for the presence of lead-based paint and/or lead-based paint hazards.

VII. PURCHASER'S CERTIFICATION OF ACCURACY

Purchaser(s) have reviewed the Purchaser's Acknowledgment in Section VI and certify, to the best of his/her/their knowledge, that the information they have provided is true and accurate.

Purchaser ____________________ Date / / Purchaser ____________________ Date / /

VIII. SELLING/BUYER'S AGENT'S CERTIFICATION OF ACCURACY

Selling/Buyer's Agent certifies that the purchaser has received the information in section VI (a) and (b).

Selling/Buyer's Agent ______________________________________ Date / /

NJAR Addendum A-6/01

NOTES

CHAPTER 14
Review Questions
(Answers on page 555)

1. An offer may be terminated by:
   (A) lapse of agreed period of time.
   (B) acceptance of offer.
   (C) counteroffer.
   (D) All of the above.

2. An option is:
   (A) a unilateral contract.
   (B) binding only on one party.
   (C) accepted by performance.
   (D) All of the above.

3. A real estate licensee may legally prepare which of the following contracts?
   (A) A contract for the sale of a three-family house with no attorney review wording.
   (B) A contract for the sale of a vacant one-family lot with no attorney review wording.
   (C) A month-to-month apartment lease with no attorney review wording.
   (D) A six-month lease for a candy store.

4. Which of the following is an essential element of any contract?
   (A) Written instrument.
   (B) Words of conveyance.
   (C) Consideration.
   (D) Acknowledgment.

5. All of the following are true concerning an option contract EXCEPT:
   (A) the optionee can enforce the sale.
   (B) the option money is usually forfeited if the purchase is not completed.
   (C) the optionee must sign the contract.
   (D) the optionor cannot require specific performance.

6. Which of the following is NOT a necessary element in the formation of a contract?
   (A) Offer.
   (B) Consideration.
   (C) Acceptance.
   (D) Performance.

7. Generally, a contract between a competent adult and a minor is:
   (A) voidable at the option of the minor.
   (B) voidable at the option of the adult.
   (C) voidable at the option of either party.
   (D) enforceable.

8. Which of the following parties are NOT competent to enter into a contract?
   (A) Minors.
   (B) Mental defectives.
   (C) Drunks.
   (D) All of the above.

9. The withdrawal of an offer before acceptance is called:
   (A) rescission.
   (B) revocation.
   (C) reversion.
   (D) rejection.

10. A contract made for an illegal purpose is:
    (A) valid.
    (B) void.
    (C) unilateral.
    (D) voidable.

11. The Latin phrase *"et vir"* means:
    (A) and others.
    (B) and wife.
    (C) and husband.
    (D) and alternatives.

12. Earnest money may be held in escrow by all BUT ONE of the following:
    (A) A real estate broker.
    (B) An attorney.
    (C) An escrow agent.
    (D) A real estate salesperson.

13. Which of the following is NOT an essential element of a contract?
    (A) Consideration.
    (B) Offer and acceptance.
    (C) Competent parties.
    (D) Earnest money deposit.

14. The transfer of rights under a contract without the release from obligation by the assignor is known as:
    (A) novation.
    (B) supercedence.
    (C) assignment.
    (D) succession.

15. Failure to perform or fulfill a contract is termed a:
    (A) defect.
    (B) fault.
    (C) breach.
    (D) delinquency.

16. All BUT ONE of the following result in a termination of an offer to purchase real property:
    (A) Marriage of buyer.
    (B) Death of buyer.
    (C) Destruction of property.
    (D) Revocation of offer.

17. A person who secured the right to purchase a property at a fixed price for a designated period of time and has paid a consideration for this privilege would own:
    (A) a lease.
    (B) an agreement to buy.
    (C) an assignment of interest.
    (D) an option.

18. X gives Y a check for $4,000 at the time X signs a contract to purchase Y's real property. The terms of the purchase are $95,000 sales price paid as follows: $30,000 in cash from X and $65,000 by way of a first mortgage for 30 years at 10% interest. Which of the following terms best describes the $30,000?
    (A) Down payment.
    (B) Hand money.
    (C) Earnest money deposit.
    (D) Binder.

19. One of the following is NOT a method by which a contract can be discharged:
    (A) Divorce of either party.
    (B) Operation of law.
    (C) Agreement.
    (D) Performance or breach.

20. When there is a "meeting of the minds" which of the following has (have) been accomplished?
    (A) Offer and acceptance.
    (B) All elements of the contract have been satisfied.
    (C) Settlement has been held.
    (D) Acknowledgment and delivery.

21. An optionee, by reason of the option contract:
    (A) has the right to collect rents during the option period.
    (B) can legally enforce the exercise of the option if the optionor changes his mind about selling.
    (C) can occupy the property during the option period.
    (D) cannot legally enforce the exercise of the option if the optionor objects.

22. A rescission of a contract is:
    (A) a ratification.
    (B) a return to the status quo.
    (C) an amendment to the terms of a contract.
    (D) an escrow arrangement.

23. A seller agreed to sell a tract of land to a buyer and the usual contract was signed by both parties. Before the transaction was completed, the seller learned that a sports complex would greatly increase the value of the property. The seller told the broker to return the buyer's deposit since he would not honor the contract. The buyer refused to accept the return of the deposit and is contemplating legal action. Of the following, the buyer's least desirable course of action would seem to be:
    (A) action for compensatory damages.
    (B) unilateral rescission.
    (C) action for specific performance.
    (D) accept a settlement.

24. In an option contract:
    (A) the buyer is bound to buy.
    (B) the seller is bound to sell.
    (C) a consideration is unnecessary.
    (D) the optionee must sign.

25. A remedy in court which could compel a party to a valid contract to sign a deed is:
    (A) specific performance.
    (B) foreclosure.
    (C) execution.
    (D) equity of redemption.

26. A portion of a printed form contract is changed by typing in contrary provisions and initialing by all parties. Which takes precedence?
    (A) The printed portion of the contract
    (B) The contract is void because of the changes.
    (C) The typewritten portion of the form.
    (D) The parties may void the contract because of the changes.

27. A contract for the sale of real estate is:
    (A) an executed agreement.
    (B) an expected agreement.
    (C) an executory agreement.
    (D) an aleatory agreement.

(Quiz continues on next page)

28. From the following list, check the statute or act which creates the need for a deed to be in writing:
    (A) The Statute of Descent.
    (B) The Recording Act.
    (C) The Statute of Frauds.
    (D) The Statute of Proof of Execution.

29. In connection with the sale of real estate, a rider is a(n):
    (A) amendment.
    (B) people.
    (C) lien.
    (D) contract.

30. Which of the following is NOT a remedy available to the parties when a contract is breached?
    (A) Unilateral rescission.
    (B) Court action for specific performance.
    (C) Sue for money damages and reimbursement of expenses.
    (D) File a criminal complaint.

31. When a contract of sale fails to mention the existence of a mortgage on a piece of real estate, but there is such a mortgage:
    (A) Seller can compel the buyer to complete the transaction if the seller allows a deduction from the sale price equal to the amount due on the mortgage.
    (B) The signing of the contract of sale automatically makes the mortgage void.
    (C) The buyer has the right to demand a title free and clear of mortgage.
    (D) Buyer must take title subject to the mortgage.

32. Prospective purchasers of property, as evidence of good faith, frequently make a deposit called:
    (A) consideration.
    (B) earnest money.
    (C) collateral security.
    (D) a deferred purchase money trust.

33. A contract which would permit an investor to purchase or not to purchase a property, as he saw fit, for a stated sum within a limited period of time is called:
    (A) an assignment.
    (B) an option.
    (C) a deposit receipt.
    (D) an agreement of sale.

34. In an option, the optionee is the:
    (A) legal owner of record.
    (B) prospective purchaser.
    (C) assignor.
    (D) assignee.

35. When a buyer and seller enter into a definite purchase agreement except that no closing date is specified, the contract is:
    (A) void for vagueness.
    (B) voidable.
    (C) enforceable.
    (D) not acceptable.

36. If, after the signing of the contract for sale of land and before the closing, the seller dies, then:
    (A) the contract is voidable at the option of the seller's representative.
    (B) the contract is voidable at the option of the buyer.
    (C) the contract is terminated by operation of law.
    (D) the death of the seller normally does not terminate the contract.

37. A contract, the terms of which have not been fully performed, is known as:
    (A) an executed contract.
    (B) an executory contract.
    (C) a unilateral contract.
    (D) a bilateral contract.

38. Which of the following is NOT true?
    (A) Once an agreement of sale is signed, there is no way to avoid completing the transaction.
    (B) A sales contract must include a legal description of the property being sold.
    (C) A sales contract should include a closing date.
    (D) A lawful purpose is an essential element of a contract.

39. Under the Statute of Frauds, certain contracts for the sale of real estate must be in writing. The principal reason for this statute is to:
    (A) prevent the buyer from defrauding the seller.
    (B) prevent the fraudulent proof of a fictitious oral contract.
    (C) protect the buyer from the broker.
    (D) protect the general public from fraud due to unrecorded deeds.

40. Which of the following is an essential element of any contract?
    (A) written instrument.
    (B) consideration.
    (C) deposit.
    (D) date.

41. Reality of consent may be lacking in a contract due to:
    (A) duress.
    (B) misrepresentation.
    (C) mistake.
    (D) All of the above.

42. Acceptance is accomplished when:
    (A) salesperson signs sale contract.
    (B) offeree signs sale contract.
    (C) offeror signs sale contract.
    (D) broker signs sale contract.

43. The phrase "time is of the essence" means:
    (A) the lawyer is in a hurry for his client to take possession.
    (B) the closing must be held in a hurry.
    (C) things required to be accomplished on dates set forth in the agreement must be done on or before those dates.
    (D) time is unimportant.

44. A clause in the contract or a mortgage which requires punctual performance is described as:
    (A) specific performance clause.
    (B) time is of the essence.
    (C) performance clause.
    (D) subrogation.

45. Assume that a contract to purchase for all cash is signed by the unmarried seller and by Mrs. Smith only as buyer. The method of ownership will be tenancy by the entirety. The contract is:
    (A) enforceable.
    (B) void.
    (C) voidable.
    (D) unenforceable.

46. If the buyer withdraws the offer before it has been accepted, the deposit money goes:
    (A) one-half to broker and one-half to buyer.
    (B) to the buyer.
    (C) to the seller.
    (D) to the broker.

47. John has signed a contract to purchase Vera's house but the closing will not take place for 90 days. During the 90-day period, John has:
    (A) legal title.
    (B) an encumbrance.
    (C) no legal interest in the property.
    (D) equitable title.

48. After securing an option to purchase Binky's property, Terry sells the option to Ed. Ed is:
    (A) an assignor
    (B) a donee.
    (C) a vendor.
    (D) an assignee.

49. A contract of sale cannot exist unless there has been an offer and:
    (A) an assignment.
    (B) an assessment.
    (C) an exception.
    (D) an acceptance.

50. A buyer withdraws a written offer before the seller has signed. The broker:
    (A) splits earnest money with seller
    (B) gets nothing.
    (C) is entitled to her commission.
    (D) can sue the buyer for damages.

51. The law which bars legal claims after certain time periods is known as the:
    (A) Statute of Frauds.
    (B) Statute of Limitations.
    (C) Administrative Procedures Act.
    (D) Real Estatc Law.

52. Fire damages a home after the contract of sale is signed by both parties but prior to closing:
    (A) The party in possession generally bears the risk of loss, according to the terms of the contract
    (B) The seller generally bears the risk of loss, according to the terms of the contract.
    (C) The buyer generally bears the risk of loss, according to the terms of the contract.
    (D) The contract is voidable by the seller.

53. Amos and Bernie have entered into a contract for the sale of Amos's house. Therefore:
    (A) Bernie now has legal title.
    (B) Bernie now has equitable title.
    (C) Bernie has no interest until the closing.
    (D) Bernie has legal title, Amos equitable title.

54. Which of the following information would NOT generally be found in the purchase and sale agreement?
    (A) The closing date.
    (B) The type of financing.
    (C) A description of the property.
    (D) The name of the mortgagee.

(Quiz continues on next page)

55. A real estate seller's agent has a responsibility to inform her client about:
    (A) The terms of financing.
    (B) The form of deposit.
    (C) The customer's willingness to pay more than originally offered.
    (D) All of the above.

56. The attorney review clause:
    (A) must be included in all contracts prepared by real estate licensees (except residential leases for less than one year) and in all post-contract addenda or revisions.
    (B) must be included in all contracts prepared by real estate licensees but not in any revisions thereof.
    (C) may be waived by agreement of the parties.
    (D) cannot be extended by agreement of the parties.

CHAPTER FIFTEEN

DEEDS

A **deed** is a written instrument which transfers an interest, right or title in realty. According to our system of land ownership, title to real property can be transferred from one person to another by four general methods: (1) by descent; (2) by will; (3) by involuntary alienation; and (4) by voluntary alienation.

1. A person who dies without a will is said to have died intestate and title to property owned at death is transferred by operation of law to the decedent's heirs by the **law of descent**. New Jersey's statutes pertaining to the rights and priorities of distribution for disposing of properties of the deceased are outlined in Chapter 8.

2. A person who dies leaving a will is said to have died **testate**, and the decedent's property is transferred and distributed according to the provisions of the will.

3. Transfer of title by **involuntary alienation** is a transfer without the owner's consent. Examples include: (a) adverse possession; (b) condemnation; (c) tax sales or public sales in actions to enforce liens (foreclosures); and (d) escheat.

4. The common means of transferring title to real property from one person to another is by **voluntary alienation**. In general the conveyance of real estate is accomplished by the execution and delivery of a deed, which is a legal instrument in writing, duly executed and delivered, whereby the owner of the land (grantor) conveys to another (grantee) some right, title or interest in or to the real estate. Where the property is a leasehold, the conveyance instrument used in place of a deed is an Assignment of Lease. Voluntary alienation may occur either by gift or by sale.

The transfer of privately owned lands from an individual to the government, without consideration, followed by an acceptance of the donation by the government, is called a **dedication**. Dedication may occur when the landowner transfers the entire fee simple interest or when only certain areas are set apart for public use, such as streets in a subdivision plat.

TYPES OF DEEDS

There are four major types of deeds: (1) Full Covenant and Warranty deed; (2) Bargain and Sale (Covenant vs. Grantor) deed; (3) Bargain and Sale deed; and (4) Quitclaim deed.

1. Warranty Deed. The warranty deed, also known as a full covenant and warranty deed, is the one considered to offer the purchaser of real estate the greatest protection of any deed. The grantor in a warranty deed warrants or guarantees the title against defects existing before the grantor acquired title or arising during the grantor's period of ownership.

The warranties in a deed are commonly called covenants, and are grouped in headings as follows:

a. Covenant of Seisin. Here the grantor states that he or she actually owns and possesses the land and has the right to convey it to another.

b. Covenant Against Encumbrances. This is a guarantee that if there are any encumbrances except those specifically mentioned in the deed, then the covenant is violated and the grantee can sue the grantor. Examples of encumbrances are tax liens, easements, deed restrictions, encroachments, etc.

c. Covenant of Quiet Enjoyment. This is a promise by the grantor that the grantee can use and enjoy the property without interference of possession by someone with a superior title.

d. Covenant of Further Assurance. By this covenant the grantor promises to perform any reasonable acts necessary to make the title good. For example, if the legal description in the original deed is flawed, the grantor must correct it.

e. Covenant of Warranty Forever. Here the grantor promises to pay for defense of the grantee's title if it is challenged by a third party. Under this covenant, the grantor is also liable to the grantee for the value of the property if the grantee is evicted by a third party who had a superior title.

The full covenant and warranty deed is rarely used today, mainly because of the increasing prominence of title insurance as a substitute for the protection given to the grantee by the covenants and warranties, and the grantor's desire to limit his liability.

2. Bargain and Sale Deed with Covenants Against Grantor's Acts. A bargain and sale deed (W/C/A/G) is a deed which supports a conveyance of property, but does not carry with it all of the warranties found in a warranty deed. Thus, the grantor's liability is limited to defects arising after title is acquired and not against defects arising before that time. This deed is the customary form of conveyance used today in New Jersey (also called **special warranty**).

3. Bargain and Sale Deed. This deed conveys any right, title or interest the grantor possesses and asserts by implication that the grantor possesses a claim to or an interest in the property. Such an assertion to a claim or interest is not present in a quitclaim deed.

4. Quitclaim Deed. The quitclaim deed provides the least protection of all deeds, and is one in which the grantor transfers to the grantee the grantor's rights, if any, in the property described. If the grantor has good title to the described property the grantee gets good title. If the grantor owns nothing, the grantee gets nothing.

A quitclaim deed is frequently used to cure a technical defect in the chain of title to a property. For example, if A wishes to clear all clouds from the title to his property, and she thinks (although she may not be certain) that B, who is a distant heir, may have a possible claim to the property, she would then ask B to give her a quitclaim deed and release any interest B may have in the land.

Deeds for Special Purposes

Although the following deeds are used for special purposes as indicated by their titles, they do not represent additional deed types. They generally take the form of a Bargain and Sale (CVG) deed.

1. Administrator's Deed. An administrator's deed is used by a court-authorized administrator to convey title to property of a person who dies intestate.

2. Correction Deed. A correction deed serves to correct mistakes such as misspelled names or an incorrect property description contained in a prior deed. This deed is also known as a *deed of confirmation.*

3. Deed of Trust. A deed of trust is used to convey legal title from a grantor to a third party trustee as security for a debt owed by the trustor (borrower) to the beneficiary (lender). At the closing, the borrower executes a deed to the trustee who holds title for the benefit of the lender, although the instrument itself may remain in the lender's possession. When the loan is paid off, the trustee deeds the property back to the borrower. If, however, the borrower defaults, the trustee sells the property and pays the proceeds of the sale to the lender to the extent of the loan balance. Any excess is paid to the borrower. Trust deeds are not generally used in New Jersey transactions.

4. Executor's Deed. An executor's deed is used to convey title to real estate owned by a decedent who dies testate, and generally contains only the covenant against the grantor's acts.

5. Gift Deed. A gift deed is one where the consideration is love and affection, and is considered valid unless the purpose of the gift deed is to defraud creditors. However, since the covenants are not supported by valuable consideration, often a donee cannot enforce the covenants of warranty against the donee.

6. Guardian's Deed. This deed is used by a guardian with permission of the court to transfer title to property owned by a minor, insane person or a spendthrift. As with all other fiduciary types of deeds, the actual consideration must be stated.

7. Sheriff's Deed. A deed given by a sheriff to the highest bidder at a public sale conducted upon foreclosure of a mortgage, unpaid taxes or a judgment.

Elements of a Deed

In general, the usual elements of a deed are: (1) written instrument; (2) date; (3) legal capacity of grantor; (4) grantee; (5) recital of consideration; (6) words of conveyance (granting clause); (7) habendum clause: (8) legal description; (9) exceptions and reservations; (10) warranties and covenants; (11) grantor's signature; (12) delivery and acceptance; (13) acknowledgment; and (14) recording.

1. Written Instrument. To be effective and to comply with the statute of frauds, a deed must be in writing. There is no prescribed form that must be used, and the wording is immaterial as long as the intent is clear. A deed should not be altered in any manner after delivery or it may be set aside by the courts. Even restoration to its original form will not make it valid again.

2. Date. Although a date is not essential to the validity of a deed, it is customarily included. Inclusion of the date frequently prevents any question as to the time of its delivery.

3. Legal Capacity of the Grantor. A grantor must be of legal age and sound mind, and must be named or clearly designated in the deed. Although the name in a deed should be identical to that appearing in the conveyance by which title was received, a discrepancy, such as a misspelling, will not invalidate the deed.

Corporation Grantors. A corporation can only conduct business through its authorized officers, and corporate business includes the ownership and sale of real estate. Corporate action is generally undertaken by a **corporate resolution** passed by the Board of Directors. In some cases, the certificate of incorporation may require shareholder approval to dispose of corporate property. Legal counsel must be sought in these transactions.

4. Grantee. To be effective a deed must designate an actual person capable of receiving as grantee, who is named or sufficiently identified. Misspelling or mistakes in the grantee's name will not invalidate the deed if the identity of the grantee is obvious. Unlike the requirements of a grantor, a grantee may be a minor or an insane person. The grantee's marital status, residence and post office address must appear on all deeds presented for recording.

5. Recital of Consideration. Under New Jersey law, the full and actual consideration must be stated in the deed. A deed which recites the consideration as "one dollar and other good valuable consideration" must be accompanied by an affidavit which stipulates an allowable exclusion such as "love and affection."

6. Words of Conveyance. Since a deed transfers a present interest in real estate, the words of conveyance found in the granting clause must show an intent to transfer such an interest now. Thus, words of intent to convey at some future time are inadequate. Although no specific words of conveyance are required, those usually used are "convey and warrant," "grant, bargain and sell," or "remise, release and quitclaim." It is by this clause that the interest or title is transferred, therefore great care should be taken to make sure these words clearly indicate the intentions of the grantor.

7. Habendum Clause. The habendum clause, which begins with the words "to have and to hold," restates the grantor's intention to convey the quantity of the estate (such as fee simple or a life estate) shown in the granting clause.

8. Description. The description clause must unquestionably describe the real estate conveyed. Therefore, a description of a more permanent nature than an address, and one that can be readily found in years to come is necessary, because a deed is part of the permanent record in the chain of title. To avoid discrepancies in the records, it is normal practice to use the same description as found in the previous deeds or in documents evidencing title.

9. Exceptions and Reservations. Often a deed will contain certain exceptions or reservations of the real estate being conveyed which withholds some right or interest which otherwise would pass with the deed. A grantor may wish to withhold from the deed some part of the estate, conveying all the land except a particular, specified portion. This is an exception. A reservation, on the other hand, is the creation of a new right created by the grantor in his own favor. For example, a parent might convey the property described to his son, reserving a life estate for the parent in the property. Following the exceptions and reservations, the grantor would set forth any restrictions on the use of the land.

10. Warranties and Covenants. These are specific assurances or guarantees given by the grantor that the deed conveys good and unencumbered title (see Warranty Deed).

11. Grantor's Signature. To be valid, a deed must be signed by the grantor. If there is more than one grantor, such as ownership by a multiple tenancy, each must sign the deed or their separate deeds. If the grantor is married, the wife's dower rights may be released by reciting her name in the deed and having her sign with her spouse.

12. Delivery and Acceptance. In order for a deed to be effective, it must be delivered by the grantor and accepted by the grantee. Delivery is the act by which the deed takes effect and passes title. Delivery is not necessarily the act of manually handing over, but rather the intention that the grantor, by his final act, signifies that he wishes the deed to become effective. Thus, if a deed is given to the grantee (or his lawyer or other agent) for purposes of inspection for accuracy, there has been no delivery. The necessary intent is absent. If it had been delivered to the grantor's attorney, there has not been a delivery because it is still in control of the grantor. Likewise, the grantee must actually intend to accept ownership of the property, though acceptance may be presumed by the courts if the deed would benefit the grantee. Often a deed may be delivered to a third party, such as an attorney, with intent to pass ownership here and now. Acceptance by such an agent for the grantee constitutes a valid delivery.

13. Acknowledgment. Although acknowledgment by the grantor on the deed is not essential to its validity, it is essential before the deed can be recorded. (See Chapter 11).

14. Recording. (See Chapter 10).

To be valid, however, a deed need not contain all of the elements listed above, as only seven are essential for a valid deed: (1) written instrument; (2) legal capacity of grantor; (3) grantee; (4) words of conveyance (granting clause); (5) legal description; (6) grantor's signature; and (7) delivery and acceptance.

Lost or Destroyed Deeds

The existence of a lost or destroyed deed may be confirmed by a judgment of the Superior Court. However, the court must receive "clear and convincing evidence" before judgment will be entered. A certified copy of the judgment is then recorded in the county clerk's or registrar's office, in lieu of the missing deed.

If there has been an error in a deed, the grantor may execute a quitclaim deed with a clause stating the purpose of the deed. Such a deed is often called a correction deed. Another alternative is to follow the description clause in the correction deed with a statement saying that the realty conveyed is the same as that conveyed by a certain deed, naming the parties, date of record, etc.

Realty Transfer Fee

A realty transfer fee based on the actual consideration must be paid by the grantor (Seller) and the deed cannot be recorded until this fee is paid. The fee is collected by the county recording officer at the time the deed is offered for recording. 28.6% of the proceeds is retained by the county for use by the county, and the balance is paid to the state treasurer for use by the state.

Realty Transfer Fee Rates

Standard transactions and new construction:
- $2.00 per $500 of consideration up to $150,000
- $3.35 per $500—$150,000 to $200,000
- $3.90 per $500—amounts over $200,000.

Senior citizens, blind, disabled, low- and moderate-income housing:
- $0.50 per $500—up to $150,000
- $1.25 per $500—amounts over $150,000.

The following title transfers are exempt from payment of the fee:

1. Transfers with a true consideration of less than $100 (requires filing of an Affidavit of Consideration, Form RTF-1).
2. Transfers involving the United States, the State of New Jersey or any agency or subdivision thereof.
3. Transfers which have the sole purpose of satisfying a debt or obligation.
4. Transfers that confirm or correct a previously recorded deed.
5. Transfers involving a merger of corporations.
6. Transfers involving a partition of property.
7. Transfers involving a sale of property for taxes or assessments.
8. Transfers between husband and wife and between parent and child.
9. Transfers involving "low and moderate income housing" as defined in P.L. 1985, Chapter 225.

Filing of Real Estate Transactions

Under a revision to the Internal Revenue Code 6045, persons closing a real estate transaction are required to report the names, social security numbers and amount of the transaction to the IRS on a 1099 B form. In New Jersey, the primary filing responsibility falls on the closing attorney or title company; however, if the closing agent is not going to file, the responsibility lies with the following parties, in this order: the mortgage lender, the seller's broker, the buyer's broker, or any other party designated responsible by the IRS regulations.

While brokers are not primarily responsible for filing, they can assist the closing agent by securing the social security numbers of the buyers and sellers at the time of contract. By doing so, the broker can assure that closing will not be delayed or postponed because of missing information.

Specimen Deed

The specimen deed on the following pages has been numbered in the margin to note the significance of certain portions. It should be noted that these numbers are not meant to correspond with numbers of items listed previously under "Elements of a Deed."

Key to Specimen Deed

1. If grantor is married, spouse's name must be given.
2. Marital status of grantee is required.
3. Grantee's address must be shown.
4. These are the "words of conveyance" or "granting clause." The Plain Language Deed has effectively merged the habendum clause and the granting clause by use of the language, "transfers ownership of."
5. Consideration.
6. Legal description of property.

7. This is a notation regarding encumbrances.
8. These are the covenants of Warranty:
   a. and b. Covenant of Seisin.
   c. Covenant of Quiet Enjoyment and Covenant Against Encumbrances.
   d. Covenant of Further Assurance.
   e. Covenant of Warranty Forever.
9. Signatures.
10. The acknowledgments are made by the signers and taken by the notary public or other authorized officer of the court. The authorized officer states that the signer appeared before him or her, that they identified themselves and that they signed the document of their own free will.

KEY WORDS

Administrator's Deed
Alienation
Bargain & Sale Deed
Cloud on Title
Conveyance
Correction Deed
Covenant
Deed
Deed of Trust
Delivery and Acceptance
Exception
Full Covenant and Warranty Deed
Grantee
Grantor
Habendum Clause
Quiet Enjoyment
Quitclaim Deed
Realty Transfer Fee
Reservation
Seisin
Special Warranty Deed
Warranties
Warranty Deed

FIGURE 15.1

Sample Deed

107—DEED - WARRANTY (With Statutory Covenants) IND OR CORP. — Plain Language

ADGRVS -1

Copyright© 1982 By ALL-STATE LEGAL SUPPLY CO. One Commerce Drive, Cranford, N.J. 07016

DEED

Prepared by: (Print signer's name below signature)

Robert A. Gaccione

This Deed is made on May 2 1985

BETWEEN
Joseph P. Travers and Helen Travers, husband and wife

whose address is 935 Amaryllis Avenue, North Caldwell, New Jersey
referred to as the Grantor,

AND
Clyde J. Paul and Margaret Paul, husband and wife

whose post office address is 115 Cortlandt St., Belleville, New Jersey
referred to as the Grantee.
The words "Grantor" and "Grantee" shall mean all Grantors and all Grantees listed above.

(1) (2) (3)

Transfer of Ownership. The Grantor grants and conveys (transfers ownership of) the property described below to the Grantee. This transfer is made for the sum of Two hundred twenty-five thousand dollars ($225,000.00)
The Grantor acknowledges receipt of this money.

(4) (5)

Tax Map Reference. (N.J.S.A. 46:15-2.1) Municipality of North Caldwell, New Jersey
Block No. 704 Lot No. 18 Account No.

☐ No property tax identification number is available on the date of this Deed. (Check box if applicable.)

Property. The property consists of the land and all the buildings and structures on the land in the Borough of North Caldwell County of Essex and State of New Jersey. The legal description is:

(6)

Shown and designated as lot 9 on map entitled "Map of Section 5, Tall Timbers Subdivision, Borough of North Caldwell, Essex County, New Jersey, property of Sheridan Brothers" dated January 1951, Made by Haight & Medvecky, Inc. Engineers, filed in the Register's Office of Essex County, New Jersey, April 15, 1951 in Case #181 which premises are particularly described as follows:

Beginning at a point in the Southerly side of Amaryllis Ave; Therein distant westerly 125 feet from where the same would intersect the westerly side of Timber Road if both sides were produced; thence (1) South 4 degrees 46 minutes 59 seconds East 175 feet; thence (2) South 85 degrees 13 minutes 01 seconds west 125 feet; thence (3) North 4 degrees 46 minutes 59 seconds west 175 feet to said Southerly side of Amaryllis Ave; thence (4) along the same line North 85 degrees 13 minutes 01 seconds East 125 feet to the point and place of BEGINNING.

Being known as 935 Amaryllis Ave.
In accordance with survey made by Haight & Medvecky, Inc. Engineers dated August 23, 1951.

Subject However, to the following:

(7)

This conveyance is made subject to restrictions of record, if any, easements of record, if any, zoning ordinances of the Borough of North Caldwell and such facts as an accurate survey may disclose.

Being the same property conveyed to the Grantor herein by deed from Joseph and Virginia Purcell, husband and wife, dated April 24, 1954 recorded in the Essex County Clerk's office in deed book 693 at page 711 on April 26, 1954.

FIGURE 15.1 (cont'd)

CHAPTER 15 DEEDS

Promises by Grantor. The Grantor's promises are listed below. Each promise is expressed in the language of a New Jersey law (with a reference to the law) and is followed by an explanation in plain language. The Grantor promises that:

a. the Grantor is lawfully seized of the said land (N.J.S.A. 46:4-3) - the Grantor is the legal owner;

b. the Grantor has the right to convey the said land to the Grantee (N.J.S.A. 46:4-4) - the Grantor has the right to convey (sell) this property;

c. the Grantee shall have quiet possession of the land free from all encumbrances (N.J.S.A. 46:4-5) - the Grantee will not be disturbed by others with claims against this property and the property is free of all encumbrances;

d. the Grantor will execute such further assurances of the said lands as may be requisite (N.J.S.A. 46:4-10) - the Grantor will comply with the Grantee's reasonable requests to correct any title defect; and

e. the Grantor will warrant generally the property hereby conveyed (N.J.S.A. 46:4-7) - the Grantor guarantees the Grantee's ownership of the property.

(8)

Who is Bound. The promises made in this Deed are legally binding upon the Grantor and all who lawfully succeed to the Grantor's rights and responsibilities. These promises can be enforced by the Grantee and all future owners of the property.

Signatures. The Grantor signs this Deed as of the date at the top of the first page. If the Grantor is a corporation, this Deed is signed and attested to by its proper corporate officers and its corporate seal is affixed.

Witnessed or Attested by:

.... Joseph P. Travers (Seal)
Joseph P. Travers

Helen Travers (Seal)
Helen Travers

STATE OF NEW JERSEY, COUNTY OF Essex SS.:
I CERTIFY that on May 2 1985

Joseph P. Travers and Helen Travers personally came before me and acknowledged under oath, to my satisfaction, that this person (or if more than one, each person):

(a) is named in and personally signed this Deed;
(b) signed, sealed and delivered this Deed as his or her act and deed; and
(c) made this Deed for $ 225,000.00 as the full and actual consideration paid or to be paid for the transfer of title. (Such consideration is defined in N.J.S.A. 46:15-5.)

....
(Print name and title below signature)
Robert A. Gaccione
an attorney-at-law of New Jersey

STATE OF NEW JERSEY, COUNTY OF SS.:
I CERTIFY that on 19

personally came before me and this person acknowledged under oath, to my satisfaction, that:

(a) this person is the secretary of the corporation named in this Deed;
(b) this person is the attesting witness to the signing of this Deed by the proper corporate officer who is the President of the corporation;
(c) this Deed was signed and delivered by the corporation as its voluntary act duly authorized by a proper resolution of its Board of Directors;
(d) this person knows the proper seal of the corporation which was affixed to this Deed;
(e) this person signed this proof to attest to the truth of these facts; and
(f) the full and actual consideration paid or to be paid for the transfer of title is $
(Such consideration is defined in N.J.S.A. 46:15-5.)

Signed and sworn to before me on 19

....
(Print name of attesting witness below signature)

....

CHAPTER 15
Review Questions
(Answers on page 556)

(Answers on page 556)

1. Which of the following may prepare a deed?
   (A) A real estate broker.
   (B) The grantor.
   (C) The grantee.
   (D) A notary public.

2. The grantor delivers a signed deed but the grantee's name is omitted. The deed is:
   (A) invalid when made but valid when grantee fills in his name.
   (B) invalid when made but valid when recorded.
   (C) valid if the deed is delivered to the grantee.
   (D) invalid.

3. In a deed the grantee:
   (A) must be of legal age.
   (B) must sign the deed.
   (C) must be of sound mind and memory.
   (D) must be named.

4. Carol executes a deed of her farm to Betty. Carol keeps the deed in her safe deposit box. Upon her death, the box is opened and attached to the deed is a note to give the deed to Betty. Who has title to the farm?
   (A) Betty.
   (B) Carol's heirs.
   (C) The state.
   (D) Betty's heirs.

5. A quitclaim deed might be used to:
   (A) remove a cloud on a title.
   (B) remove an escrow.
   (C) terminate a lease.
   (D) evict a tenant.

6. In which of the following deeds is it possible that the grantee may receive no ownership rights?
   (A) Warranty deed.
   (B) Bargain and sale deed (CVG).
   (C) Bargain and sale deed without covenants.
   (D) Quitclaim deed.

7. A quitclaim deed transfers the interest of the:
   (A) grantee.
   (B) mortgagee.
   (C) grantor.
   (D) lessee.

8. If there is an exception in a deed, it would be:
   (A) for the benefit of the grantee.
   (B) for the benefit of the grantor.
   (C) related strictly to the legal description.
   (D) unconstitutional.

9. In a deed, the buyer is referred to as the:
   (A) grantee.
   (B) grantor.
   (C) vendee.
   (D) vendor.

10. The covenant in a deed which states that the grantor has full possession of the premises in fee simple and has the right to convey the property is called the covenant of:
    (A) seisin.
    (B) habendum.
    (C) quiet enjoyment.
    (D) further assurance.

11. In the transfers of real property, ownership changes hands when the deed is:
    (A) signed.
    (B) delivered and accepted.
    (C) recorded.
    (D) notarized.

12. The clause which defines or limits the quantity of the estate being conveyed is the:
    (A) partition clause.
    (B) revocation clause.
    (C) habendum clause.
    (D) reversion clause.

13. Which of the following is NOT necessary for the validity of a deed?
    (A) Execution.
    (B) Delivery to grantee.
    (C) Recording the deed.
    (D) Designating the grantee.

14. A deed which limits the liability of the grantor to his or her own acts and all persons claiming by, through and under the grantor, is known as:
    (A) special warranty deed.
    (B) general warranty deed.
    (C) quitclaim deed.
    (D) deed of trust.

15. If the grantor delivers to the grantee a deed in which the name of the grantee has inadvertently been left out, the deed is:
    (A) invalid.
    (B) voidable.
    (C) valid.
    (D) forged.

16. Abraham sold his property to Ben. Ben did not record his deed. Abraham then sold the same property to Clara, a purchaser in good faith for value. Clara recorded her deed.
    (A) Clara has a good title to the property.
    (B) Ben has a title that is superior to the title of Clara.
    (C) The conveyance to Clara is void.
    (D) Ben does not have a cause of action against Abraham.

17. The covenant against encumbrances in a deed of conveyance warrants against the existence of all of the following undisclosed matters except:
    (A) mortgages against the land.
    (B) judgment liens against the land.
    (C) easements that adversely affect the land.
    (D) zoning ordinances that limit the use of the land.

18. If a deed is not dated, acknowledged or recorded, it:
    (A) may be invalid because of these omissions.
    (B) is void.
    (C) may be revoked by the grantor.
    (D) would not be invalid as between the parties because of these omissions.

19. To be valid, a deed:
    (A) must be acknowledged.
    (B) must be recorded.
    (C) must have a competent grantee.
    (D) must have grantor's signature.

20. Which of the following would NOT appear in a deed?
    (A) Acceleration clause.
    (B) Habendum clause.
    (C) Granting clause.
    (D) Legal description.

21. To be valid a deed must:
    (A) name the buyer and seller.
    (B) recite the date signed.
    (C) be signed by buyer and seller.
    (D) be recorded.

22. The deed that imposes the greatest liability on the grantor is the:
    (A) quitclaim deed.
    (B) full covenant and warranty deed.
    (C) bargain and sale deed.
    (D) special warranty deed.

23. The recording of the deed benefits which of the following?
    (A) Grantor.
    (B) Grantee.
    (C) Grantor's creditors.
    (D) Selling broker.

24. Deeds may be prepared by:
    (A) any licensed real estate broker.
    (B) an attorney or the owner of the property being conveyed.
    (C) any knowledgeable person.
    (D) an attorney in fact acting under authority from the grantee.

25. The responsibility of recording a deed lies with:
    (A) the grantor.
    (B) the grantee.
    (C) the mortgagee.
    (D) the state.

26. A house in Mt. Laurel, NJ sold for $560,000. How much was the Realty Transfer Fee paid by the seller?
    (A) $4,850.00
    (B) $4,734.00
    (C) $3,743.00
    (D) $3,850.00

27. Persons closing a real estate transaction are required to report the names, social security numbers and amount of the transaction to the Internal Revenue Service. In New Jersey the PRIMARY filing responsibility falls on:
    (A) the buyer's broker.
    (B) the seller's broker.
    (C) the closing attorney or title company.
    (D) the mortgage lender.

28. How many times can the same deed be used?
    (A) Once.
    (B) Twice.
    (C) As often as necessary.
    (D) It varies from state to state.

29. In New Jersey a valid general warranty deed need NOT contain:
    (A) a recital of consideration.
    (B) a written statement of the warranties.
    (C) an execution by the grantee.
    (D) a granting clause.

(Quiz continues on next page)

30. If a deed conveys title to one person, the form of ownership being conveyed is:
    (A) severalty.
    (B) joint tenancy.
    (C) tenancy in common.
    (D) tenancy by the entirety.

31. Which of the following is NOT necessary for a valid transfer of title to real estate?
    (A) Competent grantee.
    (B) Grantor's signature.
    (C) Delivery of the deed.
    (D) Written deed.

32. An acknowledgment is taken by:
    (A) the grantee.
    (B) the grantor.
    (C) both of the above.
    (D) none of the above.

Chapter XVI

Eminent Domain: Power: government to take private property for public use.
Condemnation: The process taking from the person.
Key Fair market Compensation Value
$ if its in discrepancy is going to be valued x appraisal,

ENCROACHING: Si la persona dueña de una casa abarca una porción de la otra casa

TAKING ON: diferente de adverse posesión es que si relaciona con el deed travels c̄ it.
Fences travel with the deed belongs to the property no to the owner.

CHAPTER SIXTEEN

CONDEMNATION AND ADVERSE POSSESSION

CONDEMNATION

The power of eminent domain may be exercised to acquire any interest in land, as well as a right over land, such as an easement, but the taking must be for a public purpose and not merely for a private benefit. The act or process by which this power is exercised is called **condemnation**.

The power to condemn may be exercised by public bodies, such as the United States government, the state government where the property is located, counties and municipalities, as well as public utilities and railroads. The party seeking to acquire the land is the condemnor; the owner is the condemnee.

The use of this power is subject to two important conditions:

- The use to which the property is devoted must be a public one; and
- Just compensation must be paid. Just compensation means the fair market value of the land at the time of the taking of the land.

Prior to commencing suit, the condemnor is required to enter into negotiations with the condemnee. If the negotiations are successful it will result in the filing of a *deed in lieu of condemnation* in favor of the condemnor, subject to liens of record unless they are released. If negotiations are not successful, the condemnor must file a notice of *Lis Pendens* and file suit in the Superior Court, Law Division.

The procedure is as follows: The complaint asks for the appointment of three condemnation commissioners who hold hearings and determine the amount of compensation to be paid. The decision of the commissioners is then reported to the Superior Court, and either or both parties have the right to appeal the amount of the award. If no appeal is taken, the commissioners' report is the equivalent of a final judgment of the court. Title will vest in the condemnor when the commissioners' report is recorded in the county clerk's or registrar's office, and the award is paid. If there are several parties of interest, the award is apportioned among them according to their respective claims.

Where there is a *partial taking* of property under the state's power of eminent domain, any loss in value to the owner's remaining property would necessitate the additional compensation of **severance damages**. These damages are compensable where the partial taking lowers the highest and best use or otherwise limits the use of the remainder of the property. The amount of these damages would be determined by the "before and after method," or a determination of the value of the land before the condemnation, and a revaluation of its worth after the condemnation.

When the fee title of property is condemned for public use, the general rule is that the previous owner retains no reversionary or other interests in the realty. After proper abandonment by the government agency, the land can be disposed of with no limitations as to the rights of the former owner. However, in the case of condemnation for an easement, the title to the fee remains with the landowner, and after abandonment of the public use the original owner, his heirs or assigns still own the land, free from the public use.

Inverse Condemnation. Inverse condemnation is the process by which a property owner may require the payment of just compensation when the property value is lessened by the activities of a governmental authority, even though there has been no exercise of the power of eminent domain. For example, inverse condemnation may be sought if the actions of a public authority amount to a "taking" of the property, such as the zoning of land as a wetland or flood plain.

ADVERSE POSSESSION

As noted earlier, an abstract of title shows the chain of title from the original grant or government patent down to the present owner. What it may not show is title to real property that has been acquired through adverse possession. This is a title acquired by a person who has taken possession of the land without permission and has remained in possession for a specified number of years. This fixed period is 20 years in New Jersey. A person may have entered the property with no legal right whatsoever, but after the 20-year period, and the fulfillment of other requirements, he may acquire good title to the land, and not even the previous owner of good title can evict him.

The mere possession of land for the prescribed period alone is not enough to acquire title. The other requirements for title by adverse possession are that it be open, exclusive, continuous, uninterrupted, visible and notorious.

Open. Possession must have been visible and could not be hidden. For example, possession of a cave under an owner's land of which the owner is not aware would not meet this requirement.

Exclusive. The property may have been used only by the claimant or others having a direct connection to him and not by the public in general.

Continuous and Uninterrupted. For adverse possession to ripen into actual title, the term of possession must be continuous and unbroken for the 20-year period. If the occupant were to abandon the property for a period of time, possession would automatically be restored to the true owners, and the occupant would have to begin the adverse possession period over again.

The requirement of continuity of possession may be broken during the 20-year period by:

- re-entry into possession by the true owner;
- the commencement of an action in ejectment or to quiet title by the true owner; or
- acts on the part of the claimant that admit to the superior title of the true owner (e.g., the adverse possessor accepts a lease from the owner).

Continuous adverse possession by different persons may result in title being acquired by the person in possession at the end of the statutory period. This process of receiving the benefit of another's adverse possession is called "tacking."

Open and Notorious. Actual possession of the land must be of such a nature that the rightful owner knows about the stranger's occupancy, or would be likely to know about it if he kept himself informed about his land. Originally, knowing and intentional hostility were essential ingredients for adverse possession. Today, conscious hostility is no longer necessary. Thus, any entry that is exclusive, continuous, uninterrupted, visible and notorious, even under mistaken claim of title, will support a claim of title by adverse possession. However, there is an exception for a claim of title through adverse possession resulting from a minor encroachment along a common boundary. In this case, the true owners or their predecessors in title must have had actual knowledge of the minor encroachment for possession to be open and notorious.

Although one has satisfied all the requirements to acquire title by adverse possession, such title is not considered to be marketable title which a purchaser can be compelled to accept. Title must be established by judicial proceedings against the record owner. This is accomplished by a *quiet title proceeding*. After recording the decree quieting title, the adverse possessor's title becomes part of the public record.

Limitations and Exceptions

Among the limitations and exceptions governing acquisition of title by adverse possession are those which prevent acquiring property devoted to public use and certain government-owned property. Nor may one co-tenant obtain title in this manner against another co-tenant.

At first glance, adverse possession may appear to be very inequitable for the true owner. However, the law is recognized to encourage productive use of land which otherwise stands useless. Since the true title to property is sometimes difficult to prove because of the absence of records and witnesses, it is often better to enable persons to acquire title through strict adherence of the laws rather than to allow the property to remain useless and under no claim of ownership.

KEY WORDS

Adverse Possession
Before and After Method
Condemnation
Condemnee
Eminent Domain
Just Compensation
Marketable Title
Partial Taking
Quiet Title
Tacking

CHAPTER 16
Review Questions
(Answers on page 556)

1. "Quieting a title" most nearly means:
   (A) to obtain title by adverse possession.
   (B) to color a title.
   (C) to mortgage the property.
   (D) to settle a cloud on the title by court action.

2. To establish a claim of title of a parcel of realty by adverse possession, a claimant must hold the parcel for the required time and such possession must be:
   (A) either exclusive or in common with others, provided substantial enclosure and improvement or annual cultivation can be proved.
   (B) uninterrupted for the statutory period, with or without owner's consent.
   (C) under any circumstances, provided a claim for color of title is filed.
   (D) exclusive, continuous, uninterrupted, visible and notorious.

3. Joe, Helen and Mary Travers own a large home on a ten-acre parcel of land, all of which is needed by the state due to the creation of a new state highway. Regarding this case, all of the following statements are correct EXCEPT:
   (A) The Travers may voluntarily agree to sell the land to the state.
   (B) If the state needs the land for a public purpose, it may obtain title to it even if the Travers refuse to sell.
   (C) If the state acquires the land, the owners must be justly compensated for it.
   (D) Severance damages may be awarded.

4. Which of the following elements is NOT required for adverse possession?
   (A) The possession must be without permission.
   (B) The possession must be notorious.
   (C) The possession must be under claim of right.
   (D) The possession must be held by tacking.

5. The right of eminent domain refers to:
   (A) the right of every American citizen to own property.
   (B) an institution to condemn property pending an improvement that is for the good of the community.
   (C) an institution or individual to acquire land by grant from the government.
   (D) the government right to acquire or authorize others to acquire title for public use with just compensation.

6. A landowner can prevent an adverse claim by all of the following methods EXCEPT:
   (A) ousting the trespasser.
   (B) giving the trespasser permission to stay.
   (C) preventing trespassers from entering.
   (D) observing the trespasser.

7. Compensation usually follows a court action relating to which of the following?
   (A) Trustee's sale.
   (B) Police power.
   (C) Eminent domain.
   (D) Quiet title.

8. Adverse possession will be valid against:
   (A) the lawful owner.
   (B) the state.
   (C) the county.
   (D) the federal government.

9. An adverse possession claim may not be brought against which of the following?
   (A) Government-owned land.
   (B) Industrial property.
   (C) Agricultural land.
   (D) Commercial property.

10. A claim for adverse possession is most nearly valid where:
    (A) the person occupies the premises for the statutory period with or without the owner's consent.
    (B) the adverse possessor occupied continuously for the statutory period.
    (C) the land is state-owned.
    (D) the possessor paid just compensation.

11. Which of the following is necessary to acquire title by adverse possession?
    (A) 20 years' continuous use against the will of the owner.
    (B) Pay fair market value.
    (C) A condemnation hearing.
    (D) A color of title action.

12. The act or process of taking private property for a public purpose is called:
    (A) eminent domain.
    (B) police power.
    (C) escheat.
    (D) condemnation.

NOTE: Upon completion of Chapters 14, 15 and 16 you should complete Review Quiz 2 on page 513, and compare your solutions with the Quiz Answers at the back of the book.

giving mortgage - you - mortgager.
Lender - ~~buyer~~. bank.

Right + interes on a real property - = mortgage.

Mortgage : Secure the debt.
Note : Secure the terms of repayment.

Conveine is when you sell

mortgage are assumable because banks ~~wha~~ wants to make sure that

if you don't pay 20%. as downpayment you have to pay Insurance. → PMI.

c government - 10% - FHA.

Mortgage Instrument.
deed : doesn't need a full description mortgage do.

BLANKET MORTGAGE : it es un prestamo para construccion de por ej: 5 casas en un lote para vender uno no puede comprar una casa del mismo condominio hasta que no relarease el prestamo
→ release clause

CHAPTER SEVENTEEN

MORTGAGES

MORTGAGES

Most real estate transactions require some sort of financing of a portion of the purchase price. The most common method is with a mortgage loan. It is a rare case in which a buyer is financially able to acquire a property out of personal funds. Even buyers who have adequate funds available from their own assets often prefer to advance only part of the purchase price, and then borrow the balance, repay it over a period of years, and use the money under their immediate control to better advantage elsewhere.

A borrower who gives the mortgage is called the **mortgagor** and the lender who receives it is called the **mortgagee**. It is important to understand that the mortgage is given to the lender by the borrower. After the mortgagee makes a commitment to make a loan, the mortgagor is required at closing to sign a mortgage and **promissory note** or bond. The promissory note or bond is the primary financing obligation and makes the mortgagor personally liable for the debt. It is the written evidence of the debt's existence and includes the payment schedule agreed to by the mortgagor. The mortgage is the secondary financing obligation in which the mortgagor pledges the property to secure the debt represented by the note. Thus, even a mortgagor who decides to abandon a mortgaged property is still personally liable for the debt, and the mortgagee can obtain a personal judgment against the mortgagor for any deficiency between the foreclosure sale price and the amount of the mortgage debt. This personal judgment is called a **deficiency judgment**.

The amount of the mortgagee's loan commitment is based on the sales price or the appraised value, whichever is lower. From this appraisal the lender commits or agrees to lend a certain amount of money, usually a percentage of the property's value, at a fixed or variable interest rate over a definite period.

A mortgage loan is commonly repaid in installments and amortized over a period of years at a fixed rate of annual interest. Interest rates and terms vary greatly between different types of mortgages and different types of property. Due to the many complex facets of the money market and national and economic forces, the supply of mortgage money and interest rates are constantly in a state of flux.

There are two basic theories regarding the ownership position of the mortgagor and the mortgagee. Some states, called "title theory states," take the view that through the mortgage instrument the title is actually conveyed to the mortgagee. The more recent and more widely accepted concept is the lien theory, which holds that the mortgage is not a conveyance of land but only a security. Both of these theories have evolved for the purpose of defining the actual ownership of a mortgaged piece of property so that in the event a mortgagor should default, the mortgagee has legal means by which to recover his debt through foreclosure. While the evolution of New Jersey law has technically created a hybrid theory between lien and title, we still are predominantly a lien theory state.

In some states a form of mortgage called a "deed of trust" or "trust deed" is used. In a deed of trust a debtor (trustor) conveys land to a disinterested person (trustee) in trust for the benefit of a creditor (beneficiary) as security for the payment of a debt. Trust deeds are rarely used in New Jersey.

Mortgage Instruments

Broadly defined, a mortgage is a written instrument which hypothecates land as security for a debt. "Hypothecate" means to pledge property as security for a loan without giving possession of the property to the lender. There is no particular form required, although there are certain basic contract elements that must be present to make a mortgage valid. The requirements for the creation of a valid mortgage are as follows:

1. It must be in writing.

2. The parties to the contract must possess the legal capacity to contract. If the mortgagor is a co-owner of the property, the co-owner(s) or spouse should also join in the mortgage.

3. There must be a precise legal description of the property.

4. There must be an appropriate mortgaging clause. In New Jersey, since a mortgage is given to secure a debt by means of a lien, the mortgaging clause may simply be the verb "mortgages."

5. A statement of the debt. This is a statement reciting the exact amount of money being loaned. It states the amount of money being loaned and the specifics of how, when and in what amounts, including interest, it shall be repaid.

6. A mortgageable estate. Generally, any interest in realty that can be passed by purchase or descent is capable of being pledged for mortgage purposes.

7. Foreclosure provisions. There must be provisions specifying the procedures pertaining to foreclosure of the mortgage.

8. Signature of the parties. Signature of the mortgagor must be in the instrument, and if married, the mortgagor's spouse should join in the mortgage.

9. Voluntary delivery and acceptance. The mortgage instrument must be delivered voluntarily by the mortgagor and willingly accepted by the mortgagee for the mortgage to be valid.

10. Acknowledgment and recording. Although the mortgage does not require an acknowledgment for validity, it is necessary in order for it to be recorded. Prior to recording, the mortgage operates only as a contract between the parties and creates no lien. Therefore, since an unrecorded mortgage is void as to subsequent purchasers, mortgagees should record the mortgage as soon as possible after execution.

The priority of successive liens is determined by the time of recording unless subordinated (see item 3 below). Thus, the first mortgage recorded becomes a first lien on the property; the second mortgage, a second lien, and so on. The mortgage lien is always inferior to liens for property taxes and improvement assessments.

Factors Affecting Mortgages

In addition to the essential elements of a mortgage, numerous clauses and covenants also have their effect. Some of the most commonly used are (1) acceleration clause; (2) defeasance clause; (3) subordination clause; (4) release clause; (5) covenant to pay taxes; (6) insurance clause; and (7) good repair clause.

1. Acceleration Clause. This allows the lender to demand immediate payment of the entire loan if the borrower defaults. A due on sale clause **(alienation clause)** is a type of acceleration clause that makes all future payments due when a property is sold. This clause would prevent an assumption of the loan.

2. Defeasance Clause. The defeasance clause provides that the rights of the mortgagee will come to an end, if and when the debt is repaid in full.

3. Subordination Clause. A subordination clause may be included in a mortgage agreement in which the lender agrees to allow a subsequently acquired mortgage to have legal priority. This clause is often included in a purchase money mortgage (owner financing) used to acquire land for development requiring a later construction loan. For example, land is sold to a developer who plans to develop the tract. The seller receives a $200,000 down payment and agrees to hold a $2,000,000 purchase money mortgage for the balance of the purchase price. But the developer needs to mortgage the land immediately, with the first priority going to the lender for construction money to build the project. In this case, the land seller may agree to subordinate his position to a $5,000,000 construction loan issued by a commercial bank. Thus, the commercial bank has a first lien and the land seller has a second "junior lien."

4. Release Clause. In mortgages covering more than one property (blanket mortgages), a release clause is used to allow individual parcels to be released from the underlying mortgage. This type of clause is often used by a developer/mortgagor so that a parcel can be delivered free and clear to a purchaser once it has been released from the blanket mortgage. This is also known as a "partial release clause."

5. Covenant to Pay Taxes. If the mortgagor agrees to pay all taxes, yet in fact does not, the mortgagee can advance the amount due and add this amount to the principal indebtedness. However, if the mortgage is silent on taxes, the burden to pay them still legally falls on the mortgagor.

6. Insurance Clause. The mortgage should provide that the mortgagor keep the property insured to protect the mortgagee against loss in case the improvements are damaged by fire, windstorm, etc. The mortgagor generally promises to keep the insurance effective on the mortgaged premises in an amount equal to its value.

7. Good Repair Clause. The mortgagor promises to provide maintenance on the property so as to prevent waste and keep it in a state of good repair at all times, thereby protecting the mortgagee's security.

There are many other covenants and clauses which may be written in particular mortgages. The degree to which a mortgagee can require that he be protected is virtually unlimited. The mortgagee can request that any clauses or covenants deemed necessary to adequately protect the mortgagee in any given transaction are written into the mortgage instrument.

Loan-to-Value Ratio

The loan-to-value ratio is the ratio between the amount borrowed and the sales price or appraised value of the property, whichever is lower. For example, a loan in the amount of $80,000 on a property valued at $100,000 would represent an 80% loan-to-value ratio. Generally, loan-to-value ratios for residential properties are higher than for commercial properties. The greater the loan-to-value ratio, the higher the risk involved for the lending institution. The down payment represents the borrower's equity on the day of the closing.

Assignment of Mortgage

An assignment of a mortgage is the transfer of a mortgage to a third party called an **assignee**. Since it is a form of a contract, this assignment must be written and should be recorded. In relation to the mortgagor, the assignee then takes exactly the same position as the mortgagee. In a transaction requesting an assignment of a mortgage, the assignee may require an **estoppel certificate** (certificate of no defense) from the mortgagor for protection. In this certificate, the mortgagor admits that he or she actually owes the mortgagee an outstanding debt of a certain amount. The original mortgage would usually provide that the mortgagor must furnish the estoppel certificate upon request of the mortgagee. In addition to declaring the amount of the outstanding debt, it also states the terms by which the debt is to be repaid, validates the obligation and declares that the mortgagor has no defense against the mortgagee that he might later assert against the assignee. The use of estoppel certificates in conjunction with the assignment of one- to four-family residential mortgages has been largely outmoded by practice.

Mortgage Takeover

The most common method of conveying property with an existing mortgage is for the buyer to obtain a new mortgage loan. With the proceeds of the sale, the seller pays off the remaining balance of the old mortgage, and the new mortgage becomes the first lien against the property. However, mortgaged property can also be sold, with the buyer taking over the existing mortgage of the seller. When the mortgaged realty is conveyed to another in this manner, title is taken either: (1) "subject to" the mortgage or (2) by way of "assumption" of the mortgage.

1. "Subject to" the Mortgage. When an existing mortgage is not satisfied when a property is sold because the debt is not paid, the deed will recognize the existence of the mortgage and state that the grantee takes title "subject to" the mortgage. The seller still remains personally liable for the payment of the mortgage debt, while the buyer assumes the payment of the principal and interest. However, the buyer does not become personally liable to pay the debt. As a practical matter, the buyer will see that the debt is paid to protect the investment represented by the down payment. In other words, if the buyer defaults, causing a foreclosure, the buyer would lose the realty taken for satisfaction of the debt, and the seller would be liable for any deficiency remaining between the price obtained at the foreclosure sale and the actual mortgage debt. When taking title "subject to" an existing mortgage, the buyer should obtain a "reduction certificate" from the mortgagee verifying the amount due and the terms of the mortgage.

2. "Assumption" of the Mortgage. If the language in the deed states "by accepting this deed, the buyer assumes and agrees to pay," the result is very different, because now the buyer agrees to become personally liable for any deficiency after the foreclosure sale. Thus, in the event of a foreclosure due to the buyer's default, the buyer becomes primarily liable for any deficiency, and the seller remains secondarily liable, unless released from the obligation through a **novation**. (A novation is the substitution of one party for another in a contract wherein the original contract is extinguished and the new party undertakes a new obligation).

Prepayment Penalties

A prepayment penalty is a special charge or penalty demanded of a mortgagor when a mortgage is repaid before it becomes due. In New Jersey, state-chartered banks and savings and loan lenders are statutorily prohibited from charging prepayment penalties.

Usury

Usury is an interest rate in excess of the legally permitted rate. Usury limits were removed by federal enactment in 1980. Consequently, there is no interest limitation on loans that are made by institutional lenders. However, the state does limit the interest rate that may be charged when a seller or when a third party (relative, private investor, etc.) holds the mortgage. A seller may not lawfully charge more than 17% on a first mortgage loan unless the transaction involves the purchase of the seller's primary residence. In this case the rate may be negotiated as high as 30%. On second mortgage loans the maximum legal rate is 16% for loans under $50,000 and 30% for loans over $50,000, negotiable by buyer and seller.

Release of Mortgage

Upon full payment of a mortgage debt as per the mortgage instrument, a release or discharge of mortgage (satisfaction piece) or an instrument indicating discharge of the mortgage is given the mortgagor stating that the obligation to the mortgagee has been fulfilled. To clear off the mortgage of record, the release of mortgage should be recorded; otherwise, there will be a cloud on the title. The mortgagor has the legal right to insist upon receiving this release of mortgage. The normal sequence is tender of payment in full by the mortgagor and simultaneous delivery of the release by the mortgagee containing statements which prove that he definitely intended to discharge the debt. If a mortgage has been assigned by recorded assignment, the release must be executed by the assignee/mortgagee and then recorded. In New Jersey the mortgagee is required by statute to record the satisfaction of the mortgage. The fee for recording is paid by the mortgagor.

Private Mortgage Insurance (PMI)

Private mortgage insurance, or PMI, is insurance that mortgage lenders require from most homebuyers who take out a mortgage loan in an amount in excess of 80% of a home's appraised value. In other words, buyers with less than a 20% down payment are normally required to have private mortgage insurance. The borrower pays for mortgage insurance on a monthly basis in addition to the principal and interest payments that are made on a loan. The cost of PMI can vary significantly, with monthly payments that may range from $45 to $65 per $100,000 dollars borrowed.

Homeowners Protection Act of 1998. The Homeowners Protection Act of 1998, which became effective in 1999, establishes rules for automatic termination and borrower cancellation of private mortgage insurance on home mortgages. For mortgages signed on or after July 29, 1999, PMI must (with certain exceptions) be terminated automatically when equity in the home reaches 22%, based on the original property value, but only if the mortgage payments are current. Private mortgage insurance also can be cancelled upon request (with certain exceptions) when the owner's equity in the home reaches 20%, based on the original property value, providing the mortgage payments are current.

An owner who signed a mortgage before July 29, 1999 can ask to have the PMI cancelled once his equity exceeds 20%. However, federal law does not require the lender or mortgage servicer to cancel the insurance. There are, however, some additional disclosures for mortgages signed before this time period.

At the time the policy is issued, the homeowner should carefully determine what procedures are required for cancellation.

Conventional Loans

A conventional loan is one that is not insured or guaranteed by any government agency. It is a "two-party" transaction. The exact amount that will be loaned will depend on the lending policy of the financial institution, its perception of the borrower and the property as "good risks" and any state or federal laws regulating "loan-to-value" ratios.

There are two types of conventional mortgages: fixed-rate mortgages (FRMs) and adjustable-rate mortgages (ARMs). With a fixed-rate mortgage, the interest rate does not change over the life of the loan. As a consequence, neither does the monthly payment. For more than 40 years, this was the predominant type of loan. However, in the early 1980s money lenders became unwilling to deal only in fixed-rate mortgages because they found themselves holding long-term loans at interest rates far below the rates prevailing at that time. In addition, many families were priced out of the market when interest rates rose sharply.

Adjustable-rate mortgages were developed and offered as a solution to meet the needs of homebuyers and lenders. Today, more than half of all conventional home sales are financed with ARMs. The ARM adjusts the monthly payments based on changes in either a national or regional index and borrowers get a lower initial interest rate than they normally could obtain with a fixed-rate, long-term mortgage.

Because ARMs carry this lower initial rate, buyers can usually qualify for this mortgage with a lower annual income than would be needed for a fixed-rate mortgage. Another advantage is that the borrower effectively gets automatic, free refinancing when interest rates decline. The main disadvantage, of course, is that the monthly payments will increase if interest rates rise.

Affordability, or simply qualifying for a loan, is a problem many homebuyers face these days. The lower initial payments on ARMs can help solve this problem.

Adjustable Rate Mortgages (ARMs)

With a fixed-rate mortgage, the interest rate remains constant over the life of the loan, but with an ARM, the interest rate changes periodically in relation to an index, and payments go up and down accordingly. Lenders charge lower initial interest rates for ARMs than for fixed-rate mortgages. This makes the ARM more affordable than a fixed-rate loan for the same amount. It also means that the borrower may qualify for a larger loan because lenders qualify buyers on the basis of their current income and the first year's payments. In addition, an ARM could be less expensive over a long period, particularly if interest rates remain steady or go down.

On the other hand, borrowers must weigh the risk that an increase in interest rates will lead to higher monthly payments in the future.

A borrower who is considering an adjustable-rate mortgage should ask herself the following questions: (a) will my income increase enough to cover higher mortgage payments if interest rates rise?; (b) will I be incurring other sizeable debts, such as car payments or tuition, in the near future?; and (c) how long do I plan to own this home? (If the borrower plans to sell soon, rising interest rates may not pose the same problem as they would for someone who plans to own the house for a long time.)

How ARMs Work

The Adjustment Period. With an adjustable-rate mortgage, the interest rate and monthly payment change every one, three or five years. And the interest rate can change every year. The period from one rate change to the next is called the "adjustment interval." So, a loan with an adjustment interval of one year is called a one-year ARM. The borrower has some flexibility in choosing how often the rate will change, but lenders will charge a higher rate for longer adjustment intervals.

The Index. One of the protections afforded to a borrower with an ARM is that rate changes must be tied to a regulator-approved index, one that is not under the control of the lender. The rate for the borrower must follow that indicated by the index, which must be disclosed in the repayment clause of the note. How much the rate will change depends on the changes in the index the lender uses and the margin on the mortgage. When the index rate moves up or down, so do the payments at the time of the adjustment. Some of the more commonly used indexes are:

- **Treasury Yields**. Among the most popular indexes are one-, three- or five-year Treasury securities because they are easily monitored and reflect general changes of interest rates in the economy.

- **Average Cost of Funds.** Another common index is the national or regional average cost of funds to savings and loan associations.

- **National Average Interest Rate on New Mortgages.** This rate may be based on mortgages to purchase new or used houses. Use of this index makes the loan act as if you refinanced it at the going rate at each adjustment interval.

The borrower should ask what index will be used, how often it changes, how it has performed in the past and where it is published.

Margin. The margin is added to the index rate to determine the interest rate that will be charged. Margins are constant for the life of the loan. A margin is applied to all ARMs and it can differ from one lender to another. A margin is part of the competitive pricing of mortgages and represents the lender's cost of doing business and profit. For example, if a borrower has an ARM tied to one-year Treasury yields of 6% and the margin is 2%, the loan rate will be 8%. Margins are one of the important ARM features and something that the borrower will need to discuss with the lender.

Let's say, for example, that a borrower is comparing two ARMs offered by two different lenders. Everything looks equal. But the first lender says that when the interest rate is changed after the first adjustment period, the new rate will be determined by adding 2% to the Treasury Index. The second lender sets the change at 3% over the same index. The difference per month can amount to thousands of dollars over the life of the loan.

Interest Rate Caps. Interest rate caps are limitations on how much a payment can be changed at any one adjustment period and over the life of the loan. Two caps are commonly used:

1. Periodic caps limit the interest rate and increase from one adjustment interval to the next.

2. Overall caps limit the increase in the interest rate over the life of the loan.

By law, all ARMs must have an overall cap. Many have a periodic cap.

Negative Amortization. Negative amortization occurs when the monthly payments on a loan are insufficient to pay the interest due. When an ARM has a payment cap that results in monthly payments that are not high enough to cover the interest due, the unpaid interest is added on to the principal that is owed, resulting in a debt that increases, rather than decreases.

When home prices are appreciating rapidly, which has been the case in recent years, negative amortization does not pose much of a problem. On the other hand, in a market in which home prices decrease, the combination of declining prices and negative amortization could result in a loan balance that is higher than the market value of the home. Negative amortization is not included in all mortgage plans, but it should be understood by the borrower and discussed with the lender.

Prepayment and Conversion

Prepayment. Some agreements may require the borrower to pay special fees or penalties if the ARM is paid off early. Many ARMs allow the loan to be paid in full or in part without penalty whenever the rate is adjusted. Prepayment conditions are sometimes negotiable.

Conversion. The agreement with the lender may have a clause that allows the borrower to convert the ARM to a fixed-rate mortgage at designated times. Upon conversion, the new rate is usually set at the prevailing market rate for fixed-rate mortgages. The interest rate or up-front fees may be somewhat higher for a convertible ARM. In addition, a convertible ARM may require a special fee at the time of conversion.

Mortgages Classified According to Purpose

1. Second Mortgage (Junior Mortgage). A second mortgage is secured by a property previously encumbered by a first mortgage or lien. A second mortgage is inferior to the first lien because the priority of mortgages depends on the time and date of recording. Priority becomes extremely important in the event of foreclosure because mortgages will be paid off in the order in which they were recorded. Second mortgages are sometimes used in loan assumptions, with the seller taking the second mortgage to fund a portion of the equity, enabling the buyer to make a smaller cash down payment. Another common application is a home-improvement loan. Usually a junior mortgage bears a higher interest rate to compensate for the increased risk.

2. Purchase Money Mortgage. A purchase money mortgage may be any first or junior mortgage given concurrently with a conveyance of land to secure the unpaid balance of the purchase price. It is usually a mortgage given by a purchaser to a seller in lieu of purchase money. However, a mortgage given to a person or institution other than the seller does not prevent its being a purchase money mortgage. When a landowner gives a mortgage on one piece of property to finance the purchase of another parcel, it is not a purchase money mortgage.

This kind of mortgage is often used when other financing cannot be found and a seller's desire to sell the property is great enough that he is willing to handle all or part of the financing himself.

3. Construction Loans. A construction loan is a short-term loan that provides money for the development of a real estate project. For example, a builder owns a lot valued at $25,000. He contacts a lender and arranges a construction loan of $75,000 to put a house on the lot. The builder plans to sell the house and lot for $120,000. The existing security for the construction loan is the $25,000 lot. The builder and lender sign an agreement giving the lender a first mortgage lien on the lot and any later improvements added to the lot in exchange for construction funds. The agreement is a loan commitment that provides for funds to be disbursed at designated intervals during the construction period. The construction loan term may vary from six to 18 months. Interest rates for construction loans are normally based on short-term credit rates rather than long-term mortgage rates.

When the loan agreement is concluded, disbursements are made in installments or "draws" which will only be paid after a specified amount of construction has been completed. A lender representative usually inspects and approves the progress prior to each payment. This practice is used to ensure that the improvements have increased the value of the land in an amount that will exceed the money disbursed. Disbursements are usually made in either four or five draws, for example, when the slab is poured, when the walls are up, when the building is topped off and so on.

When all construction has been completed and inspected by the lender's representative, the final disbursement is made. When the builder sells the house and lot, he will pay the construction lender from the proceeds of the sale. The buyer will either pay cash or arrange for a long-term, permanent (take-out) loan, but in either case, the builder receives his money and is able to repay the lender.

4. Blanket Mortgage. This mortgage creates a lien on two or more parcels of property that are pledged as security for a debt. The blanket mortgage is most commonly used in financing the development of residential subdivisions.

Example

A developer buys a tract of land containing 100 acres, planning to subdivide the tract into 175 one-half acre lots (allowing 25 acres for roads, etc.) and build 175 houses. Instead of going to the expense of obtaining 175 separate mortgages, the developer may be able to negotiate a blanket mortgage. The blanket mortgage will include a **partial release clause**, meaning that as the debt is repaid, individual lots will be released from the mortgage. This enables the developer to pay off part of the loan, have a certain number of lots released, build on the lots and then sell them free and clear of the lien that still exists on the unreleased lots.

---

5. Package Mortgage. A package mortgage is a real estate loan secured by both real property and personal property. Items that often are financed and included in a package mortgage include refrigerators, stoves, ovens, washers, dryers and freezers. The advantage to the purchaser is that these items can be financed at the same rate as the real estate. This rate is usually lower than if a separate security agreement was used. Now and then, upon completion of sales in a residential subdivision, the developer will sell the "model homes" and will include in the sale price items of personalty, such as furniture, carpeting, refrigerator, etc. A package mortgage may be used for this purpose.

6. Wraparound Mortgage. A wraparound (wrap) mortgage may be used by a property owner who has a large amount of equity in a property that he wishes to convert into cash without paying off an existing mortgage. It is created when a lender who did not originate the existing first mortgage writes a second mortgage. The wraparound lender takes over the payments on the first mortgage and the face amount of the wrap equals the funds advanced by the wraparound plus the remaining balance of the first loan. The new loan wraps around the old loan and the borrower makes payments to the wrap lender only, who forwards the payment on the first loan, and retains the balance.

Although wraparound mortgages are a type of second mortgage, they often carry interest rates that are lower than the prevailing rates for first mortgages. The following example illustrates how this can occur: Parker acquired a property financed with an 8% fixed rate mortgage with Bank A. The property value has doubled since it was purchased. There is a loan balance of $200,000. Parker would like to convert $50,000 of the equity into cash, but interest rates have risen to 12%. Bank B is willing to advance the $50,000 if Parker signs a wraparound mortgage carrying an interest rate of 10%. Bank B is willing to make the loan at less than the prevailing rate because it will be charging 12% on $250,000, but it will only have to disburse $50,000. Therefore, Bank B will be earning 2% (the 10% they are collecting minus the 8% they are paying Bank A) on $200,000 that they did not loan. This gives Bank B an actual yield of 20% on its $50,000. The calculation is as follows:

$50,000 x 12% = $6,000
$200,000 x 2% = $4,000
$6,000 + $4,000 = $10,000 ÷ $50,000 = 20% Rate of Return

Wraparound mortgages are not limited to third-party lenders. In the above example, a seller could provide $50,000 to a buyer and take back a wraparound mortgage.

7. Bridge Loan (GAP Financing). A bridge loan involves short-term, interest-only financing of real estate and is available for any type of real property. It is used to purchase residential property when a property owner has signed a contract for purchase of one property in anticipation of selling another currently held property prior to closing on the purchased property. This short-term funding allows a home to be purchased prior to the sale of a party's present home. When the existing home is sold, the bridge loan is paid in full. Bridge financing also is used for funding a project between the maturity of a construction loan and the issuance of permanent financing.

8. Reverse Annuity Mortgage (RAM). This type of mortgage was designed to enable elderly homeowners on fixed incomes to convert some of the equity in their homes into cash to meet living expenses. The homeowner continues to live in the property and borrows each month from a lender until a ceiling amount or loan-to-value ratio is reached. The loan balance increases each month by the amount borrowed plus interest on the entire debt. While a reverse mortgage loan is outstanding, the borrower owns the home but does not make any mortgage payments. To qualify for a reverse mortgage, the borrower must be at least 62 years of age and own a home or condominium unit. There are no income or medical requirements to qualify. The borrower can choose to receive lump-sum fixed monthly payments for life, a line of credit, or a combination of a line of credit and monthly payments. The loan amount depends on the borrower's age, prevailing interest rates and the property value.

The money received from a reverse mortgage is tax-free. However, the funds received may affect the borrower's eligibility for certain kinds of public assistance, so these loans should not be used without careful consideration and legal advice.

The loan becomes due and payable when the borrower ceases to occupy the home as a principal residence. This can occur if the senior (or last remaining spouse) passes away, sells the home or permanently moves out of the house. Naturally, the house does not have to be sold to pay off the loan. At any time the borrower or the borrower's heirs can simply pay off the reverse mortgage and keep the home.

9. Home Equity Loans. When tax law changes in 1986 eliminated deductions for most consumer purchases, home equity loans became a way to buy personal property and still get a deduction. When the property is sold, or the first mortgage is refinanced, the home equity loan has to be satisfied. Home equity loans usually have a higher interest rate than first mortgages, but the interest rates are considerably lower than the rates on credit card or department store charge cards.

There are two types of home equity loans: term loans and lines of credit. Both are in fact second mortgages because they are secured by the property, just like the first mortgage.

A *term loan* is a one-time lump sum that is paid off over a set period of time, with a fixed interest rate and fixed payments each month. A *line of credit* works like a credit card. The homeowner borrows up to a certain amount for the life of the loan, with the time limit set by the lender. During that time the borrower can withdraw money as it is needed. As the principal is reduced, the credit revolves and it can be used again. For example, if a homeowner with a $10,000 line of credit borrows $5,000 and then repays $3,000, he would still have $8,000 of available credit. The line of credit gives the borrower more flexibility than the term loan.

Lines of credit carry a variable rate of interest that fluctuates over the life of the loan. Payments will vary depending on the interest rate and how much credit has been used. When the life of the line of credit expires, everything must be paid off. Specially issued checks or credit cards access lines of credit. Lenders generally require the borrower to take an initial advance when the loan is originated, withdraw a minimum amount each time a withdrawal is made and keep a minimum balance outstanding.

Although home equity loans offer the advantage of tax deductibility on loans up to $100,000 to purchase goods, and carry a much lower interest rate than credit cards and unsecured personal loans, there are some potential down sides that should be considered. For example, a defaulting borrower could lose his home, his biggest asset. Home equity loans could be risky for younger homeowners who may lack experience in owning a home and managing money; variable rate equity loans can go up during inflationary periods while income remains the same; and there may be a substantial balloon payment.

10. Shared Appreciation Mortgage (SAM). A SAM is a mortgage loan in which the borrower agrees to share the property's appreciation with the lender in return for an interest rate below that on a standard mortgage. SAMs have a contingent interest feature—a portion of the total interest due is contingent or dependent on the appreciation of the property. At either the sale or the transfer of the property or the refinancing or on loan maturity, the borrower must pay the lender a share of the appreciation of the mortgaged property. For example, if the prevailing interest rate is 10%, a lender might agree to make a loan at 8% plus 20% of the property appreciation after ten years.

11. Buy Down. The buy down is a method by which a home builder pays cash to a lender, who in turn makes a loan to the buyer of the builder's property at a below-market interest rate. Usually the builder pays a certain number of points to the lender to "buy down" the rate of interest on the loan for a certain time period. This allows homebuyers to purchase homes with lower payments for an initial period of time, usually three to five years. After this time the homeowner pays the full interest charge.

The Federal Housing Administration also has a buy down program that allows the seller or builder to open an escrow account to be used to reduce the monthly payment of the buyer or borrower.

Mortgages Classified by Manner of Repayment

Amortized Mortgage. An amortized mortgage is one that provides for the gradual paying off of a debt by periodic installments. The payments of principal and interest are projected for the entire term of the mortgage, and the monthly payment remains constant over the entire term of the mortgage, which is then said to liquidate itself. There are equal payments on each due date, which are applied first to interest and the balance to principal. Thus, as the principal is reduced, the amount of tabulated interest also decreases, and each subsequent payment has a larger portion applied to the principal.

Example: A monthly payment of $1,176 is required to amortize a $120,000 loan, at 11% interest for a term of 25 years. (See Amortization Chart on page 434). The following payment schedule shows the distribution of principal and interest for the first five payments.

No.	Monthly Payment	Payment on Interest	Payment on Principal	Principal Balance
1	1,176	1,100.00	76.00	119,924.00
2	1,176	1,099.30	76.70	119,847.30
3	1,176	1,098.60	77.40	119,769.90
4	1,176	1,097.89	78.11	119,691.79
5	1,176	1,097.17	78.83	119,612.96

2. Straight (Term) Loan. A straight mortgage is usually a short-term or medium-term loan requiring the payment of interest only during its term. The total amount of the principal is repayable at the end of the term. Prior to the 1930s, straight mortgages were the most common method of financing residential real estate. However, the Great Depression of that time caused more than a million homeowners to lose their properties because of their inability to pay the principal upon maturity. Today, straight mortgages are generally used only in the financing of construction loans.

3. Graduated Payment Mortgage (GPM). A GPM is one in which payments begin at a lower level than with a standard, fixed-rate mortgage of the same amount. Then, the payments level off, usually after five, seven or ten years at a fixed payment which will be higher than the standard fixed-rate loan.

The plan was developed primarily to help young first-time homebuyers, and assumes that their income will increase. Borrowers generally can qualify for these loans with less income than is required for conventional loans that build up little equity during the first stages of repayment.

4. Balloon Mortgage. A balloon mortgage is a mortgage whose payout is longer than the term for which the loan was granted. With this arrangement the monthly payments are not sufficient to fully amortize the debt, calling for one final payment at the end, substantially larger than all the others, to pay off the remaining principal balance. Since this payment is very large, relative to the previous ones, it is called a balloon payment and mortgages containing this feature are called balloon mortgages.

Example

Nancy Britt is purchasing a home from Mr. and Mrs. Warren for $160,000. Nancy is making a down payment of $40,000, the balance to be financed by a $120,000 purchase money, balloon mortgage given to the Warrens. The term of the loan will be ten years, but Nancy's payments will be made as if it were a 20-year mortgage. Another way of describing the terms would be to say that it is a "10-year mortgage with a 20-year payout". The arrangement has benefit for both parties. For Nancy, it allows her to make mortgage payments as if it were a 20-year loan, reducing her payments from what they would have been on a shorter schedule. At the end of ten years, however, the full remaining principal balance at that time will have to be satisfied by paying the Warrens off in cash or by refinancing with them or a commercial lender. The balloon arrangement gives the Warrens the opportunity to revise the interest rate based upon then current market conditions, rather than being tied to the same terms for the full 20 years.

---

5. Bi-Weekly Mortgage Loan. The bi-weekly mortgage gets its name from the frequency of its payments, which are made every two weeks. Each payment is approximately one-half the amount of the usual monthly payment. The 26 bi-weekly payments are equal to 13 monthly payments a year. So the borrower is actually making one "extra monthly payment" as compared to a regular 30-year fixed-rate mortgage. This "extra payment," along with its more frequent application of payments to the loan balance (amortization), greatly increases the speed with which the loan pays off and saves the borrower a significant amount of interest. For example, a 30-year mortgage for $120,000 at 8% interest requires monthly payments of $880. A bi-weekly loan for the same amount and rate requires a payment of $440 every two weeks. However, the bi-weekly loan will be paid off in less than 23 years, and will save the borrower $56,794 in interest.

6. Open-End Mortgages. These are mortgages written to provide for additional monies to be loaned in the future for such things as additions, alterations or improvements to the property without rewriting the mortgage. By writing such a mortgage, the lender eliminates the time and paperwork involved in processing and approving a new loan. When additional monies are loaned, the lender may agree to charge the prevailing rate at the time the mortgage was signed, but it is more common to charge the market rate at the time of disbursement.

Points

If the current true cost of money is higher than the going rate for mortgage loans, lenders will not make the loan unless they are compensated for the difference in the form of a one-time, upfront loan fee called points or *discount points*. Since points are deducted from the principal when the loan is made, they represent prepaid interest. One point is 1% of the loan amount. For example, a 2% discount on a $100,000 loan would be $2,000. Thus, the borrower will receive only $98,000, but will still have to repay the entire $100,000. The lender's yield is increased 1/8% for each point charged. Thus, eight points will increase the yield 1%.

For federal income tax purposes, the cost of points is fully deductible from income in the year a home is purchased. Deductions for points paid in a refinancing must be spread over the life of the loan. In order for the points to be deductible, they should be paid to the lender by separate check. If the cost of points is being financed, the borrower should request that the lender provide a separate check in the amount of the points upon closing of the loan.

Mortgages Classified as Government-insured or Government-guaranteed

1. *Federal Housing Administration (FHA)*

The Federal Housing Administration (FHA) was created by the National Housing Act of 1934 and was made a part of the Department of Housing and Urban Development by an Act of Congress in 1965.

The primary function of the FHA is to provide insurance protection to private lenders who provide mortgage financing to homebuyers. FHA insurance encourages lenders to provide long-term, high loan-to-value mortgage loans, thereby broadening the market for home purchases.

The FHA is not a lender; it is an insurance agency. The borrower obtains the loan from a bank, savings and loan, mortgage company or other FHA-approved lender. In addition to collecting principal and interest payments, the lender collects a mortgage insurance premium from the borrower, which it forwards to the FHA. FHA then insures payment of the loan. As a result of the insurance, the lender is willing to make loans on terms not otherwise possible.

Mortgage Insurance. The FHA charges a one-time up-front mortgage insurance premium (MIP) of 2.25%. In addition, FHA charges an annual MIP of 1/2% of the annual loan balance. If the down payment exceeds 10%, the term for the premium payment is 11 years. However, if the down payment is 10% or less, the premium is paid for 30 years.

Down Payment. Most FHA loan programs offered by private lenders require between 3%-5% down payment, with a minimum of 3% coming from the borrower's own funds.

FHA Loan Limits. FHA loan limits vary throughout the state, ranging from $144,336 in Cumberland County to $261,609 in the counties of Bergen, Essex, Morris, Passaic, Sussex, Union and Warren. Therefore, borrowers should ask the lender about the maximum loan amount in a particular area.

Most Frequently Used FHA Mortgage Insurance Programs:

- Section 203(b) is the most commonly used HUD single-family program. It is available in all areas of the country, provided the property and the home meet HUD's minimum property standards. This program can be used to purchase a new or used one- to four-family home in both urban and rural areas.

- Section 234(c) provides mortgage insurance for buyers who wish to purchase a unit in a condominium project. Rules are similar to 203(b) loans, except that there is no up-front MIP charged.

- Section 203(k) allows a borrower to purchase or refinance and rehabilitate a home at least one year old. A portion of the funds is used to pay off the existing mortgage, and the remaining funds are held in escrow and released as the rehabilitation is completed.

- Section 245(a) insures graduated payment mortgages (GPMs). FHA offers five GPM plans, which vary in the rate of payment increases and the number of years over which the payments will increase.

- Section 251 insures ARMs. The interest rate cannot increase or decrease more than 1% in any one year. Over the life of the loan, the interest rate may not increase or decrease more than 5% from the initial interest rate. Lenders must inform borrowers at least 25 days in advance if there is an adjustment in the monthly payment.

Assumability. FHA loans may be assumed, but the rules vary depending on when the loan is made.

An investor or owner-occupant with no qualification of the buyer can assume loans originated prior to December 1, 1986. This is called a "simple assumption." It assigns the right to pay to the new buyer, but the liability to repay the loan remains with the first borrower in the event the assumer of the loan defaults.

If the FHA loan was originated between December 1, 1986 and February 4, 1988, credit approval of the buyer (owner-occupant or investor) is required. The seller remains liable unless released.

If the loan was originated after December 15, 1989, the FHA requires credit approval of the buyer-occupant (no investors) before conveyance of title involving assumption loans. If the borrower assumes the loan, the lender cannot refuse to release the original borrower from liability on the loan.

Steps Involved in the FHA Loan Process. The first step in a FHA transaction is to have the house appraised. Only a FHA-approved lender can order a FHA appraisal. The FHA appraiser then submits an appraisal report that may require that certain repairs be made. A certification from a termite inspection company is also usually required. Finally, the FHA appraisal report will require a letter from the municipal code enforcement officer to the effect that there are no code violations. If code violations exist they must be corrected. These repairs may be different from those required by the FHA appraiser. In addition, in all contracts involving FHA-insured loans, a FHA **amendatory clause** must be added. The purpose of the amendatory clause is to make certain that the sales price warrants the allowable FHA-insured loan. The amendatory clause enables the buyer to withdraw from the agreement without any penalty (such as forfeiture of the earnest money deposit) in the event the FHA appraisal is lower than the price the buyer agreed to pay. If, despite the "under-appraisal" by the FHA, the buyer chooses to proceed with the purchase, he may do so by paying the additional down payment resulting from the lower appraisal.

Special Features of FHA Loans:

1. Unlike VA loans, they are available for both owner-occupied and rental housing;
2. Borrowers can finance 100% of the closing costs;
3. Secondary financing to provide cash for the down payment is prohibited;
4. Either seller or buyer can pay closing costs, as long as the buyer does not pay more than the allowed fee;
5. There is no prepayment penalty;
6. The interest rate is a floating rate fixed by the marketplace;
7. The usual term of the loan is 30 years; and
8. Since the FHA loan is insured under a mutual mortgage insurance plan, the borrower pays an insurance premium.

The monthly payments also include hazard insurance premiums, 1/12 of the annual taxes, and, in the case of leasehold property, 1/12 of the annual ground rent.

2. *Department of Veteran Affairs (VA) (GI) Guaranteed Loans*

The Veterans Administration (VA) was established as an independent agency in 1930. Under the Serviceman's Readjustment Act of 1944, the VA was authorized to guarantee veterans' loans secured by real property. In 1989, the VA was elevated to Cabinet level and is now officially called the Department of Veteran Affairs.

The Act provides for a first mortgage real estate loan that is partially guaranteed by the VA, which is subject to rules pertaining to the borrower, the lender, the property, the interest, the loan amount and term, and collections and foreclosures. The amount of money the VA guarantees for the veteran is termed *entitlement*.

Unlike FHA loans, VA loans do not require mortgage insurance. They do, however, include a funding fee. A basic funding fee of 2% must be paid to VA by all except certain exempt veterans. A down payment of 5% or more will reduce the fee to 1.5% and a down payment of 10% will reduce it to 1.25%. Either the buyer or seller can pay the fee at closing, or the buyer can roll the fee into his mortgage. Lenders will waive the fee for veterans disabled in service and for widows and widowers of those who died in service.

The VA loan programs assist veterans in obtaining home, mobile home and condominium loans at more favorable financing terms than are available to non-veterans. VA officials appraise properties, supervise construction of new homes and see that lenders comply with regulations governing access to credit.

Maximum VA Mortgage. The VA guarantees the top 25% of loans. With the current maximum guaranty of $60,000, a veteran who has not previously used the benefit may be able to obtain a no-down-payment VA loan up to $240,000, depending on the borrower's income level and the appraised value of the property.

Special Features of the VA Loan:

1. Although the FHA programs are open to all permanent residents who can qualify for the mortgage, only eligible veterans can qualify for a VA loan.
2. Like FHA-insured loans, the VA program enables a qualified veteran to purchase a home with a small amount of cash, as stated earlier, for there is no limitation on the amount of the VA loan. In fact, VA lenders by law are allowed to loan as high as 100% of the appraised value of the property, although the amount of the guaranty remains limited, as stated above.

3. The VA borrower is permitted to use secondary financing to obtain additional money for the purchase of the dwelling. However, the interest rate cannot exceed the interest on the first mortgage, and the second mortgage term must be at least as long as that of the first mortgage. Because of these and other restrictions, secondary financing is rarely used in VA loans. After closing, however, the veteran can place a second mortgage on the property. Co-mortgagors are not accepted by the VA without a reduction in the guaranteed loan amount and in the amount of guaranty. Before a loan is processed, an appraisal of the property in question is made, and the VA sends to both the veteran and the lender a **Certificate of Reasonable Value (CRV)**. It is this certificate which will show the appraised value of the property for loan purposes. While there is no down payment required by the VA, in the event the veteran agrees to purchase the property for a price in excess of the VA appraisal, the veteran must pay that excess plus any closing costs in cash. The appraisal is always the sell price.

4. A VA loan to purchase, construct, alter, improve or repair a home cannot be approved by the Department of Veteran Affairs unless the veteran certifies that he or she **occupies or intends to occupy the property**. This certification must be given both at the time of loan application and again at closing. At a later time, however, the veteran can rent the home.

5. There is no prepayment penalty on a VA loan.

6. The veteran may sell his home mortgaged with a VA loan and permit the buyer (whether veteran or non-veteran) to **assume the mortgage**. A veteran can have his mortgage benefit fully restored if the home is sold and the VA mortgage is paid off, or when another veteran with as much VA entitlement as the owner assumes the loan and can qualify for the VA income, credit and occupancy requirements.

7. The VA has a limited direct loan program, but only to supplement a grant to get a specially adapted home for certain veterans who have a permanent and total service-connected disability.

8. Contracts involving VA-guaranteed loans must contain an **amendatory clause** similar to the one discussed earlier in connection with FHA loans.

General Rules for Eligibility

Veterans with active duty service that was not dishonorable during World War II and later periods are eligible for VA loan benefits. World War II (September 16, 1940 to July 25, 1947), Korean Conflict (June 27, 1950 to January 31, 1955), and Vietnam era (August 5, 1964 to May 7, 1975) veterans must have at least 90 days service. Veterans with service only during peacetime periods and active duty military personnel must have had more than 180 days active service. Veterans of enlisted service that began after September 7, 1980, or officers with service beginning after October 16, 1981, must in most cases have served at least two years.

Persian Gulf Conflict. Basically, reservists and National Guard members who were activated on or after August 2, 1990, served at least 90 days and were discharged honorably are eligible. VA regional office personnel may assist with eligibility questions.

Members of the selected reserve, including National Guard, who are not otherwise eligible and who have completed six years of service and have been honorably discharged or have completed six years service and are still serving, may be eligible. The expanded eligibility for Reserve and National Guard individuals will expire September 30, 2003. The VA should be contacted to determine what is needed to establish eligibility. Reservists will pay a slightly higher funding fee than regular veterans.

Also eligible are unremarried widows of veterans who died in service or from service-connected causes, and in-service military personnel.

Remaining Entitlement

Veterans who had a VA loan before may still have "remaining entitlement" to use for another VA loan. The current amount of entitlement available to each eligible veteran is $36,000. This was much lower in years past and has been increased over time by changes in the law. For example, a veteran who obtained a $25,000 loan in 1974 would have used $12,500 guaranty entitlement, the maximum then available. Even if that loan is not paid off, the veteran could use the $23,500 difference between the $12,500 entitlement originally used and the current maximum of $36,000 to buy another home with VA financing. An additional $10,000, up to a maximum entitlement of $46,000, is available for loans above $144,000 to purchase or construct a home.

Most lenders require that a combination of the guaranty entitlement and any cash down payment must equal at least 25% of the reasonable value or sales price of the property, whichever is less. Thus, in the example, the veteran's $23,500 remaining entitlement would probably meet a lender's minimum guaranty requirement for a no-down payment loan to buy a property valued at and selling for $94,000. The veteran could also combine a down payment with the remaining entitlement for a larger loan amount.

Restoration of Entitlement

Veterans who have previously used their VA entitlement may have it "restored" to purchase another home with a VA loan if (a) the property purchased with the prior VA loan has been sold and the loan paid in full; or (b) a qualified veteran-transferee (buyer) agrees to assume the VA loan and substitute his or her entitlement for the same amount of entitlement originally used by the veteran seller. Remaining entitlement and restoration of entitlement can be requested through the nearest VA office by completing VA Form 26-1880. The entitlement may also be restored (one time only) if the veteran has repaid the prior VA loan in full but has not disposed of the property purchased with the prior VA loan.

COMPARISON OF FHA AND VA LOAN PROGRAMS

Department of Veteran Affairs

1. Financing available to veterans (and certain unremarried widows).
2. VA financing limited to owner-occupied residential (I to 4 family) dwellings; must sign occupancy certificate on two separate occasions.
3. Does not require down payment, though lender may request small down.
4. Methods of valuation differ; VA issues a Certificate of Reasonable Value.
5. With regard to home loans, the law requires the VA loan may not exceed the reasonable value of the home.
6. No prepayment penalty.
7. Guarantees 50% of the loan on loans of $45,000 or less. For loans between $45,000 and $56,250, the guaranty will not exceed $22,500. For loans between $56,250 and $144,000, the guaranty is 40% of the loan. For loans in excess of $144,000, the VA guarantees 25% of the loan up to a maximum guaranty of $50,750.
8. Secondary financing permitted in special cases.
9. Buyer or seller may pay discount points.
10. Loan can be assumed by non-veterans. If the lender or the VA finds the purchaser is not a good credit risk, the unpaid balance may be declared immediately due and payable. If the purchaser is acceptable, the veteran will be released from liability to the VA.

Federal Housing Administration

1. Financing is available to both veterans and non-veterans alike.
2. Financing programs for owner-occupied, rental and other types of construction. Owner-occupied has greater loan-to-value ratio.
3. Requires a larger down payment than VA.
4. Different evaluation methods; like VA there are prescribed valuation procedures for the approved appraisers to follow.
5. FHA valuation sets the maximum loan FHA will insure but does not limit the sales price.
6. No prepayment penalty. (Lenders may require that any partial prepayments be in the amount of at least one monthly installment of principal or $100, whichever is less.)
7. Insures 100% of the loan by way of mutual mortgage insurance; premiums paid by buyer in cash at closing or added to the mortgage amount. The insurance premiums average approximately 2.25% of the mortgage amount.
8. No secondary financing permitted until after closing.
9. Buyer or seller may pay discount points.
10. Loans issued before December, 1986 can be assumed without prior approval of the FHA. For loans underwritten after December, 1986, credit approval of the buyer is required.

KEY WORDS

Acceleration Clause
Adjustable Rate Mortgage
Alienation Clause
Amortization
Assignment of Mortgage
Assumption of Mortgage
Balloon Mortgage
Blanket Mortgage
Bridge Loan
Construction Mortgage
Conventional Mortgage
C.R.V.
Defeasance Clause
Deficiency Judgment
Discount Points
Due-on-Sale Clause
Estoppel Certificate
FHA Insured Loan
Graduated Payment Mortgage (GPM)
Hypothecate
Junior Mortgage
Loan-to-Value Ratio
Mortgage
Mortgage Insurance Premium (MIP)
Mortgagee
Mortgagor
Novation
Open End Mortgage
Package Mortgage
Prepayment
Principal
Private Mortgage Insurance (PMI)
Promissory Note
Purchase Money Mortgage
Release Clause
Release of Mortgage
Reverse Annuity Mortgage (RAM)
Second Mortgage
Subordination Clause
Usury
VA Guaranteed Loan
Wraparound Mortgage

CHAPTER 17
Review Questions
(Answers on page 556)

1. When a buyer "assumes and agrees to pay" an existing loan on the property:
   (A) the seller is relieved from liability.
   (B) the buyer, together with the seller, is liable on the loan.
   (C) only the seller is liable.
   (D) only the buyer is liable.

2. In a purchase money mortgage:
   (A) the seller takes back a mortgage as part of the purchase price.
   (B) the seller is disposing of a mortgage loan.
   (C) the buyer is denied the prepayment privilege.
   (D) the seller is denied the prepayment privilege.

3. The loan-value ratio relates the loan to:
   (A) sales price.
   (B) appraised value.
   (C) A or B, whichever is higher.
   (D) A or B, whichever is lower.

4. The dollar value of a discount point is:
   (A) 1% of the appraised value.
   (B) 1% of the loan amount.
   (C) 1% of the down payment.
   (D) 1% of the selling price.

5. A mortgage is discharged by all of the following EXCEPT:
   (A) satisfaction.
   (B) execution of a quitclaim deed by the mortgagee.
   (C) death.
   (D) release.

6. A clause in a mortgage which permits the lender to call the entire balance due if the property is sold or otherwise conveyed by the mortgagor is called:
   (A) defeasance clause.
   (B) alienation clause.
   (C) habendum clause.
   (D) subrogation clause.

7. A statement from a borrower setting forth the amount of the unpaid balance, the interest rate and any claims he or she may have against the lender is called a(n):
   (A) lender's certificate.
   (B) title certificate.
   (C) estoppel certificate.
   (D) financial certificate.

8. A prospective home purchaser:
   (A) cannot pay more than the CRV for a home.
   (B) can pay more than the CRV or the FHA appraisal.
   (C) can pay more than the CRV but not more than the FHA appraisal.
   (D) cannot pay more than the CRV but can pay more than the FHA appraisal.

9. Where a seller is relieved of all obligations under a mortgage which the buyer is assuming, this would be best described as which of the following?
   (A) Subordination.
   (B) Novation.
   (C) Acceleration.
   (D) Subrogation.

10. The acceleration clause in a promissory note provides:
    (A) payments must be made more frequently at a future specified date.
    (B) payments may not be made more frequently than specified.
    (C) upon the happening of a certain event the entire amount of the unpaid balance becomes due.
    (D) None of the above.

11. Of the following, whose interest is benefited by an acceleration clause in a mortgage note?
    (A) The borrower.
    (B) The lender.
    (C) A future purchaser upon resale of property.
    (D) The trustee.

12. Which of the following mortgage plans would provide the purchaser with the lowest down payment?
    (A) Veterans Administration (VA).
    (B) Conventional.
    (C) Federal Housing Administration (FHA).
    (D) Conventional with PMI.

13. Discount points paid in connection with conventional loans are paid to the:
    (A) borrower.
    (B) lender.
    (C) real estate broker.
    (D) seller.

(Quiz continues on next page)

14. Which of the following mortgage plans would provide the homeowner with monthly payments from the mortgagee?
    (A) Veterans Administration (VA).
    (B) Reverse annuity mortgage.
    (C) Federal Housing Administration (FHA) 203B.
    (D) Conventional with private mortgage insurance (PMI).

15. When a mortgage is taken over by assumption:
    (A) the seller is relieved of responsibility under the mortgage and note.
    (B) the buyer becomes personally liable for payment of the debt.
    (C) the buyer becomes secondarily liable for the debt.
    (D) it is referred to as a "novation."

16. The note, as distinguished from the mortgage, creates:
    (A) an obligation to rent.
    (B) a personal obligation.
    (C) a double obligation.
    (D) a lien.

17. The money for making Federal Fair Housing Administration (FHA) loans is supplied by:
    (A) qualified lending institutions.
    (B) the Federal Fair Housing Administration.
    (C) a government agency.
    (D) the Federal Home Loan Bank.

18. The interest an owner of property has over and above the mortgage indebtedness is called:
    (A) redemption.
    (B) equity.
    (C) proportionate.
    (D) current value.

19. Under a Veterans Administration loan:
    (A) the veteran can transfer the VA loan to another home.
    (B) the veteran can sell the home and allow a nonveteran buyer to assume the loan.
    (C) the mortgage may contain a "due on sale" clause.
    (D) women are not eligible.

20. A function of the FHA is to:
    (A) build housing.
    (B) lend money.
    (C) guarantee loans.
    (D) insure loans.

21. A mortgage that covers several parcels of land and that could contain a provision for sale of an individual property, called a release clause, is:
    (A) a direct reduction mortgage.
    (B) a blanket mortgage.
    (C) an amortized mortgage.
    (D) a declining balance mortgage.

22. Sally Prebble borrowed $50,000. Over the term of the loan she paid $15,000 in interest and then made a final payment of $50,000. Sally's mortgage can best be described as a:
    (A) straight mortgage.
    (B) blanket mortgage.
    (C) open-end mortgage.
    (D) package mortgage.

23. A junior mortgage is:
    (A) always a second mortgage.
    (B) subordinate to mortgages recorded ahead of it.
    (C) a mortgage in which the interest rate is subject to periodic renegotiation during its term.
    (D) a mortgage given to a minor.

24. A second mortgage is:
    (A) equal in standing and value with a first mortgage.
    (B) a junior lien on real estate which has a prior mortgage on it.
    (C) always made by the seller.
    (D) used in practically all real estate purchases.

25. A promissory note that provides for payment of interest only during the term of the note would be:
    (A) an installment note.
    (B) a straight note.
    (C) an amortized note.
    (D) a non-negotiable note.

26. A buyer agrees to buy a home for $200,000 with a $40,000 down payment, the balance to be financed by a conventional loan. If the seller agrees to pay the discount fee of 2%, how much will he have to pay?
    (A) $2,800.
    (B) $3,200.
    (C) $4,000.
    (D) $4,200.

27. Which of the following clauses would NOT appear in a mortgage?
    (A) A subrogation clause.
    (B) A due on sale clause.
    (C) An alienation clause.
    (D) A defeasance clause.

28. "Subject to mortgage" is:
   (A) a college course on mortgage finance
   (B) a mortgage bought by FNMA and sold to GNMA.
   (C) the taking of title to property wherein the grantee is not responsible to the holder of the promissory note for the payment of any portion of the amount due.
   (D) the right to foreclose without going to court.

29. A conventional mortgage is:
   (A) guaranteed by FHA.
   (B) a commercial loan.
   (C) approved by the VA.
   (D) a two-party transaction.

30. The discount charged by a lender and paid by the seller on a federal VA loan is a percent of:
   (A) sales price.
   (B) loan amount.
   (C) appraised value.
   (D) assessed value.

31. The penalty for complete prepayment of an FHA-insured loan during the first ten years is:
   (A) 2% of the face value of the note at time of payment.
   (B) 90 days interest on the remaining balance.
   (C) 1% of the original amount of the loan.
   (D) Nothing.

32. A promissory note:
   (A) may not be executed in connection with a loan on real property.
   (B) is an agreement to do or not to do a certain thing.
   (C) is the primary evidence of a loan.
   (D) is one which is guaranteed or insured by a governmental agency.

33. A mortgage is released by:
   (A) reversion.
   (B) reconveyance.
   (C) discounting the loan.
   (D) satisfaction.

34. A clause in a mortgage or lease, stating that rights of the holders shall be secondary to a subsequent encumbrance, is:
   (A) a subordination clause.
   (B) a habendum clause.
   (C) a subrogation clause.
   (D) an inferiority clause.

35. When the amortized payment of a mortgage remains constant over the period of the loan but leaves an outstanding balance to be paid at the end, this payment of the balance is called:
   (A) a balloon payment.
   (B) an acceleration payment.
   (C) a straight payment.
   (D) kiting.

36. When you use real property as security for a loan you:
   (A) demise it.
   (B) hypothecate it.
   (C) assign it.
   (D) devise it.

37. All but one of the following is a purpose of FHA:
   (A) Insure titles.
   (B) Stabilize the mortgage market.
   (C) Encourage improvement in housing standards.
   (D) Encourage home financing.

38. Upon the completion of a sale of mortgaged property, the seller must:
   (A) pay off the mortgage.
   (B) deliver the deed to the grantee.
   (C) record the satisfaction of the mortgage.
   (D) inform the Department of Banking.

39. Conventional loans are:
   (A) guaranteed by the federal government
   (B) insured by the federal government.
   (C) not originated as often as FHA and VA loans.
   (D) loans that are not guaranteed or insured by any agency of the federal government.

40. The Veterans Administration is authorized to make direct loans where:
   (A) the veteran agrees not to occupy the property.
   (B) a disabled veteran gets a supplemental grant to get a specially adapted home.
   (C) the veteran has trouble qualifying for the loan.
   (D) the FHA refuses to insure the loan.

41. When a loan is approved by FHA:
   (A) the appraised value may be less than the sale price.
   (B) the government guarantees the value of the property.
   (C) the FHA lends the money.
   (D) the Director of HUD sets the maximum interest rate.

Mortgage : Rights & Intrs on real property

Lien : Each mortgage goes in subsecuensi recorded.

Taxes also creats a lien.

Lis pendens : pending action Can be x TEPE *'

↳ notification (gets recorded)

*' T E P E : 4 Powers of goverment to take your property.

- Escheat (when someone dies intested. - no will -)
- police power.
- Eminent Doman thru condennation. x public purpuse.
- Taxes

attachment:

General Liens: - Judgments Liens

CHAPTER EIGHTEEN

LIENS, FORECLOSURE AND REDEMPTION

LIENS

Various types of encumbrances which affect the physical condition or use of property, notably easements, restrictions and encroachments, were considered in Chapter 9. We now look at those encumbrances which affect the title to property, notably liens.

A **lien** is a right given by law to a creditor (lienor) to have a debt or charge satisfied out of the property belonging to the debtor. Liens on property may be either **voluntary**, arising from an act of the owner, such as the execution of a mortgage, or they may be **involuntary** and created by operation of law, such as tax liens or judgment liens recorded by the creditor of the owner. Involuntary liens do not require the owner's consent.

Once there has been a forced sale of the property subject to the lien, title passes to the purchaser at the sale. Ordinarily such transfer of title will be considered to relate back to the time when the lien originally arose, and thereby convey the title held by the debtor at the date the lien attached, cutting off rights of third parties that may have arisen since the creation of the lien.

A **lis pendens**, technically speaking, is not a lien upon property, but is a public notice, filed against specific lands, that an action at law is pending that may affect the title to the land. Lis pendens is a notice to a prospective purchaser, mortgagee or any other interested party that a claim against the property exists, and that future title to the property can be taken only subject to the outcome of the court action.

The foregoing are general principles affecting all liens. Naturally, there are special rules that apply to each type of lien which need to be discussed. For purposes of convenience, liens may be classified into two groups: (1) specific liens, and (2) general liens.

1. Specific Liens. These are liens which attach to and affect only a specific piece or pieces of property, such as: (a) mortgages; (b) taxes and assessments; (c) mechanics' liens; and (d) attachments. Note that a specific lien identifies the property which is the target of the lien.

a. Mortgages. When one borrows funds to finance the purchase of a home, he or she signs a mortgage on the property in order to secure or guarantee repayment of the amount due the lender. The mortgage is a conditional transfer of an interest in the property, and becomes a specific lien or claim against said property. The priority of mortgage liens, in the absence of a **subordination clause**, is according to the time of recordation, with the first mortgage recorded or registered having superior status to one subsequent in time. All mortgage liens, however, are considered inferior to those for real estate taxes or assessments. The lien becomes null and void upon payment of the debt, though a **satisfaction of mortgage** should be recorded to clear the record.

b. Real Property Taxes and Assessments. In New Jersey, real estate taxes are payable in four quarterly installments on February 1, May 1, August 1 and November 1 of each year. If they are not paid at that time, they become delinquent. Property taxes become a lien on and after the first day of January of the year for which the taxes are assessed. When taxes remain unpaid on July 1 of the year following the calendar year when the taxes were due, the tax collector can enforce the lien by selling the real property in accordance with the provisions of the Tax Sale Law.

After preparing a list of tax delinquents as of December 31st of the prior year, the tax collector advertises and holds a public auction for the sale of properties on which taxes remain unpaid. Interest and costs up to the time of sale are added to the taxes owed. The owners should be advised of the impending sale by mail, but if they are not, the sale is still valid. If taxes and charges are not paid by the date of sale, the municipality will sell its tax lien to the successful bidder who will pay the amount owed on the property. Bidding is conducted on the basis of the amount of interest the bidder will charge the delinquent property owner. The successful bidder is the party bidding the lowest amount of interest. The highest rate that may be bid is 18%. The successful bidder receives a **tax sale certificate** from the tax collector under which the purchaser acquires title and a lien, subject to the statutory right of redemption, a right that can be foreclosed.

If the owner does not exercise the statutory right of redemption and redeem the property within **two years** from the date of sale, the holder of the certificate may, through court action, initiate a foreclosure to legally bar the owner's right to redeem the property. The certificate holder has no right of use, entry or possession of the property during the redemption period, but only holds a lien against it and the potential right to gain title. If no one bids on the property at the tax sale, the municipality becomes the holder of the certificate and must hold it for at least **six months** before it could bar the owner's right to redeem. A privately held tax sale certificate has a life of 20 years and may be extended if the holder continues to pay the taxes. However, tax sale certificates held by a municipality are enforceable forever.

c. Mechanics' Liens. New Jersey law expressly provides that any persons furnishing labor or material for the improvement of real estate may file a lien upon the property affected if they are not fully compensated. Mechanics, material suppliers, contractors, sub-contractors, builders and all other persons rendering professional or skilled service, performing labor upon, or repair of any structure upon land, who are not compensated for their work may protect their interest by filing a lien against the property in a manner prescribed by law. It should be noted that real estate brokers cannot file a mechanics' lien against a property.

New Jersey practice with regard to mechanics' liens changed with enactment of the "Construction Lien Law," P.L. 1993, c. 318 (hereafter the "Lien Law"). Under preexisting law, a contractor or material supplier could only obtain a lien if a "Notice of Intention" was filed before the work was done for which the lien might be needed. In many cases, usually by the time the work had already been performed or the materials furnished and payment not received, it was too late to perfect the lien because a notice of intention had not been filed at the outset. Moreover, if the owner or contractor filed the general contract, subcontractors and suppliers were required to follow a "stop notice" procedure with no opportunity to obtain a mechanics' lien.

Under current law, the need to file a pre-claim notice of intention has been abolished. A lien claim may now be filed directly with the county clerk at any time within 90 days following the date of last work, service performed or last material furnished. Thus, any contractor, subcontractor or supplier who provides work, services, material or equipment pursuant to a written contract for an improvement to real property can decide upon, and then obtain, a lien for the value of the unpaid contract price which attaches to the interest of the owner in the realty (or for contracts with a tenant, to the leasehold interest of the tenant) after the work has ended.

The statute adds a complex set of additional requirements for lien claims arising under residential construction contracts. For purposes of this law, "residential" projects are those which involve construction or alteration of any one- or two-family dwelling or to any portion of a residential unit in a condominium, co-op or attached townhouse.

d. Attachment. Under some circumstances, a plaintiff may attach the property of a defendant by obtaining a **writ of attachment**. The writ is a lien on the defendant's real estate from the time it is issued. The defendant may not convey the attached property and if such a conveyance did occur, it would be void against the plaintiff. The writ is generally used against an absconding or fraudulent debtor by a judgment creditor or used by a plaintiff in a civil court action to prevent a defendant from disposing of property prior to the conclusion of a lawsuit.

A defendant who wishes to convey, mortgage or lease his real estate during the pendency of the suit may post a bond or arrange with plaintiff's counsel for release of the premises in question from the lien created by the attachment.

2. General Liens. These are liens that attach to and affect all property of the debtor, such as (a) judgment liens; (b) federal and state estate tax liens; (c) federal and state tax liens; and (d) decedents' debts.

a. Judgments. A judgment is a decree of court issued at the conclusion of a lawsuit stating that one individual is indebted to another, and fixing the amount of the indebtedness. A judgment of the Superior Court is a lien upon all the lands of the judgment debtor in the state of New Jersey from the time it is recorded in the county clerk's office where the property is located. A judgment is enforced by a **writ of execution** which authorizes a court officer (sheriff, constable, etc.) to seize the property and to sell as much of it as is necessary to satisfy the judgment, plus any additional costs. The lien can continue for up to 20 years, or until the debtor has made payment of the amount due under the judgment. When it has been satisfied, the debtor will obtain a "Release and Satisfaction of Judgment" from the creditor, which, when properly recorded, will remove the encumbrance from the records.

b. Federal and State Estate Tax Liens. Federal **estate taxes** are those levied by the United States on the right of an individual to transfer property at the time of death. These taxes are not "inheritance taxes." The estate of the decedent pays the federal estate tax before any property is distributed to the beneficiaries of the estate. Barring an extension, the estate tax is due within nine months after death. The duration of the lien is ten years from the date of death. The **New Jersey Transfer Inheritance Tax** is a tax imposed on the right or privilege of receiving property from a decedent at death. Taxes owed upon the transfer of a property of a deceased person encumber the real and personal property of the decedent and prevent clear title from being conveyed. The duration of the lien is 15 years.

c. Federal and State Tax Liens. These are liens imposed against real property for failure to pay various federal and state taxes. Federal tax liens result from a failure to pay any Internal Revenue tax (including income tax and payroll tax), and become a general lien against all property and property rights. Liens for state taxes, such as income taxes or general excise taxes, become general liens on all property.

d. Decedent's Debts. When a person dies, the decedent's property passes to his or her heirs or devisees, subject to any existing liens, encumbrances or rights of creditors of the estate. Debts against the estate are first paid by way of any personal property which is not specifically bequeathed. If the property is insufficient to satisfy all the debts, the real property may then be sold to pay the balance owing. Thus, title to a decedent's real estate may be subject to a lien in favor of the creditors of the estate.

Foreclosure

If the mortgagor fails to make loan payments as agreed, or otherwise violates certain covenants of the mortgage contract, the mortgagee may institute foreclosure proceedings to have the property sold at a forced sale. Foreclosure is a legal process, instituted by a mortgagee or any lienholder, to have real property sold by the sheriff of the county in which the property is located to satisfy an unpaid debt. New Jersey uses a judicial foreclosure in which the lender must appear in court to prove default in order to obtain a court judgment ordering the property to be sold. The foreclosure is broadly outlined below.

The attorney for the lender seeking to foreclose the mortgage files suit. A title search is conducted to determine all parties in interest who are advised of the pending sale. A **lis pendens**, a notice of pending legal action, is recorded giving notice of the suit. Any purchasers of the property are bound by any subsequent judgment as if they had been served with process and made party to the suit. The practical effect of a lis pendens is that title effectively becomes unmarketable until the legal matter involved is settled by the parties or decided by the court.

If the court determines that the property is to be sold, the sheriff, following the directive of the court, will advertise the public auction at which anyone may bid. The foreclosure sale (sheriff's sale) must be advertised in two local newspapers for four consecutive weeks, and a notice of sale must be posted in the sheriff's office and the premises in question at least three weeks prior to the sale. In addition, a notice must be mailed to the owner of record and to every party named as a defendant in the complaint at least ten days prior to the sale. The notice informs the defendants that if they do not appear to defend their interests, they will be foreclosed from any future rights by judgment of the court. Junior lienholders who are not notified of the foreclosure would not be able to participate in the property auction and would therefore acquire the right to file suit on their own at some future time.

The highest bidder is required to post a deposit of 20% of the total bid price in cash, certified or cashier's check immediately after the closing of the sale. The balance of the purchase price plus the fee for drawing the deed must be paid within 30 calendar days from the date of sale. If the balance is not paid in 30 days, the purchaser must pay default interest at the current prevailing rate as dictated by the State of New Jersey on the full amount of the bid up to the date that full payment is made.

Prior to the sale, the delinquent owner may redeem the property by paying the full amount of the judgment and all charges. This right is called **equity of redemption**. The equitable right of redemption terminates once the sheriff's deed has been delivered to the successful bidder.

A **sheriff's deed** is used to convey any right, title or interest that was held by the delinquent owner at the time of the sale. Thus, if the mortgagor held less than a fee simple absolute at the time the mortgage was made, the purchaser will receive the same title. For example, if an easement or a deed restriction encumbered the mortgaged property, the purchaser's title will also be encumbered. On the other hand, if the mortgagor owned an appurtenant easement over adjoining lands, the purchaser will acquire the mortgagor's rights in the easement as well.

If the sale proceeds satisfy the first mortgage, any residue is used to satisfy subsequent liens in their order of priority. If there is an excess remaining after taxes, costs of sale and debts have been paid (which is unlikely), it is called **equity**, and will be remitted to the owner. If the sale does not bring enough to cover the debt, the lender may seek a **deficiency judgment** against the borrower because of default on the promissory note or bond. The mortgagee may then be able to recover any money still owing by moving against other real and personal property owned by the debtor. In the event that a satisfactory bid on the property is not received, title will be conveyed to the lender to satisfy its lien. The lender would then sell the property in an attempt to recover the balance on the loan.

Deed in Lieu of Foreclosure

In an effort to eliminate a costly and time-consuming foreclosure action, a deed in lieu of foreclosure may be given by the mortgagor to the mortgagee, voluntarily relinquishing title to the property. A deed used for this purpose presents two problems:

1. The mortgagee acquires title subject to junior liens and other encumbrances (foreclosure eliminates these), and

2. If the mortgagor declares bankruptcy, the action is vulnerable to attack by a bankruptcy trustee as a preference or fraudulent conveyance.

New Jersey Fair Foreclosure Act (FFA)

The New Jersey Fair Foreclosure Act applies to residential mortgage foreclosure lawsuits involving owner-occupied one-, two-, three- and four-family dwellings. Under FFA the lender must send the borrower a *notice of intention to foreclose* before it can accelerate the mortgage debt or file a foreclosure complaint. The notice of intention gives the mortgagor 30 days to cure the default. If the required payment is not made within 30 days, the lender can then accelerate the loan and file a lawsuit to foreclose the mortgage.

Soldiers and Sailors Civil Relief Act (SSCRA)

The nature of military service often compromises the ability of service members to fulfill their financial obligations and to assert many of their legal rights. Congress has long recognized the need for protective legislation. The Soldiers and Sailors Civil Relief Act, among other things, operates to protect servicemen and women, including reservists and members of the National Guard (when in active service) from the loss of their homes through tax or mortgage foreclosures. If a service member's military obligation has affected his or her ability to pay on financial obligations such as mortgages, the service member can have his or her interest rate capped at 6% for the duration of the military obligation. Qualifying debts are debts that were incurred prior to the service member coming on active duty. In foreclosure proceedings, a default judgment may not be entered against a defendant unless it is accompanied by an affidavit of non-military service. If a default judgment has been entered, the defendant can apply to have it vacated until 90 days after his or her discharge. A career military person is not entitled to the protection or benefit of this act.

KEY WORDS

Assessment
Attachment
Deficiency Judgment
Equity
Equity of Redemption
Foreclosure
General Lien
Involuntary Lien
Judgment
Lien
Lis Pendens
Mechanic's Lien
Notice of Intention
Soldier's and Sailor's Civil Relief Act
Specific Lien
Statutory Right of Redemption
Writ of Execution

CHAPTER 18
Review Questions
(Answers on page 557)

1. The right by which a creditor has a claim against a borrower's property is most broadly described as:
   (A) a judgment.
   (B) an attachment.
   (C) a writ of execution.
   (D) a lien.

2. Which of the following statements is most correct concerning liens and encumbrances?
   (A) The owner cannot encumber his property.
   (B) Encumbrances lower the value of the property.
   (C) An easement is both a lien and encumbrance.
   (D) A mortgage is an encumbrance but not a lien.

3. Which of the following is NOT an encumbrance?
   (A) A mechanics' lien.
   (B) A mortgage.
   (C) An easement.
   (D) Dominant owner's easement.

4. Which of the following is NOT a voluntary lien?
   (A) A mortgage.
   (B) A deed of trust.
   (C) A mechanics' lien.
   (D) All the above.

5. The lien having priority over all others is:
   (A) the one first created and recorded.
   (B) a federal income tax lien.
   (C) a mechanics' lien.
   (D) a property tax lien.

6. In New Jersey the redemption period for the property owner after a tax sale is:
   (A) ten days.
   (B) two years.
   (C) six years.
   (D) 20 years.

7. Which of the following may NOT file a mechanics' lien for completed work that remains unpaid:
   (A) Carpenter.
   (B) Real estate broker.
   (C) Electrician.
   (D) Architect.

8. Which of the following statements is true?
   (A) All liens are encumbrances.
   (B) All encumbrances are liens.
   (C) Specific liens affect all property of the debtor located in the state.
   (D) Judgments are specific liens.

9. When the court issues an order to sell property to satisfy a judgment, it is known as a (an):
   (A) easement.
   (B) encumbrance.
   (C) attachment.
   (D) writ of execution.

10. Which of the following encumbrances would constitute a lien on real property?
    (A) Encroachment.
    (B) Restriction.
    (C) Easement.
    (D) Judgment.

11. If the proceeds of a foreclosure sale are less than the outstanding debt and foreclosure expenses, which of the following remedies are available?
    (A) There is no remedy.
    (B) The mortgagee must absorb the loss since the mortgagor is liable only for foreclosure expenses.
    (C) The owner has a statutory right of redemption.
    (D) The mortgagee may obtain a deficiency judgment against the mortgagor.

12. A lien filed by a sub-contractor is:
    (A) a claim against the general contractor.
    (B) a claim against the mortgage lender.
    (C) a claim against the broker handling the sale.
    (D) a claim against the property.

13. Which of the following is an encumbrance, but NOT a lien?
    (A) Mortgage.
    (B) Restriction.
    (C) Trust Deed.
    (D) Taxes.

(Quiz continues on next page)

14. A recorded notice of a current lawsuit involving title to real property is termed:
    (A) a lis pendens.
    (B) an attachment.
    (C) an acknowledgment.
    (D) suitus currentia.

15. A mechanics' lien takes precedence over which of the following?
    (A) A subsequently recorded judgment.
    (B) A lien for delinquent real property taxes.
    (C) Both A and B.
    (D) Neither A nor B.

A- If you live in a house x 2 consecutive
years when you sell your house and make
a profit up to 250.000 if you are single
up to 500.000 if you are married.

5075709

CHAPTER NINETEEN

FINANCING

Sources of Financing—Institutional

The ability and desire of major institutions active in the real estate market to invest funds at a given time in long- or short-term real estate loans is determined by operating policies, by the availability of money, and by the many other factors related to the national and international money market. Persons wanting to borrow money using real estate as collateral have a wide variety of sources to which they can apply. Today, these sources include homebuilders, real estate brokerage firms, financial services companies, automobile credit companies and mortgage companies. Of these, institutional lenders constitute the major source of mortgage money for residential loans, comprising two-thirds of all mortgage loans originated.

The three major institutional sources of real estate mortgage financing are (1) savings and loan associations; (2) federal and state banks; and (3) life insurance companies.

Savings and Loan Associations. Historically, savings and loan associations (also known as "thrifts") have been the method by which an individual with a small amount of money could indirectly invest in real estate and receive a financial benefit. When individuals deposit an amount of money with a savings and loan association, they are paid a specified amount of interest for the money in their savings account. The S&L in turn invests the money in real estate, from which it hopefully derives a profit, or return, providing interest for depositors and income for the association.

Savings and loan associations are a leading **primary lender** of home mortgage loans. The term "primary lender" refers to those lenders who originate loans directly to borrowers. S&Ls are an important source of mortgage funds for single-family homes, investing primarily in home purchase loans in their communities, home improvement loans, new home construction and home equity loans.

Savings and loans are either federally or state chartered. Federal associations must be a member of the Federal Home Loan Bank System (FHLBS), and the Federal Savings and Loan Insurance Corporation (FSLIC) must insure their funds up to $100,000 per account. Federally chartered associations are mutually owned (by depositors) and the word "federal" must appear in their title. State S&Ls may be either mutually owned or stock associations. In stock associations, investors buy stock to provide the capital. State chartered associations have optional membership in both the FHLBS and the FSLIC.

National and State Banks. Commercial banks are institutions that carry on their books demand deposits (checking accounts) and time deposits (savings accounts). Commercial banks in New Jersey are either chartered by the State of New Jersey and controlled by state statute, or are national banks, which are required to be members of the Federal Reserve System. The comptroller of the currency regulates their activities. The chartering agency prescribes the rules and regulations that govern the business operations of a bank.

While these institutions also provide long-term residential mortgage loan funds, their participation is not as focused as savings and loans. Banks offer a wider variety of loans, such as business and consumer loans, and other varied services.

Life Insurance Companies. Among the primary interests of life insurance companies is the investment of the funds held in trust for the benefit of their policyholders and beneficiaries of policyholders. They have great diversity of investments, with their portfolios including such things as government bonds, real estate and corporate securities of many types.

Life insurance companies are in a position to make loans on almost any type of real estate, and they supply most of the larger loans with long-term payments on commercial properties, shopping centers, industrial properties and hotels. They have also in recent years become increasingly active in residential real estate, and have provided great amounts of funds for single-family mortgages. Life insurance companies deal mainly through loan correspondents such as mortgage bankers, rather than individual borrowers.

Sources of Financing—Non-Institutional

In addition to the institutional sources of mortgage financing, there are a number of non-institutional sources of real estate financing from the private sector that deserve discussion. These are (1) loan correspondents; (2) purchase money mortgages; (3) land contracts; (4) sale and leaseback transactions; and (5) pension funds and credit unions.

Loan Correspondents. Certain sources of mortgage funds, such as insurance companies and the secondary sources discussed below, do not always deal with the borrower directly, but instead work through a **loan correspondent**. Loan correspondents are either mortgage brokers or mortgage bankers, depending on the type of loan being sought.

1. Mortgage Brokers. Mortgage brokers are not direct or primary suppliers of mortgage money, but they do play an important and necessary role in the financing process. They screen the property, secure prospects for the loans, qualify those prospects and present the mortgage loan application to the potential lender. The mortgage broker does not have the authority to approve or reject a loan on behalf of a lender. Upon acceptance of the application the mortgage broker's assignment is complete, in contrast to the mortgage banker, who normally remains in the picture and services the loan. The closing is done in the name of the lender and the mortgage broker is compensated by a finder's fee paid by the lender based on a percentage of the loan amount. The mortgage broker does not advance any part of the mortgage loan.

2. Mortgage Banking Companies. Mortgage banking companies (also called mortgage companies) are loan correspondents, but the services they provide go beyond those of the mortgage broker. Mortgage bankers originate loans with their own funds or money borrowed from other institutions (as opposed to depositors' funds) and then package these loans and sell them to primary and secondary investors. For example, a mortgage banker might accumulate a portfolio of 30 loans totaling $3,000,000 and sell them to an investor for $3,005,000. The mortgage banker usually continues to service the loan (collect monthly payments, pay taxes and insurance, pursue delinquent payments) and generally provides information on the status of the loan even after the loan has been sold. A "servicing fee" is charged before remitting the balance to the investor. Today, mortgage companies provide financing for more than half of all single-family home purchases.

Purchase Money Mortgage. Although all mortgage loans for real estate purchases are designated "purchase money mortgages" by lenders, the term is usually used to describe what happens when the seller agrees to take back all or a part of the selling price in the form of a mortgage. The purchase money mortgage is usually a junior lien because the primary lender will require a first lien position before making the loan. (See Chapter 17.)

Land Contract. A land contract, sometimes called a "contract for deed," is an installment contract for the sale of real property, often providing for a relatively small down payment, with the balance of the purchase price generally payable in monthly installments of principal and interest to the seller (called the vendor). It contains a provision that the deed and legal title to the property will not be delivered to the purchaser (called the vendee) until all or a specified part of the sale price has been paid. If the buyer defaults, the seller can normally cancel the contract and keep all payments as rent. The buyer takes possession, assumes all the risks and responsibilities of ownership, and generally covenants to keep the premises insured, repaired, pay taxes and assessments, etc.

When the contract becomes binding, the buyer thus has an equitable interest in the real estate, which is described as **equitable title**, and the seller still retains legal title. The buyer's interest in a land contract is considered to be real property, and generally the interest may be sold to a third party. If the contract has a nonassignability clause, the seller's consent must be secured first.

At the signing of the contract a deed is prepared and signed by the seller. The deed, along with a copy of the contract, is then placed in the hands of a third person, called an **escrow agent**, whose instructions are to deliver the deed to the buyer after the contract price has been met. Generally, payments are made to the escrow agent, who forwards the funds to the seller after deducting a small fee for services. An escrow agent is used to avoid complications in the event the seller dies or becomes divorced before the contract price has been paid. Since a land contract is treated as a conveyance, the buyer should demand evidence of title (even though the legal title will not be delivered until the buyer fulfills the terms of the contract), and should also record the land contract.

It is to the buyer's advantage to be given the right to prepay. This is usually done by way of a contract provision which stipulates that the monthly payments will be a certain amount "or more." Unless the contract has such a provision for prepayment, the buyer has no right to prepay.

Some of the advantages to the buyer in using the land contract are: (1) it provides a means of financing when mortgage money may be difficult to obtain or unavailable; (2) the buyer can both improve the property and take advantage of its appreciation in value; (3) a purchaser can consummate the transaction with a relatively small down payment, as opposed to the usual percent required by most lenders; and (4) since only the approval of the seller is needed for the financing, a sale can be made even when a buyer might not be able to meet the loan-to-income ratio requirements of an institutional lender.

Some of the advantages to the seller in using the land contract are: (1) a wider selection of buyers; (2) deferral of capital gains tax (by taking less than the full sales price in the year of sale); (3) maintaining reasonable control over the use of the property; (4) the ability to sell an interest by land contract without causing the mortgagee to accelerate any underlying mortgage; and (5) the opportunity of finding a buyer who might not otherwise be able to purchase a home due to an inability to qualify for new mortgage financing.

Land contracts are often used by the Veterans Administration to dispose of properties it has acquired through foreclosure.

Sale-Leaseback. Under this type of financing, the owner of an industrial or commercial property who wants capital to use in his business sells the property (or an interest therein) to an investor, and in turn leases it back for a long term.

Under the terms of the lease, the former owner becomes the lessee (tenant) under a **net lease**, and is therefore required to pay all real estate taxes, property insurance, repairs and so forth, so that all the rental paid is net to the landlord.

Among the advantages of the sale-leaseback transaction as a means of real estate financing are the following: (1) in computing income for tax purposes, the seller-lessee deducts lease payments as a business expense. Were the seller-lessee a mortgagor, the only permitted deductions would be interest and depreciation; (2) by selling the property for its full value, the seller-lessee obtains more cash than could be raised on a mortgage, since no mortgagee will loan 100% of the value of the property; and (3) existing mortgages or other documents binding on the seller-lessee may place restrictions on its rights to borrow money. Since a lease is not a loan, the leaseback transaction permits a method of getting around these restrictions.

The purchaser-lessor also gains some advantages in the sale and leaseback. For example: (1) since the seller-lessee assumes all operating expenses and burden of management, the net income (rent) provides a rate of return for the purchaser-lessor that is generally more attractive than that obtainable under a mortgage debt investment; and (2) equity ownership provides an excellent hedge against inflation, and if the property appreciates in value, the purchaser-lessor will reap the benefit of this increased value when the lease expires.

Pension Funds and Credit Unions. In recent years pension funds and credit unions have increasingly become a source of funds for real estate financing, often through mortgage brokers and bankers.

Mortgage Markets—Primary and Secondary

The **primary mortgage market** is the financial market where loans are made directly from the lender to the borrower. It is the market where the security is created. For instance, if a bank lends a homebuyer money to buy a house, that is a primary activity. But if that same bank sells the mortgage after it has been originated, the transaction would be a **secondary market** activity.

The secondary market achieves two objectives. First, it provides *liquidity* to originators of mortgage loans and enables institutions to invest in the mortgage market without having to be involved with making direct mortgage loans. Liquidity refers to the ease with which owners can sell their investments for cash. Because of the long-term nature of mortgages, the secondary market is an essential factor in maintaining lender liquidity. Second, it has led to the standardization of loan documents. Unlike corporate securities, each mortgage represents a loan made to a borrower with unique property and income characteristics. Without some form of standardization, the buyer of a loan would be reluctant to purchase the loan without evaluating each mortgage separately.

Recognizing this problem, the secondary market has standardized mortgage documents like the mortgage contract itself, the note, closing statements, property appraisal forms, loan applications and credit reports. Lenders who wish to sell mortgages in the secondary market must use the standard forms and follow the guidelines established by government regulations, such as limits on loan amounts and loan-to-value ratios.

Federally Related Agencies

Three governmentally related agencies have become increasingly important as sources of mortgage loans. Even though they deal almost exclusively in the secondary market, and buy mostly residential mortgages on one- to four-family homes, they provide funds to primary lenders who can then use the funds for income property loans. These agencies are the Federal National Mortgage Association (FNMA or Fannie Mae), the Government National Mortgage Association (GNMA or Ginnie Mae) and the Federal Home Loan Corporation (FHLMC or Freddie Mac). The role of each is discussed below.

Federal National Mortgage Association (FNMA or Fannie Mae)

The FNMA is a government-sponsored, **privately owned** corporation that specializes in buying mortgage loans, mostly from mortgage bankers. It was originally created to provide a secondary mortgage market for FHA-insured loans on homes. Since then, the company has become a shareholder-owned, privately managed corporation supporting the secondary market for VA and conventional loans as well. In 1968 it changed from a public agency to a private corporation, with its stock traded on the New York Stock Exchange.

The FNMA buys a large block or pool of mortgages from lenders and then issues *mortgage-backed securities* (MBS) to investors. The investor owns an undivided interest in the pool of mortgages that serves as the underlying asset for the security. As a MBS holder, the investor receives a pro rata share of the cash flows from the pool of mortgages.

A nationwide network of lenders, including mortgage bankers, savings and loan associations and commercial banks, originates the loans backing the MBS. Lenders submit a group of similar mortgage loans to the FNMA for securitization. If the loans meet the Fannie Mae credit quality guidelines, the pool of mortgages is then converted into an MBS which carries a guarantee of timely payment of principal and interest to the investor, whether or not there is sufficient cash flow from the underlying group of mortgages.

Loans that fall within the maximum dollar limit for loans that Fannie Mae or Freddie Mac (discussed below) purchase, and which meet their underwriting standards, are called **conforming loans**. **Non-conforming loans (jumbo loans)** are those that are over the maximum limit for loans which these entities will purchase, and which must be held by the originating lender in its own loan portfolio or sold to other secondary lenders. Due to the lessened marketability of non-conforming loans and the increased risk to the originating lender, such loans have higher interest rates than those found on conforming loans.

After the loan has been delivered to Fannie Mae, the loan originator continues to service the loan (collect payments, escrow property taxes, etc.), for which it receives a service fee. Fannie Mae's obligation is solely its own and is not backed by the full faith and credit of the U.S. government.

Government National Mortgage Association (GNMA, "Ginnie Mae")

The GNMA is a federal agency that operates as part of the U.S. Department of Housing and Urban Development (HUD) to make loans available in areas of higher risk, such as for urban development, subsidy programs and low- and moderate-income housing. Funds are generated through the sale of "pass-through securities" that provide their purchasers with a share in principal and interest from these mortgages which is "passed through" to Ginnie Mae certificate holders by lending institutions which originated the loan pools. These securities, commonly referred to as "Ginnie Maes", are issued in set denominations, although smaller investments are possible through unit investment trusts. Investor payments of principal and interest are guaranteed by the full faith and credit of the U.S. government.

Federal Home Loan Mortgage Corporation (FHLMC or Freddie Mac)

A third major participant in the secondary market is the Federal Home Loan Mortgage Corporation. It was created in 1970 to provide a secondary market for member savings and loan associations. FHLMC functions as a secondary market through the purchase and sale of mortgages, primarily conventional loans. Freddie Mac has authority to purchase conventional mortgages, pool them and sell **mortgage participation certificates (PCs)** and **guaranteed mortgage certificates (GMCs)** in the open market, with the mortgages as security. However, the FHLMC does not guarantee payment of these conventional mortgages. It contributes significantly to the vitality of the savings and loan industry by allowing that industry to use Freddie Mac to convert mortgages to cash, then to use the cash to make new mortgage loans.

The Mortgage Loan Application

When a lender receives a loan application, the main objective of both parties is to see that loan requests that show a high probability of being paid in full and on time are approved, while requests that are likely to result in default are rejected. To accomplish this, the lender will evaluate the buyer's income and credit history as well as the property being pledged to determine if it offers sufficient collateral value. The approval process varies, but most lenders use the **Uniform**

Residential Loan Application for all loans (including FHA and VA) secured by one- to four-family residences.

When qualifying borrowers, lenders look for two things: ability to pay, as evidenced by sufficient, stable and continuing income, and willingness to pay as demonstrated by the applicant's credit history. After making application. the borrower's income, assets and employment will be verified and a credit check will be done to ascertain this information. Lenders use qualifying ratios to determine whether borrowers will qualify for the amount they have applied for. While ratios are modified periodically and may be higher and less stringent with certain types of mortgage loans, generally one's monthly payment for housing expenses (principal, interest, taxes and insurance) should not exceed approximate 28% of monthly gross income. This is called the **payment-to-income ratio**. When combined with other long-term debt (child support, revolving charge accounts, etc.), housing expenses should not exceed 36% **(the total debt-to-income ratio)**. The lender will approve a loan for the lesser of the two amounts after calculating both ways.

The lender may also evaluate such factors as the income prospects of the borrower, such as a doctor who has just completed residency and is soon to begin private practice. While current income may not be high, the brighter financial prospects in the future may be considered. The projected stability of the borrower's income will definitely be considered. A lender will be more conservative with an applicant who has fluctuating or largely commission-based income versus the income of a teacher, for example, who is under contract for the same income.

If the property is income-producing, the application should be accompanied by balance sheet listing the applicant's assets, liabilities and net worth and a statement of the income from the property. The application will also inquire into whether the applicant can provide any supplemental security.

Property Inspection

The purpose of the property inspection is to determine if its value is sufficient as the security for the payment of the debt. The inspection will determine the potential rent from the property, the size, shape, topography and fitness of the site for the purpose intended, the sales prices of comparable properties, amenities, the competence of management if it is an income-producing property and the depreciation due to any cause.

Illegal Discrimination in Lending Practices

Equal Credit Opportunity Act (ECOA). The Equal Credit Opportunity Act makes it illegal to discriminate against credit applicants on the basis of race, color, gender, religion, age, national origin, marital status or because all or part of an applicant's income is derived from a public assistance program, or alimony, or child support, or because of an applicant's exercise of his or her rights under the Consumer Credit Protection Act. A lender must respond to credit applications within 30 days. If the application is rejected, reasons must be given.

The Federal Trade Commission enforces the provisions of the Act. Exceptions to the law include individuals who do not have contractual capacity (minors) and noncitizens whose status might affect a creditor's rights and remedies in the event of default. The purpose of the law is to assure that lenders will not treat one group more favorably then another group except for reasonable and justifiable reasons. For example, a creditor cannot require an applicant to disclose income from child support or alimony unless the applicant wants the creditor to include that income in deciding on the applicant's creditworthiness. Nor can a creditor inquire about birth control practices, intentions about childbearing or childbearing capability, or require female applicants to have a co-signer unless the same requirement is imposed on male applicants under the same circumstances. A lender can only ask the applicant if he or she is married, unmarried or separated.

Redlining. Redlining is an unlawful practice by which a lender or an insurance company refuses to approve loan applications or grant insurance in certain geographic areas, usually on the basis of the ethnic or racial makeup of the area surrounding the property. It is a violation of the New Jersey Law Against Discrimination and the Federal Fair Housing Act of 1968 to discriminate in the making of loans or the granting of insurance on the grounds of race, color, religion, sex, handicap, familial status or national origin.

KEY WORDS

- Federal Home Loan Mortgage Assn.
- Federal National Mortgage Assn.
- Government National Mortgage Assn.
- Institutional Lender
- Land Contract
- Mortgage Banker
- Mortgage Broker
- Non-Institutional Lender
- Primary Mortgage Market
- Redlining
- Secondary Mortgage Market

CHAPTER 19
Review Questions
(Answers on page 558)

1. Which of the following federal agencies does NOT participate in the secondary mortgage market?
   (A) FHA.
   (B) FNMA.
   (C) GNMA.
   (D) FHLMC.

2. The agency of the Department of HUD that buys and sells low-income mortgages is:
   (A) Federal Deposit Insurance Corp.
   (B) Ginnie Mae.
   (C) Federal Home Savings and Loan.
   (D) Mutual Mortgage Insurance Corp.

3. Which of the following conveys legal title and possession?
   (A) Deed.
   (B) Mortgage.
   (C) Purchase and Sale Agreement.
   (D) Option.

4. A financing arrangement by which the buyer does not become the owner of record would be a:
   (A) trust deed.
   (B) land contract.
   (C) purchase money mortgage.
   (D) quitclaim deed.

5. A federal savings and loan company must insure its deposits for at least:
   (A) $10,000.
   (B) $50,000.
   (C) $20,000.
   (D) $100,000.

6. The seller under a land contract is called the:
   (A) grantor.
   (B) grantee.
   (C) vendor.
   (D) vendee.

7. The Federal National Mortgage Association (Fannie Mae):
   (A) insures FHA loans.
   (B) guarantees VA loans.
   (C) buys and sells mortgages.
   (D) originates loans to home buyers.

8. Which of the following would be classified as an "institutional lender"?
   (A) Pension fund.
   (B) Credit union.
   (C) Life insurance company.
   (D) Real estate investment trust.

9. Under a sale-leaseback, the occupant of the property would be which of the following?
   (A) Buyer.
   (B) Seller.
   (C) Grantee.
   (D) Mortgagee.

10. A private corporation which purchases mortgages in the secondary mortgage market is called:
    (A) Government National Mortgage Association.
    (B) Federal Home Loan Corporation.
    (C) Federal National Mortgage Association.
    (D) Federal Home Loan Mortgage Association.

11. During the term of a land contract, the buyer does not have:
    (A) the right to live on the property.
    (B) the right to lease the property.
    (C) the right of possession.
    (D) legal title to the property.

12. "Redlining" is:
    (A) refusal by a lender to make loans in minority populated areas and is legal.
    (B) refusal by a lender to make loans to unqualified buyers.
    (C) refusal by a lender to make loans in minority populated areas and is unlawful.
    (D) lending more than the market value of the property.

When you advertise Int & APR have to be big.

Discount Points.

APR: Everything is included.

if you borrowing 100000 loan.

Point	Int	~~APR~~
0	6.25	⇒ 0
1.5	5.75	⇒ 1500
2.5	5.25	→ 2500.

→ depending on time
For ex: 6.25% it will be the best if you are going to stay only for one year 1/2.

CHAPTER TWENTY

TRUTH-IN-LENDING

Truth-in-Lending (TIL) refers to a federal law which became effective in July 1969 as part of the Consumer Credit Protection Act, implemented by the Federal Reserve Board's **Regulation Z**.

The purpose of the law is twofold: (1) to assure a meaningful disclosure of credit terms so that consumers can compare costs among various credit sources; and (2) to allow a borrower to rescind a transaction in certain cases. The law requires sellers and lenders to disclose credit terms and interest rates in an identical manner.

Coverage

The act generally applies to credit transactions under $25,000 that involve:

- individuals (not corporations, associations or partnerships);
- the offering or extension of credit on a regular basis, meaning more than five real estate loans or 25 consumer loans in a calendar year;
- a finance charge or repayment in at least four installments; and
- credit extended primarily for personal, family or household or agricultural purposes.

The $25,000 limitation does not apply to consumer real estate loans, including refinancing or consolidation loans, which are covered regardless of amount.

Creditors and Arrangers of Credit

Creditors are persons who must comply with Regulation Z. A creditor is a person who *arranges* or *extends* credit on a regular basis as described above. Under the Depository Institutions Deregulation Act of 1982, real estate brokers are generally exempt from the provisions of Regulation Z. However, brokers are not automatically exempt simply because they have a real estate license. If they meet the definition of a creditor, or if they act as an arranger of credit, they must comply with Regulation Z. An *arranger of credit* is a person who regularly arranges for consumer credit by another person if a finance charge is imposed. And of course, real estate licensees are subject to the advertising restrictions in Regulation Z that are discussed below.

Disclosure Statement

As stated previously, the primary purpose of Truth-in-Lending is to give full disclosure of the cost and terms of the credit. To accomplish this, the creditor or arranger is required to provide the borrower with a disclosure statement containing such information. This statement is required to be given clearly, conspicuously and in meaningful sequence, and must be printed on only one side of a single sheet of paper. The disclosure is designed to give consumers information about the costs of the loan so that they can compare these costs with those of other loan programs or lenders.

There are two types of credit under the act: *open-end credit* and *closed-end credit*. Open-end credit is extended when the amount of the credit is not fixed. For example, when a department store opens a charge account for a customer, it is open-end credit. On the other hand, closed-end credit is characterized by a fixed amount. Generally, the Truth in Lending Act requires disclosure in an open-end transaction before the credit is actually used. In a closed-end transaction, the disclosure must be made before a consumer enters into the contract.

The four most important items required in the disclosure statement are: (1) the amount financed; (2) the finance charge; (3) the annual percentage rate; and (4) the total of payments.

1. Amount Financed. The amount financed is the amount of credit provided to the buyer.

2. Finance Charge. The *finance charge* is the total dollar amount the loan will cost over its entire life and includes such costs as interest, loan fee, loan finder's fee, time-price differential, discount points, service fee and premium for credit life insurance (if it is made a condition for granting credit). Not included in the finance charge, but still itemized and disclosed to the customer, would be the real estate purchase costs, which would be paid whether or not credit is extended. These would include legal fees, appraisals, surveys, title examination, taxes not included in the cash price, recording fees, title insurance premiums, the investigation of credit report fee and the like, provided of course that they are bona fide, reasonable in amount and are not excluded for the purpose of circumvention or evasion of the law. Some of these charges may be paid by the seller, some by the buyer. In the case of first mortgages to purchase residential dwellings, the total dollar finance charge need not be stated, although the annual percentage rate must be disclosed.

3. The Annual Percentage Rate (APR). APRs are a way to calculate the annual cost of loans, taking into consideration loan origination fees (points) and the other costs associated with securing a loan. The other costs include appraisal, credit report, processing and document fees. The APR protects consumers from lenders who may not have disclosed the fees associated with a low start rate on an adjustable-rate loan or below-market rate on a fixed-rate loan. It provides a way for consumers to check the true cost of the loan.

Example: In a $100,000 loan with $2,750 prepaid finance charges (2 points, + $750 for appraisal and other charges), a 30-year term, and a fixed rate of 8%, the payments will be $733.36 (principal and interest). Since the APR is based on the amount financed ($97,250), while the payment is based on the actual amount given ($100,000), the APR (8.3%) is higher than the interest rate. Under the Truth in Lending Law, the APR must be computed to the nearest 1/8 of 1%.

4. The Total of Payments. This figure represents the total amount the borrower will have paid after all scheduled payments have been made for the entire term of the loan. This includes principal, interest and mortgage insurance premiums, but does not include payments for real estate taxes or property insurance premiums.

Other Required Disclosures

In addition to the above requirements, a lender must make the following disclosures:

- identity of the lender;
- the payment schedule;
- prepayment penalties, if any;
- insurance required;
- late payment charges;
- filing fees required;
- description of collateral required;
- deposits required;
- prohibitions on assumption of the obligation;
- demand features of the note;
- total sales price (including interest);
- adjustable rate features;
- itemization of the financed amount; and
- reference to any items shown on the loan contract, but not on the disclosure statement.

Right of Rescission (Cooling-off Period)

The customer has a limited right to rescind or cancel a credit transaction if it involves placing a lien against real estate that is his principal residence. This right is intended to protect the homeowner from losing a home to unscrupulous sellers of home improvements, appliances, furniture, etc., where the credit to purchase is secured by a mortgage on the purchaser's home. The borrower has three business days (including Saturdays) to cancel the transaction after signing the credit documents. Vacant lots sold on credit to buyers who intend to use them for principal residences are included in the rescission privileges. Credit used to acquire or construct the buyer's principal residence is not eligible for the right of rescission. However, the right of rescission does apply in a transaction that is separate from the purchase, such as a home improvement loan.

The customer may waive his right to rescind a credit transaction if the extension of credit is needed to meet a bona fide personal financial emergency before the end of the rescission period.

Advertising

Advertising rules under TIL apply not only to real estate licensees, but to owners acting on their own behalf as well. All types of advertising are covered, including Internet ads, window displays, flyers, billboards, direct mail literature and multiple listing cards if shown to the public. Real estate advertising in general terms, such as "small down payment OK," "compare our reasonable rates" or "owner will carry," is permitted. However, if an ad mentions particular points called **trigger terms**, then a number of additional disclosures must be made. These trigger terms include:

- The percentage or the amount of down payment;
- The amount of any installment payment;
- The dollar amount of the finance charge; or
- The number of installments or the period of repayment.

If an ad contains any of the information mentioned above, then the following information must be disclosed:

- Cash price or amount of a loan;
- Amount of required down payment;

- The number, amount and frequency of payments;
- The amount of the finance charge expressed as an annual percentage rate; and
- The total of all payments (except for a first mortgage on a dwelling in which the customer expects to reside).

Compliance

The federal agency in charge of enforcing Regulation Z is the Federal Trade Commission. Creditors should keep records of all compliance with the disclosure requirements of the federal Truth-in-Lending Law for at least two years after the transaction. Where joint ownership is involved, the right to receive disclosures, the right to rescind and the need to sign a waiver of such right apply to each joint owner who is a party to the transaction.

A lender who fails to make proper disclosures as required may be sued for actual damages plus twice the amount of the finance charge, as well as court costs and attorney's fees. The finance charge portion of damages is subject to a minimum of $100 and a maximum of $1,000. In addition, if lenders are convicted in a criminal action for willfully or knowingly violating the act or regulation, they can be fined up to $5,000, imprisoned for up to one year, or both.

In addition, if the required disclosures were not made, the borrower's right to rescind continues for **three years** or until the property is sold, whichever comes first. When a borrower exercises his right to rescind, he must tender any property received to the creditor, and the creditor must return all money paid by the borrower.

KEY WORDS

Annual Percentage Rate
Arranger
Creditor
Finance Charge
Regulation Z
RESPA
Right of Rescission
Total of Payments
Truth-in-Lending

CHAPTER 20
Review Questions
(Answers on page 558)

1. A broker must make Regulation Z disclosure:
   (A) in every transaction.
   (B) only if selling his own property.
   (C) only if paid for arranging the loan.
   (D) if he takes his commission by an installment note payable in four or more installments.

2. All but one of the following is included in the "finance charge" under the Truth-in-Lending provisions:
   (A) Points.
   (B) Loan finder fee.
   (C) Attorney fee.
   (D) Service charges.

3. Under Truth-in-Lending it is permissible to advertise which of the following statements alone?
   (A) $2,000 down.
   (B) 4% interest.
   (C) Reasonable monthly terms.
   (D) No closing costs.

4. Truth-in-Lending laws apply to:
   (A) commercial loan transactions involving real property.
   (B) residential real estate mortgages.
   (C) all personal property transactions.
   (D) unconscionable contracts.

5. Under Truth-in-Lending, the borrower (consumer), except in cases of a first purchase money mortgage to acquire or construct a home, has a right of rescission upon notice for:
   (A) two calendar days.
   (B) 24 hours.
   (C) three business days.
   (D) 72 hours.

6. Under Truth-in-Lending, it is permissible to have an ad which only states:
   (A) the interest rate.
   (B) the down payment.
   (C) "easy payment terms available."
   (D) the monthly payment.

7. Which of the following statements is NOT true?
   (A) The annual percentage rate combines the interest rate with other costs of the loan.
   (B) Refinanced loans are covered regardless of amount.
   (C) The Truth-in-Lending Law is a federal law.
   (D) Advertising rules under TIL do not apply to owners acting without real estate agents.

8. The primary purpose of the Truth-in-Lending Act is to:
   (A) save the general public money in their installment purchases.
   (B) disclose to the consumer the cost and conditions of the installment purchase.
   (C) limit interest rates.
   (D) protect creditors in financing transactions.

9. The annual percentage rate must be revealed to:
   (A) an applicant for a residential first mortgage loan.
   (B) an applicant for a commercial first mortgage loan.
   (C) The Federal Trade Commission.
   (D) The Federal Housing Administration.

10. Regulation Z prohibits:
    (A) the advertising of credit terms.
    (B) advertising in general terms such as "reasonable monthly payments."
    (C) Both A and B.
    (D) Neither A nor B.

NOTE: Upon completion of Chapters 17-20, you should complete Review Quiz 3 on page 517 and compare your answers with the solutions at the back of the book.

CHAPTER TWENTY-ONE

REAL ESTATE CLOSING (SETTLEMENT) PROCEDURES

When all conditions necessary to complete a transaction are met, the time comes to finalize the sale and transfer ownership from seller to buyer in accordance with the sales contract. Normally, this takes place at a meeting called a **closing** after various preliminary procedures have been completed. The closing is usually attended by: the seller and buyer, or their representatives; attorneys for the parties; a representative of the lender; and a representative of the broker. The time and place for the closing is agreed upon in the sales contract. It may take place at the attorney's office, the lender's office, at the title company or at the office of a real estate broker. In the majority of cases, the most convenient place is at the office of the attorney closing the mortgage loan, usually the attorney for the purchaser.

Closing practices vary from one part of the state to another. In the northern part of the state the process is almost always conducted by an attorney, but in the southern counties, starting somewhere below Trenton, title companies usually handle the function.

Laws Affecting Real Estate Closings

Several laws govern the conduct of closing the real estate transaction. Principally these laws include the Law of Agency, which is common law, the New Jersey Real Estate Commission Rules, which are administrative law as adopted by the New Jersey Real Estate Commission to Title 45, Chapter 15 of the New Jersey Statutes, and the Real Estate Settlement Procedures Act (RESPA), a federal regulation.

Agency Law. Agency law deals with the legal relationship and duties of the parties when one acts on behalf of another, as does the broker who represents a seller in the sale of the seller's home. The relationship is legally described as **fiduciary**, which means a position of confidence and trust. These duties at law require the agent to keep his principal informed and to account for money or property coming into the agent's possession.

New Jersey Real Estate Commission Rules. NJSA 45:15, commonly known as the New Jersey Real Estate License Laws, gives authority and responsibility for protecting the public to the New Jersey Real Estate Commission. This is accomplished through regulating the activities of licensees. To accomplish its purpose the Commission adopted Rules and Regulations which became administrative law when approved by the New Jersey Legislature. The record-keeping requirements of real estate licensees are covered in 11:5-1.12 of the Real Estate Commission Rules.

The Real Estate Settlement Procedures Act (RESPA). This federal law is designed to ensure that buyers and sellers in residential real estate transactions are informed of all settlement costs.

Transactions covered by RESPA:

1. Loans on one- to four-family residential properties, including cooperatives and condominiums.

2. Real estate transactions when the property is sold or refinanced with a new first mortgage provided by an institutional lender.

3. Federally related first mortgages including:

    - Loans made by lenders insured by the Federal Deposit Insurance Corporation (FDIC);
    - Loans insured by the FHA or guaranteed by the VA; and
    - Loans intended to be sold in the secondary market to FNMA, GNMA or FHLMC. The secondary market is discussed in Chapter 19.

Transactions NOT covered by RESPA:

1. A transaction in which the only financing is by the seller.

2 An all-cash purchase.

3. A transaction in which the mortgage is assumed by the buyer.

RESPA Requirements

RESPA mandates certain pre-closing procedures by lenders to borrowers, and regulates certain abuses by prohibiting "kickbacks" and "unearned fees." Basically, the Act was designed to provide adequate disclosure of closing costs so that prospective buyers can shop around and compare various settlement services.

Special Information Booklet. RESPA requires the lender to give the applicant a copy of a booklet prepared by the U.S. Department of Housing and Urban Development (HUD) entitled *Settlement Costs and You.* If the booklet is not made available by the lender on the day of application for the loan, it must be mailed to the applicant within three business days after the application is filed. The booklet describes the settlement process and the kinds of charges, and alerts the applicant to unfair and illegal trade practices. It also provides an explanation of settlement services and costs, with sample forms to help the applicant compare costs.

Good Faith Estimates of Closing Costs. When the loan application is made, the lender must provide good faith estimates of settlement costs which are likely to be incurred in financing the property. If these estimates are not provided when the application is made, they must be mailed within three business days. The good faith estimates must include the lender's estimate of charges for each item payable in connection with Section L on the HUD-1 Uniform Settlement Statement. The lender is not, however, required to estimate paid-in-advance items such as prepaid hazard insurance, mortgage insurance, prepaid taxes or other reserves deposited with the lender.

Uniform Settlement Statement. RESPA requires use of the HUD-1 Uniform Settlement Statement (or RESPA Statement) as the standard settlement for closings covered by the Act (see Figure 21.3).

One day before the scheduled closing, the borrower has the right to inspect the Settlement Statement, which gives an itemized account of all fees charged by the lender.

If a lender specifies use of a particular closing attorney, title examiner or title insurance company, the following additional requirements must be met:

1. The borrower must be told of this requirement;

2. Cost estimates for the service must be furnished and the good faith estimate must clearly state that the charge is based on a particular provider;

3. The name, address and telephone number of each designated provider must be furnished; and

4. The lender must specify if a business relationship exists with any of the aforementioned providers of services.

Prohibition Against Kickbacks. RESPA prohibits secret kickbacks or the payment of unearned fees from any of the aforementioned providers of services. Basically, it provides that no compensation be paid unless a service is rendered or a fee earned. The penalty under this violation is a $10,000 fine or one-year imprisonment and triple damages of the illegal compensation, plus court costs and attorney fees. This requirement does not prohibit the payment of fees to attorneys, title companies or others for services actually performed. It specifically permits cooperative brokerage splits, referral fees and commission splits through multiple listing arrangements. Brokers must therefore be certain that any fees received, other than commissions, be for services actually performed.

Other RESPA Provisions. These RESPA provisions also apply:

- Lenders are prohibited from requiring escrow deposits exceeding that amount required to pay insurance and taxes, plus two additional months' deposit.

- Sellers (builders and developers) are prohibited from requiring buyers to purchase title insurance from a particular title company. The penalty for violation of this provision is three times the cost of the insurance.

- Lenders are prohibited from charging a fee for the preparation and distribution of the required RESPA forms.

- Settlement statements must be delivered at the time of closing unless (1) the mortgagor waives this right in writing, or (2) the mortgagor or agent does not attend the closing. In these cases, the settlement statement must be mailed or delivered expeditiously to the mortgagor and seller, if applicable.

- Lenders are required to keep records on settlement statements for a two-year period, during which time the mortgagor has the right of inspection.

The Title Closing

The **title closing** is the part of the closing process in which the deed and other closing documents are delivered to the purchasers in exchange for payment of the balance of the purchase price. The other part of the procedure is the **mortgage closing**, in which the mortgage transaction is closed by delivery of the mortgage and note to the lender and the disbursement of the mortgage funds to the mortgagor.

The basic closing documents are:

- The sales contract;
- The closing statement;
- The deed of conveyance;
- The affidavit of title; and
- The survey

Conditions of the sales contract could necessitate additional documents, as each real estate transaction is different. For example, a note and mortgage would be required if financing is used in order to consummate the purchase, and a bill of sale would be used to transfer any personal property included in the sale.

Sales Contract. The sales contract, as discussed in Chapter 14, is the order or specific instructions for the closing attorneys to follow in consummating the sale. It is the legal agreement between the parties as to the sales price, terms of finance, who pays various expenses, inspections of property, repairs if any, furnishing of marketable title, proration of continuing items of expense and any special conditions and provisions in the event of default by either party. The binding sales contract, when presented to the closing attorneys, initiates the action to achieve all the terms and conditions of the sales contract before the closing date agreed upon in the contract.

Typical provisions include:

1. Buyer making loan application;

2. Property inspection of plumbing, heating and air conditioning to determine if all are in working order and make arrangements for repairs, if any; and

3. An inspection of the property for termite infestation or possible violation of environmental laws.

The attorneys for the buyer and seller usually arrange for various pre-closing tasks and each one completes certain documents. Typically the buyer's attorney will:

1. Review the purchase and sale agreement;

2. Review the mortgage commitment;

3. Order a title search and survey to determine the status of title and have available the title insurance binder so the purchaser can obtain title insurance as of the date of acquisition;

4. Order a termite inspection (if required); and

5. Prepare the closing statement.

The seller's attorney will usually do the following:

1. Review the purchase and sale agreement;

2. Prepare the deed;

3. Prepare the affidavit of title; and

4. Obtain certificate of occupancy (if required).

Closing Statement. The closing statement is similar to a balance sheet, and is an itemized summary of all details of the entire transaction. Upon closing, it becomes necessary to make adjustments, or prorations, in the amount of money owed or received by each party. The closing statement is thus the written form of final accounting, showing buyer and seller the cash requirements, the proceeds, the expense or charge allotments and the proration in relation to each of their respective positions in the transaction.

If the respective attorneys have agreed upon the closing figures in advance, the closing statement may be prepared prior to the closing. However, many attorneys prefer not to fill in the totals until all parties assemble and agree upon the figures. This minimizes problems with last-minute items, such as fuel oil adjustments. The secretary can then type the balance of the closing statement and draw the checks from the attorney trust account while the closing is taking place. A detailed discussion of the closing statement follows later in this chapter.

Deed of Conveyance. As the closing statement is being completed and the checks are being drawn, the parties can review the closing documents, including the deed. In most cases, the type of deed given by the seller is a bargain and sale deed with covenants vs. grantor. In this deed the seller does not make any representations regarding the condition of the title but merely states that he has not done anything to encumber the property. The seller's attorney often submits an unsigned copy of the deed to the buyer's attorney prior to the closing for review. The grantees, if more than one, elect the type of interest they wish to hold as co-owners; for example, as joint tenants with survivorship rights, tenants in common or tenants by the entirety. The real estate licensee should not advise which interest would be most advantageous to the buyers, leaving this type of advice to the attorney.

Affidavit of Title. In New Jersey it has become standard practice for the seller to provide an affidavit of title in which he states the existence of any known liens or facts relating to the title that were not included in the title binder and specifies any judgments against him which were not revealed in the search. If the property is owned by one spouse and was acquired after May 28, 1980, it is important for the affidavit to state whether it was occupied as the principal marital residence. The affidavit should also contain statements as to bankruptcies, marital status, repairs or improvements on the property that have not been paid for, unrecorded deeds or contracts and other facts which may affect title. The title company insuring on the basis of such an affidavit has recourse against the seller if known facts are not disclosed.

Survey. The buyer is usually required to obtain a current survey.

Financing. If the sales contract contains a provision for financing, the buyer(s) will sign a mortgage and a note or bond and will receive the loan proceeds from the mortgagee's representative. After endorsing the check, the buyer will turn it over to the person conducting the closing. This sum, plus the earnest money and cash or certified check for the balance brought by the buyer, will be paid to the seller. When the transaction involves financing, the Truth-in-Lending law must be followed. This federal law requires lenders to make meaningful credit disclosures for certain types of consumer loans (see Chapter 20).

Insurance. The lender will require the borrower to obtain hazard insurance on the property and to name the lender as an additional insured in the policy. The insurance is usually in the amount of replacement cost of the improvements, and liability insurance covering property damage and personal injury arising from the property. Hazard insurance protects both the owner and the lender against loss by fire, lightning, windstorm and other natural perils. Coverage is generally provided by a package **homeowner's policy** which insures against additional risks, including personal liability and theft.

If the loan is federally insured or guaranteed and the property is in a flood-prone area as identified by the Federal Emergency Management Agency (FEMA), the buyer may be required by federal law to carry **flood insurance**. The insurance may be purchased in participating communities under the National Flood Insurance Act of 1968. The program is designed to provide flood insurance at low rates through federal subsidy. In order to qualify for this benefit, communities must adopt and administer local measures that protect lives and new construction from future flooding by instituting or agreeing to institute some flood plain management program. If a change in flood insurance maps brings the property within a flood insurance area after the loan is made, the lender or servicer may require the owner to buy flood insurance at that time.

Day of Closing. Generally, all of the closing proceeds, including any money from a lender, are deposited into the trust account of the buyer's attorney who then issues trust checks to the seller, the title company, the attorneys, the brokers and any lien holders. In order to issue checks out of the trust account the attorney must receive checks far enough in advance to provide time for clearance, or the checks must be in the form of a certified or bank cashier's check.

Upon agreement of all appropriate adjustments, fees and charges, the parties sign the RESPA settlement statement, the sellers sign and give the deed to the buyers and the checks representing the balance of the purchase price are given to the sellers. Copies of all relevant documents should be provided to the buyer and seller for their records. At this point the broker's commission should be disbursed. The final act in the closing process is usually the turning over of keys by the seller to the buyer.

The buyer's attorney should record the deed as soon as possible after the closing. This is important for two reasons: (1) If there is a subsequent fraudulent transfer to a bona fide purchaser for value, and the subsequent purchaser records his deed before the first purchaser, the second conveyance will take priority; and (2) an intervening lien, such as a judgment against the seller, would take priority if recorded prior to the recording of the buyer's deed (see Chapter 10).

Truth-In-Lending Act

If the transaction involves financing, the provisions of the Truth-In-Lending Act must be followed. The purpose of this law is to advise buyers of the exact cost of obtaining credit. This important law was covered in Chapter 20.

Preparation of the Settlement Statement Worksheet

The closing statement (sometimes called a "settlement statement") is similar to a balance sheet, and is an itemized summary of all details of the entire transaction. Upon closing, it becomes necessary to make adjustments, or prorations, in the amount of money owed or received by each party. These are called **closing costs**. The closing statement is thus the written form of final accounting showing buyer and seller the cash requirement, the proceeds, the expense or charge allotments and the proration in relation to each of their respective positions in the transaction.

Unlike some other states in which the real estate licensee prepares the closing statement, New

Jersey closing statements are usually prepared by the purchaser's attorney, after the parties have agreed upon the appropriate adjustments. Nevertheless, real estate licensees should be familiar enough with the rules, computations and methods to be able to explain the closing statement to all parties concerned. The inexperienced seller and buyer cannot readily understand the figures and their applicability with regard to the closing statement. Satisfaction in a sale is to be had only when the buyer knows exactly what he has bought in terms of his costs, and the seller knows what has been sold in terms of the final check received. The competent salesperson or broker should be able to serve his or her client from the preliminary steps in a transfer of ownership to the final culmination of the transaction.

Closing statements are made up in "debit" and "credit" form. If any item is owed by the seller, it is debited (charged) to him; if it is owed to the seller, it is credited. On the other hand, if the item is owed to the buyer, the buyer is credited; and if owed by the buyer, it is debited to him or her. Remember, debits will always reduce a party's cash at closing, and credits will always increase cash at closing.

Rules and Customs in Computations

1. All computations for adjustments or prorations of insurance premiums, rents, taxes, interest, lease rents, etc., shall be made as of the day of closing, unless otherwise stated.

2. Insurance, rents, taxes, interest, etc. shall be computed on a 360-day year method, and a 30-day month, each month representing one-twelfth of the yearly charge, and each day representing one-thirtieth of the monthly charge.

3. How to compute the credit: Inasmuch as all prepaid items are a credit to the seller and a debit to the buyer, the "unused" period can be computed by listing the months and simply crossing off the "used" period. The period of time remaining constitutes the unused period of time. The seller will receive a credit for the unused period, and the buyer will be debited for the same period.

EXAMPLE: Closing June 20, 2002, **taxes paid** for calendar year.

~~January~~
~~February~~
~~March~~
~~April~~
~~May~~
June 20 (10 days remain in June)
July (6)
August (5)
September (4)
October (3)
November (2)
December (1)
(count back)

Answer: 6 months, 10 days. (Credit seller; debit buyer).

4. Computation when items are unpaid.

EXAMPLE: Closing June 20, 2002, **taxes unpaid** for calendar year.

(1) January
(2) February
(3) March
(4) April
(5) May
June 20 (20 days have expired in June)
~~July~~
~~August~~
~~September~~
~~October~~
~~November~~
~~December~~

Answer: 5 months, 20 days. (Credit buyer; debit seller.)

Sample Settlement Statement Worksheet

In the following pages a typical settlement statement worksheet is shown. There are many other forms but the results of the computations are the same, no matter what form is used. The worksheet is not a closing statement. It is only used by the attorney who prepares the closing statement to check computations and entries. After the worksheet is completed, the information is then transposed to a disclosure/settlement statement. The listing contract (page 215), the sales contract (page 232), the worksheet (page 301) and the HUD-1 RESPA statement (page 305) were prepared using information from the following transaction (case):

Case

Rocco Balboa and Adrian Balboa, his wife, listed their home with your firm, New Jersey Good Realty, Inc., on March 21, 2002, under a six-month exclusive right-to-sell listing. The property is located at 114 Yantacaw Brook Road, Wyckoff, New Jersey. The sellers agreed to pay a 6% sales commission for selling their home at a listed amount of $185,000.

On April 15, 2002, Apollo Creed, and Ruby Creed,

his wife, entered into a purchase and sale agreement with the Balboas for the listed amount. The Creeds deposited $1,000 with your firm and agreed to post an additional cash deposit of $17,500 within 10 days, a provision with which they complied. The buyers secured a conventional loan of $129,500 with an interest rate of 9% per annum.

The contract states that the sellers agree to pay off the existing mortgage with related expenses. The buyers will assume the hazard insurance policy. All prorations are through the closing date, May 15, 2002.

Working Data

Annual Taxes: $2,560 paid through July, 2002.
Realty Recording Fee: as required by NJ law.
Buyer's Attorney Fees: $750.
Discount: 2 points paid by buyer.
Survey: $120.
Title Insurance: $3.50 per $1,000.
Recording Documents: $46.00 (Deed $24, Mortgage $22).
Existing Mortgage Balance as of 5/15/02: $44,000.
Monthly Interest on Existing Mortgage: $275. Last paid 4/20/02.
Hazard Insurance: paid to 3/15/04, 3-yr. premium $432.
Title Search: $160.
Interest on Mortgage to 6/1/02: paid to lender in advance.

Solution and Explanations

The following entries and calculations were made. Each numbered item is equivalently numbered on the HUD-1, RESPA statement (Figure 21-3). Due to the limited space on the sample worksheet, many items not included here would ordinarily be part of an actual transaction. These include credit report fee, appraisal fee, acknowledgments on mortgage, etc.

1. **Selling Price:** $185,000 as per sales contract. The full amount was debited to the buyer and credited to the seller.

2. **Earnest Money Deposit:** $1,000 as per sales contract. This amount is credited to the buyer.

3. **Additional Deposit:** $17,500. Initial deposits plus any additional deposits often are equal to 5 to 10% of the purchase price. Credit to buyer.

4. **Survey:** $120. Usually required by lender when making loan. Debit buyer.

5. **New First Mortgage:** $129,500 as per sales contract. This amount is a credit to the buyer since it will be applied to the purchase price of the property.

6. **Title Insurance:** $647.50. The title policy is for the protection of the buyer. The premium, therefore, is a debit to his account.

7. **Interest Paid in Advance to Lender:** $485.70. The lender generally requires that interest be paid through the month of the closing. This is a debit to the buyer. The calculation is as follows: $129,500 x 9% = $11,655 ÷ 360 = $32.38 x 15 = $485.70.

8. **Recording Documents:** $46. The fee for recording the deed is a debit to the buyer, as the instrument is recorded for his benefit. The mortgagee also generally requires the buyer to pay for the recording of the mortgage as a condition to granting the loan.

9. **Existing Mortgage Payoff to Best Banking Co.:** $44,000. This amount is a debit to the seller, since it must be paid off to clear the title.

10. **Interest on Existing Mortgage Balance:** $229.16. Since interest is generally paid in arrears, the seller must pay the interest from the date of his last payment (April 20, 2002) up to the date of closing (May 15, 2002), or 25 days. The interest due on May 15, 2002 is therefore $229.16. ($275 ÷ 30 = $9.17 x 25 = $229.16.) Debit the seller.

11. **Commission:** $11,100. ($185,000 x 6% = $11,100) This amount is a debit to the seller.

12. **Taxes:** $533.33. The closing is May 15. Annual taxes of $2,560.00 are paid through July. Therefore, the taxes are prepaid 75 days. This prorated amount is a credit to the seller and a debit to the buyer. ($2,560 ÷ 360 = $7.11 x 75 = $533.33.)

13. **Insurance:** $264. Three-year policy $432 expires March 15, 1999. Daily premium = $432 ÷ 1,080 = $.40. Unused period = 660 days x $.40 = $264. Debit buyer; credit seller.

14. **Title Search:** $160. The title search is for the benefit of, and a charge to, the buyer.

15. **NJ Realty Transfer Fee:** To calculate this amount first divide $150,000 of sale price by 500 and multiply by $2.00; divide balance by 500 and multiply by $3.35. ($150,000 ÷ 500 = 300 x $2.00 = $600; $35,000 ÷ 500 = 70 x $3.35 = $234.50; $600.00 + $234.50 = $834.50).

16. **Discount Points:** This amount is calculated by multiplying the loan amount by the discount rate ($129,500 x .02 = $2,590).

FIGURE 21.1
Settlement Statement Worksheet

SETTLEMENT DATE:	BUYER'S STATEMENT		SELLER'S STATEMENT	
	DEBIT	CREDIT	DEBIT	CREDIT
1. PURCHASE PRICE	$185,000.00			$185,000.00
2. EARNEST MONEY DEPOSIT		1,000.00		
3. ADDITIONAL DEPOSIT		17,500.00		
4. SURVEY	120.00			
5. FIRST MORTGAGE PROCEEDS		129,500.00		
6. TITLE INSURANCE	647.50			
7. INTEREST PREPAID TO 6/1/97	485.70			
8. RECORDING DOCUMENTS	46.00			
9. PAY OFF EXISTING MORTGAGE			44,000.00	
10. INTEREST ON EXISTING MORTGAGE BALANCE			229.16	
11. COMMISSION TO BROKER			11,100.00	
12. TAXES, PRORATED	533.33			533.33
13. INSURANCE, PRORATED	264.00			264.00
14 TITLE SEARCH	160.00			
15. N. J. REALTY TRANSFER FEE			834.50	
16. LOAN DISCOUNT	2,590.00			
17. ATTORNEY'S FEE	750.00			
18. SUB-TOTAL, BUYER	190,596.53	148,000.00		
19. BALANCE DUE FROM BUYER		42,596.53		
20. SUB-TOTAL, SELLER			56,163.66	185,797.33
21. BALANCE DUE SELLER			129,633.67	
22. TOTALS	$190,596.53	$190,596.53	$185,797.33	$185,797.33

This amount is debited to the buyer.

17. **Buyer's Attorney Fees:** $750.00. This amount is debited to the buyer.

18. **Sub-Total Buyer:** The total of the column of debits ($190,596.53) and the total of credits ($148,000) is made only for convenience in determining the balance or difference between the debits and credits of the buyer.

19. **Balance Due from Buyer:** $42,596.53. This amount is the difference between the total of the buyer's credits and his debits. This is the amount of cash the buyer must have to close the transaction.

20. **Subtotal, Seller:** The totals of the seller's debits ($56,029.16) and credits ($185,797.33) are again only for convenience, and for determining the balance or difference between his debits and credits.

21. **Net Proceeds Paid to Seller:** $129,768.17. This amount is the difference between the total of the seller's credits and debits. This is the amount the seller will actually receive in cash for his home. There are instances in which the seller must actually pay cash in order to accomplish the sale and closing, but these instances are the exception.

TOTALS: $185,797.33 Seller. $190,596.53 Buyer. The total of the debits and the total of the credits, as they pertain to each party, must equal each other.

Explanation of Other Possible Charges and Adjustments

No single real estate transaction will contain every type of charge or adjustments. All closings are similar, but each is different. The following will explain some of the more common types of charges and adjustments that will be encountered in practice, but are not included in the example.

1. Assumption of Present Mortgage. If the transaction is made with the buyer assuming the seller's present mortgage, the amount of the mortgage to be assumed is a debit to the seller, and a credit to the buyer. In that case, the interest due from the date of the last payment to the date of the closing is a debit to the seller and the same amount is a credit to the buyer.

2. Assumption Fee. In a transaction where the existing loan is being assumed, the lending institution normally requires a fee for changing the loan records. Unless there is another agreement, this charge would be a debit to the buyer.

3. Second Mortgage. When there is to be a second mortgage involved, if the mortgage is through a lending institution, it is handled the same as a new first mortgage, with the amount shown only as a credit to the buyer.

4. Purchase Money Mortgage-Second Mortgage. If the second mortgage is to be carried by the seller, the total amount of the second mortgage is shown as a debit to the seller and a credit to the buyer.

5. FHA Mortgage Insurance Premium. This item is involved only when an FHA loan is assumed. The premium is paid by the loan company to FHA for FHA's charge to insure the lender against loss in the event the borrower defaults on the loan. The lender then bills the borrower annually, in arrears. Thus, the seller would be debited pro rata for the part of the premium accruing from the date the last premium was due and paid to the date of settlement. The buyer would be credited this amount.

6. Prepayment Penalty on Old Mortgage Payoff. If the old mortgage is to be paid off, any prepayment penalty would be a charge to the seller.

7. Special Assessments. These are special assessments on properties such as sidewalks, sewers, etc. If the special assessments have been levied, it is normal to debit only the seller since the buyer has contracted for the clear title other than named exceptions. If the assessments are to be assumed, interest due from the last date of payment is prorated.

8. Tax and Insurance Escrows. On many loans, lending institutions require that real property taxes, insurance, lease rent (if property is leased), and maintenance (if the property is a condominium) be paid with each monthly installment. This is to be placed in the mortgagor's trust account to insure that monies will be available for payment of these items when due. In a transaction where the existing loan is being assumed and there is a customer trust fund, this amount is credited to the seller and debited to the buyer.

9. Rental Income. Adjustment should be made on any rental if paid by a tenant in advance. The rent is prorated from the date of closing to the next due date and that amount is debited to the seller and credited to the buyer.

10. Security Deposits. If the seller does not (1) return the security deposit plus interest to the tenants at the time of the sale, or (2) does not hold the deposits plus interest in trust for the tenants and notify them of the sale, then the seller is required to deliver all deposits and interest to the buyer and notify the tenants. This is required because the security deposits are held in trust and must be returned to the tenant at the termination of the lease, at which time the buyer will be the lessor. If the security deposits are turned over to the buyer, debit the seller and credit the buyer.

11. Acknowledgments. A rule to follow on acknowledgments is "he who signs, pays." Thus, the seller pays for acknowledgments on deeds, assignments of lease and mortgage releases, and the buyer pays for acknowledgments on new first or second mortgages.

KEY WORDS

Affidavit of Title
Arrears
Debit
Closing
Closing Statement
Credit
Homebuyer's Guide to Settlement Costs
HUD-1 Uniform Settlement Statement
Proration
RESPA
Settlement

FIGURE 21.2

Debit/Credit Checklist

The following form is to be used as a checklist for the student, indicating whether the figures for each entry will appear in the buyer's or seller's debit or credit column. Naturally, any of these items can be changed by agreement between the parties.

	THE ENTRY:	BUYER'S STATEMENT		SELLER'S STATEMENT	
		DEBIT	CREDIT	DEBIT	CREDIT
	Consideration (purchase price)	X			X
	Initial deposit		X		
Financing	New 1st or 2nd mortgage		X		
Financing	Existing mortgage payoff			X	
Financing	2nd purchase money mortgage		X	X	
Financing	Mortgage assumed		X	X	
Financing	Agreement of sale		X	X	
Proration	Interest arrears		X	X	
Proration	Interest advance	X			X
Proration	Interest on mortgage payoff			X	
Proration	Taxes arrears		X	X	
Proration	Taxes advance	X			X
Proration	Interest assumed	X			X
Proration					
Proration	Insurance – new policy	X			
Proration	Lease rent – advance	X			X
Proration	Lease rent – arrears		X	X	
Proration	Rental (income from property) advance		X	X	
Proration	Rental income – arrears	X			X
Miscellaneous Charges	Survey & Staking (new construction)	X			
Miscellaneous Charges					
Miscellaneous Charges	Continuation of title	X			
Miscellaneous Charges	Title search	X			
Miscellaneous Charges	Title insurance	X			
Miscellaneous Charges	Drawing deed or lease			X	
Miscellaneous Charges	Acknowledgments on a deed or lease	Negotiable			
Miscellaneous Charges	Recording deed or lease	X			
Miscellaneous Charges	New mortgage loan fee	X			
Miscellaneous Charges	Discount points VA			X	
Miscellaneous Charges	Prepayment penalty			X	
Miscellaneous Charges	Conveyance tax			X	
Miscellaneous Charges	Discount Points FHA or Conventional	Negotiable			
Miscellaneous Charges					
Miscellaneous Charges	Mortgage release			X	
Miscellaneous Charges	Acknowledgment & recording or release			X	
Miscellaneous Charges					
Miscellaneous Charges	Commission			X	

FIGURE 21.3
HUD-1 Uniform Settlement Statement

FIGURE 21-4

1401—PAGE 1 HUD-1
OMB No 2502-0265 (Exp 12-31-86)

HUD-1 UNIFORM SETTLEMENT STATEMENT
(Rev August 1987)

ALL-STATE LEGAL SUPPLY CO.
One Commerce Drive, Cranford, N J 07106

A. U.S. DEPARTMENT OF HOUSING AND URBAN DEVELOPMENT			SETTLEMENT STATEMENT	
B. TYPE OF LOAN	1. ☐ FHA	2. ☐ FmHA	6 File Number:	7. Loan Number
3 ☒ CONV UNINS	4 ☐ VA	5. ☐ CONV. INS	8. Mortgage Insurance Case Number.	

C. NOTE: *This form is furnished to give you a statement of actual settlement costs. Amounts paid to and by the settlement agent are shown. Items marked "(p.o.c.)" were paid outside the closing; they are shown here for informational purposes and are not included in the totals.*
NOTE: TIN = Taxpayer's Indentification Number.

D. NAME AND ADDRESS OF BORROWER:	E. NAME, ADDRESS AND TIN OF SELLER:	F. NAME AND ADDRESS OF LENDER:
Apollo & Ruby Creed 123 Main Street Bayonne, NJ 07002	Rocco & Adrian Balboa 114 Yantacaw Brook Rd. Wyckoff, NJ 07481	Pilgrim State Bank 85 Pompton Avenue Cedar Grove, NJ 07009

G. PROPERTY LOCATION:	H. SETTLEMENT AGENT: NAME, ADDRESS AND TIN	
114 Yantacaw Brook Road Wyckoff, NJ 07481	Abraham Kinstlinger, Esq. 9 Atlantic Street, Hackensack, NJ 07601	
	PLACE OF SETTLEMENT: 9 Atlantic Street Hackensack, NJ 07601	I. SETTLEMENT DATE: May 15, 1997

	J. SUMMARY OF BORROWER'S TRANSACTION	
①	**100. GROSS AMOUNT DUE FROM BORROWER:**	
	101. Contract sales price	$185,000.00
	102. Personal property	
	103. Settlement charges to borrower *(line 1400)*	4,799.20
	104.	
	105.	
	Adjustments for items paid by seller in advance	
	106. City/town taxes to	533.33
	107. County taxes to	
	108. Assessments to	
	109. Insurance	264.00
	110.	
	111.	
	112.	
	120. GROSS AMOUNT DUE FROM BORROWER	$190,596.53
	200. AMOUNTS PAID BY OR IN BEHALF OF BORROWER:	
② ③	201. Deposit or earnest money	$ 18,500.00
	202. Principal amount of new loan(s)	129,500.00
⑤	203. Existing loan(s) taken subject to	
	204.	
	205.	
	206.	
	207.	
	208.	
	209.	
	Adjustments for items unpaid by seller	
	210. City/town taxes to	
	211. County taxes to	
	212. Assessments to	
	213.	
	214.	
	215.	
	216.	
	217.	
	218.	
	219.	
⑱	**220. TOTAL PAID BY/FOR BORROWER**	$148,000.00
	300. CASH AT SETTLEMENT FROM/TO BORROWER	
	301 Gross amount due from borrower *(line 120)*	$190,596.53
⑲	302. Less amounts paid by/for borrower *(line 220)*	(148,000.00)
	303. CASH (☒ FROM) (☐ TO) BORROWER	42,596.53

K. SUMMARY OF SELLER'S TRANSACTION		
400. GROSS AMOUNT DUE TO SELLER:		
401. Contract sales price	$185,000.00	
402. Personal property		
403.		
404.		
405.		
Adjustments for items paid by seller in advance		
406. City/town taxes to	533.33	⑫
407. County taxes to		
408. Assessments to		
409. Insurance	264.00	⑬
410.		
411.		
412.		
420. GROSS AMOUNT DUE TO SELLER	$185,797.33	
500. REDUCTIONS IN AMOUNT DUE TO SELLER:		
501. Excess deposit *(see instructions)*		
502. Settlement charges to seller *(line 1400)*	11,800.00	
503. Existing loan(s) taken subject to		
504. Payoff of first mortgage loan	44,000.00	⑨
505. Payoff of second mortgage loan		
506. Interest on mortgage		
507. balance	229.16	⑩
508.		
509.		
Adjustments for items unpaid by seller		
510. City/town taxes to		
511. County taxes to		
512. Assessments to		
513.		
514.		
515.		
516.		
517.		
518.		
519.		
520. TOTAL REDUCTION AMOUNT DUE SELLER	$ 56,029.16	⑳
600. CASH AT SETTLEMENT TO/FROM SELLER		
601. Gross amount due to seller *(line 420)*	$185,797.33	㉒
602. Less reductions in amount due seller *(line 520)*	(56,029.16)	
603. CASH (☒ TO) (☐ FROM) SELLER	129,768.17	㉑

SUBSTITUTE FORM 1099 SELLER STATEMENT

The information contained in Blocks E, G, H and I and on line 401 (or, if line 401 is asterisked, line 403 and 404) is important tax information and is being furnished to the Internal Revenue Service If you are required to file a return, a negligence penalty or other sanction will be imposed on you if this item is required to be reported and the IRS determines that it has not been reported. If this real estate is your principal residence, file Form 2119, *Sale or Exchange of Principal Residence*, for any gain, with your income tax return; for other transactions, complete the applicable parts of Form 4797, Form 6252 and/or Schedule D (Form 1040). You are required to provide the Settlement Agent (named above) with your correct taxpayer identification number If you do not provide the Settlement Agent with your correct taxpayer identification number, you may be subject to civil or criminal penalties imposed by law. Under penalties of perjury, I certify that the number shown on this statement is my correct taxpayer identification number.

____
(Seller's Signature)

FIGURE 21.3 (cont'd)

1401 – Page 2 SETTLEMENT STATEMENT HUD-1 ALL-STATE LEGAL SUPPLY CO., One Commerce Drive, Cranford, N. J 07016

L. SETTLEMENT CHARGES	PAID FROM BORROWER'S FUNDS AT SETTLEMENT	PAID FROM SELLER'S FUNDS AT SETTLEMENT	
700. TOTAL SALES/BROKER'S COMMISSION based on price $185,000 @ 6 %=11,100			
Division of Commission (line 700) as follows:			
701. $ to			
702. $ to			
703. Commission paid at Settlement to New Jersey Good Realty, Inc.		$11,100.00	(11)
704.			
800. ITEMS PAYABLE IN CONNECTION WITH LOAN			
801. Loan Origination Fee %			
802. Loan Discount 2%	$2,590.00		(16)
803. Appraisal Fee to			
804. Credit Report to			
805. Lender's Inspection Fee			
806. Mortgage Insurance Application Fee to			
807. Assumption Fee			
808.			
809.			
810.			
811.			
(7) 900. ITEMS REQUIRED BY LENDER TO BE PAID IN ADVANCE			
901. Interest from 5/15 to 6/1/97 @ $32.38 /day	485.70		
902. Mortgage Insurance Premium for months to			
903. Hazard Insurance Premium for years to			
904. years to			
905.			
1000. RESERVES DEPOSITED WITH LENDER			
1001. Hazard insurance months @ $ per month			
1002. Mortgage insurance months @ $ per month			
1003. City property taxes months @ $ per month			
1004. County property taxes months @ $ per month			
1005. Annual assessments months @ $ per month			
1006. months @ $ per month			
1007. months @ $ per month			
1008. months @ $ per month			
1100. TITLE CHARGES			
1101. Settlement or closing fee to			
1102. Abstract or title search to Arrow Title Insurance Agency	160.00		(14)
1103. Title examination to Abraham Kinstlinger			
1104. Title insurance binder to Abraham Kinstlinger			
1105. Document preparation to Abraham Kinstlinger			
1106. Notary fees to			
1107. Attorney's fees to Abraham Kinstlinger	750.00		(17)
(includes above items numbers;)			
(6) 1108. Title insurance to Arrow Title Insurance Agency	647.50		
(includes above items numbers;)			
1109. Lender's coverage $			
1110. Owner's coverage $			
1111.			
1112.			
1113.			
1200. GOVERNMENT RECORDING AND TRANSFER CHARGES			
(8) 1201. Recording fees: Deed $24.00 ; Mortgage $ 22.00 ; Releases $	46.00		
1202. City/county tax/stamps: Deed $; Mortgage $			
1203. State tax/stamps: Deed $; Mortgage $			
1204. Realty Transfer Fee		700.00	(15)
1205.			
1300. ADDITIONAL SETTLEMENT CHARGES			
(4) 1301. Survey to Alfred J. Clark, Prof. Land Surveyors	120.00		
1302. Pest inspection to			
1303.			
1304.			
1305.			
1400. TOTAL SETTLEMENT CHARGES *(enter on lines 103, Section J and 502, Section K)*	$4,799.20	$11,800.00	

CERTIFICATION

I have carefully reviewed the HUD-1 Settlement Statement and to the best of my knowledge and belief, it is a true and accurate statement of all receipts and disbursements made on my account or by me in this transaction. I further certify that I have received a copy of the HUD-1 Settlement Statement.

.... Seller .... Borrower

.... Seller .... Borrower

To the best of my knowledge the HUD-1 Settlement Statement which I have prepared is a true and accurate account of the funds which were received and have been or will be disbursed by the undersigned as part of the settlement of this transaction.

.... Settlement Agent .... Date

WARNING: It is a crime to knowingly make false statements to the United States on this or any other similiar form. Penalties upon conviction can include a fine and imprisonment. For details see: Title 18 U.S. Code Section 1001 and Section 1010.

CHAPTER 21
Review Questions
(Answers on page 558)

1. Which of the following would appear as a credit on the buyer's statement?
   (A) The first mortgage proceeds.
   (B) Prepaid taxes.
   (C) Cost of deed preparation.
   (D) Title insurance.

2. Cash due from buyer at closing is:
   (A) debit to seller.
   (B) credit to buyer.
   (C) credit to seller.
   (D) debit to buyer.

3. Balance due seller at closing is:
   (A) credit to seller and debit to buyer.
   (B) debit to seller.
   (C) credit to seller.
   (D) debit to buyer.

4. Which of the following would appear as a debit on seller's statement?
   (A) Rental income arrears.
   (B) Purchase price.
   (C) Mortgage payoff.
   (D) Insurance assumed.

5. The realty transfer fee is:
   (A) debit to seller.
   (B) debit to buyer.
   (C) credit to seller.
   (D) credit to buyer.

6. The following would appear as a debit to seller and credit to buyer:
   (A) Prepaid realty taxes.
   (B) Mortgage payoff.
   (C) Interest on mortgage payoff.
   (D) Unpaid realty taxes.

7. The following would appear as a debit to seller and credit to buyer:
   (A) Points.
   (B) Purchase money mortgage proceeds.
   (C) Loan origination fee.
   (D) Interest advance.

8. The following would be a debit to buyer and a credit to seller:
   (A) Purchase price.
   (B) Unpaid realty taxes.
   (C) Interest arrears.
   (D) Purchase money mortgage.

9. The security deposit would appear as:
   (A) only a debit to seller.
   (B) only a credit to buyer.
   (C) debit to seller and credit to buyer.
   (D) debit to buyer and credit to seller.

10. Which of the following statements is TRUE?
    (A) The realty transfer fee is paid by the purchaser.
    (B) If the buyer demands title insurance it is an additional cost for the seller.
    (C) The proceeds of the first mortgage will appear as a debit to the buyer.
    (D) A purchase money mortgage will be shown as a debit to the seller and credit to the buyer.

11. Which of the following statements is (are) TRUE?
    (A) A mortgage given to a bank would appear on the closing statement as a credit to the buyer.
    (B) A purchase money mortgage given to the seller would appear on the closing statement as a credit to the buyer and a debit to the seller.
    (C) Both A and B.
    (D) Neither A nor B.

Real estate Lic is required when you manage a real estate property x Money

Leasor → give the lease

Leasee → receive the lease

Life tenant - if finish when the tenant die. the property reverse back to ower or remainer man.

all contract in order to be enforceable → needs to be in writing.

documents

① Periodic Tenancy → you can put anything in a contract.
if you buy any property they are subject to the lease that exist

③ Tenant at sufferance: ~~[illegible]~~ tenants stay after the lease is ended.
if you cash a check after the termination of the lease you are creating month to month tenancy. and you can't kick out the tenant. if you don't accept the rent the landlord can re-entry in possession and start the ~~[illegible]~~ evict process.

④ Estate of years: if tenant moves before the termination tenants are responsible to pay for the time unrented until the termination date and also if the landlord finds another tenant that pays less rent the tenant is responsible x time unrented + the difference in $.

" The Nat. Association of Realtors is different from Real Est. commin. ~~be~~ We have to joing this in order to get the listings

- Net + gross lease are refered to the owner.

is illegal → VOID CONTRACT
Mentally insane ↗

eviction: either party can creat it.
tenant → no payment.
landlord → no oil, no gas

LESSOR
|
800/mos LESSEE/~~L~~ESSOR
|
LESSEE

as lessee
if you assigned ~~to~~ a lease to another persone:
if you charge same amount is assignment of lease, but if you charge for ex: 1,400 = is called Sublease

CHAPTER TWENTY-TWO

LEASES AND THE LANDLORD-TENANT RELATIONSHIP

A **lease** is an agreement whereby the landlord/lessor gives the tenant/lessee the right to use specific realty for a definite period, with consideration being the payment of rent. As compared to the indefinite duration of a freehold estate, leasehold estates always exist for a limited period of time. During the term of a lease the lessor has a future interest called a **reversionary interest**. This means that upon expiration of the lease, the rented premises will automatically revert to the lessor. Reversions are inheritable and freely transferred during the life of the person who owns the reversionary interest.

The lease is often called both a "contract" and a "conveyance." It is a contract in that it sets forth the rights and obligations of the parties, and it is a conveyance transferring the right to the use and possession of the property for a certain period of time. Leases may be of short duration, such as one month, or they may be substantial, such as a 99-year lease. Under New Jersey's Statute of Frauds an oral lease, in some cases, may be enforceable in court. A note of caution, however: no matter how short the duration, a written lease is the only way that the parties can truly support the terms of the agreement. Oral agreements should always be discouraged.

Leasehold estates or tenancies may be classified into four types: (1) periodic tenancy; (2) tenancy at will; (3) tenancy at sufferance; and (4) estate for years.

1. Periodic Tenancy. A periodic tenancy exists when the rental period is from period to period, such as week-to-week, month-to-month or year-to-year. All terms and conditions of the tenancy are automatically carried over from period to period and continue until one of the parties gives proper notice of termination. A periodic tenancy may be created by agreement of the parties, but usually arises out of implication where no definite time period has been agreed upon but rent has been fixed at a certain amount per week, per month or per year.

There is no specific termination date, since a periodic tenancy continues until one of the parties gives proper notice of termination. If the tenancy is from month-to-month, the amount of notice must be at least one month. If the tenancy is year-to-year, notice must generally be given at least three months prior to the termination date.

2. Tenancy at Will. A tenancy at will is an uncommon arrangement that allows a tenant to use or occupy lands and buildings at the will of the owner/lessor. In New Jersey, it can be terminated at any time by either party giving 90 days notice and will continue indefinitely until one of the parties takes action to terminate the tenancy. A tenancy at will might be used when a homeowner is selling a house occupied by a tenant, because a tenancy at will is terminated by a sale of the property or by death of either party.

3. Tenancy at Sufferance. A tenancy at sufferance arises when a tenant comes into possession of property lawfully, then wrongfully remains in possession after his lease has expired without the consent of the landlord. Since there is no notice requirement to terminate such a tenancy, the landlord may re-enter into possession and have the tenant evicted, or the landlord may elect to accept the tenant for similar terms and conditions as stipulated in the prior lease. If the landlord accepts rent from the tenant after expiration of a lease, the tenant becomes a statutory month-to-month tenant.

4. Estate for Years. An estate for years (tenancy for years), by far the most common lease, is one for a fixed or definite period of time by an agreement between lessor and lessee. The name is often misleading, because the period may be for less than a year, measured in weeks or months. This type of tenancy ends on the last day of the term of the lease, without the necessity of giving advance notice. However, if the tenant remains on the property with the landlord's consent after the expiration of his or her lease, all the terms and conditions of the original lease can be continued during this "holdover" tenancy. In a residential leasehold situation, and in the absence of any agreement to the contrary, when the landlord accepts the rent in advance after the first month of a holdover tenancy, it then creates a month-to-month tenancy, as noted in the preceding paragraph.

GROUND LEASES AND COMMERCIAL LEASES

Since the estate for years is the most commonly used leasehold, it is generally under this type of tenancy that two major types of leases are written: (a) ground leases; and (b) commercial leases.

a. Ground Leases. The ground lease is usually a tenancy for years whereby the parcel of real property is leased, usually for a long period of time. In New Jersey, leases of this nature are common. The terms of these leases may be of any length, but normally they are for 50, 55, 75 or 99 years. Ground leases usually have a specific period of time in the lease (the "fixed period") such as 30 years wherein the rent remains the same, and then provide for predetermined increases at stated intervals. These periodic increases were designed to offset inflation and led to the terms "step-up" or "graduated lease." Since the tenant pays the operating expenses, a ground lease is also a net lease.

The rent for the balance of the term is then renegotiated on or before the expiration of that term. Such negotiations between lessor and lessee are normally based on current market value of the land, using existing prevailing percentage factors or those being commonly used at the time the lease is up for renegotiation.

The ground lease generally provides that a building shall be erected on the land by the tenant, and a provision is also made as to the disposition of this building at the end of the lease term. This provision is called the "reversionary clause" and determines whether ownership of the improvements shall revert to the lessee or to the lessor at the end of the lease.

In the absence of an agreement, the building legally becomes part of the property and belongs to the landowner, who is not required to reimburse the tenant for the cost of the improvement. However, since most ground leases are for long periods, the building has generally outlived its usefulness when the lease comes to an end, and the landlord wants neither the cost nor the responsibility of removing the building from his land. Consideration should be given to a "no reversion" clause, making the improvements the lessee's responsibility.

b. Commercial Leases. A commercial lease is also normally written as a tenancy for years. The three major types of commercial leases are: (i) net lease; (ii) gross lease; and (iii) percentage lease.

i. Net Lease. The net lease requires the tenant to pay, in addition to the fixed rent, all of the property expenses which normally would be paid by the owner. These include expenses such as real estate taxes, insurance, maintenance, repairs and utilities.

ii. Gross Lease. In a gross lease, the tenant pays a flat rental amount and the landlord pays for all property charges regularly incurred by ownership. Most apartment leases are gross leases.

iii. Percentage Lease. A percentage lease is an agreement whereby the rent of the lessee is typically a fixed minimum rent plus a percentage of the gross volume of business done on the leased premises. Occasionally the rental amount in a percentage lease is based exclusively on a straight percentage, with no fixed minimum rent. The percentage factors used vary with the type of business being conducted.

The National Association of Realtors periodically publishes a list of commonly accepted percentages charged for various types of retail establishments.

When the lease is a straight percentage type with no fixed minimum, it often includes protection clauses such as the **recapture clause**, allowing the landlord to cancel if the volume of business falls below a stated fixed minimum.

iv. Reappraisal Lease. The reappraisal lease calls for property appraisals every five to ten years as the basis for periodic adjustment in the rent.

ESCALATION CLAUSES

Some leases contain escalation clauses that permit rent increases to reflect increased operating expenses such as higher taxes, maintenance costs, fuel oil, etc. Another common escalation provision ties rent increases to changes in the Consumer Price Index (CPI). Inasmuch as the increase is tied to a variable, the tenant does not know the amount of the increase at the inception of the lease.

ELEMENTS OF A LEASE

The usual elements of a lease are: (1) date; (2) contractual ability of the named parties; (3) mutual agreement with consideration; (4) description of the property; (5) use of the premises; (6) legal purpose; (7) signatures; (8) acknowledgment; and (9) recording.

1. Date. Although not essential, it is important in determining the proper prorations of rents, or priorities of the lessee's rights.

2. Contractual Ability of the Named Parties. It

is essential that the parties be named and their positions be clearly indicated, and that they have full contractual ability to enter into a contract.

3. Mutual Agreement with Consideration. The parties must reach a mutual agreement, and evidence this with valid consideration, which is the agreed-upon amount of the lessee's payment.

4. Description of the Property. This should be sufficient enough to identify the leased premises so there can be no mistaking the property or portion of property in question.

5. Use of Premises. The lease should clearly state the extent and nature of the interest being conveyed to the tenant, including the duration of the terms and the use for which the lease is intended.

6. Legal Purpose. A lease, like any other contract, must have a valid legal objective.

7. Signatures. A lease for a period longer than three years must be in writing and signed by the party to be charged. It is essential that it be signed by the landlord, since he is conveying an interest in real estate. The tenant's signature is not essential, since his possession gives actual notice of the existence of a lease. It is definitely good practice, however, to have both parties and their spouses sign the lease document.

8. Acknowledgment. A lease, like most other documents, need not be acknowledged unless it is to be recorded.

9. Recording. Recording is not necessary for a lease to be valid. However, since many long-term leases involve important property rights, it is normally recommended that the lease and any assignments be recorded. Recordation of such a lease is required, however, if the lessee intends to mortgage his leasehold interest.

TERMINATION OF LEASES

Leases are usually terminated in one of the following ways: (l) expiration of the term; (2) surrender; (3) breach of conditions of the lease; (4) eviction; (5) prior right; (6) destruction of the premises; and (7) abandonment.

1. Expiration of the Term. An estate for years ends upon the last day of the term stipulated in the lease. There is therefore no necessity of advanced written notice. A periodic tenancy requires the giving of proper notice by either the landlord or the tenant, whichever party desires to terminate the lease. Unless the landlord indicates that he elects to renew the lease of the holdover tenant, the tenant is treated, in effect, as little more than a trespasser, and is not entitled to notice, for the tenant does not have any rights in such a case.

2. Surrender. When the landlord and tenant mutually agree to terminate the lease, followed by a delivery of possession of the leased premises, the tenant is released from any obligation. This mutual agreement is termed a "surrender and acceptance."

3. Breach of Conditions. When either the landlord or tenant fails to perform according to the conditions of the lease, this constitutes a breach of lease, and the injured party may be permitted to cancel the lease.

4. Eviction. There are two types of evictions: (a) actual eviction; and (b) constructive eviction.

a. Actual Eviction. If the tenant is ousted from the premises by an act of the landlord or a stranger having superior title to the property, the tenant is removed from the premises, and is no longer liable for the rent accruing after such eviction.

The legal remedy of the landlord is called a "summary possession" proceeding, a term which is synonymous with "dispossess action" or "unlawful detainer," a term originating in early English common law. Summary possession in New Jersey is used against a tenant who holds over after expiration of the lease term, continues in possession after default of the rental payment or continues in possession after failure to perform conditions or covenants of the lease agreement, provided he is given adequate and proper notice of the default.

b. Constructive Eviction. If the landlord allows the premises to become uninhabitable, or violates the covenant of quiet enjoyment, the tenant may then remove himself from the premises and declare constructive eviction. This is a legal means in which a tenant may break a lease. However, no claim of constructive eviction will be allowed unless the tenant actually removes himself from the premises while the condition exists.

5. Prior Right. Occasionally others with a superior right or claim than that of the lessee can terminate a lease. The following are reasons this might occur: (a) foreclosure of a mortgage or other lien, if the lease were entered into after a mortgage had been placed on the property (conversely, if the mortgage were to be placed on the property after the lease was entered into—and if the lease does not contain a subordination clause—the mortgagee who forecloses would have to take the property subject to the lease); (b) condemnation of the leased premises; or (c) in the case of a lease given by a life tenant, at the life tenant's death all rights given to the lessee under the lease are terminated.

6. Destruction of the Premises. The destruction of leased property involving agricultural land, land upon which the tenant constructed his own building, or land where the tenant rents the entire building, does not generally relieve the tenant from his obligation to pay the rent for the remainder of his term. However, if a tenant leases only a portion of the building, such as an apartment, office or commercial space, destruction of the premises would normally release him from continued payment of rent.

7. Abandonment. Although abandonment does not legally terminate the lease, it does have the effect of a termination, since the premises are vacant and the rent is not being received. Most leases provide that if the lessee abandons the premises before the completion of his rental term, he is still liable for the rent until expiration of the lease. The landlord may elect to retake possession and consider the lease terminated, or he may retake possession, re-rent the premises and thus reduce the amount for which the lessee is still liable. The landlord has an obligation to mitigate damages by attempting to re-let the premises.

Mitigated damages -> responsability for landlord (Find another tenant)

Sublease vs. Assignment of Lease

If a lessor transfers to a third party the entire remaining balance of the lease term for all of the leased property, it is called an **assignment of lease**. If the lessee transfers a portion of the leased property to another, or transfers all of the leased property for a portion of the lease term term, it is called a **sublease**. In a sublease, the original tenant retains a reversionary interest in the leasehold, but in an assignment he does not.

Under an assignment of lease, either lessor or lessee assigns the lease to a third party, who is bound by all covenants that bound the assignor. When a lessee assigns a lease, the new tenant (assignee) is directly obligated to the landlord to pay rent. When a lease is assigned the assignor remains secondarily liable. Thus, if the assignee defaults and the landlord cannot recover from him, the landlord could look to the assignor to recover lost rent or other damages.

It is customary for a lease to provide that the premises must not be subleased or assigned without the written consent of the landlord or the landlord's agent.

Often, a lease contains an option to renew or extend the lease for an additional period. An **option** is an offer which, because it is secured by a consideration, cannot be revoked. An option is defined as a right that is given for consideration to purchase or lease property within a specified time at a specified price and terms. The tenant must serve proper notice of his intent to exercise the option within the specified time, thereby remaining in occupancy after the old lease expires and the new one takes effect. The lease may also provide for a **right of first refusal**. This provision gives the tenant the opportunity to match the terms of a proposed contract to purchase, before the contract is executed.

The primary difference between the option and the right of first refusal is this: if the tenant has an option, the landlord cannot deal with a third party should the tenant decide to exercise the option. However, with a first refusal right, the landlord is free to sell or lease to a third party if the tenant fails to meet the terms offered to the landlord by the third party.

OBLIGATIONS OF THE PARTIES

As a general rule, the person occupying the property is liable to others for injury caused to them while on the premises, because he alone has control and is the one in the most logical position to correct any dangerous condition. However, it is prudent for any landlord to have liability insurance of some nature to protect himself in such instances.

A tenant's primary obligation is that he be required to surrender the premises at the expiration of the term in as good a condition as they were at the commencement of the lease, reasonable wear and tear and damage by the elements excepted. A clearly drafted lease will set forth all of the duties and responsibilities of the lessor and lessee, thus avoiding ambiguities that might lead to controversy.

Security Deposits for Ten or More Residential Rental Units

A residential landlord holding a security deposit for ten or more rental units must either invest that money in an insured money market fund established by an investment company based in New Jersey or deposit it in a state or federally chartered savings bank or savings and loan institution, in an account bearing a variable rate of interest, established at least quarterly, and which is similar to the rate of interest on active interest-bearing money market transaction accounts. In the case of buildings with less than ten rental units, the landlord is required to place the money in an interest-bearing account in a state or federally chartered bank, savings bank or savings and loan institution which is in the State of New Jersey, in a time or savings deposit account. Another basic change to the law is that now the landlord, as his fee for handling the account, is entitled to retain a sum equal to the greater of 1% per annum on the amount deposited, or 12.5% of the aggregate interest yield on the deposit. For example, this would work out as follows:

Amount deposited = $10,000
Annual deposit rate = 5.25%
5.25% = $525.00 total interest for the year.

Interest of 1% on the amount deposited = $100.00, which would be retained by the landlord and $425.00 passed on to the tenants.

Therefore 12.5% of the interest yield would equal $65.62 for the landlord, with the remainder going to the tenants, so the greater amount would be the 1% per annum. The portion that is to be returned to the tenant shall either be left in the account to earn interest to the benefit of the tenant, paid to the tenant in cash on a yearly basis or credited to the payments of rent due on the renewal or anniversary date of the lease.

THE "TRUTH IN RENTING" ACT

The "Truth in Renting" Act was signed into law on February 19, 1976, as Chapter 310 of the New Jersey Public Laws of 1975. The Act requires the New Jersey Department of Community Affairs to prepare, distribute and update annually a statement in English and in Spanish of the established rights and responsibilities of residential tenants and landlords in the state. The Act calls for distribution of the statement to all tenants with a rental term of at least one month living in residences with more than two dwelling units (or more than three if the landlord occupies one). The landlord is required to give a copy of the current statement to each tenant when a lease is entered into, and to make available the current statement in the building where tenants can easily find it.

A landlord who does not properly distribute the statement can be subject to a penalty of up to $100 for each offense. Enforcement of this statute is handled through the Superior Court, Special Civil Part, Landlord-Tenant Section in the county in which the building is located or in the county in which the defendant resides. The landlord may represent himself or hire an attorney.

About the Current Statement

The Truth in Renting statement is available from the Department of Community Affairs, Office of Landlord-Tenant Information, CN 805, Trenton, NJ 08625-0805. The Office of Landlord-Tenant Information does not have jurisdictional authority over the administration of the courts, nor can the Office render legal advice. Any change in the size of print or content of the booklet that is not approved in writing by the Office of Landlord-Tenant Information will be considered to be in violation of the Act. The deadline for posting and distributing this current statement is 30 days after the Department of Community Affairs makes it available for distribution.

The statement is based on existing state laws, regulations and court cases. Its purpose is for information and reference only, not for legal advice. It is not a complete summary of all laws and court decisions that concern landlord-tenant relations. Any person who plans to take any legal action in a landlord-tenant dispute may wish to consult with the appropriate enforcing agency, a county legal services agency, a private attorney, or an owners, tenants or mobile home organization.

Special Note on Applicability

The information contained in this statement should be generally useful to all residential tenants and landlords in New Jersey. However, not all the laws apply to all types of buildings. Any person can find out if a law applies to his or her situation by carefully reading the section describing that law. If it does not say that there are exceptions, then the law applies to all residential tenants and landlords.

THE LEASE

General Provisions

A landlord-tenant relationship is formed when a landlord allows another person to use a dwelling unit for a specified period of time in return for rent. A dwelling unit may be an apartment, a house, a room or a mobile home or mobile home space. Parties to a lease must be at least 18 years old and mentally competent.[1]

A lease may be either oral or written. If written, it must be in plain language.[2] This means that it must be written so that an average person can understand it. The Division of Consumer Affairs can review leases to see if they comply with the Plain Language Law. This review is only available to landlords, who must request the review in writing. A fee is charged for this service. For more information, write to the Division of Consumer Affairs, P.O. Box 45027, Newark, NJ 07102, or call (973) 504-6339.

The Truth-in-Renting Act[3] provides that any written lease entered into or offered to a tenant must not violate any New Jersey State laws in effect at the time the lease is made. Agreements in a lease must be reasonable. Once a lease has been made, neither party can be made to accept any new agreements while it is in effect. Any fees that the landlord intends to charge should be clearly stated. This can prevent confusion and possible dispute later. A lease may permit a "late charge" when the rent is not paid by a certain date, although this charge may not be made when the five-day senior citizen grace period[4] applies, and may also provide for payment by the tenant of the landlord's attorney fees and court costs in the event of eviction for non-payment of rent or for other causes.

A landlord can require a written lease or rental agreement at the beginning of the rental or at any time after that. There is no law that requires the landlord to give the tenant a copy of the lease. The tenant should read the lease or rental agreement before signing. It is advisable for the tenant to get a copy of the lease for his or her own records at the time that it is signed. If a new landlord takes over the building, both the new landlord and the tenant must honor the lease or rental agreement until it expires.

Later disputes can be avoided if tenant and landlord (or landlord's representative) walk through the unit together and make a list (which both should sign) of all items that are in need of repair or replacement. Neither a tenant nor a landlord has the right to damage the other's property and either can be sued by the other for any property damage.

To be enforceable, obligations of the landlord or the tenant must be stated in writing, either in the lease itself or in separate rules and regulations of the landlord that are accepted, in writing, by the tenant.

Some provisions found in leases are a matter of preference by the landlord. Examples of such provisions are: (1) A landlord may restrict subletting or assigning of the leased unit; (2) A landlord may forbid or limit the keeping of domesticated animals; however, in senior citizens housing projects or senior citizens planned real estate developments (senior citizens must be 62 years of age or older) having three or more rental units, landlords must permit domesticated animals unless they become a nuisance or the tenant does not fulfill rules and regulations concerning their care and maintenance[5]; (3) A landlord may require tenants to give copies of keys; (4) A landlord may require a tenant to obtain rental insurance.

If a lease contains provisions that are against state statutes, local ordinances or governmental regulations, or a tenant feels provisions are unreasonable, a tenant has the right to enter an action in Superior Court, Special Civil Part, Landlord-Tenant Section in the county where the building is located or in the county the defendant resides, asking the court to remove this provision from the lease.[6] If a tenant and landlord cannot agree on a lease provision prior to acceptance of the document, the tenant may pursue a court action for clarification of this provision.

Generally, it is the responsibility of the landlord to obtain any certificate of occupancy that may be required by the municipality before a new tenant moves into a unit, although this responsibility is not always made clear in local ordinances and some leases provide that this cost is passed on to the tenant. (Note: Not all municipalities require a certificate of occupancy when a unit is rented.)

A landlord may not forbid or prevent installation of cable television and may not require advance payment from tenants for permission to install it.[7]

Mobile Home Leases—Private Residential Leasehold Communities

A mobile home park or private residential leasehold community landlord or operator is required: (1) to offer a written lease for at least 12 months to each mobile home dweller within the park or to a person who has purchased a mobile home from the landlord or operator.[8] The lease must be offered within 30 days from the time the purchaser lawfully moved in; (2) to give the mobile home dweller a copy of all park rules and regulations prior to signing a lease; (3) to post a copy of park rules and regulations in a recreation hall or some other place within the park where they can be easily found; and (4) to fully disclose any fees, charges and assessments, which must be based on actual costs incurred, and all rules and regulations, before the dweller moves in. Written notice of any changes must be given at least 30 days before the changes become effective.

No mobile home park landlord or operator may move, or require anyone else to move, any mobile home owned by someone else, unless he or she is able to show that it is reasonably necessary to do so and 30 days written notice is given, except in the case of an emergency. All costs of moving a mobile home at the request of the park landlord or operator, including any loss or damage, must be paid or reimbursed by the park landlord or operator. Any bribe or other payment to get into a mobile park accepted by a park landlord or operator makes the landlord or operator a disorderly person and the person making the payment can recover double its amount plus costs in Superior

Court, Special Civil Part, Landlord-Tenant Section in the county the mobile home park is located or in the county the defendant resides.

No landlord or operator may deny any resident the right to sell the resident's home within the park/community or require the unit to be moved solely on account of being sold. The landlord or operator can reserve the right to approve the purchaser, but permission cannot be unreasonably withheld. The posting of a "For Sale" sign on a mobile home may not be forbidden,[9] nor can the landlord or operator charge a commission or fee for the sale unless he or she acted as the sales agent under a written agreement with the mobile home owner.

The Private Residential Leasehold Community section[10] has new restrictions for those communities fitting the statutes' definition that outlines rights and responsibilities in the areas of community homeowner associations, first sales and removal of the community from residential use or sale of the entire community.

Public Housing Leases

Public housing authorities must follow lease regulations developed by the U.S. Department of Housing and Urban Development (HUD) as well as existing state laws. These HUD regulations list both provisions that must be included in housing authority leases and provisions that may not be included. Any questions regarding public housing can be directed to HUD at (973) 622-7900, ext. 3622, or by writing to the U.S. Dept. of Housing and Urban Development, New Jersey State Office, 1 Newark Center, Attn: Public Housing, 12th Floor, Newark, NJ 07102-5260.

Lease Renewal and Breaking

A lease is a binding contract between the landlord and the tenant and cannot be broken for any reason by either party except as detailed below. No landlord of residential rental properties, except those in owner-occupied two- or three-family dwellings, motels, hotels, transient or seasonal units, may fail to renew any lease, regardless of whether it is written or oral, except for one of the good-cause reasons described in detail under the section entitled "Eviction."[11] Tenants of owner-occupied buildings should refer to the section entitled "Other Evictions." In certain circumstances, a tenant in a yearly lease can break a lease due to disabling illness or accident, if the tenant can show a loss of income, using a prescribed form.[12] Termination will take place on the 40th day following receipt of the form by the landlord.

Certain tenants in yearly leases can terminate a lease due to the death of a spouse upon notice duly given to the landlord. Such termination shall take place by the 40th day. However, the property shall be vacated and possession turned over to the landlord at least five days prior to the 40th day following receipt of the notice by the landlord.[13] Please note, however, the provisions of this Act shall not apply to any lease the terms of which shall explicitly provide otherwise.

A tenant who breaks a lease could be required to make rental payments until the expiration date of the lease, unless the tenant can demonstrate that either: (1) "constructive eviction" (unlivable conditions) exists, meaning that the tenant notified a landlord of unlivable conditions or disturbances by other tenants and received no help to correct those conditions[14]; or (2) the landlord had re-rented. A landlord may sue the tenant who breaks a lease in the appropriate court for any damages (loss of rent, structural damage, monies extended to advertise, etc., to obtain a new tenant) caused to the dwelling unit by the tenant.

Once a unit is re-rented, there is no further obligation to pay rent unless the landlord has had to re-rent at a lower rental rate. The landlord must be able to demonstrate that he or she tried to mitigate damages by making a reasonable effort to re-rent.[15]

Tenants who remain in a unit after giving their landlord notice of their intent to leave may be held responsible for double rent payments for the months that the tenant shall continue to occupy the unit.[16]

Sailors and Soldiers Civil Relief Act

A person leasing an apartment *before* entering the military has the legal right under this Act[17] to give a 30-day notice to the landlord and break the lease with no further monetary responsibility. He or she is also entitled to the return of his or her security deposit.

If a serviceperson leases an apartment *after* entering the military, he or she is still legally responsible for the rent payments up to the end of the lease if no tenant is found to re-rent the unit.

Another thing to be aware of is that no dependents of a serviceperson may be evicted from the unit in the case of non-payment of rent where the rent does not exceed the greater amount of $1,200 per month, unless a court order for removal is obtained through the New Jersey Eviction Statute; however, suits could be delayed or postponed when a serviceperson is not under the jurisdiction of the court.

For further help, you should contact the Legal Assistance Section of Fort Dix at (609) 562-3043 or the Reserve Office of Fort Monmouth at (908) 532-4371.

Security Deposits

The following applies to all residential rental properties, including mobile homes, except owner-occupied two- or three- family dwellings. (A tenant in an owner-occupied two- or three-family dwelling may, however, make this provision applicable to his or her tenancy 30 days after sending a written request to the landlord that the landlord fulfill the requirements of the Security Deposit Law.)[18] The security deposit cannot be more than one and one-half times one month's rent.[19] It can be less. This money continues to be the property of the person making the deposit and must be held in trust by the person receiving the money. This means that the person who receives the money must make sure that no use is made of the money that is not permitted by law.

The security money must be deposited in a bank or savings and loan association in New Jersey in an account bearing interest at the current rate. However, a person who receives security deposit money for ten or more units must invest that money in an insured money market fund of a New Jersey-based investment company or deposit it in a money market account at a New Jersey bank, savings bank or savings and loan association. To pay for his or her administrative expenses, the person who received the security deposit is entitled to keep either 1% of the amount deposited or 12-1/2% of the interest, whichever is greater, minus any service fee charged by the investment company, bank, savings bank or savings and loan association. This section of the Security Deposit Law does not apply to rentals of seasonal use or rental, migrant or temporary workers where the rental is in connection with work or the place where work is being performed. "Seasonal rentals" are rentals that do not exceed 60 consecutive days by persons having a permanent residence elsewhere.

After all administrative expenses are deducted, the balance of the accrued interest is referred to as the "tenant's portion" and shall be permitted to compound to the benefit of the tenant, be paid to the tenant in cash or be credited toward the payment of rent due on the renewal or anniversary of the tenant's lease, as the tenant decides.

A person who receives a security deposit may not combine security deposit money with his or her own funds.

A tenant must be notified in writing of the name and address of the banking institution or investment company at which the money is deposited and the amount of the deposit. This must be done within 30 days after the first deposit is received. If a tenant does not receive this notice, the tenant may use the security deposit for rent payments. A tenant who wants to use the security deposit for payment of rent must give written notice to the landlord that the security money should be used for rent payments due or to become due from the tenant. After giving this notice the landlord cannot make further demand for a security deposit. However, it is possible that the new owner would be entitled to a security deposit upon demand.[20]

If a tenant is forced to move from a dwelling as a result of fire, flood, evacuation or condemnation by a municipal or state agency, and will not be able to move back in for at least seven days, the landlord must return the security deposit, minus any rent that may be due and owing. Within three business days after receiving notice that the tenant has had to move, the landlord must let the tenant know that the security deposit will be returned and tell the tenant where it can be collected. The landlord may arrange to have the municipal clerk hold the security deposit so that the tenant may collect it at the clerk's office. If the tenant has not collected the deposit within 30 days, the landlord can redeposit it with the same banking institution or investment company with which it was deposited before. If the tenant is later able to move back into the apartment but has already collected the deposit, the tenant must again pay a security deposit (one-third will be due immediately, another one-third in 30 days and the last one-third in 60 days) to the landlord.

Within 30 days after the end of a tenancy, a landlord must return to a tenant the money made as a deposit plus the interest that has been earned. The landlord may deduct from this sum the cost of any damages to the property or any other money due to him or her under the terms of the lease or agreement. The landlord must return this money either by personal delivery or by registered or certified mail. If there are any deductions made from the security deposit by the landlord, an itemized list of these deductions must also be sent to the tenant by registered or certified mail within 30 days. If the amount of money owed to the landlord for damages or unpaid rent is greater than the amount of the security deposit, the landlord may sue for the difference.

If a landlord fails to return the security deposit within 30 days, the tenant may sue. If the tenant is successful, the court may award the tenant double the amount owed, together with court costs and reasonable attorney's fees.[21]

If a building is sold, the original landlord is required to turn over the deposit plus any interest owed to the new landlord and then to notify the tenant by registered or certified mail that the new landlord will be responsible for the security deposit.[22] A recent court decision held that it is the responsibility of the new landlord to get the deposited security from the old landlord and the new landlord will be held responsible for the return of the security money even if he or she does not get it from the old landlord.[23]

The Small Claims section of the Special Civil Part of the Superior Court Law Division in the county the building is located or in the county the defendant resides has jurisdiction in actions involving security deposits where the amount does not exceed $2,000. For actions over $2,000 but not to exceed $10,000, you must file in the Special Civil Part of the Superior Court Law Division.[24]

Any person who unlawfully uses security deposit monies may be criminally charged as a disorderly person and may be subject to a fine of not less than $200.00 or imprisonment for not more than 30 days, or both.[25]

See page 329 for information on new security deposit law for residential rental properties.

Discrimination

The New Jersey Law Against Discrimination requires equal treatment in the sale or rental of housing regardless of race, creed, color, national origin, ancestry, sex, marital status or physical condition.[26] The Law applies to all landlord-tenant relationships, except those involving owner-occupied dwellings and residences planned exclusively and occupied by one sex (for example, a YMCA).[27] Discrimination complaints should be reported to the field office of the Division on Civil Rights, New Jersey Department of Law and Public Safety, which is responsible for the area where the property is located. (See back of the booklet for proper addresses.)

Refusal to rent to a family that includes children under 14 years of age and refusal to rent because of the source of any legal income are prohibited by another New Jersey law,[28] while discrimination based on age is, with certain exceptions, forbidden by the federal "Fair Housing Act." Retirement communities, especially those with minimum ages below 55, are affected by the 1988 amendments to the federal "Fair Housing Act."[29] Also prohibited is an agreement that a lease is cancelled upon the birth of a child. A complaint against a person who refuses to rent, or who tries to cancel a lease, on any of these grounds may be filed with the municipal court in the community in which the discrimination occurred. Violations of federal law may be reported to the United States Department of Housing and Urban Development or the United States Attorney. It is not illegal to refuse to rent if illegal overcrowding would result, or if an applicant has a poor credit rating or does not have enough income to afford the rent.

Consumer Fraud Protection

Since 1976, deception, fraud, misrepresentation or knowing failure or refusal to provide important information in connection with the sale or advertisement of real estate have been illegal in New Jersey.[30]

The Department of Law and Public Safety, Division of Consumer Affairs, Office of Consumer Protection, P.O. Box 45025, 124 Halsey Street, Newark, NJ 07102, (973) 504-6200 (then press 8 for a Consumer Service Representative), is responsible for enforcing the Consumer Fraud Act. An individual can also sue for triple damages for consumer fraud.[31]

Identity of Landlord

A landlord who owns a one- or two-family non-owner-occupied house is required by law to file a registration statement with the clerk of the municipality in which the building is located.[32] If the building has three or more units, the statement must be filed with the Bureau of Housing Inspection, CAN 810, Trenton, New Jersey 08625-0810, on a registration form provided by the Bureau. The Bureau sends a validated copy of the filed registration form to the municipal clerk. No filing is required for owner-occupied two-family houses.

The registration statement must also be given to each tenant and posted in a place in the building where it can be easily seen. The document must state the date of preparation and contain the names and addresses of the following: (a) the owner or owners of the building and the owners of the rental business if not the same person; (b) the registered agent and corporate officers if the owner is a corporation; (c) a person who resides in or has an office in the same county as the building and is authorized to accept service of process, if the owner is not located in the county; (d) the managing agent; (e) regular maintenance personnel; (f) the owner's representative who must be available and able to act in an emergency (the representative's telephone number must be listed); (g) every holder of a recorded mortgage on the building. If fuel oil is used to provide heat to the building and it is furnished by the owner, the name and address of the fuel oil dealer and the grade of oil used must also be included.

If there is any change in any of this information, a landlord must file an amended registration with the Bureau of Housing Inspection or, in the case of a one- or two-family dwelling, with the clerk of the municipality, within 20 days, correct the information posted in the building and notify each tenant in writing within seven days after filing. No fee is charged by the Bureau for the filing of amended registration statements.

In any eviction action by a landlord who has failed to follow the provisions of this law, the court is required by law to reserve judgment and continue the case—that is, to keep the case open and not issue a judgment for eviction—for up to 90 days to allow the landlord time to comply. If the owner has not complied within this time, the court must dismiss the case, which means that the tenant is not evicted.

A landlord who violates this act is liable for a penalty of not more than $500.00 for each offense. The penalty may be enforced in a summary proceeding in the Special Civil Part of the Superior Court Law Division in the county the building is located or in the county the defendant resides or in the municipal court under the Penalty Enforcement Law upon a complaint by the attorney general or any other person. If there is a money judgment, the amount will be paid to the State Treasurer of New Jersey if the attorney general brings suit, or to the municipality if anyone else brings suit.

RENT

A tenant has the responsibility to pay the full amount of rent on time. In exchange, an owner has the responsibility to maintain the dwelling in a livable condition.

Nonpayment and Distraint

When a tenant threatens to leave the unit without payment of rent, and a landlord has not yet received judgment from the court, the landlord may seek a temporary restraining order to prohibit the tenant from leaving the jurisdiction of the court without paying rent.[33]

A landlord is prohibited from taking or holding a residential tenant's possessions for nonpayment of rent. The legal term for this practice is "distraint." A landlord cannot use distraint for money owed on a lease or other agreement for a unit used only as a residence.[34]

A tenant may sue for damages resulting from distraint for nonpayment of rent in Superior Court, Special Civil Part, Landlord-Tenant Section, in the county the building is located or the county the defendant resides. The court may award double damages and costs of action to a tenant whose property was wrongfully distrained.

Rent Increases and Rent Control

The State of New Jersey has no laws that establish, govern or control rents. Each municipal governing body in this state may pass an ordinance establishing rent control or rent leveling. These ordinances are enforced by locally created boards. They have been upheld as a valid exercise of the municipal police power where there is a housing shortage.[35]

Notice requirements for rent increases are contained in the Eviction Law.[36] This law provides that before an owner can evict a tenant for nonpayment of an increased rent, he or she must first serve the tenant with a valid notice to quit and increase of rent.[37] *(This notice does not mean that the tenant must actually leave; the tenant has the right to remain as long as he or she pays any legal increase in rent.)* The increase in rent must not be unconscionable—that is, it must not be so unreasonable as to shock the conscience of a fair and honest person—and must comply with state laws and any municipal ordinances governing rent increases. If a tenant does not agree that a rent increase is legal and the landlord sues to evict the tenant for not paying the increase, it will be up to the court to decide if the increase is legal. If the court finds that the increase is legal, the tenant will have to pay it in order to avoid being evicted.

When a building is converted to a condominium or cooperative form of ownership, or to fee simple ownership of units, rents may not be increased to cover costs resulting solely from the conversion.[38] (This does not mean that rents may not be increased to cover the cost of new services or amenities.) This protection applies to all tenants, regardless of whether they are eligible for protected tenancy as senior citizens or disabled persons.

When a landlord follows the requirements for increasing rent and a tenant refuses to pay the increased amount, the landlord may begin an eviction action. If an increase is unconscionable or a tenant has not received proper notice, the tenant may file a complaint with a municipal rent control board where one exists.

Where there is no municipal rent control and a rent increase is charged that a tenant does not pay on the grounds that it is unconscionable, the landlord may seek to evict the tenant by court action and prove that the increase is not unconscionable.

Public-Financed and Subsidized Housing

Housing developments owned or subsidized by the U.S. Department of Housing and Urban Development (HUD), as well as unsubsidized developments with HUD-insured mortgages determined by HUD to have certain economic problems, are not subject to municipal rent control ordinances. For further information on the proper notice of a rent increase (the allowable amount of each rent increase in HUD buildings), write to U.S. Department of Housing and Urban Development, New Jersey State Office, 1 Newark Center, 12th floor, Newark, NJ 07102-5260, or call (973) 622-7900 ext. 3400. Likewise, rents fixed and controlled by the New Jersey Housing and Mortgage Finance Agency (NJHMFA) in projects it finances are not subject to municipal rent control ordinances. For further information on the proper notice of a rent increase or the allowable amount of rent increase in a NJHMFA project, please write to New Jersey Housing and Mortgage Finance Agency, 637 South Clinton Ave., P.O. Box 18550, Trenton, NJ 08650-2805, or call (609) 278-7400.

Property Tax Rebate For Tenants

The Tenant Property Tax Rebate Act of 1990[39] requires owners to pass through to their tenants, as a rent credit or cash rebate, the full amount of any current property tax reduction. The amount is derived by comparison of current year taxes with any previous year or with 1990, whichever shows the larger rebate amount.

In each municipality where a rebate is due, a Rebate Notice will be sent from the local tax collector within 30 days after tax bills are issued to the building owner. Generally, rebates are to be in monthly installments at rent payment dates, beginning within 30 days after receipt of the Rebate Note. But the first rebate is to be cumulative from January 1, and all are to be completed by December 31. If the notice is received after November 1, the rebate is to be completed by June 30 of the following year.

Exceptions to the Tenant Property Tax Rebate are made for owner-occupied two- and three-family dwellings, including separate units on a single parcel; for hotels, motels and other guest houses serving transient or seasonal tenants; and buildings or agencies subject to payments in lieu of taxes, and cooperatives, mutual housing corporations or continuing care retirement communities subject to the Limited Dividend and Non-Profit Housing Corporations or Associations Law. However, unit owners who qualify for a rebate in such places must remit the rebate to the tenant.

This information is a summary of the 1990 Act. It is conceivable that this information may change each year. For this reason, please direct all questions about this program to the Tenant Property Tax Rebate Program, New Jersey Division of Local Government Services (DLGS) Department of Community Affairs, CN 803, Trenton, NJ 08625 0803, (609) 984-5076, to ascertain any current changes between reprints of this book. DLGS makes available a booklet titled "Tenant and Landlord Guide to the Tenant Property Tax Rebate Act," that may be obtained by contacting that office.

State Homestead Credit for Tenants

Tenants may also be eligible for a rebate entitled "Homestead Credit for Tenants"[40] if they were tenants during the year for which the tax return is filed. This is not a credit on rent payments and is not paid by or through the landlord. A tenant may receive payment from the New Jersey Division of Taxation by completing the information required on the New Jersey Gross Income Tax form under HA-1040. This form must be filed by April 15 of each year with the New Jersey Division of Taxation. Even tenants who are not required to file a return for income taxes should file this form. They may still be eligible for this rebate. Questions concerning this credit should be directed to the New Jersey Division of Taxation, Taxpayers Information Service, 50 Barrack Street, Trenton, NJ 08646, (609) 588-2200 or (800) 323-4400.

MAINTENANCE

Both landlords and tenants have certain obligations for the maintenance of dwelling units. These are based on lease provisions, New Jersey statutes, local municipal ordinances and court decisions.

In general, a tenant must protect and preserve a landlord's property. Generally acceptable housekeeping practices must be followed. Proper and timely notice must be given to a landlord when there are conditions that must be repaired or corrected. A property should be returned to the landlord in the same condition as it was received, except for normal wear and tear.

A landlord, in turn, must maintain the property in livable condition. The New Jersey Supreme Court has held that a landlord offering a dwelling unit for rent implies that it is in livable condition and agrees to keep it in that condition. A landlord must repair damage to vital facilities caused by normal wear and tear after being properly notified in writing and after being given a reasonable amount of time.

Federal Lead-based Paint Disclosure

In 1992 Congress passed the Residential Lead-based Paint Hazard Reduction Act, which requires the Environmental Protection Agency (EPA) and the Department of Housing and Urban Development (HUD) to disclose and educate the public of the necessity to prevent lead poisoning in homes that may contain lead-based paint hazards. Beginning in the fall of 1996 most homebuyers and renters must receive information on lead-based paint and low-cost tips on identifying and controlling lead-based paint hazards in public and private housing built before 1978. This information must include the Consumer Product Safety Commission's (CPSC) pamphlet titled "Protect Your Family from Lead in Your Home." Sellers, landlords and their agents must provide this information before ratification of a contract of sale or a lease agreement. Most leases must include a federal disclosure form about lead-based paint.

For specific questions after reviewing the information call the National Lead Information Clearing House (NLIC) at (800) 424-5323 or (800) 638-8270 for the hearing-impaired.

For bulk copies of the pamphlet call (202) 512-1800. Ask for "Protect Your Family from Lead in Your Home" or stock number 055-000-006326. Camera-ready copies of the pamphlet are also available.

For single copies of the pamphlet, forms and the rules contact the NLIC at (800) 424-5323 or TDD: 1-800-638-8270 for the hearing-impaired or fax a request to (202) 512-2250.

Health, Safety and Maintenance Standards

By state statute and/or municipal ordinances, certain state and local agencies have the power to adopt and enforce standards for the condition of dwelling units. These powers are outlined in the following three subsections.

State Inspection and Enforcement

The Bureau of Housing Inspection (BHI) in the Department of Community Affairs is responsible for the statewide enforcement of the Hotel and Multiple Dwelling Law and the Regulations for the Maintenance of Hotels and Multiple Dwellings. Every owner of a multiple dwelling that has three or more units in a building structure or a hotel must file a certificate of registration with the Bureau. Multiple dwellings and hotels are required to be inspected at least once every five years.

The Hotel and Multiple Dwelling Law gives the Commissioner of the Department of Community Affairs power to issue and enforce regulations and to levy penalties to assure that multiple dwellings are maintained so that they do not endanger the health, safety or welfare of the tenants or the general public.[41] Both landlords and tenants must maintain buildings so that there is no violation of these regulations. Tenants must take care of their units and report any code violations to the landlord or superintendent and must,[42] upon one-day notice, allow the landlord or his representative to enter the unit to make any inspections, repairs or alterations required in order to meet code requirements. The landlord must keep the property in good repair, clean, free of infestation and free of any hazards or nuisances that might be harmful to the health or safety of the occupants, and must provide basic maintenance, including heat, building security, smoke alarm systems and properly functioning plumbing and electrical systems, etc.

Tenants who occupy one- or two-family dwellings should be aware that an amendment to the Uniform Fire Safety Act requires working smoke detectors in these residences; and that a certificate of smoke detector compliance must be obtained by the owner before any change of occupancy occurs.[43] Any person needing additional information should contact the local, (i.e., town, borough, township) FIRE OFFICIAL who administers the Uniform Fire Safety Act.

State Heat and Utility Requirements

The Hotel and Multiple Dwelling Regulations establish heating standards for buildings with three or more units. (For buildings with fewer than three units, tenants need to contact their local building or health offices for enforcement of local ordinances regarding heating.) Every unit or dwelling space must have a heating system that will provide and maintain heat at a temperature of 68° F. From October 1 to May 1, the landlord is responsible for maintaining a temperature of at least 68° F. from 6:00 a.m. to 11:00 p.m. and 65° F. at other hours, supplying the required fuel or energy, and maintaining the heating system in good condition so that it can provide the required amount of heat. However, a landlord and a tenant may agree that the tenant will supply heat to a dwelling unit when the unit is served by separate heating equipment and the source of that heat can be separately computed and billed.

The State Board of Regulatory Commissioners (BRC) enforces regulations that prohibit utility companies from shutting off utilities in tenant-occupied buildings whose owners have failed to make payments until tenants have been notified and given an opportunity to agree to make future payments.[44] The two offices of the BRC are located at 2 Gateway Center, Newark NJ 07101, (973) 648-2350 or 1-800 624-0241, and at 44 S. Clinton Avenue, CN 350, Trenton, NJ 08625, (609) 777-3300.

State Department of Health and Municipal Authority

The State Department of Health requires that local boards of health conduct a housing code enforcement program that meets state standards. The local, regional or county board of health must adopt an ordinance at least equivalent to the New Jersey State Housing Code or HIV regulations, both published by the New Jersey Department of Community Affairs, or equivalent to the maintenance codes published by BOCA (Building Officials and Code Administrators, Inc.) or APHA (American Public Health Associations). The board of health must conduct complaint inspections in any building within its jurisdiction and follow up with any necessary court enforcement.[45]

A local board of health has the authority to order the removal of lead paint from the interior of a dwelling unit when it causes a danger to occupants. When the heating equipment in a residential unit fails and the landlord does not take appropriate action after receiving proper notice from the tenant, the local board of health may act as agent for the landlord and order the repairs necessary to restore the equipment to operating condition.[46]

For emergency action in the event of failure to provide required heat, a tenant can contact the local health officer immediately after giving, or attempting to give, notice to the landlord.

"Repair and Deduct" and Rent Withholding

"Repair and deduct" and rent withholding are remedies available to a tenant only when there is a defect in a vital facility, that is, something necessary for living does not work, or a hazardous condition threatening the safety of residents. A maintenance problem that does not make something necessary for living unusable and does not threaten residents' safety is not a "defect in a vital facility." In any particular case, the courts may have to decide if the reason for using either remedy is justified. It is important that any rent that is withheld be set aside and not used for any other purpose until the court has decided the matter. Legal assistance, or the assistance of a tenants' or mobile home organization, in the use of these remedies is advisable.

The New Jersey Supreme Court has allowed the self-help remedy of repair and deduct.[47] A landlord promises at the beginning of a lease that the vital facilities needed to make the dwelling unit livable are in good condition and the property will be maintained. When there are defects in the vital facilities, A TENANT MUST FIRST NOTIFY THE LANDLORD OF THE SITUATION AND ALLOW A REASONABLE AMOUNT OF TIME FOR THE LANDLORD TO MAKE REPAIRS OR REPLACEMENTS. If a landlord fails to take action, a tenant may have the repairs made and deduct the cost from future rents. However, a landlord may take a tenant to court for nonpayment of rent. As a defense, the tenant would have to prove the presence of defects, the failure of the owner to act despite having received reasonable notice and the need to make repairs. In case the matter goes to court, the tenant may be required to demonstrate that the deducted amount is in hand. This is not required by statute but it is the practice in some courts. If there is a finding in favor of the landlord, the unpaid rent must be paid by the end of the court day to avoid eviction.

Rent withholding was authorized when the New Jersey Supreme Court[48] held that the obligation of a tenant to pay rent and the obligation—whether written or not—on the part of a landlord to maintain the property in a livable condition are mutually dependent.

If there are defects in the vital facilities and the landlord has not fixed them after receiving proper and timely notice from the tenant, the tenant may either seek a decrease in rent by court action or simply withhold rent. A landlord may bring an eviction action for nonpayment of rent. As a defense, the tenant must prove the necessity to make repairs and the failure of the landlord to act despite having received reasonable notice. To avoid possible eviction in the event the court finds in favor of the landlord, the tenant should save the amount of money withheld so that he will be able to pay it by the end of the day. It is a good idea to set up a separate bank account for this purpose.

RENT RECEIVERSHIP

In the event that a dwelling unit fails to meet minimum standards of safety and sanitation, the Rent Receivership Law permits the public officer of a municipality or tenant(s) of a dwelling to petition the court for a judgment directing the deposit of rents into court and the appointment of an administrator who must use the money to correct the unsafe conditions.[49]

Crime Insurance Information

The Federal Crime Insurance Program previously summarized in past editions of this booklet is no longer available. Crime insurance is available for tenants in all habitable property through the New Jersey Underwriters Association, Crime Insurance Indemnity Plan. To apply for crime insurance, contact the New Jersey Underwriters Association, Crime Insurance for Habitable Property, 744 Broad Street, Newark, NJ 07102 directly for an application. This insurance is applicable to theft and/or burglaries.

Locks

In order for a dwelling unit to be insurable, it must be equipped with locks that meet federal standards as described below.

State law requires that every landlord of a multiple dwelling equip the building with locks meeting federal standards. These standards are the same as those required under the New Jersey Hotel and Multiple Dwelling Regulations.

The regulations call for each exterior doorway to be protected by a door which, if not a sliding door, is equipped with a dead lock using either an interlocking vertical bolt and striker, or a minimum 1/2-inch throw dead bolt, or a minimum 1/2-inch throw self-locking latch. For further information on locks, write to the Code Administrator, Bureau of Housing Inspection, Department of Community Affairs, CN 810, Trenton, NJ 08625-0810. In buildings of fewer than three units, the tenant should contact the municipal building inspector or health officer for enforcement of any existing local ordinances.

Penalties for Damaged Property

Destruction, damage or injury to the premises by a tenant, whether done willfully or through gross negligence, is a cause for eviction.[50] The landlord may institute a summary dispossess action in the Landlord-Tenant Section, Special Civil Part of the Superior Court Law Division in the county the building is located to obtain possession of the premises three days after giving written notice to the tenant.[51]

A landlord may sue a destructive tenant in a civil action in Superior Court for costs resulting from damage. The Landlord-Tenant Section, Special Civil Part of the Superior Court Law Division in the county the building is located has jurisdiction in actions between a landlord and a tenant when the amount is $7,500 or less.

A tenant who is maliciously destructive can be brought to municipal court on charges of being a disorderly person.[52]

Public Housing Maintenance

Public Housing Authority leases must contain the rights and responsibilities of both the authority and the tenant in the event there is extensive damage to a property and conditions are created that are hazardous to life, health or safety of the occupants. A lease must include a provision for standard alternative accommodations, if available, where necessary repairs cannot be made within a reasonable time and a provision for reduction of rent in proportion to the seriousness of the damage and loss in value as a dwelling.[53]

EVICTION

A landlord may recover possession of a dwelling unit used only as a residence by consent of the tenants or through the legal process of eviction. When a landlord obtains a judgment of possession from a court, the landlord is entitled to a warrant of removal. This warrant will direct an officer of the court to remove all persons from the dwelling unit and give the landlord full possession. The warrant may also direct the officer of the court to remove tenants and belongings.

"Self-Help" Evictions

"Self-help" evictions—that is, entry into a dwelling unit and removal of tenants without their permission or without a judgment from a court—are not permitted in New Jersey under any circumstances.[54] A landlord or any other person who enters an apartment or property without a court order authorizing such entry and/or holds a tenant's belongings unlawfully by force or threat of monies owed may be liable to damages to the tenant.[55]

A person evicted in this manner may file a complaint with the Clerk of the Landlord-Tenant Section, Special Civil Part of the Law Division, or the Chancery Division of the Superior Court, in the county in which the act was committed. In a successful action by a tenant evicted through forcible entry and detainer, the court may award possession of the dwelling unit and all damages, including court costs and reasonable attorney's fees. If the dwelling unit cannot be returned to the tenant, the court may award damages.

Causes for Eviction

The eviction for good cause law applies to all residential rental properties, including mobile homes and land in a mobile home park, except owner-occupied two- or three-family dwellings, hotels, motels and other dwellings housing transient or seasonal tenants, or a unit held in trust on behalf of a member of the immediate family where one member of the immediate family permanently occupies the unit and this person has a developmental disability.[56] The Rooming and Boarding House Regulations adopted by the Department of Community Affairs make it applicable to rooming and boarding houses as well and also provide that notice for residents of those buildings must be given to the county welfare board three days before an eviction action is instituted.[57]

There are a number of causes for eviction. Each cause, except for nonpayment of rent, must be described in detail by a landlord in a written notice to a tenant.[58] No residential landlord may evict or fail to renew a lease, whether written or oral, unless the landlord can prove in court one of the 16 causes listed below.[59] Depending on the cause, a certain amount of time must pass after delivery of written notice before a landlord may begin eviction action by filing a complaint in the Landlord-Tenant Section, Special Civil Part of the Superior Court Law Division in the county the building is located. When a complaint is filed, a tenant will receive a summons to appear in court on a certain date. FAILURE TO APPEAR MAY RESULT IN LOSING THE CASE BY DEFAULT.

In some cases a landlord is required to give a tenant a preliminary written notice (written notice to cease) to stop certain acts. Only when a tenant continues such acts after the first notice does a landlord have a cause for eviction.

CAUSES FOR EVICTION, NOTICE REQUIREMENTS, AND TIME BEFORE LEGAL ACTION FOR EVICTION MAY BE INSTITUTED, ARE AS FOLLOWS:

A. **A TENANT FAILS TO PAY RENT, DUE AND OWING, ON AN ORAL OR WRITTEN LEASE.** No written notice is required and legal action may be started immediately.

B. **A TENANT CONTINUES DISORDERLY CONDUCT THAT DENIES PEACE AND QUIET TO OTHER TENANTS OR TO OTHER PEOPLE IN THE NEIGHBORHOOD AFTER A WRITTEN NOTICE TO STOP.** Legal action may be instituted three days after a second written notice.

C. **A TENANT CAUSES DESTRUCTION, DAMAGE, OR INJURY TO THE PREMISES, WILLFULLY OR THROUGH GROSS NEGLIGENCE.** Legal action may be started three days after a written notice.

D. **A TENANT CONTINUES TO VIOLATE ANY REASONABLE RULES AND REGULATIONS AFTER A WRITTEN NOTICE TO STOP. (THE RULES AND REGULATIONS MUST HAVE BEEN ACCEPTED IN WRITING BY THE TENANT OR MADE PART OF THE LEASE OR RENTAL AGREEMENT AT THE BEGINNING OF THE LEASE TERM.)** Legal action may be instituted one month after a second written notice. (Note: Month-to-month leases begin on the day rent is due and end one month later. Any rules and regulations for this type tenancy would be given on or before the start of the new month and continue after that.)

E. **A TENANT CONTINUES A SUBSTANTIAL BREACH OF ANY REASONABLE COVENANT OR AGREEMENT IN A LEASE AFTER A WRITTEN NOTICE TO STOP.** Legal action may be instituted one month after a second written notice.

F. **A TENANT FAILS TO PAY RENT AFTER A VALID NOTICE TO QUIT AND NOTICE OF RENT INCREASE.[60] THE INCREASE MUST NOT BE UNCONSCIONABLE AND MUST COMPLY WITH ANY LAWS OR MUNICIPAL ORDINANCE GOVERNING RENT INCREASES.[61]** No written notice is required and legal action may be started immediately. (Note: The "notice to quit" the premises that accompanies a rent increase does not mean that the tenant must actually leave the unit—although he or she may do so if the court determines that the rent increase is unconscionable—or that the landlord is bringing an eviction action.)

Note: Tenants evicted under the following "G" provisions may be eligible for financial and other assistance for relocation. If they are eligible, this assistance must be provided before they can be evicted. Copies of the Eviction/Relocation Regulations can be obtained from the Office of Landlord/Tenant Information, CN 805, Trenton, NJ 08625-0805, (609) 530-5423. Information on relocation assistance can be obtained from the Relocation Assistance Program[62] of the Bureau of Housing and Community Development, CN 806, Trenton, NJ 08625-0806. (609) 633-6258.

G. **(1) A LANDLORD OR OWNER WHO HAS BEEN CITED FOR VIOLATIONS OF LOCAL OR STATE HOUSING CODES WANTS TO PERMANENTLY BOARD UP OR DEMOLISH THE PREMISES OR CAN PROVE IT IS ECONOMICALLY UNFEASIBLE FOR THE OWNER TO ELIMINATE THE VIOLATIONS.**

Legal action may be instituted three months after a written notice. No warrant for possession will be issued until the requirements of the relocation law have been met.

G. (2) **A LANDLORD OR OWNER HAS BEEN CITED FOR VIOLATIONS OF LOCAL OR STATE CODES AND IT IS NOT FEASIBLE TO REMEDY THE CONDITIONS WITHOUT REMOVING THE TENANTS.** Legal action may be started three months after a written notice. No warrant for possession will be issued until the requirements of the relocation law have been met. In addition, notice must be given by the landlord to the Department of Community Affairs Office of Landlord-Tenant Information, CN 805, Trenton, NJ 08625-0805, so that the Department may prepare a report advising the court and the parties as to the feasibility of remedying the conditions without removing the tenants.

G. (3) **A LANDLORD OR OWNER WHO HAS BEEN CITED FOR VIOLATIONS OF LOCAL OR STATE CODES SEEKS TO CORRECT AN ILLEGAL OCCUPANCY.** Legal action may be instituted three months after a written notice. No warrant for possession will be issued until the requirements of the relocation laws have been met.

G. (4) **A LANDLORD OR OWNER IS A GOVERNMENTAL AGENCY THAT WANTS TO REMOVE THE PROPERTY FROM THE RENTAL MARKET TO CARRY OUT A REDEVELOPMENT OR LAND CLEARANCE PLAN.** Legal action may be instituted three months after a written notice. No warrant for possession will be issued until the requirements of the relocation law have been met.

H. **AN OWNER IS PERMANENTLY REMOVING A BUILDING OR A MOBILE HOME PARK FROM RESIDENTIAL USE.** Legal action may be instituted 18 months after written notice. When a lease is in effect, no legal action may be taken until the lease expires.

I. **A LANDLORD OR OWNER AT THE TERMINATION OF A LEASE PROPOSES REASONABLE CHANGES OF SUBSTANCE IN THE TERMS OR CONDITION OF THE LEASE (WHICH COULD INCLUDE A CHANGE IN TERM), AND THE TENANT REFUSES TO ACCEPT THE CHANGES AFTER RECEIVING A WRITTEN NOTICE DESCRIBING THE CHANGES.** Legal action may be started one month after a second written notice.

J. **A TENANT HABITUALLY FAILS TO PAY RENT DUE AND OWING WITHOUT LEGAL JUSTIFICATION AFTER RECEIVING A WRITTEN NOTICE TO CEASE.** Legal action may be instituted one month after a second written notice. (Note: The second written notice in this and the other cases where the phrase "second written notice" is used is usually entitled a "notice to quit." A "notice to cease" must come first in order to warn the tenant that action such as habitual late payment or the causes in sections B, D or E is no longer acceptable, and if continued will serve as a cause for eviction.)

K. **A LANDLORD OR OWNER OF A BUILDING IS CONVERTING FROM THE RENTAL MARKET TO A CONDOMINIUM OR COOPERATIVE.** Legal action may be instituted three years after written notice, except that tenants who qualify for protection under the Senior Citizen and Disabled Protected Tenancy Act (see below) cannot be evicted for 40 years. When a lease is in effect, no legal action may be taken until the lease expires. The landlord must comply with the regulations governing conversion to condominiums and cooperatives. At any time within 18 months of receiving notice demanding possession of the unit, a tenant may request, in writing, that the landlord provide an opportunity to rent comparable housing. ("Comparable housing" is housing that is decent, safe and sanitary and does not violate any housing codes; that is open to all people regardless of race, creed, national origin, ancestry, marital status or sex; that is similar to the unit from which the tenant is being evicted with regard to size, number of rooms, rent range, major kitchen and bathroom facilities and any special facilities needed for a handicapped or infirm person; is located in an area that is as desirable with regard to closeness to the tenant's job or business, closeness to shopping and community facilities and the quality of the general surroundings; and that meets such additional reasonable requirements as the tenant has included in his or her written request for comparable housing.) Up to five one-year stays of eviction shall be granted by the court until the court is satisfied that the tenant has been offered a reasonable opportunity to examine and rent comparable housing, except that not more than one one-year stay shall be granted if the landlord allows the tenant five months' free rent as compensation for hardship in relocation. (Note: Further information concerning condominium and cooperative conversion and application for senior citizen and disabled protected tenancy may be obtained from the Office of Landlord-Tenant Information, P.O. Box 805, Trenton, NJ 08625, or fax your request to (609) 292-2839).

L. (1) **An OWNER OF A BUILDING OR MOBILE HOME PARK THAT IS CONSTRUCTED AS**

OR IS BEING CONVERTED TO A CONDOMINIUM, COOPERATIVE OR FEE SIMPLE OWNERSHIP OF UNITS HAS CONTRACTED TO SELL THE UNIT TO A BUYER WHO WANTS TO OCCUPY IT. (THE TENANT MUST HAVE MOVED IN AFTER THE RECORDING OF THE CONDOMINIUM MASTER DEED, COOPERATIVE AGREEMENT OR SUBDIVISION MAP.) Legal action may be instituted two months after written notice. (When a lease is in effect, no legal action may be taken until the lease expires. In addition, the statement concerning conversion as required by law must be provided to the tenant.)[63]

L. **(2) AN OWNER OF THREE OR FEWER CONDOMINIUM OR COOPERATIVE UNITS IN A BUILDING WANTS TO PERSONALLY OCCUPY THE UNIT OR HAS SOLD IT TO A BUYER WHO WISHES TO PERSONALLY OCCUPY IT. (THE TENANT MUST HAVE MOVED IN AFTER THE RECORDING OF THE MASTER DEED OR COOPERATIVE AGREEMENT AND MUST HAVE RENTED THE UNIT FROM AN OWNER OF THREE OR FEWER UNITS.)** Legal action may be instituted two months after written notice. (When a lease is in effect, no legal action may be taken until if expires. In addition, the statement concerning conversion required by law must be provided to the tenant.)[64]

L. **(3) AN OWNER OF A BUILDING WITH THREE OR FEWER UNITS WISHES TO PERSONALLY OCCUPY A UNIT OR HAS CONTRACTED TO SELL THE BUILDING TO A PERSON WHO WISHES TO PERSONALLY OCCUPY IT AND THE CONTRACT CALLS FOR THE UNIT TO BE VACANT AT CLOSING.** Legal action may be instituted two months after written notice. (When a lease is in effect, no legal action may be taken until it expires.)

M. **A LANDLORD OR OWNER CONDITIONED A TENANCY UPON THE TENANT'S EMPLOYMENT BY THE LANDLORD AS A SUPERINTENDENT, JANITOR OR IN SOME OTHER CAPACITY AND THE EMPLOYMENT IS BEING TERMINATED.** Legal action may be instituted three days after written notice.

N. **THE PERSON, INCLUDING A JUVENILE ADJUDICATED DELINQUENT OR TENANT WHO KNOWINGLY HARBORS SUCH PERSON, HAS BEEN CONVICTED OF OR PLEADED GUILTY TO AN ACT WHICH CONSTITUTES AN OFFENSE UNDER THE COMPREHENSIVE DRUG ACT OF 1987 WITHIN THE LEASED PREMISES OR ON THE LAND APPURTENANT THERETO AND HAS NOT, IN CONNECTION WITH HIS SENTENCE FOR THAT OFFENSE, EITHER SUCCESSFULLY COMPLETED OR BEEN ADMITTED TO, AND CONTINUED WITH WHILE ON PROBATION, A DRUG REHABILITATION PROGRAM.** Legal action may be instituted three days after a second written notice. Legal action may not be sought where more than two (2) years after adjudication or conviction or release from incarceration has occurred.

O. **THE PERSON, INCLUDING A JUVENILE ADJUDICATED DELINQUENT OR TENANT WHO KNOWINGLY HARBORS SUCH PERSON, HAS BEEN CONVICTED OF OR PLEADED GUILTY TO AN OFFENSE INVOLVING ASSAULT OR TERRORISTIC THREATS AGAINST THE LANDLORD, THE LANDLORD'S FAMILY OR AN EMPLOYEE OF THE LANDLORD.** Legal action may be instituted three days after a second written notice. Legal action, however, may not be sought where more than two years after adjudication or conviction or release from incarceration has occurred.

P. **THE PERSON, OR TENANT WHO KNOWINGLY HARBORS SUCH PERSON WHO HAS BEEN FOUND TO BE LIABLE IN A CIVIL ACTION FOR REMOVAL COMMENCED FOR AN OFFENSE UNDER (N) OR (O) OF THIS SECTION, EXCEPT THAT THIS SECTION SHALL NOT APPLY TO A PERSON WHO HARBORS OR PERMITS A JUVENILE TO OCCUPY THE PREMISES IF THE JUVENILE HAS BEEN ADJUDICATED DELINQUENT UNDER THE COMPREHENSIVE DRUG ACT OF 1987.** Legal action may be instituted three days after a second written notice.

Other Evictions

Tenants of non-residential or commercial premises, or landlord-occupied two- and three-family dwellings, can be removed only when a court issues an order for eviction. However, in these cases, none of the good causes listed above needs to be proven and the landlord must only show that the tenant (a) is staying after the expiration of the terms of the lease and receipt of a written notice to leave, (b) is staying after a failure to pay rent, (c) is disorderly so as to destroy the peace and quiet of other tenants, (d) willfully destroys or damages the premises, (e) constantly violates the written rules and regulations or (f) violates any lease provision where the lease provides a right of re-entry reserved. No further notice is required before bringing action in court to evict in the first two causes, but a three-day written notice is required for any of the causes described as disorderly, destructive or violative of written rules or lease provisions.[65]

Rooming and Boarding House Evictions

The Regulations Governing Rooming and Boarding Houses, which are enforced by the Bureau of Rooming and Boarding House Standards of the Department of Community Affairs, require owners of rooming and boarding houses to follow the good causes and notice requirements of the Eviction Law[66] when evicting residents, except if otherwise ordered by the Bureau. There is a further requirement that the owner give at least three days' notice to the County Welfare Board before starting the eviction action.[67]

Any building having at least two living units without private kitchens and bathrooms is a rooming or boarding house if it does not meet one of the exceptions in the Rooming and Boarding House Act.[68] These exceptions include hotels with more than 85% temporary occupancy by people with homes elsewhere, school and college dormitories, buildings housing only college students and certain residences for the disabled. For additional information concerning rooming and boarding houses, contact the Bureau of Rooming and Boarding House Standards, CN 804, Trenton, NJ 08625-0804.

Penalties for Eviction Law Violations

When a tenant vacates a dwelling unit after having been given notice that the landlord wishes personally to occupy the unit and the landlord then arbitrarily fails to occupy the unit for at least six months, but instead permits personal occupancy of the unit by another tenant or registration of conversion of the property to a planned real estate development, the landlord is liable to the former tenant for three times the damages plus attorney fees and costs.

When a tenant vacates a dwelling unit after having been given notice that the landlord seeks to permanently board up or demolish the building or to permanently retire it from residential use, and the landlord does not do any of these, but instead allows any residential use of the unit for a period of five years from the date the unit became vacant, the landlord, or the former landlord, may be liable to the tenant for three times the damages plus attorney fees and costs. Additionally, the landlord or former landlord may be liable to a civil penalty of from $2,500 to $10,000 for each violation of this law and the property may not be registered as a planned real estate development during the five-year period following the date on which any dwelling unit in the property became vacant as a result of an eviction notice stating that the property was being permanently removed from residential use.[69]

Reprisal– Civil Rights of Tenants

A landlord cannot take reprisal against a tenant by eviction, substantial alteration of a lease or its terms, or refusal to renew a lease when a tenant exercises certain civil rights.[70] The law against reprisal applies to all rental properties used for dwelling purposes, including mobile homes, except owner-occupied two- or three-family dwellings.

These civil rights are:

1. A tenant attempts to enforce any rights under the lease or state or local laws.

2. A tenant has made a good faith complaint to a governmental authority about a landlord's violation of any health or safety law, regulation, code or ordinance. (A TENANT MUST HAVE FIRST NOTIFIED THE LANDLORD AND GIVEN THE LANDLORD A REASONABLE TIME TO CORRECT THE VIOLATION BEFORE MAKING THE COMPLAINT.)

3. A tenant has been an organizer, or member, of any lawful organization, including a tenant organization.

4. A tenant refuses to comply with changes in the lease or agreement, if the changes have been made by the owner because the tenant took any of the above actions.

If a landlord does take reprisal action against a tenant, a tenant may sue the landlord for damages in a civil action.

Procedures for Recovery of Premises

A landlord may recover possession of a dwelling unit through a summary dispossess action in the Landlord-Tenant Section, Special Civil Part of the Superior Court Law Division in the county the building is located. Monetary damages must be recovered in a separate civil action in Superior Court. Actions for rent in the Special Civil Part cannot exceed $10,000.

When a landlord obtains a judgment for possession from the Special Civil Part, the warrant of removal cannot be issued until three days after judgment and only between the hours of 8:00 a.m. and 6:00 p.m. This warrant of removal cannot be executed until a minimum of three days (two days for seasonal tenants in buildings with five or fewer units) have elapsed since it was issued.[71] The Fair Eviction Notice Act requires any warrant for removal to include a notice that the tenant has a right to request more time (called a "stay of execution").[72] The court will continue the case for up to ten days after the execution of the warrant for the purpose of hearing applications by the tenant for lawful relief.

Public Housing Evictions

Public housing authorities must follow state laws regarding evictions as well as the regulations of the U.S. Department of Housing and Urban Development (HUD). In the case of an eviction, a public housing tenant may request a hearing from the housing authority after receiving a notice of termination of tenancy. A housing authority may not begin an eviction action in court until the decision of the hearing officer or the hearing panel has been mailed or delivered to the tenant and a notice to vacate has been served.[73]

SENIOR CITIZENS AND DISABLED TENANTS

Senior Citizen Grace Period

Any senior citizen receiving a social security old age pension, a railroad retirement pension or any other governmental pension in lieu of social security, must be given a five-day grace period for payment when the rent is due on the first of the month. No delinquency or late charge may be made for this five-day grace period. Any person who fails to allow this grace period may be criminally prosecuted as a disorderly person.[74]

Senior Citizen and Disabled Protected Tenancy

Tenants who are at least 62 years of age by the date of the conversion recording or who are permanently disabled or a person who has been honorable discharged or released under honorable circumstances from active service in any branch of the U.S. Armed Forces who is rated as 60% disabled or higher as a result of service who live in a building being converted to a condominium, cooperative or fee simple ownership of units may be protected from eviction for 40 years if they have lived in the building for at least one year prior to the conversion recording date and have a family income that is not more than three times the average per person income in their county or $50,000, whichever is greater. *(The "conversion date" is the date on which a master deed or deed to a cooperative corporation, or a subdivision deed or map legally establishing separate lots, is filed.)* The landlord or converter is required to notify all tenants of their right to file for protected tenancy if they may be eligible. Generally, applications for protected tenancy must be filed with the designated municipal official or board within 60 days, although later filings may be accepted if there is good reason for the late filing and the conversion has not yet taken place. Tenants in Hudson County may be eligible for an additional protected tenancy established under the Tenant Protection Act of 1992. For copies of the law, regulations or forms, landlords or converters, tenants and local officials may write the Office of Landlord-Tenant Information, CN 805, Trenton, NJ 08625-4805, (609) 530-5423. For help in filling out the forms, please contact your appropriate municipal administrative agent who sent you the forms.

Tenant Protection Act of 1992

This amendment to the Eviction Law became effective on June 1, 1992.[75] It replaced the eviction moratorium for tenants in buildings being converted to condominiums, cooperatives or fee simple units of dwelling space established by PAL. 1991, Chapter 45. The 1992 amendment extends protections to **qualified** tenants in **qualified** counties in buildings converted or being converted who were not eligible for protected tenancy as either senior citizens or disabled persons under the "Senior Citizens and Disabled Protected Tenancy Act of 1987." At the present time, the only qualified county is Hudson County. Tenants in Hudson County with questions or in need of assistance in filling out the required forms should contact the administrative agent of their municipality.

Senior Citizen Rental Housing Project

This new law defines the association, governing board or body of nonprofit corporations, condominium associations or cooperative associations owning or operating a Senior Citizen Rental Housing Project in which units are rented solely to tenants 65 years of age or older (including surviving spouses 55 years or older) as the landlord and requires that the association distribute at the time of signing or any renewal of a lease copies of the following: (1) Truth-In-Lending; (2) Landlord-Identify Statement; (3) a statement that specifies the telephone numbers of the state and local offices for the municipality designated to receive reports of housing emergencies or complaints; and (4) the Public Offering Statement and the Bylaws in the case of condominiums or cooperatives.[76]

RIGHT OF ENTRY

There are no statutes in New Jersey governing the issue of a landlord keeping a key to the residential unit. In practice, this issue should be addressed within a lease provision. The landlord may want to request a key for emergency use or for making repairs. The tenant may want to request that reasonable and timely notice be given prior to entry by the landlord. Courts generally approve of arrangements specified within the lease because there are instances where the lack of a key could result in loss of life or property to others in the building if an emergency occurs when the tenant is not at home. A dispute between a landlord and tenant over the use of a key that cannot be settled by mutual agreement might have to be settled in the Superior Court. The court may or may not deny the landlord the right to have a key; however, the landlord may be liable for monetary damages to a tenant should a tenant be able to prove damage or theft of personal belongings.

A tenant disputing a landlord's right to a key can simply refuse to provide the landlord with one. The landlord, however, may seek an action for eviction for refusal to comply with reasonable lease provisions. The landlord has the burden of taking the court action and proving that the request is not unreasonable.

Tenants should note that the Regulations for Maintenance of Hotels and Multiple Dwellings, NJAC 5:10-5.1(c), provides that "every occupant of each unit of dwelling space shall give the owner thereof or his agent or employees, access to any part of the unit of dwelling space upon reasonable notification, which under ordinary circumstances shall be one day for multiple dwellings except immediately for hotels, for the purpose of making such inspection and such repairs or alterations as are necessary to effect compliance with the law and these regulations. In case of safety or structural emergencies immediate access shall be given."

Disputes that arise regarding a landlord's right of entry must be decided on a case-by-case basis in court.

FOOTNOTES FOR TRUTH-IN-RENTING

1. NJSA 9:17B1 (1973) Legal Age Requirement
2. NJSA 56:12-1 (1980) Plain Language Review Law
3. NJSA 46:8-43 thru 49 (1976) Truth in Renting Act
4. NJSA 2A:42-6.1 thru 6.3 Senior Citizen Grace Period
5. NJSA 2A:24-42 thru 112 Pets in Senior Housing
6. NJSA 46:8-48 (1976) Truth in Renting Act
7. NJSA 48:5A-49 (1972) CATV Law
8. NJSA 46:8C-2 thru 21 amended 1973 and 1975 Mobile Home/Private Residential Leasehold Communities
9. NJSA 2A:18-61.3a Eviction Law
10. NJSA 46:8C-10 thru 20 Mobile Home/Private Residential Leasehold Communities
11. NJSA 2A:18-61.3 Eviction Law
12. NJSA 46:8-9.2, Disabling Illness NJAC 5 29-2.1 and 2.2 For copies of the form write to: Office of Landlord-Tenant Information, CN 805, Trenton, NJ 08625; fax (609) 292-2839.
13. NJSA 46:8-9.1 Death of lessee
14. *Reste Realty v Corp. v. Cooper* 53 NJ 444 (March 7, 1969)
15. *Sommer v. Kridel* 74 NJ 446 (1977) Mitigate damage court dec.
16. NJSA 2A:42-5 Double Rent and Holdover Tenant Law
17. 50 U.S.C. App. 510 Sailors and Soldiers
18. NJSA 46:8-26 Security Deposit Law
19. NJSA 46:8-21.2 Security Deposit Law
20. NJSA 46:8-19 Security Deposit Law
21. NJSA 46:8-21.1 Security Deposit Law
22. NJSA 46:8-20 Security Deposit Law
23. *Hunter v. Weissberger* 212 NJ Super. 262 (June 25, 1986)
24. Court Rule 6:1 et seq. Small Claims section Special Civil Part
25. NJSA 46:8-25 Security Deposit Law
26. NJSA 10:5-12(g)(h) 1945 Law Against Discrimination
27. NJSA 10:5-5(n) Law Against Discrimination
28. NJSA 2A 42-100 thru 102 Law Against Discrimination Against Children
29. 42 USC 3601 Federal Fair Housing Act
30. NJSA 56:8-1(e) Consumer Fraud
31. NJSA 56:8-19 Consumer Fraud
32. NJSA 46:8-27 thru 37 Landlord Identity Law
33. NJSA Court Rule 4:51-1 thru 4:51-5 Writ of *Ne Exeat*
34. NJSA 2 A:33-1 thru 23 (1971) Distraint Law
35. *Inganamort v. Borough of Fort Lee*, 120 NJ Super. 286,293 (Law Division, 1973) See also *Helmsley v. Borough of Fort Lee*, 78 NJ 200 (1978) Rent Increase Case.
36. NJSA 2A 18-61.1(f) Eviction Law
37. Definition of a valid notice to quit can be found in *Gretkowski v. Wojiechowski*, 26 NJ Super 245 (App. Div. 1953) Valid Rent Increase Notice
38. NJSA 2A:18-61.31 Eviction Law
39. NJSA 54:4-6.3 thru 6.13 Tenants Property Tax Rebate NJAC 5:30 3.3 Law and Tenants Property Tax Rebate Program Administrative Regulations
40. See your NJ Income Tax return form or contact the Division of Taxation (609) 588-2200 or (800) 323-4400.
41. The New Jersey Hotel and Multiple Dwelling Law NJSA 55:13A-1 (1967) and the New Jersey Administrative Code (NJAC) 5:10-1, which define the maintenance regulations, are available for

$5.00. You may write for copies to the Bureau of Housing Inspection, Department of Community Affairs, CN 810, Trenton, NJ 08625-0810, (609) 633-6225.

42. NJAC 5:10-5.1 Multiple Dwelling Regs. for entry of units
43. NJSA 52:27D-192 State Uniform Fire Safety Act
44. NJAC 14:3-7.14 Board of Regulatory Commissioners
45. NJAC Title 8:51 Board of Health Regulations
46. NJSA 26:3 31 to 31.10 Board of Health Regulations
47. *Marini v. Ireland*, Repair and Deduct Case 56 NJ 130 (1970)
48. *Berzito v. Gambino*, 114 NJ Super 124 (1971) and 63 NJ 460 (1973)
49. NJSA 2A 42-85 thru 93 (1971) Rent Receivership Law
50. NJSA 2A:18-61.1(c) Eviction Law
51. NJSA 2A 18-61.2(a) Eviction Law
52. Anyone found to be a disorderly person will be guilty of a petty offense and may be imprisoned for not more than six months or fined not more than $500 or both unless otherwise noted. A disorderly person complaint is made to a municipal court. NJSA 2C:1-4.
53. See Section entitled Rent Increases and Rent Control; last paragraph.
54. NJSA 2A:39-1 Forcible Entry and Detainer Law (amended 1971)
55. NJSA 2A:33.1 Distress Law
56. JSA 2A:18-61.1 (1967) Eviction Law
57. NJAC 5.27-3.3(c) Rooming and Boarding House Regulations
58. NJSA 2A:18.61.2 Eviction Law
59. JSA 2A:18-61.3 Eviction Law
60. NJSA 2A:18-61.1(f) Definition of valid notice to quit can be found in *Gretkowksi v. Wojiechowski*, 26 NJ Super 245 (1953) Valid Rent Increase.
61. NJSA 2A:18-61.1(f) Unconscionability is an indefinite standard. It has been defined in terms of "action which would not be acceptable to any fair and honest man or conduct which is monstrously harsh and shocking to the conscience." *Black's Law Dictionary*, 4th Ed.: *Toker v. Westerman* 113 NJ Super 452(Dist. Court)(1970). See also *Edgemere at Somerset v. Barbara Jean Johnson*, March 23, 1976, Somerset County District Court, and see *Philip Sgroi v. Ricky L. Rosenbaum and Karen Arkenau*, May 10, 1978, Union Cty Dist Court. (The judge in the latter case decided that an increase of more than 10% in a calendar year may be considered "unconscionable," depending on the facts of the situation.)
62. NJSA 52:31B-1, NJSA 20:4-1 or NJAC 5:11-1
63. NJSA 2A:18-61.9(1976) Eviction Law and NJAC 5:24-1 Section 9
64. NJSA 2A:18-61.9(1976) Eviction Law and NJAC 5:24-1 Section 9
65. NJSA 2A:18-53 Eviction Law
66. NJAC 5:27-3.3(c) Rooming and Boarding House Regulations
67. JAC 5:27-3.4 (c) Rooming and Boarding House Law
68. JSA 55:13B-3 Rooming and Board House Law
69. NJSA 2A:18-61.6 and 61.1(a-f) Eviction Law
70. NJSA 2A:42-10.10(1970) Reprisal Law
71. NJSA 2A:18-57 (1976) Eviction Law and court rules
72. NJSA 2A:42-10.16 & 17 (1974) Summary Dispossess: warrant for removal
73. Title 24, Code of Federal Regulations, Part 866, *Federal Register*, August 7, 1975, pp. 33402-33408. Public Housing Lease Regulations.
74. NJSA 2A:42--6.1 thru 6.3 Senior Grace Period Law
75. NJSA 2A:18-61.40 thru 61.59 Eviction Law
76. P.L. 1995, C.144 (C.2A:42-113)

New Security Deposit Law. On January 1, 2004, a state law took effect providing increased protection for tenants' security deposits. The law lifted the court limit for small claims from $2,000 to $5,000. Tenants can sue for twice their deposit if the landlord fails to return the money within 30 days after a lease ends. However, the former law made such action impossible for most tenants because the average deposit is $1,350, according to state officials. Landlords also are no longer able to charge a 1% fee for managing the account and they must notify tenants about where the deposit is held and the interest rate. If a building is sold, the new landlord must obtain the existing deposit from the old landlord, rather than asking the tenant for a new deposit, as was allowed previously.

KEY WORDS

Actual Eviction
Assignment of Lease
Commercial Lease
Constructive Eviction
Demise
Dispossess Proceedings
Escalation Clause
Estate for Years
Eviction
Graduated Lease
Gross Lease
Ground Lease
Holdover Tenancy
Lease
Lessor
Net Lease
Notice to Quit
Percentage Lease
Periodic Tenancy
Recapture Clause
Security Deposit
Step-Up Lease
Sub-lease
Summary Possession
Surrender
Tenancy at Sufferance
Tenancy at Will
Waste

FIGURE 22.1

Apartment Lease

003-N.J LEASE OF RESIDENTIAL PROPERTY
PLAIN LANGUAGE

COPYRIGHT © 1984 BY COLOR PROCESS PRINTING CO.
402 PALISADE AVENUE, CLIFFSIDE PARK, N.J. 07010

REPRODUCTION OF THIS DOCUMENT WITHOUT EXPRESS WRITTEN CONSENT CONSTITUTES VIOLATION OF UNITED STATES COPYRIGHT LAW

"THIS IS A LEGALLY BINDING LEASE THAT WILL BECOME FINAL WITHIN THREE BUSINESS DAYS. DURING THIS PERIOD YOU MAY CHOOSE TO CONSULT AN ATTORNEY WHO CAN REVIEW AND CANCEL THE LEASE. SEE SECTION ON ATTORNEY REVIEW FOR DETAILS."

APARTMENT LEASE

This Agreement, Made the ______________________ day of ______________ in the year one thousand nine hundred and ______________ BETWEEN ____ as LANDLORD, and ____

____ as Tenant, witnesses that the Landlord has agreed to LET to the Tenant, and the Tenant has agreed to TAKE, from the Landlord the ______________________ apartment on the ____________ floor of the house known as ______________________________ in the City of ______________________,

County of ______________________ State of New Jersey, for the term of ______________ to commence ______________ 19____ and to end ______________ 19____, to be occupied as a strictly private dwelling apartment by the above named individuals and no other persons. And the Tenant hereby covenants and agrees to pay to the Landlord the term rent of

____

Dollars payable in equal monthly payments of $______________ in advance on the first day of each and every calendar month during the term at the office of the Landlord or the Landlord's agent, (or to whomever the Landlord may from time to time direct, in writing).

____

____

____

____

____

____

____

____

____

____

____

____

____

The premises are also Leased upon the further Covenants and Conditions:

1. **Security Deposit.** The Tenant has this day deposited with the Landlord the sum of $______________ as security for the faithful performance of this lease. It is agreed that this sum will be returned to the Tenant after Tenant has vacated the apartment, provided the Tenant has fully complied with all terms and conditions in this lease. Security may not be applied to payment of the rent.

2. **Care of the Apartment.** That the Tenant shall take good care of the Apartment and fixtures, and cause no waste or injury; shall not drive nails into the walls or woodwork of the premises, nor allow the same to be done; and shall at his own cost and expense make and do all repairs required to walls, ceilings, paper, glass and glass globes, plumbing-works, ranges, pipes and fixtures whenever damage or injury to the same shall have resulted from misuse or neglect.

3. **Signs.** That the Tenant shall not expose any sign, advertisement, illumination or projection in or out of the windows or exterior, or from the building, or upon it in any place, unless it is approved and permitted in writing by the Landlord or his authorized agent, and the Tenant shall use only such shades in the front windows of the apartment as are put up or approved by the Landlord.

4. **No Sublease or Assignment.** That the Tenant, heirs, executors or administrators shall not sublease or assign the premises, or any part of the premises, without the Landlord's or agent's consent in writing.

5. **Hazard and Health Rules.** The Tenant shall comply with all the rules and regulations of the Board of Health and City

FIGURE 22.1 (cont'd)

Ordinances applicable to the premises; and the Tenant will not use or permit to be used the premises or any part of the premises for any purpose other than that of a private dwelling apartment for himself and his immediate family.

6. **Fire.** That the Tenant shall, in case of fire, give immediate notice to the Landlord, who shall thereupon cause the damage to be repaired as soon as reasonably and conveniently may be, but if the premises are so damaged that the Landlord decides to rebuild, the term shall cease, and the rent shall be paid up to the time of the fire.

7. **Rules and Regulations.** That the Tenant shall consult and conform to the regulations governing the house and to any reasonable alterations or regulation that may be deemed necessary for the protection of the building and the general comfort and welfare of its occupants.

8. **Default.** That in case of default in any of the Covenants, the Landlord may resume possession of the premises, and relet them for the remainder of the term, at the best rent that he can obtain for account of the Tenant, who shall make good any deficiency.

9. **Access to Apartment.** That three months before the expiration of the rental term, applicants shall be admitted at reasonable hours of the day to view the premises until rented; and the Landlord or his agents shall also be permitted at any time during the term to visit and examine them at any reasonable hour of the day, and whenever necessary for any repairs to same or any part of the building, the Landlord, his servants and agents shall be permitted to make them.

10. **Interruption of Services.** The Landlord is not responsible for any inconvenience or interruption of services due to improvements, repairs or for any reason beyond the Landlord's control.

11. **No Waiver.** The failure of the Landlord to insist upon a strict performance of any of the terms, conditions and covenants in this agreement, shall not be deemed a waiver of any rights or remedies that the Landlord may have, and shall not be deemed a waiver of any subsequent breach or default in the terms, conditions and covenants of this agreement.

12. **Pets.** No dogs or other pets shall be permitted in the premises without the consent, in writing, of the Landlord.

13. **Damages.** If Landlord has to incur any legal expenses to enforce his right or recover damages due, pursuant to this lease, Landlord shall be entitled to add legal expenses in the amount which he has to spend for attorney's fee.

14. **No Alterations or Installation of Equipment.** No outdoor washline shall be permitted on the premises other than in designated areas. No automobile shall be parked in such a manner as to obstruct a walk, entrance, driveway or garage door. The Tenant will not place any aerials or any other connections to the roof or any other portion of the premises.

The Tenant shall not install or use a laundry machine, dish washing machine, air conditioning or ventilating equipment, or other mechanical equipment in the apartment or outside of the apartment without the consent of the Landlord in writing. The Tenant shall not affix wallpaper to the walls or ceilings or apply paint with colors or tints which vary from the colors or tints applied to the walls and ceilings by the Landlord.

15. **Subordination.** This Lease and Tenant's rights are subject to present and future mortgages which includes the Apartment.

16. **End of Term.** It is understood and agreed that upon the expiration of the term of this lease, or any renewal of this lease, the Tenant shall quit and surrender the apartment to the Landlord in a broom clean condition. The refrigerator, oven and stove shall also be in a clean condition; ordinary wear and tear excepted. In the event that the Tenant fails to comply with this paragraph, Landlord may at its option complete the work, clean or repair and deduct the cost from any security deposit held by Landlord. Nothing in this lease shall in any way prevent Landlord's right to recover any sum due it in excess of the security deposit.

17. **Attorney Review.**

A. STUDY BY ATTORNEY
The Tenant or the Landlord may choose to have an attorney study this lease. If an attorney is consulted, the attorney must complete his or her review of the lease within a three-day period. This lease will be legally binding at the end of this three-day period unless an attorney for the Tenant or the Landlord reviews and disapproves of the lease.

B. COUNTING THE TIME
You count the three days from the date of delivery of the signed lease to the Tenant and the Landlord. You do not count Saturdays, Sundays or legal holidays. The Tenant and the Landlord may agree in writing to extend the three-day period for attorney review.

C. NOTICE OF DISAPPROVAL
If an attorney for the Tenant or the Landlord reviews and disapproves of this lease, the attorney must notify the REAL ESTATE BROKERS and the other party named in this lease within the three-day period. Otherwise this lease will be legally binding as written. The attorney must send the notice of disapproval to the REAL ESTATE BROKERS by certified mail, by telegram, or by delivering it personally. The telegram or certified letter will be effective upon sending. The personal delivery will be effective upon delivery to the REAL ESTATE BROKERS office. The attorney may also, but need not, inform the REAL ESTATE BROKERS of any suggested revision(s) in the lease that would make it satisfactory.

____

____

____

____

IT IS HEREBY EXPRESSLY UNDERSTOOD AND AGREED that the character of the occupancy of the premises, as above expressed, is an especial consideration and inducement for the granting of this lease by the Landlord to the Tenant, and in the event of a violation by the Tenant of the restrictions against subletting the premises, or permitting the same to be occupied by parties other than the tenant, or of a violation of any other condition of this agreement, the Lease shall, at the option of the Landlord, his agents or assigns,

SPECIMEN

FIGURE 22.1 (cont'd)

cease and terminate and be at an end.

In Witness Whereof, the parties to this agreement have hereunto set their hands and seals, the day and year first above written.

Sealed and Delivered in the presence of

______________________ Landlord (L.S.)

____

______________________ Tenant (L.S.)

____

______________________ Tenant (L.S.)

CHAPTER 22
Review Questions
(Answers on page 558)

1. A tenancy for years can be for:
   (A) a certain number of days.
   (B) a certain number of months.
   (C) a certain number of years.
   (D) any of the above.

2. A landlord orally leases a store to a tenant for one year. The lease is:
   (A) valid.
   (B) invalid due to the Statute of Frauds.
   (C) a tenancy from year to year.
   (D) a periodic tenancy.

3. A lease which is based on gross revenues is a:
   (A) gross lease.
   (B) net lease.
   (C) percentage lease.
   (D) annual lease.

4. A lease held by a tenant in an apartment building project is usually a:
   (A) ground lease.
   (B) gross lease.
   (C) net lease.
   (D) percentage lease.

5. Which lease provides for certain adjustments in rent?
   (A) Ground lease.
   (B) Net lease.
   (C) Graduated lease.
   (D) Long-term lease.

6. A lease of fixed time that automatically renews itself until the landlord or tenant takes action to terminate it is:
   (A) an estate at will.
   (B) a periodic tenancy.
   (C) a tenancy at sufferance.
   (D) a holdover tenancy.

7. If the lease requires the landlord to provide repairs and the landlord refuses to do so, the tenant, after giving proper notice, may:
   (A) serve the landlord with a notice to quit.
   (B) take an ejectment action against the landlord.
   (C) have the repairs made and deduct them from the rent.
   (D) pay a reduced rent reflecting the value of the rented premises without the required repairs.

8. A sublease is:
   (A) an assignment of the lease.
   (B) a transfer of the entire leasehold.
   (C) a transfer of less-than-entire leasehold.
   (D) void after 15 years.

9. Under a net lease, the lessee is responsible for all of the following EXCEPT:
   (A) taxes.
   (B) repairs.
   (C) water charges.
   (D) mortgage payments.

10. When a tenant is unable to occupy his leased premises for the purpose intended because of a physical condition, this is called:
    (A) actual eviction.
    (B) constructive eviction.
    (C) dispossess eviction.
    (D) passive eviction.

11. Assume a mortgaged property is leased. Because of default in payment, the mortgagee forecloses on the mortgage. Which of the following statements is TRUE regarding rights under the lease?
    (A) The lessee is automatically released from any further obligation on the lease.
    (B) The lease continues in effect despite the foreclosure.
    (C) The lease is void because the mortgagor has no right to give a lease on mortgaged property.
    (D) The lease may be terminated by the mortgagee but not by the lessee.

12. The term that best describes a tenant's interest in the property is:
    (A) a life estate.
    (B) a reversionary interest.
    (C) a remainder interest.
    (D) a leasehold estate.

13. Landlord-tenant laws for residential properties provide for:
    (A) one month's notice to terminate a month-to-month tenancy.
    (B) limitations on the amount of the security deposit.
    (C) a prohibition against eviction unless there is a "good cause."
    (D) all of the above.

(Quiz continues on next page)

14. A lease which calls for a series of predetermined rent increases designed to offset inflation is called a:
    (A) graduated lease.
    (B) step-up lease.
    (C) Both A and B.
    (D) Neither A nor B.

15. A landlord and a tenant agreed to terminate a lease. This is known as:
    (A) rescission.
    (B) surrender.
    (C) release.
    (D) abandonment.

16. A lessee rents a building from February 1 to September 1. His tenancy is:
    (A) month-to-month.
    (B) periodic tenancy.
    (C) fee simple estate.
    (D) estate for years.

17. The person who most likely would make use of the remedy called "Summary Possession" would be:
    (A) the trustor.
    (B) the holder of a note in default.
    (C) the lessor.
    (D) the grantor.

18. A clause in a contract that permits an upward or downward adjustment of the obligation should certain events occur is known as a(n):
    (A) escalation clause.
    (B) acceleration clause.
    (C) penalty clause.
    (D) habendum clause.

19. The interest of a tenant who came rightly into possession by permission of the owner but continues to occupy the premises without permission is called:
    (A) a sandwich lease.
    (B) an estate at sufferance.
    (C) an estate at will.
    (D) an estate in remainder.

20. All but which one of the following are necessary parts of a lease?
    (A) Parties to the lease.
    (B) Terms of the lease.
    (C) Option to purchase.
    (D) Terms of the rental payment.

21. An oral contract for the lease of real estate for one year in New Jersey is:
    (A) voidable.
    (B) valid.
    (C) void.
    (D) invalid.

22. In the event the landlord in a New Jersey residential month-to-month lease wishes to raise the rent, he must give the tenant how many consecutive days' notice?
    (A) 72
    (B) 30
    (C) 28
    (D) 45

23. A tenant who is actually or constructively evicted by a landlord may consider his lease as being:
    (A) renewed.
    (B) terminated.
    (C) assigned.
    (D) sold.

24. Which of the following statements in reference to a residential lease is FALSE?
    (A) The security deposit is the property of the lessor during the term of the lease.
    (B) Unless a contrary agreement is in effect, the lessee may sublet.
    (C) A security deposit remains the property of the lessee until actual damage occurs.
    (D) The rental of a bungalow at the shore from August 1 to August 31 is a tenenacy for years.

25. Which of the following does NOT possess a leasehold estate?
    (A) Tenancy at sufferance.
    (B) Tenancy at will.
    (C) Life tenant.
    (D) Tenant for years.

26. A percentage lease is:
    (A) one which provides for the percentage that will be paid the broker as a commission.
    (B) one where the usual rent is based upon the net receipts of the tenant.
    (C) one which always allows the tenant to cancel his lease if his income falls below a desired amount.
    (D) one in which the rent is determined by a percentage of sales made in the leased premises.

27. A lease which ends without notice on the last day of the term is called:
    (A) a tenancy for years.
    (B) an estate at sufferance.
    (C) an estate at will.
    (D) an estate in remainder.

28. Which one of the following involves a landlord-tenant relationship?
    (A) Tenancy in common.
    (B) Periodic estate.
    (C) Joint tenancy.
    (D) Tenancy by the entireties.

29. When the premises reach a physical condition whereby the tenant is unable to occupy them for the purposes intended, the situation is legally recognized as:
    (A) a dispossess eviction.
    (B) an actual eviction.
    (C) a constructive eviction.
    (D) a passive eviction.

30. By definition, an "estate for years":
    (A) must last for a year or more.
    (B) must last for at least two years.
    (C) is for a fixed term, whether a week, a month, a decade.
    (D) requires a written lease.

31. During the term of a lease, the landlord has which of the following?
    (A) Reversion interest.
    (B) Tenancy at sufferance.
    (C) Right of reentry.
    (D) Remainder interest.

32. If it is not stipulated in the lease and the leased property is sold, the lease:
    (A) has to be renewed.
    (B) is binding on the new owner.
    (C) creates a tenancy from month-to-month.
    (D) materially affects the tenant.

33. The lessor under a net lease pays the:
    (A) taxes.
    (B) special assessments.
    (C) maintenance.
    (D) mortgage principal payments.

34. Under the terms of a typical lease, when the lessor dies:
    (A) the lease terminates.
    (B) the lessee has the option to terminate the lease.
    (C) the lease is void.
    (D) the lease is not affected.

35. A lease of land alone specifically providing for a new rental for the construction of a building by the tenant is known as a:
    (A) ground lease.
    (B) net lease.
    (C) gross lease.
    (D) sandwich lease.

36. The term "lessor" is most likely to be used to describe:
    (A) a tenant.
    (B) an owner.
    (C) a vendor.
    (D) an optionor.

37. A leasehold interest lying between the primary lease and the sublease is known as:
    (A) a percentage lease.
    (B) a sandwich lease.
    (C) an inactive lease.
    (D) an uncapitalized lease.

38. A graduated lease can best be defined as a lease:
    (A) that includes an option to purchase.
    (B) in which there may be an increase or decrease in rent at a stated future time.
    (C) under which the owner or landlord pays all ownership charges such as taxes.
    (D) that is passed intact from one owner to the next owner under terms of a contract.

39. The normal shopping center lease is a:
    (A) net lease.
    (B) percentage lease.
    (C) gross lease.
    (D) sublease.

40. When a lease provides that the lessor shall be responsible for expenses such as taxes, insurance, heat, utilities and maintenance, it is known as which of the following?
    (A) Gross lease.
    (B) Net lease.
    (C) Indexed (escalated) lease.
    (D) Graduated (step-up) lease.

41. Which of the following is true when a lease is assigned?
    (A) The assignment cannot be made without the consent of the lessor.
    (B) The assignee will pay rent directly to the lessor.
    (C) It automatically extends the term of the lease.
    (D) The lease is not assignable unless it specifically states that it is.

42. If a landlord takes legal action to evict a tenant for non-payment of rent, it is called a (an):
    (A) assignment.
    (B) constructive eviction.
    (C) self-help eviction.
    (D) actual eviction.

43. An example of a non-freehold estate is:
    (A) fee simple.
    (B) defeasible fee.
    (C) determinable fee.
    (D) a lease.

(Quiz continues on next page)

44. Which of the following is a non-freehold estate?
    (A) Tenancy by the entirety.
    (B) Tenancy in common.
    (C) Tenancy for years.
    (D) Tenancy in severalty.

45. Which of the following is NOT a leasehold estate?
    (A) Estate at will.
    (B) Estate at sufferance.
    (C) Estate for years.
    (D) Life estate.

46. A net lease:
    (A) generally requires the lessor to pay operating expenses.
    (B) is usually used for apartments.
    (C) cannot be used for industrial properties.
    (D) generally requires the lessee to pay operating expenses.

47. A tenant who transfers part of the remaining term of his or her lease is:
    (A) assigning the lease.
    (B) subleasing the premises.
    (C) a sublessee.
    (D) an assignee.

48. In New Jersey, if a landlord refuses to rent to a family because they have a child under 18 years old, it would be:
    (A) a violation of the New Jersey Law Against Discrimination.
    (B) a violation of the Federal Fair Housing Law.
    (C) a violation of license laws.
    (D) both A and B.

49. Mark rents a dwelling unit to Susan, who in turn transfers a portion of her lease term to Katy. Concerning this example, all of the following statements are correct EXCEPT:
    (A) Katy is the sublessee.
    (B) Mark is the lessor in the original lease.
    (C) Susan is the lessee in the original lease.
    (D) Katy is the lessor in her lease with Susan.

50. In New Jersey a landlord may legally evict a tenant for which of the following reasons?
    (A) The tenant joined a tenant organization.
    (B) The tenant failed to pay rent on an oral lease.
    (C) The tenant is too old.
    (D) The tenant of a two-bedroom apartment gave birth to a child.

CHAPTER TWENTY-THREE

PROPERTY MANAGEMENT

Property management is a specialized branch of the real estate business that involves the operation, supervision and execution of management policies pertaining to a given property. As an organized profession, property management dates back to 1933, when the Institute of Real Estate Management was formed under the auspices of the National Association of Realtors®. Historically, the need for property management can be traced to three factors: urbanization, technological advances in building construction and absentee ownership. In recent years the field has grown rapidly due to the increase of housing laws and regulations at all levels, and the development of new forms of multifamily ownership, including condominiums and cooperative apartments.

Management Objectives

The basic objectives of the property manager are twofold: to attain the highest possible net return for the property owner, and to protect his capital investment at all times. Each objective has a direct effect on the other. For example, it would be possible to maximize net income over a short period of time simply by cutting back on maintenance and repairs. But over the long term, this approach would have the opposite effect, leading to tenant dissatisfaction, a decrease in net income and a lessening of the property's value.

Specialized Fields

Because of the complexity and diversity of property management, areas of specialization have developed with respect to the types of properties being managed. The skills of the apartment building manager are somewhat different from those required to manage an office building, a shopping center or an industrial park. Hotels, retail buildings and single-purpose buildings such as theaters, restaurants and hospitals require still other skills. Expertise learned in one type of property is not always transferable to another. Nevertheless, the work involves a number of functions that are common to the management of all types of properties. These include:

1. Qualifying and investigating tenant's credit.
2. Marketing the space and collecting rents.
3. Establishing and maintaining trust accounts for rental income and security deposits.
4. Purchasing supplies and auditing and paying bills.
5. Hiring, training and supervising employees.
6. Inspecting vacant space frequently.
7. Arranging and paying for adequate insurance coverage.
8. Scrutinizing taxes and assessments.
9. Analyzing depreciation deductions.
10. Developing tenant relations policies.
11. Maintaining proper records and making periodic reports (usually monthly) to the owner.
12. Preparing and executing leases.
13. Advertising vacancies through selected media.
14. Planning and supervising alteration and modernization programs.
15. Having knowledge of health, building code and safety standards.
16. Providing adequate security to safeguard tenants.
17. Preparing an annual budget.

The Property Management Agreement

As with any kind of business arrangement, the property manager or management company should enter into a formal contract that clearly states the rights and obligations of both parties. A typical property management agreement is shown in Figure 23-3. It contains the minimum points of agreement necessary for the property manager to do his work and can easily be adapted to any situation with the help of an attorney. It covers the work to be performed, the frequency of reports to the owner and fees for management. The agreement is very specific about the authority of the property manager to enter into agreements on behalf of the owner, but it is less specific about daily operations. By necessity, this part of the contract should be flexible. Larger properties will require more detailed contracts.

Management agreements will normally take one of two forms. The manager may be hired as an *employee* of an owner or corporation to handle large commercial buildings. Under this arrangement, the corporation generally pays the manager a salary. This employer-employee relationship is very common. The other arrangement involves a principal-agent relationship similar to that found in the seller-broker or buyer-broker relationship.

The typical items that should be covered in a management agreement include:

1. A legal description of the property.
2. A time period for the agreement to exist.
3. A definition of the responsibilities of the manager.
4. The authority of the manager.
5. The reporting requirements (both frequency and detail).
6. Compensation of the manager.
7. A limit on how much the manager can spend without expressed authority except in a case of emergency.

There may be other clauses in a management agreement, but these are the most frequently used. As a fiduciary, the property manager is bound not only by the contractual provisions of the management agreement, but as well by the legal obligations imposed on all agents that were discussed in Chapter 12.

The management agreement typically assigns the role of **general agent** to the property manager. As a general agent the manager's authority includes the general powers associated with the operation of the business. The property manager must set up an administrative office and staff. The hiring (and firing) of either employees or outside contractors who provide services are part of the general agent's functions for the management and administration of properties. The manager will attempt to get the best possible arrangement for the provision of these services in order to maximize the net income available for distribution to the owners. Any personal relationships with contractors or vendors must be disclosed to the property owner.

Licensing Requirements

The definitions of "real estate broker" and "real estate salesperson" include property managers as set forth in NJSA 45:15-3. The legal effect is that those who manage property for others must be licensed, subject to certain exceptions. The exceptions are: (a) resident managers (often called *superintendents*) of residential property who supervise the care of an apartment complex while living in one of the units in the complex; and (b) managers who manage property as a salaried employee of the property owner, providing the employee is paid, based on the employer's obligation to pay compensation in the absence of any rental activity. Licensing is discussed in more detail below.

Office and Equipment

Office requirements for each of the above vary according to the circumstances. The nature and extent of the manager's clientele will determine the location and "image" of an office. The type of office equipment required, particularly for bookkeeping and accounting, will be dictated by the size and complexity of the managed properties.

Personnel

Personnel requirements of a property management office parallel those of any well-organized business. Provisions must be made for the management of the properties, of course, and in addition there must be accounting, clerical, purchasing and logistical support. There is no universal terminology by which one may determine responsibilities based upon title in the property management field. Each organization will have its own system. A "real estate manager" or "vice president-real estate" may have the same duties as a "property manager," "property administrator," etc.

Management Fees

Normally, a property manager's compensation is an agreed-upon percentage of gross collectible income. The percentage generally varies from 5 to 10%. In many cases, additional charges are made for non-routine services such as leasing, supervising major repairs, etc. Direct employee expenses, such as salaries for superintendents, maintenance supervisors and others, are charged directly to the owner.

OPERATING RESPONSIBILITIES OF A PROPERTY MANAGER

The operating responsibilities of a property manager can be placed in the following categories:

- Establishing a management plan
- Budget preparation
- Preparing a rental schedule and leasing space
- Rent collection
- Record-keeping
- Maintenance
- Communicating with the owner
- Handling tenant requests.

The Management Plan

Before taking on a property management assignment, a visual inspection of the property must be made. The inspection will reveal the scope of the work required of the manager. During discussion of the management plan and objectives with the owner, the property manager should review the results of the inspection and suggest a priority of maintenance expenditures. A long-range plan can then be developed based on the owner's objectives.

If the owner wishes to maximize income by minimizing maintenance, constraints will be placed on the manager's decisions. Owners also differ considerably regarding the degree of authority they are willing to delegate. Some want to be consulted about the smallest of details while others only want to be involved in major decisions. If it appears that the owner's goals are not compatible with the manager's, the business should be declined, because once employment is accepted, the manager has a fiduciary responsibility to promote the owner's interests to the best of his or her ability.

Budget Preparation

Once a management plan has been established, a budget is prepared that will include a projection of expected income, vacancies and operating expenses. These target projections provide a basis for monitoring the performance of a property and controlling the expenses associated with its operation. Periodic review of the budget and comparisons with actual operations will point out areas that will need attention and correction. For example, if projected income is lower than expected because of vacancies, the rental schedule should be reviewed, in addition to other possible reasons for the unexpected vacancies. When operating income and expenses are significantly lower than projected, owners will expect the manager to account for the differences.

Expenses are usually shown as either *fixed expenses* or *variable expenses*. Fixed expenses can be either regularly recurring costs or periodic costs. Regularly recurring costs arise each month. Employee wages, basic operating costs and maintenance expenditures fall into this category. Periodic costs such as property taxes and insurance premiums recur at longer intervals. Variable expenses, which are associated with the level of occupancy, include decorating costs, replenishment of supplies and minor repairs.

The budget should also provide for the maintenance of a working capital account so that the manager will have the ability to meet required payments at various points in time. Often reserves are set up for this purpose. The amount of working capital required can usually be estimated from previous operating experience.

Leasing Space

Securing desirable tenants at attractive rates is an important property management function. A successful property manager must have the ability to select tenants that will be able to meet the financial obligation being undertaken in the lease. Every prospective tenant should be required to fill out a thorough application form and a seasoned manager or rental agent should personally interview the applicant.

Rents are based on supply and demand for the type of property and are generally established on the basis of market comparison. A good strategy is to rate rental units by comparing them with comparable properties in similar neighborhoods for which accurate data is available. Rents for apartments will vary because of area of floor space, number of bathrooms, floor locations, available services, recreation facilities and transportation to and from the area. The rental schedule may also be affected by the owner's leasing policies, meaning that rents will vary depending on the length of leases, and whether or not the units are furnished. Tenant *retention* is at least as important as tenant selection, because tenants will move at the end of a lease if the rent is not as acceptable to them as it would be to a prospective tenant.

Since leases can be quite complex, the property manager must have an understanding of the numerous lease provisions applicable to different tenants. For example, flat monthly rate rents may be in effect for residential properties while percentage leases will be in effect for commercial properties in regional malls. Lease provisions were discussed in Chapter 22.

Rent Collection

If tenants have been properly screened and the lease is clearly worded, rent collection should be an easy task. The lease generally states that rent payments are due in advance on the first day of each and every calendar month. Since the owner depends on a steady flow of income to meet expenses and achieve a positive net income, rent payments must not be allowed to become delinquent. The requirement of a security deposit is also an effective screening device. If a prospective tenant wants to rent space but does not have the money for a security deposit, it is not likely that he or she will be able to pay the rent each month. New Jersey allows a security deposit equal to 1.5 months rent on residential leases. (See the "Truth in Renting Act" in Chapter 22 for detailed information regarding security deposits.)

When the rent is not paid on time the manager must decide on a course of action. Typically the tenant will be sent a reminder on the 5th day of the month. If rent is not received by the 10th day, a second reminder is sent and the tenant is requested to personally call on the property manager. Only by visiting with the tenant can the manager discover the underlying problem and decide whether the rent can be collected or if eviction is required.

When it is apparent that the delinquent rent will not be paid, action must be taken to recover possession of the premises through the legal process of eviction. The process begins with the landlord serving the tenant with a **notice to quit**. If the tenant fails to vacate the premises, the landlord takes the matter to court. If the landlord wins the case, or if the tenant fails to appear, the court will issue a **Judgment of Possession** under which the tenant is ordered to vacate the premises. If the tenant refuses to move, the landlord is entitled to a **Warrant for Removal** under which an officer of the court such as a constable is directed to remove all persons and belongings from the premises and to give the landlord full possession.

Record-keeping

The property manager must produce records that are accurate, precise and easy to understand. These reports will serve as the basis for the income and expense report, which generally is presented to the owner on a monthly basis. By comparing the report with the budget, the owner will be able to see items that may be exceeding amounts budgeted for them. A property manager must make periodic reports to the owner of the property, and the owner, in turn, must make periodic reports to the state and federal governments for tax purposes. The property manager can provide a valuable service by reporting the information in a manner that will satisfy the owner's need for information and also provide the information needed for tax purposes. A basic income and expense report is shown in Figure 23-1.

Maintenance

One of the main responsibilities of the property manager is to see that the building and its grounds are properly serviced and maintained. The building must be kept clean and attractive at all times. If the property is not kept in good condition, vacancies will occur which will decrease the property's value and injure the reputation of the property management company.

The property manager's responsibility for maintenance falls into three categories:

- Preventive maintenance;
- Corrective maintenance (repairs); and
- New or rehabilitation construction.

Preventive maintenance includes those regularly scheduled activities that will maintain the structure from a capital point of view so that the long-range value and physical integrity of the building will be preserved. Most authorities agree this is the most important but most neglected maintenance responsibility. Examples are vacuuming hallway carpets, periodic lubrication of gears and motors, regular maintenance schedules, etc. An in-house staff may carry out preventive maintenance, or the work may be contracted out to independent contractors. Generally, a combination of the two will be used. For example, employees usually handle routine items such as daily housekeeping chores and small repairs, while independent contractors are used for large, difficult or technical jobs such as air conditioning failures or paving repairs. Primarily, the decision is based on an analysis of the cost-effectiveness of the solution as applied to the particular problem.

Inspection of the property should be made on a regular basis. The property manager and the maintenance staff should constantly be on the lookout for possible defects around the property. Problems and hazards should be checked for in sidewalks, stairs, wiring, plumbing, roofing, boiler rooms or anywhere that inattention may cause an accident.

New or rehabilitation construction involves the addition of new areas to a project or physical remodeling in order to change use or to modernize. This has become an increasing responsibility of managers of large properties as buildings mature through their life cycles. An example is remodeling a kitchen to replace freestanding appliances with modern built-in equipment.

The entire maintenance program must be in line with the owner's objectives. Although property managers usually have authority to have repairs made, they still must stay within the budget.

Handling Tenant Requests

Closely related to the maintenance function is the servicing of tenant requests. Usually these involve routine repairs and maintenance, but there are times when the functional requirements of a tenant may require alterations to the tenant's premises. The manager must evaluate all such requests from tenants, and, based upon the economics of the requests, make recommendations to the owner as to whether or not the work should be undertaken.

Routine service requests are generally written on carbon copy forms that will serve as a basis for accounting and record-keeping. The work orders usually contain the following information:

1. The nature of the request, when it was made and by whom.

2. Detailed instructions to the person who is to carry out the request.

3. Report completion of the request to both the tenant and the property manager.

When tenants complain of some condition in the building there are a number of reasons the property manager should act promptly. First, quick attention creates good will and encourages future tenant cooperation in reporting problems. Next, it reduces liability suits from tenants, guests or employees who might be injured as a result of the defect. Once a complaint has been filed it is easier for an injured person to prove negligence against an owner or agent who fails to correct the condition. Finally, prompt attention can save the owner money because the condition might be one that could worsen rapidly.

Communicating with the Owner

The key to effective relations between owners, property managers and tenants is communication. Under the law of agency, knowledge of the agent is imputed to be knowledge of the principal. In practice, however, owners know only what property managers tell them orally and in written reports. If the reports are incomplete, owners may not even be aware of tenant complaints and maintenance problems.

The property manager is responsible for establishing the means and frequency of communication. Generally, telephonic or written communication is always necessary when any of the following occur:

1. A disaster such as fire or flood, or serious damage or injury to a tenant, a guest or employee.
2. Tenant requests that exceed the manager's authority.
3. Notices of commercial tenants vacating or a change in the tenant's ownership or financial status.
4. Recommendations for long-range programs, such as modernization.
5. Any change in the community affecting tenancy, such as the withdrawal of a major industry or the construction of a competitive property.
6. Inquiries for the purchase of the property.

STATE AND LOCAL LAWS AFFECTING PROPERTY MANAGEMENT

License Laws

The New Jersey Real Estate License Law is set forth in Title 45, Chapter 15 of the Statutes. Persons who manage properties other than their own or that of their employers must be licensed under the law. The definitions of "real estate broker" and "real estate salesperson" include property managers as set forth in 45:15-3. Certain exceptions are made in 45:15-4. One of these exceptions deals with property managers. An employee engaged by an owner to "manage" his property is not required to have a real estate license if: (a) the employee engages in property management activity in pursuit of the employer's general business; (b) the employee performs additional activities for the employer such as bookkeeping, purchasing, etc., and (c) the employee is paid based upon the employer's obligation to pay compensation in the absence of any rental activity.

Other sections of the License Laws and the Rules and Regulations of the Real Estate Commission deal with the operation of the property management office, maintenance of trust accounts and residential landlord/tenant relations.

Police Power

The exercise of police power through state law and local ordinances has had a significant impact on a private landowner's ability to use his real property. Discrimination laws, zoning, city planning, subdividing, building codes and environmental protection laws are all based on the exercise of the police power.

Eminent Domain

The government at all levels has the right to terminate a lease, but it must provide just compensation. Both the property owner and the tenants would be entitled to compensation.

FEDERAL LAWS AFFECTING PROPERTY MANAGEMENT

There are several federal laws with which a property manager may be concerned, depending on the nature and the extent of property managed. A brief discussion of major legislation is therefore in order.

Environmental Protection

Federal environmental laws and regulations have been passed to control both public and private pollution. The primary regulating body at the federal level is the Environmental Protection Agency (EPA). The agency sets standards of acceptable pollution and provides advice and assistance to state, regional and municipal environmental control agencies. (See Chapter 33, Environmental Laws.)

The Federal Fair Housing Act

Although this law is titled "The Fair Housing Act," and therefore is of primary interest to property managers in the residential field, all property managers must be aware that discrimination based on race in the leasing of any type of property is a violation of federal law. The Fair Housing Act of 1968, contained in Title VIII of the Civil Rights Act of 1968, provides that it is unlawful to discriminate on the basis of race, color, religion, sex, national origin, physical and mental handicap and familial status when selling or leasing residential property.

The Internal Revenue Code

Property managers have responsibility for proper reporting of wages and withholding taxes and social security contributions of employees.

The Occupational Safety and Health Act (OSHA)

The Secretary of Labor has prescribed federal standards for workplace health and safety and imposed fines for failure to meet them. Property managers should check this law to determine the extent of its applicability to their operation.

FINANCIAL RESPONSIBILITIES OF A PROPERTY MANAGER

The financial responsibilities of a property manager will vary according to the amount and type of property managed, the services offered by the property manager to various owners and the size of the property management organization. A licensee who manages only a few houses will be responsible mainly for accounting and reporting, but very little budgeting or sophisticated financial management. A property manager in a large organization, on the other hand, may be required to prepare involved financial reports and analyses, including long-term budgets and forecasts.

Due to the fiduciary nature of the business, the selection and maintenance of an adequate trust fund accounting system is essential. The records of all funds passing through the property manager's hands must be kept and made available for periodic review by an accountant and the owner.

Regardless of the extent of their responsibilities or the size of their companies, all licensees must conform to New Jersey License Law and Real Estate Commission Rules and Regulations. The accounting responsibilities of licensees were covered in Chapter 3.

Income and Expense Report

Basic to all property management is the **income and expense report**, which is the principal document by which the property manager communicates with the owner. Figure 23-1 shows a basic outline that can be expanded to meet the needs of a particular property. For a small property, the property manager may simply photocopy the ledger sheet and send it to the owner, as in Figure 23-2.

Periodic Profit and Loss (P&L) Statement

No less than yearly, the property manager will summarize the activity concerning a property for a given period, and submit to the owner a **profit and loss statement**. Usually the P&L report is prepared on a calendar year basis, unless the owner is a corporation or entity filing income tax returns on a fiscal year basis.

The format of a profit and loss statement is very much like the income and expense statement and can also follow the example shown in Figure 23-1.

Cash Flow

Probably the most important single computation the property manager makes is the determination of the cash flow from a property. This is essential in all property, from a single-family residence to huge complexes held by multi-state organizations. The cash flow represents the sum of money generated by an income-producing property after all operating expenses and debt-service (mortgage payments), including principal and interest, have been paid. It can be calculated on either a before-tax or after-tax basis.

Professional Property Management Organizations

A number of professional societies and organizations have been formed to help the public identify

FIGURE 23.1 Income and Expense Report

GEORGIAN GARDENS APARTMENTS INCOME AND EXPENSE REPORT

INCOME	
Maximum Possible Income	$250,000
Less Vacancy	- 12,500
Net Rental Income	237,500
Other Income (Laundry, Vending Machines)	3,000
Total Operating Income	$240,500
EXPENSES	
Administrative, Office, Legal & Audit	$ 10,000
Electricity	5,000
Gas	2,000
Water	3,000
Garbage Removal	2,000
Maintenance	16,000
Insurance	6,000
Taxes	12,600
Management Fee 5% (5% x $237,500)	11,875
Total Operating Expenses	$ 68,475
Reserve for Replacement	12,000
Total Expenses	- 80,475
Net Operating Income (NOI)	$160,025

responsible real estate property managers. They offer seminars, courses and publications that prepare people for the profession. Thus, the necessary skills do not have to be acquired by experience alone. These organizations issue professional designations to members who, through education and experience, have demonstrated proficiency in the management of income-producing properties. Some of the organizations with their designations are listed below:

Institute of Real Estate Management (IREM), with the individual designation of Certified Property Manager (CPM). Phone: (800) 837-0706.

Building Owner's and Manager's Association (BOMA), with the individual designation of Real Property Administrator (RPA). Phone: (202) 408-2662.

National Association of Home Builders (NAHB), Apartment Council, with the individual designation of Registered Apartment Manager (RAM). Phone: (202) 822-0200.

National Apartment Association (NAA), with the individual designation of Certified Apartment Manager (CAM). Phone: (202) 955-1142.

International Council of Shopping Centers (ICSC). Phone: (646) 728-3800.

REFERENCE BOOKS ON PROPERTY MANAGEMENT

The following books are general property management texts. Licensees interested should write the publisher for descriptive information.

Principles of Real Estate Management, James C. Downs, Jr., CPM, Institute of Real Estate Management, 430 North Michigan Avenue, Chicago, IL 60611.

Property Management, Robert C. Kyle and Floyd M. Baird, Real Estate Education Company, 500 North Dearborn Street, Chicago, IL 60610.

FIGURE 23.2
Property Manager's Ledger Report

SEPARATE RECORD FOR EACH PROPERTY MANAGED

Owner	RANDY GARRISON	Deposit	
Address	260 MILL ST. BELLEVILLE, N.J.	Monthly Rent	$880.
Property	GEORGIAN GARDENS APTS.	Commission:	
Tenant's Name	MOYES #1; WALKER #2	Leases	
Units	2	Collection	INCLUDED
Remarks		Management	$60.

Date	Received From or Paid To	Description	Receipt or Check No.	Amount Received	Date Deposited	Amount Disbursed	Balance
5/5/89	GEORGE MOYES	MAY RENT APT. 1	RCPT. 2	$400.	5/5/89		$400
5/5/89	MARSHA WALKER	MAY RENT APT. 2	RCPT. 3	$480.	5/5/89		$880
5/6/89	PUBLIC SERVICE ELEC.	APRIL ELEC BILL	CK.001			$55	$825
5/7/89	PAUL LISTER	MNGT. FEE	CK.002			$60	$765
5/7/89	RANDY GARRISON	MAY RENTAL PROCEEDS	CK.003			$765	-0-

FIGURE 23.3
Property Management Agreement

NCR (No Carbon Required)

MANAGEMENT AGREEMENT

IN CONSIDERATION of the covenants herein contained, ____________________

____________________, hereinafter designated as Owner,
agrees to employ ____________________, hereinafter designated as Agent,
to rent, lease, operate and manage the real property situated in the City of ____________________,
County of ____________, State of ____________, Known as ____________________

____

for a period commencing this date and terminating at midnight of ____________, and continuing on a month to month basis thereafter subject to ________ days written notice of intent to terminate by either party, upon the following TERMS AND CONDITIONS:

AGENT'S AUTHORITIES AND OBLIGATIONS

Owner hereby confers upon Agent the following authorities and obligations, where initialed by Owner:

________ To advertise the availability "for rent" or "for lease" of the premises and to display "For Rent" or "For Lease" signs. To screen and use diligence in the selection of prospective tenants and to abide by all fair housing laws.

________ To negotiate leases as may be approved by Owner. Lease terms not to exceed ____________________.

________ To execute leases and rental agreements on behalf of Owner.

________ To collect rents, security deposits, and all other receipts, and to deposit such monies in a trust account with a qualified banking institution.

________ To serve notice of termination of tenancies, notices to quit or pay rent, and such other notices as Agent may deem appropriate.

________ To employ attorneys approved by Owner for the purpose of enforcing Owner's rights under leases and rental agreements and instituting legal action on behalf of Owner.

________ To provide all services reasonably necessary for the proper management of the property including periodic inspections, supervision of maintenance, and arranging for such improvements, alterations and repairs as may be required of Owner.

________ To hire, supervise and discharge all employees and independent contractors required in the operation and maintenance of the property. Compensation shall be in such amounts as approved by Owner and the employment of any employee shall be terminable at will. It is agreed that all such employees are employees of the Owner and not of the Agent. To prepare payroll tax returns for Owner, where applicable, and to make payments of such taxes to the appropriate agencies from gross revenues.

________ To contract for repairs or alterations at a cost to Owner not to exceed $____________________.

________ To contract for emergency repairs at a cost to Owner not to exceed $____________________ per repair.

________ In the event Owner is not available for consultation, to contract for such repairs and expenditures as are necessary for the protection of the property from damage, or to perform services to the tenants provided for in their leases.

________ To execute service contracts for utilites and services for the operation, maintenance, and safety of the property as Agent deems necessary or advisable. Provided that the terms of any such contract shall not exceed ____________ months and the amount payable each month shall not exceed $____________ without written approval of Owner.

To pay from gross receipts all operating expenses and such other expenses as may be authorized by Owner, including:

________ Mortgage Payments

________ Property Taxes

________ Payroll Taxes

________ Insurance Premiums

________ Other: ____________________

____________________.

________ To maintain accurate records of all monies received and disbursed in connection with the management of the property. Said records shall be open for inspection by Owner during regular business hours and upon reasonable notice.

________ To submit monthly statements of all receipts and disbursements not later than the ________ day of the following month.

OWNER'S OBLIGATIONS

Owner agrees to pay to Agent fees for services rendered at the rates hereinafter set forth. Such compensation is due and payable on demand and may be deducted by the Agent from receipts.

COMPENSATION FOR MANAGEMENT SERVICES (initial where applicable):

________ $____________ per month for each single family residence.

________ ________% of gross monthly collections, provided that the minimum compensation is at least $____________ per month.

________ $____________ flat fee per unit per month.

COMPENSATION FOR LEASING:

________ New leases: ____________________.

________ Renegotiated leases: ____________________.

COMPENSATION FOR MODERNIZATION OR CAPITAL IMPROVEMENTS: ____________________

____________________.

COMPENSATION FOR REFINANCING: ____________________.

COMPENSATION FOR OTHER SERVICES: ____________________.

Owner shall indemnify and save the Agent harmless from any and all costs. expenses, attorney's fees, suits, liabilities. damages from or connected with the management of the property by Agent, or the performance or exercise of any of the duties, obligations, powers, or authorities herein or hereafter granted to Agent.

Owner shall not hold Agent liable for any error of judgement, or for any mistake of fact or law, or for anything which Agent may do or refrain from doing hereinafter, except in cases of willful misconduct or gross negligence.

Owner agrees to carry, at Owner's expense, Workers Compensation Insurance for Owner's employees. Owner also agrees to carry, at Owner's expense, bodily injury, property damage and personal injury public liability insurance in the amount of not less than $500,000 combined single limit for bodily injury and property damage. The policy shall be written on a comprehensive general liability form and shall name the Agent as additional insured.

Owner shall immediately furnish Agent with a certificate of insurance evidencing that the above coverage is in force with a carrier acceptable to Agent. In the event Agent receives notice that said insurance coverage is to be cancelled, Agent shall have the option to immediately cancel this agreement.

Owner assumes full responsibility for the payment of any expenses and obligations incurred in connection with the exercise of Agent's duties set forth in this agreement.

Owner shall deposit with Agent $____________ as an initial operating reserve and will cover any excess of expenses over income within ten days of any request by Agent. The Agent may terminate this agreement immediately if the request for additional funds is not paid. Owner understands that it is not Agent's obligation to advance its own funds for payment of Owner's operating expenses.

FIGURE 23.3 (cont'd)

OTHER TERMS

All notices required to be given hereunder shall be in writing and mailed to the parties hereto at the addresses set forth below.

In the event of any legal action by the parties arising out of this agreement, the prevailing party shall be entitled to reasonable attorney's fees and costs, to be determined by the court in which such action is brought.

ADDITIONAL TERMS:

____

____

____

____

Agent accepts the employment under the terms hereof and agrees to use diligence in the exercise of the obligations, duties, authorities and powers conferred herein upon Agent.

Dated: ______________

______________ **Agent** ______________ **Owner**

By ______________ ______________ **Owner**

Title ______________ **Soc. Sec. #** ______________

Address ______________ **Address** ______________

Phone ______________ **Phone** ______________

FORM 115 (3-85)

COPYRIGHT © 1985, BY PROFESSIONAL PUBLISHING CORP, 122 PAUL DR, SAN RAFAEL, CA 94903

PROFESSIONAL PUBLISHING

KEY WORDS

Budget
Certified Property Manager
Effective Gross Income
Operating Expenses
Proft & Loss Statement
Property Management
Management Plan
Resident Manager

CHAPTER 23
Review Questions
(Answers on page 559)

(Answers on page 559)

1. In inflationary times, a property manager would NOT want a long-term lease with rents based on:
   (A) graduated amounts.
   (B) the consumer price index.
   (C) the cost-of-living index.
   (D) a fixed rate.

2. All but one of the following should be included as fixed operating expenses in the budget for property management:
   (A) property manager's fees.
   (B) ceiling replacement.
   (C) fuel costs.
   (D) maintenance.

3. A property manager's duties include which of the following?
   (A) Advertising.
   (B) Investing clients' monies.
   (C) Both A and B.
   (D) Neither A nor B.

4. In addition to providing the owner with a good income, one of the most effective ways for a property manager to advertise his management abilities is through a well-run building which has:
   (A) as high or higher rents than other similar buildings.
   (B) satisfied tenants served by competent employees.
   (C) the most complete and up-to-date accounting reports.
   (D) the lowest-paid employees.

5. Which of the following should NOT be a consideration in selecting a tenant?
   (A) The size of the space versus the tenant's requirements.
   (B) Tenant's ability to pay.
   (C) Racial and ethnic backgrounds of the tenants.
   (D) Compatibility of the business to other tenants.

6. Certified Property Manager (CPM) is a designation awarded to qualified applicants by:
   (A) local boards of Realtors.
   (B) BOMA.
   (C) state associations of real estate boards.
   (D) The Institute of Real Estate Management.

7. A broker who is employed under a property management contract is a:
   (A) trustee.
   (B) fiduciary.
   (C) assignee.
   (D) beneficiary.

8. A property manager, to secure the best return for the investment, would establish rental income by:
   (A) long-term rental at high of present economic period.
   (B) long-term contract with middle of present-day rentals.
   (C) long-term with built-in escalation clause.
   (D) month-to-month rental.

9. In negotiating a property management agreement with the owner of an apartment building, the property manager would most likely base his fee upon which one of the following?
   (A) Percentage of gross collectible income.
   (B) Percentage of net income.
   (C) The value of the property.
   (D) Gross income fully rented.

10. Assume that a broker is a property manager. He is able to buy merchandise needed for the property through a relative at a lower price than from any other source. He should:
    (A) proceed with the purchases.
    (B) proceed with the purchases, charging the owner a portion of the costs saved for work done in securing a better price.
    (C) discuss the matter with the owner and receive his permission to purchase the merchandise from the relative.
    (D) not purchase from a relative.

11. In management of real estate a broker may:
    (A) personally accept rebates from suppliers for himself.
    (B) commingle rents received with his own funds.
    (C) invest security deposits in an interest-bearing account for his own benefit.
    (D) not make a secret profit.

CHAPTER TWENTY-FOUR

ANTI-DISCRIMINATION AND FEDERAL FAIR HOUSING

NEW JERSEY LAW AGAINST DISCRIMINATION

Title 10, Chapter 5, N.J.S.A. states that it is against public policy to discriminate against any individual because of "race, creed (religion), color, national origin, ancestry, marital status, familial status, atypical hereditary cellular or blood trait, and liability for military service, sex, nationality, affectional or sexual orientation, or mental and physical handicap (including AIDS and HIV infection)." The law protects individuals against discrimination in employment, housing, public accommodations and certain business transactions. The law also prohibits certain nursing homes or intermediate care facilities from discriminating against an individual because he or she is eligible for Medicaid. Our focus in this chapter will be on unlawful discrimination in housing.

"Affectional or sexual orientation" is defined as male or female heterosexuality, homosexuality or bisexuality by inclination, practice, identity or expression, having a history thereof or being perceived presumed or identified by others as having such an orientation. "Heterosexuality" means affectional, emotional or physical attraction or behavior which is primarily directed towards persons of the other gender; "homosexuality" means affectional, emotional or physical attraction or behavior which is primarily directed towards persons of the same gender; and "bisexuality" is affectional, emotional or physical attraction or behavior which is directed towards persons of either gender.

The New Jersey Law Against Discrimination is one of the broadest anti-discrimination laws in the country. It has been developing over 30 years, with the latest amendment being enacted in 1993. All real estate brokers and other persons engaged in the sale or rental of real property (i.e., apartment complexes and builders) must display the official poster of the New Jersey Division on Civil Rights in a conspicuous manner in their places of business (Figure 24.3).

The sale or rental of all property, including open land, whether for residential or business purposes, is covered by the law.

The law forbids the following acts:

1. Refusing to sell, lease, assign, sublease or to deny or withhold real property or any part or portion thereof from any person or group of persons because of race, creed, color, national origin, ancestry, marital status or sex.

2. Any differential treatment in providing realty services related to the sale or rental of property such as changing the terms, conditions, privileges, facilities or services provided to any person or group of persons who are protected by the law as noted in the above paragraph. Deliberate use of tactics of discouragement, whether by delay, credit investigations, withholding of material information, or by more subtly suggesting that the customer is unwelcome, constitutes a violation of the Law Against Discrimination by an apartment owner, broker or salesperson if the practice is applied selectively to member(s) of a particular unwanted race, sex, creed, etc. and for the purpose of preventing a consummation of a sale or rental transaction.

3. Any statements, ads, publications, signs or any form of application for the purchase, rental, lease, assignment or sublease of any real property or portion thereof which expresses a preference or limitation based upon race, creed, color, national origin, ancestry, sex or marital status would violate the law. It is also against the law for newspapers published in the state of New Jersey to publish any advertisement which expresses any limitation specification, or discrimination in the sale, rental or lease of property.

4. Refusing to grant, extend or renew a loan or extend credit or changing any terms, services or conditions because of any reason stated in paragraph 1 above.

5. Using an application form for a loan or extension of credit that expresses directly or indirectly any limitation or specification based on race, creed, color, etc.

6. The practice of **blockbusting** (panic peddling)—a racially discriminatory and illegal

practice by which homeowners are induced to sell their properties by making representations that prices will drop because of the entry into the neighborhood of a minority group or groups. Furthermore, a real estate licensee cannot indicate that the entry into a neighborhood of diverse groups will or may result in other undesirable consequences, such as increase in crime and anti-social behavior or a decline in the quality of schools or other public facilities.

7. Directing minority customers to predominantly minority neighborhoods and directing white customers to predominantly white neighborhood without mentioning other opportunities in their price range. This practice is called **racial steering**.

Enforcement Provisions

The provisions of the Law Against Discrimination apply to all persons in the state (not just to licensed real estate brokers and salespersons), and are enforced by the Division of Civil Rights in the Department of Law and Public Safety. Furthermore, the aggrieved renter or buyer may choose to sue the broker, salesperson and/or owner engaged in discriminatory conduct, in state or federal court, for substantial money damages as well as attorneys' fees.

Any person may file a complaint with the Division within 180 days of the date of the alleged violation. The complaint must be filed at one of the Division's five regional offices located in Newark, Trenton, Paterson, Camden and Atlantic City. Alternatively, a person may file a complaint in New Jersey Superior Court within two years of the alleged violation.

If the Division accepts the complaint, the person who filed the complaint is referred to as the **complainant** in the matter. The complaint is then assigned to a Division investigator. The Division investigator serves the complaint on the **respondent** who is alleged to have committed the unlawful discrimination. Within 20 days of being served the complaint, the respondent must file an answer to the complaint.

The investigator assigned to the case will conduct an investigation, which may include interviews and field visits. Based on the investigation, the investigator makes a recommendation to the Division's director as to whether or not probable cause exists to believe the allegations of discrimination are true.

If there is a finding of probable cause, the complainant and the respondent are notified of the finding and the Division schedules a **conciliation conference** with the respondent. The purpose of the conciliation is to determine if the respondent is interested in settling the matter without the need for further proceedings. If the Division can work out an agreement with the respondent and the complainant accepts the agreement, then the matter will be closed. Conciliation could result in financial compensation and obtaining housing.

If an agreement cannot be reached, the director will transmit the case to the Office of Administrative Law for a hearing. A deputy attorney general may be assigned to prosecute the case on behalf of the Division or the complainant may retain his/her own counsel. After the hearing, the administrative law judge (ALJ) will render an initial decision which can be accepted, modified or rejected by the director.

If the initial decision is accepted, the director will issue an order adopting the decision. If the initial decision is rejected, the director may reverse the findings of the ALJ or remand (send back) the case to the ALJ for further consideration.

The director, among other things, can order the respondent to cease and desist from engagement in the discriminatory conduct. The director may also award attorney's fees and assess penalties of up to $2,000 for the first offense and $5,000 for each subsequent offense.

The final order of the director may be appealed to the Appellate Division of the New Jersey Superior Court, located in Trenton. A notice of appeal must be filed with the Appellate Division within 45 days of the director's order.

Prior to accepting the seller's authorization to list his home for sale, a copy of the Attorney General's Memorandum, shown in Figure 24.2, must be given and explained to each such homeowner.

New Jersey Antidiscrimination Poster

All real estate and rental offices in New Jersey must display an antidiscrimination poster, as shown in Figure 24.1. Failure to display the poster may result in a fine of $100 or more.

FEDERAL FAIR HOUSING LAWS

Civil Rights Act of 1866

After the Civil War, Congress passed this Act which "prohibits all racial discrimination, private or public, in the sale and rental of property." The Civil Rights Act of 1866 was brought to the forefront in 1968 in the U.S. Supreme Court case of

FIGURE 24.1 New Jersey Antidiscrimination Poster

New Jersey Law Prohibits

DISCRIMINATION

in

HOUSING

ON THE BASIS OF: Race, Creed, Color, National Origin, Ancestry, Marital or Familial Status, Gender, Affectional or Sexual Orientation, or Disability

BY: Real Estate Agents or Brokers, Financial Institutions, Property Owners, Landlords, or Building Superintendents

WITH RESPECT TO: the Sale, Rental, or Lease of Real Property, Including the Listing or Advertisement, or the Receipt or Transmittal of Offers to Purchase or Rent, or the Application and Terms of a Mortgage or Other Loan for the Purchase, Construction or Rehabilitation of Real Property

REMEDY MAY INCLUDE: An Order Restraining Unlawful Discrimination, Reimbursement for Financial Loss and Monetary Compensation for Pain and Humiliation Experienced as a Result of Unlawful Discrimination, and Attorney's Fees

Newspapers cannot publish real estate advertisements which express any discrimination against persons protected by the New Jersey Law Against Discrimination, N.J.S.A. 10:5-1 et seq.

VIOLATIONS SHOULD BE REPORTED TO THE NEAREST OFFICE

CAMDEN
(856) 614-2550

PATERSON
(973) 977-4500

NEWARK
(973) 648-2700

ATLANTIC CITY
(609) 441-3100

TRENTON
(609) 292-4605

TTY Users may contact the New Jersey Division on Civil Rights through the New Jersey Relay Operator. **Dial 711** and ask the Relay Operator to contact the Division at **(609) 292-7701**.

All real estate brokers and persons who engage in the business of selling or renting real property who are covered by the New Jersey Law Against Discrimination N.J.S.A. 10:5-1 shall display the official poster of the New Jersey Division on Civil Rights in places easily visible to all prospective tenants and purchasers N.J.A.C. 13:8-1.3.

LPS New Jersey Dept. of Law & Public Safety

CIVIL RIGHTS

FIGURE 24.2
New Jersey Attorney General's Memorandum

State of New Jersey
DEPARTMENT OF LAW AND PUBLIC SAFETY
OFFICE OF THE ATTORNEY GENERAL
PO Box 080
TRENTON, NJ 08625-0080
(609) 292-4925

JAMES E. MCGREEVEY
Governor

DAVID SAMSON
Attorney General

April, 2002

TO: Owners of Real Property

SUBJECT: New Jersey Law Against Discrimination and Federal Fair Housing Laws

The rules of the New Jersey Real Estate Commission require every licensed broker or salesperson with whom you are listing your property for sale or for rent to give you a copy of this legal memorandum. The purpose of this is to help you comply with the New Jersey Law Against Discrimination ("LAD") and federal laws which prohibit discrimination in the sale or rental of real property. Together, the LAD and the Fair Housing Amendments Act of 1988 prohibit you from discriminating against a prospective buyer or tenant because of his/her race, creed, color, national origin, sex, marital status, affectional or sexual orientation, familial status, actual or perceived physical or mental handicap, ancestry or nationality. (Note: "familial status" refers to families with a child or children under 18 years old and/or pregnant women. "Handicapped" includes persons afflicted with AIDS or HIV or perceived to be afflicted with AIDS.)

The following are some of the requirements which apply to the sale or rental of your property:

1. All persons, regardless of their membership in one of the protected classes stated above, are entitled to equal treatment in the terms, conditions or privileges of the sale or rental of any real property (e.g. it is illegal to deny that housing is available for inspection, sale or rent when it really is available).
2. No discriminatory advertising of any kind relating to the proposed sale or rental is permitted.
3. The broker or salesperson with whom you list your property must refuse the listing if you indicate any intention of discriminating on any of the aforesaid bases.
4. The broker or salesperson with whom you list your property must transmit to you every written offer he/she receives on your property.
5. Any provision in any lease or rental agreement prohibiting maintenance of a pet or pets on the premises is not applicable to a service or guide dog owned by a handicapped, blind or deaf tenant.
6. A landlord may not charge a handicapped, blind or deaf tenant an extra fee for keeping a service or guide dog.
7. As landlord, you must permit a handicapped tenant, at his/her own expense, to make reasonable modifications to the existing premise if such modifications are necessary to afford such person full enjoyment of the premises.

New Jersey Is An Equal Opportunity Employer • Printed on Recycled Paper and Recyclable

FIGURE 24.2 (cont'd)

Page 2

The sale or rental of all property including open land, whether for business or residential purposes, is covered by the LAD, with the following exceptions:

1. The rental of a single apartment or flat in a two-family dwelling, the other occupancy unit of which is occupied by the owner as his/her residence or the household of his/her family at the time of such rentals.
2. The rental of a room or rooms to another person or persons by the owner or occupant of a one-family dwelling occupied by him/her as his/her residence or the household of his/her family at the time of such rental.
3. In the sale, lease or rental of real property, preference given to persons of the same religion by a religious organization.

However, these exceptions do not apply if the dwelling was built or substantially rebuilt with the use of public funds, or financed in whole or part by a loan, or a commitment for a loan, guaranteed or insured by any agency of the federal government. The term "any agency of the federal government" includes, but is not limited to, the Federal Housing Administration (FHA) or the Veterans Administration (VA), which are most commonly used in such matters. In addition, discrimination in connection with some of the transactions covered by the above exceptions is nevertheless prohibited under the Federal Civil Rights Act of 1866 (42 U.S.C. §1981, 1982). However, the prohibition against discrimination on the basis of familial status does not apply to housing for older persons (as defined in the "Law Against Discrimination" at N.J.S.A. 10:5-5 mm) where at least one occupant of the dwelling is at least 55 years old.

Brokers and salespersons are licensed by the New Jersey Real Estate Commission. Their activities are subject to the general real estate laws of the state and the Commission's own rules and regulations. The New Jersey Law Against Discrimination applies to all people in the State and is enforced by the Division on Civil Rights in the Department of Law and Public Safety.

Should you require additional information or have any questions, please contact the Division on Civil Rights, Bureau of Prevention and Citizens' Rights at (609) 292-2918.

Sincerely yours,

DAVID SAMSON
ATTORNEY GENERAL OF NEW JERSEY

Jones vs. Alfred H. Mayer Co. In this landmark case, a builder refused to sell a house an African-American. Upon a decision for the plaintiff, the builder was ordered to sell the house to the plaintiff in 1968 at 1965 prices. The court's decision was based on its interpretation of the Civil Rights Act of 1866 as prohibiting discrimination based on race.

Although the 1866 law offers extensive relief from racial discrimination, it does not address important areas which were covered by later legislation. For example, it does not:

1. prohibit discriminatory advertising or other preference representations;
2. specifically deal with discrimination by real estate firms or in financing arrangements;
3. prohibit discrimination based on religion, national origin, sex, familial status, or physical or mental handicap; and
4. provide for damages of wrongfully rejected tenants or purchasers (although courts have indicated they will take into consideration the intent of the law).

Exemptions

The New Jersey Law Against Discrimination does NOT apply to:

1. The rental of a single apartment in a two-family dwelling, if the other unit is occupied by the owner as his residence or the household of family at the time of the rental.
2. The rental of a room or rooms to a person or persons by the owner or occupant of a one-family dwelling (boarding house, rooming house) occupied by the owner as a residence or the household of his family at the time of the rental.
3. Preference given to persons of the same religion by a religious organization in the sale or rental of real property.

The above exemptions do not apply if the dwelling was built or substantially rebuilt with the use of public funds, or was financed by a government-insured or guaranteed loan. New Jersey's law does not include an exemption for a homeowner who sells without a broker, and there never is an exemption based on race.

Federal Fair Housing Law (Title VIII, Civil Rights Act of 1968)

A person who has been injured by a discriminatory act also has the right to bring action under certain federal laws. In 1968, Congress passed Title VIII of the Civil Rights Act, called the Federal Fair Housing Law, which declared a national policy of providing fair housing throughout the United States. This law makes discrimination based on race, color, sex, religion or national origin illegal in connection with the sale or rental of most housing and any vacant land offered for residential construction or use. This law must be posted in a broker's office (Figure 24.3). The notice lists the protected classes and the activities that constitute violations of the law.

The Fair Housing Amendments of 1988 added protections for physically or mentally handicapped people and people with children under the age of 18. Unlike New Jersey's anti-discrimination law, the federal law does not prohibit discrimination in other types of real estate transactions, such as those involving commercial or industrial properties.

The Fair Housing Law prohibits the following acts, if they are based in part on race, color, sex, religion, national origin, physical or mental handicap, or having children under 18:

1. Refusing to sell or rent to or deal or negotiate with any person;
2. Discriminating in terms or conditions for buying or renting housing;
3. Discriminating by advertising that housing is more readily available to persons of a certain race, color, sex, religion or national origin;
4. Denying that housing is available for inspection, sale or rent when it actually is available;
5. Blockbusting-for-profit, that is, persuading owners to sell or rent housing by telling them that minority groups are moving into the neighborhood or by any communications, such as mailings or door-to-door canvassing, which would cause a reasonable person to believe that he should sell due to the prospective entry into the neighborhood of persons of a race, sex, creed, or nationality other than his own.
6. Denying or making different terms or conditions for home loans by commercial lenders; and
7. Denying to anyone the use or participation in any real estate service, such as broker's organi-

zations, multiple listing services or other facilities, related to the selling or renting of housing.

Exemptions

The Fair Housing Law does NOT apply to:

1. The sale of real property if neither a broker nor discriminatory advertising is used. Only one sale is exempt in any two-year period.

2. The rental of a room or rooms in owner-occupied dwellings with four or fewer units as long as unlawful discriminatory advertising is not used, and the services of a broker are not employed.

3. The sale, rental or occupancy of dwellings owned or operated by a religious organization for other than a commercial purpose. Membership in that religious organization may not be limited on the basis of race, color, sex, national origin, handicap or familial status.

4. The rental or occupancy of dwellings owned or operated by a private club that are limited to its own members, as long as the lodgings are not operated for commercial purposes.

The above exemptions, however, do not apply to the provisions of the Civil Rights Act of 1866 that prohibits discrimination on the basis of race.

THE 1988 AMENDMENT

On March 12, 1989 the Civil Rights Act was expanded to include housing for the handicapped and "familial status" (people with children under 18 years of age). The amendment had been passed in 1988.

The Handicapped

"Handicapped" is defined as anyone having a physical or mental impairment that substantially limits one or more major life activities. This has been interpreted to include persons with AIDS or HIV infection, but does not include current, illegal use of or addiction to a controlled substance. The definitions of "handicapped" are consistent under state and federal laws.

It is illegal to refuse to permit, at the expense of the handicapped person, reasonable modifications to existing housing units. The landlord may, where it is reasonable to do so, require the renter to restore the premises to the original condition, reasonable wear and tear excepted. Landlords must make reasonable accommodations in rules, policies, practices or services to afford a handicapped person an equal opportunity to enjoy a dwelling. The Act includes an exception: the handicapped person's tenancy must not pose a threat to the health and safety of the other tenants or their property.

It is illegal to design and construct multifamily dwellings with four or more units, for first occupancy after March 13, 1991, in a manner that makes them inaccessible to handicapped persons. Doors and hallways into and within the premises must be wide enough to accommodate wheelchairs; light switches, thermostats, etc. must be in accessible locations; public use and common areas must be readily accessible to and usable by handicapped persons; and bathroom walls must be reinforced to allow later installation of grab bars. In buildings with elevators, all units and common areas must comply. In "walk-up" buildings only the ground floor areas must comply.

Familial Status

Familial status means one or more persons under the age of 18 who are living with a parent or another person having legal custody of them or a person who has been designated in writing by the parent or guardian as having custody. Persons who are pregnant or in the process of securing legal custody of an individual under 18 years of age are also protected under the Act.

Housing for the elderly is exempted from the obligation to rent to families with children. Housing for the elderly is defined in three ways:

1. Housing constructed with the assistance of federal or state programs and which is specifically built and operated to assist elderly persons;

2. Housing which is intended for and solely occupied by persons over 62 years of age (persons under 62 years of age in occupancy prior to September 13, 1988 will not prevent exemption, but "all new" occupants must be over 62 years of age); and

3. Housing which is intended and operated for occupancy by at least one person 55 years of age or older per unit and: (a) has significant facilities and services designed to meet the social and physical needs of older persons; or (b) is impractical to provide significant facilities for older persons, but the housing is necessary to provide important housing opportunities for older persons; and (c) at least 80% of the units are currently occupied by at least one person 55 years of age or older and publishes and adheres to policies and procedures

which demonstrate an intent to serve this population.

HUD Fair Housing Poster

An amendment to the 1968 Fair Housing Act requires that an equal opportunity poster (shown in Figure 24.3) be displayed at real estate brokerage offices, mortgage lender's offices, model home sites and other related locations. If the poster is not displayed, HUD will consider any charges of discrimination to be true in the absence of evidence to the contrary.

VIOLATION, COMPLAINTS AND ENFORCEMENT OF THE FAIR HOUSING ACT OF 1968

The Fair Housing Act provides an enforcement system that allows parties in a dispute the choice of having the case brought before an administrative law judge (ALJ) or Federal District Court. Consequently, a person charged with unlawful discrimination can choose a trial by jury rather than having HUD decide.

Enforcement Provisions

Title VIII allows an aggrieved person one year to file a complaint with HUD and two years in which to bring a federal suit. Once a complaint is filed, HUD must investigate the complaint and render a decision within 100 days. During the 100-day period, HUD may be able to resolve the complaint and have the parties sign a conciliation agreement. HUD is required to refer a complaint to state agencies if their fair housing laws are "substantially equivalent" to Title VIII. HUD can also seek preliminary or temporary relief, including temporary restraining orders where such actions are necessary to carry out the purpose of the law.

If HUD issues a charge following an investigation of a discrimination complaint, either the complainant (which can be HUD), aggrieved person or the respondent would have 20 days to have the charge heard in a Federal District Court. If no choice for a court procedure is made, HUD would be authorized to automatically bring the complaint before an administrative law judge (ALJ) within HUD. The ALJ would continue proceedings as long as the aggrieved person did not begin a separate action in federal court that related to the charge.

The ALJ may impose a penalty against the respondent up to a maximum of $10,000 if there is no prior violation; $25,000 is there has been one prior violation within the preceding five-year period; and $50,000 if there have been two or more violations within the preceding seven-year period.

If a single individual rather than a real estate corporation engages in more than one discriminatory housing practice, the judge can levy the $25,000 or $50,000 fine without regard to the time limits. Either party can appeal the ALJ's decision to a U.S. District Court within 30 days.

In addition to the penalties mentioned above, anyone found guilty of unlawful discrimination may be required to pay the other party's legal fees and court costs.

"Testing"

Gathering evidence for any of the above approaches can be complex. One of the techniques used by the government or plaintiffs is "testing." Courts have ruled that testing is an acceptable practice to see if unlawful discrimination by real estate offices is taking place. The following steps are usually involved in the testing procedure following a complaint by a prospective buyer or tenant:

1. A white couple of a certain socio-economic status is sent to the suspected broker and shows interest in the property in question.

2. Soon after, a minority couple of the same socio-economic status will come to the same real estate broker. They will answer the same essential questions, with the same essential answers, as did the white couple.

3. After the minority couple has finished, a different white couple will come in and repeat the procedure.

4. The attitudes and representations of the broker to all three couples will be compared. These findings will all be admissible in court.

Americans with Disabilities Act (ADA)

The Americans with Disabilities Act was signed into law on July 16, 1990. The ADA is federal civil rights law for people with disabilities, comparable to civil rights law passed in the 1960s for other minorities. It provides that Americans with physical and mental disabilities, including AIDS and alcoholism, are entitled to legal protections that ensure them equal opportunities under the law.

The ADA covers all people with disabilities, visible and hidden, including:

- A person with a physical or mental impair-

FIGURE 24.3 Federal Fair Housing Law Poster

U.S. Department of Housing and Urban Development

EQUAL HOUSING OPPORTUNITY

We Do Business in Accordance With the Federal Fair Housing Law

(The Fair Housing Amendments Act of 1988)

It is Illegal to Discriminate Against Any Person Because of Race, Color, Religion, Sex, Handicap, Familial Status, or National Origin

- In the sale or rental of housing or residential lots
- In advertising the sale or rental of housing
- In the financing of housing
- In the provision of real estate brokerage services
- In the appraisal of housing
- Blockbusting is also illegal

Anyone who feels he or she has been discriminated against may file a complaint of housing discrimination with the:
1-800-424-8590 (Toll Free)
1-800-424-8529 (TDD)

U.S. Department of Housing and Urban Development
Assistant Secretary for Fair Housing and Equal Opportunity
Washington, D.C. 20410

Previous editions are obsolete

form **HUD-928.1** (3-89)

ment that substantially limits one or more major life functions (eating, breathing, caring for one-self, working, walking, etc.);

- A person with a record of such an impairment (even if that record is inaccurate); and
- A person who is regarded as having such an impairment.

Some people are explicitly excluded from coverage, including:

- Current users of illegal drugs (but those with a history of drug or alcohol abuse are covered and an employer can continue to conduct drug tests on employees for illegal drugs); and
- Those with sexual behavior disorders such as transvestitism or transsexualism, and those who have conditions of compulsive gambling, kleptomania or pyromania.

The ADA does not cover housing, except for hotels and other temporary housing. Housing discrimination is covered by federal and state fair housing laws. The ADA also prohibits discrimination against a person who is "associated with a person with a disability". For example, it would be illegal for a restaurant to refuse to serve a non-disabled person just because that person was with a person with a disability.

The Act has five titles, each dealing with a particular aspect of life that affects the lives of people with disabilities. A brief discussion of each of the titles follows.

TITLE I. EMPLOYMENT. Title I prohibits employment discrimination against qualified individuals. Employers with 15 or more full- or part-time employees are subject to the provisions of the ADA. Employment agencies, labor unions and agencies providing fringe benefits or training programs are also covered. In general, the ADA prohibits discrimination against a qualified person with a disability.

TITLE II: STATE AND LOCAL GOVERNMENT. Title II states that "no qualified individual with a disability shall, by reason of such disability, be excluded from participation in, or be denied the benefits of, or be subject to discrimination by a department, agency, special purpose district or other instrumentality of a state or local government." This title impacts on public transportation such as rail systems and bus services and obligates transit authorities to provide paratransit (door-to-door) services to disabled persons with service response time, cost and availability comparable to the main-line service. Air transporation is not covered by the ADA, but is covered under the federal Air Carriers Act.

TITLE III: PUBLIC ACCOMMODATIONS. Title III prohibits discrimination based on disability by businesses that are public accommodations. Public accommodations are any place, building or outdoor space that a member of the public can enter with or without a fee. Public accommodations do *not* include "private clubs" (those for which membership must be voted on by other members) and operations owned or operated by religious entities.

ADA requires that all-new construction on public accommodations and common facilities are accessible. Physical barriers in existing facilities must be removed. If this is not possible, alternative methods of providing the services must be offered when such is "readily achievable," meaning able to be carried out without much difficulty or expense (e.g., free delivery, taped tours of inaccessible exhibits, disposable cup dispensers on water fountains).

In addition, a public accommodation must make reasonable modifications in policies, practices and procedures unless it would fundamentally alter the nature of the goods and the services offered. Although pets are not allowed, service animals must be allowed in gardens or other public accommodations. However, a "no-touching" policy may be necessary for delicate artwork or fragile plants, even though people with visual impairments may be denied the full enjoyment of these objects.

TITLE IV: TELECOMMUNICATIONS FOR THE DEAF. Under this service people with TDD/TTYs who are calling a party without a TDD/TTY, and vice-versa, can make the call through a relay service, which will transmit the call via TDD/TTY or voice, depending on need. In addition, Title IV requires that all public service announcements funded in whole or in part with federal funds must be close-captioned, meaning that a person with a special TV decoder will see the captioning.

TITLE V: MISCELLANEOUS PROVISIONS. Other provisions of the ADA include the following:

- Disability is defined as a physical or mental impairment that substantially limits one or more of the major activities of life. The government defines some 900 variations of disability.
- Employers may not use tests or job requirements that tend to screen out the disabled.
- Program sponsors cannot charge people with disabilities an extra fee or surcharge to participate in any recreational or educational activity, seminar or workshop.

- There is a prohibition against retaliation for filing a charge or opposing a discriminatory practice; retaliation will constitute a separate offense.

- The ADA will not prohibit an insurance company from using sound actuarial data to administer risks, even if the effect is that people with disabilities will be charged more or denied coverage, but it must not be used as a subterfuge to deny coverage.

Penalties for violation of the Americans with Disabilities Act include fines of up to $50,000 for the first offense and up to $100,000 for subsequent offenses, as well as injunctions against operations that do not comply. The Act is enforced by the U.S. attorney general.

KEY WORDS

Americans with Disabilities Act (ADA)
Attorney General's Memorandum
Blockbusting
Civil Rights Act of 1866
Complainant
Discrimination
Familial Status
Federal Fair Housing
HUD
New Jersey Law Against Discrimination
Racial Steering
Respondent
Testing

COMPARISON OF FEDERAL FAIR HOUSING LAW & NEW JERSEY DISCRIMINATION LAW

Federal Fair Housing Law	New Jersey Discrimination Law
1. Outlaws discrimination based on race, color, religion, sex, national origin, physical or mental handicap or having children under age 18.	1. Outlaws discrimination based on race, sex, color, religion, ancestry, marital status, familial status, physical handicap, national origin, mental handicap (with medical approval), nationality and sexual or affectional orientation.
2. Only applies to discrimination in housing.	2. Broadly covers all real estate transactions.
3. The financial practice section applies only to lending institutions.	3. The financing practice section applies to anyone rendering financial aid to someone in connection with a real estate transaction.
4. Specifically covers refusal to admit broker and salesperson to membership in a professional organization or multiple listing service.	4. No such specific provision; probably not a violation since a "real estate transaction."
5. Complaint must be filed within one year. Since the burden of proof is on the complainant, most discrimination cases involve "testers" hired by lawyers or fair housing organizations.	5. Complaint must be filed within 180 days.
6. Exemption for owner-occupant of four-unit multi-dwelling building.	6. Exemption for rental of duplex (two-family dwelling) where lessor or member of his immediate family occupies one unit.
7. Exemption for single-family house where services of broker and/or discriminatory advertising are not used.	7. No similar exemption.
8. Allows religious-related organizations to discriminate on basis of religion.	8. Allows religious-related organizations to discriminate on basis of religion.
9. Exemption for preferences given by private clubs.	9. This area of the law is not definitive.
10. HUD is in charge, but if it can't get parties to conciliate, then party must go to court (state court) where the state has similar fair housing legislation.	10. Division of Civil Rights is in charge and has power to set up administrative hearing and take affirmative action if it is decided that a violation has taken place.

CHAPTER 24
Review Questions
(Answers on page 559)

1. If, when you are taking a listing on an owner-occupied single-family residence, the owner states that you are not to show the property to unmarried people, you should:
   (A) ignore the request and proceed with the listing.
   (B) comply with your principal's request.
   (C) make note of the fact in the listing and continue to list, hoping that no unmarried people want to see the property.
   (D) refuse to take the listing.

2. Which is the federal agency that administers fair housing laws?
   (A) FHA.
   (B) NAR.
   (C) HUD.
   (D) Attorney General.

3. A landlord refused to rent to a blind person who used a guide dog. The landlord claimed that the refusal was based on a lease restriction prohibiting pets.
   (A) The action was lawful but unethical.
   (B) The action was unlawful, because federal law requires reasonable accommodations to the needs of handicapped persons in rules, policies, etc. to allow the handicapped an equal opportunity to use or enjoy a dwelling.
   (C) The action was lawful and ethical.
   (D) The action would be allowed because of the restriction in the lease.

4. Under Federal Fair Housing, which of the following is exempt?
   (A) Private clubs operating a commercial boarding house.
   (B) Religious organizations.
   (C) Owner-occupied six-family houses.
   (D) Builder-developers.

5. Blockbusting is acceptable:
   (A) with approval of the buyer and seller.
   (B) with approval of HUD.
   (C) with approval of the New Jersey Division of Civil Rights.
   (D) under no circumstances.

6. Under the New Jersey Law Against Discrimination, which of the following would be exempt from the law?
   (A) The rental of a single apartment or flat in a two-family dwelling, the other occupancy unit of which is occupied by the owner as his residence at the time of the rental.
   (B) The owner of a single-family house with respect to its sale.
   (C) Both A and B.
   (D) Neither A nor B.

7. The Federal Fair Housing Act of 1968 does NOT apply to which of the following?
   (A) Religion.
   (B) Physical handicap.
   (C) Sex.
   (D) Marital status.

8. A chanting religious group bought a house in a subdivision and organized it into a commune. A broker eager to make some quick profits began to canvass this neighborhood soliciting listings by inquiring whether residents knew who had just moved into the area and leaving his business card. Which term best describes the broker's marketing program?
   (A) Redlining.
   (B) Lawful solicitation.
   (C) Blockbusting.
   (D) Steering.

9. The Civil Rights Act of 1866 prohibits discrimination in housing on the basis of:
   (A) race.
   (B) color.
   (C) religion.
   (D) all of the above.

10. John Medvecky lives on the first floor of a two-family house which he owns in Cedar Grove, NJ. In renting the second floor apartment Medvecky may lawfully reject an applicant because of:
    (A) race.
    (B) marital status.
    (C) Both A and B.
    (D) Neither A nor B.

(Quiz continues on next page)

11. Under the Discrimination Law, among the powers of the Division of Civil Rights is the power to:
    (A) impose money penalties.
    (B) suspend licenses.
    (C) imprison.
    (D) revoke licenses.

12. Under the New Jersey Law Against Discrimination, which of the following penalties may be imposed by the Division of Civil Rights for a first offense?
    (A) A fine of not more than $5,000.
    (B) Revocation of a broker's or salesperson's real estate license.
    (C) Suspension of a broker's or salesperson's real estate license.
    (D) Issuance of cease and desist orders.

13. The practice of directing minority customers to minority areas is known as:
    (A) steering and is legal.
    (B) steering and is illegal.
    (C) panic peddling.
    (D) blockbusting.

14. Under the New Jersey Discrimination Law, discrimination for which of the following reasons would NOT be unlawful?
    (A) Religion.
    (B) National origin.
    (C) Marital status.
    (D) Age.

15. The unlawful practice of a lending institution refusing to approve loans in a particular town because of the number of properties that are owned by members of minority groups is called:
    (A) blockbusting.
    (B) redlining.
    (C) panic peddling.
    (D) disintermediation.

16. If Mrs. Murphy lives in a rooming house that she owns across the street from a college, she may lawfully do all of the following EXCEPT:
    (A) refuse to rent to members of a certain religion.
    (B) refuse to rent to families with children under 18 years of age.
    (C) discriminate on the basis of physical handicap.
    (D) advertise "Female Students Only."

17. You are violating the Federal Fair Housing Act of 1968 if you:
    (A) establish a multiple listing service that excludes members on the basis of race.
    (B) refuse to sell a vacant lot zoned commercial because of the buyer's nationality.
    (C) refuse to rent an office because of the prospective tenant's religion.
    (D) refuse to rent an apartment because of the applicant's marital status.

18. The authority under the Federal Fair Housing Act rests with:
    (A) the Secretary of the Interior.
    (B) the Attorney General.
    (C) the Federal Housing Authority.
    (D) the Secretary of Housing and Urban Development.

19. An owner wants to sell his property without the aid of a real estate broker. He may legally do all but one of the following:
    (A) Establish the purchasing power of the buyer.
    (B) Write up the sales contract between himself and the buyer.
    (C) Require that the buyer assume the present mortgage.
    (D) Reject a buyer on account of race.

20. A New Jersey developer is offering lots for sale in a subdivision zoned "light industry." The asking price is $50,000. The developer receives a full-price, all-cash offer from a minority buyer with the following contingency: "This offer will become void if not accepted within 10 days." On the 11th day, the developer sells the lot in question to a Caucasian buyer for $40,000. Which of the following statements is true?
    (A) The developer violated the Federal Fair Housing Act.
    (B) The developer's action was legal because the contingency expired.
    (C) New Jersey developers are exempt from the law.
    (D) A violation of the New Jersey Law Against Discrimination has occurred.

21. A complaint under the New Jersey Discrimination Law must be submitted within:
    (A) 180 days.
    (B) 60 days.
    (C) 45 days.
    (D) two years.

22. A New Jersey landlord cannot refuse to rent to a family because:
    (A) of marital status.
    (B) they have a pet.
    (C) of familial status.
    (D) of both A and C.

23. Evelyn and Walter Jenkins, an African-American couple, visit the office of XYZ Real Estate Co. After discussing their housing needs and financial information, the agent shows them homes in their price range, but only ones located in areas with a high percentage of African-American residents. The agent is engaging in the unlawful practice of:
    (A) steering.
    (B) redlining.
    (C) blockbusting.
    (D) panic peddling.

CHAPTER TWENTY-FIVE

REAL ESTATE TAXES AND TAX ASPECTS OF REAL ESTATE OWNERSHIP

REAL ESTATE TAXES

Similar to the governmental control inherent in zoning, the ownership of real property is subject to certain other governmental limitations, among which is the state's right to levy taxes. The costs of government are recurring and the levying of taxes helps defray these costs. The primary sources of state tax revenue are income tax (both corporate and personal), sales tax, general excise tax and real property tax. Our interest here will be in the latter.

Real Property Taxes

In order to support government services, property taxes are levied against real property according to the property's **assessed value**. Real property taxes are referred to as **ad valorem** taxes, that is, taxes paid "according to the value" of the property.

The assessed value of the property is based upon the value determined by the tax assessor for the purpose of determining annual taxes. The assessed value is based upon the market value of the property at the time the assessment is done. However, this does not mean that the market value and the assessed value are usually the same. The assessed value will remain in effect until a new assessment is made. Meanwhile, the market value may have risen or fallen.

Land and improvements are assessed separately, with the resultant assessments being added together to form the total assessment. After the assessor completes the assessment, a **tax roll** will be prepared showing the assessments of all taxable property.

Real estate taxes become a lien on real estate for the entire year, beginning on January 1. Taxes are payable in four quarterly installments on the first day of the middle month of each quarter. Thus, taxes are due on the first of February, May, August and November.

Tax Rate Computation

Each taxing district (municipality) in the state prepares a budget early in each calendar year, determining the total amount of money that will be required to pay for the public services such as administration, improvements, police and fire protection, schools, roads, parks, etc. The budget is reviewed by the mayor and council and adjusted if necessary. The council determines the amount to be raised from real property taxes by deducting from the total budget the funds which will be received from other sources, such as state funds for educational purposes, federal grants, state and federal welfare assistance, income from fees, licenses and permits, etc. The local property tax rate is then determined by dividing the amount of revenue to be raised by the assessed valuation of all properties in the municipality (ratable).

For example, if the total amount needed for next year's budget is $5 million and the total assessments of all real estate in the town is $125 million, the tax rate for the town is $5 million ÷ $125 million = .04, or 4%. This rate can be expressed in many ways, but in New Jersey it is usually expressed as an amount per $100. In the example above, the rate would be expressed as $4.00 per $100 of assessed value. In some jurisdictions the tax rate is expressed in mills. A mill is 1/1000 of a dollar, or $.001.

Determining Annual Tax

To determine the annual taxes to be paid on a specific property, divide the assessed valuation by 100 and then multiply by the tax rate. For example, if a property is assessed at $40,000 with a tax rate of $4.00 per hundred, the annual taxes would be $1,600 ($40,000 ÷ 100 = 400 x $4.00 = $1,600).

Although assessments are levied on the basis of 100% of value in all 21 counties in New Jersey, it would not be possible for a municipality to maintain that level without an annual revaluation. Consequently, the local assessor will try to maintain a common level of assessments based on the costs and values of the year in which the last formal revaluation was made. For tax purposes, a property is assessed at full and fair value, that is, the price that, in the assessor's opinion, a willing seller would accept from a willing buyer.

Equalization

Although real estate taxes are levied on a local basis, each tax district (town, township, borough, city, etc.) must in turn pay taxes to the county for maintenance of county roads and to help to cover the cost of administering county courts, police, parks, prisons and other county institutions.

The county bases the taxes on the total assessments that were made by assessors in each tax district to avoid duplication in the assessment process. The purpose of equalization is to see that all county residents pay a tax in the same proportion to market value. For instance, if assessments in Town A are based on 27% of value, and Town B assesses properties at 97% of value, the residents in Town B would pay far more than their fair share to the county.

Thus, if assessments in a tax district turn out to be 20% below the state average, the underassessment can be adjusted by applying an equalization rate of 125% to all assessments in that district. For example, a property assessed for tax purposes at $100,000 would have an equalized value of $125,000 ($100,000 x 1.25). Each year the State Board of Taxation publishes tables of Equalization Rates based on the ratio of assessments to sales in each tax district during the previous year.

Tax Appeals

Every taxpayer that believes the assessment is unequal, excessive or illegal has the right to a tax appeal. The first step would be an appeal to the local tax assessor for possible adjustment. The assessor can reduce the assessment until January 10. If rejected at that level, the owner has until April 1 to appeal to the County Board of Taxation. The County Board must rule on appeals by November 10. The taxpayer has 45 days from the date of the County Tax Board judgment to appeal to the New Jersey Tax Court.

The tax appeal can only question the assessment or tax method, not the amount of tax or the tax rate. If it can be established that comparable neighboring properties have been selling for less than the property in question, the taxpayer stands a good chance of getting a reduction in the assessed value.

Tax Sale

When taxes are delinquent six months after the end of the tax year, the tax collector will put the property up for tax sale. A list of tax delinquents will be prepared as of December 31 of the prior year. Interest and costs up to the time of sale are added to the taxes owed. The owner will be advised of the impending sale, which will be advertised on a tax sale list indicating the date, place and time of sale, owner of record, property identification and amount owed. A tax sale is a public sale and anyone may bid. If taxes and charges are not paid by the date of sale, the municipality will sell its tax lien to the successful bidder who will pay the amount owed on the property.

Bidding is conducted on the basis of the amount of interest the bidder will charge the delinquent property owner. The successful bidder is the party bidding the *lowest* amount of interest. The highest rate that may be bid is 18%. The successful bidder will receive a **tax sale certificate** from the tax collector setting forth the tax lien to the bidder, date of sale and amount paid by the purchaser and rate of redemption. The certificate should be recorded.

If the owner does not exercise the **statutory right of redemption** and redeem the property within **two years** from the date of sale, the holder of the certificate may, through court action, initiate a foreclosure action to legally bar the owner's right to redeem the property, whereupon the certificate holder would become the owner of the property in fee simple as of a final deadline date established by the court. All rights of the previous owner would then be terminated. The certificate holder has no right of use, entry or possession of the property during the redemption period, but only holds a lien against it and the potential right to gain title.

If no one bids on the property at the tax sale, the municipality becomes the holder of the certificate and it may foreclose by a procedure called foreclosure **in rem**, meaning "against the property." The municipality must have held the tax sale certificate for at least **six months**. Notice of the suit is provided by publication in a newspaper and by personal service or registered or certified mail upon the assessed owner and all other persons having an ownership or lien interest in the property. If no one contests the foreclosure, a final judgment is entered in favor of the municipality. When the judgment is recorded, the municipality acquires fee simple title to the foreclosed property

Tax sale certificates held by an individual have a life of 20 years, but that period can be extended if the holder of the certificate continues to pay taxes beyond the 20-year period. Tax sale certificates held by a municipality are enforceable forever.

Special Property Tax Treatments

Senior Citizens. There is an annual deduction of $250 for homeowners age 65 or older, or disabled, who have incomes under $10,000 per year from all sources except social security and who have lived in a house for the past two years. The municipality administers this benefit.

Veterans. Eligible veterans and their unmarried surviving spouses are entitled to a flat deduction of $250 for the year 2003 and thereafter. If both husband and wife are veterans, a total deduction of $500 is allowed. A person may qualify for both the senior citizen and veteran reductions.

NJ SAVER Rebate

Eligibility: Residents who owned and paid property taxes on a home in New Jersey that was their principal residence on October 1. The Division of Taxation will review all applications to determine if eligibility requirements have been met. Call 1-877-658-2972 (toll-free within New Jersey, New York, Pennsylvania, Delaware and Maryland) or 609-826-4288. Applications can also be filed on the Division's Web site at: www.njsaverrebate.com.

Homestead Rebate

Eligibility: Homeowners and tenants who pay property taxes on their principal residence in New Jersey, either directly or through rent, and whose gross income does not exceed $100,000 ($40,000 for homeowners who are not 65 years of age or disabled). Rebates range from $90 to $775, and are adjusted to reflect changes in the cost of living. Use Form HR-1040 (and Form NJ-1040, if required), or Homestead Rebate Application section of Form NJ-1040EZ, or file electronically using NJ Web/PC File, NJ TeleFile, or approved vendor software by April 15.

Property Tax Reimbursement

Eligibility: Homeowners, including owners of mobile homes located in mobile home parks, age 65 or older, or receiving federal social security disability benefits, who paid property taxes on their principal residence in New Jersey either directly or through mobile home park site fees. Applicants must be New Jersey residents for at least the past ten years, and lived in the home for which reimbursement is claimed for at least the last three years, and must meet certain income limits. Applicants must meet all requirements for both base year and reimbursement year. The benefit is reimbursement of the difference between the amount of property taxes paid for the base year and the amount paid for the reimbursement year. Form PTR-1 is used for first-time reimbursement and Form PTR-2 is used thereafter.

Farmland Assessment Act

The goal of the Act is to preserve farmland and open space, save the family farm and provide farmers with economic relief by permitting qualified farmland to be assessed at a substantially lower agricultural use rate. Provisions to qualify are that a minimum of **five acres** must be actively devoted to agricultural purposes or to the production of plants or animals useful to man, for **two successive years** prior to application. Standards for annual gross sales of resultant output must be met and application must be made to the municipal tax assessor. If the application is approved by the local tax assessor, the assessment will be based on the use of the land for agriculture or horticulture use and not on its value to a developer.

If the agricultural use is later terminated, it is subject to the payment of **rollback taxes**, the additional taxes that would have been due in the current year and the previous two years. The agreement of sale should state who would be responsible for any possible rollback taxes from loss of a farmland assessment.

Exemptions

The tax assessor, on a tabular list known as the "tax assessment list," separately assesses each parcel of land. The assessor prepares the list on October 1 for the following year. Certain properties are entitled to exemptions, such as government-owned property and lands owned by charitable, religious or non-profit institutions. Some properties are entitled to partial tax abatements, e.g., "Fox-Lance abatements," which were used to encourage investments in deteriorating neighborhoods. If, however, a tax-exempt property is leased to an entity that is not entitled to an exemption, the leasehold can be taxed.

Special Assessments

In addition to the above-mentioned taxes on real property, special assessments covering costs such as sidewalks, curbs, paving, drainage or other improvements may be levied by municipalities to cover improvements to properties in a limited area. In such a case, the cost of the improvement is paid for only by those taxpayers that directly benefit from the improvement. A special assessment may be paid in full during one tax year or by installments over a period of time.

TAX ASPECTS OF REAL ESTATE OWNERSHIP

The federal government grants certain income tax advantages to individuals through real estate investment and ownership. The following will attempt to set forth some of the basics that should be understood by every real estate broker and salesperson, as well as by anyone considering an investment in real estate.

Since we will make only brief mention of these few principles regarding the tax aspects of ownership, these should serve only as a possible guide to areas needing more detailed inquiry, or to the seeking of legal counsel or the advice of a tax consultant.

RULES ON PERSONAL RESIDENCES

Real estate held as a personal residence has a number of peculiarities that distinguish it from properties held for investment. An owner is not permitted an allowance for depreciation, nor are deductions permitted for expenses of repair and maintenance. Exceptions to this rule usually involve using the premises or some part thereof for purposes other than as a residence. If the residence, or a portion thereof, is rented or used for business purposes, the owner may claim a depreciation allowance and a deduction for expenses. A home that is rented, or used for business purposes, ceases to be a home in the legal sense and becomes a rental unit or an adjunct of the business.

The most beneficial of the tax advantages associated with home ownership are deductions for property taxes and mortgage interest; deferment of taxes on capital gains; a $250,000 exclusion; and installment sales treatment.

Mortgage Interest

With respect to an individual's interest expense, no deduction is allowed for personal consumer interest, such as interest on car loans and credit cards.

The rules, however, are different when a homeowner's residence is pledged as the security for payment of a debt. Homeowners may deduct the interest portion of all payments on residential mortgage loans used to purchase a principal and second residence, provided the total residential debt does not exceed $1 million ($500,000 for each spouse filing separately). In addition, interest is deductible on loans of up to $100,000 ($50,000 for each spouse filing separately) on the equity in a residence, regardless of how the proceeds are used. Home equity debt is debt other than the acquisition indebtedness secured by the home, to the extent that the total amount of debt does not exceed the fair market value of the home reduced by the acquisition indebtedness. For example, a home with a fair market value of $150,000 and a purchase money mortgage of $120,000 could support a home equity loan up to $30,000 on which the interest is deductible.

Discount Points. Discount points paid by a borrower or seller for a mortgage loan to purchase a residence are deductible in full in the year paid, the same as interest. If, however, the points are paid to refinance an existing loan, the discount must be deducted over the term of the loan, not in the year paid. For example, if the discount amounts to $3,600 on a 30-year loan, only $120 may be deducted each year. If the house is sold before the refinanced loan has been paid, the owner can deduct the remaining points not yet deducted.

Real Estate Taxes. Real estate taxes paid by the property owner are deductible without limitation in determining net taxable income. Although mortgage interest deductions are limited to only a principal and second residence, there is no such limitation for property taxes.

The taxpayer's gross income is reduced by the amount of realty taxes paid, thereby reducing the amount of income that will be taxed as ordinary income.

Casualty Losses. Casualty losses are another deduction that results from home ownership. Four rules apply: (1) the deduction is limited to (a) the decrease in fair market value of the property resulting from the loss or (b) the adjusted basis in the property, whichever is less; (2) the first $100 is not deductible; (3) insurance proceeds must be used to reduce the amount of the loss; and (4) casualty losses must be reduced by 10% of the taxpayer's adjusted gross income.

Repairs, Maintenance and Capital Improvements

Routine repair and maintenance expenses are not deductible on the taxpayer's residence as they are with an income-producing property.

The expense of a capital improvement, such as

the addition of a room, may not be deducted in the year it is made, but it may produce a benefit in the future. (If the house sells for more than the original price, the cost of the improvement can be deducted from the amount of capital gain).

Capital Gain on Sale of Principal Residence

When a taxpayer sells a personal residence for more than the price originally paid, there is a capital gain. If the sale of a personal residence results in a loss, the owner cannot take the loss when filing a tax return. The amount of the capital gain is the difference between the **adjusted basis** of the property value and the **realized selling price**.

Adjusted Basis. The adjusted basis is the owner's original cost plus any additions or improvements, plus buying expenses, less certain deductions including any nontaxable gain from the sale of a former residence and casualty losses taken.

Since any increase in the adjusted basis will reduce the amount of taxable capital gain when the property is sold, it is important that the taxpayer keep accurate records of all relevant transactions. IRS will require proof that the adjusted basis was properly calculated.

Realized Selling Price. The realized selling price is the total consideration received (including cash, notes, mortgages and real and personal property), less (1) selling expenses, and (2) fixing-up expenses.

Selling expenses include sales commission, advertising paid for by the seller, legal fees and discount points paid by seller.

Fixing-up expenses include decorating and repair costs incurred solely to assist in the sale of the property. The expenses must have been incurred for work performed within 90 days prior to the signing of the sales contract and must have been paid no more than 30 days after the sale. Capital improvements cannot be included as a fixing-up expense. Fixing-up expenses may be deducted from the contract sale price of the house in order to determine the adjusted sale price, provided they are not deducted elsewhere on the return.

Example: A couple purchased a home in 1980 for $120,000 and then added a bedroom at a cost of $20,000. They are now selling the home for $180,000. They have agreed to pay a broker's fee of 5% of the sales price and two discount points for the buyer's $144,000 mortgage loan. Closing costs amount to $1,000.

Selling price			$180,000
Less:			
5% commission		$ 9,000	
Closing costs		+ 1,000	
Points		+2,880	
		$12,880	- 12,880
Realized selling price			$167,120
Basis			
Original cost	$120,000		
Improvements	+20,000		
Adjusted basis	$140,000		-140,000
Capital gain			$ 27,120

The main point about the tax deferral is this: Any gain realized from the sale must be subtracted from the value of the new residence, thus lowering its basis. Lowering the basis increases the amount of the gain that will result from the eventual sale of the new home.

Capital Gains Exemption

The current capital gains law allows homeowners to avoid paying taxes on the first $500,000 profit if they are married, or on the first $250,000 if they are single. The gain on the sale of a home is not currently taxable if two simple tests are met:

1. In the five-year period just before the sale, the taxpayer must have owned the home and used it as a principal residence for at least 24 months within the period (second homes and summer homes do not qualify). If the home is sold in less than two years, a prorated portion of the gain will be taxed.

2. In the two years prior to the sale, the taxpayer must not have claimed this benefit on a prior sale.

Homeowners are allowed to use the provision as often as they like as long as it fits in that two-year period. The tax may be deferred for many years and for many houses. When the final residence is sold, the taxpayer must substantiate the adjusted basis and a capital gains tax at the rate of 15% must be paid if the gains exceed the exclusion limit. If, however, the owner dies first, the basis of the property becomes the fair market value at the time of death and the heirs are not liable for payment of any of the deferred gain.

The exclusion applies only to federal income tax. New Jersey residents are still subject to a state tax on any gain unless they roll over the profit into a replacement residence within two years.

Installment Sales

A taxpayer can minimize the payment of income taxes by use of an **installment sale**. An installment sale is defined as any sale in which the seller receives at least one payment after the year of the sale. Under this method, the seller accepts a mortgage as part of the purchase price, and the tax on the gain is paid as the mortgage principal is collected each year. A land contract (see Chapter 19) is often used for this purpose.

When property is sold on the installment basis, the amount of gain subject to tax must be determined. Figuring what percent of the sale price represents a capital gain does this. Remember that capital gain is the difference between realized selling price and the adjusted basis of the property.

Example

A property sold for $105,000. The buyer made a down payment of $20,000 and gave the seller a purchase money mortgage and note for $85,000 payable at 10% over 10 years. The seller's basis in the property is $50,000 and selling expenses are $7,000.

Gross selling price:	$105,000	
Less selling expenses:	7,000	
Realized selling price:	98,000	
Less adjusted basis:	50,000	
Gain		$48,000

The seller's taxable gain under this installment method is computed as follows:

48,000 ÷ 105,000 = 46%

In the year of sale the seller pays a capital gain tax on 46% of $20,000, or $9,200. Assuming a capital gain rate of 20%, this would be a tax of $1,840. In each subsequent year the taxpayer will pay a capital gain tax on 46% of the principal amounts received.

The current exclusion of gains of $250,000 and $500,000 has made the installment sale less attractive than it has been in the past. When questions arise regarding which approach is most beneficial, the real estate agent should advise the taxpayer to seek the advice of an accountant or tax attorney.

Penalty-Free IRA

The Tax Code allows penalty-free early withdrawals of up to $10,000 from an IRA to help with the down payment on a first-time home purchase. The IRA could be the home purchaser's own account or can be a parent's or grandparent's.

RULES ON INVESTMENT PROPERTIES

Depreciation Allowance

Economic depreciation is covered in Chapter 27. This chapter deals with the depreciation allowances for tax purposes.

A depreciation allowance is a permissible deduction from income that works the same way as a charitable deduction or a deduction for interest or real property taxes paid. The primary difference between the depreciation deduction and the interest or property tax deduction is that the taxpayer does not have to spend dollars in order to claim a deduction.

What Can Be Depreciated

Property is depreciable if it meets these requirements:

1. It must be used in business or held for the production of income;
2. It must have a limited and determinable useful life, and that life must be longer than one year; and
3. It must be something that wears out, decays, gets used up, becomes obsolete or loses value from natural causes.

Real estate that would qualify for depreciation is property used in a trade or business or in the production of income, including equipment, furniture, and so on used in connection with the depreciable property. Thus, there must be an allocation between land and improvements before depreciation is taken.

When depreciating a real estate investment, the total investment value is allocated between land and building, since only the building portion of the investment can be depreciated. Land does not depreciate. In making such an allocation the appraiser may (a) use the tax assessor's ratio, which involves the use of a ratio derived from the tax assessor's assessment of the property; or (b) use the sales comparison approach for estimating the value of the vacant land.

Once the value has been allocated between land and building, the next step is to determine the period of time over which the improvement can be depreciated. This period is the building's **economic (useful) life**. Economic life should not be confused with physical life. Economic life is the remaining period for which improvements are expected to generate more income than operating expenses cost. The fact that more buildings are torn down than fall down illustrates that most improvements have a physical life that is far longer their useful life.

After estimating the economic life of the improvements and determining their value relative to that of the land, the depreciation allowance will depend on whether the investment property is residential or non-residential, as will be explained below.

Formerly, several methods of depreciation were available to owners of income-producing properties. One was **straight line**, where the depreciable basis is written off at a constant rate over the estimated life of the investment. Several accelerated methods that allowed faster write-offs were also available and investors used these methods whenever possible. The problem with the straight-line method was that the taxpayer had to negotiate the useful life with the IRS and justify that the time selected was proper. In 1981, the disputes were eliminated with the introduction of the Accelerated Cost Recovery System (ACRS).

The ACRS system was modified in 1986, and today depreciation allowances are governed by the Modified Accelerated Cost Recovery System (MACRS). However, for investment property owners, the word "accelerated" is misleading. Non-residential investment properties, such as office buildings, must be written off over 39 years and residential investment properties, such as apartment buildings, over 27.5 years, *both on a straight-line basis*. The straight-line method assumes that the only kind of depreciation is physical deterioration that causes a constant wearing out of property over its useful life. The useful life for property placed in service before January 1, 1987 varies, depending on the date of service.

Example

If a residential investment property is purchased for $360,000 with a land value of $60,000, and placed in service after January 1, 1987, the depreciable basis would be $300,000 ($360,000 minus $60,000 land value). Using straight-line depreciation, the allowable yearly depreciation deduction would be $10,909 ($300,000 ÷ 27.5 years).

Calculation of Gain upon Sale of Investment Property

The calculation of a gain upon the sale of an investment property follows the same pattern as that for a personal residence. The primary difference is that the *basis* of the investment property will be reduced by an amount equal to any depreciation or rehabilitation tax credits the investor claims. Thus, a larger taxable gain (or smaller loss that may be used to offset other passive income) results than if the owner had not claimed these items. Investment property owners can postpone the payment of income tax on gains by using a *tax-deferred exchange* or an *installment sale*.

Tax-deferred Exchange

Investment property does not qualify for the capital gains exemption allowed for principal residences, which was discussed earlier. Owners of investment properties are, however, eligible for a similar tax shelter if the property is traded for like-kind property. Real property qualifies for a tax-deferred exchange if it is traded for other real property, although not necessarily the same type of real property. For example, an exchange of a condominium in Atlantic City for a farm in Warren County, or the exchange of a mall in Brick Township for a ranch in Montana, would both qualify as a like-kind exchange. The exchange of real property for any kind of personal property does not qualify.

Although an exchange may occur simultaneously, most exchanges are of the deferred type. To qualify as a like-kind exchange, the replacement property must be identified within 45 days after the transfer of the relinquished property; and must actually be received within 180 days of the relinquished property. Part of the gain may be taxable if any "unlike property" (boot) is included to balance the value of the properties exchanged. For example, if one property is exchanged for another plus $25,000, the party receiving the cash will owe tax on the boot received up to the realized gain on the exchange. Tax-deferred exchanges will be discussed in Chapter 26.

Installment Sales Treatment

The details provided earlier about postponement of capital gains tax by application of an installment sale plan also apply to investment properties.

Dealers of real estate, however, are not entitled to installment deferment and must pay any tax on gains at the time of the sale. Dealers are persons or companies who buy on their own account. Examples include subdividers who sell lots and builders/developers who sell houses.

Passive Loss Rules

In 1986 Congress passed passive loss rules to eliminate so-called "tax shelters." Tax sheltering is achieved when a loss from one investment is used to offset income from another source and thus "shelter" it from tax.

The rules limit the amount of loss a taxpayer is allowed to report on his tax return each year. The rules allow the taxpayer to only take losses from rental real estate to the extent that he had income from other rental real estate properties. Thus if an investor owns two properties, one of which produces income of $3,000 per year, and the other generates a loss of $3,000, he could offset the income from the first property with the loss of the second.

However, the rules provide that losses from passive activities (those in which the investor does not materially participate) may not be used to offset other active income or portfolio income. Active income is income derived from salary or personal services. Portfolio income includes interest, dividends, royalties and capital gains on the sale of investment property.

Passive investments include all real estate limited partnerships, all rental real estate investments and all other investments in which the investor does not materially participate.

Unused passive losses may be carried over to later years indefinitely. Unused passive losses may come about because they exceed passive income, or because there were only passive losses and there was no passive income to offset.

Currently there is an exception for small investors. They can deduct up to $25,000 of loss against their ordinary income, providing the investor actively participated in the management of the property, holds at least a 10% interest in the investment, and has taxable income of no more than $100,000 before the deduction is made. Active participation would include approving new tenants, deciding on rental terms, making decisions about expenditures for capital improvements and approving repairs. The deduction is reduced by $1 for every $2 of income up to $150,000. No losses are allowed for income over $150,000.

Alternative Minimum Tax (AMT)

The Alternative Minimum Tax is a complex calculation designed to insure that high-income taxpayers pay a minimum amount of tax. The AMT takes effect when the taxpayer's taxable income is reduced below a certain level. In order to determine whether to pay regular tax liability or AMT liability, taxes must be calculated under the current IRS regulations and the AMT rules. The taxpayer then pays the tax liability, which is the greater of these two amounts.

Tax Credits

The tax credit is the greatest of all the tax advantages granted by the federal government to individuals through real estate investment and ownership. It reduces taxes dollar-for-dollar. A credit is worth a lot more than a deduction, particularly for people in a low tax bracket. For example, a $100 deduction will save $15 for anyone in the 15% tax bracket and $30 for anyone in the 30% bracket. However, a $100 credit will save a full $100. A credit is worth the same amount regardless of the tax bracket. Tax credits may be claimed to build housing for low-income residents and for rehabilitation of older buildings and historic structures.

KEY WORDS

Ad Valorem
Assessment Taxes
Assessed Valuation
Basis
Capital Gains Tax
Depreciation
Installment Sales Tax Rule
Passive Losses
Personal Residence Tax Rule
Real Property Taxes
Special Assessments
Straight-Line Depreciation
Tax Sale

CHAPTER 25
Review Questions
(Answers on page 560)

1. The compulsory taxes the government imposes against benefiting property owners for street improvements or road repairs are called:
   (A) special excise taxes.
   (B) special assessments.
   (C) general assessments.
   (D) capital gains tax.

2. A seller who sells his principal residence must have occupied the house for at least what period of time to avoid paying taxes on the gain up to the allowable limit?
   (A) Six months.
   (B) 12 months.
   (C) 18 months.
   (D) 24 months.

3. In regard to senior citizen tax reductions in New Jersey:
   (A) the senior citizen must occupy the property to qualify.
   (B) the reduction is $50 per year.
   (C) the reduction is $450 if both spouses qualify.
   (D) the senior citizen would not qualify if income exceeds $5,000 per annum.

4. A tax sale:
   (A) vests possession in the successful bidder at the time of the sale.
   (B) is conducted by the sheriff in the county where the property is located.
   (C) may be held as soon as the taxes are overdue.
   (D) is subject to the delinquent taxpayer's right of redemption.

5. Taxes may be increased or decreased by adjusting the:
   (A) assessment.
   (B) tax rate.
   (C) Both of the above are correct.
   (D) Neither of the above is correct.

6. Which of the following is true?
   (A) If taxes are delinquent, the property will be taken by the government by escheat.
   (B) Real property assessment for tax purposes is determined by the state and county.
   (C) The redemption period is two years after a tax lien sale.
   (D) Tax liens are satisfied before all liens except mechanics' liens.

7. The federal income tax law allows an investor to gradually write off his original investment. What method is used?
   (A) Exchanges.
   (B) Installment buying.
   (C) Depreciation.
   (D) Land contract.

8. A couple buys a residence for $80,000. During the first year they have expenses of $4,100 in mortgage interest, $4,500 in real property taxes, depreciation of $3,300 and fire insurance of $520. They also added a guest room for $6,400. Deductions on their tax return for the year will be:
   (A) $6,120.
   (B) $8,600.
   (C) $12,520.
   (D) $1,500.

9. Which of the following is NOT an eligible tax deduction on a personal residence?
   (A) Discount points paid by a purchaser.
   (B) Depreciation.
   (C) Property taxes.
   (D) Mortgage interest.

10. Local government programs and services are financed primarily through:
    (A) federal income taxes.
    (B) state income taxes.
    (C) state sales taxes.
    (D) property taxes.

11. A town may recover the costs of curbs or sidewalks by:
    (A) a state income tax.
    (B) a sewer assessment.
    (C) a special assessment.
    (D) a personalty tax.

12. To qualify for a depreciation deduction for income tax purposes, the property must be:
    (A) improved.
    (B) unencumbered.
    (C) purchased prior to tax reform.
    (D) old.

13. The investor's down payment represents:
    (A) debt.
    (B) capital gain.
    (C) equity.
    (D) passive loss.

(Quiz continues on next page)

14. In Thelma's last will and testament, she devised a house to her daughter, Louise. After the death of Thelma, if Louise decides to sell the property, the cost basis for tax purposes will be:
    (A) Thelma's adjusted basis at the time the gift was made.
    (B) Thelma's adjusted basis, after adjusting for inflation.
    (C) the fair market value of the property at the time of Thelma's death.
    (D) the market value of the property at the time of the sale.

15. Alex purchased an apartment building in 1994. For tax purposes, he may depreciate the building over what period of time?
    (A) 15 years.
    (B) 27.5 years.
    (C) 29.5 years.
    (D) 39 years.

16. If a $300,000 office building is built on a lot that cost $75,000, what is the amount of straight-line depreciation the first year?
    (A) $7,692.
    (B) $10,909.
    (C) $11,905.
    (D) $13, 636.

17. The 1986 Tax Reform Act permits a homeowner to deduct which of the following when filing a federal tax return?
    (A) Mortgage amortization.
    (B) Property taxes.
    (C) Depreciation on a personal residence over 27.5 years.
    (D) All of the above.

18. Which of the following would NOT be considered a capital improvement?
    (A) Installation of a new roof.
    (B) Replacement of the furnace.
    (C) Addition of a garage.
    (D) Repair to central air conditioning unit.

19. Depreciation on a property:
    (A) represents an out-of-pocket expense to an investor.
    (B) is a reduction against income taxes.
    (C) increases the property's basis of value.
    (D) is not recaptured when the property is sold.

20. Which of the following is NOT an allowable expense deduction on an income-producing property?
    (A) Depreciation.
    (B) Maintenance costs.
    (C) Principal payments.
    (D) Interest expense.

21. If you pay $5,000 in interest and you are in the 28% tax bracket, how much can you deduct against taxable income?
    (A) $1,400.
    (B) $1,080.
    (C) $1,040.
    (D) $5,000.

22. Which of the following statements is NOT true regarding capital gains treatment on a personal residence?
    (A) Single persons filing a tax return are entitled to a $250,000 exclusion.
    (B) Married filers are eligible for a $500,000 exclusion.
    (C) Homeowners must have owned and occupied the property as their residence for at least three of the five years immediately preceding the sale.
    (D) There is no limit on the number of times the exemption may be used as long as eligibility requirements are met.

23. A house valued at $205,000 is assessed at 80% of value. If the tax rate is $5.40 per $100, the monthly taxes will be:
    (A) $738.00.
    (B) $822.00.
    (C) $903.80.
    (D) $997.97.

24. If the quarterly taxes on a property are $1,750 and the assessed value is $22,000 for the land and $80,000 for improvements, what is the tax rate per $100?
    (A) $5.42
    (B) $6.86
    (C) $7.27
    (D) $8.35

CHAPTER TWENTY-SIX

TAX-DEFERRED EXCHANGES UNDER SECTION 1031

OVERVIEW

The complicated and diverse nature of today's tax laws produces an atmosphere that demands imaginative real estate techniques to solve burdensome tax situations. Investors often discover that tax consequences make selling their properties for cash inadvisable due to their diminished net return after taxes. These and other potential tax problems that arise can often be solved through a well-structured exchange.

The 1986 Tax Act did not affect Section 1031 of the Internal Revenue Code, but other changes in the 1986 Tax Act and the 1984 Tax Act encourage use of this section. Section 1031 provides a mechanism through which real estate investors can exchange property they hold for property they want. If an investor does not receive "**boot**," appreciated property can be exchanged tax-free and the realized gain on such property will be deferred until an eventual sale. The realized gain, however, will be taxable to the extent of any "unlike property" (boot) that was included to balance the value of the properties exchanged.

Investors can use a tax-deferred exchange to: (a) achieve leverage, meaning that by having more money to put down, a higher valued property can be acquired; (b) take advantage of the time value of money—a dollar today is worth more than a dollar tomorrow, so instead of paying a large capital gain tax today, they can pay it in the future when it is worth less; (c) exchange property from a run-down location to a better location; and (d) to achieve other goals, such as exchanging one large property into multiple properties to leave to heirs.

An exchange is not always a good idea. Both gains and losses are deferred under 1031. Therefore, a taxpayer who wishes to report a loss must be sure his sale does not accidentally become an exchange. In addition, if a taxpayer has only a small gain, the cost of the exchange may exceed the tax savings. An exchange may also not be appropriate where the taxpayer is selling real property on contract and is eligible for installment treatment on payments received. Because of these complex issues, potential exchangors should always consult with their tax attorney or CPA before deciding to do a tax-deferred exchange.

The 1984 Tax Act sanctioned, within limits, delayed exchanges. Until then, to accomplish an exchange, investors had to first locate a replacement property. Because it was unlikely that the owner of a replacement property wanted the property held by the exchangor, a third party who owned a replacement property was needed to complete the exchange.

In 1991, the IRS published regulation Section 1.1031 (k) that provides clear guidance for the conduct of a deferred exchange. This regulation covers the role of the qualified intermediary, assignment of contracts, control of escrow funds, identification requirements, earning of interest and who is disqualified to act as a qualified intermediary or control the escrow account.

IRS RATIONALE FOR ALLOWING TAX-DEFERRED EXCHANGES

The federal income tax law is intended to levy a tax based on all current sources of income. Because the sale of an asset whose value has appreciated provides a source of income, the resulting gain is taxable. A taxable gain will occur also when property is sold for more than its adjusted tax basis, which has been reduced by depreciation allowances. But a problem arises when properties are exchanged for something other than cash. In these cases, it is difficult to determine the exact amount of gain or loss.

Section 1031 provides a simple mechanism to defer gains and thus avoid the valuation issue. If an exchange produces no change in the nature of property held, no tax is due. The deferred taxes are, however, attached to the new property, in the form of a carryover of the old tax basis. The tax basis of the replacement property is essentially the purchase price of the replacement property minus the gain that was deferred on the sale of the relinqished property as a result of the exchange. This provides a method for accounting for all taxes deferred in the past. When the newly acquired property is eventually sold for cash or exchanged for "unlike" property, the low tax basis that was carried over from the old property serves to increase the recognized gain, and effectively "settles up" the past tax deferrals.

Effect of Tax Reform

Under the 1986 Tax Reform Act, there was no distinction in tax rates for capital gains as compared to ordinary income. Also, the purchase of new property generates less depreciation than the previous law allowed because the required life is longer. Thus, the motivation to exchange rather than sell property was enhanced by the 1986 Tax Reform Act.

Tax-free Means Tax-deferred

Exchanges are called tax-free because gains are not subject to income taxation at the time of the exchange. However, because exchanges merely defer taxation, they are called "tax-deferred exchanges."

Definitions

Acquisition Cost: The contract price plus the acquisition expenses to acquire the property. These expenses do not include prepaid items such as real estate taxes and hazard insurance, or expenses involved with financing, such as discount points.

Adjusted Basis: The "unadjusted basis" (see below), adjusted or modified by additions or subtractions. Additions to "basis" include improvements and betterments made to the property since its acquisition. Subtractions from "basis" include depreciation and depletion deductions.

Adjusted Sales Price: Selling price less selling expenses.

Boot: Additional consideration of unlike property included in a transaction to equalize the value of property exchanged. Most often cash, boot may also include net mortgage relief, and unlike property such as cars, jewelry or other property.

Dealer Property: Dealer property is property held for resale, not for appreciation and/or income. For instance, a developer who purchases and resells lots could be considered a dealer. Dealer property cannot be exchanged under Section 1031.

Disqualified Person: In an exchange transaction, a person who cannot hold the escrow account, receive identification notice or serve as a qualified intermediary. A disqualified person is any person who:

(a) is an agent of the taxpayer at the time of the transaction, including anyone who acted as the taxpayer's employee, attorney, accountant, investment broker or real estate agent or broker within the two-year period ending on the date of transfer of the first relinquished property;

(b) is a family member; or

(c) is any person who, together with the exchangor or the exchangor's agent, "bears a relationship described in either Section 267 (b) or Section 707 (b)—determined by substituting in each section '10%' for '50%' each place it appears."

Note: If a totally independent person or qualified intermediary is not being used to insure proper control of the escrow funds, the exchangor should seek legal review of Section 1.1031(k)-1(k) to be sure a "disqualified person" is not involved.

Exchangor: The investment property owner who does an exchange by disposing of the relinquished property and acquiring a replacement property of like kind.

Investment Property: Generally, an investment that is passive and held for appreciation over time.

Like Kind: Refers to the nature and character of property, not the grade or quality. Under Section 1031, like-kind property is any property used for business or investment purposes.

Property Used in Trade or Business: Property that generates income as a result of a business activity. For instance, if a real estate broker owns the building in which his real estate office is located, the building would be considered business real estate.

Qualified Escrow Agent: A qualified escrow agent is a corporation that holds the cash from the settlement of the relinquished property. The escrow agent could be the intermediary, a title company or a bank.

Qualified Intermediary: A specially formed company that facilitates the 1031 exchange by acquiring and transferring the relinquished and replacement properties. The intermediary also prepares the required 1031 documentation. IRS requires a qualified intermediary in all 1031 exchanges except "direct exchanges."

Realized Gain: Upon an exchange, the difference between the adjusted basis of the property originally held and the fair market value of the property (including cash) received. Also, the profit on the sale plus all depreciation taken.

Recognized Gain: The portion of realized gain that is subject to immediate taxation.

Relinquished Property: In an exchange, the property held for productive use in a trade or business or for investment that is transferred. Not limited to just one relinquished property.

Replacement Property: The property received in an exchange to be held either for productive use in a trade or business or for investment. Not limited to just one replacement property.

Selling Expenses: Expenses incidental to the sale of property, such as points, attorney fees and commissions. Selling expenses are deducted from the selling price to arrive at the adjusted sale price.

Substituted Basis: Where "basis" is continued or carried through from one taxpayer to another or from one piece of property to another.

Tax Due: The combined federal and state tax rates.

Unadjusted Basis: The starting point for determining depreciation and gain or loss. In most situations, it is the original cost of the property to the taxpayer.

Unlike Property: Property that is not real estate, or property that does not qualify as like-kind in an exchange.

Tax-deferred Exchange: Definition

Section 1031 of the Internal Revenue Code defines a tax-deferred exchange as follows:

"A deferred exchange is defined as an exchange in which, pursuant to an agreement, the taxpayer transfers property held for productive use in a trade or for investment (the 'relinquished property') and subsequently receives property to be held either for productive use in a trade or business or for investment (the 'replacement property')."

General Requirements

The three basic requirements of a tax-deferred exchange of like-kind property under Section 1031 are:

1. There must be an exchange (a delayed exchange may qualify if identification and settlement time limits are met).

2. Both the asset relinquished and the one received in the exchange must be **held for investment purposes or used in a taxpayer's trade or business**. Investment property includes real estate, improved or unimproved, held for investment or income-producing purposes. Property used in a taxpayer's trade or business includes his place of doing business, as well as equipment used in his trade or business.

3. The exchange must involve property deemed to be of **like-kind**.

There must be an exchange or a qualified delayed exchange. An exchange is a reciprocal transfer of property. Generally, when property is sold and replacement property bought from a third party, there is a sale. However, under certain conditions a delayed exchange qualifies. When a sale and purchase are effected with the same party, the Internal Revenue Service might contend that the substance of the transaction was an exchange rather than a sale and treat the taxpayers accordingly.

Both the asset surrendered and the one received in the exchange must be held for productive use in a trade or business or held as an investment. It cannot be property for personal use, such as a home or an automobile. It cannot be stock in trade or property held for sale in an inventory. Property that is used for farming, manufacturing or income-producing purposes generally would qualify when exchanged for like-kind property. The property can be any kind used in the taxpayer's business for a productive purpose. It can be a leasehold for real estate if the leasehold has 30 or more years to run, including options.

The exchange must involve property deemed to be of **like-kind**. Real estate has an advantage in meeting the like-kind requirement, because any real property held for business or investment purposes qualifies as like-kind.

To qualify as like-kind under Section 1031, the following criteria must be met:

1. Both exchanged properties must be in the United States.

2. The relinquished property must be used by the exchangor for investment, business or production of income. **It is not important how the buyer intends to use the property.**

3. The exchangor must use the replacement property for investment, business and/or production of income. **It is not important how the property is currently being used by the seller of the replacement property.**

4. The replacement property must be identified within **45 days**.

5. The replacement property must be received within **180 days** of settlement of the relinquished property or by the tax return due date, whichever is earlier.

Property NOT Qualified for a 1031 Exchange

1. A **principal residence** does not qualify for the benefits of a tax-deferred exchange under the provisions of Section 1031. However, Section 1034 gives personal residences more liberal tax treatment in a sale if replaced.

2. A **second home** does not qualify as an investment property. For instance, a vacation property may be rented out, but if the owner uses it for personal reasons for more than 14 days, or more than 10% of the days actually rented (whichever is greater), it will be treated as a second home for that tax year. In any given tax year a vacation home can change from investment property to second home, depending upon use.

3. **Dealer property** cannot be exchanged under Section 1031. Lots or homes held primarily for sale by a developer do not qualify for an exchange because they are inventory. Also, a contractor in the business of buying homes and renovating them for resale could be considered a dealer.

4. **Partnership interests** may not be exchanged under Section 1031. If a business property is owned in the name of the partnership, for example, "ABC Properties Partnership," then all of the partners must do the exchange. Individual partners may not exchange their respective interests because their interest in the partnership is personalty, not real property. On the other hand, if the partnership is dissolved, the property is deeded to individual partners as tenants in common, and each partner can either exchange his or her separate interest, or pay the tax.

The Basic Types of Exchanges

A **simultaneous exchange** is an exchange in which the closing of the relinquished property and the replacement property occur on the same day.

A **delayed exchange** is one in which the replacement property is closed on at a later date than the closing of the relinquished property. This type of exchange might be desirable when a suitable property to exchange has not been located, or when certain financing is to be arranged, or when improvements to the property are to be built prior to the exchange. In a delayed exchange there are two closings, with a delay between the first closing of the relinquished property and the subsequent closing of the replacement property.

Prior to the *Starker* decision (*Starker vs. U.S.*, 602 F. 2d 1341, 9th Cir., 1979) the IRS took the position that a taxpayer could not use Section 1031 for a delayed exchange.

In *Starker*, a major corporation acquired land from Starker under a contract in which the corporation agreed to acquire other real estate in the future and deed it to Starker. The corporation had up to five years to find suitable property or pay in cash a certain amount which had a 6% growth factor. During the next year the corporation conveyed to Starker a contract right to purchase another property. The property was subject to a life estate and could not pass to Starker until the life estate expired. Starker, however, had immediate possession of the property, subject to certain restrictions. The IRS argued that the transaction did not qualify for Section 1031 because (1) the transfers were not simultaneous and (2) Starker received immediately in the exchange a right, which was not like the real property Starker transferred.

The Ninth Circuit held that simultaneity is not required and that rights of ownership are no different from ownership rights. Thus, a delayed exchange was provided for Starker. The 1984 Tax Reform Act, Section 77, amended IRC Section 1031 permits non-simultaneous exchanges if identification and settlement time limits are met.

A **reverse exchange** is an exchange in which the replacement property is acquired before settlement of the relinquished property. A replacement property may be placed under contract at any time, but the investor may not close on the replacement property until settlement on the relinquished property.

Usually the intermediary takes title to the replacement property and holds title until the taxpayer can find a buyer for his exchange property and close on the sale under an exchange agreement with the intermediary. Subsequent to the closing of the exchange property (or simultaneous with this closing), the intermediary conveys title to the replacement property to the taxpayer.

An **improvement exchange** is an exchange in which a taxpayer desires to acquire a property and arrange for construction of improvements on the property before it is received as replacement property. The improvements are usually a building on an unimproved lot, but also include enhancements made to an already improved property in order to create adequate value to close on the exchange with no boot occurring. The Code and Regulations do not permit a taxpayer to construct improvements on a property as part of a 1031 Exchange after he has taken title to property as replacement property in an exchange. Therefore, it is necessary for the intermediary to close on, take title and hold title to the property until the improvements are constructed and then convey title to the improved property to the taxpayer as replacement property. Improvement exchanges are done in the context of both delayed exchanges and reverse exchanges, depending on the circumstances. Improvement exchanges are not covered by the Safe Harbor Regulations but are common across the country.

Delayed Exchanges– The Exchange Process and the Time Rules

A taxpayer desiring to do a 1031 Exchange lists and/or markets his property for sale in the normal manner without regard to the contemplated 1031 Exchange. A buyer is found and a contract to sell the property is executed. Accommodation language is usually placed in the contract securing the cooperation of the buyer to the seller's intended 1031 Exchange, but such accommodation language is not mandatory.

When contingencies are satisfied and the contract is scheduled for a closing, the services of an intermediary are arranged for. The taxpayer enters into an exchange agreement with the intermediary which permits the intermediary to become the "substitute seller" in accordance with the requirements of the Code and Regulations.

The Exchange Agreement usually provides for:

- An assignment of the seller's Contract to Buy and Sell Real Estate to the Intermediary.
- A closing where the Intermediary receives the proceeds due the seller at closing. Direct deeding is used. The Exchange Agreement will comply with the requirements of the Code and Regulations wherein the taxpayer can have no rights to the funds being held by the Intermediary until the exchange is completed or the Exchange Agreement terminates. The taxpayer "cannot touch" the funds.
- An interval of time where the seller proceeds to locate suitable replacement property and enter into a contract to purchase the property. The interval of time is subject to the 45-day and 180-day rules, covered in more detail below.
- An assignment of the contract to purchase replacement property to the Intermediary.
- A closing where the Intermediary uses the exchange funds in his possession and direct deeding to acquire the replacement property for the seller.

Tax Implications of a Sale vs. Exchange

The first step in deciding whether to sell an investment property and pay the tax, or do an exchange, is to estimate the tax due and the net proceeds after tax. The Tax-free Exchange Analysis Worksheet shown in Figure 26.1 is an excellent tool for this purpose. A brief description follows:

1. **Adjusted Basis.** The owner's original basis is the purchase price plus acquisition costs. Any improvements to the property are added to the original basis. From that basis, depreciation taken over the years is subtracted to arrive at the tax basis. The worksheet example shows an adjusted basis of $75,000 and total depreciation of $21,600. Therefore:

Adjusted Basis	$ 75,000
Less: All Depreciation Taken	- 21,600
Tax Basis	$ 53,400

2. **Realized Gain.** The realized gain is computed by subtracting the tax basis from the adjusted sales price. Continuing the example:

Adjusted Sales Price	$117,000
Less: Tax Basis	- 53,400
Realized Gain	$ 63,600

If the property is sold, the capital gain of $63,600 will be added to the taxpayer's taxable income.

3. **Tax Due.** To determine the tax due, it is necessary to combine the federal and state tax rates. Under the 1997 Taxpayer Relief Act, the maximum federal capital gains tax rate was reduced from 28% to 20% for the higher bracket and from 20% to 15% for the lower bracket.

The state rate must be added to the federal rate. In New Jersey the rate varies from 1.5% to 7%, depending upon income. The example used here assumes a 5.5% state rate.

$21,600 x 30.5% = $6,588
$42,000 x 25.5% = $10,710

If the property is sold, the TAX DUE will be $17,298.

If the property is EXCHANGED, $15,900 of taxes can be deferred, and the funds that are saved, fully reinvested.

4. **Net Sales Proceeds After Tax.** Part C of the worksheet indicates that $52,000 would be available before tax or $34,702 after tax.

5. **Investor Options.** When the worksheet is completed the investor can clearly see the options available:

   - SELL, pay taxes of $17,298 and have $34,702 to reinvest; or

   - EXCHANGE, pay no taxes now, defer $63,600 of gain, and have $52,000 to reinvest.

Using the Worksheet

Clearly, the Tax-free Exchange Analysis Worksheet is useful in assisting small investors and real estate agents to decide if an investment property should be exchanged or sold and to estimate the amount of cash proceeds that will be available for reinvestment. The investor and agent can then work together to plan what types of properties might be acquired to complete the exchange.

Reinvestment Requirements

One of the main objectives of a tax-deferred exchange is to defer paying any tax on the gain realized. If, however, an exchange is to be totally tax-free, the following four requirements must be met:

1. The acquisition cost of the replacement property or properties must be equal to, or more expensive than, the adjusted sales price for the relinquished property.

2. No cash may be returned to the exchangor. All the proceeds in the qualified escrow account must be reinvested.

3. Any new or assumed mortgage total on the replacement property must be equal to or greater than the debt paid off on the relinquished property, or new cash must be added to offset the difference.

4. The exchangor may not receive non-like property, including owner-held notes or personal property.

If we extend the worksheet example, the exchangor would have to:

(a) pay at least $117,000 for the replacement property or properties;

(b) reinvest the entire $52,000 that was placed in escrow; and

(c) have new or assumed mortgages of at least $65,000 or add or substitute new cash to reach that total.

Partial Tax-free Exchange

At times, an exchange may not meet all conditions necessary to be totally tax-free, and the exchangor is left with taxable income called "boot." The three main types of boot are described next:

1. **Cash.** If any cash is received in the transaction, it is taxable. Using the worksheet, suppose the investor needs $25,000 in cash and receives it at settlement of the relinquished property:

Sales Proceeds (Before Tax)	$52,000
Cash Received (Taxable Income)	$25,000
Cash Reinvested	$27,000

2. **Mortgage Boot.** Mortgage relief also becomes boot and taxable income. In an exchange where both properties have mortgage debts, the two mortgages are "netted out" and the amount of mortgage boot is the amount that the mortgage debt on the relinquished property exceeds the amount of the mortgage on the replacement property. Adding new cash to the down payment can offset mortgage relief. In the above example, if the total new mortgage debt on the replacement properties is only $50,000, then $15,000 mortgage boot will result.

Total Current Mortgages	$65,000
Total New Mortgages	$50,000
Mortgage Boot (Taxable)	$15,000

3. **Non-like Property.** If the exchangor receives non-like property (car, mobile home, etc.) as part of the consideration in an exchange, it is taxable income at market value. Another source of non-like property is a mortgage taken back by the exchangor. If the exchangor takes back financing on the relinquished property and creates an installment sale, the value of the note is considered boot and will be taxed.

OTHER SOURCES OF TAXABLE INCOME

Depreciable Property. If depreciable property is exchanged for non-depreciable property (land), the accelerated portion of any depreciation taken is considered taxable income.

Interest Earned on Escrow Funds. At the end of the exchange period, the exchangor can receive

FIGURE 26.1
Tax-free Exchange Analysis Worksheet

LIKE – KIND EXCHANGE ANALYSIS

The purpose of this form is to determine the tax impact if a property is sold and not exchanged.

A. TAXABLE GAIN IF PROPERTY IS SOLD

1.	**SELLING PRICE**	$ 130,000	
2.	Less: Selling Costs	- 13,000	
3.	**ADJUSTED SELLING PRICE**		$ 117,000
4.	Original Cost Basis	$ 60,000	
5.	Plus: Improvements	+ 15,000	
6.	**ADJUSTED COST BASIS**	= 75,000	
7.	Less: All depreciation authorized/taken	- 21,600	
8.	Less: **TAX BASIS**		- 53,400
9.	**TOTAL TAXABLE GAIN** or (LOSS) if property is sold		$ 63,600

B. FEDERAL TAX ON GAIN

10.	a. Excess accelerated appreciation (taxed as ordinary income)	______
	b. Recapture of Section 1250 depreciation $ 21,600 x 25% + 5.5% state	+ 6,588
	c. Capital gain on Profit (Adj. Selling Price - Adj. Cost Basis) $ 42,000 x 25.5%	+ 10,710
11.	**Total Federal Tax If Property Is Sold**	$ 17,298

C. BEFORE AND AFTER TAX PROCEEDS

12.	SELLING PRICE (line 1)	$ 130,000
13.	Less: Balance Due on all Loans	- 65,000
14.	EQUITY	= 65,000
15.	Less: Selling Costs (line 2)	- 13,000
16.	**Proceeds Before Tax** (cash to escrow in exchange)	$ 52,000
17.	Less: Total Tax Due (Line 11)	- 17,298
18.	**Net Sale Proceeds After Tax** if property is sold	$ 34,702

D. OPTION –

1. **Sell and pay taxes** of $ 17,298 (line 11) and have $ 34,702 (line 18) to reinvest; or
2. **Exchange—pay zero tax** now, defer $ 63,600 (line 9) of gain and have $ 52,000 (line 16) to invest in real estate.

ALWAYS CONSULT WITH YOUR OWN TAX/LEGAL ADVISOR

interest on the funds that were held in escrow. The interest is treated as normal interest and is taxable.

DOCUMENTATION

The IRS may look more closely at a tax-free exchange than a taxable sale, so it is important that the exchangor carefully follow the requirements set down in the regulations. Five elements are essential:

1. **Intent.** The investor must show that from the start to the end of the transaction, the disposal of one property and the acquisition of another was intended to be an exchange. Intent can be demonstrated by adding the following provision to the standard listing agreement:

   "It is the intent of the owner(s) to dispose of this property as a tax-deferred exchange in accordance with IRC Section 1031, and the owner requires the buyer to cooperate in a tax-deferred exchange."

2. **Form and Documentation.** IRS regulations for an exchange must be followed precisely and the exchange process must be properly documented. If documentation is improper, the transaction could be considered a sale instead of an exchange.

3. **Control of Funds.** At no time in the delayed exchange process can the exchangor have any control or otherwise obtain any benefits from the cash held in the escrow account. Gain or loss occurs when the exchangor actually or constructively receives money or other property before receiving the like-kind replacement property. Actual receipt means the money or other property has been received by the exchangor. Constructive receipt means the money is credited to the exchangor's account or otherwise made available to him or her.

4. **Like-kind Properties.** The properties exchanged must be investment or business properties that meet the like-kind criteria.

TIME LIMITS

As a result of the *Starker* cases, the Tax Reform Act of 1984 established two time limits that require strict compliance. These are:

1. **Identification Period.** The replacement property or properties to be acquired in the exchange must be identified before the end of the identification period. The identification period begins on the date the taxpayer transfers the relinquished property and ends at midnight on the 45th day thereafter.

Rules for Identifying Replacement Properties. The IRS regulations published in 1991 provide the following guidelines:

(a) The identification of possible replacement properties must be by written notice (the identification notice) signed by the taxpayer and hand-delivered, mailed, faxed or otherwise sent to the Intermediary. The identification notice must contain an unambiguous description of the replacement property. This includes, in the case of real property, the legal description, street address or a distinguisable name. The written identification may be separate, or contained in the contract/agreement for the replacement property. A replacement property received before the end of the identification period will be considered as identified.

(b) The exchangor may identify more than one replacement property under one of the three following conditions:

- **The Three Property Rule.** Any three properties regardless of their market values.
- **The 200% Rule.** Any number of properties as long as the aggregate fair market value of identified does not exceed 200% of the fair market value of all relinquished properties as of the initial transfer date.
- **The 95% Rule.** Any number of replacement properties if the fair market value of the properties actually received by the end of the exchange period is at least 95% of the aggregate FMV of all the potential replacement properties identified.

(c) Identification may be revoked in writing at any time during the 45-day identification period.

(d) Incidental property is disregarded in the identification if in a commercial transaction it is typically transferred with the larger property, and the aggregate fair market value of the incidental property does not exceed 15% of the fair market value of the larger property.

Identification of Property to be Built. The regulations for identifying and receiving replacement property not yet built are contained in paragraph 1.1031k-1(e) of the Code. The identification requirement for the property to be built will be met if the identification provides "a legal description" for the underlying land and as much detail as is practical regarding construction of the improvements at the time identification is made.

Improvements made to property already owned by

the exchangor are not considered like-kind and cannot be used as a replacement property.

2. **Exchange Period.** The identified replacement property must be received by the end of the exchange period. The exchange period begins on the date the taxpayer transfers the relinquished property and ends at midnight on the 180th day thereafter or the due date (including extensions) for the taxpayer's return.

Because the replacement property must be settled within 180 days or the tax return due date, whichever is earlier, it may be necessary for the exchangor to file an extension, if the closing on the relinquished property takes place late in the year. For instance, if the closing on the relinquished property takes place on December 10, and the tax return is due on April 15, the exchangor would have to file an extension in order to get the full 180 days before closing on the replacement property. Failure to file an extension can cause the replacement period to end on the due date of the return. This can be a trap for the unwary.

THE TAX-DEFERRED EXCHANGE PROCESS

The exchange process set forth in the new regulations is often called a delayed or Starker exchange. It works well for real estate licensees because it permits use of standard listing and purchase contracts, such as the Realtor® form, used by licensees on a daily basis. It provides time to sell the exchangor's property, find a replacement property and close on the new property in an orderly fashion. And by using a qualified intermediary, the exchangor does not have to depend on the buyer or seller being involved in the process.

THE QUALIFIED INTERMEDIARY

The most important part of the 1991 IRS regulations is the "safe harbor" provision for use of a qualified intermediary in this kind of exchange. Generally, the qualified intermediary will be recommended by the owner's real estate agent, accountant, or attorney.

IRS defines a qualified intermediary as follows:

"A person who is not the taxpayer or a disqualified person, and enters into a written agreement with the taxpayer and, as required by the exchange agreement, acquires the relinquished property from the taxpayer, transfers the relinquished property, acquires the replacement property, and transfers the replacement property to the taxpayer."

Steps in the Delayed Exchange Process

The first step in the exchange process is for the qualified intermediary (generally a corporation set up specially to do exchanges) to prepare an exchange agreement outlining each step in the exchange process. Usually, the exchange agreement is prepared after there has been a written offer and acceptance on the property to be relinquished.

Prior to closing, the exchangor assigns to the qualified intermediary the sales contract for the relinquished property. The regulations require that the assignment be written and that all parties be notified of the assignment before closing.

At the first closing, the relinquished property is transferred from the exchangor to the qualified intermediary. The qualified intermediary immediately transfers the property to the buyer and receives the funds from the buyer. These funds are placed in a **qualified escrow account** by the qualified intermediary so that the exchangor has no control over them.

When new properties are located and identified, and contract terms are agreed upon, the exchangor can assign the contract or the qualified intermediary can sign the contract as purchaser. At closing, the qualified intermediary provides the settlement agent the necessary funds from the escrow account.

CONTRACT TO PURCHASE THE EXCHANGOR'S PROPERTY

As noted earlier, in this type of exchange it is not important if the buyers are investors or plan to use the property as a principal residence. When the contract is presented, it will most likely be on a standard form. Accommodation language is usually placed in the contract securing the cooperation of the buyer to the seller's intended 1031 Exchange, but such accommodation language is not mandatory. An example follows:

"Notwithstanding anything in this purchase agreement to the contrary, the Owner/Exchangor will transfer the property to the Purchaser as part of a Tax Deferred Like-Kind Exchange. It is the intent of the parties that the Owner/Exchangor be allowed to use Section 1031 of the Internal Revenue Code to exchange this property for other property to be identified and acquired later in accordance with Section 1031 regulations.

"This contract may be assigned to a qualified intermediary solely for the purpose of completing the exchange. The purchaser will be notified in writing when the assignment is made. Title, however, will be conveyed directly from the Owner/ Exchangor to the Purchaser as authorized by Revenue Ruling 90-34.

"The Purchaser will be held harmless, and no additional expense or liability will be incurred by the Purchaser as a result of this like-kind exchange. All other items and conditions of this contract remain in full force and effect."

Note: Listing agents may wish to include in the contract a statement that the exchangor acknowledges that he or she has received independent professional advice regarding the tax-free exchange and is not relying on the listing agent for advice.

The addendum serves three purposes. First, it shows the owner's intent to do an exchange. Second, it permits assignment of the contract to a qualified intermediary. Third, it assures the purchasers that there is no additional expense or liability on their part. If the contract is silent on the matter of assignment, it may be assigned without the need for an addendum. It should be emphasized that once the purchasers sign the initial exchange addendum, there is normally no need for them to sign any other documents relative to the exchange.

ACQUIRING REPLACEMENT PROPERTY

As soon as the exchangor's property is listed, the owners should begin their search for a replacement property or properties. They should decide what type of property they want, the location, price, down payment, type of financing and negative cash flow that can be handled, before they start to look for replacement properties and make the 45-day identification. This information must be transmitted to the real estate agent wherever the replacement property is to be purchased.

If the replacement property is under construction and new financing will be required, the time limits can present a problem. The lender needs to be identified early and made aware of the exchange transaction to insure there are no underwriting problems.

Replacement Property Contract Addendum

When the replacement property is located and the terms and conditions are agreed upon, it is necessary to add an addendum to the standard contract. A sample follows:

"The Purchaser/Exchanger is acquiring this property to complete a deferred Like-Kind Exchange under Section 1031 of the Internal Revenue Code; and in accordance with the Exchange Agreement with ________________ (Qualified Intermediary), who has full authority to complete the Exchange.

"Solely for the purpose of completing the Exchange, this contract may be assigned to the Qualified Intermediary. The seller will be notified in writing when this assignment is made. Title, however, shall be conveyed directly from the Seller to the Exchangor in accordance with Revenue Ruling 90-34.

"Seller will be held harmless and there will be no additional expense to the Seller as a result of this Like-Kind Exchange."

Transfer of Title Using a Qualified Intermediary

Under the terms of the required exchange agreement, the qualified intermediary acquires the relinquished property from the exchangor, transfers the relinquished property to the buyer, acquires the replacement property, and at the second closing, transfers the replacement property to the exchangor.

The regulations (§1.1031(k)-1(g) (4)(iv) provide two methods by which the qualified intermediary can acquire and transfer property:

1. The qualified intermediary may acquire and transfer legal title to the property; or

2. The qualified intermediary may enter into a contract agreement with the buyer to transfer the relinquished property to the buyer; the qualified intermediary may enter into a contract agreement with the seller to transfer the replacement property to the exchangor; and the properties are transferred in accordance with the agreements.

The regulation provides the authority under which the qualified intermediary may enter into the contract agreements. It states:

"An intermediary is treated as entering into an agreement if the rights of a party (exchanger) to the agreement are assigned to the intermediary and all parties to the agreement are notified in writing of the assignment on or before the date of relevant transfer of the property."

Settlement Instructions

In the exchange process an important responsibility of the qualified intermediary is to provide exchange settlement instructions to the settlement agent (escrow agent, settlement attorney, closing agent). The regulations do not specify the format to be used, but the goal is to have the settlement statement (HUD-1) indicate that the transaction is an exchange rather than a sale.

The instructions to the settlement agent should include notice that the property will be transferred through the qualified intermediary, provisions for direct wire transfer of all trust funds (proceeds) to the qualified intermediary and deeding instructions.

Transfer of Title

In April 1990, the IRS authorized the use of a direct deed in an exchange transaction. As a result, almost all exchanges using a qualified intermediary use this method to transfer title. The use of a direct deed keeps the qualified intermediary from being in the chain of title and reduces the intermediary's liability. Three methods have been used to transfer title in an exchange. These are:

Double Deed. Title to the exchangor's property is transferred to the qualified intermediary on one deed, and on another deed the qualified intermediary transfers title to the buyer. To acquire title to the replacement property, the seller transfers title to the qualified intermediary on one deed and in turn, the qualified intermediary transfers title to the exchangor on a separate deed. This method results in higher costs because of the need to record two deeds for each transaction, as well as additional legal and transfer fees.

Sequential or Three-party Deed. A single deed is used to transfer the relinquished property from the exchangor to the qualified intermediary and then in turn to the buyer. Also, a single deed is used to transfer title from the seller to the qualified intermediary and then to the exchangor. When this method is used, only one deed is recorded for each transaction.

Direct Deed. A direct deed transfers title to the property directly from one party (seller) to the other (exchangor) without the third party in the exchange ever being shown in the deed.

Certification of Funds

After assignment of the contract, the certification of the availability of funds, and, if required, the earnest money deposit and the down payment, must come from the qualified intermediary who is holding the funds, because the exchangor has no control of the funds.

Simultaneous Exchange with a Qualified Intermediary

Although the use of a qualified intermediary is most often associated with a delayed exchange, buyers and sellers generally use a qualified intermediary to effect the transfer of title even when the settlements are simultaneous. The regulations give specific approval to the use of a qualified intermediary in a simultaneous exchange. A simultaneous exchange, like the delayed exchange, involves two closings, but they usually happen at the same time and at the same place.

Exchange Fees

In addition to the normal costs associated with the financing and settlements of the exchange properties, the following costs should be considered: any additional legal or settlement fees and the qualified intermediary fee. Costs will vary, but for planning purposes, approximately $1,000 should be used as the fee for preparation of documentation, securing the trust funds and acting as a qualified intermediary.

Compliance with FIRPTA

If the seller in an exchange transaction, including the exchangor, is a nonresident alien or foreign corporation, the reporting and withholding requirements of the Foreign Investment in Real Property Tax Act of 1980 (FIRPTA) must be followed. If the seller (transferor) is a foreign person or corporation, the buyer (transferee) must withhold and forward to the IRS 10% of the sales price.

Withholding may be reduced or eliminated if a "withholding certificate" is obtained. To comply with the law a qualified intermediary will normally require a "Certification of Nonforeign Status" from the seller of the replacement property.

Summary

The delayed exchange involves four parties: (1) the exchangor; (2) the buyer of the relinquished property; (3) the seller of the replacement property; and (4) a qualified intermediary. The exchange takes place in the following steps:

1. The exchangor lists his property, indicating his intention to do an exchange.

2. The exchangor finds a buyer, adds the exchange addendum, and assigns the purchase agreement to a qualified intermediary.

3. At the first closing, the exchangor transfers the property to the intermediary who transfers

it to the buyer. The intermediary holds the proceeds from the buyer in a qualified escrow account.

4. The exchangor finds a replacement property within time limits and signs a contract to purchase.

5. At the second closing, the intermediary pays the seller of the replacement property, using the money from the sale of the relinquished property. The property is transferred from the seller to the intermediary, then from the intermediary to the exchangor.

6. The exchange is complete and the exchangor reports the exchange (see below).

Safe Harbor Example

The new regulations include an excellent "safe harbor" example to explain the proper use of the qualified intermediary. This example is included as a case study of the tax deferred exchange process later on this page.

New Basis—Depreciation: Reporting the Exchange

1. **Basis in New Properties.** When an investor buys a new property, the basis is usually the purchase price plus some acquisition costs. However, in the case of an exchange, determining the basis requires an additional step.

Assume a purchase of two replacement properties having an acquisition cost of $132,000 and $122,000, for a total of $254,000. To determine the total basis in the new properties, subtract from the acquisition cost the realized gain deferred.

Acquisition Costs of New Properties	$254,000
Less: Realized Gain Deferred	- 63,600
Total New Basis	$ 190,000

2. **Depreciation.** The new basis for the replacement properties is needed to set up the depreciation schedule. To establish the depreciation schedule for each new property, allocate basis to the properties in the ratio of their relative market value.

	Market Value	Ratio
Exchange Property #1	$130,000	52%
Exchange Property #2	120,000	48%
Total	$250,000	100%

The new depreciation schedule for analysis purposes may then be computed as follows:

	Exchange Property #1	#2
Allocation	52%	48%
New Basis ($190,400)	$99,008	$91,392
Less: Land (20%)	-19,802	-18,278
Improvements	79,206	73,114
Annual Depreciation (27.5 years - S.L.)*	2,880	2,659
Monthly Depreciation	240	222

* If the property was nonresidential and was placed in service after 5/13/93, the depreciation would be straight-line for 39 years.

3. **Reporting the Like-kind Exchange.** The like-kind exchange is reported on IRS Form 8824. In addition, Schedule D, Capital Gains and Losses, is completed for exchanges of investment property and IRS Form 4797, Sale of Business Property, is required for exchanges of business property and any recapture of depreciation.

Case Study: Tax-deferred Exchange

The following deferred exchange example is based on the example in the IRS Regulations covering "safe harbor" procedures (see 1.1 031 k-1 (g)(8) Example 4, dated April 12, 1991).

Situation

On May 1, 1991, Mr. Smith enters into an agreement to sell his property to Mr. & Mrs. Jones for $100,000 on May 17, 1991. However, Mr. & Mrs. Jones are unwilling to participate in a like-kind exchange.

Mr. Smith thus enters into an exchange agreement with the Realty Exchange Corporation whereby Mr. Smith retains the Realty Exchange Corporation to facilitate an exchange with respect to exchangor's property. The Realty Exchange Corporation is not a disqualified person. In the exchange agreement between Mr. Smith and the Realty Exchange Corporation, Mr. Smith assigns to the Realty Exchange Corporation all of Mr. Smith's rights in the agreement with Mr. & Mrs. Jones. The exchange agreement expressly limits Mr. Smith's rights to receive, pledge, borrow or otherwise obtain the benefits of money or other property held by the Realty Exchange Corporation.

On May 17, 1991, Mr. Smith notifies Mr. & Mrs. Jones in writing of the assignment. On the same date, Mr. Smith executes and delivers to Mr. & Mrs. Jones a deed conveying his property to Mr. & Mrs. Jones. Mr. & Mrs. Jones pay $10,000 to Mr. Smith and $90,000 to the Realty Exchange

FIGURE 26.2
Like-kind Deferred Exchange

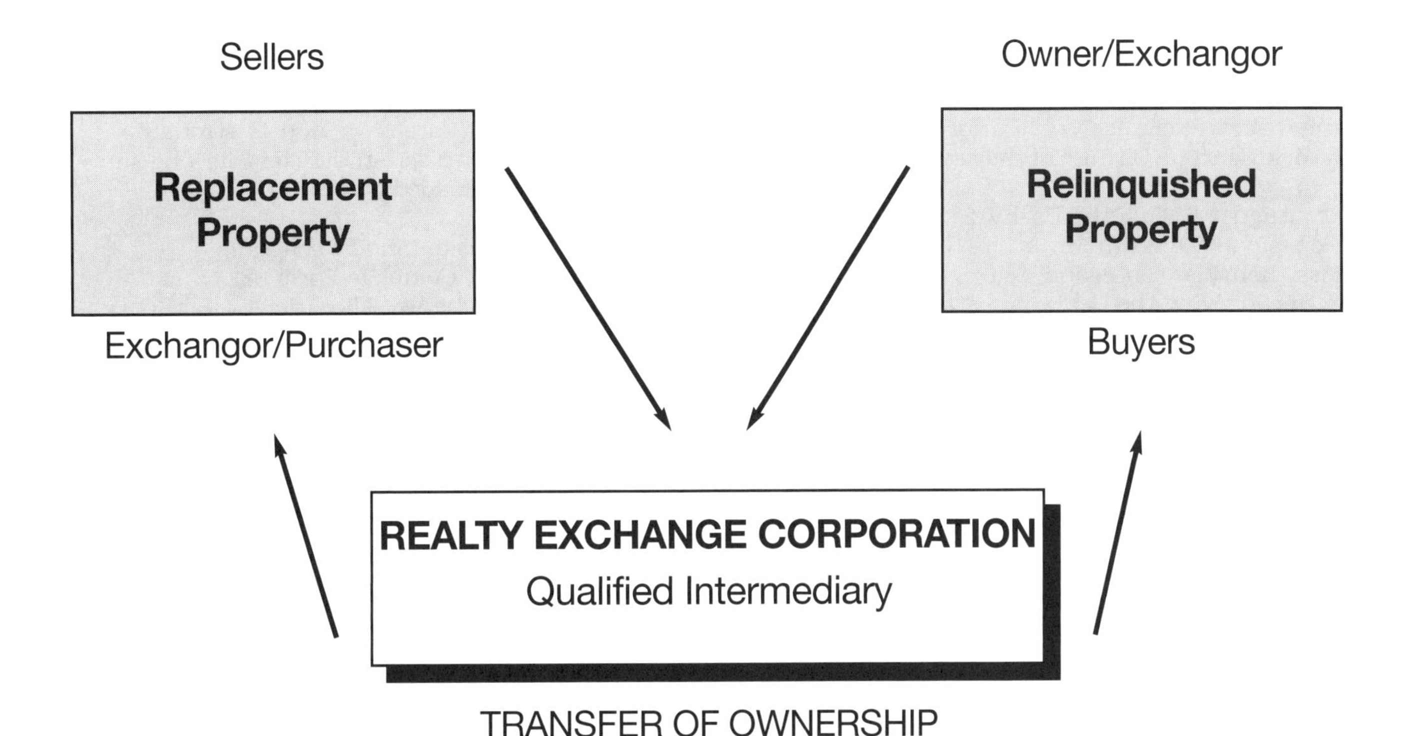

Steps:

1. Identify replacement property(ies) in writing within 45 days
2. Add exchange addendum to replacement property contract(s)
3. Assign contract to qualified intermediary
4. Notify sellers
5. Provide settlement instructions
6. Funds wired to settlement agent
7. Settle within 180 days
8. Report on IRS Form 8824

Steps:

1. Show intent in listing agreement
2. Add exchange addendum to buyers' offer
3. Sign exchange agreement
4. Assign contract to qualified intermediary
5. Notify buyers
6. Provide settlement instructions
7. Direct deed property to buyers
8. Exchange funds wired to qualified escrow account

Corporation. [Note: the $10,000 is cash boot to Mr. Smith.]

On June 1, 1991, Mr. Smith identifies the Henry property as a replacement property. On July 5, 1991, Mr. Smith enters into an agreement to purchase the Henry property from Mr. & Mrs. Henry for $90,000, assigns his rights in that agreement to the Realty Exchange Corporation and notifies Mr. & Mrs. Henry in writing of the assignment.

On August 9, 1991, the Realty Exchange Corporation pays $90,000 to Mr. & Mrs. Henry, and Mr. & Mrs. Henry execute and deliver to Mr. Smith a deed conveying the Henry property to Mr. Smith.

Analysis:

The exchange agreement entered into by Mr. Smith and the Realty Exchange Corporation satisfied the requirements of paragraph (g)(4)(iii)(B) for written exchange agreements. Because Mr. Smith's rights in his agreements with Mr. & Mrs. Jones and Mr. & Mrs. Henry were assigned to the Realty Exchange Corporation, and Mr. & Mrs. Jones and Mr. & Mrs. Henry were notified in writing of the assignment on or before the transfer of the properties, the Realty Exchange Corporation is treated as entering into those agreements.

Because the Realty Exchange Corporation is treated as entering into an agreement with Mr. & Mrs. Jones for the transfer of exchangor's property and, pursuant to that agreement, exchangor's property was transferred to Mr. & Mrs. Jones, the Realty Exchange Corporation is treated as acquiring and transferring exchangor's property.

Similarly, because the Realty Exchange Corporation is treated as entering into an agreement with Mr. & Mrs. Henry for the transfer of the Henry property and, pursuant to that agreement, the Henry property was transferred to Mr. Smith, the Realty Exchange Corporation is treated as acquiring and transferring the Henry property.

This result is reached for purposes of Section 1031 regardless of whether the Realty Exchange Corporation was Mr. Smith's agent under state law and regardless of whether the Realty Exchange Corporation is considered, under general tax principles, to have acquired title or beneficial ownership of the properties. Thus, the Realty Exchange Corporation was a qualified intermediary.

ACKNOWLEDGMENT

The information on tax-deferred exchanges using a qualified intermediary was drawn from *Tax Deferred Exchange of Investment Property* by The Horan Group, and is used with permission. The Horan Group's excellent workbook gives a detailed explanation of the exchange process in plain language, and is strongly recommended for further study. The following sample forms are included:

- Form 8824: Like-kind Exchanges
- Worksheet to Complete Form 8824
- Deferred Exchange Allocation of Settlement Costs
- Estimating Total Depreciation Taken
- Depreciation Tables
- Exchange and Escrow Account Agreement
- Fee Schedule
- Like-kind Property Exchange Addendum
- Assignment of Contract
- Notification of Assignment of Contract
- Like-kind Property Exchange Addendum
- HUD-1 Settlement Statement

The book is available from:

The Horan Group
3501 Delashmutt Drive
Haymarket, Virginia 22069
(703) 754-9411

The exchange agreement between Mr. Smith and the Realty Exchange Corporation expressly limited Mr. Smith's rights to receive, pledge, borrow or otherwise obtain the benefits of the money held by the Realty Exchange Corporation. Thus, Mr. Smith did not have the immediate ability or unrestricted right to receive money or other property held by the Realty Exchange Corporation before Mr. Smith received the Henry property. For purposes of Section 1031 and this section, therefore, Mr. Smith is determined not to be in actual or constructive receipt of the $90,000 held by the Realty Exchange Corporation before Mr. Smith received the Henry property. In addition, the transfer of exchangor's property by Mr. Smith and Mr. Smith's acquisition of the Henry property qualify as an exchange under Section 1031.

CHAPTER 26
Review Questions
(Answers on page 560)

1. "Boot" is a factor to be taken into consideration in a:
   (A) transfer by conditional sales contract.
   (B) percentage lease on commercial property.
   (C) purchase of FHA loans by FNMA.
   (D) tax-deferred exchange.

2. The property acquired by the exchangor is called the:
   (A) acquired property.
   (B) new property.
   (C) substituted property.
   (D) replacement property.

3. "Boot" is the:
   (A) same as equity.
   (B) difference in value between two properties traded.
   (C) difference in equity between two properties traded.
   (D) amount which is due at maturity date of a partially amortized note.

4. Which of the following statements concerning exchanges in real property is true?
   (A) They are always tax-free.
   (B) Tax must be immediately paid on any gain.
   (C) They are tax-favored.
   (D) They are unlawful.

5. If mortgage boot exists, the taxable amount is:
   (A) the total mortgages on the relinquished property minus the total mortgages on the replacement property.
   (B) the total mortgages on the relinquished property plus the total mortgages on the replacement property.
   (C) the total mortgages on the replacement property.
   (D) the total mortgages on the relinquished property.

6. An exchangor relinquished a property for $120,000 and received a replacement property for $180,000. The buyer of the relinquished property obtained first mortgage financing of $100,000 and the exchangor took back a purchase money second mortgage of $20,000 payable at 9.75% over 10 years. What is the amount of boot in this exchange?
   (A) $20,000.
   (B) $40,000.
   (C) $60,000.
   (D) $80,000.

7. Ginger completes an exchange in which she receives $225,000. She had taken depreciation of $45,000 on her relinquished property and she had a capital gain of $80,000, $50,000 of which was tax-deferred. What is her basis in the replacement property?
   (A) $100,000.
   (B) $125,000.
   (C) $130,000.
   (D) $150,000.

8. Binky purchases the exchangor's property for $185,000, out of which the exchangor's net proceeds are $118,000. The exchangor completes the exchange by acquiring a replacement property for $187,000 with an investment of $111,000. How much is the cash boot?
   (A) 0.
   (B) $2,000.
   (C) $7,000.
   (D) $38,000.

9. Which of the following properties would NOT qualify for a 1031 Exchange?
   (A) An office condominium.
   (B) A vacation home rented out for the month of August.
   (C) A business property.
   (D) An investment property.

10. If the original basis of a property was $90,000, and total depreciation taken was $23,000, what is the adjusted basis?
    (A) $23,000.
    (B) $67,000.
    (C) $113,000.
    (D) Not enough information supplied.

11. What is the realized gain on sale of an investment property if the adjusted sales price is $130,000 and the adjusted basis is $40,000?
    (A) $40,000.
    (B) $90,000.
    (C) $80,000.
    (D) $170,000.

12. If the owner's equity is $55,500 and selling costs are $5,500, what are the sale proceeds before tax?
    (A) $5,500.
    (B) $50,000.
    (C) $61,000.
    (D) $55,500.

(Quiz continues on next page)

13. Real estate used in a building owner's business activity is considered:
    (A) operating real estate.
    (B) investment real estate.
    (C) principal real estate.
    (D) business real estate.

14. Within 180 days of relinquishing a property, the exchangor must:
    (A) identify the replacement property.
    (B) report the exchange to the IRS on Form 8824.
    (C) pay taxes on the realized gain.
    (D) take title to the replacement property.

15. The written document that identifies the replacement property in an exchange should be signed by:
    (A) the exchangor.
    (B) the owner of the replacement property.
    (C) both A and B.
    (D) neither A nor B.

16. Within the 45-day identification period, the exchangor may identify:
    (A) only one potential replacement property.
    (B) any property that does not exceed the value of the relinquished property.
    (C) three properties of any fair market value.
    (D) any number of properties without restriction.

17. With a federal tax rate of 28%, what is the total tax due if the realized gain on a sale is $75,000, and the taxpayer must pay a state tax rate of 6%?
    (A) $3,550.
    (B) $4,500.
    (C) $21,000.
    (D) $25,500.

18. If depreciable property is exchanged for non-depreciable property (land), taxes will be due on:
    (A) the price paid for the land.
    (B) the accelerated portion of any depreciation taken on the depreciable property.
    (C) the fair market value of the land.
    (D) the fair market value of the depreciable property.

CHAPTER TWENTY-SEVEN

APPRAISING

Introduction

An appraisal is best defined as an estimate or opinion of value of an adequately described property, as of a specific date, by a competent appraiser, supported by factual and relevant data. The valuation or appraisal of real estate is utilized in all phases of the real estate business and in practically every real estate transaction. It is important that a real estate broker or salesperson have a working knowledge of the functions of an appraisal, its elements and its utilization. While the broker or salesperson need not qualify as an expert appraiser, he or she should be qualified to render an estimate of value or probable market value of a property which he or she proposes to list and sell. The broker or salesperson should also be familiar with the concepts of value, the forces that influence value and the methods by which value may be estimated.

Value, Price and Cost

Value may be described as the worth of an item in money or goods at a certain time. The value most commonly sought by brokers and appraisers is market value, or the probable sales price of the property if it were offered in the open market. **Market value** may be defined as the most probable price a ready, willing and able buyer, not forced to buy, will pay to a ready, willing and able seller, not forced to sell, allowing a reasonable time for exposure in the open market. The **cost** of a property is the amount of money used to construct improvements plus the value of the land. **Market price** is generally what a person pays for a property, and may differ widely from its market value. For example, a seller under pressure to sell may accept a price considerably lower than the market value.

Types of Value

Some of the various types of value include: (1) market value, which is based on the willing seller, willing buyer concept as stated above; (2) assessed value, or the value used for property tax purposes; (3) book value, or the value according to the owner's books, usually for income tax purposes, which is determined by taking original cost, less depreciation, plus capital improvements, often called "basis" or "adjusted cost basis"; (4) loan value, or the value as established by a lender for loan purposes; and (5) insurance value, or the value based on the cost of restoration, replacement or reimbursement for loss.

Economic Characteristics of Value

For real estate to have value, it must also possess certain economic characteristics, which are referred to as the "four elements of value." The elements are demand, utility, scarcity and transferability (DUST).

1. **Demand,** which implies both a need and the existence of monetary power to satisfy that need. Demand alone (as can be seen by our need for air and water) will not create a marketable commodity.

2. **Utility,** which is broadly defined as the power to render a service or fill a need. If a property has no use, regardless of how scarce it is, it will not have value.

3. **Scarcity,** which can only be considered in relation to supply and demand. As with utility, in order for scarcity to affect value, one has to determine the other factors involved, such as utility and demand. An item might have great utility and be in high demand, and yet not create value. The air we breathe is a good example of this.

4. **Transferability,** which is physical mobility together with possession and control of the rights of ownership. Even if the factors of utility, scarcity and demand are present, but the item is not transferable, very little value will exist.

Principles of Value

Since an understanding of the basic economic principles of value are essential to an understanding of the purpose, techniques and procedures of an appraisal, they may be listed as follows:

1. **Principle of Supply and Demand.** The value of any commodity is created both by demand and scarcity. Generally, the greater the scarcity, the greater the demand, hence, the greater the value.

2. Principle of Change. Change is a constant, ever-present force which affects all properties, and is a part of the law of cause and effect. The changes affect land use, which in turn changes the value of the land. Most real estate passes through four life cycles: *growth, stability, decline* and *renewal.* After land passes through the fourth stage, the process will repeat itself.

3. Principle of Substitution. This principle states that the maximum value of a parcel of real estate is set by the cost of acquiring an equally desirable and valuable substitute property, assuming there is no delay in making the substitution. For example, a house would not sell for $180,000 if equally desirable substitutes could be purchased for $140,000 without costly delay.

4. Principle of Highest and Best Use. This may be expressed as that use which at the time of appraisal is most likely to produce the greatest net return over a given period of time. This is usually expressed in terms of net income. The appraiser must consider that the present use of a parcel may not be the use that would attribute the highest value to the land. For example, a single-family house in a commercial area would be unlikely to represent the highest and best use for the property.

5. Principle of Increasing and Decreasing Returns. This affirms that money spent on improvements to land and structures will produce greater and greater net income (increasing returns) up to a point (surplus productivity). When this point is reached, any additional investment will produce lower returns, indicating that the point of diminishing returns has been reached.

6. Principle of Contribution. This follows the same principle as increasing and decreasing returns, but is only applied to a portion of the real estate and its overall contribution to value. For example, if a fireplace adds $15,000 to the value of a house, then its contribution is $15,000 regardless of the cost to build it. In some cases, the value added by an addition is less than its cost. This should be basic in any feasibility study of remodeling or modernization.

7. Principle of Competition. This principle is based on the theory that competition arises from profits, and that excess profit will bring about ruinous competition. For example, one too many real estate brokerage firms in the same town will likely result in losses for one or more of the competing firms.

8. Principle of Conformity. This principle affirms that maximum value is realized when there is a reasonable amount of social and economic homogeneity present. Related to the principle of conformity are the principles of **regression** and **progression**. The principle of regression states that when properties of dissimilar value are placed together in the same neighborhood, the value of the superior property is decreased. The principle of progression states the opposite view: If a property of lower value is placed in a neighborhood of more valuable homes, the value of the inferior property is increased. Zoning regulations and private deed restrictions help to sustain reasonable uniformity.

9. Principle of Anticipation. This principle holds that value is the worth of all present and future benefits arising from ownership and use of real property. Thus, an investor in income property invests in anticipation of future income benefits.

10. Principle of Plottage. This principle holds that a value increment can be realized by bringing two or more smaller parcels of land under one ownership through a process known as "assemblage." Plottage means the value of the parcels, when combined, is greater than the sums of the values of the individual tracts under separate owners. For example, two adjacent lots are each worth $20,000. By combining them under one owner, the assembled tract becomes large enough for use as an apartment building site, worth $75,000. The plottage value is $35,000.

The importance of each will vary depending on the type of property being appraised and market conditions.

There are four more considerations that influence value:

1. Social considerations, which include such elements as prestige, attitudes toward law and order, family sizes and homogeneity of social and economic characteristics.

2. Physical considerations, which might include street patterns and widths, convenience to schools, shopping, parks, churches and recreation, topographical features, relation to the rest of the city, shape and size of lots, etc.

3. Economic considerations, including rent and income levels, vacancy of living units, new construction and vacant land, growth patterns of the neighborhood, etc.

4. Governmental considerations, such as special assessments, taxes, zoning and building codes.

The Appraisal Process

The creation of an appraisal is a problem-solving technique which requires an orderly procedure. The following will outline the basic steps in an appraisal process:

1. Define the problem. This involves establishing at the beginning exactly what is to be appraised, the purpose of the appraisal and the date of the appraisal.

2. Inspect the neighborhood and the subject property. In addition to conducting an inspection of the neighborhood and the property in question, the appraiser will consider the age and physical condition of typical properties; the convenience of the subject property to churches, schools, transportation and shopping; the apparent rate and direction of growth; vacancies, zoning and trends towards other uses; and any favorable (or unfavorable) characteristics which might affect the value of the subject property.

3. Collect the pertinent data. Some of this data will be gathered during an inspection of the property and neighborhood, and the rest will be relevant factual data about the region, city and neighborhood. Together they will form the foundation of the appraisal. Which data are relevant will naturally be dependent upon the type of property being appraised and the purpose of the appraisal.

4. Apply each approach to value. The appraiser will now classify the data, and indicate the value by as many methods as possible.

5. Correlate the value estimate. This is not accomplished by simply averaging the estimates, but rather by once again considering the purpose of the appraisal, assessing the type of property in question, and evaluating the adequacy of data. These considerations will influence the weight given to each estimate and thus, with emphasis which gives the most reliable solution to the purpose of the appraisal, will allow the appraiser to temper his estimate in accordance with his judgment and arrive at a supportable conclusion of value.

6. Prepare the appraisal report. The final step in the appraisal process is the preparation of the appraisal report. This report will not only contain the appraiser's conclusion of value, but also the supportive factual data that are the basis for that conclusion.

Depreciation

In appraising by either the cost or capitalization approach, the necessity for estimating depreciation becomes increasingly clear. This type of depreciation (as opposed to book depreciation related to tax shelter in investment real estate) is defined as loss in value to the improvements of a property due to any cause, and is further broken down into three distinct areas: (1) deterioration; (2) functional obsolescence; and (3) external obsolescence.

1. Deterioration. Physical deterioration is most commonly evidenced as ordinary wear-and-tear on improvements.

2. Functional Obsolescence. This may be defined as the lack of desirability due to functional shortcomings, such as floor plan, size, style, age, etc., particularly as they are compared with those existing in new, more modern and efficient structures serving the same function.

3. External Obsolescence. A loss in value that is caused by changes that are external, or outside the subject property, such as a residence in close proximity to a new high-speed highway or industrial complex or to a new airport which has its approach path over a residential area.

After separating depreciation into the above three types (deterioration, functional obsolescence and external obsolescence), each type may be further defined as (a) curable; or (b) incurable:

- **Curable.** That depreciation which can be economically repaired, replaced or corrected, and where the cost to correct the defect will not exceed the increase in property value. Examples include a worn-out roof, old-style kitchen or fixtures, etc.

- **Incurable.** That depreciation in which it is not economically feasible or profitable to replace or cure the condition. External obsolescence, for example, is normally incurable, because the owner of the subject property does not have control over it.

Accrued depreciation is the total depreciation from the time of construction to the date of appraisal due to all causes.

Three Approaches to Value

Outlined below are the three approaches or appraisal techniques used to estimate value: (1) the sales comparison approach (also called the market data approach); (2) the income approach (also called the capitalization approach); and (3) the cost approach (also called the reproduction or summation approach).

SALES COMPARISON APPROACH

Appraisal by this approach is the one most commonly used by real estate brokers and salespersons in their everyday estimation of market values. The sales comparison approach is based on the principle of substitution, by which the price of a property will not generally exceed the cost necessary to acquire a similar substitute property of equal desirability which is readily available on the open market. Thus, the value of a property is established by the prices that are currently being paid for similar or comparable properties. In order for a property to be considered similar, and thus be used for comparison, it must have the same "highest and best use" as the subject property, and be reasonably similar with respect to size, location, physical condition and the like. The comparative sale must have also taken place within a reasonably recent period of time (such as six months), and have been a bona fide transaction by parties not forced to buy or sell.

Adjustments. When the comparable property contains features that are dissimilar to the subject property, the appraiser must adjust the sales price of the comparable property in order to compensate for the differences. The objective of the sales comparison approach is to match the comparable to the subject property. The subject property cannot have adjustments made to it, because at this time it has no assigned value. Thus, if the **comparable** has a feature that is **inferior**, you **add (CIA)**. If the **comparable** has a feature that is **better** (superior), you **subtract (CBS)**.

To illustrate this concept, the above diagram consists of three glasses of water. Comparable #1 has an *inferior* amount of water, so you would add water to equate it to the subject property (CIA). Comparable #2 is *better* because it contains a superior amount of water, so you would subtract water to equate it to the subject (CBS).

Gross Rent and Gross Income Multipliers

Gross rent multipliers are a rule of thumb method for estimating the value of rental properties. Dividing the sales price of comparable properties derives the "multiplier" by their gross annual or monthly rent. The multiplier is then applied to the gross annual or monthly rent of the subject property to estimate its value.

The Gross Rent Multiplier (GRM) relates the sales price to gross monthly rental income, while the **Gross Income Multiplier (GIM)** uses gross annual income. Generally, the GRM is used for appraising residential properties (e.g., one- to four-family dwellings) and the GIM is used for commercial and industrial properties and large apartment buildings, which often derive income from sources other than rent, such as vending machines and concessions.

Sales Price ÷ Gross Monthly Income = GRM
Sales Price ÷ Gross Annual Income = GIM

Gross Monthly Rent x GRM =
Estimated Value of Subject Property
Gross Annual Income x GIM =
Estimated Value of Subject Property

Example

	Sale Price	÷	Gross Annual Income	=	Gross Income Multiplier
Property A	$155,000		$22,000		7.05
Property B	$137,500		17,200		7.99
Property C	$195,000		21,700		8.99
Property D	$215,000		33,000		6.52

Based upon the information gathered, the appraiser will use his judgment to determine the multiplier that he feels is most representative for use in the calculation of the subject property's value, giving particular consideration to multipliers for the most comparable properties. (The resultant multipliers are not simply taken and averaged.)

If the subject property being appraised had annual gross income of $60,000 and the appraiser had determined that a gross income multiplier of "8" would be used, these figures would be multiplied to produce an estimated value of $480,000.

Some of the advantages of the sales comparison approach are that it is direct, easily understood by non-appraisers and effective and accurate in the appraisal of land or residential properties that are frequently sold in the marketplace. The major disadvantage is that it requires an active market for the type of property that is being appraised, and thus would be difficult to use for unique properties, such as houses of worship or schools which are not actively sold.

INCOME APPROACH

The income approach is based on the assumption that the value of a property may be determined by the amount of net income it can reasonably produce over its remaining **economic life**. The economic life is the period of time for which a building is expected to yield a return in excess of that obtainable from the bare land. The economic life cannot exceed the **physical life** although, due to external factors such as changes in the environment of the building, it may be shorter. Thus, the value of an income-producing property is equal to the present worth of its future income. Stated another way, an income-producing property is worth what someone will pay for it in order to have the right to receive the income. It can therefore be said that the income approach is an evaluation of a projected income stream, or an attempt to determine the present worth of future income.

There are five basic steps used to determine value using the income approach. These are:

1. Estimate potential gross income. Gross income refers to the total annual income the property would likely produce if it were fully occupied, or its potential annual income from all sources. In determining the potential gross income of a building, one must also consider the type of rent involved. "Economic rent" is the rent which the property would command if it were vacant and available for rent in the open market, while "contract rent" is the rent presently being paid by the existing tenants. An investor would also look to the "quality" of the income, or the manner in which it meets the requirements of a good investment in terms of safety of principal and certainty of yield; the "quality" of the income, as it relates to the financial responsibility of the tenant (usually reflected in the interest rate, for the greater the risk, the higher the interest rate); and the "durability" of the income, which refers to the remaining length of time it will continue.

2. Estimate effective gross income. Potential gross income less an allowance for vacancy and collection losses is termed "effective gross income."

3. Deduct annual expenses to arrive at net operating income (NOI). These are expenses chargeable to the operation of the property, and may be either: (a) **fixed expenses**, which remain the same whether or not the units are rented, such as property taxes, insurance, etc.; (b) **operating expenses**, which cover operating costs such as management fee, utilities, advertising, interior and exterior maintenance, janitorial services, grounds care, etc.; and (c) **reserves for replacements**, which constitute the annual allowance for replacement of equipment and building components such as stoves, refrigerators, air conditioners, carpets, drapes, water heaters, etc. **Note:** principal and interest payments on existing mortgages, income tax on the return on the investment, capital improvements and depreciation are not considered operating expenses and cannot be considered in this step.

Rate of return

4. Estimate the Capitalization (Cap) Rate. The capitalization rate is the rate of return (or yield) that an investor expects on the purchase price. The cap rate is found by comparing the NOI of the subject property with the sales prices of comparable properties that have sold in the current market. For example, a comparable property that was producing annual net income of $28,000 recently sold for $200,000. The cap rate is $28,000 ÷ $200,000, or 14%. If other comparable properties sold at prices that yielded essentially the same rate, the appraiser should use a 14% rate for the subject property.

5. Estimate the Property Value. The fifth and final step is to apply the capitalization rate to the property's NOI (annual net income ÷ cap rate = value).

Some valuable points to remember are that (1) the higher the risk, the higher the capitalization rate; (2) as interest rates increase, capitalization rates increase; and (3) if capitalization rates increase but the net income remains constant, the value of the property will decrease.

An example of the income approach to estimate property value follows: An appraiser is estimating the value of a property that has a gross annual income of $18,000. Expenses and the reserve for replacements amount to $9,000 and there is an outstanding mortgage balance of $50,000 payable at $400 per month, including principal and interest at 9%. He is using 5% of the gross annual income as the vacancy factor, and will use a capitalization rate of 12%.

Potential Gross Annual Income	
5 units @ $300 month x 12 months	$18,000
Less vacancy factor (5%)	- 900
Effective Gross Income	$ 17,100
Less expenses and reserves	- 9,000
Net Income	$ 8,100

Capitalize Net Income
Income ÷ Rate = Value
$8,100 ÷ 12% = $67,500

If an appraiser already knows the value and the income, to determine the rate he would divide the income by the value:

Income ÷ Value = Rate
$8,100 ÷ $67,500 = 12%

Or if he knows the value and rate, but wishes to determine the income:

Value x Rate = Income
$67,500 x 12% = $8,100

Often an investor will want to know the cash flow he can expect from the property. This is the income remaining from the gross income after deducting

FIGURE 27.1
Basic Steps in the Appraisal Process

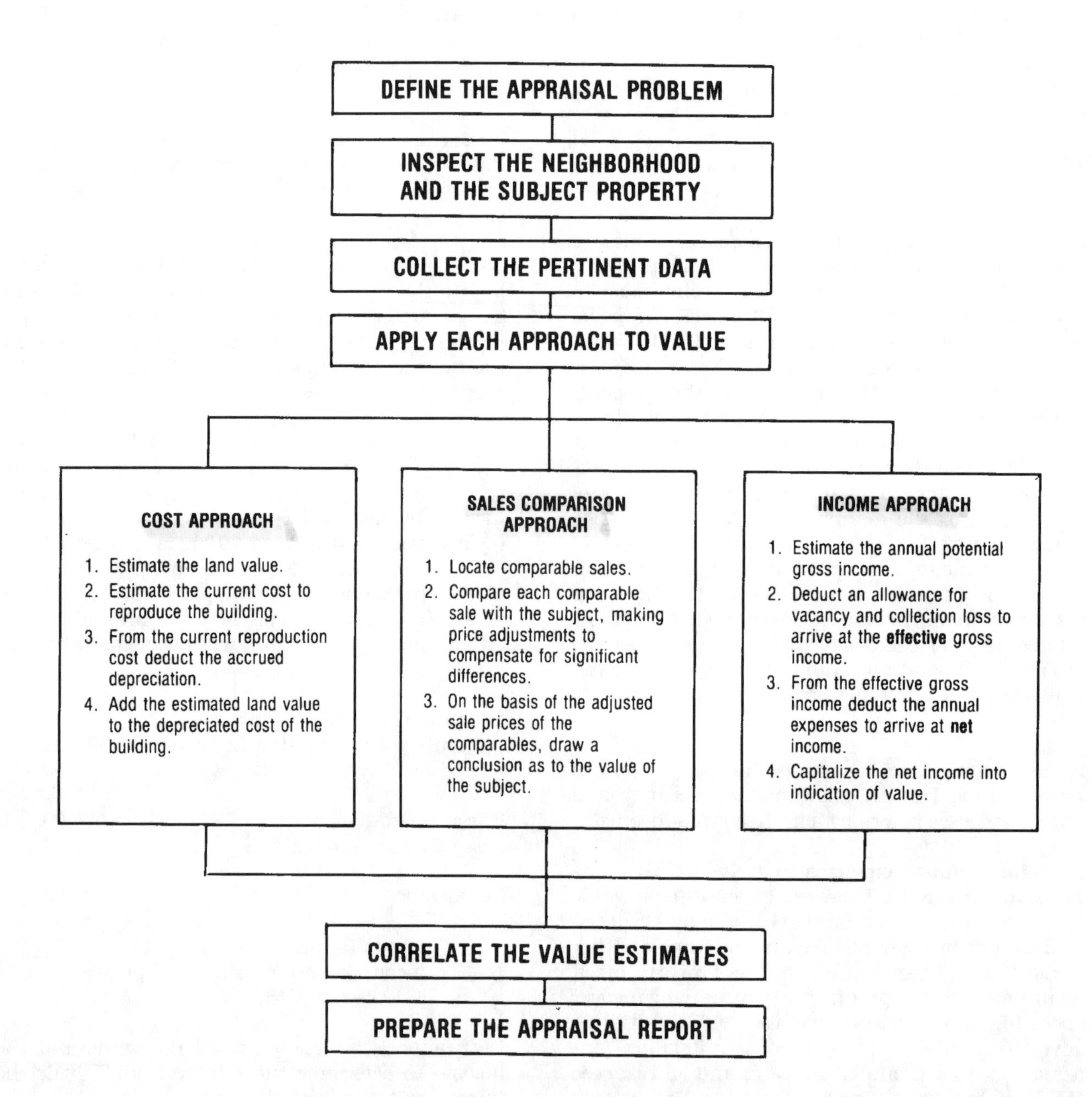

Reprinted from the excellent source *Real Estate Appraising (Step-by-Step)* by Paul G. Creteau, published by Castle Publishing Company, Portland, Maine.

the operating expenses, principal and interest payments, and any income taxes attributable to the investment.

Net Income	$8,100
Less principal and interest payments ($400 x 12)	- 4,800
Cash flow before personal income taxes	$ 3,300

COST APPROACH

The cost approach consists of four basic steps:

1. Estimate the value of the land as if vacant.
2. Estimate the current cost of replacing or reproducing the building, which is usually done by a square or cubic foot measurement of the exterior of the improvement. (Note the distinction between the reproduction cost, which is the present cost of reproducing the improvement with one of an exact replica, and the replacement cost, which is the present cost of replacing the improvement with one of similar utility).

TABLE 27.1: The Cost Approach

1. Estimated cost of vacant land:		$30,000
2. Estimated replacement cost of improvement:		
House: 30' x 50' = 1,500 s.f. x $35 =	52,500	
Garage: 12' x 20' = 240 s.f. x $10.75 =	2,580	
	$55,080	
3. Less depreciation:		
$55,080 ÷ 40yrs. = 1,377 x 10yrs. =	13,770	$41,310
4. Indicated value by cost approach:		$71,310

3. Estimate and deduct the amount of depreciation.
4. Add the estimated land value to the depreciated reproduction or replacement cost of the building to arrive at an indication of the total value of the property.

The methods used in estimating replacement costs are (1) quantity survey method; (2) unit-cost-in-place method; (3) cubic foot method; (4) square foot method; and (5) index method.

1. Quantity Survey Method. Determine the quantity and grade of materials used to replace the subject property (lumber, brick, shingles, etc.), their current prices and the labor hours required to install them. The appraiser adds to these direct costs the indirect costs of building permits, surveys, payroll taxes and contractor's overhead and profit to estimate the cost of the structure. Although this method is accurate, it is extremely time-consuming and its use is generally restricted to the appraisal of historical properties. This is also known as the "contractor's method."

2. Unit-Cost-in-Place Method. Estimate the cost of labor and material combined for each component part of the building, i.e., roof, walls, floor, foundation, etc. When this method is used, some components like roofs and floors are priced on the basis of square feet while others, like plumbing fixtures and windows, are estimated on the basis of price per unit.

3. Square Foot Method. The total cost per square foot of recently constructed buildings comparable to the subject property is multiplied by the floor area of the subject property (computed by measuring the outside perimeter of the building).

4. Cubic Foot Method. Estimate cubic foot area of building (computed by measuring the outside of the building) and apply the cost per cubic foot.

5. Index Method. When this method is used, a factor that represents a percentage increase in construction costs (the index) is applied to the original cost of the subject property. Because it fails to account for individual property variables, it is generally used only as a check on the estimate reached by the other methods.

The principal advantage of using the cost approach is that the replacement cost of a structure will at least establish its **upper limit of value**. In the appraisal of special-purpose or unique properties such as schools, churches, libraries, etc., it becomes the appraiser's most accurate approach, since these property types seldom produce a rental income and are rarely bought or sold in the open market. The principal disadvantage of the cost approach lies in the fact that the cost to create something does not always indicate true value, as there may be a considerable difference between the current cost of replacement of a structure and its actual value in the open market. Also, since physical deterioration and functional and economic obsolescence cannot be precisely measured, it is often difficult to accurately estimate the value of an older structure.

Appraiser Licensing Requirements

As of April 1, 1992, New Jersey's Appraisal Licensing Law requires that appraisers must be licensed or certified to make fee appraisals for federally related transactions. Licensing and certification are handled by the state Real Estate Appraisers Board in the Department of Law and Public Safety, Division of Consumer Affairs, 124 Halsey St., 6th floor, Newark, NJ 07102; telephone (973) 504-6480.

Residential License. In order to become a State-Licensed Real Estate Appraiser (SLREA), an applicant must complete 90 classroom hours approved by the state Real Estate Appraisers Board; have at least 2,000 hours appraisal experience in no fewer than 24 months; be at least 18 years of age; have a high school diploma or equivalency certificate; and pass a state examination. SLREAs may appraise non-complex one- to four-family units having a **transaction value** of less than $250,000. Transaction value is defined as "the amount of the loan" (for loans) or "the market value of the real property interest involved" (for sales, leases, exchanges, etc.).

Residential Certification. In order to become licensed as a State-Certified Residential Real Estate Appraiser (SCRREA), an applicant must possess the same qualifications as a SLREA, and in addition must complete 30 classroom hours approved by the state Real Estate Appraisers Board and must have accumulated 2,500 hours of appraisal experience in no fewer than 24 months. A SCRREA may appraise one- to four-family residential units without regard to the transaction value or complexity. A SCRREA may also appraise commercial property having a transaction value of less than $250,000.

General Certification. In order to become licensed as a State-Certified General Real Estate Appraiser (SCGREA), an applicant must first qualify as a SCRREA and then successfully complete an additional 60 classroom hours in courses approved by the state Real Estate Appraisers Board. In addition, applicants must demonstrate 3,000 hours of appraisal experience in no fewer than 30 months, of which at least 50% must be in non-residential appraisal work. SCGREAs may appraise all types of real property, regardless of transaction value or complexity.

Apprentice Program. An apprentice permit may be issued to an individual who will work under the direct supervision of a licensed or certified appraiser who certifies that he or she will directly supervise and be responsible for work performed by the apprentice appraiser. Applicants for the apprentice program must be: at least 18 years old; of good moral character; have a high school diploma or its equivalent; and successfully complete a Board-approved course of 15 hours on the Uniform Standards of Appraisal Practice within six months prior to filing application for the apprentice permit.

Continuing Education. As of January 1, 1998, licensees are required to successfully complete the Uniform Standards of Professional Appraisal Practice course every other biennial renewal period. This 15-hour course qualifies as continuing education credit as part of the 28 hours of recertification credit. Licensees are required to maintain continuing education records for at least four years.

Please call the Real Estate Appraisers Board concerning any revisions to rules and regulations.

KEY WORDS

Accrued Depreciation
Appraisal
Basis
Capitalization
Capitalization Rate
Comparable
Cost
Cost Approach
Depreciation
Deterioration
Economic Life
Economic Obsolescence
Effective Gross Income
Functional Obsolescence
Gross Income Multiplier
Highest and Best Use
Income Approach
Market Data Approach
Market Value
Net Income
Physical Depreciation
Price
Recapture Rate
Reproduction Cost
Value

CHAPTER 27
Review Questions
(Answers on page 560)

1. Which of the following might be classified as functional obsolescence?
   (A) Exterior needs painting.
   (B) Property fronts on a busy expressway.
   (C) Very small bedroom closets.
   (D) Neighborhood is 35 to 50 years old.

2. When capitalization is sought, a person is particularly interested in:
   (A) the potential future value.
   (B) cost value.
   (C) total capital invested.
   (D) converting income into value.

3. In estimating the value lost by a structure due to physical deterioration, the appraiser places greatest emphasis on:
   (A) the condition of the surrounding buildings.
   (B) the zoning of the neighborhood.
   (C) the original cost of the building.
   (D) the observed condition of the subject building.

4. Of the three methods of appraising properties, reproduction cost approach is particularly appropriate and would give the most accurate value in the appraisal of a(n):
   (A) new home.
   (B) multiple dwelling.
   (C) old home.
   (D) medium-age home.

5. The formula used in direct capitalization of income property valuation is:
   (A) value equals cap rate divided by income.
   (B) value equals annual net income divided by cap rate.
   (C) value equals income multiplied by cap rate.
   (D) value equals income divided by net assets.

6. The economic life of a building has come to an end when:
   (A) the building ceases to represent the highest and best use of the land.
   (B) the value of the land and the building equals the value of the land only.
   (C) the rent produced is valued at less than a similar amount of money invested elsewhere could produce.
   (D) the reserve for depreciation equals the cost to replace the building.

7. An appraiser's fee is typically based on which of the following?
   (A) Time and expenses.
   (B) Percent of value estimate.
   (C) Percent of assessed valuation.
   (D) Percent of income.

8. All but one of the following is used to estimate value:
   (A) Improvements.
   (B) Deterioration.
   (C Livelihood.
   (D) Economic life.

9. In regard to the capitalization rate:
   (A) as it increases, value of property increases.
   (B) as it decreases, value of property decreases.
   (C) as it increases, value of property decreases.
   (D) changing capitalization rate has no effect on value of the property.

10. The difference between the cost of replacement and current valuation is equal to:
    (A) accrued depreciation.
    (B) assessed valuation.
    (C) market value.
    (D) book value.

11. The most widely used approach to appraisal of real property is the:
    (A) income approach.
    (B) sales comparison approach.
    (C) cost approach.
    (D) SWAG approach.

12. The useful life of a building, or period of time after which the income provided by it is not sufficient to warrant its maintenance, is called:
    (A) recapture limit.
    (B) economic life.
    (C) reversion limit.
    (D) investment duration.

13. Which of the following is NOT an example of physical deterioration?
    (A) Poor floor plan.
    (B) Peeling paint.
    (C) Cracked patio.
    (D) Missing shingles.

(Quiz continues on next page)

14. Physical deterioration most closely means:
    (A) obsolescence.
    (B) wear and tear.
    (C) repair.
    (D) recapture.

15. The sales comparison approach to value gives:
    (A) indication of the lowest value.
    (B) indication of the highest value.
    (C) indication of the future value.
    (D) range of probable value.

16. A homogeneous community has what effect on real estate values?
    (A) Stabilizes them.
    (B) Causes the value to increase.
    (C) Causes the value to decrease.
    (D) Doesn't have any effect.

17. A house with four bedrooms and one bath is an example of:
    (A) economic obsolescence.
    (B) functional obsolescence.
    (C) physical deterioration.
    (D) all of the above.

18. Real estate values are most affected by:
    (A) location.
    (B) availability of money.
    (C) appraisal.
    (D) national trends.

19. The trend in architectural design in a neighborhood is toward more contemporary styled homes. Because of this trend a conservatively designed home will tend to:
    (A) depreciate in value more rapidly.
    (B) depreciate in value less rapidly.
    (C) stay the same value.
    (D) appreciate in value.

20. A residence located in an area where there are factories and plants, and where there is much smoke and dust, is suffering from:
    (A) physical depreciation.
    (B) external obsolescence.
    (C) functional obsolescence.
    (D) None of the above.

21. All but which one of the following would be considered in the cost approach appraisal method?
    (A) Operating expenses.
    (B) Depreciation.
    (C) Land value.
    (D) Replacement cost.

22. In estimating value, the before and after method is used most often with:
    (A) condemnation.
    (B) exchange.
    (C) cost of reproduction.
    (D) option.

23. Functional obsolescence is a decrease in value due to:
    (A) being "outdated."
    (B) decline in neighborhood.
    (C) something wearing out.
    (D) excessive cost.

24. Market value is most closely related to:
    (A) selling price.
    (B) replacement price.
    (C) analysis.
    (D) reproduction price.

25. With respect to an appraisal, which of the following is NOT correct?
    (A) It is the appraiser's opinion of market value.
    (B) It is the appraiser's conclusion of market value.
    (C) It is the appraiser's estimate of market value.
    (D) It is the appraiser's determination of market value.

26. The method most frequently used to determine value for a fire insurance policy is:
    (A) sales comparison.
    (B) cost approach.
    (C) income approach.
    (D) declining balance.

27. Which of the following factors would have little or no effect in determining the value of a commercial property?
    (A) Purpose of the appraisal.
    (B) Income from property.
    (C) Original cost of the property.
    (D) Zoning.

28. The use of the gross multiplier to assist in appraising real property leased to various tenants is based upon:
    (A) gross income in relation to capitalized value.
    (B) relationship between rental value and sales price of property.
    (C) gross income and anticipated gross income.
    (D) scheduled gross income and expected net income.

29. In appraising a house, the appraiser finds that Comparable A is similar to the subject property and sold for $180,000. Comparable B is also similar except it has one additional bedroom and sold for $200,000. In regard to the extra bedroom, what adjustment is made?
    (A) Add $20,000 to the subject property.
    (B) Add $20,000 to Comparable A.
    (C) Subtract $20,000 from the subject property.
    (D) Subtract $20,000 from Comparable B.

30. The amount which a seller who does not have to sell will accept from a buyer who does not have to buy is called:
    (A) market value.
    (B) market price.
    (C) assessed value.
    (D) appraised value.

31. The definition of market value assumes that:
    (A) the buyer is not under pressure to buy and the seller is not under pressure to sell.
    (B) the property has been on the market for a reasonable length of time.
    (C) Both A and B.
    (D) Neither A nor B.

32. Which of the following statements is true?
    (A) Market price and market value are interchangeable terms.
    (B) An appraiser would most likely use the cost approach to estimate the value of a church.
    (C) The income approach is used for most appraisals.
    (D) The cost approach is used to estimate the value of vacant land.

33. If the subject property has central air conditioning valued at $2,000, and the comparable does not, the sales price of the comparable is adjusted by:
    (A) + $2,000.
    (B) - $2,000.
    (C) - $1,000.
    (D) Can't be computed based on the information given.

34. Accrued depreciation may be defined as:
    (A) future depreciation.
    (B) the total depreciation from the time of construction to the date of appraisal from all causes.
    (C) deferred maintenance.
    (D) none of the above.

CHAPTER TWENTY-EIGHT

LAND DESCRIPTION

Every parcel of land that becomes the object of a sale or lease, or the security of an obligation, must be properly identified or described. These descriptions are often referred to as **legal descriptions**, and are based on a land survey of the property consisting of research of the property boundary and adjoining property boundaries, field notes, measurements, analysis of the record title and the resulting survey plan. In New Jersey, the only person permitted by law to perform a survey is a licensed Professional Land Surveyor.

A survey, therefore, is the process by which a parcel of land is measured to identify the exact boundaries of the property and determine if all structures are completely within those boundaries. When a survey is performed in connection with a conveyance of land, the surveyor is required to furnish the client with a new property description based on the results of the survey, unless the survey and record description of the property are identical.

Land descriptions in New Jersey are developed through one or more of the following techniques: (1) metes and bounds; (2) boundary system; (3) lot and block number on a recorded map; (4) monuments; (5) street address; and (6) tax identification.

METES AND BOUNDS DESCRIPTION

Metes are the bearings (direction and angle) and distance of the course, and the bounds refer to monuments and boundaries. Metes and bounds are commonly used in the legal descriptions found in deeds and are used when it is necessary or desirable to describe a tract of land with irregular boundaries. They are also used when the property referred to is not covered by a duly-recorded map or when it is of such an irregular shape as to make it impractical to describe otherwise. Old descriptions of this type used trees, stones, creeks and other objects as markers which have since disappeared, moved or otherwise been altered, often making descriptions indefinite.

These physically identifiable objects are called **monuments** (described below), and would take precedence over linear measurements if there was any discrepancy. Sometimes reference is made to "benchmarks," which are monuments used to establish elevation.

Metes and bounds descriptions start at a designated point called the "point of beginning" (P.O.B.), and proceed around the boundaries of the parcel by reference to linear measurements, directions and courses, ending at the P.O.B. Metes and bounds

FIGURE 28.1

The Four Quadrants

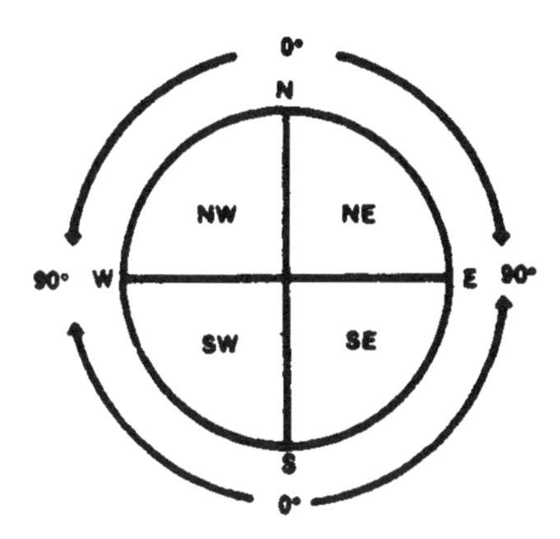

FIGURE 28.2

Metes & Bounds Description

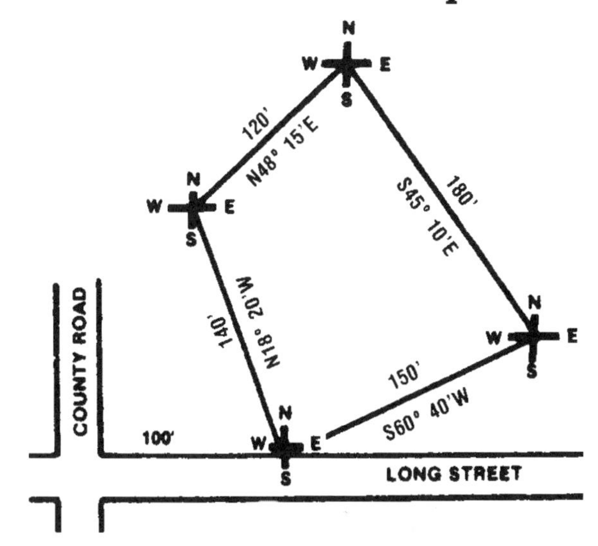

Beginning at a point on the North side of Long Street, 100 feet East from the corner formed from the North side of Long Street and the East side of County Road; thence N18°20'W, 140 feet; thence N48°15'E, 120 feet; thence S45°10'E, 180 feet; thence S60°40'W, 150 feet to the point of beginning.

descriptions are illustrated, typically with a circle on which the points of a compass have been superimposed. This circle is further divided into four quadrants (quarters), each identified according to the angle formed by its boundary lines. The quadrants are North-East, South-East, South-West and North-West. Each quadrant contains 90 degrees, measured from North toward the East or West or from South toward East or West. A bearing of the same degrees in the opposite quadrant is still describing the same line, but traveling or measured in the opposite direction. For example, a bearing of "North 45 degrees East" would be on the same line as "South 45 degrees West," depending on which direction you were traveling (see Figure 28.1). An example of a metes and bounds description can be seen in Figure 28.2.

Bounds Description

A bounds description is used to describe property and easements solely by reference to the adjoining owners. For example, a bounds description might describe a property as "bounded on the north by Jones, the east by Jenkins, the south by. . .," and so on. Many of the telephone and utility service easements and almost every title report contain at least one of these.

LOT AND BLOCK NUMBER ON A RECORDED MAP

When large tracts of land are subdivided into building lots by a licensed Professional Land Surveyor, the developer files a map of the tract in the recording offices of the county clerk of the county in which the land is located. The plan is then made part of the public record in the county courthouse. These maps must be prepared and filed in accordance with the New Jersey Map Filing Law. Each block plotted on the plan is identified with a number or letter. Each lot within the block is numbered. In describing a lot from a recorded plot, the lot and block number, the name or number of the subdivision plot and the name of the county and state would be used.

A typical description by lot number on a recorded map might read as follows:

"Shown and designated as Lot 125 on Map entitled, 'Map of Section 5, Tall Timbers Subdivision, Borough of North Caldwell, Essex County, New Jersey, property of Ruffalo Brothers' dated June 1955 made by Miller and McGiffert, Inc. Engineers, filed in the Registrar's Office of Essex County, New Jersey, November 9, 1955 in Case No. 2145."

FIGURE 28.3
A Description Made By Monuments Alone

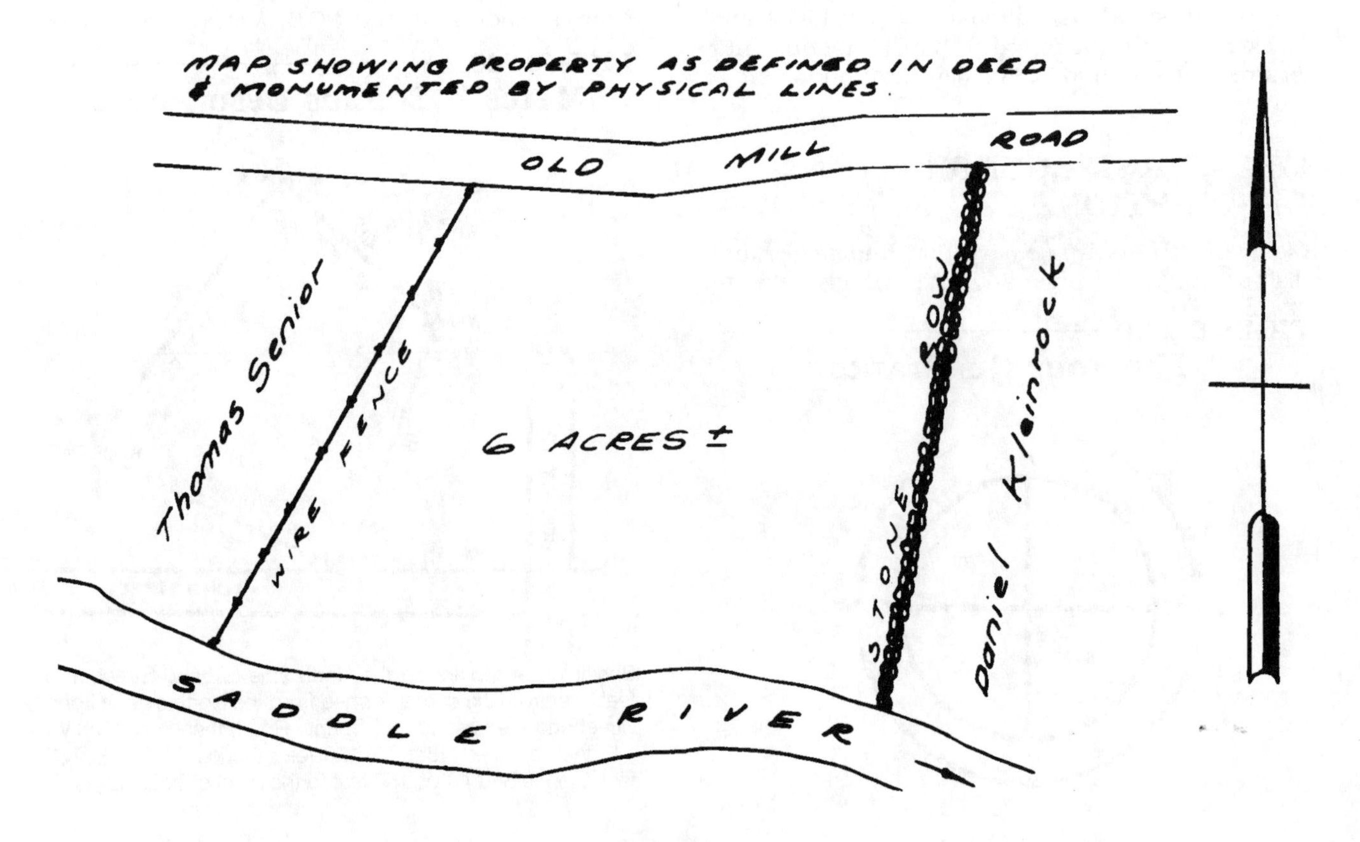

MONUMENTS

Land parcels in rural areas are sometimes described by monuments which describe the boundaries or corners of property. A monument is a marker and can be either natural, such as a river or tree, or man-made, such as a fence or cement-filled pipe. The most common survey marker today is an iron pin or an iron pipe driven in the ground. All modern survey markers are required to have identification indicating the surveyor responsible for setting the marker. The ultimate users (purchasers) must be advised of their right to have corner markers set as part of a survey and they must sign a waiver if they do not want the markers set.

The P.O.B. in a metes and bounds description is usually a monument. A description using the physical boundaries of the property as monumentation is more economical but there is no way that it can be plotted. A second problem that might be encountered is the loss of the physical boundaries by either natural or man-made forces. Without measurements these lines cannot be relocated. The following is an example of a description made by monuments alone, as depicted in Figure 28.3:

"All that tract of land situated in the Borough of Upper Saddle River, County of Bergen, State of New Jersey, more particularly bounded and described as follows:

"Beginning at a point in the southerly line of Old Mill Road, at the division line between lands of Thomas Senior to the west, and party of the first part to the east, and running from thence:

1. Easterly, along the southerly line of Old Mill Road along the several courses thereof, to the

FIGURE 28.4
A Metes & Bounds Description

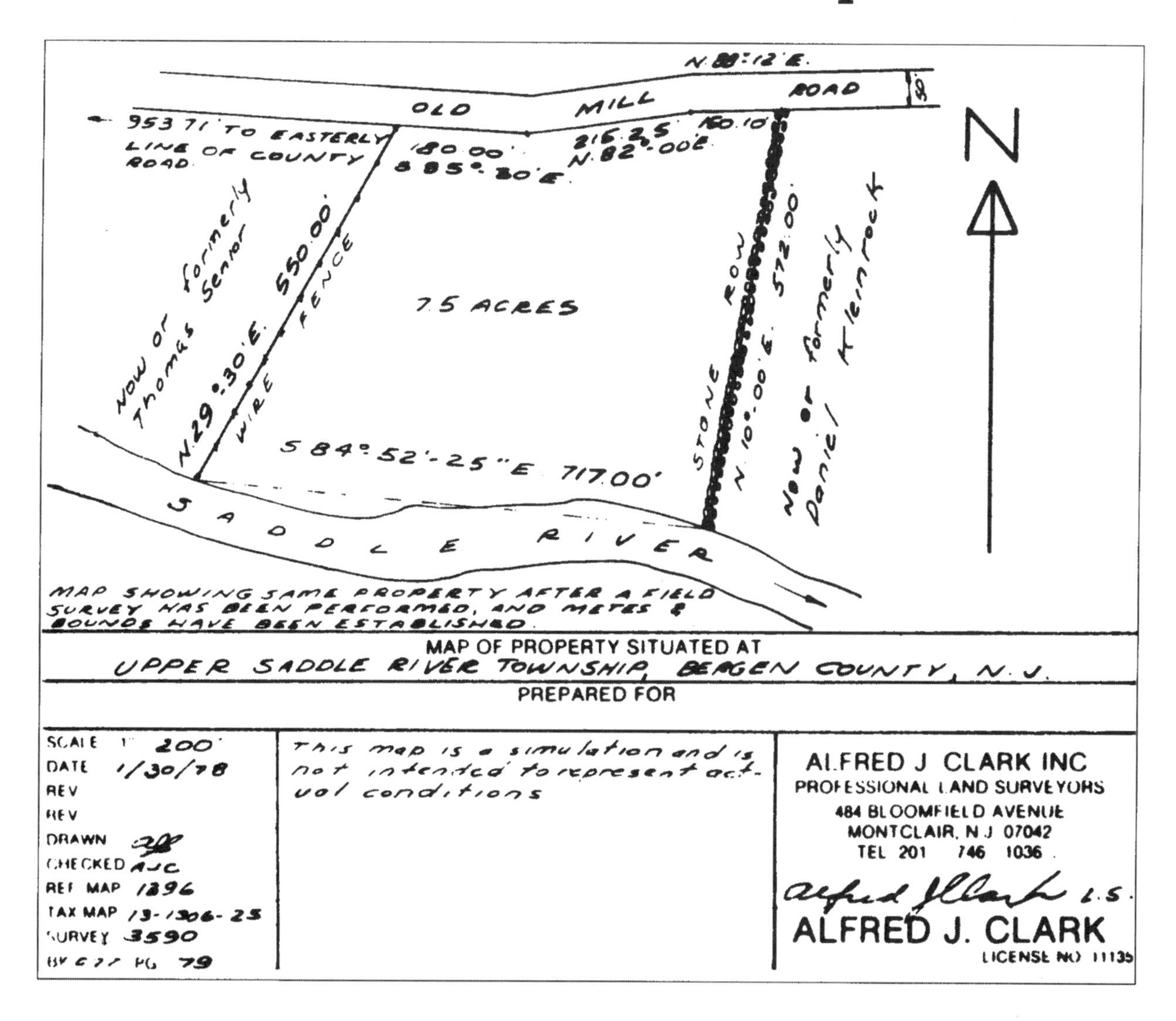

FIGURE 28.5

Tax Map Key

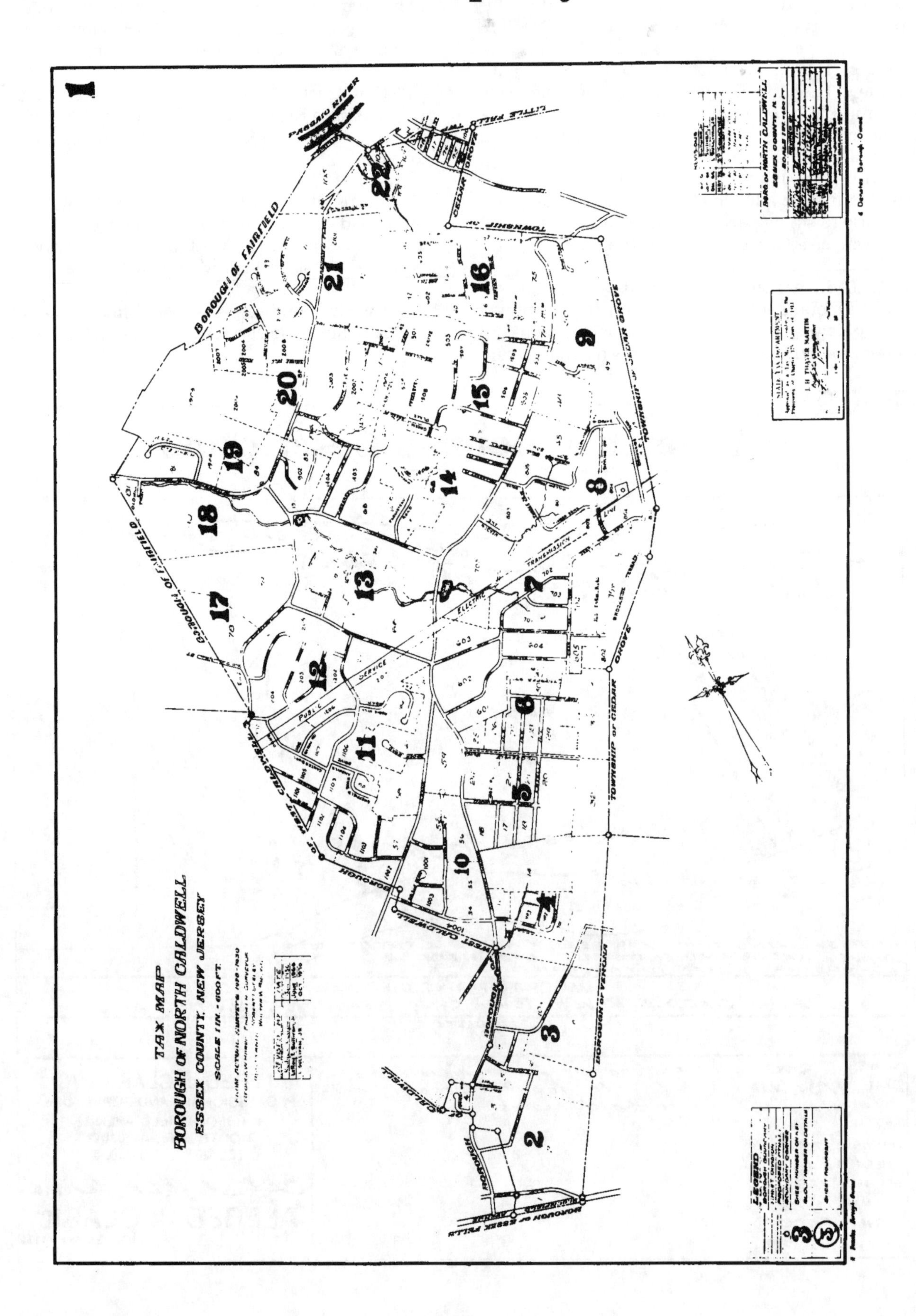

FIGURE 28.6

Lot and Block Number

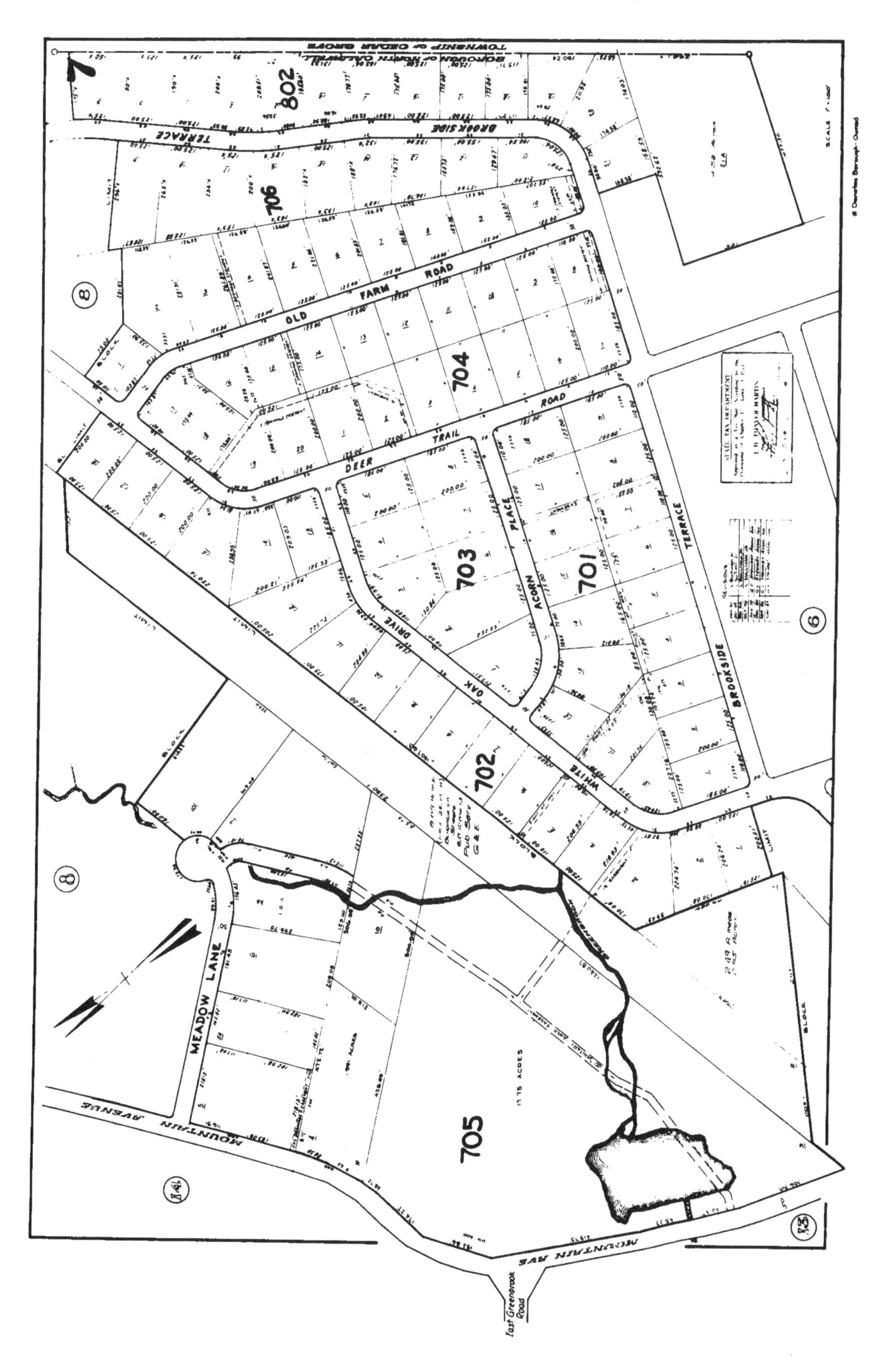

westerly line of Daniel Kleinrock, as marked by the center line of a stonewall; thence
2. Southerly, along the center line of said stonewall, to the Northerly side of the Saddle River; thence
3. Westerly, along the shore line of said river, to the said division line between Thomas Senior to the west, and party of the first part to the east; thence
4. Northerly, along said division line, and along a wire fence marking said line, to the southerly line of Old Mill Road, and the point of beginning.

"Containing six acres more or less."

A new metes and bounds description as it might be prepared by a Professional Land Surveyor is shown in Figure 28.4.

"Beginning at a point in the southerly line of Old Mill Road, distant 953.71' easterly from its intersection with the easterly line of County Road, and running from thence:

1. South 85°-30' East, along the southerly line of Old Mill Road, 180.00', to an angle; thence
2. North 82°-00' East, still along the same, 215.25', to another angle; thence
3. North 88°-12' East, still along the same, 150.10', to the northwest corner of lands now or formerly of Daniel Kleinrock; thence
4. South 10°-00' West, along the westerly line of said lands, and along the center line of a stone wall, 572.00', to the northerly side of the Saddle River; thence
5. Westerly along the various courses of the westerly line of the Saddle River (North 84°-52'-25" West, 717.00', if traversed in a straight line) to the easterly line of lands now or formerly of Thomas Senior; thence
6. North 29°-30' East, along said line, and along the center line of a wire fence, 550.00' to the southerly line of Old Mill Road, and the point of the beginning.

"Containing 7.50 acres in accordance with a survey by Alfred J. Clark, Inc., Professional Land Surveyors, dated January 30, 1978."

STREET ADDRESS

Street address is the most unreliable of all descriptions, and although it may be used to describe a property on offer forms (binders), listings and agreements of sale, this type of description should never be used in a deed or mortgage, or to describe unimproved land. The street address can appropriately be used to support a more definite description, for example one by lot and block or metes and bounds. The legal description is generally followed by a phrase such as ". . .and more commonly known as 123 Sunset Lane, Boonton, New Jersey."

This statement assures a meeting of the minds regarding the parcel being conveyed.

TAX IDENTIFICATION

Each municipality in New Jersey has a book of tax maps prepared by the licensed land surveyor, who is obligated to prepare such maps in full compliance with the legal requirements pertaining to such maps. This book first presents a "key map" showing the entire community, its boundaries, street names, patterns and road network. The key map divides the community into various areas and assigns a number to each area. This number indicates the page number in the map book on which the detail map for an area can be found.

For instance, if you want to find the lot and block number of 34 Deer Trail Road, North Caldwell, New Jersey, the key map for North Caldwell (Figure 28.5) would direct you to page 7 of the map book for the detail on 34 Deer Trail Road. By turning to page 7 of the map book (Figure 28.6) you could identify the property as lot 18, block 704. You could also determine that the dimensions of this lot are 125' x 175', which is 21,875 square feet or approximately 1/2 acre. The circled numbers on the detail map (Figure 28.6) indicate the sheet numbers of adjoining properties. The bold "No. 7" in the upper right hand corner of the key map indicates the page number of the map book. Therefore, the map book of North Caldwell contains 22 pages, page 1 of which is the key map.

FIGURE 28.7 Subdivision of Two Full Quadrangles

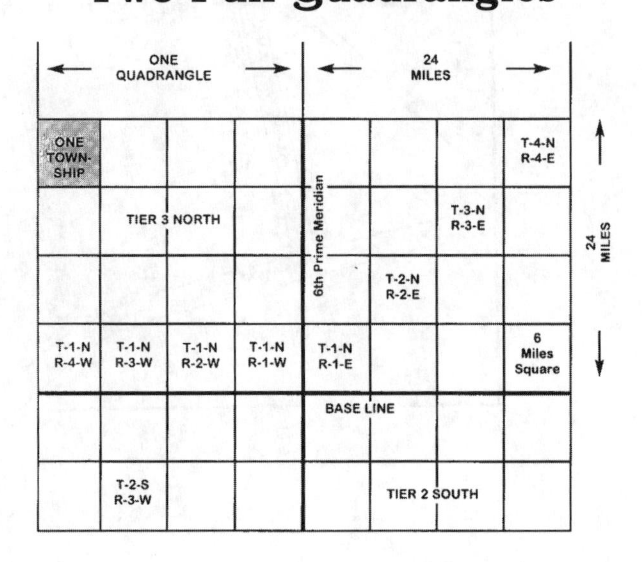

FIGURE 28.8
The Sections in a Township

36	31	32	33	34	35	36	31
1	6	5	4	3	2	1	6
12	7	8	9	10	11	12	7
13	18	17	16	15	14	13	18
24	19	20	21	22	23	24	19
25	30	29	28	27	26	25	30
36	31	32	33	34	35	36	31
1	6	5	4	3	2	1	6

6 Miles

GOVERNMENT SURVEY SYSTEM

In the late 1700s the vast regions of the West were being explored and settled, and it became apparent that a plan needed to be devised which would allow for locating specific plots of land. Thus a system of rectangular survey was eventually adopted from a plan originally formed in 1785. Generally, the states lying west of the Ohio River (except Texas) and Florida employ this system. **It is not used in New Jersey.**

The government survey was designed to create a checkerboard of identical squares covering a given area. The largest squares measure 24 miles on each side and are called "quadrangles." Each quadrangle is further divided into 16 squares called "townships" whose four boundaries each measure six miles and run north-south and east-west. The north-south line is called a **meridian**, and the east-west line is

FIGURE 28.9
Detailed Map of a Section

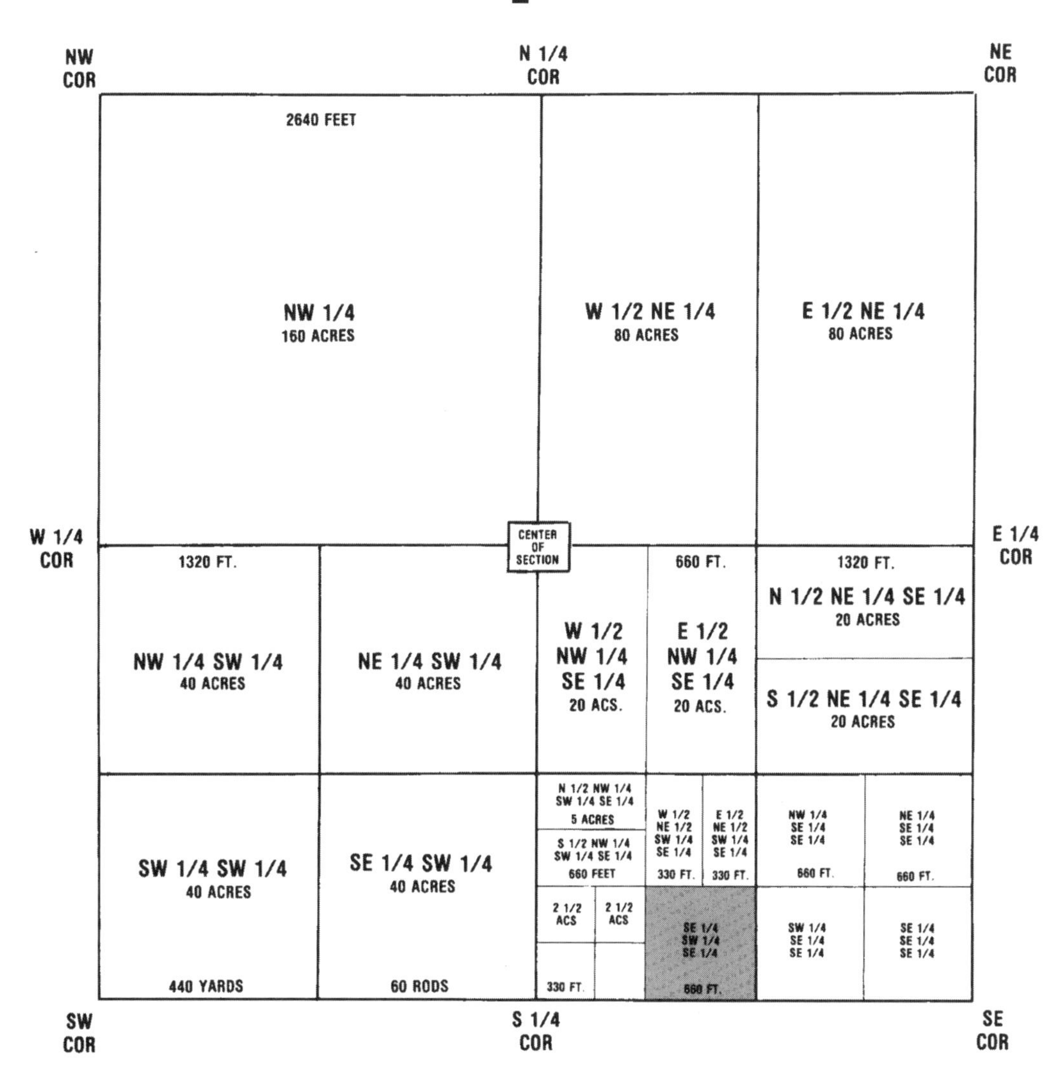

referred to as the **base line**. A column of townships running north-south is called a "range" and is numbered numerically east and west according to its distance from the principal meridian. There are now 36 principal meridians located in different parts of the United States. A row of townships running east and west is called a "tier" and is numbered according to the distance from the base line.

The sketch in Figure 28.7 shows the subdivision of two full quadrangles with the 6th Principal Meridian acting as the dividing line. A portion of two quadrangles is shown below the base line. A township is shaded in.

In Figure 28.8, note that the numbers of the sections are so positioned so that each lot is adjacent to at least one lot numbered sequentially. A section is one square mile and contains 640 acres.

In reading rectangular descriptions, one reads backwards from the general part of the description to the specific part at the beginning. For example, a tract of land described as SE1/4SW1/4SE1/4 would be identified by reading from right to left, first identifying the southeast quarter of the entire section, then the southwest quarter of that quarter, and finally, the southeast quarter of the quarter-quarter section. Thus, SE1/4SW1/4SE1/4 contains 10 acres (shaded in Figure 28.9).

IMPORTANT FACTS ABOUT LAND MEASUREMENT

Be sure to know the following land measurements as they apply to legal descriptions:

1. A square mile contains 640 acres.
2. A circle contains 360 degrees.
   Each degree contains 60 minutes (60').
   Each minute contains 60 seconds (60").
3. A mile is 5,280 feet or 1,760 yards.
4. An acre contains 43,560 square feet.
5. A chain is 66 feet.
6. A front foot is one foot on a street line or waterfront line with each front foot extending the depth of the lot.

See Appendix III in Chapter 36 for other land measurements.

KEY WORDS

- Acre
- Benchmark
- Chain
- Front Foot
- Lot and Block Number
- Legal Description
- Metes and Bounds
- Monument
- Point of Beginning
- Survey
- Tax Map Key

CHAPTER 28
Review Questions
(Answers on page 561)

1. New Jersey's system of land descriptions includes, but is not limited to:
   (A) rectangular survey.
   (B) government survey.
   (C) metes and bounds.
   (D) geodetic survey.

2. Where must you find the most complete legal description?
   (A) Listing agreement.
   (B) Closing statement.
   (C) Deed.
   (D) Lease.

3. In order for a buyer to be certain that the property being purchased has no encroachments, the buyer should obtain:
   (A) purchaser's policy of title insurance.
   (B) survey.
   (C) certificate of no defense.
   (D) warranty deed.

4. In connection with a metes and bounds description, official markers on the property used to determine elevations are called:
   (A) monuments.
   (B) benchmarks.
   (C) attachments.
   (D) meters.

5. The boundary lines of land, with their terminal points and angles, are called:
   (A) benchmarks.
   (B) geodetic survey points.
   (C) metes and bounds.
   (D) longitude and latitude.

6. Legal descriptions in New Jersey include:
   (A) a metes and bounds description.
   (B) monuments.
   (C) tax map identification.
   (D) all of the above.

7. The person most apt to use a benchmark in his profession would be a:
   (A) lawyer.
   (B) carpenter.
   (C) general contractor.
   (D) surveyor.

8. Which of the following can be natural to the environment?
   (A) Benchmarks.
   (B) Metes of survey.
   (C) Old liens.
   (D) Monuments.

9. Which of the following systems of land descriptions gives a starting point and the direction and the length of lines to be run?
   (A) Monuments.
   (B) Recorded plats.
   (C) Courses and distances.
   (D) Metes and bounds.

10. The process by which a piece of land is measured and its area ascertained, and the paper containing a statement of the course, distance and quantity of land, is called:
   (A) title search.
   (B) title insurance.
   (C) survey.
   (D) abstract.

11. Which of the following legal descriptions is NOT used in New Jersey?
   (A) Street address.
   (B) Monuments.
   (C) Government survey system.
   (D) Tax identification.

12. Which of the following terms would NOT be found in a metes and bounds description?
   (A) Point of beginning.
   (B) Minutes.
   (C) Seconds.
   (D) Quadrangle.

13. A square mile contains 640 acres. Therefore a square 1/2 mile contains:
   (A) 160 acres.
   (B) 320 acres.
   (C) 80 acres.
   (D) 120 acres.

14. What type of land description is being used in a deed that reads, "All that tract of land beginning at the Southeast corner of Cortlandt St. and William St. and proceeding South 0 degrees for 150 feet, then East 0 degrees for 80 feet, then North 0 degrees for 150 feet, then West 0 degrees for 80 feet to the point of beginning"?
   (A) Monuments.
   (B) Boundaries.
   (C) Tax map identification.
   (D) Metes and bounds.

CHAPTER TWENTY-NINE

PLANNING, ZONING AND BUILDING ORDINANCES

As noted earlier, there are four major governmental limitations on the ownership of real property: (1) the right of eminent domain exercised through a condemnation proceeding, which is the governmental seizure of property for the good of the public with just compensation; (2) escheat, or the right of the state to claim residual land abandoned or left upon the death of a person having neither a will nor heirs; (3) taxation, the right of the government to tax real estate to support services such as police departments and fire departments; and (4) the police power to regulate land use through city planning, zoning and building ordinances. It is this last limitation of public use that shall be the scope of this chapter.

Through the Fifth and Fourteenth Amendments to the United States Constitution, an individual is assured that neither the federal or state government will deprive him of "life, liberty, or property without due process of law." This, however, does not change the inherent police powers of the United States or individual states to make laws and regulations affecting privately owned land for the public good. Land use controls fall into three broad categories: planning and subdivision control, zoning and building ordinances.

PLANNING

The need for community planning, which originally evolved in the Middle Ages, has become acute in modern times due to rapid urban population growth, the remarkable advances in population and the increasing demands of commercial traffic within our cities. The constant change of today's communities parallels their rapid growth, creating a need for flexibility in the design of the overall city and county structure. The goals of planning are aimed not only at correcting existing problems, but, equally as important, are directed toward evolving positive plans to achieve a harmonious balance within a city, while providing for the extremely rapid internal growth of the future.

Although the results of land-use regulations have social, economic and fiscal implications, this chapter is principally concerned with physical or land-use planning by local governments.

Legislative Authority

The power of municipal governments to plan and regulate the development of real estate currently is set forth by the **Municipal Land Use Law** enacted in 1976 (N.J.S.A. 40:55D-1 to 129), which amended, codified and consolidated earlier statues. Under the law, municipalities are required to process and adopt a **master plan** based upon their specific economic, social, and physical features. The master plan is a "blueprint" for the development of lands within a municipality. The plan typically includes "zoning maps" of the community recommended by the planning board for adoption by the governing body. The maps designate areas of proposed uses, such as for residential, commercial, retail, industrial, recreational and open space purposes. Before the plan is approved, detailed investigation is made into relevant factors such as population densities, traffic patterns and environmental considerations.

The plan must be re-examined at least once every six years and either amended or re-adopted. Prior to the enactment of zoning ordinances by the municipal governing body, the land use and housing elements of the master plan must be approved. Ordinances conflicting with the plan may be adopted only by majority vote of the governing body, along with a statement explaining the reasons for departing from the plan.

Planning Boards

The master plan is implemented and interpreted by a **local planning board**. Municipalities may create planning boards which are given authority under state law to prepare and adopt the master plan; hear applications and make decisions on subdivisions, site plans and conditional uses; and prepare a capital improvement program of projects relating to streets, water supply and sewage treatment and other infrastructure. Planning boards may be composed of seven or nine members, with the majority comprised of citizens appointed by the mayor or governing body, along with minority representation from elected or appointed municipal officials. The primary function of the planning board thus deals with longer-term policy in the development of the master plan, and the implementation of that plan through review of site plan and subdivision ordinances and the review of applications for site plan or subdivision approval when no "use" variance is involved.

Municipal zoning ordinances designate the areas or zones of permitted uses and also establish standards for the provision of adequate physical improvements including, but not limited to, off-street parking and loading areas, marginal access roads and roadways, other circulation facilities and water sewerage and drainage facilities. To ensure that changes in land use conform to the zoning ordinance and the master plan, development proposals are subject to site plan and/or subdivision review by the planning board.

The planning board also makes recommendations to the governing body for the adoption of land use regulations, such as required front footage or minimum lot sizes. If two adjoining districts have incompatible uses, planners normally try to place a **buffer zone** between the two zoning districts. A buffer zone is a strip of land separating the incompatible uses, for example, a residential subdivision and an industrial park.

Subdivision Regulation

Planning boards are particularly active in the approval of proposed subdivisions. A **subdivision** is the division of a parcel of land into a number of smaller lots, usually for the purpose of constructing new homes. A community, as part of the master plan, generally adopts subdivision regulations. A developer planning to build homes must submit detailed plans of his project to the planning board to receive subdivision approval prior to beginning construction. Chapter 28 in this text included a discussion of the **plat maps** prepared and submitted by developers to a planning board. In preparing these maps the developer must comply with the subdivision regulations. These regulations generally set standards for building locations, street construction, curbs, sidewalks, street lighting, fire hydrants, storm and sanitary sewers, building and **setback lines** and so on. While planning boards exercise broad authority, they are bound to grant approval when a subdivider has successfully complied with the requirements of the law.

An **environmental impact statement** may also be required to determine the impact of a proposed project, as mandated by local, state or federal regulations. Such factors as population densities, noise, air and water quality traffic patterns and employment would be considered.

Applications to a planning board constitute either a **minor** or **major** subdivision. A minor subdivision is defined as "a subdivision of land for the creation of lots specifically permitted by ordinance as a minor subdivision. . . ." Therefore, a minor subdivision provision in a local ordinance will always specify the number of lots which constitutes a minor subdivision. Typically, when a tract is divided into four lots or less and a street is not extended, it is a **minor subdivision** and a public hearing is not required. If, however, a street is extended or there are more than four lots involved, it is generally a **major subdivision**, which requires a public hearing. In this case, applicants are required to notify all property owners within a radius of 200 feet. Service must be personal or by registered mail. In addition, applicants are required to file a preliminary map of the subdivision with the planning board. The planning board may then review the preliminary map and make certain recommendations to the applicant to effect changes in the number of lots, etc. prior to the filing of a final map for approval. If the property is located on a state or county road, prior approval of the county planning board is required before the local board may act.

Preparing subdivision packages to receive approvals is often an involved and time-consuming operation that involves a good deal of lead-time, as well as preliminary expense for the various kinds of information that must be provided. In addition, if the developer's plan will impact further upon the county or state, approvals from those levels must also be sought.

ZONING

Zoning is the operational arm of general planning in that it is a police power, which gives counties and municipalities the power to control their land for the most beneficial use of the population, both socially and economically.

The zoning statute states that the purpose of zoning is "to lessen congestion in the streets; secure safety from fire, flood or panic; promote health, morals and the general welfare; provide adequate light and air; prevent the overcrowding of land and buildings; and to avoid undue concentration of the population."

Zoning establishes land-use districts and sets different restrictions and standards within each district. Generally, the use districts are divided into four basic classifications: "R" for residential, "C" for commercial, "I" for industrial and "A" for agricultural. Each classification usually includes a number of sub-categories. For instance, industrial zones may be divided into light and heavy industrial zones; residential may be divided into one-family and multi-family zones; multi-family may be divided into low-rise, medium-rise, high-rise, and so on. Many large cities have dozens of different use zones, each having different restrictions and standards.

Zoning ordinances also address the manner of use permitted for lands located within a particular zoning district by regulating such items as maximum building height, minimum lot size and floor space requirements, or nuisance regulations controlling such things as signs, noise or noxious odors. Other requirements may specify the maximum building size permitted to occupy a parcel of land, off-street parking requirements, prohibitions against building in flood plains, open space requirements, restrictions favoring housing for the elderly and **setback lines**. Setbacks are imaginary lines beyond which a structure may not be built. Setbacks in the front of a property are sometimes called **building lines**; those on the side of a property, **sideyard requirements** and those in the rear of the property, **rear yard requirements**.

Non-conforming Uses

When a zoning ordinance is implemented and a zoning district is created, some uses may exist which do not conform to the zoning ordinance. These preexisting uses are called **non-conforming uses**, and result from the particular property being lawfully used prior to the passage of new zoning regulations. The non-conforming use is generally permitted to remain ("grandfathered") under the municipal land use regulations, so long as the property is used for the same purpose and it is not destroyed. If the use were to change or cease to be continuous, or if the property were destroyed, the owner would have to conform to current zoning regulation or seek a variance. Only current uses of land may qualify as nonconforming uses. Vacant land, therefore, cannot qualify as a nonconforming use. If a property is sold, the new owner may continue the nonconforming use of the property, as its sale would not be considered a discontinuance or abandonment of use.

The delicate nature of the non-conforming use is best illustrated by its comparison with a use variance. The variance is a right to a use otherwise not permitted by the zoning board. In substance, the use then becomes a non-conforming use that runs with the land. If a building allowed by a variance is substantially destroyed by fire or otherwise, the owner may rebuild it without municipal approval. If, however, the destroyed building were a non-conforming use, municipal approval would be required for the new construction.

Zoning Board of Adjustment

In contrast to the policy responsibilities of the planning board, a zoning board of adjustment in each municipality is appointed to interpret zoning questions and to grant **variances**, and to otherwise administer the ordinance. A variance is a type of relief granted by a zoning authority to allow for a specific violation of the zoning requirements, usually to alleviate a hardship. Variances are similar to zoning changes, but while a zoning change is a request to actually change the use of the land, a variance is a request to do some act contrary to the usual rule. For example, a variance might be granted to the owner of an undersized lot to reduce the sideyard requirements slightly to be able to fit a building on it. Other matters for which a variance may be sought include setback requirements, density, parking, etc.

Application for a variance is made to the zoning board of adjustment or planning board, depending on the type of variance. All hearings of the board of adjustment and planning board are public and all property owners within 200 feet must be notified of the hearing as described above in connection with application for major subdivisions.

An applicant has no vested right to obtain a variance, but must prove that his unique hardship warrants the granting of it. There is a presumption that a municipality's zoning regulations are reasonable. An applicant for a "use" variance must satisfy both "positive" criteria or "special reasons" for the grant of the variance—such as the proposed site is particularly suitable for the intended use, or the proposed project's overall contribution to the public interest—and the absence of "negative" criteria, meaning that the variance can be granted without substantial detriment to the public good and that it is not inconsistent with the intent and purpose of the master plan and zoning ordinance. A variance does not change the zoning of the property in question, but simply grants permission to exempt it from the zoning regulations in force for the balance of the zoning district. Unlike the planning board, the zoning board is composed of seven members, none of whom may be elected officials or municipal employees.

Zoning Appeals

Appeals from decisions of both planning boards or zoning boards of adjustment may be made to the municipal governing body, which is required to decide the appeal within 95 days of the published decision of the planning or zoning board. If a zoning ordinance is attacked as invalid, the challenger has the burden of proof of establishing the invalidity of the ordinance. Appeals may be made against zoning ordinances on the ground that they are illegal, discriminatory or a denial of due process and the equal protection of the laws. Appeals may also be made on the ground that the zoning office misinterpreted the code.

Amendments

An owner who is unsuccessful in obtaining a variance may attempt to have the area rezoned through a process called **amendment**. The amendment can be requested by a property owner or by the local government. The zoning board usually hears requests at a public hearing, after which the board makes a recommendation to the local governmental body, which will make the final decision.

Exclusionary Zoning

Exclusionary zoning involves zoning regulation(s) which effectively serve to limit housing opportunities to low- and moderate-income families. Such practices have been declared illegal when they serve to reduce housing opportunity for significant segments of the population in developing communities, which impact upon regional housing needs and exclude certain uses and certain types of structures from certain districts.

Formerly, zoning ordinances that required minimum lot sizes for residential use were sustained in New Jersey. For example, in *Fischer v. Bedminster Township*, 11 NJ 194 (1952) the Supreme Court held that a township ordinance which restricted construction of residences in a strictly rural area upon a plot of less than five acres was not unreasonable per se. And in *Lionshead Lake, Inc. v. Wayne Township*, 11 NJ 165 (1952) the New Jersey Supreme Court held that the ordinance, fixing a minimum living-floor space of 1,068 square feet for a one-story building and 1,300 square feet for a two-story dwelling, was reasonable and valid.

More recently, however, suits have been filed in New Jersey against various municipalities accusing them of attracting taxpaying industries while keeping out, by means of "large lot" zoning, the people who work in these industries and their families. For example, in *Molino v. Mayor and Council of Glassboro*, 116 NJ 195, a building developer challenged a local ordinance which stipulated that in multi-family dwelling units, 70% of the units had to be one bedroom, no more than 25% could be two bedrooms, and no more than 5% could contain three-bedroom units.

The court held that the borough's zoning ordinance was, in effect, an effort to restrict the population of the borough to adults while excluding children, and was therefore violative of the equal protection clause of the Constitution and invalid.

The Mount Laurel Decisions

In addition to statutory controls, the courts in New Jersey also have played a significant role in the land use process by increasing the level of state participation in local land-use decisions, particularly through a series of decisions in the "Mount Laurel" affordable housing litigation. The landmark case was *Southern Burlington County NAACP, Camden Legal Services, Ethel Lawrence, et al. v. Township of Mount Laurel.*

In **Mount Laurel I** (1975), the court determined that the township had overzoned for industry, effectively preventing any large amount of remaining land to be used for residential development. Also, residential zoning of remaining land was determined to have caused such property to be out of reach for low- and moderate-income families. Further, the community was determined not to be making an appropriate variety of housing available for all people, and in doing so was charged with failing to promote the general welfare. As a result of this decision, each municipality in the state was required to zone in such a manner to provide for the municipality's fair share of present and regional housing needs.

Mt. Laurel II (1983) was a detailed follow-up lawsuit instituted against Mt. Laurel and other communities, claiming footdragging in the implementation of the requirements of Mt. Laurel I. This decision not only reinforced the court's previous position, but specified that all municipalities were required to provide their fair share of the regional need for low- and moderate-income housing. (20% low- and moderate-income housing is the figure most often cited as the fair share.) To accomplish this purpose, if removal of exclusionary zoning restrictions alone would not provide for a reasonable opportunity for the construction of low- and moderate-income housing, municipalities were required to provide for **inclusionary zoning**. This meant that they had to encourage such development by (a) requiring mandatory set-asides of dwelling units for low- and moderate-income families; and (b) offering density bonuses to developers that would allow them to build additional housing in exchange for voluntarily providing for low- and moderate-income units. Mt. Laurel II also provided for three judges to hear all Mt. Laurel-related cases and specified that if a municipality failed to revise its zoning ordinance as directed by the court, the court could implement remedies and grant builders approvals to solve the problem (builder's remedy).

In 1985, in the midst of much criticism of the court for effectively attempting to legislate, and in a desire by many for a legislative rather than a judicial solution to the problem, the legislature passed the **Fair Housing Act** which:

- established a Council on Affordable Housing (COAH) comprised of builders, public officials and public members empowered to assign fair share quotas of low- and moderate-income housing to communities; and

- enabled municipalities to meet up to half of their fair share obligation by contributing toward the construction of qualified housing in urban areas through cash payments of $20,000 per transferred unit in lieu of building units within the municipality, subject to the fair share allocation.

Pursuant to regulations promulgated by COAH and the Department of Community Affairs, there are deed restrictions on all fair share housing units which permit the units sold or leased now or in the future to be occupied only by those who meet low-income guidelines (income up to 50% of a county's median income) or moderate-income guidelines (income from 51%-80% of a county's median income). When such units are sold or rented, they are offered at prices based upon the incomes of the prospective buyers or tenants. In addition, a restriction may further seek to recapture a portion of the profit on resale if the sale price exceeds a certain sum.

The decision in **Mt. Laurel III** (1986), *Hills Development Co. v. Township of Bernards*, upheld the constitutionality of the Fair Housing Act, the role of the Council on Affordable Housing and the regional contribution agreement concept, and also transferred pending litigation to COAH. The Council also allowed municipalities to further lower their quotas by: (1) giving credit for subsidized apartments built since 1980; (2) giving credit for environmentally sensitive land considered unbuildable; and (3) allowing communities to count renovated houses and apartments in basements and garages toward their total.

Planned Unit Developments (PUDs)

The **planned unit development** (PUD) is a specific type of zoning being used more frequently as a means of utilizing land as efficiently as possible. The purpose of the PUD is to encourage a more efficient use of land and public services by allowing a more flexible means of land development than is permissible under lot-by-lot restrictions. For example, by permitting cluster-type housing in a residential area normally zoned for 7,500 sq. ft. lots, a developer can place the units closer together, providing a smaller amount of yard space for each unit, yet at the same time reserving larger areas of open or recreational space than would normally be possible due to the limited amount of remaining land. Such a development may consist of single-family detached homes; garden apartments or high-rise apartments; industrial, commercial or mixed-use projects; or a condominium project.

A PUD is generally originated by a single developer who obtains the zoning and subdivision approvals and usually develops the streets, utilities, lighting, water supply, sewer lines, etc. Individual lots are then sold to individual homeowners or "unit holders." The unit holders may be shareholders in a corporation that holds title to the property or the ownership of the common areas may be transferred to a **homeowners' association**.

Property owners in a PUD must abide by a number of **covenants, conditions and restrictions** (CCRs). For example, the association can stipulate what color the exterior of the house can be painted, the number of residents and pets per household, what can be planted in the front yard and whether the owner can have a satellite dish. The PUD developer establishes the initial set of CCRs and then turns them over to the association when sales of units reach a stipulated percent.

In short, a PUD might be summed up as a give-and-take situation between developer and planning authorities, to derive the most satisfactory use from a tract of land, to provide the greatest benefit to the community and the most economically feasible project to the developer.

BUILDING ORDINANCES

Closely related to zoning are **building codes** or ordinances which cover specific requirements with respect to the construction and maintenance of buildings to protect the public health and safety from inferior construction practices. Building codes generally cover such things as size and location of rooms, exits, fireproofing, quality of construction materials, elevators, floor loads, electrical installation, plumbing and many other measures for the protection of the occupants and the public. The codes are usually separated into specialized areas such as electrical codes, plumbing codes and fire codes, and are administered by specific departments of the local government to ensure their compliance.

Before a landowner can demolish, repair or begin the construction of a building or other improvement, he must apply for and obtain a **building permit**. The plans and specifications of the proposed structure generally accompany the application. A building permit will be issued only after the construction official (building inspector) is satisfied that the building will conform to local zoning ordinances and will comply with all the requirements of the building codes. A fee is normally payable before a permit is issued, and in most jurisdictions a copy of the permit must be posted on the construction site while the authorized work is in progress. The building department can order the removal of the structure, or impose stiff penalties for any work begun or completed without first obtaining a building permit.

During construction, the building inspector and other municipal inspectors make inspections to determine that the work is being accomplished in the prescribed manner. When construction has been completed, a final inspection is made. If all municipal requirements have been met, the building inspector or other empowered official will issue a **certificate of occupancy** (C.O.) certifying that the premises are fit for occupancy. Lending institutions may also require a certified copy of the certificate before they will close a mortgage loan. A certificate of occupancy is always required for new construction and may, by local ordinance, be required for a change of occupancy.

Hotel and Multiple Dwelling Health and Safety Code

In 1968 New Jersey repealed the old "Tenement House Law" and replaced it with the present law. Under the old law a tenement house was defined as any building in which three or more "families" lived independently of each other and did their cooking on the premises. The new law changed "families" to "persons" and eliminated the cooking criteria. The law is enforced by the New Jersey Department of Community Affairs.

The law applies to multiple dwellings with three or more rental units and hotels with ten or more units of dwelling space or sleeping facilities for 25 persons. If a property falls into one of these categories, the purchaser should obtain a certificate of compliance concerning safety requirements from the Department of Community Affairs.

Uniform Construction Code

All New Jersey municipalities must comply with the state Uniform Construction Code. The Code is administered and enforced by local authorities under the supervision of the Department of Community Affairs through its Code Advisory Board. The Code regulates the use, occupancy, construction and alteration of all buildings. Existing buildings do not have to comply with the Code unless they become unsafe.

Smoke Detector Law

Under a New Jersey law, all one- and two-family properties are required to have installed appropriate smoke detectors prior to being sold or leased. At least one smoke detector must be present on each level of the home and outside each separate sleeping area in the immediate vicinity of the bedrooms. The detectors may be battery-operated, permanently wired or plugged in if the outlet is not controlled by a switch and the plug cannot readily be pulled out. All detectors must be listed devices that satisfy Underwriters Laboratory Standard No. 217.

Proof of the detectors' presence must be established before a change in occupancy can occur, either by an inspection by the local fire prevention official or, at the official's option, by a certification signed by an individual in one of seven regulated professions, i.e., architects, engineers, real estate agents, fire subcode officials, attorneys, an employee of a New Jersey licensed title insurance company or a certified New Jersey fire official/inspector.

Municipalities that enforce the state's Fire Code locally can enact ordinances containing more stringent requirements for smoke detectors. Thus, real estate licensees should verify the applicable standard with the local fire official. The state has established a $15 application fee for the necessary certificate. Municipalities may charge more based on actual costs.

If the Fire Code enforcing agency is the state, licensees should contact the Inspections Unit at the state's Bureau of Fire Safety at (609) 633-6132. The enforcing agency with jurisdiction can be determined by consulting the Registry of Fire Code Enforcing Agencies published quarterly by the Bureau. This is available at most libraries, municipal offices or through the Bureau at (609) 633-6124.

Licensees should also be aware of N.J.S.A. 52:27D210(f). This provision of the Uniform Fire Safety Act imposes liability on purchasers for violations of record, unpaid fees and unpaid penalties. To avoid liability, purchasers must obtain a Certificate of Fire Code Status stating that none of the above exist.

KEY WORDS

Buffer Zone
Building Ordinances
Master Plan
Non-conforming Use
Planned Unit Development
Police Power
Setback
Subdivision
Variance
Zoning

CHAPTER 29
Review Questions
(Answers on page 561)

1. Government restrictions on land include all BUT ONE of the following:
   (A) Title closure.
   (B) Taxation.
   (C) Eminent domain.
   (D) Zoning.

2. Zoning ordinances usually cover such matters as:
   (A) base lines.
   (B) setback lines.
   (C) deed restrictions.
   (D) prescription.

3. There are several ways in which the use of land is regulated or controlled. Which of the following is NOT a means of regulating the use of land?
   (A) Resolutions passed by local real estate board.
   (B) Zoning ordinances.
   (C) Public ownership.
   (D) Restrictions contained in sellers' deeds.

4. Which of the following is NOT a recognized public purpose of zoning?
   (A) To prohibit nuisances from odors, signs and undue noise.
   (B) To exclude low-income families from expensive neighborhoods.
   (C) To regulate area and bulk of buildings.
   (D) To establish minimum lot sizes and degree of lot coverage.

5. An area separating two incompatible zoning districts is called a:
   (A) buffer zone.
   (B median.
   (C) divider.
   (D) setback.

6. The provisions of building codes are designed to establish minimum:
   (A) construction standards for buildings within the state.
   (B) licensing requirements for contractors.
   (C) fees for the building permits.
   (D) lot sizes.

7. B, a landowner, builds a small factory in the city of X. After the factory is built, the city of X adopts a zoning ordinance in which the area in question is designated a residential area. Therefore:
   (A) B must move his plant to a portion of the city zoned for industrial purposes.
   (B) B may continue to operate as a nonconforming use.
   (C) B should abandon his plant and sue the city for damages.
   (D) B is entitled to a variance.

8. An ordinance specifies that no permanent improvement may be built within 15 feet of the curb or other established line. Such a requirement is called:
   (A) spot zoning.
   (B) a setback.
   (C) a buffer zone.
   (D) a prescriptive easement.

9. Eminent domain, taxation, police power and escheat are:
   (A) limitations on the ownership of any property.
   (B) limited to the federal government.
   (C) benefits accruing to the owner of real property.
   (D) limited to state government.

10. A use which was lawfully established prior to the enactment of a zoning ordinance, and no longer is consistent with other uses imposed by the ordinance, is called a:
    (A) variance.
    (B) spot zoning.
    (C) deviation.
    (D) nonconforming use.

11. Municipal planning boards are generally empowered to:
    (A) draft a master plan.
    (B) control the subdivision of lands.
    (C) recommend to the governing body the adoption of amendments concerning land zoning ordinances.
    (D) All of the above.

(Quiz continues on next page)

12. Charlie wants to extend the side of his house beyond the setback boundary. Which must Charlie obtain?
    (A) Variance.
    (B) Non-conforming use.
    (C) Subordination.
    (D) Reservation.

13. Smoke detectors must be installed:
    (A) in all kitchens.
    (B) on each level of a home and outside each sleeping area.
    (C) only in commercial buildings.
    (D) only in multiple dwellings.

NOTE: Upon completion of Chapters 21-29, you should answer the questions in Review Quiz 4 on page 521 and compare your answers with the solutions at the back of the book.

CHAPTER THIRTY

REAL ESTATE MATHEMATICS

GENERAL

The importance of mathematics to the real estate broker or salesperson cannot be overemphasized. Virtually no transaction can be completed without some computations. The ability to accurately perform necessary mathematical calculations is an integral part of the skill and competency of a real estate licensee.

This chapter is intended to be a review of the basic arithmetic calculations typically encountered by the real estate licensee. Each section includes an explanation of a specific type of calculation, examples illustrating its application to real estate situations and several practice problems. You are encouraged to consider additional applications and different factual situations to supplement those presented here. Such practice can be a valuable self-testing technique and should pay dividends in improved effectiveness as a real estate professional.

The most difficult part of any arithmetic problem is not in the calculation (since you have the use of a calculator), but in defining the problem, extracting the pertinent information and selecting the proper formulas or rules to arrive at the correct solution.

CALCULATORS

The real estate licensing examination permits use of a calculator, if certain rules are followed. The calculator must be silent, battery-operated, without paper tape printing capabilities, and must not have an alphabetic key pad. A calculator capable of the four basic functions: addition, subtraction, multiplication and division, is adequate. When choosing a calculator, you should look for two other important features: (1) a percent key, and (2) "sequential capability"—the ability to perform a number of different calculations in sequence before arriving at a final answer.

The math problems discussed in this chapter assume the use of a common, inexpensive calculator that does not have an "enter" key, but does have an "equal" key. "Algebraic logic" is the lofty term used to describe calculators which have been programmed in this manner. Essentially, it means they have been formatted to solve problems by working in a straight line, using normal thought patterns (4 + 2 =; 4 - 2 =; 4 x 2 =; 4 ÷ 2 =).

Using the Calculator

The secret to using the electronic calculator is to write the problem in a straight line. Answers are then automatic. For example:

Addition:	435 + 50 = 485
Subtraction:	435 - 50 = 385
Multiplication:	435 x 50 = 21,750
Division:	435 ÷ 50 = 8.7

Note that in the each of the above examples, the numbers were entered into the calculator in a straight line and the "=" key was depressed to arrive at the solution. Hereafter when you see the equal key in parentheses (=), it indicates that the equal key has not been depressed.

Using the Percent Key

435 + 20% (=) 522
435 - 20% (=) 348
435 x 20% (=) 87
435 ÷ 20% (=) 2,175

Notice that the "=" key was not used in the above examples. The calculator displayed the solution after the "%" key was depressed.

The percent key eliminates the need to change a percent to its decimal equivalent before making a calculation. If you wanted to find the annual interest payments on a $100,000 loan at a rate of 9% without using the percent key, you would have to convert 9% to its decimal equivalent (.09), enter 100,000 x .09, and depress the "=" key to arrive at the solution, $9,000.

When using the percent key, you just enter 100,000 x 9% and the solution (9,000) will appear in the display. (Some calculators may require you to depress the "=" key after the "%" key, but the need to convert the percent to its decimal equivalent has still been eliminated.)

Sequential Calculations

Most calculators, even the simplest, least expensive ones, include a feature that allows you to perform an uninterrupted series of calculations in a desired sequence.

Example: 25 + 20 - 15 x 5 ÷ 4 = 37.5

Example: 30 + 20 - 10 x 8 ÷ 5 x 12% (=) 7.68

In the second example, if your calculator does not automatically display 7.68, depress the "=" key for the solution.

ARITHMETIC REVIEW

Nearly all of the mathematical problems encountered in real estate deal with decimal or percentage numbers. A brief review of the fundamentals involved in such problems follows.

I. Fractions appear in different forms, depending on the use that is made of them.

A. Fractions such as 1/2, 1/3, 2/3 and 5/6 are known as **common fractions**. They are for everyday common use. For example, a person buys 1/2 of an acre of land, or measures a board to sixteenths of an inch.

B. Fractions in the decimal form, as 0.8 or 0.07 or 0.135, are known as **decimals**. They are for precise measurement.

C. Fractions in the percent form are the fractions of business and are very much like decimal fractions. The sign for this way of writing hundredths is %. Thus, we can see the sign that means hundredths in place of the decimal that shows hundredths. 7 ÷ 100 = .07 = 7%. Because a percent is a decimal whose denominator is 100, you can write a decimal as a percent, or a percent as a decimal. You can also write a percent as a common fraction or a common fraction as a percent, provided you can express it with 100 as the denominator.

1. To change a decimal to a percent, move the decimal two places to the right, and write the sign (%) for percent. Thus .08 = 8%.

2. To change a percent to a decimal, drop the percent sign and move the point two places to the left. Thus 65% = .65; 2% = .02.

3. To change a fraction to a percent, divide the numerator (top number) by the denominator (bottom number), then move the point two places to the right and write the sign (%) for percent.

1/2 = 1 ÷ 2 = 0.5 = 50%
1/8 = 1 ÷ 8 = .125 = 12.5%

II. The application of these fundamentals is not difficult.

A. To find the percent of a number, multiply the number by the percent. Example: Brown saves 15% of his salary, which is $18,000 per year. How much does he save each year?

18,000 x 15% (=) $2,700

B. To find what percent one number is of another, the number asked about is the dividend (numerator) of the division problem. Example: 20 is what percent of 25? When you write the problem, place 20, the number asked about, in the dividend. 20 ÷ 25 = .80 or 80%.

III. Base, Rate and Part

A. The area of main interest to understand in real estate mathematics is that dealing with base, part and rate. Every percentage problem contains these three elements. (Technically "part" should be called "percentage.")

B. Given any two of these elements the unknown one can be found by using one of the following formulas:

BASE = PART ÷ RATE
PART = BASE x RATE
RATE = PART ÷ BASE

The following mnemonic (memory device) will prove helpful in solving problems dealing with percent and provides the same information as the above equations.

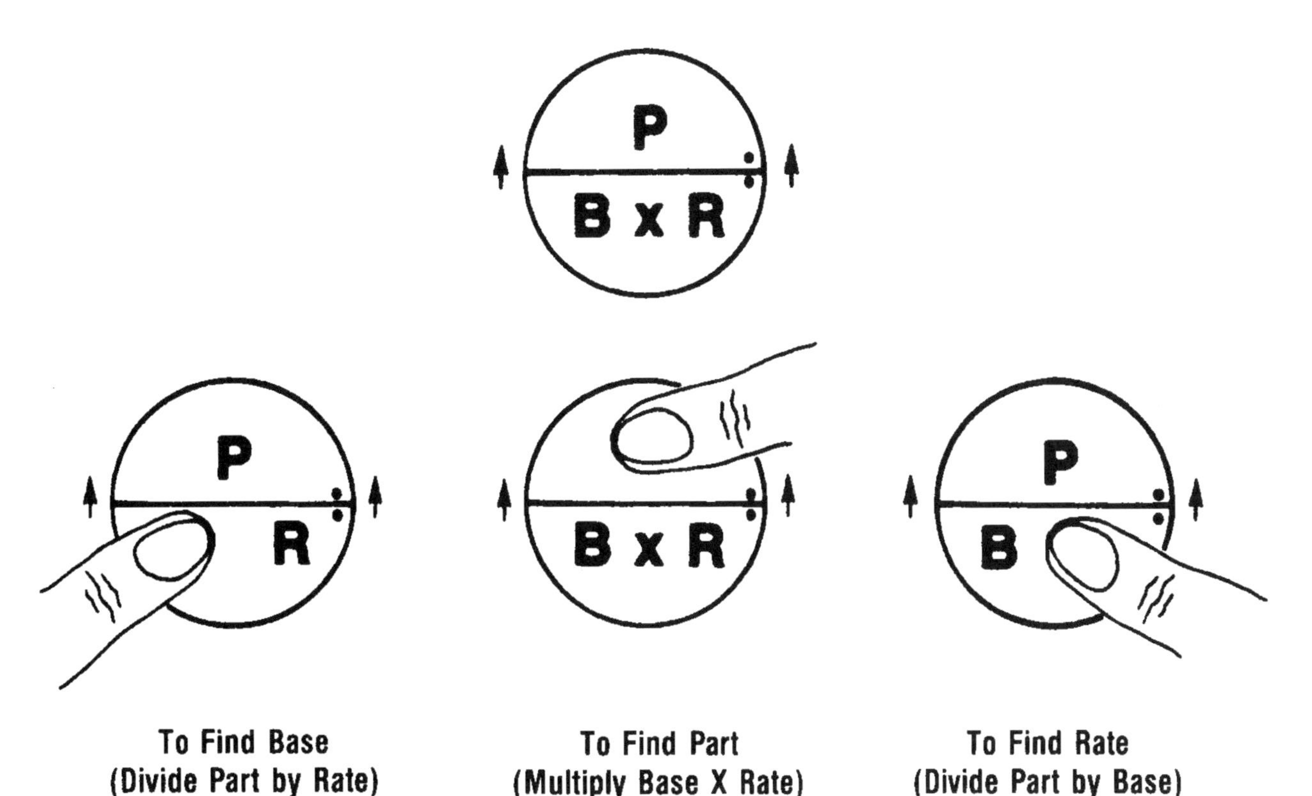

Identifying the Missing Element

Obviously, little is achieved by learning the formula if you cannot identify the missing element. On the other hand, if you learn the formula and you can identify the missing element, the solution becomes easy.

Identification of RATE rarely presents a problem, because the question generally states "tax rate," "interest rate," etc. If the word "rate" does not appear, look for a fraction, a decimal or a percent (1/5, .20, 20%), as RATE must always be expressed in one of these ways.

The BASE is the whole amount being dealt with in a particular problem. For example, in a mortgage problem the BASE is the amount of the loan (principal). The mortgage payments will be a PART of the loan. In a tax problem the BASE amount is the assessed valuation. The annual taxes will be a PART of the assessed value. In a sales price problem the BASE is the selling price and the PART will be the commission.

Typical terms used when applying the relationship to problem situations are:

BASE	PART	RATE
Selling Price	Commission	Rate of Commission
Depreciable Base	Depreciation	Rate of Depreciation
Investment	Net Income Per Year	% of Return
Investment	Profit (Loss)	% of Profit (Loss)
Principal	Interest Per Year	Rate of Interest
Assessed Value	Annual Taxes	Tax Rate
Amount of Insurance	Annual Premium	Insurance Rate

Common Unit of Expression

In all arithmetic problems, the units used in the calculation must be the same. Inches cannot be multiplied by feet, nor can feet be multiplied by inches. Annual rates cannot be divided into monthly payments nor can monthly payments be divided by annual rates of interest. You must either change inches to feet, or feet to inches; monthly payments to annual payments or vice versa; and so on.

Now consider these examples:

A house and lot are selling for $200,000. The lot is valued at $50,000. The lot value is what percent of the selling price? The BASE in this example is the selling price. The PART is the value of the lot.

Part	÷	Base	=	Rate
$50,000	÷	$200,000	=	.25 = 25%

A rate is usually expressed as a percent. Remember that percent means "per hundred." In the above example the lot is valued at 25% of the total selling price; or you could say the house is 75% of the selling price.

Try these practice exercises in finding percents.

1. PART = 2 BASE = 5 RATE = ?
2. PART = 1 BASE = 8 RATE = ?
3. PART = 30 BASE = 50 RATE = ?

Solutions:

1. 2 ÷ 5 = .4 = 40%
2. 1 ÷ 8 = .125 = 12.5%
3. 30 ÷ 50 = .6 = 60%

In some problems the RATE will be given and either the PART or the BASE will be unknown. To find the PART, do the following:

BASE x RATE = PART

Example:

A farmer had 40 acres of land for sale. Brown bought 20% of the farm. You can find the number of acres purchased (the PART) by multiplying the total area (the BASE) by the percent (RATE).

Brown's Purchase = Total Area x RATE = PART
40 acres x 20% (=) 8 acres

Example: A lot was selling for $4,000. Greene bought it for $3,000. What was the percent of discount?

In this case you are looking for the RATE. The selling price ($4,000) is the BASE and the discount ($1,000) is the PART. To find the RATE, this is what you have to do:

PART ÷ BASE = RATE
1,000 ÷ 4,000 = .25 = 25%

Example:

A certain property is being depreciated at the rate of 5% per year. The amount of depreciation this year is $6,000. What is the value upon which this depreciation is based?

In this case we are looking for the BASE. The depreciation ($6,000) is the PART and the 5% is the RATE.

PART ÷ RATE = BASE
$6,000 ÷ 5% (=) $120,000

Commission

The importance of being able to calculate one's commission need not be stressed. The general formula for determining commission is:

Gross Sales Price x Rate of Commission = Commission
(BASE) (RATE) (PART)

Example:

A broker is to receive a 5% commission on a $200,000 sale. What commission will the broker receive?

(BASE)	x	(RATE)	=	(PART)
$200,000	x	5%	(=)	$10,000

Now try these practice problems. Check your answers with the solutions given at the end of this section.

1. The 5% commission received by a broker at closing was $3,000. What was the gross sales price of the lot sold?

2. The broker received a commission of $2,793 on a sale price of $39,900. What was the broker's rate of commission?

3. The owner would like to receive $23,500 net after sale of a lot. She agrees to pay the broker a 6% commission. For what amount must the broker list the property in order for the owner to net $23,500?

4. A broker is to be paid a commission of 7% on a sale of a $30,000 property:

   a. How much will the broker receive?

   b. The broker will retain 50% of the commission, 20% will go to the listing salesperson and 30% to the selling salesperson. How much will the salespersons get as a result of this sale?

5. A property manager has contracted with a client to receive 5% of the gross rents collected. The property is a three-family, with two units renting for $500 per month and one unit for $600 per month. What monthly commission will the broker receive if all three units are rented for the entire month?

Solutions:

1. $3,000 ÷ 5% (=) $60,000

2. $2,793 ÷ $39,900 = .07 = 7%

3. If the owner nets $23,500 after paying a 6% commission, then $23,500 is 94% of the sales price.
$23,500 ÷ 94% (=) $25,000

4. a. $30,000 x 7% (=) $2,100
b. Seller's Commission: $2,100 x 30% (=) $630 Lister's Commission: $2,100 x 20% (=) $420

5. $1,600 x 5% (=) $80

Depreciation

The value of property usually fluctuates over time. Factors which influence property values include physical wear and tear, damage, obsolescence, inflation, neighborhood changes, supply and demand and so on.

Depreciation refers to an allocation procedure which may be used for any of three purposes:

A. As one factor in determining the market value of a building (replacement cost less an allowance for years of use).

B. Determining a deductible amount for income tax purposes.

C. Determining the book value of a structure for accounting purposes. The topic of depreciation may well require several chapters in an accounting textbook. The purpose here is to review the basic computational methods involving percents. For a more detailed discussion of depreciation methods, consult the appropriate tax manual or accounting text.

The simplest method of depreciation is called the "straight line" method. Using this method, the depreciation is spread evenly over the estimated life of the property. In the case of improved properties, depreciation is computed only on physical structures (buildings), never on the land itself.

Example:

A 10-year-old residence is totally destroyed by fire. At present prices, the building will cost $150,000 to replace. If the house had a useful life of 40 years when it was built, how much has it depreciated?

Base Cost	x	Percent of Remaining Life	=	Depreciation
$150,000	x	25% (10 yrs ÷ 40 yrs.)	(=)	$37,500

(Note that the original purchase price was not considered, nor was the price of the land.)

In the example above, the annual depreciation rate is 1/40th of the total cost or 2.5%. Thus the house is determined to have depreciated in value $3,750 for each year of its 10-year life. The accumulated depreciation is therefore $37,500 or 25% of the current replacement cost.

Example:

A duplex is purchased for income purposes at a cost of $90,000. The value of the land is determined to be $6,000. If tax guidelines allow an annual deduction of 2.5% for depreciation on this particular type of rental property, what deduction may be taken for depreciation this year?

Depreciable Base x Rate of Depreciation = Deduction
$84,000 x 2.5% (=) $2,100

(Note that the value of the land was deducted from the original cost to determine the depreciable base.)

Try these practice problems :

1. A rental property was purchased for $135,000. The land was valued at $27,000. The owner claimed a depreciation deduction of $2,700 for income tax purposes this year. What rate of depreciation is he using?

2. A 26-year-old building is being depreciated by the straight-line method over an estimated 39-year life. The accumulated depreciation has decreased the book value of the building to $210,000. What was the original construction cost of this building?

3. A building is being depreciated at a rate of 4% per year. The amount depreciated this year was $5,000. What is the value upon which this depreciation is based?

4. The book value of a building is $270,000. It was constructed five years ago at a cost of $360,000. What was the yearly rate of depreciation?

Solutions:

1. $135,000 - $27,000 = $108,000 Building Value
   $2,700 ÷ $108,000 = .025 = 2.5%

2. 13 ÷ 39 = .333
   $210,000 ÷ 33.3% (=) $630,000 Original Cost

3. $5,000 ÷ 4% (=) $125,000 Value

4. $360,000 - $270,000 = $90,000 Total Depreciation
   $90,000 ÷ 5 years = $18,000 Yearly Depreciation
   $18,000 ÷ 360,000 = .05 = 5% Per Year Depreciation

Annual Return on Investment and Capitalization

A. Annual Return on Investment

Anyone considering an investment in property will be interested in determining the rate of return that can be expected from that investment. The rate of return is the relationship between the investment and the net income it produces each year. The formula used to calculate the rate of return on an investment is:

Annual Net Income ÷ Investment = Rate of Return
(PART) (BASE) (RATE)

It is important to use the **annual net income** in this calculation. The net income is calculated by deducting all of the owner's property chargeable expenses from the gross income. Such expenses include real estate taxes, insurance, maintenance, utilities and other operating expenses.

An understanding of the relationship between gross income, net income, investment and rate of return is essential if you are to deal with questions which are frequently asked in real estate transactions, such as:

"How much rent must I charge in order to get a 10% rate of return per year?"
"How much must I invest to provide an annual net income of $20,000 at a rate of 9%?"

B. Capitalization

In appraising the value of an investment, the capitalization rate serves a function very much like an interest rate. Just as savers will not be attracted to a bank offering 5% interest if other banks are giving 6%

interest, informed investors are not likely to invest in property returning 8% if the market capitalization rate is 10%.

Methods used to determine the capitalization rate for a given property are beyond the scope of this chapter, but keep in mind that it is a composite of several factors, including a rate of return ON an investment and a rate of return OF the investment through depreciation.

The general formula for calculating the value of a property given the capitalization rate is:

Annual Net Income ÷ Capitalization Rate = Value
PART) (RATE) (BASE)

Example:

Brown owns an apartment building. His net income from the property is $36,000, which represents a 12% return on his investment. How much has he invested in the property?

Net Income ÷ Rate of Return = Investment
$36,000 ÷ 12% (=) $300,000

Example:

Green wants to invest in income property. She wants a rate of return of at least 12%. Will she be interested in a property priced at $125,000 which produces a yearly net income of $9,000?

Net Income ÷ Investment = Rate
$9,000 ÷ $125,000 = .072 = 7.2%

Practice Problems:

1. Milligan bought a rental property for $55,000. The rent for each of the four units is $190 per month and each unit is rented for the entire year. Expenses on the building average $200 per month and taxes are $1,000 per year. What is the annual rate of return on this property?

2. If a business property valued at $60,000 earns 12% on the total investment annually, what is the monthly income?

3. Travers owns a property valued at $45,000. Her annual gross income from renting it to Mr. and Mrs. Peters is $5,460. Her rate of return is 8%. What is the amount of her annual expenses?

Solutions:

1. Gross Income = 4 x 12 x $190 = $9,120
Expenses = $200 x 12 + 1,000 = $3,400
Net Income = $9,120 - $3,400 = $5,720
$5,720 ÷ $55,000 = .104 = 10.4% Rate of Return

2 $60,000 x 12% (=) $7,200 Net Income Per Year
$7,200 ÷ 12 months = $600 Monthly Income

3. $45,000 x 8% (=) $3,600 Net Income
$5,460 - $3,600 = $1,860 Expenses

PROFIT OR LOSS PROBLEMS

"If we sell at that price, we will make 20% over our cost."
"How much do I have to sell my home for in order to make a 15% profit?"
"If I sell for $20,000 instead of $25,000, what percent will I lose?"

Often a seller wants to know what profit or loss he will realize by selling a parcel of real estate at a given price. Frequently a sale will not even be made if a certain profit will not be realized or if a loss will occur.

The broker is also interested in profit and loss figures because maximizing profit or minimizing loss is one way to promote a principal's interest.

The general formula for profit and loss rates is:

Original Investment x % of Profit (Loss) = Profit (Loss)

Example:

A lot was purchased for $25,000 and sold for $32,500. What percent of profit was made on the sale?

$32,500 - $25,000 = $7,500 Profit
$ 7,500 ÷ $25,000 = .3 = 30% Profit

It is important to remember that the calculation compares the amount of profit to the ORIGINAL INVESTMENT. Sometimes the selling price will be given and the percent of profit or loss. In such situations, it is best to think of the original cost and selling price in terms of percents before calculating.

Example: If there is a 15% profit, then think:

Original Cost + Profit = Selling Price
100% + 15% (=) 115%

or, if there is a 15% loss:

Original Cost - Loss = Selling Price
100% - 15% (=) 85%

Example:

If Barry sold a lot for $48,000 and made a 20% profit, what was Barry's original cost? Original Cost (100%) + Profit (20%) = Selling Price. 100% + 20% = 120%.

Now that you have calculated the proper rate, you can calculate the original cost.

$48,000 ÷ 120% (=) $40,000 Original Cost

Try these practice exercises:

1. Mary bought a property for $34,000 and sold it one year later at a 10% profit. What was the selling price?

2. Jack Green, a broker, has a property listed at $35,000. Jim Black purchases it for $32,500 and later sells it for $30,000. What percent of loss did Jim take on the exchange?

3. The Gardners recently sold a lot for $25,200. This was a 5% profit over their original cost. How much did they pay for the home originally?

Solutions:

1. $34,000 x 110% (=) $37,400 Selling Price

2. $2,500 ÷ $32,500 = .0769 = 7.69% Loss

3. $25,200 ÷ 105% (=) $24,000 Original Cost

INTEREST

Few real estate buyers are able to purchase a home without the use of money borrowed from a bank, savings and loan association or other financial source. The rent paid by the borrower for the use of borrowed funds is called **interest**. This charge is usually expressed as a rate or percent, and is an annual rate unless otherwise indicated. Thus, reference to "interest at 9%" means that the borrower will be charged $9 interest for each $100 borrowed for a 12-month period.

The type of interest calculation usually used in real estate transaction is called **simple interest**. Using this method of calculation, interest is charged only on the unpaid balance of the principal.

The formula for simple interest is:

Principal x Rate of Interest x Time = Interest

This formula differs from others in this section because of the "Time" factor. You need this factor to calculate interest for periods other than one full year.

Example:

The amount of a loan is $4,000 and the annual rate of interest is 9%. How much interest will be paid on the loan in one year?

Principal	x Rate	x Time	= Interest
$4,000	x 9%	x 1	= $360

What if the loan is to be paid off in two months? Since two months is 2/12 of a year, the interest charged should be 2/12 or 1/6 of the yearly interest. You can calculate this as follows:

Principal x Rate x Time = Interest
Interest = $4,000 x 9% x 1 ÷ 6 (.1666)
Interest = $360 x .1666
Interest = $60

The period of a loan may be for a certain number of days. The business world generally considers a year to have 360 days when calculating interest. The 360-day year is commonly known as a "business year" or a "banker's year." The United States government calculates interest based on a 365-day year. Interest calculated using a 365-day year is called "accurate" or "exact" interest. Whether a 360- or 365-day year is used in the calculation of interest may be a matter for negotiation between the parties to a transaction. For exam purposes a business year is used.

Calculate the interest for 35 days on the $4,000 loan in the previous example, using a business year.

Interest = Principal x Rate x Time
Interest = $4,000 x 9% ÷ 360 x 35
Interest = $4,000 x 9% x 1 = $35

Now try these practice exercises:

1. If the rate of interest is 7% per annum and the quarterly interest payments are $525.00, what is the amount of the loan?
2. $2,000 is borrowed at 9% interest per year. The loan is made on May 1 and is to be paid back on August 31. Compute the interest charge based on a business year.

Solutions:

1. $525 x 4 = $2,100
   $2,100 ÷ 7% (=) $30,000

2. $2,000 x 9% (=) $180
   $180 x 1/3 (.333) = $60

PRORATION

At the time a sale of property is closed, there may be certain financial benefits and/or responsibilities which will pass from seller to buyer along with the property. It is important that such benefits and responsibilities be allocated to the parties involved in proportion to the time they owned or will own the property. The calculation involved in allocating these benefits and responsibilities properly is called **proration**.

The following are examples of items which must be prorated in closing a real estate transaction: real estate taxes, insurance premiums, rents, and water and utility bills.

In New Jersey prorations are made up to and including the day of closing. The seller is responsible for the day of closing and the buyer becomes responsible the day after closing. Use a 30-day month for all calculations.

A. Real Estate Taxes

Property taxes become a lien on January 1. Taxes are due quarterly on the 1st day of February, May, August and November. If taxes are owed, you must determine the number of months and days in the tax year(s) for which the seller has not paid taxes. Such charges will be prorated as a credit to the buyer and a debit to the seller.

Example:

The annual property taxes for the current year were $3,200 and were unpaid. The property was sold and the transaction closed on August 20. What amount in taxes should be credited to the buyer and debited to the seller?

The seller owes taxes for 7 months and 20 days. Therefore, the prorated taxes are $2,067.70 (credit buyer; debit seller).

$3,200 ÷ 360 days = $8.99 per day
$8.99 x 230 days = $2,067.70

B. Insurance Premiums

Existing insurance policies are seldom transferred to the buyer, but when they are, the buyer will reimburse the seller for the prepaid premiums by way of a credit on the closing statement. This amount is computed from the day of closing through the date of expiration of the policy.

Example:

A property settlement takes place on May 20, 2002. An existing fire insurance policy, written for five years on October 14, 1999, is to be transferred to the buyer. The paid-up premium was $1,080. Determine the amount of premium that should be credited to the seller and debited to the buyer.

Solution:

The policy expires October 14, 2004, so the buyer is covered for 28 months plus 24 days (864 days), May 20, 2002 thru October 14, 2004.

Yearly Premium = $960 ÷ 1,800 days = $.60 per day
Prepaid Coverage: 864 days x $.60 per day = $518.40 (credit seller; debit buyer)

C. Practice Exercises

The owner of a property contracts with a broker to sell a property for $250,000 and agrees to pay a commission of 5% on the selling price. The closing date is September 15, 2002. Use this information to answer the following questions:

1. What is the amount of commission due the broker?

2. If the seller has not paid the 2002 taxes of $3,600, what amount will be prorated as a credit to the buyer and a debit to the seller?

3. The property is insured through February 5, 2003 for 90% of the current selling price. The prepaid three-year premium was $17.60 per $1,000. What is the amount that will be credited to the seller and debited to the buyer?

Solutions:

1. $250,000 x 5% (=) $12,500

2. Total time seller owned property in 2002 = 8.5 months (255 days)
   $3,600 ÷ 360 x 255 = $2,550

3. $250,000 x 90% (=) $225,000 (amount of policy)
   225 x $17.60 = $3,960 (3-year premium)
   $3960 ÷ 1,080 days = $3.66 (daily premium)

   Total number of days covered beyond September 15, 2002:

   2002 - 105
   2003 - 35
   140 days (unused)

   $3.66 x 140 = $512.40

Property Taxes

The major source of local government revenue is the property tax. Knowledge of how this tax is computed is extremely important to the real estate broker or salesperson. The first step in the process is an appraisal of the market value of the property by the local tax assessor. It is assumed that this appraisal is uniform throughout the district and free of bias. Procedures for appeal are available to the property owner who feels that his property value has been appraised too high.

Example:

A municipality requires a total revenue from property tax of $3,987,000. The assessed valuation of all property in the district is $45,986,000. The tax rate for that municipality is computed as follows:

Total Tax Levy ÷ Total Assessed Valuation = Tax Rate
$3,987,000 ÷ $45,986,000 = $.087

The tax rate in New Jersey is generally expressed as an amount "per hundred dollars." Therefore, in the example above, the tax rate would be expressed as $8.70 per $100.

Practice Exercises:

1. A property is assessed at $120,000. The tax rate is $5.40. What are the annual taxes on this property?

2. The annual taxes on a house are $5,300. The tax rate is $4.60. What is the assessed valuation?

3. Assessed valuation is $24,000; taxes are $811.20. Determine the rate.

Solutions:

1. Assessed Valuation ÷ 100 x Tax Rate = Annual Taxes
   $120,000 ÷ 100 = 1,200 x $5.40 = $6,480.

2. Annual Taxes ÷ Tax Rate = Assessed Valuation
   $5,300 ÷ 4.6% = $115,217

3. Annual Taxes ÷ Assessed Valuation = Tax Rate
   $811.20 ÷ $24,000 = .0338 x 100 = $3.38 per hundred (3.38%)

Home Mortgages

Few people pay the purchase price of a piece of property outright. The most common means of payment is a mortgage plan from a lending institution. The **mortgage** is a contract in which the borrower pledges the property as security for the loan and promises to repay the money. Almost all mortgage contracts call for repayment in equal monthly payments (called **amortizing** the mortgage). As payments are made, they are applied first to the interest due and then to reduce the unpaid balance (principal).

The monthly payment a mortgage will require is often a major factor in a prospective buyer's decision, so you will frequently be called upon to compute the amount needed to amortize the mortgage. An invaluable aid in such computations is an amortization chart such as the one shown on the next page.

Example:

A loan of $1,000 at 12% interest to be paid off in 25 years will require monthly payments of $10.53 per $1,000. What monthly payments would be needed to amortize a 25-year mortgage of $23,000 at 12% interest?

Since the monthly payment per $1000 is $10.53 (taken from the Amortization Chart on the next page), simply multiply the number of thousands (23 in this example) by $10.53. The payment needed is $242.19.

Another question that frequently arises in real estate transactions is how much of the monthly payment goes to pay interest due and how much goes to reduce the premium. The lending institution will prepare a complete loan payment schedule for the mortgagor, but you should understand the principles involved and be able to construct one also.

Continuing the example of a $23,000 mortgage at 12% for 25 years, calculate how much of the first payment goes for interest.

Principal x Rate x Time = Interest
$23,000 x 2% x 1 ÷ 12 = $230.00

The balance of the $242.19 payment ($12.19) is used to reduce the principal:

New Principal = $23,000 - $12.19 = $22,987.81

The calculations for the second month are:

Interest = $22,987.81 x 12% x 1 ÷ 12 = $229.88
Payment on Principal = $12.31

The following chart shows the first five monthly payments on a loan schedule to amortize a $23,000 loan at 12% for 25 years:

No.	Monthly Payment	Payment on Interest	Payment on Principal	Principal Balance
1	242.19	230.00	12.19	22,987.81
2	242.19	229.88	12.31	22,975.50
3	242.19	229.75	12.44	22,963,06
4	242.19	229.63	12.56	22,950.50
5	242.19	229.50	12.69	22,937.81

AMORTIZATION CHART
Monthly Payment Per $1,000

Years	8%	9%	10%	11%	12%	13%	14%	15%
1	86.99	87.45	87.92	88.39	88.85	89.32	89.79	90.26
2	45.23	45.69	46.15	46.61	47.08	47.54	48.01	48.49
3	31.34	31.80	32.27	32.74	33.22	33.70	34.18	34.67
4	24.41	24.89	25.36	25.85	26.34	26.83	27.33	27.83
5	20.28	20.76	21.25	21.74	22.25	22.75	23.27	23.79
6	17.53	18.03	18.53	19.04	19.55	20.07	20.61	21.14
7	15.59	16.09	16.60	17.12	17.65	18.19	18.74	19.30
8	14.14	14.65	15.17	15.71	16.25	16.81	17.37	17.95
9	13.02	13.54	14.08	14.63	15.18	15.75	16.33	16.92
10	12.13	12.67	13.22	13.78	14.35	14.93	15.53	16.13
11	11.42	11.96	12.52	13.09	13.68	14.28	14.89	15.51
12	10.82	11.38	11.95	12.54	13.13	13.75	14.37	15.01
13	10.33	10.90	11.48	12.08	12.69	13.31	13.95	14.60
14	9.91	10.49	11.08	11.69	12.31	12.95	13.61	14.27
15	9.56	10.14	10.75	11.37	12.00	12.65	13.32	14.00
16	9.25	9.85	10.46	11.09	11.74	12.40	13.08	13.77
17	8.98	9.59	10.21	10.85	11.51	12.19	12.87	13.58
18	8.75	9.36	10.00	10.65	11.32	12.00	12.70	13.42
19	8.55	9.17	9.81	10.47	11.15	11.85	12.56	13.28
20	8.36	9.00	9.65	10.32	11.01	11.72	12.44	13.17
21	8.20	8.85	9.51	10.19	10.89	11.60	12.33	13.07
22	8.06	8.71	9.38	10.07	10.78	11.50	12.24	12.99
23	7.93	8.59	9.27	9.97	10.69	11.42	12.16	12.92
24	7.82	8.49	9.17	9.88	10.60	11.34	12.10	12.86
25	7.72	8.39	9.09	9.80	10.53	11.28	12.04	12.81
26	7.63	8.31	9.01	9.73	10.47	11.22	11.99	12.76
27	7.54	8.23	8.94	9.67	10.41	11.17	11.95	12.73
28	7.47	8.16	8.88	9.61	10.37	11.13	11.91	12.70
29	7.40	8.10	8.82	9.57	10.32	11.09	11.88	12.67
30	7.34	8.05	8.78	9.52	10.29	11.06	11.85	12.64

Multiply the cost per $1,000 by the amount of the loan (in thousands). The result will be the monthly payment, including principal and interest. For example, for a $100,000 loan for 30 years at 9%, multiply 100 x 8.05 = 805.

Practice Exercises:

1. Calculate the monthly payments for each of the following mortgages:

   A) $32,000 at 11% for 20 years.
   B) $28,500 at 11% for 25 years.
   C) $21,900 at 12% for 23 years.

2. Wellington has enough for a $25,000 down payment on a house and can pay $800 per month toward interest and principal. The interest rate is 11%. If Wellington can obtain a 25-year mortgage, approximately what price range is he looking for?

3. Simon bought a house for $150,000. After making a down payment of $30,000, he obtained a mortgage loan for the balance at 11% for 25 years.

   A) Find the amount of the monthly payment.
   B) Make a loan payment schedule for the first five payments.

Solutions:

1. A) $1,000 at 11% for 20 years requires $10.32 per month. Payment = 32 x $10.32 = $330.24
   B) $1,000 at 11% for 25 years requires $9.80 per month. Payment = 28.5 x $9.80 = $279.30
   C) $1,000 at 12% for 23 years requires $10.69 per month. Payment = 21.9 x $10.69 = $234.11

2. $1,000 at 11% for 25 years requires $9.80 per month.

   He can afford $800 per month, so divide 800 by 9.80 to find the size of the mortgage. (800 ÷ 9.80 = $81,632). Maximum loan = $81,632. Add to this amount his down payment and he is looking in the $106,630 price range.

3. A) Principal = $120,000 ($150,000 - $30,000); Payment = 120 x $9.80 = $1,176.

   B)

No.	Monthly Payment	Payment on Interest	Payment on Principal	Principal Balance
1	1,176	1,100.00	76.00	119,924.00
2	1,176	1,099.30	76.70	119,847.30
3	1,176	1,098.60	77.40	119,769.90
4	1,176	1,097.89	78.11	119,691.79
5	1,176	1,097.17	78.83	119,612.96

PERIMETER, AREA, AND VOLUME

Perimeter (Linear Measurement)

Perimeter is the distance around a figure. To find the perimeter, add the length of all sides.

Example: Compute the perimeter of the following figures:

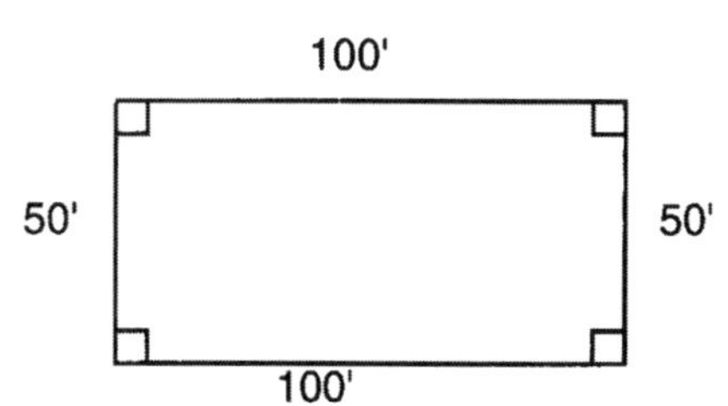

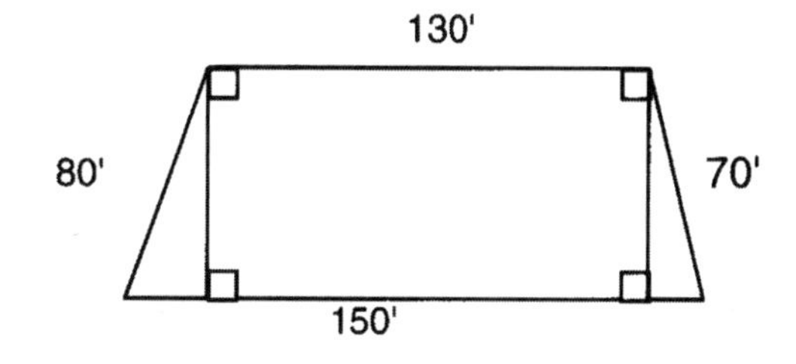

P = 50' + 100' + 50' + 100'
P = 300'

P = 80' + 130' + 70' + 150'
P = 430'

Area

Area is the measurement of a flat surface, such as a floor, wall or field. Real estate licensees are frequently called upon to describe a property in terms of its physical dimensions. How large is the lot? How big is the master bedroom? Which house has the larger kitchen? This section will review the basic methods of calculating area measurements to describe a building or lot.

A. Rectangles

Any flat surface with four straight sides is called a quadrilateral. The most common quadrilateral is a **rectangle**. The opposite sides of a rectangle are the same length and are parallel to each other, and all corner angles measure 90 degrees. The area of a rectangle can be found by multiplying one side by any other side perpendicular to it.

Formula: Area = Length x Width (A = L x W)

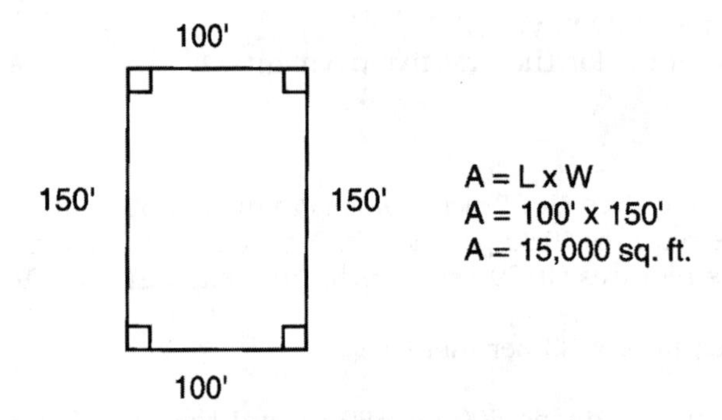

Example:

Find the areas of these rooms:

1. Kitchen: 9 ft. x 12 ft.
2. Den: 9 ft. x 8 ft.-6 in.

Solution:

The area of the kitchen is 108 sq. ft. (9 x 12). Before calculating the area of the den, you must express the dimensions with a common unit. For most purposes it will be easier to work with the larger unit, so you should use feet as the common unit in this problem. 8 ft. 6 in. = 8.5 ft. 9 x 8.5 = 76.5. The area of the den is 76.5 sq. ft.

Sometimes a room will be nearly rectangular, but will have an alcove attached such as the two rooms pictured below.

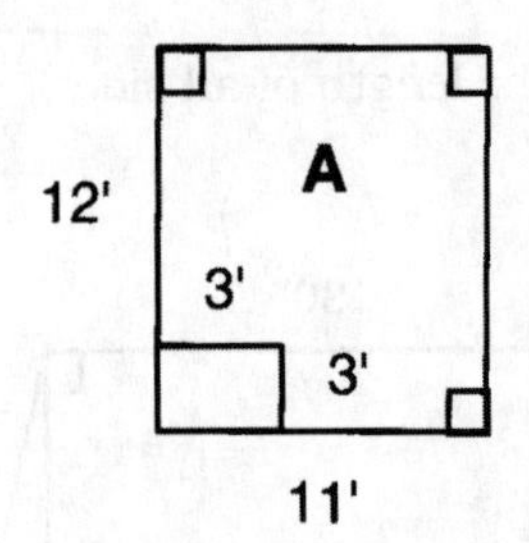

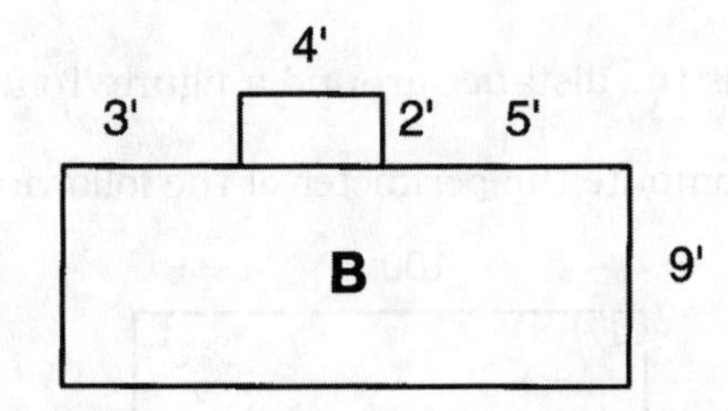

The dotted lines suggest two methods commonly used to find such areas. For room A, you can compute the large area (11' x 12') and subtract the "missing" area (3' x 3'). The result is 123 sq. ft. For room B, the method suggested is to add the small area (4' x 2') to the area of the larger part (12' x 9'). The result is 116 sq. ft.

B. Squares

A **square** is a flat surface having four equal sides, all of which are parallel, and all corner angles measure 90 degrees. To find the area of a square you multiply one side by any other side.

Formula: Area = Length x Width (A = L x W)

Example:

Find the area of a room that is 20 ft. square.

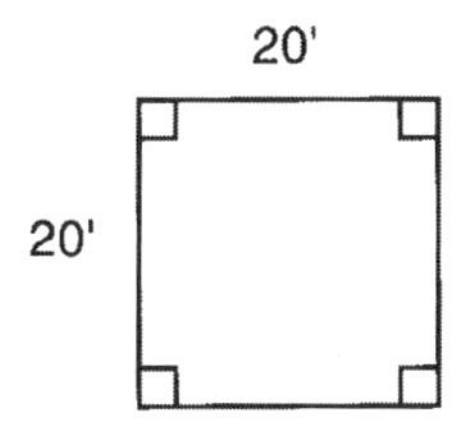

Solution:

20' x 20' = 400 square feet.

Geometric Method

The geometric method uses a circle to find the area of rectangles and squares. As with percentages, multiply across and divide upward. Note that area is always on the top of the equation (numerator).

Area = Length x Width

Example:

A rectangular lot has a frontage of 80 ft. and a depth of 125 ft. How many sq. ft. does it contain?

Solution:

Area = 80' x 125' = 10,000 sq. ft.

Example:

A lot containing 21,780 sq. ft. has a frontage of 150 ft. What is its depth?

Solution:

Area ÷ Frontage = Depth
21,780 ÷ 150 = 145.2

Example:

A parcel of land with an area of 14,520 sq. ft. has a depth of 110 ft. What is the frontage?

Solution:

Area ÷ Depth = Frontage
14,520 sq. ft. ÷ 110' = 132'

C. Triangles

A **triangle** is a figure having three sides and three angles.

Base: Either side of a triangle measuring 90 degrees to another side.

Apex: The point at which two sloping sides of a triangle intersect.

Height: The perpendicular distance from the base of a triangle to the apex.

Formula: Area = 1/2 base x height

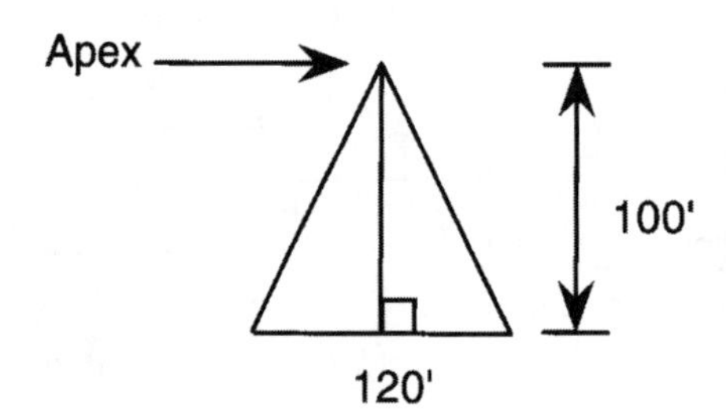

Example:

Find the area of a triangle having a base of 120 ft. and a height of 100 ft.

Solution:

Area = 1/2 base x height
Area = 60' x 100' = 6,000 sq. ft.

Example:

Find the area of a triangle having a base of 80 ft. and a height of 70 ft.

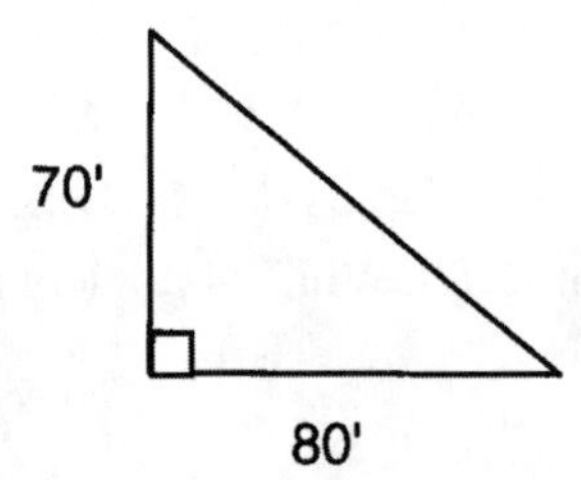

Solution:

Area = 1/2 base x height
Area = 40' x 70'
Area = 2,800 sq. ft.

D. Trapezoids

A **trapezoid** is a figure having four sides, only two of which are parallel and are of different lengths. The area of a trapezoid is computed by taking one-half the sum of the bases and multiplying by the height.

Formula: Area = 1/2 x (base + base) x height.

Base: Either of the parallel sides of a trapezoid.

Height: The vertical distance between the parallel bases.

Example: What is the area of the following trapezoid?

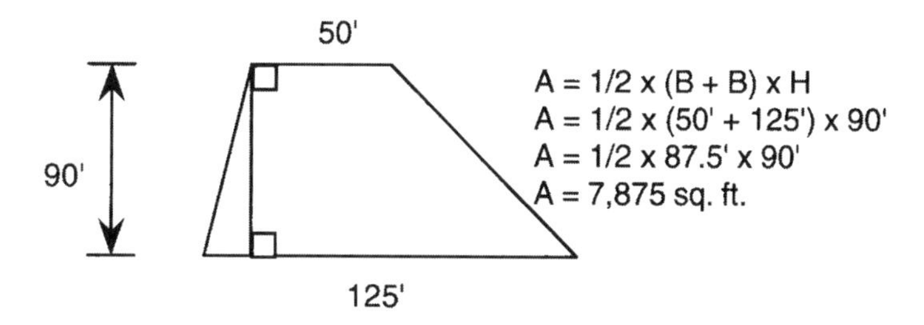

E. Irregular Figures

To find the area of an irregular figure, divide the figure into regions for which you can compute the areas. Then add the areas of each region. Be careful not to overlap.

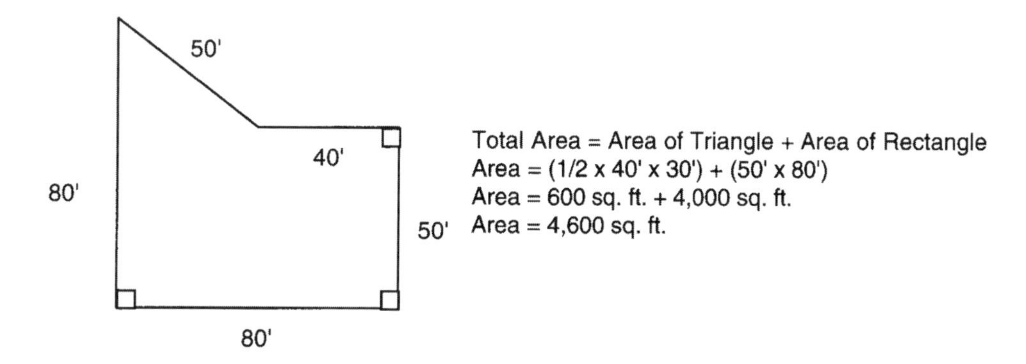

F. Circle

The **circumference** of a circle is the "distance around" the outside of a circle. The **diameter** is the distance through the center of a circle to its curve. The **radius** is the distance from the center of a circle to its curve.

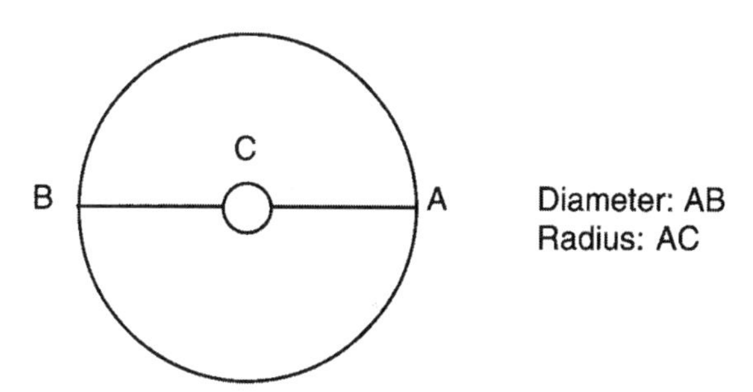

The ratio of the circumference to the diameter is the same for all circles. That is, circumference divided by diameter is a constant number. This constant number is called "Pi" (π). Thus π equals 3.14.

The following formulas are used to determine circumference (C), diameter (D), radius (r), and area (A) of a circle:

Circumference:	$C = \pi \times D$
Diameter	$D = C \div p$
Radius:	$r = D \div 2$
Area:	$A = \pi \times r^2$

Example:

Compute the following: (a) circumference, (b) radius and (c) area, of a circular swimming pool having a diameter of 24 feet.

Solution:

(a) Circumference = 3.14 x 24' = 75.36 sq. ft.
(b) Radius = 24' ÷ 2 = 12'
(c) Area = 3.14 x 12' x 12' = 452.16 sq. ft.

F. Volume

Volume adds a third dimension to area measurement, that of height or depth.

The **volume** of a rectangular space, such as a room, is the product of its length times its width times its height.

Formula:	Volume	=	Length x Width x Height
	V	=	L x W x H
	48,000 cu. ft.		60' 40' 20'

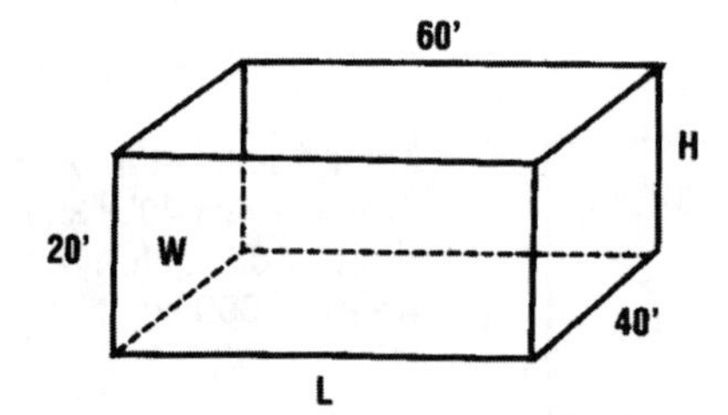

The volume of triangular space such as that in the attic space of a peaked roof can be found by multiplying the area of the triangle by the length of the attic.

Example:

To calculate the cost of providing air conditioning, you must compute the volume of air contained in the building outlined below. Find the volume in cubic feet.

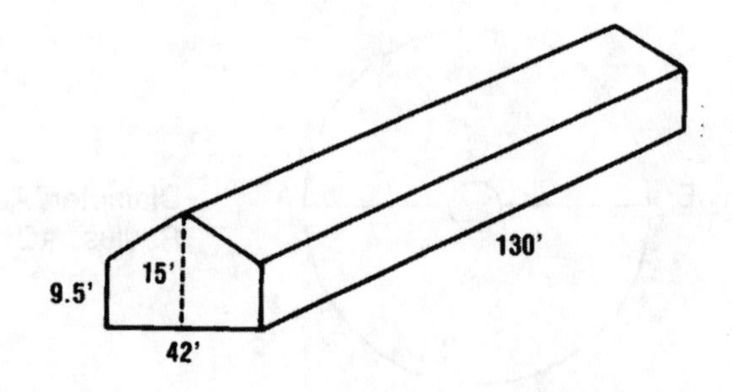

Area = Area of Triangle + Area of Rectangle
Area = (1/2 x 42' x 5.5') x (9.5' x 42')
Area = 115.5 sq. ft. + 399 sq. ft.
Area = 514.5 sq. ft.
V = A x H
V = 514.5 sq. ft. x 130'
V = 66,885 cu. ft.

Practice Exercises:

1. A house has three rectangular-shaped bedrooms. Their dimensions are: 9' by 13'; 9'6" by 12'; and 11'3" by 10'9". Find the area of each bedroom.

2. A rectangular lot measures 250' by 175'. Find its area in square feet. Express this area as square yards. How does this area compare to an acre?

3. Find the total area of the shaded lots.

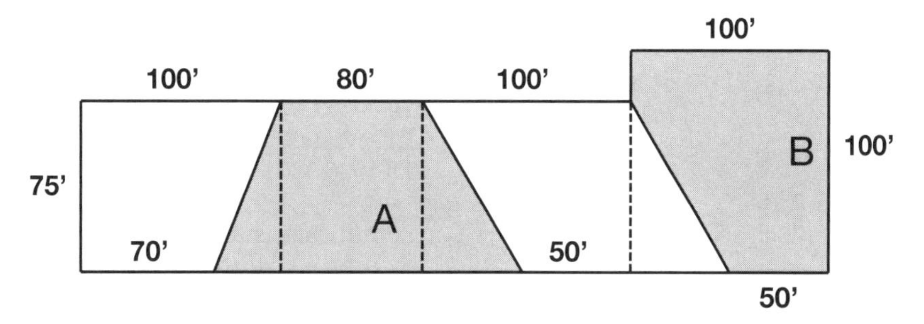

Solutions:

1. For the 9' by 13' room the area is 9' x 13' = 117 sq. ft.

   For the second room, convert 9'6" to 9.5' before multiplying. 9.5' x 12' = 114 sq. ft.

   For the third room, convert both measures to feet: 11'3" = 11.25' and 10'9" = 10.75'. 11.25' x 1.75' = 120.9 sq. ft.

2. 250' x 175' = 43,750 sq. ft.

   1 square yard = 3' x 3' = 9 sq. ft. Therefore divide by 9 to find its area in square yards:

   43,750 ÷ 9 = 4.861 sq. yds. The lot is just slightly larger than an acre. (1 acre = 43,560 sq. ft.)

3. Shaded area A:

   A = 1/2 x (b+b) x h
   A = 1/2 x (80' + 160') x 75'
   A = 120' x 75' = 9,000 sq. ft.

   Shaded area B:

   Subtract the area of a 50' x 75' triangle from area of rectangle: 100' x 100' = 10,000 sq. ft.
   Area of triangle: 1/2 x 50' x 75' = 1,875 sq. ft.
   Total area = 10,000 sq. ft. - 1,875 sq. ft. = 8,125 sq. ft.

CHAPTER 30
Review Questions
(Answers on page 562)

(Answers on page 562)

Commission and Sales Price

1. A house sold for 7/8 of the $60,000 asking price. If two brokers split the 6% commission, how much will each receive?
   (A) $3,150
   (B) $1,800
   (C) $2,225
   (D) $1,575

2. | Sales: | Commission Rate: |
   | --- | --- |
   | $48,000 | 6% |
   | $63,900 | 3% |
   | $52,500 | 6% |

   A salesperson receives 25% of all commissions listed above. How much did he earn?
   (A) $1,986.75
   (B) $2,466.00
   (C) $2,055.00
   (D) $3,178.80

3. A home was purchased three years ago for $70,000. It was listed for sale at a price which represented a 20% profit. If the seller accepted an offer which was $6,000 below list price, what did she receive after paying a 6% commission?
   (A) $73,320
   (B) $78,960
   (C) $72,960
   (D) $73,800

4. An apartment manager receives 30% of the first month's rent and 6% of each month thereafter. If the rent is $320 per month, what will his annual fee amount to?
   (A) $211.20
   (B) $307.20
   (C) $326.40
   (D) $312.20

5. A broker's commission earned on a sale was $3,800. If he charged 6% of the first $50,000 and 4% on any amount over that, what was the sales price?
   (A) $76,200
   (B) $55,000
   (C) $58,500
   (D) $70,000

6. After paying the broker's commission fee of 7% and expenses of $317, a seller desires a net amount to himself of $34,000. What will the sales price be?
   (A) $36,900
   (B) $36,697
   (C) $36,600
   (D) $36,380

7. Commissions are divided in a ratio of 3 to 2 by a broker and salesperson, respectively. On a sale of $60,000 at a 7% commission, the salesperson is paid how much less than the broker?
   (A) $600
   (B) $840
   (C) $1,680
   (D) $950

8. Clark Wink wants to realize $37,000 from the sale of his property after paying expenses of $800 and paying the broker a 10% commission. What must the sales price be?
   (A) $41,500
   (B) $41,580
   (C) $41,900
   (D) $42,000

9. A salesperson is paid on a basis of 9% commission on the first $80,000 of sales during one month plus 2.5% of any amount over $80,000. If he sold four houses during one month for $42,000, $45,500, $48,000 and $49,500, how much more would he have made if he had been paid a straight 6% commission?
   (A) $1,275
   (B) $1,450
   (C) $9,200
   (D) $3,850

10. A listing agreement provided for a commission to the broker of 6% of the first $30,000 and 3% of anything above $30,000. The commission received by the broker was $2,070. What did the property sell for?
   (A) $39,000
   (B) $32,500
   (C) $37,000
   (D) $35,500

Appreciation/Depreciation

1. A house is currently valued at $54,000. What was the value nine years ago, to the nearest $100, if it has increased in value at an average rate of 6% per year?
(A) $24,800
(B) $34,900
(C) $35,800
(D) $35,100

2. A property which cost $78,000 six years ago is now valued at $66,300. What was the average yearly depreciation?
(A) 6 2/3%
(B) 2 1/4%
(C) 2 3/8%
(D) 2 1/2%

3. If you sell a lot for $40,000 after making a 17% profit, what was the price you originally paid?
(A) $32,999
(B) $34,188
(C) $37,650
(D) $38,120

4. In eight years a property depreciated in value from $120,000 to $102,000. What was the average annual rate of depreciation?
(A) 2.16 %
(B) 1.875%
(C) 15%
(D) 1.765%

Measures (Area)

1. The house shown in the diagram below was constructed at a cost of $24 per square foot, and the cost of the lot came to $21,780 per acre. If the builder wishes to realize a 12% profit on his investment, what must the sales price be?

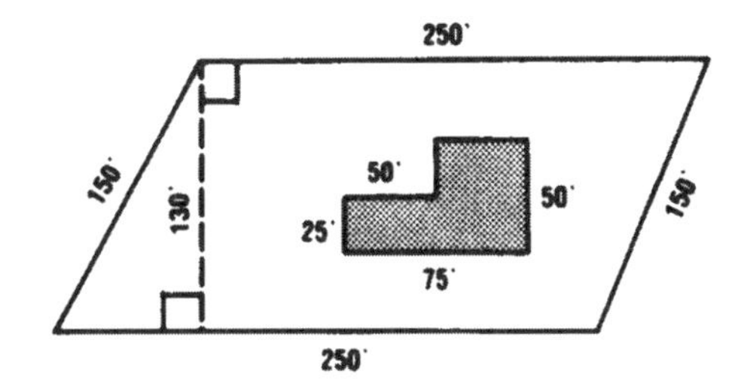

(A) $76,250
(B) $85,400
(C) $86,647
(D) $82,500

2. The original cost to build the home shown below was $18 per square foot. The cost to reproduce the same house today would be $41,472. What has been the increase in cost per square foot?

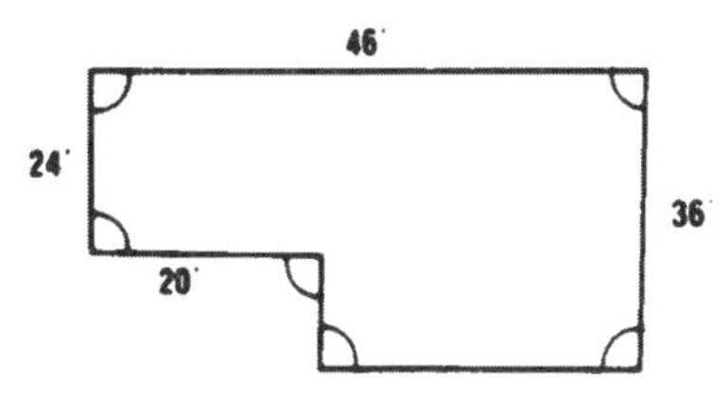

(A) $11.29
(B) $8.29
(C) $6.29
(D) $4.29

3. If 30% of the tract shown is to be used for the construction of homes, how many acres will still be available for other purposes?

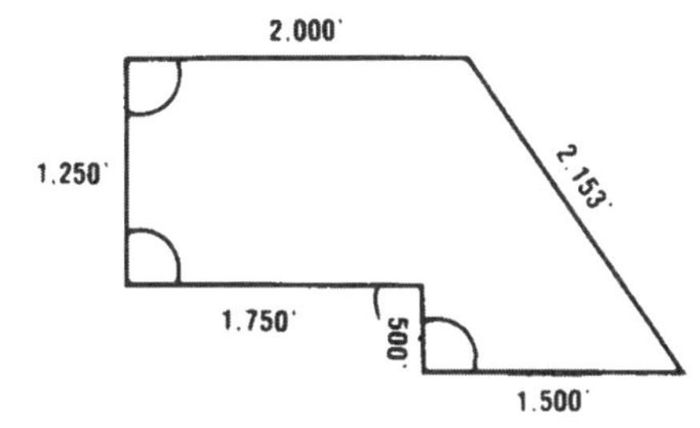

(A) 55.0
(B) 59.8
(C) 56.2
(D) 52.7

4. How many square feet are contained in the lot shown?

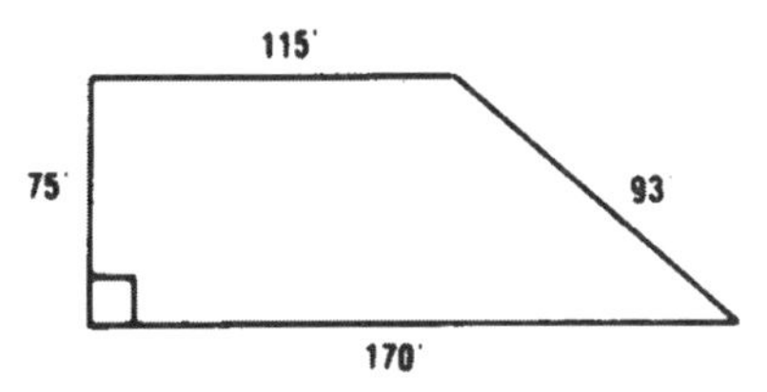

(A) 21,375.0
(B) 10,687.5
(C) 11,970.0
(D) 12,970.5

5. A rectangular lot which measures 100' x 145.2' is what percent of an acre?
(A) 25%
(B) 33.3%
(C) 80%
(D) 20%

6. Office space measuring 102' x 84' rents for $4.75 per square foot annually. What is the monthly rent payment?
   (A) $406.98
   (B) $3,391.50
   (C) $339.15
   (D) $4,069.80

7. The exterior of a ranch house measures 32 feet across the front and 26 feet front to back. If the exterior walls are 9 inches thick, what is the square footage of the interior?
   (A) 803.25
   (B) 793.00
   (C) 832.00
   (D) 747.25

Interest

1. Ken Fixit borrowed $8,400 at 8 3/4% interest. He repaid the principal and interest in one payment at the end of nine months. What amount did he pay?
   (A) $9,135.00
   (B) $8,951.25
   (C) $9,282.00
   (D) $9,851.25

2. What is the annual interest rate on a $9,200 loan if interest payments of $212.75 are paid every three months?
   (A) 7.82%
   (B) 6.93%
   (C) 10.81%
   (D) 9.25%

3. Quarterly interest payments of $160 are paid on an $8,000 loan. What is the interest rate per annum?
   (A) 8%
   (B) 2%
   (C) 24%
   (D) 5%

4. A lender charged 3 discount points on a $147,000 loan. What was the dollar amount of discount points on this loan?
   (A) $441
   (B) $490
   (C) $4,410
   (D) $4,900

5. Brown has a home improvement loan of $7,500 on which he makes quarterly interest payments of $168.75. What annual rate of interest does he pay?
   (A) 9%
   (B) 7.5%
   (C) 4%
   (D) 11%

6. A $168,000 loan at 10% interest had principal and interest payments of $1,474.32 per month. How much of the first month's payment would be applied to principal?
   (A) $74.32
   (B) $74.94
   (C) $76.25
   (D) $79.87

Proration

Note:
(1) *For testing purposes use a 30-day month (360-day year) for proration problems.*
(2) *Unless told otherwise, the seller is responsible for the day of closing.*

1. A seller sold a property to a buyer and the closing took place on April 15th. The annual taxes of $2,700 were unpaid. What would be the tax proration at closing?
   (A) $787.50 debit seller; credit buyer
   (B) $787.50 credit seller, debit buyer
   (C) $1,912.50 debit seller; credit buyer
   (D) $1,912.50 credit seller; debit buyer

2. The annual taxes of $1,320 and a three-year homeowner's policy costing $396 were paid on January 1. If the property is sold on July 15, what amount will be credited to the seller?
   (A) $907.50
   (B) $808.50
   (C) $786.50
   (D) $929.50

3. The mortgage balance after the July 1st payment was $47,500. The monthly P & I payment was $510. The interest is computed in arrears at 12.25%. What amount will the seller be debited if the closing takes place July 20th?
   (A) $323.26
   (B) $361.62
   (C) $232.26
   (D) $161.60

4. A property is assessed at 40% of its appraised value of $135,000. The tax rate is $7.40 per $100 and taxes are due and payable January 1st each year in advance. If the closing takes place on August 12th, how much will the buyer owe the seller for the prorated taxes?
   (A) $1,351.80
   (B) $1,531.80
   (C) $1,746.50
   (D) $1,831.80

5. A buyer bought a house and obtained a $100,000 loan at 8% interest. The buyer is responsible for the closing date, which will be May 18. The buyer's first mortgage payment will be June 1. How much prepaid interest will be charged to the buyer at the closing?
   (A) $266.64
   (B) $288.86
   (C) $822.14
   (D) $955.46

Investment & Appraising

1. A lot 160' x 410' sells for $16,400. What should a second lot in the same area 204' x 375' sell for?
   (A) $21,012
   (B) $18,460
   (C) $19,125
   (D) $20,500

2. An investor realizes a 12% return on his investment. If the income is $960 a month, what is the value of his property?
   (A) $8,000
   (B) $96,000
   (C) $80,000
   (D) $13,824

3. In order to realize a net profit of $750 per month, how much must be invested at a 12% rate of return per annum?
   (A) $6,250
   (B) $75,000
   (C) $108,000
   (D) $10,800

4. A property has a current land value of $60,000. Current replacement cost of improvements is $230,000. Depreciation is 25%. What is the depreciated value for this property?
   (A) $212,500
   (B) $232,500
   (C) $223,500
   (D) $253,200

5. Barry purchased a warehouse for $230,000. The property rented out for $3,200 per month with a 5% vacancy rate. Annual expenses were $4,000 for utilities; $5,200 for realty taxes; $1,500 management fee; and $9,700 for the mortgage payments. What would be the annual rate of return for this property?
   (A) 6.9%
   (B) 11%
   (C) 14.3%
   (D) 15.7%

6. The cost of building a rectangular dwelling 48 feet by 24 feet is $23.75 per square foot. What will the price be to the nearest $100 if the builder wants a gross profit of 14% on his investment?
   (A) $38,300
   (B) $36,500
   (C) $31,200
   (D) $31,100

7. A percentage lease calls for a rent equal to 2 1/2% of the gross annual sales, with a minimum annual rent of $6,000. What is the annual rent if gross sales were $190,000?
   (A) $6,000
   (B) $4,750
   (C) $7,600
   (D) $10,750

8. A home situated on a lot 75' x 100' is valued at $48,000. If the home occupies 15% of the property and similar lots are selling for $14,000, what would be the approximate cost per square foot to reproduce the house?
   (A) $40
   (B) $38
   (C) $42
   (D) $30

9. Each unit of an 18-family apartment dwelling rents for $230 per month. Annual expenses are $4,600 for maintenance, $1,050 for insurance, $5,134 for taxes, $2,400 for heat and utilities, $19,400 interest and 5% of the effective gross income for management fees. The vacancy rate is 5%. What is the owner's net rate of return the first year if he paid $211,000 for the property?
   (A) 12%
   (B) 15%
   (C) 6%
   (D) 49%

10. An apartment dwelling has a monthly gross rental income of $8,000 and the annual expenses are $6,600. If a purchaser desires an 11% return on his investment, what must the purchase price be?
    (A) $872,727.27
    (B) $812,727.27
    (C) $983,400.00
    (D) $1,056,000.00

11. Smith purchased five parcels of land for $7,000 each and sold them as eight separate parcels for $5,600 each. What percent of profit did he make on his investment?
    (A) 28%
    (B) 35.7%
    (C) 12.8%
    (D) 21.9%

12. A factory building eight years old has a depreciated value of $460,000. If the total economic life of the building is 40 years, what was its value new?
    (A) $532,000
    (B) $483,000
    (C) $575,000
    (D) $552,000

13. An apartment building has a vacancy factor of 4% and the annual expenses amount to $2,352. What is the market value if the gross income is $16,200 per year and the capitalization rate is 12%?
    (A) $194,400
    (B) $135,000
    (C) $153,400
    (D) $110,000

14. If you purchased a property for $80,000 and sold it later for $100,000, your rate of appreciation would be:
    (A) 25%
    (B) 18%
    (C) 16%
    (D) 20%

15. An investor purchased seven lots costing $8,000 each and spent $3,200 per lot for improvements. He wishes to sell the property for 15% more than he has invested. What must the sales price be?
    (A) $92,235
    (B) $94,600
    (C) $90,160
    (D) $88,200

16. A condominium complex containing 50 units was built on property costing $58,000. $48,000 was spent on roads, sidewalks and sewers. Construction costs amounted to $1,245,000 and $72,000 was spent on other expenses. All of the money was borrowed for eight months at an annual interest rate of 12%. If the developer wants a 15% net return on his total investment, what must each unit, to the nearest $100, sell for?
    (A) $30,700
    (B) $35,300
    (C) $28,500
    (D) $33,000

17. A property is purchased for $43,500. What must the minimum sales price be if annual expenses amounted to $4,000 and a gross profit of 12% on the investment is to be realized on a resale at the end of one year?
    (A) $48,720
    (B) $53,200
    (C) $53,977
    (D) $52,300

18. If a building contains 48 offices, each having an area of 900 sq. ft., what is the vacancy rate if 10 of the offices are vacant for one month, one is empty for two months, and one is empty for five months?
    (A) 2.95%
    (B) 35.4%
    (C) 14.7%
    (D) 16.3%

19. Total rent during the year amounted to $6,600 under a percentage lease calling for a base rent of $500 a month plus 3 3/4% of the annual gross in excess of $50,000. What amount did the business gross?
    (A) $52,250
    (B) $66,000
    (C) $72,250
    (D) $64,500

Taxes & Insurance

1. A building lot is valued at $40,000 and is assessed at 75%. If the tax bill is $1,200, what is the tax rate per $100?
    (A) $4.00
    (B) $400
    (C) $.25
    (D) $3.00

2. A 150' x 250' commercial lot was assessed at $140 per front foot and the building was assessed at $85,000. What was the yearly tax if the rate was $8.60 per $100?
    (A) $7,562
    (B) $7,265
    (C) $9,116
    (D) $10,320

3. A township assesses property at 80% of value. Semi-annual taxes of $902.40 are paid by the owner of a house valued at $48,000. What is the tax rate per $100?
    (A) $4.70
    (B) $2.35
    (C) $3.76
    (D) $1.88

4. If the contents of a home were valued at $12,000 and insured for $8,400, contents valued at $18,500 would be insured for:
    (A) $12,950
    (B) $12,250
    (C) $11,600
    (D) $12,400

5. In a town that has a tax rate of $5.70 per $100, a house with an annual tax bill of $5,985 is placed on the market for $180,000. What is the assessed value?
   (A) $105,000
   (B) $115,000
   (C) $130,000
   (D) $1,598

6. In question #5, the assessed value is what percent of the market value?
   (A) 17.14%
   (B) 58.3%
   (C) 171.4%
   (D) 63.4%

7. If the assessed value of a property is 80% of its market value, what are the annual taxes if the tax rate is $3.75 per $100 and the market value is $56,000?
   (A) $1,194.67
   (B) $1,680.00
   (C) $2,100.00
   (D) $1,870.50

Miscellaneous

1. A developer has determined that 1/2 of his tract will be used for the construction of single-family homes, 1/3 will be allocated for a shopping center, and 72 acres will be reserved for recreation areas. How many acres will be used for the shopping center?
   (A) 144
   (B) 432
   (C) 216
   (D) 72

2. Great Deal Realty deducts 8% of the total commission for promotional and advertising expenses and pays its listing and selling agents each 25% of the balance. What would one of its associates earn if she listed and sold a house for $160,000, with a 5.5% commission?
   (A) $1,673
   (B) $8,096
   (C) $4,048
   (D) $8,800

3. A tract of land measures 2,000' x 150'. A lot within the tract is 75' x 100'. The lot is what fraction of the entire tract?
   (A) 1/25
   (B) 1/40
   (C) 1/30
   (D) 1/50

4. Sue B. Lett and her husband bought a two-family home and want enough rent from one apartment that they can live in the other rent-free. Their annual expenses are $1,260 and taxes are $816. Their monthly loan payments are $180. What must the monthly rent be?
   (A) $383
   (B) $288
   (C) $188
   (D) $353

5. A house and lot are purchased for $70,000. The cost of the lot amounted to 25% of the purchase price. If the bank will loan 90% of the value of the house, how much will the down payment be?
   (A) $11,667
   (B) $7,000
   (C) $17,500
   (D) $22,750

6. The monthly payment on a $37,000 mortgage is $8.50 per $1,000. The annual taxes of $1,008 and a three-year insurance policy costing $432 are prorated and paid monthly. What is the total monthly payment?
   (A) $354.50
   (B) $434.50
   (C) $410.50
   (D) $420.50

7. The purchase price of a home is $44,000. The down payment is 3% of the first $25,000 and 5% of the balance. How much will the seller pay if he is to be charged 4 discount points?
   (A) $1,057
   (B) $1,760
   (C) $1,692
   (D) $1,100

8. Which of the transactions listed below will provide the seller with a net amount of $40,910?

Transaction	Sale Price	Broker's Fee	Additional Expenses
I	$43,700	6%	$126
II	$43,900	6%	$356
III	$43,500	6%	$ 40
IV	$43,900	6%	$340

(A) I (B) II (C) III (D) IV

9. A tract of land was subdivided, allowing 50% of the total area for residential use, 1/4 of the land for a shopping center, 1/8 for streets, and five acres for recreation. What is the total acreage?
(A) 40 acres
(B) 62.5 acres
(C) 52 acres
(D) 46 acres

10. A lease provides for a base rent of $750 per month plus 2.5% of all gross annual income in excess of $240,000. The lessee realized a gross annual income of $310,000. How much rent did he pay that year?
(A) $15,000
(B) $10,750
(C) $13,750
(D) $9,175

11. Nellie borrowed $4,500 at 9.75% interest per year. When she prepaid the loan, she paid $156.39 in interest. How long did she have the money?
(A) 93 days
(B) 95 days
(C) 116 days
(D) 130 days

12. The sellers have agreed to a sales price of $52,500 for their property. In addition to the 6% broker's fee, they have also consented to pay a 5-point discount fee in order that the purchasers may obtain an FHA-insured loan of $50,400. How much will the sellers net from the sale?
(A) $46,725
(B) $46,882
(C) $46,830
(D) $46,956

13. Smith has purchased Jones' home for $50,000 and is assuming Jones' mortgage balance of $40,000 at 9% interest rate. The closing takes placed August 20th and Jones has not made his August payment. What will the entry be on the seller's closing statement?
(A) $200 debit
(B) $200 credit
(C) $100 credit
(D) $100 debit

14. An investor purchased two apartment houses, paying $120,000 for the first one. The first apartment house cost 80% of what he paid for the second one. How much did he pay for the second apartment house?
(A) $150,000
(B) $96,000
(C) $144,000
(D) $154,000

15. A real estate salesperson receives 40% of the 6% fees paid to her broker on her sales. What are her average monthly sales if she earns $18,000 annually?
(A) $43,200
(B) $62,500
(C) $52,500
(D) $75,000

16. Smith pays $8.05 per $1,000 per month on his mortgage loan. He borrowed 80% of the $45,000 purchase price at 9% interest for 30 years. How much does Smith pay monthly?
(A) $362.25
(B) $299.80
(C) $289.80
(D) $325.50

17. A $42,000 mortgage loan is to be amortized at $8.05 per $1,000 per month. The semi-annual taxes of $624 and a three-year insurance premium of $396 are to be prorated and paid monthly. What is the total monthly payment?
(A) $423.10
(B) $453.10
(C) $401.10
(D) $475.10

18. Sarah sold a lot for 25% more than she paid for it. She invested the proceeds at 12%, which gave her $970 per year in interest. What did she originally pay for the lot?
(A) $2,943
(B) $11,547
(C) $6,467
(D) $5,658

19. On a scale drawing on which 1" = 4', a room shown as 7.5"x 3.75" would contain how many square feet?
(A) 351.5
(B) 112.5
(C) 1,125
(D) 450

20. Bill Buttons sold his home for $127,500 after making a profit of 35% on his purchase price. How much did he originally pay for the home?
(A) $82,875
(B) $86,750
(C) $172,125
(D) $94,444

21. A rectangular tract of land containing two acres has a frontage of 528 feet. What is the depth of the property?
(A) 165'
(B) 82.5'
(C) 121'
(D) 460'

22. A rectangular lot is 125' x 95'. The town has a required setback of 15', sideyard restrictions of 8' and a rear line of 6'. This is not a corner lot. If you are allowed to build on 75% of the unrestricted area, what is the area of the largest one-story house you could build on this lot?
    (A) 6,049 sq. ft.
    (B) 4,069 sq. ft.
    (C) 8,066 sq. ft.
    (D) 10,082 sq. ft.

23. If the tax assessment on a piece of property increased by 30% and the tax rate decreased by 30%, what happens to the taxes?
    (A) 30% increase
    (B) 30% decrease
    (C) Stay the same
    (D) Decrease by 9%

24. The property below was bought at a cost of $210,000. Mrs. Jones, the owner, is going to convert the one-family house into offices and to landscape the grounds. If it cost her $0.40 per square foot for landscaping, what must she charge per square foot of office space so that her gross return is 16% of her investment?

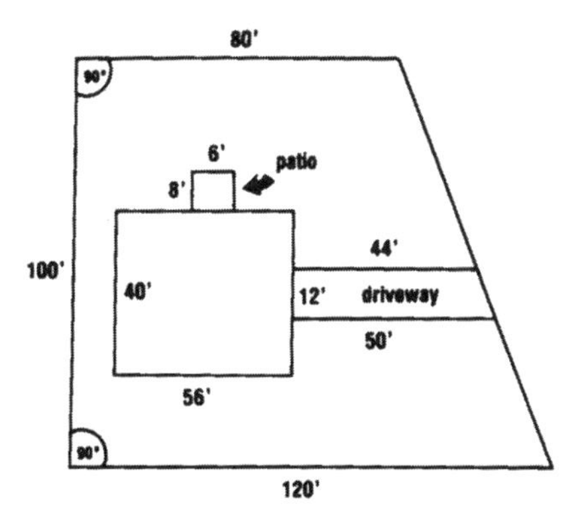

Round answer to the nearest dollar

    (A) $31.00
    (B) $15.00
    (C) $28.00
    (D) $37.00

25. Mr. Jones wants to sell his home at a 25% profit. If the selling price ends up being 20% less than the asking price, what is the net result?
    (A) 5% gain
    (B) 5% loss
    (C) 45% gain
    (D) Selling price = Original purchase price

26. A seller paid $4,235, which represented a 7 discount points fee on an FHA mortgage. What was the amount of the loan?
    (A) $60,500
    (B) $30,750
    (C) $2,965
    (D) $80,050

27. A homeowner's home appreciated 10% over the past 10 years. If he sells his home at this new price and pays a broker a commission of 10% of the selling price, which of the following is true?
    (A) 10% gain
    (B) 10% loss
    (C) Net selling price = Original cost
    (D) Net selling price is 1% less than original cost.

CHAPTER THIRTY-ONE

MOBILE AND MANUFACTURED HOMES

New Jersey's Motor Vehicle Dealer Licensing Law, 39:10-19, has been amended to provide that licensed real estate brokers, although not licensed as motor vehicle dealers, may now legally broker the resale of mobile and manufactured homes which are titled as motor vehicles. Specifically, those vehicles are mobile homes without their own motor power (other than recreational vehicles) and manufactured homes. Mobile homes and manufactured homes are required to bear motor vehicle titles.

Real estate licensees who broker transactions involving mobile homes or manufactured homes and demonstrate a lack of familiarity with all applicable laws are subject to sanctions by the New Jersey Real Estate Commission (see 11:5-1.12(i), Chapter 3).

Manufactured Home Taxation Act

The New Jersey Legislature has determined that:

A. It is in the public interest that the Legislature address the difficult questions raised in litigation over the tax status of manufactured homes;

B. Manufactured homes located in mobile home parks receive fewer public services than manufactured homes or other single-family dwelling units located on privately owned lots, and therefore require a lower level of public expenditures;

C. With respect to purchaser financing, manufactured homes located in mobile home parks are not treated in the same manner as manufactured homes located on private lots owned by a homeowner or other residential property, and are not typically financed through mortgage arrangements, but through installment credit;

D. Because of the differences in siting between manufactured homes in mobile home parks and manufactured homes located elsewhere, it is difficult to equate the two for property title purposes and for purposes of property tax enforcement;

E. Certain property owned by public utilities that would otherwise constitute real property for the purposes of taxation is not real property for such purposes, and has provided an alternate means of ensuring that the owner of such property is responsible for reasonable payment for public services which that owner receives;

F. The factors that distinguish manufactured homes in mobile home parks from other dwelling units warrant a distinction between them, similar to the distinction drawn in the case of public utility property;

G. It is necessary to draw such a distinction in a fair and equitable manner that will not penalize the owners of the manufactured homes located in mobile home parks, nor absolve them of their responsibility to pay for the public services they receive;

H. It is further necessary to ensure parity, where taxation is concerned, between manufactured homes situated outside mobile home parks and other similar dwelling units;

I. The land and improvements which constitute a mobile home park, including any improvements added as part of the private provision of otherwise public services, are subject to taxation as real property, and the revenues derived from the assessment and levy of these real property taxes contribute to the defrayal of the costs of public services provided the owner of the park and lessees of sites in the park; and

J. It is appropriate and necessary to provide a method by which a municipality may receive reasonable payment for services provided to the owners of manufactured homes in mobile home parks, the cost of which services is not defrayed by real property tax revenues. (54:4-1.3)

Definitions

Cooperative—A cooperative is a housing corporation or association that entitles shareholders or members to possess and occupy for dwelling purposes a house, apartment, manufactured home or other unit of housing owned by the corporation or association, or to purchase a unit of housing constructed or erected by the corporation or association.

Grade—Grade refers to a plane consisting of the average finished ground level adjacent to a structure, building or facility at all visible exterior walls.

Manufactured Home—A manufactured home is a unit of housing that:

1. Consists of one or more transportable sections that are substantially constructed off site and, if more than one section, are joined together on site;
2. Is built on a permanent chassis;
3. Is designed to be used, when connected to utilities, as a dwelling on a permanent or nonpermanent foundation; and
4. Is manufactured in accordance with the standards promulgated for a manufactured home by the secretary pursuant to the "National Manufactured Housing Construction Code Act," P.L. 1975, c.217.

Mobile Home Park—A mobile home park is a parcel of land, or two or more contiguous parcels of land, containing no fewer than ten sites (three sites if built before 1983) equipped for the installation of manufactured homes, where these sites are under common ownership and control, other than as a cooperative, for the purpose of leasing each site to the owner of a manufactured home for the installation thereof, and where the park owner provides services, which are provided by the municipality in which the park is located for property owners outside the park, including:

1. The construction and maintenance of streets;
2. Lighting of streets and other common areas;
3. Garbage removal;
4. Snow removal; and
5. Provision for the drainage of surface water from home sites and common areas.

A parcel, or any contiguous parcels, of land which contain no fewer than three sites equipped for the installation of manufactured homes, and which otherwise conform to the provisions of this subsection, qualifies as a mobile home park under the law.

Municipal Service Fee—This is a fee imposed on manufactured homes installed in a mobile home park for the purpose of reasonable payment for services rendered by the municipality or any other local taxing authority established by ordinance of the municipal governing body, to reimburse the municipality for educational costs associated with pupils residing in that park.

Nonpermanent Foundation—A nonpermanent foundation is one consisting of nonmortared blocks, wheels, a concrete slab, runners, or any combination thereof, or any other system approved by the commissioner for the installation and anchorage of a manufactured home on other than a permanent foundation.

Permanent Foundation—A permanent foundation is a system of support installed either partially or entirely below grade, which is:

1. Capable of transferring all design loads imposed by or upon the structure into soil or bedrock without failure;
2. Placed at an adequate depth below grade to prevent frost damage; and
3. Constructed of any material approved by the commissioner.

Trailer—A trailer is a recreational vehicle, travel trailer, camper or other transportable, temporary dwelling unit, with or without its own motor power, designed and constructed for travel and recreational purposes to be installed on a nonpermanent foundation if installation is required (54:4-1.4).

Procedure For Transferring Title to a Mobile or Manufactured Home

Licensees are advised to strictly adhere to the following DMV requirements when attempting to transfer the title to a mobile or manufactured home. To transfer the motor vehicle title to a mobile or manufactured home, a **personal appearance** at a motor vehicle agency is required. When appearing at a DMV agency/office to transfer a title, a real estate licensee must bring:

1. The properly completed (absolutely no white-outs or strike-throughs) and fully executed original title, signed by the seller and buyer;
2. Completed sales tax form (Form LS240) indicating exemption 3F;
3. Original limited dual power of attorney from seller and buyer authorizing the brokerage firm and the individual salesperson who will do so to transfer the title from the seller(s) to the buyer(s) at the agency and/or to obtain and

complete a new title in the event the original title is lost;

4. Completed application for Certificate of Ownership (Form ISM/SS7), in cases where unit is currently titled in a state other than New Jersey; and

5. Personal ID (driver's license, etc.) and license pocket card of licensee who will sign documents as the attorney-in-fact for buyer and seller. Forms (LS 240 and ISM/SS7) may be obtained from a local DMV agency.

In unusual circumstances, such as where a unit is titled in a name other than the seller, or no title was ever issued, or where an estate is involved or there has been a divorce, **before attempting to transfer a title at an agency** licensees should call the DMV's Title Unit in Trenton at (609) 984-8419 for instructions.

Titles cannot be transferred if they are encumbered. Therefore, licensees should confirm that the sellers have good title to the unit before taking a listing. DMV currently requires four to six weeks to provide a lien search after its receipt of a mailed request accompanied by the required fee of $5 per search. Requests delivered in person at the Trenton headquarters, for a maximum of three lien searches, can be responded to within a matter of hours, as you wait. Lien searches only cover the current record titleholders of the unit and liens which have attached since that owner took title. For a more comprehensive "title search," which extends further back in time and takes longer to produce, a fee of $10.50 is required. Questions on lien or title searches can be directed to the DMV at (609) 292-0466.

In cases where titles are encumbered, the liens must be satisfied before title can be transferred. The newest form of title (Red Title Form) contains spaces for the release of two liens and an indication of the total number of lienholders. The satisfaction of a lien must be evidenced either by the lienholder's signature on the title itself in the lien release location, along with the title of the person signing the release and the date of the satisfaction of the lien, or by the production of an original signed letter, on the letterhead of the lienholder, confirming satisfaction of the obligation and the release of the lien.

It should be noted that not all liens against such units are recorded with the DMV. Therefore, a UCC search at the office of the secretary of state and/or with the clerk of the county in which the unit is situated may have to be performed.

Rights of Residents in Mobile and Manufactured Homes

Purchases From Owners. Mobile home park owners or operators may not require residents to purchase from them underskirting, equipment for tying down mobile homes or any other equipment required by law or regulations of the mobile home park. The park operator may, however, stipulate by rule or regulation the style or quality of such equipment to be purchased by the tenant from a vendor of the tenant's choosing.

Electric or Gas Appliances. Mobile home park owners or operators may not charge residents who choose to install an electric or gas appliance in their mobile home an additional fee unless that fee reflects the cost to the mobile home park of such installation or its use. Nor may the installation, service or maintenance of any such appliance, or the making of any interior improvements in a mobile home be restricted, if such installation or improvement is in compliance with applicable building codes and other provisions of law (46:8C-2 a,b).

Purchases of Gas. Mobile home park owners or operators may not require residents to purchase from them or from any vendor or supplier they designate, any natural product, by-product or synthetic or petroleum gas; unless the owner or operator owns or has a possessory interest in the lines or equipment that transmits or consumes a specific fuel, and only when that system is properly operating under state and local laws using fuel that is competitively priced. If the park owner or operator does not own or have a possessory interest in the lines or equipment, the park owner or operator may, by rule or regulation, designate a specific grade or quality of petroleum or gas to be used. Specification of grade or quality is also permitted whenever reasonably necessary to maintain safety standards prescribed by state or local regulation (46:8C-2 b (2)).

Requirement to Move or Relocate. No mobile home park landlord or operator may move, or require anyone else to move, any mobile home owned by anyone else, unless he or she is able to show that it is reasonably necessary to do so and 30 days written notice is given, except in case of an emergency. All costs of moving a mobile home at the request of the park landlord or operator, including any loss or damage, must be paid or reimbursed by the park landlord or operator, and this right to reimbursement cannot be waived (46:8C-2 (3)).

Disclosure of Charges and Rules and Regulations. The law requires park owners to supply to buyers a copy of the park's rules and regulations and a list of all fees, assessments and service charges imposed upon tenants before a lease is signed or a rental agreement is entered into. No fees, charges or assessments that have been disclosed may be increased, and no rules and regulations may be changed by the park owner or operator, without specifying the date of implementation of said fees, charges, assessments or rules and regulations. Tenants must be given 30 days written notice if changes are made.

In addition, all fees, charges or assessments, including entrance, membership or association fees, disclosed by mobile home park owners or operators must be specifically related to actual costs incurred by the mobile home park owner or operator. No fee in reimbursement of the owner's or operator's costs in obtaining a prospective tenant's credit report shall exceed the actual cost to the owner or operator of obtaining such a report, including the cost of providing the prospective tenant with copies of the reports in accordance with the law. A complete and accurate copy of any report furnished to an owner or operator by a credit reporting service with respect to a prospective tenant shall be promptly forwarded to the prospective tenant by the owner or operator. All disclosures must be completed prior to the execution of any leasing agreement, or the entering into of any other contractual relationship.

Failure on the part of the mobile home park owner or operator to fully disclose all fees, charges or assessments will prevent the park owner or operator from collecting those fees, charges or assessments, and if the dweller refuses to pay any undisclosed charges, the owner or operator will not be able to use that as a cause for eviction in any court of law (46:8C-2 c).

Unlawful Gifts. Any bribe or other payment to get into a mobile home park accepted by a park landlord or operator makes the landlord or operator a disorderly person, and the person making the payment can recover double its amount plus costs in Superior Court, Special Civil Part, Landlord-Tenant Section in the county in which the mobile home park is located or in the county in which the defendant resides (46:8C-2 e,f).

Sale of Mobile Home Within Park. No mobile home park landlord or operator may deny any resident the right to sell the resident's own mobile home within the park or require the resident to remove the mobile home from the park solely on the basis of its sale. The park landlord or operator can reserve the right to approve the purchaser, but such permission may not be unreasonably withheld. To avoid disputes, licensees should include in contracts they prepare on these transactions a clause indicating that upon receipt of written notice of the tenancy application, the buyer will be entitled to a full refund of all deposit monies.

"For Sale" Signs. The posting of a "For Sale" sign by a mobile home owner may not be forbidden, but the location and size of the sign to be erected on the lot or in the park may be regulated.

Commissions or Fees. The landlord or operator may not charge a commission or fee for the sale of a mobile home unless he or she acted as the sales agent under a written agreement with the mobile home owner.

Rights of Owners of Mobile Home Parks

In addition to being familiar with the laws protecting residents, licensees must also be familiar with the rights of people who own mobile home parks, because this is where the majority of mobile and manufactured homes are located.

Notice of Sale. Park owners must be given **advance written notice** of the intended sale of any unit situated in their park. The law gives the park owner the right to approve or disapprove of new applicants for tenancy in the park, as long as the approval is not unreasonably withheld. In transactions where the parties intend that the unit will remain in the park, the law provides that no contract for the sale of a mobile home will be valid unless the seller has advised the purchaser, in writing, of the park owner or operator's right to approve the purchaser.

To avoid disputes, licensees should include in contracts they prepare on these transactions a clause indicating that upon receipt of a written notice of disapproval of the tenancy application, the buyer will be entitled to a full refund of all deposit monies.

Application for Tenancy. An application for tenancy in the park must also be provided by the seller to the prospective purchaser. Sellers can obtain application forms from the park owners or management. Prospective purchasers are required by law to personally present the application to the park owners or management, who then have the legal right to perform credit checks on the applicants. It is imperative that written approval of the tenancy application be secured **before closing**, if the buyer intends to continue to occupy space in the park.

Other Requirements. Other requirements may be imposed on resales, such as providing to the park owner copies of the title and certain other documents, and may also establish homesite standards. As this is information which is material to the entire transaction, licensees should assure that prospective purchasers are supplied with this information before they sign a contract to purchase a unit.

Licensees should also be aware that it is not uncommon for park owners to include in their lease with a unit owner a clause reserving to themselves a **right of first refusal** on the purchase of the unit.

Leases Generally Not Assignable. The leases for lots in mobile home parks generally are not assignable and prohibit the subletting of the lot. It is therefore essential that, before a licensee begins to market a unit for sale, he or she determines not only what the seller's current rental fee is, but also what the monthly rent will be for a new occupant of that space. Intentional or negligent misrepresentation by licensees of this amount can result in disastrous consequences for purchasers and will be considered serious regulatory violations by the Commission.

Licensees should obtain a copy of a park's rules and regulations for their own reference, in addition to assuring that they are supplied to a buyer.

Taxation of Manufactured Homes

A manufactured home is subject to taxation as real property under NJSA 54:4 when that home:

1. is affixed to the land on which it is sited by a permanent foundation; or

2. is affixed to that land by a nonpermanent foundation and connected to utility systems in such manner as to render the home habitable as a dwelling unit on a permanent basis (54:4-1.5).

Trailers are not covered by the law, and manufactured homes that are installed in a mobile home park are not subject to taxation as real property.

Municipal Service Fee

A municipality must establish an ordinance for the imposition of an annual municipal service fee on manufactured homes installed in a mobile home park within its corporate boundaries. In setting this fee, the municipal governing body must consider the extent to which the taxes levied against the land and improvements in the park defray the costs of services provided or paid for by the municipality, or any other taxing authority, for lessees of sites in the park. The ordinance imposing the municipal service fee must provide for the proration of that fee, as necessary, in order to account for vacancies in the mobile home park.

The mobile home landlord or operator must collect the fee each month from the owner of the mobile or manufactured home and give a receipt upon collection. The park owner must then transmit the fees collected to the tax collector of the taxing district in which the fee is imposed, along with a copy of each receipt issued.

The governing body of a municipality may, by ordinance, fix a rate of interest to be charged a homeowner by the municipality for failure to pay the municipal service fee, and to be charged a park owner for failure to transmit fees actually collected. This rate will be fixed within the limits established for interest charged for delinquent property taxes.

An ordinance adopted pursuant to this law must set forth the manner in which the municipal service fee will be allocated among the owners of manufactured homes within the mobile home park. The respective portion of the municipal service fee allocated to the owner of a manufactured home constitutes a rent surcharge, collectible in addition to any surcharge or increase permitted by any rent control or rent leveling ordinance adopted by the municipality. The respective portion of a municipal service fee allocated to the owner of a manufactured home is deemed to be rent for eviction purposes (54:4-1.6).

Sales Tax

The sales tax imposed by the "Sales and Use Tax Act" will be applied only against the manufacturer's invoice price of a manufactured home upon the first sale of that home (54:4-1.7).

Transfer Inheritance and Estate Tax

A manufactured home that is subject to real property taxation under the law will also be treated as real property for the purposes of imposing the transfer inheritance and estate tax pursuant to New Jersey law (54:4-1.9).

Certificate of Ownership

A person who has a certificate of ownership issued by the director for a mobile or manufactured home, located in a mobile home park, that will be relocated on land that the owner of the home owns or has an interest in, must, at least ten days prior to that relocation, file with the director a "notice of relocation." If the director accepts the notice, the certificate of ownership will be canceled on the date of relocation (39:10-11.1).

Truth-In-Renting Law

As is the case in all brokered rental transactions, licensees must also be aware of the requirements imposed by New Jersey's **Truth in Renting Law**, N.J.S.A. 46:8-43 (See Chapter 22). When questions arise on transactions involving mobile or manufactured homes, buyers, sellers, park owners and licensees can call the New Jersey Manufactured Housing Association at (609) 588-9040 for information. Questions about title transfer procedures should be directed to the DMV.

Confirmation of Resale Requirements

Prior to closing, confirmation that resale requirements have been met should be obtained from the park owner or management. In addition, a Smoke Detector Certificate and, where required by the municipality, a Certificate of Occupancy must be obtained. It must also be determined whether any unpaid rent or other outstanding fees are owed to the park and, if so, satisfactory arrangements for payment must be made. Where the buyer is using borrowed funds to finance the purchase, a lender-community agreement form may also need to be signed. The availability of the financing may be contingent upon the park owner's willingness to enter into a lender-community agreement.

Transfer of Title

After a closing, the title to the unit must be transferred. Where the licensee will personally transfer the title at a DMV agency, the requirements set forth earlier under "Procedure For Transferring Title. . ." must be fulfilled and the procedures described in steps 3 and 5 must be followed. In addition, notice of the change in ownership should be sent to the unit's manufacturer to assure coverage for the new owner under any warranty which may still be in effect on the unit.

Mobile Home Leases

A mobile home park landlord or operator is required to:

1. Offer a written lease for at least 12 months to each mobile home dweller within the park or to a person who has purchased a mobile home from the landlord or operator. The lease must be offered within 30 days from the time the purchaser lawfully moved in;

2. Give the mobile home owner a copy of all park rules and regulations prior to signing a lease;

3. Post a copy of park rules and regulations in a recreation hall or some other place within the park where it can easily be found; and

4. Give full disclosure of all fees, charges and assessments which must be based on (1) actual costs incurred and (2) all rules and regulations, before the dweller moves in. Written notice of any changes must be given at least 30 days before the changes become effective.

Sunday Sales

N.J.S.A. 2A:171-1.1 provides that anyone who carries on or engages in the business of selling, dealing or trading in new or used motor vehicles or who sells, deals or trades in new or used motor vehicles as a business on Sundays is guilty of a disorderly persons offense. Persons convicted of this offense are subject to fines, imprisonment or both. The attorney general's office has informally indicated that it cannot conclude that this law does not apply to real estate licensees selling mobile home or manufactured housing units on Sundays.

Compliance

Failure to comply with the various requirements described above will result in denial of a requested title transfer. The additional requirements of the Department of Community Affairs, as well as landlord/tenant obligations, must also be fulfilled as outlined above.

On the private sale of a mobile home, failure to comply with the application procedure as described, before any sales agreement is entered into, will absolve the park owner or operator from the requirement of offering a lease to the purchaser as described above in the section on "Mobile Home Leases." The preceding is not applicable if a buyer plans to immediately remove a home from the park.

Either a mobile home owner, mobile home purchaser or park owner or operator aggrieved by the failure of any person to comply with the provisions of this section may seek damages and reasonable costs and attorneys fees in a complaint, cross-claim or third-party complaint in a court of competent jurisdiction.

If the mobile home park owner or operator unreasonably withholds approval of a purchaser of a mobile home as a tenant, either the mobile home owner who is selling or the intended purchaser of the mobile home may institute an action in the Superior Court. A plaintiff who shall recover a judgment in any such action shall be awarded all damages proximately caused by the unreasonable refusal of the mobile home park owner or operator to approve the sale, together with the costs of the action and reasonable attorneys' fees. In any such action the court shall also be empowered to order the admission of the purchaser of the mobile home to the mobile home park (46:8C-3).

To obtain more information about mobile and manufactured homes, call the New Jersey Manufactured Housing Association, (609) 588-9040, and/or the Mobile Homeowners Association of New Jersey, (609) 695-3483. Questions relating to title transfer procedures and requirements should be directed to the DMV.

KEY WORDS

Manufactured Home
Mobile Home Park
Municipal Service Fee
Trailer

CHAPTER 31
Review Questions
(Answers on page 566)

1. A mobile home park is a parcel of land or two or more contiguous parcels of land containing no fewer than ____ sites equipped for the installation of manufactured homes.
   (A) 2
   (B) 10
   (C) 20
   (D) 30

2. Which of the following properties are subject to taxation as real property?
   (A) A manufactured home installed in a mobile home park.
   (B) A trailer.
   (C) A manufactured home attached to a nonpermanent foundation and not connected to utility systems.
   (D) A manufactured home attached to land and installed on a permanent foundation.

3. Which of the following statements is TRUE?
   (A) A motor vehicle dealer's license is required to sell a mobile home for a fee.
   (B) A mobile home operator can prohibit display of a "For Sale" sign in a mobile home park.
   (C) A resident of a mobile home park who plans to sell his or her home must give written notice to the park owner or operator.
   (D) A mobile home operator may require residents to buy natural synthetic gas from a particular vendor as long as the park operator does not own the lines or equipment that transmit the gas.

4. Which of the following statements is NOT true?
   (A) A mobile home park operator must offer a lease for at least 12 months to each mobile home dweller.
   (B) Written notice of rule changes must be given to residents in mobile home parks at least 30 days before becoming effective.
   (C) A mobile home landlord must give a copy of rules and regulations to home owners no later than 30 days after signing a lease.
   (D) Manufactured homes installed in mobile home parks are not subject to taxation as real property.

5. When appearing at a DMV office to transfer title of a mobile home, a real estate licensee must bring all of the following, EXCEPT:
   (A) completed application for a Certificate of Ownership where the unit is currently licensed in New Jersey.
   (B) personal ID and license, pocket card of licensee who will sign as attorney-in-fact for buyer and seller.
   (C) completed Sales Tax Form.
   (D) properly completed original title signed by seller and buyer.

6. A mobile home park landlord can:
   (A) refuse to allow a mobile home owner to assign her lease.
   (B) prohibit the posting of a "For Sale" sign in the park.
   (C) charge a commission for the sale of a mobile home because it is personal property.
   (D) not reserve a right of first refusal on the purchase of a unit.

7. Which of the following statements is FALSE?
   (A) Prior to closing, confirmation that resale requirements have been met should be obtained from the park owner.
   (B) After the closing, notice of change in ownership should be sent to the company that manufactured the mobile or manufactured home to assure coverage under warranties.
   (C) Questions relating to title transfer should be directed to the Mobile Homeowner's Association.
   (D) A mobile home operator must post a copy of the park's rules and regulations in a recreation hall or other place where it can easily be found.

CHAPTER THIRTY-TWO

BUSINESS OPPORTUNITIES

A real estate license is not required to engage in the sale of business opportunities. However, a real estate license is required if the sale involves an interest in real estate, including negotiation of a new lease with the landlord or assignment of the seller's lease. If the sale of a business for $100,000 included a $30,000 building, an unlicensed person could be paid a fee on only the $70,000 portion of that sale and could not participate in negotiations involving the sale or lease of the realty.

Since the sale of a business opportunity involves the sale of personal property, the rules and laws governing transfers of chattels apply. The usual transaction involves such going businesses as grocery stores, drug stores, gasoline stations, restaurants, bakeries, garages and bars. The sale of such businesses almost always includes the stock, fixtures and goodwill.

In handling sales of businesses a licensee will encounter new forms and documents to cover the transfer or financing of personal property such as movable equipment, inventory and accounts receivable. For example, equipment and inventory (stock in trade) are usually transferred by a "bill of sale" rather than a deed; and accounts receivable are "assigned" by a written document or assignment.

Requirement That Contract to Sell Be in Writing. The sale of a business may be much more complicated than the sale of a piece of real estate. If the transaction includes sale of an interest in land or if it involves the sale of goods of $500 or more, a written contract is required under the Uniform Commercial Code. The written contract ought to include all the terms of sale covering matters such as transfer of stock in trade, fixtures, goodwill, terms of payment, time for transfer of possession, provisions for compliance with the bulk transfers law and warranties of title on the part of the seller, training period, etc. Since every business differs and the matters to be covered in the written contract vary widely with each individual transaction, it is advisable that the broker strongly recommend that the buyer retain an attorney and an accountant who have retail brokerage experience, preferably in the specific field.

Representations and Warranties. Selling a business is sometimes a risky transaction. The buyer may find after he is in possession and has operated the business for a short period of time that he is not doing as well as he expected and will therefore look for excuses to rescind the transaction. The attorney for the seller may try to protect his client by having a clause in the agreement of sale providing that the seller has made no representations regarding the business and that the buyer has made his own inspection of the business and takes all goods, fixtures and other property "as is," without warranties of any kind. Such a clause, however, gives only limited protection to the seller and will not protect him against a clear showing of fraudulent misrepresentation.

Transfer of License, Franchise or Distributorship. Some businesses involve transfer of a franchise or license. Arrangements will have to be made to see that the franchise or license is transferred to the buyer, and in some types of enterprise he must obtain a new franchise or license from the commercial licensor or government agency. For example, suppose there is the sale of a restaurant which has been licensed to serve liquor. The seller will have a license issued annually by the local town board or the city council. The buyer will have to make application to the municipality to have the license transferred. While the broker as agent for the seller has no duty with respect to obtaining such permits and licenses, the purchase may be contingent on issuance of the license, and the broker's commission may depend on seeing the transaction through to a successful completion.

Covenant Not to Compete. Where the seller is selling a going business, the buyer may wish protection against the seller who may go back on a competitive basis at some other location. For example, if Smith buys a restaurant from Jones who says he is going to retire, Smith may seek a specific written promise from Jones that he will neither operate nor buy another restaurant in the immediate area (one mile to five miles) for a specified period of time, five years for example. This kind of clause is called a "restrictive covenant" or "covenant not to compete" and is enforceable as it is not held to be an unreasonable restraint on doing business. It should be limited as to time and territory to the extent necessary to protect the goodwill for which the buyer is paying.

Assignment of Accounts Receivable. Where the sale of the business includes all the outstanding customer accounts receivable, that is, the right to collect all outstanding bills owed to the seller by previous customers in the course of business, the seller "assigns" these accounts to the buyer. The assignment should be written and the buyer should notify each customer that he is taking over the business, that the customer's account has been assigned to him, and that all payments on the account should be made to him. Otherwise the customer may make payments on his bill to the original owner and be protected. The agreement of sale of business, however, would only cover the provisions for assignment; it is up to the buyer to protect himself by giving notice to the customer. Where the written agreement provides for assignment of accounts, it ought to provide that the seller makes no representations or warranties regarding the collectibility of such accounts. The accounts receivable are usually sold at a discount, and should be reduced by the bad debt factor shown in the operating statement of the seller. Usually, however, accounts receivable are not purchased as part of the business.

Assignment of Existing Lease or Negotiation of New Lease. Where the seller occupies the business premises under an existing lease, the buyer will usually want either an assignment of the existing lease or a new lease; and one or the other of these may be made a "condition" of the sale of the business. If the existing lease prohibits assignment without the written consent of the lessor, then of course consent will have to be obtained. From the seller's point of view, it is wise to urge the buyer to obtain a new lease because on an assignment the seller would remain liable to the lessor if the buyer should later default. On the other hand, the fact that the seller has a favorable lease may make his business more saleable. Remember that negotiation of a new lease or assignment of an existing one is an activity that requires a real estate license.

Sale of Fixtures with Business. When the sale includes fixtures, the buyer should investigate to determine that they in fact belong to the seller, or whether they are security for a loan. For example, under some lease provisions, fixtures belong to the lessor upon termination of the lease; in this case a lessee should not include those fixtures in the sale.

Compliance with Zoning Laws, Building Codes and Other Government Regulations. Particularly when the business includes a building, the buyer must assure himself that the business complies with all laws and regulations governing the business involved, including zoning and building codes. At the time of sale, government officials are likely to inspect the premises and enforce on the buyer any regulations which the seller has knowingly or unknowingly been violating. Despite the fact that these matters are beyond the scope of the broker's function, he must be aware of the problem or the transaction may fall through.

Bulk Sales and Uniform Commercial Code. A body of law which attempts to make all laws relating to commercial transactions uniform throughout the country is the Uniform Commercial Code. It primarily covers personal property transactions. Its main relevance to real property is in the area of fixtures and the sale of business opportunities.

Of particular importance to buyers and sellers of business opportunities are the requirements of Article 6 of the Uniform Commercial Code known as the Bulk Transfer Act. The problem addressed by the Bulk Transfer Act comes about when the seller of a business, who owes money to creditors, transfers his inventory (stock in trade) to some third party without any notice to creditors. By the time the creditors learn of the transaction, the debtor (seller) may have already departed, taking with him the proceeds of the sale. Article 6 requires the buyer to give at least ten days notice to creditors that a bulk transfer is about to take place so that creditors can take action to prevent dissipation of the proceeds before their claims are paid.

Under the Act, the seller must assist the buyer in preparing a list of outstanding creditors, including the amount owed to each, and a schedule of all real and personal property that will be included in the sale. A notice must list the names and addresses of both buyers and sellers of the business, and state whether or not all debts will be paid. This notice must be delivered personally or sent by registered mail to all persons on the list of creditors. The buyer may also record the list in the county clerk's office in the county where the business is located, or with the secretary of state of New Jersey. The list must be signed and sworn to by the seller or his agent and must contain the names of all persons who have possible claims against the business, even if the claims are in dispute. The seller is responsible for the completeness and accuracy of the list of creditors and it is unlawful to make false statements on such a list.

The list must be made available for ten days prior to the transfer, and the buyer must preserve the list and schedule for six months after the transfer and allow inspection by any listed creditor.

Any creditor who has not received notice in accordance with the Act may treat the transfer as ineffective. This means that such a creditor may disregard the transfer and may, after obtaining a judgment against the seller, levy against the assets as if they were still the property of the seller. Thus, if the Bulk Transfer Act is not complied with, a buyer could pay the entire purchase price to a seller, and then lose all of the purchased inventory to creditors of the seller.

The New Jersey statute of limitations on bulk transfers is six months from the date of sale unless the transfer has been concealed, in which case the statute would run six months from the date of its discovery.

Financing. Most businesses are sold by the owner accepting a down payment and carrying the balance on a security agreement or conditional sales contract. Essentially, these documents are one and the same in their purpose and have largely replaced the chattel mortgage. In both cases, the rights of the parties and third persons are determined by the Uniform Commercial Code.

In effect, the owner of the business is loaning the buyer the amount over and above the down payment necessary to acquire the business. The buyer signs an installment note for the amount he owes, together with the security agreement or conditional sales contract, and the note stipulates that in the event of default the security behind the note may be sold or foreclosed.

The business broker should insist that the monthly mortgage payments are realistic. Usually a business operator cannot pay more than 4 to 5% of his gross in monthly payments. The notes can be increased after the first few years, and a balloon note arrangement after five to ten years could be considered.

In the event the seller does not have complete title because another person has a security interest in the goods, it is possible for a buyer to take title subject to an existing security agreement or conditional sales contract.

Depreciation. The buyer should know what depreciation he make take on the items sold as part of the business. The Internal Revenue Service will furnish guidelines on estimated useful life expectancies. For a detailed explanation of depreciation, see Chapter 26. However, in connection with the sale of a business opportunity, a bonus depreciation allowed in the first year is notable. It provides an allowance of 20% on new or used personal property used in the business, over and above the regular depreciation. The maximum bonus depreciation is 20% of the first $10,000 in value. If a husband and wife file a joint return, they may take 20% of the first $20,000 in value. The property must be tangible and must have a useful life of at least six years.

KEY WORDS

Bulk Transfer Act
Covenant Not to Compete
Goodwill
Stock in Trade
Uniform Commercial Code

CHAPTER 32
Review Questions
(Answers on page 566)

1. Under the Bulk Transfer Act the buyer may record the list of the seller's existing creditors with the:
   (A) county clerk's office.
   (B) Secretary of HUD.
   (C) seller's attorney.
   (D) buyer's attorney.

2. A buyer of a business may insist that the seller sign a restrictive covenant not to:
   (A) compete in a specified territory.
   (B) compete for a specified time.
   (C) sell certain goods.
   (D) All of the above.

3. Title of inventory and equipment are transferred by:
   (A) mortgage.
   (B) bill of sale.
   (C) security agreement.
   (D) debenture.

4. A real estate license is required to engage in the sale of a business opportunity if:
   (A) the sale involves an assignment of the seller's lease.
   (B) the sale involves negotiation of a new lease with the landlord.
   (C) the sale involves the sale of the land and building.
   (D) All of the above.

5. A clause in the agreement of sale providing that the buyer has inspected the business and takes goods, fixtures and other property "as is":
   (A) protects the seller completely in the future.
   (B) will not protect the seller against a clear showing of fraudulent misrepresentation.
   (C) is required under the Bulk Transfer Act.
   (D) is for the protection of the vendee.

6. The Uniform Commercial Code:
   (A) primarily covers real property transactions.
   (B) resulted in repeal of the Bulk Transfer Act.
   (C) does not cover transactions involving an interest in land.
   (D) requires a written contract if the transaction involves the sale of goods of $500 or more.

CHAPTER THIRTY-THREE

ENVIRONMENTAL LAWS

INTRODUCTION

The disposal of hazardous waste and toxic chemicals goes on daily in many parts of the United States, both on the surface and in the subsurface of property, and also in our inland and offshore waters. The Office of Water and Waste Management, U.S. Environmental Agency estimated that in 1994 there were 750,000 hazardous waste generators in the United States and 50,000 uncontrolled, abandoned and inactive hazardous waste disposal sites in the country.

Broadly, the question raised deals with the effects of such pollution on New Jersey's environment. More specifically, questions arise as to how daily exposure to this contamination affects the average citizen of the state. The legal issues that follow are not only what harm is created by the presence of such contamination on a given landowner's property or adjacent property, but more importantly, who will be responsible?

The traditional answer was that the polluting industry would be responsible for resultant damage. However, more and more cases involve as defendants either landowners who have been conveyed contaminated property and who have allowed the contamination to inflict injury on an adjacent property owner, or real estate brokers who have knowingly aided in the conveyance of property which is affected by contamination.

The purpose of this chapter is to acquaint real estate professionals with some of the state and federal laws dealing with environmental pollution and to create an awareness of the potential for liability when a real estate broker aids in the conveyance of property adversely affected by toxic or hazardous waste. It is not intended to provide detailed guidance regarding the specific laws.

The potential for future liability for buyers, sellers and brokers requires that environmental considerations play a prominent role in virtually every real estate transaction.

ENVIRONMENTAL EXPOSURE

Hazardous substances can be found indoors and outdoors. Indoor pollutants can include cleaning chemicals, solvents and paint, pipes with lead solder, lawn and garden chemicals, pesticides, asphalt roofing, window caulking and various other elements that, without proper ventilation, can build to dangerous levels.

Although naturally occurring radon comes from an outside source—the breakdown of uranium beneath the surface of the earth—it also represents an indoor hazard, since it can creep into the lower levels of homes. As with the other hazards mentioned here, it can usually be remedied through proper ventilation.

In commercial buildings, asbestos fibers constitute a serious health hazard for people working where the fibers have been released into the air. Tenants can also suffer from "sick building syndrome," a condition caused by pollutants within the building such as carpet fibers and particulates from furniture.

Other commercial or industrial pollutants can create hazards beyond their own boundaries. Ground water and soil contamination caused by chemical leaks, landfills and other disposal sites, and industrial air and water emissions can, and often do, affect surrounding neighborhoods. Although professionals in both commercial and residential real estate may not be directly responsible for remedying such contaminants, they may be expected to know of their existence and effects. In the worst case, they may be charged for misrepresentation for selling a property in an area where hazardous substances pose a health threat. The following contaminants represent the most widely known health hazards

Ground Water Contamination. About 50% of Americans rely on ground water for their principal water supply. When the same supply is used for irrigation, drinking and industrial purposes, the effect may be long-term contamination. And once it's been contaminated, ground water is difficult to clean up, if not impossible. You can usually find out about an area's water quality from the local or county health department. Inspections may give clues to possible contamination. Prospective home buyers may also want to know about nearby industrial facilities or gasoline stations, and they may want to check with health or environmental officials for information on hazards in the area.

Recent studies have shown that drinking water wells, particularly those in the southern part of the state, sometimes contain unsafe levels of chemicals such as mercury. This led to enactment of the **Private Well Testing Act** (NJSA 58:12-A-26). Under the law, which took effect on September 14, 2002, every contract for the sale of real property with a private drinking water well must contain a requirement that the well be tested for contaminants. At every closing for a subject property, the buyer and seller must certify in writing that they have reviewed the well test results. A licensee who fails to include the required mandate may be considered to be in violation of NJSA 45:15-17 (e) (incompetence). Additional information can be obtained from the Web site of the Department of Environmental Protection, www.state.nj/dep/pwta, or the New Jersey Real Estate Commission at www.njdobi.org.

Leaking Underground Storage Tanks (USTs). The boom in automobile sales after World War II was closely followed by the construction of thousands of gasoline stations across the country. At these stations, the steel tanks that were installed underground to store gasoline had an average life expectancy of 30 to 50 years. Since the early 1980s, corrosion of steel tanks, along with faulty installation and operation, has resulted in widespread ground water contamination by gasoline. The Environmental Protection Agency (EPA) estimates that about 705,000 underground storage tanks nationwide store petroleum or hazardous substances that can harm the environment and human health if the USTs release their stored contents. In September 1999, the EPA was monitoring about 370,000 leaking underground storage tank sites in the United States.

One major problem with the leaks is that they're very difficult to detect. Yet a leak of just one gallon of gasoline per day into a ground water aquifer is enough to contaminate the water of a community of 50,000 people. The 1984 amendments to the Resource Conservation and Recovery Act (RCRA) brought underground storage tanks under the EPA's jurisdiction, and environmental experts see some hope in solving the problem of leaking tanks.

In New Jersey, heating oil USTs with an aggregate capacity of less than 2,000 gallons are exempt from UST regulations, and heating oil USTs of any size, used exclusively to heat residential buildings, are exempt from UST regulations.

Asbestos. Asbestos continues to be a costly issue for commercial property owners and lenders. Inhalation of asbestos fibers released into the air by friable asbestos (asbestos that crumbles easily) has been linked with cancer and asbestosis, a degenerative lung disease. Buildings constructed between the 1940s and the late 1970s are likely to contain asbestos insulation, since it was widely used in fireproofing. Although the federal government hasn't required asbestos removal in commercial buildings, the EPA has strict procedures for handling asbestos materials during removal, demolition and renovation.

The Asbestos Hazard Emergency Response Act (AHERA) requires that public and private primary and secondary schools are inspected for asbestos and that the discovery of asbestos be reported to both building occupants and parent-teacher associations. Also required is the development of an appropriate response to any asbestos present.

Urea-Formaldehyde Foam Insulation (UFFI). UFFI is pumped into walls and ceilings as a foam that later hardens and acts as a home insulating material. Formaldehyde in the insulation reacts with heat and humidity in the air, allowing formaldehyde gas to be released. Formaldehyde can cause symptoms such as breathing difficulties, headaches, nausea, nosebleeds, eye, nose and ear irritation and dizziness. Although formerly popular for insulating older homes, UFFI was banned from further use or sale by the Consumer Products Safety Commission (CPSC) in 1982. The courts overturned the ban, but the adverse publicity has drastically curtailed the use of UFFI. Some states require identification and disclosure of the presence of UFFI, but New Jersey is not among them.

Carbon Monoxide. Carbon monoxide or CO is an odorless and colorless gas that is produced when fuels such as gasoline, oil, propane, coal, wood and natural gas do not have an adequate supply of oxygen to burn completely. When CO is breathed into the body, it combines with the body's blood and prevents it from absorbing oxygen. High levels of carbon monoxide can be fatal.

Common sources of CO poisoning include:
- Malfunctioning heating equipment;
- Blocked chimneys;
- Indoor use of barbecue grills;
- Using cooking appliances for heating purposes;
- Sitting inside an idling vehicle for a prolonged period of time; and
- Repairing or running engines, such as vehicles, lawnmowers, and snowblowers in an attached garage.

The symptoms of CO poisoning are often mistaken for the flu—severe headaches, nausea, vomiting and drowsiness. However, with CO poisoning there is no fever and the symptoms clear up with exposure to fresh air.

Carbon monoxide detectors must be installed in all buildings that contain three or more dwelling units in New Jersey.

Waste Disposal Sites. (Landfills). Americans generate trash at the rate of four pounds per person per day, which translates to 600,000 tons per day or 210 million tons per year. Some of the trash gets recycled or recovered, but most of it is buried in landfills. A landfill is a carefully designed structure built into or on top of the ground in which trash is isolated from the surrounding environment (groundwater, air, and rain). This isolation is accomplished by using either a clay or plastic liner and daily covering with soil. Under these conditions, trash will not decompose much. It's not like a compost pile, where trash is buried in a way that will cause it to decompose quickly.

The construction and maintenance of landfills is heavily regulated by state and federal agencies. Before a city or other authority can build a landfill, an environmental impact study must be done, and when a landfill closes, the site, especially the ground water, must be monitored and maintained for up to 30 years. Despite government scrutiny, real estate licensees must be aware of these sites in their market area and take necessary investigative action when dealing with potential tenants and buyers.

Under the *Sanitary Landfill Facility Closure and Contingency Fund Act*, if a property being sold has been used as a sanitary land fill facility, the seller must include in the contract of sale a statement that the property has been so used and for what period of time. The Act includes a sole-source landfill (one which is the depository of only the waste its own commercial operation has generated). Failure to include such information will result in the contract's being void at the sole discretion of the buyer, and no equitable defenses to voiding the contract are recognized.

Lead Paint. Approximately 64 million dwellings—all built before 1978—contain some lead-based paint. Although the mere existence of lead paint does not mean it is dangerous, lead from paint, chips and dust can pose serious health hazards if not taken care of properly. Particularly at risk are families renovating older structures and low-income families living in run-down housing. In these cases hazards are created by disrupting lead-painted surfaces during renovations.

The U.S. Department of Housing and Urban Development (HUD) and the U.S. Environmental Agency (EPA) have issued disclosure rules requiring that individuals receive certain information before renting, buying or renovating housing that was built prior to 1978. The rules implement Section 1018 of the Residential Lead-Based Paint Hazard Reduction Act of 1992. Specifically, under the HUD/EPA rules:

1. Sellers and landlords must disclose any known lead-based paint hazards in homes. They are also required to give buyers or tenants any reports that are available from tests that may have been performed (such as results of a prior home inspection) before sale or lease. Once disclosure is made on a new rental it does not have to be repeated upon renewal, unless the status of lead-based paint changes.

2. Sellers and landlords must give buyers and tenants a pamphlet entitled "Protect Your Family From Lead In Your Home." The pamphlet, developed by HUD, EPA and the Consumer Product Safety Commission, is available in both English and Spanish.

3. Homebuyers receive an optional ten-day period to conduct a lead-based inspection or risk assessment at their own expense. The number of days can be changed by mutual consent. The purchaser can waive his or her right to inspect the property, but the seller cannot refuse to permit the buyer up to a ten-day period to check the house out before becoming legally bound by the sales contract.

4. Sales contracts and leases must include a federal form about lead paint in the building.

5. Sellers, landlords and real estate agents all share responsibility for ensuring compliance with the rule. (Agents should inform sellers and landlords of their obligations under this rule.)

The rule covers most public and private housing that could be occupied by children and was built before 1978—the year lead was outlawed in household paint. There are, however, some exceptions, meaning that not all pre-1978 housing qualifies as "target property" as defined by the disclosure requirements. Not covered is housing built after 1977; zero-bedroom units, such as efficiencies, lofts and dormitories; leases for less than 100 days, such as vacation houses or short-term rentals; housing for the elderly (62+); housing for the handicapped; rental housing that has been inspected by a certified inspector and found to be free of lead-based paint; and foreclosure sales.

The rule does not require any lead paint testing, removal or abatement, nor does it invalidate leasing and sales contracts. Failure to comply with the rules could subject owners to civil penalties up to $10,000, criminal prosecution and a court-

FIGURE 33.1 Property/Environmental Information Disclosure Worksheet

Property Address: ______________________________

____

To the best of (my) (our) knowledge and belief, the above-referenced property contains, as of the date hereof, only the following features or is affected by only the following environmental conditions. (Check all that apply. Use additional sheets for further explanation as necessary or for environmental conditions not listed below.)

______ Public water supply
______ Individual well-water supply
______ Asbestos insulation
______ Urea-formaldehyde foam insulation
______ Individual septic system
______ Public sewer lines
______ Settling, slippage, sliding, or other soil problems
______ Flooding, grading, or drainage problems
______ Depressions, mounds, or soft spots
______ Traces of concrete, metal, or asphalt indicating prior commercial use
______ Ravines or earth embankment that may indicate former dumping
______ Discoloring of soil or vegetation
______ Oil sheen in wet areas
______ Malfunctioning septic systems
______ Contamination of well water
______ Proximity of property to former or current waste disposal sites
______ Proximity of property to former, current, or proposed commercial establishments, such as industrial plants, gas stations, and military facilities
______ Proximity of property to former, current, or proposed mines or gravel pits
______ Proximity of property to farms
______ Elevated radon levels on the property
______ Elevated radon levels in the neighborhood
______ Pipelines carrying oil, gas, or chemicals underneath or adjacent to the property
______ Existence of pipeline rights-of-way or easements over or adjacent to the property
______ Use of lead-base paint (any paint prior to 1978) on any surfaces
______ Other (describe) ______________________________

____

____

____

Seller Date

____

Seller Date

imposed award equal to three times any damages incurred by an individual buying or renting property.

Since some buyers might be inclined to play contract negotiation games during the ten-day inspection period, the seller should be cautioned to use contingency-clause language that will clearly spell out both parties' rights and options in likely cases. The National Association of Realtors has distributed guidance to its members suggesting contingency language that allows:

- the buyer to cancel the contract if the test results reveals "unacceptable" amounts of lead-based paints in the house.
- the seller to get rid of the offending paint. In this case, the buyer would be bound to go to closing, once the buyer and seller agree the removal is complete. To prevent the buyer from simply using the ten-day period to back out of the original deal for other reasons, the contingency could require delivery of a copy of the buyer's inspection report to the seller to document the problem.
- a mutually agreed-upon statement regarding the starting and ending dates for any testing the purchaser seeks.
- clear instructions on what happens to the earnest money deposit in the event the sales contract breaks down over lead-based paint.

Radon. Radon, a radioactive gas, has always been a part of our natural environment. However, this radioactive gas, formed by the natural breakdown of uranium, is increasingly a subject of public discussion and concern. Under New Jersey law, a seller must disclose to a buyer the results of any radon testing or mitigation work when entering into a contract for the sale of real estate.

Radon can move easily through soil and tiny cracks in rock. When it reaches the surface of the soil, it disperses and is diluted to very low levels in the outdoor environment. However, when the gas takes a different route and enters homes by way of openings in the foundation, a small crack in a basement wall or through an earthen basement floor, it can build up to unacceptable levels.

Radon then decays to radioactive decay products. These decay products can attach to dust; when these dust particles are inhaled and enter the lungs, radiation is emitted. This can damage lung tissue and increase the risk of developing lung cancer.

The Environmental Protection Agency (EPA) has established levels of radon gas that are considered unsafe. Testing devices, which measure concentrations of radon gas, are reported as "picocuries per liter." A **picocurie (pc)** is a measurement of radioactivity. The EPA has recommended 4 pc as the maximum acceptable indoor level of radon. In cases where levels of radon in a home range between 4 and 20 pc, homeowners are recommended to take action to reduce the level within one to two years. If the level is between 20 and 200 pc, action should be taken within several months. A reading above 200 pc should be reported promptly to and confirmed by the New Jersey Department of Environmental Protection (DEP), which will conduct another test to confirm the reading. If confirmed, action should be taken within a few weeks.

The homeowner or a private firm can accomplish testing for radon. Two relatively inexpensive and accurate measurement devices are presently available: (1) the charcoal canister and (2) the alpha-track detector. The charcoal canister is more widely used, largely because it is placed in the home for a matter of only three to seven days, providing a result more quickly than the alpha-track detector, which must be placed for 30 to 90 days.

Usually, the elimination of radon is simple and inexpensive. It poses a problem only when if found at high levels. Proper ventilation systems or the use of exhaust fans usually move the radon gas from the concentrated area into the atmosphere, where it disappears. As part of its campaign to increase public awareness of radon, NJ DEP offers an information package that contains lists of private companies specializing in radon testing and radon remediation.

To obtain the package, and for answers to additional questions regarding radon, call NJ DEP at the following toll-free number: 1-800-648-0394.

Mold. Molds are simple, microscopic organisms that are present virtually everywhere, indoors and outdoors. Molds, along with mushrooms and yeast, are fungi and are needed to break down dead material and recycle nutrients into the environment. For molds to grow and reproduce, they need only a food source—any organic material, such as leaves, wood, paper or dirt—and moisture. Because molds grow by digesting the organic material, they gradually destroy whatever they grow on. Sometimes new molds grow on old mold colonies. Mold growths on surfaces can be seen in the form of discoloration, frequently green, gray, brown or black, but also white and other colors. Mold is most likely to grow where there is water or dampness, such as in bathrooms and basements.

Everyone is exposed to some mold on a daily basis without evident harm. However, too much exposure to mold may cause or worsen conditions such as asthma, hay fever or other allergies. The most common symptoms of overexposure are cough, congestion, runny nose, eye irritation and aggravation of asthma. Depending on the amount of exposure and a person's individual vulnerability, more serious health effects, such as fevers and breathing problems, can occur but are unusual.

When moldy material becomes damaged or disturbed, microscopic cells called **spores** are be released into the air. Live spores act like seeds, forming new mold spores (colonies) when they find the right conditions. Exposure can occur if people inhale the spores, directly handle moldy materials or accidentally ingest it. Also, mold can sometimes produce chemicals called **mycotoxins**. Mycotoxins may cause illness in people who are sensitive to them or who are exposed to large amounts in the air. Large exposures are typically associated with certain occupations, such as agricultural work.

All molds need water to grow. Mold can grow almost anywhere there is water damage, high humidity or dampness. Most often molds are confined to areas near the source of water. Removing the source of moisture—such as through repairs or dehumidification—is critical to preventing mold growth.

Stachybotrys chartarum is a type of mold that has been associated with health effects in people. It is a greenish-black mold that can grow on materials with a high cellulose content such as drywall, sheetrock, dropped ceiling tiles and wood, that become chronically moist or water-damaged due to excessive humidity, water leaks, condensation or flooding. Many molds are black in appearance but are not *Stachybotrys*. For example, the black mold commonly found between bathroom tiles is not *Stachybotrys*. Only specially trained professionals (mycologists), employing a microscopic exam, can positively identify *Stachybotrys*.

Typically, indoor air levels of *Stachybotrys* are low; however, as with other types of mold, at higher levels health effects can occur. These include cold-like symptoms, rashes, sinusitis and aggravation of asthma. Some related symptoms are more general, such as inability to concentrate and fatigue. Usually, symptoms disappear after the contamination is removed.

Although any visible mold can be sampled by an environmental consultant and/or analyzed by a laboratory specializing in microbiology, these tests can be very expensive—from hundreds to thousands of dollars. There is no simple and cheap way to sample the air in a home to find out what types of mold are present and whether they are airborne. Even if a home is tested, it is difficult to say at what levels health effects would occur. Therefore, it is more important get rid of the mold than find out more about it. The most effective way to treat mold is to correct underlying water damage and clean the affected area.

Mold should be cleaned as soon as it appears. Persons cleaning mold should be free of symptoms and allergies. Small areas of mold should be cleaned using a detergent/soapy solution or an appropriate household cleaner. Gloves should be worn during cleaning. The cleaned area should then be thoroughly dried and any sponges or rags used to clean the mold should be destroyed.

If the mold returns quickly or spreads, it may indicate an underlying problem such as a leak. Any underlying water problems must be fixed to successfully eliminate mold problems. If mold contamination is extensive, a professional abatement company may need to be consulted.

Anyone who believes that they or their children have symptoms that they suspect are caused by exposure to mold, should see a physician. Keep in mind that many symptoms associated with mold exposure may also be caused by many other illnesses. The physician should be informed about the symptoms and about when, how and for how long the exposure took place.

For more information about the health effects of mold exposure and information on the safe removal of mold, please call the New Jersey Department of Environmental Protection (DEP) at 1-800-648-0394.

Environment and the Law

The federal Environmental Protection Agency (EPA) regulates the generation, transportation and disposal of hazardous wastes. EPA's mandate comes from the Resource Conservation and Recovery Act (RCRA.)

The RCRA was created in 1976 in response to an environmental disaster that forced the permanent evacuation of Love Canal, New York. RCRA established regulations for the generation, transportation, storage, use, treatment, disposal and cleanup of hazardous waste. Under this law, the EPA regulates any business that generates more than 220 pounds per month of a hazardous chemical. Together, Congress and the EPA have worked to tighten standards on companies in an attempt to reduce the threat of contamination to the public and the surrounding environment. For example, in 1984 Congress imposed such strict safety requirements on landfills that hundreds of hazardous waste landfill operations were forced to close because they couldn't comply with the requirements.

CERCLA. The Comprehensive Environmental Response Compensation and Liability Act (CERCLA), 42 U.S.C. 9601 *et seq.*, was passed in 1980 to provide a federally-funded response to problems caused by abandoned hazardous waste sites. The statute established a multi-billion-dollar fund (commonly known as "Superfund") to pay for a wide range of cleanup actions at hazardous waste disposal sites. When Superfund money has been spent to clean up hazardous waste dumps and spills at a site, the United States may recover all such expenditures from four classes of responsible parties:

1. The present owner or operator of a site where hazardous substances have been released;
2. The owner or operator of the site at the time the hazardous substances were disposed of;
3. Any person who arranged for disposal or treatment at the site of hazardous substances owned or possessed by that person; and
4. Any person who accepted hazardous substances for transport to the site, if that person selected the site.

The liability provision of CERCLA makes all owners and transporters of hazardous waste *strictly liable* for the cost of cleanup without regard to fault, meaning the EPA does not have to prove wrongdoing to obtain cleanup or recovery costs. Furthermore, each owner is "jointly and individually" liable, which means each individual owner is personally responsible for the total damages. Thus, if only one owner is financially able to pay the entire amount, then that owner must pay the total charge and then try to recover from the other parties. In addition, owners or operators who refuse to comply with a Superfund directive can be fined up to $25,000 per day, whether or not they were responsible for the contamination. In many cases, the cost of cleanup or penalties or both far outweighs the value of the property.

Superfund Amendments and Reauthorization Act (SARA). The Superfund expired in September 1985. In 1986, Congress reauthorized the Superfund in the Superfund Amendments and Reauthorization Act (SARA). The amendment statute contains stronger clean-up standards for contaminated sites and five times the funding of the original Superfund. SARA also sought to clarify a lender's obligations. As noted earlier, liability under the Superfund extends to both present and previous owners of the contaminated site. Lenders found themselves as either the present owners or somewhere in the chain of title through foreclosure proceedings.

Innocent Landowner Immunity. The Superfund amendments also created a concept called *innocent landowner immunity*. In certain cases, a landowner in the chain of title was recognized as completely innocent of all wrongdoing and therefore not held liable. The innocent landowner immunity clause established the grounds on which a person or business could be exempted from that liability. In order to avail himself of this defense, an owner must establish that:

1. The pollution was caused by a third party;
2. The property was acquired by the owner after the placement of the hazardous substance on it;
3. At the time of acquisition the owner did not know and had no reason to know of the problem;
4. "Due care" was exercised when the property was purchased, meaning the purchaser must have made appropriate inquiry into the previous ownership and uses of the property in an effort to minimize liability (this is referred to as completing due diligence); and
5. Reasonable precautions were taken in the exercise of the ownership rights.

Disclosure

Real estate licensees have an obligation to ask clients if they know of any environmental problems on their property, and clients must disclose any known problems. (See NJAC 11:5-6.4 (b) supra.) In addition, the National Association of Realtors (NAR) has developed a sample environmental disclosure checklist for residential property transfers.

When disclosing information about environmental conditions on the property or in surrounding areas, keep in mind that environmental consulting is a highly specialized field. Real estate professionals should not claim to be experts on the environment. State and federal agencies, as well as private consulting firms, can be contacted for information and advice.

Easton v. Strassburger. The California case of *Easton v. Strassburger* illustrates the potential liability to which real estate practitioners may be exposed. This case involved the sale of a home that was built on an improperly engineered and compacted landfill. The court said that both the listing and selling agents failed to disclose "reasonably discoverable facts" that affected the value or desirability of the property. The California legislature followed up on that decision with legislation stating that salespeople must conduct a "reasonably diligent and competent inspection" of the property, looking for red flags that might signify a problem.

For brokers of commercial real estate, the issue of liability becomes even more significant. With the stiff penalties imposed under the Superfund statute, a transfer of property on which an environmental hazard is found could result in liability not only for the seller but also for the buyer, the attorneys, the title company, the lender and the broker. If environmental problems are found, the broker should recommend that an environmental consultant be engaged.

Environmental Audits. For commercial transactions, many lenders are now requiring environmental audits of properties. Besides concern over the value of their investments, lenders are protecting themselves against liability for Superfund cleanup. Lenders that get involved in the management of a troubled company and those that foreclose on bankrupt companies may be held accountable for contamination cleanup costs.

NEW JERSEY'S INDUSTRIAL SITE RECOVERY ACT (ISRA)

New Jersey's Industrial Site Recovery Act (ISRA) imposes preconditions on the sale, transfer or closure of certain "industrial establishments" involved in the generation, manufacture, refining, transportation, treatment, storage, handling or disposal of hazardous wastes or substances. The law is implemented by the New Jersey Department of Environmental Protection (NJ DEP). This program is designed to prevent abandonment of contaminated sites as well as ensure that when facilities change ownership, the new owners will receive a clean property.

Facilities that fall into the ISRA program include all whose primary activities fall into certain SIC Codes. The federal Office of Management and Budget publishes the codes in the *Standard Industrial Classification Manual (SIC Manual)*, which describes and assigns a four-digit number to each and every economic activity. Although in certain specific cases a facility may be exempted from the regulations and a letter of non-applicability may be obtained to satisfy lender requirements, buyers should always insist on some form of site audit following ISRA standards to minimize the possibility of hidden liabilities prior to purchase.

Who Must Comply With ISRA

Businesses subject to ISRA are referred to in the statute and regulations as "industrial establishments" and the regulations clearly define the businesses covered. Three criteria are used to determine ISRA compliance:

- The SIC (Standard Industrial Classification) number of the activity at the site;
- The presencc of "hazardous substances"; and
- The date of operations.

SIC Number. There are 24 major industry groups covered by ISRA. Very generally, the industries covered are involved in manufacturing, textiles, apparel, wood, furniture, paper, printing, chemicals, petroleum, rubber, leather, glass, metals, machinery, electronics, pipelines, power and the warehousing of chemicals. If the business does not have a SIC number as defined in N.J.S.A. 13:1 K-8, ISRA does not apply.

Hazardous Substances. The second criteria that may classify a business as an "industrial establishment" is the presence of "hazardous substances." If the operation in question has been engaged in the generation, manufacture, refining, transportation, treatment, storage, handling or disposal of hazardous substances, on-site, above or below ground, it is covered. Many petroleum products appear on the DEP's list of hazardous substances. Therefore, the presence of a heating oil tank may require ECRA compliance. For example, if decorative glass novelties are created in a small shop (SIC 3229), using no chemicals (only a Bunsen burner and glass rod stock), ECRA compliance would be required if they heat by oil.

Date of Operations. The third criteria involves the date of operations. If a place of business has been engaged in operations on or after December 31, 1983, it is covered.

If a business operation meets the definition of an industrial establishment, both the owner and operator of the business operation and the owner of the real property on which the business is conducted are responsible for complying with ISRA.

Events Triggering ISRA Compliance

ISRA requires owners or operators of an industrial establishment to notify the NJ DEP upon the closing of operations or upon the transfer of ownership or operations of the industrial establishment. If compliance is required because ISRA is applicable to a particular transaction, then the responsibility rests jointly and individually upon the owner and operator of the industrial establishment as well as landlords and tenants.

The first step of compliance is the preliminary assessment, which is basically a walk-through inspection of the industrial establishment. The preliminary assessment is followed by a site investigation, which involves sampling of soil, water and other media suspected to be contaminated to confirm the presence of contamination. The remedial action is the clean-up, which can involve the removal or other remediation of the contamination. A wide range of techniques and technologies exist which provide evaluation to achieve cost savings and efficiency. Once NJ DEP completes its review of all data after each step, it approves the compliance with ISRA by way of a "no further action" letter.

ISRA requires the posting of a "remediation funding source" which acts as financial assurance to NJ DEP that remediation will be completed. The remediation-funding source must be in the amount of the remediation and be posted prior to the commencement of the remediation.

PINELANDS PROTECTION ACT OF 1979 (N.J.S.A. 13:18-1 *et seq.*)

The Pinelands was recognized by Congress in 1978 to be an area of national significance because of its unique resources. Congress called upon the state to protect those resources, and in 1979 the state legislature passed the Pinelands Protection Act. The Act created a 15-member Commission composed of local, state and federal officials and directed it to develop a plan to achieve resource protection.

The New Jersey Pinelands Commission administers the Pinelands Protection Act. The jurisdiction of the Commission includes parts of Atlantic, Burlington, Camden, Cape May, Cumberland, Gloucester and Ocean Counties. Within the 937,000-acre State Pinelands Area (see Figure 33.2), the Commission regulates virtually all forms of construction. A permit must be approved by the Commission prior to construction.

Under the Act, the discharge of dredged or fill material requires a wetlands permit issued by the U.S. Army Corps of Engineers under the federal 404 permit program. However, the Pinelands Commission may provide for more stringent regulation of activities in and around freshwater wetland areas within its jurisdiction. Generally, the Act prohibits most types of development within 300 feet of a wetland.

The discharge of dredged or fill material into open waters requires an Open Water Fill Permit, which is issued by the state. Requirements under this system are similar to those of the U.S. Army Corps of Engineers.

HACKENSACK MEADOWLANDS RECLAMATION AND DEVELOPMENT ACT (N.J.S.A. 13:17-1 *et seq.*)

The Hackensack Meadowlands Development Commission (HMDC) administers the Hackensack Meadowlands Reclamation and Development Act. The Act subjects an 18,000-acre district in Bergen and Hudson counties (Hackensack Meadows) to comprehensive regional planning and zoning (see Figure 33.3).

Activities in areas under the jurisdiction of the Hackensack Meadowlands Development Commission require permits from the U.S. Army Corps of Engineers when the discharge of dredged or fill material occurs. The discharge of dredged or fill material into non-tidal open waters requires an Open Water Fill Permit. Requirements under this system are similar to those of the Corps.

To determine if a property or activity is regulated by the Hackensack Meadowlands Development Commission, contact the Commission at Hackensack Meadowlands Development Commission, One De Korte Park Plaza, Lyndhurst, NJ 07071. Telephone: (201) 460-1700.

Activities in the Hackensack Meadowlands commonly require the obtaining of a State Waterfront Development Permit. To determine which state permits may be required, you must contact the Division of Coastal Resources at (609) 292-0060.

NEW JERSEY WETLANDS ACT OF 1970 (N.J.S.A. 13:9A-1)

This act regulates all dredging, filling, removing or otherwise altering coastal and tidal wetlands. Coastal wetlands are defined as banks, marshes, swamps, flat or other low land subject to tidal action, including lands whose surface is at or below an elevation of one foot above local extreme high water. Under this Act, any construction, draining, dredging, excavation or dumping upon a wetland is prohibited unless an application is filed for a permit with the New Jersey Division of Environmental Protection (NJ DEP). Such an application must include a detailed description of the proposed work and a map showing the area of the affected wetlands, with the location of the proposed work therein. In granting a permit, the NJ DEP must attempt to prevent further deterioration or alteration of wetlands. Violations of the Act may result in penalties of $3,000 per day of violation. "Coastal wetlands" do not include any land or realty subject to the jurisdiction of the Hackensack Meadowlands Development Commission mentioned earlier.

THE PINELANDS

The following municipalities have land within the Pinelands area:

Atlantic County
Buena Borough*
Buena Vista Township
Corbin City*
Egg Harbor City*
Egg Harbor Township
Estell Manor City*
Folsom Borough*
Galloway Township*
Hamilton Township*
Hamilton Town*
Hammonton Town*
Mullica Township*
Port Republic City
Weymouth Township*

Ocean County
Barnegat Township*
Beachwood Borough*
Berkeley Township*
Englewood Township*
Jackson Township*
Lacey Township
Lakehurst Borough*
Little Egg Harbor Township*
Manchester Township*
Ocean Township*
Plumsted Township*
South Toms River Borough*
Stafford Township*

Burlington County
Bass River Township*
Evesham Township*
Medford Lakes Borough*
Medford Township*
New Hanover Township*
North Hanover Township*
Pemberton Township*
Shamong Township*
Southampton Township*
Springfield Township*
Tabernacle Township*
Washington Township*
Woodland Township*
Wrightstown Borough*

Camden County
Berlin Borough*
Berlin Township*
Chesilhurst Borough*
Waterford Township*
Winslow Township*

Cape May County
Dennis Township*
Upper Township*
Woodbine Borough*

Cumberland County
Maurice River Township*
Vineland City*

Gloucester County
Franklin Township*
Monroe Township*

*These municipalities have been certified by the Pinelands Commission as of November, 1989. This means that the zoning officer in these municipalities may give information on regulations, permitted uses, lot sizes and application procedures. The local Pinelands zoning map and ordinance revisions which were completed by local officials have been approved by the Pinelands Commission.

HISTORY OF THE PINELANDS

170 to 200 million years ago—Atlantic Coastal Plain begins to form.

100 million years ago—Start of sequence in which the Atlantic Ocean repeatedly covered the coastal plan and then withdrew, depositing layers of geologic material that now lies beneath the Pinelands.

10,000 years ago—End of the last Ice Age; present plant and animal populations begin to develop; earliest native Americans appear.

1624—Exploration of coastal inlets and bays reported.

1674—Earliest permanent European settlers occupy area north of present Burlington County line.

1760-1860 (approximate)—Iron, charcoal and glass industries flourish.

1916—Blueberries cultivated by Elizabeth White.

1917—Fort Dix established.

1955—State of New Jersey acquires 100,000-acre Wharton Tract as state forest.

1964—Pinelands Regional Planning Board proposes supersonic jetport and city of 250,000.

1971—Pinelands Environmental Counsel created and assigned to prepare master plan for 320,000 acres.

November 21,1981—Commission adopts plan for 556,000-acre Protection Area and balance of the Pinelands National Reserve.

January 14, 1981—Management plan takes effect following approval by Gov. Brendon T. Byrne.

January 16, 1981—Secretary of the Interior Cecil D. Andrus approves plan.

1977—Gov. Byrne appoints Pinelands Review Committee to define Pinelands boundaries.

1977—Casino gambling begins in Atlantic City, increasing development pressure on nearby Pinelands.

1978—National Parks and Recreation Act establishes Pinelands National Reserve; calls for preparation of Comprehensive Management Plan.

February 8, 1979—Gov. Byrne issues executive order establishing Pinelands Commission and instituting development controls while Commission prepares management plan.

June 28, 1979—Gov. Byrne signs Pinelands Protection Act, setting deadline for completion of management plans and endorsing interim development controls.

August 8,1980—Pinelands Commission adopts management plan for 368,000-acre Preservation Area (the Pinelands core).

FIGURE 33.2

New Jersey Pinelands

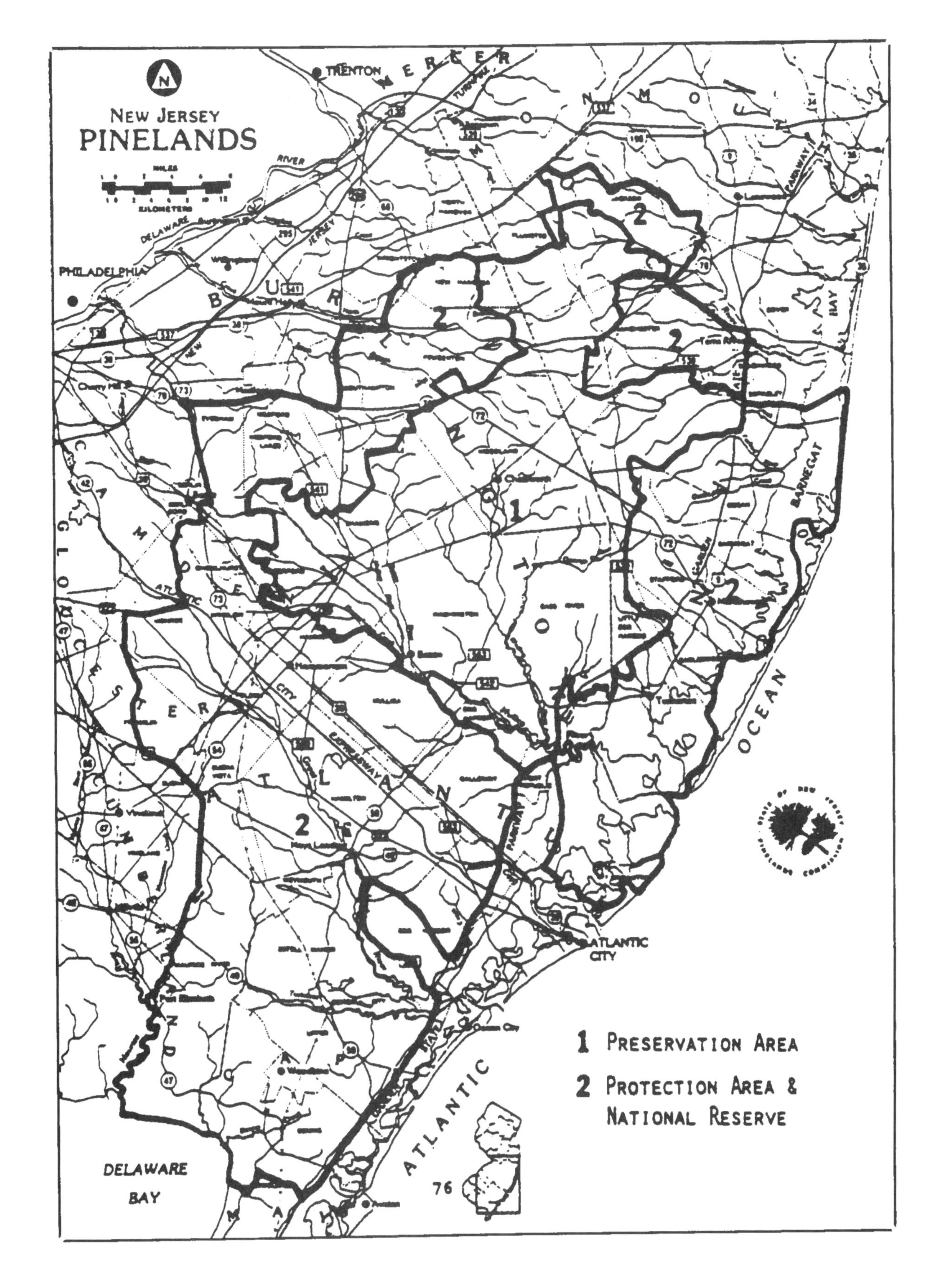

FIGURE 33.3
Hackensack Meadowlands District

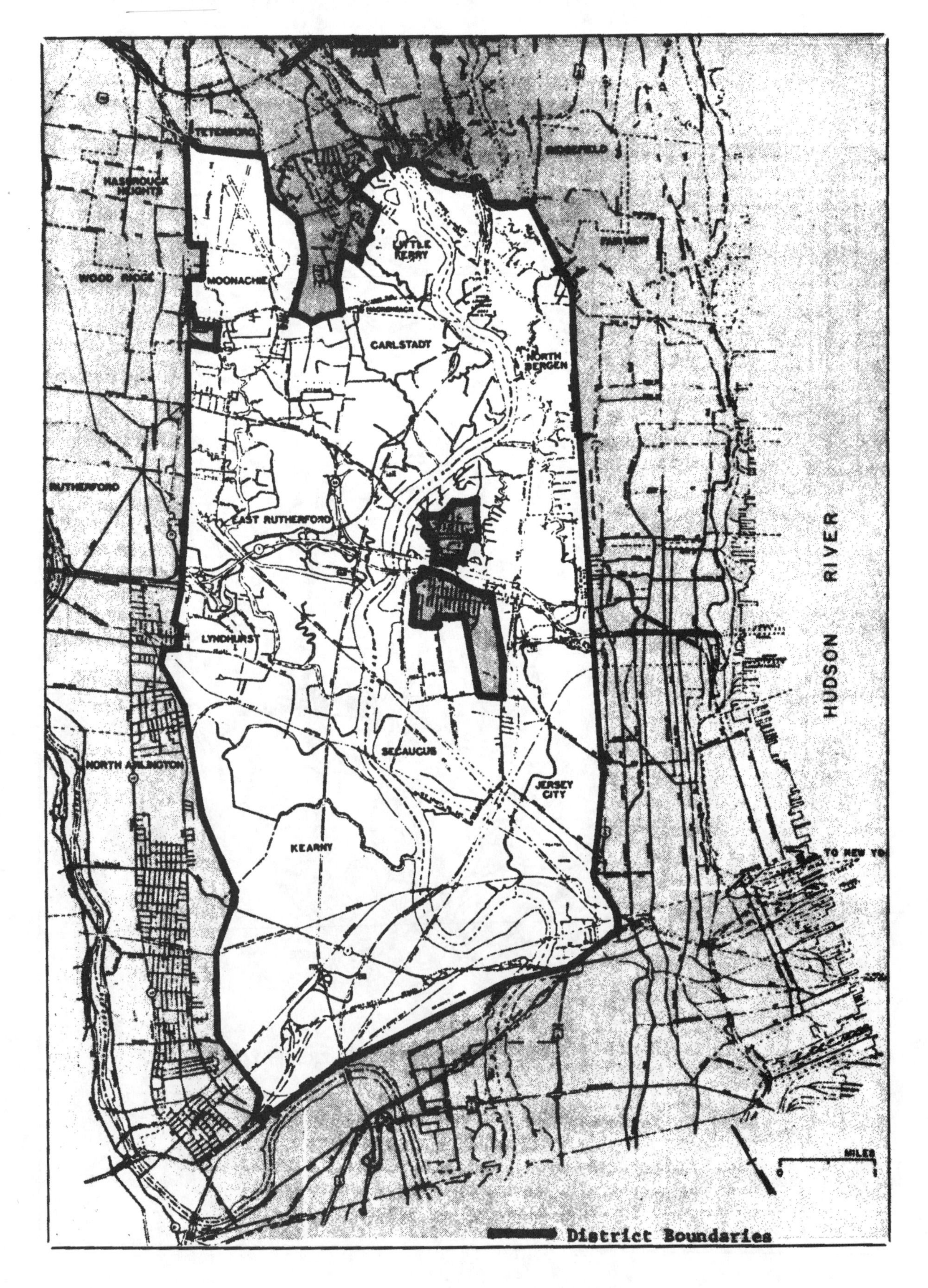

FIGURE 33.4
New Jersey Coastal Zone

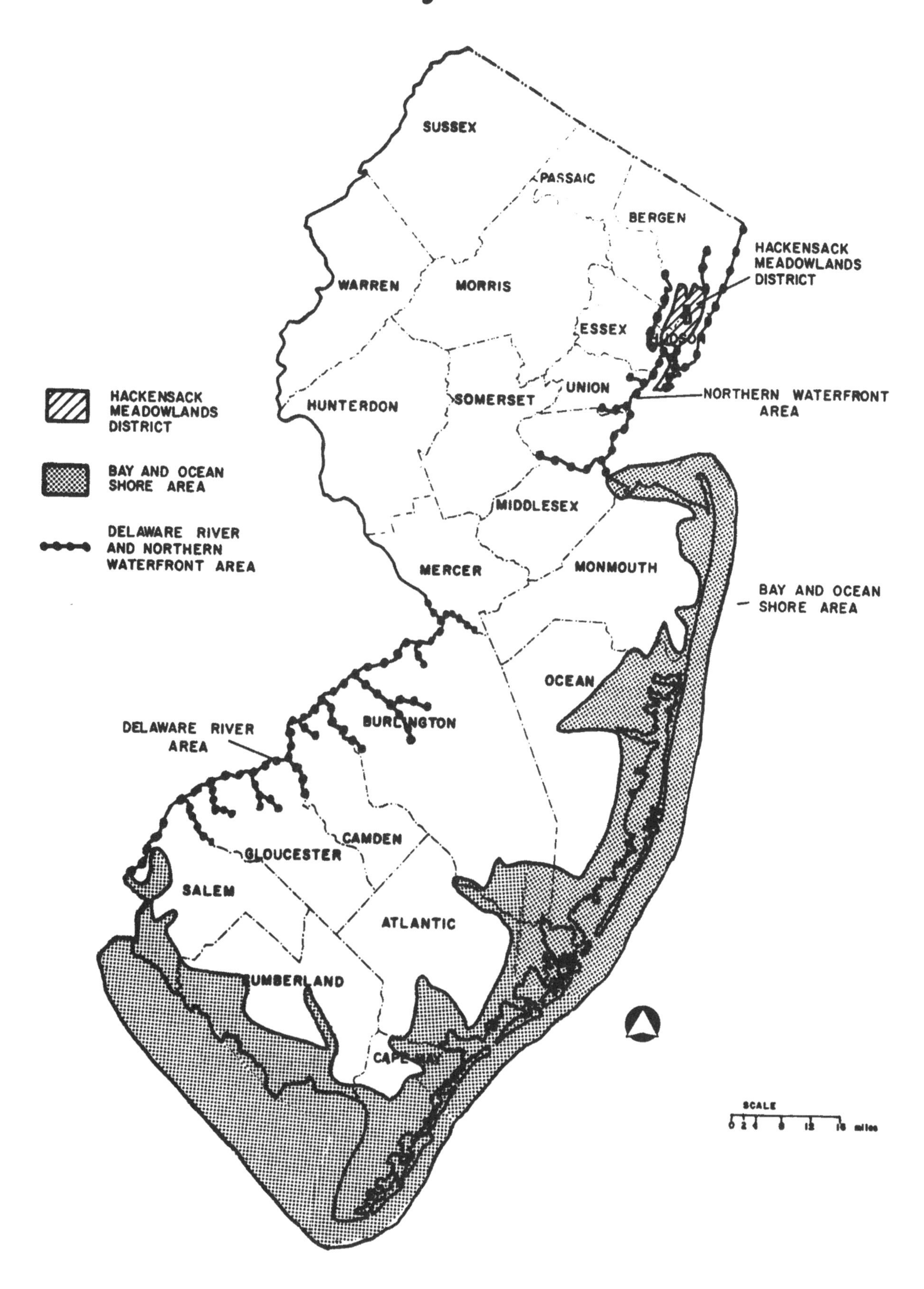

FRESHWATER WETLANDS PROTECTION ACT OF 1987 (N.J.S.A. 13:9B)

Freshwater wetlands serve a variety of important ecological functions, including: the natural purification of surface and ground waters; protection from flood and storm damage; and a habitat for the major portion of the state's fish and wildlife, including migratory birds, endangered species and commercially and recreationally important wildlife. They also maintain critical base flow to the state's surface waters by gradually releasing stored flood waters and ground water, particularly during drought periods.

The Freshwater Wetlands Protection Act is intended to preserve the purity and integrity of wetlands from random unnecessary or undesirable alteration or disturbance. State permits under this Act are required to be obtained from NJ DEP.

The Freshwater Wetlands Protection Act defines a wetland as "an area that is inundated or saturated by surface water or ground water at a frequency and duration sufficient to support, and that under normal circumstances does support, a prevalence of vegetation typically adapted for life in saturated soil conditions, technically known as 'hydrophytic vegetation.'" The Act also requires that wetlands be designated according to guidelines established in the *Wetland Identification and Delineation Manual* developed by the U.S. Environmental Protection Agency and subsequent amendments thereto. Copies of the USEPA delineation manual can be obtained by contacting:

Maps and Publications Bureau of Revenue
NJ Department of Environmental Protection
CN 402 Trenton, NJ 08625
Telephone: (609) 530-5790

NEW JERSEY COASTAL AREA DEVELOPMENT REVIEW ACT (N.J.S.A. Section 13:19-1 *et seq.*)

The Coastal Area Facility Review Act (CAFRA) was enacted in 1973 in order to protect ecologically sensitive areas and encourage the development of compatible land uses. CAFRA was amended in 1994 and is now called the Coastal Area Development Review Act (CADRA). CADRA establishes an environmental impact review process for any substantial new development in the state's "coastal area." The area designated as coastal area is described in the statute. It runs from Sandy Hook, in the North, to Cape May in the South and then North and West to the Delaware Memorial Bridge (see Figure 33.4).

Generally, CADRA requires a permit for any development on beaches and dunes and for the first development within 150 feet of the ocean, river or a bay. Beyond the first development, within the 150-foot area, a CADRA permit will be required for the building of three or more housing units. There are several other categories of development, which fall within the purview of the statute. These should be reviewed in order to determine CADRA's applicability to the subject tract.

An application for a CADRA permit is made to the New Jersey Department of Environmental Protection and in most instances must include an environmental impact statement. Generally, the grounds for issuing a permit include a showing by the applicant that there will be minimal interference with the animal life in the area and minimal deterioration of unique or irreplaceable land types.

"SUPERLIEN" STATUTES

New Jersey is one of seven states that have enacted so-called "superlien" provisions in their Superfund/Spill Fund statutes. While differing in their details, these statutes generally provide that a lien may be imposed against the real property subject to a cleanup in order to assist the state in recovering state funds expended on cleanup efforts. The liens are "superliens" because they have priority over all other liens and encumbrances, including previously filed ones (mortgages, for example).

The New Jersey "superlien" statute is called The Spill Compensation and Control Act, N.J.S.A. 58:1023.11 *et seq.* This law imposes liability for cleanup costs upon "Any person who has discharged a hazardous substance or is in any way responsible for any hazardous substance" which the Department of Environmental Protection is removing or has removed.

The Spill Act generally addresses the same types of conditions which would be addressed by CERCLA, with the addition of any releases of petroleum. An important difference in the Spill Act is that any expenditures by the government under the Act constitute a first priority lien upon property subject to the cleanup, except if the property contains six units or less and is used exclusively for residential purposes. On such property the lien is subordinate to prior liens.

CHAPTER THIRTY-FOUR

HOW TO GET THE HIGHEST SCORE

Good study techniques mean a higher score and often are the difference between passing and failing, so study the techniques below. The nice thing about most of them is that it takes little extra work to learn and use them.

PRE-TEST PREPARATION

Establish a Study Schedule. When you decide to begin studying, determine the number of days you have left before taking the test. Then set up a schedule and assign yourself a certain number of chapters to review, questions to answer, and arithmetic problems to do each day, so you'll be able to finish the entire book in the time available. This process will also enable you to gauge your overall progress so if you start to fall behind, you will quickly recognize it so you can get back on track.

Stick To the Schedule You Set. Only you can determine what your best studying time is, but when you have established it, stick to it. Once you get in the groove, you'll find that your study time will become more natural, even if you've been away from studying for a long time. Don't put off getting started. Before you know it, the time for preparation will almost be up and time lost might not be able to be made up.

My experience in teaching thousands of real estate license candidates is that the primary reason applicants fail is because they don't study enough. For some, this is the result of laziness—hoping to pass with the least amount of effort. No one can guarantee you will pass if you study, but if you don't, it is a virtual certainty that you won't pass. Others fail to study enough, even though they fully intended to do so, because time just got away from them, or because they thought they had a "valid reason" for not studying. Regardless of the reason, if you don't put in the necessary time, you can't expect to produce your best results. The cruel truth is that the test doesn't know how busy you are or what other demands you have on your time. It only knows right answers.

The licensing examination is both comprehensive and challenging and requires your full effort and concentration to be handled successfully. If you want to be successful, you must commit yourself to conscientious study. There is no easy way. Your willingness to apply yourself to learning as much as you can will not only serve you well in preparation for the test, but also as a basis for long run success in your career or personal pursuits.

Consider Studying with Others. As part of your overall studying process, you may want to occasionally get together with other students. If you decide to do so, be sure the group is small and comprised only of members who are at least as well informed, or better informed, than you are. Studying with those who know less can only serve to hold you back.

Don't Put Off Taking the Test. You should take the state examination at the earliest possible date. The longer you put it off, the more you are likely to forget.

THE DAY BEFORE THE EXAM

Know Test Time and Location. Be sure to know what time you are to be at the test center and know exactly how to get there. Students have missed the exam entirely or have arrived in a dither because they did not make sure where they were going beforehand. Gas up the day before the test so you won't waste time looking around for an open gas station on exam day.

Don't Cram. Some people are good at cramming for an exam, others are not. But even if you cram well, don't do it late the night before the exam. It can leave you tired and nervous and cancel out the advantage of whatever you learned.

Assemble Appropriate Items. Get the following items ready to take with you for test day: School completion certificate; two signature IDs, including one photo ID; a watch and a hand-held, silent, battery-operated calculator that contains no paper tape; a pencil and a money order for the exam fee. Having these items ready in one place in advance will save a last minute run around the homestead and will assist in keeping you in a relaxed frame of mind.

Get a Good Night's Sleep. The test is both mentally and physically tiring. Be sure you are well-rested.

TEST DAY

Rise and Shine. Give yourself plenty of time to get ready and have something nutritious for breakfast. You will not have eaten since the night before and won't be eating again until after the test. You want to make sure that you have enough fuel to keep you going. Otherwise, you may start to get hungry during the test and your ability to concentrate may suffer from it. Give yourself every edge.

Arrive at the Test Center ahead of time. Plan to arrive at the test center early to allow for traffic delays, car trouble, etc.

Do not talk to others about the test. While you are waiting at the test center to check in, you'll see some applicants furiously interrogating each other about potential test questions. Do not get involved in these last-minute review sessions. They will only serve to confuse the issue. If you have properly prepared yourself, you will have little to learn from such discussions anyway.

TAKING THE TEST

Pace yourself on time. You have four hours to complete the exam. Salesperson candidates must answer 122 questions (12 of which are pre-test items and don't count); broker candidates have 135 questions, including 15 pre-test items. You 'll answer some questions quickly from your basic knowledge. Others, particularly those involving math, will take longer. A good uggestion is to try to average one minute on each question except difficult questions and math questions. Glance at your watch every 30 minutes or so to see how you are doing.

Leave difficult or lengthy questions until last. When you come to a question that will take three or four minutes to answer, pass it by and come back to it later.

Stick with your first choice unless you are SURE you made a mistake. Be very wary of corrections. Corrections are of two sorts: those that follow a realization based on good reason that you made a mistake, and those where a panic impulse causes you to change. Always make the former; never make the latter. Long experience shows the odds are three-to-one that your impulsive correction will be from a right to a wrong answer. Rarely will an answer be improved by coming back to worry over it.

Handling bad questions. Every exam will include "bad" questions. When you come across a vague or ambiguous question on the exam, just do the best you can with it. Above all, don't panic, and don't let it affect your frame of mind. Examinees have a tendency to think that the outcome of the entire exam is riding on every qucstion. It is not. You can miss 30% of the questions and still pass. Don't lose sight of this fact when taking the exam. When two answers seem right, or no answer seems right, simply make an educated guess as to which answer the examiner thinks is right and make the choice.

Read each question carefully. This is a major problem in objective exams. Misinterpretation is your most serious danger. Many people "read" what they think the words say rather than what has actually been written.

Trick questions. The examiners are not out to "get you." They will not try to trap you or deceive you. The purpose of the exam is to test your competency. It is a reading comprehension examination. Don't waste your time looking for "trick questions."

"Absolute" and "Hedging" words. Be careful when a question contains an absolute word such as will, shall, cannot, always, never, only, all, etc. These questions deserve special attention. An absolute word strongly hints that the statement is wrong. On the other hand, hedging words like usually, some, many and most strongly hint that the statement is true.

Reject obviously wrong answers. It is a rare question in which you cannot reject one or two choices. If you find it necessary to guess at a question, you greatly improve your odds by rejecting answers you know are wrong.

Answer all questions. Do not leave any questions unanswered. The grade for a wrong answer is no worse than the grade for a blank answer; both are zero. But a blank answer is a sure zero. If you guess, you have a one-in-four chance of being right, and, if you reject the obviously wrong choices as suggested above, you could lower the odds to a one-in-two chance.

Don't jump to conclusions. An answer may be partly right but it may not be the correct answer. Do not select the first one that seems possible. Examine all alternative answers.

Be a "bitter ender." If you finish before the time is up, take time to review the entire exam. You may discover some you misread or misunderstood. Make sure you have answered every question, and chose the answer you intended to choose. Stay till the bitter end. (But don't change an answer unless you are sure you made a mistake.)

If you've learned real estate principles reasonably well, and if you use this text as directed, you will have little trouble passing the exam.

CHAPTER THIRTY-FIVE

INDEX & GLOSSARY

ABANDONMENT—The relinquishment of all rights and title to a property with no intention of reclaiming ownership. **9-168**

ABSTRACT OF TITLE—A condensed history of the title to a parcel of land consisting of a summary of every recorded instrument, together with a statement of all liens, charges or encumbrances affecting title to that land. **11-180**

ABUTTING OWNER—An owner whose land touches a highway or other public place.

ACCELERATED COST RECOVERY SYSTEM—A method of depreciation in which more depreciation is deducted in earlier years and less in later years. **25-371**

ACCELERATION CLAUSE—A clause in a mortgage or installment contract stating that upon default of payment due, immediate and full payment of the balance of the obligation becomes due and payable. **17-260**

ACCESSION—Acquisition of property by its joining or union with other property.

ACCESS RIGHT—The right of a property owner to have ingress and egress to and from his property.

ACCRETION—Gradual additions to land by deposits of sand or soil by bordering waters through natural causes. **4-138**

ACCRUED DEPRECIATION—The difference between the cost of a replacement new, on the date of the appraisal, and the present appraised value. **27-393**

ACKNOWLEDGEMENT—A formal declaration made before a notary public or other authorized person, by a person who has executed an instrument, that such execution is his free act and deed. **10-173**

ACQUISITION COST—The price and all related fees paid to acquire a property. **26-376**

ACRE—A measure of land equal to 160 square rods, 4,840 square yards, or 43,560 square feet. **28-410**

ACTUAL AUTHORITY—Such authority that a principal intentionally gives his agent.

ACTUAL EVICTION—A process whereby the landlord may terminate a lease for good reason and the tenant must appear and show cause why he should not be evicted. Also called dispossess proceeding, summary possession, and unlawful detainer. **22-311**

ACTUAL NOTICE—Notice received by direct communication; notice that has been brought expressly to a person's attention. **10-173**

ADJOINING OWNER—One whose property is contiguous or next to. **9-169**

ADJUSTABLE RATE MORTGAGE (ARM)—A mortgage loan that allows the interest rate to be changed at specific intervals over the term of the loan. **17-262**

ADJUSTED BASIS—For tax purposes, the original cost of property reduced by depreciation deductions and increased by the cost of capital improvements. **25-369**

ADJUSTED SALES PRICE—The amount realized on the sale of a home minus the qualified expenses of fixing up a home to sell it. **26-376**

ADMINISTRATOR—A person appointed by the court to administer the estate of a deceased person who died intestate (no will). **8-163**

ADMINISTRATOR'S DEED—A deed given by an administrator. **15-246**

AD VALOREM—Tax according to valuation. **25-365**

ADVERSE POSSESSION—The means of acquiring title to land against the real owner, where possession has been actual, open, hostile, exclusive, continuous and under claim of right for the statutory period of 20 years. **16-255**

AFFIDAVIT OF TITLE—A statement reduced to writing and sworn to before a notary public or some other authorized officer in which the seller states the existence of any known liens or facts relating to the title that were not included in the title binder, and reveals any judgments that were not revealed in the search. **11-187**

AFFIRM—To confirm or to ratify.

AGENCY—The legal relationship resulting from an agreement that the agent is authorized by a principal to perform certain acts on behalf of the principal in dealing with a third party. **12-191**

AGENT—A person who is authorized to act on behalf of another person, called the "principal." **12-191**

AIR RIGHTS—The rights vested by a grant of an estate in real property to all or any portion of the space above the ground. **4-137**

ALIENATION—The transferring of real property from one person to another. **15-245**

ALIENATION CLAUSE—A clause in a conventional mortgage calling for payment of the entire principal balance in full in the event a transfer of title to the mortgaged property takes place; also known as a "due-on-sale clause." **17-260**

ALLUVION—That increase of soil on a shore or bank of a river as the result of accretion. **4-138**

AMENITIES—Those things which are marked by such qualities as pleasantness, comfortableness and agreeableness. In appraising, the amenities of property are those qualities which increase the pleasure of ownership and are not necessarily related to monetary values. **12-201**

AMERICAN LAND TITLE ASSOCIATION (ALTA)—A national association of more than 2,000 land title companies established to encourage uniformity and quality in title insurance policies. **11-188**

AMERICANS WITH DISABILITIES ACT—A law that provides access requirements and prohibits discrimination against people with disabilities in public accommodations, state and local government, transportation, telecommunications and employment. **24-356**

AMORTIZATION—The gradual paying off of a debt on an installment basis. **17-267**

AMOUNT REALIZED—Selling price minus selling expenses. **25-369**

ANNEXATION—The act of attaching, adding, joining or uniting one thing to another.

ANNUAL PERCENTAGE RATE (APR)—The effective rate of interest for a loan per year, disclosure of which is required by the Federal Truth in Lending Law. **20-292**

ANTENUPTIAL AGREEMENT—An agreement made by a man and woman in contemplation of their marriage and to be effective on marriage. Also called prenuptial agreement.

APPRAISAL-An estimate of value of real estate; the report stating and supporting the estimated value of realty. **27-391**

APPRAISAL BY CAPITALIZATION—Determining the value of property by dividing net annual income by the capitalization rate. Used on income-producing properties. **27-395**

APPRAISAL BY COST APPROACH—Estimating the value of a piece of property by adding to the estimated land value the estimate of the replacement cost or reproduction cost of the building less depreciation. Also called "summation" or "reproduction cost" approach. **27-397**

APPRAISAL BY SALES COMPARISON—An appraisal of property through the examination and comparison of actual sales of comparable properties. **27-393**

APPRECIATION—An increased value of property due to economic or related causes which may prove to be either temporary or permanent.

APPURTENANCE—That which has been added to a property, which becomes an inherent part of the property, and will pass with it when conveyed. **5-142**

APR—See "annual percentage rate."

ARM—See "adjustable rate mortgage."

ARELLO—The Association of Real Estate License Law Officials. A federation of real estate license law officials to assist each other in the administration and enforcement of license laws in the United States and Canada.

ASSEMBLAGE—Putting together two or more lots to form a large parcel. To be distinguished from "plottage," which is the resulting value. **27-392**

ASSESSED VALUATION—An assessment of property values by the government for the purpose of taxation. **25-365**

ASSESSMENT—A charge against real estate made by a unit of government to cover the proportionate cost of improvements. **25-365**

ASSIGNEE—The person to whom an agreement or contract is transferred. **14-225**

ASSIGNMENT—The method or manner by which a right, specialty or contract is transferred from one person to another. **14-225**

ASSIGNOR—A party who assigns or transfers an agreement or contract to another. **14-225**

ASSUMPTION OF MORTGAGE—Taking of title to property by assuming liability for payment of an existing note secured by a mortgage. **17-261**

ATTACHMENT—The act of taking realty by judicial order and placing it within the custody of the court. **18-278**

ATTORNEY-IN-FACT—One who is authorized to perform certain acts for another under a power of attorney. **12-202**

ATTORNEY REVIEW CLAUSE—In New Jersey, a clause that must appear in all purchase and sale agreements and all leases prepared by real estate licensees, allowing buyers and sellers a period of three days to consult an attorney who can review and cancel the contract or lease. **3-25**

ATTRACTION PRINCIPLE—The pulling force of a commercial business center due to one or more of the various merchandising factors existing.

AVULSION—The sudden removal of land of one owner and depositing it on the land of another when a stream changes its channel. **4-138**

BALLOON PAYMENT—Final installment payment on a note which is greater than the preceding installment payments and pays the note in full. **17-267**

BARGAIN AND SALE DEED—A deed used to convey title to real property, which may or may not include warranties; if any, they are generally limited to an assertion by the grantor that he has possession of the property. **15-246**

BASELINE AND MERIDIAN—Imaginary lines used by surveyors in locating and describing land under the rectangular survey method. The north-south line is the meridian, the east-west line is the base line. Used mostly in Western states.

BASIS—Original cost of property plus value of any improvements put on by the seller and minus any depreciation taken. **27-391**

BEARING WALL—Supports any vertical load in addition to its own weight.

BEFORE AND AFTER METHOD—An appraisal method used in condemnation cases where there has been a partial taking of the property. **16-225**

BENCHMARK—A permanent reference mark or point established for use in measuring differences in elevation. **28-403**

BENEFICIARY—A person who receives and benefits from the gifts or acts of another; one who receives the proceeds from a will, insurance policy or trust.

BEQUEATH—Formerly, the giving of personal property by will. Today, the term "devise" is used. **8-163**

BEQUEST—Formerly, personal property given by a will. (See bequeath). **8-163**

BIANNUAL—Happening twice each year; semi-annual.

BIENNIAL—Happening once every two years. **3-17**

BILATERAL CONTRACT—A contract in which both parties have reciprocal obligations toward each other. **14-221**

BILL OF SALE—A written instrument which passes title of personal property from seller to buyer. **5-141**

BINDER—An agreement to cover a down payment for the purchase of real estate as evidence of good faith on the part of the purchaser; shows the receipt of a deposit and outlines the basic terms of the transaction. **14-226**

BIWEEKLY LOAN—A loan in which 26 half-size payments are made each year, resulting in the borrower saving interest and paying off the loan sooner than under a standard loan arrangement with monthly payments.

BLANKET MORTGAGE—One mortgage covering two or more specific parcels of realty. **17-260**

BLIGHTED AREA—A real estate district where the conditions of property are below standard and productivity substantially reduced as a result. "Blighted area" is very often a term of art used in federal statutes involving urban renewal, etc. An area is not so designated without official action of the governing body of the community under these statutes.

BLOCKBUSTING—The unlawful discriminatory practice of encouraging members of one race or creed to move into a neighborhood, and then exploiting the situation by persuading residents to sell their houses at deflated prices because of the alleged social deterioration of the neighborhood. **24-349**

BONA FIDE—In good faith, without fraud; genuine; real. **10-174**

BOOT—The payment to satisfy the difference in equities in an exchange, which may be in cash, personal property, note, financing or anything of agreed-upon value. **26-376**

BRANCH OFFICE—Any office other than the main office from which real estate business is conducted. **3-16**

BREACH OF CONTRACT—Violation of any of the terms or conditions of a contract; default; non-performance. **14-226**

BROKER—A licensed person who negotiates the purchase and sale of real estate for another. **3-15**

BROKER OF RECORD—The supervising broker of a partnership or corporation who is responsible for the actions and inaction of all licensed salespersons and broker-salespersons of such entities. **3-29**

BUFFER ZONE—A parcel of land separating two other parcels or areas, such as a strip of land between an industrial and a residential area. **29-414**

BUILDING CODES—Regulations defining materials and/or performance standards for structural components, as well as heights, safety features, sanitation and health requirements, and setback and sideline restrictions. **29-417**

BUILDING LINE—A line at a certain distance from the front and/or sides of a lot, beyond which no building may project.

BUNDLE OF RIGHTS—Ownership concept in real estate, which embraces the rights of possession, use, enjoyment and disposition. **4-137**

BUYER BROKER—A broker who represents a buyer in a real estate transaction. **12-193**

CADRA—New Jersey's Coastal Area Development Review Act that applies to projects near coastal waters in the southern part of the state. It regulates all development activities and all related work such as excavation, grading, shore protection, structures and site preparation. **33-476**

CAPITAL GAIN—The gain on the sale of a capital asset such as real estate. **25-369**

CAPITALIZATION—The act of converting future income into current equivalent value. **27-393**

CAPITALIZATION RATE—The relationship or ratio between the net income from a real estate investment and the value of the investment, usually expressed as a percentage; the rate of interest which is, considered a reasonable return on the investment. **27-395**

CAVEAT EMPTOR—Let the buyer beware; the buyer must examine the goods or property and buy at his or her own risk.

CERCLA—The Comprehensive Environmental Response, Compensation and Liability Act, commonly known as Superfund. This federal law established prohibitions and regulations concerning closed and abandoned hazardous waste sites, provided liability for people responsible for releases of hazardous waste at these sites and establishes funding to provide clean up when no responsible party could be identified.

CERTIFICATE OF ELIGIBILITY—The document that verifies the entitlement of an individual to the benefits of the Servicemen's Readjustment Act of 1944 by establishing his service record qualifications with the government agency.

CERTIFICATE OF NO DEFENSE—An instrument executed by the mortgagor to the assignee upon the sale of the mortgage, setting forth the present status of the mortgage and attesting to its validity; estoppel certificate. **17-261**

CERTIFICATE OF OCCUPANCY (C.O.)—A document issued by a local government indicating that the building is in compliance with public health and building codes and may be legally occupied. **29-418**

CERTIFICATE OF REASONABLE VALUE—Commonly known as a C.R.V.; this is the appraisal commitment of the Veterans Administration used to fix the value of a property being proposed for purchase by a veteran under the GI Bill of Rights. **17-270**

CERTIFICATE OF TITLE—An opinion rendered by an attorney as to the status of title to a property according to the public records.

CERTIFIED PROPERTY MANAGER—Commonly known as C.P.M., this identification is bestowed upon any property manager who has met the requirements of the Institute of Property Management operated under the auspices of the National Association of Realtors. **23-343**

CHAIN—A measurement of distance. Engineer's chain is a series of 100 wire links, each of which is one foot in length. A surveyor's chain is a series of wire links, each of which is 7.92 inches long. The surveyor's chain has a total length equal to four rods or 66 feet. Ten square chains of land is one acre. **28-410**

CHAIN OF TITLE—A sequential history of the conveyances, encumbrances and records of ownership to a piece of property through the years from the original grant to present, as revealed through the public records. **11-180**

CHATTEL—Personal property which is tangible and movable. **5-141**

CHATTEL MORTGAGE—A personal property mortgage. **5-141**

CITE—To quote an authority or an example; to call to attention or enumerate.

CLIENT—The principal to a real estate transaction who employs the agent. **12-191**

CLOSING—The time when a transaction is consummated, or the actual signing over the documents and delivery of the deed; the time after signing when the documents are recorded. **14-225**

CLOSING STATEMENT—A statement of settlement made by a broker or an escrow company that reflects the financial position of the buyer and seller in that particular real estate transaction. **21-297**

CLOUD ON TITLE—Any conditions revealed by a title search which may affect or impair the owner's title to property because of their apparent or probable validity. **15-246**

CODICIL—A supplement or addition to a will which adds to, subtracts from, alters, revokes or qualifies the provisions of a will. **8-163**

COLOR OF TITLE—That which appears to be good title but which is not in fact good title, such as title held under a defective deed.

COMMINGLING—Mixing money belonging to clients with personal funds. **3-24**

COMMISSION—An agent's compensation for performance of the duties of his agency; in real estate practice, a percentage of the selling price of the property, or percentage of rentals, etc. **13-213**

COMMITMENT—A pledge or a promise; an agreement.

COMMON ELEMENT—In a condominium, land and all parts of a building usually used by all the owners for their mutual convenience or safety; also called "common area." **7-154**

COMMON EXPENSE—In a condominium, the expenses of operation; all sums designated as such by the declaration or bylaws.

COMMON LAW—Laws that have evolved from general usage and have been legally established through court decision.

COMPARABLES—Properties that are similar to the subject property. Commonly called "comps." **27-394**

COMPARATIVE MARKET ANALYSIS—An informal estimate of value to assist property owners in establishing an asking price for their properties. **3-22**

COMPETENT PARTIES—Those who are qualified or mentally competent to enter into a contract. **14-221**

COMPOUND INTEREST—Interest paid both on the original principal and on interest accrued from the time it fell due.

CONDEMNATION—The process by which property of a private owner is taken for public use, with just compensation to the owner, under the right of eminent domain. **16-255**

CONDEMNEE—One whose property is condemned. **16-255**

CONDOMINIUM OWNERSHIP—The individual outright ownership of a single unit in a multi-unit property together with an interest in the common elements of that property. **7-154**

CONSEQUENTIAL DAMAGE—A term used to define damage arising from the acts of public bodies or adjacent owners to a given parcel of land which impairs the value of that parcel without actually condemning its use in whole or part.

CONSIDERATION—Valuable consideration, a promise or an act of legal value bargained for and received in return for a promise; good consideration, love and affection. **14-223**

CONSTRUCTIVE EVICTION—Breach of the covenant warranting quiet enjoyment in a lease; when a landlord performs an act depriving the tenant of quiet enjoyment of the premises, thereby causing the tenant to move. **22-311**

CONSTRUCTIVE NOTICE—Notice given by the public records; legal presumption of notice given by the public records. Also called "legal notice." **10-173**

CONSUMER INFORMATION STATEMENT—A statement on New Jersey Real Estate Relationships as prescribed in NJAC 11:5-1.43(h). **12-193**

CONSUMMATE—To bring to completion, perfection or fulfillment.

CONTIGUOUS—In close proximity; adjoining; e.g., parcels of land next to each other.

CONTINGENT—Dependent upon an uncertain future event.

CONTINUATION—An update of a title search, covering the period from the preliminary title report to the time of the recording of the documents. **11-184**

CONTRACT—A legal agreement between competent parties for a consideration to perform or refrain from performing certain acts. **14-221**

CONVENTIONAL MORTGAGE—A mortgage which is not FHA-insured or VA-guaranteed. **17-262**

CONVEYANCE—The transfer of the title of land from one to another; an instrument which carries from one person to another an interest in land. **15-245**

COOPERATIVE OWNERSHIP—Ownership that usually takes the form of shares of stock in a corporation owning the entire building and a proprietary lease giving the stockholder/tenant the right to occupy a unit for which he pays a proportionate share of the maintenance and operating expenses. **7-154**

CORNER INFLUENCE—The additional value attributed to a corner lot due to its various advantages for business uses.

CORPORATION—A vehicle used to carry on business, with its owners having liability only to the extent of their stock ownership; considered being an individual or separate entity. **7-156**

CORPOREAL—Rights of a visible and tangible nature. **6-145**

CORRECTION DEED—A deed used to cover a prior erroneous deed; a deed of confirmation; a reformation deed. **15-246**

COUNTER OFFER—A new offer made in response to an earlier offer.

COVENANT—An agreement written into deeds and other instruments which promises or guarantees that something shall or shall not be done; an agreement stipulating certain use or non-use of property. **15-245**

CREDIT—In closing statements, an amount entered in a person's favor.

CUL-DE-SAC—A passageway or street with only one outlet; a blind alley; a turn-around.

CURTESY—The right that a husband has in his wife's estate at her death. **8-162**

DAMAGES—The indemnity recoverable by an injured party as compensation for the loss suffered through the act or default of another. **14-221**

DEBT SERVICE—The amount needed for payment of principal and interest on an amortized debt.

DECLARATION—That which, along with the by-laws, defines the rules by which a condominium will exist. **7-155**

DEDICATION—A transfer of property from an individual to the public. **9-168**

DEED—An instrument in writing, duly executed and delivered by the grantor, that conveys to the grantee some right, title or interest in or to real estate. **15-245**

DEED OF TRUST—See "trust deed." **15-246**

DEED RESTRICTION—A private limitation in a deed, placed by a grantor limiting the use of land by future owners.

DEFAULT—Failure to meet an obligation or promise when due. **14-226**

DEFEASANCE CLAUSE—The clause in a mortgage that gives a mortgagor the right to redeem his property upon the payment of his obligation to the mortgagee, and declares the instrument null and void upon payment of debt when due. **17-260**

DEFICIENCY JUDGMENT—A judgment for the balance of a debt, issued when the difference between the indebtedness sued upon and the sale price obtained at the foreclosure sale is less than the debt. **17-259**

DELIVERY—The act or intent of transferring an instrument from one person to another in such a way that it cannot be recalled. **15-247**

DEMISE—A conveyance of an estate to another for life, for years, or at will; to lease.

DEPOSIT—Money given by one to another as evidence of good faith; evidence or security for performance of a contract. **14-223**

DEPRECIATION—Loss of value brought about by physical deterioration or functional or economic obsolescence. **27-393**

DESCENT—Ownership transferred by means of inheritance. **8-162**

DETERIORATION—Loss in value brought about by wear and tear. **27-393**

DEVISE—A gift of real or personal property by will. **8-163**

DEVISEE—One who receives a gift of real estate or personal property by will. **8-163**

DEVISOR—One who gives real or personal property by will. **8-163**

DISCOUNT POINTS—A fee paid to induce a lender to make a mortgage loan. Each point charged represents 1% of the loan amount and increases the interest rate by 1/8 of 1%. **17-267**

DISPOSSESS PROCEEDINGS—A legal process by a

landlord to remove a tenant and regain possession of real property due to some breach of the lease agreement by the tenant. **22-311**

DOMINANT ESTATE—An estate attached to and benefiting from the servient estate, e.g., an easement runs over the servient estate and serves the dominant estate; also called the "dominant tenant." **9-167**

DONEE—A person to whom a gift is made.

DONOR—A person who makes a gift.

DOWER—The one-half interest a wife has in the property of her husband; a life estate in one-half of the land the husband owns during the continuance of the marriage relationship. **8-161**

DOWER CONSUMMATE—The completed dower; the right a wife has in her husband's property upon his death. **8-161**

DOWER INCHOATE—The right a wife has in her husband's property during his life. **8-161**

DUAL AGENCY—Representing two clients in the same transaction. **12-199**

DUAL CONTRACT—The illegal practice of providing two different contracts in the same transaction, with the second contract not reflecting the true agreement of the parties. **14-222**

DUE-ON-SALE CLAUSE—See Alienation Clause. **17-260**

DURESS—Unlawful constraint or action against a person, forcing him to perform some act against his will. **14-224**

EARNEST MONEY—Initial payment made by a purchaser of real estate as evidence of good faith. **14-223**

EASEMENT—A right, privilege or interest which one party has in the land of another. **9-167**

EASEMENT APPURTENANT—An easement that is attached to and runs with the land. It cannot exist apart from the particular land to which it is attached. **9-167**

EASEMENT BY NECESSITY—The right of an owner to cross over the property of another for a special necessary purpose, such as in a landlocked situation. **9-168**

EASEMENT BY PRESCRIPTION—A method of acquiring a right to a portion of property by lapse of time, in the manner of adverse possession. **9-168**

EASEMENT IN GROSS—An easement that does not attach to the land, and is usually given to a quasi-public corporation such as the electric or phone company. **9-167**

ECONOMIC LIFE—The period of time over which a property may be profitably used. **27-394**

ECONOMIC OBSOLESCENCE—See "obsolescence." **27-397**

ECONOMIC RENT—The rental warranted to be paid in the open real estate market based upon current rentals being paid for comparable space. **27-395**

EGRESS—Means of leaving property without trespassing the property rights of other surrounding owners. **9-167**

EJECTMENT—A form of action to regain possession of real property, with damages for the unlawful retention; generally used when there is no landlord/tenant relationship.

ELECTIVE SHARE—In New Jersey, a minimum one-third share which a surviving spouse may claim in lieu of any amount specified in the deceased spouse's will. **8-162**

EMBLEMENTS—Trees or crops that are cultivated annually; the rights of a tenant to harvest the annual crop even after his tenancy has ended. **4-137**

EMINENT DOMAIN—The right of a government to take private property for public use upon the payment of just compensation. **4-137**

EMPLOYING BROKER—The supervising broker for a real estate company organized as a sole-proprietorship. **3-16**

ENCROACHMENT—A building or fixture which intrudes partly or wholly upon the property of another. **9-169**

ENCUMBRANCE—A claim, lien, charge or liability attached to and binding upon real property which affects or limits the title thereto. **9-167**

EQUAL CREDIT OPPORTUNITY ACT—A federal law prohibiting unlawful discrimination in the extension of credit. **19-287**

EQUALIZATION—The process by which the assessed values of properties are raised or lowered to correct assessment inequities, particularly between various tax districts in a county. **25-366**

EQUITABLE TITLE—Title of a purchaser under a contract of sale or agreement of sale. **14-225**

EQUITY—The interest or value which an owner has in real estate over and above the liens against it; branch of remedial justice by and through which relief is afforded to parties in courts of equity. **18-279**

EQUITY OF REDEMPTION—The right of an owner to reclaim property before it is sold through foreclosure proceedings by payment of the debt, interest and cost. **18-279**

EROSION—The gradual wearing away of land due to natural causes of wind and water. **4-138**

ERRORS AND OMISSIONS INSURANCE—Designed to protect professionals from innocent negligent acts. **12-207**

ESCALATION CLAUSE—The clause in a mortgage that permits the holder to increase or decrease the interest rate during the term of the mortgage. **17-310**

ESCHEAT—The reverting of property to the state when heirs capable of inheriting are lacking, or the property is abandoned. **4-137**

ESCROW—The deposit of instruments and funds with instructions to a third neutral party to carry out the provisions of an agreement or contract. **3-23**

ESCROW AGENT—An independent third party who acts in a fiduciary capacity and is legally bound to carry out the terms of an escrow agreement. (See Escrow). **19-284**

ESCROW HOLDER—The one who receives a deed or other item from a grantor to be delivered to the grantee upon the performance of a condition or the occurrence of a contingency.

ESTATE—The degree, quantity, nature and extent of interest a person has in real property. **6-145**

ESTATE FOR YEARS—A lease; an interest in land by virtue of a contract for the possession for a definite and limited period of time. **22-309**

ESTOPPEL CERTIFICATE—See "Certificate of No Defense." **17-261**

ESTOVERS—Wood which a lessee is permitted to use from the landlord's premises to provide minimum fuel, repairs and tools for his necessary use. (The opposite of waste).

ET AL—Latin for "and others."

ET UX—Latin for "and wife."

EVICTION—A legal proceeding by a landlord to recover possession of leased premises from a tenant due to some breach of the lease contract. **22-311**

EXCHANGE—A method of conveying real property by trading with another property. **26-375**

EXCLUSIVE AGENCY—A written instrument giving one agent the right to sell property for a specified time, but reserving the right of the owner to sell the property himself without the payment of a commission. **13-213**

EXCLUSIVE RIGHT TO SELL—A written agreement between owner and agent giving the agent the right to collect a commission if the property is sold by anyone during the term of the agreement. **13-213**

EXECUTE—To complete, to perform, to make, to do, to follow out; to execute a deed, to make a deed including especially signing; to execute a form; to perform the contract; to follow out to the end; to complete.

EXECUTED CONTRACT—A contract that is fully signed or performed. **14-222**

EXECUTOR—A person named in a will to carry out its provisions as to the disposition of the estate of a deceased person. **8-162**

EXECUTORY CONTRACT—A contract not yet fully performed. **14-232**

EXECUTRIX—Feminine of "executor." **8-163**

EXPRESS AUTHORITY—Clearly stated duties of an agent, as set forth by his or her principal.

EXTERNAL OBSOLESCENCE—Loss of value caused by factors outside the property, such as zoning. **27-393**

FACADE—The front of a building.

FEDERAL FLOOD INSURANCE—A federal program to aid in rebuilding homes destroyed by floods and designating areas where floods are most likely to occur. **21-298**

FEDERAL HOME LOAN MORTGAGE CORPORATION (FHLMC)—A federal agency which buys mortgages in the secondary money market from commercial banks and federally insured savings and loan associations; "Freddie Mac." **19-286**

FEDERAL HOUSING ADMINISTRATION (FHA)—An agency of the federal government which insures certain real estate loans. **17-268**

FEDERAL NATIONAL MORTGAGE ASSOCIATION (FNMA)—A part public, part private corporation that buys and sells mortgages in the secondary money market, known as "Fannie Mae." **19-286**

FEE CONDITIONAL—An estate granted absolutely but only so long as a specified event occurs or does not occur. **6-146**

FEE DETERMINABLE—A fee estate which exists only until a specified event does or does not occur. Upon the happening of such event, the fee automatically ends and reverts back to the original grantor, or to his estate. **6-145**

FEE SIMPLE—An estate in real property, by which the owner has the greatest power over the title which it is possible to have, being an absolute estate; an estate of inheritance belonging to the owner, that he may dispose of, trade, or will as he chooses. **6-145**

FEE TAIL—an estate that was inheritable by particular lineal heirs. Upon lack of such heirs the estate reverted back to the grantor or his heirs. No longer recognized.

FEE TITLE POLICY—The title insurance policy covering the property owner.

FHA LOAN—A mortgage loan insured by the Federal Housing Administration. **17-268**

FIDUCIARY—A person in a position of great trust and confidence, as the relationship between principal and agent. **12-192**

FINDERS' FEE—A fee paid to a person for putting together the two parties in a real estate transaction. **19-284**

FISCAL YEAR—A year, used for tax, corporate and accounting purposes, which begins on a date other than January 1.

FIXING-UP EXPENSES—Expenses incurred for physically preparing a personal residence for sale. **25-369**

FIXTURE—An article of personal property which has been installed in or attached to land or a building thereon, in such a manner that it is now considered to be a part of the real estate. **5-141**

FLASHING—Metal strips placed around roof openings to provide water tightness.

FORECLOSURE—Procedure whereby property pledged as security for a debt is sold to pay the debt in event of default in payments or terms. **18-279**

FORFEITURE—Loss of money or anything of value

due to failure to perform; a right expressly given in an installment contract whereby the seller terminates the contract for non-payment, and retains all of the payments previously made by the buyer.

FORESHORE—Land between the high-water mark and low-water mark.

FRAUD—The intentional and successful employment of deception in order to cheat or deceive another person and to thereby gain some dishonest advantage. **3-26**

FREEHOLD—An estate in real property for an indefinite and uncertain time. **6-145**

FRONT FOOT—Property measurement by the front foot on its street line or waterfront line with each front foot extending the depth of the lot.

FUNCTIONAL OBSOLESCENCE—See "obsolescence." **27-393**

GABLE—The vertical triangular end of a building.

GAMBREL ROOF—A roof with a lower steeper slope and an upper flatter one.

GENERAL LIEN—A lien which attaches to all property owned by the debtor. **18-278**

G.I. LOAN—Same as VA loan. **17-269**

GOODWILL—An intangible asset arising from the reputation of a business. **32-459**

GOVERNMENT NATIONAL MORTGAGE ASSOCIATION (GNMA)—A federal agency which provides special assistance for federally aided housing programs; active in the secondary money market for government subsidized housing programs; "Ginnie Mae." **19-286**

GRADUATED LEASE—See step-up lease. **22-310**

GRADUATED PAYMENT MORTGAGE (GPM)—A mortgage calling for lower payments in early years than in later years. Payments increase in steps each year until the installments become sufficient to amortize the loan. **17-267**

GRANDFATHER CLAUSE—See "nonconforming use." **29-415**

GRANT—A transfer of real property.

GRANTEE—The purchaser; the person to whom an interest in realty is conveyed by deed. **15-245**

GRANTOR—The seller; the person who conveys an interest in realty by deed. **15-245**

GRI—The professional designation of Graduate Realtor's Institute, earned by completion of prescribed courses of study conducted by state boards of Realtors.

GROSS INCOME—Total income derived from a business or income property before expenses are deducted. **27-394**

GROSS LEASE—A lease of property in which the lessor meets all property charges incurred through ownership. **22-310**

GROSS MULTIPLIER—A number which is used to determine approximate selling price for income property by multiplying the gross income times this number (income x multiplier = selling price). **27-394**

GROUND LEASE—A lease for the use of the land, usually providing for improvements to be placed on the land by the user. **22-310**

GROUND RENT—The net rent paid for a parcel of unimproved land; that portion of the total rental is considered to represent a return upon the land only.

GUARANTY FUND—A fund established from licensing fees for paying claims of persons who have been injured by the illegal acts of licensees. **3-19**

HABENDUM CLAUSE—The portion of a deed beginning "to have and to hold," which usually follows the granting clause and explains or limits the estate granted. **15-247**

HEIR—One who inherits property.

HEREDITAMENTS—Any property, real or personal, tangible or intangible, that may be inherited.

HIGHEST AND BEST USE—That legal use which at the time of an appraisal is most likely to produce the greatest net return over a given period of time. **27-392**

HOLDOVER TENANT—A tenant who remains in possession of a property after expiration of the lease term. **22-311**

HOLOGRAPHIC WILL—An unwitnessed will written in hand by the person leaving the will. **8-163**

HOMOGENEOUS—The same or similar kind of structure; similar; as used in appraising, homogeneity tends to stabilize values in an area. **27-392**

HORIZONTAL PROPERTY ACT—The name given to the laws that recognize condominium ownership in New Jersey; horizontal layers of ownership. **7-154**

HYPOTHECATE—To pledge property as security; to mortgage. **17-259**

I.F.A.—Abbreviation for "Independent Fee Appraiser."

IMPLIED AUTHORITY—The authority that an agent is assumed to have because of a course of conduct, or which is inferred from the fact that he has been authorized to perform certain acts.

INCAPACITY—Lack of legal qualifications making a person incapable of performing some act. Mental deficients, minors, etc. lack legal capacity to perform certain acts.

INCHOATE—Incomplete; not perfected. **8-161**

INCORPOREAL—Intangible; without physical existence. **6-145**

INDEFEASIBLE—Not capable of being annulled or voided. **6-146**

INDEPENDENT CONTRACTOR—One who is retained to perform a certain act subject to the control and direction of another as to the end result, but not as to how the act is performed. The critical feature is that an independent contractor, unlike an employee, is not subject to the control of the person who retained him or her. **12-204**

INDUSTRIAL PARKS—Tracts subdivided into usable sites for sale or lease, catering to light industry, and providing a planned and controlled environment.

INGRESS—An entrance to property which does not trespass over the property rights of others. **9-167**

INJUNCTION—A writ or order issued under the seal of a court to restrain one or more parties from performing an act which is deemed to be inequitable or unjust in regard to the rights of some other party.

IN REM—Foreclosure proceedings by a municipality against the property directly, as distinguished from a proceeding against a person, in taking property for nonpayment of taxes.

INSTALLMENT CONTRACT—A contract that provides for payment of a purchase price in installments. **25-370**

INSTRUMENT—A written legal document.

INTERIM FINANCING—A short-term loan obtained to cover financing of the construction of a building.

INTESTATE—Having made no valid will; also a person who dies without a will, or with one which is defective in form. **8-163**

INVOLUNTARY LIEN—A lien imposed against property without consent of an owner: e.g., taxes, special assessments, and federal income tax liens. **18-277**

IRREVOCABLE—Incapable of being recalled or revoked; unchangeable.

ISRA—The Industrial Site Recovery Act, a New Jersey statute that imposes certain pre-conditioning on the sale, transfer or closure of industrial establishments involved with hazardous substances or waste. **33-470**

JOINT TENANCY—Ownership by two or more persons with rights of survivorship; all joint tenants own equal interests and have equal rights in the property. Each owner is possessed of an undivided part of the whole. **7-151**

JOINT VENTURE—A joining of two or more people in a specific business enterprise; similar to a partnership, and generally with no intention of a continuing relationship beyond the original purpose. **7-154**

JUDGMENT—The final determination of the rights and liabilities of the parties by a court in an action before it. **18-278**

JUNIOR LIEN—A subordinate lien. **17-260**

JUNIOR MORTGAGE—A mortgage that is subordinate to a prior existing mortgage on the same realty. **17-264**

LACHES—Delay or negligence in asserting one's legal rights.

LAND CONTRACT—Written agreement in which buyer agrees to buy certain realty and seller agrees to sell upon terms and conditions set forth therein. Title remains with the seller until terms and conditions are fulfilled; buyer has equitable title. **19-284**

LAND PATENT—An instrument conveying government-owned lands to individuals.

LATERAL SUPPORT—The support that the soil of an adjoining owner gives to his neighbor's land. **9-169**

LEASE—A contract whereby the lawful owner of the property transfers his rights of use and possession to another for a specified term. **22-309**

LEASEHOLD—An estate or right in real property that involves possession but not ownership. **6-147**

LEGACY—A gift of personal property, usually money, by will.

LEGAL DESCRIPTION—A description, recognized by law, that will definitely locate and identify the property. **28-382**

LESSEE—One who rents property under a lease contract. **22-309**

LESSOR—An owner who enters into a lease with a tenant. **22-309**

LESS THAN FREEHOLD—A lease; a leasehold estate. Also called "non-freehold." **6-147**

LEVERAGE—The use of borrowed funds in financing, with the anticipation that the property acquired will increase in return so that the investor will realize a profit, not only on his own investment, but on the borrowed funds as well.

LICENSE—A personal privilege to enter the land of another for a specific purpose. **9-169**

LIEN—A right, given by law, whereby a creditor may satisfy a debt out of the proceeds of the sale of real or personal property belonging to the debtor; an encumbrance, usually naming property as security for payment of a debt or for the discharge of an obligation. **18-277**

LIFE ESTATE—An estate or interest in real property held for the duration of the life of a certain person. Upon the expiration of that life, the estate will automatically be vested in a remainderman or reversioner. **6-145**

LIKE-KIND PROPERTY—Property having the same nature. To qualify for a tax-deferred exchange and the resulting tax benefit, the properties being exchanged must be of "like-kind." For example, investment property traded for investment property would qualify. **26-376**

LIMITED COMMON ELEMENT—In a condominium, those common elements reserved for the use of a certain apartment, or certain apartments, to the exclusion of other apartments. **7-155**

LIMITED PARTNERSHIP—A partnership composed of general and limited partners whose contribution and liability are limited and specifically defined. **7-154**

LIQUIDATED DAMAGES—An amount predetermined by the parties to an agreement that will be forfeited as compensation for breach of contract. **14-227**

LIS PENDENS—A legal document giving constructive notice that legal action is pending. **18-277**

LISTING—A written employment agreement between a property owner and a broker authorizing the broker to sell, lease or exchange the realty. **13-213**

LITTORAL—Property that borders a large body of water, such as a lake, ocean or sea is said to be littoral property. **4-138**

LOAN COMMITMENT—A commitment by a lender as to the amount he will loan to a qualified borrower on a particular piece of real estate.

LOAN-TO-VALUE RATIO (LTV)—The ratio between a mortgage loan and the market or appraised value, whichever is lower. **17-261**

LOFT BUILDING—An industrial building formerly used by one manufacturer but now subdivided into many individual partitions, suitable for small manufacturers.

M.A.I.—Designates a person who is a member of the American Institute of Real Estate Appraisers of the National Association of Realtors.

MANSARD—A roof having two slopes on all sides, with the lower slope steeper than the upper one.

MARGINAL LAND—Land which barely pays the cost of working or using.

MARKETABLE TITLE—Title free and clear of objectionable liens or encumbrances; title which is free from reasonable doubts or defects, which can be readily sold or mortgaged. **11-185**

MARKET PRICE—The actual price paid in a given transaction. Contrast with market value. **27-391**

MARKET VALUE—The highest price a ready, willing and able buyer, not forced to buy, will pay to a ready, willing and able seller, not forced to sell, allowing a reasonable time for exposure in the open market. **27-391**

MASTER PLAN—A guide to the use of property within a community, as established by a planning board, to project the desired future growth and nature of the area covered. **29-413**

MECHANIC'S LIEN—A lien which exists against real property in favor of persons who have performed work or furnished materials for the improvement of the real estate. **18-278**

MEGAN'S LAW—A New Jersey law that establishes law registration and notification provisions and requires the classification of convicted sex offenders using a three-tier system.

MERGER OF TITLE—The absorption of one estate into another.

METES AND BOUNDS—A method of describing or locating real property; metes are measures of length and bounds are boundaries; a description starting with a well-marked point of beginning and following the boundaries of the land until it returns once more to the point of beginning. **28-403**

MILE—A linear measurement of distance equal to 1,760 yards, 5,280 feet, or 1,608 meters. **28-410**

MILL—One-tenth of one cent. Used in some states to compute property taxes. **25-365**

MINOR—A person who is under the legal age of competence; one under 18 years of age.

M.I.P.—The mortgage insurance premium collected by the FHA for insuring the mortgage. **17-268**

MISDEMEANOR—A crime of lesser consequences than a felony which is subject to minor jail terms, fines, or both. **3-27**

MISREPRESENTATION—A false statement made with the intent to induce some action by another party. **14-224**

MOBILE HOMES—Three-dimensional single-family units, built to be towed on their own chassis, not required to satisfy local building codes. **31-451**

MODULAR—A building composed of modules, joined with one another, horizontally or vertically or both, the modules themselves being self-contained sections constructed in a factory on the assembly line.

MONTH-TO-MONTH TENANCY—A periodic tenancy which automatically renews at the end of each month, unless one of the parties to the agreement (landlord of tenant) serves the other with a proper notice to cancel. **22-309**

MONUMENT—A fixed object and point established by surveyors to establish land locations; includes not only artificial objects such as posts and fences, but natural objects such as trees, mountains and water courses. **28-403**

MORTGAGE—An instrument in writing which, when recorded, creates a lien upon property pledged as security for the repayment of a debt or obligation. **17-259**

MORTGAGE BANKER—A corporation or firm which makes, delivers, and services mortgage loans. **19-284**

MORTGAGE BROKER—A person or firm which acts as an intermediary between borrower and lender. **19-284**

MORTGAGE INSURANCE PREMIUM (MIP)—The mortgage insurance premium paid by the borrower to the FHA on insured loans. The MIP can be paid in cash at closing or added to the loan amount. **17-268**

MORTGAGEE—The party who lends money and accepts a mortgage to secure the payment of the debt. **17-259**

MORTGAGOR—The party who borrows money and gives a mortgage on the property as security for his or her obligation to pay the debt. **17-259**

MULTIPLE LISTING SERVICE (M.L.S.)—An arrangement among brokers whereby they share their listings. **13-214**

NAR—The National Association of Realtors®. Only brokers who are members of local real estate boards are entitled to use the trademark name "REALTOR." **2-5**

NAVIGABLE WATERS—Those bodies of water,

which are capable of being used for public transportation. **4-137**

NEGATIVE AMORTIZATION—An increase in the outstanding balance of a loan caused by the failure of mortgage payments to cover interest charged on the loan. **17-264**

NEGOTIABLE INSTRUMENT—A written instrument, signed by its maker or drawer, containing an unconditional promise to pay a certain sum of money; can be passed freely from one person to another.

NEGOTIATE—To transact business; to arrange terms of a contract.

NET INCOME—With reference to property, the sum derived after a vacancy allowance and expenses have been deducted from the gross income; generally described as net income before depreciation, and usually defining the income a property will earn in a normal year's operation. **27-392**

NET LEASE—A lease in which the tenant pays rent for occupancy, plus maintenance and operation expenses, and usually including taxes and insurance. **22-310**

NET LISTING—A listing that provides that the agent may retain all sums received over and above a net price to the owner as compensation for his services. A prohibited practice in New Jersey. **13-214**

NOMINAL CONSIDERATION—One bearing no relation to the real value of the contract. An example is a property which is deeded for $10.00.

NONCONFORMING USE—A use which is contrary to zoning laws, but which is permitted (grandfathered) because the use was allowed before the zoning law came into effect. **29-415**

NOTARY PUBLIC—An officer of the court who is authorized to take acknowledgements to certain documents, such as deeds and mortgages, and before whom affidavits may be sworn. **10-173**

NOTE—A written instrument acknowledging a debt and promising payment. **17-259**

NOTICE TO QUIT—Notice to a tenant to vacate. **22-318**

NOVATION—The substituting of a new obligation for an old one. **17-261**

NONCULPATIVE WILL—An oral will.

OBSOLESCENCE—Functional obsolescence or lack of desirability in terms of layout, style and design as compared with that of a new property serving the same function; external obsolescence or a loss in value from causes in the neighborhood, but outside the property itself. **27-393**

OFFER—A promise by one party to act in a certain manner provided the other party would act in the manner requested. In a real estate sales contract, the offer to purchase realty according to certain stipulated terms and conditions. **14-222**

OPEN-END MORTGAGE—A mortgage containing a clause which permits the mortgagor to borrow additional money up to the original amount of the loan after the loan has been reduced, without rewriting the mortgage. **17-267**

OPEN LISTING—A listing given to any number of agents without liability to compensate any except the one who first secures a buyer ready, willing and able to meet the terms of the listing. **13-213**

OPERATING EXPENSES—Amounts paid to maintain income-producing property other than debt service and income taxes. **27-395**

OPTION—A right given for consideration to purchase or lease a property upon specified terms within a specified time. **14-225**

OPTIONEE—The one obtaining the option right. **14-225**

OPTIONOR—The one granting the option to another. **14-225**

ORDINANCE—A legislative enactment of a city or county, such as zoning.

OVER-IMPROVEMENT—An improvement that is not the highest and best use for the site on which it is placed, usually by reason of excess size or cost.

PACKAGE MORTGAGE—A mortgage commonly used in subdivision developments whereby chattels such as appliances are "packaged" into the mortgage along with the real property. **17-265**

PAROL EVIDENCE—Oral testimony rather than that reduced to writing. **14-227**

PARTIAL TAKING—The taking of a portion of a piece of property through condemnation. **16-255**

PARTITION—Court proceedings by which co-owners of commonly owned property seek to sever their common ownership. **7-152**

PARTNERSHIP—A contract between two or more persons to carry on as co-owners of a business, and to share the profits in certain proportions. **7-154**

PARTY WALL—A wall erected on the line between adjoining properties, which are under separate ownership, for the use of both owners. **9-170**

PATENT—A conveyance for the transfer of title to land owned by the government; land patent.

PERCENTAGE LEASE—A lease of property in which the rental is based upon the volume of gross sales made on the leased premises. **22-310**

PERFORMANCE BOND—A bond which provides assurance of the completion of an undertaking in accordance with an agreement, such as that supplied by a contractor guaranteeing the completion of a building project.

PERIODIC TENANCY—Tenancy of property for an indefinite period which can be terminated by either party with proper notice. **22-309**

PERSONAL PROPERTY—Any property not real property; personalty. **5-141**

PHYSICAL DETERIORATION—Any loss to property values caused by normal wear and tear or usage.

Also includes such things as termite damage, dry rot and the like. **27-393**

PLANNED UNIT DEVELOPMENT (PUD)—A development and zoning concept which is designed to produce a high density of dwelling units with maximum utilization of open spaces. **29-417**

PLANNING BOARD—The municipal body responsible for subdivision and site plan (subdivision) applications. **29-413**

PLAT—A plan or map of a certain piece or pieces of land. **29-414**

PLAT FIELD BOOK—A public record containing facts pertaining to land.

PLOTTAGE—The land increment produced by combining smaller individually owned plots into a larger tract under single ownership; see "assemblage." **27-392**

POINT OF BEGINNING (POB)—A known identifiable point at which a metes and bounds description starts and ends. Also called the "point of origin." **28-403**

POINTS—See "discount points." **17-267**

POLICE POWER—The inherent right of a government to enact such legislation as may be deemed necessary to protect and promote the health, safety and general welfare of the public. **4-137**

POWER OF ATTORNEY—A written instrument authorizing a person to act as the agent on behalf of another to the extent indicated in the instrument. **12-202**

PRE-FABS—Structural parts, fabricated in advance, and assembled on the site.

PRENUPTIAL AGREEMENT—See Antenuptial Agreement.

PREPAYMENT CLAUSE—The clause in a mortgage or note stating the penalty, if any, for payment before it actually becomes due. **17-264**

PRESCRIPTION—Title obtained by possession for a prescribed period; prescriptive rights. **9-168**

PRIMA FACIE EVIDENCE—Evidence which is good and sufficient on its face ("at first view") to establish a given fact or case, unless rebutted or contradicted.

PRIMARY MORTGAGE MARKET—The source of loan funds available directly to borrowers, whether for first or second mortgages. **19-285**

PRINCIPAL—The employer of an agent or broker. Also, a sum of money owed as a debt upon which interest is calculated. **12-191; 17-261**

PRIVATE MORTGAGE INSURANCE (PMI)—Default insurance on conventional loans, provided by private mortgage insurance companies. Usually the top 20% of the loan is insured in return for the insurance premium paid by the borrower. **17-262**

PROBATE—The legal process of determining the validity of a will, paying the debts of the estate and determining who is to receive the remainder of the estate. **8-162**

PROCURING CAUSE—The cause of a series of events, which leads to the consummation of a sale. **12-204**

PROMISSORY NOTE—A written promise to pay a certain sum of money at a definite date in the future. **17-259**

PROMULGATE—To publish, announce or declare.

PROPRIETARY LEASE—A lease in a cooperative apartment between the owner-corporation and the tenant stockholder. **7-154**

PROPRIETORSHIP—A business held by a person who has legal title or exclusive right thereto.

PRORATE—To divide or distribute proportionately; to divide monies, usually at time of closing, proportionately between seller and buyer. **21-302**

PROSPECTUS—A printed statement distributed to describe and to advertise a new business venture, a real estate project or stock issue.

PURCHASE MONEY MORTGAGE—A mortgage on property given by a buyer, either to the seller or to a third party in order to secure a portion of the purchase price. **17-260**

QUALIFIED FEE—An estate in fee simple bound by limitations imposed by the grantor.

QUIET ENJOYMENT—The right of an owner or tenant legally in possession to the use of property without interference from the landlord, or grantor, or anyone claiming through him. **15-245**

QUIET TITLE—A court action brought to establish title or to remove a cloud on the title; an action clearing tax titles or titles based upon adverse possession. **16-256**

QUITCLAIM DEED—A deed containing no warranties or covenants, which relinquishes any interest, title or claim in property the grantor may have, if any. **15-246**

QUORUM—A majority of the entire body; minimum needed to legally conduct a meeting.

RACIAL STEERING—See Steering.

RADON—A radioactive gas formed by the natural breakdown of uranium. **33-467**

RATIFICATION—The approval or confirmation by one person of an act of contract performed or entered into on his behalf by another, who at the time lacked authority to act as his agent.

READY, WILLING AND ABLE—A person who is prepared, financially able and willing to enter into a binding contract. **12-202**

REAL ESTATE—The physical land at, below and above the earth's surface with all appurtenances, including structures. **4-137**

REAL ESTATE INVESTMENT TRUST (REIT)—A method of pooling investor funds using the trust form of ownership and featuring single taxation of profits. **7-156**

REAL ESTATE SETTLEMENT PROCEDURES

ACT (RESPA)—A federal law dealing with federally related real estate loans for one- to four-family dwellings. Intended to provide borrowers with estimate of closing costs so they can comparison shop. **21-295**

REALTOR—See "NAR."

REALTOR-ASSOCIATE—A salesperson who works for a Realtor/Broker and belongs to the local Board of Realtors.

REALTY TRANSFER FEE—A transfer tax that must be paid by the seller upon passing of title. **15-248**

RECEIVER—A court-appointed custodian who holds property for the court, pending final disposition of the matter before the court. **3-16**

RECORDING—The act of writing or entering an instrument into a book of public records, which constitutes notice to all persons of the rights or claims contained in the instrument; often called "constructive notice" or "legal notice." **10-173**

RECTANGULAR SURVEY—Government system of land survey noted for accuracy, adapted to the measurement of extensive territory (not used in New Jersey). **28-409**

REDLINING—The unlawful practice of refusing to approve mortgage loans in certain neighborhoods on the basis of race or ethnic composition. **19-287**

REFORMATION—An action to correct a mistake in a deed or other document.

REGULATION Z—A federal regulation requiring creditors to provide full disclosure of the terms of a loan (Truth-in-Lending). **20-291**

RELEASE—The relinquishment or surrender of a right, claim or interest. **17-260**

RELEASE CLAUSE—A clause in a blanket mortgage which gives the property owner the right to pay off a portion of the indebtedness, thereby freeing a portion of his property from the mortgage. **17-260**

RELEASE OF MORTGAGE—The instrument given by the mortgagee to the mortgagor indicating discharge of the mortgage, stating that the obligation has been fulfilled and the debt paid off. **17-262**

RELICTION—Gradual recession of water from the usual watermark. **4-138**

REMAINDER ESTATE—An estate created by a single grant simultaneously with another which vests with a third party upon termination of the prior estate, such as a life estate. **6-147**

REMAINDERMAN—The one in whom an estate vests after termination of a prior estate. **6-147**

RENDERED—Furnished; presented; performed; made.

RESCIND—To annul; cancel. **14-226**

RESCISSION—The annulling, revocation or repealing of a contract by mutual consent of the parties, or for cause by either party to the contract, and returning the parties to their original position (the "status quo"). **14-226**

RESCISSION CLAUSE—A clause occasionally found in an agreement of sale which requires the seller to return all of the buyer's payments less costs and a fair rental value in the event the buyer defaults.

RESERVATION—A right retained by a grantor in conveying property. **15-247**

RESTRICTION—Clause in a deed or other written instrument limiting use to which the property may be put. **9-169**

REVERSE ANNUITY MORTGAGE (RAM)—A type of mortgage developed for elderly homeowners with substantial equity wherein the mortgagee makes monthly payments to the mortgagor. Consequently, the homeowner is not forced to sell the home to meet fixed living expenses. **17-265**

REVERSION—The residue of an estate left to the grantor or his heirs after termination of all prior estates and interests; the right of a lessor to recover possession of leased property upon the termination of the lease, with all subsequent rights to use and enjoy the property. **6-147**

REVERSIONARY INTEREST—A present right to future possession of an estate. **6-147**

REVOCATION—The act of recalling some agreement, power or interest previously given.

RIDER—An amendment or attachment to a contract. **14-228**

RIGHT OF WAY—An easement or right of passage over another's land.

RIPARIAN RIGHTS—The right of a landowner to the use of water on or adjacent to his land. **4-138**

RUNNING WITH THE LAND—A covenant which extends beyond the original parties to an agreement and binds all subsequent parties. **9-167**

SALE AND LEASEBACK—The sale and subsequent leasing back by the seller-lessee. **19-285**

SANDWICH LEASE—A leasehold interest of a sublessor, which lies between the primary lease (owner), and the operating lease (user).

SATISFACTION OF MORTGAGE—An instrument used when a lien is paid off and satisfied on the records; also called "satisfaction piece." See "release of mortgage." **17-262**

SEAL—An impression made to attest to the execution of an instrument.

SECONDARY MORTGAGE MARKET—The marketplace for the sale and purchase of existing mortgages. **19-286**

SECTION—A section of land established by government survey containing 640 acres, or one square mile. Also, a portion of a tax map description. **28-410**

SECURITY DEPOSIT—Deposit made to assure performance of an obligation, usually by a lessee. **22-316**

SEISIN—Possession of real property by one entitled thereto; a warranty that at the time of delivery of a deed the grantor actually has the right and capacity to convey good legal title; also "seizen." **15-245**

SERVIENT TENEMENT—The property encumbered by an easement. **9-167**

SETBACK—An ordinance prohibiting the erection of a building or structure between the curb or other established line and the setback line; the distance a house must be set back from the street in accordance with local zoning rules. **29-415**

SEVERALTY—Sole or independent ownership. **7-151**

SEVERANCE DAMAGES—Damages paid to an owner when his property has been partially taken by condemnation, thus reducing the highest and best use of the remaining land. **16-255**

SIMPLE INTEREST—Interest computed upon the declining balance of a particular amount; as principal declines so does the interest payment. **30-430**

SKY LEASE—A lease of space above a piece of real estate.

SPECIAL AGENT—A person who is authorized to perform only certain specified functions on behalf of his or her principal. **12-191**

SPECIAL ASSESSMENT—An assessment generally made against only those specific parcels of realty directly benefiting therefrom. **25-367**

SPECIAL WARRANTY DEED—A deed in which the grantor warrants title only against defects occurring during the grantor's ownership. **15-246**

SPECIFIC LIEN—A lien which is applicable to one property in particular versus a general lien, which applies to all property of the individual involved. **18-277**

SPECIFIC PERFORMANCE—A remedy which the court will grant in certain cases, compelling the defendant to perform or carry out the terms of a valid, existing agreement or contract. **14-226**

S.R.A.—Abbreviation for "Society of Residential Appraisers."

STATUTE OF FRAUDS—State law which requires, among other things, that certain contracts relating to real estate must be in writing to be enforceable at law. **14-221**

STATUTE OF LIMITATIONS—Laws setting forth the period of time in which suit can be brought for a particular act. **14-227**

STATUTORY RIGHT OF REDEMPTION—See "redemption." **18-277**

STEERING—Directing prospective buyers or tenants into or away from certain areas on illegal discrimination grounds. **24-350**

STEP-UP LEASE—A lease with fixed increases at stated intervals, or increases based upon periodic appraisals at stated times; graduated lease; graded lease. **22-310**

STIGMATIZED PROPERTY—A property on which the value is negatively influenced by a social condition (barking dog, loud neighbors, etc.) or a psychological impairment (murder, suicide, report of ghosts, etc.)

STRAIGHT-LINE DEPRECIATION—Setting aside or allowing a fixed sum of money each year to offset replacement or improvements when needed. **25-371**

STRAIGHT NOTE—A note requiring only interest payments at regular intervals until maturity, when the full balance becomes due. **17-267**

STRAW MAN—One who purchases property for another to conceal the identity of the real purchaser; a dummy purchaser; a nominee.

SUBDIVISION—A tract of land divided into lots suitable for home building purposes. **29-414**

SUBJECT PROPERTY—The property being appraised.

SUBLEASE—A lease given by a lessee for a portion of the unexpired balance of his term, or one given for a portion of the leased premises. **22-312**

SUBORDINATION CLAUSE—A clause in a mortgage or lease stating that the rights of the holder shall be secondary or subordinate to a subsequent encumbrance. **17-260**

SUBROGATION—The substitution of one person in place of another with reference to a lawful claim, demand or right, so that he succeeds to such rights of the other. **11-187**

SUMMARY POSSESSION—See Actual Possession.

SUMP PUMP—An automatic water pump used in basements to raise water to the sewer level.

SURETY—One who becomes a guarantor for another.

SURRENDER—The cancellation of a lease by an act of mutual consent of lessor and lessee. **22-311**

SURVEY—The process by which a parcel of land is measured and its area ascertained.

SYNDICATION—Multiple ownership of an investment, usually in the form of a limited partnership.

TAKE-OUT FINANCING—Permanent or long-term financing of individual condominium units for their respective buyers. **17-264**

TAX DEED—A deed for property sold by a government unit for non-payment of taxes.

TAX-DEFERRED EXCHANGE—Under Section 1031 of the Internal Revenue Code, property used in a trade or business can be exchanged for like-kind property and the tax deferred until a later date. **26-375**

TAX SALE—A sale of property, usually at auction, for non-payment of assessed taxes. **25-366**

TENANCY AT SUFFERANCE—A tenancy arising when the tenant wrongfully holds over after the expiration of his term. The landlord has the choice of evicting the tenant or accepting him for a similar term and under the conditions of the previous holding. **22-309**

TENANCY AT WILL—Possession and occupancy of land terminable at the will of either party. **22-309**

TENANCY BY THE ENTIRETY—A tenancy held by

husband and wife giving each the equal right to possession and enjoyment during their joint lives, along with the right to sole ownership upon the death of either partner. **7-152**

TENANCY FOR YEARS—Leasing of a property for a fixed period of time. **22-309**

TENANCY IN COMMON—Ownership by two or more persons who hold undivided interest, without right of survivorship. Upon the death of one tenant, his interest goes to his heirs. Interests need not be equal, and each owner is possessed of the whole of an undivided part. **7-153**

TENDER—To offer; to present.

TENEMENT—All rights in land which pass with a conveyance of the land.

TESTAMENT—The written declaration of one's last will. **8-162**

TESTATE—Leaving a will upon death. **8-163**

TESTATOR—A person who makes a will. **8-163**

TIME OF THE ESSENCE—n a contract, a requirement of punctual performance. **14-231**

TITLE—Evidence that an owner of land is in lawful possession thereof; an instrument evidencing such ownership.

TITLE INSURANCE—A policy of insurance which indemnifies the holder for loss sustained by reason of a defect in the title, provided the loss does not result from a defect excluded by the policy provisions. **11-179**

TOPOGRAPHY—The nature of the surface of land.

TORRENS SYSTEM—A system for the registration of land in some states (not New Jersey) indicating the status of the title, including ownership and encumbrances, without the necessity of additional search of the public records.

TORT—A negligent or intentional wrong; a wrongful act; violation of a legal right.

TOWN HOUSE—The architectural style of a structure whose common elements may be shared by two or more unit occupants.

TOWNSHIP—A section of land established by government survey that is six miles long, six miles wide and contains 36 sections, each one mile square. (Not in New Jersey.) **28-409**

TRADE—See Exchange. **26-375**

TRADE FIXTURE—Articles of personal property annexed to real property, but which are necessary to the carrying on of a trade and are removable by the owner or tenant when he leaves. **5-141**

TRANSACTION BROKER—Brokerage firm which works with both parties in an effort to arrive at an agreement on sale or rental of real estate and facilitates the closing of a transaction, but does not have an agency relationship with either of the parties.

TRESPASS—Wrongful invasion of land by one having no lawful right to enter.

TRUST DEED—Deed given by borrower to trustee to be held pending fulfillment of an obligation. **17-259**

TRUSTEE—One who holds property in trust for another to secure the performance of an obligation.

TRUTH-IN-LENDING—A federal law designed to let borrowers know the exact cost of obtaining credit; a disclosure device. **20-291**

UNDER-IMPROVEMENT—Construction of improvements on land which is less expensive and smaller than required for that land to produce highest use.

UNDISCLOSED DUAL AGENT—An illegal agency relationship arising when a real estate broker represents two principals in a transaction without their informed consent. **12-192**

UNDIVIDED INTEREST—Title to property owned by two or more persons, with no one co-owner having exclusive rights to any specific part. **7-156**

UNDUE INFLUENCE—Taking any advantage of another by playing on his weaknesses or distress. **14-224**

UNILATERAL CONTRACT—A contract whereby only one party is obligated to perform his obligation to another. **14-221**

UNIMPROVED LAND—Land upon which no buildings have been constructed; also called raw land.

UNITED STATES GOVERNMENT SURVEY SYSTEM—A method of describing or locating real property by reference to the governmental survey, rectangular survey system. Not used in New Jersey. **28-409**

UNITIES OF TITLE—Necessities usually required in the formation of a joint tenancy or tenancy by the entirety: time, title, interest and possession. **7-151**

UNLAWFUL DETAINER—See actual eviction.

UNLAWFUL ENTRY—See trespass.

UNMARKETABLE TITLE—A title containing substantial defects which might cause a prospective purchaser to suffer title litigation and possible loss.

UPSET PRICE—The minimum price at a foreclosure sale, below which the property cannot be sold.

USURY—Charging a rate of interest on a loan greater than that permitted by law. **17-261**

VALID—Having binding force; legally sufficient and authorized by law. **14-221**

VA LOAN—A loan guaranteed by the U.S. Department of Veteran Affairs under the Serviceman's Readjustment Act of 1944 and later. **17-269**

VALUATION—The estimated worth of property.

VARIANCE—Permission obtained from zoning authorities permitting the construction of a building or structure that is forbidden by present zoning ordinances. **29-415**

VENDEE—The purchaser; buyer, so named in the contract.

VENDOR—The seller, so named in the contract.

VENUE—The geographic area in which a court has

legal jurisdiction.

VERIFY—To confirm or substantiate by oath.

VETERANS ADMINISTRATION (VA)—An agency of the federal government, the activities of which include guaranteed repayment of certain loans in the event of default. **17-269**

VOID—To have no force or effect; that which is unenforceable. **14-221**

VOIDABLE—That, which is capable of being adjudged void, but is not void unless action is taken to make it so. Able to be made void. **14-221**

VOLUNTARY LIEN—Any lien placed on property with consent of, or as a result of, the voluntary act of the owner, e.g., a mortgage. **18-277**

WAIVE—To relinquish, or abandon. The abandonment of some claim or right.

WARRANTY DEED—A deed in which the grantor fully warrants a good clear title to the property; a deed that contains covenants of title. **15-245**

WASTE—Willful destruction of any part of the land which would injure or prejudice the landlord's or remainderman's reversionary right. **6-146**

WATER TABLE—The depth underground of the natural waters as measured from the surface.

WRAP-AROUND MORTGAGE—A wrap-around mortgage is a sometimes-used vehicle to provide secondary or additional financing. It is a mortgage which includes within its lien an existing or prior mortgage (it "wraps around" the existing obligation). The wrap-around mortgagee assumes the existing or prior mortgage, includes it with any additional financing being provided, creates a new mortgage for the total amount, and therefore, advances to a primary position. The mortgagor then makes one payment for the total amount to the wrap-around mortgagee, who in turn maintains the debt service on the prior obligation. **17-265**

WRIT OF EXECUTION—A writ or court order authorizing and directing an officer of the court to carry out the judgment or decree of the court. **18-278**

YIELD—The return on an investment; the amount of profit made as a percentage of the amount invested.

ZONE—An area set aside for specific use, subject to certain restrictions or restraints; also part of tax map description.

ZONING—An act of the city or county authorities by exercise of police power in regulating, controlling or specifying the type of use to which property may be put in specific areas. **29-414**

GLOSSARY
Review Questions
(Answers on page 566)

1. The word "cited" most nearly means:
   (A) situated.
   (B) quoted.
   (C) remarked.
   (D) located.

2. Straight-line depreciation is:
   (A) a constant rate of depreciation over the life of a wasting asset.
   (B) a form of accelerated depreciation.
   (C) the same as declining balance.
   (D) a type of depreciation that fluctuates periodically.

3. Littoral property:
   (A) is trash strewn on streets.
   (B) is property which has precise measurements.
   (C) borders an ocean.
   (D) is land beneath a non-navigable stream.

4. A commitment is a(n):
   (A) form of confinement.
   (B) pledge or promise.
   (C) order of the court.
   (D) surrender of title.

5. A court-appointed custodian who holds property for the court pending final disposition of a matter before the court is a(n):
   (A) administrator.
   (B) executor.
   (C) trustee.
   (D) receiver.

6. An agreement to cover a down payment for the purchase of real estate as evidence of good faith on the part of the purchaser is a(n):
   (A) earnest money deposit.
   (B) binder.
   (C) Both A and B.
   (D) Neither A nor B.

7. The process of computing current value from expected future income is:
   (A) capitalization.
   (B) evaluation.
   (C) bonding.
   (D) comparable.

8. A condemnee is:
   (A) someone sent to jail.
   (B) someone whose property has been taken through condemnation proceedings.
   (C) a court-appointed administrator.
   (D) a recipient of property through condemnation proceedings.

9. To hypothecate is to:
   (A) tender something of value.
   (B) acquire real property.
   (C) mortgage.
   (D) return a favor.

10. The word "revoked" most nearly means:
    (A) repealed or recalled.
    (B) rejected.
    (C) repaired.
    (D) reviewed.

11. The violation of an obligation, engagement or duty is a:
    (A) breach.
    (B) defeasance.
    (C) dismissal.
    (D) right.

12. The residue of an estate left to a grantor or a lessor after termination of a previous estate is a:
    (A) reversion.
    (B) inversion.
    (C) restitution to the rightful owner.
    (D) surrender of obligation.

13. In law, the word "tender" means:
    (A) to care for.
    (B) a sore or critical dispute.
    (C) to offer or present.
    (D) to assume an obligation.

14. "In lieu of" most nearly means:
    (A) instead of.
    (B) besides.
    (C) on account of.
    (D) unless.

15. "Hypothecate" most nearly means:
    (A) to give as security.
    (B) to negotiate.
    (C) to divulge.
    (D) to repel.

16. The word "fiduciary" is most closely related to:
    (A) indenture.
    (B) trust.
    (C) warranty.
    (D) agency.

(Quiz continues on next page)

17. An escrow is:
(A) a leasehold estate.
(B) to deposit funds with instructions to a neutral third party to carry out the terms of a contract.
(C) a remedy for a breach of contract.
(D) an essential element of a valid contract.

18. "Promulgated" most nearly means:
(A) renewed.
(B) accepted.
(C) announced.
(D) reconsidered.

19. The Equal Credit Opportunity Act is a:
(A) state law dealing with credit opportunities.
(B) law requiring uniform interest rates.
(C) federal law that prohibits discrimination against minorities for any reason.
(D) federal law prohibiting illegal discrimination in the extension of credit.

20 "Waiver" could mean all of the following except:
(A) restitution.
(B) renunciation.
(C) abandonment.
(D) surrender.

21. The distance from the curb or other established line, within which no building may be erected, is called:
(A) sidewalk easement.
(B) offset.
(C) setback.
(D) pedestrian right of way.

22. A statute is:
(A) a monument.
(B) an act of the legislature.
(C) a regulation of the REC.
(D) an ornament.

23. Homogeneity means:
(A) similar.
(B) incompatible.
(C) dissimilar.
(D) pasteurized.

24. One who has the right to sign the name of his principal to legal documents is:
(A) an optionee.
(B) a special agent.
(C) an attorney in fact.
(D) an attorney at law.

25. Certain documents must be acknowledged before they can be recorded. To acknowledge means:
(A) to declare that you signed a document voluntarily.
(B) to make an affidavit.
(C) to authenticate the contents of a document.
(D) to record.

26. The amount of value of a property above the total liens or mortgages is known as:
(A) profit.
(B) equity.
(C) deficiency.
(D) effective gross income.

27. "Divulge" most nearly means:
(A) clandestine.
(B) hide.
(C) print.
(D) disclose.

28. All of the following terms may be synonymous except:
(A) recipient-donee.
(B) mortgagor-lender.
(C) vendor-seller.
(D) vendee-purchaser.

29. A remedy in a court of equity compelling the defendant to carry out the terms of a real estate contract is a(n):
(A) judgment.
(B) injunction.
(C) surety.
(D) specific performance.

30. "Ad valorem" is:
(A) a solemn declaration in the nature of an oath.
(B) a tax according to valuation.
(C) possession inconsistent with the right of the true owner.
(D) a rental unit.

31. Court action to settle a title dispute is called:
(A) quiet title action.
(B) color of title.
(C) eminent domain.
(D) dedication.

32. In the planning and engineering of a tract for subdivision purposes, a "cul-de-sac" is frequently employed. This term is used in reference to a type of:
(A) sewage disposal plant.
(B) storm drain.
(C) street.
(D) recreation area.

33. Which of the following best describes earnest money?
    (A) The money deposited by the purchaser at the time of signing the contract.
    (B) The consideration for the sale of the property.
    (C) The money deposited by the purchaser with the broker or seller to pay for the expense of examining title.
    (D) The money paid by the seller to adjust final expenses.

34. "Quorum" most nearly means:
    (A) occupied.
    (B) the number legally constituted to conduct business.
    (C) 75%.
    (D) audience.

35. That which is capable of being adjudged void, but is not void unless action is taken to make it so, is:
    (A) voidable.
    (B) void.
    (C) invalid.
    (D) illegal.

36. The words "et ux" most nearly mean:
    (A) and all.
    (B) and others.
    (C) and me.
    (D) and wife.

37. A person to whom a bequest had been made would receive:
    (A) a devise.
    (B) mixed property in a will.
    (C) personal property in a will.
    (D) personal property from someone who died intestate.

38. A title which is free from encumbrances or clouds is a(n):
    (A) marketable or merchantable title.
    (B) clouded title.
    (C) absolute fee simple title.
    (D) abstract of title.

39. The word "consummate" most nearly means:
    (A) tender.
    (B) soup.
    (C) shut.
    (D) complete.

40. "To subordinate" most nearly means:
    (A) to subrogate.
    (B) to act as co-signer.
    (C) to occupy land belonging to others.
    (D) to cause a lien to become, or remain, junior in priority.

41. Liquidated damages are:
    (A) damages agreed to be paid by the defaulting party.
    (B) the same as specific performance.
    (C) the same as a penalty.
    (D) the same as general damages.

42. A public notice, filed against specific lands, that an action at law is pending that may affect the title of the land is:
    (A) judgment.
    (B) economic life.
    (C) lis pendens.
    (D) recording.

43. A certificate of occupancy is:
    (A) a certificate issued by the VA showing the amount of entitlement used.
    (B) a certificate issued by the VA indicating its estimate of the property's value.
    (C) a document issued by a municipal government permitting a structure to be legally occupied.
    (D) a certification given by a tenant indicating an intent to occupy a property.

44. An ownership concept which embraces the rights of possession, use, disposition and enjoyment is called:
    (A) corporeal ownership.
    (B) bundle of rights.
    (C) incorporeal ownership.
    (D) a leasehold.

45. The Real Estate Settlement Procedures Act (RESPA) is a:
    (A) state law requiring estimates of closing costs.
    (B) federal law prohibiting referral fees between brokers.
    (C) federal law dealing with environmental hazards.
    (D) federal law requiring estimates of closing costs so buyers may comparison shop.

46. Amortization means:
    (A) appreciation.
    (B) liquidation.
    (C) depreciation.
    (D) adolescence.

47. Dual agency occurs when:
    (A) a broker maintains two offices.
    (B) a real estate broker employs two agents.
    (C) a broker represents two clients in the same transaction.
    (D) a broker has dual customers in the same transaction.

(Quiz continues on next page)

48. A setback is:
    (A) a player in the NFL.
    (B) a franchised steak house occupying under a percentage lease.
    (C) a loss of commission on a consummated deal.
    (D) the distance that a building or other structure must be set back from the property line in accordance with local zoning laws.

49. A habendum clause appears in a (an):
    (A) mortgage.
    (B) agreement of sale.
    (C) lease.
    (D) deed.

50. In real estate parlance a "comp" is
    (A) a free room in Atlantic City.
    (B) a Certificate of Occupancy for Multiple Properties.
    (C) a composite of the different approaches to value.
    (D) a property similar to the subject property.

51. A printed advertisement for a new development such as a subdivision is called a(n):
    (A) reservation.
    (B) prospectus.
    (C) nomenclature.
    (D) origination.

52. An incident of land which passes with the title to the land is:
    (A) a bequest.
    (B) an appurtenance.
    (C) a hereditament.
    (D) an attachment.

53. The rights to the water thereon of a person owning land containing or bordering upon a stream are called:
    (A) bridge rights.
    (B) riparian rights.
    (C) eminent domain.
    (D) a reservation.

54. A net listing is:
    (A) a listing in which the broker's commission is any amount over an agreed-upon price to the seller, and is prohibited in New Jersey.
    (B) a listing in which the broker's commission is any amount over an agreed-upon price to the seller, and is permitted in New Jersey with the | consent of the parties.
    (C) a listing on a marina at the New Jersey shore.
    (D) a listing that states the exact amount that a broker will be paid.

55. A declaration made by a person to a qualified official that he freely and voluntarily executed a deed or other instrument is called an:
    (A) acknowledgement.
    (B) authorization.
    (C) execution.
    (D) authentication.

56. Reversion of property to the state is called:
    (A) escheat.
    (B) descent.
    (C) remainder.
    (D) dedication.

57. "Chattel" is another name for:
    (A) a wife's equity in her husband's estate.
    (B) tangible personal property.
    (C) survivorship rights.
    (D) an improvement to property.

58. "Agent" most nearly means:
    (A) one who represents another.
    (B) one who holds realty at sufferance.
    (C) one who is the source of another's authority.
    (D) one in whom complete power is vested.

59. A "due-on-sale" clause:
    (A) is a clause that makes the Realty Transfer Fee due-on-sale of the property.
    (B) requires payment of the commission at the closing.
    (C) is a covenant in a warranty deed.
    (D) is a clause in a conventional mortgage requiring payment of a mortgage balance if the mortgaged property gets sold.

60. "Irrevocable" most nearly means:
    (A) unalterable.
    (B) reversible.
    (C) illegal.
    (D) changeable.

61. An "assignee" is:
    (A) one who assigns land to another.
    (B) one who receives the assignment.
    (C) anyone who signs anything.
    (D) usually a seller.

62. A junior mortgage is:
    (A) a mortgage which is subordinate to a prior existing mortgage on the same realty.
    (B) a mortgage loan advanced to a minor.
    (C) a lien that takes precedence over a first mortgage.
    (D) a loan sold in the secondary market.

63. In a contract, the seller of real estate may be referred to as:
    (A) vendor.
    (B) vendee.
    (C) lessee.
    (D) lessor.

64. Combining adjoining parcels of land into one larger holding, providing the opportunity for more profitable development, is called:
    (A) accretion.
    (B) attachment.
    (C) highest and best use.
    (D) assemblage.

65. "Bona fide" means:
    (A) in good faith.
    (B) better than new.
    (C) willing to help.
    (D) dower.

66. "To convey" most nearly means:
    (A) to buy.
    (B) to warrant.
    (C) to obligate.
    (D) to transfer.

67. The term "prescription" is most often used in connection with:
    (A) augmented estate
    (B) an easement created by trespass for a prescribed period.
    (C) the rental of a drug store.
    (D) a license granted by a land owner.

68. "Annual percentage rate" refers to:
    (A) the maximum annual increase in an adjustable rate mortgage.
    (B) the effective rate of interest for a loan per year.
    (C) the compound interest rate on a loan per year.
    (D) the maximum rate of interest permitted by statute.

69. The action to compel the seller to execute a deed pursuant to a written agreement is an action for:
    (A) specific performance.
    (B) estoppel.
    (C) lis pendens.
    (D) certiorari.

70. "Bona fide" can mean all except:
    (A) unlawful.
    (B) genuine.
    (C) in good faith.
    (D) without fraud.

71. A clause in a New Jersey contract allowing the buyer or seller three days to consult an attorney who can review and cancel the contract is called a (an):
    (A) rescission clause.
    (B) cancellation clause.
    (C) surrender clause.
    (D) attorney review clause.

72. The giving up or abandoning of a claim or right to the person against whom the claim exists or the right is to be exercised is:
    (A) a release.
    (B) removing a cloud on the title.
    (C) a quitclaim.
    (D) quieting the title.

73. "Biennial" means:
    (A) twice a day.
    (B) two times each two years.
    (C) every two years.
    (D) semi-annually.

74. The "upset price" is the:
    (A) price that upsets the seller because it is too low.
    (B) price that upsets the buyer because it is too high.
    (C) minimum price at a foreclosure sale below which a mortgaged property cannot be sold.
    (D) maximum price at a foreclosure sale above which a mortgaged property cannot be sold.

75. A shareholder in a cooperative apartment has a:
    (A) fee simple interest.
    (B) irrevocable right of possession.
    (C) leasehold interest.
    (D) conditional life estate.

CHAPTER THIRTY-SIX

APPENDICES

• Appendix I: Abbreviations

AABR Accredited Buyer Representative
a/c Air Conditioning
AC Acre
AFLB Accredited Farm and Land Broker
AFM Accredited Farm Manager
AI All-Inclusive
AIA American Institute of Architects
AIP American Institute of Planners
AIREA American Institute of Real Estate Appraisers
aka Also Known As
A/L Assignment of Lease
ALTA American Land Title Association
A/M Assignment of Mortgage
AMA Affirmative Marketing Agreement
AMO Accredited Management Organization
ANSI American National Standards Institute
APR Annual Percentage Rate
ASREC American Society of Real Estate Counselors

BFB Bone Fide Purchaser
BIC Broker in Charge
BOM Back on Market
BOMA Building Owners & Managers Association
BTU British Thermal Unit

CAI Community Associations Institute
CBD Central Business District
CCIM Certified Commercial Investment Member
CC&Rs Covenants, Conditions & Restrictions
CDO Capital District Ordinance
CID Commercial Investment Division
CMB Certified Mortgage Banker
Co. Company
CO Certificate of Occupancy
CON Connected (Sewer)
CPA Certified Public Accountant
CPM Certified Property Manager
CRB Certified Residential Broker
CRE Counselor of Real Estate
CRV Certificate of Reasonable Value
CT Conveyance Tax
CTF Customer Trust Fund
CVG Covenants vs. Grantor
CZC Comprehensive Zoning Code

dba "Doing Business As"
DP Down Payment
DREI Distinguished Real Estate Instructor

EIS Environmental Impact Statement
EM Earnest Money Deposit
EPA Environmental Protection Agency

FAR Floor Area Ratio
FDIC Federal Deposit Insurance Corporation
FH Flood Hazard
FHA Federal Housing Administration
FHLB Federal Home Land Bank
FHLMC Federal Home Loan Mortgage Corporation (Freddie Mac)
FICA Federal Income Contributions Act
FLB Federal Land Bank
FLI Farm Land Institute
FmHA Farmers Home Administration
FMV Fair Market Value
FNMA Federal National Mortgage Association (Fannie Mae)
FRS Federal Reserve System
FS Fee Simple
FSBO For Sale by Owner
FSLIC Federal Savings and Loan Insurance Corporation
FTC Federal Trade Commission

GIT Gross Income Tax
GNMA Government National Mortgage Association (Ginnie Mae)
GP General Plan
GLA Gross Leasable Area
GRI Graduate, Realtors Institute
GRM Gross Rent Multiplier

HUD U.S. Department of Housing & Urban Development

IFA Independent Fee Appraiser
Inc. Incorporated
IRC Internal Revenue Code
IREM Institute of Real Estate Management
IRS Internal Revenue Service

J/T Joint Tenant

L Leasehold
L# Liber Number (Book Number)

LH Leasehold
LIR Land-Use Intensity Rating
Lis/P Lis Pendens
L.P. Land Patent
LS Locus Sigilli (Latin, "place of seal")
Ltd. Limited
LUI Land Use Intensity
L/V Loan-to-Value Ratio

MAGIC Mortgage Guaranty Insurance Corporation (MGIC)
MAI Member Appraisal Institute
MBA Mortgage Bankers Association of America
MF Multi-family
MGIC Mortgage Guaranty Insurance Corporation
MGRM Monthly Gross Rent Multiplier
MIP Mortgage Insurance Premium
MLS Multiple Listing Service
MPR Minimum Property Requirement

n/a Not Available, or Not Applicable
NAA National Apartment Association
NAHB National Association of Home Builders
NAR National Association of REALTORS
NAREB National Association of Real Estate Boards (now NAR)
NAREB National Association of Real Estate Brokers
NARELLO National Association of Real Estate Licensing Law Officials
NASD National Association of Securities Dealers
NC Not Connected (Sewer)
NIFLB National Institute of Farm and Land Brokers
NIREB National Institute of Real Estate Brokers
NJAR New Jersey Association of Realtors
NOI Net Operating Income
NSF Not Sufficient Funds

OE&T Operating Expenses & Taxes
OEO Office of Economic Opportunity
OILSR Office of Interstate Land Sales Registration
OIR Official Interpretation Rulings
O.L.&T. Owner's, Landlord's & Tenant's Public Liability Insurance
OTC Over-the-Counter

PB Principal Broker
PE Professional Engineer
P&I Principal & Interest
PITI Principal, Interest, Taxes & Insurance (monthly payments)
PMI Private Mortgage Insurance
POB Point of Beginning
PSC Participation Sale Certificate
PUD Planned Unit Development

R REALTOR
RA REALTOR-ASSOCIATE
REBAC Real Estate Buyer's Agent Council
REC Real Estate Commission
REIT Real Estate Investment Trust
REPAC Real Estate Political Action Committee
RESPA Real Estate Settlement Procedures Act
RESSI Real Estate Securities and Syndication Institute
RNMI REALTORS National Marketing Institute
ROI Return on Investment
R/W Right of Way

S Salesperson
S Section
SBLN Setback Line
SEC Securities and Exchange Commission
SIR Society of Industrial REALTORS
S&L Savings & Loan Association
SMSA Standard Metropolitan Statistical Area
SOYD Sum of Year's Digits
SRA Senior Realty Appraiser
SRA Senior Residential Appraiser
SREA Senior Real Estate Analyst
SREA Society of Real Estate Appraisers
SRPA Senior Real Property Appraisers
SS Namely (Latin, "scilicet")
SSCRA Soldiers and Sailors Civil Relief Act

T/C Tenant in Common
TDR Transfer Development Rights
T/E Tenancy by Entirety
TSO Time Share Ownership

UCC Uniform Commercial Code
ULI Urban Land Institute
ULSPA Uniform Land Sales Practices Act
UPA Uniform Partnership Act
USGS United States Geological Survey

VA Veterans Administration
VRM Variable Rate Mortgage
Vs Versus

WCR Women's Council of REALTORS
WROS With Right of Survivorship
W/W Wall to Wall

Z Zone

• Appendix II: House Parts Dictionary

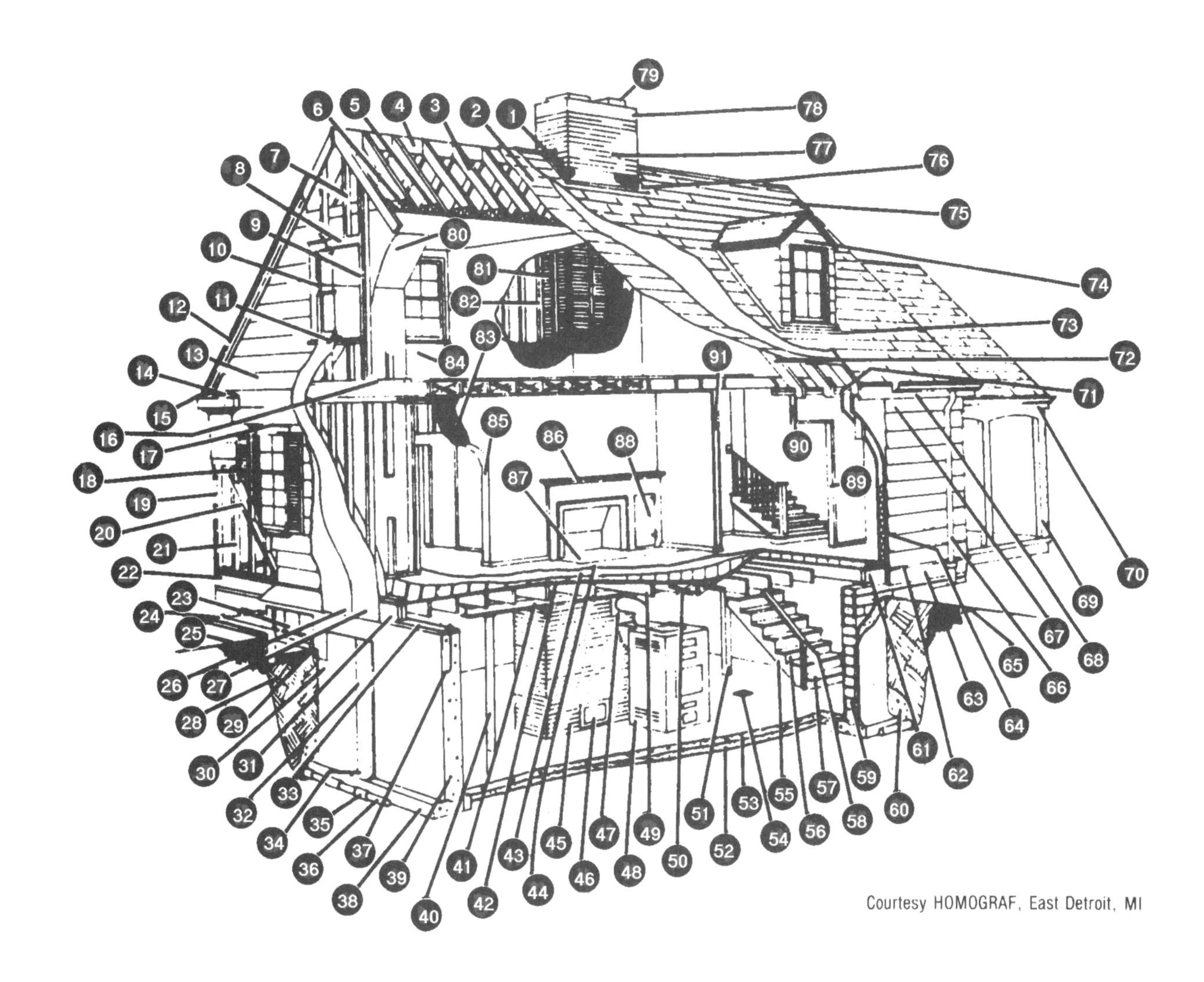

Courtesy HOMOGRAF, East Detroit, MI

1. FLASHING
2. ROOF BOARDS
3. RAFTERS
4. RIDGE BOARDS
5. CEILING JOISTS
6. CEILING INSULATION
7. GABLE STUDS
8. WINDOW HEADER
9. ROUGH WINDOW OPENING
10. WINDOW SASH
11. WINDOW SILL
12. GABLE RAKE MOLDING
13. BEVEL SIDING
14. CORNICE RETURN
15. GUTTER
16. FLOOR PLATE
17. DRIP CAP MOLDING
18. SHUTTERS
19. CORNER STUDS
20. DIAGONAL BRACING
21. WALL STUDS
22. JOIST TRIMMER
23. BASEMENT SASH
24. WINDOW AREA-WAY
25. GRADE LINE
26. BUILDING PAPER
27. SHEATHING
28. BACKFILL
29. AGGREGATE FILL
30. WATERPROOFING
31. JOIST HEADER
32. CEMENT PLASTER
33. BOND PLATE
34. CEMENT COVE
35. TARPAPER JOINT COVER
36. DRAIN TILE
37. ANCHOR BOLTS
38. CONCRETE FOOTING
39. CONCRETE FOUNDATION WALL
40. PIPE COLUMN
41. STEEL BEAM
42. WOOD SUB-FLOOR
43. FLOORING FELT
44. FINISH FLOORING
45. MASONRY CHIMNEY
46. ASH PIT CLEANOUT
47. THIMBLE
48. FURNACE
49. FLOOR JOISTS
50. BRIDGING
51. POST OR COLUMN
52. AGGREGATE FILL
53. CONCRETE FLOOR SLAB
54. FLOOR DRAIN
55. STAIR STRINGER
56. STAIR RISER
57. STAIR TREAD
58. STAIR RAIL
59. CEMENT BLOCK FOUNDATION WALL
60. AGGREGATE FILL
61. JOIST TRIMMER
62. DRIP CAP
63. WEATHER BOARD
64. WALL INSULATION
65. EARTH
66. CONDUCTOR
67. FRIEZE BOARD
68. FACIA OR CORNICE BOARD
69. PORCH POST
70. PORCH FRIEZE BOARD
71. TOP PLATES
72. RAFTERS
73. FLASHING
74. DORMER
75. SHINGLES
76. FLASHING
77. MASONRY CHIMNEY
78. CEMENT CAP
79. CHIMNEY POT OR FLUE LINING
80. ANGLED CEILING
81. MASONRY
82. FURRING STRIPS
83. LATH
84. PLASTER
85. PLASTER ARCH
86. MANTLE
87. HEARTH
88. WOOD BOX
89. CASED OPENING
90. HEADER
91. PARTITION

• Appendix III: Land Measurements

LINEAR MEASURE

1 foot = 12 inches
1 yard = 3 feet; 36 inches
1 meter = 39.37 inches
1 link = 7.92 inches
1 rod = 25 links; 51/2 yards; 161/2 feet
1 chain = 100 links; 4 rods; 66 feet
1 furlong = 40 rods
1 mile = 80 chains; 8,000 links; 8 furlongs; 1,760 yards; 5,280 ft.
100 feet = 6.6 rods

SQUARE MEASURE

1 sq. foot = 144 sq. inches
1 sq. yard = 9 sq. feet
1 sq. rod = 272.25 sq. ft (16.5' x 16.5'); 272.25/9 = 30.25 sq. yds.
1 sq. chain = 16 sq. rods; 4,356 sq. feet
1 acre = 10 sq. chains; 160 sq. rods; 4,840 sq. yards; 43,560 sq. feet
1 sq. mile = 640 acres; 1 section; 2.59 sq. km
1 section = 1 sq. mile; 640 acres
1 township = 36 sq. miles; 6 miles square
1 quarter section = 160 acres

CUBIC MEASURE

1 cubic foot = 1,728 cubic inches
1 cubic yard = 27 cubic feet

TO COMPUTE LAND MEASUREMENT

1. To find the area of a square or rectangle (a four-sided parcel of land with opposite sides parallel), multiply the length by the width.

2. To find the area of a parallelogram (a four-sided parcel of land whose opposite sides are parallel, but whose angles are not necessarily right angles), multiply the base by the perpendicular height.

3. To find the area of a triangle (a three-sided parcel), multiply the base by one-half of the perpendicular height.

4. To find the area of a trapezoid (a four-sided parcel having two of its sides parallel), multiply half of the sum of the two parallel sides by the perpendicular distance between those sides.

5. To determine the area of a trapezium (a parcel that is bounded by four straight lines, in which no two sides are parallel, the length of each line is known, and the two opposite angles are supplements of each other), add all four sides together, divide their sum in half, subtract separately each side from that sum and the four remainders thus obtained, multiply continually together, and subtract the square root of the last product. An easier method for some might be simply to divide the parcel into triangles and trapezoids, determine and add together their several areas, and the total sum will be the area of the parcel.

• Appendix IV: Registry Division Fees*

Bergen County Clerk's Office, Hackensack, N.J.

Any document for re-recording	$ 3.00 plus recording fees
for each additional page	$ 2.00
for each marginal notation (mark-off)	$ 3.00
Deed	$18.00 first page plus $2.00 each additional
Mortgage	$15.00 first page plus $2.00 each additional
Contract of Sale	$15.00 first page plus $2.00 each additional
Leases	$15.00 first page plus $2.00 each additional
Lis Pendens	$15.00 first page plus $2.00 each additional
Tax Sale Certificate	$15.00 first page plus $2.00 each additional
Power of Attorney	$15.00 first page plus $2.00 each additional
Redemption, Discharge, Assignment, Postponement, Extension, Release, Modification, Subordination of Mortgage or Tax Sale Certificate	$18.00 first page plus $2.00 each additional
Lis Pendens Foreclosure	$10.50
Discharge of Lis Pendens	$ 3.00
Cancellation of Mortgage or Tax Sale Certificate	$ 8.00
Cancellation of Re-Recorded Mortgage or Tax Sale Certificate	$ 8.00 (for each re-recording)
Financing Statements (UCC-1)	$25.00
Financing Statement with an Assignment	$25.00
Continuation (UCC-3)	$25.00
Amendment	$25.00
Subordination	$25.00
Assignment	$25.00
Assumption	$25.00
Termination	$25.00
Partial Release	$25.00
Vacation	$15.00
Notice of Settlement	$ 8.00
Disclaimer	$ 5.00
Certified Copies: any document	$ 2.00 each page plus $2.00 for certification
Military	$ 1.00

***The fees listed here may vary in other counties**

• Appendix V: New Jersey Population By County

AND CHANGE FROM 1983

COUNTY	1983	1998	CHANGE
Atlantic	197,000	243,400	46,400
Bergen	843,700	875,200	31,500
Burlington	373,600	430,100	56,500
Camden	479, 500	514,600	35,100
Cape May	87,000	100,200	13,200
Cumberland	133,200	142,900	9,700
Essex	842, 600	766,400	-76,200
Gloucester	204,900	253,900	49,000
Hudson	560, 300	570,100	9,800
Hunterdon	90,500	125,900	35,400
Mercer	312,900	337,800	24,900
Middlesex	610, 900	731,400	120,500
Monmouth	515,100	617,900	102,800
Morris	413,800	470,700	56,900
Ocean	364,000	503,200	139,200
Passaic	454,600	494,900	40,300
Salem	65,800	66,100	300
Somerset	206,800	291,300	84,500
Sussex	119,300	146,600	27,300
Union	505,900	509,900	-4,000
Warren	85,200	101,000	15,800
STATE TOTAL	**7,466,600**	**8,293,500**	**826,900**

• Appendix VI: Listing Abbreviations

Air Conditioner—AC
Apartment—apt
Appliances—appl
Appointment—appt
Attached—att
Barbeque—bbq
Basement—bsmt
Bathroom—ba
Bedroom—BR
Bi-Level—Bi-Lev
Block—blk
Breakfast Nook—BfNk
Breezeway—brzwy
Cape Cod—CC
Carpet—crpt
Center Hall—CH
Clean—cln
Colonial—Col
Condition—cond
Decorated—dec
Dishwasher—DW
Driveway—drvwy
Entrance Hall—EH
Excellent—exc
Excluded—excl
Family Room—FR
Finished—fin
Fireplace—fpl
Floor—flr
Garage—gar
Grade Level—GrdLev
Immediate—immed
Includes, Included—incl
Kitchen—K
Large—lge
Laundry—ldry
Lockbox—LB
Master Bedroom—MBR
Modern Eat-in Kitchen—MEIK
More or Less—m/l
Occupancy—occpy
Outside Entrance—o/e
Owner Carry—o/c
Panelled Family Room—PFR
Power of Attorney—POA
Powder Room—PowRm
Recreation Room—RR
Panelled Recreation Room—PRR
Screened Open Porch—SOP
Side Hall—SH
Split Level—S/L
Stairway—S/W
Tiled Bath with Stall Shower—TBw/ss
Tiled Bath with Shower over Tub—Tbw/sot
Twin Size Bedroom—TSBR
Vacant Land—VL
Vaulted (ceilings)—vltd
Wall to Wall—w/w
Washer & Dryer—W&D
With—w/
Yard—yd

• Appendix VII: Sources of Reference

The Appraisal of Real Estate, American Institute of Real Estate Appraisers
The Art of Real Estate Appraisal, by Ventolo and Williams
Banking and Insurance Quarterly, New Jersey Department of Banking and Insurance
Barrons Real Estate Handbook, by Jack C. Harris and Jack P. Friedman
Basic Real Estate Law in New Jersey, by Joseph J. De Palma, Keith A. Krauss and Elliot L. Warm
Doing the Right Thing (A Real Estate Practitioner's Guide to Ethical Decision Making), by Deborah H. Long
Essentials of New Jersey Real Estate, by Edith Lank and Joan M. Sobeck
Essentials of Real Estate Investment, by David Sirota
Federal Income Taxation, by Daniel F. Lynch
A Guide to Real Estate License Examinations, by John T. Ellis
Guide to Real Estate License Examinations, by William B. French, Stephen J. Martin and Thomas E. Battle III
Hand Book of New Jersey Title Practice, by Lawrence Joel Fineberg, A.B., J.D., CTP
Handbook of Real Estate Terms, by Dennis S. Tosh, Jr.
How to Invest in Real Estate, by Maurice A. Unger
Land Title Institute, Land Title Association
The Language of Creative Financing, by Stephen R. Mettling
The Language of Real Estate, by John W. Reilly
Mastering Real Estate Math in One Day, by John T. Ellis and Victoria R. Beam
Mastering Real Estate Principles, by Gerald R. Cortesi
Modern Real Estate Practice, by Galaty, Allaway and Kyle
The New Jersey Banking and Insurance Quarterly
New Jersey Realtor®
New Jersey Revised Statutes
Passing the Real Estate Salespersons Examination, by Lawrence J. Danks
Principles of Real Estate, by Edna L. Hebard and Gerald S. Meisel
Principles of Real Estate Management, by James C. Downes
Property Management, by Kyle and Baird
Questions and Answers on Real Estate, by Robert W. Seminow
Real Estate Appraising, by Paul G. Creteau
Real Estate Investment, by John P. Wiedemer
Real Estate Law, by Robert Kratovil
Real Estate License Course, by Anthony Schools
Real Estate Manual, Real Estate Commission, State of Colorado
Real Estate Principles, by Charles J. Jacobus and Bruce Harwood
Real Estate Principles and Practices, by Benson and North
Real Estate Principles and Practices, by James E. Larson
Reference Book, California Department of Real Estate, State of California
Residential Real Estate Law and Practice in New Jersey, by Arthur S. Horn
Super Course for Real Estate Licensing, by Julie Garton Good
Texas Real Estate Research Center

CHAPTER THIRTY-SEVEN

QUESTIONS AND ANSWERS

• Review Quiz 1
(Answers on page 567)

1. The ownership of a condominium unit differs from that of an ownership interest in a cooperative apartment project in which of the following ways?
   (A) You can be deeded fee simple title on a condominium unit.
   (B) The owner of a cooperative apartment project owns an undivided interest in the entire project.
   (C) Condominiums are subject to subdivision laws.
   (D) They are identical.

2. If you are a licensee selling your own real property, you must:
   (A) inform your principal broker of your interest in the property.
   (B) include a contract provision informing prospective buyers of your interest in the property.
   (C) inform the Real Estate Commission.
   (D) inform your broker and the buyer.

3. If an attorney also has an insurance license and a real estate broker's license, in one transaction he could legally collect:
   (A) selling fee and attorney's fee.
   (B) listing fee and attorney's fee.
   (C) broker's fee and insurance fee.
   (D) None of the above.

4. The licensing laws require which of the following to be in writing?
   (A) The listing agreement for the sale of real property.
   (B) The contract between two brokers cooperating on a real estate transaction.
   (C) Leases for longer than three years.
   (D) None of the above.

5. Before issuing a real estate salesperson's license, New Jersey requires:
   (A) minimum experience.
   (B) residency requirements.
   (C) U.S. citizenship.
   (D) minimum education requirements.

6. Brokers' real estate ads in New Jersey must include:
   (A) the street address of the property.
   (B) the name of the listing.
   (C) the name of the agent showing the property.
   (D) the name of the brokerage firm.

7. Alice purchased a two-bedroom condominium. She now holds:
   (A) fee simple interest in her unit.
   (B) shares of stock in a corporation.
   (C) a leasehold interest.
   (D) a proprietary lease.

8. Which of the following would NOT need a real estate license?
   (A) A person selling real estate pursuant to a court order.
   (B) A person auctioning real estate.
   (C) A person selling real estate on a part-time basis.
   (D) A person selling vacant lots.

9. The membership of the Real Estate Commission must include representatives of:
   (A) the legal profession.
   (B) lending institutions.
   (C) the real estate industry.
   (D) appraisers.

10. Which of the following must comply with the licensing requirements of Title 45, Chapter 15?
    (A) An officer of a real estate brokerage corporation whose only input with the corporation is money.
    (B) A lessor.
    (C) An auctioneer.
    (D) An administrator.

11. The broker must give a copy of the listing to the:
    (A) buyer.
    (B) seller.
    (C) Both A and B.
    (D) Neither A nor B.

12. The Realtor Code of Ethics is:
    (A) a code put into law by the Real Estate Commission of New Jersey.
    (B) a code obligatory upon members of the National Association of Realtors.
    (C) part of the statutes of New Jersey pertaining to licensed real estate salespersons and brokers.
    (D) part of an act pertaining to Prevention of Discrimination in Real Property Transactions.

13. In advertising a listed property for sale, a broker may NOT legally:
    (A) run an ad which does not give the listing price of the property.
    (B) state the kind of financing available.
    (C) fail to state the street address of the property.
    (D) run an ad giving the impression that he is the owner of the property.

14. The Commission may suspend or revoke a license:
    (A) when a broker charges more than 6% commission.
    (B) for splitting a commission with a broker from out-of-state here to negotiate.
    (C) for a first license law offense.
    (D) for being committed for observation in a mental institution.

15. If convicted of forgery the Commission will not grant a license within:
    (A) one year.
    (B) two years.
    (C) three years.
    (D) five years.

16. Which of the following is true of each broker licensed to operate in New Jersey?
    (A) He must be a resident of New Jersey for one year prior to licensure.
    (B) He must be a citizen of the United States.
    (C) Both A and B.
    (D) Neither A nor B.

17. A real estate deal is made between a seller and buyer, without the services of a broker. They arrange with a licensed broker, for a fee, to prepare certain instruments. The broker may lawfully prepare a(n):
    (A) agreement of sale.
    (B) deed.
    (C) purchase money mortgage.
    (D) None of the above.

18. A real estate broker hired an unlicensed individual to work in a subdivision on weekends. Which of the following could the employee do without violation of the Real Estate Law?
    (A) Type real estate documents for the salesperson.
    (B) Quote prices over the phone.
    (C) Show the houses.
    (D) Discuss terms with prospects.

19. A broker must keep permanent records of how he handled other people's funds for:
    (A) 60 days.
    (B) two years.
    (C) six years.
    (D) ten years.

20. The relationship between a broker who has a listing and the owner of the property being offered for sale is that of a:
    (A) guardian.
    (B) receiver.
    (C) fiduciary.
    (D) trustee.

21. If W. Sutton, the principal broker for Anytown Realty Co., has his license revoked:
    (A) his sales associates may continue to engage in the real estate business until their licenses expire.
    (B) his sales associates may continue to engage in the real estate business until the following July 1.
    (C) the licenses of his sales associates are automatically suspended.
    (D) his sales associates will have to transfer to another broker and pay a transfer fee.

22. After a partition of property between two tenants in common, the tenancy is:
    (A) entirety.
    (B) joint.
    (C) common.
    (D) severalty.

23. Which of the following ownerships is least likely considered real property?
    (A) Condominium.
    (B) Townhouse.
    (C) Co-operative.
    (D) Planned unit development.

24. All of the following are synonymous with land and improvements and rights therein except:
    (A) real estate.
    (B) real property.
    (C) Realtor.
    (D) realty.

25. Commingling is the opposite of:
    (A) trust fund.
    (B) mingle.
    (C) segregate.
    (D) neutral depository.

26. A broker was working with a buyer on an exclusive right to sell listing, and presented an offer at less than the listed price. At the same time, the owner was dealing with another buyer who offered more money for the property and all in cash. The owner sold to the buyer at the higher price and all cash. The broker is entitled to:
    (A) a reasonable commission based upon his offer.
    (B) stop the sale of the property.
    (C) void the sale.
    (D) a commission based upon the higher selling price.

27. In the absence of a prior agreement as to when the broker's commission is earned, such commission is earned:
    (A) at consummation of the deal.
    (B) upon a meeting of the minds of buyer and seller and expiration of attorney review period.
    (C) at time broker introduced buyer to seller.
    (D) when the deed is delivered.

28. An oral listing is:
    (A) unlawful.
    (B) good.
    (C) unenforceable.
    (D) enforceable.

29. "Reversion" most nearly means:
    (A) escheat.
    (B) land passes to grantee's heirs and assigns.
    (C) land returns to grantor, his heirs and assigns after completion of the grant.
    (D) property is alienated.

30. After the sale, the listing broker refused to split commission with the selling broker. Who is responsible to pay the selling broker?
    (A) The listor.
    (B) The listing broker.
    (C) The seller.
    (D) The MLS.

31. In an exclusive agency listing, if the owner finds a buyer, the broker gets:
    (A) full commission.
    (B) one-third commission.
    (C) one-half commission.
    (D) no commission.

32. Death of either the principal or agent terminates the:
    (A) listing contract.
    (B) power of attorney.
    (C) Both A and B.
    (D) Neither A nor B.

33. The type of listing in which a broker is least likely to know the amount of money he will receive for the sale of the property is a(n):
    (A) open listing.
    (B) exclusive authorization to sell.
    (C) closed listing.
    (D) net listing.

34. "Intestate" means:
    (A) to die leaving a will.
    (B) to die without leaving a will.
    (C) to die without leaving an heir.
    (D) the state receives your property.

35. A broker is holding an earnest money deposit equal to the amount of his commission. The seller, at the closing, refuses to pay the broker a commission and demands that the broker pay him the entire deposit. The broker should:
    (A) refuse to permit the closing of the deal.
    (B) retain the earnest money as his commission.
    (C) file a complaint with the Real Estate Commission.
    (D) pay the earnest money to the seller and then sue for his commission.

36. A declaration made by a person to an official that he freely and voluntarily executed a deed is called an:
    (A) acknowledgement.
    (B) authorization.
    (C) authentication.
    (D) execution.

37. Which of the following types of property is normally NOT real property?
    (A) Water rights.
    (B) Appurtenances.
    (C) Air space rights.
    (D) Furniture.

38. Littoral property does NOT border a(n):
    (A) ocean.
    (B) stream.
    (C) lake.
    (D) sea.

39. A real estate broker who has entered into an agency contract with a seller may delegate his responsibilities under the contract to one or more of his salespersons because:
(A) all agency contracts are assignable.
(B) the contract always contains this specific authority.
(C) this is an implied authority arising out of custom.
(D) the Real Estate Commission permits this.

40. A, B and C own property as joint tenants. C dies and B sells his interest in the property to D. The property is now owned:
(A) as joint tenants by A, D and C's widow, E, his sole heir.
(B) A and D as joint tenants.
(C) A and D as tenants in common, each with a half interest.
(D) A and D and B's wife.

41. The loss of one's real estate by the gradual wearing away of soil through the operation of natural causes is:
(A) erosion.
(B) escheat.
(C) curtilage.
(D) obsolescence.

42. When two or more owners have concurrent, unequal interests in the same property, they hold as:
(A) joint tenants.
(B) tenants in common.
(C) tenants by the entirety.
(D) tenants for years.

43. A corporation cannot hold title to real property in New Jersey with another as a joint tenant because:
(A) it is a violation of the Securities Act.
(B) of its perpetual existence.
(C) it is difficult to list all stockholders in the deed.
(D) a corporation cannot convey title to real property.

44. A joint tenant may NOT:
(A) sell his interest.
(B) give away his interest.
(C) encumber his interest.
(D) sell the property.

45. A real estate broker hires a secretary who does not have a real estate license and agrees to pay her a fixed salary. Which of the following duties may be performed by her?
(A) Giving information on the telephone, such as selling prices of the office listings.
(B) Collecting rents from lessees of property managed by the broker.
(C) Telephone solicitation of listings from prospective sellers.
(D) Typing contracts for the salesperson in the broker's office.

46. Where two unrelated brokers hold title to property, one with a one-third interest and the other a two-thirds interest, title would most likely be held as:
(A) joint tenancy.
(B) tenancy by the entirety.
(C) tenancy in common.
(D) tenancy in severalty.

47. In a typical real estate listing contract, the broker would best be described as:
(A) a general agent.
(B) a special agent.
(C) the principal for the agent.
(D) the principal for the sub-agent.

48. If you possessed a fee simple estate, the property could be:
(A) sold.
(B) subdivided.
(C) mortgaged.
(D) All of the above.

49. A real estate broker's office could NOT be located:
(A) on a farm.
(B) in the home of one of his salespersons.
(C) in a marina.
(D) in the same building with an attorney.

50. If a New Jersey broker wants to list a property in Delaware he would need authority from:
(A) the Delaware REC.
(B) the New Jersey REC.
(C) the Federal Trade Commission.
(D) the Interstate Commerce Commission.

• Review Quiz 2
(Answers on page 568)

1. Buyer made offer at less than asking price. Seller made counter-offer. Buyer would not accept counter-offer. Seller than agreed to accept the first offer, so:
   (A) buyer was legally bound to complete deal.
   (B) broker had earned his commission.
   (C) buyer was released from his offer when seller made counter-offer.
   (D) broker is liable if the contract is unenforceable.

2. The law which bars legal claims after certain time limits is known as the:
   (A) Statute of Frauds.
   (B) Statute of Limitations.
   (C) Administrative Procedures Act.
   (D) Real Estate Law.

3. In New Jersey, an oral lease of real estate for one year is:
   (A) void.
   (B) unenforceable.
   (C) illegal.
   (D) valid.

4. A contract of sale cannot exist unless there has been an offer and:
   (A) an assignment.
   (B) a mortgage.
   (C) an assessment.
   (D) an acceptance.

5. A prospective buyer who is in the locality and able to inspect the property for himself ordinarily has a right to rely on the broker's representations as to:
   (A) future value of the property.
   (B) nothing the broker says.
   (C) everything the broker says.
   (D) concealed details of construction of the building

6. A contract that is indefeasible:
   (A) cannot be voided.
   (B) is void.
   (C) is voidable.
   (D) is unenforceable.

7. Effective delivery of a deed depends upon the:
   (A) knowledge of its existence by the grantee.
   (B) mere physical transfer of the deed to grantee.
   (C) intention of the grantor.
   (D) prior acknowledgement of grantor's signature.

8. If a buyer withdraws a written offer before the seller signed, the broker:
   (A) splits earnest money with seller.
   (B) adjusts the amount of the commission.
   (C) gets nothing.
   (D) is entitled to expenses.

9. A power of attorney is not necessarily revoked if:
   (A) the principal dies.
   (B) the attorney-in-fact fails to use it for 90 days.
   (C) the principal records a declaration revoking it.
   (D) the attorney-in-fact dies.

10. Recording a deed is to the greatest benefit of the:
    (A) grantor.
    (B) public trustee.
    (C) attorney.
    (D) grantee.

11. An assignment of property rights constitutes:
    (A) a lease.
    (B) an encumbrance.
    (C) an assignee.
    (D) a conveyance.

12. A clause in the contract or a mortgage which requires punctual performance is described as:
    (A) a specific performance clause.
    (B) time is of the essence.
    (C) an acceleration clause.
    (D) an alienation clause.

13. Andy and Barry enter into a contract in which Andy orally agrees to leave the crystal chandelier in the entrance foyer if Barry purchases his house. The value of the chandelier is $450. When a written agreement is prepared the provision regarding the chandelier is left out. Which of the following is true?
    (A) Barry can sue for specific performance to recover the chandelier.
    (B) Barry cannot recover the chandelier because of the parol evidence rule.
    (C) Barry cannot sue because of the Statute of Frauds.
    (D) Barry cannot recover the chandelier because it is an ornamental fixture and therefore personal property.

14. If the optionee dies prior to the exercise of the option, the option is:
    (A) terminated.
    (B) voidable.
    (C) valid.
    (D) unenforceable.

15. When a buyer on a recorded land contract uses a quitclaim deed to extinguish his interest, who signs the deed?
    (A) the vendor.
    (B) the vendee.
    (C) the notary public who took the acknowledgement.
    (D) the broker who prepared the sales agreement.

16. Which of the following is an essential element of any contract?
    (A) Written instrument.
    (B) Consideration.
    (C) Deposit.
    (D) Date.

17. The phrase "time is of the essence" means:
    (A) the lawyer is in a hurry to take possession.
    (B) the closing must be held in a hurry.
    (C) things required to be accomplished on dates set forth in the agreement must be done on or before those dates.
    (D) time is unimportant.

18. It is common procedure to record all of the following instruments EXCEPT:
    (A) agreement of sale.
    (B) notice of completion.
    (C) an assignment of a mortgage.
    (D) a notice of intention.

19. If, after the signing of the contract for sale of land and before the closing, the seller dies:
    (A) the contract is voidable at the option of the seller's representative.
    (B) the contract is voidable at the option of the buyer.
    (C) the deal is terminated by operation of law.
    (D) the death of the seller normally does not terminate the contract.

20. A contract, the terms of which have not been fully performed, is known as:
    (A) an executed contract.
    (B) an executory contract.
    (C) a unilateral contract.
    (D) a bilateral contract.

21. If an option contract is entered into by a property owner and a prospective buyer, which of the following statements is true?
    (A) the optionor may sell or not at his option.
    (B) the optionee must buy.
    (C) the optionor must sell, but the buyer need not buy.
    (D) it is specifically enforceable by both parties.

22. The term "merchantable title" means:
    (A) that the title has no defects.
    (B) that the seller can transfer his interest by deed.
    (C) that an abstract certified to date can be prepared.
    (D) that the title appears reasonably to be free of defects.

23. If the buyer withdraws his offer before it has been accepted, the deposit money goes:
    (A) one-half to the broker and one-half to the buyer.
    (B) to the buyer.
    (C) to the seller.
    (D) to the broker.

24. "Default" is best described as:
    (A) to find fault.
    (B) the non-performance of a duty.
    (C) unstable ground.
    (D) defer payment.

25. In the event that a deed to a property was drawn to Charlie Young and he died prior to the date of the deed's delivery, which of the following statements would be true?
    (A) The property would revert to government ownership.
    (B) The property would become part of Charlie's estate and be directly conveyed to his heirs.
    (C) The deed would be considered invalid.
    (D) The deed would be considered valid but the contract would have to be renegotiated to the satisfaction of the grantor.

26. If a portion of a printed form contract is changed by typing in contrary provisions, and the changes are initialed by all parties, which of the following statements is true?
    (A) Printing takes precedence over typing.
    (B) The contract is void because of the changes.
    (C) Typing takes precedence over printing.
    (D) The parties may void the contract because of the change.

27. A contract for the sale of real estate is:
(A) an executed agreement.
(B) an expected agreement.
(C) an executory agreement.
(D) an anticipatory agreement.

28. From the following list, which statute or act creates the need for a deed to be in writing?
(A) The Statute of Descent.
(B) The Recording Act.
(C) The Statute of Frauds.
(D) The Proof of Execution Statute.

29. In connection with a contract, a rider is a(n):
(A) amendment.
(B) person.
(C) lien.
(D) prohibited.

30. If the real property owner is a corporation, who signs the listing agreement?
(A) President.
(B) Secretary.
(C) Persons authorized by corporate resolution.
(D) Treasurer.

31. Where a title search reveals that there is a broken chain of title, it can best be cured by:
(A) quitclaim deed.
(B) general warranty deed.
(C) partition.
(D) quiet title proceeding.

32. The covenant against encumbrances in a deed of conveyance warrants against the existence of all of the following EXCEPT:
(A) mortgages against the land.
(B) judgment liens against the land.
(C) easements that adversely affect the land.
(D) zoning ordinances that limit the use of the land.

33. Where a contract of sales fails to mention the existence of a mortgage on the land, but there is such a mortgage:
(A) seller can compel the buyer to complete the deal if the seller allows a deduction from the sale price equal to the amount due on the mortgage.
(B) the signing of the contract of sale automatically makes the mortgage void.
(C) the buyer has the right to demand a title free and clear of mortgage.
(D) buyer must take title subject to the mortgage.

34. Prospective purchasers of property, as evidence of good faith, generally make a deposit called:
(A) consideration.
(B) earnest money.
(C) collateral security.
(D) a deferred purchase money trust.

35. The name of a contract which would permit an investor to purchase or not to purchase a property as he saw fit, for a stated sum within a limited period of time, is known as:
(A) an assignment.
(B) an option.
(C) a deposit receipt.
(D) an agreement of sale.

36. A buyer acquires equitable title when:
(A) an offer is made.
(B) the full purchase price is paid.
(C) a purchase and sale agreement is signed by buyer and seller.
(D) the deed is recorded.

37. In an option, the optionee is the:
(A) legal owner of record.
(B) prospective purchaser.
(C) assignor.
(D) assignee.

38. After a written offer and written acceptance, earnest money deposits placed in a brokerage trust account are being held for the:
(A) buyer.
(B) seller.
(C) broker.
(D) insured depository.

39. When buyer and seller enter into a definite purchase agreement except that no closing date is specified, the contract is:
(A) void for vagueness.
(B) voidable.
(C) enforceable.
(D) not acceptable.

40. Acceptance is accomplished when:
(A) offeree signs sales contract.
(B) offeror signs sales contract.
(C) contract is acknowledged.
(D) contract is recorded.

41. Which of the following statements is true if the seller crossed out the crystal chandelier on the buyer's written offer?
(A) The broker has earned his commission.
(B) The buyer must accept the modification.
(C) The seller is making a counter offer.
(D) The buyer has become the offeror.

42. An option to purchase a farm does NOT require:
(A) the holding of a real estate license.
(B) a valuable consideration actually delivered to the optionor.
(C) that the contract be in writing.
(D) that the optionor sell if the option is exercised.

43. Under the Statute of Frauds, all contracts for the sale of real estate must be in writing. The principal reason for this statute is to:
(A) prevent the buyer from defrauding the seller.
(B) prevent fraud and perjuries.
(C) protect the buyer from the broker.
(D) protect the general public from fraud due to unrecorded deeds.

44. Which of the following is NOT an involuntary alienation?
(A) Escheat.
(B) Dedication.
(C) Adverse possession.
(D) Condemnation.

45. A person to whom real estate is conveyed, the "buyer," is also called:
(A) assignee.
(B) offeree.
(C) grantee.
(D) optionee.

46. Alex has informed Barry that he wishes to relinquish his easement across Barry's property. Barry should ask Alex to sign a:
(A) deed of trust.
(B) special warranty deed.
(C) bargain and sale deed.
(D) quitclaim deed.

47. Failure to meet an obligation when due is known as:
(A) duress.
(B) default.
(C) deficiency.
(D) defeasance.

48. A "vendee" is:
(A) one who sells or offers to sell.
(B) one who buys or offers to buy.
(C) one who leases to another.
(D) one who lends to another.

49. A contract between a competent person and an incompetent person can be voided by:
(A) the incompetent person.
(B) the competent person.
(C) either person.
(D) neither person.

50. Arnold agreed to deliver a deed to Connor in which Arnold will assure good title only through the time of his (Arnold's) ownership. The type of deed used would be:
(A) a quitclaim deed.
(B) a general warranty deed.
(C) a CVG (special warranty) deed.
(D) a bargain and sale deed without covenants.

• Review Quiz 3
(Answers on page 569)

1. Upon the completion of a sale of mortgaged property, the seller must:
   (A) pay off the mortgage.
   (B) deliver the deed to the grantee.
   (C) obtain the approval of the mortgagee.
   (D) obtain a satisfaction piece.

2. A prospective home purchaser:
   (A) can pay more than the CRV but not more than the FHA appraisal.
   (B) cannot pay more than the CRV but can pay more than an FHA appraisal.
   (C) cannot pay more than the CRV or the FHA appraisal.
   (D) can pay more than the CRV or the FHA appraisal.

3. A mortgage is released by:
   (A) reversion.
   (B) reconveyance.
   (C) quitclaim deed.
   (D) satisfaction.

4. A clause in a mortgage or lease, stating that rights of the holders shall be secondary to a subsequent encumbrance, is:
   (A) a clause in a deed to permit access to another property.
   (B) found in a tax deed.
   (C) a subordination clause.
   (D) a habendum clause.

5. The payment for mutual mortgage insurance on an FHA loan:
   (A) may be paid by buyer in cash at closing or added to the mortgage amount.
   (B) is approximately 2.25% of the mortgage amount.
   (C) Both A and B.
   (D) Neither A nor B.

6. Which of the following is NOT a requirement of a valid adverse possession claim in New Jersey?
   (A) open and visible possession.
   (B) continuous use.
   (C) exclusive use.
   (D) possession for 21 years without permission.

7. The term "refinancing" refers to:
   (A) obtaining a second mortgage on a property that already has a first mortgage.
   (B) the repayment of an existing mortgage loan from the proceeds of a new one.
   (C) changing one or more of the terms of an existing mortgage loan.
   (D) a secondary mortgage market transaction.

8. Interest calculated on the total sum of the principal and on the unpaid interest accrued thereon is called:
   (A) simple interest.
   (B) compound interest.
   (C) penalty interest.
   (D) interest rate.

9. Which of the following pieces of information may be advertised by itself, according to Regulation Z?
   (A) the total of all payments.
   (B) the amount of any installment payment.
   (C) the annual percentage rate.
   (D) the interest rate on the loan.

10. Usury means most nearly:
    (A) making loans without benefit of co-signors.
    (B) lending money at fluctuating interest rates.
    (C) capable of multiple usage.
    (D) illegal interest.

11. Which of the following is a source of primary mortgage funds?
    (A) Federal Deposit Insurance Corporation.
    (B) Federal National Mortgage Association.
    (C) Federal Home Loan Bank.
    (D) Federal Savings & Loan Association.

12. The mortgage creates the:
    (A) mode of payment.
    (B) security for repayment of the debt.
    (C) personal promise to pay.
    (D) promise to the mortgagee.

13. An installment contract for the sale of real estate does not give the buyer:
    (A) the right to live on the property.
    (B) the right to lease the property.
    (C) the right of possession.
    (D) legal title to the property.

14. Usually a mechanic's lien is satisfied by:
    (A) court order.
    (B) payment in full.
    (C) recording a release.
    (D) satisfaction of the judgment.

15. An individual, partnership or corporation to whom title to a property is conditionally conveyed as security for a loan is known as:
    (A) mortgagor.
    (B) borrower.
    (C) mortgagee.
    (D) lessee.

16. When a borrower defaults on an FHA-insured loan, any losses sustained by foreclosure are made through:
   (A) the Federal Treasury.
   (B) the Mutual Mortgage Insurance Plan.
   (C) an attachment lien against the borrower.
   (D) an assessment against the lending institution.

17. Of the following, whose interest is benefited by an acceleration clause in a mortgage or trust deed note?
   (A) The borrower.
   (B) The lender.
   (C) A future purchaser upon resale of property.
   (D) The trustee.

18. Which of the following encumbrances would constitute a lien on real property?
   (A) Easement.
   (B) Encroachment.
   (C) Deed restriction.
   (D) Unpaid realty taxes.

19. A right given by law to a creditor to have a debt or charge satisfied out of property belonging to the debtor is a(n):
   (A) mortgage.
   (B) lien.
   (C) right of way.
   (D) escheat.

20. The effect of an acceleration clause in a mortgage or a deed of trust is to:
   (A) require the mortgagor to make more payments per month.
   (B) to increase the amount of the monthly payments.
   (C) when exercised, to require that all the balance be paid at once.
   (D) to pressure the mortgagor in making his payments.

21. A written acknowledgement that a mortgage has been canceled is:
   (A) a defeasance statement.
   (B) a promissory note.
   (C) a satisfaction piece.
   (D) an estoppel certificate.

22. Which of the following mortgage types allows a builder to release lots one at a time as they are developed?
   (A) Blanket mortgage.
   (B) Package mortgage.
   (C) Open-end mortgage.
   (D) Conventional mortgage.

23. A mortgagor would be relieved of personal liability under a mortgage under which of the following circumstances?
   (A) A buyer purchases the mortgaged property subject to the existing mortgage.
   (B) A buyer assumes the existing mortgage and there is a novation.
   (C) The mortgage is assigned by the mortgagee.
   (D) A buyer assumes the existing mortgage.

24. Upon satisfaction of a mortgage, which of the following clauses is activated?
   (A) Alienation clause.
   (B) Defeasance clause.
   (C) Acceleration clause.
   (D) Release clause.

25. A written instrument creating a lien on real estate as security for repayment of a specified debt is a(n):
   (A) lien.
   (B) mortgage.
   (C) general warranty deed.
   (D) option.

26. In researching records at the county clerk's office, you can usually distinguish between a first and second mortgage by:
   (A) the date of instrument.
   (B) the amount of the mortgage
   (C) notations made by the recorder.
   (D) the recording date.

27. When you use real property as security for a loan you:
   (A) pledge it.
   (B) hypothecate it.
   (C) assign it.
   (D) devise it.

28. All BUT ONE of the following is a purpose of FHA:
   (A) insure titles.
   (B) stabilize the mortgage market.
   (C) encourage improvement in housing standards.
   (D) encourage home financing.

29. A second mortgage is:
   (A) equal in standing and value with a first mortgage.
   (B) a junior lien on real estate which has a prior mortgage on it.
   (C) always made by the seller.
   (D) used in practically all real estate purchases.

30. A promissory note that provides for payment of interest only during the term of the note would be:
    (A) an installment note.
    (B) a straight note.
    (C) an amortized note.
    (D) a non-negotiable note.

31. In real estate financing, the primary obligation to satisfy a debt is evidenced by:
    (A) a mortgage.
    (B) a promissory note.
    (C) a chattel mortgage.
    (D) a warranty deed.

32. If a house is purchased for $100,000 with an 80% mortgage, how much will the lender charge if the loan is discounted three points?
    (A) $240
    (B) $300
    (C) $2,400
    (D) $3,000

33. A "release clause" is used commonly in:
    (A) a lease.
    (B) a blanket encumbrance.
    (C) an attachment.
    (D) a judgment lien.

34. The penalty for complete prepayment of an FHA-insured loan during the first ten years is:
    (A) 2% of the face value of the note at the time of payment.
    (B) 90 days interest on the remaining balance.
    (C) 1% of the original amount of the lien.
    (D) nothing.

35. Loan discounts for FHA loans are paid to:
    (A) FHA.
    (B) HUD.
    (C) mortgagee.
    (D) seller.

36. When the seller finances the buyer's purchase of a home, it is best described as a(n):
    (A) conventional mortgage.
    (B) chattel mortgage.
    (C) purchase money mortgage.
    (D) article of agreement.

37. A "balloon payment" on a mortgage refers to:
    (A) first payment.
    (B) last payment.
    (C) middle payment.
    (D) second payment.

38. In the absence of an agreement to the contrary, the mortgage normally having priority will be:
    (A) the mortgage for the largest amount.
    (B) the mortgage which is the first mortgage.
    (C) the mortgage which is recorded first.
    (D) the mortgage which is a construction loan mortgage.

39. The maximum guarantee on a VA-guaranteed loan is limited to:
    (A) the assessed value of the property.
    (B) 40% of the loan on loans above $45,000, up to a maximum of $36,000.
    (C) $7,500
    (D) the amount shown on the CRV.

40. Which would NOT be an example of involuntary alienation?
    (A) Mortgage.
    (B) Tax sale.
    (C) Adverse possession.
    (D) Foreclosure.

41. A promissory note:
    (A) may not be executed in connection with a loan on real property.
    (B) is an agreement to do or not to do a certain thing.
    (C) is the primary evidence of a loan.
    (D) is one which is guaranteed or insured by a governmental agency.

42. The person to whom a mortgage is made is the lender, also called:
    (A) the mortgagor.
    (B) the mortgagee.
    (C) the obligor.
    (D) a dependent.

43. "Subject to mortgage" is:
    (A) a type of conditional loan.
    (B) a mortgage bought by FNMA and sold to GNMA.
    (C) the taking of title to property by a grantee, wherein he is not responsible to the holder of the promissory note for the payment of any portion of the amount due.
    (D) the right to foreclose without going to court.

44. Which of the following statements is TRUE?
    (A) All liens are encumbrances.
    (B) All encumbrances are liens.
    (C) Specific liens affect all property of the debtor located in the state.
    (D) Judgments are specific liens.

45. What accompanies a mortgage?
(A) A promissory note.
(B) A deed.
(C) Both A and B.
(D) Neither A nor B.

46. When the court has issued an order to sell property to satisfy a judgment, it is known as:
(A) an easement.
(B) an encumbrance.
(C) an attachment.
(D) a writ of execution.

47. A conventional mortgage is:
(A) guaranteed by the FHA.
(B) a two-party transaction.
(C) approved by the FHA.
(D) made at a rate of interest set by a government agency.

48. The discharge of certain property from the lien of a judgment, mortgage or claim is a:
(A) release of lien.
(B) lien binder.
(C) lien discharge.
(D) tax.

49. A mortgage that covers several parcels of land (property) and that may contain a provision for sale of an individual property and thereby reduce mortgage payments is:
(A) a direct reduction mortgage.
(B) an amortized mortgage.
(C) a blanket mortgage.
(D) a declining balance mortgage.

50. The discount charged by a lender and paid by the seller on a Federal VA loan is a percentage of the:
(A) sales price.
(B) loan amount.
(C) appraised value.
(D) assessed value.

• Review Quiz 4
(Answers on page 570)

1. Under the New Jersey Discrimination Law, a complaint must be submitted within:
   (A) 180 days.
   (B) 60 days.
   (C) 45 days.
   (D) one year.

2. Under a net lease, a tenant is least likely to pay:
   (A) taxes.
   (B) utilities.
   (C) insurance.
   (D) mortgage amortization.

3. A recapture clause is usually used in what type of lease?
   (A) Net lease.
   (B) Gross lease.
   (C) Percentage lease.
   (D) Business lease.

4. A lease that has a definite termination date is a:
   (A) tenancy for years.
   (B) periodic tenancy.
   (C) tenancy at will.
   (D) tenancy at sufferance.

5. A graduated lease can best be defined as a lease:
   (A) that includes an option to purchase.
   (B) in which there may be an increase or decrease in rent at a stated future time.
   (C) under which the owner or landlord pays all ownership charges such as taxes.
   (D) that is passed intact from one owner to the next owner under terms of a contract.

6. The normal shopping center lease is a:
   (A) graduated lease.
   (B) percentage lease.
   (C) gross lease.
   (D) sublease.

7. Norman did not vacate his apartment when his three-year lease expired on April 30. On May 1, Norman paid the rent he had been paying and the landlord accepted it. Norman's lease is now:
   (A) terminated by operation of law.
   (B) renewed for three years.
   (C) a statutory month-to-month tenancy.
   (D) renewed for a period of one year.

8. The term "lessor" is used to describe:
   (A) a tenant.
   (B) a landlord.
   (C) a vendor.
   (D) an optionor.

9. A leasehold interest lying between the primary lease and the sublease is known as:
   (A) a percentage lease.
   (B) a sandwich lease.
   (C) an inactive lease.
   (D) an uncapitalized lease.

10. A tenant who is actually or constructively evicted by a landlord may consider his lease as being:
   (A) renewed.
   (B) terminated.
   (C) assigned.
   (D) sold.

11. Which of the following statements in reference to a lease is FALSE?
   (A) The law limits the amount of security deposit on a commercial lease.
   (B) Unless contrary agreement is in effect, the lessee may sublet.
   (C) A security deposit remains the property of the lessee until actual damage occurs.
   (D) A written lease cannot be altered by oral agreement.

12. Which of the following does NOT possess a leasehold estate?
   (A) Tenancy at sufferance.
   (B) Tenancy at will.
   (C) Life tenant.
   (D) Tenant for years.

13. A percentage lease is:
   (A) one which provides for the percentage that will be paid the broker as a commission.
   (B) one where the usual rent is based upon the net receipts of the tenant.
   (C) one which always allows the tenant to cancel his lease if his income falls below a desired amount.
   (D) one in which the tenant's usual rent is based upon the gross receipts.

14. The interest of a tenant who came rightly into possession by permission of the owner but continues to occupy the premises without permission is called:
   (A) a sandwich lease.
   (B) an estate at sufferance.
   (C) an estate at will.
   (D) an estate in remainder.

15. When the premises reach a physical condition whereby the tenant is unable to occupy them for the purposes intended, the situation is legally recognized as:
    (A) a dispossess eviction.
    (B) an actual eviction.
    (C) a constructive eviction.
    (D) a passive eviction.

16. By definition, an "estate for years":
    (A) must last for a year or more.
    (B) must be for at least two years.
    (C) is for a fixed term, whether a week, a month, a decade.
    (D) requires a written lease.

17. The deprivation of the possession of lands or tenements is called:
    (A) covenant.
    (B) avulsion.
    (C) eviction.
    (D) default.

18. At the end of tenancy for years the landlord has which of the following?
    (A) Reversion interest.
    (B) Tenancy at sufferance.
    (C) Right of re-entry.
    (D) Remainder interest.

19. If it is not stipulated in the lease and the leased property is sold, the lease:
    (A) has to be renewed.
    (B) is binding on the new owner.
    (C) creates a tenancy from month to month.
    (D) materially affects the tenant.

20. The lessor under a net lease pays the:
    (A) taxes.
    (B) special assessments.
    (C) maintenance.
    (D) mortgage principal payments.

21. When the lessor dies:
    (A) the lease terminates.
    (B) the lessee has the option to terminate the lease.
    (C) the lease is void.
    (D) the lease is not affected.

22. A long-term lease of land under which the tenant erects a building which goes to the lessor at the end of the lease is called a:
    (A) ground lease.
    (B) net lease.
    (C) gross lease.
    (D) sandwich lease.

23. If an area is rezoned industrial and a commercial establishment is allowed to continue its operation in that area, this is an example of which of the following?
    (A) Variance.
    (B) Nonconforming use.
    (C) Instability.
    (D) Homogeneity.

24. Which of the following best describes the concept of highest and best use?
    (A) Gross return.
    (B) Natural and legal use.
    (C) Greatest net return over a given period.
    (D) Homogeneous use.

25. An appraiser usually appraises to determine:
    (A) assessed value.
    (B) book value.
    (C) market value.
    (D) insurance value.

26. The combining of two or more parcels of land is called:
    (A) annexation.
    (B) appreciation.
    (C) assemblage.
    (D) integration.

27. Thelma had two years to go on her lease and she rents it to Louise for six months. This is called a (an):
    (A) assignment.
    (B) net lease.
    (C) interim lease.
    (D) sublease.

28. A properly drafted property management agreement should contain which of the following?
    (A) Names of owner and manager.
    (B) Requirement that the manager provide periodic reports to the owner.
    (C) Description of property.
    (D) All of the above.

29. If a mortgaged property is leased with a subordination clause, and because of default in payment the mortgagee forecloses on the mortgage:
    (A) the lessee is released from any further obligation on the lease.
    (B) the lease continues in effect despite the foreclosure.
    (C) the lease is void because the mortgagor has no right to give a lease on mortgaged property.
    (D) the lease may be terminated by the mortgagee but not the lessee.

30. Assume that a broker is a property manager. He is able to buy merchandise needed for the property through a relative at a lower price than from any other source. He should:
    (A) proceed with the purchases.
    (B) proceed with the purchases, charging the owner a portion of the costs saved for work done in securing a better price.
    (C) proceed with the purchases but inform the owner in writing of the fact that a relative owned the company from which the purchases were made.
    (D) not purchase from a relative.

31. In management of real estate a broker may:
    (A) personally accept rebates from suppliers for himself.
    (B) commingle rents received with his own funds.
    (C) invest security deposits in an interest-bearing account for his own benefit.
    (D) not make a secret profit.

32. When a broker signs a contract to manage an owner's property he becomes a:
    (A) lessor.
    (B) trustee.
    (C) receiver.
    (D) fiduciary.

33. Which of the following is NOT a valid operating expense for an income-producing property?
    (A) Heating oil.
    (B) Cleaning supplies.
    (C) Ceiling replacements.
    (D) Management fees.

34. The authority for enforcement of the Federal Fair Housing Act rests with:
    (A) the Secretary of the Interior.
    (B) the Attorney General.
    (C) the Federal Housing Authority.
    (D) the Secretary of Housing and Urban Development.

35. An "estate for years" in real estate can also be called:
    (A) a leasehold estate.
    (B) a fee simple conditional.
    (C) a fee.
    (D) a joint tenancy.

36. Charlie wants to extend the side of his house beyond the setback boundary. Which must Charlie obtain?
    (A) Variance.
    (B) Non-conforming use.
    (C) Subordination.
    (D) Reservation.

37. If the reproduction cost shows a higher value than the appraised value, which of the following has occurred?
    (A) Accrued depreciation.
    (B) Excessive appraisal.
    (C) External obsolescence.
    (D) Capitalization.

38. In evaluating an appraisal, the before-and-after method is used most often with:
    (A) condemnation.
    (B) exchange.
    (C) cost of reproduction.
    (D) option.

39. The term over which a property gives benefits to its owner is:
    (A) investment duration.
    (B) physical life.
    (C) value duration.
    (D) economic life.

40. Market value is most closely related to:
    (A) selling price.
    (B) replacement price.
    (C) income analysis.
    (D) reproduction price.

41. All but one of the following is an example of external obsolescence. Name the exception.
    (A) Population density.
    (B) Direct effect of the elements.
    (C) Zoning.
    (D) Special assessments.

42. In the sales comparison approach, the value of a feature found in the subject property but not in the comparable would be treated as:
    (A) added to the sales price paid for the comparable.
    (B) subtracted from the price of the subject property.
    (C) a negative adjustment to the subject property.
    (D) a positive adjustment to the subject and a negative to the comparable.

43. In appraising a library building, the appraiser would emphasize the:
    (A) cost approach.
    (B) sales comparison approach.
    (C) income approach.
    (D) market data approach.

44. When operating expenses are deducted from effective gross income, the investor is left with:
    (A) gross collectible income.
    (B) gross income.
    (C) net operating income.
    (D) net effective income (NEI).

Gross Income - op

45. Under Regulation Z, which of the following may NOT be advertised alone?
    (A) "No money down."
    (B) "Easy monthly payments."
    (C) "Excellent loan for assumption."
    (D) "Check our reasonable rates."

46. Which of the following is exempt from giving notice to a consumer purchasing a home, according to the Truth-in-Lending Act?
    (A) A second mortgagee.
    (B) A seller carrying back a first mortgage.
    (C) A broker arranging credit for a fee.
    (D) A home builder.

47. The primary purpose of the Truth-in-Lending Act is to:
    (A) save members of the general public money in their installment purchases.
    (B) establish a more uniform set of charges.
    (C) disclose to the consumer the cost and conditions of the installment purchase.
    (D) assist the federal government in controlling "shady" lending practices.

48. Under Truth-in-Lending, the borrower (consumer) has a right of rescission upon notice for:
    (A) seven calendar days.
    (B) 24 hours.
    (C) three business days.
    (D) 72 hours.

49. In a residential lease, the security deposit:
    (A) can't be more than the first month's rent.
    (B) is held by the lessor in an interest-bearing account for the duration of the lease.
    (C) remains the property of the lessor during the term of the lease.
    (D) All of the above.

50. An example of a less-than-freehold estate is:
    (A) a life estate.
    (B) a leasehold estate.
    (C) a fee simple estate.
    (D) a mortgaged property.

• Review Quiz 5
(Answers on page 571)

1. All but one of the following are examples of government limitations on ownership:
   (A) Police power.
   (B) Encroachment.
   (C) Eminent domain.
   (D) Taxation.

2. An instrument which transfers possession of real property but does not transfer ownership is a:
   (A) deed.
   (B) mortgage
   (C) satisfaction piece.
   (D) lease.

3. A mortgage is usually released by:
   (A) reversion.
   (B) reconveyance.
   (C) quitclaim deed.
   (D) satisfaction piece.

4. The word "severable" most closely means:
   (A) sole ownership of property.
   (B) capable of division into separate rights.
   (C) more than one.
   (D) harsh.

5. If title to real property remains in seller's name after he has sold it on a monthly payment plan, the buyer would have purchased it under:
   (A) FHA financing.
   (B) a guaranteed loan.
   (C) a land contract.
   (D) an option.

6. A promissory note providing for payment of interest only to be paid during its term is a(n):
   (A) installment note.
   (B) straight note.
   (C) amortized note.
   (D) non-interest-bearing note.

7. Which of the following is NOT a type of legal description?
   (A) Metes and bounds.
   (B) Plottage.
   (C) Tax map identification.
   (D) Monuments.

8. The gradual retirement of a debt by equal payments is known as:
   (A) amortization.
   (B) capitalization.
   (C) liquidation.
   (D) balloon payment.

9. "Usury" means most nearly:
   (A) making loans without benefit of co-signors.
   (B) lending money.
   (C) capable of multiple usage.
   (D) illegal interest.

10. The word "revoked" most nearly means:
    (A) rescinded.
    (B) released.
    (C) reviewed.
    (D) repaired.

11. A party wall would be found:
    (A) along a property line.
    (B) between the dining and living rooms.
    (C) facing the direction from which bad weather usually comes.
    (D) between the upper and lower stories of a structure.

12. Which of the following deeds offer the least protection to the grantee?
    (A) Bargain and sale.
    (B) Special warranty.
    (C) General warranty.
    (D) Quitclaim.

13. When the amortized payment of a mortgage does remain constant over the period of the loan but leaves an outstanding balance to be paid at the end, this payment of the balance is called a(n):
    (A) escalation payment
    (B) balloon payment.
    (C) satisfaction payment.
    (D) acceleration payment.

14. Which term best describes a court order to carry out the terms of a signed real estate contract?
    (A) Specific performance.
    (B) Lis pendens.
    (C) Attachment.
    (D) Judgment.

15. The owner wants to sell his property without the aid of a real estate broker. He may legally do ALL BUT ONE of the following:
    (A) Establish the purchasing power of the buyer.
    (B) Write up the sale contract between himself and the buyer.
    (C) Require that the buyer assume the present mortgage.
    (D) Post a notice that he prefers a buyer of a certain religion.

16. In a lease, the right of first refusal most nearly means:
(A) tenant can cancel.
(B) tenant can extend.
(C) tenant can buy a foreclosure sale.
(D) tenant can match an offer to purchase made to the owner.

17. Where the seller defaults, the earnest money:
(A) belongs to the broker.
(B) should be returned to the buyer.
(C) should be placed in an escrow fund.
(D) should be retained by the seller.

18. Which of the following funds should NOT be placed in the real estate trust account?
(A) Installment land contract collection.
(B) Earnest monies.
(C) Rental collections.
(D) Petty cash.

19. "Appurtenances" can include all but one of the following:
(A) Easements.
(B) Fences
(C) Chattels.
(D) Improvements.

20. The turning over of land by a developer to a public use is called:
(A) subordination.
(B) escalation.
(C) condemnation.
(D) dedication.

21. A contract signed by an unmarried minor is:
(A) void.
(B) voidable.
(C) unenforceable.
(D) indefeasible.

22. The broker owes an obligation to:
(A) divide the commission with another broker chosen or preferred by the buyer.
(B) divulge to the buyer the lowest price at which the seller will sell.
(C) present to his principal all written offers he receives, including all of the terms and conditions of each offer signed by a prospective buyer.
(D) nobody.

23. The kind of estate that is inheritable and freely transferable is:
(A) an estate in remainder.
(B) a life estate.
(C) a fee simple estate.
(D) an estate in reversion.

24. A licensed real estate broker selling a property on which he holds an option must notify the purchaser that he is the:
(A) optionee.
(B) optionor.
(C) tenant.
(D) lessee.

25. A broker owes certain fiduciary duties to his principal. Which one of the following is NOT included?
(A) Loyalty to his principal.
(B) Must obey instructions.
(C) Maintain the property.
(D) Account for money and property.

26. Which of the following does NOT involve a freehold estate?
(A) Life estate.
(B) Defeasible fee.
(C) Unrecorded vendor's deed.
(D) Estate for years.

27. Of the following, the largest estate or ownership in real property is:
(A) estate at sufferance.
(B) estate at will.
(C) life estate.
(D) fee simple.

28. A salesperson may advertise a property for sale only:
(A) if he personally listed the property.
(B) if the name of the broker is included in the ad.
(C) if his broker is entitled to use the term "Realtor."
(D) if he pays for the ad himself out of his commission.

29. Which of the following is NOT a fiduciary relationship?
(A) Agent to seller.
(B) Agent to customer.
(C) Attorney to client.
(D) Attorney-in-fact to principal.

30. Unless there is a stipulation to the contrary, when real property under a lease is sold, the lease:
(A) must be renewed.
(B) is immediately canceled.
(C) remains binding on the new owner.
(D) becomes a tenancy from month to month.

31. Which of the following activities is considered an act of fraud?
(A) Buyer agent exclusively.
(B) Undisclosed dual agency.
(C) Seller agent exclusively.
(D) Transaction broker.

32. A private corporation which purchases mortgages in the secondary mortgage market is called:
   (A) Government National Mortgage Association.
   (B) Federal Home Loan Corporation.
   (C) Federal National Mortgage Association.
   (D) Federal Home Loan Mortgage Association.

33. Where two brothers hold title to property, one with a one-third interest and the other a two-thirds interest, title would most likely be held as:
   (A) joint tenancy.
   (B) tenancy by the entirety.
   (C) tenancy in common.
   (D) tenancy in severalty.

34. The broker owes a fiduciary responsibility to:
   (A) the customer.
   (B) the client.
   (C) the Real Estate Commission.
   (D) the Board of Realtors.

35. When mortgage rates increase:
   (A) the money supply increases.
   (B) vacancy rates increase.
   (C) demand for apartment rental units increases.
   (D) disintermediation increases.

36. Zoning ordinances usually cover such matters as:
   (A) base lines.
   (B) setback lines.
   (C) deed restrictions.
   (D) prescription.

37. A soil test to determine if the soil will take sufficient water seepage for use of a septic tank is called a:
   (A) percolation test.
   (B) defeasance survey.
   (C) plottage test.
   (D) reversion test.

38. The boundary lines of land, with their terminal points and angles, are called:
   (A) bench marks.
   (B) geodetic survey points.
   (C) metes and bounds.
   (D) longitude and latitude.

39. The main purpose of the license law is to:
   (A) protect the public.
   (B) limit competition.
   (C) increase revenue.
   (D) limit the number of licensees.

40. A property is deeded to "Al Stine, et ux." The phrase "et ux" means:
   (A) and wife.
   (B) and others.
   (C) over and above.
   (D) without recourse.

41. A will, written by hand, dated and signed, is:
   (A) intestate.
   (B) a legacy.
   (C) nonculpative.
   (D) holographic.

42. An appurtenance is a(n):
   (A) rude remark.
   (B) fixture.
   (C) right, privilege or improvement that passes with the land.
   (D) permanent repair to property.

43. A deed wherein the grantor limits his liability to his tenure is a:
   (A) quitclaim deed.
   (B) special warranty deed.
   (C) general warranty deed.
   (D) None of the above.

44. A non-conforming use is:
   (A) a variance.
   (B) a use which can be re-established.
   (C) at variance with zoning laws.
   (D) indefeasible.

45. In the application of the income approach, when the rate increases:
   (A) the value increases.
   (B) the value decreases.
   (C) the income increases.
   (D) the income decreases.

46. The term over which a property gives benefits to its owner is called:
   (A) useful life.
   (B) remaining life.
   (C) economic life.
   (D) All of the above.

47. An option without valid consideration is:
   (A) void.
   (B) voidable.
   (C) valid.
   (D) enforceable.

48. The distance from the curb or other established line, within which no building may be erected, is called:
(A) public easement.
(B) side-yard.
(C) building line.
(D) setback.

49. Under Regulation Z all of the following must be in the disclosure statement except:
(A) total finance charges.
(B) pay-off penalties.
(C) attorney's fees.
(D) annual percentage rate.

50. To qualify for a depreciation deduction for income tax purposes, the property must be:
(A) mortgaged.
(B) improved.
(C) unencumbered.
(D) a personal residence.

General Real Estate Examination Content Outline
Salesperson and Broker Examinations
The exams have 80 scored questions and 12 pretest questions. Ten percent of the scored questions will involve mathematical computations.

I. Real property characteristics, definitions, ownership, restrictions, and transfer (16 questions - 20%)

A. Definitions, descriptions, and ways to hold title
1. Elements of real and personal property
2. Property description and legal description
3. Estates in real property
4. Forms, rights, interests, and obligations of ownership

B. Land use controls and restrictions
1. Public (e.g., zoning, taxation, police power)
2. Private (e.g., liens, encumbrances, recording and priorities, subdivision/association rules)

C. Transfer/alienation of title to real property
1. Voluntary and involuntary
2. Deeds, warranties, and defects in title

II. Assessing and explaining property valuation and the appraisal process (12 questions - 15%)

A. Principles, types, and estimates of property value

B. Influences on property value

C. Approaches to property valuation and investment analysis

III. Contracts, agency relationships with buyers and sellers, and federal requirements (20 questions - 25%)

A. Contract elements, types (e.g., valid, enforceable) and terminology

B. Agency employment contracts, listing and buyer agency agreements, and required elements

C. Purchase/Sales contracts and contingencies

D. General agency relationships and fiduciary responsibilities

E. Property conditions and disclosures (e.g., property, environmental)

F. Procedures and laws governing real estate activities (e.g., Federal Fair Housing Act, Americans with Disabilities Act, antitrust, marketing controls)

VI. Financing the transaction and settlement (20 questions - 25%)

A. Financing components
1. Financing instruments (e.g., notes, mortgages, contract for deed, deed or trust)
2. Sources (e.g., primary and secondary mortgage markets, seller financing
3. Types of loans
4. Financing concepts and terminology

B. Lender requirements and obligations

C. Settlement Procedures

D. Settlement documents (e.g., title review, RESPA)

E. Financing costs, property taxation, proration calculations and other closing costs

V. Leases, rents, and property management (12 questions - 15%)

A. Types and elements of leasehold estates, leases, lease clauses, and rental agreements

B. Lessor and lessee rights, responsibilities, and recourse

C. Management contracts and obligations of parties

Source: Promissor (formerly ASI)

about the SALESPERSON PRACTICE FINAL

The practice test on the following pages is patterned after the actual test. The best way to prepare for the state exam is to work with questions similar to those which appear on the actual test. The actual test and this practice test have the same types of questions, time limit and level of difficulty. This practice test is not a copy of the actual test. The actual test is copyrighted and may not be duplicated. The primary purpose of your taking the practice test is to help you realize your weak areas so you can concentrate your studies on those areas.

General Information

1. Specific information about the actual test may be found in the Candidate Guide provided by your license preparation school.

2. Be sure to keep track of questions of which you are uncertain. When you complete answering all the ones of which you're certain, go back and try again on the uncertain ones. Do **not** leave any blank answers.

	Questions	Minimum Number Needed to Pass	Candidate's Score Number Right
PART I–GENERAL TEST	80	56	________
PART II–STATE TEST	30	21	________

3. Do not answer any questions until you have read them through carefully.

4. The General Test contains 80 scored questions and 12 pretest questions.

5. Ten percent (8) of the scored questions on the General Test will involve mathematical computations.

6. The allotted time for the salesperson's exam is three and one-half hours. Applicants are not permitted to continue the test beyond the established time limit.

EXPro Electronic Testing System

The New Jersey State examination will be administered by Promissor (ASI) on an electronic testing system called EXPro. This system eliminates the use of paper and pencil answer sheets and enables the testing service to give you the results of your exam. as soon as you complete it. Questions and answers are presented on a touch sensitive screen. A computer memory card records your responses and automatically times the exam.

EXPro allows you to change your answers, skip questions, and mark questions for review. **Knowledge of computers and typing is absolutely NOT required.**

• Salesperson Practice Final
(Answers on page 571)

PART I— GENERAL TEST

1. The law which requires that transfers of real property ownership be in writing is known as the:
   (A) law of evidence.
   (B) statute of liberties.
   (C) statute of frauds.
   (D) statute of limitations.

2. In a VA loan:
   (A) a down payment is required.
   (B) there must be an approved appraisal.
   (C) one must be a veteran to assume the loan.
   (D) the maximum term is 25 years.

3. When a land contract is entered into:
   (A) legal title passes to the buyer.
   (B) the seller executes the deed.
   (C) the buyer cannot occupy property.
   (D) the buyer acquires equitable title.

4. A five bedroom, one bath residence is an example of what type of depreciation?
   (A) Functional.
   (B) Economic.
   (C) Physical.
   (D) All of the above.

5. One of the following is NOT an essential requirement for a valid deed:
   (A) The buyer and seller be named.
   (B) Words of conveyance.
   (C) Acknowledgement and recording.
   (D) Competent grantor.

6. If two married brothers own property as joint tenants and one brother dies, his wife owns:
   (A) a one-third life estate in half of the undivided interest her husband owned.
   (B) a one-half life estate in the entire property.
   (C) fee simple estate in half of the property.
   (D) no interest.

7. In a lease:
   (A) the original lessee could be liable for rent payments even though he sublets the premises.
   (B) a tenancy for years is one which continues indefinitely until one of the parties elects to terminate it by giving proper notice.
   (C) a residential security deposit is the property of the lessor during a lease term.
   (D) the tenant is the lessor.

8. To use property for the best net return to the property is:
   (A) functional value.
   (B) appreciation.
   (C) highest and best use.
   (D) economic value.

9. What is the best way to find a cloud on title?
   (A) Application for title insurance.
   (B) Appraisal.
   (C) Warranty deed.
   (D) Title search.

10. A life estate is:
    (A) a freehold interest in real estate and is considered real property.
    (B) a less than freehold interest and is not considered real property.
    (C) inheritable.
    (D) a non-freehold estate.

11. Where a title search reveals that there is a broken chain of title it can best be cured by:
    (A) quitclaim deed.
    (B) general warranty deed.
    (C) partition.
    (D) welding.

12. When the lessor sells his leased property:
    (A) the lease is binding on the seller.
    (B) the lease is binding on the buyer.
    (C) the lease is voidable by the buyer.
    (D) the lease is voidable by the seller.

13. The phrase "principals only" excludes:
    (A) disinterested buyers.
    (B) real estate brokers.
    (C) prospective buyers.
    (D) financially weak buyers.

14. A mechanic's lien may not be levied by:
    (A) an architect.
    (B) a real estate broker.
    (C) a subcontractor.
    (D) a plumber.

15. The covenant in a deed in which the grantor guarantees he has title is:
    (A) the habendum.
    (B) seizen.
    (C) the conveyance.
    (D) quiet enjoyment.

16. A judgment becomes effective when:
    (A) the debt is incurred.
    (B) the suit is delivered.
    (C) the verdict is rendered.
    (D) it is recorded.

17. Which of the following is a private agency that buys and sells in the secondary mortgage market?
    (A) FNMA.
    (B) GNMA.
    (C) FHLMC.
    (D) HUD.

18. If title is indefeasible it can't be:
    (A) recorded.
    (B) conveyed.
    (C) voided.
    (D) alienated.

19. When a broker signs a contract to manage an owner's property, he becomes:
    (A) a lessor.
    (B) a trustee.
    (C) a receiver.
    (D) a fiduciary.

20. A blanket mortgage:
    (A) covers several parcels of land.
    (B) must be settled in full when one parcel is sold.
    (C) cannot be assigned.
    (D) must be on contiguous lots.

21. The holder of a life estate can do all of the following EXCEPT:
    (A) pay the taxes.
    (B) commit waste.
    (C) lease.
    (D) mortgage.

22. Recording acts passed by the various states:
    (A) require that all documents pertaining to real estate transfers be recorded in the public records.
    (B) provide for the recording of any instrument by which an estate in land is created.
    (C) provide for constructive notice.
    (D) provide for recording offices in municipalities.

23. In estimating the value of real estate, you should consider all except:
    (A) market data information.
    (B) deterioration of the property.
    (C) income of the property.
    (D) income of the buyer.

24. If you possessed a fee simple estate, the property could be:
    (A) sold.
    (B) subdivided.
    (C) mortgaged.
    (D) All of the above.

25. The recovery of the cost of improvements to a property over a set period of time is called:
    (A) amortization.
    (B) capitalization.
    (C) recapture.
    (D) reformation.

26. An abstract of title is best described as:
    (A) a brief history of the title to a particular property.
    (B) a summary of each deed in a title search.
    (C) an appraisal of the lands and the improvements.
    (D) a summary of all the improvements and encroachments on the property.

27. The right of a water company to lay and maintain mains along the rear of a lot is called:
    (A) an appurtenance.
    (B) a right of encroachment.
    (C) easement in gross.
    (D) riparian right.

28. Which is correct for restrictive covenants?
    (A) They may not be at variance with zoning ordinances.
    (B) They restrict the use of the property.
    (C) They are imposed by government.
    (D) They are not encumbrances.

29. In a residential lease, the security deposit:
    (A) can't be more than the first month's rent.
    (B) belongs to the lessor for the duration of the lease.
    (C) must be deposited in an insured depository.
    (D) must be returned to the lessee if the property is sold.

30. When a husband and wife purchase a property jointly, and it is their intention that upon the death of either one the share of the deceased would pass to their heirs, they would elect:
    (A) a tenancy by the entirety.
    (B) a joint tenancy.
    (C) tenancy in common.
    (D) tenancy by will.

31. A bonafide purchaser is a purchaser who:
 (A) has put up an earnest money deposit with his offer.
 (B) has qualified for a mortgage plan.
 (C) has entered into the purchase in good faith.
 (D) has made a contingent offer.

32. A change made to an existing will is known as:
 (A) an addendum.
 (B) an amendment.
 (C) a supplement.
 (D) a codicil.

33. The Bonanza Savings Bank makes a 30-year conventional loan at an annual interest rate of 8.5%. If it wishes to earn a yield of 9%, how many points must it charge?
 (A) One.
 (B) Two.
 (C) Three.
 (D) Four.

34. The abbreviation APR stands for:
 (A) approximate percentage rate.
 (B) annual percentage rate.
 (C) annual proration.
 (D) adjustable percentage rate.

35. A mortgage given by the purchaser to the seller in partial payment of the purchase price of the property is known as:
 (A) trust mortgage.
 (B) purchase money mortgage.
 (C) installment land contract.
 (D) construction loan.

36. The right of the government to place reasonable restrictions on the use of privately held land is known as:
 (A) eminent domain.
 (B) police power.
 (C) condemnation.
 (D) dedication.

37. A lien granted in favor of a person who furnished labor or materials for an improvement to land is a:
 (A) property lien.
 (B) mechanic's lien.
 (C) general lien.
 (D) non-money encumbrance.

38. The actual act of transferring ownership of land is known as:
 (A) a grant.
 (B) an easement.
 (C) a demise.
 (D) a curtesy.

39. It may be said that homogeneity in a neighborhood:
 (A) creates stability in values.
 (B) increases prices.
 (C) decreases values.
 (D) has no effect on value.

40. In which case would a custodian need a real estate license?
 (A) He rents a condominium building for the association of owners.
 (B) He rents property for more than one owner.
 (C) Both A & B.
 (D) Neither A nor B.

41. Chad L. Morgidge leases a commercial warehouse to Sollum Lee Sware for two years. Which is true?
 (A) The lease must be in writing.
 (B) The rights of Morgidge and Sware are regulated by the New Jersey "Truth in Renting" law.
 (C) The security deposit does not have to be placed in an interest-bearing account.
 (D) This is called a devise.

42. According to the Law of Agency:
 (A) a broker must always charge a commission and put the amount on the listing form.
 (B) a broker may sue and collect a commission even though he has no written employment contract.
 (C) principal must be competent.
 (D) both principal and agent must be competent.

43. A person who assumes an existing mortgage:
 (A) becomes the mortgagee.
 (B) becomes a co-guarantor along with the original maker.
 (C) does not assume any responsibility for mortgage payments.
 (D) relieves the original maker of his obligation.

44. The word "hypothecate" means:
 (A) to institute.
 (B) to delay.
 (C) to enter into a written agreement.
 (D) to pledge without giving up possession.

45. Who is legally entitled to use real estate which has been sold at a tax sale during the two-year period of redemption that follows?
 (A) Mortgagee.
 (B) Lien holder.
 (C) Sheriff.
 (D) Owner of record.

46. Conventional loans include:
(A) ARMs and VA.
(B) Fixed Rate and FHA.
(C) FHA and VA.
(D) ARMs and Fixed Rate.

47. A writ which authorizes and directs the proper officer of the court (usually the sheriff) to carry into effect the judgment or decree of the court is known as a(n):
(A) instrument.
(B) injunction.
(C) writ of execution.
(D) lien.

48. If a seller prepays taxes and insurance on a property, the process used to reimburse the seller for the unused portion is called:
(A) capitalization.
(B) proration.
(C) rebate.
(D) amortization.

49. A charge levied against real estate to cover the proportionate cost of a sewer installation is:
(A) an ad valorem tax.
(B) a special assessment tax.
(C) a county tax.
(D) a pollution tax.

50. A young couple wants to buy a home. Their income is low now, but prospects are good for future earnings increases. They will apply for:
(A) an FHA 203.
(B) a conventional insured loan.
(C) an FHA 245 (Graduated Payment Mortgage).
(D) an FNMA.

51. The repayment of principal and interest within a specified period of time is a characteristic of a(n):
(A) delinquent loan.
(B) amortized loan.
(C) accelerated loan.
(D) equalized loan.

52. Which fee would a condominium owner be least likely to be expected to pay?
(A) Recreation fee.
(B) Maintenance fee.
(C) Stock transfer fee.
(D) Hazard insurance fee.

53. Who is the final tenant on a sale and leaseback?
(A) The buyer.
(B) The seller.
(C) The optionor.
(D) The optionee.

54. The physical characteristics of land include all of the following EXCEPT:
(A) scarcity.
(B) fixity.
(C) permanence.
(D) non-homogeneity.

55. The responsibility of recording a deed lies with:
(A) the state.
(B) the county.
(C) the grantor.
(D) the grantee.

56. To the owner of the dominant property, an easement is:
(A) an encumbrance.
(B) an appurtenance.
(C) a common interest.
(D) an attachment.

57. Options and "first refusals":
(A) are bilateral contracts.
(B) are interchangeable terms.
(C) must be written to be enforceable.
(D) cannot be enforced by the offeree.

58. John and Mary own and occupy a single-family house. They are entitled to deduct the following from their federal income tax:
(A) mortgage interest expense and real estate taxes.
(B) principal and interest payments on the mortgage.
(C) depreciation.
(D) All of the above.

59. Isaac died and left a 1,000-acre farm in Warren County to David. This is called a:
(A) devise.
(B) legacy.
(C) bequest.
(D) miracle.

60. Which of the following is a unilateral contract?
(A) Lease.
(B) Purchase and sale agreement.
(C) Marriage contract.
(D) Option.

61. The process of taking private property for public use is referred to as:
(A) condemnation.
(B) eminent domain.
(C) escheat.
(D) dedication.

62. To the owner of the servient property an easement is:
(A) an encumbrance.
(B) an appurtenance.
(C) a common interest.
(D) an attachment.

63. Utilizing a property to its greatest economic advantage is commonly referred to as:
(A) mobilization.
(B) economic utility.
(C) highest and best use.
(D) market value.

64. The cost approach to value:
(A) sets the lower limit of value.
(B) sets the upper limit of value.
(C) is best applied to income-producing property.
(D) is best applied to older properties.

65. A house and lot are priced at $15,000 and $1,000 respectively. How much cash is needed to purchase the property if the bank will loan 80% of the cost of the house only?
(A) $5,200
(B) $12,000
(C) $4,000
(D) $13,000

66. An investor bought a 75-acre plot for $1,450 per acre. Taxes and other expenses amounted to $6,842 per year. At the end of five years the property was sold for a net price of exactly twice the original cost. What was the net profit on the sale?
(A) $183,290
(B) $74,540
(C) $108,750
(D) $101,908

67. A couple bought a duplex and plan to live in one half while renting out the other to cover costs. Expenses for one year are $1,133, taxes are $115, and the loan payments are $195 per month. What must the monthly rent be?
(A) $300
(B) $121
(C) $406
(D) $275

68. The sale of a parcel of real estate owned by a corporation is authorized by:
(A) a corporate charter.
(B) the president of the corporation.
(C) a corporate resolution.
(D) the attorney general.

69. On January 1, a seller paid $130 for a three-year insurance policy and $625 in annual property taxes. If the home was then sold the following August 1, what was the unused portion for taxes and insurance?
(A) $261.00
(B) $407.00
(C) $338.00
(D) $365.40

70. An option is an example of a(n):
(A) executory contract.
(B) anticipatory contract.
(C) executed contract.
(D) voidable contract.

71. A lot 270' x 390' sells for $45,000. Another lot in close proximity is 90' x 130'. What will the second lot sell for?
(A) $15,000
(B) $5,000
(C) $7,500
(D) $3,750

72. A $20,000 loan is being paid off at a monthly rate of $7.50 per $1,000. Taxes are $54 per year, and the three-year insurance has a $360 premium. What was the first month's payment?
(A) $161.50
(B) $167.10
(C) $164.50
(D) $263.20

73. How many square feet are in a lot whose scale dimensions on a blueprint are 13 1/2" by 17 3/4" (scale: 1/8" = 1')?
(A) 15,336
(B) 13,536
(C) 1,534
(D) 1,354

74. A leasehold interest:
(A) lasts forever.
(B) may be created out of a fee simple interest.
(C) lasts for a lifetime.
(D) is the same as tenancy for years.

75. A fiduciary relationship is established by a(n):
(A) option.
(B) mortgage.
(C) deed.
(D) power of attorney.

76. A legal instrument that creates a lien against personal property is called a(n):
(A) security agreement.
(B) estoppel certificate.
(C) bill of sale.
(D) note.

77. A term used to describe the status of a "holdover tenant" is a(n):
    (A) tenancy at sufferance.
    (B) tenancy at will.
    (C) periodic tenancy.
    (D) estate for years.

78. Title vested in one person is said to be in:
    (A) common.
    (B) severalty.
    (C) singularity.
    (D) unity.

79. All of these are examples of involuntary alienation EXCEPT:
    (A) eminent domain.
    (B) adverse possession.
    (C) devise.
    (D) escheat.

80. A bag of fertilizer contains 210 lbs. of nitrates and 90 lbs. of moss. What percentage of the mix is nitrates?
    (A) 70%
    (B) 30%
    (C) 20%
    (D) 40%

PART II– NEW JERSEY STATE LAWS

81. John Lesser owns a two-family house in Bayonne, New Jersey. He occupies one of the apartments and has a conventional mortgage. If he discriminates against a prospective tenant on account of race, it would be:
    (A) a violation of the Federal Fair Housing Law.
    (B) lawful because he is exempt from the law.
    (C) unlawful.
    (D) a violation of the New Jersey Law Against Discrimination.

82. A broker could properly advertise:
    (A) "free TV if you buy a house through our office."
    (B) free market study.
    (C) free appraisal.
    (D) free cooking gas and electricity.

83. A New Jersey broker had been practicing for five years with a clean record, but then was charged with three violations of the license laws and brought before the Real Estate Commission. He would be subject to a maximum fine of:
    (A) $1,000
    (B) $25,000
    (C) nothing; the REC cannot enforce money penalties without court action.
    (D) $500

84. The Real Estate Commission is funded by:
    (A) federal and state grants.
    (B) license fees.
    (C) the general treasury.
    (D) examination fees.

85. Regarding the Real Estate Sales Full Disclosure Act, which of the following is NOT correct?
    (A) A subdivision of 90 lots is usually exempt from the Act.
    (B) Photographs of the subject property need not be submitted.
    (C) The fee for an initial registration shall not exceed $1,000.
    (D) The rescission period is 7 calendar days.

86. By statutory definition, which of the following activities, if done for compensation, does NOT constitute real estate brokerage?
    (A) Soliciting for prospective buyers.
    (B) Making a real estate appraisal.
    (C) Auctioning real estate.
    (D) Trading or exchanging real estate.

87. Under the New Jersey Law Against Discrimination:
    (A) complaints must be filed within 60 days of the alleged discrimination.
    (B) licensees are required to provide owners with a copy of the Attorney General's memorandum on the law against discrimination.
    (C) discrimination because of age is unlawful.
    (D) discrimination on account of marital status is prohibited.

88. A real estate salesperson:
    (A) can never be in charge of a branch office.
    (B) cannot recover from the Guaranty Fund if his broker fails to pay him.
    (C) cannot sue a client for compensation.
    (D) All of the above statements are true.

89. A promissory note as an earnest money deposit with an offer to purchase is acceptable with the written authorization of:
(A) the broker.
(B) the vendee (buyer).
(C) the vendor (seller).
(D) the buyer's attorney.

90. If a licensee is found guilty of a third violation of the license law, the Commission may:
(A) impose a 90-day jail sentence.
(B) direct that no real estate license ever again be issued to that person.
(C) impose a $30,000 fine for the third violation.
(D) hold the licensee in contempt of court.

91. The Real Estate Commission settles commission disputes between:
(A) brokers and salespersons.
(B) brokers and their clients.
(C) Both A and B.
(D) Neither A nor B.

92. The person who files a complaint under the Federal Fair Housing Act is:
(A) the respondent.
(B) the complainant.
(C) HUD.
(D) the Attorney General.

93. All places of business maintained by a real estate broker must:
(A) be open to the public during usual business hours.
(B) be independent of living quarters if said office is less than 14 years old.
(C) state "Licensed Real Estate Broker" on the exterior.
(D) All of the above.

94. In New Jersey there is a right of redemption in connection with:
(A) mortgage foreclosure.
(B) tax sale.
(C) executed judgment.
(D) conveyance by deed.

95. Functional obsolescence would least likely include:
(A) poor architecture.
(B) poor design.
(C) an outdated kitchen.
(D) rotting wood.

96. In estimating the value of a church, the appraiser would use:
(A) the market data approach.
(B) the cost approach.
(C) the capitalization approach.
(D) the "before and after" approach.

97. The most important factor influencing value is:
(A) floor plan.
(B) age.
(C) location.
(D) tax basis.

98. All of the following are types of depreciation except:
(A) straight-line.
(B) sum-of-the-years digits.
(C) cost reproduction.
(D) double-declining balance.

99. With regard to the senior citizen tax reduction, which of the following is NOT true?
(A) The senior citizen must occupy the property to qualify.
(B) The senior citizen is not eligible if his or her income exceeds $10,000 per year.
(C) application for same is made at the local level.
(D) the reduction is allowed on any New Jersey real estate owned by the senior citizen.

100. A one-year temporary broker's license may be issued:
(A) in the event of the death of a broker.
(B) if a broker's license is suspended.
(C) to the widow of a broker who has held a salesperson's license for one year.
(D) in the event a broker's license is revoked.

101. The primary purpose of the license laws is to:
(A) protect the public in real estate transactions.
(B) increase revenues to the state.
(C) limit the number of licensees.
(D) protect brokers and salespersons.

102. Sally, a licensed salesperson, resigned from the ABC Agency. Her broker must give her an accounting of earned, but unpaid commissions within what period of time?
(A) ten days.
(B) 30 days.
(C) Immediately upon termination of employment.
(D) The broker does not have to account because Sally is not entitled to compensation after she leaves his employment.

103. Ben Broker had a lease signed by a landlord and tenant. He must provide all parties with copies of the lease within what period of time?
(A) Immediately.
(B) Ten days.
(C) 30 days.
(D) Five business days.

104. A New York broker wishes to obtain a nonresident broker's license in New Jersey. He must:
    (A) file a surety bond with the Commission.
    (B) pass the New Jersey broker's exam, make application and pay the fee.
    (C) file an "irrevocable consent" form with the New Jersey Real Estate Commission.
    (D) receive a waiver from the New York REC.

105. All members of the New Jersey Real Estate Commission are:
    (A) appointed by the secretary-director of the Real Estate Commission.
    (B) appointed by the governor.
    (C) required to be brokers for 10 years.
    (D) responsible for promulgating real estate laws.

106. FHA mortgage insurance is paid by the:
    (A) seller.
    (B) borrower.
    (C) lender.
    (D) broker.

107. A real estate broker can legally prepare:
    (A) a deed.
    (B) an abstract of title.
    (C) a purchase and sale agreement.
    (D) None of the above.

108. Title to real property may be conveyed:
    (A) to a minor.
    (B) by a minor.
    (C) by bill of sale.
    (D) by demise.

109. For services performed in connection with a real estate transaction, the New Jersey broker who handled the transaction may give part of his or her commission to which of the following?
    (A) A New Jersey attorney.
    (B) The seller.
    (C) A salesperson employed by another broker.
    (D) A licensed broker of another state for the referral.

110. To be licensed as a broker in New Jersey you must:
    (A) be a resident of New Jersey.
    (B) be a citizen of the United States.
    (C) be of legal age.
    (D) All of the above.

about the BROKER'S PRACTICE FINAL

The practice test on the following pages is patterned after the actual test. The best way to prepare for the state exam is to work with questions similar to those which appear on the actual test. The actual test and this practice test have the same types of questions, time limit and level of difficulty. This practice test is not a copy of the actual test. The actual test is copyrighted and may not be duplicated. The primary purpose of your taking the practice test is to help you realize your weak areas so you can concentrate your studies on those areas.

General Information

1. Specific information about the actual test may be found in the Candidate Guide provided by your license preparation school.

2. Be sure to keep track of questions of which you are uncertain. When you complete answering all the ones of which you're certain, go back and try again on the uncertain ones. Do **not** leave any blank answers.

	Questions	**Minimum Number Needed to Pass**	**Candidate's Score Number Right**
PART I–GENERAL TEST	**80**	**56**	________
PART II–STATE TEST	**40**	**28**	________

3. Do not answer any questions until you have read them through carefully.

4. The General Test contains 80 scored questions and 12 pretest questions.

5. Ten percent (8) of the scored questions on the General Test will involve mathematical computations.

6. The allotted time for the broker's exam is three and one-half hours. Applicants are not permitted to continue the test beyond the established time limit.

EXPro Electronic Testing System

The New Jersey State examination will be administered by Promissor (ASI) on an electronic testing system called EXPro. This system eliminates the use of paper and pencil answer sheets and enables the testing service to give you the results of your exam. as soon as you complete it. Questions and answers are presented on a touch sensitive screen A computer memory card records your responses and automatically times the exam.

EXPro allows you to change your answers, skip questions, and mark questions for review. **Knowledge of computers and typing is absolutely NOT required.**

• Broker's Practice Final
(Answers on page 573)

PART I– GENERAL TEST

1. The Federal Fair Housing Law does NOT apply to:
   (A) rooms or units in a six-family dwelling where the owner actually resides in one of the units.
   (B) denying a person access to a multiple listing service on account of race.
   (C) religious organizations.
   (D) private clubs operated for profit.

2. When computing an annual percentage rate for disclosure purposes under the Truth-in-Lending Law, you would include as finance charges the:
   (A) service charge for making the loan.
   (B) survey fee.
   (C) attorney's fee.
   (D) hazard insurance premium.

3. When a loan is approved by the FHA:
   (A) the appraised value must not be less than the sale price.
   (B) the government guarantees the value of the property.
   (C) the borrower must be an owner-occupant.
   (D) the FHA charges an insurance premium.

4. The Veterans Administration:
   (A) regularly makes direct loans up to certain amounts.
   (B) does not apply to women.
   (C) will only guarantee loans for borrowers who intend to occupy the property.
   (D) will not allow a non-veteran to assume the loan.

5. Under the Federal Fair Housing Law, it is an unlawful act of discrimination:
   (A) for members of one religion to refuse to rent rooms in one of its retirement homes to a person of a different religion, where membership in the religion owning the retirement home is restricted on account of race, color or national origin.
   (B) where the discrimination is based on marital status.
   (C) where the discrimination is based on age.
   (D) if the transaction involves vacant land.

6. When a purchaser signs an offer allowing the seller three days in which to accept the offer:
   (A) the purchaser may not withdraw before the expiration of the three days.
   (B) the purchaser may withdraw the offer at any time prior to seller's acceptance.
   (C) the Statute of Limitations applies.
   (D) acceptance will not terminate the offer.

7. A professional appraiser can render ALL BUT ONE of the following:
   (A) An opinion of value.
   (B) A conclusion of value.
   (C) A judgment of value.
   (D) A determination of value.

8. The formula used in direct capitalization of income property valuation is:
   (A) value equals cap rate divided by income.
   (B) value equals income divided by cap rate.
   (C) value equals income multiplied by cap rate.
   (D) value equals income divided by net assets.

9. The economic life of a building has come to an end when:
   (A) the building ceases to represent the highest and best use of the land.
   (B) the value of the rent for the land and the building equals the value of the land only.
   (C) the rent produced is valued at less than a similar amount of money invested elsewhere could produce.
   (D) the reserve for depreciation equals the cost to replace the building.

10. A mortgage which allows for advances to a mortgagor up to a certain maximum is a:
    (A) package mortgage.
    (B) open-end mortgage.
    (C) purchase money mortgage.
    (D) wrap-around mortgage.

11. Constructive notice of a fact is established by:
    (A) entering it on the public record.
    (B) acting openly in accordance with the fact.
    (C) direct communication of the fact to each interested party.
    (D) testifying to the existence of the fact under oath in open court.

12. Equity in a property is:
    (A) the value over and above the mortgage.
    (B) during the period of ownership, the cash payment made at time of acquisition.
    (C) the interest a buyer acquires when he signs a contract to purchase real estate.
    (D) the difference between the price paid for a property and the price at which it is sold.

13. Highest and best use is concerned with all of the following except:
    (A) new yield to owner.
    (B) utility of surrounding area.
    (C) relationship to regional development.
    (D) interest rate on investment loans.

14. Title passes:
    (A) on closing.
    (B) on recordation.
    (C) on signing.
    (D) on delivery.

15. What goes with a mortgage?
    (A) Deed.
    (B) Trust deed.
    (C) Lease.
    (D) Promissory note or bond.

16. An example of constructive eviction is:
    (A) tenant is evicted to construct a new building which lessor will not occupy.
    (B) tenant vacates because landlord has allowed premises to deteriorate and become untenantable.
    (C) landlord has followed due process to evict.
    (D) when landlord serves tenant with "notice to quit."

17. Which of the following liens takes precedence over all the others?
    (A) Judgment against seller.
    (B) Judgment against buyer.
    (C) Delinquent real property tax.
    (D) First mortgage or first deed of trust.

18. A coal furnace in a single-family house is an example of:
    (A) external obsolescence.
    (B) functional obsolescence.
    (C) economic obsolescence.
    (D) physical deterioration.

19. If there is a break in the chain of title, the best approach is:
    (A) get a new warranty deed.
    (B) start a suit to quiet title.
    (C) get a new abstract of title.
    (D) get a letter of explanation from the grantor.

20. Which of the following terms pertain to the process of estimating the value of property?
    (A) Capitalization.
    (B) Equalization.
    (C) Deficiency.
    (D) Alienation.

21. On a first mortgage to purchase an existing home, the lender must show which of the following?
    (A) The annual percentage rate.
    (B) The total of all interest payments and finance charges.
    (C) Rescission period.
    (D) All of the above.

22. The holder of a life estate may do all but one of the following:
    (A) Mortgage.
    (B) Make improvements.
    (C) Waste.
    (D) Make alterations.

23. Eminent domain is the right which enables:
    (A) an institution to condemn property for use for the public.
    (B) the state to escheat.
    (C) the government to allow condemnation of private property for public use with just compensation.
    (D) the fire department to destroy your house to prevent the spread of fire.

24. When a husband and wife desire to buy real property in both their names for cash and the husband is not available to sign the purchase contract:
    (A) the purchase contract is voidable if only the wife signs.
    (B) both husband and wife must sign the contract.
    (C) the agreement is valid if only the wife signs.
    (D) the seller may sue both spouses in the event of default.

25. It is an unethical practice for a broker representing the seller to:
    (A) advise the seller of the highest price he believes a prospective purchaser is willing to pay.
    (B) advise a prospective purchaser of the lowest price the seller is willing to accept.
    (C) Both A and B.
    (D) Neither A nor B.

26. To be valid a deed need NOT:
    (A) name buyer and seller.
    (B) have words of conveyance.
    (C) be acknowledged and recorded.
    (D) be delivered and accepted.

27. The "before and after" method is used in:
    (A) condemnation.
    (B) replacement cost approach.
    (C) plastic surgery.
    (D) rehabilitation.

28. Gable wants to sell his property without the aid of a real estate broker. He may legally do all but one of the following:
    (A) establish the purchasing power of the buyer.
    (B) write up the sale contract between himself and the buyer.
    (C) require that the buyer assume the present mortgage.
    (D) post a notice that he prefers a buyer of a certain religion.

29. A riparian owner is one who owns land bounding on:
    (A) a municipal property.
    (B) a waterway.
    (C) a national forest.
    (D) unsurveyed public lands.

30. Under the Federal Fair Housing Law it is permissible to:
    (A) approve a loan to a person who intends to rent the property only to members of a minority group.
    (B) refuse to grant loans on the basis of the financial condition of an applicant who is a member of a minority group.
    (C) reject an applicant for MLS because of religion.
    (D) reject a prospective tenant for a unit in a four-family house on Maple Avenue if the owner lives on Elm Avenue.

31. All but one of the following are examples of valuable consideration. Name the exception.
    (A) Any movable object with cash value.
    (B) Extension of time.
    (C) Mutual promises of performance.
    (D) Love and affection.

32. An individual, partnership or corporation to whom title is conditionally conveyed as security is a:
    (A) trustor.
    (B) beneficiary.
    (C) mortgagee.
    (D) offeree.

33. The purchase and putting together of several pieces of land which results in making the property more valuable is:
    (A) annexation.
    (B) appreciation.
    (C) assemblage.
    (D) integration.

34. Physical deterioration most closely means:
    (A) obsolescence.
    (B) wear and tear.
    (C) repair.
    (D) recapture.

35. The right of a water company to lay and maintain water mains along the rear of a lot is called:
    (A) an appurtenance.
    (B) riparian right.
    (C) easement in gross.
    (D) a right of encroachment.

36. When something of value is held by a disinterested third party to be delivered upon the fulfillment of some condition, it is called:
    (A) a deed of trust.
    (B) a promissory note.
    (C) a dedication.
    (D) an escrow.

37. A shopping center operator rents a store to a boutique on a percentage lease. The percentage is usually based on:
    (A) market value.
    (B) tenant's gross sales.
    (C) tenant's net income.
    (D) assessed valuation.

38. A foreign language instrument:
    (A) is unlawful.
    (B) can be recorded with an English translation attached.
    (C) cannot be recorded.
    (D) is void.

39. All but one of the following is a method of depreciation for tax purposes:
    (A) Sum-of-the-years digits.
    (B) Straight-line.
    (C) Double-declining balance.
    (D) Cost appreciation.

40. One who is NOT incompetent to contract is one who:
    (A) is adjudicated insane.
    (B) is a minor incapable of acting for himself.
    (C) is a drunkard.
    (D) is illiterate.

41. How would a purchase money second mortgage given by the purchaser to the seller appear on the settlement statement upon closing the real estate sale?
    (A) Credit to purchaser and debit to seller.
    (B) Debit to purchaser and credit to seller.
    (C) Only debit to purchaser.
    (D) Only credit to seller.

42. If the reproduction cost shows a higher value than the appraised value, which of the following most probably has occurred?
    (A) Accrued depreciation.
    (B) Excessive appraisal.
    (C) Economic obsolescence.
    (D) Capitalization.

43. Which of the following would not be considered in the cost approach to value?
    (A) Reproduction cost.
    (B) Depreciation.
    (C) Land value.
    (D) Operating expenses.

44. A property manager should recognize that an increase in mortgage rates usually is accompanied by an increase in:
    (A) vacancy rates.
    (B) demand for apartments.
    (C) house sales.
    (D) money supply.

45. When a paved driveway for one house trespasses on the adjoining property:
    (A) an easement is created.
    (B) it is an encroachment.
    (C) a lien is created.
    (D) the owner who did the paving is the encroachee.

46. An optionee can:
    (A) mortgage the property.
    (B) assign the option to another person if the option agreement is silent on the matter.
    (C) occupy the property.
    (D) collect rents.

47. Which of the following would NOT be a way in which coverage can be added to a regular fire insurance policy?
    (A) An endorsement.
    (B) An addendum.
    (C) An assignment.
    (D) A rider.

48. All property which is not considered to be real estate is called:
    (A) littoral property.
    (B) personal property.
    (C) emblement property.
    (D) realty.

49. Which of the following is a non-freehold estate?
    (A) A fee simple estate.
    (B) An estate for years.
    (C) A life estate.
    (D) A statutory estate.

50. An adverse influence on title to real property is called:
    (A) an appurtenance.
    (B) a plot.
    (C) an encumbrance.
    (D) progression.

51. An easement acquired by constant, open and adverse use is called an easement by:
    (A) subscription.
    (B) adverse possession.
    (C) prescription.
    (D) necessity.

52. Prior to the death of the spouse, dower and curtesy rights are:
    (A) consummate.
    (B) vested.
    (C) inchoate.
    (D) assigned.

53. Which of the following is out of place?
    (A) Easement.
    (B) Land.
    (C) Building.
    (D) Trees and shrubs.

54. Property is owned in severalty when:
    (A) three or more persons have concurrent interests.
    (B) the deed is in one name.
    (C) husband and wife jointly own the property.
    (D) the interests of the joint owners can be severed.

55. Which of the following could NOT take title as a joint tenant?
    (A) An alien.
    (B) A corporation.
    (C) A married person.
    (D) An unmarried person.

56. John and Mary owned as tenants by the entirety. Upon divorce, in lieu of any other agreement:
    (A) they remain tenants by the entirety.
    (B) the divorce converts their method of ownership to a tenancy in common.
    (C) their method of ownership is not affected.
    (D) the ex-wife owns in severalty.

57. Arnold and Bill, each of whom are married, purchased a property as joint tenants in 1983. If Arnold pre-deceases Bill:
    (A) Arnold's heirs will inherit the property.
    (B) Bill will own the property in severalty.
    (C) Bill will acquire the property subject to the dower interest of Arnold's wife.
    (D) Bill will hold title in severalty and his (Bill's) spouse now has an inchoate dower interest.

58. When the high-water mark permanently recedes, exposing dry land, it is called:
(A) reliction.
(B) addiction.
(C) alluvion.
(D) avulsion.

59. A brief history of title to a specific parcel of land is called:
(A) affidavit of title.
(B) chain of title.
(C) abstract of title.
(D) report of title.

60. A court action to compel the party in default to carry out the terms of a real estate purchase and sale agreement is called:
(A) an "In Rem" suit.
(B) a liquidated damages suit.
(C) a lis pendens suit.
(D) a specific performance suit.

61. A buyer defaults under the terms of a contract to buy real estate. The seller may:
(A) sue for specific performance.
(B) rescind.
(C) sue for damages.
(D) Any of the above.

62. A farmer has 50 acres of apple orchards netting him $13,120 a year. What cost per acre must he sell the orchard for in order to net the same amount if invested at 8.2% annually?
(A) $2,152
(B) $1,076
(C) $16,000
(D) $3,200

63. The party who pledges property under a mortgage in a mortgage loan transaction is the:
(A) mortgagee.
(B) mortgagor.
(C) obligee.
(D) vendor.

64. The buyer under a contract for the sale of real estate is the:
(A) vendee.
(B) offeree.
(C) mortgagee.
(D) grantor.

65. A house depreciated at 2 1/2% per year for the past five years and the lot has increased from $5,000 to $8,000 during the same period. If the original combined value of house and lot was $42,000, what is the current value of the house?
(A) $24,375
(B) $32,375
(C) $40,375
(D) $36,750

66. The process by which property is pledged as security for a debt with the borrower retaining possession of the pledged property is called:
(A) amortization.
(B) distress.
(C) alienation.
(D) hypothecation.

67. A form of land description that describes land on the basis of its location on a recorded map is called:
(A) lot and block description.
(B) metes and bounds description.
(C) street address description.
(D) description by monuments.

68. The government's right to take private lands for public purposes is called:
(A) condemnation.
(B) confiscation.
(C) escheat.
(D) eminent domain.

69. An office building requires an excavation 10 ft. deep, 90 ft. wide and 110 ft. long. The cost will be $24 per cubic yard. How much will the excavation cost?
(A) $56,000
(B) $88,000
(C) $90,000
(D) $48,000

70. Exercises of police power include all of the following EXCEPT:
(A) building codes.
(B) planning.
(C) liens.
(D) rent control.

71. A man paid $100,000 for 27 lots, each with a frontage of 100 feet. He decides to keep two of the lots for himself. If he has expenses of $5,000, $5,000 and $10,000 and he wants to realize a 50% profit of his total investment, how much must he sell each lot for?
(A) $7,200
(B) $5,200
(C) $6,000
(D) $6,800

72. A store was leased with the agreement that rental will be $300 per month plus 4 1/2% of the gross annual income over $200,000. If the total rent was $4,725 for the year, what was the gross amount of business for the year?
(A) $225,000
(B) $25,000
(C) $280,000
(D) $80,000

73. A property is bought for $11,200 by four persons. Two owners each hold 1/7 of the property and the third owner holds 1/14 of the property. What amount of money did the fourth owner contribute to buy the property?
(A) $8,800
(B) $8,000
(C) $7,200
(D) $6,200

74. A developer wants to divide five acres into 60' x 125' lots. If the town requires 300 ft. of roads, 40 ft. wide, how many full lots will the developer be able to obtain?
(A) 27
(B) 28
(C) 32
(D) 274

75. A two-story colonial-style home has four bedrooms, two of which are very small. This would serve to reduce the property's value and would be an example of:
(A) external obsolescence.
(B) functional obsolescence.
(C) physical deterioration.
(D) diminishment.

76. A house sells for $9,900. If that price is 10% over what the seller paid last year, and he paid $175 in taxes and paid off the 4% interest on the original cost of the house, how much did he net?
(A) $5,585
(B) $365
(C) $449.60
(D) $419

77. The Real Estate Sales Full Disclosure Act applies to covered out-of-state land sales for all of the following circumstances EXCEPT:
(A) cooperatives.
(B) single, isolated transactions.
(C) time shares.
(D) condominiums.

78. A home is assessed at 80% of the appraised value. If the appraised value is 90% of the selling price, what are the annual taxes if the selling price was $230,000 and the tax rate is $2.75 per $100?
(A) $6,125
(B) $5,126
(C) $4,125
(D) $4,554

79. Which of the following processes would be used in estimating value by the income approach?
(A) Subordination.
(B) Amortization.
(C) Capitalization.
(D) Equalization.

80. Which of the following is not an involuntary alienation of property?
(A) Eminent domain.
(B) Escheat.
(C) Mortgage foreclosure.
(D) Dedication.

PART II— NEW JERSEY STATE LAWS

81. A broker agreed to pay a bonus to all associates who sold five houses in any calendar month. Al Dente sold five houses the following month and received the bonus. This is an example of:
(A) a voidable contract.
(B) an option.
(C) a unilateral contract.
(D) a bilateral contract.

82. Mr. Gross, a tenant, occupies under an estate for years. Therefore:
(A) his lease must be written in New Jersey if the term exceeds one year.
(B) his lease must state the name of the insured depository in which the security money is deposited.
(C) the term of the lease must be for at least one year.
(D) no notice is required to terminate the lease.

83. The clause in a mortgage that allows the mortgagee to demand the full amount of the debt in the event of default is called a(n):
(A) alienation clause.
(B) acceleration clause.
(C) "due on sale" clause.
(D) escalation clause.

84. When you sign a contract to purchase real estate you have:
    (A) an insurable interest.
    (B) an equitable interest.
    (C) an assignable interest.
    (D) All of the above.

85. When taxes on your property are delinquent:
    (A) the state can sell the property after the expiration of three years.
    (B) you have one year to redeem after the tax sale.
    (C) the unpaid taxes constitute a "first lien."
    (D) the property cannot be sold.

86. It is permissible under state law for the owner of a duplex to discriminate in the rental of one unit where:
    (A) the owner-lessor resides in the other unit.
    (B) the owner has a VA loan.
    (C) the owner has an FHA loan.
    (D) an employee of the owner-lessor resides in the other unit.

87. The New Jersey Law Against Discrimination is regulated by:
    (A) HUD.
    (B) New Jersey Division of Civil Rights.
    (C) New Jersey Department of Regulatory Agencies.
    (D) New Jersey Fair Housing Council.

88. The New Jersey Law Against Discrimination prohibits discrimination on account of:
    (A) age.
    (B) children.
    (C) color.
    (D) All of the above.

89. A racially discriminatory provision in a deed:
    (A) is void.
    (B) voids the deed.
    (C) is voidable.
    (D) is enforceable if the restriction pre-dates the 1968 Federal Fair Housing Law.

90. A real estate license is required for:
    (A) sale of a farm, including farm equipment, by father to son.
    (B) receiver in bankruptcy.
    (C) executor to convey title to estate property.
    (D) one who solicits listings.

91. An associate broker is defined as:
    (A) a self-employed broker.
    (B) a member of a trade association.
    (C) a licensed broker who works for a principal broker.
    (D) a partnership of a principal broker.

92. Real estate license laws are an example of:
    (A) police powers of the state.
    (B) restraint of trade.
    (C) federal restriction on free enterprise.
    (D) eminent domain.

93. Ernest and Julio owned a piece of property jointly, but the deed was silent as to the method of ownership. Ernest died leaving a will. The court will presume:
    (A) joint tenancy.
    (B) tenancy in common.
    (C) tenancy by the entirety.
    (D) tenancy by will.

94. A square mile contains 640 acres. Consequently, a square half-mile would contain:
    (A) 160 acres.
    (B) 320 acres.
    (C) 80 acres.
    (D) 240 acres.

95. Which of the following is not essential for a valid lease?
    (A) Term of lease.
    (B) Amount of rental payments.
    (C) Description of property.
    (D) Statement that rental payments be made in advance.

96. A primary source of funds for residential mortgage financing is:
    (A) Federal Home Loan Bank.
    (B) Federal Savings and Loan Corporation.
    (C) Federal Savings and Loan Association.
    (D) Federal Housing Administration.

97. When a lender advances funds for a loan, the discount points that are usually charged are equivalent to:
    (A) taxes.
    (B) prepaid interest.
    (C) discounts to the buyers.
    (D) prepayment penalties.

98. Under what type of employer other than a licensed broker may a salesperson be licensed?
    (A) Attorney.
    (B) Associate broker.
    (C) Property owner.
    (D) None of the above.

99. What type of competence of knowledge is NOT tested on the license examination?
    (A) Understanding of license laws.
    (B) Ability to sell real estate.
    (C) Nature of deeds, abstracts, contracts and mortgages.
    (D) Land description and other details of the law.

100. After an applicant has passed the license examination, he is so notified. The applicant has how long to apply for a license?
(A) One year from completion of the course.
(B) One year from the date of the examination.
(C) 30 days.
(D) No time limit.

101. One "mill" equals:
(A) one-tenth of a dollar.
(B) one-hundredth of a dollar.
(C) one-tenth of a cent.
(D) one-hundredth of a cent.

102. A property owner whose taxes are in default is subject to tax sale after:
(A) one year.
(B) two years.
(C) six months.
(D) 30 days.

103. A broker cannot execute a contract on behalf of his principal unless:
(A) the broker is a lawyer.
(B) he has been granted power of attorney.
(C) he cannot locate the principal.
(D) None of the above.

104. If a broker collects a fee from more than one party in a transaction:
(A) he forfeits his commission.
(B) he is subject to suspension.
(C) he must make full disclosure to both parties.
(D) he is guilty of commingling fees.

105. On a closing statement the realty transfer fee is customarily charged to:
(A) the seller.
(B) the closing attorney.
(C) the buyer.
(D) the title insurance company.

106. In the secondary mortgage market:
(A) second mortgages are made to risky borrowers.
(B) second mortgages are sold to banks and savings and loans.
(C) first mortgages are bought and sold.
(D) first mortgages are bought but cannot be sold.

107. The problem with a description of land by monuments is:
(A) monuments may be moved.
(B) description is imprecise.
(C) references may be destroyed.
(D) A, B and C.

108. Which of the following is NOT TRUE regarding quitclaim deeds?
(A) The grantor cannot convey fee simple title.
(B) It is usually used to clear a cloud from the title.
(C) The grantor transfers and releases all title, rights and interest in the property that he had previously or now has.
(D) The grantee's title cannot be defeated by unrecorded titles which may be later brought to light.

109. Amos, Bob and Debbie own a tract of land as joint tenants. Debbie sells her interest to Juan. Amos and Bob own the land with Juan as:
(A) joint tenants.
(B) tenants in common.
(C) tenants by the entireties.
(D) tenants at sufferance.

110. The Real Estate Commission is a division of:
(A) Department of Banking and Insurance.
(B) Department of Banking.
(C) Department of Community Affairs.
(D) Department of Professional Regulatory Agencies.

111. Which of the following events will result in automatic revocation of a real estate license?
(A) Payment out of the Guaranty Fund.
(B) Fraud.
(C) Commingling.
(D) Embezzlement.

112. A broker receiving an advance fee of more than $25.00 must account to the client for expenditures within:
(A) 30 days.
(B) 60 days.
(C) 90 days.
(D) six months.

113. With regard to the statement outlining the 7-day rescission (cooling off) period provided for in the Real Estate Sales Full Disclosure Act, which of the following statements is true?
(A) The rescission period runs for 7 business days.
(B) The statement must be printed in English and Spanish.
(C) The statement must be printed in English only.
(D) Some contracts must be printed in English, others in Spanish.

114. If a real estate broker submitted a customer's offer to a seller and the seller rejected it, which of the following statements is true?
   (A) The broker must keep a record of the transaction for six months.
   (B) Brokers are not required to keep records of unaccepted offers.
   (C) The broker must keep a record of the transaction for six years.
   (D) None of the above statements is true.

115. If a house has a market value of $72,750, and the contract rent for the house is $712.50, the gross rent multiplier is:
   (A) 108.
   (B) 106.
   (C) 104.
   (D) 102.

116. Which of the following is NOT a radon remediation technique?
   (A) Natural ventilation.
   (B) Forced ventilation.
   (C) Disintermediation.
   (D) Sub-slab ventilation.

117. A New Jersey real estate licensee can legally prepare (fill in the blank spaces) on a form contract for which of the following transactions?
   (A) A five-family house.
   (B) A lease for an office building containing less than 10,000 square feet.
   (C) A subdivision containing eight lots.
   (D) A four-family, non-owner-occupied house.

118. In lieu of any agreement to the contrary, a real estate broker must pay a salesperson within:
   (A) ten days after the broker is paid.
   (B) ten days after closing.
   (C) ten days after the broker deposits the commission check.
   (D) ten days after the check clears.

119. Which of the following is NOT TRUE regarding broker-salespersons?
   (A) They have passed the broker's examination.
   (B) They are working under the supervision of a principal broker.
   (C) They could be a principal broker if they chose to be.
   (D) They have fewer license law restraints than salespersons.

120. In New Jersey, it is permissible for a licensee to:
   (A) earn interest on trust accounts.
   (B) use the trust account for the broker's benefit.
   (C) work for more than one broker at the same time.
   (D) work out of two offices at the same time.

Answers To Quiz Questions

CHAPTER 3
New Jersey License Laws

1. **C** A, B, and D are false statements.
2. **A** As long as the licensee does not misrepresent or defraud, he is free to exercise his talents of persuasion.
3. **B** 45:15-14
4. **D** 45:15-17
5. **C** 11:5-5.5
6. **C** 11:5-6.4
7. **D** The contracts remain in force.
8. **C** 11:5-4.4(c)
9. **B** 45:15-17
10. **C** The other practices are restricted to attorneys.
11. **A** 11:5-4.1(a)2
12. **B** This came about as a result of a REC rule.
13. **A** The REC may demand an accounting but will not settle contractual disputes between licensees.
14. **B** Meaning all real estate licenses expire at midnight of June 30, once every two years.
15. **A** 45:15-12
16. **A** 45:15-17(m)
17. **A** 11:5-1.18(a)
18. **B** 11:5-1.15(b)
19. **C** 11:5-6.1(h)
20. **B** 45:15-11.3
21. **B** See "memorandum" page 352, first paragraph.
22. **C** 45:15-17(j)
23. **D** 11:5-6.1(b) An ad which does not clearly indicate that the advertising licensee is engaged in the real estate brokerage business is referred to as a "blind ad" and is improper conduct.
24. **B** See Chapter 2.
25. **D** 45:15-3
26. **C** 11:5-4.2(a)1
27. **D** 45:15-17(m)
28. **D** Preparation of the sales contract would constitute the illegal practice of law, because the broker was not acting as the broker in this transaction.
29. **D** 45:15-12.1
30. **A** Citizenship and residency are not requirements for licensing.
31. **D** 11:5-1.15(m;2)
32. **D** 45:15-12.5
33. **D** Broker must provide pocket card.
34. **A** See p. 19, "Guaranty Fund."
35. **D** The legislature sets the license fees and promulgates laws. The testing service sets the exam fees.
36. **C** 45:15-17(m)
37. **C** 11:5-6.4(g)
38. **C** 11:5-1.23(e)
39. **D** 45:15-3. In practice, most broker's secretaries are licensed so they can perform the other tasks.
40. **B** 11:5-6.1(b)
41. **C** 11:5-5.4
42. **D** 11:5-6.4(g)
43. **D** 11:5-6.5
44. **C** 45:15-16.27, 2(5)
45. **B** 11:5-6.4(c)
46. **D** 11:5-6.4(f)
47. **D** 45:15-16.27, 20(b)
48. **A** 11:5-6.2(a)4
49. **D** See p. 19, "Guaranty Fund."
50. **A** 11:5-5.4(d)

CHAPTER 4
Land, Land Elements and Water

1. **C** The term Realtor® is a registered word which may only be used by members of the state and local boards affiliated with the National Association of Realtors.
2. **C** Emblements are crops and thus personal property.
3. **C** These rights are received in addition to the physical property.
4. **B** Riparian rights are water rights.
5. **B** Personal property is usually movable.
6. **B** Rights of possession, use, enjoyment and disposition.
7. **D** Avulsion is sudden tearing away of land.
8. **A** The buyer receives sub-surface rights unless specifically reserved by seller.
9. **A** When avulsion occurs, the property line does not change.
10. **A** Perennial plantings are realty.
11. **C** Government at all levels places limitations on the use of property.
12. **C** Avulsion is sudden; alluvion gradual.
13. **A** Reliction is the opposite of submergence.
14. **A** Air rights may be sold, leased or retained.

Chapter 5
Personal Property and Fixtures

1. **A** B, C, and D are realty.
2. **A** A chattel mortgage (now called a security agreement) is used to finance the purchase of personal property.
3. **C** A, B and D are real property.
4. **C** Personalty is movable.
5. **C** Appurtenances include only real property.
6. **A** Bill of Sale conveys title to personal property.
7. **D** A trade fixture (barber chair, hair washing sinks, etc.) is personalty.
8. **D** Method of annexation is important, but not key. Main test is "intention."
9. **C** All property that is not real property is personal property and vice versa.

10. **B** The mortgage pledges the realty as security for the debt, but the mortgage itself is personal property.
11. **B** For example, a tree, when cut down.
12. **B** See explanation to #9.
13. **B** A, C and D are real property.
14. **B** A refrigerator is personalty, a fixture is realty.

Chapter 6
Estates and Interests in Real Property

1. **C** Such as fee simple absolute as opposed to a conditional fee.
2. **C** Not a fixed term but measured by the life of a person or persons.
3. **C** Devise is to transfer by will.
4. **D** Widow has a life estate; children, a remainder,
5. **C** A, B and D are false statements.
6. **C** A remainder is a future interest that passes to a third party at the end of a life estate.
7. **C** An estate defines the nature, degree, extent and duration of a person's ownership in land.
8. **B** A remainder vests with a third party upon termination of a prior interest.
9. **B** Inasmuch as it will be "defeated" if he does not marry.
10. **C** Gilligan has no right to object to the sale.
11. **C** In this situation, the life estate passes to heirs of grantee until death of the measuring life.
12. **A** With remainder, upon death of grantee, property goes to designated third party.
13. **D** With reversion, upon death of grantee, property returns to grantor.
14. **D** The type of estate is not affected.
15. **B** A life estate can be created by law, i.e., dower, curtesy.
16. **B** A, C and D are false statements.
17. **D** Only government may condemn property.
18. **A** A life estate is not an inheritable estate.
19. **C** Fee simple is the highest degree of ownership.
20. **A** B, C and D are leasehold estates.

Chapter 7
Methods of Ownership

1. **B** B and C held as tenants in common.
2. **B** In tenancy by the entirety, the marital unit owns the property; therefore, both spouses must act to partition or sell.
3. **C** Sole ownership is called "severalty."
4. **D** Each tenant has undivided interest to possess the whole.
5. **D** For example, where two people own land as tenants in common until they partition it. Then they each own a particular tract of land.
6. **B** Only allowed in tenancy in common or severalty.
7. **D** At death there is no interest in his estate to will.
8. **C** Real estate licensees should not give legal advice.
9. **B** It is the unauthorized practice of law for a broker to determine the tenancy, though he should discuss the various differences.
10. **A** The buyer could not obtain specific performance without both signatures. A creditor would have to be a creditor of both spouses.
11. **B** Testate means having made a valid will.
12. **B** Tenancy by the entirety is limited to husband and wife.
13. **C** A, B and D are true of joint tenancy.
14. **D** If it were joint tenancy, the shares must be equal.
15. **B** The brother has a one-half undivided tenancy in common interest.
16. **C** The property passes outside the probate estate.
17. **B** No survivorship rights.
18. **D** He may sell his interest but not "the property."
19. **C** Equal shares required with joint tenancy.
20. **B** The corporation would always be the last survivor.
21. **C** Upon the death of C, A and B owned the property as joint tenants. When B sold his interest to D, A and D became tenants in common.
22. **D** Because of no survivorship rights.
23. **A** Cannot be joint tenancy because of unequal shares. Cannot be severalty because of two owners.
24. **A** Automatic in New Jersey.
25. **D** Divorce terminates dower.
26. **C** Automatic in New Jersey unless spouses indicate otherwise.
27. **D** The permissive legislation that created condos.

Chapter 8
Dower, Curtesy, Wills and Descent

1. **B** Property goes to legal heirs of person who died.
2. **C** Heirs receive nothing until all estate debts have been paid. Remember, the decedent's contracts are still binding on his estate (not necessarily his relatives).
3. **D** It takes effect upon the testator's death.
4. **B** Administrator is appointed by probate court in the case of intestacy.
5. **D** Executrix is female "executor."
6. **C** Do not confuse devise with demise (to lease).

7. **D** Note that in addition to no will there are also no heirs.
8. **D** A, B and C could be used while the owner is alive.
9. **D** Inchoate means not yet perfected.
10. **A** Right of possession only applies to the matrimonial residence.
11. **B** See explanation to #10.
12. **C** Condemnation and adverse possession are examples of involuntary alienation.
13. **D** A testator is a person who makes a will.
14. **D** A demise is a transfer of an estate by lease.
15. **C** A minor lacks capacity to be a vendor, vendee or grantor.

Chapter 9 Easements, Restrictions and Rights of Adjoining Owners

1. **D** An easement by prescription is created by trespass.
2. **C** The easement is an appurtenance to the dominant property and an encumbrance to the servient.
3. **D** Called restrictive covenants.
4. **B** Covenants are private
5. **C** A restriction is an encumbrance, but not a lien, because there is no creditor involved.
6. **B** Generally the way a town acquires the land for streets in a subdivision.
7. **B** An encroachment arises when a building intrudes upon the land of another.
8. **B** An encumbrance is any interest in land that adversely affects its value.
9. **C** With an easement in gross, no dominant estate exists, only a servient estate.
10. **B** Unlike an easement, a license is revocable.
11. **A** Because the owner of the dominant property owns the easement right.
12. **B** Ingress is the right of entry; egress is the right of exit.
13. **B** A typical example of an easement in gross.
14. **D** The surveyor would determine the intrusion of a building or part of a building from another property.

Chapter 10 Acknowledgements, Recording and Constructive Notice

1. **C** In the other cases (A and B) the grantee with the prior unrecorded deed would prevail.
2. **C** Each of New Jersey's counties has a recording office at the county seat.
3. **B** Buyer has an obligation to make a title search and a visual inspection of the property.
4. **B** The acknowledgment is given "to" the other parties.
5. **D** All records are public information.
6. **A** An unrecorded deed is valid between the parties as well as valid against third parties who knew of the conveyance.
7. **B** Constructive notice is notice imputed by law.
8. **A** Actual notice consists of express information of a fact.
9. **B** Acknowledgement is essential for recording.
10. **B** Possession of property gives constructive notice.
11. **B** A quitclaim deed conveys only the grantor's rights with no warranties of ownership.
12. **D** Recording does not guarantee validity, only gives constructive notice.
13. **C** Month-to-month leases are not recorded.
14. **D** The grantee (buyer) is protected by recording.
15. **B** Purchase and sale contracts usually are not recorded.
16. **D** Recording gives constructive notice, but does not guarantee or insure title.

Chapter 11 Title Insurance

1. **A** An extended coverage policy would cover B and C.
2. **B** Title insurance is single-premium insurance.
3. **D** The county clerk enters documents into the records. The person signing provides the acknowledgment.
4. **C** The mortgagee's policy protects the lender, but is paid for by the borrower.
5. **A** B and C are exceptions.
6. **A** A brief history of title, rarely used today.
7. **D** The title policy will not cover defects which arise after the grantee takes title.
8. **D** It traces the title from the time of the original grant and is used by the attorney to prepare the opinion of title.
9. **B** Title insurance protects the holder from any loss suffered because of a title defect.
10. **A** The owner's policy is not assignable.
11. **A** Estimating value is the appraiser's responsibility.
12. **B** See explanation to #6.
13. **D** A, B and C are all terms for "seller."
14. **B** Alienation is any transfer of title and possession of property. May be voluntary (sale) or involuntary, such as condemnation or adverse possession.

Chapter 12 Agency

1. **D** An executor owes a duty to the estate. A mortgagor is a debtor.
2. **C** A broker is an agent with limited authority.
3. **C** Salesperson can only accept compensation from broker.
4. **C** Not spelled "principle."
5. **C** If the seller defaults, the agent may sue the seller for the commission. If the buyer defaults, the agent may take a direct action against the buyer.
6. **D** All statements are true.
7. **C** A salesperson may not accept compensation from anyone other then his or her employing broker.
8. **D** Compensation is arrived at by agreement between the broker and owner.
9. **C** Employees do not owe fiduciary obligations to an employer.
10. **D** See NJAC 11:5-1.23.
11. **D** Broker and salesperson have fiduciary obligations; seller must disclose defects under case law.
12. **C** The agent must disclose material facts to the client.
13. **A** A principal agent relationship exists between the broker and his or her salespersons.
14. **B** The power of attorney is the instrument creating the authority. The attorney-in-fact is the person to whom the authority was given.
15. **A** The broker is the agent and the salesperson is a sub-agent.
16. **A** An agent is a fiduciary for a principal, not vice-versa.
17. **C** The authority of the broker is limited to finding a buyer or tenant.
18. **C** The purchaser can ascertain this himself. The broker must disclose information about A, B or D.
19. **B** See explanation to #17. A real estate property manager is usually a general agent.
20. **B** Non-use will not revoke a power of attorney.
21. **A** Necessary for recording.
22. **A** B, C, and D are not agency agreements as is the listing.
23. **D** Also by mutual agreement, accomplishment of objective and expiration of agreed period of time.
24. **C** A, B and D will terminate an agency relationship.
25. **D** Patience is not a fiduciary obligation.
26. **A** An oral authorization to sell real estate is unenforceable.
27. **A** The death of the agent will terminate the listing. In this question, the agent is XYZ Realty Corporation, not Mr. Case.
28. **C** Written agreement and compensation are not requisites to create an agency relationship.
29. **B** Real estate agents work "for" clients and "with" customers. Fiduciary obligations are owed to the client, not the customer.
30. **D** Undisclosed dual agency is an act of fraud.

Chapter 13 Listings

1. **D** The principal may also be referred to as the "client."
2. **B** To avoid the situation where the seller sells to a buyer with whom the broker has formerly worked, the broker should "register" the prospect by giving written notice.
3. **C** With an exclusive right to sell listing, the broker has the right to a commission if the property is sold by anyone, including the owner, during the term of the contract.
4. **D** She was not the procuring cause.
5. **C** The commission paid to the salesperson is negotiable.
6. **C** As the seller's agent, the broker should argue for the best price.
7. **C** Don't confuse open listing with multiple listing. In a multiple listing only one broker is employed.
8. **B** MLS involves a situation where the exclusive listing agent pools his listing with other member brokers.
9. **B** The salesperson is directly responsible to his or her employing broker and is a subagent for the seller.
10. **B** The exclusive agency agreement allows the owner alone to find a buyer without paying a commission. If any other broker procures a buyer, the listing broker is entitled to the commission.
11. **D** As a special agent, the broker's authority is limited to finding a buyer or a tenant.
12. **C** Net listings are prohibited. With a multiple listing or exclusive agency, only one broker is employed.
13. **B** In this case the owner wants to deal only with prospective buyers or tenants.
14. **B** An exclusive agency must be written. The other statements are false.
15. **C** No commission is due if the property does not get sold.
16. **C** See explanation to #3.
17. **A** The broker must advise the buyer about property defects.
18. **D** Death, insanity or bankruptcy of the property owner or agent will terminate the listing, but not marriage.
19. **D** A listing agreement is an agency agreement and can be terminated for any of

the reasons stated.
20. **B** This is a contractual dispute.
21. **C** See explanation to #10.
22. **D** Both listings will achieve the owner's objective.
23. **B** An oral listing is unenforceable.
24. **A** The listing is signed by the broker and the client.
25. **B** Generally, brokers do not offer or accept sub-agency as a business relationship. Thus, the participating (cooperating) broker is usually the buyer's agent.

Chapter 14 Contracts

1. **D** Any of these will terminate an offer.
2. **D** All statements are true.
3. **C** Only the property owner or a lawyer may prepare the contracts involving A, B and D.
4. **C** A is only required for contracts falling within the Statute of Frauds; B is only required in a deed; D is only required to record.
5. **C** Only the optionor must sign.
6. **D** Performance is not essential in forming contract.
7. **A** Only the minor may disaffirm the contract.
8. **D** All lack legal capacity to contract.
9. **B** Rescission could take place after acceptance. Rejection would be an act of offeree, not offeror.
10. **B** A void contract has no legal force or effect, for example a contract to commit an illegal act.
11. **C** The Latin term for "and wife" is "*et ux.*"
12. **D** A salesperson cannot establish a trust account.
13. **D** Earnest money is strongly recommended but is not essential to the validity of a contract.
14. **C** If the party transferring rights was released, it would be a novation.
15. **C** Also called default.
16. **A** Marriage will not terminate an offer.
17. **D** The seller must sell, the buyer does not have to buy.
18. **A** The $4,000 is the earnest money deposit.
19. A Divorce will not affect enforceability of a contract.
20. **A** An essential element for a valid contract.
21. **B** An optionee does not have the right do any of the things mentioned in A, C, or D.
22. **B** Rescission is the act of canceling a contract either by mutual agreement or unilaterally when the other party defaults.
23. **B** Rescission is generally considered the least desirable remedy for breach of contract.
24. **B** See explanation to #17.
25. **A** Used in real estate because each parcel of land is nonhomogeneous.
26. **C** Typewritten additions indicate clear intent of parties.
27. **C** Because a number of things remain to be done, such as payment of purchase price, delivery of deed, etc.
28. **C** Descent deals with distribution of property when owner dies intestate.
29. **A** A rider is an amendment or attachment to a contract.
30. **D** All of the other remedies are available to the party who is not in default.
31. **C** Buyer does not have to take title to mortgaged property.
32. **B** The consideration in a real estate contract is the promise to pay the full purchase price.
33. **B** Typical terms of option contract.
34. **B** Optionee is potential buyer; optionor is owner.
35. **C** The court will presume a reasonable period of time.
36. **D** Death does not normally terminate a contract for the sale of real estate, as it is not an agency agreement.
37. **B** Executed contract is one in which terms have been completely carried out.
38. **A** After execution, completion of a contract can be avoided by rescission or mutual assent.
39. **B** Oral contracts for the sale of real estate are unenforceable under the Statute of Frauds.
40. **B** A contract does not have to be written, dated or accompanied by a deposit, although all are recommended.
41. **D** Because there could not be a meeting of the minds.
42. **B** When offeror signs, it constitutes an offer. When offeree signs, it indicates acceptance and becomes a contract.
43. **C** "Time is of the essence" makes the closing date definite.
44. **B** When a "time is of the essence" clause is included in a contract, all dates in the agreement must be interpreted exactly.
45. **A** Mrs. Smith could seek specific performance against the seller in the event of default. The seller could not, however, sue Mr. Smith if Mrs. Smith defaults.
46. **B** Because there is no contract.
47. **D** Vera retains legal title until closing.
48. **D** An assignee is someone who receives an assignment.
49. **D** Offer and acceptance are essential elements of a contract.
50. **B** See explanation to #46.
51. **B** After the statutory period, the creditor is barred from bringing a suit to enforce a claim.

52. **B** In the absence of such a provision, the buyer would bear the risk because of his equitable title.
53. **B** Buyer has equitable title from time contract is signed until closing. Buyer acquires legal title at closing.
54. **D** All of the information in A, B and C should be included in the contract.
55. **D** All of these are material to the transaction.
56. **A** The attorney review clause can be extended, but cannot be waived.

Chapter 15
Deeds

1. **B** Although the deed may legally be prepared by the grantor, it should be prepared by an attorney.
2. **D** Such a deed can only be made valid by the grantor (or agent) filling in names.
3. **D** The grantee can lack legal capacity and does not sign the deed.
4. **B** There was no delivery service. Carol has control over the deed and did not give it irrevocably.
5. **A** Such as an unreleased dower interest of a former owner's wife.
6. **D** Grantor makes no promises in a quitclaim deed.
7. **C** The quitclaim deed makes no warranties of ownership, only transfers any interest the grantor has.
8. **B** Because the grantor is conveying his land for a specific portion described in the deed.
9. **A** In the contract, buyer is called "vendee."
10. **A** A covenant in a General Warranty deed. It states that the grantor owns the property and has the right to sell it.
11. **B** Not when the deed is signed, because the grantor may change his mind before delivery.
12. **C** Called the "to have and to hold" clause. Generally outmoded by the plain language deed.
13. **C** Recording only gives notice; it does not validate a deed.
14. **A** Also called a CVG deed.
15. **A** See explanation, Answer 2.
16. **A** Because she recorded prior to Ben, Abraham's conveyance to Clara was fraudulent. Therefore, Ben has a cause of action against Abraham.
17. **D** Zoning ordinances are not encumbrances.
18. **D** Date, acknowledgement and recording are customary and recommended, but not essential.
19. **D** Acknowledgement and recording are recommended but are not essential to validity of deed. Grantor must be competent, but not required of grantee.
20. **A** Acceleration clause appears in a mortgage.
21. **A** Deed must name buyer and seller, but only seller must sign.
22. **B** Because it contains covenants of title.
23. **B** Grantee (buyer) is protected by recording.
24. **B** Only an attorney or the property owner can legally prepare a deed.
25. **B** Grantor's attorney usually prepares deed, which is recorded by buyer's attorney after closing.
26. **C** \$150,000 ÷ 500 = 300 x 2.00 = \$600
    \$50.000 ÷ 500 = 100 x 3.35 = \$335
    \$360,000 ÷ 500 = 700 x 3.90 = \$2,808
    \$600 + \$335 + \$2,808 = \$3,743
27. **C** After that, in this order; lender, seller's agent, buyer's agent.
28. **A** With each title transfer, a new deed is prepared.
29. **C** Grantee never signs deed.
30. **A** In severalty ownership.
31. **A** Title can be conveyed to a minor, but not by a minor.
32. **D** The acknowledgment is taken by an attorney, notary public, judge, etc.

Chapter 16
Condemnation and Adverse Possession

1. **D** Often used to settle adverse possession or prescriptive easement disputes.
2. **D** Needs to be hostile; if with owner's consent, then claimant would be a licensee.
3. **D** Severance damages are paid only when there is a partial taking.
4. **D** Could be one claimant for 20 years.
5. **D** An inherent right of government.
6. **D** Knowledge of the trespasser will not be a defense to a claim for adverse possession.
7. **C** No compensation is paid when government exercises police power.
8. **A** An adverse possession claim will only be valid against the lawful owner.
9. **A** A claim for adverse possession is not valid against property devoted to public use and certain government-owned land.
10. **B** For adverse possession to ripen into title, possession must be unbroken for 20 years.
11. **A** See explanation to #10.
12. **D** Eminent domain is the *power* and condemnation is the *process* of taking the property.

Chapter 17
Mortgages

1. **B** Unless there is a novation, the seller is not released under an assumption.
2. **A** A is generally true, however, all loans for real estate purchases are referred to as "purchase money mortgages."

3. **D** The ratio between the amount borrowed and the lesser of the contract price or appraised value.
4. **B** One point is 1% of the loan amount, not 1% of the selling price.
5. **C** Death does not terminate contractual obligations; they are binding on the estate.
6. **B** A form of acceleration clause.
7. **C** After execution of the estoppel certificate the borrower is prevented from denying the existence of its terms.
8. **B** But the loan will be based on the lower appraisal value and the borrower must pay the difference in cash.
9. **B** A novation is a substitution of new parties for the original parties to a contract.
10. **C** Default in mortgage payments, for example.
11. **B** It allows the lender to demand the total unpaid balance in the event of default.
12. **A** No down payment required for VA loans.
13. **B** Points are paid to the mortgagee, not the seller.
14. **B** Designed for older homeowners on fixed incomes, with substantial equity in their home.
15. **B** The buyer assumes personal liability by taking over the mortgage and the note.
16. **B** The note is the primary evidence of the loan and makes the borrower personally liable for the debt.
17. **A** The FHA does not lend money, it insures loans.
18. **B** Two things account for equity build-up: debt reduction and property appreciation.
19. **B** However, the veteran does not restore his eligibility for a new loan until the old loan is paid off or it is assumed by a veteran buycr who substitutes his eligibility.
20. **D** The FHA does not lend money or build housing. The VA guarantees loans.
21. **B** Often used by developers.
22. **A** Because the principal was not reduced, only interest was paid. Do not confuse with balloon mortgage, where balance drops.
23. **B** A, C and D are buyers. B is a lender.
24. **B** Junior lien would be satisfied after the prior lien in the event of foreclosure.
25. **B** No principal reduction during the term of the loan.
26. **B** \$200,000 - \$40,000 = \$160,000 x 2% = \$3,200.
27. **A** A subrogation clause is found in an insurance policy.
28. **C** In the event of a deficiency, the lender can look only to the seller.
29. **D** The two parties are the lender and borrower. Government insured or guaranteed loans involve three parties: lender, borrower and a government agency (FHA or VA).
30. **B** Loan discounts are called points. Each discount point is 1% of the loan amount.
31. **D** Prepayment penalties are no longer charged with FHA loans.
32. **C** As previously noted.
33. **D** Also called "discharge."
34. **A** The subordination clause permits a mortgage recorded at a later date to take priority over an existing mortgage.
35. **A** This occurs because the payments were calculated on a longer payment period than the actual term of the loan.
36. **B** A hypothecation occurs when property is pledged as the security for a loan, and the borrower retains possession of the pledged property.
37. **A** Title companies insure titles. The FHA insures mortgage payments.
38. **B** If the buyer assumes the mortgage, it would not be paid off and a satisfaction would not be recorded.
39. **D** Only two parties are involved – lender and borrower.
40. **B** The VA would not make a loan to an unqualified borrower.
41. **A** FHA insures the loan. Interest rates are determined by the market, not by HUD.

Chapter 18
Liens, Foreclosure and Redemption

1. **D** A writ of execution is the remedy if the debtor does not pay.
2. **B** All liens are encumbrances, but not all encumbrances are liens. Encumbrances always lower value.
3. **D** An easement encumbers the servient property.
4. **C** A voluntary lien is a debt that the property owner agrees to have recorded, such as a mortgage or trust deed.
5. **D** An exception to the rule that liens are satisfied in the order of recording.
6. **B** 20 years statute of limitations for judgments.
7. **B** The lien is given as security for payment of work performed and materials furnished to improve real estate.
8. **A** B, C and D are false statements.
9. **D** An attachment is a court order tying up defendant's property until completion of a court suit.
10. **D** The others do not involve a creditor.
11. **D** By taking action for default on the promissory note.
12. **D** Property owner can prevent this by recording contract with the general contractor.
13. **B** No creditor involved.
14. **A** A title search would discover notice of the pending suit.
15. **A** The tax lien would always be satisfied first, but subsequently recorded liens would stand in line.

Chapter 19 Financing

1. **A** VA and FHA guarantee and insure loans but do not engage in secondary market.
2. **B** Such as urban renewal projects and elderly housing.
3. **A** A purchase and sale agreement conveys equitable title.
4. **B** Buyer does not get title until last payment is paid. Can also be used to purchase improved real estate.
5. **D** Deposits are insured by FSLIC.
6. **C** Seller is vendor in contract; grantor in deed.
7. **C** Fannie Mae operates in the secondary market.
8. **C** The others would be classified as non-institutional.
9. **B** The buyer is the former owner.
10. **C** Created as a government agency in 1938; reorganized and became private in 1968.
11. **D** The buyer can do all of the other things.
12. **C** A violation of state and federal laws.

Chapter 20 Truth-in-Lending

1. **C** The law applies only to creditors and arrangers of credit.
2. **C** Such fee would be incurred regardless of whether credit was extended.
3. **C** Advertising in general terms is permissible by itself. If any specific credit information is given, additional information must be provided.
4. **B** The law applies only to "consumer" loans.
5. **C** A "cooling off" period.
6. **C** See explanation to #3.
7. **D** Owners acting on their own behalf are not subject to TIL.
8. **B** To allow comparison shopping.
9. **A** Commercial transactions are not covered.
10. **D** Advertising in general terms is permitted.

Chapter 21 Real Estate Closing (Settlement) Procedures

1. **A** It measures buyer's cash at closing.
2. **B** It increases buyer's cash at closing.
3. **B** This is the seller's net proceeds.
4. **C** It reduces seller's cash at closing.
5. **A** It reduces seller's cash but does not affect buyer's cash.
6. **D** Because it will reduce the seller's cash and increase the buyer's cash.
7. **B** It reduces seller's cash and increases buyer's cash.
8. **A** It reduces buyer's cash and increases seller's cash.
9. **C** Security deposits would decrease seller's cash and increase buyer's cash at closing.
10. **D** A purchase money mortgage reduces seller's cash and increases buyer's cash.
11. **C** Both statements are true.

Chapter 22 Leases and the Landlord-Tenant Relationship

1. **D** The interest conveyed is leasehold.
2. **A** Leases for longer than three years must be written.
3. **C** The excess rent is based on gross sales.
4. **B** Because the landlord usually pays the operating expenses.
5. **C** Also called step-up lease.
6. **B** For example, a month-to-month lease.
7. **C** The New Jersey Supreme Court has allowed the self-help remedy of "repair and deduct" (*Marini v. Ireland*, 56 N.J. 130 (1970).
8. **C** A sublease is for part of the term or part of the premises.
9. **D** Lessor pays mortgage payments.
10. **B** Tenant may be freed from further obligation to pay rent.
11. **D** The subordination clause in the lease states that the lease is subordinate to the mortgage.
12. **D** Landlord has a reversionary interest.
13. **D** A, B, and C are required by law.
14. **C** Used for long-term rentals.
15. **B** Termination by mutual consent is technically called "surrender and acceptance."
16. **D** Any lease for a definite period of time is a tenancy for years.
17. **C** Summary possession is also called "actual eviction."
18. **A** For instance, where tenant agrees to pay proportionate share of real estate tax increases.
19. **B** In this case tenant is called "holdover tenant."
20. **C** An option to purchase, however, may be included.
21. **B** New Jersey Statute of Frauds requires leases for longer than three years to be written to be enforceable.
22. **B** Notice must be served personally or by registered mail.
23. **B** After actual eviction, tenant's obligation to pay rent may continue.
24. **A** In a residential lease the security deposit remains the property of the lessee during the lease term.
25. **C** A life estate is a freehold estate.
26. **D** A, B and C are false statements.
27. **A** The most common tenancy.
28. **B** A, C, and D are freehold estates.
29. **C** Generally, the tenant must vacate while the condition exists.

30. **C** Don't be misled by the term. Any lease allowing possession for a fixed term is a tenancy for years.
31. **A** The premises "revert" to the lessor when the lease ends.
32. **B** Also important to disclose the terms of the lease in the purchase and sale agreement as the purchase is subject to the lease.
33. **D** The tenant (lessee) usually pays the rest.
34. **D** Lessor's death will not affect the tenant's rights.
35. **A** Building goes to lessor at end of lease.
36. **B** Tenant is lessee.
37. **B** Sandwich lease is held by someone who neither owns nor occupies the premises. For instance, a lease held by a tenant who subleases to another tenant.
38. **B** This lease provides for graduated changes in the amount of rent at predetermined intervals. Used for long-term leases.
39. **B** With excess rent based on a percent of gross sales.
40. **A** Tenant pays expenses in net lease.
41. **B** Tenant has the right to sublease if lease is silent on the matter.
42. **D** An assignment is for all of the premises for all of the term.
43. **D** Non-freehold is also called less-than-freehold.
44. **C** All of the others are ownership methods under freehold estates.
45. **D** A life estate is freehold.
46. **D** Not used in apartments because of difficulty in apportioning expenses.
47. **B** An assignment would transfer *all* of the remaining term.
48. **D** Familial status violation.
49. **D** Katy is the lessee in her lease with Susan.
50. **B** The others are not "just causes" for eviction.

Chapter 23
Property Management

1. **D** The property manager would want to be able to adjust rents to account for inflation.
2. **B** This item might be handled by a special account called "reserves for replacement."
3. **A** Investing client's funds is not a property manager's function.
4. **B** High rents may not produce good net income if there are unnecessary expenses.
5. **C** Violation of federal and state laws.
6. **D** IREM is an affiliate of the National Association of Realtors.
7. **B** Handling the client's money and property in a position of confidence and trust.
8. **C** The best of both worlds.
9. **A** Called "effective gross income": gross potential income minus vacancy and collection losses.
10. **C** To avoid inference of self-interest.
11. **D** A secret profit would be a breach of the property manager's fiduciary duties.

Chapter 24
Anti-Discrimination and Federal Fair Housing

1. **D** Marital status is a protected class under the N.J. Law Against Discrimination
2. **C** Dept. of Housing and Urban Development.
3. **B** The 1988 amendments added protections for physically and mentally handicapped persons.
4. **B** Private clubs cannot operate for a profit.
5. **D** Blockbusting is a violation of federal and state laws.
6. **A** The owner of a single-family house cannot discriminate.
7. **D** The Federal Fair Housing Act only applies to discrimination in housing.
8. **C** This is an unlawful practice.
9. **A** The other classes became protected by later laws.
10. **B** Racial discrimination would be a violation of the Civil Rights Act of 1866.
11. **A** Revocation or suspension requires action by the REC.
12. **D** The Division of Civil Rights cannot revoke or suspend a real estate license. But it can inform the Commission, which can then take disciplinary action.
13. **B** Called "racial steering."
14. **D** Age discrimination is not a fair housing violation. Don't confuse with familial status.
15. **B** A violation of federal and state laws.
16. **D** Mrs. Murphy may legally refuse to rent to male students, but cannot advertise in a discriminatory manner.
17. **A** The Federal Fair Housing Act applies only to housing; marital status is a protected class under the state law.
18. **D** Commonly called "HUD."
19. **D** A violation of federal and state laws.
20. **D** By using delaying tactics, the developer violated the N.J. Law Against Discrimination which broadly covers all real estate transactions. The federal law deals only with housing and does not cover lots zoned "light industry."
21. **A** One year to file under the federal law.
22. **D** Discrimination because of familial status violates federal law. Marital status is covered by N.J. law.
23. **A** Racial steering is a violation of state and federal laws.

Chapter 25
Real Estate Taxes and Tax Aspects of Real Estate Ownership

1. **B** Special assessments are paid for only by property owners who benefit from the improvement. General assessments are paid by all property owners through the ad valorem tax.
2. **D** His tax is deferred.
3. **A** Veteran's deduction is $50 per year. Senior citizens qualify if income is under $10,000 per year.
4. **D** Six months if the municipality holds the lien; two years if the lien is held by an individual.
5. **C** The rate is generally adjusted to reflect budget changes. The assessment is adjusted only upon revaluation.
6. **C** Real estate taxes are levied on a local basis.
7. **C** The investor can recapture his investment in improvements through depreciation.
8. **B** Only interest expense and real estate taxes are deductible items.
9. **B** Depreciation deduction is only allowed on rental properties.
10. **D** Property taxes are levied by municipalities.
11. **C** Paid only by benefiting property owners.
12. **A** Vacant land cannot be depreciated.
13. **C** Equity is the value that the owner has in property over and above the liens against it.
14. **C** If property is inherited, the basis of value becomes the market value as of the date of the grantor's death.
15. **B** 27.5 years residential; 39 years non-residential.
16. **A** $300,000 ÷ 39 = $7,692. (The land may not be depreciated.)
17. **B** The homeowner may deduct only mortgage interest and real estate taxes.
18. **D** Repairs are expenses which are "recurring" and "predictable."
19. **B** Depreciation is recaptured when property is sold.
20. **C** The other items are deductible.
21. **D** You get to deduct all the interest. Your net taxable income is taxed.
22. **C** The residency requirement is two of the five years preceding the sale.
23. **A** $205,000 x 80% = $164,000 x 5.4% = $8,856 ÷ 12 = $738.00
24. **B** $1,750 x 4 = $7,000 ÷ $102,000 = .068 = $6.80

Chapter 26
Tax-deferred Exchanges Under Section 1031

1. **D** It is the payment to satisfy the difference in equities in an exchange.
2. **D** The property transferred by the exchangor is the "relinquished" property.
3. **C** See explanation to #1.
4. **C** The exchange is tax-favored because it allows the investor to postpone payment of the capital gains tax.
5. **A** Mortgage boot is the amount by which the mortgage debt on the property given up exceeds the amount of the mortgage on the property received.
6. **A** The value of the note is considered boot and will be taxed.
7. **C** $225,000 – $95,000 = $130,000. The basis in the replacement property is equal to the price of the replacement property less any untaxed gain. Untaxed gain consists of any capital gains not subject to taxation, plus any depreciation taken on the relinquished property.
8. **C** $118,000 – $111,000 = $7,000. The cash boot is taxable.
9. **B** The vacation home would be considered a "second home" because it was rented out for more than 14 days.
10. **B** Basis + Improvements – Depreciation = Adjusted Basis. $90,000 – $23,000 = $67,000.
11. **B** Adjusted Selling Price – Adjusted Basis = Realized Gain. $130,000 – $40,000 = $90,000.
12. **B** Equity – Selling Costs = Sales Proceeds Before Tax. $55,500 – $5,500 = $50,000.
13. **D** Business real estate is any real estate used in a business activity.
14. **D** The investor must identify the replacement property within 45 days and receive the property within 180 days.
15. **A** No need for owner of replacement property to sign.
16. **C** Also, any number of properties if their fair market value does not exceed 200% of FMV of all relinquished properties.
17. **D** 28% + 6% = 34%. $75,000 x 34% = $25,500.
18. **B** IRS recaptures the accelerated depreciation when depreciable property is exchanged for non-depreciable property.

Chapter 27
Appraising

1. **C** Functional obsolescence is a loss in value due to any cause within the property except for physical deterioration.
2. **D** It is the process whereby expected future income is converted to value.
3. **D** A and B are external; C is irrelevant.
4. **A** Because there is no income and no depreciation.
5. **B** Make sure the income is annual and net.
6. **B** Because the building has been totally depreciated.

7. **A** A fee contingent on the value estimate would be unethical.
8. **C** Livelihood has no bearing on value.
9. **C** Because a higher rate indicates a higher risk and the higher the risk, the lower the value.
10. **A** Accrued depreciation is total depreciation from all causes.
11. **B** Because most improved real estate consists of used single-family houses which are appraised by this method.
12. **B** Since the building is a wasting asset, it is necessary to factor in an amount to recapture the money lost when the building reaches the end of its economic life.
13. **A** The investment in the building can be recaptured through depreciation, but the land may not be depreciated.
14. **B** Obsolescence may cause a property to lose value while the property remains perfectly sound.
15. **D** The upper limit of value is established by the cost approach.
16. **A** Areas with similar homes, family make-up, facilities, etc.
17. **B** Because value is adversely affected, but the structure remains sound.
18. **A** Location, location, location.
19. **A** Because of lack of homogeneity.
20. **B** Because of influences outside the property line.
21. **A** Using cost approach, appraiser estimates current reproduction cost, deducts depreciation and adds value of vacant land.
22. **A** Used when there is a "partial taking."
23. **A** B is external; C is physical deterioration.
24. **A** Market value is the price that a willing seller will accept from a willing buyer.
25. **D** An appraiser can estimate value, give an opinion, or come to a conclusion of value, but he or she cannot determine value; only the market can do that.
26. **B** The insurance company is concerned with neither the income produced by an insured property nor its market value.
27. **C** All of the other information is relevant.
28. **B** Sales price divided by monthly contract rent.
29. **D** If the comparable is better, subtract (CBS).
30. **A** Price is what a property sells for; value is what it's worth.
31. **C** If either of the parties is under pressure to act or the property has not been on the market for a reasonable time, the seller may be receiving market price instead of market value.
32. **B** Because there is no income and because there are no comparables.
33. **A** If the comparable is inferior, add (CIA).
34. **B** It is total depreciation from all causes: physical, functional and external.

Chapter 28
Land Description

1. **C** Also, tax map identification, and lot and block number on a recorded map.
2. **C** The deed must unquestionably describe the real estate conveyed.
3. **B** Title insurance policies usually do not cover defects in boundaries and survey, or encroachments.
4. **B** Monuments are used by surveyors to determine land locations but do not establish elevations.
5. **C** Metes refers to measures; bounds to boundaries.
6. **D** Also street address and lot and block number on a recorded map.
7. **D** Surveyors use benchmarks to measure elevations.
8. **D** Monuments may be natural such as a tree or the edge of water, or man-made such as a cement-filled pipe, or a brass plaque in a sidewalk to serve as a benchmark.
9. **D** The starting point is called the point of beginning. The description must begin and end at the same identical point.
10. **C** Usually included as part of a title search.
11. **C** This method of land description is not used in N.J.
12. **D** A quadrangle is a 24-square-mile area used in connection with the Government Survey System.
13. **A** A square 1/2 mile is 1/4 of a square mile. 640 ÷ 4 = 160.
14. **D** A metes and bounds description starts at a well-marked point of beginning and proceeds in distances and directions until it returns to the same beginning point.

Chapter 29
Planning, Zoning and Building Ordinances

1. **A** Title closing is the process of transferring title, not a restriction.
2. **B** Base lines are used with Government Survey; deed restrictions are private limitations.
3. **A** Real estate boards have no control over land uses.
4. **B** Area and volume of buildings are controlled by zoning, not building codes.
5. **A** A buffer zone is a transitional area separating a residential area from a less desirable contiguous use such as commercial or industrial.
6. **A** To provide for safe and sound construction.
7. **B** The use is "grandfathered."
8. **B** Setback provisions are intended to keep buildings away from streets to provide

more light and air and less noise for homeowners.

9. **A** All except escheat can be exercised by municipal, county, state or federal governments.
10. **D** The use can continue.
11. **D** Only the legislature can enact laws.
12. **A** Application is made to Zoning Board or Planning Board, depending on type.
13. **B** Required by state law.

Chapter 30
Real Estate Mathematics

Commission and Sales Price

1. **D** 7/8 = 7 ÷ 8 = .875 = 87.5%
$60,000 x 87.5% = $52,500 sales price
$52,500 x 6% = $3,150 total commission
$3,150 ÷ 2 = $1,575 for each broker

2 **A** $48,000 x 6% = $2,880; $63,900 x 3% = $1,917; $52,000 x 6% = $3,150
$2,880 + $1,917 + $3,150 = $7,947 total commissions
$7,947 x 25% = $1,986.75 salesperson's earnings

3. **A** 100% + 20% = 120%
$70,000 x 120% = $84,000 list price
$84,000 - $6,000 = $78,000 selling price
$78,000 x 6% = $4,680 commission
$78,000 - $4,680 = $73,320 net to seller

4. **B** $320 x 30% = $96 first month
$320 x 6% = $19.20 each month thereafter
$19.20 x 11 months = $211.20
$96 + $211.20 = $307.20 annual fee

5. **D** $50,000 x 6% = $3,000 commission on first $50,000
$3,800 - $3,000 = $800 commission at 4%
$800 ÷ 4% = $20,000 amount over $50,000
$50,000 + $20,000 = $70,000 sales price

6. **A** $34,000 + $317 = $34,317
100% - 7 = 93%
$34,317 ÷ 93% = $36,900 sales price

7. **B** $60,000 x 7% = $4,200
3 + 2 = 5 parts
$4,200 ÷ 5 parts = $840 per part
$840 x 3 = $2,520 broker's share
$840 x 2 = $1,680 salesperson's share
$2,520 - $1,680 = $840 less to salesperson

8. **D** Must get $37,000 + $800 + 10% commission
$37,800 = 90% of sales price
$37,800 ÷ 90% = $42,000 sales price

9. **A** $42,000 + $45,500 + $48,000 + $49,500 = $185,000 total sales
$80,000 x 9% = $7,200 commission on first $80,000
$105,000 x 25% = $2,625 commission on amount in excess of $80,000
$7,200 + $2,625 = $9,825 total commission
$185,000 x 6% = $11,100 commission at 6%
$11,100 - $9,825 = $1,275 more at 6%

10. **A** $30,000 x 6% = $1,800 commission on first $30,000
$2,070 - $1,800 = $270 commission on amount over $30,000
$270 ÷ 3% = $9,000 sales price above $30,000
$30,000 + $9,000 = $39,000 sales price

Appreciation/Depreciation

1. **D** 9 years x 6% = 54% increase in value
100% original value + 54% = 154% current value
$54,000 ÷ 154% = $35,064.94 original value. Rounded = $35,100

2. **D** $78,000 - $66,300 = $11,700 depreciation over 6 years
$11,700 ÷ $78,000 = 15% depreciation over 6 years
15% ÷ 6 = 2.5% average depreciation per year

3. **B** $40,000 ÷ 117% = $34,188

4. **B** $120,000 - $102,000 = $18,000 amount of depreciation
$18,000 ÷ $120,000 = 15% depreciation in 8 years
15% ÷ 8 = 1.875% annually

Measures (Area)

1. **B** Divide the house into one rectangle (25' x 75') and one square (25' x 25')
25' x 75' = 1,875 sq. ft.; 25' x 25' = 625 sq. ft.
1,875 sq. ft. + 625 sq. ft. = 2,500 sq. ft. area of house
2,500 sq. ft. x $24 per sq. ft. = $60,000 cost of house
Property is a parallelogram: Area = 1/2 (base + base) x height
Area of lot = 1/2 (250' + 250') x 130' = 1/2 (500') x 130' = 250' x 130' = 32,500 sq. ft.
$21,780 per acre = $21,780 ÷ 43,560 sq. ft. = $.50 per sq. ft.
32,500 sq. ft. x $.50 per sq. ft. = $16,250 cost of lot
$60,000 cost of house + $16,250 cost of lot = $76,250 total cost
$76,250 x 12% = $9,150 profit
$76,250 + 9,150 = $85,400 sales price

2. **A** 24' x 46' = 1,104 sq. ft.
12' x 26' = 312 sq. ft.
1,104 + 312 = 1,416 sq. ft. total area
1,416 x $18 = $25,488 original cost
$41,472 present cost ÷ 1,416 sq. ft. = $29.29 per sq. ft.
$29.29 per sq. ft. present cost - $18 per sq. ft. original cost = $11.29 per sq. ft. increase

3. **B** A = 1,750' x 1,250' = 2,187,500 sq. ft.
B = (2,000' - 1,750) x (1,250' + 500') = 250' x 1,750' = 437,500 sq. ft.
C = 1/2 (1,500' - 250') x (1,250' + 500') = 1/2 (1,250) x 1,750' = 625' x 1,750 = 1,093,750 sq. ft.
2,187,500 sq.ft. + 437,500 + 1,093,750 = 3,718,750 sq. ft.
3,718,750 x 70% (for use other than homes) = 2,603,125 sq. ft.
2,603,125 sq. ft. ÷ 43,560 (sq. ft. per acre) = 59.76 acres

4. **B** Area of a trapezoid = 1/2 (base + base) x height
Area = 1/2 (115' + 170') = 1/2 (285') x 75' = 142.5 x 75' = 10,687.5 sq.ft.

5. **B** 100' x 145.2 = 14,520 sq. ft.
14,520 ÷ 43,560 sq. ft. (1 acre) = .333 = 33.3%

6. **B** 102' x 84' = 8,568 sq. ft.
8,568 sq. ft. x $4.75 = $40,698 annual rent
$40,698 ÷ 12 months = $3,391.50 per month

7. **D** 9 inches thickness on each side = 18 inches or 1.5 ft.
32' - 1.5' = 30.5'
26' - 1.5' = 24.5'
30.5' x 24.5' = 747.25 sq. ft.

Interest

1. **B** $8,400 x 8.75% = $735 annual interest
$735 ÷ 12 = $61.25 interest per month
$61.25 x 9 = $551.25 interest for nine months
$8,400 + $551.25 = $8,951.25

2. **D** $212.75 x 4 = $851 annual interest
$851 ÷ $9,200 = 9.25% annual interest rate

3. **A** $160 x 4 = $640 annual interest
$640 ÷ $8,000 = 8% annual interest rate

4. **C** $147,000 x 3% = $4,410

5. **A** $168.75 x 4 = $675 annual interest amount
$675 ÷ $7,500 = 9% annual interest rate

6. **A** $168,000 x 10% = $16,800 ÷ 12 = $1,400 interest first payment.
$1,474.32 - $1,400 = $74.32 principal first payment.
$168,000 - $74.32 = $167,925.68 new loan balance.

Proration

1. **A** $2,700 ÷ 360 = $7.50 cost/day
$7.50 x 105 = $787.50 prorated taxes

2. **D** $1,320 ÷ 12 months = $110 taxes per month
12 months - 6.5 months = 5.5 months tax credit to seller
5.5 months x $110 = $605 credit to seller
$396 ÷ 36 months = $11 insurance per month
36 months - 6.5 months = 29.5 months insurance credit to seller
29.5 x $11 = $324.50 credit to seller
$605 + $324.50 = $929.50 total credit to seller

3. **A** $47,500 x 12.25% = $5,818.75 annual interest
$ 5,818.75 ÷ 360 = $16.16 interest per day
$16.16 x 20 = $323.26

4. **B** $135,000 x 40% = $54,000 assessed value
$7.40 per $100 = 7.4%
$54,000 x 7.4% = $3,996 annual taxes
$3,996 ÷ 360 = $11.10 daily taxes
$11.10 x 138 days (4 months, 18 days) = $1,531.80

5. **B** $100,000 x 8% = $8,000 annual interest
$8,000 ÷ 365 = $21.91 interest per day
$21.91 x 13 = $284.83 prepaid interest

Investment & Appraising

1. **C** 160' x 410' = 65,600 sq.ft.
$16,400 ÷ 65,600 = $.25 per sq.ft.
204' x 375' = 76,500 sq. ft.
76,500 x $.25 = $19,125 sales price

2. **B** $960 x 12 months = $11,520 annual income
$11,520 ÷ 12 % = $96,000 value of property

3. **B** $750 x 12 months = $9,000 net profit annually
$9,000 ÷ 12% = $75,000 required investment

4. **B** $230,000 x 25% = $57,500 depreciation
$230,000 - $57,500 + $60,000 (land) = $232,500 depreciated value

5. **B** $3,200 x 12 = $38,400 gross annual income
$38,400 - $1,920 (vacancy) - $4,000 (utilities) - $5,200 (taxes) - $1,500 (management fee)

= $25,780 net operating income (NOI)
$25,780 ÷ $230,000 = 11.2 cap. rate

6. **C** 48' x 24' = 1,152 sq. ft.
1,152 x $23.75 per sq. ft. = $27,360 total cost
$27,360 x 14% = $3,830.40 gross profit
$27,360 + $3,830.40 = $31, 190.40
or
$27,360 x 114% (100% + 14% profit) = $31,190.40
$31,190.40 rounded to nearest $100 = $31,200

7. **A** $190,000 x .025 = $4,750
$6,000 minimum rent must be paid.

8. **D** 75' x 100' = 7,500 sq. ft.
7,500 x .15 = 1,125 sq. ft. occupied by home
$48,000 - $14,000 costs of land = $34,000 cost of home
$34,000 ÷ 1,125 sq. ft. = 30.22 per sq. ft.

9. **B** $230 x 18 = $4,140 per month gross rent
$4,140 x 12 = $49,680 annual gross income
$49,680 x .05 vacancy = $2,484 vacancy factor
$49,680 - $2,484 = $47,196 gross effective income
$47,196 x .10 = $47,196 gross effective income
$4,600 + $1,050 + $2,400.40 + $19,400 + $4,719.60 = $34,570 total expenses
$47,196 gross income - $34,570 expenses = $12,622 net income
$12,626 ÷ $85,600 = .1475 = 14.75% net return

10. **B** $8,000 x 12 months = $96,000 annual income
$96,000 - $6,600 annual expenses = $89,400 annual net income
$89,400 ÷ 11% rate of return = $812,727.27 sales price

11. **A** $7,000 x 5 = $35,000 investment
$5,600 x 8 = $44,800 sales price
$44,800 - $35,000 = $9,800 profit
$9,800 ÷ $35,000 = .28 = 28% profit

12. **C** 100%÷ 40 years = .025 = 2.5% per year
2.5% x 8 years = 20% depreciation to date
100% - 20% = 80% of remaining value
$460,000 ÷ 80% = $575,000 value new

13. **D** $16,200 x 4% = $648 vacancy factor
$16,200 - $648 = $15,552 effective gross income
$15,552 - $2,352 = $13,200 net income
$13,200 ÷ 12% = $110,000 market value

14. **A** $20,000 ÷ $80,000 = 25%

15. **C** $8,000 x 7 = $56,000 purchase price
$3,200 x 7 = $22,400 cost of improvements
$56,000 + 22,400 = $78,400 total investment
$78,400 + 115% = $78,400 x 115% = $90,160 sales price

16. **B** $58,000 + $48,000 + $1,245,000 + $72,000 = $1,423,000
12% annual interest rate ÷ 12 = 1% per month
8 months x 1% = 8% interest paid on loan
$1,423,000 x 8% = $113,840 interest for 8 months
$1,423,000 + $113,840 = $1,536,840 total investment
$1,536,840 x 15% profit = $230,526 profit
$1,536,840 + 230,526 = $1,767,366
$1,767,366 ÷ 50 units = $35,347.32 per unit
$35,347.32 to nearest $100 = $35,300 per unit

17. **B** $43,500 purchase price + $4,000 expenses = $47,500 total investment
$47,500 x 12% = $5,700 gross profit on investment
$47,500 + $5,700 = $53,200 sales price
or
$47,500 x 112% = $53,200 sales price

18. **A** 48 offices x 12 months = 576
10 + 2 + 5 = 17 months vacant
17 ÷ 576 = 2.95%

19. **B** $500 x 12 months = $6,000 annual base rent
$6,600 - $6,000 = $600 rent in excess of base rent
$600 ÷ 3.75% = $16,000 gross over $50,000
$50,000 + $16,000 = $66,000 total annual gross

Taxes/Insurance

1. **A** $40,000 x 75% = $30,000
$1,200 ÷ $30,000 = .04
$100 x 4% = $4.00

2. **C** 150' x 140' = $21,000 land assessment
$21,000 = $85,000 (building assessment) = $106,000 assessed value
$106,000 x 8.6% = $9,116 annual taxes

3. **A** $48,000 x 80% = $38,400 assessed value
$902.40 x 2 = $1,804.80 annual taxes
$1,804.80 ÷ $38,400 = $0.047 tax rate per dollar
$0.047 per dollar = $4.70 per $100

4. **A** $8,400 ÷ $12,000 = .70 or 70% of value
$18,500 x 70% = $12,950 insured value

5. **A** $5,985 ÷ 5.7% = $105,000.

6. **B** \$105,000 ÷ \$180,000 = 58.3%

7. **B** \$56,800 x 80% = \$44,800 assessed value
\$3.75 per \$100 = 3.75%
\$44,800 x 3.75% = \$1,680 annual taxes

Miscellaneous

1. **A** Single family homes = 1/2 or 50% of entire tract
Shopping center = 1/3 or 33.333% of entire tract
100% (entire tract - 83.333% = 16.666%)
Therefore 16.666% = 72 acres
72 ÷ 16.666% = 432 acres entire tract
432 x 33.333% = 144 acres used for shop ping center

2. **C** \$160,000 x 5.5% = \$8,800
\$8,800 x 92% = \$8,096
\$8,096 ÷ 2 = \$4,048

3. **B** 2,000' x 150' = 300,000 sq. ft.
75' x 100' = 7,500 sq. ft.
7,500 ÷ 300,000 = .025 = 2.5/100 = 1/40 of entire tract

4. **D** \$1,260 ÷ 12 = \$105 monthly expense
\$816 ÷ 12 = \$68 taxes monthly
\$105 + \$68 + \$180 = \$353 rent to cover total expense

5. **D** \$70,000 x 25% = \$17,500 value of lot
\$70,000 - \$17,500 = \$52,500 value of house
\$52,500 x 90% = \$47,250 bank loan
\$70,000 - \$47,250 = \$22,750 down payment

6. **C** \$37,000 ÷ 1,000 = 37
37 x \$8.50 = \$314.50 per month for mort-gage
\$1,008 taxes ÷ 12 = \$84 per month taxes
\$432 insurance ÷ 36 = \$12 per month insurance
\$314.50 + \$84 + \$12 = \$410.50 total monthly payment

7. **C** \$44,000 - \$25,000 = \$19,000
\$25,000 x 3% = \$750
\$19,000 x 5% = \$950
\$750 + \$950 = \$1,700 down payment
\$44,000 - \$1,700 = \$42,300 amount financed
\$42,300 x 4% = \$1,692

8. **B** \$43,900 x 6% = \$2,634 commission amount
\$43,900 - \$2,634 = \$41,266 sales price less commission
\$41,266 - \$356 = \$40,910 net to seller (Transaction II)

9. **A** 50% = residential use; 1/4 = 25% shopping center; 1/8 = 12.5% for streets
50% + 25% + 12.5% = 87.5%
12.5% remaining = 5 acres for recreation
5 acres ÷ 12.5% = 40 acres total

10. **B** \$750 x 12 months = \$9,000 annual base rent
\$310,000 - \$240,000 = \$70,000 excess over minimum
\$70,000 x 2.5% = \$1,750 additional rent
\$9,000 + \$1,750 = \$10,750 annual rent

11. **D** \$4,500 x 9.75% = \$438.75 annual interest
\$438.75 ÷ 365 days = \$1.20 daily interest
\$156 ÷ \$1.20 = 130 days

12. **C** \$52,500 x 6% = \$3,150 broker's fee
\$50,400 x 5% = \$2,520 discount fee
\$3,150 + \$2,520 = \$5,670
\$52,500 - \$5,670 = \$46,830 net to sellers

13. **A** \$40,000 x 9% = \$3,600 annual interest
\$3,600 ÷ 360 days = \$10 per day
\$10 x 20 days = \$200 debit

14. **A** 120,000 ÷ 80% = \$150,000

15. **B** 40% of 6% = 40% x 6% = 2.4%
\$18,000 ÷ 2.4% = \$750,000 per year
\$750,000 ÷ 12 months = \$62,500 average monthly sales

16. **C** \$45,000 x 80% = \$36,000 mortgage amount
\$36,000 ÷ 1,000 = 36
\$8.05 x 36 = \$289.80 per month

17. **B** \$42,000 ÷ 1,000 = 42
\$8.05 x 42 = \$338.10 per month mortgage payment
\$624 ÷ 6 = \$104 tax per month
\$396 ÷ 36 = \$11 insurance per month
\$338.10 + \$104 + \$11 = \$453.10 total monthly payment

18. **C** \$970 ÷ 12% = \$8,083.33
\$8,083.33 ÷ 125% = \$6,466.66

19. **D** 7.5" x 4 = 30'
3.75" x 4 = 15'
30' x 15' = 450 sq. ft.

20. **D** \$127,500 ÷ 135% = \$94,444

21. **A** Area of rectangle = base x height
43,560 sq. ft. x 2 = 87,120 sq. ft. in tract
87,120 sq. ft. ÷ 528' frontage = 165' depth

22. A 109' x 74' = 8,066 sq. ft.
8,066 x 75% = 6,049 sq. ft.

23. **D** 70% x 130% = 91% (91% = 9% decrease)

24. **B** Lot = 10,000 sq. ft.

(1/2(B + B) x H = 100' x 100')
Office space = 2,240 sq. ft.
Driveway = 564 sq. ft.
Patio = 48 sq. ft.
Landscaped area = 7,148 sq. ft. (10,000 - 2,852)
7,148 sq. ft. x .4 = $2,859.20 landscaping cost
$210,000 cost + $2,859.20 = $212,859.20
$212,859.20 x 16% = $34,057.47
$34,057.47 ÷ 2,240 = $15.20 charge per sq. ft. of office space

25. **D** 125% x 80% = 100%

26. **A** $4,235 ÷ 7% = $60,500

27. **D** 110% x 90%= 99%

Chapter 31
Mobile and Manufactured Homes

1. **B** 3 sites if built before 1983.
2. **D** Trailers are exempt as well as manufactured homes in a mobile home park.
3. **C** In addition, seller must give buyer an application for park tenancy.
4. **C** Rules and regulations must be given to mobile home dwellers prior to occupancy.
5. **A** The application for Certificate of Ownership of the unit is required if the unit is currently titled in a state other than NJ.
6. **A** These leases generally are not assignable.
7. **C** Questions about title transfer should be directed to the DMV.

Chapter 32
Business Opportunities

1. **A** Also with the N.J. Secretary of State.
2. **D** Called a "covenant not to compete."
3. **B** A security agreement would be used to finance the inventory and any other personal property.
4. **D** A fee can be legally paid to, and received by, an unlicensed person for the sale of the business itself.
5. **B** The "as is" clause gives only limited protection to the seller and is not a defense against fraudulent misrepresentation.
6. **D** The Uniform Commercial Code primarily covers personal property transactions.

Glossary Review Questions

1. **B** For example, quoting an authority.
2. **A** For instance, $100,000 ÷ 27.5 years (economic life) = 3.64% straight line depreciation.
3. **C** Littoral property differs from riparian property which borders waterways such as lakes and streams.
4. **B** Also a promise or agreement.
5. **D** Pending final disposition of court proceedings.
6. **C** Generally, 10% of the sale price.
7. **A** Used to estimate the value of income-producing properties.
8. **B** The condemning authority is the condemnor.
9. **C** To pledge without giving up possession.
10. **A** To revoke is to recall an interest or power previously granted. For instance, license revocation.
11. **A** Also called "default."
12. **A** For example, at end of lease or life estate.
13. **C** As in tendering or presenting earnest money.
14. **A** A seller may agree to pay a buyer's discount points in lieu of reducing the price.
15. **A** Without giving up possession.
16. **B** For instance real estate brokers, lawyers and property managers are fiduciaries because they handle client's property as trustees.
17. **B** Often used with installment land contracts.
18. **C** For instance, the legislature promulgates laws; the REC promulgates rules and regulations.
19. **D** Prohibits credit discrimination based on race, color, religion, national origin, sex, marital
status, age and receipt of public assistance funds.
20. **A** Restitution means to make good. For example, the Commission may impose restitution of money owed to others as a condition of restoration of a license after revocation or suspension.
21. **C** Established by zoning laws.
22. **B** Statutes are enacted by the legislature. Regulations are adopted by the Commissioner of Banking and Insurance. Violation of a
regulation is cause for any disciplinary action permitted by statute.
23. **A** Homogeneity in lot sizes and architectural styles stabilizes values.
24. **C** A special agent lacks such authority.
25. **A** In presence of an officer of the court (notary public, attorney, various judges, county clerk, etc.)
26. **B** Equity and profit are not synonymous.
27. **D** A real estate broker must divulge to all parties whom he or she represents.
28. **B** Mortgagor is borrower, not lender.
29. **D** For example, a seller who refuses to sell can be required to sell.
30. **B** Real estate taxes are levied on an ad valorem basis.

31. **A** For example, the settling of a dispute involving an adverse possession claim.
32. **C** A street with an intersection at one end and a place to turn around on the other.
33. **A** The earnest money deposit is not the consideration. The consideration is the buyer's promise to pay the full purchase price and the seller's promise to convey title.
34. **B** The by-laws of a cooperative corporation may specify how many members of the board of directors constitute a quorum for voting purposes.
35. **A** For example a contract between an adult and a minor is voidable by the minor, but not by the adult.
36. **D** The Latin term for "and others" is "*et al.*"
37. **C** One bequeaths personalty in a will.
38. **A** A clouded title would contain encumbrances.
39. **D** For example, a real estate transaction is consummated when the seller signs and delivers the deed.
40. **D** For example, a subordination clause permits a subsequently recorded mortgage to take priority over an existing mortgage.
41. **A** The attorney drafting the liquidated damages clause must exercise care that it is not construed to be a penalty which the court will disallow.
42. **C** For example, when a mortgagee starts a foreclosure proceeding, the action would be recorded in the lis pendens index.
43. **C** A Certificate of Occupancy is always required for new construction, sometimes for a change of occupancy; depends upon municipality.
44. **B** Thc owner in fee simple has the right to sell, devise, give, or lease, all or any part of these rights.
45. **D** Applies to one- to four-family houses financed by federally related loans.
46. **B** An amortizing mortgage is gradually liquidated as principal payments are made.
47. **C** Disclosed dual agency is legal; undisclosed dual agency is illegal.
48. **D** Choice D defines a setback.
49. **D** The "to have and to hold" clause appearing in a deed.
50. **D** Used with sales comparison approach.
51. **B** Under the Real Estate Sales Full Disclosure Act, the prospectus is called the "public offering statement."
52. **B** Any right, privilege or improvement that passes with the property (mineral rights, easements, buildings, etc.)
53. **B** Rights to water adjoining a property are called "riparian rights."
54. **A** Illegal in N.J., discouraged in most states.
55. **A** Necessary for recording.
56. **A** If no will and no legal heirs.
57. **B** Title to chattels is passed from seller to buyer by a bill of sale.
58. **A** Real estate brokers are special agents of the client.
59. **D** The due-on-sale clause is also called the "acceleration clause."
60. **A** Irrevocable interests "run with the land."
61. **B** The one who assigns an interest to another is the assignor.
62. **A** Satisfied after another mortgage.
63. **A** Seller is designated vendor in contract; buyer is vendee.
64. **D** The value of the one large holding is higher than the total value of the individual parcels. The increment resulting from the assemblage is called "plottage."
65. **A** A bona fide purchaser for value would most likely win a title dispute against a donee.
66. **D** As in a transfer of title from a seller to a buyer.
67. **B** The prescribed period is 20 years in New Jersey. Varies in other states.
68. **B** Federal Truth In Lending Law requires disclosure of the APR.
69. **A** An allowable action for breach of real estate contract because each parcel is unique.
70. **A** Nothing unlawful could be bona fide.
71. **D** Must be in all contracts prepared by licensees for sale of residential real estate containing
one to four dwelling units and vacant one-family lots.
72. **A** For example, relinquishing an easement.
73. **C** Semi-annual would be biannual.
74. **C** A minimum price set by a court.
75. **C** Because of the proprietary lease.

Review Quiz 1

1. **A** In a co-op there is no deed, just a proprietary lease.
2. **B** See 45:15-17(g)
3. **C** In the other cases he would be acting in a dual capacity in violation of 45:15-17(i).
4. **D** The agreements must be written pursuant to the Statute of Frauds, not because of the license law.
5. **D** A, B and C are not required.
6. **D** 11:15-1:15(b)
7. **A** B, C and D involve cooperative apartments.
8. **A** 45:15-4
9. **C** Five members must be brokers.
10. **C** 45:15-3
11. **B** The buyer does not get a copy.
12. **B** Realtors are licensees who belong to a trade association.
13. **D** It is called a "blind ad" and would be a violation of 11:15-1.45(C).

14. **C** 45:15-17
15. **D** 45:15-12.1
16. **D** No residency or citizenship requirement.
17. **D** Under these circumstances, preparation of any of the agreements would constitute the practice of law.
18. **A** The other activities require a license.
19. **C** This ties in with the Statute of Limitations for a suit involving money damages.
20. **C** See 11:15-1.23 (a)
21. **C** 45:15-15
22. **D** Now each owns a particular tract of land.
23. **C** The shareholder in a co-op has a leasehold interest.
24. **C** A Realtor is a licensee who belongs to a real estate trade association (NAR).
25. **C** Commingling is mixing; segregating is separating.
26. **D** As provided in the listing contract.
27. **B** If a seller defaults, broker can sue for the commission. If buyer defaults, broker can take direct action against buyer.
28. **C** Statute of Frauds requires listing to be written to be enforceable.
29. **C** For example, at the end of a lease or a life estate.
30. **B** This is a contractual dispute between the cooperating brokers.
31. **D** Exclusive agency relieves owner of commission payment if he finds his own buyer.
32. **C** Both are terminated because both are agency agreements.
33. **D** Net listings are prohibited in New Jersey.
34. **B** Court then appoints administrator to handle disposition of property in accordance with Law of Descent.
35. **D** The broker's contractual dispute is separate and apart from the real estate transaction.
36. **A** Required for recording.
37. **D** Furniture is personal property.
38. **B** Littoral property adjoins any of the other bodies of water.
39. **C** But he couldn't assign entire contract to another brokerage firm.
40. **C** No dower or curtesy rights in property which spouse owns as joint tenant.
41. **A** For example, by the action of streams or winds.
42. **B** Joint tenants; interest must be equal.
43. **B** It would always be the last surviving tenant.
44. **D** His interest can be transferred and result in a severance of the joint tenancy.
45. **D** The other activities require a license.
46. **C** A. requires equal shares; B. requires marriage; D. requires only one owner.
47. **B** Because of limited authority.
48. **D** An owner in fee simple can do all of the activities described.
49. **B** See 11:5-1.19(b)
50. **A** A license is required in the state in which the land is located.

Review Quiz 2

1. **C** Counter-offer is a rejection of the original offer.
2. **B** For example, six years for money damages.
3. **D** Leases for longer than three years must be written to be enforceable. An oral lease for one year is valid.
4. **D** Also called "mutual agreement" or "meeting of the minds."
5. **D** For example, buyer has a right to rely on broker's representation regarding type of insulation.
6. **A** Such as a contract to purchase with no conditions.
7. **C** Grantee does not even have to know about it, since acceptance is often presumed.
8. **C** There was no contract.
9. **B** Non-use will not terminate power of attorney.
10. **D** Recording protects grantee (buyer).
11. **D** It is a transfer of property rights.
12. **B** Terms must be carried out by a precise time and without deviation.
13. **B** The officer taking the acknowledgement cannot be an "interested party."
14. **C** It is enforceable by his heirs.
15. **B** Vendee is buyer; vendor is seller.
16. **B** Only certain contracts need be in writing under the Statute of Frauds. Deposit and date are recommended but not required.
17. **C** Requires punctual performance. See explanation to #12.
18. **A** The agreement of sale generally is not recorded.
19. **D** Death will terminate an agency agreement, but not a contract between a buyer and seller.
20. **B** For example, a contract for the sale of real estate.
21. **C** Because it is unilateral.
22. **D** Defects are undisclosed clouds on the title.
23. **B** Because there is no contract.
24. **B** Also called "breach."
25. **C** For valid delivery you need an alive beneficiary (grantee).
26. **C** The intent of the parties would be clear.
27. **C** Because a number of things remain to be done such as payment of price, delivery of deed, etc.
28. **C** Under the Statute of Frauds certain agreements must be written to be enforceable in court.
29. **A** For example, a lease prohibited pets but a rider allowed the tenant to have a dog.
30. **C** To prevent a fraudulent transfer of title by corporate officers.

31. **A** Easiest method is to have the possible title claimant release his disputed interest; if that fails, then expensive method is quiet title suit.
32. **D** Zoning ordinances are matters of public knowledge.
33. **C** The seller lacks "marketable title" and can be sued for damages.
34. B Sometimes called a "binder" or "hand money."
35. **B** The seller must sell if the buyer decides to buy. However, the buyer does not have a corresponding obligation to buy.
36. **C** The buyer has equitable title between signing of the contract and closing.
37. **B** The optionor is the property owner.
38. **B** The deposit becomes the property of the seller when the offer is accepted.
39. **C** Courts will imply a reasonable date to close.
40. **A** When offeror signs contract it constitutes an offer. When offeree signs contract it indicates acceptance and creates a contract.
41. **C** And the original offer is terminated.
42. **A** A license is not required to enter into an option agreement.
43. **B** The statute applies only to executory oral agreements. Fully executed contracts are not covered by the statute.
44. **B** A dedication is a voluntary transfer of real estate from an individual to the government.
45. **C** Buyer is grantee; seller is grantor.
46. **D** By signing the quitclaim deed, Alex clears the cloud from the title.
47. **B** Also called "breach."
48. **B** The contract identifies seller as vendor, and buyer as vendee.
49. **A** Called a "voidable contract."
50. **C** Used by fiduciaries who wish to limit their liability to the time of their tenure.

Review Quiz 3

1. **B** The mortgage could be assumed.
2. **D** A purchaser can pay more than the CRV or FHA appraisal, but must make up difference at closing.
3. **D** A trust deed is released by reconveyance.
4. **C** Permitting a mortgage recorded at a later date to take priority over an earlier recorded mortgage.
5. **C** Both statements are true.
6. **D** Possession must be for 20 years.
7. **B** Refinancing is the substitution of an old loan with a new loan. The placing of a second mortgage on a property does not involve refinancing.
8. **B** Contrast with simple interest, where interest is paid only on the principal.
9. **C** The ad can state the annual percentage rate without any other disclosure.
10. **D** Usury limits vary depending on the type of loan and lender.
11. **D** Fannie Mae is in the secondary market.
12. **B** The note creates the personal promise to pay.
13. **D** The buyer (vendee) has all of the other rights.
14. **C** Payment is not enough to clear the record.
15. **C** Mortgagee is lender, mortgagor is borrower.
16. **B** The premium paid by the borrower is called the "mortgage insurance premium" (MIP).
17. **B** This allows the lender to demand the unpaid balance of a debt in the event of default.
18. **D** The others are encumbrances, but not liens.
19. **B** A mortgage simply would be an example of a lien.
20. **C** Allowing the mortgage to foreclose once, rather than each month as payments become due.
21. **C** Also called "discharge."
22. **A** Often used by developers.
23. **B** Novation is substitution of new parties for the original parties to an agreement.
24. **B** Terminates the rights of the mortgagee when the debt is paid.
25. **B** The written instrument itself is called a "mortgage."
26. **D** In the event of default, mortgages are satisfied in the order in which they were recorded.
27. **B** Unlike a true pledge, you do not surrender possession.
28. **A** It insures loans, not title (title insurance).
29. **B** The second mortgage would be satisfied second if default occurred.
30. **B** Amortized has both interest and principal.
31. **B** The mortgage creates the lien, the note is evidence of the debt and creates the personal promise to pay.
32. **C** $100,000 x 80% x 3% = $2,400.
33. **B** Allowing specific lots to be removed from the blanket mortgage held by the lender.
34. **D** No prepayment penalty on FHA loans.
35. **C** It is a cost incident to acquiring the loan.
36. **C** A common interpretation, although any loan used as part of the purchase price is a purchase money mortgage.
37. **B** Always larger then preceding payments.
38. **C** A mortgage labeled a first mortgage will not have priority over a prior recorded mortgage.
39. **B** The CRV is the VA's opinion of the property's value but does not limit the loan amount.
40. **A** A mortgage is a voluntary lien placed by the property owner.

41. **C** The note is the personal promise to pay.
42. **B** Mortgagee-lender; mortgagor-borrower.
43. **C** If a deficiency occurs the lender is limited to an action against the seller only.
44. **A** Judgments result in a general lien.
45. **A** The promissory note or bond accompanies the mortgage.
46. **D** Allows the creditor to levy against the property to satisfy the debt.
47. **B** The two parties are the lender and borrower. When a loan is insured or guaranteed by the federal government, a government agency becomes a third party.
48. **A** The release must be recorded to clear the title.
49. **C** The mortgaged parcels do not have to be contiguous.
50. **B** Commonly called "points."

Review Quiz 4

1. **A** One year under the federal law.
2. **D** Landlord pays mortgage payments.
3. **C** Allows landlord to cancel if volume of business falls below stated fixed minimum.
4. **A** A lease for any fixed period of time such as two weeks, six months, three years, ten years, etc.
5. **B** Also called a "step-up lease."
6. **B** Rent is based on a percentage of gross sales.
7. **C** Automatically.
8. **B** Lessor is landlord; lessee is tenant.
9. **B** The lease held by a sublessor who subleases to another tenant.
10. **B** With an actual eviction the tenant would remain responsible for unpaid rent that accrues.
11. **A** Security deposit law applies only to residential leases.
12. **C** Life tenant possesses freehold estate.
13. **D** Common in shopping center leases.
14. **B** Tenant is called a "holdover tenant."
15. **C** Tenant must move while condition exists.
16. **C** The term is misleading because period could be less than a year.
17. **C** Could be actual or constructive.
18. **A** A reversion occurs when property goes back to the original owner at the end of an interest such as a life estate or a lease.
19. **B** Property is always purchased subject to the rights of existing tenants.
20. **D** The other expenses are usually paid by the tenant.
21. **D** Lessor's death will not affect tenant's rights.
22. **A** Buildings belong to lessor at end of lease.
23. **B** The commercial use is "grandfathered".
24. **C** An appraisal term indicating the legal use that will produce the greatest net return to a property over its economic life.
25. **C** The price that a willing seller will accept from a willing buyer.
26. **C** The resulting parcel is worth more than the total value of the individual parcels before the assemblage occurred. The increment in value is called "plottage."
27. **D** Because it was for less than the unexpired term.
28. **D** All standard provisions in a Property Management Contract.
29. **D** The tenant's rights are subordinate to the rights of the mortgagee.
30. **C** To avoid any inference of self-dealing.
31. **D** This would be a breach of the property manager's fiduciary duty to the client.
32. **D** With the attendant legal duties.
33. **C** Ceiling repairs are an operating expense. Ceiling replacement is a capital improvement.
34. **D** Commonly called "HUD."
35. **A** Also called "non-freehold" or "less than freehold."
36. **A** An exception granted by a zoning board permitting a violation of the zoning ordinance.
37. **A** Accrued depreciation is total depreciation from all causes, physical, functional and external.
38. **A** Used in connection with a partial taking of property.
39. **D** Also called "useful life."
40. **A** Market value is what a property is worth. Replacement price is what it would cost to reproduce a building.
41. **B** B would be an example of physical deterioration.
42. **A** The value of the subject property goes up or down for each feature that differs from the comparable.
43. **A** Because there is no income and there are no comparables.
44. **C** Gross potential income minus vacancies and collection losses = effective gross income. Effective gross income minus operating expenses = net operating income.
45. **A** The fact of no down payment is a specific financing term thus requiring disclosure of all credit terms.
46. **B** First liens are exempt.
47. **C** So that buyers can comparison shop.
48. **C** Seven calendar days is the rescission period under the Real Estate Sales Full Disclosure Act.
49. **B** If a commercial lease, C would be correct.
50. **B** A, C and D are freehold estates.

Review Quiz 5

1. **B** An encroachment not a governmental limitation.
2. **D** The tenant acquires a leasehold interest.
3. **D** Also called "discharge."
4. **B** Do not confuse with sole ownership, which is severalty.
5. **C** Title does not pass until last payment is made. Also called "contract for deed."
6. **B** Principal is not reduced during term of the loan.
7. **B** Plottage is an increase in value resulting from an assemblage.
8. **A** Amortization is the gradual retirement of a debt by a series of principal and interest payments over a definite period of time, leaving a zero balance at the end.
9. **D** Usury laws vary based on types of loans and types of lenders.
10. **A** As when a real estate license is revoked for unworthy conduct.
11. **A** D would be correct under condominium ownership.
12. **D** No covenants of title.
13. **B** The balloon payment is larger than preceding payments and pays the loan in full.
14. **A** Specific performance is allowable with real estate because each parcel is unique.
15. **D** Discriminatory advertising violates state and federal laws.
16. **D** The owner must submit to the tenant any offer from a third party. The tenant has the right to match that offer. If the tenant fails to match the offer, the owner is free to sell to the third party.
17. **B** Because there was no contract.
18. **D** Could be construed to be commingling.
19. **C** Chattels are personal property.
20. **D** Usually used to convey title to portion of subdivision for use as streets.
21. **B** Only by the minor.
22. **C** See 11:5-1.23(d).
23. **C** The only inheritable estate.
24. **A** See 45:15-17(p).
25. **C** All of the others are fiduciary duties.
26. **D** Estate for years is leasehold.
27. **D** Life estate is freehold, but less than fee simple.
28. **B** See 11:5-1.15 (b).
29. **B** Not a principal-agent relationship.
30. **C** New owner cannot alter terms.
31. **B** Disclosed dual agency is permitted with informed consent.
32. **C** Formerly a government agency.
33. **C** Because of unequal shares and relationship of parties.
34. **B** The broker works "for" the client and "with" the customer.
35. **C** Because fewer prospective buyers could qualify for financing.
36. **B** Deed restrictions are private limitations.
37. **A** Should be contingency in contract to purchase, if there are no city sewers.
38. **C** Metes are measures; bounds are boundaries.
39. **A** Because of fiduciary obligations of licensees.
40. **A** "And others" is "*et al.*"
41. **D** Holographic wills are legal in New Jersey, but are not recommended.
42. **C** Any, right, privilege or improvement that passes with the land.
43. **B** The type of deed used by an executor or administrator.
44. **C** May have been granted by zoning board or "grandfathered."
45. **B** Because a higher rate indicates a higher risk.
46. **D** 100% ÷ economic life = straight-line depreciation.
47. **A** Consideration is an essential element of all contracts.
48. **D** Established by zoning ordinance.
49. **C** Attorney's fee would be paid even if there was no financing.
50. **B** Vacant land is not a wasting asset and therefore cannot be depreciated for tax purposes.

Salesperson Practice Final

1. **C** Statute of limitations places time limits to bring suit.
2. **B** The VA issues a CRV.
3. **D** Legal title does not pass until last payment is made.
4. **A** Classic example.
5. **C** Recommended but not essential.
6. **D** The property would pass to the surviving brother.
7. **A** The original tenant remains liable.
8. **C** Assumes legal use.
9. **D** This is the purpose of the title search.
10. **A** The only inheritable interest is fee simple.
11. **A** The quitclaim deed is commonly used for this purpose.
12. **B** New owner cannot alter terms.
13. **B** Owner waits to deal only with prospective buyers or tenants.
14. **B** Only persons furnishing labor or materials for improvement of real estate.
15. **B** A representation that grantor owns the property and has the right to sell it.
16. **D** Called "docketed."
17. **A** Formerly a government agency.
18. **C** For example, absolute fee simple.
19. **D** Because he handles owner's property in a position of confidence and trust.
20. **A** Often used by developers.
21. **B** Willful destruction of land or improvements.

22. **C** Recording is recommended but not required.
23. **D** All of the other information is pertinent.
24. **D** All are commonly done.
25. **C** The tax code permits an investor to recapture the cost of improvements through depreciation.
26. **A** Rarely used any more.
27. **C** With an easement in gross there is no dominant tenement.
28. **B** Restrictive covenants are private restrictions.
29. **C** In an interest-bearing account.
30. **C** Otherwise a tenancy by entirety would be created automatically.
31. **C** Earnest money is recommended but not required.
32. **D** Could be an addition or deletion.
33. **D** Since eight points will increase the yield by 1%, four points would increase it 1/2%.
34. **B** Truth-in-lending law requires disclosure of this.
35. **B** Common use of term, although any mortgage to secure part of the purchase price is a purchase money mortgage.
36. **B** For example, zoning, building codes, and fire department regulations.
37. **B** A specific lien against property.
38. **A** A demise is a transfer of an interest by lease.
39. **A** Homogeneous means similar.
40. **C** Both activities require a license.
41. **C** The security deposit law only covers residential.
42. **C** The principal must have legal capacity but technically, not the agent.
43. **B** The buyer and seller are jointly and individually responsible.
44. **D** As in a mortgage.
45. **D** The lien holder has a lien but no right of possession.
46. **D** FHA and VA are insured/guaranteed.
47. **C** The process by which the creditor levies against the debtor's property.
48. **B** Prepaid items are credits; unpaid items are debits.
49. **B** Special assessments are paid for only by benefiting property owners.
50. **C** Allows more buyers to qualify.
51. **B** Most common mode of payment.
52. **C** Shares of stock would be involved with co-ops.
53. **B** The grantor becomes the lessee.
54. **A** Scarcity is an economic characteristic.
55. **D** The grantee is the buyer.
56. **B** It is an encumbrance to the servient property.
57. **C** Under the Statute of Frauds.
58. **A** Principal payments are not deductible. Depreciation deductions are allowable only for investment properties.
59. **A** Personal property left in a will is a bequest.
60. **D** All the others involve an exchange of promises.
61. **A** Eminent domain is the right of the government to take the property. Condemnation is the act of taking it.
62. **A** It is an appurtenance to the owner of the dominant property.
63. **C** Results in the greatest net return.
64. **B** Generally used for a new property or where there is no income or no comparables.
65. **C** $15,000 x 80% = $12,000
$16,000 – $12,000 = $4,000
66. **B** 75 x $1,450 = $108,750
$ 6,842 x 5 = $34,210
$108,750 + $34,210 = $142,960
$108,750 x 2 – $142,960 = $74,540
67. **A** $1,133 + $115 + $1240
$195 x 12 + $1,240 = $3,580
$3,850 ÷ 12 = $298.33 (rounded to $300)
68. **C** A corporate resolution authorizes sale of corporate property.
69. **D** $130 ÷ 1,080 days = $.12 per day (insurance)
$625 ÷ 360 = $1.74 per day (taxes)
870 x $.12 = $104.40 insurance credit
150 x $1.74 = $261.00 tax credit
$104.40 + $261.00 = $365.40
70. **A** An option is executory because it is still to be brought into effect, and unilateral, because only the optionee makes a promise.
71. **B** 270' x 390' = 105,300 sq. ft.
$45,000 ÷ $105,300 = .427
90' x 130' = 11,700 sq. ft. x .427 = $4,995.90
72. **C** $7.50 x $20 = $ 150
$54 ÷ 12 = $4.50
$360 ÷ 36 = $10
$150 + $450 + $10 = $164.50
73. **A** If 1/8" = 1', then 1" = 8'
13.5 x 8 = 108'
17.75 x 8 = 142'
108' x 142' = 15,336 sq. ft.
74. **B** A leasehold is not the same as a tenency for years, because a leasehold may also be periodic or at sufferance.
75. **D** A power of attorney creates a fiduciary relationship between the principal and the attorney-in-fact.
76. **A** A security agreement is used to finance personal property. The bill of sale transfers title to personalty.
77. **A** The tenancy created is called a tenancy at sufferance. The tenant who fails to vacate is called a holdover tenant.
78. **B** Ownership by one person is called severalty because it is "severed" from the rights of all others.
79. **C** A devise is a voluntary transfer of real estate by gift or will.
80. **A** 210 ÷ 300 = 70%

81. **C** A violation of the Civil Rights Act of 1866.
82. **B** Under the license law, a market study is not an appraisal.
83. **B** $5,000 + $10,000 + $10,000
84. **C** See 45:15-29.
85. **C** $3,000 maximum.
86. **B** However, an appraiser's license is required.
87. **D** All of the other statements are false.
88. **D** Only the principal broker may sue a client. See 45:15-3.
89. **C** The vendor is the seller (client).
90. **B** The Commission may refuse to ever again grant a license after a third violation.
91. **D** The Real Estate Commission can demand an explanation but will not settle a contractual dispute.
92. **B** The alleged violator must respond to the complaint and is called the "respondent."
93. **D** All statements are true.
94. **B** Two years.
95. **D** Rotting would indicate physical deterioration.
96. **B** The value of the land plus the reproduction cost, minus depreciation.
97. **C** Location, location, location.
98. **C** Cost reproduction is a method of estimating value, not a type of depreciation.
99. **D** It is only allowed on one piece of real estate.
100. **A** Also for mental or physical incapacity. See 45:15-11.3.
101. **A** Because of the fiduciary nature of a broker's activities.
102. **B** See 45:15-17, last paragraph.
103. **A** See 11:5-1.16 (a) 4.
104. **C** See 45:15-21.
105. **B** Five of the eight members are brokers.
106. **B** Called mortgage insurance premium (MIP).
107. **C** On one- to four-family houses providing he is the broker in the transaction.
108. **A** The grantor must be competent, but not necessarily the grantee.
109. **D** See 45:15-3.1.
110. **C** Residency and citizenship are not required.

Broker's Practice Final

1. **C** Religious organizations are allowed to discriminate on basis of religion.
2. **A** None of the other changes are connected with financing costs.
3. **D** Owner must occupy if loan is guaranteed by VA.
4. **C** Non-veterans can assume VA loans.
5. **A** Membership in the religion may not be restricted on account of race, color or nationality.
6. **B** An offer may be withdrawn any time before accepted.
7. **D** Only the market can determine value.
8. **B** Income must be annual and net.
9. **B** Because the building has been totally depreciated for tax purposes.
10. **B** Advances are made at the original interest rate.
11. **A** Deeds and mortgages are recorded at the county clerk's office.
12. **A** Upon signing contract buyer acquires equitable title, not equity.
13. **A** Highest and best use is concerned with use.
14. **D** Usually at closing.
15. **D** A deed does not necessarily accompany a mortgage (for example when a property is refinanced).
16. **B** Tenant must vacate while condition exists.
17. **C** A lien for real estate taxes will be satisfied first.
18. **B** Functional obsolescence is a loss in value from any cause within the property except physical deterioration.
19. **B** Because generally a person can acquire no better title then that held by the previous grantor.
20. **A** Annual net income ÷ cap rate = value.
21. **A** (B) and (C) are exempt from the provisions of TIL.
22. **C** Willful destruction of any part of landlord's land or improvements.
23. **C** An inherent government right.
24. **C** In event of default seller is limited to action against wife only.
25. **B** (A) is required, (B) is a breach of loyalty to client.
26. **C** All of the others are essential.
27. **A** When there is a partial taking.
28. **D** Discriminatory advertising is prohibited.
29. **B** Riparian rights refer to the use of water on, under or adjacent to an owner's land.
30. **B** A lender may refuse a loan to a person who is a member of a minority group, but not because a person is a minority.
31. **D** Love and affection are considered good consideration.
32. **C** Mortgagee – lender; mortgagor – borrower.
33. **C** Annexation is one of the tests of a fixture.
34. **B** Physical deterioration is loss of value caused by age and action of the elements.
35. **C** With a gross easement there is no dominant estate, only a servient estate.
36. **D** As in a land contract.
37. **B** And also may include a base rent.
38. **B** Also must contain an acknowledgment.
39. **D** Appreciation is an increase in value.
40. **D** Persons who cannot read may enter into a valid contract.

41. **A** Because it increases the purchaser's cash and decreases the seller's cash.
42. **A** Accrued depreciation is the total depreciation from all causes: physical, functional and external.
43. **D** Operating expenses would only be figured in the income approach.
44. **B** Because fewer prospective buyers can qualify for mortgage financing.
45. **B** And would generally be found by survey.
46. **B** The assignee then acquires the assignor's rights.
47. **C** An assignment would transfer the policy to another insured.
48. **B** And vice-versa.
49. **B** Also called less-than-freehold.
50. **C** An appurtenance would be a positive influence.
51. **C** 20 years required in N.J.
52. **C** Upon the spouse's death, the rights become consummate.
53. **A** (A) is incorporeal; the others are corporeal.
54. **B** Severalty is sole ownership,
55. **B** Because of its perpetual existence.
56. **B** Each with a 1/2 interest.
57. **B** Because of survivorship rights.
58. **A** Exposed land belongs to riparian owner.
59. **C** Rarely used under current practice.
60. **D** Allowed for real estate suits because each parcel of land is unique.
61. **D** All are valid remedies for default.
62. **D** \$13,000 ÷ 8.2% = \$ 160,975.61 ÷ 50 = \$3,219.51
63. **B** The mortgagor (borrower) gives the mortgage to the mortgagee (lender). Don't confuse the mortgage with the loan.
64. **A** The buyer is referred to as the vendee in the contract, and as the grantee in the deed.
65. **B** \$42,000 – \$5,000 = \$37,000 original cost of house
\$37,000 x 2 1/2% x 5 = \$4,625 depreciation on house
\$37,000 – \$4,625 = \$32,375
66. **D** In other words, hypothecate means to mortgage.
67. **A** Metes and bounds means by distances and directions.
68. **D** Eminent domain is the right to take private lands. Condemnation is the act or process by which the property is taken.
69. **B** 10' x 90' x 110' = 99,000 cu. ft.
99,000 ÷ 27 = 3,667 cu. yds.
3,667 x \$24 = \$88,000
70. **C** Police powers are exercised by government. Liens are rights imposed by creditors.
71. **A** \$100,000 + \$20,000 = \$120,000 investment
\$120,000 + 50% = \$\$180,000
\$180,000 ÷ 25 lots = \$7,200 per lot
72. **A** \$300 x 12 = \$3,600
\$4,725 – \$3,600 = \$1,125 excess rent
\$1,125 ÷ 4.5% = \$25,000
\$200,000 + \$25,000 = \$225,000 gross sales
73. **C** 1/7 = 14.29%; 1/14 = 7.14%
14.29% + 14.29% + 7.14% = 35.72%
100% – 35.72% = 64.28% owned by 4th owner
\$11,200 x 64.28% = \$7,200 (rounded)
74. **A** 43,560 x 5 = 217,800 sq. ft.
60' x 125' = 7,500 sq. ft. per lot
300' x 40' = 12,000 sq. ft. of roads
217,800 – 12,000 = 205,800 sq. ft.
205,800 ÷ 7,500 = 27
75. **B** Small bedrooms, small closets, etc. are examples of functional obsolescence.
76. **B** \$9,900 ÷ 110% = \$9,000 cost last year
\$9,000 x 4% = \$360 interest lost
\$360 + \$175 = \$535
\$9,900 – \$535 – \$9,000 = \$365
77. **B** The Act only applies to subdivided properties, not to single, isolated transactions.
78. **D** \$230,000 x 90% = \$207,000 appraised value
\$207,000 x 80% = \$165,000 assessed value
\$165,000 ÷ 100 x \$2.75 = \$4,554
79. **C** Annual net income ÷ cap. rate = value.
80. **D** Dedication is a voluntary alienation.
81. **C** Only the broker is making a promise.
82. **D** Ends automatically on the last day of the term.
83. **B** Allows the mortgagee to foreclose.
84. **D** The vendee has all of the interests described.
85. **C** Redemption period is two years.
86. **A** Or the household of the owner-lessor's family.
87. **B** HUD enforces the federal law.
88. **C** Familial status is covered by the federal law.
89. **A** The deed is valid but the racial restriction is void.
90. **D** Owners, receivers and executors are exempt.
91. **C** Requirement to be branch office supervisor.
92. **A** In order to protect the public.
93. **B** Court will always presume tenancy in common when ownership method is not specified.
94. **A** A square half-mile contains 160 acres. One-half of a square mile contains 320 acres.
95. **D** If not stated, rent is due at end of month.
96. **C** FHA insures loans.
97. **B** To increase yield by 1% = 8 discount points.
98. **D** A salesperson must work under the supervision of a principal broker.
99. **B** Salesmanship is not tested.
100. **A** The course completion certificate is good for one year.

101. **C** Or one-thousandth of a dollar; expressed .001.
102. **A** The redemption period after the tax sale is two years.
103. **B** Broker has no such authority without the power-of-attorney.
104. **C** See 45:15-17(b).
105. **A** Deed cannot be recorded unless the fee is paid.
106. **C** The secondary market is the mechanism available for buying and selling first mortgages.
107. **D** A, B and C illustrate the problems with monument descriptions.
108. **A** The grantor conveys any interest he or she may have, including fee simple.
109. **B** Amos and Bob remain joint tenants.
110. **A** Formerly Banking and Insurance.
111. **A** All of the others could result in revocation, but revocation is automatic when payment is made out of guaranty fund.
112. **C** Must account for how the money was spent.
113. **C** The rescission period is seven calendar days.
114. **A** Six-month record-keeping requirement for rejected offers.
115. **D** $72,750 ÷ $712.50 = 102.
116. **C** Disintermediation involves removal of deposits from lending institutions and investing them in other assets.
117. **D** Only the owner or an attorney can prepare the other contracts.
118. **A** See 11:5-1.10 (a,2).
119. **D** The other statements are true.
120. **D** Two offices, not two different brokers.

REAL ESTATE CROSSWORD PUZZLE

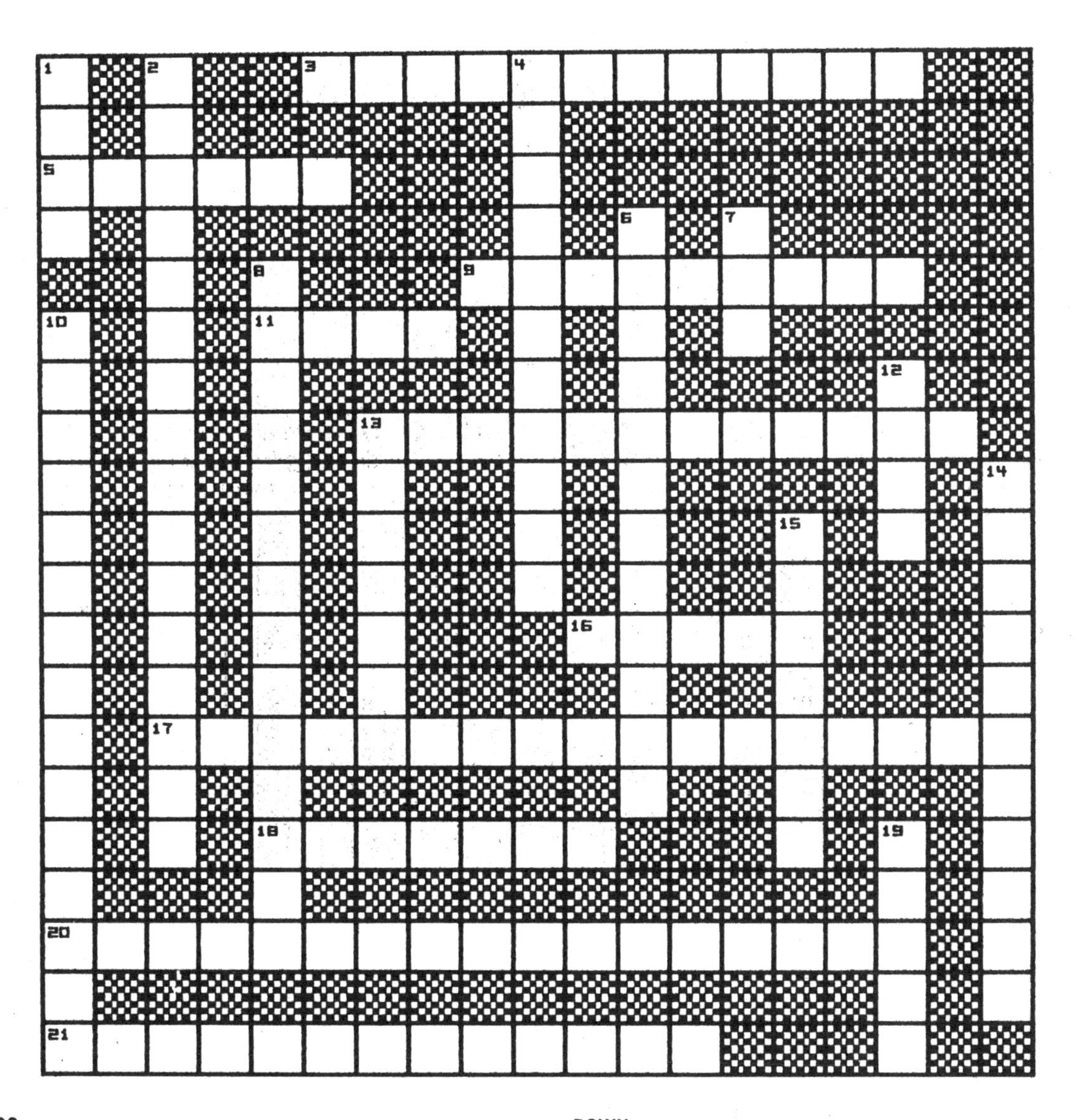

ACROSS

3. Secondary place of business.
5. Means of leaving property without trespassing the property rights of other surrounding owners.
9. A person in a position of great trust and confidence.
11. Latin for "and others."
13. Collecting broker's commission and representing either part in a different capacity for a fee.
16. Given by offeror.
17. Government fee which the seller pays when real estate changes hands.
18. A deed for property sold by a government unit for non-payment of taxes.
20. Squatter's rights.
21. Government right to take private property for public use upon payment of just compensation.

Answers on the next page

DOWN

1. An instrument in writing conveying title or interest in or to real estate.
2. Must be kept by brokers for at least six years.
4. Mixing client's funds with your own.
6. Fund established to pay claim of persons injured by the illegal acts of licensees.
7. The premium collected by the FHA for insuring the mortgage.
8. An appraisal method used where there has been a partial taking of the property.
10. A personal property mortgage. Now called a "security agreement."
12. Latin for "and wife."
13. The law that describes the distribution of property in the case of an intestate death.
14. Right of the government to enact legislation necessary for the welfare of the public.
15. The statutory right which a husband has in his wife's estate at her death.
19. A person to whom a gift is made.

For more educational real estate crossword puzzles, get your copy of "The Crosswords of Real Estate".

Answers to
REAL ESTATE CROSSWORD PUZZLE
on previous page

D		P			B	R	A	N	C	H	O	F	F	I	C	E		
E		E							O									
E	G	R	E	S	S				M									
D		M							M		G		M					
		A		B				F	I	D	U	C	I	A	R	Y		
C		N		E	T	A	L		N		A		P					
H		E		F					G		R					E		
A		N		O		D	U	A	L	C	A	P	A	C	I	T	Y	
T		T		R		E			I		N					U		P
T		R		E		S			N		T			C		X		O
E		E		A		C			G		Y			U				L
L		C		N		E				O	F	F	E	R				I
M		O		D		N					U			T				C
O		R	E	A	L	T	Y	T	R	A	N	S	F	E	R	F	E	E
R		D		F							D			S				P
T		S		T	A	X	D	E	E	D				Y		D		O
G				E												O		W
A	D	V	E	R	S	E	P	O	S	S	E	S	S	I	O	N		E
G																E		R
E	M	I	N	E	N	T	D	O	M	A	I	N				E		

For more educational real estate crossword puzzles, get your copy of "The Crosswords of Real Estate".

Additional Study Aids. . .

The Crosswords of Real Estate
by Frank J. Kovats and Frank W. Kovats

This **Crosswords of Real Estate** Puzzle Book is an interesting way to learn some of the most frequently used real estate terms. These 20 puzzles contain hundreds of real estate terms and are guaranteed to be challenging, educational and entertaining. **$12.00**

Thesaurus of Real Estate Exam Terms
by Frank W. Kovats

Now, close to 2 hours of easy-to-listen-to, easy-to-learn, real estate exam terms are defined and discussed by New Jersey educator and real estate author, Frank W. Kovats.

Plus: Packaged with the cassettes in a long lasting attractive vinyl album is a special 8-section, 60 page progress guide, complete with helpful review quizzes. **$39.00**

STUDY SMART™ Real Estate Math Made Easy!

This two tape audio cassette program covers all the math skills necessary to pass the exam. It includes a math workbook with BOTH completed examples as well as practice problems. PLUS, it has an appendix with keyed answers. It uses basic arithmetic skills that we all learned in school (no algebra necessary). Using the "T" formula, it covers commissions, taxes, pro-rations, area & volume, financing, appraisal, closing and seller net. With this book and a calculator, real estate math truly is MADE EASY. **$39.00** plus postage & handling

Glosario De Terminos Del Examen De Bienes Raices
by Frank W. Kovats

GLOSARIO DE TERMINOS DEL EXAMEN DE BIENES RAICES
Frank W. Kovats
GUIA DE PROGRESOS

"Glosario De Terminos Del Examen De Bienes Raices" has been prepared in response to numerous requests from students for whom English is a second language. It contains 402 key real estate terms and 39 review quizzes. 86 pages. **$14.95** plus postage & handling.

ORDER FORM

Quantity	Item	Total
	The Crosswords of Real Estate **$12.00** Plus $2.00 Postage & Handling	
	Thesaurus of Real Estate Exam Terms **$39.00** Plus $3.00 Postage & Handling	
	Study Smart **$39.00** Plus $3.00 Postage & Handling	
	Glosario Del Terminos Examen Raices **$14.95** Plus $3.00 Postage & Handling	

Fill in quantity section and enclose total amount of order plus appropriate postage & handling. Enclose check or money order payable to: Kovco Publications Inc. Mail to: Kovco Publications, Inc.,
230 W. Passaic Street,
Maywood, NJ 07607 or call **(201)843-PASS**

To Order by Fax: (201)843-0715
To Order by Phone: (201)843-9099

Name ______________________

Address ______________________

City ______________ State ________ Zip ________

Phone ______________________

Form of Pmt: ☐ Visa ☐ Mastercard ☐ American Express

Card Number ______________ Exp. Date ________

Order Form

Additional Study Aids. . .

The Crosswords of Real Estate

by Frank J. Kovats and Frank W. Kovats

This **Crosswords of Real Estate** Puzzle Book is an interesting way to learn some of the most frequently used real estate terms. These 20 puzzles contain hundreds of real estate terms and are guaranteed to be challenging, educational and entertaining. **$12.00**

Thesaurus of Real Estate Exam Terms

by Frank W. Kovats

Now, close to 2 hours of easy-to-listen-to, easy-to-learn, real estate exam terms are defined and discussed by New Jersey educator and real estate author, Frank W. Kovats.

Plus: Packaged with the cassettes in a long lasting attractive vinyl album is a special 8-section, 60 page progress guide, complete with helpful review quizzes. **$39.00**

STUDY SMART™ Real Estate Math Made Easy!

This two tape audio cassette program covers all the math skills necessary to pass the exam. It includes a math workbook with BOTH completed examples as well as practice problems. PLUS, it has an appendix with keyed answers. It uses basic arithmetic skills that we all learned in school (no algebra necessary). Using the "T" formula, it covers commissions, taxes, pro-rations, area & volume, financing, appraisal, closing and seller net. With this book and a calculator, real estate math truly is MADE EASY. **$39.00** plus postage & handling

Glosario De Terminos Del Examen De Bienes Raices

by Frank W. Kovats

GLOSARIO DE TERMINOS
DEL EXAMEN DE BIENES RAICES
Frank W. Kovats
GUIA DE PROGRESOS

"Glosario De Terminos Del Examen De Bienes Raices" has been prepared in response to numerous requests from students for whom English is a second language. It contains 402 key real estate terms and 39 review quizzes. 86 pages. **$14.95** plus postage & handling.

Order Form

ORDER FORM

Quantity	Item	Total
	The Crosswords of Real Estate **$12.00** Plus $2.00 Postage & Handling	
	Thesaurus of Real Estate Exam Terms **$39.00** Plus $3.00 Postage & Handling	
	Study Smart **$39.00** Plus $3.00 Postage & Handling	
	Glosario Del Terminos Examen Raices **$14.95** Plus $3.00 Postage & Handling	

Fill in quantity section and enclose total amount of order plus appropriate postage & handling. Enclose check or money order payable to: Kovco Publications Inc. Mail to: Kovco Publications, Inc.,
230 W. Passaic Street,
Maywood, NJ 07607 or call **(201)843-PASS**

To Order by Fax: (201)843-0715
To Order by Phone: (201)843-9099

Name ______________________

Address ______________________

City ______________ State __________ Zip __________

Phone ______________________

Form of Pmt: ☐ Visa ☐ Mastercard ☐ American Express

Card Number ______________ Exp. Date __________

Additional Study Aids. . .

The Crosswords of Real Estate

by Frank J. Kovats and Frank W. Kovats

This **Crosswords of Real Estate** Puzzle Book is an interesting way to learn some of the most frequently used real estate terms. These 20 puzzles contain hundreds of real estate terms and are guaranteed to be challenging, educational and entertaining. **$12.00**

Thesaurus of Real Estate Exam Terms

by Frank W. Kovats

Now, close to 2 hours of easy-to-listen-to, easy-to-learn, real estate exam terms are defined and discussed by New Jersey educator and real estate author, Frank W. Kovats.

Plus: Packaged with the cassettes in a long lasting attractive vinyl album is a special 8-section, 60 page progress guide, complete with helpful review quizzes. **$39.00**

Order Form

STUDY SMART™ Real Estate Math Made Easy!

This two tape audio cassette program covers all the math skills necessary to pass the exam. It includes a math workbook with BOTH completed examples as well as practice problems. PLUS, it has an appendix with keyed answers. It uses basic arithmetic skills that we all learned in school (no algebra necessary). Using the "T" formula, it covers commissions, taxes, pro-rations, area & volume, financing, appraisal, closing and seller net. With this book and a calculator, real estate math truly is MADE EASY. **$39.00** plus postage & handling

Glosario De Terminos Del Examen De Bienes Raices

by Frank W. Kovats

GLOSARIO DE TERMINOS
DEL EXAMEN DE BIENES RAICES
Frank W. Kovats
GUIA DE PROGRESOS

"Glosario De Terminos Del Examen De Bienes Raices" has been prepared in response to numerous requests from students for whom English is a second language. It contains 402 key real estate terms and 39 review quizzes. 86 pages. **$14.95** plus postage & handling.

ORDER FORM

Quantity	Item	Total
	The Crosswords of Real Estate **$12.00** Plus $2.00 Postage & Handling	
	Thesaurus of Real Estate Exam Terms **$39.00** Plus $3.00 Postage & Handling	
	Study Smart **$39.00** Plus $3.00 Postage & Handling	
	Glosario Del Terminos Examen Raices **$14.95** Plus $3.00 Postage & Handling	

Fill in quantity section and enclose total amount of order plus appropriate postage & handling. Enclose check or money order payable to: Kovco Publications Inc. Mail to: Kovco Publications, Inc.,
230 W. Passaic Street,
Maywood, NJ 07607 or call **(201)843-PASS**

To Order by Fax: (201)843-0715
To Order by Phone: (201)843-9099

Name ______________________

Address ______________________

City ____________ State ________ Zip ________

Phone ______________________

Form of Pmt: ☐ Visa ☐ Mastercard ☐ American Express

Card Number ______________ Exp. Date ________